July 25-27, 2017
Washington, DC, USA



Association for
Computing Machinery

*Advancing Computing as a Science & Profession*

# PODC'17

Proceedings of the ACM Symposium on

## Principles of Distributed Computing

*Sponsored by:*

***ACM SIGACT & ACM SIGOPS***

*Supported by:*

***Amazon Web Services, IBM Research, Orcale Labs, & VMware***

Association for
Computing Machinery

*Advancing Computing as a Science & Profession*

**The Association for Computing Machinery**
**2 Penn Plaza, Suite 701**
**New York, New York 10121-0701**



**ISBN:** 978-1-4503-4992-5 (Digital)

**ISBN:** 978-1-4503-5205-5 (Print)

Additional copies may be ordered prepaid from:

**ACM Order Department**
PO Box 30777
New York, NY 10087-0777, USA

Phone: 1-800-342-6626 (USA and Canada)
+1-212-626-0500 (Global)
Fax: +1-212-944-1318
E-mail: acmhelp@acm.org
Hours of Operation: 8:30 am – 4:30 pm ET

# PODC 2017 Program Chair's Preface

The ACM Symposium on Principles of Distributed Computing (PODC) is one of the premier international conferences on algorithms for distributed computation, including the theory, design, analysis, implementation, and application of such algorithms to domains stretching from traditional long-haul networks to mobile and sensor networks. PODC is sponsored by the ACM Special Interest Group on theoretical computer science, SIGACT, and the ACM Special Interest Group operating systems, SIGOPS.

This volume contains the papers presented at PODC 2017, the 36th Symposium on Principles of Distributed Computing, held on July 25–27, 2017 in Washington, DC. The volume also includes the citations for two awards jointly sponsored by PODC and the EATCS Symposium on Distributed Computing (DISC): the Edsger W. Dijkstra Prize in Distributed Computing, and the Principles of Distributed Computing Doctoral Dissertation Award.

The 2017 Edsger W. Dijkstra Prize in Distributed Computing will be presented at DISC 2017 in Vienna, Austria, to Elizabeth Borowsky and Eli Gafni for their paper "Generalized FLP Impossibility Result for t-resilient Asynchronous Computations" published in the *Proceedings of the 25th Annual ACM Symposium on Theory of Computing* (STOC) in 1993.

The 2017 Principles of Distributed Computing Doctoral Dissertation Award is presented to Mohsen Ghaffari, for his dissertation "Improved Distributed Algorithms for Fundamental Graph Problems," written under the supervision of Nancy Lynch at MIT.

There were 154 papers submitted to the symposium, and in addition there were 14 brief announcement submissions. The Program Committee selected 38 contributions, or less than 25% of the 154 submissions, for regular presentations at the symposium. Each presentation is accompanied by a ten-page paper in this volume. The Program Committee also selected 21 papers for presentation as brief announcements (some of which came from the regular paper submissions that could not be accepted due to paucity of space). Each brief announcement is accompanied by a three-page paper in this volume. These announcements present ongoing work or recent results, and it is expected that these results will appear as full papers in other conference proceedings or journals. Every submitted paper was read and evaluated by at least three members of the Program Committee. The committee was assisted by more than 140 external reviewers. The Program Committee made its final decisions during the April 24–25, 2017 meeting hosted by Nancy Lynch at MIT. Revised and expanded versions of several selected papers will be considered for publication in a special issue of the journal *Distributed Computing* and in the *Journal of ACM.*

The program included three keynote lectures by Guy Blelloch (CMU, USA), Maurice Herlihy (Brown University, USA), and Rosario Gennaro (CUNY, USA).

The Best Paper Award was presented to Michael Elkin for the paper "A Simple Deterministic Distributed MST Algorithm, with Near-Optimal Time and Message Complexities." The Best Student Paper Award was presented to Peter Davies for the paper "Exploiting Spontaneous Transmissions for Broadcasting and Leader Election in Radio," coauthored with Artur Czumaj.

This year PODC was co-located with 2017 ACM SPAA (Symposium on Parallelism in Algorithms and Architectures). There were also two workshops co-located with PODC: the *4th Workshop on Adaptive Resource Management and Scheduling for Cloud Computing*, and the *5th Workshop on Biological Distributed Algorithms.* The broader program also included two tutorials:

Recent Advances in R/W Computability with Speculations by Eli Gafni, and High-Level Specification of Distributed Algorithms by Y. Annie Liu, Scott D. Stoller, and Bo Lin.

We also celebrated David Peleg's $60^{th}$ birthday at a pre-conference event.

Putting together PODC 2017 was a team effort. We first thank the authors for providing the content of the program. We are grateful to the Program Committee and the external reviewers, who worked very hard in reviewing papers and providing feedback for authors. The guidance of the Steering Committee and the help of the Conference Committee was timely and invaluable. Finally, we thank our sponsors, ACM SIGACT and ACM SIGOPS, and our corporate supporters, Amazon Web Services, IBM Research, Oracle Labs and VMware.

Alexander A. Schwarzmann
*PODC 2017 Program Chair*

# Table of Contents

## Session 3

Session Chair: Kishori Konwar *(Massachusetts Institute of Technology)*



## Keynote 2



## Session 4

Session Chair: Calvin Newport *(Georgetown University)*

## Session 5

Session Chair: Nancy Lynch *(Massachusetts Institute of Technology)*



## Session 6

Session Chair: Gadi Taubenfeld *(IDC Herzliya)*



## Keynote 3



## Session 7

Session Chair: Lorenzo Alvisi *(Cornell University and University of Texas)*

## Session 8



## Session 9

# PODC 2017 Symposium Organization

**General Chair:** Elad Michael Schiller *(Chalmers University of Technology, Sweden)*

**Program Committee Chair:** Alexander A. Schwarzmann *(University of Connecticut, USA)*

**Organizing Chair:** Jeremy Fineman *(Georgetown University, USA)*

**Treasurer:** Calvin Newport *(Georgetown University, USA)*

**Publicity Chair:** Mark Tuttle *(Amazon, Canada)*

**Communication Chair:** Jukka Suomela *(Aalto University, Finland)*

**Workshop Coordinator:** Leonid Barenboim *(Open University, Israel)*

**Proceedings Coordinator:** Theophanis Hadjistasi *(University of Connecticut, USA)*

**Travel Grant Coordinator:** Bapi Chatterjee (Chalmers University of Technology, Sweden)

**Steering Committee Chair:** Nitin Vaidya *(University of Illinois, USA)*

**Steering Committee:**
Pierre Fraigniaud *(CNRS, Université Paris-Diderot, France)*
Calvin Newport *(Georgetown University, USA)*
Andrzej Pelc *(Université du Québec en Outaouais, Canada)*
Alexander A. Schwarzmann *(University of Connecticut, USA)*
Paul Spirakis *(University of Liverpool, UK)*
Elad Michael Schiller *(Chalmers University of Technology, Sweden)*

**Program Committee:**
Lorenzo Alvisi *(University of Texas Austin and Cornell University, USA)*
Hagit Attiya *(The Technion, Israel)*
Michael Bender *(Stony Brook University, USA)*
Borzoo Bonakdarpour *(McMaster University, Canada)*
Silvia Bonomi *(Sapienza Università di Roma, Italy)*
Christian Cachin *(IBM Research, Switzerland)*
Irina Calciu *(VMware Research, USA)*
Bogdan Chlebus *(University of Colorado Denver, USA)*
Carole Delporte-Gallet *(Université Paris Diderot, Paris 7, France)*
Shlomi Dolev *(Ben-Gurion University, Israel)*
Greg Eisenhauer *(Georgia Tech, USA)*
Faith Ellen *(University of Toronto, Canada)*
Panagiota Faturu *(University of Crete, Greece)*
Antonio Fernandez Anta *(IMDEA, Spain)*
Paola Flocchini *(University of Ottawa, Canada)*
Chryssis Georgiou *(University of Cyprus, Cyprus)*
Andreas Haeberlen *(University of Pennsylvania, USA)*
Magnus Halldorsson *(Reykjavik University, Iceland)*
Anne-Marie Kermarrec *(INRIA, Rennes, France)*

**Program Committee: (continued)**

Aggelos Kiayias *(Edinburgh University, UK)*
Kishori Konwar *(MIT, USA)*
Nancy Lynch *(MIT, USA)*
Calvin Newport *(Georgetown University, USA)*
Cristina Nita-Rotaru *(Northeastern University, USA)*
Merav Parter *(Weizmann Institute, Israel)*
Andrzej Pelc *(University of Quebec, Canada)*
Franck Petit *(Université Pierre-et-Marie-Curie, Paris 6, France)*
Maria Potop-Butucaru *(Univ. Pierre-et-Marie-Curie, Paris 6, France)*
Michel Raynal *(IRISA, Rennes, France)*
Andrea Richa *(Arizona State University, USA)*
Luis Rodrigues *(IST, ULisboa, Portugal)*
Elad Schiller *(Chalmers University Technology, Sweden)*
Robert Soulé *(USI, Lugano, Switzerland)*
Paul Spirakis *(University Liverpool, UK and CTI, Greece)*
Gadi Taubenfeld *(IDC Herzliya, Israel)*
Nitin Vaidya *(University of Illinois, USA)*
Robbert van Renesse *(Cornell University, USA)*
Jennifer Welch *(Texas A&M University, USA)*

**External Reviewers:**

Amr Abdelnabi
Andres Abeliuk
Chrysovalandis Agathangelou
Dan Alistarh
Luciana Arantes
Maya Arbel
Sergio Arevalo
James Aspnes
Chen Avin
Mathias Bæk Tejs Knudsen
Leonid Barenboim
Joffroy Beauquier
Luca Becchetti
Oren Becker
Allan Borodin
Sébastien Bouchard
Marjorie Bournat
Zohir Bouzid
Quentin Bramas
Janna Burman
Costas Busch
Eleni C. Akrida
Roberto Calvo-Palomino
Armando Castañeda
Arnaud Casteigts
Himanshu Chauhan
Vicent Cholvi
Koen Claessen
Andrea Clementi
Natacha Crooks
Andrzej Czygrinow
Shantanu Das
Ajoy Datta
Gianluca De Marco
Antonella Del Pozzo
Argyrios Deligkas
Roman Dementiev
Stéphane Devismes
Giuseppe Di Luna
Yoann Dieudonne
Anaïs Durand
Adem Efe Gencer
Michael Elkin
Yuval Emek
Ittay Eyal
Luis F. Chiroque
Sergey Frenkel
Leszek Gasieniec
Cyril Gavoille
Rati Gelashvili
Ran Gelles
Golnaz Ghasemiesfeh
Nikolaos Kallimanis
Xiaohan Kang
Liran Katzir
Idit Keidar

**External Reviewers: (continued)**

Alex Kogan
Christian Konrad
Amos Korman
Petr Kuznetsov
Arnaud Labourel
Ioannis Lamprou
Theodoros Gkountouvas
Alexey Gotsman
Vincent Gramoli
Theophanis Hadjistasi
Nicolas Hanusse
Maurice Herlihy
Lisa Higham
Heidi Howard
Justin Hsu
Nicole Immorlica
Taisuke Izumi
Colette Johnen
Christoph Lenzen
Nikos Leonardos
Quanquan Liu
Zhiyu Liu
Adrian Loch
Federico Lombardi
Zvi Lotker
Bernardo M. David
Víctor M. López Millán
Mahyar Malekpour
Frederik Mallmann-Trenn
Ioannis Marcoullis
Darryl Mcadams
Themistoklis Melissourgos
Hammurabi Mendes
George Mertzios
Othon Michail
Matthew Milano
Adam Morrison
Achour Mostéfaoui
Cameron Musco
Danupon Nanongkai
Prakash Narayana Moorthy
Ofer Neiman
Nicolas Nicolaou
Rotem Oshman
Roberto Palmieri
Giorgos Panagiotakos
Gopal Pandurangan
David Peleg
Richard Peng
Thomas Petig
Seth Pettie
Tsvetomira Radeva
Sergio Rajsbaum
Christoforos Raptopoulos
Netanel Raviv
Peter Robinson
Paolo Romano
Thomas Ropars
Stephane Rovedakis
Alexander Russell
Joel Rybicki
Jared Saia
Nicola Santoro
Vikram Saraph
Nicholas Schiefer
Johannes Schneider
Gregory Schwartzman
Michele Scquizzato
Kevin Sekniqi
Andres Sevilla
Isaac Sheff
Umair Siddique
Shikha Singh
Yannis Stamatiou
Aikaterini-Panagiota Stouka
Hsin-Hao Su
Jukka Suomela
Nathalie Sznajder
Sebastien Tixeuil
Corentin Travers
Lewis Tseng
José Verschae
Laurent Viennot
Giovanni Viglietta
Vincent Villain
Wojciech Wawrzyniak
Qin Xin
Thomas Zacharias
Akka Zemmari
Hong-Sheng Zhou
Leqi Zhu
Dionysis Zindros

# Sponsors & Supporters of PODC 2017

Sponsors: SIGACT SIGOPS

Supporters: amazon web services IBM Research Oracle Labs vmware

# The 2017 Edsger W. Dijkstra Prize in Distributed Computing

The Edsger W. Dijkstra Prize in Distributed Computing was created to acknowledge outstanding papers on the principles of distributed computing whose significance and impact on the theory or practice of distributed computing have been evident for at least a decade. The Prize is sponsored jointly by the ACM Symposium on Principles of Distributed Computing (PODC) and the EATCS Symposium on Distributed Computing (DISC). This award is presented annually, with the presentation taking place alternately at PODC and DISC.

The 2017 Award Committee, composed of Alexander Schwarzmann (Chair), Marcos K. Aguilera, Alessandro Panconesi, Andrzej Pelc, Andrea Richa, and Roger Wattenhofer, has selected

**Elizabeth Borowsky and Eli Gafni**

to receive the 2017 Edsger W. Dijkstra Prize in Distributed Computing for the outstanding paper:

Elizabeth Borowsky, Eli Gafni:
**Generalized FLP impossibility result for t-resilient asynchronous computations.**
Proceedings of the 25th Annual ACM Symposium on Theory of Computing (STOC 1993), pages 91–100, 1993.
http://dl.acm.org/citation.cfm?doid=167088.167119

This is a fundamental paper in the original sense. It contains two breakthrough contributions. First, it lays a new concept of read-write simulations in the very foundation of distributed computing. Second, it introduces the *immediate-snapshot* model. For the first contribution, the paper argues that, even though distributed systems exhibit multiple seemingly incomparable instantiations, they operate on the same fundamental principles. By deriving these principles, we could obtain computability and complexity results concerning a given specific distributed system via simulations and reductions.

The paper illustrates this approach by proposing an ingenious simulation tool, now commonly referred to as the *BG Simulation*. The tool allows a system of $k + 1$ processes to consistently *simulate* algorithms designed for any *k-resilient* system. The BG Simulation proved to be instrumental in establishing impossibility results and building reductions between them. In particular, this paper uses the BG Simulation to derive the fundamental impossibility of $k$-resilient $k$-set consensus from the impossibility of *wait-free* set consensus.

The second key contribution, the immediate-snapshot model, leads to a simple and elegant combinatorial characterization of the set of runs of a protocol. This characterization then leads to the impossibility of wait-free set consensus through a simple application of Sperner's Lemma.

These two points—the use of a simpler model of computation to establish the wait-free set-consensus impossibility and the use of simulation to derive the generalized $k$-resilient impossibility from the wait-free one—distinguishes this paper from two concurrent papers appeared at STOC 1993, by Herlihy and Shavit and by Saks and Zaharoglou, journal versions of which were later awarded the prestigious Gödel prize.

Since 1993, both contributions of this paper were widely adopted by the distributed-computing community. The illuminating BG Simulation technique gave rise to a broad spectrum of results in various contexts: from adversarial shared-memory computing to mobile Byzantine robots. The BG simulation and abstractions around it establish now the very basis of the state-of-the-art research field of distributed computability theory. The (iterated) immediate-snapshot model is widely adopted nowadays in combinatorial representations of distributed computations. As was correctly conjectured by the authors in a concurrent paper, the *protocol complex* of this model is precisely captured by the *standard chromatic subdivision*, enabling straightforward reasoning about the model's computability. The two contributions also help us in *teaching* the foundations of resilience: it is much easier to deal with the wait-free model, and deduce computability of other models via simulation.

In summary, this paper turned out to be crucial for our understanding of fault-tolerant distributed computing. It proposed a powerful reduction technique, the BG simulation, it introduced the immediate-snapshot model, and it established the fundamental impossibility of $k$-resilient $k$-set consensus.

Yehuda Afek, *Tel Aviv University, Israel*
Rachid Guerraoui, *EPFL, Switzerland*
Taisuke Izumi, *Nagoya Institute of Technology, Japan*
Petr Kuznetsov, *Télécom ParisTech, France*

# The 2017 Principles of Distributed Computing Doctoral Dissertation Award

The winner of the 2017 Principles of Distributed Computing Doctoral Dissertation Award is Dr. **Mohsen Ghaffari**, for his dissertation **"Improved Distributed Algorithms for Fundamental Graph Problems**," written under the supervision of Prof. Nancy Lynch at the Massachusetts Institute of Technology.

Ghaffari's thesis represents an extraordinary study of network algorithms which is, at the same time, both deep and extensive. Many of the results included in this thesis (5, to be precise) have already been awarded "Best Student Paper" award or "Best Paper" award (and sometimes both) in top-notch conferences. The number of publications produced by Ghaffari while working on his thesis is also staggering (over 35 papers!): the thesis covers only a small part of his work. Most important, Ghaffari made a very significant contribution to the Theory of Network Algorithms, particularly to randomized network algorithms.

Specifically, the thesis contains three parts. In the first part, a new randomized algorithm for the Maximal Independent Set (MIS) problem is developed. The algorithm is simple and local in a strong sense: the termination time of a node depends only the coin-tosses within distance 2. This algorithm improves on all previous results and thus leads to improved time complexity in the many applications that use MIS as a building block. In the second part, Ghaffari presents results concerning vertex- and edge-connectivity in graphs, with applications to different problems such as Connected Dominated Set and Minimum Spanning Tree computation. And in the last part of the thesis, following classical packet routing results, scheduling multiple network tasks concurrently is considered. It is shown that in fact, there may be an unavoidable logarithmic gap between the case of packet routing and general tasks, but on the positive side, we never need to pay more than a single logarithmic factor (beyond the "congestion+dilation" lower bound) to schedule multiple tasks.

**The award.** The award is sponsored jointly by the ACM Symposium on Principles of Distributed Computing (PODC) and the EATCS Symposium on Distributed Computing (DISC). This award is presented annually, with the presentation taking place alternately at PODC and DISC. The 2017 award will be presented at PODC 2017, to be held in Washington DC, USA.

The 2017 Principles of Distributed Computing Doctoral Dissertation Award Committee:

Cyril Gavoille, *LaBRI, U. Bordeaux*
Boaz Patt-Shamir, *Chair, Tel Aviv University*
Michel Raynal, *IRISA, U. Rennes 1*
Gadi Taubenfeld, *IDC*

# Invited Talk: Some Sequential Algorithms are Almost Always Parallel

Guy E. Blelloch
Carnegie Mellon University
Pittsburgh, PA, USA
guyb@cs.cmu.edu

## ABSTRACT

Over the years many interesting and efficient parallel algorithms have been developed to solve a wide variety of problems, but not much attention has been paid to studying the inherent parallelism in sequential algorithms—i.e., understanding the depth of their dependence structure, and how shallow dependence structures might be used to develop efficient parallel implementations.

In this talk I will describe recent work on analyzing the dependence depth of iterative sequential algorithms—ones that loop over a collection of elements. Many of these algorithms have deep dependence chains in the worst case, but shallow chains (polylog w.h.p.) if the elements are randomly ordered. Examples include many fundamental algorithms: the Knuth shuffle for random permutations, sorting by insertion into a binary search tree, greedy maximal independent set (MIS), greedy maximal matching, greedy graph-coloring, counting cycles in a permutation, incremental k-dimensional linear programming, and incremental 2d Delaunay triangulation. An advantage of the approach is that it can lead to very simple and efficient parallel algorithms. Our MIS algorithm, for example can be coded in a dozen or so lines, and is significantly faster than Luby's algorithm on modern multicore machines. Also the approach encourages snapping the view that sequential and parallel algorithms are distinct, and instead thinking of algorithms, in general, as collections of instructions with dependences among them


*PODC'17 & SPAA'17, July 24-27, 2017, Washington, DC, USA.*

ACM ISBN 978-1-4503-4992-5/17/07 & 978-1-4503-4593-4/17/07.
DOI: http://dx.doi.org/10.1145/3087801.3087871

## BIOGRAPHY

Guy Blelloch is a Professor of Computer Science at Carnegie Mellon University. He received a BA in Physics and BS in Engineering from Swarthmore College in 1983, and a PhD in Computer Science from MIT in 1988. His research interests are in algorithms and programming languages and how they interact, with an emphasis on parallel computation. He has worked on programming-language based cost models along with provable implementation bounds, on bounding costs in runtime scheduling and parallel garbage collection, and designed the Nesl programming language. He has developed a variety of parallel algorithms, including algorithms for graph connectivity, set cover, semi sorting, suffix trees, balanced trees, hashing, shortest paths, and Delaunay triangulation. His work has both been in models that are communication conscious, e.g. accounting for caching, and not. He is most proud of developing a sophomore level algorithms and data structures course at Carnegie Mellon in which parallelism is taught from the start. He is an ACM Fellow for his contributions in parallel computation, and was general chair of the ACM Symposium on Parallelism in Algorithms and Architecture (SPAA) from 2011-2015.

# Exploiting Spontaneous Transmissions for Broadcasting and Leader Election in Radio Networks*

Artur Czumaj
Centre for Discrete Mathematics and its Applications
Department of Computer Science
University of Warwick
A.Czumaj@warwick.ac.uk

Peter Davies
Centre for Discrete Mathematics and its Applications
Department of Computer Science
University of Warwick
P.W.Davies@warwick.ac.uk

## ABSTRACT

We study two fundamental communication primitives: *broadcasting* and *leader election* in the classical model of multi-hop radio networks with unknown topology and without collision detection mechanisms. It has been known for almost 20 years that in undirected networks with $n$ nodes and diameter $D$, randomized broadcasting requires $\Omega(D \log \frac{n}{D} + \log^2 n)$ rounds in expectation, assuming that uninformed nodes are not allowed to communicate (until they are informed). Only very recently, Haeupler and Wajc (PODC'2016) showed that this bound can be slightly improved for the model with spontaneous transmissions, providing an $O(D\frac{\log n \log\log n}{\log D} + \log^{O(1)} n)$-time broadcasting algorithm. In this paper, we give a new and faster algorithm that completes broadcasting in $O(D\frac{\log n}{\log D} + \log^{O(1)} n)$ time, with high probability. This yields the first optimal $O(D)$-time broadcasting algorithm whenever $D$ is polynomial in $n$.

Furthermore, our approach can be applied to design a new leader election algorithm that matches the performance of our broadcasting algorithm. Previously, all fast randomized leader election algorithms have been using broadcasting as their subroutine and their complexity have been asymptotically strictly bigger than the complexity of broadcasting. In particular, the fastest previously known randomized leader election algorithm of Ghaffari and Haeupler (SODA'2013) requires $O(D \log \frac{n}{D} \min\{\log\log n, \log \frac{n}{D}\} + \log^{O(1)} n)$-time with high probability. Our new algorithm requires $O(D\frac{\log n}{\log D} + \log^{O(1)} n)$ time with high probability, and it achieves the optimal $O(D)$ time whenever $D$ is polynomial in $n$.

## CCS CONCEPTS

• **Theory of computation** → **Distributed algorithms**; • **Networks** → *Network algorithms*;

## KEYWORDS

Broadcasting; Leader Election; Radio Networks

*Research partially supported by the Centre for Discrete Mathematics and its Applications (DIMAP) and by EPSRC award EP/N011163/1.


*PODC '17, July 25-27, 2017, Washington, DC, USA*

ACM ISBN 978-1-4503-4992-5/17/07...$15.00
http://dx.doi.org/10.1145/3087801.3087825

## 1 INTRODUCTION

### 1.1 Model of communication networks

We consider the classical model of *ad-hoc radio networks* with *unknown structure*. A *radio network* is modeled by an *undirected* network $\mathfrak{N} = (V, E)$, where the set of nodes corresponds to the set of transmitter-receiver stations. An edge $\{v, u\} \in E$ means that node $v$ can send a message directly to node $u$ and vice versa. To make propagation of information feasible, we assume that $\mathfrak{N}$ is connected.

In accordance with the standard model of unknown (ad-hoc) radio networks (for more elaborate discussion about the model, see, e.g., [1, 3, 4, 6, 7, 11–13, 15, 17, 19]), we make the assumption that a node does not have any prior knowledge about the topology of the network, its in-degree and out-degree, or the set of its neighbors. We assume that the only knowledge of each node is the *size* of the network $n$ and the *diameter* of the network $D$. For our algorithms, knowledge of only a linear upper bound for these values will suffice.

Nodes operate in discrete, synchronous time steps. When we refer to the "running time" of an algorithm, we mean the number of time steps which elapse before completion (i.e., we are not concerned with the number of calculations nodes perform within time steps). In each time step a node can either *transmit* a message to all of its out-neighbors at once or can remain silent and *listen* to the messages from its in-neighbors. We do not make any restriction on the size of messages, though the algorithms we present can easily be made to operate under the condition of $O(\log n)$-bit transmissions.

A further important feature of the model considered in this paper is that it allows *spontaneous transmissions*, that is, any node can transmit if it so wishes. In some prior works (see, e.g., [4, 10, 17]), it has been assumed (typically for the broadcasting problem) that uninformed nodes are not allowed to communicate (until they are informed). While this assumption is natural for the broadcasting problem, it is meaningless for the leader election problem, and so, throughout the paper we will allow spontaneous transmissions.

The distinguishing feature of radio networks is the interfering behavior of transmissions. In the most standard radio networks model, the *model without collision detection* (see, e.g., [1, 3, 7, 19]), which is studied in this paper, if a node $v$ listens in a given round and precisely one of its in-neighbors transmits, then $v$ receives the message. In all other cases $v$ receives nothing; in particular, the lack of collision detection means that $v$ is unable to distinguish between zero of its in-neighbors transmitting and more than one.

The model without collision detection describes the most restrictive interfering behavior of transmissions; also considered in the literature is a less restrictive variant, the model with collision detection, where a node listening can distinguish between zero of its in-neighbors transmitting and more than one (cf. [12, 19]).

## 1.2 Key communications primitives: Broadcasting, leader election, and COMPETE

In this paper we consider two fundamental communications primitives: *broadcasting* and *leader election*. We present randomized algorithms that perform these tasks *with high probability* (i.e., $1 - n^{-c}$ for an arbitrary constant $c$), and analyze worst-case running time.

*Broadcasting* is one of the most fundamental problems in communication networks and has been extensively studied for many decades (see, e.g., [19] and the references therein). The premise of the broadcasting task is that one particular node, called the *source*, has a message which must become known to all other nodes. As such, broadcasting is one of the most basic means of global communication in a network.

*Leader Election* is another most fundamental problems in communication networks that aims to ensure that all nodes agree on such a designated leader. Specifically, at the conclusion of a leader election algorithm, all nodes should output the same node ID, and precisely one node should identify this ID as its own. Leader election is a fundamental primitive in distributed computations and, as the most basic means of breaking symmetry within radio networks, it is used as a preliminary step in many more complex communication tasks. For example, many fast multi-message communication protocols require construction of a breadth-first search tree (or some similar variant), which in turn requires a single node to act as source (for more examples, cf. [5, 11], and the references therein).

To design efficient algorithms for broadcasting and leader election, we will be studying an auxiliary problem that we call COMPETE. COMPETE has a similar flavor to broadcasting, but instead of transmitting a single message from a single source to all nodes in the network, it takes as its input a source set $S \subseteq V$, in which every source $s \in S$ has a message (of integer value) it wishes to propagate, and guarantees that upon completion all nodes in $\mathfrak{N}$ know the highest-valued source message.

It is easy to see how the COMPETE process generalizes broadcasting: it is simply invoked with the source as the only member of the set $S$. To perform leader election, one can probabilistically generate a small set (e.g., of size $\Omega(\log n)$) of candidate leaders, and then perform COMPETE using this set, with *IDs* as the messages to be propagated. Therefore, to design an efficient randomized broadcasting and leader election algorithms, it is sufficient to design a fast randomized algorithm for COMPETE (cf. Section 5).

## 1.3 Previous work

As a fundamental communications primitive, the task of *broadcasting* has been extensively studied for various network models, see, e.g., [19] and the references therein.

For the model studied in this paper, undirected radio networks with unknown structure and without collision detection, the first non-trivial major result was due to Bar-Yehuda et al. [3], who, in a seminal paper, designed an almost optimal randomized broadcasting algorithm achieving the running time of $O((D + \log n) \cdot \log n)$ with high probability. This bound was later improved by Czumaj and Rytter [10], and independently Kowalski and Pelc [16], who gave randomized broadcasting algorithms that complete the task in $O(D \log \frac{n}{D} + \log^2 n)$ time with high probability. Importantly, all these algorithms were assuming that nodes are not allowed to transmit spontaneously, i.e., they must wait to receive the source message before they can begin to participate. Indeed, for the model with no spontaneous transmissions allowed, it has been known that any randomized broadcasting algorithm requires $\Omega(D \log \frac{n}{D} + \log^2 n)$ time [1, 17]. Only very recently, Haeupler and Wajc [13] demonstrated that allowing spontaneous transmissions can lead to faster broadcasting algorithms, by designing a randomized algorithm that completes broadcasting in $O(D \frac{\log n \log\log n}{\log D} + \log^{O(1)} n)$ time, with high probability. This is the only algorithm (that we are aware of) that beats the lower bound of $\Omega(D \log \frac{n}{D} + \log^2 n)$ [1, 17] in the model with no spontaneous transmissions. Given that for the model that allows spontaneous transmissions any broadcasting algorithm requires $\Omega(D + \log^2)$ time (cf. [1, 19]), the algorithm due to Haeupler and Wajc [13] is *almost optimal* (up to an $O(\log \log n)$ factor) whenever $D$ is polynomial in $n$.

Broadcasting has been also studied in various related models, including directed networks, deterministic broadcasting protocols, models with collision detection, and models in which the entire network structure is known. For example, in the model with collision detection, an $O(D + \log^6 n)$-time randomized algorithm due to Ghaffari et al. [12] is the first to exploit collisions and surpass the algorithms for broadcasting without collision detection. For deterministic protocols, the best results are an $O(n \log D \log \log D)$-time algorithm in directed networks [9], and an $O(n \log D)$-time algorithm in undirected networks [14].

For more details about broadcasting in various model, see, e.g., [19] and the references therein.

The problem of *leader election* has also been extensively studied in the distributed computing community for several decades. For the model considered in this paper, it is known that a simple reduction (see, e.g., [2]), involving performing a network-wide binary search for the highest ID using broadcasting as a subroutine every step, requires $O(T_{BC} \log n)$ time. Here $T_{BC}$ is time taken to perform broadcasting (provided the broadcasting algorithm used can be extended to work from multiple sources). This yields leader election randomized algorithms taking time $O(D \log \frac{n}{D} \log n + \log^3 n)$ using the broadcasting algorithms of [10, 16], or $O(D \frac{\log^2 n \log\log n}{\log D} + \log^{O(1)} n)$ using the broadcasting algorithm of [13]. This approach has been improved only very recently by Ghaffari and Haeupler [11], who took a more complex approach to achieve an $O(D \log \frac{n}{D} + \log^3 n) \cdot \min\{\log \log n, \log \frac{n}{D}\}$ time algorithm based on growing clusters within the network. Notice that in the regime of large $D$ being polynomial in $n$, when $D \approx n^c$ for a constant $c$, $0 < c < 1$, the fastest leader election algorithm achieves the (high probability) running time of $O(D \log n \log \log n)$.

Leader election has also been studied in various related settings. For example, one can achieve $O(T_{BC})$ expected (rather than worst case) running time [8], or time $O(T_{BC}\sqrt{\log n})$ with high probability even for directed networks [8], and deterministically time $O(n \log n \log D \log\log D)$ [9] or $O(n \log^{3/2} n \sqrt{\log\log n})$ [5].

## 1.4 New results

In this paper we extend the approach recently developed by Haeupler and Wajc [13] to design a fast randomized algorithm for COMPETE, running in time $O(D\frac{\log n}{\log D} + |S|D^{0.125} + \log^{O(1)} n)$, with high probability (Theorem 4.1). By applying this algorithm to the broadcasting problem (Theorem 5.1) and to the leader election problem (Theorem 5.2), we obtain randomized algorithms for both these problems running in time $O(D\frac{\log n}{\log D} + \log^{O(1)} n)$, with high probability. For $D = \Omega(\log^c n)$ for a sufficiently large constant $c$, these running time bounds improve the fastest previous algorithms for broadcasting and leader election by factors $O(\log\log n)$ and $O(\log n \log\log n)$, respectively. More importantly, whenever $D$ is polynomial in $n$ (i.e., $D = \Omega(n^\varepsilon)$, for some positive constant $\varepsilon$), this running time is $O(D)$, which is asymptotically optimal since time $D$ is required for any information to traverse the network.

Our algorithms are the first to achieve optimality over this range of parameters, and are also the first instance (in our model) of leader election time being asymptotically equal to fastest broadcasting time, since the former is usually a harder task in radio network models.

Finally, even though the current lower bounds for the randomized broadcasting and leader election problems are $\Omega(D+\log^2 n)$, we would not be surprised if our upper bounds $O(D\frac{\log n}{\log D} + \log^{O(1)} n)$ were tight for $D = \Omega(\log^c n)$ for some sufficiently large constant $c$.

*Note:* We assume throughout that $D = \Omega(\log^c n)$ for some sufficiently large constant $c$. If this is not the case, then the $O(D \log \frac{n}{D} + \log^2 n)$-time algorithm of [10, 16] should be used instead.

# 2 APPROACH

Our approach to study COMPETE (and hence also broadcasting and leader election problems) follows the methodology recently applied for fast distributed communication primitives by Ghaffari, Haeupler, and others (see, e.g., [11, 13]). In order to solve the problem, we split computations into three parts. First, all nodes in the network will communicate with their local neighborhood to create some clustering of the network. Then, using this clustering, the nodes will perform some computations within each cluster, so that all nodes in the cluster share some useful knowledge. Finally, the knowledge from the clusters will be utilized to efficiently perform global communication.

## 2.1 Clusterings, PARTITION, and schedulings

To implement this approach efficiently, we follow a similar line to that of Haeupler and Wajc [13] and rely on a clustering procedure of Miller et al. [18], adapted for the radio network model.

LEMMA 2.1 (LEMMA 3.1 OF [13]). *Let $0 < \beta \leq 1$. Any network on $n$ nodes can be partitioned into clusters each with strong diameter $O(\frac{\log n}{\beta})$ with high probability, and every edge cut by this partition with probability $O(\beta)$. This algorithm can be implemented in the radio network setting in $O(\frac{\log^3 n}{\beta})$ rounds.*

The network being partitioned into clusters means that each node identifies one particular node as its *cluster center*, the subgraph of nodes identifying any particular node as their cluster center is connected, and any node which is a cluster center to anyone must be cluster center to itself. Here the term *"strong diameter"* refers to diameter using only edges within the relevant cluster.

The clustering provided by the application of Lemma 2.1 will be denoted by PARTITION($\beta$).

This framework will be used in our central result, Theorem 2.2, which states that upon applying PARTITION($\beta$) with $\beta$ randomly chosen from some range polynomial in $D$, with constant probability the expected distance from some fixed node to its cluster center is $O(\frac{\log n}{\beta \log D})$.

THEOREM 2.2. *Let $j$ be an integer chosen uniformly at random between $0.01 \log D$ and $0.1 \log D$, and let $\beta = 2^{-j}$. For any node $v$, with probability at least $0.55$ (over choice of $j$), the expected distance from $v$ to its cluster center upon applying PARTITION($\beta$) is $O(\frac{\log n}{\beta \log D})$.*

We will sketch the very technical proof of this result in Appendix, in Section A; for a complete proof of Theorem 2.2, we refer to the full version of this paper[1]. This result applies to the clustering method in any setting, not just radio networks, and hence may well be of independent interest. It improves over the result of [13] that expected distance to cluster center is $O(\frac{\log n \log\log n}{\beta \log D})$.

The approach described above is combined with a means of communicating within clusters from [12] using the notion of *schedules*.

LEMMA 2.3 (LEMMA 2.1 OF [13]). *A network of diameter $D$ and with $n$ nodes can be preprocessed in $O(D \log^{O(1)} n)$ rounds, yielding a* ***schedule*** *which allows for one-to-all broadcast of $k$ messages in $O(D + k \log n + \log^6 n)$ rounds with high probability. This schedule satisfies the following properties:*

- *for some prescribed node $r$, the schedule transmits messages to and from nodes at distance $\ell$ from $r$ in $O(\ell + \log^6 n)$ rounds with high probability;*
- *the schedule is periodic with period $O(\log n)$: it can be thought of as restarting every $O(\log n)$ steps.*

Whenever we refer to computing or using *schedules* during our algorithms, we mean using the method from Lemma 2.3. We note that, as shown in Lemma 4.2 of [13], we can perform this preprocessing in such a way that it succeeds with high probability despite collisions, at a multiplicative $O(\log^{O(1)} n)$ time cost.

## 2.2 Algorithm structure

The general approach then proceeds as follows: first there is a preprocessing phase, in which we partition the network using PARTITION($\beta$) from Lemma 2.1, and compute schedules within the clusters using Lemma 2.3. Then we broadcast the message through the network using these computed schedules within clusters. Any shortest $(u, v)$-path $p$ crosses $O(|p|\beta)$ clusters in expectation, and communication within these clusters takes $O(\frac{\log n}{\beta \log D})$ expected time, so total time required should be $O(|p|\frac{\log n}{\log D}) = O(D\frac{\log n}{\log D})$.

[1] Available at https://arxiv.org/abs/1703.01859.

Of course, this omits many of the technical details, and we encounter several difficulties when trying to implement the approach. Firstly, Theorem 2.2 only bounds expected distance to cluster center with constant probability. However, by generating many different clusterings, with different random values of $\beta$, and curtailing application of the schedules after $O(\frac{\log n}{\beta \log D})$ time, we can ensure that we do make sufficient progress with high probability. A second issue is that these values of $\beta$ must somehow be coordinated, which we solve by using an extra layer of "coarse" clusters, similarly to [13]. Thirdly, collisions can occur between nodes of different clusters during both precomputation and broadcasting phases. We take several measures to deal with these collisions in our algorithms and analysis.

## 2.3 Advances over previous works

The idea of performing some precomputation locally and then using this local knowledge to perform a global task occurs frequently in distributed computing. In our setting, the most similar prior work is the $O(D\frac{\log n \log\log n}{\log D} + \log^{O(1)} n)$-time broadcasting algorithm due to Haeupler and Wajc [13]. Here we summarize our main technical differences from that paper and other related works:

- It was known from [13] that when PARTITION($\beta$) is run with $1/\beta$ randomly selected from a range polynomial in $D$, the expected distance from a node to its cluster center is $O(\frac{\log n \log\log n}{\beta \log D})$. We improve this result with Theorem 2.2, which states that with constant probability this distance is $O(\frac{\log n}{\beta \log D})$.
- We demonstrate how, by switching clusterings frequently and curtailing their schedules after $O(\frac{\log n}{\beta \log D})$ time, we can improve the fastest time for broadcasting in radio networks.
- We show that, with a different method of analysis and an algorithmic background process to deal with collisions, we can extend this method to also complete leader election, a task usually more difficult.

# 3 ALGORITHM FOR COMPETE

Since our broadcasting and leader election protocols require the same asymptotic running time and use similar methods (cf. Section 5), we can combine their workings into a single generalized procedure COMPETE.

COMPETE takes as input a source set $S$, in which every source $s \in S$ has a message it wishes to propagate, and guarantees, with high probability, that upon completion all nodes know the highest-valued source message. The process takes $O(D\frac{\log n}{\log D} + |S|D^{0.125} + \log^{O(1)} n)$ time (cf. Theorem 4.1), which is within the $O(D\frac{\log n}{\log D} + \log^{O(1)} n)$ time claimed for broadcasting and leader election, as long as $|S| = O(D^{0.875})$.

Our efficient algorithm for COMPETE consists of two processes which run concurrently, alternating between steps of each. The main COMPETE process is designed to propagate messages quickly through most of the network, and the background process is slower, with the purpose of "papering over the cracks" in the main process; in this case that means passing messages across coarse cluster boundaries.

**Algorithm 1** COMPETE($S$)

1) Compute a *coarse clustering* using PARTITION($\beta$) with $\beta = \frac{1}{\sqrt{D}}$.
2) Compute a schedule within each coarse cluster.
3) Within each coarse cluster, for each integer $j$, $0.01 \log D \leq j \leq 0.1 \log D$, compute $D^{0.2}$ different *fine clusterings* using PARTITION($\beta$) with $\beta = 2^{-j}$.
4) Compute schedules within all fine clusterings.
5) Each coarse cluster center computes a $D^{0.99}$-length sequence of randomly chosen fine clusterings to use.
6) Transmit this sequence within each coarse cluster, using the coarse cluster schedules.
7) For each fine clustering in the sequence perform INTRA-CLUSTER PROPAGATION($O(\frac{\log n}{\beta \log D})$) (with the value of $\beta$ corresponding to the fine clustering).

In the main process, we first compute a *coarse clustering*, that is, one with comparatively large clusters, which we need to spread shared randomness. Then, within the coarse clusters we compute many different *fine clusterings*, i.e., sub-clusterings with smaller clusters. These are the clusterings we will use to propagate information through the network. The coarse clusters generate and transmit a random sequence of these fine clusterings, which tells their members in what order to use the fine clusterings for this propagation (this was the sole purpose of the coarse clustering). We show that, when applying INTRA-CLUSTER PROPAGATION($O(\frac{\log n}{\beta \log D})$) on a clustering with $\beta$ chosen at random, we have a constant probability of making sufficient progress towards our goal of information propagation. We can treat the progress made during each application of INTRA-CLUSTER PROPAGATION as being independent, since we use a different random clustering each time (and with high probability, whenever we choose a clustering we have used before, we have made sufficient progress in between so that the clusters we are analyzing are far apart and behave independently). Therefore we can use a Chernoff bound to show that with high probability we make sufficient progress throughout the algorithm as a whole.

An issue with the main process, though, is that at the boundaries of the coarse clustering, collisions between coarse clusters can cause INTRA-CLUSTER PROPAGATION to fail. To rectify this, *we interleave steps of the main process with steps of a background process* (Algorithm 2), e.g., by performing the main process during even time-steps and the background process during odd time-steps.

**Algorithm 2** COMPETE($S$) - BACKGROUND PROCESS

1) Compute $D^{0.2}$ different *fine clusterings* using PARTITION($\beta$) with $\beta = D^{-0.1}$.
2) Compute a schedule within each cluster, for each clustering.
3) Cycling through clusterings in round-robin order, perform INTRA-CLUSTER PROPAGATION($O(\frac{\log n}{\beta})$).

The background process is simpler: it follows a similar line to the main process, but does not use a coarse clustering, only fine clusterings. This means that we do not have the shared randomness we use in the main process, so we cannot choose $\beta$ randomly (we instead fix $\beta = D^{-0.1}$) and we cannot use a random ordering of fine clusterings (we instead use a round-robin order). As a result, we must run Intra-Cluster Propagation for longer to achieve a constant probability of making good progress, and so the propagation of information is slower (if we were to rely on the background process alone, we would only achieve $O(D \log n + \log^{O(1)} n)$ time).

However, the upside is that there are no coarse cluster boundaries, and so the progress is made consistently throughout the network. Therefore, we can analyze the progress of our algorithm using the faster main process most of the time, and switching to analysis of the background process when the main process reaches a coarse cluster boundary. Since the coarse clusters are comparatively large, their boundaries are reached infrequently, and so we can show that overall the algorithm still makes progress quickly.

Both Compete processes make use of Intra-Cluster Propagation as a primitive, which makes use of the computed clusters and schedule to propagate information. Specifically, the procedure facilitates communication between the cluster center and nodes within $\ell$ hops.

**Algorithm 3** Intra-Cluster Propagation($\ell$)

1) Broadcast the highest message known by the cluster center to all nodes within $\ell$ distance.
2) All such nodes which know a higher message participate in a broadcast towards the cluster center.
3) Broadcast the highest message known by the cluster center to all nodes within $\ell$ distance.

Here we apply Lemma 2.3: after computing schedules, it is possible to broadcast between the cluster center and nodes at distance at most $\ell$ in time $O(\ell + \log^{O(1)} n)$. That is, on an outward broadcast all nodes within distance $\ell$ of the cluster center hear its message, and on an inward broadcast the cluster center hears the message of at least one participating node. This would be sufficient in isolation, but since we perform Intra-Cluster Propagation within all fine clusters at the same time, we will describe a background process (Algorithm 4) to deal with collisions between fine clusters in the same coarse cluster. As before, we intersperse the steps of the main process and background process, performing one step of each alternately.

**Algorithm 4** Intra-Cluster Propagation Background Process

Repeat until main process is complete:
**for** $i = 1$ to $\log n$ **do**
  with probability $2^{-i}$ (coordinated in each cluster) perform one round of Decay;
  otherwise remain silent for $\log n$ steps.
**end for**

The background process aims to individually inform nodes that border other fine clusters, and therefore may have collisions that prevent them from participating properly in the main process. The goal is to ensure that eventually (we will bound the amount of time that we may have to wait), such a node's cluster will be the only neighboring cluster to perform Decay (Algorithm 5), which ensures that the node will then hear its cluster's message (with constant probability).

The Decay protocol, first introduced by Bar-Yehuda et al. [3], is a fundamental transmission primitive employed by many randomized radio network communication algorithms.

**Algorithm 5** Decay at a node $v$

**for** $i = 1$ **to** $\log n$, in time step $i$ **do**:
  $v$ transmits its message with probability $2^{-i}$.

Lemma 3.1 ([3]). *After a single round of Decay, a node $v$ with at least one participating in-neighbor receives a message with constant probability.* □

## 4 ANALYSIS OF COMPETE ALGORITHM

In this section we prove the following guarantee on the behavior of Compete:

Theorem 4.1. *Compete(S) informs all nodes of the highest message in S within $O(\frac{D \log n}{\log D} + |S|D^{0.125} + \log^{O(1)} n)$ time-steps, with high probability.*

The precomputation phase of Compete, that is, steps 1-6 of the main process and steps 1-2 of the background process, requires $O(D^{0.99} \log^{O(1)} n) = O(D)$ time, and upon its completion we have all the schedules required to perform Intra-Cluster Propagation. As in [13], we can ignore collisions during these precomputation steps, since we can simulate each transmission step with $O(\log n)$ rounds of Decay to ensure their success without exceeding $O(D)$ total time.

We first prove a result that allows us to use Intra-Cluster Propagation to propagate messages through the network. During a fixed application of Intra-Cluster Propagation, we call a node *valid* if it can correctly send and receive messages to/from its cluster center despite collisions between fine clusters.

Lemma 4.2. *For some constant c, upon applying Intra-Cluster Propagation($\ell$) with $\ell = D^{\Omega(1)}$, a fixed node u at distance at most $\frac{\ell}{c}$ from its cluster center is valid with probability at least* 0.99.

Proof. Let $u$ be a node at distance $d$ from its cluster center, and call nodes on the shortest path from $u$ to the cluster center who border another fine cluster *risky*. We make use of a result of [13] (a corollary of Lemma 3.6 used during proof of Lemma 4.6) which states that any node is risky with probability $O(\beta)$. Therefore the expected number of risky nodes on the path is $O(d\beta)$.

Let $v$ be a risky node bordering $q$ fine clusters, and consider how long $v$ must wait to be informed if it has a neighbor in its own cluster who wishes to inform it. Whenever $2^{-i}$ is within a constant factor of $\frac{1}{q}$ during the background process, Decay has $\Omega(\frac{1}{q})$ probability of informing $v$ from its own cluster. This is because with probability $\Omega(\frac{1}{q})$, $v$'s cluster is the only cluster bordering $v$ to perform Decay, and in this case $v$ is informed with constant probability. Since this value of $2^{-i}$ recurs every $O(\log^2 n)$ steps, the time needed to inform $v$ is $O(q \log^2 n)$ in expectation.

We use another result from [13], Corollary 3.9, which states that with high probability all nodes border $O(\frac{\log n}{\log D}) = O(\log n)$ clusters. Therefore the total amount of time spent informing risky nodes is $O(d\beta \cdot \log^3 n) = O(d)$ in expectation, and since $O(d + \log^{O(1)} n)$ time is required to inform non-risky nodes using the main process, $u$ can communicate with its cluster center in $O(d + \log^{O(1)} n)$ expected time. By choosing sufficiently large $c$, by Markov's inequality $v$ is valid with probability at least 0.99. □

This will allow us to use Intra-Cluster Propagation to propagate information locally. To make a global argument, we will analyze the Compete algorithm's progress along paths by partitioning said paths into length $D^{0.12}$ subpaths. We call the set of all nodes within distance $D^{0.11}$ of a subpath its *neighborhood*, and we call a subpath *good* if all nodes in its neighborhood are in the same coarse cluster (and *bad* otherwise). We will show that we pass messages along good subpaths quickly under the main Compete process, and along bad subpaths more slowly under the background process.

To show that there are not too many bad subpaths, we make use of the following result from [13]:

Lemma 4.3 (Corollary 3.8 of [13]). *After running Partition($\beta$) the probability of a fixed node $u$ having nodes from $t$ distinct clusters at distance $d$ or less from $u$ is at most $(1 - e^{-\beta(2d+1)})^{t-1}$.* □

Therefore the probability of a node $u$ having nodes from two different coarse clusters within $D^{0.11}$ distance is at most

$$1 - e^{-D^{-0.5}(2D^{0.11}+1)} \leq 1 - e^{-3D^{-0.39}} \leq 3D^{-0.39} .$$

Taking the union bound over all nodes in a path, we find that any length-$D^{0.12}$ path is bad with probability upper bounded by $D^{0.12} \cdot 3D^{-0.39} \leq D^{-0.26}$.

Lemma 4.4. *All shortest paths $p$ between two vertices have $O(D^{0.63})$ bad subpaths, with high probability.*

Proof. Fix some shortest path $p$. As in the proof of Lemma 4.3 of [13], we first condition on the event that all exponentially distributed random variables $\delta_v$ used when computing the coarse clustering are at most $2D^{0.5} \log n$, which is the case with high probability (for details of how the clustering algorithm works see [13, 18]). Then, the events that two length-$D^{0.12}$ subpaths of distance at least $5D^{0.5} \log n$ apart are bad are independent, since they are not affected by any of the same $\delta_v$. If we label the length-$D^{0.12}$ subpaths of $p$ in order from one end of the path to the other, and group them by label mod $6D^{0.38} \log n$, then the badness of every subpath is independent from all the others in its group. Hence, the number of bad subpaths in each group is binomially distributed, and is $O(\frac{D}{D^{0.12} \cdot 6D^{0.38} \log n} \cdot D^{-0.26}) = O(D^{0.24})$ with high probability by a Chernoff bound. By the union bound over all of the groups, the total number of bad subpaths is $O(D^{0.62})$ with high probability. If we allow this amount to be as high as $O(D^{0.63})$, we can reduce the probability that we exceed it to $n^{-c}$ for an arbitrarily large constant $c$. We can then take a union bound over all $n^2$ shortest paths, and find that they all have $O(D^{0.63})$ bad subpaths with high probability. □

Having bounded the number of bad subpaths, we can show we can pass messages along them using the background process, quickly enough that we do not exceed the algorithm's stated running time in total. Note that here, and henceforth, we will refer to messages by their place in increasing order out of all messages of nodes in $S$. That is, by *message $j$* we mean the $j^{th}$ highest message in $S$.

Lemma 4.5 (***Bad subpaths***). *Let $p$ be any $(u, v)$-path of length at most $D^{0.12}$. Let $j$ be the minimum, over all nodes $v$ in $p$'s neighborhood, of the highest message known by $v$ at time-step $t$. If, at timestep $t$, $u$ knows a message higher than $j$, then by time-step $t' = t + O(D^{0.121})$ all nodes in $p$ know a message at least as high as $j + 1$ with high probability.*

Proof. We analyze only the background process, and consider separately each fine clustering used in the sequence between time-steps $t$ and $t'$. For any such clustering, let $w$ be the furthest node along $p$ which knows a message at least as high as $j + 1$. We call the clustering *good* if:

- all nodes in $w$'s cluster are $O(D^{0.1} \log n)$ distance from the cluster center;
- the node $x$ which is $\frac{D^{0.1}}{c}$ nodes along $p$ from $w$ is in its cluster as $w$;
- $x$ and $w$ are valid (recall that this means they succeed in Intra-Cluster Propagation).

By Lemma 2.1 the first event occurs with high probability, by Corollary 3.7 of [13], we can make the probability of the second event an arbitrarily high constant by our choice of $c$, and by Lemma 4.2 and the union bound, the third event occurs with probability at least $1 - 2(1 - 0.99) = 0.98$, conditioned on the first. Therefore the clustering is good with probability at least $\frac{1}{2}$, by applying the union bound again.

By a Chernoff bound, $\Omega(D^{0.02})$ of the clusterings applied between times $t$ and $t'$ will be good. Consider each good clustering in turn. After applying such a clustering, $w$'s cluster will be informed of an ID higher than $j$. Every time this occurs, $w$ advances at least $\frac{D^{0.1}}{c}$ steps, and so by time $t'$ the entire path knows a message at least as high as $j + 1$. □

We now make a similar argument for the good subpaths, but since we can use the main Compete process without fear of collisions from other coarse clusters, we get a better time bound:

Lemma 4.6 (***Good subpaths***). *Let $p$ be any good $(u, v)$-path of length at most $D^{0.12}$. Let $j$ be the minimum, over all nodes $v$ within $D^{0.11}$ distance $p$, of the highest message known by $v$ at time-step $t$. If, at timestep $t$, $u$ knows a message higher than $j$, then by time-step $t' = t + O(D^{0.12} \frac{\log n}{\log D})$ all nodes in $p$ know a message at least as high as $j + 1$ with high probability.*

Proof. We analyze only the main procedure, and consider separately each fine clustering used in the sequence between time-steps $t$ and $t'$. For any such clustering, let $w$ be the furthest node along $p$ which knows a message at least as high as $j + 1$. We call the clustering *good* if:

- $w$ is at distance at most $c_1 \frac{\log n}{\beta \log D}$ from its cluster center;

- the node $x$ which is $\frac{D^{0.1}}{c}$ nodes along $p$ from $w$ is in the same cluster as $w$;
- $x$ and $w$ are valid (recall that this means they succeed in Intra-Cluster Propagation).

By Theorem 2.2, and using Markov's inequality, we can choose $c_1$ such that the first event occurs with probability at least 0.54, conditioned on all previous randomness. By Corollary 3.7 of [13], we can choose $c_2$ so that the second event occurs with probability at least 0.99, also conditioned on all previous randomness. By Lemma 4.2 the probability that $x$ and $w$ are valid, conditioned on the first event, is at least 0.98. Therefore each fine clustering is good with probability at least $\frac{1}{2}$ (by the union bound).

Let $S$ be the set of all clusterings applied between time-steps $t$ and $t'$. We are interested in the quantity $\sum_{s \in S \text{ is good}} \beta_s^{-1}$. Note that this majorizes the quantity $\sum_{s \in S} x_s$, where the $x_s$ are independent Bernoulli variables which take value $\beta_s^{-1}$ with probability $\frac{1}{2}$ and 0 otherwise. The expected value of this quantity is $\frac{1}{2}\sum_{s \in S \text{ is good}} \beta_s^{-1} \geq \frac{c}{3} D^{0.12}$. By Hoeffding's inequality,

$$\mathbb{P}\left[\sum_{s \in S} x_s \leq \frac{c}{6} D^{0.12}\right] \leq e^{-\frac{2|S|^2(\frac{c}{6}D^{0.12})^2}{\sum_{s \in S} \beta_s^{-2}}} \leq e^{-\frac{2|S|(\frac{c}{6}D^{0.12})^2}{D^{0.1}}} \leq e^{-\log^2 n}.$$

By time $t'$, $w$ has advanced at least $\frac{\sum_{s \in S}}{c_2} \geq \frac{cD^{0.12}}{6c_2}$ steps along $p$, and so by choosing a sufficiently large constant in the big-Oh notation for $t'$, we can ensure that every node in $p$ knows a message at least as high as $j + 1$. □

We combine the results from Lemmas 4.4–4.6 to show how to propagate messages along any shortest path between two nodes.

Lemma 4.7 (***All shortest paths***). *Let $u$ and $v$ be any nodes in $\mathfrak{N}$, $p$ be some shortest $(u, v)$-path, and let $b$ be the number of bad length-$D^{0.12}$ subpaths of $p$. If $u$ knows a message at least as high as $i$ at time-step $t$, then after $t + 2k(\frac{|p|\log n}{\log D} + (2i + b)D^{0.125})$ steps, $v$ knows a message at least as high as $i$ with high probability.*

Proof. We prove the lemma using double induction. Our 'outer' induction shall be on the value $i$.
**Base case:** $i = 1$. By Lemma 4.4, $p$ contains at most $D^{0.63}$ bad subpaths. Applying Lemmas 4.5 and 4.6, the time taken to inform $v$ of a message at least as high as 1 is at most $D^{0.63} \cdot O(D^{0.121}) + D^{0.88} \cdot O(D^{0.12}\frac{\log n}{\log D}) \leq kD\frac{\log n}{\log D}$.
**Inductive step:** We can now assume the claim for $i = \ell - 1$ (inductive assumption 1), and prove the inductive step $i = \ell$. We do this using a second induction, on $|p|$.

**Base case:** $|p| \leq D^{0.12}$. $p$ is a single subpath. If $p$ is good, then by inductive assumption 1, all nodes within $D^{0.11}$ of $p$ know an ID at least as high as $\ell - 1$ by time-step $t + k(\frac{(|p|+D^{0.11})\log n}{\log D} + (2(\ell - 1) + 1)D^{0.125})$. Then, by Lemma 4.6, $v$ knows an ID at least as high as $\ell$ by time-step

$$t + k\left(\frac{(|p| + D^{0.11})\log n}{\log D} + (2\ell - 1)D^{0.125}\right) + cD^{0.12}\frac{\log n}{\log D} \leq t + k\left(\frac{|p|\log n}{\log D} + 2\ell D^{0.125}\right).$$

If $p$ is bad then by inductive assumption (1), all nodes within $D^{0.11}$ of $p$ know an ID at least as high as $\ell - 1$ by time-step $t + k(\frac{(|p|+D^{0.11})\log n}{\log D} + (2(\ell - 1) + 2)D^{0.125})$. Then, by Lemma 4.5, $v$ knows an ID at least as high as $i$ by time-step

$$t + k\left(\frac{(|p| + D^{0.11})\log n}{\log D} + 2\ell D^{0.125}\right) + cD^{0.121} \leq t + k\left(\frac{|p|\log n}{\log D} + (2\ell + 1)D^{0.125}\right).$$

**Inductive step:** Having proved the base case, we can now assume the claim for $i = \ell$ and $|p| < q$ (inductive assumption 2), and prove the inductive step $|p| = q$.

Let $u'$ be the start node of the last subpath of $p$. If this subpath is good, then by inductive assumption 2, $u'$ knows an ID at least as high as $\ell$ by time-step $t + k(\frac{(|p|-D^{0.12})\log n}{\log D} + (2i + b)D^{0.125})$. By inductive assumption (1), all nodes within $D^{0.11}$ of $p$ know a message at least as high as $\ell - 1$ by time-step $t + k((|p| + D^{0.11})\log n\log D + (2(\ell - 1) + (b + 1)))D^{0.125} \leq t + k(\frac{(|p|-D^{0.12})\log n}{\log D} + (2\ell + b))D^{0.125}$ Therefore, by Lemma 4.6, $v$ knows a message at least as high as $\ell$ by time-step

$$t + k\left(\frac{(|p| - D^{0.12})\log n}{\log D} + (2\ell + b)D^{0.125}\right) + cD^{0.12}\frac{\log n}{\log D} \leq t + k\left(\frac{|p|\log n}{\log D} + (2\ell + b)D^{0.125}\frac{\log n}{\log D}\right).$$

If the subpath is bad, then by inductive assumption (2), $u'$ knows an ID at least as high as $\ell$ by time-step $t+k(\frac{(|p|-D^{0.12})\log n}{\log D}+(2\ell+b-1)D^{0.125}) \leq t+k(\frac{(|p|+D^{0.11})\log n}{\log D}+(2(\ell-1)+b)D^{0.125})$. By inductive assumption (1), all nodes within $D^{0.11}$ of $p$ know a message at least as high as $\ell-1$ by time-step $t+k(\frac{(|p|+D^{0.11})\log n}{\log D}+(2(\ell-1)+b)D^{0.125})$ Therefore, by Lemma 4.5, $v$ knows a message at least as high as $\ell$ by time-step

$$t + k\left(\frac{(|p| + D^{0.11})\log n}{\log D} + (2(\ell - 1) + b)D^{0.125}\right) + cD^{0.121} \leq t + k\left(\frac{|p|\log n}{\log D} + (2\ell + b)D^{0.125}\frac{\log n}{\log D}\right).$$

This completes the proof by induction. □

We are now ready to prove Theorem 4.1:

Proof of Theorem 4.1. The precomputation phase takes at most $O(D + \log^{O(1)})$ time. Upon beginning the Intra-Cluster Propagation phase, one node $u$ knows the highest message. Therefore by Lemma 4.7, all nodes $v$ know this message within $2k(\frac{|dist(u,v)|\log n}{\log D} + (2|S|+b)D^{0.125}) = O(\frac{D\log n}{\log D} + |S|D^{0.125} + \log^{O(1)} n)$ time-steps, with high probability. □

# 5 APPLYING COMPETE TO BROADCASTING AND LEADER ELECTION

It is not difficult to see that Compete can be used to perform both broadcasting and leader election.

Theorem 5.1. *Compete$(\{s\})$ completes broadcasting in $O(D\frac{\log n}{\log D} + \log^{O(1)} n)$ time with high probability.*

Proof. Compete informs all nodes of the highest message in the message set in time $O(D\frac{\log n}{\log D} + \log^{O(1)} n)$, with high probability. Since this set contains only the source message, broadcasting is completed. □

**Algorithm 6** Leader Election

Nodes choose to become candidates in $C$ with probability $\frac{100 \log n}{n}$.
Candidates randomly generate $\Theta(\log n)$-bit IDs.
Perform Compete($C$).

Theorem 5.2. *Algorithm 6 completes leader election within time* $O(D\frac{\log n}{\log D} + \log^{O(1)} n)$, *with high probability*

Proof. With high probability $|C| = \Theta(\log n)$ and all candidate IDs are unique. Conditioning on this, Compete informs all nodes of the highest candidate ID within time $O(D\frac{\log n}{\log D} + \log^{O(1)} n)$, with high probability. Therefore leader election is completed. □

## 6 CONCLUSIONS

The tasks of broadcasting and leader election in radio networks are longstanding, fundamental problems in distributed computing. Our main contribution are new algorithms for these problems that improve running times for both to $O(D\frac{\log n}{\log D} + \log^{O(1)} n)$, with high probability. For $D = \Omega(\log^c n)$ for a sufficiently large constant $c$, these running time bounds improve the fastest previous algorithms for broadcasting and leader election by factors $O(\log \log n)$ and $O(\log n \log \log n)$, respectively. More importantly, whenever $D$ is polynomial in $n$ (i.e., $D = \Omega(n^\varepsilon)$, for some positive constant $\varepsilon$), the obtained running time is $O(D)$, which is asymptotically optimal since time $D$ is required for any information to traverse the network.

There is no better lower bound than $\Omega(D + \log^2 n)$ for broadcasting or leader election when spontaneous transmissions are allowed, so the most immediate open question is to close that gap. While a tighter analysis of our method might trim the additive polylog($n$) term significantly, it is difficult to see how $\log^2 n$ could be reached without a radically different approach. Similarly, the $D\frac{\log n}{\log D}$ term seems to be a limit of the clustering approach, and reducing it to $D$ would likely require significant changes. In fact, we would not be surprised if our upper bounds $O(D\frac{\log n}{\log D})$ were tight for $D = \Omega(\log^c n)$ for a sufficiently large constant $c$.

The main focus of this paper has been to study the impact of spontaneous transmissions for basic communication primitives in randomized algorithms undirected networks. An interesting question is whether spontaneous transmissions can help in *directed* networks, which would be very surprising, or for *deterministic* protocols.

## REFERENCES


[1] Noga Alon, Amotz Bar-Noy, Nathan Linial, and David Peleg. 1991. A Lower Bound for Radio Broadcast. *Journal of Computer and System Sciences* 43, 2 (October 1991), 290–298.
[2] Reuven Bar-Yehuda, Oded Goldreich, and Alon Itai. 1991. Efficient Emulation of Single-hop Radio Network with Collision on Multi-hop Radio Network with no Collision Detection. *Distributed Computing* 5, 1 (September 1991), 67–71.
[3] Reuven Bar-Yehuda, Oded Goldreich, and Alon Itai. 1992. On the Time-complexity of Broadcast in Multi-hop Radio Networks: An Exponential Gap between Determinism and Randomization. *Journal of Computer and System Sciences* 45, 1 (August 1992), 104–126.
[4] Bogdan S. Chlebus, Leszek Gąsieniec, Alan Gibbons, Andrzej Pelc, and Wojciech Rytter. 2002. Deterministic Broadcasting in Unknown Radio Networks. *Distributed Computing* 15, 1 (January 2002), 27–38.
[5] Bogdan S. Chlebus, Dariusz R. Kowalski, and Andrzej Pelc. 2012. Electing a Leader in Multi-hop Radio Networks. In *Proceedings of the 16th International Conference on Principles of Distributed Systems (OPODIS) (Lecture Notes in Computer Science)*, Vol. 7702. Springer, Berlin, Heidelberg, 106–120.
[6] Marek Chrobak, Leszek Gąsieniec, and Wojciech Rytter. 2002. Fast Broadcasting and Gossiping in Radio Networks. *Journal of Algorithms* 43, 2 (May 2002), 177–189.
[7] Andrea E. F. Clementi, Angelo Monti, and Riccardo Silvestri. 2003. Distributed Broadcasting in Radio Networks of Unknown Topology. *Theoretical Computer Science* 302, 1-3 (April 2003), 337–364.
[8] Artur Czumaj and Peter Davies. 2016. Brief Announcement: Optimal Leader Election in Multi-Hop Radio Networks. In *Proceedings of the 35th Annual ACM Symposium on Principles of Distributed Computing (PODC)*. ACM Press, New York, NY, 47–49.
[9] Artur Czumaj and Peter Davies. 2016. Faster Deterministic Communication in Radio Networks. In *Proceedings of the 43rd Annual International Colloquium on Automata, Languages and Programming (ICALP)*. Leibniz International Proceedings in Informatics (LIPICS), Schloss Dagstuhl – Leibniz-Zentrum für Informatik, Dagstuhl Publishing, Germany, 139:1–139:14.
[10] Artur Czumaj and Wojciech Rytter. 2003. Broadcasting Algorithms in Radio Networks with Unknown Topology. *Journal of Algorithms* 60, 2 (August 2003), 115–143.
[11] Mohsen Ghaffari and Bernhard Haeupler. 2013. Near Optimal Leader Election in Multi-hop Radio Networks. In *Proceedings of the 24th Annual ACM-SIAM Symposium on Discrete Algorithms (SODA)*. SIAM, Philadelphia, PA, 748–766.
[12] Mohsen Ghaffari, Bernhard Haeupler, and Majid Khabbazian. 2015. Randomized Broadcast in Radio Networks with Collision Detection. *Distributed Computing* 28, 6 (December 2015), 407–422.
[13] Bernhard Haeupler and David Wajc. 2016. A Faster Distributed Radio Broadcast Primitive. In *Proceedings of the 35th Annual ACM Symposium on Principles of Distributed Computing (PODC)*. ACM Press, New York, NY, 361–370.
[14] Dariusz R. Kowalski. 2005. On Selection Problem in Radio Networks. In *Proceedings of the 24th Annual ACM Symposium on Principles of Distributed Computing (PODC)*. ACM Press, New York, NY, 158–166.
[15] Dariusz R. Kowalski and Andrzej Pelc. 2004. Faster Deterministic Broadcasting in Ad Hoc Radio Networks. *SIAM Journal on Discrete Mathematics* 18, 2 (2004), 332–346.
[16] Dariusz R. Kowalski and Andrzej Pelc. 2005. Broadcasting in Undirected ad hoc Radio Networks. *Distributed Computing* 18, 1 (July 2005), 43–57.
[17] Eyal Kushilevitz and Yishay Mansour. 1998. An $\Omega(D \log(N/D))$ Lower Bound for Broadcast in Radio Networks. *SIAM Journal on Computing* 27, 3 (1998), 702–712.
[18] Gary L. Miller, Richard Peng, and Shen Chen Xu. 2013. Parallel Graph Decompositions Using Random Shifts. In *Proceedings of the 25th Annual ACM Symposium on Parallelism in Algorithms and Architectures (SPAA)*. ACM Press, New York, NY, 196–203.
[19] David Peleg. 2007. Time-efficient Broadcasting in Radio Networks: A Review. In *Proceedings of the 4th International Conference on Distributed Computing and Internet Technology (ICDCIT) (Lecture Notes in Computer Science)*, Vol. 4882. Springer, Berlin, Heidelberg, 1–18.


## A APPENDIX: CLUSTERING PROPERTY (PROOF OF THEOREM 2.2)

In this section we provide main ideas needed to prove a key property of the clustering method in our algorithm Partition($\beta$), Theorem 2.2. Partition($\beta$) is based on a method first introduced by Miller et al. [18]. The concept is as follows: each node $v$ independently generates an exponentially distributed random variable $\delta_v$, that is, a variable taking values in $\mathbb{R}_{\geq 0}$ with $\mathbb{P}[\delta_v \leq y] = 1 - e^{-\beta y}$. Then, each node chooses its cluster center $u$ to be the node maximizing $\delta_u - dist(u, v)$. It can be seen by the triangle inequality that a node which is cluster center to any node is also cluster center to itself. For details of how to implement this in the radio network setting, see [13].

The rest of this section is now devoted to a sketch of the proof of Theorem 2.2; for a complete and very technical proof of Theorem 2.2, we refer to the full version of this paper.

## A.1 Bounding expected distance by $O(S_{x,\beta})$

Our first step in proving Theorem 2.2 is to obtain a bound for distance to cluster center which is based upon the number of nodes at each distance layer from $v$. To this purpose, let $A_i(v)$ be the set of nodes at distance $i$ from $v$ and denote $x_i = |A_i(v)|$. Denote $\boldsymbol{x} \in \mathbb{N}_0^D$ to be the vector with these $x_i$ as coefficients.

Denote $T_{\boldsymbol{x},\beta} = \sum_{i=0}^{D} i x_i e^{-i\beta}$ and $B_{\boldsymbol{x},\beta} = \sum_{i=0}^{D} x_i e^{-i\beta}$. Denote $S_{\boldsymbol{x},\beta} = \frac{T_{\boldsymbol{x},\beta}}{B_{\boldsymbol{x},\beta}} = \frac{\sum_{i=0}^{D} i x_i e^{-i\beta}}{\sum_{i=0}^{D} x_i e^{-i\beta}}$. These quantities will be used in the following key auxiliary lemma describing the expected distance from any fixed $v$ to its cluster center after applying PARTITION($\beta$).

LEMMA A.1. *For any fixed node $v$ and value $\beta$ with $D^{-0.01} \leq \beta \leq D^{-0.1}$, the expected distance from $v$ to its cluster center upon applying PARTITION($\beta$) is at most* $\frac{5\sum_{i=0}^{D} i x_i e^{-i\beta}}{\sum_{i=0}^{D} x_i e^{-i\beta}} = 5S_{\boldsymbol{x},\beta}$.

PROOF. We compute the expected distance to cluster center:

$$\begin{aligned}
&\mathbb{E}[\text{distance from } v \text{ to its cluster center}] \\
&= \sum_{i=0}^{D} i \cdot \mathbb{P}[v\text{'s cluster center is distance } i \text{ away}] \\
&= \sum_{i=0}^{D} i \cdot \left( \sum_{u \in A_i(v)} \mathbb{P}[u \text{ is } v\text{'s cluster center}] \right) .
\end{aligned}$$

We concentrate on this latter probability and henceforth fix $u \in A_i(v)$ to be some node at distance $i$ from $v$. For simplicity of notation, let $\mathcal{P}_{u,v}$ denote $\mathbb{P}[u \text{ is } v\text{'s cluster center}]$. We note that,

$$\mathcal{P}_{u,v} = \int_i^\infty \beta e^{-\beta p} \mathbb{P}[u \text{ is } v\text{'s cluster center} | \delta_u = p] \, dp$$

by conditioning on the value of $\delta_u$ over its whole range and multiplying by the corresponding probability density function (we can start the integral at $i$ since if $\delta_u < i$ then $\mathcal{P}_{u,v} = 0$).

Having conditioned on $\delta_u$, we can evaluate the probability that $u$ is $v$'s cluster center based on the random variables generated by other nodes, since the probabilities that each other node 'beats' $u$ are now independent, $\mathcal{P}_{u,v}$ is equal to:

$$\int_i^\infty \beta e^{-\beta p} \prod_{w \neq u} \mathbb{P}[\delta_w - dist(v,w) < \delta_u - dist(v,u) | \delta_u = p] \, dp \ .$$

We can simplify by grouping the nodes $w$ based on distance from $v$, though we must be careful to include a $\frac{1}{\mathbb{P}[\delta_u < p]}$ term to cancel out $u$'s contribution to the resulting product:

$$\mathcal{P}_{u,v} = \int_i^\infty \frac{\beta e^{-\beta p}}{\mathbb{P}[\delta_u < p]} \prod_{k=0}^{D} \prod_{w \in A_k(v)} \mathbb{P}[\delta_w - k < p - i] \, dp \ .$$

Plugging in the cumulative distribution function yields:

$$\mathcal{P}_{u,v} = \int_i^\infty \frac{\beta e^{-\beta p}}{1 - e^{-\beta p}} \prod_{k=0}^{D} \prod_{w \in A_k(v)} 1 - e^{-\beta(p-i+k)} dp \ .$$

We use the standard inequality $1 - y \leq e^{-y}$ for $y \in [0, 1]$, here setting $y = e^{-\beta(p-i+k)}$, and account for the second product by taking the contents to the power of $x_k$:

$$\begin{aligned}
\mathcal{P}_{u,v} &\leq \int_i^\infty \frac{\beta e^{-\beta p}}{1 - e^{-\beta p}} \prod_{k=0}^{D} \prod_{w \in A_k(v)} e^{-e^{-\beta(p-i+k)}} dp \\
&= \int_i^\infty \frac{\beta e^{-\beta p}}{1 - e^{-\beta p}} \prod_{k=0}^{D} e^{-e^{-\beta(p-i+k)} x_k} dp \ .
\end{aligned}$$

We can also remove the remaining product by taking it as a sum into the exponent, and re-arranging some terms yields:

$$\begin{aligned}
\mathcal{P}_{u,v} &\leq \int_i^\infty \frac{\beta e^{-\beta p}}{1 - e^{-\beta p}} e^{-e^{\beta(i-p)} \sum_{k=0}^{D} x_k e^{-\beta k}} dp \\
&= \int_i^\infty \frac{\beta e^{-\beta p}}{1 - e^{-\beta p}} e^{-e^{\beta(i-p)} B_{\boldsymbol{x},\beta}} dp \ ,
\end{aligned}$$

where for succinctness we use our definition $B_{\boldsymbol{x},\beta} = \sum_{i=0}^{D} x_i e^{-i\beta}$.

At this point we split the integral and bound the parts separately, since they exhibit different behavior:

$$\mathcal{P}_{u,v} \leq J + K \ ,$$

where,

$$\begin{aligned}
J &= \int_i^{\frac{1}{\beta}} \frac{\beta e^{-\beta p}}{1 - e^{-\beta p}} e^{-e^{\beta(i-p)} B_{\boldsymbol{x},\beta}} dp \ , \\
K &= \int_{\frac{1}{\beta}}^\infty \frac{\beta e^{-\beta p}}{1 - e^{-\beta p}} e^{-e^{\beta(i-p)} B_{\boldsymbol{x},\beta}} dp \ .
\end{aligned}$$

To bound $J$, we make use of the following bound on $B_{\boldsymbol{x},\beta}$:

$$\begin{aligned}
B_{\boldsymbol{x},\beta} &= \sum_{k=0}^{D} x_k e^{-k\beta} \geq \sum_{k=0}^{\lceil \frac{D}{2} \rceil} e^{-k\beta} \geq \int_{-1}^{\frac{D}{2}} e^{-z\beta} dz \\
&= \frac{-1}{\beta}(e^{-\frac{\beta D}{2}} - e^{-\beta}) \geq \frac{1}{2\beta} \ .
\end{aligned}$$

This gives

$$J \leq \int_i^{\frac{1}{\beta}} \frac{\beta e^{-\beta p}}{1 - e^{-\beta p}} e^{-e^{\beta(i-p)} \frac{1}{2\beta}} dp \ .$$

Since $e^{\beta(i-p)} \geq e^{-1}$, we obtain,

$$J \leq \int_1^{\frac{1}{\beta}} \frac{\beta e^{-\beta p}}{1 - e^{-\beta p}} e^{-\frac{1}{2e\beta}} dp = \beta e^{-\frac{1}{2e\beta}} \int_1^{\frac{1}{\beta}} \frac{e^{-\beta p}}{1 - e^{-\beta p}} dp \ .$$

We can then use that $\int_a^b \frac{e^{-\beta p}}{1 - e^{-\beta p}} = \frac{1}{\beta} \log \frac{(1-e^{\beta b})}{(1-e^{\beta a})} + a - b$ to evaluate $J \leq e^{-\frac{1}{2e\beta}} \log \frac{(1-e)}{(1-e^{\beta})}$. Since $e^{\beta} > 1 + \beta$, re-arranging yields $J \leq e^{-\frac{1}{2e\beta}} \log \frac{e-1}{\beta}$. Finally, since we can assume that $\frac{1}{\beta} \geq \log^c n$ for some sufficiently large $c$, we obtain,

$$J \leq e^{-\frac{\log^2 n}{2e}} \log \frac{e-1}{\beta} \leq n^{-2} \ .$$

We now turn our attention to $K = \int_{\frac{1}{\beta}}^\infty \frac{\beta e^{-\beta p}}{1 - e^{-\beta p}} e^{-e^{\beta(i-p)} B_{\boldsymbol{x},\beta}} dp$. Since $1 - e^{-\beta p} \geq 1 - e^{-1} > \frac{1}{2}$, we get

$$K < \int_{\frac{1}{\beta}}^\infty 2\beta e^{-\beta p} e^{-e^{-\beta p} e^{\beta i} B_{\boldsymbol{x},\beta}} dp \ .$$

Using that $e^{-e^{-\beta p}} \le 1 - \frac{1}{2}e^{-\beta p}$ (since $0 \le e^{-\beta p} \le 1$), we obtain,

$$K < \int_{\frac{1}{\beta}}^{\infty} 2\beta e^{-\beta p}(1 - \frac{1}{2}e^{-\beta p})^{e^{\beta i}B_{x,\beta}} dp \ .$$

Evaluating the integral, using

$$\int_a^{\infty} e^{-\beta p}(1 - \frac{1}{2}e^{-\beta p})^c = \frac{(e^{-a\beta} - 2)(1 - \frac{1}{2}e^{-a\beta})^c + 2}{\beta(1 + c)} \ ,$$

we obtain,

$$K < 2\frac{(e^{-1} - 2)(1 - \frac{1}{2}e^{-1})^{e^{\beta i}B_{x,\beta}} + 2}{1 + e^{\beta i}B_{x,\beta}} \le \frac{4}{e^{\beta i}B_{x,\beta}} \ .$$

We can now combine our calculations to prove the lemma. Since $x_i = |A_i(v)|$, we have,

$\mathbb{E}$[distance from $v$ to its cluster center]

$$= \sum_{i=0}^{D} i \sum_{u \in A_i(v)} \mathcal{P}_{u,v} \le \sum_{i=0}^{D} i x_i (J + K)$$

$$< \sum_{i=0}^{D} i x_i \left( n^{-2} + \frac{4}{e^{\beta i}B_{\boldsymbol{x},\beta}} \right) \le n^{-2} \sum_{i=0}^{D} D x_i + \frac{4\sum_{i=0}^{D} i x_i e^{-\beta i}}{B_{\boldsymbol{x},\beta}}$$

$$\le \frac{D}{n} + 4S_{\boldsymbol{x},\beta} \le 5S_{\boldsymbol{x},\beta} \ . \qquad \square$$

## A.2 Simplifying the form of $x$ to bound $S_{x,\beta}$

By Lemma A.1, we must now bound the value of $S_{\boldsymbol{x},\beta} = \frac{\sum_{i=0}^{D} i x_i e^{-i\beta}}{\sum_{i=0}^{D} x_i e^{-i\beta}}$. To simplify our analysis, we will apply two transformations to $\boldsymbol{x}$ which will provide us with useful properties for bounding, while not increasing any $S_{\boldsymbol{x},\beta}$ by more than a constant factor.

The first transformation we apply will be to collate coefficients of $\boldsymbol{x}$ into indices which are just the powers of 2. That is, we sum the coefficients of $\boldsymbol{x}$ over regions of doubling size.

Let $f : \mathbb{R}^{D+1} \to \mathbb{R}^{D+1}$ be given by

$$f(\boldsymbol{x})_i = \begin{cases} \sum_{\ell=2i}^{4i-1} x_\ell & \text{if } i = 2^k \text{ for some } k \in \mathbb{N}_0, \\ 0 & \text{otherwise.} \end{cases}$$

We can bound $S_{\boldsymbol{x},\beta}$ in terms of $S_{f(\boldsymbol{x}),\beta}$.

Lemma A.2. *For all* $\boldsymbol{x} \in \mathbb{N}_0^D$, $S_{\boldsymbol{x},\beta} \le 11 S_{f(\boldsymbol{x}),\beta}$.

Having applied $f$ to ensure that only power-of-2 coefficients of $\boldsymbol{x}$ are non-zero, we apply a second transformation to ensure that the coefficients are not "too decreasing"; in particular, we guarantee that each non-zero coefficient is at least half the previous one.

Let $g : \mathbb{R}^{D+1} \to \mathbb{R}^{D+1}$ be given by

$$g(\boldsymbol{x})_i = \begin{cases} \sum_{\ell \le i} \frac{\ell x_\ell}{i} & \text{if } i = 2^k \text{ for some } k \in \mathbb{N}_0, \\ 0 & \text{otherwise.} \end{cases}$$

This definition achieves our aim since when $i$ is a power of 2,

$$2g(\boldsymbol{x})_{2i} = 2\sum_{\ell \le 2i} \frac{\ell x_\ell}{2i} = \sum_{\ell \le 2i} \frac{\ell x_\ell}{i} \ge \sum_{\ell \le i} \frac{\ell x_\ell}{i} = g(\boldsymbol{x})_{2i} \ .$$

Similarly to Lemma A.2, we can bound $S_{\boldsymbol{x},\beta}$ in terms of $S_{g(\boldsymbol{x}),\beta}$.

Lemma A.3. *For all* $\boldsymbol{x} \in \mathbb{N}_0^D$ *which have* $x_i = 0$ *for all* $i \notin \{2^k : k \in \mathbb{N}_0\}$, $S_{\boldsymbol{x},\beta} \le 2S_{g(\boldsymbol{x}),\beta}$.

## A.3 Bounding $S_{x,\beta}$ for simplified $x$

Now that we have shown in Lemmas A.2 and A.3 that the transformations $f$ and $g$ do not increase $S_{\boldsymbol{x},\beta}$ by more than a constant factor, we show how they help to bound the value of $S_{\boldsymbol{x},\beta}$. Let $\boldsymbol{x}'$ be the vector obtained after applying the two transformations to $\boldsymbol{x}$, i.e., $\boldsymbol{x}' = g \circ f(\boldsymbol{x})$. We begin with the following lemma.

Lemma A.4. $\boldsymbol{x}'$ *has the following properties:*

- $x'_i = 0$ *for all* $i \notin \{2^k : k \in \mathbb{N}_0\}$;
- $x'_1 \ge 2$;
- $||\boldsymbol{x}'||_1 = \sum_{i=0}^{D} x'_i \le 2n$, ;
- $2x'_{2i} \ge x'_i$ *for all* $i$, *due to transformation* $g$.

Our argument will be based on examining the ratios between consecutive non-zero coefficients in $\boldsymbol{x}'$. To that end, define $k_i = \log \frac{x'_{2^{i+1}}}{x'_{2^i}}$ for all $0.01 \log D \le i \le 0.1 \log D$, and note that $k_i \ge \log \frac{1}{2} = -1$ for all $i$ and $\sum_{i=0}^{\log D} k_i \le \log n$ by Lemma A.4.

We first show a condition on these $k_i$ which guarantees that $S_{\boldsymbol{x}',\beta}$ (and hence $S_{\boldsymbol{x},\beta}$) is $O(\frac{\log n}{\beta \log D})$ for some particular value of $\beta$:

Lemma A.5. *If for fixed* $j$ *and for all* $m \ge 8$ *we have*

$$\sum_{\ell=j+\log\frac{\log n}{\log D}}^{j+\log\frac{\log n}{\log D}+m} k_\ell \le 2^m \frac{\log n}{\log D}$$

*then* $S_{\boldsymbol{x}',2^{-j}} = O(\frac{2^j \log n}{\log D})$.

Finally, we can show that there are many $j$ for which the condition of Lemma A.5 holds.

Lemma A.6. *The number of integers* $j$, $0.01 \log D \le j \le 0.1 \log D$, *for which there is* $i \ge 8$ *satisfying* $\sum_{\ell=j+\log\frac{\log n}{\log D}}^{j+\log\frac{\log n}{\log D}+i} k_\ell > 2^i \frac{\log n}{\log D}$ *is upper bounded by* $0.04 \log D$.

We are now ready to prove our main result, Theorem 2.2.

Proof of Theorem 2.2. With probability at least $1 - \frac{0.04}{0.1-0.01} \ge 0.55$, for all $i \ge 8$ we have that

$$\sum_{\ell=j+\log\frac{\log n}{\log D}}^{j+\log\frac{\log n}{\log D}+i} k_\ell \le 2^i \frac{\log n}{\log D} \ .$$

Then, $S_{\boldsymbol{x}',2^{-j}} = O(\frac{2^j \log n}{\log D})$ by Lemmas A.5 and A.6. Applying Lemmas A.2 and A.3, we get $S_{\boldsymbol{x},2^{-j}} = O(\frac{2^j \log n}{\log D})$. Finally, applying Lemma A.1, we find that the expected distance from $v$ to its cluster center is at most $O(\frac{2^j \log n}{\log D})$. $\square$

# The Space Requirement of Local Forwarding on Acyclic Networks*

Boaz Patt-Shamir
Tel Aviv University
Tel Aviv, Israel
boaz@tau.ac.il

Will Rosenbaum
Tel Aviv University
Tel Aviv, Israel
will.rosenbaum@gmail.com

## ABSTRACT

We consider packet forwarding in acyclic networks with bounded adversarial packet injections. We focus on the model of adversarial queuing theory, where each packet is injected into the network with a prescribed path to its destination, and both the long-range average rate and the short-range burst size are bounded. Each edge has an associated buffer that stores packets while they wait to cross the edge. Our goal is to minimize the buffer space required to avoid overflows.

Previous results for local forwarding protocols required buffers of size $\Omega(n)$. In the case of single destination trees, it is known that for centralized protocols, buffers of size $O(1)$ are sufficient. We show that for local protocols, buffers of size $\Theta(\log n)$ are necessary and sufficient for single destination trees. The upper bound is achieved by a novel protocol which we call Odd-Even Downhill forwarding (OED). We also show that even slightly more general networks—such as path graphs with multiple destinations, or DAGs with a single destination—require buffers of size $\Omega(n)$ to avoid overflows, even if forwarding is done by centralized, offline protocols.

## 1 INTRODUCTION

Object movement, be it physical or virtual, is arguably the fundamental trait of any process. In computer networks, object movement is usually reduced to packet routing and forwarding. In this context, a packet represents an atomic unit of data which must be moved from its origin to its destination. Packets are injected at their source node by the environment. While traversing the network, they are stored in buffers in intermediate nodes. The movement of packets is restricted by the network topology, as well as link capacities, buffer sizes and possibly other factors.

It is common practice (e.g., [20]) to distinguish between packet *routing*, whose function is to determine a route for each packet from its source to destination, and packet *forwarding*, which determines when each packet is transmitted over a link. The adversarial queuing theory (AQT) model [11] analyzes the effect of forwarding when the route of each packet is chosen (adversarially) at the time of injection.

*This research is supported in part by the Israel Science Foundation (grant No. 1444/14).


*PODC '17, July 25-27, 2017, Washington, DC, USA*

ACM ISBN 978-1-4503-4992-5/17/07...$15.00
https://doi.org/10.1145/3087801.3087803

The quality of a forwarding protocol is judged by the maximal injection rate (in a given network, or over a class of networks) under which the protocol can guarantee that buffer loads remain bounded. When edge capacities are bounded, there is a maximal rate of packets the network can process. A common way of restricting the rate of packet injections is the "leaky bucket" model of Cruz [12]. This model defines a *$(\rho, \sigma)$-bounded adversary* to be an injection pattern such that for any edge $e$, the number of packets injected in any time window of size $t$ and whose routes contain $e$ is at most $t\rho + \sigma$. Intuitively, $\rho$ is an upper bound on the long-term average demand for $e$ and $\sigma$ is an upper bound on its instantaneous burstiness.[1]

The goal of this work is to understand *quantitatively* the worst-case buffer loads inflicted by adversarial packet injections for various network topologies and forwarding strategies. This viewpoint was taken in [1] for directed acyclic graphs (DAGs) and [22], for single-destination trees.[2] In [22], it was shown that a simple protocol can guarantee maximal load of $O(\rho + \sigma)$. However, the protocol of [22] is not local: forwarding decision depend on the state of nodes arbitrarily far away. In this paper, we propose a new *local* forwarding protocol, called *Odd-Even Downhill* (*OED*) forwarding. OED forwarding guarantees worst-case loads of size $O(\rho \log(\operatorname{diam} G) + \sigma)$, where $\operatorname{diam} G$ is the length of the longest path in the network $G$. The $O(\log(\operatorname{diam} G))$ upper bound for OED forwarding exponentially outperforms all local protocols of which we are aware. In particular, all "greedy" protocols (in which all non-empty buffers always forward a packet) are known to have worst case loads of size $\Omega(\operatorname{diam} G)$ [1, 22]. When the network is a single destination path and $\rho \leq 1$, OED forwarding can be described a follows: a nonempty buffer forwards a packet if (1) its load is strictly larger than the load of the next buffer, or (2) its load is equal to the next buffer and the loads are *odd*. We prove that the upper bound achieved by OED is tight for local protocols, as for any local protocol there is a corresponding injection pattern that incurs loads of size $\Omega(\log(\operatorname{diam} G) + \sigma)$.

We also show that apparently minor generalizations of the topology may increase the worst case load exponentially. Specifically, even in the case of a directed $n$-node path, if packets may have arbitrary origin and destination, the worst-case load can reach $\Omega(n)$ for a $(\rho, 2)$-bounded adversary for any $\rho > 1/2$. This result generalizes to single source, single destination DAGs. Moreover, the lower bound holds even if the algorithm is centralized and offline (and,

[1] Historically, the AQT adversary is parametrized by an average rate $r$ and a "window size" $w$ with a similar interpretation. This model is essentially equivalent to the the $(\rho, \sigma)$ model we use. See [24] for a detailed comparison of the two models.
[2] That is, the union of the routes of all packets forms a directed tree, such that all packets are destined for the root.

*a fortiori*, for local and online protocols). Interestingly, a matching upper bound is achieved in the case of DAGs by the greedy "longest-in-system" protocol [1], which is local.

*Related Work.* Adversarial queuing theory (AQT) was introduced in the seminal work of Borodin *et al.* [11]. Starting in [11], AQT considers only *greedy* (a.k.a. *work-conserving*) protocols, where a buffer must forward a packet whenever it is not empty. They define a protocol to be stable (for a family of networks and adversaries) if the maximum buffer size is bounded by some function of the network and the parameters of the adversary, independent of the number of injection rounds. They prove that all greedy protocols are stable for the family of DAGs and arbitrary adversaries of rate 1.[3] If the network contains a cycle, however, some greedy protocols are stable against rate-1 adversaries, while others are not. Andrews *et al.* [5] prove that there exist greedy forwarding protocols which are stable for all networks. They also prove that some greedy protocols incur worst-case exponential loads, even in DAGs. Adler and Rosén [1] analyze the performance of the "longest-in-system" (LIS) greedy protocol in DAGs. They prove that LIS achieves optimal $\Theta(\operatorname{diam} G)$ buffer size (and delay) on DAGs.

Aiello *et al.* [3] considered AQT with finite buffers. In their model, packets injected or forwarded to a full buffer are dropped. The goal of a protocol is to maximize the number of packets successfully delivered to their destination. The performance of a protocol is determined by competitive analysis—that is, its performance is compared to the performance of an optimal offline protocol (for the given injection pattern). They show that all greedy protocols are $O(n)$-competitive on DAGs (with $n$ nodes), while some greedy protocols are not competitive on cycle graphs. For the $n$-node path, they prove an $\Omega(\sqrt{n})$-competitive lower bound for greedy protocols. To our knowledge, there are no known competitive lower bounds for non-greedy protocols in this model. Overflows are further studied in [4, 16], in the single buffer case.

Non-greedy protocols, not considered in AQT, were studied in different contexts. For example, the *downhill algorithm*, where packets have "heights" according to their location in the buffer, and may be forwarded only if their height drops, has been used for many objectives, including deadlock avoidance [21], max-flow computation [14], multicommodity flow computation [8, 9], and routing in dynamically changing topology [2, 6, 10, 19]. The buffer size in a downhill algorithm is typically linear (in the number of nodes, or in the length of the longest simple path).[4] Another popular non-greedy forwarding paradigm is the *credit-based flow control*, whose main objective is to avoid overflows in various contexts, such as ATM networks [18], or NoCs [23].

The paper most relevant to our work is [22], where the authors consider AQT on single destination trees. They describe a centralized protocol which achieves maximum loads of size $O(\rho+\sigma)$. They further prove that any greedy or downhill forwarding protocol incurs loads of size $\Omega(n)$ on an $n$-node path where all packets have destination at one end of the path. They ask (1) if a local forwarding protocol can achieve performance similar to their centralized protocol, and (2) if any protocol can achieve sublinear worst-case loads on more general topologies than single-destination trees.

[3] In AQT literature, it is common to assume that all links have rate 1.

[4] In [19], a buffer's height is accounted for by counters, so that each node needs to hold only a constant number of packets and $O(\log n)$-bit counters.

| Topology/Locality | greedy | local | global |
|---|---|---|---|
| Single Destination Trees | $\Theta(n)$ [1, 22] | $\Theta(\log n)$ †‡ | $\Theta(1)$ [22] |
| General DAGs | $\Theta(n)$ [1] | $\Theta(n)$ ‡ | $\Theta(n)$ ‡ |

**Table 1:** *Summary of worst-case buffer sizes for different network topologies and forwarding protocols. New upper and lower bounds are marked by † and ‡ (respectively).*

*Our Contributions.* Our work answers the two open questions posed in [22]. In particular we show:

(1) There exists a local forwarding protocol—Odd-even downhill (OED) forwarding—which achieves worst-case loads of size $O(\rho \log(\operatorname{diam} G) + \sigma)$. Further, OED achieves delay of $O(\operatorname{diam} G)$ for $\rho < 1$.
(2) Any local forwarding protocol on single destination trees has worst-case loads of size $\Omega(\log(\operatorname{diam} G))$ when all edges have unit capacity, for any constant $\rho > 0$ and $\sigma \geq 1$.
(3) Any local forwarding protocol on the single destination undirected ring or path has worst-case loads of size
$$\Omega\left(\frac{\log(\operatorname{diam} G)}{\log\log(\operatorname{diam} G)}\right)$$
even if edges have unlimited capacity.
(4) Any (local or centralized, offline or online) protocol incurs loads of size $\Omega(\operatorname{diam} G)$ on the multiple destination path or single source, single destination DAGs for rates $\rho > 1/2$ and unit capacities.

We remark that lower bounds (3) and (4) above also hold in a less restrictive model where a packet need not follow its prescribed path to its destination. Such a model is indeed more natural, for example, in the context of dynamic networks [7, 17], where the prescribed edges may not remain in the network.

Table 1 shows the complete picture of matching upper and lower bounds for the three classifications of forwarding protocols and two families of networks we consider in this paper.

**Postscript.** Following the completion of this work, we have learned of an independent work which significantly overlaps our results. More specifically, in [13], Dobrev et al. describe an algorithm that is identical (!) to our OED forwarding protocol, along with matching lower bounds for all local forwarding protocols. Interestingly, the analysis of the algorithm in [13] is very different from our analysis.

*Paper organization.* Section 2 contains a formal description of our computational model and gives more background. In Section 3 we analyze single destination trees: upper bounds on the load for the OED algorithm, lower bounds on the load for any local protocol. We also analyze the delay in Section 4. Section 6 proves general load lower bounds for DAGs. Finally Section 7 contains some concluding remarks and open questions.

## 2 MODEL AND BACKGROUND

*Network.* We model a network as a directed graph $G = (V, E)$. Each edge $e = (u, v) \in E$ has an associated buffer. We use $e$ to refer to both an edge and the buffer associated with the edge. At any given time, this buffer stores packets currently residing at $u$ which must cross $e$ to ingress $v$. Each edge $e \in E$ has a *capacity* $C(e) \in \mathbf{N}$, that determines the number of packets which can be forwarded across $e$ in a single step. Unless otherwise noted, we assume that edge capacities are uniform, i.e., $C(e) = 1$ for all $e \in E$.

*Adversarial Model.* New packets spontaneously appear in the network in discrete steps via *injections*. Each packet $p$ has an associated route $R(p) = (e_0, e_1, \ldots, e_k)$. The tail of $e_0$ is $p$'s *origin* and the head of $e_k$ is $p$'s *destination*. We assume that the route $R(p)$ is chosen by an adversary, and that $p$ must follow $R(p)$ to its destination.

The adversary is limited in how many packets can be injected in each injection step. We use the "leaky bucket" model of adversarial injections described by Cruz [12]. Such an adversary is characterized by two parameters: a *rate* $\rho$ and a *burstiness* $\sigma$.

*Definition 2.1.* Let $G = (V, E)$ be a directed network and $A$ an adversarial injection pattern. For an interval $I = [t_0, t_1]$ and edge $e \in E$, let $N_I(e)$ denote the number of packets injected by $A$ at times $t \in I$ whose path contains $e$. We say that $A$ is *$(\rho, \sigma)$-bounded* if for all $I$ and for all $e \in E$, we have $N_I(e) \leq \rho\,|I| + \sigma$. Here, $|I|$ is the number of steps in the interval $I$ so that $|[t_0, t_1]| = t_1 - t_0 + 1$. We denote the set of all $(\rho, \sigma)$-bounded adversaries by $\mathcal{A}(\rho, \sigma)$.

*Forwarding Protocols.* A forwarding protocol proceeds in synchronous *rounds*. Each round consists of three *steps*:

(1) A *communication step*, during which each vertex may exchange messages with its neighbors and perform local computations. Here, edges serve as bi-directional communication links for protocol control messages, as opposed to data packets.
(2) A *forwarding step*, in which each (non-empty) buffer may forward a packet across its corresponding edge. Forwarded packets arrive at the other endpoint of the link, and are placed in the buffer corresponding to their next edge traversal, or if they have reached their destination, they are removed from the network.
(3) An *injection step*, in which new packets are injected into the network by an adversary.

A forwarding algorithm consists of a *forwarding policy* and a *scheduling policy*. The forwarding policy is a rule which determines whether or not each buffer in the network forwards some packet during a given round. If a buffer $e$ is to forward a packet, the scheduling policy determines *which* packet gets forwarded along $e$. We say that a forwarding policy is *greedy* if $e$ always forwards a packet whenever the buffer is non-empty.[5]

The forwarding and scheduling policies for a buffer $e$ in a node $v$ may depend on the contents of buffers in other nodes. Thus, we allow vertices to communicate with neighbors in the communication step before the forwarding step. We call a protocol *$d$-local* if in each round $t$ the behavior of a buffer in a node $v$ only depends on the contents of buffers up to distance $d$ from $v$. A policy is *local* if it is $d$-local for some fixed constant $d$ independent of the size of $G$. If $d = \mathrm{diam}(G)$ we call the policy *global*. We shall be mostly concerned with local policies.

[5] In Adversarial Queuing Theory, only greedy protocols are considered, and consequently, in AQT there is no distinction between forwarding and scheduling policies. Note that in the context of single-destination trees, the *scheduling* is immaterial except for individual latency.

**Algorithm 1** OED forwarding policy into a node $v \in V \setminus \{r\}$

```
e ← argmax_{(u,v)∈E} {L((u, v))}                 // break ties arbitrarily
f ← (v, w)                   // f is the single edge outgoing from v
if (L(e) > L(f)) or (L(e) = L(f) and L(f) is odd) then
    e forwards a packet to f
end if
```

In this work, our primary objective is to bound the maximum number of packets stored in any buffer at any given time. For an edge $e \in E$ and round $t$ we define the *load* of $e$ at time $t$—denoted $L^t(e)$—to be the number of packets stored in $e$ at the *beginning* of round $t$, i.e., before the forwarding and injection steps of round $t$. The *configuration* of a network $G$ at time $t$ is the map $L^t : E \to \mathbf{N}$. For a fixed network $G = (V, E)$, forwarding protocol $F$, and adversary $A$, we define the *cost* of $F$ on $G$ for $A$ to be $\mathrm{cost}(F, G, A) = \sup\left\{L^t(e) \mid e \in E, t \in \mathbf{N}\right\}$, i.e., the maximal load of any buffer over the course of the execution. The *delay* of a packet is the number of steps since its injection until it reaches its destination. The delay of an execution, denoted $\mathrm{delay}(F, G, A)$, is the supremum of packet delays over all packets in the execution of $F$ on $G$ with injections $A$ (if some packet $p$ is never delivered, then $\mathrm{delay}(F, G, A) = \infty$).

*Single Destination Trees.* Here, we state our main results for the problem of forwarding packets on single destination trees. Let $G = (V, E)$ be a directed tree, where all edges $e \in E$ are directed towards the root, $r \in V$. We denote the parameter $n = |V|$. For simplicity, we assume that each edge $e \in E$ has unit capacity $C(e) = 1$ and that the adversary has rate $\rho \leq 1$. In Section 3.1 we relax this restriction to arbitrary uniform capacities $c \geq 1$ and $\rho \leq c$.

Theorem 2.2. *Let $\mathcal{G}$ be the family of single destination trees, and $\mathcal{A} = \mathcal{A}(\rho, \sigma)$ with $\rho, \sigma > 0$ and $\rho \leq 1$. There exists a 2-local forwarding protocol* OED *such that for all $G \in \mathcal{G}$ and $A \in \mathcal{A}(\rho, \sigma)$ we have* $\mathrm{cost}(\mathrm{OED}, G, A) = O(\log(\mathrm{diam}\, G) + \sigma)$. *The protocol* OED *is optimal in the sense that for any $d$-local protocol $F$ with $d = O(1)$, there exists $A \in \mathcal{A}(\rho, \sigma)$ such that* $\mathrm{cost}(F, G, A) = \Omega(\rho \log(\mathrm{diam}\, G) + \sigma)$.

The lower bound of Theorem 2.2 implies a gap between the worst-case performance of local and global protocols, due to the upper bound of $O(\rho + \sigma)$ on the cost of the global protocol of [22].

## 3 THE OED ALGORITHM

In this section, we prove the upper bound of Theorem 2.2 by introducing the Odd-Even Downhill (OED) protocol, whose pseudo code is presented in Algorithm 1.

Theorem 3.1. *Let $\mathcal{G}$ be the family of single destination trees, and $\mathcal{A} = \mathcal{A}(\rho, \sigma)$ with $\rho \leq 1$. There exists a local protocol* OED *such that* $\mathrm{cost}(\mathrm{OED}, G, \mathcal{A}) \leq 2\log_3(\mathrm{depth}(G)) + 2\sigma + 2$.

We note that OED is not greedy, as it is known that any greedy protocol has cost at least $\Omega(\mathrm{diam}(G))$ in the worst case [22]. Moreover, OED exponentially outperforms all local protocols of which we are aware for single destination trees.

The OED protocol works as follows. Consider first a node $v$ with one incoming edge $e = (u, v)$. The OED protocol says that at any time $t$, $u$ forwards a packet to $v$, i.e., to $v$'s outgoing link $f = (v, w)$ if either $L^t(e) > L^t(f)$, or if $L^t(e) \geq L^t(f)$ and $L^t(e)$ is odd (the load of the destination is defined to be $-\infty$). In the general case, there are multiple incoming edges, and the rule is applied after $v$ chooses the incoming edge with the highest load; all other incoming edges are idle. Forwarding from an edge $e$ depends only on the loads of $e$'s siblings and the load of $e$'s parent, and hence OED is 2-local.

Before proving Theorem 3.1, we introduce some notation. Let $H = (V', E')$ be a directed forest, i.e., a disjoint union of directed trees. For a buffer $e = (v, w) \in E'$ with $v, w \in V'$, the *depth* of $e$, denoted depth$(e)$, is the length of the (unique) path from $v$—the node further from the root—to the root of the connected component containing $v$. By abuse of notation, for a tree $T = (V'', E'')$ we denote $\text{depth}(T) = \sup\{\text{depth}(e) \mid e \in E''\}$. We define the *level* of $e$, denoted lv$(e)$, by $\text{lv}(e) = \text{depth}(T_e) - \text{depth}(e)$, where $T_e$ is the connected component of $H$ containing $v$. We denote the set of all edges at level at most $\ell$ by $\text{Far}_\ell(H)$: $\text{Far}_\ell(H) = \{e \in E' \mid \text{lv}(e) \leq \ell\}$.

We think of packets as arranged vertically in a buffer, so that the first packet has height 1, the next one height 2 etc. We define the *j-load* of a buffer $e$ at time $t$ to be the number of packets in $e$ at height at least $j$, at the *beginning* of round $t$. Formally, for $e \in E$ and $t, j \in \mathbf{N}$, define

$$L_j^t(e) = \max\left\{L^t(e) - j + 1,\ 0\right\},$$

and for a set $S \subseteq E$, the $j$-load of $S$ at time $t$ is $L_j^t(S) = \sum_{e \in S} L_j^t(e)$. For $j, t \in \mathbf{N}$ define $H_j^t$ to be the set of buffers $e$ satisfying $L^t(e) \geq j$. Define a *j-plateau* to be a connected component of $H_j^t$ (cf. [22]).

The key to our analysis of OED is to understand the dynamics of plateaus. Under OED, in every round the root of each 1-plateau moves closer to the destination until the root of the plateau is a child of the destination. From this time and on, one packet will leave the plateau in each step.

The persistent movement of plateaus toward the destination is a feature OED shares with greedy protocols. Unlike greedy protocols, however, OED forwarding never pushes packets to buffers with a greater load. Thus under OED, plateaus cannot grow vertically due to forwarding. Consider the dynamics of a $j$-plateau for $j$ even. No buffer of load at most $j$ will forward a packet to a $j$-plateau, so the dynamics of the buffers of height at least $j+1$ in a $j$-plateau mimic the dynamics of the same configuration with $j$ packets removed from each buffer. Thus, each $(j+1)$-plateau in $H_j^t$ moves closer to the root of its connected component in each round. As a consequence, we are able to bound the total $j+1$ load of $H_j^t$ by the depth of $H_j^t$ at any time. Lemma 3.4 formalizes this bound.

Before we start the analysis, let us make the following preliminary simplification for convenience: We assume that there is exactly one edge, denoted $e_r$, incoming into the root. No generality is lost because if there is no such edge, consider the distinct subtrees rooted at the children of the root: each of the subtrees has one edge incoming to the root, and since packets injected into different subtrees do not interfere with one another, we may consider these subtrees separately.

Using the notion of $e_r$, we make the following natural definition (cf. [12]).

*Definition 3.2.* The *excess* at time $t \in \mathbf{N}$ is

$$\xi(t) = \max\left\{N_{[s,t]}(e_r) - (t - s + 1) \mid s \leq t\right\} \cup \{0\}.$$

A simple consequence of this definition is that during the $t$-th round, at most $\xi(t+1) - \xi(t) + 1$ packets were injected. Further, by the assumption that the adversary is $(\rho, \sigma)$-bounded, we have $\xi(t) \leq \sigma$ for all $t$.

*Notation 3.3.* Let $t, j, \in \mathbf{N}$. Then $H_j^t$ is the forest of buffers whose load at time $t$ is at least $j$. Formally, $H_j^t = (V_j^t, E_j^t)$, where $E_j^t = \left\{e \in E \,\middle|\, L^t(e) \geq j\right\}$ and $V_j^t = \left\{v \,\middle|\, (v, u) \in E_j^t\right\}$.

We now state the main lemma used in our proof of Theorem 3.1.

Lemma 3.4. *For all even heights $j$ and all $t$,*

$$L_{j+1}^t(H_j^t) \leq \text{depth}(H_j^t) + \sigma.$$

To see why the lemma implies the theorem, consider a buffer $e$ with maximum load $m$. Then for any even $j < m$ there are at least $m - j$ packets at height greater than $j$ in $H_j^t$ (in particular, there are $m - j$ such packets in $e$). Thus, the lemma implies that $\text{depth}(H_j^t) \geq m - j - \sigma$. Now consider the plateaus $H_{j-2}^t$. There are at least $2\,\text{depth}(H_j^t) + m - j \geq 3m - 3j - 2\sigma$ packets at height greater than $j - 1$, so the lemma implies that $\text{depth}(H_{j-2}^t) + \sigma$ is at least this large. Continuing in this way, $\text{depth}(H_j^t)$ increases exponentially as $j$ decreases. Thus, $m$ must be logarithmic in the depth of $G$.

Proof of Theorem 3.1. Let us denote $D = \text{depth}(G)$ and $D_j^t = \text{depth}(H_j^t)$. Applying Lemma 3.4, for all $t, j$ we have

$$L_{2j+1}^t(H_{2j}^t) \leq D_{2j}^t + \sigma.$$

On the other hand, for any $m > j$, we have

$$L_{2j+1}^t(H_{2j}^t) \geq \sum_{i=1}^{2m-2j} |E_{2j+i}^t| \geq 2\sum_{i=1}^{m-j} |E_{2j+2i}^t| \geq 2\sum_{i=1}^{m-j} D_{2j+2i}^t.$$

The first inequality holds because for all $k \geq 0$ there are $\left|E_k^t\right|$ packets at height $k$; thus the sum counts the number of packets at heights between $2j+1$ and $2m$. The second inequality holds because $|E_{2j+2i-1}^t| \geq |E_{2j+2i}^t|$ for all $t$ (if a buffer has load at least $2j + 2i$, then it also has load at least $2j + 2i - 1$). Combining the previous two expressions, we find that for all $m > j$, we have $2\sum_{i=1}^{m-j} D_{2j+2i}^t - \sigma \leq D_{2j}^t$. A simple induction argument then gives that for all $k < m$,

$$2 \cdot 3^{k-1} D_{2m}^t - 3^{k-1}\sigma \leq D_{2m-2k}^t. \tag{1}$$

Taking $k = m$ gives $2 \cdot 3^{m-1} D_{2m}^t - 3^{m-1}\sigma \leq D$ for all $m$. Let $m$ be the largest value for which $D_{2m} \geq \sigma$.[6] Then we have $3^{m-1}\sigma \leq D$, hence $m \leq \log_3(D) - \log_3(\sigma) + 1$. Further,

$$L_{2m+3}^t(H_{2m+2}^t) \leq D_{2m+2}^t + \sigma < 2\sigma.$$

Since the maximum load can be at most $2m + 2 + L_{2m+3}(H_{2m+2})$, combining the previous two expressions gives $\sup_{e \in E}\left\{L^t(e)\right\} \leq 2\log_3(D) + 2\sigma + 2 = O(\log D + \sigma)$, as desired. □

[6]If no such $m$ exists, (i.e., $D < \sigma$), then Lemma 3.4 with $j = 0$ gives that the total load satisfies $L(g) \leq D + \sigma = O(\sigma)$ so that the theorem follows.

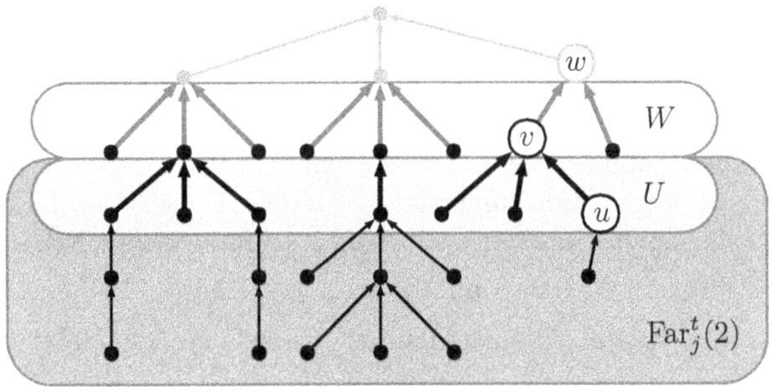


**Figure 1:** *An illustrative example for* $\text{Far}_j^t(k)$ *in some connected component of* $H_j^k$ *with* $k = 2$. *The crux of the inductive step in the proof of Lemma 3.6 is the following observation. If no buffer in U forwards, then either (1) all buffers in U have load at most j, or (2) some buffer in W has load at least* $j + 2$.

Lemma 3.4 is a consequence of the following four sub-lemmas. Lemma 3.6 analyzes the $(j + 1)$-loads above $j$-plateaus without considering the movement of the underlying $j$-plateaus. Lemmas 3.7, 3.8, and 3.9 describe the dynamics of $j$-plateaus as they shrink, grow, and collide. Before stating and proving Lemma 3.4, we introduce some notation.

*Notation 3.5.* For $k \geq 0$, $\text{Far}_j^t(k)$ denotes the set of edges in $H_j^t$ at level at most $k$, i.e., $\text{Far}_j^t(k) = \{e \in H_j^t \mid \text{lv}(e) \leq k\}$. See Figure 1 for an illustration.

LEMMA 3.6. *For t, and even j, suppose that for all* $\ell \leq \text{depth}(H_j^t)$

$$L_{j+1}^t(\text{Far}_j^t(\ell)) \leq \ell + \xi(t) .$$

*Let* $v \leq \xi(t+1) - \xi(t) + 1$ *be the number of packets injected during round t. For a fixed* $k \leq \text{depth}(H_j^t)$, *let* $v = v_{in} + v_{out}$ *where* $v_{in}$ *is the number of packets injected into buffers in* $\text{Far}_j^t(k)$, *and* $v_{out}$ *is the number of packets injected to buffers* $u \notin \text{Far}_j^t(k)$. *Then*

$$L_{j+1}^{t+1}(\text{Far}_j^t(k)) \leq k + \xi(t+1) - v_{out}. \tag{2}$$

PROOF. Suppose to the contrary that (2) fails, and choose the minimum $k$ for which it fails. By the definition of $\text{Far}_j^t(k)$, no leaf in $\text{Far}_j^t(k)$ receives a packet from a child (in $G$) during round $t$, because packets are never forwarded to buffers with greater load. Further, since $j$ is even, no buffer with load $j$ receives a packet from another buffer of load $j$ in round $t$. Therefore, $L_{j+1}(\text{Far}_j^t(k))$ can only increase if packets are injected into $\text{Far}_j^t(k)$ during the injection step of the $t$-th round.

Since we assume (2) fails, $L_{j+1}(\text{Far}_j^t(k))$ must have increased by at least $v_{in}$ during round $t$. However, $L_{j+1}(\text{Far}_j^t(k))$ can increase by at most $v_{in}$. Thus, by the hypothesis of the lemma,

$$L_{j+1}^{t+1}(\text{Far}_j^t(k)) \geq k + \xi(t+1) + 1 - v_{out} \geq k + \xi(t) + v_{in} . \tag{3}$$

Let $U$ be the set of edges in $\text{Far}_j^t(k)$ at level exactly $k$, and let $W$ denote the set of edges in $H_j^t$ at level exactly $k + 1$. By the definition of level, $U$ contains all edges in $H_j^t$ leading out of $\text{Far}_j^t(k)$. We claim that there exists $e \in U$ such that $L^t(e) \geq j + 1$. (Otherwise, $L_{j+1}^t(\text{Far}_j^t(k-1)) = L_{j+1}^t(\text{Far}_j^t(k)) = k + \xi(t) > (k-1) + \xi(t)$ contradicting the hypothesis of the lemma.) Let $e = (u, w) \in U$ with $L^t(e) \geq j + 1$, and let $f = (w, v)$ be the (unique) edge out of $w$. By (3), no edge $e' \in U$ with $L^t(e') \geq j + 1$ can forward a packet in round $t$. Thus, the edge $e$ does not forward in round $t$. Therefore, either (a) $L^t(f) \geq j + 2$, or (b) there exists $e' = (u', w) \in U$ such that $L^t(e') \geq L^t(e)$. In case (a), we have $L_{j+1}^t(\text{Far}_j^t(k+1)) \geq L_{j+1}^t(\text{Far}_j^t(k)) + 2 \geq k + 3 + \xi(t)$, which contradicts the hypothesis of the lemma. Thus (a) cannot occur. However, if (b) occurs but not (a), the edge $(u', w)$ forwards in round $t$ contradicting (3). Thus, (2) occurs. □

LEMMA 3.7. *Let* $e = (u, v) \in E_j^t$ *where* $v \in V_j^t$ *is not a root in* $H_j^t$ *(i.e.,* $\text{depth}(e) > 0$*). Then* $L^{t+1}(e) \geq j$. *In particular,* $(u, v) \in V_j^{t+1}$.

PROOF. Since $v$ is not a root, let $f = (v, w) \in E_j^t$. By definition, $L^t(e), L^t(f) \geq j$. If $L^t(e) = j$, then $e$ will not forward a packet in round $t$, as $j$ is even. On the other hand, if $L^t(e) \geq j+1$, $e$ can forward at most one packet in a single round, hence $L^{t+1}(e) \geq j$. □

LEMMA 3.8. *If* $e \in H_j^t \cap H_j^{t+1}$, *then* $\text{lv}_j^{t+1}(e) \geq \text{lv}_j^t(e)$, *where* $\text{lv}_j^t(e)$ *denotes the level of e in* $H_j^t$.

PROOF. Fix $e \in E_j^t \cap E_j^{t+1}$. Let $T^t$ and $T^{t+1}$ be the trees containing $e$ at times $t$ and $t + 1$, respectively. By Lemma 3.7, $T^{t+1}$ can be obtained from $T^t$ by applying one or more of the following operations:

(a) removing the root $r$ from $T^t$,
(b) attaching a tree $T$ as a child of some node $u$ in $T^t$,
(c) attaching $T^t$ as a subtree of another tree $T$.

We will show that each of these operations can only increase the level of $e$. For (a), both the depth of $e$ and the depth of $T^t$ are decreased by 1, so $\text{lv}(e)$ is unchanged. For operation (b), attaching $T$ can only increase the depth of $T^t$ while leaving $\text{depth}(e)$ unchanged. Thus the $\text{lv}(e)$ can only increase. Finally, for operation (c), suppose the root $r$ of $T^t$ becomes a child of a vertex $u$ in $T$. Then the depth of $v$ (and every other vertex in $T^t$) increases by $\text{depth}((u, w)) + 1$ where $w$ is $u$'s parent (if any). Since the depth of the new tree is at least $\text{depth}(T^t) + \text{depth}((u, w)) + 1$, $\text{lv}(e)$ cannot decrease. □

LEMMA 3.9. *Let* $S = H_j^{t+1} \setminus H_j^t$, *and let* $v_{out}$ *denote the number of packets injected to edges* $e \notin H_j^t$ *in round t. Then* $L_{j+1}^{t+1}(S) \leq v_{out}$.

PROOF OF LEMMA 3.9. Suppose $e \in S$ so that $L^{t+1}(e) \geq j$ but $L^t(e) < j$. Let $L_{\text{fwd}}^t(e)$ denote the load of $e$ during round $t$ after the forwarding step, but before the injection step. Observe that $L_{\text{fwd}}^t(e) \leq j$ because $v$ could have received at most one packet from a child in the forwarding step. Therefore, $e$ must have received at least $L_{j+1}^{t+1}(e)$ packets during the injection step of round $t$. Thus $L_{j+1}^{t+1}(S) = \sum_{v \in S} L_{j+1}^{t+1}(v) \leq v_{\text{out}}$. □

PROOF OF LEMMA 3.4. We will prove the more general statement that for all even heights $j$, all times $t$ and all levels $k \geq 0$ we have $L_{j+1}^t(\text{Far}_j^t(k)) \leq k + \xi(t)$. Lemma 3.4 follows taking $k = \text{depth}(H_j^t)$, and using the fact that $\xi(t) < \sigma$.

We argue by induction on $t$. The case $t = 1$ is trivial as no packets have been injected at the beginning of the first round. Suppose the lemma holds at time $t-1$. Let $S = H_j^t \setminus H_j^{t-1}$. By Lemma 3.8, $\mathrm{Far}_j^t(k) \cap H_j^{t-1} \subseteq \mathrm{Far}_j^{t-1}(k)$. Therefore, we have $\mathrm{Far}_j^t(k) \subseteq S \cup \mathrm{Far}_j^{t-1}(k)$. As before, let $v_{\mathrm{in}}$ and $v_{\mathrm{out}}$ be the number of packets, respectively, injected into $\mathrm{Far}_j^{t-1}(k)$ and its complement in round $t-1$. It follows that

$$\begin{aligned} L_{j+1}^t(\mathrm{Far}_j^t(k)) &\leq L_{j+1}^t(S \cup \mathrm{Far}_j^{t-1}(k)) \\ &= L_{j+1}^t(S) + L_{j+1}^t(\mathrm{Far}_j^{t-1}(k)) \\ &\leq v_{\mathrm{out}} + k + \xi(t) - v_{\mathrm{out}} \qquad \text{(Lemmas 3.9 \& 3.6)} \\ &= k + \xi(t). \end{aligned}$$

□

## 3.1 General Uniform Capacities

In this section we describe a modification of OED forwarding for general uniform edge capacities. That is, we assume that every edge has capacity $c \geq 1$. In this case, the adversary may have any rate $\rho \leq c$. For simplicity, we assume that $\rho$ is an integer and that $\rho = \Theta(c)$. We define the *virtual load* of a buffer $e$ to be $\mathrm{VL}(e) = \lceil L(e)/\rho \rceil$. The idea of generalized OED is to apply the OED forwarding rule to *virtual* loads, and forward packets $\rho$ at a time. If $v$ has multiple children $u_1, \ldots, u_k$ with the same virtual load, $v$ accepts the $\rho$ "highest" packets stored in $(u_1, v), \ldots, (u_k, v)$. We formally describe the modified version of OED forwarding in Algorithm 2.

**Algorithm 2** OED for general uniform $c \geq 1$ for a node $v \in V$

```
X ← {(u, v) ∈ E}                              // set of incoming edges
f ← (v, w)                                     // outgoing edge
if ∃e ∈ X such that (VL(e) > VL(f)) or (VL(e) = VL(f) and
VL(f) is odd) then
    q ← L_{ρ VL(f)+1}(X) if VL(f) is odd, and L_{ρ(VL(f)+1)+1}(X) otherwise
    P ← set of min{ρ, q} highest packets in buffers in X
    each e ∈ X forwards |e ∩ P| packets
end if
```

With the generalization of OED forwarding described in Algorithm 2, we obtain the following performance guarantee.

Theorem 3.10. *Let $\mathcal{G}$ be the family of single destination trees with uniform capacities $c \geq 1$, and $\mathcal{A} = \mathcal{A}(\rho, \sigma)$ with $\rho \leq c$. Then the generalized OED in Algorithm 2 achieves* $\mathrm{cost}(\mathrm{OED}, G, \mathcal{A}) = O(\rho \log n + \sigma)$.

The proof of Theorem 3.10 (omitted) is analogous to the proof of Theorem 3.1. The main difference is that in the analysis, we classify plateaus by *virtual* load rather than true load. In particular, we obtain the following analogue of Lemma 3.4, from which Theorem 3.10 follows.

Lemma 3.11. *For a fixed time $t$ and even height $j$, let $H_j^t$ be the forest of nodes containing buffers in $G$ whose* virtual *load is at least $j$. Then $L_{\rho j+1}^t(H_j^t) \leq \rho \cdot \mathrm{depth}(H_j^t) + \xi(t)$.*

# 4 DELAY

In this section, we analyze the delay experienced by packets under OED forwarding—that is, the amount of time it takes for a packet to reach its destination. In the case where $\rho = c = 1$, OED forwarding may incur infinite delay. Indeed, we will show that for *any* forwarding protocol with maximum loads less than $\mathrm{diam}(G) - 1$, there is a $(1, 0)$-bounded adversary which incurs infinite delays. Nonetheless, for $\rho$ strictly less than 1, the delay for OED is $O\left(\frac{\mathrm{diam}(G)}{1-\rho} + \sigma\right)$ assuming first in, first out (FIFO) or longest in system (LIS) scheduling.

*Definition 4.1.* Let $G$ be a network, $F$ a forwarding protocol, and $A$ an adversary. The *delay* of $F$ on $G$ with adversary $A$ is the maximum amount of time that any packet remains in $G$ before being delivered to its destination. For a packet $p$, let $t_p$ denote the time $p$ was injected. Then

$$\mathrm{delay}(F, G, A) = \sup_{t,p}\{t - t_p \mid p \text{ not delivered by time } t\}.$$

Observe that if some packet $p$ is never delivered to its destination, then $\mathrm{delay}(F, G, A) = \infty$.

Proposition 4.2. *Consider the line network $G = (V, E)$ where $V = \{v_1, \ldots, v_n\}$, $E = \{e_1, \ldots, e_{n-1}\}$ and $e_i = (v_i, v_{i+1})$, and assume each edge has capacity 1. Suppose that for all $A \in \mathcal{A}(1, 0)$, $\mathrm{delay}(F, G, A) < \infty$. Then there exists $A \in \mathcal{A}(1, 0)$ such that $\mathrm{cost}(F, G, A) \geq n - 2$.*

Proof. Consider the adversary $A$ which in each of the first $n-2$ rounds injects one packet per round at $v_1$ destined for $v_n$. For all $t > n-2$, $A$ injects a single packet at $v_{n-1}$ destined for $v_n$. This concludes the description of $A$.

We now analyze the load. Call the packets injected at $v_1$ *initial* packets. At the end of round $n-2$, all initial packets are in buffers $e_1, \ldots, e_{n-2}$. Since $\mathrm{delay}(F, G, A) < \infty$, there is a time $t$ such that all initial packets reach $v_n$ by time $t$. Thus, during the time interval $I = [n-1, t]$, all $n-2$ initial packets crossed the edge $e_{n-1}$. But during $I$, a packet is injected into $e_{n-1}$ in each round, and since at most one packet reaches $v_n$ from $v_{n-1}$ in each round, it must be the case that $L^t(e_{n-1}) \geq n-2$. □

Proposition 4.2 shows that finite delay and sublinear cost are mutually exclusive for any protocol when the rate of the adversary is equal to the capacity of the edges. The following result bounds the delay incurred by OED when the rate is strictly smaller than the capacity. For simplicity, we assume that $c = 1$.

Proposition 4.3. *Let $G$ be a single destination tree. Consider OED forwarding where each queue is first in, first out (FIFO) or longest in system (LIS). For any $A \in \mathcal{A}(\rho, \sigma)$ with $\rho < 1$, $\mathrm{delay}(\mathrm{OED}, G, A) = O\left(\frac{\mathrm{diam}(G)}{1-\rho} + \sigma\right)$.*

Before proving Proposition 4.3, we state and prove two lemmas. Suppose $g$ is a buffer on the path between $p$ and its destination. We say that $p$ is *connected to* $g$ at time $t$ if each buffer $e$ on the path from $p$ to $g$ satisfies $L^t(e) \geq 1$. That is, $p$ is connected to $g$ if $p$ resides in $g$'s connected component in $H_1^t$.

LEMMA 4.4. *Suppose $p$ is connected to $g$ at time $t$, and $p$ has not been forwarded to $g$ by time $t+w$ for some $w \geq 0$. Then $p$ is connected to $g$ at time $t + w$.*

PROOF. We induct on $w$. The case $w = 0$ holds by the hypothesis. Suppose $p$ is connected $g$ at time $t + w$, and suppose to the contrary that $p$ becomes disconnected from $g$ at time $t + w + 1$. That is, there is some buffer $e$ in the path from $p$ to $g$ satisfying $L^{t+w}(e) \geq 1$ but $L^{t+w+1}(e) = 0$. If there are multiple such buffers $e$, choose the one closest to $p$ at time $t + w$. Then we must have had $L^{t+w}(e) = 1$ and $e$ forwarded a packet in round $t + w$, but not received a packet. Let $f$ be $e$'s child on the path from $p$ to $e$. By the inductive hypothesis, $L^{t+w}(f) \geq 1$. Therefore, the activated edge $(f', e)$ in round $t + w$ must have satisfied $L^{t+w}(f') \geq 1$. Since $L^{t+w}(e) = 1$, $f'$ would have forwarded a packet to $e$ in round $t + w$, a contradiction. Thus, $p$ remains connected to $g$ at time $t + w + 1$. □

LEMMA 4.5. *Suppose $p$ is injected at time $r$. Then for some $w \leq \text{diam}(G)$, $p$ is connected to the destination at time $r + w$.*

PROOF. For $w \geq 0$, let $g_w$ be the furthest buffer from $p$ along the path from $p$ to the destination to which $p$ is connected. We will show that for all $w$ such that $g_w$ is not the destination, $\text{depth}(g_{w+1}) \leq \text{depth}(w_r) - 1$. To this end, by Lemma 4.4, it suffices to show that if $f$ is $g_w$'s parent, then $L^{r+w+1}(g_w) \geq 1$. By the definition of $g_w$, $L^{r+w}(f) = 0$. Since at least one of $f$'s children—namely, $g_w$—has a positive load at time $r + w$, $f$ receives a packet during this round. Thus, $L^{r+w+1}(f) \geq 1$. Therefore, $g_{w+1}$ is either $f$ or one of $f$'s ancestors and the desired result follows. □

PROOF OF PROPOSITION 4.3. We prove the proposition for FIFO queues, then describe how to modify the argument for LIS scheduling. Suppose $p$ is a packet in the system at time $t$. We we define the *position* of $p$ at time $t$, denoted $\text{pos}^t(p)$, to be the number of packets which could potentially delay $p$. Such packets reside in $p$'s current buffer, buffers on the path from $p$ to the destination, or buffers in different branches of $G$ than $p$'s current location.

Suppose $p$ is injected at time $r$ and becomes connected to the destination at time $s \geq r$. By Lemma 4.5, $s - r \leq \text{diam}(G)$. For $w \geq 0$, the adversary can inject at most $\rho(w+1)+\sigma$ packets during the interval $[s, s+w]$. However, during the interval $[s, s+w]$, as long as $p$ is connected to its destination, one packet will leave the system in each round. Thus there is a net loss of $(1-\rho)w - \rho - \sigma$ packets, and each lost packet decreases $\text{pos}^t(p)$ by 1. By Lemma 3.4 with $j = 0$, we have $\text{pos}^s(p) \leq \text{diam}\, G + \sigma$. Therefore, $p$ must have been delivered by time $s+w$ for any $w$ satisfying $(1-\rho)w - \rho - \sigma > \text{diam}\, G + \sigma$. Solving this inequality for $w$ gives that $p$ was delivered by time $s + w$ for $w = \frac{1}{1-\rho}\,\text{diam}(G) + \rho + 2\sigma + 1$. Combining this expression with with Lemma 4.5 above, $p$ is delivered by time $t = r + \text{diam}(G) + w$, whence the proposition follows for FIFO queues.

To modify the proof of Proposition 4.3 for LIS scheduling, we need only modify the definition of $\text{pos}^t(p)$ to include packets in buffers $f \prec e$ which were injected before time $r$. The rest of the argument is exactly the same. □

## 5 LOWER BOUNDS ON LOCAL ALGORITHMS

In this section we prove lower bounds on the space requirement of local algorithms. We start with the model of unit capacity links, and then extend the bound to infinite capacity links.

THEOREM 5.1. *Consider the line network $G = (V, E)$ where $V = \{v_1, \ldots, v_n\}$, $E = \{e_1, \ldots, e_{n-1}\}$ where $e_i = (v_i, v_{i+1})$. For every constant $\rho > 0$, $\sigma \geq 1$ and for all deterministic protocols $F$ with locality $d$, there exists an adversary $A_F \in \mathcal{A}(\rho, \sigma)$ such that $\text{cost}(F, G, A_F) = \Omega(\frac{1}{d}\log n + \sigma)$.*

To simplify presentation, we assume that $\rho > 1/2$ and $\sigma \geq 2$. For general $\rho$ and $\sigma = 1$, the same proof techniques described below can be applied using $k = O(1/\rho)$ sub-intervals instead of 2. We start with a helper lemma which we state without proof.

LEMMA 5.2. *For any fixed $\rho > 1/2$ and $\sigma \geq 2$, there exist constants $M \in \mathbf{N}$ and $\varepsilon > 0$ such that a $(\rho, \sigma)$- adversary $A$ can inject, in any $M$ consecutive time steps, $(\frac{1}{2} + \varepsilon)M$ packets, all crossing the same edge $e$.*

We now describe the adversary $A_F$ which achieves the lower bound of Theorem 5.1 against a deterministic local protocol $F$. Without loss of generality, we assume $n$ is a power of two. The idea is that $A_F$ initially injects packets into $v_1$ until the average load in the system is at least 1/2. $A_F$ then breaks the network into two subintervals of size $n/2$. In the next phase lasting roughly $n/4d$ rounds, $A_F$ injects roughly $n/8d + \varepsilon n/4d$ packets[7] into the middle of one of the subintervals.

The adversary chooses which subinterval to inject into by simulating the protocol $F$ for roughly $n/4d$ steps assuming no new injections, and picking the subinterval $I$ with larger average load. In $n/4d$ steps, at most $n/4d$ packets could have left the network. Thus the average load in $I$ is at least $1/2 - 1/4d$ after $n/4d$ rounds without injections. Since $A_F$ injects packets into the middle of $I$, the locality of $F$ guarantees that nodes at the boundary of $I$ will not detect that the packets were injected until after roughly $n/4d$ rounds have elapsed. Thus, the net gain or loss of packets from forwarding across $I$'s boundary will be the same in the simulation with no packet injections as when $A_F$ injects the packets. When $A_F$ injects packets into $I$, its new load will be the simulated load plus the number of packets injected. Since $n/8d + \varepsilon n/4d$ packets were injected and $|I| = n/2$, the average load of $I$ increases to at least $1/2 + \varepsilon/2d$.

$A_F$ continues by iteratively applying the strategy described above to $I$: $A_F$ splits $I$ into subintervals, simulates $F$, injects into the heavier subinterval, and repeats with the heavier subinterval. This process continues for $\Theta(\log n)$ phases. Each iteration increases the average load of some interval by at least $\varepsilon/2d$, so load of some subinterval is $\Omega((\varepsilon/d)\log n)$. We give a formal description of $A_F$ as Algorithm 3.

The following lemma formalizes the effect of locality on the loads of buffers. It shows that if two configurations are identical in some neighborhood of a buffer $e$, then the actions of $e$ in both configurations are identical for some time.

[7]Throughout this section, we assume that all ratios (e.g., $n/8d$) are integers in order to simplify notation.

**Algorithm 3** Adversary $A_F$ against $F$ with locality $d$

1: $I \leftarrow \{0, \dots, n-1\}$
2: In $n$ rounds, inject $(\frac{1}{2} + \varepsilon)n$ packets into $v_0$
3: **while** $|I| \geq 4d + 2M$ **do**
4: $\quad I_0, I_1 \leftarrow$ left and right halves of $I$
5: $\quad k \leftarrow |I|/4d$
6: $\quad$ Simulate $k$ rounds of $F$ w/out injection get simulated loads $\tilde{L}$
7: $\quad I \leftarrow \arg\max \left\{\tilde{L}(I_0), \tilde{L}(I_1)\right\}$ where $\tilde{L}(I_i)$ is sim. load of $I_i$.
8: $\quad$ In $k$ rounds, inject $(\frac{1}{2} + \varepsilon)k$ packets into $m_I$, the midpt. of $I$
9: **end while**

Lemma 5.3. *Let $F$ be a deterministic protocol with locality $d$ and $G = (V, E)$ a directed network, and let $e \in E$. Let $L, K$ be two configurations of $G$ such that for some $t \in \mathbf{N}$, we have that for all $f \in E$ with $\operatorname{dist}(f, e) \leq td$, $L(f) = K(f)$. Let $L'$ be the configuration reached from $L$ after $t$ injection-free steps, and define $K'$ similarly. Then for all $g \in E$ with $\operatorname{dist}(g, e) \leq d$ we have $L'(g) = K'(g)$.*

Proof. We argue by induction on $t$. The base case $t = 0$ is trivial, as $L' = L$, $K' = K$, and $L(e) = K(e)$ by assumption.

For the inductive step, suppose the lemma holds for $t-1$, and let $\widehat{L}$ and $\widehat{K}$ denote the configurations resulting from $L$ and $K$, respectively, after $t-1$ steps. By the assumption for $t$, it holds that for any $g \in \Gamma_d(e)$, in $K$ and $L$ we have that $L(f) = K(f)$ for all $f \in E$ with $\operatorname{dist}(f, g) \leq d(t-1)$. Therefore, the induction hypothesis, applied to all such edges $g$ with $t-1$, implies that for all $g \in \Gamma_d(e)$ we have $\widehat{K}(g) = \widehat{L}(g)$. Since the configuration of any edge is a deterministic function of the state of the edges within distance $d$ (and the injections, which are non-existent in our case), we may deduce that in $K'$ and $L'$, which result from $\widehat{K}$ and $\widehat{L}$ by taking one step, we have $K'(e) = L'(e)$, and we are done. □

Corollary 5.4. *Suppose $L^t$ is a configuration at time $t$ and $e, f \in E$ with $\operatorname{dist}(e, f) \geq dk$. Let $\tilde{L}^{t+k}$ be the configuration obtained by applying $F$ without injections at times $s \in [t, t+k]$, and let $L^{t+k}$ be the configuration obtained when packets are injected only into $f$ during times $s \in [t, t+k]$. Then for all $s \in [t, t+k]$ and $g$ with $\operatorname{dist}(g, e) \leq d$ we have $\tilde{L}^s(g) = L^s(g)$. In particular, $e$ forwards precisely the same (number of) packets during rounds $t, \dots, t+k$ regardless of whether or not packets are injected into $f$.*

Proof. By induction, it is easy to shows that for all $\ell \in [0, k]$, at time $t + \ell$ we have $\tilde{L}^s(g) = L^s(g)$ for all $g$ with $\operatorname{dist}(g, e) \leq (k-\ell)d$. For the inductive step, apply Lemma 5.3 to all $g'$ with $\operatorname{dist}(g', e) \leq (k-\ell)d$. □

The following lemma shows that $A_F$ increases the average load of some sub-interval in each iteration of Algorithm 3.

Lemma 5.5. *Consider a single iteration of the "while" loop in Algorithm 3. Let $I$ be the active interval at the beginning of the loop, and $I' \subseteq I$ the interval chosen in line 7. Suppose the loop begins during round $t$ and ends immediately before round $t + k$ where $k = |I|/4d$. Then $\bar{L}^{t+k}(I') \geq \bar{L}^t(I) + \varepsilon/2d$ where $\bar{L}^t(I) = L^t(I)/|I|$ is the average load of $I$ at time $t$.*

Proof. We must show that

$$\bar{L}^{t+k}(I') \geq \bar{L}^t(I) + \frac{\varepsilon}{2d} \tag{4}$$

Where $\bar{L}^t(I) = L^t(I)/|I|$ is the average load of $I$ at time $t$. First observe that in $k$ rounds, at most $k$ packets could have left $I$. Thus, the simulated load of $I$ at time $t + k$ satisfies

$$\tilde{L}^{t+k}(I) \geq L^t(I) - k = L^t(I) - \frac{|I|}{4d}\,.$$

By the choice of $I'$, the simulated average load of $I'$ satisfies

$$\tilde{L}^{t+k}(I')/\left|I'\right| \geq \bar{L}^t(I) - 1/4d\,.$$

Let $f$ and $g$ be the edges which, respectively, enter and leave $I'$ (i.e., $I'$'s left and right endpoints), and let $e$ be the middle buffer of $I'$. By Corollary 5.4, in $k$ rounds, $f$ and $g$ will forward the same number of packets regardless of whether packets are injected into $e$. By Lemma 5.2, the adversary $A_F$ injects at least $(1/2+\varepsilon)k$ packets into $e$. Therefore, the average load of $I'$ increases by at least

$$\frac{(1/2+\varepsilon)k}{|I'|} = \frac{1/2+\varepsilon}{|I|/2} \cdot \frac{|I|}{4d} = \frac{1}{4d} + \frac{\varepsilon}{2d}\,.$$

Thus, we have $\bar{L}^{t+k} \geq \bar{L}^t(I) - (1/4d) + (1/4d) + (\varepsilon/2d)$, which gives the desired result. □

Proof of Theorem 5.1. Initially $|I| = n$. Each iteration of the while loop in Algorithm 3 halves $|I|$. Since the loop only terminates when $|I| < 4d + 2M$ (where $M$ is determined by Lemma 5.2), it continues for $\Omega(\log n)$ steps. Therefore, by Lemma 5.5, at the end of the final iteration, the load of $I$ satisfies $\bar{L}(I) \geq \Omega\left(\frac{\varepsilon}{d} \log n\right)$. In particular, some buffer has load at least this large. □

**Extensions.** Theorem 5.1 assumes that packet movement is restricted by the routes determined by the adversary with channel capacities that are a constant factor larger than the rate $\rho$. Here we describe more general, albeit slightly weaker lower bounds which do not rely upon these assumptions. Thus locality alone—without capacity constraints or assuming that the routes are given in advance—is enough to allow a $(\rho, \sigma)$-adversary to inflict nearly logarithmic loads. The lower bounds apply to a bi-directional ring network with unlimited capacities and a single destination, and also to any network with a large induced cycle or path.

Theorem 5.6. *Let $C_n$ be the (un directed) cycle network with $n$ vertices, $v_1, \dots, v_n$ where $v_n$ is the destination of all packets and all edges have infinite capacity. Then for every deterministic $d$-local protocol and $\rho > 0$, there exists a $(\rho, 1)$-adversary $A_F$ such that $\operatorname{cost}(F, C_n, A_F) = \Omega(\log n / \log\log n)$.*

To prove Theorem 5.6, the adversary adopts a similar strategy as the adversary in the proof of Theorem 5.1. Starting from an interval $I = \{v_i, v_{i+1}, \dots, v_m\}$ with average load $\bar{L}(I) = \alpha$, $A_F$ breaks $I$ into $k$ disjoint consecutive subintervals $I = I_1 \cup I_2 \cup \dots \cup I_k$. The goal of $A_F$ is to perform injections so that there exists some subinterval $I_j$ whose average load is $\alpha + \varepsilon$ for some constant $\varepsilon$ which depends only on $d$ and $\rho$. The adversary continues setting $I \leftarrow I_j$ and iteratively applying this procedure until $|I|$ is constant. After $\ell$ levels of recursion, the average load of $I$ is $\ell\varepsilon$. We show that it is sufficient to choose $k = O(\log n)$. Thus, the adversary continues for $\Omega(\log n / \log\log n)$ iterations, and the desired result follows.

**Algorithm 4** Injection procedure for adversary $A_F$

```
1: if There exists I_j with L̄(I_j) ≥ α + ε then
2:     I ← I_j
3: else
4:     t ← |I| /2kd
5:     simulate F for t rounds
6:     I_j ← arg max {L̃(I_i) | 1 ≤ i ≤ k}
7:     in t rounds, inject ρt packets into the middle of I_j
8:     I ← I_j
9: end if
```

Proof of Theorem 5.6. Let $\varepsilon > 0$ and $k \geq 2$ be parameters to be chosen later. Without loss of generality, we assume that $1/\rho$ is an integer.[8] Thus, in any any $1/\rho$ consecutive steps, a $(\rho, 1)$-bounded adversary can inject a packet. For any interval $I = \{v_i, \ldots, v_\ell\}$, write $I$ as $k$ consecutive intervals $I = I_1 \cup I_2 \cup \cdots \cup I_k$ with $|I_j| = |I|/k$. Suppose $I$ has average load $\bar{L}(I) = \alpha$. Then $A_F$ repeats the injection procedure of Algorithm 4 until $|I| \leq 2dk$.

Suppose $\bar{L}(I) = \alpha$ before some call to Algorithm 4. We will show that there exists $k = O(\log n)$ and $\varepsilon > 0$ depending only on $\rho$ and $d$ such that after a call to Algorithm 4 we have $\bar{L}(I) \geq \alpha + \varepsilon$. Clearly this is the case if line 2 is executed, so we focus on the case where lines 4–8 are executed.

Since $t < |I_1|, |I_k|$, any packets which left $I$ after $t$ simulated rounds must have been in $I_1$ or $I_k$. Since $\bar{L}(I_1), \bar{L}(I_k) < \alpha + \varepsilon$, the number of packets which could have left $I$ is at most $\frac{2}{k}|I|(\alpha + \varepsilon)$. Therefore, the simulated load after $t$ rounds satisfies $\tilde{L}(I) \geq |I|(\alpha - \frac{2}{k}(\alpha + \varepsilon))$. In particular, the average simulated load of $I_j$ chosen in line 6 is at least $\alpha - \frac{2}{k}(\alpha + \varepsilon)$. Applying Corollary 5.4, the average load of $I_j$ after line 7 is $\alpha - \frac{2}{k}(\alpha + \varepsilon) + \frac{\rho}{2d}$, as $\rho t = \rho|I_j|/2d$ packets were injected in line 7. In order to obtain the claimed load increase, we must find $k$ and $\varepsilon$ such that

$$\frac{\rho}{2d} - \frac{2}{k}(\alpha + \varepsilon) \geq \varepsilon,$$

or equivalently

$$k \geq \frac{4d(\alpha + \varepsilon)}{\rho - 2d\varepsilon}. \tag{5}$$

Choosing $\varepsilon = \rho/4d$, (5) is satisfied for any $k \geq 8d\alpha/\rho + 2$. Observe that if $\alpha$ is ever larger than $\log n$, then then Theorem 5.6 follows. Thus it suffices to consider $\alpha \leq \log n$. Therefore (5) is satisfied for $\varepsilon = \rho/4d$ and $k = 8(d/\rho)\log n + 2$.

To finish the proof, $A_F$ initially chooses $I = \{v_1, \ldots, v_n\}$. Since $|I|$ decreases by a factor of $1/k = \Theta(\log n)$ each iteration of Algorithm 4, the procedure continues for $\ell = \Theta(\log n / \log\log n)$ iterations. Each iteration increases the average load of $I$ by at least $\varepsilon$. Thus after $\ell$ iterations, some buffer has a load which is $\Omega(\log n / \log\log n)$, as desired. □

## 6 GENERAL DAGS

In this section, we consider local forwarding protocols on general directed acyclic graphs (DAGs). In this context, Adler and Rosén prove the following theorem.

[8] If $1/\rho$ is not an integer, we can decrease $\rho$ to $1/\lceil 1/\rho \rceil$.

**Algorithm 5** A $(1, 0)$-adversary against all forwarding protocols.

```
for i ← 1 to n/2 do
    for j ← 1 to n − i − 1 do
        Inject one packet at e_1 with destination v_{n−i}.
        Inject one packet at e_{n−i} with destination v_n.
    end for
end for
```

Theorem 6.1 (Adler & Roseén [1]). *Let $\mathcal{F}$ be the family of DAGs, and let* LIS *be the greedy longest-in-system scheduling policy. Then for every $G \in \mathcal{F}$ and $\rho, \sigma > 0$, $\rho \leq 1$ and $A \in \mathcal{A}(\rho, \sigma)$ we have* $\mathrm{cost}(\mathrm{LIS}, G, A) = O(\mathrm{diam}(G) + \sigma)$, *where* $\mathrm{diam}(G)$ *is the length of the longest path in G. Further, this bound is tight as there exists an adversary $A \in \mathcal{A}(\rho, \sigma)$ such that* $\mathrm{cost}(\mathrm{LIS}, G, A) = \Omega(\mathrm{diam}(G))$.

In [22] it is proved that the lower bound of $\Omega(\mathrm{diam}(G))$ holds for *any* greedy protocol. Here, we generalize these lower bounds further to all protocols on DAGs. We emphasize that the following lower bound (which matches the upper bound of the greedy LIS protocol) holds even for global, offline, dynamic, and randomized protocols.

Theorem 6.2. *Let $\mathcal{F}$ be the family of multiple destination paths. For every $G \in \mathcal{F}$, $\rho > 1/2$, and $\sigma \geq 2$, there exists an adversary $A \in \mathcal{A}(\rho, \sigma)$ such that for every forwarding protocol F (possibly global, offline, and randomized),* $\mathrm{cost}(F, G, A) = \Omega(n)$. *Further, the lower bound holds even if packets need not follow prescribed routes to their destinations.*

Proof. Let $G = (V, E)$ be the path graph with $V = \{v_1, \ldots, v_n\}$ and $E = \{e_1, \ldots, e_{n-1}\}$ where $e_i = (v_i, v_{i+1})$. Consider the adversary $A$ whose injection pattern is given in Algorithm 5. For simplicity of presentation, we assume that $\rho = 1$, though an application of Lemma 5.2 gives the general result. To further simplify notation for each $i < j$, we associate the buffers $e_i, e_{i+1}, \ldots, e_j$ with the interval $[i, j]$

**Observation.** Suppose a packet $p$ is injected at $v_1$ during the $i$-th iteration of the outer loop. Then at the end of the $i$-th iteration, $p$ is in the interval $[1, n - i - 1]$. In particular, $p$ is not delivered to its destination during the $i$-th iteration.

Let $\alpha_i$ denote the average load of $[1, n - i]$ at the beginning of iteration $i$, and $\beta_i$ be the average load of $[1, n - i]$ at the end of iteration $i$. Note that $2(n - i - 1)$ packets were injected into $[1, n - i]$ during this iteration. However, only $n - i - 1$ packets could have left $[1, n - i]$, as (by the observation above) no packet with a destination in $[1, n - i]$ reached its destination during the $i$-th iteration. Therefore, we have

$$\beta_i - \alpha_i \geq \frac{n - i - 1}{n - i} \geq \frac{1}{2} \quad \text{for} \quad i \leq n - 2. \tag{6}$$

We claim that for each $i < n/2$, at the end of the $i$-th iteration either (a) $L(e_{n-i}) \geq \frac{n}{8}$, or (b) $\alpha_{i+1} \geq \alpha_i + \frac{1}{4}$. To see this, note that if $L(e_{n-i}) < n/8$, then removing $e_{n-i}$ from $[1, n - i]$ can decrease the average load by less than $1/4$ because we assume that $i < n/2$. Then (b) follows from (6). Therefore, after $n/2$ iterations of the outer loop of Algorithm 5, either we had $L(e_{n-i}) \geq n/8$ for some $i < n/2$, or the average load of $[1, n/2]$ satisfies $\alpha_{n/2} \geq n/8$. In either case, the maximum load is $\Omega(n)$, as desired. □

*Remarks.* In the case where packets must follow their prescribed routes, the lower bound of Theorem 6.2 can be extended to single-source, single-destination DAGs as well. To achieve this lower bound, one can modify each directed path network by adding a single source vertex $u$ and a single destination vertex $w$. For every vertex $v$ in the path, add directed edges $(u, v)$ and $(v, w)$. We can then simulate injections at $v$ by injections into the buffer $(u, v)$. Similarly, a packet $p$ with destination $v$ is simulated by requiring that $v$ cross $(v, w)$.

Somewhat interestingly, the same adversary $A$ achieves the $\Omega(n)$ cost against any protocol. Theorem 6.2 also implies that there is a large difference in how locality affects the worst-case behavior of forwarding protocols on single destination trees and multiple destination paths. In the case of single destination trees (for fixed $\sigma$), global, local, and greedy policies (which can be viewed as 0-local policies) achieve worst case bounds of $O(1)$, $O(\log n)$, and $O(n)$, respectively. For multiple destinations, locality has no effect whatsoever on the worst case behavior, as all incur loads which are $\Omega(n)$. Further, the greedy LIS protocol achieves an optimal upper bound of $O(n)$.

## 7 CONCLUSIONS AND FUTURE WORK

In this work we have shown that in the case of a single destination tree, the maximal buffer load under a $(\rho, \sigma)$-adversary can be bounded by $\Theta(\rho \log(\operatorname{diam} G) + \sigma)$ for local algorithms: the lower bound holds for any $O(1)$-local algorithm, and the upper bound holds for the OED algorithm. In contrast, we have also shown that if we relax the single-destination assumption (even in a line network), or if we relax the tree assumption (even with a single destination), the maximal load jumps to $\Omega(\operatorname{diam}(G))$. These results seem to more-or-less settle the question of the maximal load in the $(\rho, \sigma)$-adversary case. The $\Omega(\operatorname{diam}(G))$ lower bound of Theorem 6.2 holds for randomized protocols, however we did not consider lower bounds for randomized local forwarding protocols on single destination trees. We conjecture that the $\Omega(\frac{1}{d} \log(\operatorname{diam} G) + \sigma)$ lower bound of Theorem 5.1 holds in expectation for randomized local protocols as well. The lower bound of Theorem 5.1 is valid for non-constant locality $d$, but it is nontrivial only for $d = O(\log(\operatorname{diam} G))$. We conjecture that the bound is tight for all $d = O(\log(\operatorname{diam} G))$.

It is interesting to understand the *competitive ratio* of the load for unrestricted adversaries: what is the worst-case ratio, over all injection patterns, of the buffer load generated by a forwarding algorithm to the optimal buffer load?

Another interesting question is to understand the case of overflows for unrestricted adversaries (see [15] for a survey of this model). In this case the algorithm needs also to say which packet to drop. The question is, assuming that buffers have some finite capacity $B$, what is the worst case ratio of the number of packets delivered by the algorithm to the best possible number of packets deliverable for the same injection pattern?

## REFERENCES


[1] Micah Adler and Adi Rosén. Tight bounds for the performance of longest-in-system on dags. In Helmut Alt and Afonso Ferreira, editors, *STACS 2002: 19th Annual Symposium on Theoretical Aspects of Computer Science Antibes - Juan les Pins, France, March 14–16, 2002 Proceedings*, pages 88–99, Berlin, Heidelberg, 2002. Springer Berlin Heidelberg.

[2] Yehuda Afek, Baruch Awerbuch, Eli Gafni, Yishay Mansour, Adi Rosén, and Nir Shavit. Slide-the key to polynomial end-to-end communication. *J. Algorithms*, 22(1):158–186, 1997.

[3] William Aiello, Rafail Ostrovsky, Eyal Kushilevitz, and Adi Rosén. Dynamic routing on networks with fixed-size buffers. In *Proc. 14th Ann. ACM-SIAM Symp. on Discrete Algorithms*, SODA '03, pages 771–780, Philadelphia, PA, USA, 2003. SIAM.

[4] William A. Aiello, Yishay Mansour, S. Rajagopolan, and Adi Rosén. Competitive queue policies for differentiated services. *J. Algorithms*, 55(2):113–141, May 2005.

[5] Matthew Andrews, Baruch Awerbuch, Antonio Fernández, Tom Leighton, Zhiyong Liu, and Jon Kleinberg. Universal-stability results and performance bounds for greedy contention-resolution protocols. *J. ACM*, 48(1):39–69, January 2001.

[6] Baruch Awerbuch, Petra Berenbrink, André Brinkmann, and Christian Scheideler. Simple routing strategies for adversarial systems. In *42nd Ann. Symp. on Foundations of Computer Science, FOCS 2001, 14-17 October 2001, Las Vegas, Nevada, USA*, pages 158–167, 2001.

[7] Baruch Awerbuch and Shilmon Event. Reliable broadcast protocols in unreliable networks. *Networks*, 16(4):381–396, 1986.

[8] Baruch Awerbuch and Tom Leighton. A simple local-control approximation algorithm for multicommodity flow. In *Foundations of Computer Science, 1993. Proceedings., 34th Annual Symposium on*, pages 459–468. IEEE, 1993.

[9] Baruch Awerbuch and Tom Leighton. Improved approximation algorithms for the multi-commodity flow problem and local competitive routing in dynamic networks. In *Proceedings of the twenty-sixth annual ACM symposium on Theory of computing*, pages 487–496. ACM, 1994.

[10] Baruch Awerbuch, Boaz Patt-Shamir, and George Varghese. Self-stabilizing end-to-end communication. *J. High Speed Networks*, 5(4):365–381, 1996.

[11] Allan Borodin, Jon Kleinberg, Prabhakar Raghavan, Madhu Sudan, and David P. Williamson. Adversarial queuing theory. *J. ACM*, 48(1):13–38, January 2001.

[12] R. L. Cruz. A calculus for network delay. i. network elements in isolation. *IEEE Transactions on Information Theory*, 37(1):114–131, Jan 1991.

[13] Stefan Dobrev, Manuel Lafond, Lata Narayanan, and Jaroslav Opatrny. Optimal local buffer management for information gathering with adversarial traffic. In *Proceedings of the 29th ACM Symposium on Parallelism in Algorithms and Architectures*, SPAA '17, New York, NY, USA, 2017. ACM.

[14] Andrew V. Goldberg and Robert E. Tarjan. Finding minimum-cost circulations by successive approximation. *Math. Oper. Res.*, 15(3):430–466, July 1990.

[15] Michael H. Goldwasser. A survey of buffer management policies for packet switches. *SIGACT News*, 41(1):100–128, March 2010.

[16] Alexander Kesselman, Zvi Lotker, Yishay Mansour, Boaz Patt-Shamir, Baruch Schieber, and Maxim Sviridenko. Buffer overflow management in QoS switches. *SIAM Journal on Computing*, 33(3):563–583, 2004.

[17] Fabian Kuhn, Nancy A. Lynch, and Rotem Oshman. Distributed computation in dynamic networks. In Leonard J. Schulman, editor, *Proceedings of the 42nd ACM Symposium on Theory of Computing, STOC 2010, Cambridge, Massachusetts, USA, 5-8 June 2010*, pages 513–522. ACM, 2010.

[18] HT Kung and Robert Morris. Credit-based flow control for ATM networks. *IEEE Network*, 9(2):40–48, 1995.

[19] Eyal Kushilevitz, Rafail Ostrovsky, and Adi Rosén. Log-space polynomial end-to-end communication. *SIAM J. Comput.*, 27(6):1531–1549, 1998.

[20] Tom Leighton, Bruce Maggs, and Satish Rao. Universal packet routing algorithms. In *29th Ann. Symp. on Foundations of Computer Science*, pages 256–269, White Plains, NY, October 1988.

[21] Philip M. Merlin and Paul J. Schweitzer. Deadlock avoidance in store-and-forward networks—I: store and forward deadlock. *IEEE Trans. on Communications*, 28(3):345–354, March 1980.

[22] Avery Miller and Boaz Patt-Shamir. Buffer size for routing limited-rate adversarial traffic. In *Distributed Computing: 30th International Symposium, DISC 2016, Paris, France, September 27-29, 2016. Proceedings*, pages 328–341, Berlin, Heidelberg, 2016. Springer Berlin Heidelberg.

[23] Umit Y Ogras and Radu Marculescu. Analysis and optimization of prediction-based flow control in networks-on-chip. In *Modeling, Analysis and Optimization of Network-on-Chip Communication Architectures*, pages 105–133. Springer, 2013.

[24] Adi Rosén. A note on models for non-probabilistic analysis of packet switching networks. *Information Processing Letters*, 84(5):237 - 240, 2002.

# Communication Primitives in Cognitive Radio Networks

Seth Gilbert
National University of Singapore
seth.gilbert@comp.nus.edu.sg

Fabian Kuhn
University of Freiburg
kuhn@cs.uni-freiburg.de

Chaodong Zheng*
Nanjing University
chaodong@nju.edu.cn

## ABSTRACT

Cognitive radio networks are a new type of multi-channel wireless network in which different nodes can have access to different sets of channels. By providing multiple channels, they improve the efficiency and reliability of wireless communication. However, the heterogeneous nature of cognitive radio networks also brings new challenges to the design and analysis of distributed algorithms.

In this paper, we focus on two fundamental problems in cognitive radio networks: neighbor discovery, and global broadcast. We consider a synchronous network containing $n$ nodes, each of which has access to $c$ channels. We assume the network has diameter $D$, and each pair of neighbors have at least $k \geq 1$, and at most $k_{max} \leq c$, shared channels. We also assume each node has at most $\Delta$ neighbors. For the neighbor discovery problem, we design a randomized algorithm called CSeek which has time complexity $\tilde{O}((c^2/k)+(k_{max}/k)\cdot\Delta)$. CSeek is flexible and robust, which allows us to use it as a generic "filter" to find "well-connected" neighbors with an even shorter running time. We then move on to the global broadcast problem, and propose CGCast, a randomized algorithm which takes $\tilde{O}((c^2/k) + (k_{max}/k)\cdot\Delta + D\cdot\Delta)$ time. CGCast uses CSeek to achieve communication among neighbors, and uses edge coloring to establish an efficient deterministic schedule for fast message dissemination.

Towards the end of the paper, we give lower bounds for solving the two problems. These lower bounds demonstrate that in many cases CSeek and CGCast are near optimal.

## CCS CONCEPTS

• **Theory of computation → Distributed algorithms;**

## KEYWORDS

Cognitive radio networks, neighbor discovery, broadcast

**ACM Reference format:**
Seth Gilbert, Fabian Kuhn, and Chaodong Zheng. 2017. Communication Primitives in Cognitive Radio Networks. In *Proceedings of ACM Symposium on Principles of Distributed Computing, Washington, DC, USA, July 25–27, 2017 (PODC '17)*, 10 pages.
https://doi.org/10.1145/3087801.3087805

*Also with State Key Lab for Novel Software Technology, Nanjing University, Nanjing, 210093, P.R. China.


*PODC '17, July 25–27, 2017, Washington, DC, USA*

ACM ISBN 978-1-4503-4992-5/17/07...$15.00
https://doi.org/10.1145/3087801.3087805

## 1 INTRODUCTION

*Cognitive radio networks* are a new type of wireless network in which different devices have access to different (but overlapping) frequency bands. This asymmetry might be a result of interference (e.g., from disruptive devices or from prioritized users) or due to regulatory concerns. Cognitive radio networks provide a potential answer to the continuously increasing bandwidth needs of wireless communication, as they enable more graceful sharing of the available bandwidth. For example, two commonly discussed scenarios are: (1) they allow the general public to use idle spectrum in the licensed bands that are assigned to primary users (e.g., television broadcasters) [21, 23]; (2) they can increase the number of radio networks that can practically coexist in one area.

Although cognitive radio networks are not a particularly new concept, our understanding of them remains limited when compared with the extensive research that has been done on classical single-channel or multi-channel wireless networks. In cognitive radio networks, the core challenge comes from its heterogeneous nature: different pairs of transceivers can share different sets of channels. Such unpredictable overlapping patterns (among transceivers) makes it very difficult to design and analyze efficient algorithms. In fact, much interesting work in this area has focused primarily on simulations to demonstrate effectiveness, see, e.g., [14, 24, 26].

In this paper, we focus on two important problems that are still not well understood: *neighbor discovery*, and *global broadcast*. These problems are fundamental primitives for any network: neighbor discovery is typically a bootstrapping procedure, and broadcast is a key building block for accomplishing many more complex tasks. We are interested in developing randomized algorithms with provable performance guarantees that can solve them efficiently.

More specifically, we consider a synchronous cognitive radio network containing $n$ nodes, each of which has a transceiver that can access $c$ channels. If two nodes are within the transmission radius of each other and share some communication channels, then they are *neighbors*. We assume each pair of neighbors share at least $k \geq 1$ channels. As a result, we can model the network as a simple graph by letting each node denote a vertex, and connect two vertices if they are neighbors.

*Neighbor discovery.* To solve the neighbor discovery problem, each node must learn the identities of all of its neighbors. A simple and straightforward strategy would be for each node to randomly hop among the set of channels that are available to it, and then broadcast (its identity) or listen each with some probability (e.g., using a backoff procedure to resolve contention). This simple algorithm yields a time complexity of approximately $\tilde{O}((c^2/k)\cdot\Delta)$, where $\Delta$ is the maximum number of neighbors a node can have. By contrast, $\Omega(\Delta)$ is a trivial lower bound since in the worst-case, a node may receive information from only one neighbor per time slot, and nodes sharing a common neighbor may not be able to communicate with each other directly (e.g., a star network).

In this paper, we devise a new algorithm called CSEEK that is much more efficient. In particular, CSEEK can solve the neighbor discovery problem in $\tilde{O}((c^2/k) + (k_{max}/k) \cdot \Delta)$ time, w.h.p.[1] Here, $k_{max}$ denotes the maximum number of channels two neighbors share. Notice, if all pairs of neighbors share the same (or a similar) number of overlapping channels, then CSEEK only costs $\tilde{O}(c^2/k+\Delta)$ time. As we shall later see, this nearly matches the lower bound for solving neighbor discovery in our model.

The intuition behind CSEEK is that a node, instead of hopping among channels uniformly at random (e.g., in the trivial approach described above), should spend more time on channels on which it overlaps with more neighbors. Unfortunately, the pattern of overlaps is not known to the nodes in advance. Hence, in the first part of the algorithm, nodes hop among channels uniformly at random, sampling the "*density*" of channels; a key component of our solution is an efficient procedure for estimating density. In the second part, nodes visit dense channels more often, assuming they can hear more neighbors on these channels. By properly dividing the time between sampling and seeking, we obtain an efficient algorithm.

We have also devised a variant of CSEEK that can solve the $\hat{k}$-*neighbor-discovery* problem. In real networks, nodes may only concern with neighbors that have strong connections with them. This motivates the $\hat{k}$-neighbor-discovery problem, in which the goal is to find (at least) all neighbors that share at least $\hat{k} \geq k$ channels with you. A variant of CSEEK—which is called CKSEEK—can solve the $\hat{k}$-neighbor-discovery problem in $\tilde{O}((c^2/\hat{k}) + (k_{max}/\hat{k}) \cdot \Delta_{\hat{k}} + \Delta)$ time. Here, $\Delta_{\hat{k}}$ is the maximum number of neighbors a node can have that share at least $\hat{k}$ channels with it. The similarity between CKSEEK and CSEEK demonstrates the robustness of the general strategy we have employed.

*Global broadcast.* In this problem, a designated *source* node needs to disseminate a message to all other nodes in the network. Again, one can devise a straightforward solution in which nodes hop among channels randomly and wait for the message if uninformed, or broadcast it (using a backoff procedure) if they are already informed. Such naive solution would cost approximately $\tilde{O}((c^2/k) \cdot D)$ time, where $D$ is the diameter of the network.

We propose a new algorithm called CGCAST that can solve global broadcast in $\tilde{O}((c^2/k)+(k_{max}/k)\cdot\Delta+D\cdot\Delta)$ time, w.h.p. Again, when $k_{max} = \Theta(k)$, the complexity of CGCAST is reduced to $\tilde{O}((c^2/k) + D \cdot \Delta)$. The performance improvements of CGCAST comes from two design decisions. First, for an informed node to quickly disseminate the message to its neighbors, we do an edge coloring and use the solution to establish an efficient deterministic schedule. Secondly, in order to solve edge coloring efficiently, we use CSEEK as a primitive for communication. This once again demonstrates the flexibility and robustness of CSEEK.

*Lower bounds.* In the last part of the paper, we devise lower bounds for solving neighbor discovery and global broadcast in the considered model. (The techniques were originally from [22].)

[1]We use "w.h.p." to abbreviate "with high probability with respect to $n$", which means an event happens with probability at least $1 - 1/n^{\alpha}$, for arbitrary constant $\alpha \geq 1$.

More specifically, to prove the $\Omega(c^2/k+\Delta)$ lower bound for neighbor discovery, we consider a combinatorial game which captures the core difficulty of the problem, and then do a reduction argument to prove our claim. The combinatorial game has been previously used to prove other lower bounds in cognitive radio networks (see, e.g., [8]), but the reduction argument is tailored for our purpose. On the other hand, we also show a $\Omega((c^2/k) + D \cdot \min\{c, \Delta\})$ lower bound for global broadcast. Proving this bound is quite straightforward, and we include it mainly for the sake of completeness.

As can be seen, when $k_{max} = \Theta(k)$, CSEEK matches the lower bound within poly-logarithmic factor; and for global broadcast, when $k_{max} = \Theta(k)$ and $c \geq \Delta$, again our bounds are near tight.

## 2 RELATED WORK

There is much ongoing work in the area of cognitive radio networks, both in terms of low-level implementation issues (e.g., [1] and [29]) and in terms of algorithms. In this paper, we focus on the latter part: designing efficient distributed algorithms for key communication primitives in this type of network.

*Neighbor discovery.* In traditional single-channel or multi-channel wireless networks, neighbor discovery is a problem that has been extensively studied under various different models (w.r.t., e.g., synchrony and availability of collision detection), from both theoretic perspective and system perspective. Interested readers can, e.g., refer to the survey paper from Khan et al. [13], and from Chen et al. [5], for more details. On the contrary, for cognitive radio networks, limited focus has been put on this problem. (Interested readers can refer to related parts in [13] and [30] for a brief survey.) Moreover, among the works that do tackle this problem, most only use experiments or simulations to evaluate the performance of their proposed solutions. In fact, we are only able to identify one work from Zeng et al. [19, 30] that explicitly targets this issue and provides provable theoretical results.

In this interesting paper, the authors design and analyze several algorithms for neighbor discovery in cognitive radio networks under a variety of assumptions for both synchronous and asynchronous systems. In particular, using our terminology/model, their algorithm takes $\tilde{O}(c^2/k + c \cdot \Delta/k)$ time. Recall CSEEK has time complexity $\tilde{O}((c^2/k) + (k_{max}/k) \cdot \Delta)$. Therefore, when $c \geq \Delta$, our algorithm performs (asymptotically) as well as theirs; and when $c \leq \Delta$, CSEEK outperforms their algorithm. In particular, when $c \leq \Delta$, CSEEK is faster by a factor of $c/k_{max}$, which can be of order $\Theta(c)$ in the extreme case.

We also note here that neighbor discovery can potentially be solved using other algorithms that were originally designed for other purposes. For example, solutions to rendezvous [6, 10, 11, 16, 25]—a popular problem which requires each pair of neighbors in the network to meet every so often—can be helpful. The only problem is, contention may exist when meeting happens, thus simple meeting does not alway imply successful exchange of identities. Indeed, most recent (also shown to be near optimal) results [6, 10] can solve rendezvous in $\tilde{O}(c^2)$ time. When ignoring contention and assuming $k = O(1)$, this bound matches the simple algorithm we described in the introduction section. (Notice, however, that the algorithms presented in [6, 10] are deterministic, while the simple one we introduced earlier is randomized) The difficult part, and what CSEEK achieves, is to resolve contention when meeting happens, and maintain low time complexity in the meantime.

*Broadcast.* The goal of a broadcast is to distribute information in a network. Typically, there are two kinds of broadcast: local broadcast, in which the objective is to disseminate the message to your immediate neighbors; and global broadcast, in which all nodes in the network need to receive the message.

Similar to the case of neighbor discovery, in traditional wireless networks, broadcast is a problem that has been extensively studied. Take the single channel case as an example. In early days, in a seminal paper, Bar-Yehuda et al. [4] proposed an algorithm with time complexity $O(D \cdot \log n + \log^2 n)$. Lower bounds of $\Omega(D + \log^2 n)$ and $\Omega(D \cdot \log(n/D))$ were also derived in [2, 15]. In recent years, significant progress was made from the upper bound side: Ghaffari et al. provided an algorithm with run time $O(D + \log^6 n)$ in [7]. (In fact, a most recent result suggests an $O(D + \log^2 n)$ algorithm [3].)

In the cognitive radio network setting, there are a few papers addressing the broadcast problem, and the models and approaches they employed are highly diverse. For example, in a series of papers by Song and Xie [26–28], by carefully constructing channel hopping sequences, the authors are able to accomplish broadcast in multi-hop cognitive radio networks. These works analyze the probability that a broadcast will be successful, but do not provide a theoretical guarantee on broadcast time. Instead, they focus on simulations to show the effectiveness. In this paper, we take a full-on algorithmic approach, guaranteeing successful global broadcast with high probability and analyzing our algorithms for worst-case performance. For the local broadcast problem, in a paper by Gilbert et al. [8], the authors propose a simple randomized algorithm that is shown to be near optimal. In another paper by Kondareddy et al. [14], the authors use "minimal neighbor graph" to achieve local broadcast, which in turn helps to disseminate control information. Finally, another approach to tackle the broadcast problem is to assume that all necessary information (e.g., channel availability, network topology) is known in advance, and then focus on developing efficient algorithms which can find good broadcast schedules. Both [17] and [12] belong to this category. In this paper, by contrast, we assume minimal a priori environmental knowledge.

## 3 MODEL

In this section, we describe the system model in detail.

We consider a synchronous wireless network containing $n$ nodes, each of which has a unique identity.

Each node has a radio transceiver that can access $c$ channels, and different nodes can potentially access different sets of channels. Moreover, we assume for each channel, different nodes may have different labels for it. That is, we do not assume *global channel labels* exist. Instead, nodes have *local channel labels.*

For two nodes, if they are within the transmission range of each other and share some channels, then they are *neighbors.* For each pair of neighboring nodes, we assume they share at least $k \geq 1$ channels, and at most $k_{max} \leq c$ channels. For each node, it does not know the identities of its neighbors, it also does not know the set of channels on which it can communicate with its neighbors.

Now, we can model the network as a simple graph $\mathcal{G}$, in which each vertex denotes a node, and there is an edge connecting two nodes iff they are neighbors. We assume $\mathcal{G}$ is connected, and has diameter $D$. We also assume the maximum degree of $\mathcal{G}$ is $\Delta$, which implies a node can have at most $\Delta$ neighbors.

We divide time into discrete *slots.* In each time slot, each radio transceiver can only operate on one of the $c$ available channels. For a node $u$, if it decides to broadcast a message in a time slot, then it only "receives" that message in that slot. If $u$ decides to listen on a channel and no neighbors of $u$ broadcast on that channel in that slot, then $u$ hears nothing (i.e., silence). If $u$ decides to listen on a channel and among the neighbors of $u$, exactly one broadcasts on that channel in that slot, then $u$ hears the message from that node. Finally, if $u$ decides to listen on a channel and multiple neighbors of $u$ broadcast on that channel in that slot, then $u$ again hears nothing. That is, nodes cannot distinguish between silence and multiple nodes broadcasting simultaneously. (Alternatively, we can say we assume collision detection is *not* available.) We also note here that the messages generated in our neighbor discovery algorithms are always quite small ($O(\log n)$ in particular). However, in the global broadcast algorithm CGCAST, in the extreme case, the message size can reach $\tilde{O}(\Delta^2)$.

Finally, we assume nodes start execution simultaneously, and can independently generate random bits. We also assume nodes know the aforementioned key parameters: $n, c, k, k_{max}, D, \Delta$.

## 4 ALGORITHMS FOR NEIGHBOR DISCOVERY

In this section, we introduce CSEEK, an efficient randomized algorithm that can solve neighbor discovery. We will also present a variant of CSEEK that can solve $\hat{k}$-neighbor-discovery.

### 4.1 COUNT: A Counting Procedure

Before presenting CSEEK and CKSEEK, we first introduce a simple counting algorithm COUNT that allows a node to get an estimate on how many other nodes are on the same channel. In particular, the estimate given by COUNT is guaranteed to be within a small constant factor of the actual value. Algorithm COUNT is generic and can easily be plugged into other wireless network algorithms.

More specifically, COUNT solves the following problem: On a channel, there is one listening node and an unknown number of broadcasters. The listener wants to learn the count of broadcasters. Notice, since the degree upper bound $\Delta$ is known, nodes know the actual number of broadcasters will not exceed $\Delta$.

To solve this problem, COUNT needs $\lg \Delta$ rounds, each of which contains $\Theta(\lg n)$ time slots. Hence, the total time complexity is $O(\lg^2 n)$. At a high level, the algorithm takes the classical "guess and verify" approach. More specifically, in each round, nodes will have an estimate of the actual count. The estimate starts from one, and doubles after each round. In each round, each broadcaster will broadcast with probability that is proportional to the reciprocal of the estimate, and the listener will count how many messages it can receive within this round. When the estimate is close to the actual count, the fraction of time slots within a round in which messages are received by the listener will reach a certain peak value. As a result, the listener can obtain a relatively accurate count.

Due to space constraint, detailed description and analysis of COUNT is left in the full version of the paper [9]. Here, we only states the guarantees provided by it.

LEMMA 4.1. *The counting procedure* COUNT *takes* $O(\lg^2 n)$ *time slots, and allows the listener to obtain a count that is in* $[m, 4m]$, *w.h.p. Here,* $m$ *is the actual number of broadcasters.*

## 4.2 The CSEEK Algorithm

We now present the CSEEK algorithm, which contains two parts. Intuitively, it is designed in the following way. In part one, each node samples all the channels that are available to it to get an idea about how many of its neighbors have access to each channel. Moreover, as we shall later see, for a node $u$, part one also offers an opportunity for it to learn the identities of the neighbors that overlap with it primarily on less crowded channels (i.e., channels on which $u$ does not overlap with many neighbors). In part two, $u$ will go to more crowded channels more often, so that neighbors that mostly overlap with it on these channels—even though there may exist many neighbors on each such channel—get enough chances to introduce themselves to $u$.

More specifically, part one contains $\Theta((c^2/k)\cdot \lg n)$ steps, each of which contains $O(\lg^2 n)$ slots. This implies the total time complexity of part one is $O((c^2/k)\cdot \lg^3 n)$. In each step, each node will go to one of the $c$ channels that is available to it uniformly at random, and then choose to be a broadcaster or listener each with probability $1/2$. Then, within current step, each node will run the counting procedure COUNT on the selected channel. Listeners will record the count, and any identities they have heard. Broadcasters, on the other hand, will broadcast their identities when necessary (i.e., according to COUNT.)

The second part of CSEEK contains $\Theta((k_{max}/k)\cdot \Delta \cdot \lg n)$ steps, each of which contains $\lg \Delta$ slots. Hence, the total time complexity of part two is $O((k_{max}/k)\cdot \Delta \cdot \lg^2 n)$. In each step, each node will choose to be a broadcaster or listener each with probability $1/2$. If a node $u$ chooses to be a broadcaster, then it will pick one of the $c$ available channels uniformly at random and go to that channel. However, if $u$ chooses to be a listener, then it will pick an available channel according to the total count it has obtained during part one. More specifically, if the total count $u$ has obtained for channel $ch$ during part one is $x_{ch}$, then it will choose $ch$ in a step in part two with probability $x_{ch}/\sum_{ch'\in C_u} x_{ch'}$. Here, $C_u$ is the set of channels that are available to $u$. Once nodes have picked channels, in a step, a listener will listen in every slot and record any identity it has heard; a broadcaster, on the other hand, will broadcast its identity with probability $2^{i-1}/\Delta$ in the $i^{\text{th}}$ slot of current step. The pseudocode of CSEEK is shown in Figure 1.

## 4.3 Analysis of the CSEEK Algorithm

In this part, we prove the correctness of CSEEK.

Consider a node $u$ and one of its neighbors $v$. The first key technical result states that if for most of the channels on which $u$ and $v$ overlap, at most $O(c)$ neighbors of $u$ overlap with $u$ on each of these channels, then by the end of part one, $u$ will know $v$'s identity, w.h.p. That is, if most of the channels $u$ and $v$ share are not too "crowded", then $u$ will know $v$'s identity after part one. More precisely, we have the following lemma.

LEMMA 4.2. *Assume* $v$ *is one of* $u$*'s neighbors, also assume* $u$ *and* $v$ *overlap on* $k_{u,v}$ *channels. Assume among these channels, there exist at least* $k_{u,v}/2$ *channels such that for each of these channels, at most* $8c$ *of* $u$*'s neighbors overlap with* $u$ *on this channel. Then, during part one, after* $O((c^2/k_{u,v})\cdot \lg n)$ *steps each of which containing* $O(\lg^2 n)$ *slots,* $u$ *will hear* $v$*'s identity, w.h.p.*

We now sketch the proof of Lemma 4.2. (Due to space constraint, if not otherwise stated, detailed proofs of lemmas and theorems are provided in the full version of the paper [9].) In each step in part one, for $u$ to hear $v$'s identity, three conditions must hold: (a) $u$ is a listener and $v$ is a broadcaster; (b) $u$ and $v$ choose the same channel; and (c) $v$ broadcasts alone in some slot during the counting procedure. According to protocol description, clearly condition (a) holds with probability $1/4$. Moreover, it is not hard to see that condition (b) holds with probability $k_{u,v}/c^2$. Hence, the tricky part is to calculate the probability that condition (c) holds. Assume (a) and (b) indeed happen, we know there is at least a fifty percent chance that for the channel $u$ and $v$ have chosen, there are at most $8c$ neighbors of $u$ that can access this channel. If this is indeed the case, then in expectation, at most $(8c-1)\cdot(1/c)\cdot(1/2) = O(1)$ neighbors of $u$ (beside $v$) are acting as broadcasters on this channel in this step. That is, there is only a *constant* number of broadcasters. Since the counting procedure COUNT that is executed within the step contains a rounds in which the estimate (approximately) matches the number of broadcasters, and since each round in COUNT contains $\Theta(\lg n)$ slots, this "constant level contention" can be fully resolved. Therefore, conditioned on (a) and (b) indeed happening, (c) will happen with at least some constant probability. As a result, we can conclude in each step, $u$ will hear $v$'s identity with probability at least $\Omega(k_{u,v}/c^2)$. Since each step is independent, the lemma follows.

In the second key technical result, we consider the case in which most of the channels on which $u$ and $v$ overlap are crowded. (I.e., the "complement" of the previous case.) In this scenario, we claim that $u$ will hear $v$'s identity during part two.

LEMMA 4.3. *Assume* $v$ *is one of* $u$*'s neighbors, also assume* $u$ *and* $v$ *overlap on* $k_{u,v}$ *channels. Assume among these channels, there exist at least* $k_{u,v}/2$ *channels such that for each of these channels, at least* $8c$ *of* $u$*'s neighbors overlap with* $u$ *on this channel. Then, during part two, after* $O((\sum_{w\in N_u} k_{u,w})/k_{u,v}\cdot \lg n)$ *steps each of which containing* $\lg \Delta$ *slots,* $u$ *will hear* $v$*'s identity, w.h.p. Here,* $N_u$ *denotes the set of* $u$*'s neighbors.*

The proof for Lemma 4.3 is more involved than that of Lemma 4.2, and we provide the full version of it here.

PROOF. Assume node $u$ has $\Delta_u$ neighbors, call this set of neighbors $N_u$. Assume the set of channels on which $u$ and $v$ overlap is $\mathcal{K}_{u,v}$. Let $\mathcal{K}'_{u,v}$ be a subset of $\mathcal{K}_{u,v}$ which is of size at least $k_{u,v}/2$, such that for each channel in $\mathcal{K}'_{u,v}$, node $u$ overlaps with at least $8c$ of its neighbors.

Before proving the lemma, we show two simple facts.

Firstly, notice that after part one of protocol execution, for a channel $ch$, if the count obtained by $u$ is $x_{ch}$, then the actual count $\hat{x}_{ch}$ is in range of $[x_{ch}/4, 4x_{ch}]$, w.h.p. This is because, according to Lemma 4.1, the counting procedure COUNT can provide a relatively accurate count that is within constant factor of error.

**Pseudocode of CSeek executed at node $u$:**

```
sum ← 0, ids ← ∅
for (i = 1 to c) do counts[i] ← 0          ▷ counts is a dictionary used to store the count for each channel
PART I
for (i = 1 to Θ((c^2/k) · lg n)) do
    ch ← random(1, c)          ▷ Choose channel, where random(x, y) returns a uniformly distributed random integer in [x, y]
    role ← random(0, 1)          ▷ Choose to be broadcaster or listener
    ⟨count_ch, ids_ch⟩ ← count(ch, role)          ▷ Execute COUNT with specified role on specific channel
    sum ← sum + count_ch, counts[ch] ← counts[ch] + count_ch          ▷ Update counts
    if (ids_ch ≠ ∅) then ids ← ids ∪ ids_ch          ▷ Update identities
PART II
for (i = 1 to Θ((k_max/k) · Δ · lg n)) do
    role ← random(0, 1)          ▷ Choose to be broadcaster or listener
    if (role == 0) then          ▷ If u is a broadcaster
        ch ← random(1, c)          ▷ Choose channel
        for (j = lg Δ to 1) do          ▷ Do backoff style broadcast
            if (random(1, 2^j) == 1) then broadcast(ch, id_u)          ▷ id_u is the identity of u
    else          ▷ If u is a listener
        rnd ← random(1, sum), ch ← 1
        while (rnd > counts[ch]) do          ▷ Choose channel ch with probability count_ch / Σ_{ch'∈C_u} count_ch'
            rnd ← rnd − counts[ch], ch ← ch + 1
        for (j = lg Δ to 1) do          ▷ Listen on the chosen channel and record identities
            id ← listen(ch)
            if (id ≠ null) then ids ← ids ∪ {id}
RETURN RESULT
return ids
```

**Figure 1: Pseudocode of the CSeek algorithm.**

The above fact further implies another conclusion: $\sum_{ch\in C_u} x_{ch} = \Theta(\sum_{w\in N_u}(k_{u,w}/k)\cdot\lg n)$, where $C_u$ is the set of channels that is available to $u$, w.h.p. This is because, in one step in part one, for $u$ to meet a neighbor $w$ (but not necessarily hear $w$'s identity) while $u$ is a listener and $w$ is a broadcaster, the probability is $(1/2)\cdot(1/2)\cdot(k_{u,w}/c)\cdot(1/c) = k_{u,w}/(4c^2)$. Since part one contains $\Theta((c^2/k)\cdot\lg n)$ steps, we know $u$ will meet $w$ while $u$ is a listener and $w$ is a broadcaster for $\Theta((k_{u,w}/k)\cdot\lg n)$ times, w.h.p. Therefore, we know $\sum_{ch\in C_u}\hat{x}_{ch} = \Theta(\sum_{w\in N_u}(k_{u,w}/k)\cdot\lg n)$, w.h.p. Since $\sum_{ch\in C_u} x_{ch}$ is a constant factor estimate of $\sum_{ch\in C_u}\hat{x}_{ch}$, we can conclude $\sum_{ch\in C_u} x_{ch} = \Theta(\sum_{w\in N_u}(k_{u,w}/k)\cdot\lg n)$, w.h.p.

With the above facts, we now proceed to prove the lemma.

Consider a step in part two, we calculate the probability that $u$ hear $v$'s identity on one of the channels in $\mathcal{K}'_{u,v}$ in this step.

To calculate this probability, we first consider the probability that $u$ meets $v$ on a specific channel $ch\in\mathcal{K}'_{u,v}$ while $u$ is a listener and $v$ is a broadcaster. For this to happen, first, $u$ must choose to listen and $v$ must choose to broadcast, which happens with probability $1/4$. Secondly, $u$ and $v$ must choose the same channel $ch\in\mathcal{K}'_{u,v}$, and this happens with probability $(x_{ch}/(\Theta(\sum_{w\in N_u}(k_{u,w}/k)\cdot\lg n)))\cdot(1/c) = \Theta(x_{ch}/(c\cdot\lg n\cdot\sum_{w\in N_u}(k_{u,w}/k)))$.

We now calculate the value of $x_{ch}$. In one step in part one, for $u$ and one of its neighbor $w$ which overlaps with $u$ on channel $ch$, the probability that $u$ meets $w$ on channel $ch$ while $u$ is a listener and $w$ is a broadcaster is $(1/2)\cdot(1/2)\cdot(1/c)\cdot(1/c) = 1/4c^2$. Hence, in expectation, the actual count $u$ should have is $n_{ch}\cdot(1/4c^2)\cdot\Theta((c^2/k)\cdot\lg n) = \Theta(n_{ch}/k\cdot\lg n)$. Here, $n_{ch}$ is the number of neighbors that overlap with $u$ on channel $ch$. Notice, $ch$ is a channel in $\mathcal{K}'_{u,v}$, thus $n_{ch}\geq 8c\geq 8k$. Moreover, in part one, nodes make choices independently in each step, and each node makes choices independently in different steps. Hence, apply a Chernoff bound [20], we know the actual count $u$ should have is $\Theta(n_{ch}/k\cdot\lg n)$, w.h.p. Since the counting procedure can provide constant factor estimate, we know $x_{ch} = \Theta(n_{ch}/k\cdot\lg n)$, w.h.p.

At this point, we know in one step in part two, with probability at least $\Theta(x_{ch}/(c\cdot\lg n\cdot\sum_{w\in N_u}(k_{u,w}/k))) = \Theta(n_{ch}/(c\cdot\sum_{w\in N_u}k_{u,w}))$: node $u$ and $v$ will both choose channel $ch\in\mathcal{K}'_{u,v}$, and $u$ will be a listener, and $v$ will be a broadcaster.

The next key factor that needs to be taken into consideration is the level of contention, as other broadcaster may try to broadcast on channel $ch$ as well. To quantify such contention, consider another neighbor of $u$ which also overlaps with $u$ on channel $ch$. We call this neighbor $w$, and calculate the probability that $w$ broadcasts on $ch$ in this step. For this to happen: (a) $w$ must choose to broadcast, which happens with probability $1/2$; and (b) $w$ must choose channel $ch$, which happens with probability $1/c$. Notice, we have assumed there are $n_{ch}\geq 8c$ neighbors of $u$ that overlap with it on channel $ch$. Hence, in expectation, beside $v$, in one step in part two, there will be $(n_{ch}-1)\cdot(1/2)\cdot(1/c)$ other broadcasters on channel $ch$. Notice, $3\leq 3n_{ch}/(8c)\leq(n_{ch}-1)\cdot(1/2)\cdot(1/c)\leq n_{ch}/(2c)$, and each node makes choices independently. Hence, apply a Chernoff bound and we know, with at least some constant probability, there are $\Theta(n_{ch}/c)$ other neighbors of $u$ that will broadcast on channel $ch$ in one step during part two.

Since there is a backoff procedure within each step in part two, we can now conclude: in one step in part two, with probability at least $\Theta(n_{ch}/(c \cdot \sum_{w \in N_u} k_{u,w})) \cdot \Theta(c/n_{ch}) \cdot \Theta(1) = \Theta(1/\sum_{w \in N_u} k_{u,w})$, $u$ will hear $v$'s identity on channel $ch \in \mathcal{K}'_{u,v}$. Define $e_{ch_i}$ to be the event that $u$ hears $v$'s identity on channel $ch_i \in \mathcal{K}'_{u,v}$, we know $\mathbb{P}(e_{ch_i}) = \Omega(1/\sum_{w \in N_u} k_{u,w})$. Notice, $\{e_{ch_i} | ch_i \in \mathcal{K}'_{u,v}\}$ is a set of disjoint events. Moreover, we have assumed $|\mathcal{K}'_{u,v}| \geq k_{u,v}/2$. Therefore, in one step in part two, the probability that $u$ will hear $v$'s identity is at least $(k_{u,v}/2) \cdot \Omega(1/\sum_{w \in N_u} k_{u,w}) = \Omega(k_{u,v}/\sum_{w \in N_u} k_{u,w})$. Since each step in part two is independent, we know after $\Theta((\sum_{w \in N_u} k_{u,w})/k_{u,v} \cdot \lg n)$ steps, $u$ will know $v$'s identity w.h.p. This completes our proof for the lemma. □

Combine Lemma 4.2 and Lemma 4.3 will immediately lead to the following theorem.

THEOREM 4.4. *CSEEK can solve the neighbor discovery problem in* $O((c^2/k) \cdot \lg^3 n + (k_{max}/k) \cdot \Delta \cdot \lg^2 n) = \tilde{O}((c^2/k) + (k_{max}/k) \cdot \Delta)$ *time slots, w.h.p.*

## 4.4 CKSEEK: Using CSEEK as a General Filter

The CSEEK algorithm allows nodes to discover all neighbors. However, sometimes, it may be desirable to discover "well connected" neighbors. In particular, it is possible that a node may only need to find neighbors that overlap with it on sufficiently many channels. In this part, we show that the CSEEK algorithm can solve this problem as well, even with a shorter running time! This demonstrates CSEEK can be used a flexible filter: on the one hand, a long execution guarantees all neighbors will be discovered; yet on the other hand, if only "well connected" neighbors are concerned, then the running time can be reduced. Nonetheless, one point worth noting is that our proposed solution is guaranteed to find all "well connected" neighbors (w.h.p.), but it may also return other neighbors. I.e., the proposed solution finds *at least* all "well connected" neighbors.

To be concrete, we consider the $\hat{k}$-neighbor-discovery problem, in which the goal is to let each node find (at least) all neighbors that overlap with it on at least $\hat{k} \geq k$ channels. For a node $u$, if a neighbor $v$ overlaps with it on at least $\hat{k}$ channels, then we say $v$ is a *good neighbor* of $u$.

To solve the $\hat{k}$-neighbor-discovery problem, we only need to make small adjustments to the execution time of CSEEK, resulting a protocol called CKSEEK. More specifically, in CKSEEK, part one contains only $\Theta((c^2/\hat{k}) \cdot \lg n)$ steps, and part two contains only $\Theta(((k_{max}/\hat{k}) \cdot \Delta_{\hat{k}} + \Delta + c) \cdot \lg n)$ steps. Here, $\Delta_{\hat{k}}$ denotes the maximum number of good neighbors a node can have. Notice, if an estimate of $\Delta_{\hat{k}}$ is not available, we can simply run part two longer, making it containing $\Theta(((k_{max}/\hat{k}) \cdot \Delta + c) \cdot \lg n)$ steps.

The high level intuition of why CSEEK has such an extension (i.e., CKSEEK) is that, during part two, well connected neighbors get to meet more often. Hence, they can also discover each other quicker. More specifically, consider a node $u$ and one of its good neighbors $v$, we now prove the correctness of CKSEEK. Similar to the analysis of CSEEK, we still consider two complement cases. In the first case, we claim that if for at least half of the channels on which $u$ and $v$ overlap, at most $8c$ neighbors of $u$ overlap with it on each of these channels, then by the end of part one of CKSEEK, $u$ will know $v$'s identity, w.h.p. This is a direct application of Lemma 4.2. In the second case, we assume most of the channels $u$ and $v$ share are crowded. In such scenario, $u$ will know $v$'s identity during part two of CKSEEK. In particular, we have the following lemma.

LEMMA 4.5. *Assume $v$ is one of $u$'s good neighbors, also assume $u$ and $v$ overlap on $k_{u,v}$ channels. Assume among these channels, there exist at least $k_{u,v}/2$ channels such that for each of these channels, at least $8c$ of $u$'s neighbors overlap with $u$ on this channel. Then, during part two of CKSEEK, after $O(((k_{max}/\hat{k}) \cdot \Delta_{\hat{k}} + \Delta + c) \cdot \lg n)$ steps each of which containing $\lg \Delta$ slots, $u$ will hear $v$'s identity, w.h.p.*

Lemma 4.5 looks very similar to Lemma 4.3, and it is tempting to use the same idea to prove it. At a high level, this is indeed the case: we still calculate the probability that $u$ hears $v$'s identity in one step during part two. However, the detailed approach is different. Among the differences, the most significant one is how to bound the sum of the counts $u$ obtained during part one. In CSEEK, part one is sufficiently long, and we can claim during part one $u$ will meet each of its neighbor $v$ for $\Theta((k_{u,v}/k) \cdot \lg n)$ times, in expectation, and w.h.p. This immediately tells us the counts sum to $\Theta(\sum_{w \in N_u} (k_{u,w}/k) \cdot \lg n)$, w.h.p. In CKSEEK, however, part one is shorter, and we can only claim during part one $u$ will meet its neighbor $v$ for $\Theta((k_{u,v}/\hat{k}) \cdot \lg n)$ times in expectation, but not w.h.p. To overcome this difficulty, we come up with a more careful way to calculate the sum, allowing us to bound it from above by $O(((k_{max}/\hat{k}) \cdot \Delta_{\hat{k}} + \Delta + c) \cdot \lg n)$, w.h.p. Again, due to space constraint, we leave the complete proof to the full version of the paper.

Based on the above analysis, we can easily obtain the following theorem. Notice, it implies when $\hat{k} > k$, the (asymptotic) runtime of CKSEEK is strictly shorter than that of CSEEK.

THEOREM 4.6. *CKSEEK can solve the $\hat{k}$-neighbor-discovery problem in* $O((c^2/\hat{k}) \cdot \lg^3 n + ((k_{max}/\hat{k}) \cdot \Delta_{\hat{k}} + \Delta) \cdot \lg^2 n) = \tilde{O}((c^2/\hat{k}) + (k_{max}/\hat{k}) \cdot \Delta_{\hat{k}} + \Delta)$ *time slots, w.h.p.*

# 5 ALGORITHM FOR GLOBAL BROADCAST

In this part, we introduce CGCAST, an algorithm for solving global broadcast in cognitive radio networks. We will begin with an overview, then proceed to the details, and finally show its correctness.

## 5.1 Overview

The key reason that the simple global broadcast algorithm described in the introduction section is inefficient is that nodes are *randomly* hopping among channels, making it slow to propagate the message among neighbors. To solve this issue, in CGCAST, we let neighbors establish a *deterministic* schedule of meeting, so that once a node is informed, it can quickly disseminate the message.

More specifically, to establish a communication schedule among neighbors, we reduce the problem to *edge coloring*. In this graph problem, each vertex will color each edge that is connected to it from a set of $\Theta(\Delta)$ colors, while guaranteeing that each neighboring edge has a unique color. Once this is done, we can imagine a broadcast protocol which proceeds in steps, each of which contains $\Theta(\Delta)$ rounds. By mapping each round in a step to a color, each pair of neighbors have a "dedicated" round for communication in each step, without congestion. In this way, informed nodes can quickly disseminate the message to their neighbors.

However, to solve edge coloring, more efforts are needed. First, by using the *line graph*, we can reduce edge coloring to node coloring (i.e., vertex coloring), in which a node and all of its neighbors are quired to have unique colors. There are many efficient algorithms for this task. However, one problem is that these algorithms usually assume a node can send a potentially different message to every neighbor in one time slot. This is not true in our model. To solve this issue, we need to leverage the neighbor discovery algorithm developed in previous sections. In particular, notice that to solve neighbor discovery, a node needs to receive some information from each of its neighbors. Therefore, if we can solve neighbor discovery in $T$ time, then we can use the same procedure to allow each pair of neighbors to exchange one message in $T$ time.

## 5.2 The CGCAST Algorithm

We now proceed to describe the details of the CGCAST algorithm, which can be divided into three main parts: the neighbor discovery part, the edge coloring part, and the message dissemination part.

Firstly, we will run the CSEEK neighbor discovery algorithm, so that each node can know its neighbors. This process will take $\tilde{O}((c^2/k) + (k_{max}/k) \cdot \Delta)$ time slots, as Theorem 4.4 suggests.

Once neighbor discovery is done, we will work on the line graph of the original network graph $\mathcal{G}$, so that we can solve edge coloring in $\mathcal{G}$ by solving node coloring in its line graph. More specifically, the line graph $\mathcal{G}_L$ of $\mathcal{G}$ is defined in the following way: each edge $(u, v)$ in $\mathcal{G}$ is a node $w_{u,v}$ in $\mathcal{G}_L$, and two nodes in $\mathcal{G}_L$ are connected if and only if they share one common endpoint in $\mathcal{G}$. Also notice, in the line graph $\mathcal{G}_L$, for a (virtual) node $(u, v)$, it is simulated by the (physical) node in $\mathcal{G}$ which has the smaller identity. (For example, nodes' identities may be a set of binary strings, which can be compared like numbers.) Since each node in $\mathcal{G}$ knows the identities of its neighbors, such simulation can be correctly done in a consistent manner. That is, for each edge $(u, v)$ in $\mathcal{G}$ (i.e., each virtual node in $\mathcal{G}_L$), it will be simulated by one node in $\{u, v\}$, and both $u$ and $v$ know which node that is (i.e., either itself or the other endpoint).

We now describe how to obtain a valid node coloring of $\mathcal{G}_L$, which is an implementation of the classical algorithm described in [18] under our model.[2] The node coloring procedure contains $\Theta(\lg n)$ phases, each of which contains two steps, and each step contains $\tilde{\Theta}((c^2/k) + (k_{max}/k) \cdot \Delta)$ time slots. Initially, each (virtual) node in $\mathcal{G}_L$ has an identical palette containing $2\Delta$ different colors, and all nodes in $\mathcal{G}_L$ are active. At the beginning of the first step of each phase, for each active node in $\mathcal{G}_L$, with probability $1/2$, it chooses to do nothing in this step. Otherwise, it randomly chooses a color that is still available in its palette. Then, during the $\tilde{\Theta}((c^2/k) + (k_{max}/k) \cdot \Delta)$ time slots within the current step, neighboring active nodes in $\mathcal{G}_L$ will exchange the colors they have chosen. (This is possible as one execution of CSEEK allows neighboring nodes in $\mathcal{G}$ to exchange information once. Moreover, for any two physical nodes simulating two neighboring virtual nodes in $\mathcal{G}_L$, they are at most two hops away.) If two active neighboring nodes in $\mathcal{G}_L$ have chosen the same color, then both of them will give up their choices. Otherwise, they will keep their choices. In the second step within current phase, neighboring active nodes in $\mathcal{G}_L$ will use the $\tilde{\Theta}((c^2/k) + (k_{max}/k) \cdot \Delta)$ time slots to exchange their choices on the colors. If an active node has decided on a color, then it will become inactive after the current phase. Otherwise, an active node will remember which colors have already been chosen by its neighbors, remove these colors, and then continue into the next phase.

Once the node coloring procedure is done, we need to run CSEEK one more time, so that for each virtual node $w_{u,v}$ in $\mathcal{G}_L$, the physical node (in $\mathcal{G}$) which simulates this virtual node can transmit the choice of color (of edge $(u, v)$) to the other physical node. At this time point, we have a $2\Delta$ edge coloring of $\mathcal{G}$.

The next, and final part would be to leverage the edge coloring result to quickly disseminate the message. The message dissemination part contains $D$ phases, each of which contains $2\Delta$ steps. Each step has $\Theta(\lg n)$ rounds, and each round costs $\lg \Delta$ time slots. Therefore, the total time complexity of the message dissemination part is $O(D \cdot \Delta \cdot \lg^2 n) = \tilde{O}(D \cdot \Delta)$ time slots. The message dissemination part proceeds in the following way. Nodes map the $2\Delta$ colors to the $2\Delta$ steps within each phase according to some predefined rule. Moreover, for each pair of neighboring nodes, among the set of channels that is available to both of them, they can fix a special "dedicated communication channel" during the initial neighbor discovery part. (We discuss how to fix such special channels in the next paragraph.)

Now, consider a node $u$. In each phase, in the $i^{\text{th}}$ step, assume the corresponding color is $\mathcal{K}_i$. If $u$ is not adjacent to an edge with color $\mathcal{K}_i$, then it will stay idle in this step. Otherwise, assume edge $(u, v)$ has color $\mathcal{K}_i$. In such case, in this step, $u$ will go to the special channel that it has agreed with $v$. Now, if $u$ does not know the message yet, it will listen during this step. Otherwise, if $u$ is already informed, then within each of the $\Theta(\lg n)$ rounds in current step, it will do a backoff style broadcast on the chosen channel. (This is why each round costs $\lg \Delta$ time slots). This completes our description of the CGCAST algorithm.

Before proceeding to the analysis, we describe one possible method which allows two neighbors to fix a dedicated communication channel despite the absence of global channel label. During the initial neighbor discovery part, when $u$ hears $v$ for the first time, it records the number of the current time slot. Then, after the neighbor discovery part, and before the edge coloring part, nodes will run CSEEK once more. This time, in the message, $u$ includes not only its identity, but also the numbers of time slots in which it heard its neighbors for the first time in the previous execution of CSEEK. Now, for a pair of neighboring nodes $u$ and $v$, assume $u$ hears $v$ for the first time in slot $t_{u,v}$, and $v$ hears $u$ for the first time in slot $t_{v,u}$. Then, $u$ and $v$ will fix the channel they used in slot $\min\{t_{u,v}, t_{v,u}\}$ as their dedicated communication channel. Since all nodes start executing CGCAST simultaneously, we know both $u$ and $v$ can correctly determine $\min\{t_{u,v}, t_{v,u}\}$.

[2]There exist better node coloring algorithms which are faster, or use less colors. However, these algorithms are more complex, and usually do not provide significantly better results (for our setting). Moreover, node coloring is not the focus of this paper. Therefore, we only use a simple and relatively efficient algorithm here.

## 5.3 Analysis of the CGCast Algorithm

To show the correctness of CGCast, firstly notice that a valid $2\Delta$ node coloring of $\mathcal{G}_L$ gives a valid $2\Delta$ edge coloring for network graph $\mathcal{G}$. This follows from the definition of line graph.

Fact 5.1. *For a simple graph $\mathcal{G}$ with maximum degree $\Delta$, if we have a valid $2\Delta$ node coloring for its line graph $\mathcal{G}_L$, then we can obtain a valid $2\Delta$ edge coloring for $\mathcal{G}$.*

We then prove our algorithm can correctly generate a $2\Delta$ node coloring for line graph $\mathcal{G}_L$. In particular, we adopt the proof in Section 3.3 of [18] to our model. The high level idea of the proof is that after each phase, with some constant probability, a constant fraction of the remaining nodes in $\mathcal{G}_L$ will decide their colors and become inactive. As a result, within $O(\lg n)$ phases, all nodes in $\mathcal{G}_L$ will terminate, w.h.p.

Lemma 5.2. *In CGCast, after executing the coloring procedure, we have a $2\Delta$ node coloring of $\mathcal{G}_L$, w.h.p.*

Proof. We clarify some points before proving the lemma.

Firstly, consider two neighboring (virtual) nodes in $\mathcal{G}_L$: node $w_{u_1,u_2}$ and node $w_{u_1,u_3}$. Here, $w_{u_1,u_2}$ denotes the edge $(u_1, u_2)$ in $\mathcal{G}$ and $w_{u_1,u_3}$ denotes the edge $(u_1, u_3)$ in $\mathcal{G}$. If these two virtual nodes are simulated by the same physical node (in particular, $u_1$), then for every step in each phase of the coloring procedure, they can (locally) exchange information. Otherwise, if these two virtual nodes are simulated by different physical nodes, then these two physical nodes must be directed connected or are two hops away from each other (in $\mathcal{G}$). Since each step of each phase is long enough for running CSeek twice, the two physical nodes simulating these two virtual nodes can still exchange one piece of information.

Secondly, notice the maximum degree of $\mathcal{G}$ is $\Delta$, this implies for each pair of neighbors in $\mathcal{G}$, excluding the edge that connects them, there are at most $2\Delta - 2$ other edges which are adjacent to them. Hence, in the line graph $\mathcal{G}_L$, the maximum degree is $2\Delta - 2$, which implies $2\Delta$ colors is enough to color the nodes in $\mathcal{G}_L$.

We are now ready to prove the lemma. We first calculate the probability that a node $w_1$ in $\mathcal{G}_L$ becomes inactive after one phase.

Assume $w_1$ is still active at the beginning of phase $i$. If none of its neighbors are active at the beginning of phase $i$, then with probability $1/2$, node $w_1$ will choose a color that has not been used by any of its neighbors. (There is always some color available, as $w_1$ has at most $2\Delta - 2$ neighbors while there are $2\Delta$ colors available initially.) Moreover, after this phase, $w_1$ will decide on this color and become inactive.

Otherwise, some neighbors of $w_1$ are still active at the beginning of phase $i$. Assume $W$ denotes this set of active neighbors. Consider a node $w_2 \in W$. At the beginning of phase $i$, with probability $1/2$, node $w_1$ will choose a color that has not been used by any neighbors previously. Assume this event indeed happens. In such case, with probability $1/2$, node $w_2$ will choose not to pick any color in this phase. Otherwise, if node $w_2$ chooses a color, then with probability at most $1/k_{i,w_1}$, node $w_1$ and $w_2$ will choose identical colors. Here, $k_{i,w_1}$ denotes the number of colors that is available for $w_1$ to choose during phase $i$. As a result, we know conditioned on the event that $w_1$ chooses a color, the probability that $w_1$ chooses same color with some of its neighbors is at most $\sum_{w \in W}((1/2) \cdot (1/k_{i,w_1})) = \sum_{w \in W} 1/(2 \cdot k_{i,w_1})$. Notice that for $w_1$, the number of remaining available colors is always at least as large as the number of remaining active neighbors, thus we know $|W| \le k_{i,w_1}$. Hence, we know conditioned on the event that $w_1$ chooses a color, the probability that $w_1$ chooses the same color with some of its neighbors is at most $1/2$.

At this time point, we can conclude that the probability that node $w_1$ becomes inactive after one phase is at least $(1/2) \cdot (1/2) = 1/4$. As a result, we know in expectation, after each phase, at least $1/4$ fraction of remaining nodes will decide their colors and become inactive. Let $x_i$ be the number of active nodes at the beginning of phase $i$, and let $y_i$ be the number of nodes that turn from active to inactive after phase $i$. We know $\mathbb{E}(y_i) \ge x_i/4$. Now, according to the definition of expectation, we know $\mathbb{E}(y_i) \le x_i \cdot \mathbb{P}(y_i \ge x_i/10) + (x_i/10) \cdot \mathbb{P}(y_i < x_i/10) \le x_i \cdot \mathbb{P}(y_i \ge x_i/10) + x_i/10$. Hence, we know $x_i/4 \le x_i \cdot \mathbb{P}(y_i \ge x_i/10) + x_i/10$. This implies $\mathbb{P}(y_i \ge x_i/10) \ge 3/20$, which is saying after each phase, with some constant probability, a constant fraction of remaining nodes in $\mathcal{G}_L$ will decide their colors and become inactive. Since each phase is independent, by using a Chernoff bound, we know after $\Theta(\lg n)$ phases, all nodes in $\mathcal{G}_L$ will decide and become inactive, w.h.p. □

The last step is to show the effectiveness of the message dissemination part. In essence, after each phase, the message will propagate one hop. Since the network has diameter $D$, we know all nodes in the network will know the message after $D$ phases. This concludes our analysis and leads to the following theorem.

Theorem 5.3. *CGCast can solve the global broadcast problem in $O((c^2/k) \cdot \lg^4 n + (k_{max}/k) \cdot \Delta \cdot \lg^3 n + D \cdot \Delta \cdot \lg^2 n) = \tilde{O}((c^2/k) + (k_{max}/k) \cdot \Delta + D \cdot \Delta)$ time slots, w.h.p.*

# 6 LOWER BOUNDS

## 6.1 Lower Bound for Neighbor Discovery

In this part, we will derive a $\Omega((c^2/k) + \Delta)$ lower bound for the neighbor discovery problem in cognitive radio networks. It demonstrates CSeek is near optimal (within poly-logarithmic factor) when the number of overlapping channels for different pairs of neighbors are same or similar (i.e., $k_{max} = \Theta(k)$).

To begin with, we argue the $\Omega(\Delta)$ factor in the lower bound. Imagine a star network and consider the node at the center. Call this node $u$. In each time slot, we know $u$ can receive at most one message. Moreover, in each message, there is at most one neighbor's identity. This is due to the topology of the network. Hence, we know at least $\Delta$ time slots is needed for $u$ to learn all neighbors' identities.

We then focus on the $\Omega(c^2/k)$ factor, which needs more efforts. Our strategy is to first derive a lower bound for winning a combinatorial game which captures the core difficulty of unknown channel overlapping pattern in cognitive radio networks, and then connect the game to the neighbor discovery problem by a reduction argument. We have previously studied this game and used it to derive lower bounds for the local broadcast problem in cognitive radio networks [8]. Here, we will reuse some of the results.

To obtain the needed $\Omega(c^2/k)$ bound, the game we considered is slightly different when $k \le c/2$ and $c/2 < k \le c$. We first focus on the $k \le c/2$ scenario.

*The $k \le c/2$ scenario.* In this setting, we consider the $(c, k)$-*bipartite hitting game*. In this game, the input is two integers $c, k$

such that $1 \leq k \leq c/\beta$, where $\beta \geq 2$ is a constant. Consider two sets of nodes each of size $c$: $A = \{a_1, a_2, \cdots, a_c\}$ and $B = \{b_1, b_2, \cdots, b_c\}$. Let $\mathcal{H}$ be a complete bipartite graph on bipartition $(A, B)$. The game is played between a *player* and a *referee*. At the beginning of the game, the referee privately selects a matching $M$ of size $k$ from $\mathcal{H}$. The game then proceeds in rounds. In each round, the player proposes an edge $e$ in $\mathcal{H}$. If $e \in M$ the player *wins*, otherwise it moves on to the next round.

In the lemma below, a lower bound is shown for winning the $(c, k)$-bipartite hitting game.

LEMMA 6.1 (LEMMA 11 FROM [8]). *Let $\mathcal{P}$ be a player that guarantees to win the $(c, k)$-bipartite hitting game in $f(c, k)$ rounds with probability at least $1/2$, for some $1 \leq k \leq c/\beta$, and some constant $\beta \geq 2$. It follows that $f(c, k) \geq c^2/(\alpha k) = \Theta(c^2/k)$, where $2 < \alpha = 2(\beta/(\beta - 1))^2 \leq 8$.*

We then reduce $(c, k)$-bipartite hitting to neighbor discovery. In particular, we construct a network containing only two nodes and then simulate an algorithm $\mathcal{A}$ running in it. We demonstrate that if $\mathcal{A}$ can achieve neighbor discovery fast, then we can use the simulation process to solve $(c, k)$-bipartite hitting fast.

LEMMA 6.2. *Let $\mathcal{A}$ be an algorithm that guarantees to solve neighbor discovery in $g(c, k)$ slots with probability at least $1/2$. Then, one can use $\mathcal{A}$ to construct a player $\mathcal{P}_{\mathcal{A}}$ that guarantees to win the $(c, k)$-bipartite hitting game in $O(g(c, k))$ rounds, for any $1 \leq k \leq c$, with probability at least $1/2$.*

PROOF. We construct our player $\mathcal{P}_{\mathcal{A}}$ to simulate a network containing two nodes: $u$ and $v$. Assume $u$ and $v$ share exactly $k$ channels. Moreover, since we consider the local channel label model, let $A = \{a_1, a_2, \cdots, a_c\}$ be $u$'s channel set and $B = \{b_1, b_2, \cdots, b_c\}$ be $v$'s channel set.

The first key observation for our simulation is that a $k$-matching $M$ over the complete bipartite graph with bipartition $(A, B)$ also describes a valid overlap of $k$ channels between $u$ and $v$. The second key observation for our simulation is that in order for $\mathcal{A}$ to solve neighbor discovery in such a network, there must exist a time slot in which $u$ lands on a shared channel with $v$. When the overlaps are viewed as a matching, this is the same as saying that there must exist a time slot in which $u$ chooses some $a_i$ and $v$ chooses some $b_j$ such that $(a_i, b_j) \in M$.

We are now ready to describe our simulation and establish its correctness. The player $\mathcal{P}_{\mathcal{A}}$ simulates $u$ running with channel set $A$, and $v$ running with channel set $B$, and the (unknown to the player) matching $M$ chosen by the referee for this execution defining the $k$ overlapping channels. In each simulated time slot $r$, player $\mathcal{P}_{\mathcal{A}}$ guesses $(a_r, b_r)$, where $a_r$ is the channel selected by $u$ in this time slot, and $b_r$ is the channel selected by $v$ in this time slot. If a guess does not win the game, it follows that $u$ has failed to land on a shared channel with $v$, so $\mathcal{P}_{\mathcal{A}}$ can correctly complete the simulated time slot by simulating no communication between $u$ and $v$.

As noted, to complete neighbor discovery, there must exist a time slot in which $u$ shares a channel with $v$. In that simulated time slot, $\mathcal{P}_{\mathcal{A}}$'s guess will win the bipartite hitting game. Because $\mathcal{P}_{\mathcal{A}}$ gets at most one guess per simulated time slot, we can immediately have the lemma. □

*The $k > c/2$ scenario.* In this setting, we use a similar strategy as the $k \leq c/2$ scenario, but focusing on a different hitting game called the *c-complete bipartite hitting game*. The input to this game is an integer $c \geq 1$. Consider two sets of nodes $A = \{a_1, a_2, \cdots, a_c\}$ and $B = \{b_1, b_2, \cdots, b_c\}$. Let $\mathcal{H}$ be a complete bipartite graph on bipartition $(A, B)$. The game is again played between a *player* and a *referee*. At the beginning of the game the referee privately selects a *maximum* matching $M$ in $\mathcal{H}$. The game then proceeds in rounds. In each round, the player proposes an edge $e$ in $\mathcal{H}$. If $e \in M$ the player *wins*, otherwise it moves on to the next round. Again, we can show a lower bound for winning this hitting game.

LEMMA 6.3 (LEMMA 14 FROM [8]). *Let $\mathcal{P}$ be a player that guarantees to win the c-complete bipartite hitting game in $f(c)$ rounds with probability at least $1/2$, for some positive integer $c$. It follows that $f(c) \geq c/3$.*

Now, notice Lemma 6.2 is also applicable to the $k > c/2$ scenario (as the $(c, k)$-bipartite hitting game becomes the $c$-complete bipartite hitting game when $k = c$). This implies there exists a strategy for using a fast neighbor discovery algorithm to solve $c$-complete bipartite hitting fast. Therefore, by combining Lemma 6.1, 6.3, and Lemma 6.2, along with the $\Omega(\Delta)$ lower bound we previously discussed, Theorem 6.4 follows.

THEOREM 6.4. *For any algorithm, to solve the neighbor discovery problem under the considered model with probability at least $1/2$, the time consumption is at least $\Omega((c^2/k) + \Delta)$.*

## 6.2 Lower Bounds for Global Broadcast

In this part, we give a $\Omega((c^2/k) + D \cdot \min\{c, \Delta\})$ lower bound for solving global broadcast in cognitive radio networks. More precisely, we have the following theorem.

THEOREM 6.5. *For any algorithm, to solve the global broadcast problem under the considered model with probability at least $1/2$, the time consumption is at least $\Omega((c^2/k) + D \cdot \min\{c, \Delta\})$.*

Proving this theorem is not too difficult. The argument for the $\Omega(c^2/k)$ part is similar to the one we used when proving the lower bound for neighbor discovery. In particular, we can reduce the $(c, k)$-bipartite hitting game discussed earlier to two node broadcast (i.e., one source node and one uninformed node). For the $\Omega(D \cdot \min\{c, \Delta\})$ part, we consider the case where the network graph $\mathcal{G}$ is a complete tree with each non-leaf node having $\Delta$ children. Then, for the message to propagate one hop, we show it will take at least $\Theta(\min\{c, \Delta\})$ time slots. Since the network diameter is $D$, we can obtain the bound as desired.

# 7 SUMMARY AND DISCUSSION

In this paper, we focus on providing algorithms that can act as key communication primitives in cognitive radio networks. In particular, we propose several randomized algorithms that can solve neighbor discovery and global broadcast efficiently. Unlike many previous work, our algorithms provide provable performance guarantees, and we show these upper bounds are near optimal in many cases by deriving corresponding lower bounds. Nevertheless, we suspect there is still room for improvements, from either the algorithmic side or the lower bound side.

Consider the neighbor discovery problem as an example, the upper and lower bound can still have a big gap when different pairs of neighbors share significantly different number of channels. This is a result of how we design CSEEK. In particular, in part two of CSEEK, for a node $u$, the algorithm gives priority to the more crowded channels. On the other hand, for nodes that overlap with $u$ on more channels, during part one, $u$ will meet them more often, creating the impression that certain channels are more crowded. Moreover, in the backoff procedure within each step in part two, all nodes are competing fairly. As a result of these design decisions, during part two, node $u$ is more likely to hear nodes that overlap with it on many channels. This slows down the algorithm's progress. To solve this issue, one possible way is to somehow give priority to nodes that overlap with $u$ on less channels. However, this is not easy, as node $u$ has no information about these neighbors before discovering them. More importantly, even if $u$ knows a neighbor $v$ overlaps with it on many channels, it may not be feasible to simply ask $v$ to reduce it's broadcasting probability, as another neighbor of $v$ may only overlap with $v$ on few channels. Alternatively, we may try to improve the lower bound based on these observations. However, this again seems highly non-trivial.

On the other hand, for the global broadcast problem, we also suspect it may be possible to improve the lower bound. In particular, for the tree we constructed in the proof of Theorem 6.5, since each node (except the leaves) has $\Delta$ children, the hight of the tree is actually $O(\lg n)$. This implies $O(D \cdot \min\{c, \Delta\})$ is really just $O(\min\{c, \Delta\} \cdot \lg n)$. To extend this argument—which is essentially saying if propagating one hop is expensive then we can't have large diameter—to the generic case, unfortunately, seems quite difficult.

## ACKNOWLEDGMENTS

This work is supported by State Key Lab for Novel Software Technology at Nanjing University ZZKT2017D03, by ERC Grant No. 336495 (ACDC), and by NUS FRC T1 251RES1404.

## REFERENCES

[1] Ian F. Akyildiz, Won-Yeol Lee, Mehmet C. Vuran, and Shantidev Mohanty. 2008. A survey on spectrum management in cognitive radio networks. *IEEE Communications Magazine* 46, 4 (2008), 40–48.

[2] Noga Alon, Amotz Bar-Noy, Nathan Linial, and David Peleg. 1991. A lower bound for radio broadcast. *J. Comput. System Sci.* 43, 2 (1991), 290–298.

[3] Ny Aina Andriambolamalala and Vlady Ravelomanana. 2017. An Optimal Randomized Broadcasting Algorithm in Radio Networks with Collision Detection. (2017). arXiv:1701.01587

[4] Reuven Bar-Yehuda, Oded Goldreich, and Alon Itai. 1992. On the time-complexity of broadcast in multi-hop radio networks: An exponential gap between determinism and randomization. *J. Comput. System Sci.* 45, 1 (1992), 104- 126.

[5] Lin Chen and Kaigui Bian. 2016. Neighbor discovery in mobile sensing applications: A comprehensive survey. *Ad Hoc Networks* 48 (2016), 38–52.

[6] Sixia Chen, Alexander Russell, Abhishek Samanta, and Ravi Sundaram. 2014. Deterministic Blind Rendezvous in Cognitive Radio Networks. In *Proceedings of the 34th International Conference on Distributed Computing Systems (ICDCS '14)*. IEEE, Madrid, Spain, 358–367.

[7] Mohsen Ghaffari, Bernhard Haeupler, and Majid Khabbazian. 2015. Randomized broadcast in radio networks with collision detection. *Distributed Computing* 28, 6 (2015), 407–422.

[8] Seth Gilbert, Fabian Kuhn, Calvin Newport, and Chaodong Zheng. 2015. Efficient Communication in Cognitive Radio Networks. In *Proceedings of the 2015 ACM Symposium on Principles of Distributed Computing (PODC '15)*. ACM, Donostia, Spain, 119–128.

[9] Seth Gilbert, Fabian Kuhn, and Chaodong Zheng. 2017. Communication Primitives in Cognitive Radio Networks. (2017). arXiv:1703.06130

[10] Zhaoquan Gu, Qiang-Sheng Hua, and Weiguo Dai. 2014. Fully Distributed Algorithms for Blind Rendezvous in Cognitive Radio Networks. In *Proceedings of the 15th ACM International Symposium on Mobile Ad Hoc Networking and Computing (MOBIHOC '14)*. ACM, Philadelphia, PA, USA, 155–164.

[11] Zhaoquan Gu, Qiang-Sheng Hua, Yuexuan Wang, and Francis C.M. Lau. 2013. Nearly optimal asynchronous blind rendezvous algorithm for Cognitive Radio Networks. In *Proceedings of the 10th IEEE Communications Society Conference on Sensor, Mesh and Ad Hoc Communications and Networks (SECON '13)*. IEEE, New Orleans, LA, USA, 371–379.

[12] Shouling Ji, Raheem Beyah, and Zhipeng Cai. 2013. Minimum-Latency Broadcast Scheduling for Cognitive Radio Networks. In *Proceedings of the 10th IEEE Communications Society Conference on Sensor, Mesh and Ad Hoc Communications and Networks (SECON '13)*. IEEE, New Orleans, LA, USA, 389–397.

[13] Athar Ali Khan, Mubashir Husain Rehmani, and Yasir Saleem. 2015. Neighbor discovery in traditional wireless networks and cognitive radio networks: Basics, taxonomy, challenges and future research directions. *Journal of Network and Computer Applications* 52 (2015), 173–190.

[14] Yogesh R. Kondareddy and Prathima Agrawal. 2008. Selective Broadcasting in Multi-Hop Cognitive Radio Networks. In *Proceedings of the 2008 IEEE Sarnoff Symposium*. IEEE, Princeton, NJ, USA, 1–5.

[15] Eyal Kushilevitz and Yishay Mansour. 1993. An $\Omega(D \cdot \log(n/D))$ Lower Bound for Broadcast in Radio Networks. In *Proceedings of the 12th Annual ACM Symposium on Principles of Distributed Computing (PODC '93)*. ACM, Ithaca, NY, USA, 65–74.

[16] Zhiyong Lin, Hai Liu, Xiaowen Chu, and Y-W Leung. 2011. Jump-stay based channel-hopping algorithm with guaranteed rendezvous for cognitive radio networks. In *Proceedings of the 30th International Conference on Computer Communications (INFOCOM '11)*. IEEE, Shanghai, China, 2444–2452.

[17] Chanaka J. Liyana Arachchige, S. Venkatesan, R. Chandrasekaran, and Neeraj Mittal. 2011. Minimal Time Broadcasting in Cognitive Radio Networks. In *Proceedings of the 12th International Conference on Distributed Computing and Networking (ICDCN '11)*. Springer, Bangalore, India, 364–375.

[18] Michael Luby. 1993. Removing randomness in parallel computation without a processor penalty. *J. Comput. System Sci.* 47, 2 (1993), 250–286.

[19] Neeraj Mittal, Yanyan Zeng, S. Venkatesan, and R. Chandrasekaran. 2011. Randomized Distributed Algorithms for Neighbor Discovery in Multi-hop Multichannel Heterogeneous Wireless Networks. In *Proceedings of the 31st International Conference on Distributed Computing Systems (ICDCS '11)*. IEEE, Minneapolis, MN, USA, 57–66.

[20] Michael Mitzenmacher and Eli Upfal. 2005. *Probability and computing: Randomized algorithms and probabilistic analysis*. Cambridge University Press.

[21] Erika Morphy. 2015. How new 'white space' rules could lead to an urban superWiFi. (2015). http://www.computerworld.com/article/2970867

[22] Calvin Newport. 2014. Radio Network Lower Bounds Made Easy. In *Proceedings of the 28th International Symposium on Distributed Computing (DISC '14)*. Springer, Austin, TX, USA, 258–272.

[23] IEEE 802.22 Working Group on Wireless Regional Area Networks. 2017. IEEE 802.22. (2017). http://www.ieee802.org/22

[24] Mubashir Husain Rehmani, Aline Carneiro Viana, Hicham Khalife, and Serge Fdida. 2013. SURF: A distributed channel selection strategy for data dissemination in multi-hop cognitive radio networks. *Computer Communications* 36, 10-11 (2013), 1172–1185.

[25] Jongmin Shin, Dongmin Yang, and Cheeha Kim. 2010. A Channel Rendezvous Scheme for Cognitive Radio Networks. *IEEE Communications Letters* 14 (2010), 954–956.

[26] Yi Song and Jiang Xie. 2012. A distributed broadcast protocol in multi-hop cognitive radio ad hoc networks without a common control channel. In *Proceedings of the 31st International Conference on Computer Communications (INFOCOM '12)*. IEEE, Orlando, FL, USA, 2273–2281.

[27] Yi Song and Jiang Xie. 2014. $QB^2IC$: A QoS-Based Broadcast Protocol Under Blind Information for Multihop Cognitive Radio Ad Hoc Networks. *IEEE Transactions on Vehicular Technology* 63, 3 (2014), 1453–1466.

[28] Yi Song and Jiang Xie. 2015. BRACER: A Distributed Broadcast Protocol in Multi-Hop Cognitive Radio Ad Hoc Networks with Collision Avoidance. *IEEE Transactions on Mobile Computing* 14, 3 (2015), 509–524.

[29] Tevfik Yucek and Huseyin Arslan. 2009. A survey of spectrum sensing algorithms for cognitive radio applications. *IEEE Communications Surveys Tutorials* 11, 1 (2009), 116–130.

[30] Yanyan Zeng, K. Alex Mills, Shreyas Gokhale, Neeraj Mittal, S. Venkatesan, and R. Chandrasekaran. 2016. Robust neighbor discovery in multi-hop multi-channel heterogeneous wireless networks. *J. Parallel and Distrib. Comput.* 92 (2016), 15–34.

# Broadcasting in Noisy Radio Networks*

Keren Censor-Hillel
Technion
Haifa 32000, Israel
ckeren@cs.technion.ac.il

Bernhard Haeupler
Carnegie Mellon University
Pittsburgh, PA 15213
haeupler@cs.cmu.edu

D. Ellis Hershkowitz
Carnegie Mellon University
Pittsburgh, PA 15213
dhershko@cs.cmu.edu

Goran Zuzic
Carnegie Mellon University
Pittsburgh, PA 15213
gzuzic@cs.cmu.edu

## ABSTRACT

The widely-studied radio network model [Chlamtac and Kutten, 1985] is a graph-based description that captures the inherent impact of collisions in wireless communication. In this model, the strong assumption is made that node $v$ receives a message from a neighbor if and only if exactly one of its neighbors broadcasts.

We relax this assumption by introducing a new *noisy radio network model* in which random faults occur at senders or receivers. Specifically, for a constant noise parameter $p \in [0, 1)$, either every sender has probability $p$ of transmitting noise or every receiver of a single transmission in its neighborhood has probability $p$ of receiving noise.

We first study *single-message broadcast* algorithms in noisy radio networks and show that the Decay algorithm [Bar-Yehuda et al., 1992] remains robust in the noisy model while the diameter-linear algorithm of Gasieniec et al., 2007 does not. We give a modified version of the algorithm of Gasieniec et al., 2007 that is robust to sender and receiver faults, and extend both this modified algorithm and the Decay algorithm to robust *multi-message broadcast* algorithms, broadcasting $\Omega\left(\frac{1}{\log n \log\log n}\right)$ and $\Omega\left(\frac{1}{\log n}\right)$ messages per round, respectively.

We next investigate the extent to which (network) coding improves throughput in noisy radio networks. In particular, we study the coding cap – the ratio of the throughput of coding to that of routing – in noisy radio networks. We address the previously perplexing result of Alon et al. 2014 that worst case coding throughput is no better than worst case routing throughput up to constants: we show that the worst case throughput performance of coding is, in fact, superior to that of routing – by a $\Theta(\log(n))$ gap – provided receiver faults are introduced. However, we show that sender faults have little effect on throughput. In particular, we show that any coding or routing scheme for the noiseless setting can be transformed to be robust to sender faults with only a constant throughput overhead. These transformations imply that the results of Alon et al., 2014 carry over to noisy radio networks with sender faults as well. As a result, if sender faults are introduced then there exist topologies for which there is a $\Theta(\log\log n)$ gap, but the worst case throughput across all topologies is $\Theta\left(\frac{1}{\log n}\right)$ for both coding and routing.

## CCS CONCEPTS

• **Theory of computation → Distributed computing models; Distributed algorithms**; *Graph algorithms analysis*;

## KEYWORDS

radio networks, robust radio networks, network gossip, random linear network coding, network coding gaps

**ACM Reference format:**
Keren Censor-Hillel, Bernhard Haeupler, D. Ellis Hershkowitz, and Goran Zuzic. 2017. Broadcasting in Noisy Radio Networks. In *Proceedings of ACM Symposium on Principles of Distributed Computing, Washington, DC, USA, July 25–27, 2017 (PODC '17)*, 10 pages.
https://doi.org/http://dx.doi.org/10.1145/3087801.3087808

*Supported in part by the Israel Science Foundation (grant 1696/14), the Binational Science Foundation (grant 2015803), and the National Science Foundation through grants CCF-1527110 and CCF-1618280


*PODC '17, July 25–27, 2017, Washington, DC, USA*

ACM ISBN 978-1-4503-4992-5/17/07...$15.00
http://dx.doi.org/10.1145/3087801.3087808

## 1 INTRODUCTION

Broadcasting messages throughout a network is one of the most important network communication primitives. The classic radio network model of Chlamtac and Kutten [8] was designed as a mathematical model to study broadcasting in a wireless setting. In this model, a radio network is represented by an undirected graph of $n$ nodes that communicate by transmitting messages during synchronized rounds. During each round, every node can either listen to the radio channel or transmit a message. A listening node $v$ receives a message if and only if exactly one of its neighbors transmits during that round. If more than a single neighbor transmits in a certain round, a collision occurs and node $v$ does not receive any of the transmitted messages.

The broadcast task in the classic radio network model – in which a single message or multiple messages need to be disseminated throughout the network – has been studied extensively [2, 4, 5, 10, 26, 34]. Classic algorithms [4, 20] typically employ *routing*. That is, nodes only transmit one of the messages the algorithm is disseminating. Alternatively, *(network) coding* approaches, in which nodes transmit multiple messages coded together, have been of recent interest [1, 3, 6, 17, 23, 25, 32].

Despite having been extensively studied, a notable deficit of the classic radio network model is its inability to model random noise. Specifically, the classic model assumes that a message that is sent without collisions is correctly received. However, this assumption is overly optimistic for real environments, in which noise may impede communication.

*Our contribution.* In this paper, we introduce the *noisy radio network model*, in which the classic graph-based model of Chlamtac and Kutten [8] is augmented with random faults. In particular, for a constant fault parameter $p \in [0, 1)$, every transmission may be noisy with probability $p$ (*sender fault*), or a node $v$ that would otherwise receive a message with probability $p$ receives noise instead (*receiver fault*). The faults occur independently at each node.

We begin by studying the extent to which the performance of existing single-message broadcasting algorithms deteriorates: we show that while the Decay algorithm of Bar-Yehuda, Goldreich and Itai [4] is robust to faults, the diameter-linear algorithm of Gąsieniec, Peleg and Xin [20] (which we call FASTBC) deteriorates considerably. We then develop a new single-message, diameter-linear algorithm for the noisy radio network model. Moreover, we describe how to extend both Decay and our modified algorithm to multi-message broadcasting algorithms, achieving throughputs of $\Omega\left(\frac{1}{\log n}\right)$ and $\Omega\left(\frac{1}{\log n \log\log n}\right)$ messages per round, respectively.

The main challenge that arises when designing fault-robust algorithms is avoiding careful deterministic round synchronization; that is, random faults prevent nodes from knowing exactly which other nodes have a message in any given round. Prior algorithms used round synchronization of this nature but can be made fault-robust by repeating certain otherwise fragile subroutines.

Additionally, we study the power of (network) coding in the new noisy radio network model. In particular, we examine the *coding gap* in this model: roughly the ratio between the throughput of coding to the throughput of routing. For the classic radio network model, recent work of Alon et al. [3] demonstrated an $\Omega(\log\log n)$ coding gap on certain networks. However, the same work shows that up to constant factors, in worst case topologies, coding performs no better than routing, when one broadcasts a very large number of messages. This runs contrary to the intuition that coding ought to improve the throughput of communication.

We resolve these counterintuitive results by showing that coding is, in fact, much more powerful than routing, *provided receiver faults occur*. Not only do we show that with receiver faults coding throughput is superior to routing by a $\Theta(\log n)$ gap on certain topologies, but we prove that the worst case performance of coding is superior to that of routing by a $\Theta(\log n)$ gap. These results emphasize that in practical settings coding can, in fact, significantly improve broadcast efficiency.

Lastly, we show that any algorithm for the classical radio network model can be made robust to sender faults at the price of a constant factor in throughput. This implies that the counterintuitive results of Alon et al. [3] carry over to the noisy radio network model *with sender faults*.

## 2 RELATED WORK

The radio network model was introduced more than 30 years ago in the pioneering work of Chlamtac and Kutten [8]. Since then computation in radio networks has been extensively studied. An excellent survey is given by Peleg [34]. Below, we discuss the most related work.

**Single-message broadcasting in radio networks:** In Bar-Yehuda et al. [4], it was shown that single-message broadcast in a known topology can be achieved in $O(D\log n + \log^2 n)$ rounds, where $D$ is the diameter of the network. This was improved by Gąsieniec et al. [20] and Kowalski and Pelc [27] who showed that if the topology is known broadcast can be completed in $O(D + \log^2 n)$ rounds. If the topology is not known, Czumaj and Rytter [10] show that $O(D\log(n/D) + \log^2 n)$ rounds suffice. By the $\Omega(\log^2 n)$ and $\Omega(D\log(n/D))$ lower bounds of Alon et al. [2] and Kushilevitz and Mansour [30], respectively, the above complexities are optimal. Lastly, if *collision detection* is available – a stronger assumption than known topology – a $O(D + \operatorname{poly}\log n)$-round algorithm is achievable as shown by Ghaffari et al. [17].

**Multi-message broadcasting in radio networks:** The earliest work for broadcasting $k$ messages is Bar-Yehuda and Israeli [5], who gave an algorithm that used $O((n + (k + D)\log n)\log\Delta)$ rounds, where $\Delta$ is the maximum node degree. A deterministic algorithm that works in $O(n\log^4 n + k\log^3 n)$ rounds was given by Chlebus et al. [9]. The first algorithm to beat the performance of Bar-Yehuda and Israeli [5] and to achieve an optimal $O(k\log n)$ dependence on the number of messages was given by Ghaffari and Haeupler [15]. This algorithm completes in $O(k\log n + D\log n/D + \operatorname{poly}\log n)$ rounds. The $\Omega(k\log n)$ lower bound for the number of rounds is given by Alon et al. [3]. Ghaffari et al. [17] provided an algorithm that completes in $O(k\log n + D + \log^2 n)$ rounds if the topology is known. Both of the latter algorithms crucially rely on (network) coding.

**Network coding and coding gap:** Network coding was first studied outside of the radio broadcast model by Ahlswede et al. [1]. For multiple-message broadcast, network coding algorithms by Ghaffari et al. [17] and Khabbazian and Kowalski [25] achieved a throughput of $\Omega(1/\log n)$. A network coding gap of $\Omega(\log\log n)$ on certain topologies for the radio network model was demonstrated by Alon et al. [3] as was a $\Theta(1)$ worst case gap.

In wired undirected networks, Li et al. [32] show the network coding gap to be at most 2. For directed wired networks, Halperin et al. [23] shows that the coding gap corresponds to the integrality gap of directed Steiner-tree LP. For the wired vertex-congest model, in which messages sent at the same time do not collide, a tight coding gap of $\Theta(\log n)$ was given by Censor-Hillel et al. [6].

**Robust communication models:** The noisy broadcast model, introduced by El-Gamal. [12], resembles our model as it assumes random errors. This model was mostly studied in the context of computing functions of the inputs of nodes [14, 21, 31, 33]. However, this model assumes a complete communication network and single-bit transmissions. An extension of this line of work for random planar networks was also studied [11, 24, 36]. Unlike our own model, in this model a node can receive a message from multiple neighbors in a single round.

Another model that captures unreliability in radio networks is the *dual graph* model [7, 18, 19, 28, 29]. In this graph-based model, there is a static set of edges that form the network graph $G$ as well as an additional graph $G'$ which consists of edges that may or may not be present in each round, as chosen by an adversary. While an excellent way to capture an environment where some links are reliable and others are not, the dual graph model fails to model random noise.

# 3 PRELIMINARIES

In this section, we review the classic radio network model, define our generalization of it, define throughput, explain how we quantify the coding gap and describe existing broadcast algorithms.

## 3.1 The (Noisy) Radio Broadcast Model and $k$-Message Broadcast

The classic radio network model consists of an undirected graph $G = (V, E)$ with $n$ nodes and diameter $D$. Nodes communicate in synchronized time steps (rounds) by either remaining silent (listening) or locally broadcasting a **packet** (each neighbor gets the same packet). A node $u$ receives a packet from a neighbor in round $r$ if and only if exactly one of its neighbors broadcasts in $r$ and $u$ remains silent. We term this model the **faultless** model.

We build on the classic model and introduce a **noisy radio network** model. Our model is the same as the classic radio broadcast model but with one of two modifications. In the **receiver faults** model, a node that is listening and has only one broadcasting neighbor receives noise with constant probability (independently of other nodes). In the **sender faults** model, a broadcasting node has a constant probability of transmitting noise (independently of other senders failing). We use $p \in [0, 1)$ to denote the fault probability and expose it in results where appropriate. In both variations of the model, we assume that if a node $u$ receives noise due to collisions, faults, or none of its neighbors broadcasting, the node does not mistake this noise for a legitimate packet from a neighbor.

The most commonly studied algorithmic problem in the radio network model is the $k$-message broadcast problem. This problem consists of a **source** $s \in V$ and $k$ **messages**. $(G, s)$ is often referred to as the **topology**. Each message is of size $O(\log(nk))$ and each packet is of size $O(\log(nk))$.[1] The source $s$ begins in the first round as the only node that knows the messages. The problem is solved once all nodes have all $k$ messages.

A **schedule** is defined by the assignment of a function $b_u^r(\cdot)$ to each node $u$ in each round $r$, which, intuitively, governs the behavior of node $u$ in round $r$. The schedule is static and does not change during rounds. The domain and co-domain of the function depend on the setting as follows. In a **routing** setting, the function $b_u^r$ takes no input (except the implicit arguments $u$ and $r$) and outputs either a *stay silent token* or the index in $\{1, 2, ..., k\}$ of the message to broadcast. If the output of $b_u^r$ is the index of a message which $u$ has not received by round $r$, the node remains silent. In a **(network) coding** setting, the function $b_u^r$ takes as input the entire history of packets node $u$ received and outputs either a *stay silent token* or an arbitrary packet of length $O(\log nk)$. We informally refer to an **algorithm** as a procedure that outputs a schedule.

## 3.2 Throughput

The throughput of a given topology is roughly the maximum number of messages that can be transmitted per round as the number of messages, $k$, goes to infinity.

*Definition 3.1 (Topology Throughput).* The routing throughput of a topology $(G, s)$ is defined as

$$\tau(G, s) = \limsup_{k\to\infty} \frac{k}{\min_{\mathcal{S}_k} |\mathcal{S}_k|}$$

where $|\mathcal{S}_k|$ is the number of rounds taken by the schedule $\mathcal{S}_k$. In the faultless setting, the minimum is taken over schedules that broadcast $k$ messages from $s$ to all nodes in $G$. In the faulty setting, the minimum is taken over schedules that succeed with probability at least $1 - \frac{1}{k}$.[2]

Given a set of schedules, we define the **throughput of the set of schedules** as above but where we minimize over the set (rather than all possible schedules).

In general, we show topology throughput lower bounds of $\tau$ in the noisy model by showing that, for any $\epsilon > 0$ and any

[1] Papers more commonly define the message and packet size to be $O(\log n)$. However, this choice leads to tedious technical difficulties in the noisy setting. Our choice of message and packet size as $O(\log(nk))$ is reasonable for two reasons: (1) $k = \text{poly}(n)$ is the most practical setting and (2) without using $O(\log k)$ bits one cannot even send a message identifier. This assumption will become particularly important for us when providing coding schedules, as it is what enables us to use Reed-Solomon coding to create packets that can be broadcast in a single round.

[2] In the faulty setting $\min_{\mathcal{S}_k} |\mathcal{S}_k|$ could be replaced by the minimum of the *expected number of rounds* taken by any schedule that succeeds with probability 1. While our results can be adapted to this definition, this definition introduces various technical issues which we wish to avoid in order to simplify the presentation.

$k$, there is a $k_0 > k$ such that there exists a schedule that broadcasts $k_0$ messages in $k_0 X$ rounds, where $|\frac{1}{X} - \tau| \le \epsilon$. Similarly, to show a throughput upper bound of $\tau$ in the noisy model we demonstrate that, for sufficiently large $k$, any schedule that broadcasts with a probability of failure of at most $1/k$ requires at least $k\tau^{-1}$ rounds.

## 3.3 Comparing Routing and Network Coding

There are a couple of natural ways to quantify the advantage that coding offers over routing. First, one might be interested in finding a fixed topology where the ratio of coding throughput to routing throughput is largest. Second, one might be interested in the worst case performance of coding compared to the worst case performance of routing. We formalize these two quantities as the *shared topology gap* and the *worst case topology gap* respectively. Let $\tau^R(G,s)$ and $\tau^{\text{NC}}(G,s)$ be the throughputs of $(G,s)$ when using routing schedules and when using network coding schedules respectively.

*Definition 3.2 (Shared Topology Gap).* The shared topology gap is:

$$\mathcal{G}_s = \max_{G,s} \left[\tau^{\text{NC}}(G,s)/\tau^R(G,s)\right]$$

*Definition 3.3 (Worst Case Topology Gap).* The worst case topology gap is defined as

$$\mathcal{G}_w = \left[\min_{G,s} \tau^{\text{NC}}(G,s)\right] / \left[\min_{G,s} \tau^R(G,s)\right]$$

We will also sometimes refer to the coding gap of a fixed network $(G,s)$ defined as $\tau^{\text{NC}}(G,s)/\tau^R(G,s)$. Note that any lower bound on the coding gap of a network is a lower bound on $\mathcal{G}_s$.

## 3.4 Broadcast Algorithms for Faultless Radio Networks

In this section, for completeness, we present the broadcast algorithms for the faultless setting whose performance in the noisy setting are addressed in Section 4.

*3.4.1 Decay.* Here we describe the classic Decay algorithm [4] for broadcasting **a single message** from the source $s$ to every other node. For each round, we define the set of **informed nodes** as all the nodes that received the message up to that round.

**Algorithm:** Divide the rounds into phases of $O(\log n)$ rounds. During the $i^{th}$ round of each phase, where $i \le O(\log n)$, each **informed** node broadcasts the message independently with probability $2^{-i}$. A simple calculation yields the following.

LEMMA 3.4. *If a node $v$ has an informed neighbor at the start of the phase, it becomes informed by the end of the phase with constant probability.*

The round complexity of Decay then follows [4].

LEMMA 3.5 (BAR-YEHUDA ET AL. [4]). *In the faultless setting, Decay spreads a single message in $O(D\log n + \log n(\log n + \log \frac{1}{\delta}))$ rounds with a probability of failure of at most $\delta$.*

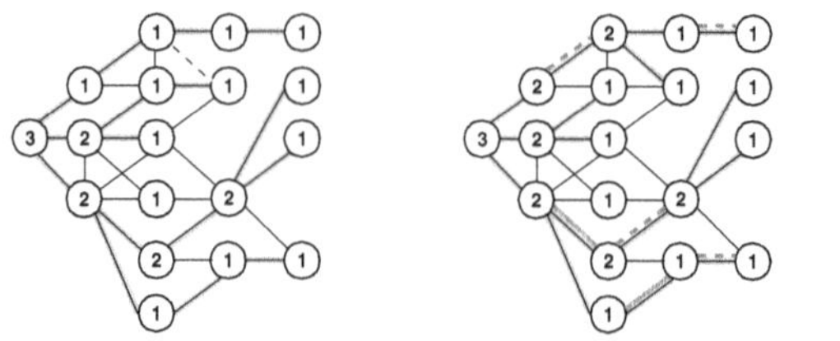

(a) A ranked BFS Tree that is not a GBST. (b) A ranked BFS Tree that is a GBST.

**Figure 1: Black lines indicate edges in $G$; pink lines indicated edges in $\mathcal{T}$; the dashed yellow line indicates the edge which makes Figure 1(a) not a GBST; dashed green lines indicate a fast node and the corresponding child in the GBST. Example taken from Ghaffari et al. [17].**

*3.4.2 FASTBC.* We next describe an optimal algorithm for single-message broadcast when all the nodes **know the topology** beforehand, given by Gąsieniec et al. [20], which we refer to as the FASTBC algorithm. FASTBC works by first decomposing the graph into a **gathering-broadcasting spanning tree** (GBST) and then utilizing this structure to broadcast a message in $D + O(\log^2 n)$ rounds.

We need the following notion in order to describe the algorithm. A **ranked breadth-first search (BFS) tree** $\mathcal{T}$ for a graph $G$ is a BFS tree rooted at a source node $s$ where every node in the tree is assigned an integral rank. The ranks are assigned inductively, as follows. Every leaf node has rank 1. A non-leaf node $v$ with a maximum child rank of $r$ is assigned a rank of $r$ if exactly one child of $v$ has rank $r$. Otherwise, if two or more children have rank $r$, then $v$ is assigned a rank of $r+1$. Additionally, we define the level of node $v$ in a BFS tree as the distance from $s$ to $v$. The maximum rank can be bounded as follows.

LEMMA 3.6 (GABER AND MANSOUR [13]). *The largest rank $r_{\max}$ in a ranked BFS tree of size $n$ is no greater than $\lceil \log_2 n \rceil$.*

**GBST:** A ranked BFS tree $\mathcal{T}$ of a graph $G$ is a **gathering-broadcasting spanning tree** (GBST) if and only if no two distinct nodes on the same level and of the same rank $r$ have two distinct $\mathcal{T}$-parents both with rank $r$. See Figure 1 for a comparison of a ranked BFS tree that is not a GBST with a ranked BFS tree that is a GBST. Note that we assume nodes agree on a common GBST before the start of the algorithm because of the known topology assumption.

**Fast nodes in a GBST:** We call node $u$ **fast** if one of its GBST-children has the same rank as $u$, and that tree-edge is called a **fast edge**. Any GBST-path from the source to a node has nonincreasing ranks. Hence it is composed of at most $O(\log n)$ **fast stretches** of consecutive fast nodes of the same rank connected by fast edges.

**The FASTBC Algorithm [20]:** At a high level, FASTBC divides the rounds into odd and even numbered rounds. On odd-numbered rounds (called **slow transmission rounds**) it performs a standard Decay algorithm that pushes a message from a higher ranked node to a lower ranked one. During even-numbered rounds (called **fast transmission rounds**) it pushes a message along fast stretches.

More formally, during a fast transmission round $2t$, only **fast** nodes on level $l$ and rank $r$ broadcast if $t \equiv l - 6r \pmod{6r_{\max}}$. During a slow transmission round $2t+1$, all nodes broadcast with probability $2^{-(t \bmod O(\log n))}$.

Intuitively, messages on a fast stretch ride a **wave** from the start of the stretch to its tail. More formally, when a messages gets transmitted along a fast stretch for the first time, it never gets interrupted until it reaches the tail. This non-interference along fast stretches is ensured by the properties of the GBST. The round complexity of FASTBC is given as follows.

Lemma 3.7 (Gąsieniec et al. [20]). *In the faultless setting, FASTBC spreads a single message in $D+O(\log n(\log n + \log \frac{1}{\delta}))$ rounds with a probability of failure of at most $\delta$.*

# 4 ROBUST BROADCAST ALGORITHMS

In this section we describe how we adapt algorithms from the faultless setting to the sender or receiver faults setting in order to obtain robust broadcast algorithms.

## 4.1 Robust Algorithms for Single-Message Broadcast

Decay [4] – which spreads a message in $O(D\log n + \log^2 n)$ rounds with high probability[3] in the faultless setting – is a classic faultless broadcasting algorithm. We now prove that the Decay algorithm works as-is with faults.

Lemma 4.1. *With sender or receiver faults with fault probability p, the Decay algorithm spreads a single message in $O\left(\frac{\log n}{1-p}(D + \log n + \log \frac{1}{\delta})\right)$ rounds with a probability of failure of at most $\delta$.*

Proof. Fix a path $s = u_0, u_1, ..., u_l = v$ from the source $s$ to any node $v$ (the length $l$ of the path is at most the diameter $D$). At round $t$, let $\phi$ be the largest $i$ such that $u_i$ knows the message (initially, $\phi = 0$). After one phase of $O(\log n)$ rounds $\phi$ either remains the same or increases by 1 with probability $c(1-p)$ for a particular constant $c > 0$ by an analogue of Theorem 3.4 which appears in Section 3.4.1. Hence, after $O(\frac{1}{1-p}(D + \log n + \log \frac{1}{\delta}))$ phases, the probability of failure can be bounded via a Chernoff bound:

$$Pr[\Phi < l] < \exp\left(-\Omega\left(\log n + \log \frac{1}{\delta}\right)\right).$$

Applying a union bound over all $n$ nodes gives that the failure probability is at most $n \cdot \exp(-\Omega(\log n + \log \frac{1}{\delta})) < \exp(-\Omega(\log \frac{1}{\delta})) < \delta$. □

[3]We denote "with high probability" when the probability of success is at least $1 - \frac{1}{n}$.

While the Decay algorithm is very simple and does not require nodes to know the topology in advance, the number of rounds it takes depends super-linearly on the diameter. However, if the topology is known in advance, it is possible to achieve linear dependence on the diameter in the faultless setting, as shown by the FASTBC algorithm [20]. FASTBC succeeds with high probability in $O(D + \log^2 n)$ rounds.

However, in contrast to the Decay algorithm, the performance of FASTBC deteriorates in the faulty setting. In particular, FASTBC uses a fragile round counting mechanism to synchronize message passing along its fast stretches which does not translate well to the faulty setting. The following result quantifies this performance deterioration.

Lemma 4.2. *FASTBC takes $\Theta\left(\frac{p}{1-p}D\log n + \frac{1}{1-p}D\right)$ rounds in expectation to broadcast a message along a single path of length $D$.*

Proof. Consider a path of length $D$ with a message on its left endpoint. Let $f(x)$ be the expected number of rounds to traverse the path of length $x$ with FASTBC under the condition that the leftmost node broadcasts in the next round. With probability $1-p$ the broadcast is successful, leading to a subproblem with length $x-1$. Alternatively, with probability $p$, it can be unsuccessful – leading to a waiting time of $\Theta(\log n)$ until the leftmost node broadcasts again and without reducing the path length $x$. The resulting recurrence is $f(x) = 1 + (1-p)f(x-1) + p[f(x) + \Theta(\log n)]$ which can be rewritten as $f(x) = f(x-1) + \frac{1}{1-p} + \frac{p}{1-p}\Theta(\log n)$, leading to $f(x) = \Theta(\frac{p}{1-p}x\log n + \frac{1}{1-p}x)$. □

One simple way to construct a robust broadcast algorithm is to perform FASTBC but repeat each round $\Theta(\log n)$ times for a total of $O(D\log n + \log^{O(1)} n)$ rounds. This approach works because the probability that any message gets dropped is at most $\frac{1}{n^{\Omega(1)}}$, which allows one to apply a union bound over the entire algorithm (of length at most poly$(n)$). However, this approach loses the linear dependence on $D$ and therefore performs no better than Decay. A better approach, inspired by Theorem 4.2, would be to repeat each message $\Theta(\log\log n)$ times, giving $p = \frac{1}{\log^{\Omega(1)} n}$ and a $O(D\log\log n + \text{poly}\log n)$-round algorithm.

We further refine this approach in the following **Robust FASTBC** algorithm, which gives a linear dependence on $D$ in the noisy setting.

**Robust FASTBC Algorithm:** As in FASTBC, a gathering-broadcasting spanning tree is constructed from the source node. Let the round number of the algorithm be $t$. When $t$ is odd, each node will perform a standard Decay step (a node broadcasts with probability $2^{-(t-1)/2 \bmod O(\log n)}$). Let $S = \Theta(\log\log n)$ and $c$ be a sufficiently large constant. At even-numbered rounds $t$, a node in the fast set with level $l$ and rank $r$ will broadcast if $\lfloor \frac{l}{S} \rfloor - 6r = \lfloor \frac{t/2}{cS} \rfloor \pmod{6r_{\max}}$ and $l \equiv t \pmod 3$.

The following is our main result for this section.

THEOREM 4.3. *Robust FASTBC spreads a single message in $O(D + \log n \log\log n(\log n + \log \frac{1}{\delta}))$ rounds with a probability of failure of at most $\delta$ if sender or receiver faults occur with probability $p$.*

PROOF. Fix a GBST path $P = (s = u_0, u_1, u_1, ..., u_l = v)$ from the source $s$ to a node $v$. Partition the edges on the path into fast stretches (consecutive edges connecting two nodes of the same rank) and non-fast edges. There can be at most $O(\log n)$ non-fast edges interconnecting $O(\log n)$ fast stretches.

Assuming a message is on a non-fast edge, during the next $\Theta(\log n)$ rounds it is transmitted along that edge with constant probability. Given that there are only $O(\log n)$ such edges, a Chernoff bound gives us that after $O(\log n(\log n + \log \frac{1}{\delta}))$ such rounds (where a message is waiting to be transmitted along a non-fast edge), the message is transmitted along all the non-fast edges on $P$ with probability at least $1 - \frac{\delta}{2n}$.

Next, we turn to counting the number of rounds that a message spends on fast stretches (during even-numbered rounds). Note that from the design of the algorithm and the properties of the GBST no two broadcasting nodes ever interfere with each other (hence the only failures come from constant probability faults).

Call a fast node from the path $P$ a **barrier** if its level is divisible by $S$ and call a message **active** if it is on a fast stretch and the node it is currently at is broadcasting. Note that a message that enters a fast stretch has to wait $r_{\max} cS = O(\log n \log\log n)$ rounds until it becomes active. Once it is active, consider its behavior during the next $cS = O(\log\log n)$ rounds. The message can either exit the stretch, remain active (meaning it reaches the next barrier) or become inactive (by failing $(c-1)S$ out of $cS$ transmissions). The probability of becoming inactive is at most $\frac{1}{\log^3 n}$ by Chernoff with an appropriate constant $c$. Every time a message becomes inactive, it waits $O(\log n \log\log n)$ rounds before it becomes active.

Let $d_1, d_2, ..., d_q$ (note that $q \le O(\log n)$) be the lengths of the fast stretches in the path $P$. When a message is active, it traverses the paths in at most $\sum_{i=1}^{q} \lceil d_i/S \rceil \cdot cS = \sum_{i=1}^{q} O(d_i + 1) = O(D + \log n)$ rounds. The number of rounds it takes for a message to become active is at most

$$\left(q + \frac{T}{cS} Pr[\text{msg inactive in } cS \text{ rounds}]\right) \cdot$$
$$\cdot\, O(\log n \log\log n)$$
$$\le O(\log^2 n \log\log n) + \frac{T}{\Theta(\log\log n)} \frac{1}{\log^3 n} O(\log n \log\log n)$$
$$= O(\log^2 n \log\log n) + \Theta\left(\frac{T}{\log^2 n}\right),$$

where $T$ is the length of the entire protocol. The $q$ term comes from becoming active each time a message enters a fast stretch. The $\frac{T}{cS}$ accounts for the possibility of a message becoming inactive in between barriers. A Chernoff bound proves that if $T = \Theta(D + \log n \log\log n(\log n + \log \frac{1}{\delta}))$, the message gets passed along the path with a probability of at least $1 - \frac{\delta}{2n}$.

Putting together the behavior during the odd-numbered and even-numbered rounds and applying a union bound over all $n$ nodes gives that the protocol forwards the message from the source to all other nodes in the claimed number of rounds with probability at least $1 - \delta$. □

## 4.2 Robust Algorithms for Multi-Message Broadcast

A pleasant feature of single-message broadcasting algorithms that are robust to sender failures is that they can be used in a black-box manner to transmit $k$ messages with random linear network coding [22], provided some minor technical conditions are satisfied. For instance, a node cannot change its behavior based on whether it receives a message or not. However, all of our algorithms can be made to satisfy these conditions using methods similar to [17]. We state the results that can be achieved and refer the reader to Ghaffari et al. [17] and Haeupler [22] for details.

LEMMA 4.4. *Decay with random linear network coding can broadcast $k$ messages in $O(D \log n + k \log n + \log^2 n)$ rounds if sender or receiver faults occur with constant probability. It follows that any topology has a coding throughput of $\Omega\left(\frac{1}{\log n}\right)$.*

LEMMA 4.5. *Robust FASTBC with random linear network coding can broadcast $k$ messages in $O(D + k \log n \log\log n + \log^2 n \log\log n)$ rounds if sender or receiver faults occur with constant probability. It follows that any topology has a coding throughput of $\Omega\left(\frac{1}{\log n \log\log n}\right)$.*

We leave as an open problem the existence of an algorithm that is robust to sender and receiver faults and can broadcast $k$ messages in $O(D + k \log n + \operatorname{poly}\log(n))$ – this would be optimal up to additive poly log factors.

# 5 THROUGHPUT GAPS WITH NOISY BROADCAST

We now study the gaps between (network) coding and routing in the noisy radio network model. In the faultless setting, by Theorem 4.4, coding can send $k$ messages in $O(D \log n + k \log n + \log^2 n)$ rounds. Moreover, in the faultless setting, no routing scheme with $k$ polynomial in $n$ is known to send $k$ messages in fewer than $\Omega\left(k \log^2 n\right)$ rounds. The apparent disparity of what is achievable with coding versus routing demands a formal explanation.

Previous work of Alon et al. [3] attempts to formalize this gap. Although this work shows a shared topology gap of $\Omega(\log\log n)$ in the faultless setting, it also shows a counterintuitive worst case topology gap of $\Theta(1)$.

Our new model and results give a more satisfactory explanation. We formally show in what sense the high throughput routing schemes of Alon et al. [3] are not robust; namely, they cease to be efficient for random receiver failures. Moreover, in the noisy radio network model we prove that coding is indeed necessary for high throughput broadcasting by exhibiting a worst case topology gap of $\Theta(\log n)$ and a shared topology gap of $\Omega(\log n)$ in the receiver fault setting. All of our routing lower bounds, and therefore all of our gaps, are particularly strong as we prove them in a setting where routing is allowed to be **adaptive**, as we later define.

Additionally, we show that with coding or adaptive routing, sender faults have little impact on throughput: every coding (resp. routing) schedule that assumes no faults can be transformed into a coding (resp. adaptive routing) schedule in the sender faults setting with the same throughput up to constants. These transformations allow us to conclude the following: (1) interestingly, the worst case topology gap is highly sensitive to whether sender or receiver faults are examined – we show it to be $\Theta(1)$ for sender faults with adaptive routing; (2) the $\Omega(\log\log n)$ shared topology gap of the faultless setting also exists in the sender fault setting.

We now define an adaptive routing schedule wherein all nodes are allowed to adapt to all faults.

*Definition 5.1 (Adaptive Routing Schedule).* An adaptive routing schedule is a sequence of functions $b_r(\cdot)$ – one for each every round $r$ – that takes as input *i)* the entire topology $(G, s)$ and *ii)* all tuples $(u, i)$ where node $u$ received message $m_i$ in some round $r' < r$. Each $b_r(\cdot)$ outputs a sequence of length $n$ directing each node to either remain silent or to broadcast a message they know.

In practice, a distributed routing algorithm might receive some feedback as to when faults occur but it will certainly not receive as much as our adaptive routing schedules. Thus, our definition is sufficiently strong for proving meaningful gaps. Moreover, if routing is non-adaptive, it is not difficult to show a $\Theta(\log k)$ gap on a single-link topology. However, with adaptive routing the gap can be shown to be $\Theta(1)$ on the single-link topology. Thus, adaptivity can considerably improve routing throughput, further motivating adaptive routing as a strong model for proving gaps.

Lastly, we use Reed-Solomon coding [35] as a black box for our coding schedules throughout this section. Given $k$ input packets, Reed-Solomon coding constructs poly$(nk)$ coded packets such that any $k$ of the coded packets is sufficient to reconstruct the original $k$ packets.

## 5.1 Gaps for Receiver Faults with Adaptive Routing

In this section we study the coding gaps with receiver faults and adaptive routing.

*5.1.1 Star Topology: $\Theta(\log n)$ Gap for Receiver Faults with Adaptive Routing.* We first show a $\Theta(\log n)$ gap in the receiver fault setting on a star topology. A **star topology** consists of a node $s$ and $n$ other adjacent nodes.[4]

LEMMA 5.2. *The adaptive routing throughput of the star topology with receiver faults is $\Theta(1/\log n)$.*

[4]We use $n$ instead of $n-1$ other nodes to simplify calculations.

PROOF SKETCH. A lower bound of $\Omega\left(\frac{1}{\log n}\right)$ on throughput follows from applying a Chernoff bound to the schedule that broadcasts message $m_1$ from $s$ until it is received by all nodes, then $m_2$ and so forth up to message $m_k$. The schedule stops after $13k + k\log n$.

An upper bound of $O\left(\frac{1}{\log n}\right)$ on throughput can be shown roughly by the fact that each message requires $O(\log n)$ rounds in expectation to be received.

□

LEMMA 5.3. *The coding throughput of the star topology with receiver faults is $\Theta(1)$.*

PROOF SKETCH. A throughput of $O(1)$ trivially follows because $\Omega(k)$ rounds are strictly necessary. A coding throughput of $\Omega(1)$ by applying a Chernoff bound to a schedule that uses Reed-Solomon coding.

□

Theorem 5.2 and Theorem 5.3 give the claimed gap on the star topology.

THEOREM 5.4. *In the receiver faults setting there is a $\Theta(\log n)$ coding gap for the star topology with adaptive routing. A shared topology gap of $\Omega(\log n)$ in the receiver faults setting follows.*

*5.1.2 Worst Case Topology: $\Theta(\log n)$ Gap for Receiver Faults with Adaptive Routing.* Having shown a shared topology gap of $\Omega(\log n)$ in the receiver fault setting we now show a worst case topology gap of $\Theta(\log n)$ with receiver faults. Recall that we define the worst case topology gap as $\min_{G,s}\tau^{\text{NC}}(G,s)/\min_{G,s}\tau^{R}(G,s)$. To prove the $\Theta(\log n)$ gap, we show that with receiver faults and adaptive routing, $\min_{G,s}\tau^{\text{NC}}(G,s) = \Theta(1/\log n)$ and $\min_{G,s}\tau^{R}(G,s) = \Theta(1/\log^2 n)$.

We first describe the topology, $\mathcal{WCT}$, that has minimal throughput for both coding and adaptive routing with receiver faults. The $\mathcal{WCT}$ topology is based on a construction of Ghaffari et al. [16]; Ghaffari et al. [16] demonstrate the existence of a bipartite network of radius 2 with $\tilde{\Theta}(\sqrt{n})$ nodes. These $\tilde{\Theta}(\sqrt{n})$ nodes consist of a source node, $\tilde{\Theta}(\sqrt{n})$ receiver nodes and $\Theta(\sqrt{n})$ sender nodes. Every receiver node is connected to a subset of the sender nodes by a probabilistic construction. See Figure 2(a) for a sketch of the network. We duplicate each of the $\tilde{\Theta}(\sqrt{n})$ receiver nodes to induce $\tilde{\Theta}(\sqrt{n})$ star-like topologies which we term clusters. More formally, $\mathcal{WCT}$ is as follows.

**Worst case topology ($\mathcal{WCT}$) for receiver faults:** We begin with the construction of Ghaffari et al. [16]. Instead of each receiver node, $r$, we construct a **cluster** of $\tilde{\Theta}(\sqrt{n})$ nodes. Each node in the cluster that replaces receiver $r$ has an edge to sender node $s$ if and only if $\{s, r\}$ is an edge of the original network of Ghaffari et al. [16]. We use the symbol $\mathcal{WCT}$ for the resulting network. See Figure 2(b) for an illustration of $\mathcal{WCT}$.

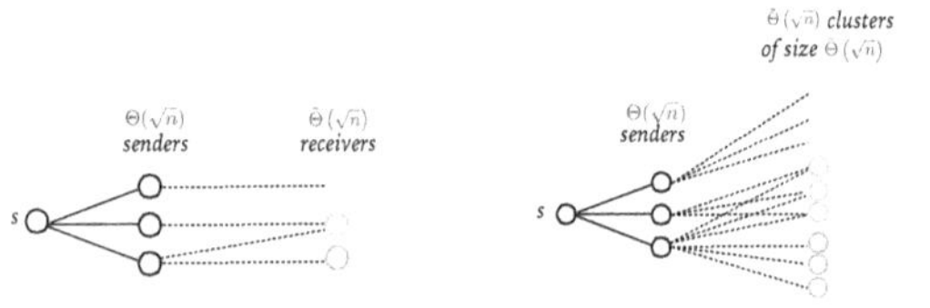


(a) The lower bound network from Ghaffari et al. [16]. (b) The modified lower bound network, $\mathcal{WCT}$.

**Figure 2: We modify the network from [16] to a worst case topology in the receiver fault setting; dotted lines refer to edges from the probabilistic construction, solid lines refer to definite edges and clusters are colored according to the receiver node from which they are derived.**

Since nodes in a cluster are connected to the same sender nodes, a node in a cluster is sent a packet without collision if and only if all other nodes in the cluster are sent the same packet without collision. Moreover, Ghaffari et al. [16] prove that at most $O(1/\log n)$ of all receiver nodes receive a packet without collision in any one round, so the following holds.

LEMMA 5.5. *At most $O(1/\log n)$ of clusters of $\mathcal{WCT}$ receive a packet without collision per round.*

We now use this topology to prove the following claim.

LEMMA 5.6. *Adaptive routing on $\mathcal{WCT}$ has a throughput of $O(1/\log^2 n)$ in the receiver fault setting.*

PROOF. Consider the above described $\mathcal{WCT}$. Since in each round every node in a cluster is sent the same message without collision or no message, we can interpret each as a star of $\tilde{\Theta}(\sqrt{n})$ nodes. By Theorem 5.2, each cluster must receive a packet without collision at least $\Omega(k \log(\sqrt{n})) = \Omega(k \log n)$ times, in order to receive $k$ messages with a probability of failure of at most $1/k$. Thus, in order for every node to receive a message such that the probability of failure is at most $1/k$, every cluster must receive a message without collision at least $\Omega(k \log n)$ times. By Theorem 5.5, $O\left(\frac{1}{\log n}\right)$ clusters are sent a packet without collision each round and so at least $\Omega((\log n)(k \log n)) = \Omega(k \log^2 n)$ rounds are necessary to have a failure probability of at most $1/k$. Thus, the throughput is at most $O(1/\log^2 n)$. □

We next move to the $\Omega(1/\log^2 n)$ adaptive routing throughput in the receiver fault setting. To prove this possibility result we first sketch an intermediate result for bipartite networks.

LEMMA 5.7. *Consider bipartite network $V = L \cup R$ where every node in $L$ knows the same $k$ messages. There exists an adaptive routing schedule of length $O(k \log^2 n)$ that broadcasts the $k$ messages to all the nodes in $R$ with probability at least $1 - \exp(-\Omega(k))$ in the receiver fault setting.*

PROOF. We show that there exists an adaptive routing schedule, $\mathcal{S}_j$, that succeeds in broadcasting $k$ messages from all nodes in $L$ to all nodes in $R$ with a probability of failure of at most $\exp(-\Omega(k))$. By Theorem 4.1, Decay can route all $k$ messages to $R$ in $O(\log^2 n)$ rounds with a failure probability of at most $1/n$. Denote by $\mathcal{S}_{m_i}$ this schedule provided by Decay when it is used for message $m_i$. The schedule $\mathcal{S}_j$ runs the schedule $\mathcal{S}_{m_1}$ repeatedly until it succeeds, then it runs $\mathcal{S}_{m_2}$ until it succeeds and so forth until $\mathcal{S}_{m_k}$. However, $\mathcal{S}$ never runs more than $\frac{2k}{1-1/n}$ of these schedules in total.

Let $C_i$ be the random variable that stands for the number of times $\mathcal{S}_{m_i}$ must be run and let $C = \sum_i C_i$. Note that $C_i$ is a geometric random variable with probability of success $1 - 1/n$ and that $\mathbb{E}[C] = k/(1 - \frac{1}{n})$. By a Chernoff bound for geometric random variables, we have that the probability that $\mathcal{S}$ does not succeed is

$$\begin{aligned} \Pr\left(C \geq \frac{(1+1)k}{1-1/n}\right) &\leq \exp\left(-\frac{1^2(k-1)}{2(1+1)}\right) \\ &= \exp(-\Omega(k)). \end{aligned}$$

Thus, $\mathcal{S}_j$ succeeds in sending $k$ messages in $\frac{2k}{1-1/n}(\log^2 n) = \Omega(k \log^2 n)$ rounds with a probability of failure of at most $\exp(-\Omega(k))$. □

LEMMA 5.8. *Adaptive routing on any network has a throughput of $\Omega(1/\log^2 n)$ with receiver faults.*

PROOF. We now prove that the worst case adaptive routing throughput is $\Omega(1/\log^2 n)$ by providing an adaptive routing schedule. Roughly, our schedule works by **pipelining** schedules given by Lemma 5.7. We first note that any broadcast problem given a source $s$ and graph $G$ can be broken into a series of broadcast problems on bipartite graphs. In particular, it can be broken into the BFS layering of $G$ where the $i^{th}$ layer contains all nodes with distance exactly $i$ from $s$. Let $L_i$ be the set of nodes in the $i^{th}$ layer. Note that each pair of consecutive layers $L_i$, $L_{i+1}$ defines a bipartite network. Next, we divide $k$ into $D$ batches of size $k' = \frac{k}{D}$ (assume, without loss of generality, that $D$ divides $k$), which we pipeline.

By Theorem 5.7, we can broadcast batch $j \in [D]$ of $k'$ messages in $O(k' \log^2 n)$ rounds with a failure probability of at most $\exp(-\Omega(k'))$. Let $\mathcal{S}_j$ be the schedule that broadcasts batch $j$ in this manner.

We now describe our schedule for broadcasting through the entire network. We divide rounds into meta-rounds of size $\Omega(k' \log^2 n)$. The $k$-th layer runs $\mathcal{S}_j$ in meta-round $3j + k - 3$. In other words, we pipeline batches through the network using the above schedule for bipartite graphs, working layers of 3 apart so we do not incur extra collisions. We run $4(D + \frac{k}{k'})$ meta-rounds.

We argue that this schedule achieves a throughput of $\Omega(1/\log^2 n)$. A fixed $\mathcal{S}_j$ fails in a meta-round with a probability of at most $\exp(-\Omega(k')) = \exp(-\Omega(k/D)) \leq 1/k^c$, for sufficiently large $k$. By a union bound over the diameter, the probability that any $\mathcal{S}_j$ fails in a meta-round is at most $1/k^{c-1}$. Moreover, we run $4(D + \frac{k}{k'})$ meta-rounds and so by another union bound over meta-rounds, an $\mathcal{S}_j$ fails in any meta-round with a probability of at most $1/k^{c-2} \leq 1/k$, for an appropriate $c$. Lastly, if every $\mathcal{S}_j$ in every meta-round succeeds, then every node receives every batch, meaning that every node receives all messages. Since each meta-round is of length $\frac{2k'}{1-1/n}\log^2 n$ and we run $4(D+\frac{k}{k'})$ meta-rounds, we use a total of $4(D+\frac{k}{k'})(\frac{2k'}{1-1/n}\log^2 n) \leq 24k\log^2 n$ rounds to succeed with probability at least $1-1/k$, for $n \geq 2$.

Finally, it trivially holds that for any $\epsilon > 0$ and $k$ there exists a $k_0$ such that $|\frac{k_0}{24k_0\log^2 n} - \frac{1}{24\log^2}| \leq \epsilon$. □

The impossibility result of Theorem 5.6 and the possibility result of Theorem 5.8 yield the following.

LEMMA 5.9. *The worst case adaptive routing throughput with receiver faults is $\Theta(1/\log^2 n)$, i.e.* $\min_{G,s}\tau^R(G,s) = \Theta(1/\log^2 n)$.

Next, we show that coding in the receiver fault setting can always achieve a throughput of $\Omega(1/\log n)$, and that no better bound exists.

LEMMA 5.10. *The worst case coding throughput in the receiver fault setting is $\Theta(1/\log n)$, i.e.* $\min_{G,s}\tau^{NC}(G,s) = \Theta(1/\log n)$.

PROOF. We first prove that the worst case coding throughput is $O(1/\log n)$ with receiver faults. Consider the above worst case topology. In any given round at most $O(1/\log n)$ clusters receive a message. Each cluster forms a star and, similarly to *Theorem* 5.3, each star must be sent the message $\Theta(k)$ rounds, in order to decode all $k$ messages. Thus, $\Omega(k\log n)$ rounds are strictly necessary and in particular are necessary to succeed with probability at least $1-1/k$. We conclude a coding throughput of $O(1/\log n)$ on this topology.

By Theorem 4.4, the worst case coding throughput is $\Omega(1/\log n)$ with receiver faults. □

By Theorem 5.9 and Theorem 5.10, we conclude our strong worst case topology gap.

THEOREM 5.11. *The worst case topology gap is $\Theta(\log n)$ for receiver faults with adaptive routing.*

## 5.2 Transformations from the Faultless Setting to the Faulty Setting

Having shown that there is a strong $\Theta(\log n)$ gap in the receiver fault setting, we now turn our attention to the sender fault setting. We begin by presenting explicit transformations of schedules from the faultless setting into schedules that are robust to faults.

LEMMA 5.12. *A set of routing schedules with throughput $\tau$ in the faultless setting can be transformed into a set of adaptive routing schedules with throughput $\tau(1-p)$ for the sender fault setting.*

PROOF SKETCH. One can use the schedule from the faultless setting that sent $k$ messages to send $kx$ for sufficiently large $x$. □

LEMMA 5.13. *A set of coding schedules from the faultless setting with throughput $\tau$ can be transformed into a set of coding schedules with throughput $\tau(1-p)$ in the sender or receiver fault setting.*

PROOF SKETCH. A proof similar to that of 5.12 along with Reed-Solomon coding yields the desire claim. □

## 5.3 Gaps for Sender Faults with Adaptive Routing

We now use our transformations to derive a shared topology gap of $\Omega(\log\log n)$ and a worst case topology gap of $\Theta(1)$ in the *sender fault setting* if routing is adaptive. This is a stark departure from the $\Theta(\log n)$ worst case topology gap of the *receiver fault setting.*

THEOREM 5.14. *The shared topology gap is $\Omega(\log\log n)$ with senders faults and adaptive routing.*

PROOF. In Alon et al. [3], a network that has a routing throughput of $O(1/\log\log n)$ in the faultless setting is given. A throughput upper bound of $O(1/\log\log n)$ in the faultless setting clearly implies a throughput upper bound of $O(1/\log\log n)$ in the sender fault setting. The work of Alon et al. [3] also provides a set of coding schedules that achieves a throughput of $\Omega(1)$ on the same network in the faultless setting. By Theorem 5.13, we conclude a coding throughput of $\Omega(1)$ in sender fault setting. Thus, we conclude an $\Omega(\log\log n)$ gap on this topology and so a shared topology gap of $\Omega(\log\log n)$. □

THEOREM 5.15. *The worst case topology gap is $\Theta(1)$ in the sender fault setting with adaptive routing.*

PROOF. Recall that the worst case topology gap is

$$\min_{G,s}\tau^{\mathrm{NC}}(G,s)/\min_{G,s}\tau^R(G,s).$$

We first show that $\min_{G,s}\tau^{\mathrm{NC}}(G,s) = \Theta(1/\log n)$. It is shown in Alon et al. [3] that there exist topologies where coding requires a throughput of $O(1/\log n)$ in the faultless setting. Note that a throughput upper bound in the faultless setting clearly implies one for the sender fault setting. Additionally, coding can achieve a throughput of $\Omega(1/\log n)$ in the sender fault setting, by Theorem 4.4.

We now show $\min_{G,s}\tau^R(G,s) = \Theta(1/\log n)$. It is shown in Alon et al. [3] that there exist topologies where routing requires a throughput of $O(1/\log n)$ in the faultless setting, and again we note that a throughput upper bound in the faultless setting clearly implies one for the sender fault setting. The work of Alon et al. [3] also shows that in the faultless setting there exists a set of routing schedules with a throughput of $\Omega(1/\log n)$. We conclude, by Theorem 5.12, a routing throughput of $\Omega(1/\log n)$ is achievable in the sender fault setting.

Thus, $\min_{G,s}\tau^{\mathrm{NC}}(G,s) = \Theta(1/\log n)$ and $\min_{G,s}\tau^R(G,s) = \Theta(1/\log n)$ and so with sender faults and adaptive routing the worst case topology gap is $\Theta(1)$. □

## REFERENCES


[1] R. Ahlswede, Ning Cai, S. Y.R. Li, and R. W. Yeung. 2006. Network Information Flow. *IEEE Trans. Inf. Theor.* 46, 4 (Sept. 2006), 1204–1216. https://doi.org/10.1109/18.850663

[2] Noga Alon, Amotz Bar-Noy, Nathan Linial, and David Peleg. 1991. A lower bound for radio broadcast. *J. Comput. System Sci.* 43, 2 (1991), 290–298.

[3] Noga Alon, Mohsen Ghaffari, Bernhard Haeupler, and Majid Khabbazian. 2014. Broadcast Throughput in Radio Networks: Routing vs. Network Coding. *ACM-SIAM Symposium on Discrete Algorithms (SODA) 2014* (2014), 1831–1843. https://doi.org/10.1137/1.9781611973402.132

[4] Reuven Bar-Yehuda, Oded Goldreich, and Alon Itai. 1992. On the time-complexity of broadcast in multi-hop radio networks: An exponential gap between determinism and randomization. *J. Comput. System Sci.* 45, 1 (1992), 104–126.

[5] R. Bar-Yehuda and A. Israeli. 1989. Multiple Communication in Multi-hop Radio Networks. In *Proceedings of the Eighth Annual ACM Symposium on Principles of Distributed Computing (PODC '89)*. ACM, New York, NY, USA, 329–338. https://doi.org/10.1145/72981.73005

[6] Keren Censor-Hillel, Mohsen Ghaffari, and Fabian Kuhn. 2014. A New Perspective on Vertex Connectivity. In *Proceedings of the Twenty-fifth Annual ACM-SIAM Symposium on Discrete Algorithms (SODA '14)*. Society for Industrial and Applied Mathematics, Philadelphia, PA, USA, 546–561. http://dl.acm.org/citation.cfm?id=2634074.2634115

[7] Keren Censor-Hillel, Seth Gilbert, Fabian Kuhn, Nancy A. Lynch, and Calvin C. Newport. 2014. Structuring unreliable radio networks. *Distributed Computing* 27, 1 (2014), 1–19. https://doi.org/10.1007/s00446-013-0198-8

[8] I. Chlamtac and S. Kutten. 1985. On Broadcasting in Radio Networks - Problem Analysis and Protocol Design. *IEEE Transactions on Communications* 33, 12 (December 1985), 1240–1246. https://doi.org/10.1109/TCOM.1985.1096245

[9] Bogdan S Chlebus, Dariusz R Kowalski, Andrzej Pelc, and Mariusz A Rokicki. 2011. Efficient distributed communication in ad-hoc radio networks. In *International Colloquium on Automata, Languages, and Programming*. Springer, 613–624.

[10] Artur Czumaj and Wojciech Rytter. 2006. Broadcasting algorithms in radio networks with unknown topology. *Journal of Algorithms* 60, 2 (2006), 115 – 143. https://doi.org/10.1016/j.jalgor.2004.08.001

[11] Chinmoy Dutta and Jaikumar Radhakrishnan. 2008. Lower Bounds for Noisy Wireless Networks using Sampling Algorithms. In *49th Annual IEEE Symposium on Foundations of Computer Science, FOCS 2008, October 25-28, 2008, Philadelphia, PA, USA*. 394–402. https://doi.org/10.1109/FOCS.2008.72

[12] Abbas El-Gamal. 1984. Open problems presented at the 1984 workshop on specific problems in communication and computation. *Sponsored by bell communication research* (1984).

[13] Iris Gaber and Yishay Mansour. 2003. Centralized Broadcast in Multihop Radio Networks. *J. Algorithms* 46, 1 (Jan. 2003), 1–20. https://doi.org/10.1016/S0196-6774(02)00292-4

[14] Robert G. Gallager. 1988. Finding parity in a simple broadcast network. *IEEE Trans. Information Theory* 34, 2 (1988), 176–180. https://doi.org/10.1109/18.2626

[15] Mohsen Ghaffari and Bernhard Haeupler. 2013. Fast structuring of radio networks large for multi-message communications. In *International Symposium on Distributed Computing*. Springer, 492–506.

[16] Mohsen Ghaffari, Bernhard Haeupler, and Majid Khabbazian. 2013. A bound on the throughput of radio networks. *arXiv preprint arXiv:1302.0264* (2013).

[17] Mohsen Ghaffari, Bernhard Haeupler, and Majid Khabbazian. 2015. Randomized broadcast in radio networks with collision detection. *Distributed Computing* 28, 6 (2015), 407–422.

[18] Mohsen Ghaffari, Bernhard Haeupler, Nancy A. Lynch, and Calvin C. Newport. 2012. Bounds on Contention Management in Radio Networks. In *Distributed Computing - 26th International Symposium, DISC 2012, Salvador, Brazil, October 16-18, 2012. Proceedings*. 223–237. https://doi.org/10.1007/978-3-642-33651-5_16

[19] Mohsen Ghaffari, Nancy A. Lynch, and Calvin C. Newport. 2013. The cost of radio network broadcast for different models of unreliable links. In *PODC '13, Montreal, QC, Canada, July 22-24, 2013*. 345–354. https://doi.org/10.1145/2484239.2484259

[20] Leszek Gąsieniec, David Peleg, and Qin Xin. 2007. Faster communication in known topology radio networks. *Distributed Computing* 19, 4 (2007), 289–300.

[21] Navin Goyal, Guy Kindler, and Michael E. Saks. 2008. Lower Bounds for the Noisy Broadcast Problem. *SIAM J. Comput.* 37, 6 (2008), 1806–1841. https://doi.org/10.1137/060654864

[22] Bernhard Haeupler. 2011. Analyzing network coding gossip made easy. In *Proceedings of the forty-third annual ACM symposium on Theory of computing*. ACM, 293–302.

[23] Eran Halperin, Guy Kortsarz, Robert Krauthgamer, Aravind Srinivasan, and Nan Wang. 2003. Integrality Ratio for Group Steiner Trees and Directed Steiner Trees. In *Proceedings of the Fourteenth Annual ACM-SIAM Symposium on Discrete Algorithms (SODA '03)*. Society for Industrial and Applied Mathematics, Philadelphia, PA, USA, 275–284. http://dl.acm.org/citation.cfm?id=644108.644155

[24] Yashodhan Kanoria and D. Manjunath. 2007. On distributed computation in noisy random planar networks. In *Proceedings of the IEEE International Symposium on Information Theory (ISIT)*. 626–630.

[25] Majid Khabbazian and Dariusz R. Kowalski. 2011. Time-efficient Randomized Multiple-message Broadcast in Radio Networks. In *Proceedings of the 30th Annual ACM SIGACT-SIGOPS Symposium on Principles of Distributed Computing (PODC '11)*. ACM, New York, NY, USA, 373–380. https://doi.org/10.1145/1993806.1993884

[26] Dariusz R. Kowalski and Andrzej Pelc. 2005. Broadcasting in Undirected Ad Hoc Radio Networks. *Distrib. Comput.* 18, 1 (July 2005), 43–57. https://doi.org/10.1007/s00446-005-0126-7

[27] Dariusz R. Kowalski and Andrzej Pelc. 2007. Optimal Deterministic Broadcasting in Known Topology Radio Networks. *Distributed Computing* 19, 3 (2007), 185–195.

[28] Fabian Kuhn, Nancy A. Lynch, and Calvin C. Newport. 2011. The abstract MAC layer. *Distributed Computing* 24, 3-4 (2011), 187–206. https://doi.org/10.1007/s00446-010-0118-0

[29] Fabian Kuhn, Nancy A. Lynch, Calvin C. Newport, Rotem Oshman, and Andréa W. Richa. 2010. Broadcasting in unreliable radio networks. In *Proceedings of the 29th Annual ACM Symposium on Principles of Distributed Computing, PODC 2010, Zurich, Switzerland, July 25-28, 2010*. 336–345. https://doi.org/10.1145/1835698.1835779

[30] Eyal Kushilevitz and Yishay Mansour. 1993. An Omega(D Log(N/D)) Lower Bound for Broadcast in Radio Networks. In *Proceedings of the Twelfth Annual ACM Symposium on Principles of Distributed Computing (PODC '93)*. ACM, New York, NY, USA, 65–74. https://doi.org/10.1145/164051.164059

[31] Eyal Kushilevitz and Yishay Mansour. 1998. Computation in Noisy Radio Networks.. In *SODA*, Vol. 98. 236–243.

[32] Z. Li, B. Li, and L. C. Lau. 2009. A Constant Bound on Throughput Improvement of Multicast Network Coding in Undirected Networks. *IEEE Transactions on Information Theory* 55, 3 (March 2009), 1016–1026. https://doi.org/10.1109/TIT.2008.2011516

[33] Ilan Newman. 2004. Computing in Fault Tolerance Broadcast Networks. In *19th Annual IEEE Conference on Computational Complexity (CCC 2004), 21-24 June 2004, Amherst, MA, USA*. 113–122. https://doi.org/10.1109/CCC.2004.1313813

[34] David Peleg. 2007. *Time-Efficient Broadcasting in Radio Networks: A Review*. Springer Berlin Heidelberg, Berlin, Heidelberg, 1–18. https://doi.org/10.1007/978-3-540-77115-9_1

[35] Stephen B. Wicker. 1994. *Reed-Solomon Codes and Their Applications*. IEEE Press, Piscataway, NJ, USA.

[36] Lei Ying, R. Srikant, and Geir E. Dullerud. 2006. Distributed symmetric function computation in noisy wireless sensor networks with binary data. In *4th International Symposium on Modeling and Optimization in Mobile, Ad-Hoc and Wireless Networks (WiOpt 2006), 3-6 April 2006, Boston, Massachusetts, USA*. 336–344. https://doi.org/10.1109/WIOPT.2006.1666455

# Gossip in a Smartphone Peer-to-Peer Network

Calvin Newport
Georgetown University
Washington, DC, USA
cnewport@cs.georgetown.edu

## ABSTRACT

In this paper, we study the fundamental problem of gossip in the *mobile telephone model*: a recently introduced variation of the classical *telephone model* modified to better describe the local peer-to-peer communication services implemented in many popular smartphone operating systems. In more detail, the mobile telephone model differs from the classical telephone model in three ways: (1) each device can participate in at most one connection per round; (2) the network topology can undergo a parameterized rate of change; and (3) devices can advertise a parameterized number of bits about their state to their neighbors in each round before connection attempts are initiated. We begin by describing and analyzing new randomized gossip algorithms in this model under the harsh assumption of a network topology that can change completely in every round. We prove a significant time complexity gap between the case where nodes can advertise 0 bits to their neighbors in each round, and the case where nodes can advertise 1 bit. For the latter assumption, we present two solutions: the first depends on a shared randomness source, while the second eliminates this assumption using a pseudorandomness generator we prove to exist with a novel generalization of a classical result from the study of two-party communication complexity. We then turn our attention to the easier case where the topology graph is stable, and describe and analyze a new gossip algorithm that provides a substantial performance improvement for many parameters. We conclude by studying a relaxed version of gossip in which it is only necessary for nodes to each learn a specified fraction of the messages in the system. We prove that our existing algorithms for dynamic network topologies and a single advertising bit solve this relaxed version up to a polynomial factor faster (in network size) for many parameters. These are the first known gossip results for the mobile telephone model, and they significantly expand our understanding of how to communicate and coordinate in this increasingly relevant setting.

## KEYWORDS

gossip; mobile telephone model; smartphone; peer-to-peer


*PODC'17, , July 25–27, 2017, Washington, DC, USA.*

ACM ISBN 978-1-4503-4992-5/17/07...$15.00.
http://dx.doi.org/10.1145/3087801.3087813

## 1 INTRODUCTION

This paper describes and analyzes new gossip algorithms in the mobile telephone model: an abstraction that captures the local device-to-device communication capabilities available in most smartphone operating systems; e.g., as implemented by services such as Bluetooth LE [16], WiFi Direct [2], and Apple's Multipeer Connectivity framework [20].

*Motivation.* Smartphones are a ubiquitous communication platform: there are currently over 3.9 billion smartphone subscriptions worldwide [18]. Most smartphone communication leverages one-hop radio links to cell towers or WiFi access points. In recent years, however, the major smartphone operating systems have included increasingly stable and useful support for local peer-to-peer communication that allows a device to talk directly to a nearby device (using local radio broadcast) while avoiding cellular and WiFi infrastructure.

The ability to create these local links, combined with the ubiquity of smartphones, enables scenarios in which large groups of nearby smartphone users run applications that create peer-to-peer meshes supporting infrastructure-free networking. There are many possible motivations for these smartphone peer-to-peer networks. For example, they can support communication in settings where network infrastructure is *censored* (e.g., government protests), *overwhelmed* (e.g., a large festival or march), or *unavailable* (e.g., after a disaster or at a remote event). In addition, in developing countries, cellular data minutes are often bought in blocks and carefully conserved—increasing interest in networking operations that do not require cellular infrastructure.

To further validate the potential usefulness of smartphone peer-to-peer networks, consider the FireChat application, which implements group chat using smartphone peer-to-peer services. In the few years since its initial release, it has been widely adopted in over 120 countries and has been used successfully in multiple government protests, festivals (e.g., at Burning Man, which is held far from cell towers), and disaster scenarios [9].

Developing useful applications for this smartphone peer-to-peer setting requires distributed algorithms that can provide global reliability and efficiency guarantees on top of an unpredictable collection of local links. As detailed below, the models that describe this emerging setting are sufficiently different from existing models that new algorithms and analysis techniques are required. This paper addresses this need by describing and analyzing new gossip algorithms for this important setting.

*The Mobile Telephone Model.* The mobile telephone model studied in this paper was introduced in recent work [10, 23]. It is a variant of the classical telephone peer-to-peer model (e.g., [3, 6–8, 11–15]) modified to better describe the capabilities and constraints of existing smartphone peer-to-peer services. The details of the mobile telephone model are inspired, in particular, by the current specifications of Apple's Multipeer Connectivity framework [20]: a peer-to-peer service available in every iOS version since iOS 7 that allows nodes to advertise services, discover nearby advertisers, and attempt to connect to nearby advertisers, using only local radio broadcast. (The definition of the classical telephone model, and differences between the classical telephone and mobile telephone model, are detailed and discussed below in the related work section.)

In more detail, the mobile telephone model abstracts the basic *scan-and-connect* dynamics of the Multipeer framework as follows. Time proceeds in synchronous rounds. In each round, a connected graph describes the underlying network topology for that round. At the beginning of each round, each device (also called a *node* in the following) learns its neighbors in the topology graph (e.g., as the result of a scan). Each device can then attempt to initiate a connection with a neighbor. Each node can support at most one connection—so if multiple nodes attempt to connect with the same target, only one connection will succeed. If two nodes connect, they can perform a bounded amount of reliable communication before the round ends.

We parameterize this model with a *tag length* $b \geq 0$. At the beginning of each round, each node can choose a *tag* consisting of $b$ bits to advertise. When performing a scan, each node learns both the ids and chosen tags of its neighbors (where $b = 0$ means there are no tags). These tags can change from round to round. In our previous study of rumor spreading with parameter $b = 1$ [10], for example, at the beginning of a given round, each node that already knows the rumor advertises a 1 with its tag, while other nodes advertise a 0. This simplified the rumor spreading task by enabling nodes that know the rumor to only attempt to connect to nodes that do not. This capability of nodes to use tags to deliver limited information to their neighbors is motivated by the ability of devices to choose and change their service advertisements in the Multipeer framework.

We also parameterize the model with a *stability factor* $\tau \geq 1$. The underlying network topology must stay stable for at least $\tau$ rounds between changes. For $\tau = 1$, for example, the network topology can change completely in every round, while for $\tau = \infty$, the topology never changes. There exist finer-grained approaches for capturing intermediate levels of stability (e.g., $T$-interval connectivity [19]), but in this paper we study only the two extreme cases of fully dynamic and fully stable topologies, so our simpler stability factor definition is sufficient. The need to model topology changes is motivated by the inherently mobile nature of the smartphone setting.

*Results.* In this paper, we describe and analyze new algorithms for the *gossip* problem in the mobile telephone model with respect to different model parameter and algorithm assumptions. This problem assumes a subset of nodes start with messages (also called *tokens*). The goal is to spread these messages to the entire network. Gossip is fundamental in distributed computing and is considered particularly important for ad hoc networks such as the smartphone meshes studied in this paper (c.f., the introductory discussion in [24]).

Below (and in Figure 1) we state and discuss our main results. In the following, let $n > 1$ be the network size and $k, 1 \leq k \leq n$, be the number of tokens in the system. For a given topology graph,

| Assumptions | Algorithm | Gossip Round Complexity |
|---|---|---|
| Standard Gossip | | |
| $b = 0, \tau \geq 1$ | BlindMatch | $O((1/\alpha)k\Delta^2 \log^2 n)$ |
| $b = 1, \tau \geq 1$ | SharedBit* | $O(kn)$ |
| $b = 1, \tau \geq 1$ | SimSharedBit** | $O(kn + (1/\alpha)\Delta^{1/\tau} \log^6 n)$ |
| $b = 1, \tau = \infty$ | CrowdedBin | $O((k/\alpha) \log^6 n)$ |
| $\epsilon$-Gossip ($0 < \epsilon < 1$) | | |
| $b = 1, \tau \geq 1$ | SharedBit* | $O\left(\frac{n\sqrt{\Delta \log \Delta}}{(1-\epsilon)\alpha}\right)$ |

**Figure 1: A summary of gossip and $\epsilon$-gossip round complexity bounds proved in this paper. (In the $\epsilon$-gossip problem, it is assumed that every node starts with a message, but each node need only learn an $\epsilon$-fraction of the $n$ total messages.) In the following: $n$ is the network size, $k$ is the number of gossip messages, $\alpha$ and $\Delta$ are the vertex expansion and maximum degree, respectively, of the network topology graph, $b$ is the tag length, and $\tau$ is the stability factor. All results hold with high probability in $n$ (i.e., at least $1 - 1/n$). Notice, the result for $b = 0$ and $\tau \geq 1$ is the best known result even for the easier case of $b = 0$ and $\tau = \infty$. (*) The SharedBit algorithm (alone among all algorithms studied) requires shared randomness. (**) The SimSharedBit algorithm is existential in the sense that it depends on a pseudorandomness generator that we prove exists in Section 5.**

we use $\alpha$ to describe its vertex expansion (see the model discussion below) and $\Delta$ to describe its maximum degree.[1] We assume the topologies are connected. All round complexity results hold with high probability in $n$ (i.e., probability at least $1 - 1/n$).

We start by considering the difficult setting where $b = 0$ and $\tau = 1$; i.e., nodes cannot use tags and the network topology graph can change completely in each round. In Section 4, we describe and analyze a natural strategy for this setting called BlindMatch, which has nodes select neighbors with uniform randomness to send connection attempts.[2] We prove that BlindMatch solves gossip in $O((1/\alpha)k\Delta^2 \log^2 n)$ rounds. This bound might seem pessimistic at first glance, but it is known that disseminating even a single message in the mobile telephone model with this strategy can take $\Omega(\Delta^2/\sqrt{\alpha})$ rounds in some networks [23]. Indeed, this lower bound holds even for the easier assumption that $\tau = \infty$. Accordingly, we do not consider $b = 0$ and $\tau = \infty$ as a distinct case in this paper. (To provide intuition for why $\Omega(\Delta^2)$ rounds are sometimes necessary, consider two stars centered on $u$ and $v$, respectively, where each star has around $\Delta$ points and $u$ and $v$ are connected by an edge. Assume $u$ starts with a gossip message. For $v$ to receive this message two events must happen: (1) $u$ selects $v$ for a connection; and (2) $v$ accepts $u$'s connection from all incoming connections in that round. The first event occurs with probability $\approx 1/\Delta$, and because $v$ can expect a constant fraction of its neighbors to send it connection

[1]If the topology is dynamic, then $\alpha$ is defined as the minimum expansion over all rounds, and $\Delta$ is defined as the largest maximum degree over all rounds.

[2]This is essentially the well-known PUSH-PULL strategy from the classical telephone model with the key exception that in our model if a node receives multiple connection attempts, only one succeeds. As discussed in the related work and Section 4, this well-motivated model change requires new analysis techniques to understand information propagation.

attempts in any given round, the second event also occurs with probability $\approx 1/\Delta$.) Our BlindMatch result provides the benchmark against which we attempt to improve with the algorithms that follow.

In Section 5, we consider the case where $b = 1$ and $\tau \geq 1$; i.e., the network can still change completely in each round, but now nodes can advertise a single bit to their neighbors. We begin by describing and analyzing an algorithm called SharedBit. This algorithm assumes a shared randomness source which is used to implement (essentially) a random hash function that allows nodes to hash their current set of known messages to a single bit to be used as their one-bit advertising tag. The key guarantee of this function is that nodes with the same sets advertise the same bit, and nodes with different sets have a constant probability of advertising different bits. This helps nodes seek out productive connections with neighbors (e.g., connections in which at least one node learns something new). We prove that SharedBit solves gossip in $O(kn)$ rounds.

We next seek to eliminate the shared randomness assumption. To do so, we describe SimSharedBit which solves gossip in $O(kn + (1/\alpha)\Delta^{1/\tau}\log^6 n)$ rounds, without assuming a shared randomness source. Notice, because $\alpha \geq 2/n$ and $\Delta \leq n$, this solution is always within log factors of the SharedBit for large $k$, and for small $k$ it is still comparable for many values of $\alpha$, $\Delta$, and/or $\tau$.

The SimSharedBit algorithm depends on a novel generalization of *Newman's Theorem* [21]—a well-known result on public randomness simulation from the study of two-party communication complexity. We prove that there exists an appropriate pseudorandom number generator that can provide sufficient randomness for the SharedBit strategy. We then elect a leader in $O((1/\alpha)\Delta^{1/\tau}\log^6 n)$ rounds using an algorithm from [23], and use this leader to disseminate a small generator seed. We note that our generalization of Newman's Theorem is potentially of standalone interest as the techniques we introduced can be used to study pseudorandomness in many different graph algorithm settings.

In Section 6, we consider the impact of topology changes on gossip time. In particular, we consider the case where $b = 1$ and $\tau = \infty$; i.e., the network topology is stable. We describe and analyze CrowdedBin, an algorithm that solves gossip in $O((1/\alpha)k\log^6 n)$ rounds. This algorithm matches or outperforms the $O(kn)$ round complexity of SharedBit for all $\alpha$ values (ignoring log factors). For well-connected networks (e.g., constant $\alpha$), it performs almost a factor of $n$ faster. These results hint that large increases to stability are more valuable to gossip algorithms than large increases to tag length (for most of our solutions, increasing $b$ beyond 1 only improves performance by at most logarithmic factors).

The benefit of stable network topologies is that nodes can transmit larger amounts of information about their current state to their neighbors by using their single bit advertisement tag over multiple rounds. CrowdedBin leverages this capability to help nodes efficiently converge on an accurate estimate of $k$—which is not known in advance. This process depends on nodes testing guesses by throwing their tokens into a number of bins corresponding to the current guess, and then seeking/spreading evidence of crowding (as established by a new balls-in-bins algorithm described in Section 6). Once all nodes learn an appropriate guess of $k$, CrowdedBin deploys an efficient parallel rumor spreading strategy to efficiently disseminate the $k$ tokens.

Finally, we consider the $\epsilon$*-gossip* problem, which is parameterized with a fraction $\epsilon$, $0 < \epsilon < 1$, assumes that $k = n$, and relaxes the gossip problem to require only that every node receives at least $n\epsilon$ of the $n$ total tokens. This variation is useful for settings where it is sufficient for nodes to learn *enough* rumors to complete the task at hand; e.g., when an algorithm requires responses from only a majority quorum of nodes.

In Section 7, we re-analyze the SharedBit gossip algorithm from Section 5. Deploying a novel argument based on finding productive "coalitions" of nodes, we show that SharedBit solves $\epsilon$-gossip in $O\left(\frac{n\sqrt{\Delta\log\Delta}}{(1-\epsilon)\alpha}\right)$ rounds. Recall that SharedBit solves regular gossip in $O(n^2)$ rounds under the $k = n$ assumption. Therefore, when $\epsilon$ is a constant fraction and the network is well-connected ($\alpha$ is large), SharedBit solves $\epsilon$-gossip up to a (sub-linear) polynomial factor faster than the standard gossip problem.

*Related Work.* The mobile telephone model used in this paper was first introduced in a study of rumor spreading by Ghaffari and Newport [10]. We also recently studied leader election in this same model [23]. As noted, the mobile telephone model is a variation of the classical telephone model (first introduced by Frieze and Grimmett [7]) adapted to better describe smartphone peer-to-peer networks. The mobile model differs from the classical model in two ways: (1) the classical model implicitly fixes $b = 0$ and (typically) $\tau = \infty$; and (2) the classical model allows nodes to accept an unbounded number of incoming connections.

It is important to emphasize that most of the well-known bounds in the classical model depend on this assumption of unbounded connections, and removing this assumption requires new analysis techniques; c.f., the discussion in [10]. We note that work by Daum et al. [4] (which preceded [10, 23]) also pointed out the dependence of existing telephone model bounds on unbounded concurrent connections.

A fundamental problem in peer-to-peer networks is *rumor spreading*, in which a single message must be disseminated from a designated source to all nodes (this is equivalent to gossip with $k = 1$). This problem is well-understood in the classical telephone model, where spreading times are often expressed with respect to spectral properties of the network topology graph such as graph conductance (e.g., [12]) and vertex expansion (e.g., [3, 6, 13, 15]). This existing work established that efficient rumor spreading is possible with respect to both graph properties in the classical model. In [10], we studied this problem in the mobile telephone model. We proved that efficient rumor spreading with respect to conductance *is not* possible in the mobile telephone model, but efficient spreading with respect to vertex expansion *is* possible. We then proved that for $b = 1$ and $\tau \geq 1$, a simple random spreading strategy solves the problem in $O((1/\alpha)\Delta^{1/\tau}\text{polylog}(n))$ rounds—matching the tight $\Theta((1/\alpha)\log^2 n)$ result from the classical telephone model within log factors for $\tau \geq \log\Delta$. In [23], we built on these results to solve leader election in similar asymptotic time.

Though gossip is well-studied in peer-to-peer models (see [24] for a good overview), little is known about how to tackle the problem in the mobile telephone model, where concurrent connections are now bounded but nodes can leverage advertising tags.[3] Finally, we note that there are application similarities between gossip in the mobile telephone model and existing reliable multicast solutions for mobile ad hoc (e.g., [17]) and delay-tolerant (e.g., [1]) networks. These existing solutions, however, tend to be empirically evaluated and depend on the ability to predict information about link behavior (e.g., estimated link duration or an advance schedule of when given links will be present).

## 2 MODEL AND PROBLEM

We describe a smartphone peer-to-peer network using the *mobile telephone model*. As elaborated in the introduction, the basic properties of this model—including its scan-and-connect behavior, dynamic topologies, and the ability to advertise a bounded tag—are inspired in particular by the behavior of the Apple Multipeer Connectivity framework for smartphone peer-to-peer networking.

In more detail, we assume executions proceed in synchronous rounds labeled $1, 2, \ldots$. We describe a peer-to-peer network topology in each round $r$ as an undirected connected graph $G_r = (V, E_r)$ that can change from round to round, constrained by the stability factor (see below). We call the sequence of graphs $G_1, G_2, \ldots$ that describe the evolving topology a dynamic graph. We assume the definition of the dynamic graph is fixed at the beginning of the execution.

We assume a computational process (also called a *node* in the following) is assigned to each vertex in $V$, and use $n = |V|$ to indicate the network size. We assume all nodes start during round 1. At the beginning of each round $r$, we assume each node $u$ learns its neighbor set $N(u)$ in $G_r$. Node $u$ can then select at most one node from $N(u)$ and send a connection proposal. A node that sends a proposal cannot also receive a proposal. If a node $v$ does not send a proposal, and at least one neighbor sends a proposal to $v$, then $v$ can *accept* an incoming proposal. There are different ways to model how $v$ selects a proposal to accept. In this paper, for simplicity, we assume $v$ accepts an incoming proposal selected with uniform randomness from the incoming proposals. If node $v$ accepts a proposal from node $u$, the two nodes are *connected* and can perform a bounded amount of interactive communication to conclude the round. We leave the specific bound on communication per connection as a problem parameter.

*Model Parameters.* We parameterize the mobile telephone model with two integers, a *tag length* $b \geq 0$ and a *stability factor* $\tau \geq 1$. We allow each node to select a *tag* containing $b$ bits to advertise at the beginning of each round. That is, if node $u$ chooses tag $b_u$ at the beginning of a round, all neighbors of $u$ learn $b_u$ before making their connection decisions in this round. A node can change its tag from round to round.

We also allow for the possibility of the network topology changing between rounds. We bound the allowable changes with a stability factor $\tau \geq 1$. For a given $\tau$, the dynamic graph describing the changing topology must satisfy the property that at least $\tau$ rounds must pass between any changes to the topology. For $\tau = 1$, the graph can change arbitrarily in every round. We use the convention of stating $\tau = \infty$ to indicate the graph never changes.

*Vertex Expansion and Maximum Degree.* Several of our results express time complexity bounds with respect to the *vertex expansion* $\alpha$ of the dynamic graph describing the network topology. To define $\alpha$, we first review a standard definition of vertex expansion for a fixed static unconnected graph $G = (V, E)$.

For a given $S \subseteq V$, define the *boundary* of $S$, indicated $\partial S$, as follows: $\partial S = \{v \in V \setminus S : N(v) \cap S \neq \emptyset\}$: that is, $\partial S$ is the set of nodes not in $S$ that are directly connected to $S$ by an edge in $E$. Next define $\alpha(S) = |\partial S|/|S|$. As in [10, 13], we define the *vertex expansion* $\alpha(G)$ of our static graph $G = (V, E)$ as follows:

$$\alpha(G) = \min_{S \subset V, 0 < |S| \leq n/2} \alpha(S).$$

Notice that despite the possibility of $\alpha(S) > 1$ for some $S$, we always have $\alpha(G) \leq 1$. We define the vertex expansion $\alpha$ of a *dynamic* graph $G_1, G_2 \ldots$, to be the minimum vertex expansion over all of the dynamic graph's constituent static graphs (i.e., $\alpha = \min\{\alpha(G_i) : i \geq 1\}$).

Similarly, we define the maximum degree $\Delta$ of a dynamic graph to be the maximum degree over all of the dynamic graph's constituent static graphs.

*The Gossip Problem.* The gossip problem assumes each node is provided an upper bound[4] $N \geq n$ on the network size and a unique ID (UID) from $[N]$. The problem assumes some subset of nodes begins with a gossip message to spread (which we also call a *token*). We use $k$ to describe the size of this subset and assume that $k$ is not known to the nodes in advance. A given node can start the execution with multiple tokens, but no token starts at more than one node. We treat gossip tokens as comparable black boxes that can only be communicated between nodes through connections (e.g., a node cannot transmit a gossip token to a neighbor by spelling it out bit by bit using its advertising tags). If a node begins an execution with a token or has received the token through a connection, we say that the node *owns*, *knows* or has *learned* that token. We assume that a pair of connected nodes can exchange at most $O(1)$ tokens and $O(\text{polylog}(N))$ additional bits during a one round connection.

*Solving the Gossip Problem.* The gossip problem requires all nodes to learn all $k$ tokens, Formally, we say a distributed algorithm *solves the gossip problem in* $f(n, k, \alpha, b, \tau)$ *rounds*, if with probability at least $1 - 1/n$, all nodes know all $k$ tokens by round $f(n, k, \alpha, b, \tau)$ when executed in a network of size $n$, with $k$ tokens, vertex expansion $\alpha$, tag length $b$, and stability factor $\tau$. We omit parameters when not relevant to the bound.

*Probability Preliminaries.* The analyses that follow leverage the following well-known probability results:

THEOREM 2.1. *For* $p \in [0, 1]$: $(1 - p) \leq e^{-p}$ *and* $(1 + p) \geq 2^p$.

[3]It might be tempting to simply run $k$ parallel instances of the rumor spreading strategy from [10] to gossip $k$ messages, but this approach fails for three reasons: (1) our model allows only $O(1)$ tokens to be sent per connection per round; (2) each of the $k$ instances requires its own advertising tag bit, whereas all of our new gossip results focus on the case where $b \leq 1$; and (3) nodes do not know $k$ in advance. Accordingly, most results presented in this paper require substantial technical novelty.

[4]For the sake of concision, the results described in the introduction and Figure 1 make the standard assumption that $N$ is a polynomial upper bound on $n$, allowing us to replace $N$ with $n$ within logarithmic factors inside asymptotic notation. In the formal theorem statements for these results, however, we avoid this simplification and leave $N$ in place where used—enabling a slightly finer-grained understanding of the impact of the looseness of network size estimation on our complexity guarantees.

Theorem 2.2 (Chernoff Bound: Lower Bound Form). *Let $Y = \sum_{i=1}^{t} X_i$ be the sum of $t > 0$ i.i.d. random indicator variables $X_1$, $X_2$,..., $X_t$, and let $\mu = E(Y)$. Fix some fraction $\delta$, $0 < \delta < 1$. It follows:*

$$\Pr(X \leq (1-\delta)\mu) \leq e^{-\frac{\delta^2 \mu}{2}}.$$

Theorem 2.3 (Chernoff Bound: Upper Bound Form). *Let $Y = \sum_{i=1}^{t} X_i$ be the sum of $t > 0$ i.i.d. random indicator variables $X_1$, $X_2$,..., $X_t$, and let $\mu = E(Y)$. Fix some value $\delta > 1$. It follows:*

$$\Pr(X \geq (1+\delta)\mu) \leq e^{-\frac{\delta \mu}{3}}.$$

Theorem 2.4 (Chernoff-Hoeffding Bound). *Let $X_1, X_2, ..., X_t$, be $t \geq 1$ i.i.d. random indicator variables. Let $\mu = E(X_i)$ and fix some $\delta > 0$. It follows:*

$$\Pr\left(\frac{1}{t}\sum_{i=1}^{t} X_i \geq \mu + \delta\right) \leq e^{-2\delta^2 t}.$$

Theorem 2.5 (Markov's Ineqւailty). *Let $X$ be a nonnegative random variable and $a > 0$ be a real number. It follows:*

$$\Pr(X \geq a) \leq \frac{E(X)}{a}.$$

# 3 TOKEN TRANSFER SUBROUTINE

An obstacle to solving gossip in the mobile telephone model is deciding which tokens to exchange between two connected nodes. In more detail, once two nodes $u$ and $v$ with respective token sets $T_u$ and $T_v$ connect, even if they *know* $T_u \neq T_v$, they must still identify at least one token $t \notin T_u \cap T_v$ to transfer for this round of gossip to be useful. Complicating this task is the model restriction that $u$ and $v$ can only exchange $O(\text{polylog}(N))$ bits before deciding which tokens (if any) to transfer. This is not (nearly) enough bits to encode a full token set (a simple counting argument establishes that every coding scheme will require $\Omega(N)$ bits for some sets). Therefore, a more efficient routine is needed to implement this useful token transfer.

Here we describe a *transfer subroutine* that solves this problem and is used by multiple gossip algorithms described in this paper. This routine, which we call $Transfer(\epsilon)$, for an error bound $\epsilon$, $0 < \epsilon < 1$, is a straightforward application of an existing algorithmic tool from the literature on two-party communication complexity. It guarantees the following: if $Transfer(\epsilon)$ is called by two connected nodes $u$ and $v$, with respective token sets $T_u$ and $T_v$, and $T_u \neq T_v$, then with probability at least $1 - \epsilon$ the smallest token $t$ (by a predetermined token ordering) that is *not* in $T_u \cap T_v$, will be transferred by the node that knows $t$ to the node that does not. This routine requires $u$ and $v$ to exchange only $O(\log^2 N \cdot \log(\frac{\log N}{\epsilon}))$ controls bits in addition to token $t$. It also assumes some fixed ordering on tokens.

*Equality Testing.* We use one of the many known existing solutions to the *set equality* (EQ) problem from the study of two-party communication complexity. In our setting with $u$ and $v$ (described) above, these existing solutions provide $u$ and $v$ a way to test the equality of $T_u$ and $T_v$, and they offer the following guarantee: if $T_u = T_v$, then $u$ and $v$ will correctly determine their sets are equal with probability 1, else if $T_u \neq T_v$ then $u$ and $v$ will *erroneously* determine their sets are equal with probability no more than 1/2. These existing solutions assume only private randomness and require $u$ and $v$ to exchange no more than $O(\log N)$ bits. A nice property of most such solutions is that each trial is independent. Therefore, if $u$ and $v$ repeat this test $c$ times, for some integer $c \geq 1$, then the error probability drops exponentially fast with $c$ to $2^{-c}$. Let us fix one such equality testing routine and call it $EQTest(c)$, where parameter $c \geq 1$ determines how many trials to execute in testing the equality.

*The Transfer Subroutine.* We now deploy $EQTest(\epsilon')$, for $\epsilon' = \lceil \log(\frac{\log N}{\epsilon}) \rceil$, as a subroutine to implement the $Transfer(\epsilon)$ routine. In particular, recall that for a given $u$ and $v$, we can understand $T_u$ and $T_v$ to both be subsets of the values in $[N]$ (as each node in the network can label each token with its UID from $[N]$ at the beginning of the execution). Our goal is to identify the smallest location value in $[N]$ that is in $T_u \cup T_v$ but not in $T_u \cap T_v$. To do so, we can implement a binary search over the interval $[N]$, using $EQTest(\epsilon')$ to test the equality of the interval in question between $u$ and $v$. In more detail:

**Transfer**($\epsilon$):
  $a \leftarrow 1; b \leftarrow N$
  **while** $a \neq b$
    *result* $\leftarrow$ **EQTest**($\epsilon'$) executed on $T_u \cap [a, \lfloor b/2 \rfloor]$ and $T_v \cap [a, \lfloor b/2 \rfloor]$
    **if** *result* = *notequal* **then** $b \leftarrow \lfloor b/2 \rfloor$ **else** $a \leftarrow \lfloor b/2 \rfloor + 1$
  *transfer* token $a$ to the other node if you know token $a$

The above logic implements a basic binary search over the interval $[N]$ to identify the smallest value in this interval that is in exactly one of the two sets $T_u$ and $T_v$. If every call to $EQTest$ succeeds then the search succeeds and $Transfer$ behaves correctly. There are at most $\log N$ calls to $EQTest$, each of which fails with probability $2^{-\epsilon'} \leq \epsilon / \log N$. Therefore, by a union bound, the probability that at least one of the $\log N$ calls to $EQTest$ fails is less than $\epsilon$, as claimed. From a communication complexity perspective, each call to $EQTest(\epsilon')$ requires $O(\log N \cdot \epsilon') = O(\log N \cdot \log(\log N/\epsilon))$ bits, and we make $\log N$ such calls. Therefore, the total communication complexity is in $O(\log^2 N \cdot \log(\frac{\log N}{\epsilon}))$, as claimed.

# 4 GOSSIP WITH 0-BIT TAGS AND DYNAMIC TOPOLOGY

Here we consider the most difficult case for gossip in our model: nodes cannot advertise any information to their neighbors ($b = 0$), and the network topology graph can change arbitrarily in every round ($\tau = 1$). We study the performance of a straightforward random token propagation strategy.

A detailed treatment of this algorithm, including the full proof details, are deferred to the full version of this paper [22].

*The BlindMatch Gossip Algorithm.* At the beginning of each round $r \geq 1$, each node $u \in V$ flips a fair coin to decide whether to be a *sender* or a *receiver* in $r$. If $u$ decides to be a sender, it selects a neighbor uniformly from among its neighbors in this round and sends it a connection proposal. If $u$ decides to be a receiver it waits to receive proposals. If two nodes $u$ and $v$ connect, they execute the token transfer subroutine.

*Analysis.* Our goal is to prove the following theorem regarding the performance of BlindMatch:

THEOREM 4.1. *The BlindMatch gossip algorithm solves the gossip problem in $O((1/\alpha)k\Delta^2 \log^2 N)$ rounds when executed with tag length $b = 0$ in a network with stability $\tau \geq 1$.*

This time bound might seem pessimistically large at first glance, but as shown in [23], there are networks in which simple random connection strategies require $\Omega(\Delta^2/\sqrt{\alpha})$ rounds to spread even a single message. The proof details adapt our recent analysis of leader election strategies in the mobile telephone model under the assumption that $b = 0$ [23] to account for multiple gossip messages.

## 5 GOSSIP WITH 1-BIT TAGS AND DYNAMIC TOPOLOGY

Here we describe and analyze two gossip algorithm that now assume $b = 1$ (i.e., nodes can advertise a single bit to their neighbors in each round). The graph, however, can still change arbitrarily in every round (i.e., the algorithms must work for any $\tau \geq 1$). Our goal is exploit the shift from $b = 0$ to $b = 1$ to solve gossip more efficiently in most cases. Our first algorithm, called SharedBit, assumes shared randomness. Our second algorithm, called SimSharedBit, does not, but it relies on an existential pseudorandomness generator.

### 5.1 Shared Randomness

Below we provide a condensed description of the SharedBit gossip algorithm and discuss its performance. A detailed treatment of this algorithm, including the full proof details, are deferred to the full version of this paper [22].

*The SharedBit Gossip Algorithm (Overview).* The algorithm assumes each node has access to a shared random bit string $\hat{r}$ of length $O(N^3 \log N)$, where each bit in $\hat{r}$ is generated with independent and uniform randomness. At the beginning of each round $r$, each node $u$ uses fresh bits from $\hat{r}$ to hash the set of tokens it knows at the beginning of this round to a single bit $b_u(r)$. This bit $b_u(r)$ is what $u$ advertises to its neighbors in round $r$. If $b_u(r) = 0$, then $u$ will receive connection proposals in this round. If $b_u(r) = 1$ and $u$ has at least one neighbor advertising 0, then $u$ will choose one these neighbors with uniform randomness and send it a connection proposal. If two nodes $u$ and $v$ connect in round $r$, they use the token transfer subroutine to attempt to exchange tokens. If a node runs out of fresh bits $\hat{r}$ to use it can cycle back to the beginning of this shared string.

*Analysis.* Our goal is to prove the following theorem regarding the SharedBit gossip algorithm:

THEOREM 5.1. *The SharedBit gossip algorithm solves the gossip problem in $O(kn)$ rounds when executed with shared randomness and tag length $b = 1$ in a network with stability $\tau \geq 1$.*

The proof of this theorem begins by establishing the following key property of the token hash strategy used by SharedBit (where $T_u(r)$ is set of tokens known by node $u$ at the beginning of round $r$):

LEMMA 5.2. *Fix two nodes $u, v \in V$, $u \neq v$, and a round $r$, $1 \leq r \leq cN^2$. Fix a $r - 1$ round execution of SharedBit, and let $p = \Pr(b_u(r) \neq b_v(r))$ be the probability (defined over the random selection of the relevant bits in $\hat{r}$) that $u$ and $v$ generate different advertising bits in round $r$. If $T_u(r) = T_v(r)$ then $p = 0$, else if $T_u(r) \neq T_v(r)$, then $p = 1/2$.*

This property ensures that any successful connection created by SharedBit is *productive* in the sense that at least one endpoint will learn a new token. The remainder of the proof first notes that with constant probability there will be *some* productive connections in any given round. It then leverages a stochastic dominance argument (to sidestep inter-round dependencies) to show that $\Theta(kn)$ rounds are sufficient to guarantee enough productive rounds to solve the gossip problem for $k$ tokens.

### 5.2 Eliminating the Shared Randomness Assumption

Shared randomness is not always a reasonable assumption. With this in mind, we describe and analyze SimSharedBit, a variation of SharedBit that does not require shared randomness. A detailed description and analysis of SimSharedBit is deferred to the full version of this paper [22]. Here we summarize the algorithm's strategy and state its main performance guarantee.

*SimSharedBit Strategy.* The high-level strategy for SimSharedBit is to first elect a leader that disseminates a *seed* string that can be used to generate sufficient randomness to run SharedBit. This leader election uses a strategy from [23], and requires an additional $O((1/\alpha)\Delta^{1/\tau}\text{polylog}(N))$ rounds. Notice, however, this time is asymptotically dominated by $kn$ (ignoring log factors) for many parameter values.

We emphasize that the number of shared bits required by SharedBit is much too large to be efficiently disseminated directly: our model restricts connections to deliver polylog($N$) bits per round, while SharedBit requires $\Omega(N^3)$ shared bits. The seed selected and disseminated by the leader, by contrast, will be small enough to be fully transmitted over a single round connection.

To prove that there exists a randomness generator that can extract sufficient randomness for our purpose from seeds of this small size, we adapt the technical details of Newman's Theorem [21] from the simpler world of two-party communication to the more complicated world of $n$ parties on a distributed and changing network topology. In more detail, we prove the existence of a multiset $\mathcal{R}'$, containing only poly($N$) bit strings of the length required for SharedBit, that is *sufficiently* random to guarantee that if a leader chooses $\hat{r}$ uniformly from $\mathcal{R}'$, the SharedBit algorithm using shared randomness $\hat{r}$ is still likely to solve gossip efficiently. Because $\mathcal{R}'$ contains only poly($N$) strings, the leader can identify the string it selected using only polylog($N$) bits (this selection is the *seed* it disseminates)—enabling efficient propagation of this information. The existential nature of SimSharedBit is entirely encapsulated in the existence of this set $\mathcal{R}'$.

*Analysis.* Our goal is to prove the following theorem regarding SimSharedBit:

THEOREM 5.3. *There exists a bit string multiset $\mathcal{R}'$ of size $N^{\Theta(1)}$, such that the SimSharedBit gossip algorithm using this $\mathcal{R}'$ as its* *source of simulated shared bit strings solves the gossip problem in $O(kn + (1/\alpha)\Delta^{1/\tau}\log^6 N)$ rounds when executed with tag length $b = 1$ in a network with stability $\tau \geq 1$.*

The key technical novelty in proving this theorem is the proof of the existence of a sufficiently random $\mathcal{R}'$. Our argument generalizes the strategy deployed to prove Newman's Theorem [21]. Whereas the classical Newman's Theorem result applies the probabilistic method to prove the existence of a sufficiently random bit string multiset for all possible inputs for two players, we have to account for $n \geq 2$ players, all possible different dynamic graphs, assignments of tokens, and rounds required for the leader election to complete. These counts, however, are of sizes no more than exponential in $N$, allowing the probabilistic method argument to proceed with proper adjustments to constants. Our generalization is potentially of standalone interest as it can be used to provide similar public randomness simulation results for other dynamic network algorithms.

# 6 GOSSIP WITH 1-BIT TAGS AND STABLE TOPOLOGY

The preceding gossip algorithms make no assumptions about the stability of the underlying network topology. Their analysis holds for every $\tau \geq 1$. In some settings, this assumption might be pessimistic. Here we seek better performance when the network topology graph does not change (i.e., $\tau = \infty$).

In more detail, we describe and analyze the CrowdedBin algorithm, which solves gossip in $\tilde{O}(k/\alpha)$ rounds with $b = 1$ and $\tau = \infty$ (where $\tilde{O}$ hides polylog$(N)$ factors). This algorithm is comparable to the trivial $\Omega(k)$ lower bound for gossiping $k$ tokens in a model where a node can only send one token per round. It also outperforms our best result for $\tau = 1$—the $O(kn)$ round complexity of SharedBit—for every $\alpha \in \omega(1/n)$ (ignoring log factors).

*Discussion: Crowded Bins.* The name CrowdedBin comes from a core behavior in the algorithm in which nodes toss their tokens into a fixed number of bins corresponding to their current estimate $\hat{k}$ of $k$ (the number of tokens in the network). Nodes do not know $k$ in advance. Determining this value is crucial to enabling efficient parallel dissemination of their tokens. Leveraging a new balls-in-bins analysis, we upper bound the number of tokens in any given bin *if* the estimate $\hat{k}$ is sufficiently large. The nodes therefore search for crowded bins as evidence that they need a larger estimate of $k$. This mechanism provides a way to check that a current guess $\hat{k}$ is too small while only paying a time complexity price relative to $\hat{k}$ (as there are only $\hat{k}$ bins required to check for crowding). Because the sequence of guesses we try are geometrically increasing, the cost of checking estimates smaller than $k$ will sum up to $\tilde{O}(k)$.

*Discussion: Spreading Bits versus Spreading Tokens.* We also emphasize that the CrowdedBin algorithm makes a clear distinction between propagating information using the advertising bits and propagating the tokens themselves (which are treated as black boxes, potentially large in size, that require a pairwise connection for transfer). Combining the stability of the network with each node's ability to advertise a bit to *all* its neighbors in each round, nodes first attempt to stabilize to a consistent and accurate estimate of $k$, and a consistent set of *tags* describing the network's tokens. Once stabilized, this information can then support the efficient spreading of the tokens, link by link, to the whole network. Accordingly, CrowdedBin can be understood to occur in two phases (which, in practice, might substantially overlap). During the first phase, nodes use their advertising bits to efficiently learn about the network. During the second phase, nodes use this knowledge to efficiently spread gossip tokens. The first phase depends on network stability as this is what allows a node to communicate complicated information to its neighborhood using its small advertising tag over many rounds.

*The PPUSH Rumor Spreading Strategy.* The CrowdedBin algorithm uses a simple rumor spreading strategy called PPUSH as a subroutine to help spread tokens once the network has stabilized. This algorithm was introduced in our earlier study of rumor spreading in the mobile telephone model [10]. PPUSH assumes a subset of nodes start with a common rumor $m$, and the goal is to spread $m$ to all nodes. It requires $b \geq 1$.

In more detail, the strategy PPUSH works as follows: (1) at the beginning of each round, if a nodes knows $m$ (i.e., it is *informed*), it advertises bit 1, otherwise if it does not know $m$ (i.e., it is *uninformed*), it advertises bit 0; (2) each informed node that has at least one uninformed neighbor in this round, chooses an uninformed neighbor with uniform randomness and attempts to form a connection to spread the rumor. In [10], we proved the following key result about the performance of PPUSH:

THEOREM 6.1 (ADAPTED FROM [10]). *With high probability in $N$: PPUSH succeeds in spreading the rumor to all nodes in $O(\log^4 N/\alpha)$ rounds when executed in the mobile telephone model with $b \geq 1$, $\tau = \infty$, and a topology graph with expansion $\alpha$.*

We will leverage this theorem in our analysis of our gossip algorithm. We also use the following useful property proved in [10] which relates network diameter to expansion:[5]

THEOREM 6.2 (ADAPTED FROM [10]). *Fix a connected graph with $n$ nodes, expansion $\alpha$, and diameter $D$. It follows that $D = O(\log n/\alpha)$.*

## 6.1 The CrowdedBin Gossip Algorithm

We are now ready to describe our CrowdedBin algorithm. We present it here in its own section with its description divided into parts to clarify its presentation.

In the following, we assume each node $u \in V$ identifies itself with a *tag* $t_u$ chosen uniformly from the space $\{1, 2, ..., N^{\beta}\}$, where $\beta \geq 2$ is constant we fix in our analysis. Let $\ell = \beta \log N$ be the number of bits needed to describe a tag. To simplify notation, we assume in the following that $N$ is a power of 2.

*Parallelizing Instances.* Nodes do not know in advance the value of $k$ (the number of tokens in the system). They consider $\log N$ *estimates* of $k$: $k_1, k_2, ..., k_{\log N}$, where each $k_i = 2^i$. The nodes run in parallel a separate gossip *instance* for each estimate. We use the notation *instance i* to refer to the instance corresponding to estimate

[5]The actual result we proved in [10] is that it is always possible to spread a rumor in $O(\log n/\alpha)$ rounds in the mobile telephone model in a graph with expansion $\alpha$. The rumor spreading time in a given network can never be smaller than the network diameter, which provides a trivial lower bound on the problem.

$k_i$. In order to run $\log N$ instances in parallel, each node uses $\log N$ rounds to simulate one round each of the $\log N$ instances. That is, nodes divide rounds into *simulation groups* consisting of $\log N$ rounds. Round $j$ of simulation group $i$ is used to simulate round $i$ of instance $j$.

*Instance Schedules.* Each instance $i$ groups its rounds into *blocks* containing $\ell + \log N$ rounds each. It then groups these blocks into *bins* containing $\gamma \log N$ blocks each, where $\gamma > 1$ is a constant we fix in our analysis below. Finally, it groups the bins into *phases* consisting of $k_i$ bins each. In other words, the schedule for instance $i$ is made up of phases, where each phase has $k_i$ bins, which are each made up of $\gamma \log N$ blocks, which each contain $\ell + \log N$ rounds: adding to a total of $\gamma(\beta + 1)k_i \log^2 N$ total rounds per phase.

*Initialization.* Each node $u \in V$ that begins an execution of the CrowdedBin algorithm with a gossip token, independently selects a bin for its token for each of the $\log N$ instances. That is, for each instance $i$, $u$ selects a bin $b_u(i)$ with uniform independent randomness from $\{1, 2, ..., k_i\}$. Each node $u$ also maintains, for each instance $i$, and each bin $j$ for this instance, a set $T_u(i, j)$ containing the tags it has seen so far for tokens in bin $j$ in instance $i$. For each instance $i$, if node $u$ has a token it initializes $T_u(i, b_u(i)) = \{t_u\}$ (i.e., it places its own tag in the bin it selected for that instance). Node $u$ also maintains a set $Q_u$ containing the tokens it has received so far, where each token in $Q_u$ is also labeled with its tag. Finally, each node $u$ maintains a variable $est_u$, initialized to 1, which describes the current instance node $u$ is participating in.

*Participation.* Each node will only participate in a single instance at a time, and it will only participate in complete phases of an instance. In more detail, if some instance $i$ starts a new phase in round $r$, and some node $u$ has $est_u = i$ at the start of round $r$, node $u$ is now committed to participate in this full phase of instance $i$. As we will detail, its estimate cannot change again until this phase completes.

To participate in a phase of instance $i$, node $u$ does the following. First, for each bin $j$, $1 \leq j \leq k_i$, $u$ orders the tags in $T_u(i, j)$ (if any) in increasing order. It will use the first $\ell$ rounds of the first block to spell out the smallest such tag, bit by bit, using its advertising bits (here the assumption that $b \geq 1$ is needed). It will then use the first $\ell$ rounds of the second block to spell out the second smallest tag, and so on. There are $\gamma \log N$ total blocks in this bin. If $u$ knows more than this many tags for this bin, it transmits only the first $\gamma \log N$. Node $u$ transmits all 0's during the blocks in this bin for which it has no tags to advertise (here is where we use the assumption that the smallest possible tag is 1—preventing a block of all 0's from being mistaken for a tag.)

During the rounds dedicated to bin $j$, node $u$ also collects the bits advertised by its neighbors in each block. If it learns of a tag $t_v$ that is not currently in $T_u(i, j)$, it will put it aside and then add it to this set once the rounds dedicated to bin $j$ in this phase conclude.

We have only so far described what node $u$ does during the first $\ell$ rounds for each block in our fixed instance $j$. During the remaining $\log N$ rounds in these blocks, $u$ will attempt to disseminate the actual tokens corresponding to the tags advertised (here we emphasize the difference between spelling out the bits of a tag using advertising bits and actually transmitting a token, which requires two nodes to form a connection). In more detail, $u$ executes the PPUSH rumor spreading strategy from [10] (see above) during the last $\log N$ rounds of each block in the current bin. In more detail, for a given block $h$ in this bin, if $u$ advertised tag $t$ in the first $\ell$ rounds of this block, *and* $u$ actually has the token corresponding to tag $t$ in $Q_u$, it executes PPUSH in the remaining rounds of this block using this token as the rumor and advertising 1 (i.e., it runs PPUSH with the status of an already informed node). Otherwise, node $u$ runs PPUSH advertising 0 (i.e., it runs the PPUSH as an uniformed node).

*Increasing Size Estimates.* A core behavior in this algorithm is how nodes upgrade their current estimate of the value $k$ (stored in $est_u$ for each node $u$). As described above, each node initializes their estimate to 1. As described below, these estimates can only grow during an execution. We call an increase in this estimate at a given node an *upgrade*. There are two events that trigger an upgrade at a given node $u$.

The first event is that node $u$ sees "activity" on an instance $i' > est_u$, where $est_u$ is its current estimate. The term "activity" in this context means seeing a 1-bit advertised in an instance $i'$ round. If this event occurs, then $u$ knows that some other node has already increased its estimate beyond $est_u$, so $u$ should upgrade its estimate as well. The second event is that node $u$ fills a bin in its current estimate. That is, there is some bin $j$ such that $|T(est_u, j)| \geq \gamma \log N$. We call this event a *crowded bin*, and $u$ can use this as evidence that $est_u$ does not have enough bins for the number of tags in the system and therefore $est_u$ is too small of an estimate for $k$. If this event occurs, $u$ will increase $est_u$ by 1 (unless $est_u$ is already at its maximum value in which case it will remain unchanged.).

Recall, as specified above, that if a node $u$ increases its estimate $est_u$ to a new value, it will complete the phase of whatever instance it was participating in before switching to the new estimate moving forward. This restriction simplifies the algorithmic analysis.

## 6.2 Analysis

Our goal in this section is to prove the below theorem regarding CrowdedBin. Some proof details have been deferred to the full version of this paper [22].

THEOREM 6.3. *The CrowdedBin gossip algorithm solves the gossip problem in $O((1/\alpha)k \log^6 N)$ rounds when executed with tag length $b = 1$ in a network with stability $\tau = \infty$.*

At the beginning of an execution each node randomly assigns a tag from $\{1, 2, ..., N^\beta\}$ to its token, and then randomly assigns the token to a bin in each of the $\log N$ instances. We call the global collection of these assignments for a given execution a *configuration*. Fix a configuration. We call a given instance $i$ of this configuration, $1 \leq i \leq \log N$, *crowded*, if the configuration has an instance $i$ bin with at least $\gamma \log N$ unique tags assigned to it. The *target* instance for our fixed configuration is the smallest instance $i$ that is *not* crowded. If every instance is crowded, then we say the *target* instance is *undefined*. We begin our analysis by defining what it means for a configuration to be *good* with respect to these terms:

*Definition 6.4.* A configuration is *good* if and only if it satisfies the following two properties: (1) every token is assigned a unique tag; and (2) the target instance $i$ is defined, and $k_i \leq 2k$.

A direct corollary of the above definition is that if a configuration is good, and $i$ is the target, then $k_i > k/(\gamma \log N)$. We now bound the probability that the nodes generate a good configuration. We will show that increasing the constant $\beta$, used to define the space $\{1, 2, ..., N^\beta\}$ from which tags are drawn, and the constant $\gamma$, used to define the number of blocks per bin, increases the high probability that a configuration is good. To make this argument we begin by establishing a non-standard balls-in-bins argument applicable to our specific algorithm's behavior.

LEMMA 6.5. *Fix some constant $\gamma \geq 9$. Assume $k$ balls, $1 \leq k \leq N$, are thrown into $k' \geq k$ bins with independent and uniform randomness. The probability that at least one bin has at least $\gamma \log N$ balls, is less than $1/N^{(\gamma/3)-2}$.*

We apply the above balls-in-bin argument to prove the following lemma which argues that good configurations are likely.

LEMMA 6.6. *Fix some constant $c \geq 1$. For a tag space constant $\beta \geq c+3$, and a bin size constant $\gamma \geq 3c+9$, the nodes generate a good configuration with probability at least $1 - 1/N^c$.*

The below lemma follows directly from the definition of good and the mechanism by which our algorithm updates estimates:

LEMMA 6.7. *In an execution with a good configuration with target instance $i$, no node ever sets its local estimate to a value larger than $i$. That is, for all $u$ and all rounds, $est_u \leq i$.*

We now continue our analysis by bounding the time required for all nodes to reach the target instance. We do so with two arguments: the first concerning the rounds required for nodes to learn of a larger estimate existing in the system, and the second concerning the rounds required for the largest estimate to increase if it is still less than the target. For the following results, let $D$ describe the diameter of the static network topology:

LEMMA 6.8. *Fix an execution with a good configuration with target instance $i$. Assume that at the beginning of round $r$ of this execution the largest estimate in the system is $i_{max} \leq i$. By round $r' = r + O(Dk_{i_{max}} \log^3 N)$ either: the largest estimate in the system is larger than $i_{max}$, or all nodes have estimate $i_{max}$.*

LEMMA 6.9. *Fix an execution with a good configuration with target instance $i$. Assume that at the beginning of round $r$ of this execution the largest estimate in the system is $i_{max} < i$. By round $r' = r + O(Dk_{i_{max}} \log^3 N)$ the largest estimate in the system is larger than $i_{max}$.*

We now leverage Lemmas 6.8 and 6.9 to bound the rounds required for all nodes to permanently stabilize to the target instance.

LEMMA 6.10. *Fix an execution with a good configuration with target instance $i$. By round $r = O(Dk_i \log^3 N)$, every node has estimate $i$. That is, for every node $u$, $est_u = i$ by round $r$.*

PROOF. By the definition of our algorithm, estimates never decrease. By Lemma 6.7, no node will ever adopt an estimate greater than $i$. Combined, it follows that we can keep applying Lemma 6.9 to increase the largest estimate until the largest estimate reaches $i$. We can then apply a single instance of Lemma 6.8 to ensure all nodes have this estimate, permanently satisfying the lemma.

To bound the time required for these applications of the above lemmas, we leverage our observation that the largest estimate can only increase. It follows that in the worst case we apply Lemma 6.9 exactly once for each of the estimates leading up to the target $i$. Because these estimates form a geometric sequence (e.g., 2, 4, 8, ...), the total rounds needed for these applications of Lemma 6.9 is upper bounded by:

$$\begin{aligned} O(Dk_1 \log^3 N) + ... + O(Dk_i \log^3 N) &= \\ O\left((D \log^3 N)(k_1 + k_2 + ... + k_i)\right) &= O(Dk_i \log^3 N) \end{aligned}$$

The final application of Lemma 6.8 to spread estimate $i$ to all remaining nodes once it exists in the system adds only a single an additional $O(Dk_i \log^3 N)$ rounds. The lemma statement follows. □

The preceding arguments bound the rounds required for useful information to propagate through the network via the nodes' advertising bits. We now conclude our proof by turning our attention to the rounds required for the actual tokens (which must be passed one at a time through pairwise connections) to spread.

PROOF OF THEOREM 6.3. Assume for now that the configuration is good and $i$ its target instance. Let round $r = O(Dk_i \log^3 N)$ be the round specified by Lemma 6.10 for the network to converge its estimate. That is, every node has the same estimate $i$ by round $r$. By definition, no bin is crowded for instance $i$ in a good configuration. It follows that *every* tag for *every* bin in this instance will be spread in *every* round by the nodes that know that tag in that round. Following the same propagation arguments used in Lemmas 6.8 and 6.9, after at most $D$ more phases of instance $i$, all nodes will know all tags. This requires at most $O(Dk_i \log^3 N)$ rounds. Therefore by some round $r' = O(Dk_i \log^3 N)$, the system will have reached a *stable* state in which every node has the same estimate $i$ and knows the tag for every token in the system. This information will never again change so we can turn our attention for the rounds required to finish propagating the actual tokens after this point of stabilization.

To bound this token propagation time, fix an arbitrary token $t$ with tag $q$ in instance $i$. Because we assume the system has stabilized, every node has $q$ assigned to the same block of the same bin in their instance $i$ phase. It follows that if we append together the last $\log N$ rounds from these blocks (i.e., the rounds in which nodes run PPUSH for the tag described in the first $\ell$ rounds of the block), we obtain a proper execution of PPUSH rumor spreading for token $t$ during these rounds. That is, every time we come to the last $\log N$ rounds of $q$'s block, all nodes are running PPUSH for rumor $t$, picking up where they left off in the previous instance.

Applying Theorem 6.1 from above, it follows that with high probability in $N$, $O(\log^4 N/\alpha)$ rounds are sufficient for $t$ to spread to all nodes after stabilization. Each phase provides $\log N$ rounds of PPUSH, so $O(\log^3 N/\alpha)$ phases are sufficient after stabilization.

The key observation is that each execution of instance $i$ services *all* $k$ rumors after stabilization, as each rumor has its own fixed bin in the instance $i$ phase. Therefore, $O(\log^3 N/\alpha)$ phases are sufficient to spread *all* $k$ rumors in parallel. A union bound establishes that all $k \leq N$ instances succeed with a slightly reduced high probability.

From a probability perspective, we know from Lemma 6.6 that the configuration is good with high probability. We just argued above that if the configuration is good, then with an additional high probability the tokens will all spread in the stated time, once the system stabilizes. We can increase both high probabilities to the desired exponent by increasing the constant $\beta$ and $\gamma$ used in the definition of crowded bins, and the constant factor in the time bound for PPUSH. A union bound then shows that both good events occur with high probability.

From round cost perspective, we established that the time to stabilization is at most $O(Dk_i \log^3 N)$ rounds, while the time to complete propagation after stabilization is at most $O(\log^3 N/\alpha)$ instance $i$ phases, which each require $O(k_i \log^3 N)$ rounds. The final time complexity is then in: $O(Dk_i \log^3 N + (k_i \log^6 N)/\alpha)$.

By the definition of a good configuration, we know $k_i \leq 2k$, and by Theorem 6.2, we know $D = O(\log N/\alpha)$. We can therefore simplify this complexity to $O((k \log^6 N)/\alpha)$ rounds, as required. □

## 7 $\epsilon$-GOSSIP WITH 1-BIT TAGS AND DYNAMIC TOPOLOGY

Here we consider $\epsilon$-Gossip: a relaxed version of the gossip problem that is parameterized with some $\epsilon$, $0 < \epsilon < 1$ (e.g., as also studied in [5]). In more detail, the problem assumes all $n$ nodes start with a token. To solve $\epsilon$-gossip there must be a subset $S$ of the $n$ nodes in the system, where $|S| \geq \epsilon n$ *and* for every $u, v \in S$, $u$ knows $v$'s token and $v$ knows $u$'s token. Our goal here is to prove that for reasonably well-connected graphs and constant $\epsilon$, *almost* solving gossip can be significantly faster than *fully* solving gossip.

Crucially, we do not present a new algorithm to tackle this new problem. We instead reanalyze SharedBit gossip to study how quickly it achieves $\epsilon$-Gossip for a given $\epsilon$ bound. Our goal is to prove the following result (in the full version of this paper [22] we also prove a corollary about SimSharedBit achieving a similar result without requiring shared randomness):

THEOREM 7.1. *Fix some $\epsilon$, $0 < \epsilon < 1$. The SharedBit gossip algorithm solves the $\epsilon$-gossip problem in $O\left((n\sqrt{\Delta \log \Delta})/((1-\epsilon)\alpha)\right)$ rounds when executed with shared randomness and tag length $b = 1$ in a network with stability $\tau \geq 1$.*

Given that $\Delta \leq n$, this new time complexity is faster than the $O(n^2)$ rounds required by SharedBit (for $k = n$) when $\epsilon$ is a constant fraction and $\alpha = \omega(\log \Delta/(\sqrt{\Delta \log \Delta}))$.

The full details of this result are provided in the full version of this paper [22]. The core idea behind this analysis is to first prove that in any round such that the problem is not solved, there exists a *coalition* of nodes such that: (1) the size of the coalition is $\approx \epsilon n$; and (2) no node *not in* the coalition has the same token set as a node *in* the coalition. Because of the large size of this coalition, we can then prove that there exist many links from this coalition to nodes outside its boundaries. By definition, each of these links, if transformed into a connection, would productively transfer a token. We can then study the expected number of these links to transform in this manner. Put another way, for constant $\epsilon$, this proof leverages the intuition that until a constant fraction of the messages have spread, there is potential for lots of spreading.

## REFERENCES


[1] Scott Burleigh, Adrian Hooke, Leigh Torgerson, Kevin Fall, Vint Cerf, Bob Durst, Keith Scott, and Howard Weiss. 2003. Delay-tolerant networking: an approach to interplanetary internet. *IEEE Communications Magazine* 41, 6 (2003), 128–136.

[2] Daniel Camps-Mur, Andres Garcia-Saavedra, and Pablo Serrano. 2013. Device-to-device communications with Wi-Fi Direct: overview and experimentation. *IEEE wireless communications* 20, 3 (2013), 96–104.

[3] Flavio Chierichetti, Silvio Lattanzi, and Alessandro Panconesi. 2010. Rumour Spreading and Graph Conductance.. In *Proceedings of the ACM-SIAM symposium on Discrete Algorithms (SODA)*.

[4] Sebastian Daum, Fabian Kuhn, and Yannic Maus. 2016. Rumor Spreading with Bounded In-Degree. In *International Colloquium on Structural Information and Communication Complexity (SIRROCO)*.

[5] Shlomi Dolev, Seth Gilbert, Rachid Guerraoui, and Calvin Newport. 2007. Gossiping in a multi-channel radio network. In *Proceedings of the Symposium on Distributed Computing (DISC)*.

[6] Nikolaos Fountoulakis and Konstantinos Panagiotou. 2010. Rumor spreading on random regular graphs and expanders. In *Approximation, Randomization, and Combinatorial Optimization. Algorithms and Techniques*. Springer, 560–573.

[7] Alan M Frieze and Geoffrey R Grimmett. 1985. The shortest-path problem for graphs with random arc-lengths. *Discrete Applied Mathematics* 10, 1 (1985), 57–77.

[8] Alan M Frieze and Geoffrey R Grimmett. 1985. The shortest-path problem for graphs with random arc-lengths. *Discrete Applied Mathematics* 10, 1 (1985), 57–77.

[9] Open Garden. Accessed: Feb., 2017. FireChat Phone-to-Phone App. (Accessed: Feb., 2017). http://www.opengarden.com/FireChat.

[10] Mohsen Ghaffari and Calvin Newport. 2016. How to Discreetly Spread a Rumor in a Crowd. In *Proceedings of the International Symposium on Distributed Computing (DISC)*.

[11] George Giakkoupis. 2011. Tight bounds for rumor spreading in graphs of a given conductance. In *Proceedings of the Symposium on Theoretical Aspects of Computer Science (STACS)*.

[12] George Giakkoupis. 2011. Tight bounds for rumor spreading in graphs of a given conductance. In *Proceedings of the Symposium on Theoretical Aspects of Computer Science (STACS)*.

[13] George Giakkoupis. 2014. Tight bounds for rumor spreading with vertex expansion. In *Proceedings of the ACM-SIAM Symposium on Discrete Algorithms (SODA)*.

[14] George Giakkoupis and Thomas Sauerwald. 2012. Rumor spreading and vertex expansion. In *Proceedings of the ACM-SIAM symposium on Discrete Algorithms (SODA)*. 1623–1641.

[15] George Giakkoupis and Thomas Sauerwald. 2012. Rumor spreading and vertex expansion. In *Proceedings of the ACM-SIAM symposium on Discrete Algorithms (SODA)*. SIAM, 1623–1641.

[16] Carles Gomez, Joaquim Oller, and Josep Paradells. 2012. Overview and evaluation of bluetooth low energy: An emerging low-power wireless technology. *Sensors* 12, 9 (2012), 11734–11753.

[17] Thiagaraja Gopalsamy, Mukesh Singhal, D Panda, and P Sadayappan. 2002. A reliable multicast algorithm for mobile ad hoc networks. In *Proceedings of the IEEE International Conference on Distributed Computing Systems (ICDCS)*. IEEE, 563–570.

[18] Ericsson Inc. Accessed: Feb., 2017. Latest mobile statistics: key figures (Ericsson Mobility Report). (Accessed: Feb., 2017). https://www.ericsson.com/mobility-report/latest-mobile-statistics.

[19] Fabian Kuhn, Nancy Lynch, and Rotem Oshman. 2010. Distributed computation in dynamic networks. In *Proceedings of the Symposium on Principles of Distributed Computing (PODC)*. ACM, 513–522.

[20] David Mark, Jayant Varma, Jeff LaMarche, Alex Horovitz, and Kevin Kim. 2015. Peer-to-Peer Using Multipeer Connectivity. In *More iPhone Development with Swift*. Springer, 239–280.

[21] Ilan Newman. 1991. Private vs. common random bits in communication complexity. *Information processing letters* 39, 2 (1991), 67–71.

[22] Calvin Newport. 2017. Gossip in a Smartphone Peer-to-Peer Network. In *Proceedings of the Symposium on Principles of Distributed Computing (PODC)*. Full version available on arXiv and at: http://people.cs.georgetown.edu/~cnewport/pubs/gossipmobile-full.pdf.

[23] Calvin Newport. 2017. Leader Election in a Smartphone Peer-to-Peer Network. In *Proceedings of the IEEE International Parallel and Distributed Processing Symposium (IPDPS)*. Full version available online at: http://people.cs.georgetown.edu/~cnewport/pubs/le-IPDPS2017.pdf.

[24] Devavrat Shah et al. 2009. Gossip algorithms. *Foundations and Trends in Networking* 3, 1 (2009), 1–125.

# Analyzing Contention and Backoff in Asynchronous Shared Memory

Naama Ben-David
Carnegie Mellon University
nbendavi@cs.cmu.edu

Guy E. Blelloch
Carnegie Mellon University
guyb@cs.cmu.edu

## ABSTRACT

Randomized backoff protocols have long been used to reduce contention on shared resources. They are heavily used in communication channels and radio networks, and have also been shown to greatly improve the performance of shared memory algorithms in real systems. However, while backoff protocols are well understood in many settings, their effect in shared memory has never been theoretically analyzed. This discrepency may be due to the difficulty of modeling asynchrony without eliminating the advantage gained by local delays.

In this paper, we introduce a new cost model for contention in shared memory. Our model allows for adversarial asynchrony, but also provides a clear notion of time, thus enabling easy calculation of contention costs and delays. We then consider a simple use case in which $n$ processes try to update a single memory location. Using our model, we first show that a naïve protocol, without any backoff, requires $\Omega(n^3)$ work until all processes successfully update that location. We then analyze the commonly used exponential delay protocol, and show that it requires $\Theta(n^2 \log n)$ work with high probability. Finally, we show that the exponential delay protocol is suboptimal, by introducing a new backoff protocol based on adaptive probabilities and showing that, for the same use case, it requires only $O(n^2)$ work with high probability.

**ACM Reference format:**
Naama Ben-David and Guy E. Blelloch. 2017. Analyzing Contention and Backoff in Asynchronous Shared Memory. In *Proceedings of PODC'17, July 25-27, 2017, Washington, DC, USA, ,* 10 pages.
DOI: 10.1145/3087801.3087828

## 1 INTRODUCTION

Exponential backoff protocols are commonly used in many settings to avoid contention on a shared resource. They appear in transactional memory [27], communication channels [9, 10, 14, 15], radio and wireless networks [6, 8], local area networks [25], and even shared memory algorithms [3, 22]. Many backoff protocols have been developed and proved efficient for these communication tasks. The general setting is that many processes want to send a message over a channel (or a network), but the transmission fails if more than one message is sent at the same time. Usually, transmissions are assumed to happen in synchronous rounds, and time is measured by the number of rounds until all messages are successfully transmitted. A round is wasted if more than one process attempts to transmit, but the cost remains constant regardless of how many processes attempted to transmit in that round.

The situation is different in a shared memory setting. If many processes attempt to access the same memory location, they all suffer *contention*, which slows down their response time, and becomes worse as the number of conflicting processes increases. For example, if $P$ processes all access the same memory location at the same time, this can require $\Theta(P)$ 'wait time' for each process, for a total of $\Theta(P^2)$ total work. Several theoretical models have been developed to try to capture these costs [12, 13, 17, 18, 21]. However, none of these models have been applied to analyze backoff protocols. The reason is, at least in part, that these models are not well suited for the task. In general, shared memory contention and performance is more difficult to model than channel communication because of the inherent asynchrony in shared memory systems.

Asynchrony in shared memory algorithms is usually modeled by assuming a powerful adversary that determines the schedule of instructions. Some models capturing contention, like those of Dwork, Herlihy, and Waarts [12] and Fich, Hendler and Shavit [13], give too much power to the adversary to be able to get any meaningful worst case bounds on backoff protocols. The model of Dwork *et al.* assumes every instruction has an invocation and a response, and each instruction suffers contention equivalent to the number of responses to other instructions that occurred between its own invocation and response. Fich *et al.* assign cost differently; in particular, they assume only modifying instructions that immediately precede a given instruction $i$ can have an effect on $i$'s running time. While these models are reasonable for obtaining lower bounds, they are impractical for attaining meaningful upper bounds. Because of the great power the adversary is given, the advantage of backoff protocols is lost in these models.

Further work by Hendler and Kutten [21] restricts the power of the adversary in an attempt to capture more likely executions. They present a model similar to that of Dwork *et al.* [12], but add the notion of $k$-synchrony on top of it. This requirement states that an execution is $k$-synchronous if in any subexecution, no process can do $k + 1$ operations before all other processes do at least one. This property, while attractively simple, does not succeed in capturing all possible real executions. Asynchrony in real systems often arises from processes being swapped out. In such cases, one process can be delayed a great deal with respect to the others, and no reasonable value of $k$ allows for such delays.


*PODC'17, July 25-27, 2017, Washington, DC, USA*

DOI: 10.1145/3087801.3087828

All of these models have an additional problem: there is no clear notion of time. This further complicates the analysis of time-based protocols such as exponential delay, where processes delay themselves for increasingly longer amounts of time.

A different line of work aiming to create a more realistic model for shared memory has focused on relaxing the adversarial scheduler to a stochastic one, leading to tractable analysis of the step complexity of some lock-free algorithms [1, 2]. However, this line of work also relies on strong assumptions on the behavior of the scheduler. Furthermore, it has not directly accounted for contention, rendering the analysis of backoff under this model meaningless.

In spite of the difficulty of theoretically analyzing backoff, these protocols have been shown to be effective in combating shared memory contention. Many systems benefit greatly from the application of an exponential backoff protocol for highly contented memory [3, 19, 22, 24, 26]. For about 30 years, exponential delay has been successfully used in practice to significantly reduce running time in algorithms that suffer from contention.

In this paper, we take a first step towards closing this gap between theory and practice. We define a model for analyzing contention in shared memory protocols, and use it to analyze backoff. Our model allows for asynchrony, but maintains a clear notion of time. We do this by giving the adversary full power on one part of the processes' delay, but taking it away in another part. In particular, we allow each process to have up to one *ready* instruction, and the adversary determines when to invoke, or *activate*, each ready instruction. However, once active, instructions have a priority order that the adversary can no longer control. This models the difference between delays caused by the system between instructions of a process (e.g. caused by an interrupt), and delays incurred after the instruction has been invoked in the hardware (assuming an instruction cannot be interrupted midstream). We then define *time steps*, in which all active instruction attempt to execute. Furthermore, we define *conflicts* between instructions; two conflicting instructions cannot be executed in the same time step. An active instruction will be executed in the first time step in which it does not conflict with any higher-priority instruction. In this paper, we say that modifying instructions (such as compare-and-swap) conflict with all other instructions on the same location, but any two non-modifying instructions do not conflict. This reflects the fact that in modern systems, multiple reads to the same location can go through in parallel, but a modifying instruction requires exclusive access to the memory, sequentializing other instructions behind it. This is due to cache coherency protocols.

We then consider a situation in which $n$ processes want to update the same memory location. Such a situation arises often in the implementations of various lock-free data structures such as counters and stacks. We use our model to analyze various protocols that achieve such an update. We first show that a naïve approach, which uses a simple read-modify-write loop with no backoff, can lead to a total of $\Omega(n^3)$ work, while a classic exponential delay protocol improves that to $\Theta(n^2 \log n)$. To the best of our knowledge, this is the first analysis of exponential delay for shared memory. Perhaps surprisingly, we show that this protocol is suboptimal. We propose a different protocol, based on adapting probabilities, that achieves $O(n^2)$ work.

The key to this improvement stems from using read operations to get a more accurate estimate of the contention that the process is facing. Recall that in our model, reads can go through in parallel, while modifying instructions conflict with others. In our protocol, instead of delaying for increasingly long periods of time when faced with recurring contention, a process becomes increasingly likely to choose to read rather than write. Intuitively, reading the value of a memory location allows a process to gauge the level of contention it's facing by comparing the new value to the previous value it read. Each process keeps a write-probability that it updates after every operation. It uses this probability to determine its next instruction; i.e. whether it will attempt a compare-and-swap or only read. If the value of the memory does not change between two consecutive reads, the process raises its write-probability. Otherwise, the process lowers it. This constant feedback, and the possibility of raising the probability back up when necessary, is what allows this protocol to do better than exponential delay.

In summary, the contributions of this paper are as follows: (1) We define a new time-based cost model to account for contention in shared memory; (2) We provide the first analysis of the commonly used exponential delay protocol; and (3) We propose a new backoff protocol that is asymptotically better than the classic one.

## 2 MODEL

Our model aims to separate delays caused by contention from other delays that may occur in shared memory systems. In most known shared memory models, all types of delays (or causes of asynchrony) are grouped into one, and are treated by assuming an adversary that controls the order of execution. However, we note that once an instruction is successfully invoked in the hardware, its performance, while it could greatly vary because of contention, is relatively predictable. Throughout this paper, we only consider instructions that are applied on shared memory.

Thus, we say that each process $p \in P$ may have up to one pending instruction $I_t(p)$ at any time $t$. Each pending instruction may either be *ready* or *active*. The ready instructions represent instructions that are ready to run, but have not yet been invoked in the hardware; they might be delayed because the calling process is swapped out, failed or otherwise delayed by the system. Active instructions are instructions that have already started executing in the hardware, and are now delayed by contention (e.g. executing the cache coherency protocol). The adversary controls when each instruction moves from ready to active, and then instructions are moved from active to 'done' as soon as they do not contend with any earlier instruction, not under the control of the adversary.

We thus divide the set of pending instructions at time $t$, denoted $I_t$, into two subsets; an unordered set of *ready* instructions $R_t$ and an ordered set of *active* instructions $A_t$, such that $A_t \cup R_t = I_t$ and $A_t \cap R_t = \emptyset$. There is a priority order, denoted $<$ (less is higher priority), among instructions in $A_t$ that corresponds to the order in which they were invoked in the hardware. Furthermore, to model contention, we define *conflicts* between instructions. For any pair of operations $i, j \in I_t$, the predicate $C(i,j)$ is *true* if $i$ conflicts with $j$, and is *false* otherwise. For the purpose of this paper, we say that $C(i,j)$ is true if and only if $i$ and $j$ both access the same memory location and at least one of them is a modifying instruction. This function can also represent other types of conflicts, such as false sharing, depending on the behavior of the system we want to model.

In each time step $t$, each instruction may undergo at most one of the following transitions: it may be moved from $R_t$ to $A_{t+1}$, it may be removed from $A_t$, or it may be inserted into $R_{t+1}$. More specifically, the adversary chooses a (possibly empty) subset $S_t \in R_t$ to activate. It gives a priority order among the instructions in $S_t$, and places them in priority order behind elements already in $A_t$. Furthermore, in time step $t$, we define the set of *executed* instructions to be $E_t = \{i \in A_t | \nexists j \in A_t.C(i,j) \wedge j < i\}$. That is, an instruction $i \in A_t$ is executed in time $t$ if and only if there is no other instruction in $A_t$ that conflicts with $i$ and is ahead of $i$ in the priority order. In addition, every process $p \in P$ may add a new instructionto $R_{t+1}$ as long as there is only one instruction per process in $I_{t+1}$. The set of newly ready instructions is called $N_t$. The next time step, $t+1$ has the following sets: $R_{t+1} = (R_t \setminus S_t) \cup N_t$, $A_{t+1} = (A_t \setminus E_t) \cup S_t$ and $I_{t+1} = (I_t \setminus E_t) \cup N_t = R_{t+1} \cup A_{t+1}$. Furthermore, for all instructions $i \in S_t$ and all instructions $j \in A_t$, $j < i$.

An *execution* $E$ is a sequence of the instructions executed by processes in the system, which defines a total order on the instructions. This total order must be an extension of the partial order defined by time steps; that is, for any two instructions $i$ and $j$, executed in time $t$ and $t'$ respectively, if $t < t'$ then $i$ appears before $j$ in the execution $E$. $E|p$ is the projection of $E$ onto the process $p$; that is, it is the subsequence of $E$ that contains only instructions by process $p$, and no other instruction.

We consider two measurements of efficiency for algorithms evaluated by this model. One measurement is immediate: we say the running time of an execution is the number of time steps taken until termination. Another measurement is called *work*. Intuitively, this measures the total amount of cycles that all processes spent on the execution. We say that a process spends one cycle for every time step $t$ in which $I_t(p) \in A_t$. Thus, the amount of work taken by an execution is given by the sum over all time steps $t$ of the size of $A_t$ (i.e. $W = \sum_t |A_t|$). All of the bounds in this paper are given in terms of work. We feel that work better represents the demands of these protocols on the resources of the machine, as inactive processes could be asleep or making progress on some unrelated task.

*Adversary.* We assume an oblivious adversary [5]. That is, the adversary does not see processes' local values before making them active, and thus cannot make decisions based on that knowledge. Such values include the results of any random coin flips and the type of operation that the process will perform. The adversary can, however, know the algorithm that the processes are following and the history of the execution so far. We also assume that once an instruction is made active, the adversary may see its local values. However, at that point, the adversary is no longer allowed to make changes to the priorities, and thus cannot use that knowledge.

*Protocols.* In the rest of this paper, we analyze and compare different backoff protocols. To keep the examples clean and the focus on the backoff protocols themselves rather than where they are used, we consider a simple use case: a read-modify-write update as defined in Algorithm 1. A *read* instruction takes a memory location $x$, and, if it is executed at time $t$, will return the value stored in $x$ at $t$. A *CAS* instruction takes three arguments; a memory location $x$, an expected value $v_e$ and a new value $v_n$. As usual, a CAS executed at time $t$ is *successful* if and only if the value stored in $x$ at $t$ is the expected value $v_e$. In that case, the CAS instruction changes the value in $x$ to the new value $v_n$. Otherwise, it is a *failed* CAS, and does not change the value stored in $x$. The CAS returns a boolean indicating whether it was successful.

An *update attempt* by process $p$ is one iteration of Algorithm 1. In every update attempt, $p$ reads the current value, then uses the *Modify* function provided to it to calculate the new value it will use for its CAS instruction. The Modify function can represent any change a process might need to make in an algorithm that uses such updates. A *successful update attempt* is one in which the CAS succeeds and the loop exits. Otherwise, we say that the update attempt *failed*. For simplicity, we assume that every CAS instruction has a distinct $v_n$, and thus an update attempt fails if and only if there was a successful CAS by a different process between its read and its CAS. We assume that CAS instructions conflict with all other instructions on the same location. However, read instructions do not conflict with each other. Note that such an update protocol is commonly used in the implementation of shared objects such as counters and stacks.

**Algorithm 1** Update Loop

```
procedure UPDATE(x, Modify)
    while True do                ▷ One iteration is an update attempt
        currnetVal ← Read(x)
        val ← Modify(currentVal)
        if CAS(x, currentVal, val) then return
```

## 3 EXPONENTIAL BACKOFF

Exponential backoff protocols are widely used in practice to improve the performance of shared-memory concurrent algorithms [3, 22, 24]. However, to the best of our knowledge, there has been no running time analysis of these algorithms that shows why they do so well. In this section, we provide the first analysis of the standard exponential delay algorithm for concurrent algorithms.

In general, the exponential backoff protocol works as follows. Each process starts with a maxDelay of 1 (or some other constant), and attempts an update. If it fails, it doubles its maxDelay, and then picks a number $d$ uniformly at random in the range [1, maxDelay]. It then delays for $d$ time units, and attempts another update. We refer to this approach as the *exponential delay* protocol.

Exponential delay is common in the literature and is applied in several settings to reduce running time; for example, Mellor-Crummey and Scott use it for barriers [24], Herlihy uses it between successive attempts of lock-free operations [22], and Anderson used it for spin locks [3]. The pseudo-code for exponential delay on an update protocol is given in Algorithm 2.

Using our model, as defined in section 2, we show that in an asynchronous but timed setting, the exponential delay protocol does indeed significantly improve the running time. In particular, we show that for $n$ processes to each successfully update the same memory location once, the naïve (no-backoff) approach requires $\Theta(n^3)$ work, but using exponential delay, this is reduced to

**Algorithm 2** Exponential Delay

```
procedure UPDATE(x, Modify)
    maxDelay ← 1
    while True do            ▷ One iteration is an update attempt
        currentVal ← Read(x)
        val ← Modify(currentVal)
        if CAS(x, currentVal, val) then return
        maxDelay ← 2 · maxDelay
        d ← rand(1, maxDelay)
        Wait d steps
```

$\Theta(n^2 \log n)$. For simplicity, we assume that each process only needs to successfully write once; after its first successful write, it will not rejoin the ready set. To show the upper bound for exponential delay, we rely on one additional assumption, which is not used in the proofs of the lower bounds.

Assumption 1. *In any time step $t$ where the active set $A_t$ is empty and the ready set $R_t$ is not, the adversary* must *move a non-empty subset of $R_t$ to $A_t$.*

*Analyzing the naïve protocol.* We consider $n$ processes trying to update the same memory location using a naïve update loop with no backoff. The pseudocode of this protocol is given in Algorithm 1. To give a lower bound for this protocol, we imagine a very simple adversarial behavior; whenever any instruction is ready, the adversary immediately activates it. Note that this is not a contrived or improbable adversary. Nevertheless, this scheduling strategy is enough to show a $\Omega(n^3)$ work bound.

The intuition is as follows: the active set has around $n$ instructions at all times. A successful update attempt can only happen about once every $n$ time steps, because CAS attempts always conflict, and the active queue is long. The average process will thus have to make around $n/2$ update attempts before succeeding, and wait around $n/2$ time steps for each one, thus needing $\Omega(n^2)$ work. This gives us the bound of $\Omega(n^3)$ work for all processes together.

Theorem 3.1. *The naïve update protocol requires $\Omega(n^3)$ work for $n$ processes to each successfully update one location once.*

Proof. Consider an adversary that simply activates every instruction as soon as it becomes ready, and assume that $n$ instructions are ready at the start. Recall that an update attempt can only succeed if there was no successful CAS by any other process between that update attempt's read and CAS instructions. Furthermore, all CAS instructions conflict with each other, and for a CAS attempt to be successful, there have to be no other successful CAS instructions while it waits in the active set to be executed.

We partition the execution into *rounds*. Each round has exactly one successful CAS in it (the $i$th successful CAS is in round $R_i$), and ends immediately after this CAS. The execution ends after round $R_n$. Note that $R_1$ is short; all processes start with their read instructions, which takes one time step since reads do not conflict with each other, and in the next time step there is a successful CAS. However, after $R_1$, all processes that have not yet terminated will have a failed CAS instruction in each round. In particular, every round $R_i$ for $i \geq 2$ has at least $n - i$ failed CAS attempts in it. Furthermore, note that in each round $R_i$, there are at least $n - i$ instructions in the active set at every time step during $R_i$. This is because each process immediately returns to the active set with a new instruction.

Recall that the work of an execution is equal to the sum over all time steps of the size of the active set. Thus, we sum over all rounds and all time steps in them, to get

$$W = \sum_{i=1}^{n} R_i = \sum_{i=1}^{n} (n-i)^2 < \sum_{i=1}^{n/2} \left(\frac{n}{2}\right)^2 = \Omega(n^3). \qquad \square$$

## 3.1 Analyzing Exponential Delay

To analyze the exponential delay protocol, we assume that when a process delays itself for $d$ time, it waits $d$ time steps between leaving the active set and rejoining the ready set.

*The lower bound.* To show a lower bound of $\Omega(n^2 \log n)$ on the running time of an update loop using the exponential delay protocol, we simply need to present a strategy for the adversary that forces the algorithm to take that long.

Theorem 3.2. *The standard exponential delay algorithm takes $\Omega(n^2 \log n)$ work for $n$ processes to each successfully update one location once.*

Proof. Consider an adversary that simply places every operation in the active set as soon as it becomes ready, and assume that $n$ operations are ready at the start. Recall that work is defined as the sum over all time steps of the length of the active set.

For every process $p$, let $M_r$ be $p$'s maxDelay and $D_r$ be its actual delay after its $r$th update attempt. Note that the adversary's strategy is to activate $p$ immediately after $D_r$ steps. However, regardless of $D_r$, in this proof we only start charging work for $p$'s presence in the active set $M_r$ steps after its $r$th update attempt, or we charge zero if the process already finished after $M_r$ steps. Thus, we actually charge for less work than is being done in reality.

Note that at time step $t$, there will be $n - d_t$ processes in the active set, where $d_t$ is the number of processes that are done by time $t$ or are delayed at time $t$. Then note that any single process $p$ can only do at most one update attempt per $n$ time steps. This is because all update attempts contain a CAS, and thus conflict with each other under our model. Furthermore, after $p$ executes one update attempt, it must delay for maxDelay time steps, and then wait behind every other instruction in the active set. The active set starts with $n$ instructions at the beginning of the execution. This also means that successful CAS instructions happen at most once every $n$ time steps.

Every time a process executes an update attempt, assuming it does not terminate, it doubles its maxDelay. As noted above, for every process $p$, this happens about once every $n$ time steps. As delays grow, there are proportionally many processes that are delayed at any given time $t$. We can model this as $d_t \leq 2^{\lceil t/n \rceil + 1}$. We now calculate the amount of work $W$ this execution will take.

$$\begin{aligned} W &= \sum_t |A_t| = \sum_t \max\{n - d_t, 0\} \\ &\geq \sum_t \max\{n - 2^{\lceil t/n \rceil + 1}, 0\} \\ &= n \cdot (n-4) + n \cdot (n-8) + \ldots + n \cdot (n-n) \\ &= \Omega(n^2 \log n). \end{aligned} \qquad \square$$

*The upper bound.* Recall that for the purpose of this analysis, we use Assumption 1. Given this assumption, we show that once every process's max delay reaches $12n$, the algorithm terminates within $O(n \log n)$ work w.h.p.. This is because sufficiently many time slots are empty to allow quick progress. Thus, the adversary can only expand the work while not all processes' maxDelays have reached at least $12n$. We show that the adversary cannot prevent this from happening for more than $O(n^2 \log n)$ work w.h.p..

LEMMA 3.3. *Consider n processes attempting to update the same memory location, using the exponential delay algorithm, and assume all of them have a max delay of at least S by some time t. Then in any segment of length S starting after time t in the execution, there will be at most 2n update attempts in expectation and w.h.p..*

PROOF. For each process $p$, let $R(p,k)$ be the event that process $p$ was ready with a new update attempt $k$ times during the segment. Then the probability that $p$ will attempt $k$ updates in the segment is bounded by:

$$P[R(p,k)] \leq \prod_{j=1}^{k} \frac{S}{2^{j-1} \cdot S} = \prod_{j=1}^{k} \frac{1}{2^{j-1}} = \frac{1}{2^{k(k-1)/2}}$$

The above calculation assumes that every time $p$ attempts to execute and then restarts its delay, it gets to start over at the beginning of the segment. This assumption is clearly too strong, and means that in reality the probability of attempting $k$ updates within one segment decays even faster as $k$ grows. However, for our purposes, this bound suffices. Furthermore, note that the probability that any single process $p$ is ready at least $2 \cdot (\sqrt{\log n} + 1)$ times is:

$$P[R(p, 2 \cdot (\sqrt{\log n} + 1))] \leq \frac{1}{2^{(\sqrt{\log n}+1)\sqrt{\log n}}} < \frac{1}{n}.$$

Thus, no process will be ready in any one segment more than $O(\sqrt{\log n})$ times w.h.p.. Let $N$ be the number of update attempts by all the processes during the segment. We can calculate the expected number of update attempts in the segment as follows:

$$E[N] < \sum_{k=1}^{S} n \cdot P[R_i(p,k)] = n \sum_{k=1}^{S} \frac{1}{2^{k(k-1)/2}} < \frac{7}{4} n$$

Using Hoeffding's inequality, we can similarly bound the number of update attempts in the segment with high probability:

$$P(X - E[X] \geq \delta) \leq \exp\left(-\frac{2n^2\delta^2}{\sum_{i=1}^{n}(\max_i - \min_i)^2}\right)$$

$$P(X \geq \frac{15}{8}) \leq \exp\left(-\frac{n^2}{32n(\sqrt{\log n})^2}\right) = \exp\left(-\frac{n}{32 \log n}\right)$$

Therefore, the number of update attempts ready by processes with max delay at least $S$ during any segment of length $S$ is bounded by $\frac{15}{8}n < 2n$ in expectation and with high probability. □

LEMMA 3.4. *Consider n processes attempting to update the same memory location, using the exponential delay algorithm. Within $O(n \log n)$ time steps and $O(n^2 \log n)$ work, all processes will have a max delay of at least 12n, with high probability.*

PROOF. We partition the set of processes $P$ into three subsets – small-delay, large-delay and done – according to the processes' state in the execution, and update these sets as the execution proceeds.

For a given time step $t$, let $S_t$ be the set of *small-delay* processes, whose max delay is small, i.e. maxDelay $< 12n$. Similarly, let $L_t$ be the set of *large-delay* processes whose, max delay is large, i.e. maxDelay $\geq 12n$, and let $D_t$ be the set of processes that are *done* (i.e., have already CASed successfully and terminated by time $t$). Note that $S_0 = P$, $L_0 = D_0 = \emptyset$, that is, at the beginning of the execution, all processes have a small max delay. Furthermore, by definition, the execution ends on the first time step $t$ such that $D_t = P$ and $S_t = L_t = \emptyset$.

We want to bound the amount of work in the execution until the first time step $t$ such that $L_t \cup D_t = P$. To do so, we need to show that small-delay processes make progress regularly. That is, we need to show that the adversary cannot prevent small-delay processes from raising their delays by keeping them in the ready set for long. By Assumption 1, if only small-delay processes are in the ready set $R_t$ at some time $t$, then the adversary must activate at least one of them. Thus, we show that in any execution, a constant fraction of the time steps have no large-delay processes ready.

We split up the execution into segments of length $12n$ time steps each. By Lemma 3.3, in each such segment $S_t$ that starts at time $t$, there are at most $2|L_t|$ update attempts by processes in $L_t$ with high probability. Thus, even if $|L_t| = \Theta(n)$, in every segment of size $12n$, there is a constant fraction of time steps (at least $10n$ with high probability) in which no process in $L_t$ is ready. Furthermore, note that since their max delays are $< 12n$, every process in $S_t$ must be ready at least once in every segment. Recall that the adversary must make at least one instruction active in every step in which there is at least one instruction that is ready. Thus, allowing for processes in $S_t$ to 'miss' the empty time steps in one segment, we have the following progress guarantee: at least once every two segments of length $12n$, at least $n$ instructions of processes with small delays will be executed.

Note that every process needs to execute $\log 12n$ instructions in order to have a large delay. Therefore, for all processes to arrive at a large delay, we need $n \log 12n$ executions of instructions that belong to processes with a small delay. By the above progress guarantee, we know that every $24n$ time steps, at least $n$ such instructions are executed. Thus, in at most $24n \log 12n$ time steps, all processes will reach a delay of at least $12n$, with high probability. Note that in every time step $t$, there can be at most $n$ instructions in the active set, $A_t$. Thus, the total work for this part of the execution is bounded by $W = \sum_t^{24n \log 12n} |A_t| = O(n^2 \log n)$ with high probability. □

LEMMA 3.5. *Consider n processes attempting to update the same memory location, using the exponential delay algorithm. If the max delay of every process is at least 12n, then the algorithm will terminate within $O(n \log n)$ additional work with high probability.*

PROOF. We can apply the analysis of linear probing in hash tables [23] to this problem. Every process has to find its own time slot in which to execute its instruction, and if it collides with another process on some time slot, it will remain in the active set, and try again in the next one.

We think of the update attempts of the processes as elements being inserted into a hash table, and the time slots as the bins of the hash table. If a process's instruction collides with another's then it will 'probe' the next time slot, until it finds an empty slot in which to execute. Counting the number of probes that each instruction does gives us exactly the amount of work done in the execution.

For the purpose of this analysis, we assume that an update attempt succeeds if and only if neither its read nor its CAS collide with any other instruction. If either one of them does, we assume that this process will have to try again. Furthermore, since each update attempt involves two instructions, we put two time slots in a bin; that is, we assume the number of bins is half of the minimum max delay of the processes (in this case, we know all processes have max delay $\geq 12n$). Thus, we effectively double the load factor in our analysis to account for the two instructions of the update attempts.

Thus, if we have $k \leq n$ update attempts, and all of their processes have max delay at least $m$, then the maximum amount of work for one update attempt of any process is at most the number of probes an element would require to be inserted into a hash table with load factor $\alpha = 2k/m$.

We start with $n$ processes participating, all of them having a max delay of at least $12n$. By Lemma 3.3, we know that there are at most $2n$ update attempts in $12n$ time steps, with high probability. Thus, our load factor is $\alpha = (2 \cdot 2n)/12n = 1/3$. Let $X_i$ be the amount of work that process $p_i$ does for one update attempt. Let $X = \frac{1}{n}\sum_i E[X_i]$. It is well known [23] that in this case, the expected number of probes an insertion does in linear probing is at most

$$E[X] = \frac{1}{2}\left(1 + \left(\frac{1}{1-\alpha}\right)^2\right) = \frac{1}{2}\left(1 + \frac{9}{4}\right) = \frac{13}{8}.$$

Thus, by Markov's inequality,

$$P[X \geq \frac{15}{8}] \leq \frac{8E[X]}{15} = \frac{13}{15}.$$

Thus, $X < \frac{15}{8}$ with probability at least $\frac{2}{15}$. Note that the amount of work per process is integral and at least one (when it experiences no collisions). Therefore, a simple averaging argument shows that at least $\frac{1}{8}$ of the processes cost only 1, and thus experience no collisions, with probability at least $\frac{2}{15}$. Any process that experiences no collisions terminates in that step. Therefore, with constant probability, a constant fraction of the processes terminate out of every $n$ update attempts.

We can imagine repeatedly having rounds in which the remaining processes are inserted into a hash table of size. Note that the expected cost for $n$ processes to do one update attempt is at most $\frac{16n}{13}$. Furthermore, note that this cost is in reality even better, since process delays increase and the number of inserted instructions decreases, both causing less collisions as the load factor $\alpha$ decreases. However, even if we do not take the decreasing load factor into account, a constant factor of the processes terminate in every such 'round'. Note that since we do not account for the improvements from the previous rounds when calculating the expected cost of round $i$, the rounds are independent. Thus, we can apply the Chernoff bound to show that within $O(\log n)$ rounds, all processes successfully update, costing a total of $O(n \log n)$ work with high probability. □

The lemmas above immediately lead to the following theorem.

Theorem 3.6. *The standard exponential delay algorithm takes $O(n^2 \log n)$ work with high probability for $n$ processes to each successfully update the same location once.*

We can further strengthen this result by showing that the time that processes spend delaying does not asymptotically increase the work of the algorithm. That is, even if we account for process delays as part of the total work, exponential delay still achieves $O(n^2 \log n)$ work in expectation. Due to lack of space, we leave this to the full version of the paper.

# 4 A NEW APPROACH: ADAPTIVE PROBABILITY

We present a new protocol that beats the standard exponential delay protocol under our model. The pseudocode for our algorithm is given in Algorithm 3. We say that every iteration of the while loop executed by process $p$ is an update attempt, or a *step* by $p$.

Each process maintains a probability *prob*, which it updates in every step. All processes start with $prob = 1$. Each process also keeps track of the value *val* that was returned by its most recent read. On each step, $p$ tries to CAS with probability *prob* into location $x$and if successful it is done. Otherwise it re-reads the value at $x$ and if changed (indicating contention) it halves its probability, and if not changed it doubles its probability. Intuitively, this protocol lets processes receive more frequent feedback on the state of the system than exponential delay (by reading the contended memory), and hence processes can adjust to different levels of contention faster. Furthermore, 'backing-on' allows processes to recover more quickly from previous high loads. Since reads do not conflict with each other in our model, reads between CASes are coalesced into a single time step, and do not significantly affect work, as our analysis will show. In particular, we show that for $n$ processes to successfully update a single memory location following our protocol, it takes $O(n^2)$ work in expectation and with high probability.

**Algorithm 3** Adaptive Probability

```
procedure UPDATE(x, Modify)
    currentVal ← Read(x)
    prob ← 1
    while True do                ▷ One iteration is an update attempt
        heads ← flip(prob)
        if heads then
            val ← Modify(currentVal)
            if CAS(x, currentVal, val) then return
        newVal ← Read(x)
        if newVal = currentVal then
            prob ← max(1, 2 · prob)
        else
            prob ← prob/2
            currentVal = newVal
```

## 4.1 Analysis

The most important factor for understanding the behaviour of our algorithm is the CAS-probabilities of the processes. These probabilities determine the expected number of reads and CAS attempts each

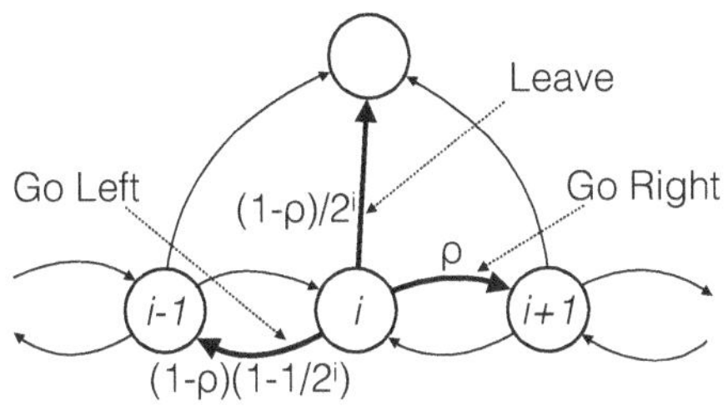


**Figure 1: Simple state transition system for one process's execution. The transitions $p$ can make are labeled with their name and their transition probability. The probability $\rho$ is determined by the adversary.**

process does during the execution, and thus they greatly influence the overall work.

We first analyze an execution for a single process in isolation, and then consider the progress of the execution as a whole, when all processes participate. Consider any process $p \in P$ as it executes Algorithm 3. Let $E$ be any legal execution, and $E|p$ be the execution restricted to only $p$'s instructions. For the rest of this discussion, and for the proof of Lemma 4.1, when we discuss numbered steps, we mean $p$'s steps in $E|p$. Recall that a step is defined to be a single iteration of the while loop (or a single update attempt), and thus every step may contain more than one instruction. For every process $p \in P$, we define $p$'s *state* at step $t$, $s(t)$, to be $i$ if $p$'s probability at step $t$ is $2^{-i}$. Note that $p$'s state is never the same in two consecutive steps. Furthermore, as long as $p$ doesn't terminate, $p$'s state can only change by one in every step. That is, if $s(t) = i$, then $s(t+1) = i+1$ or $s(t+1) = i-1$. We can model a process $p$'s states over the execution using a simple state transition system (Figure 1). In addition to these states, we need one state in the chain to represent $p$ terminating.

The transition probabilities between $p$'s probability states depend on the other processes in the system. Note that in our algorithm, $p$ decreases its probability in step $t$, or transitions to the right, if and only if there has been a successful update by some other process between $p$'s read and its CAS. Otherwise, $p$'s state transition will depend on its own CAS-probability—if it CASes, its successfully updates and terminates, and otherwise it goes left. Thus, $p$'s state transition depends on whether other processes successfully update. This is heavily controlled by the adversary.

Recall that we assume an oblivious adversary. That is, the adversary cannot base its decision of which processes to activate on their local values. In particular, that means that we do not allow the adversary to know the result of a process's coin flips, and thus whether it will read or CAS in the next step. However, we do allow the adversary to observe the instruction being done once that instruction is in the active set, and thus keep track of each process's history to know its state at every time step.

Therefore, the adversary can decide which instructions to activate given the probability states of their process. In particular, when considering a single process $p$'s state transition, the adversary can decide how many processes it activates between two consecutive steps of $p$ and how likely those processes are to successfully update. Thus, we can abstract the adversary's power by saying it can pick any probability $\rho$ for how likely the state will go right, i.e., conflict with another process and decrease its probability. Note that in reality, if all participating processes are using the same protocol, the adversary will be more restricted than this, however despite the power we are giving the adversary this abstraction still allows us to prove the first important lemma of our analysis.

Lemma 4.1. *Every process executes at most 4 CAS attempts in expectation before terminating.*

For this Lemma, we will focus on any one process $p \in P$, and track its movement in the state transition system during a given execution $E$. In the rest of this section, unless otherwise indicated, all analysis refers to process $p$ and execution $E$ of Algorithm 3.

We denote by $R(i)$ the number of 'right' state transitions of $p$ from state $i$ to state $i+1$ in $E$, and by $L(i)$ the number of 'left' state transitions of $p$ from $i$ to $i-1$ in $E$. We first make an observation about these state transitions.

Observation 1. *For every state $i$, $L(i+1) \le R(i) + 1$.*

That is, the number of transitions from $i+1$ to $i$ is at most the number of transitions from $i$ to $i+1$, plus 1. This can be easily seen by considering, for every time $p$ transitions from $i$ to $i+1$, how it got to state $i$. $p$ starts at state 0. Thus, for every state $i > 0$, the first time $p$ reaches state $i+1$ is by going right from state $i$. However, for every subsequent time $p$ transitions right from $i$ to $i+1$, it must have, at some point, gone left from $i+1$ to $i$. Thus, the number of times $p$ transitions from $i$ to $i+1$ is at most one more than the number of times it transitions from $i+1$ to $i$.

Proof of Lemma 4.1. Consider execution $E|p$; that is, the execution $E$ restricted to just the instructions of $p$, and let $C_E$ be the number of CAS attempts in this execution. We partition $E|p$ into two buckets, and analyze each separately; for every state $i$, we place the first time $p$ reaches $i$ into the first bucket, denoted *Init*, and place every remaining instruction in the execution into the second bucket, called *Main*. Thus, $C_E = C_I + C_M$, where $C_I$ and $C_M$ correspond to the cost (number of CAS attempts) of *Init* and *Main* respectively.

Note that *Init* corresponds to an execution in which $p$ only goes down in probability. In every state $i$ it reaches, it has probability $\frac{1}{2^i}$ of attempting a CAS, and thus expected cost of $\frac{1}{2^i}$ for that state. Thus, we can easily calculate its expected cost.

$$E[C_I] = \sum_{i=0}^{\infty} 2^{-i} \le 2.$$

We now consider the *Main* bucket of the execution $E|p$. There are two random variables that affect the steps that $p$ takes. The adversary can affect whether $p$ goes right or not, by picking a value for $\rho$ (see Figure 1). However, if $p$ does not go right, then only $p$'s coin flip determines whether it will go left or leave (this is independent of any choice of the adversary). We will charge the right transitions, that the adversary can affect, against the left-or-leave transition that the adversary cannot. We can do this since for every left transition from a state $i$ in the main bucket, there is at most one corresponding right transition from $i$ when it goes back to the right through state $i$ (there might be none if it terminates at a position to the left).

We define $D$ to be the sequence of times $t$ in *Main* in which $p$ does not go right, and use $j$ to indicate indices into this sequence (to avoid confusion with $i$ for state and $t$ for position in $E|p$). Let $C_{M,j}$ to be the random variable for the remaining cost of *Main*, after the $j$th step in $D$, but not including the final successful CAS. If just before the $j$th step in $D$, the process is at state $i$, there is a $c_j = \frac{1}{2^i}$ probability that the process will CAS and terminate. Thus, there is a $1 - c_j$ probability that the execution will continue. We let $R_j$ be the random variable indicating that the future right transition assign to $j$ does a CAS. The expected cost (probability) of CASing when going right from state $i$ is $\frac{1}{2^i}$, but since there might not be a future right transition, $E[R_j] \leq c_j$. We now have the following recurrence for the expectation of $C_{M,j}$:

$$\begin{aligned} E[C_{M,j}] &= E[R_j] + \left(1 - c_j\right) E[C_{M,j+1}] \\ &\leq c_j + \left(1 - c_j\right) E[C_{M,j+1}] \end{aligned}$$

The $c_j$'s represent the results of independent coin flips, and therefore the expectations can be multiplied. We therefore have:

$$\begin{aligned} E[C_{M,1}] &\leq c_1 + (1 - c_1) \cdot E[C_{M,2}] \\ &= c_1 + (1 - c_1)(c_2 + (1 - c_2)(c_3 + (1 - c_3)(\ldots))) \\ &= 1 - (1 - c_1) + (1 - c_1) \cdot c_2 + (1 - c_1)(1 - c_2) \cdot c_3 + \ldots \\ &= 1 - (1 - c_1)(1 - c_2) + (1 - c_1)(1 - c_2) \cdot c_3 + \ldots \\ &= 1 - (1 - c_1)(1 - c_2)(1 - c_3) \ldots \\ &\leq 1 \end{aligned}$$

Recall that in addition to this cost, there is exactly one successful CAS that causes $p$ to terminate, so $C_M = C_{M,1} + 1$. Adding this to the cost of the two buckets of the execution, we can bound the total expected cost of $E|p$ by $E[C_E] = E[C_I + C_M] \leq 2 + 1 + 1 = 4$. □

We now consider the total number of steps that $p$ does in $E$. Recall that a step, or an update attempt, is defined as an iteration of the loop in Algorithm 3, even if the process doesn't execute a CAS. We first show that the maximum number of steps of $p$ depends on the number of successful updates by other processes. For this purpose, we stop considering $E|p$ in isolation, and instead look at the execution $E$ as a whole.

Lemma 4.2 (Throughput lemma). *For any process $p$ and state $i$, let $t$ and $t'$ be two times in $E$ at which $p$ executes a read instruction that causes it to transition to state $i$. Then the number of steps $p$ takes between $t$ and $t'$ is at most $2k$, where $k$ is the number of successful updates in the execution between $t$ and $t'$.*

Proof. Let $E' \subseteq E$ be a sub-execution where the first and last instructions in $E'$ are by process $p$, and both bring $p$ to state $i$. Let $k$ be the number of successful updates that occur during $E'$.

We say that $p$ *observes* a successful update $w$ if $p$ decreased its probability due to the value written by $w$. We note that for $p$ to return to a state $i$, it has to raise its probability exactly as many times as it decreases it, when counting starting at the last time it was at state $i$. Note that $p$ can only decrease its probability if it observes a new successful update. Since it must change its probability on every step, $p$ raises its probability on every step where it does not observe a new update. Thus, one observed update's effect gets 'canceled out' by one update attempt of $p$ in which it did not observe any successful updates. Clearly, $p$ can observe at most $k$ successful updates during $E'$. Thus, it can make at most $k$ update attempts raising its probability, for a total of at most $2k$ steps during $E'$. □

Corollary 4.3. *Every process makes at most $2n$ update attempts during an execution of Algorithm 3, where $n$ is the number of successful updates in the execution.*

Proof. Consider any process $p \in P$ and recall that every process starts the execution at state $i = 0$. At this state, $p$ has probability 1 of attempting a CAS. If, at any time, $p$ is in state 0, and no successful update happens before its next step, then $p$ succeeds and terminates. Note that there are at most $n - 1$ successful updates by other processes during $p$'s execution, since each process only updates once. By Lemma 4.2, if $p$ takes $2n - 2$ steps without terminating, then $p$ is back at state 0, and all other processes have executed successful updates. Thus, $p$'s next step is a CAS that succeeds, since all other processes have terminated. Therefore, $p$ can make at most $2n$ update attempts before it succeeds. □

We are now ready to analyze the entire execution.

Theorem 4.4. *Algorithm 3 takes $O(n^2)$ work in expectation for $n$ processes to each successfully update the same location once.*

Proof. Note that by Corollary 4.3, every process executing Algorithm 3 does at most $O(n)$ instructions until it terminates. Thus, in the entire execution, there are $O(n^2)$ instructions. Furthermore, by Lemma 4.1, only $O(n)$ of these are CAS attempts in expectation. The rest must be read instructions.

Recall that $W = \sum_t |A_t|$, and that for all times $t$, $|A_t| \leq n$. Furthermore, recall that CAS instructions conflict with every other instruction, but read instructions do not conflict with each other. Thus, a CAS instruction $w$ executed at time $t$ can cause every instruction $i \in A_t$ such that $i <_A w$ to be delayed one time step. There are at most $O(n)$ such delayed instructions per CAS instruction. In addition, any read instruction will be active for exactly one time step if there is no CAS instruction in front of it. Thus, we have: $W = O(n) \cdot O(n) + O(n^2) = O(n^2)$. □

We can extend our results to be with high probability. For this, the key is to show that there is a linear number of CAS attempts with high probability in every execution, and then the rest of the results carry through.

Lemma 4.5. *There are $O(n)$ CAS attempts in any execution with high probability.*

Proof. We first show that, with high probability, no process attempts more than $O(\log n)$ CAS instructions. To do this, we define an indicator variable $X_i = 1$ if $p$ executes a CAS instruction in its $i$th update attempt, and $X_i = 0$ otherwise. Note that $X_i$ is independent from $X_j$ for all $i \neq j$. Furthermore, let $X = \sum_i X_i$. In Lemma 4.1, we show that $E[X] \leq 4$. We can now use the Chernoff inequality to bound the probability of a single process attempting more than $c \log n$ CAS instructions for any constant $c$.

$$P[X > (1 + c \log n) \cdot 4] \leq e^{\frac{-4c \log n}{3}} = \frac{1}{n^{4c/3}}$$

Thus, every process attempts at most $O(\log n)$ CAS instructions w.h.p. We can now use this bound on the number of CAS attempts per process when bounding the probability of getting more than a linear number of CAS attempts in the system in any execution.

We can now number the processes, and define, for each process $p_i$, $Y_i = w_i$ where $w_i$ is the number of CAS attempts $p_i$ executes in E. We assume that for every $i$, $Y_i \in [0, c \log n]$ for some constant $c$. Let $\bar{Y} = 1/n \sum_{i=1}^{n} Y_i$. Then by Lemma 4.1, $E[\bar{Y}] = 4$. Plugging this into Hoeffding's inequality, we get

$$P[\bar{Y} \geq 5] \leq e^{\frac{-2n}{c \log^2 n}}$$

Therefore, with high probability, there are at most $5n$ CAS attempts in the execution $E$. □

We thus have the following theorem.

THEOREM 4.6. *Algorithm 3 takes $O(n^2)$ work in expectation and with high probability for n processes to each successfully update the same location once.*

## 5 OTHER CONTENTION MODELS

Contention has been the subject of a lot of research in the past 25 years. Many researchers noted its effect on the performance of algorithms in shared memory and used backoff to mitigate its cost [3, 19, 22, 24]. Anderson [3] used exponential delay to improve the performance of spin locks. Herlihy [22] used a very similar exponential delay protocol in read-modify-write loops of lock-free and wait-free algorithms. However, all of these studies, while showing empirical evidence of the effectiveness of exponential delay, do not provide any theoretical analysis.

Studying the effect of contention in theory requires a good model to account for its cost. Gibbons, Matias and Ramachandran first introduced contention into PRAM models [17, 18]. They observed that the CRCW PRAM is not realistic, and instead defined the QRQW PRAM. This model allows for concurrent reads and writes, but queues them up at every memory location, such that the cost incurred is proportional to the number of such operations on location. Their model also allows processes to pipeline instructions. That is, processes are allowed to have multiple instructions enqueued on the memory at the same time. Instructions incur a delay at least as large as the length of the queue at the time they join.

Dwork, Herlihy and Waarts [12] defined memory *stalls* to account for contention. In their model, each atomic instruction on a base object has an *invocation* and a *response*. An instruction experiences a stall if, between its invocation and response, another instruction on the same location receives its response. Thus, if many operations access the same location concurrently, they could incur many stalls, capturing the effect of contention. In this model, the adversary is given more power than in ours. In particular, we can imagine our model's 'activation' of an instruction as its invocation. Our model then allows the adversary to control the order of invocations of the instructions, but not their responses. Furthermore, Dwork *et al.*'s model does not distinguish between different types of instructions—all are assumed to conflict if they are on the same location. Thus, our model is similar to a version of Dwork *et al.*'s model that restricts the allowed executions according to instructions' invocation order and only considers conflicts with modifying instructions. However, they still cannot deal with exponential delay since they have no direct measure of time.

Fich, Hendler and Shavit [13] defined a different version of memory stalls, based on Dwork et al.'s work. Their model distinguishes between instructions, or *events*, that may modify the memory and ones that may not. An instruction is only slowed down by *modifying* instructions done by different processes on the same memory location. They show a lower bound on the number of stalls incurred by a single instruction in any implementation of a large class of objects. In our model, we consider the same types of conlicts as Fich *et al.* do. However, Fich *et al.* use the same fully adversarial model as in Dwork *et al.*'s work. Thus, our model allows only a subset of the executions allowed by theirs. However, even given the same execution, the two models do not assign it the same cost. In particular, in Fich *et al.*'s model, the only instructions that stall a given instruction $i$ are the modifying instructions *immediately* preceding it. Thus, if there is at least one read instruction between any constant number of modifying instructions, each will only suffer a constant number of stalls. The same is not true for our model.

Further work in this area was done by Hendler and Kutten [21]. Their work introduces a model that restricts the power of the adversary. They define the notion of *k-synchrony*, which, intuitively, states that no process is allowed to be more than a $k$ factor faster than any other process. They consider a model which assigns a cost to a given linearized execution by considering the dependencies between the instructions. While in their analysis they assume that all instructions on the same location contend, they discuss the possibility of treating read instructions differently than writes.

Atalar *et al.* [4] also address conflicts in shared memory and their effect on algorithm performance. They consider a class of lock-free algorithms whose operations do some local work, and then repeat a 'Read-CAS loop' (similar to our definition of an update attempt) until they succeed. Their proposed model divides conflicts into two types; hardware and logical conflicts. This division is reminiscent of our model's ready vs. active instructions. However, the two classifications do not address the same sources of delays.

Contention has been studied in many settings other than shared memory as well. Bar-Yehuda, Goldreich and Itai [8] applied exponential backoff to the problem of broadcasting a message over multi-hop radio networks. In this setting, there are synchronous rounds in which nodes on a graph may transmit a message to all of their neighbors. A node gets a message in a given round if and only if exactly one of its neighbors transmitted in that round. They show that using exponential backoff, broadcast can be solved exponentially faster than any deterministic broadcast algorithm. Radio networks have since been extensively studied, and many new algorithms using backoff have been developed [7, 16, 20].

Similar backoff protocols have been considered for communication channels. Bender *et al.* [9] consider a simple channel with adversarial disruptions. They show that using a back-off/back-on approach, in which probability of transmission is allowed to rise in some cases, achieves better throughput. This is similar to the approach taken by our adaptive probability protocol. An in-depth study of backoff on multiple access channels is given by Bender *et al.* in [10]. They introduce a new backoff protocol which achieves good throughput, polylog transmission attempts, and robustness to a disruptive adversary. Further work has been done on different varieties of communication channels [6, 11, 14, 15].

The models considered in these papers are similar to each other (with some variations on the initial state of the system, how collisions are handled, and the adversary's power), but differ from shared memory in several important ways. Firstly, these communication networks generally assume synchronous rounds, whereas this is not reasonable for shared memory. Furthermore, unlike shared memory, running time in networks and communication channels is measured by the number of rounds for an algorithm to complete, regardless of how many transmissions are sent per round. However, in shared memory the cost grows with the number of attempted operations. Another difference is the behavior upon collision; in shared memory, one modifying operation still goes through, and slows down the rest, whereas in other communication models, no message can be transmitted in that round. Furthermore, a single 'message' in shared memory can take multiple steps (such as an update that is implemented with two instructions). These differences make it hard to apply results from other models directly to shared memory.

## 6 CONCLUDING REMARKS

We've presented a new cost model for contention in shared memory. Using insights from this model, we've proposed the adaptive probabilities algorithm and analyzed the work it requires when all processes update the same location. Furthermore, we've shown that in this situation, it beats the classic exponential backoff approach.

We believe that our work is a step in the direction of truly being able to analyze the performance of shared memory algorithms, and leaves many interesting open questions. Although we've only discussed the performance of these protocols on one specific use case, we believe that our results can be generalized to other scenarios. We note that update loops such as those we consider are common in many algorithms; they are used in implementations of many important objects such as locks, counters, and stacks. It would be interesting to see how these results transfer to implementations of lock-free data structures, and their performance with and without backoff mechanisms in place. One could also apply our analysis and adaptive probabilities approach to lock free algorithms that iterate on a more complicated procedure until they succeed. We also believe key ideas from our approach can be applied to early-exit protocols, such as test-and-set, where processes that fail may choose to leave without successfully updating.

## 7 ACKNOWLEDGEMENTS

This work is supported by the National Science Foundation under grant number CCF-1314590, and the Natural Sciences and Engineering Research Canada post graduate scholarship. We thank Mor Harchol-Balter for insightful discussions that led to the proof of Lemma 4.1.

## REFERENCES


[1] Dan Alistarh, Keren Censor-Hillel, and Nir Shavit. Are lock-free concurrent algorithms practically wait-free? *Journal of the ACM (JACM)*, 63(4):31, 2016.

[2] Dan Alistarh, Thomas Sauerwald, and Milan Vojnović. Lock-free algorithms under stochastic schedulers. In *Proceedings of the 2015 ACM Symposium on Principles of Distributed Computing*, pages 251–260. ACM, 2015.

[3] Thomas E. Anderson. The performance of spin lock alternatives for shared-money multiprocessors. *IEEE Transactions on Parallel and Distributed Systems*, 1(1):6–16, 1990.

[4] Aras Atalar, Paul Renaud-Goud, and Philippas Tsigas. Analyzing the performance of lock-free data structures: A conflict-based model. In *Distributed Computing - 29th International Symposium, DISC 2015, Tokyo, Japan, October 7-9, 2015, Proceedings*, pages 341–355, 2015.

[5] Yonatan Aumann and Michael A Bender. Efficient asynchronous consensus with the value-oblivious adversary scheduler. In *International Colloquium on Automata, Languages, and Programming*, pages 622–633. Springer, 1996.

[6] Baruch Awerbuch, Andrea Richa, and Christian Scheideler. A jamming-resistant mac protocol for single-hop wireless networks. In *Proceedings of the twenty-seventh ACM symposium on Principles of distributed computing*, pages 45–54. ACM, 2008.

[7] R. Bar-Yehuda, A. Israeli, and A. Itai. Multiple communication in multi-hop radio networks. *SIAM Journal on Computing*, 22(4):875–887, 1993.

[8] Reuven Bar-Yehuda, Oded Goldreich, and Alon Itai. On the time-complexity of broadcast in multi-hop radio networks: An exponential gap between determinism and randomization. *Journal of Computer and System Sciences*, 45(1):104–126, 1992.

[9] Michael A Bender, Martin Farach-Colton, Simai He, Bradley C Kuszmaul, and Charles E Leiserson. Adversarial contention resolution for simple channels. In *Proceedings of the seventeenth annual ACM symposium on Parallelism in algorithms and architectures*, pages 325–332. ACM, 2005.

[10] Michael A Bender, Jeremy T Fineman, Seth Gilbert, and Maxwell Young. How to scale exponential backoff: Constant throughput, polylog access attempts, and robustness. In *Proceedings of the Twenty-Seventh Annual ACM-SIAM Symposium on Discrete Algorithms*, pages 636–654. Society for Industrial and Applied Mathematics, 2016.

[11] Michael A Bender, Tsvi Kopelowitz, Seth Pettie, and Maxwell Young. Contention resolution with log-logstar channel accesses. In *STOC*, pages 499–508, 2016.

[12] Cynthia Dwork, Maurice Herlihy, and Orli Waarts. Contention in shared memory algorithms. *Journal of the ACM (JACM)*, 44(6):779–805, 1997.

[13] Faith Ellen, Danny Hendler, and Nir Shavit. On the inherent sequentiality of concurrent objects. *SIAM Journal on Computing*, 41(3):519–536, 2012.

[14] Jeremy T Fineman, Seth Gilbert, Fabian Kuhn, and Calvin Newport. Contention resolution on a fading channel. In *Proceedings of the 2016 ACM Symposium on Principles of Distributed Computing*, pages 155–164. ACM, 2016.

[15] Jeremy T Fineman, Calvin Newport, and Tonghe Wang. Contention resolution on multiple channels with collision detection. In *Proceedings of the 2016 ACM Symposium on Principles of Distributed Computing*, pages 175–184. ACM, 2016.

[16] Mohsen Ghaffari, Bernhard Haeupler, and Majid Khabbazian. Randomized broadcast in radio networks with collision detection. *Distributed Computing*, 28(6):407–422, 2015.

[17] Phillip B Gibbons, Yossi Matias, and Vijaya Ramachandran. The queue-read queue-write asynchronous PRAM model. In *European Conference on Parallel Processing*, pages 277–292. Springer, 1996.

[18] Phillip B Gibbons, Yossi Matias, and Vijaya Ramachandran. The queue-read queue-write PRAM model: Accounting for contention in parallel algorithms. *SIAM Journal on Computing*, pages 638–648, 1997.

[19] Gary Graunke and Shreekant Thakkar. Synchronization algorithms for shared-memory multiprocessors. *Computer*, 23(6):60–69, 1990.

[20] Bernhard Haeupler and David Wajc. A faster distributed radio broadcast primitive. In *Proceedings of the 2016 ACM Symposium on Principles of Distributed Computing*, pages 361–370. ACM, 2016.

[21] Danny Hendler and Shay Kutten. Constructing shared objects that are both robust and high-throughput. In *International Symposium on Distributed Computing*, pages 428–442. Springer, 2006.

[22] Maurice Herlihy. A methodology for implementing highly concurrent data structures. In *ACM SIGPLAN Notices*, volume 25, pages 197–206. ACM, 1990.

[23] Donald Ervin Knuth. *The art of computer programming: sorting and searching*, volume 3. Pearson Education, 1998.

[24] John M Mellor-Crummey and Michael L Scott. Algorithms for scalable synchronization on shared-memory multiprocessors. *ACM Transactions on Computer Systems (TOCS)*, 9(1):21–65, 1991.

[25] Robert M Metcalfe and David R Boggs. Ethernet: Distributed packet switching for local computer networks. *Communications of the ACM*, 19(7):395–404, 1976.

[26] Maged M Michael and Michael L Scott. Nonblocking algorithms and preemption-safe locking on multiprogrammed shared memory multiprocessors. *journal of parallel and distributed computing*, 51(1):1–26, 1998.

[27] William N Scherer III and Michael L Scott. Advanced contention management for dynamic software transactional memory. In *Proceedings of the twenty-fourth annual ACM symposium on Principles of distributed computing*, pages 240–248. ACM, 2005.

# A Layered Architecture for Erasure-Coded Consistent Distributed Storage

Kishori M. Konwar
EECS, MIT
kishori@csail.mit.edu

N. Prakash
EECS, MIT
prakashn@mit.edu

Nancy Lynch
EECS, MIT
lynch@csail.mit.edu

Muriel Médard
EECS, MIT
medard@mit.edu

## ABSTRACT

Motivated by emerging applications to the *edge computing* paradigm, we introduce a two-layer erasure-coded fault-tolerant distributed storage system offering atomic access for read and write operations. In edge computing, clients interact with an edge-layer of servers that is geographically near; the edge-layer in turn interacts with a back-end layer of servers. The edge-layer provides low latency access and temporary storage for client operations, and uses the back-end layer for persistent storage. Our algorithm, termed Layered Data Storage (LDS) algorithm, offers several features suitable for edge-computing systems, works under asynchronous message-passing environments, supports multiple readers and writers, and can tolerate $f_1 < n_1/2$ and $f_2 < n_2/3$ crash failures in the two layers having $n_1$ and $n_2$ servers, respectively. We use a class of erasure codes known as regenerating codes for storage of data in the back-end layer. The choice of regenerating codes, instead of popular choices like Reed-Solomon codes, not only optimizes the cost of back-end storage, but also helps in optimizing communication cost of read operations, when the value needs to be recreated all the way from the back-end. The two-layer architecture permits a modular implementation of atomicity and erasure-code protocols; the implementation of erasure-codes is mostly limited to interaction between the two layers. We prove liveness and atomicity of LDS, and also compute performance costs associated with read and write operations. In a system with $n_1 = \Theta(n_2), f_1 = \Theta(n_1), f_2 = \Theta(n_2)$, the write and read costs are respectively given by $\Theta(n_1)$ and $\Theta(1) + n_1\mathcal{I}(\delta > 0)$. Here $\delta$ is a parameter closely related to the number of write operations that are concurrent with the read operation, and $\mathcal{I}(\delta > 0)$ is 1 if $\delta > 0$, and 0 if $\delta = 0$. The cost of persistent storage in the back-end layer is $\Theta(1)$. The impact of temporary storage is minimally felt in a multi-object system running $N$ independent instances of LDS, where only a small fraction of the objects undergo concurrent accesses at any point during the execution. For the multi-object system, we identify a condition on the rate of concurrent writes in the system such that the overall storage cost is dominated by that of persistent storage in the back-end layer, and is given by $\Theta(N)$.


*PODC '17, July 25-27, 2017, Washington, DC, USA*

ACM ISBN 978-1-4503-4992-5/17/07...$15.00
https://doi.org/10.1145/3087801.3087832

## CCS CONCEPTS

• **Mathematics of computing** → **Coding theory**; • **Information systems** → **Distributed storage**; • **Theory of computation** → **Distributed algorithms**;

## KEYWORDS

object storage; asynchronous distributed network; edge computing; consistency; liveness; storage cost; communication cost; erasure codes; regenerating codes; fault tolerance

## 1 INTRODUCTION

We introduce a two-layer erasure-coded fault-tolerant distributed storage system offering atomic access [23] for read and write operations. Providing consistent access to stored data is a fundamental problem in distributed computing. The most desirable form of consistency is atomicity, which in simple terms, gives the users of the data service the impression that the various concurrent read and write operations take place sequentially. Our work is motivated by applications to decentralized *edge computing*, which is an emerging distributed computing paradigm where processing of data moves closer to the users instead of processing the entire data in distant data centers or cloud centers [4, 12, 24, 29]. Edge computing is considered to be a key enabler for Internet of Things. In this form of computing, the users or clients interact with servers in the edge of the network, which forms the first layer of servers. The edge servers in turn interact with a second layer servers in the back-end, which is either a distant data-center or a cloud center. Geographic proximity of edge servers to clients permits high speed operations between clients and the edge layer, whereas communication between the edge and the back-end layer is typically much slower [24]. Thus, it is desirable whenever possible to complete client operations via interaction only with the edge layer. The edge servers however are severely restricted in their total storage capacity. We envisage a system that handles millions of files, which we call objects; the edge servers clearly do not have the capacity to store all the objects for the entire duration of execution. In practice, at any given time, only a tiny fraction of all objects undergo concurrent accesses; in our system, the limited storage space in the edge layer acts as a temporary storage for those objects that are getting accessed. The second layer of servers provide permanent storage for all the objects for the entire duration of execution. The servers in the first layer act as virtual clients of the second layer servers.

An important requirement in edge-computing systems is to reduce the cost of operation of the back-end layer, by making efficient use of the edge layer [29]. Communication between the two layers, and persistent storage in the second layer contribute to the cost of operation of the second layer. We address both these factors in our system design. The layered approach to implementing an atomic storage service carries the advantage that, during intervals of high concurrency from write operations on any one object, the edge layer can be used to *retain* the more recent versions of the object that are being (concurrently) written, while *filtering* out the outdated versions. The ability to avoid writing every version to the second layer decreases the overall write communication cost between the two layers. Our architecture also permits the edge layer to be configured as a *proxy cache* layer for objects that are frequently read, and thus avoids the need to read from the back-end layer for such objects.

In this work, we use a recent class of erasure codes known as *regenerating codes* [8] for storage of data in the back-end layer. From a storage cost view-point, these are as efficient as popular erasure codes like Reed-Solomon codes [27]. In our system, usage of regenerating codes, instead of Reed-Solomon codes, provides the extra advantage of reducing read communication cost when the object needs to be recreated from the coded data in the cloud layer. Specifically, we rely on class of regenerating codes known as *minimum bandwidth regenerating codes* for simultaneously optimizing read and storage costs.

While this may be the first work that explicitly uses regenerating codes for consistent data storage, the study of erasure codes—like Reed-Solomon codes—in implementations of consistent distributed storage, is an active area of research by itself [6, 7, 11, 17, 30]. In the commonly used single-layer storage systems, for several regimes of operation, cost metrics of Reed-Solomon-code based implementations [1, 6, 11, 17] outperform those of replication based implementations [3]. In comparison with single layer systems, the layered architecture naturally permits a layering of the protocols needed to implement atomicity, and erasure code in the cloud layer. The protocols needed to implement atomicity are largely limited to interactions between the clients and the edge servers, while those needed to implement the erasure code are largely limited to interactions between the edge and cloud servers. From an engineering viewpoint, the modularity of our implementation makes it suitable even for situations that does not necessarily demand a two-layer system.

## 1.1 Our Algorithm for the Two-Layer System

We propose the *Layered Distributed Storage* (LDS) algorithm for implementing a multi-writer, multi-reader atomic storage service over a two-layer asynchronous network. The algorithm is designed to address the various requirements described above for edge computing systems. A write operation completes after writing the object value to the first layer; it does not wait for the first layer to store the corresponding coded data in the second layer. For a read operation, concurrency with write operations increases the chance of it being served directly from the first layer; otherwise, servers in the first layer *regenerate* coded data from the second layer, which are then relayed to the reader. Servers in the first layer interact with those of second layer via the well defined actions (which we call as *internal operations*) *write-to-L2* and *regenerate-from-L2* for implementing the regenerating code in the second layer. The algorithm is designed to tolerate $f_1 < n_1/2$ and $f_2 < n_2/3$ crash failures in the first and second layers, having $n_1$ and $n_2$ servers, respectively. We prove liveness and atomicity properties of the algorithm, and also calculate various performance costs. In a system with $n_1 = \Theta(n_2), f_1 = \Theta(n_1), f_2 = \Theta(n_2)$, the write and read costs are respectively given by $\Theta(n_1)$ and $\Theta(1) + n_1 \mathcal{I}(\delta > 0)$. Here $\delta$ is a parameter closely related to the number of write or internal *write-to-L2* operations that are concurrent with the read operation, and $\mathcal{I}(\delta > 0)$ is 1 if $\delta > 0$, and 0 if $\delta = 0$.. Our ability to reduce the read cost to $\Theta(1)$, when $\delta = 0$ comes from the usage of minimum bandwidth regenerating (MBR) codes (see Section 2). In order to ascertain the contribution of temporary storage cost to the overall storage cost, we carry out a multi-object (say $N$) analysis, where each of the $N$ objects is implemented by an independent instance of the LDS algorithm. The multi-object analysis assumes bounded latency for point-to-point channels. We identify conditions on the total number of concurrent write operations per unit time, such that the permanent storage cost in the second layer dominates the temporary storage cost in the first layer, and is given by $\Theta(N)$. Further, we compute bounds on completion times of successful client operations, under bounded latency.

## 1.2 Related Work

Replication based algorithms for implementing atomic shared memory appears in [3], [13]. The model in [13] uses a two-layer system, with one layer dedicated exclusively for meta-data, and other layer for storage. The model is suitable when actual data is much larger than meta-data, and permits easy scalability of the storage layer. However, clients interact with servers in both layers, and thus is not directly comparable to our model, where clients only interact with the first layer. Both [3], [13] use quorums for implementing atomicity; variations of these algorithms appear in practical systems like Cassandra [21]. Replication based algorithms in single-layer systems, for dynamic settings appear in RAMBO [22], DynaStore [2]. Dynamic setting allow servers to leave and enter the system; these algorithms rely on reconfiguration of quorums. Erasure-code based implementations of consistent data storage in single layer systems appear in [1, 6, 11, 17, 30]. Bounds on the performance costs for erasure-code based implementations appear in [7, 30]. In [5], [10], [15], erasure codes are used in algorithms for implementing atomic memory in settings that tolerate Byzantine failures. In [11, 14, 18], authors provide algorithms that permit repair of crashed servers (in a static setting), while implementing consistent storage. In the content of our work, it is of future interest to develop protocols for recovery of crashed servers in the second-layer, which implements permanent coded storage.

We rely on regenerating codes which were introduced in [8] with the motivation of enabling efficient repair of failed servers in distributed storage systems. For the same storage-overhead and resiliency, the communication cost for repair, termed repair-bandwidth, is substantially less than what is needed by popular codes like Reed-Solomon codes. There has been significant theoretical progress since the work of [8]; a survey appears in [9]. Several systems works show usefulness of these codes or their variations in practical systems for immutable data [20, 25, 28]. In this work, we cast internal read operations by virtual clients in the first layer as repair operations, and this enables us to reduce the overall read cost. We rely on code constructions from [26] for the existence of MBR codes needed in our work, and these codes offer *exact repair.* A different class of codes known as Random Linear Network Codes [16] permit implementation of regenerating codes via *functional repair.* These codes offer probabilistic guarantees, and permit near optimal operation of regenerating codes for any choice of operating point suggested by [8]. In the context of our work, it will be interesting to find out the probabilistic guarantees that can be obtained if we use RLNCs instead of the codes in [26].

System Model and definitions appear in Section 2. The pseudo code of the LDS algorithm, along with its description is presented in Section 3. In Section 4, we state several properties of the algorithm, which are tied together to prove its liveness and atomicity properties. Performance cost analysis appears in Section 5. Our conclusions appear in Section 6. Proofs of various claims can be found in an extended version of the paper [19].

## 2 SYSTEM MODEL AND DEFINITIONS

*Model of Computation.* We assume a distributed storage system consisting of asynchronous processes of three types: writers ($\mathcal{W}$), readers ($\mathcal{R}$) and servers ($\mathcal{S}$). The servers are organized into two logical layers $\mathcal{L}_1$ and $\mathcal{L}_2$, with $\mathcal{L}_i$ consisting of $n_i, i = 1,2$ servers. Each process has a unique id, and the ids are totally ordered. Client (reader/writer) interactions are limited to servers in $\mathcal{L}_1$, the servers in $\mathcal{L}_1$ in turn interact with servers in $\mathcal{L}_2$. Further, the servers in $\mathcal{L}_1$ and $\mathcal{L}_2$ are denoted by $\{s_1, s_2, \ldots, s_{n_1}\}$ and $\{s_{n_1+1}, s_{n_1+2}, \ldots, s_{n_1+n_2}\}$, respectively. We assume the clients to be well-formed, i.e., a client issues a new operation only after completion of its previous operation, if any. The $\mathcal{L}_1$-$\mathcal{L}_2$ interaction happens via the well defined actions *write-to-L2* and *regenerate-from-L2.* We will refer to these actions as internal operations initiated by the servers in $\mathcal{L}_1$. We assume a crash failure model for processes. Once a process crashes, it does not execute any further steps for the rest of the execution. The LDS algorithm is designed to tolerate $f_i$ crash failures in layer $\mathcal{L}_i, i = 1,2$, where $f_1 < n_1/2$ and $f_2 < n_2/3$. Any number of readers and writers can crash during the execution. Communication is modeled via reliable point-to-point links between any two processes. This means that as long as the destination process is non-faulty, any message sent on the link is guaranteed to eventually reach the destination process. The model allows the sender process to fail after placing the message in the channel; message-delivery depends only on whether the destination is non-faulty.

*Liveness and Atomicity.* We implement one object, say $x$, via the LDS algorithm supporting read/write operations. For multiple objects, we simply run multiple instances of the LDS algorithm. The object value $v$ come from the set $\mathcal{V}$; initially $v$ is set to a distinguished value $v_0$ ($\in \mathcal{V}$). Reader $r$ requests a read operation on object $x$. Similarly, a write operation is requested by a writer $w$. Each operation at a non-faulty client begins with an *invocation step* and terminates with a *response step.* An operation $\pi$ is *incomplete* in an execution when the invocation step of $\pi$ does not have the associated response step; otherwise we say that $\pi$ is *complete.* In an execution, we say that an operation (read or write) $\pi_1$ *precedes* another operation $\pi_2$, if the response step for $\pi_1$ precedes the invocation step of $\pi_2$. Two operations are *concurrent* if neither precedes the other.

By liveness, we mean that during any well-formed execution of the algorithm, any read or write operation initiated by a non-faulty reader or writer completes, despite the crash failure of any other client and up to $f_1$ server crashes in $\mathcal{L}_1$, and up to $f_2$ server crashes in $\mathcal{L}_2$. By atomicity of an execution, we mean that the read and write operations in the execution can be arranged in a sequential order that is consistent with the order of invocations and responses. We refer to [23] for formal definition of atomicity. We use the sufficient condition presented in Lemma 13.16 of [23] to prove atomicity of LDS.

*Regenerating Codes.* We introduce the framework as in [8], and then see its usage in our work. In the regenerating-code framework, a file $\mathcal{F}$ of size $B$ symbols is encoded and stored across $n$ servers such that each server stores $\alpha$ symbols. The symbols are assumed to be drawn from a finite field $\mathbb{F}_q$, for some $q$. The content from any $k$ servers ($k\alpha$ symbols) can be used to decode the original file $\mathcal{F}$. For repair of a failed server, the replacement server contacts any subset of $d \geq k$ surviving servers in the system, and downloads $\beta$ symbols from each of the $d$ servers. The $\beta$ symbols from a *helper* server is possibly a function of the $\alpha$ symbols in the server. The parameters of the code, say $C$, shall be denoted as $\{(n,k,d)(\alpha,\beta)\}$. It was shown in [8] that the file-size $B$ is upper bounded by $B \leq \sum_{i=0}^{k-1} \min(\alpha, (d-i)\beta)$. Two extreme points of operation correspond to the minimum storage overhead (MSR) operating point, with $B = k\alpha$ and minimum repair bandwidth (MBR) operating point, with $\alpha = d\beta$. In this work, we use codes at the MBR operating point. The file-size at the MBR point is give by $B_{MBR} = \sum_{i=0}^{k-1}(d-i)\beta$. We also focus on exact-repair codes, meaning that the content of a replacement server after repair is identical to what was stored in the server before crash failure (the framework permits *functional repair* [8] which we do not consider). Code constructions for any set of parameters at the MBR point appear in [26], and we rely on this work for existence of codes. In this work, the file $\mathcal{F}$ corresponds to the object value $v$ that is written.

In this work, we use an $\{(n = n_1 + n_2, k, d)(\alpha, \beta)\}$ MBR code $C$. The parameters $k$ and $d$ are such that $n_1 = 2f_1 + k$ and $n_2 = 2f_2 + d$. We define two additional codes $C_1$ and $C_2$ that are derived from the code $C$. The code $C_1$ is obtained by restricting attention to the first $n_1$ coded symbols of $C$, while the code $C_2$ is obtained by restricting attention to the last $n_2$ coded symbols of $C$. Thus if $[c_1\ c_2\ \ldots c_{n_1}\ c_{n_1+1}\ \ldots c_{n_1+n_2}], c_i \in \mathbb{F}_q^{\alpha}$ denotes a codeword of $C$, the vectors $[c_1\ c_2\ \ldots c_{n_1}]$ and $[c_{n_1+1}\ \ldots c_{n_1+n_2}]$ will be codewords of $C_1$ and $C_2$, respectively. We associate the code symbol $c_i$ with server $s_i$, $1 \leq i \leq n_1 + n2$.

The usage of these three codes is as follows. Each server in $\mathcal{L}_1$, having access to the object value $v$ (at an appropriate point in the execution) encodes $v$ using code $C_2$ and sends coded data $c_{n_1+i}$ to server $s_{n_1+i}$ in $\mathcal{L}_2, 1 \le i \le n_2$. During a read operation, a server say $s_j$ in $\mathcal{L}_1$ can potentially reconstruct the coded data $c_j$ using content from $\mathcal{L}_2$. Here we think of $c_j$ as part of the code $C$, and $c_j$ gets reconstructed via a repair procedure (invoked by server $s_j$ in $\mathcal{L}_1$) where the $d$ helper servers belong to $\mathcal{L}_2$. By operating at the MBR point, we minimize the cost that need by the server $s_j$ to reconstruct $c_j$. Finally, in our algorithm, we permit the possibility that the reader receives $k$ coded data elements from $k$ servers in $\mathcal{L}_1$, during a read operation. In this case, the reader uses the code $C_1$ to attempt decoding the object value $v$.

An important property of the MBR code construction in [26], which is needed in our algorithm, is the fact the a helper server only needs to know the index of the failed server, while computing the helper data, and does not need to know the indices of the other $d-1$ helpers whose helper data will be used in repair. Not all regenerating code constructions, including those of MBR codes, have this property that we need. In our work, a server $s_j \in \mathcal{L}_1$ requests for help from all servers in $\mathcal{L}_2$, and does not know a priori, the subset of $d$ servers that will form the helper servers. As we shall see in the algorithm, the server $s_j$ simply relies on the first $d$ responses that it receives, and considers these as the helper data for repair. In this case, it is crucial that any server in $\mathcal{L}_2$ that computes its $\beta$ symbols does so without any assumption on the specific set of $d$ servers in $\mathcal{L}_2$ that will eventually form the helper servers for the repair operation.

*Storage and Communication Costs.* The communication cost associated with a read or write operation is the (worst-case) size of the total data that gets transmitted in the messages sent as part of the operation. While calculating write-cost, we also include costs due to internal *write-to-L2* operations initiated as a result of the write, even though these internal *write-to-L2* operations do not influence the termination point of the write operation. The storage cost at any point in the execution is the worst-case total amount of data that is stored in the servers in $\mathcal{L}_1$ and $\mathcal{L}_2$. The total data in $\mathcal{L}_1$ contributes to temporary storage cost, while that in $\mathcal{L}_2$ contributes to permanent storage cost. Costs contributed by meta-data (data for book keeping such as tags, counters, etc.) are ignored while ascertaining either storage or communication costs. Further the costs are normalized by the size of $v$; in other words, costs are expressed as though size of $v$ is 1 unit.

## 3 *LDS* ALGORITHM

In this section, we present the *LDS* algorithm. The protocols for clients, servers in $\mathcal{L}_1$ and servers in $\mathcal{L}_2$ appear in Figs. 1, 2 and 3 respectively. Tags are used for version control of object values. A tag $t$ is defined as a pair $(z, w)$, where $z \in \mathbb{N}$ and $w \in \mathcal{W}$ denotes the ID of a writer. We use $\mathcal{T}$ to denote the set of all possible tags. For any two tags $t_1, t_2 \in \mathcal{T}$ we say $t_2 > t_1$ if $(i)$ $t_2.z > t_1.z$ or $(ii)$ $t_2.z = t_1.z$ and $t_2.w > t_1.w$. The relation $>$ imposes a total order on the set $\mathcal{T}$.

Each server $s$ in $\mathcal{L}_1$ maintains the following state variables: $a)$ a list $L \subseteq \mathcal{T} \times \mathcal{V}$, which forms a temporary storage for tag-value pairs received as part of write operations, $b)$ $\Gamma \subseteq \mathcal{R} \times \mathcal{T}$, which indicates the set of readers being currently served. The pair $(r, t_{req}) \in \Gamma$ indicates that the reader $r$ requested for tag $t_{req}$ during the read operation. $c)$ $t_c$: committed tag at the server, $d)$ $K$ : a key-value set used by the server as part of internal *regenerate-from-L2* operations. The keys belong to $\mathcal{R}$, and values belong to $\mathcal{T} \times \mathcal{H}$. Here $\mathcal{H}$ denotes the set of all possible helper data corresponding to coded data elements $\{c_s(v), v \in \mathcal{V}\}$. Entries of $\mathcal{H}$ belong to $\mathbb{F}_q^{\beta}$. In addition to these, the server also maintains three counter variables for various operations. The state variable for a server in $\mathcal{L}_2$ simply consists of one (tag, coded-element) pair. For any server $s$, we use the notation $s.y$ to refer its state variable $y$. Further, we write $s.y|_T$ to denote the value of $s.y$ at point $T$ of the execution. Following the spirit of I/O automata [23], an execution fragment of the algorithm is simply an alternating sequence of (the collection of all) states and actions. By an action, we mean a block of code executed by any one process without waiting for further external inputs.

In our algorithm, we use a *broadcast* primitive for certain meta-data message delivery. The primitive has the property that if the message is consumed by any one server in $\mathcal{L}_1$, the same message is eventually consumed by every non-faulty server in $\mathcal{L}_1$. An implementation of the primitive, on top of reliable communication channels (as in our model), can be found in [17]. In this implementation, the idea is that the process that invokes the broadcast protocol first sends, via point-to-point channels, the message to a fixed set $S_{f_1+1}$ of $f_1+1$ servers in $\mathcal{L}_1$. Each of these servers, upon reception of the message for first time, sends it to all the servers in $\mathcal{L}_1$, before consuming the message itself. The primitive helps in the scenario when the process that invokes the broadcast protocol crashes before sending the message to all servers.

### 3.1 Write Operation

The write operation has two phases, and aims to temporarily store the object value $v$ in $\mathcal{L}_1$ such that up to $f_1$ failures in $\mathcal{L}_1$ does not result in loss of the value. During the first phase *get-tag*, the writer $w$ determines the new tag for the value to be written. To this end, the writer queries all servers in $\mathcal{L}_1$ for maximum tags, and awaits responses from $f_1+k$ servers in $\mathcal{L}_1$. Each server that gets the *get-tag* request responds with the maximum tag present in the list $L$, i.e. $\max_{(t,*) \in L} t$. The writer picks the maximum tag, say $t$, from among the responses, and creates a new and higher tag $t_w = tag(\pi)$.

In the second phase *put-data*, the writer sends the new (tag, value) pair to all severs in $\mathcal{L}_1$, and awaits acknowledgments from $f_1+k$ servers in $\mathcal{L}_1$. A server that receives the new (tag, value) pair $(t_{in}, v_{in})$ as a first step uses the *broadcast* primitive to send a data-reception message to all servers in $\mathcal{L}_1$. Note that this message contains only meta-data information and not the actual value. Each server $s \in \mathcal{L}_1$ maintains a committed tag variable $t_c$ to indicate the highest tag that the server either finished writing or is currently writing to $\mathcal{L}_2$. After sending the broadcast message, the server adds the pair $(t_{in}, v_{in})$ to its temporary storage list $L$ if $t_{in} > t_c$. If $t_{in} < t_c$, the server simply sends an acknowledgment back to the writer, and completes its participation in the ongoing write operation. If the server adds the pair $(t_{in}, v_{in})$ to $L$, it waits to hear the *broadcast* message regarding the ongoing write operation from at least $f_1+k$ servers before sending acknowledgment to the writer $w$. We implement this via the *broadcast-resp* action. It may be noted

**Fig. 1** The *LDS* algorithm for a writer $w \in \mathcal{W}$ and reader $r \in \mathcal{R}$.

*LDS* steps at a writer $w$:

<u>*get-tag*</u>:
  Send QUERY-TAG to servers in $\mathcal{L}_1$
  Wait for responses from $f_1 + k$ servers, and select max tag $t$.

<u>*put-data*</u>:
  Create new tag $t_w = (t.z + 1, w)$.
  Send (PUT-DATA, $(t_w, v)$) to servers in $\mathcal{L}_1$
  Wait for responses from $f_1 + k$ servers in $\mathcal{L}_1$, and terminate

*LDS* steps at a reader $r$:

<u>*get-commited-tag*</u>:
  Send QUERY-COMM-TAG to servers in $\mathcal{L}_1$
  Await $f_1 + k$ responses, and select max tag $t_{req}$

<u>*get-data*</u>:
  Send (QUERY-DATA, $t_{req}$) to servers in $\mathcal{L}_1$
  Await responses from $f_1 + k$ servers such that at least one of them is a (tag, value) pair, or at least $k$ of them are (tag, coded-element) pairs corresponding to some common tag. In the latter case, decode corresponding value using code $C_1$. Select the $(t_r, v_r)$ pair corresponding to the highest tag, from the available (tag, value) pairs.

<u>*put-tag*</u>:
  Send (PUT-TAG, $t_r$) to servers in $\mathcal{L}_1$
  Await responses from $f_1 + k$ servers in $\mathcal{L}_1$. Return $v_r$

that a server sends acknowledgment to writer via the *broadcast-resp* action only if it had added the (tag, value) pair to $L$ during the *put-data-resp* action.

## 3.2 Additional Steps during *broadcast-resp*

The server performs a few additional steps during the *broadcast-resp* action, and these aid ongoing read operations, garbage collection of the temporary storage, and also help to offload the coded elements to $\mathcal{L}_2$. The execution of these additional steps do not affect the termination point of the write operation. We explain these steps next.

<u>*Update committed tag $t_c$:*</u> The server checks if $t_{in}$ is greater than the committed tag $t_c$, and if so updates the $t_c$ to $t_{in}$. We note that even though the server added $(t_{in}, v_{in})$ to $L$ only after checking $t_{in} > t_c$, the committed tag might have advanced due to concurrent write operations corresponding to higher tags and thus it is possible that $t_{in} < t_c$ when the server does the check. Also, if $t_{in} > t_c$, it cab be shown that $(t_{in}, v_{in}) \in L$. In other words the value $v_{in}$ has not been garbage collected yet from the temporary storage $L$. We explain the mechanism of garbage collection shortly.

<u>*Serve outstanding read requests:*</u> The server sends the pair $(t_{in}, v_{in})$ to any outstanding read request whose requested tag $t_{req} \leq t_{in}$. In this case, the server also considers the read operation as being served and will not send any further message to the corresponding reader. We note this is only one of the various possibilities to serve a reader. Read operation is discussed in detail later.

<u>*Garbage collection of older tags:*</u> Garbage collection happens in two ways in our algorithm. We explain one of those here, the other will be explained as part of the description of the internal *write-to-L2* operation. The server replaces any (tag, value) pair $(t, v)$ in the list $L$ corresponding to $t < t_c = t_{in}$ with $(t, \perp)$, and thus removing the value associated with tags which are less than the committed tag. The combination of our method of updating the committed tag and garbage collection described here ensures that during intervals of concurrency from multiple write operations, we only offload the more recent (tag, value) pairs (after the tags get committed) to the back-end layer. Also the garbage collection described here eliminates values corresponding to older write operations which might have failed during the execution (and thus, which will not get a chance to get garbage collected via the second option which we describe below).

<u>*Internal write-to-L2 operation:*</u> The server computes the coded elements $\{c_{n_1+1}, \ldots, c_{n_1+n_2}\}$ corresponding to value $v_{in}$ and sends $(t_{in}, c_{n_1+i})$ to server $s_{n_1+i}$ in $\mathcal{L}_2$, $1 \leq i \leq n_2$. In our algorithm, each server in $\mathcal{L}_2$ stores coded data corresponding to exactly one tag at any point during the execution. A server in $\mathcal{L}_2$ that receives (tag, coded-element) pair $(t, c)$ as part of an internal *write-to-L2* operation replaces the local pair (tag, coded-element) pair $(t_\ell, c_\ell)$ with the incoming one if $t > t_\ell$. The *write-to-L2* operation initiated by server $s \in \mathcal{L}_1$ terminates after it receives acknowledgments from $f_1 + d$ servers in $\mathcal{L}_2$. Before terminating, the server also garbage collects the pair $(t_{in}, v_{in})$ from its list.

A pictorial illustration of the events that occur as a result of an initiation of a *put-data* phase by a writer is shown in Fig. 4.

## 3.3 Read operation

The idea behind the read operation is that the reader gets served (tag, value) pairs from temporary storage in $\mathcal{L}_1$, if it overlaps with concurrent write or internal *write-to-L2* operations. If not, servers in $\mathcal{L}_1$ regenerate (tag, coded-element) pairs via *regenerate-from-L2* operations, which are then sent to the reader. In the latter case, the reader needs to decode the value $v$ using the code $C_1$. A read operation consists of three phases. During the first phase *get-commited-tag*, the reader identifies the minimum tag, $t_{req}$, whose corresponding value it can return at the end of the operation. Towards this, the reader collects committed tags from $f_1 + k$ servers in

**Fig. 2** The *LDS* algorithm for any server in $\mathcal{L}_1$.

```
LDS state variables & steps at an L1 server, s_j:
State Variables:
    L ⊆ T × V, initially {(t_0, ⊥)}
    Γ ⊆ R × T, initially empty
    t_c ∈ T initially t_c = t_0
    commitCounter[t] : t ∈ T, initially 0 ∀t ∈ T
    readCounter[r]: r ∈ R, initially 0 ∀r ∈ R
    writeCounter[t]: t ∈ T, initially 0 ∀t ∈ T
    K : key-value set; keys from R, values from T × H

get-tag-resp (QUERY-TAG) from w ∈ W:
    send max{t : (t, *) ∈ L} to w

put-data-resp (PUT-DATA, (t_in, v_in)) received:
    broadcast(COMMIT-TAG, t_in) to L1
    if t_in > t_c then
        L ← L ∪ {(t_in, v_in)}
    else
        send ACK to writer w of tag t_in

broadcast-resp (COMMIT-TAG, t_in) received:
    commitCounter[t_in] ← commitCounter[t_in] + 1
    if (t_in, *) ∈ L ∧ commitCounter[t_in] ≥ f_1 + k then
        send ACK to writer w of tag t_in
        if t_in > t_c then
            t_c ← t_in
            for each γ ∈ Γ such that t_c ≥ γ.t_req,
                send (t_in, v_in) to reader γ.r
                Γ ← Γ − {γ}
            for each (t, *) ∈ L s.t. t < t_c //delete older value
                L ← L − {(t, *)} ∪ {(t, ⊥)}
            initiate write-to-L2(t_in, v_in) // write v_in to L2

write-to-L2(t_in, v_in):
    for each s_{n1+i} ∈ L2
        Compute coded element c_{n1+i} for value v
        send (WRITE-CODE-ELEM, (t_in, c_{n1+i})) to s

write-to-L2-complete (ACK-CODE-ELEM, t) received:
    writeCounter[t] ← writeCounter[t] + 1
    if writeCounter[t] = n_2 − f_2 then
        L ← L − {(t, *)} ∪ {(t, ⊥)}

get-commited-tag-resp (QUERY-COMM-TAG) from r ∈ R:
    send t_c to r

get-data-resp (QUERY-DATA, t_req) from r ∈ R:
    if (t_req, v_req) ∈ L then
        send (t_req, v_req) to reader r
    else
        if t_c > t_req ∧ (t_c, v_c) ∈ L then
            send (t_c, v_c) to reader r
        else
            Γ ← Γ ∪ {(r, t_req)}
            initiate regenerate-from-L2(r)

regenerate-from-L2(r):
    for each s ∈ L2
        send (QUERY-CODE-ELEM, r) to s

regenerate-from-L2-complete(SEND-HELPER-ELEM, (r, t, h_{n1+i,j})) recv:
    readCounter[r] ← readCounter[r] + 1
    K[r] ← K[r] ∪ {(t, h_{n1+i,j})}
    if readerCounter[r] = n_2 − f_2 = f_2 + d then
        (t̂, ĉ_j) ← regenerate highest possible tag using K[r]
        //(⊥, ⊥) if failed to regenerate any tag
        clear K[r]
        if ĉ_j ≠ ⊥ ∧ t̂ ≥ γ.t_req then // where γ = (r, t_req)
            send (t̂, ĉ_j) to r
        else
            send (⊥, ⊥) to r

put-tag-resp (PUT-TAG, (t_in)) received from r ∈ R:
    Γ ← Γ − {γ'} // γ' = (r, t_req)
    if t_in > t_c then
        t_c ← t_in
        if (t_c, v_c) ∈ L then
            for each γ ∈ Γ s. t. t_c ≥ γ.t_req
                send (t_c, v_c) to reader γ.r,
                Γ ← Γ − {γ}.
            initiate write-to-L2(t_in, v_in)
        else
            L ← L ∪ {(t_c, ⊥)}
            t̄ ← max{t : t < t_c ∧ (t, v) ∈ L}
            // t̄ =⊥, if none exists
            for each γ ∈ Γ such that t̄ ≥ γ.t_req,
                send (t̄, v̄) to reader γ.r
                Γ ← Γ − {γ}
        for each (t, *) ∈ L s.t. t < t_c
            L ← L − {(t, *)} ∪ {(t, ⊥)}
    send ACK to r
```

$\mathcal{L}_1$, and computes the requested tag $t_{req}$ as the maximum of these $f_1 + k$ committed tags.

During the second *get-data* phase, the reader sends $t_{req}$ to all the servers in $\mathcal{L}_1$, awaits responses from $f_1 + k$ distinct servers such that 1) at least one of the responses contains a tag-value pair, say $(t_r, v_r)$, $t_r \geq t_{req}$ or 2) at least $k$ of the responses contain coded elements corresponding to some fixed tag, say $t_r$ such that $t_r \geq t_{req}$. In the latter case, the reader uses the code $C_2$ to decode the value $v_r$ corresponding to tag $t_r$. If more than one candidate is found for the (tag, value) pair that can be returned, the reader picks the pair

**Fig. 3** The *LDS* algorithm for any server in $\mathcal{L}_2$ .

*LDS* state variables & steps at an $\mathcal{L}_2$ server $s_{n_1+i}$:

State Variables:

$(t, c) \in \mathcal{T} \times \mathbb{F}_q^{\alpha}$, initially $(t_0, c_0)$

*write-to-L2-resp* (WRITE-CODE-ELEM, $(t_{in}, c_{in})$) from $s_j$:

**if** $t_{in} > t$ **then**

$(t, c) \leftarrow (t_{in}, c_{in})$

send (ACK-CODE-ELEM, $t_{in}$) to $s_j$

*regenerate-from-L2-resp*(QUERY-CODE-ELEM, $r$) from $s_j$:

Compute helper data $h_{n_1+i,j} \in \mathbb{F}_q^{\beta}$ for repairing $c_j$

send (SEND-HELPER-ELEM, $(r, t, h_{n_1+i,j})$) to $s_j$

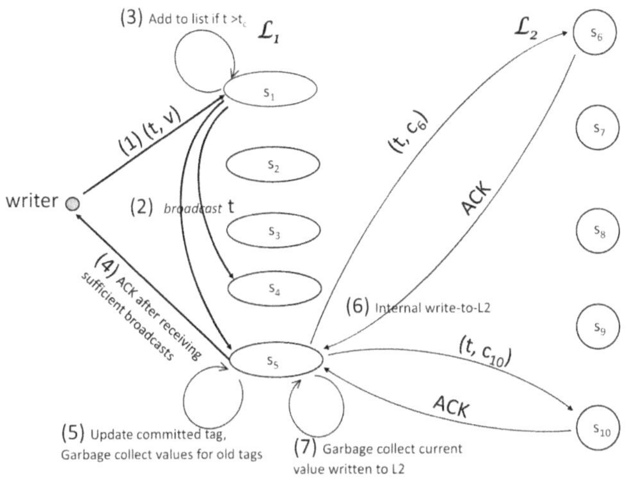


**Figure 4: An illustration of the events that occur as a result of an initiation of a *put-data* phase by a writer. The illustration is only representative, and does not cover all possible executions. In this illustration, the steps occur in the order** (1), (2) **and so on. Steps** (5), (6), (7) **occur after sending ACK to the writer, and hence does not affect the termination point of the write operation.**

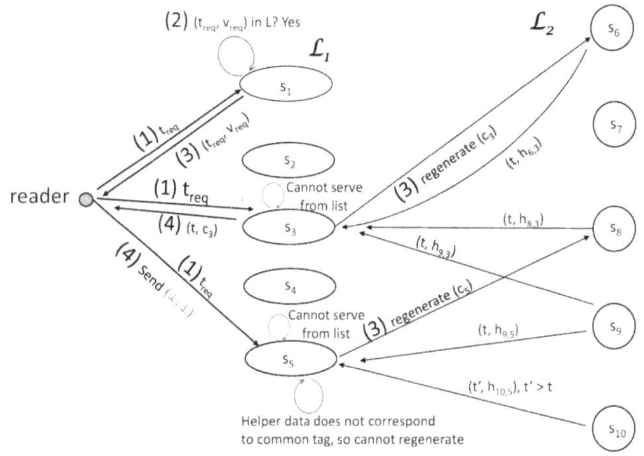


**Figure 5: An illustration of the events that occur as a result of an initiation of a *get-data* phase by a reader. Once again, the illustration is only representative, and does not cover all possible executions. Server $s_1$ responds to the reader using content from local list, server $s_3$ regenerates successfully, server $s_5$ fails to regenerate successfully.**

corresponding to the maximum tag. From the servers' point of view, a server $s \in \mathcal{L}_1$ upon reception of the *get-data* request checks if either $(t_{req}, v_{req})$ or $(t_c, v_c), t_c > t_{req}$ is in its list; in this case, $s$ responds immediately to the reader with the corresponding pair. Otherwise, $s$ adds the reader to its list $\Gamma$ of outstanding readers, initiates an internal *regenerate-from-L2* operation in which $s$ attempts to regenerate a tag-coded data element pair $(t', c'_s), t' \geq t_{req}$ via a repair process taking help from servers in $\mathcal{L}_2$. Towards this, the server $s$ contacts all servers in $\mathcal{L}_2$, and each server $\bar{s} \in \mathcal{L}_2$, using its state variable $(\bar{t}, \bar{c}_s)$, computes and sends the helper data $(\bar{t}, \bar{h}_s)$ back to the server $s$. We note that the MBR code that we use (from [26]) has the property that $\bar{h}_s$ can be uniquely computed given $\bar{c}_s$ and the id of the server $s$ which invokes the *regenerate-from-L2* operation. The server $s$ waits for $d + f_2$ responses, and if at least $d$ responses correspond to a common tag, say $t', t' \geq t_{req}$, regenerates the pair $(t', c')$, and sends $(t', c')$ back to the reader. It is possible that regeneration fails, and this can happen in two ways: 1) the server $s$ regenerates a pair $(t'', c'')$, however $t'' < t_{req}$, 2) among the $f_2 + d$ responses received by the server $s$, there is no subset of $d$ responses corresponding to a common tag. In our algorithm, if regeneration from $\mathcal{L}_2$ fails, the server $s$ simply sends $(\perp, \perp)$ back to the reader. The reader interprets the response $(\perp, \perp)$ as a sign of unsuccessful regeneration. We note that irrespective of if regeneration succeeds or not, the server does not remove the reader from its list of outstanding readers. In the algorithm, we allow the server $s$ to respond to a registered reader with a tag-value pair, during the *broadcast-resp* action as explained earlier. It is possible that while the server awaits responses from $\mathcal{L}_2$ towards regeneration, a new tag $t$ gets committed by $s$ via the *broadcast-resp* action; in this case, if $t \geq t_c$, server $s$ sends $(t, v)$ to $r$, and also unregisters $r$ from its outstanding reader list. A pictorial illustration of the events that occur as a result of an initiation of a *get-data* phase by a writer is shown in Fig. 5.

In the third phase *put-tag*, the reader *writes-back* tag $t_r$ corresponding to $v_r$, and ensures that at least $f_1 + k$ servers in $\mathcal{L}_1$ have their committed tags at least as high as $t_r$, before the read operation completes. However, the value $v_r$ is not written back in this third phase, and this is important to decrease the read cost. When a server $s \in \mathcal{L}_1$ receives the *put-tag* request for tag $t_r$, it checks if $(t_r, v_t)$ is in its list. In this case, the server thinks of the *put-tag* request simply as a proxy for having encountered the event $commitCounter[t_r] = f_1 + k$ during the *broadcast-resp* action, and carries out all the steps that it would have done during the the *broadcast-resp* action (except sending an ACK to the writer). However, if the server sees the tag $t_r$ for the first time during the execution, it still updates its committed tag to $t_r$, and simply adds $(t_r, \perp)$ to its list. Further, the server carries out a sequence of steps similar to the case when $(t_r, v_r) \in L$ (except initiating *write-to-L2*) before sending ACK to reader. The third phase also helps in unregistering the reader from the servers in $\mathcal{L}_1$.

# 4 PROPERTIES OF THE ALGORITHM

We state several interesting properties of the LDS algorithm. These will be found useful while proving the liveness and atomicity properties of the algorithm. We let $S_a \subset \mathcal{L}_1, |S_a| = f_1 + k$ to denote the set of $f_1 + k$ servers in $\mathcal{L}_1$ that never crash fail during the execution. The following lemmas are only applicable to servers that are alive at the concerned point(s) of execution appearing in the lemmas.

For every operation $\pi$ in $\Pi$ corresponding to a non-faulty reader or writer, we associate a $(tag, value)$ pair that we denote as $(tag(\pi), value(\pi))$. For a write operation $\pi$, we define the $(tag(\pi), value(\pi))$ pair as the message $(t_w, v)$ which the writer sends in the *put-data* phase. If $\pi$ is a read, we define the $(tag(\pi), value(\pi))$ pair as $(t_r, v)$ where $v$ is the value that gets returned, and $t_r$ is the associated tag. We also define tags, in a similar manner for those failed write operations that at least managed to complete the first round of the write operation. This is simply the tag $t_w$ that the writer would use in *put-data* phase, if it were alive. In our discussion, we ignore writes that failed before completion of the first round.

For any two points $T_1, T_2$ in an execution of LDS, we say $T_1 < T_2$ if $T_1$ occurs earlier than $T_2$ in the execution. The following three lemmas describe properties of committed tag $t_c$, and tags in the list.

LEMMA 4.1 (**Monotonicity of committed tag**). *Consider any two points $T_1$ and $T_2$ in an execution of LDS, such that $T_1 < T_2$. Then, for any server $s \in \mathcal{L}_1$, $s.tc|_{T_1} \leq s.tc|_{T_2}$.*

LEMMA 4.2 (**Garbage collection of older tags**). *For any server $s \in \mathcal{L}_1$, at any point $T$ in an execution of LDS, if $(t, v) \in s.L|_T$, we have $t \geq s.t_c|_T$.*

LEMMA 4.3 (**Persistence of tags corresponding to completed operations**). *Consider any successful write or read operation $\phi$ in an execution of LDS, and let $T$ be any point in the execution after $\phi$ completes. For any set $S'$ of $f_1 + k$ servers in $\mathcal{L}_1$ that are non-faulty at $T$, there exists $s \in S'$ such that $s.t_c|_T \geq tag(\phi)$ and $\max\{t : (t, *) \in s.L|_T\} \geq tag(\phi)$.*

The following lemma shows that an internal *regenerate-from-L2* operation respects previously completed internal *write-to-L2* operations. Our assumption that $f_2 < n_2/3$ is used in the proof of this lemma.

LEMMA 4.4 (**Consistency of Internal Reads with respect to Internal Writes**). *Let $\sigma_2$ denote a successful internal write-to-L2$(t, v)$ operation executed by some server in $\mathcal{L}_1$. Next, consider an internal regenerate-from-L2 operation $\pi_2$, initiated after the completion of $\sigma_2$, by a server $s \in \mathcal{L}_1$ such that a tag-coded-element pair, say $(t', c')$ was successfully regenerated by the server $s$. Then, $t' \geq t$; i.e., the regenerated tag is at least as high as what was written before the read started.*

The following three lemmas are central to prove the liveness of read operations.

LEMMA 4.5 (**If internal** *regenerate-from-L2* **operation fails**). *Consider an internal regenerate-from-L2 operation initiated at point $T$ of the execution by a server $s_1 \in \mathcal{L}_1$ such that $s_1$ failed to regenerate any tag-coded-element pair based on the responses. Then, there exists a point $\widetilde{T} > T$ in the execution such that the following statement is true: There exists a subset $S_b$ of $S_a$ such that $|S_b| = k$, and $\forall s' \in S_b$ $(\widetilde{t}, \widetilde{v}) \in s'.L|_{\widetilde{T}}$, where $\widetilde{t} = \max_{s \in \mathcal{L}_1} s.tc|_{\widetilde{T}}$.*

LEMMA 4.6 (**If internal** *regenerate-from-L2* **operation regenerates a tag older than the request tag**). *Consider an internal regenerate-from-L2 operation initiated at point $T$ of the execution by a server $s_1 \in \mathcal{L}_1$ such that $s_1$ only manages to regenerate $(t, c)$ based on the responses, where $t < t_{req}$. Here $t_{req}$ is the tag sent by the associated reader during the get-data phase. Then, there exists a point $\widetilde{T} > T$ in the execution such that the following statement is true: There exists a subset $S_b$ of $S_a$ such that $|S_b| = k$, and $\forall s' \in S_b$ $(\widetilde{t}, \widetilde{v}) \in s'.L|_{\widetilde{T}}$, where $\widetilde{t} = \max_{s \in \mathcal{L}_1} s.tc|_{\widetilde{T}}$.*

LEMMA 4.7 (**If two Internal** *regenerate-from-L2* **operations regenerate differing tags**). *Consider internal regenerate-from-L2 operations initiated at points $T$ and $T'$ of the execution, respectively by servers $s$ and $s'$ in $\mathcal{L}_1$. Suppose that $s$ and $s'$ regenerate tags $t$ and $t'$ such that $t < t'$. Then, there exists a point $\widetilde{T} > T$ in the execution such that the following statement is true: There exists a subset $S_b$ of $S_a$ such that $|S_b| = k$, and $\forall s' \in S_b$ $(\widetilde{t}, \widetilde{v}) \in s'.L|_{\widetilde{T}}$, where $\widetilde{t} = \max_{s \in \mathcal{L}_1} s.tc|_{\widetilde{T}}$.*

THEOREM 4.8 (**Liveness**). *Consider any well-formed execution of the LDS algorithm, where at most $f_1 < n_1/2$ and $f_2 < n_2/3$ servers crash fail in layers $\mathcal{L}_1$ and $\mathcal{L}_2$, respectively. Then every operation associated with a non-faulty client completes.*

THEOREM 4.9 (**Atomicity**). *Every well-formed execution of the LDS algorithm is atomic.*

# 5 COST COMPUTATION: STORAGE, COMMUNICATION AND LATENCY

In this section we discuss storage and communication costs associated with read/write operations, and also carry out a latency analysis of the algorithm, in which estimates for durations of successful client operations are provided. We also analyze a multi-object system, under bounded latency, to ascertain the contribution of temporary storage toward the overall storage cost. We calculate costs for a system in which the number of servers in the two layers are of the same order, i.e., $n_1 = \Theta(n_2)$. We further assume that the parameters $k, d$ of the regenerating code are such that $k = \Theta(n_2), d = \Theta(n_2)$. This assumption is consistent with usages of codes in practical systems.

In this analysis, we assume that corresponding to any failed write operation $\pi$, there exists a successful write operation $\pi'$ such that $tag(\pi') > tag(\pi)$. This essentially avoids pathological cases where the execution is a trail of only unsuccessful writes. Note that the restriction on the nature of execution was not imposed while proving liveness or atomicity.

Like in Section 4, our lemmas in this section apply only to servers that are non-faulty at the concerned point(s) of execution appearing in the lemmas. Also, we continue to ignore writes that failed before the completion of the first round.

LEMMA 5.1 (**Temporary Nature of $\mathcal{L}_1$ Storage**). *Consider a successful write operation $\pi \in \beta$. Then, there exists a point of execution $T_e(\pi)$ in $\beta$ such that for all $T' \geq T_e(\pi)$ in $\beta$, we have $s.t_c|_{T'} \geq tag(\pi)$ and $(t, v) \notin s.L|_{T'}, \forall s \in \mathcal{L}_1, t \leq tag(\pi)$.*

For a failed write operation $\pi \in \beta$, let $\pi'$ be the first successful write in $\beta$ such that $tag(\pi') > tag(\pi)$ (i,e., if we linearize all write operations, $\pi'$ is the first successful write operation that appears after $\pi$ - such a write operation exists because of our assumption in this section). Then, it is clear that for all $T' \geq T_e(\pi')$ in $\beta$, we have $(t, v) \notin s.L|_{T'}, \forall s \in \mathcal{L}_1, t \leq tag(\pi)$, and thus Lemma 5.1 indirectly applies to failed writes as well. Based on this observation, for any failed write $\pi \in \beta$, we define the termination point $T_{end}(\pi)$ of $\pi$ as the point $T_e(\pi')$, where $\pi'$ is the first successful write in $\beta$ such that $tag(\pi') > tag(\pi)$.

*Definition 5.2* (**Extended write operation**). Corresponding to any write operation $\pi \in \beta$, we define a hypothetical extended write operation $\pi_e$ such that $tag(\pi_e) = tag(\pi)$, $T_{start}(\pi_e) = T_{start}(\pi)$ and $T_{end}(\pi_e) = \max(T_{end}(\pi), T_e(\pi))$, where $T_e(\pi)$ is as obtained from Lemma 5.1.

The set of all extended write operations in $\beta$ shall be denoted by $\Pi_e$.

*Definition 5.3* (**Concurrency Parameter $\delta_\rho$**). Consider any successful read operation $\rho \in \beta$, and let $\pi_e$ denote the last extended write operation in $\beta$ that completed before the start of $\rho$. Let $\Sigma = \{\sigma_e \in \Pi_e | tag(\sigma) > tag(\pi_e)$ and $\sigma_e$ overlaps with $\rho\}$. We define concurrency parameter $\delta_\rho$ as the cardinality of the set $\Sigma$.

LEMMA 5.4 (**Write, Read Cost**). *The communication cost associated with any write operation in $\beta$ is given by $n_1 + n_1 n_2 \frac{2d}{k(2d-k+1)} = \Theta(n_1)$. The communication cost associated with any successful read operation $\rho$ in $\beta$ is given by $n_1(1 + \frac{n_2}{d})\frac{2d}{k(2d-k+1)} + n_1 I(\delta_\rho > 0) = \Theta(1) + n_1 I(\delta_\rho > 0)$. Here, $I(\delta_\rho > 0)$ is 1 if $\delta_\rho > 0$, and 0 if $\delta_\rho = 0$.*

REMARK 1. *Our ability to reduce the read cost to $\Theta(1)$ in the absence of concurrency from extended writes comes from the usage of regenerating codes at MBR point. Regenerating codes at other operating points are not guaranteed to give the same read cost. For instance, in a system with equal number of servers in either layer, also with identical fault-tolerance (i.e., $n_1 = n_2, f_1 = f_2$), it can be shown that usage of codes at the MSR point will imply that read cost is $\Omega(n_1)$ even if $\delta_\rho = 0$.*

LEMMA 5.5 (**Single Object Permanent Storage Cost**). *The (worst case) storage cost in $\mathcal{L}_2$ at any point in the execution of the LDS algorithm is given by $\frac{2dn_2}{k(2d-k+1)} = \Theta(1)$.*

REMARK 2. *Usage of MSR codes, instead of MBR codes, would give a storage cost of $\frac{n_2}{k} = \Theta(1)$. For fixed $n_2, k, d$, the storage-cost due to MBR codes is at most twice that of MSR codes. As long as we focus on order-results, MBR codes do well in terms of both storage and read costs; see Remark 1 as well.*

## 5.1 Bounded Latency Analysis

For bounded latency analysis, we assume the delay on the various point-to-point links are upper bounded as follows: 1) $\tau_1$, for any link between a client and a server in $\mathcal{L}_1$, 2) $\tau_2$, for any link between a server in $\mathcal{L}_1$ and a server in $\mathcal{L}_2$, and 3) $\tau_0$, for any link between two servers in $\mathcal{L}_1$. We also assume that the local computations on any process take negligible time when compared to delay on any of the links. In edge computing systems, $\tau_2$ is typically much higher than both $\tau_1$ and $\tau_0$.

LEMMA 5.6 (**Write, Read Latency**). *A successful write operation in $\beta$ completes within a duration of $4\tau_1 + 2\tau_0$. The associated extended write operation completes within a duration of $\max(3\tau_1 + 2\tau_0 + 2\tau_2, 4\tau_1 + 2\tau_0)$. A successful read operation in $\beta$ completes within a duration of $\max(6\tau_1 + 2\tau_2, 5\tau_1 + 2\tau_0 + \tau_2)$.*

#### 5.1.1 *Impact of Number of Concurrent Write Operations on Temporary Storage, via Multi-Object Analysis.*

Consider implementing $N$ atomic objects in our two-layer storage system, via $N$ independent instances of the LDS algorithm. The value of each of the objects is assumed to have size 1. Let $\theta$ denote an upper bounded on the total number of concurrent extended write operations experienced by the system within any duration of $\tau_1$ time units. We show that under appropriate conditions on $\theta$, the total storage cost is dominated by that of permanent storage in $\mathcal{L}_2$. We make the following simplifying assumptions: 1) System is symmetrical so that $n_1 = n_2, f_1 = f_2 (\implies k = d)$ 2) $\tau_0 = \tau_1$, and 3) All the invoked write operations are successful. We note that it is possible to relax any of these assumptions and give a more involved analysis. Also, let $\mu = \tau_2/\tau_1$.

LEMMA 5.7 (**Relative Cost of Temporary Storage**). *At any point in the execution, the worst case storage cost in $\mathcal{L}_1$ and $\mathcal{L}_2$ are upper bounded by $\lceil 5 + 2\mu \rceil \theta n_1$ and $\frac{2Nn_2}{k+1}$. Specifically, if $\theta << \frac{Nn_2}{kn_1\mu}$, the overall storage cost is dominated by that of permanent storage in $\mathcal{L}_2$, and is given by $\Theta(N)$.*

An illustration of Lemma 5.7 is provided in Fig. 6. In this example, we assume $n_1 = n_2 = 100, k = d = 80, \tau_2 = 10\tau_1$ and $\theta = 100$, and plot $\mathcal{L}_1$ and $\mathcal{L}_2$ storage costs as a function of the number $N$ of objects stored. As claimed in Lemma 5.7, for large $N$, overall storage cost is dominated by that of permanent storage in $\mathcal{L}_2$, and increases linearly with $N$. Also, for this example, we see that the $\mathcal{L}_2$ storage cost per object is less than 3. If we had used replication in $\mathcal{L}_2$ (along with a suitable algorithm), instead of MBR codes, the $\mathcal{L}_2$ storage cost per object would have been $n_2 = 100$.

# 6 CONCLUSION

In this paper we proposed a two-layer model for strongly consistent data-storage, while supporting read/write operations. Our model and LDS algorithm were both motivated by the proliferation of edge computing applications. In the model, the first layer is closer (in terms of network latency) to the clients and the second layer stores bulk data. In the presence of frequent read and write operations,

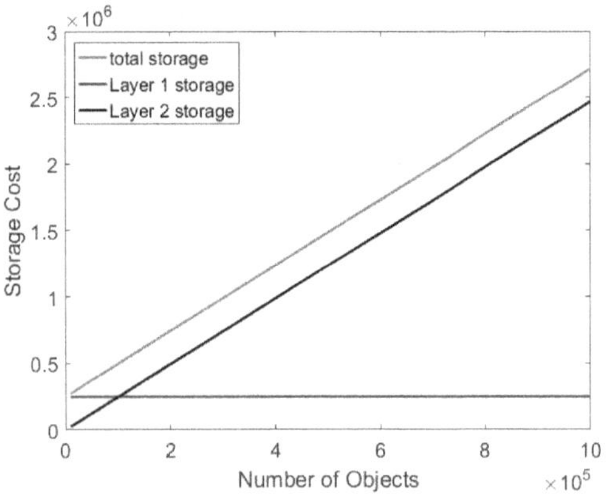


**Figure 6: Illustration of the variation of $\mathcal{L}_1$ and $\mathcal{L}_2$ storage costs as a function of the number of objects stored. In this example, we assume $n_1 = n_2 = 100, k = d = 80, \tau_2 = 10\tau_1$ and $\theta = 100$.**

most of the operations are served without the need to communicate with the back-end layer, thereby decreasing the latency of operations. In this regard, the first layer behaves as a proxy cache. In our algorithm, we use regenerating codes to simultaneously optimize storage and read costs. Several interesting avenues for future work exist. It is of interest to extend the framework to carry out repair of erasure-coded servers in $\mathcal{L}_2$. A model for repair in single-layer systems using erasure codes was proposed in [18]. The modularity of implementation possibly makes the repair problem in $\mathcal{L}_2$ simpler that the one in [18]. Furthermore, we would like to explore if the modularity of implementation could be advantageously used to implement a different consistency policy like regularity without affecting the implementation of the erasure codes in the back-end. Similarly, it is also of interest to study feasibility of other codes from the class of regenerating codes (like RLNCs [16]) in the back-end layer, without affecting client protocols.

## 7 ACKNOWLEDGMENTS

The work is supported in part by AFOSR under grants FA9550-13-1-0042, FA9550-14-1-043, FA9550-14-1-0403, and in part by NSF under awards CCF-1217506, CCF-0939370.

## REFERENCES


[1] M. K. Aguilera, R. Janakiraman, and L. Xu. 2005. Using erasure codes efficiently for storage in a distributed system. In *Proceedings of International Conference on Dependable Systems and Networks (DSN)*. 336–345.

[2] M. K. Aguilera, I. Keidar, D. Malkhi, and A. Shraer. 2011. Dynamic atomic storage without consensus. *J. ACM* (2011), 7:1–7:32.

[3] H. Attiya, A. Bar-Noy, and D. Dolev. 1996. Sharing Memory Robustly in Message Passing Systems. *J. ACM* 42(1) (1996), 124–142.

[4] Flavio Bonomi, Rodolfo Milito, Jiang Zhu, and Sateesh Addepalli. 2012. Fog Computing and Its Role in the Internet of Things. In *Proceedings of the First Ed. MCC Workshop Mobile Cloud Computing (MCC 12)*. 13âĂŞ–16.

[5] C. Cachin and S. Tessaro. 2006. Optimal Resilience for Erasure-Coded Byzantine Distributed Storage. In *Proceedings of International Conference on Dependable Systems and Networks (DSN)*. 115–124.

[6] V. R. Cadambe, N. A. Lynch, M. Médard, and P. M. Musial. 2014. A Coded Shared Atomic Memory Algorithm for Message Passing Architectures. In *Proceedings of 13th IEEE International Symposium on Network Computing and Applications (NCA)*. 253–260.

[7] Viveck R Cadambe, Zhiying Wang, and Nancy Lynch. 2016. Information-theoretic lower bounds on the storage cost of shared memory emulation. In *Proceedings of the 2016 ACM Symposium on Principles of Distributed Computing*. ACM, 305–313.

[8] Alexandros G Dimakis, P Brighten Godfrey, Yunnan Wu, Martin J Wainwright, and Kannan Ramchandran. 2010. Network coding for distributed storage systems. *Information Theory, IEEE Transactions on* 56, 9 (2010), 4539–4551.

[9] A. G. Dimakis, K. Ramchandran, Y. Wu, and C. Suh. 2011. A survey on network codes for distributed storage. *Proc. IEEE* 99, 3 (2011), 476–489.

[10] D. Dobre, G. Karame, W. Li, M. Majuntke, N. Suri, and M. Vukolić. 2013. PoWerStore: proofs of writing for efficient and robust storage. In *Proceedings of the 2013 ACM SIGSAC conference on Computer & communications security*. 285–298.

[11] P. Dutta, R. Guerraoui, and R. R. Levy. 2008. Optimistic Erasure-Coded Distributed Storage. In *Proceedings of the 22nd international symposium on Distributed Computing (DISC)*. Berlin, Heidelberg, 182–196.

[12] Dave Evans. 2011. The Internet of Things: How the Next Evolution of the Internet Is Changing Everything. *Cisco Internet Business Solutions Group (IBSG)* (2011).

[13] R. Fan and N. Lynch. 2003. Efficient Replication of Large Data Objects. In *Distributed algorithms (Lecture Notes in Computer Science)*. 75–91.

[14] R. Guerraoui, R. R. Levy, B. Pochon, and J. Pugh. 2008. The collective memory of amnesic processes. *ACM Trans. Algorithms* 4, 1 (2008), 1–31.

[15] J. Hendricks, G. R. Ganger, and M. K. Reiter. 2007. Low-overhead byzantine fault-tolerant storage. In *ACM SIGOPS Operating Systems Review*, Vol. 41. 73–86.

[16] T. Ho, M. Medard, R. Koetter, D. R. Karger, M. Effros, J. Shi, and B. Leong. 2006. A Random Linear Network Coding Approach to Multicast. *IEEE Transactions on Information Theory* 52, 10 (Oct 2006), 4413–4430.

[17] K. M. Konwar, N. Prakash, E. Kantor, N. Lynch, M. Medard, and A. A. Schwarzmann. 2016. Storage-Optimized Data-Atomic Algorithms for Handling Erasures and Errors in Distributed Storage Systems. In *30th IEEE International Parallel & Distributed Processing Symposium (IPDPS)*.

[18] Kishori M Konwar, N Prakash, Nancy Lynch, and Muriel Médard. 2016. RADON: Repairable atomic data object in networks. In *The International Conference on Distributed Systems (OPODIS)*.

[19] Kishori M. Konwar, N. Prakash, Nancy A. Lynch, and Muriel Médard. 2017. A Layered Architecture for Erasure-Coded Consistent Distributed Storage. *CoRR* abs/1703.01286 (2017). http://arxiv.org/abs/1703.01286

[20] M Nikhil Krishnan, N Prakash, V Lalitha, Birenjith Sasidharan, P Vijay Kumar, Srinivasan Narayanamurthy, Ranjit Kumar, and Siddhartha Nandi. 2014. Evaluation of Codes with Inherent Double Replication for Hadoop.. In *HotStorage*.

[21] Avinash Lakshman and Prashant Malik. 2010. Cassandra: A Decentralized Structured Storage System. *SIGOPS Oper. Syst. Rev.* 44, 2 (April 2010), 35–40.

[22] N. Lynch and A. A. Shvartsman. 2002. RAMBO: A reconfigurable atomic memory service for dynamic networks. In *Proceedings of 16th International Symposium on Distributed Computing (DISC)*. 173–190.

[23] N. A. Lynch. 1996. *Distributed Algorithms*. Morgan Kaufmann Publishers.

[24] Erik Nygren, Ramesh K. Sitaraman, and Jennifer Sun. 2010. The Akamai network: a platform for high-performance internet applications. *Operating Systems Review* 44 (2010), 2–19.

[25] K. V. Rashmi, P. Nakkiran, J. Wang, N. B. Shah, and K. Ramchandran. 2015. Having Your Cake and Eating It Too: Jointly Optimal Erasure Codes for I/O, Storage, and Network-bandwidth. In *13th USENIX Conference on File and Storage Technologies (FAST)*. 81–94.

[26] Korlakai Vinayak Rashmi, Nihar B Shah, and P Vijay Kumar. 2011. Optimal exact-regenerating codes for distributed storage at the MSR and MBR points via a product-matrix construction. *IEEE Transactions on Information Theory* 57, 8 (2011), 5227–5239.

[27] I. S. Reed and G. Solomon. 1960. Polynomial codes over certain finite fields. *Journal of the society for industrial and applied mathematics* 8, 2 (1960), 300–304.

[28] M. Sathiamoorthy, M. Asteris, D. Papailiopoulos, A. G. Dimakis, R. Vadali, S. Chen, and D. Borthakur. 2013. XORing elephants: novel erasure codes for big data. In *Proceedings of the 39th international conference on Very Large Data Bases*. 325–336.

[29] Weisong Shi, Jie Cao, Quan Zhang, Youhuizi Li Li, and Lanyu Xu. 2016. Edge Computing: Vision and Challenges. *IEEE INTERNET OF THINGS* 3, 5 (October 2016).

[30] Alexander Spiegelman, Yuval Cassuto, Gregory Chockler, and Idit Keidar. 2016. Space Bounds for Reliable Storage: Fundamental Limits of Coding. In *Proceedings of the 2016 ACM Symposium on Principles of Distributed Computing (PODC '16)*. ACM, New York, NY, USA.

# Seeing is Believing: A Client-Centric Specification of Database Isolation

Natacha Crooks
The University of Texas at Austin and Cornell University

Youer Pu
Cornell University

Lorenzo Alvisi
The University of Texas at Austin and Cornell University

Allen Clement
Google, Inc.

## ABSTRACT

This paper introduces the first *state-based* formalization of isolation guarantees. Our approach is premised on a simple observation: applications view storage systems as black-boxes that transition through a series of states, a subset of which are observed by applications. Defining isolation guarantees in terms of these states frees definitions from implementation-specific assumptions. It makes immediately clear what anomalies, if any, applications can expect to observe, thus bridging the gap that exists today between how isolation guarantees are defined and how they are perceived. The clarity that results from definitions based on client-observable states brings forth several benefits. First, it allows us to easily compare the guarantees of distinct, but semantically close, isolation guarantees. We find that several well-known guarantees, previously thought to be distinct, are in fact equivalent, and that many previously incomparable flavors of snapshot isolation can be organized in a clean hierarchy. Second, freeing definitions from implementation-specific artefacts can suggest more efficient implementations of the same isolation guarantee. We show how a client-centric implementation of parallel snapshot isolation can be more resilient to *slowdown cascades*, a common phenomenon in large-scale datacenters.

**ACM Reference format:**
Natacha Crooks, Youer Pu, Lorenzo Alvisi, and Allen Clement. 2017. Seeing is Believing: A Client-Centric Specification of Database Isolation. In *Proceedings of PODC '17, Washington, DC, USA, July 25-27, 2017,* 10 pages.
http://dx.doi.org/10.1145/3087801.3087802

## 1 INTRODUCTION

Large-scale applications such as Facebook [1], or Twitter [56] offload the managing of data at scale to replicated and/or distributed systems. These systems, which often span multiple regions or continents, must sustain high-throughput, guarantee low-latency, and remain available across failures. To meet these demands, commercial databases or distributed storage systems like MySQL [45], Oracle [46], or SQL Server [42] often give up serializability [47] (the gold-standard correctness criterion: an interleaved execution of transactions must be equivalent to a serial schedule) and instead privilege weaker but more scalable correctness criteria [2, 15, 34, 45, 49, 50, 53, 61] (referred to as *weak isolation*) such as snapshot isolation [15] or read committed [15]. In fact, to the best of our knowledge, almost all SQL databases use read committed as their default isolation level [39, 42, 45, 46, 50, 51], with some only supporting read-committed or snapshot isolation [45, 51][1].

This trend poses an additional burden on the application programmer, as these weaker isolation guarantees allow for counterintuitive application behaviors: relaxing the ordering of operations yields better performance, but introduces schedules and anomalies that could not arise if transactions executed atomically and sequentially. These anomalies may affect application logic: consider a bank account with a $50 balance and no overdraft allowed. If the application runs under read-committed [15], the underlying database may allow two transactions to concurrently withdraw $45, incorrectly leaving the account with a negative balance [15].

To mitigate this increased programming complexity, many commercial databases and distributed storage systems [14, 28, 29, 39–41, 45, 46, 50] interact with applications through a front-end that gives applications the illusion of querying or writing to a logically centralized, failure-free node that will scale as much as one's wallet will allow [28, 29, 39, 40, 46]. In practice, however, this abstraction is leaky: a careful understanding of the system that implements a given isolation level is oftentimes *necessary* to determine which anomalies the system will admit and how these will affect application correctness.

Indeed, the guarantees provided by isolation levels are often dependent on specific and occasionally implicit system properties—be it properties of storage (e.g., whether it is single or multiversioned [16]); of the chosen concurrency control (e.g., whether it is based on locking or timestamps [15]); or other system features (e.g., the existence of a centralized timestamp [27]).

Consider for example serializability [47]: the original ANSI SQL specification states that guaranteeing serializability is equivalent to preventing four phenomena [15]. This equivalence, however, only holds for lock-based, single version databases. Such implicit dependencies continue to have practical consequences: current multiversioned commercial databases that prevent these four phenomenas, such as Oracle 12c, claim to implement serializability, when they in fact implement the weaker notion of snapshot isolation [11, 27, 46]. As such, they accept non-serializable schedules akin to the schedule in Figure 1(r), an anomaly commonly referred to as *write skew* [15]. In contrast, a majority reject the (serializable)


*PODC '17, July 25-27, 2017, Washington, DC, USA*

ACM ISBN 978-1-4503-4992-5/17/07...$15.00
http://dx.doi.org/10.1145/3087801.3087802

[1] As of June 2017

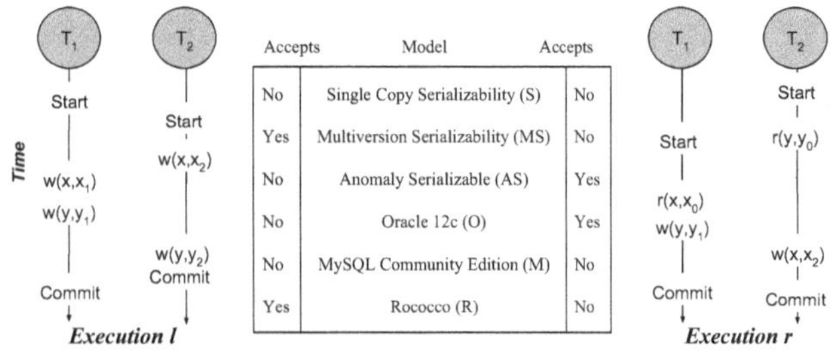


***Figure 1: Serializability. Abbreviations refer to: S[47], MS[17], AS[15] O[46], M[45], R[43].***

schedule of Figure 1(l) because, for performance reasons, these systems choose not reorder writes.

We submit that the root of this complexity is a fundamental semantic gap between how application programmers experience isolation guarantees and how they are currently formally defined. From a programmer's perspective, isolation guarantees are contracts between the storage systems and its clients, specifying the set of behaviors that clients can expect to observe—i.e., the set of admissible values that each read is allowed to return. When it comes to formally defining these guarantees, however, the current practice is to focus, rather than on the values that the clients can observe, on the *mechanisms* that can produce those values—i.e., histories capturing the relative ordering of low-level read and write operations.

Expressing isolation at such a low level of abstraction has significant drawbacks. First, it requires application programmers to reason about the ordering of operations that they cannot directly observe. Second, it makes it easy, as we have seen, to inadvertently contaminate what should be system-independent guarantees with system-specific assumptions. Third, by relying on operations that are only meaningful within one of the layers in the system's stack, it makes it hard to reason end-to-end about the system's guarantees.

To address these issues, we propose a new model that, for the first time, expresses isolation guarantees exclusively as *properties of states that applications can observe*, without relying on traditional notions—such as dependency graphs, histories, or version orders— that are instead invisible to applications. This new foundation comes at no cost in terms of generality or expressiveness: we offer below state-based and client-centric definitions of most modern isolation definitions, and prove that they are equivalent to their existing counterparts. It does, however, result in greater clarity, which yields significant benefits.

First, this model makes clear to developers what anomalies, if any, their applications can expect to observe, thus bridging the semantic gap between how isolation is experienced and how it is formalized. For example, we show (§5.1) how a state-based and client-centric definition brings immediately into focus the root cause of the write-skew anomaly, which distinguishes snapshot isolation from serializability.

Second, by removing the distorting effects of implementation artefacts, our approach makes it easy to compare the guarantees of distinct, but semantically close, isolation guarantees. The results are sometimes surprising. We prove (§5.2) that several well-known flavors of isolation in fact provide the same guarantees: *parallel snapshot isolation* (PSI) [20, 53] is equivalent to *lazy consistency* (PL-2+) [2, 3]; similarly, *generalized snapshot isolation* (GSI) [48] is actually equivalent to ANSI snapshot isolation (ANSI SI) [15], though GSI was proposed as a more scalable alternative to ANSI SI. Likewise, we also show that the lesser known *strong session SI* [24] and *prefix-consistent SI* [48] are also equivalent. Ultimately, the insights offered by state-based definitions enable us to organize in a clean hierarchy (§5.2) what used to be incomparable flavors of snapshot isolation [2, 9, 15, 24, 37, 48, 53].

Finally, by focusing on how clients perceive a given isolation guarantee, rather than on the mechanisms currently used to implement it, a state-based formalization can lead to a fresh, end-to-end perspective on how that guarantee should be implemented. Specifically, a state-based definition of parallel snapshot isolation (PSI) makes clear that the requirement of totally ordering transactions at each datacenter, which is baked into its current definition [53], is only an implementation artefact. Removing it offers the opportunity of an alternative implementation of PSI that makes it resilient to *slowdown cascades* [37], a common failure scenario in large-scale datacenters that has inhibited the adoption of stronger isolation models in industry [5].

After quickly reviewing in Section 2 the current approach to formalizing isolation guarantees, we introduce our state-based model in Section 3, and use it in Section 4 to define several isolation guarantees. We highlight the benefits of our approach in Section 5, summarize related work in Section 6 before outlining its limitations and concluding in Section 7.

## 2 BACKGROUND

Isolation guarantees have been formalized in many different ways: initial specifications of serializability [47] define correctness as a function of schedule equivalence, while weaker isolation guarantees have been defined using implementation-oriented operational specifications [13, 15, 53] or by relating the order in which transactions commit with the values that they observe [20, 21, 52]. The most prevalent approach, however, has been to formulate isolation guarantees as dependency graphs, with edges denoting conflicts between transactions: this method was introduced by Bernstein et al. to formalize serializability for both single-version [16] and multiversioned databases [17], and subsequently refined by Adya to specify weak isolation guarantees [2]. Adya's specification has since been adopted as the de-facto language for specifying isolation [25, 37, 54, 58]. We select Adya's model as a baseline and prove our definitions equivalent to his in §4.

**Adya's formalism** We summarize below some of the key definitions and results from Adya's treatment of isolation [2]; a more complete description can be found in our technical report [22].

Adya's model is expressed in terms of *histories*, which consist of two parts: a partial order of events that reflect the operations of a set of transactions, and a version order that imposes a total order on committed object versions. Every history is associated with a *directed serialization graph* DSG(H) [17], whose nodes consist of committed transactions and whose edges mark the conflicts (read-write, write-write, or write-read) that occur between them. For specific isolation levels, Adya further augments the model with logical start and commit timestamps for transactions, leading

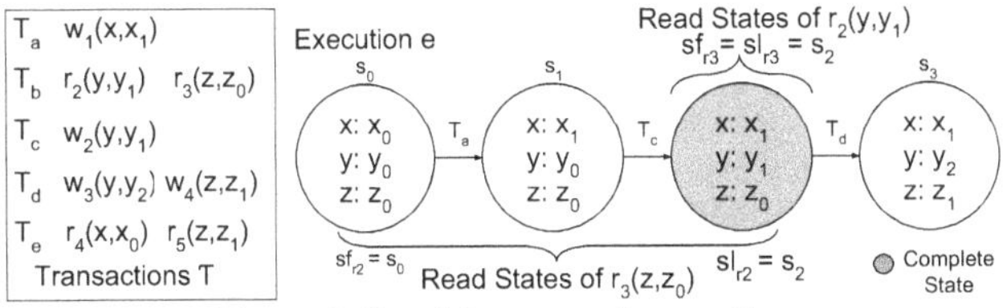


*Figure 2: Read States and execution.*

to *start-ordered serialization graphs* (*SSG(H)*) that add start-dependency edges to the nodes and edges of the corresponding DSG(H) (two transactions $T, T'$ are start-ordered if the commit timestamp of one precedes the start timestamp of the other).

An execution satisfies a given isolation level if it disallows *aborted reads*, *intermediate reads*, and *circularity*. The first two conditions prevent a transaction $T_1$ from reading, respectively, (*i*) values produced by an aborted transaction $T_2$ and (*ii*) a version of an object $x$ written by a transaction $T_2$ that $T_2$ subsequently overwrites. The third condition is more complex. Disallowing circularity prevents cycles in the serialization graph; the specific edges that compose the cycle, however, are dependent on the particular isolation level: read-uncommitted disallows cycles consisting only of write-write edges in the DSG(H) (referred to by Adya as phenomenon G0)[2], while all remaining ANSI SQL isolation levels disallow cycles consisting of write-write/write-read edges (phenomenon G1). Serializability also disallows cycles that include read-write edges (G2). In contrast, snapshot isolation disallows write-write/write-read edges without corresponding start edges (G-SI(a)) as well as cycles containing a single read-write edge in the SSG(H) (G-SI(b)).

**Towards a new formalism** Adya's formalism, like its other existing counterparts, specifies isolation guarantees as constraints on the ordering of the read and write operations that the storage system performs, and relies on low-level implementation details like timestamps or version order. Unfortunately, applications cannot directly observe this ordering: to them, the storage system is a black box. All they can observe are the values returned by the read operations they issue: they experience the storage system as if it were going through a sequence of atomic state transitions, of which they observe a subset. To make it easier for applications to reason about different levels of isolation, we adopt the viewpoint of the applications that must ultimately use their guarantees and introduce a new formalization of isolation based on *application-observable states*.

## 3 A STATE-BASED MODEL

To the best of our knowledge, our model is the first to specify isolation without relying on some notion of history. Instead, it associates with each transaction the set of candidate states (called *read states*) from which the transaction may have retrieved the values it read during its execution. Read states perform a role similar to Kripke structures [35]: they inform the application of the set of possible worlds (i.e., states) consistent with what a transaction observed during its execution.

Intuitively, a storage system guarantees a specific isolation level $I$ if it can produce an *execution* (a sequence of atomic state transitions) that satisfies two conditions. First, the execution must be consistent with the values observed by each transaction $T$; in our model, this requirement is expressed by associating every transaction $T$ with a set of read states, representing the states that the storage *could* have been in when the application executed $T$'s operations. Second, the execution must be valid, in that it must satisfy the constraints imposed by $I$; $I$ effectively narrows down which transactions' read states can be used to build an acceptable execution. If no read state proves suitable for some transaction, then $I$ does not hold.

More formally, we define a *storage system* $S$ with respect to a set $\mathcal{K}$ of keys and $\mathcal{V}$ of values; a *system state* $s$ is a unique mapping from keys to values produced by writes from aborted or committed transactions. For simplicity, we assume that each value is uniquely identifiable, as is common practice both in existing formalisms [2, 17] and in practical systems (ETags in Azure [40] and S3 [7], timestamps in Cassandra [8]). There can thus be no ambiguity, when reading an object, as to which transaction wrote its content. In the initial system state, all keys have value $\perp$; later states similarly include every key, possibly mapped to $\perp$. As is common in database systems, we assume that applications modify the storage system's state using transactions. A *transaction* $T$ is a tuple $(\Sigma_T, \xrightarrow{to})$, where $\Sigma_T$ is the set of *operations* in $T$, and $\xrightarrow{to}$ is a total order on $\Sigma_T$. Operations can be either reads or writes. *Read* operations $r(k,v)$ retrieve value $v$ by reading key $k$; *write* operations $w(k,v)$ update $k$ to its new value $v$. The *read set* of $T$ comprises the keys read by $T$: $\mathcal{R}_T = \{k | r(k,v) \in \Sigma_T\}$. Similarly, the *write set* of $T$ comprises the keys that $T$ updates: $\mathcal{W}_T = \{k | w(k,v) \in \Sigma_T\}$. For simplicity of exposition, we assume that a transaction only writes a key once. Finally, we assume the existence of a time oracle $O$ that assigns distinct real-time *start* and *commit* timestamps ($T.start$ and $T.commit$) to every transaction $T \in \mathcal{T}$. A transaction $T_1$ time-precedes $T_2$ (we write $T_1 <_s T_2$) if $T_1.commit < T_2.start$. Applying a transaction $T$ to a state $s$ transitions the system to a state $s'$ that is identical to $s$ in every key except those written by $T$. Formally,

**Definition 1** $s \xrightarrow{T} s' \equiv \Big(\big([(k,v) \in s' \wedge (k,v) \notin s] \Rightarrow k \in \mathcal{W}_T\big) \wedge \big(w(k,v) \in \Sigma_T \Rightarrow (k,v) \in s'\big)\Big)$.

We refer to $s$ as the *parent state* of $T$ (denoted as $s_{p,T}$) [3]; to the transaction that generated $s$ as $T_s$; and to the set of keys in which $s$ and $s'$ differ as $\Delta(s,s')$. An *execution* $e$ for a set of transactions $\mathcal{T}$ is a totally ordered set defined by the pair $(\mathcal{S}_e, \xrightarrow{T \in \mathcal{T}})$, where $\mathcal{S}_e$ is the set of states generated by applying, starting from the system's initial state, a permutation of all the transactions in $\mathcal{T}$. We write $s \xrightarrow{*} s'$ (respectively, $s \xrightarrow{+} s'$) to denote a sequence of zero (respectively, one) or more state transitions from $s$ to $s'$ in $e$. For example, in Figure 2, $\mathcal{T}$ comprises five transactions, operating on a state that consists of the current version of keys $x$, $y$, and $z$.

Note that while $e$ identifies the state transitions produced by each transaction $T \in \mathcal{T}$, it does not specify from which states in $\mathcal{S}_e$ each operation in $T$ reads. In particular, reading a key in replicated distributed systems will not necessarily return the value produced by the latest write to that key, as writes may become visible in different orders at different replicas. In general, multiple states in

[2]We will use Adya's shorthand for this and other phenomena in §4, when we prove that our new state-based definitions of isolation guarantees are equivalent to his.

[3]Henceforth, we will drop the subscripted $T$ unless there is ambiguity.

$\mathcal{S}_e$ may be compatible with the value returned by any given operation. We call this subset the operation's *read states*. To prevent operations from *reading from the future*, we restrict the valid read states for the operations in $T$ to be no later than $s_p$. Further, once an operation in $T$ writes $v$ to $k$, we require all subsequent operations in $T$ that read $k$ to return $v$ [2]: in this case, their set of read states by convention includes all states in $\mathcal{S}_e$ up to and including $s_p$.

**Definition 2** *Given an execution $e$ for a set of transactions $\mathcal{T}$, let $T \in \mathcal{T}$ and let $s_p$ denote $T$'s parent state. The read states for a read operation $o = r(k,v) \in \Sigma_T$ define the set of states*
$\mathcal{RS}_e(o) = \{s \in \mathcal{S}_e | s \xrightarrow{*} s_p \land$
$\big((k,v) \in s \lor (\exists w(k,v) \in \Sigma_T : w(k,v) \xrightarrow{to} r(k,v))\big)\}$.

Figure 2 illustrates the notion of read states for the operations executed by transaction $T_b$. Since $r_2$ returns $y_1$, its only possible read state is $s_2$, i.e., the only state containing $y_1$. When it comes to $r_3$, however, $z_0$ could have been read from any of $s_0$, $s_1$, or $s_2$: from the perspective of the client executing $T_b$, these read states are indistinguishable. By convention, write operations have read states too: for a write operation in $T$, they include all states in $\mathcal{S}_e$ up to and including $T$'s parent state. It is easy to prove that the read states of any operation $o$ define a subsequence of contiguous states in the total order that $e$ defines on $\mathcal{S}_e$. We refer to the first state in that sequence as $sf_o$ and to the last state as $sl_o$. For instance, in Figure 2, $sf_{r_3}$ is $s_0$ (the first state that contains $z_0$) and $sl_{r_3}$ is $s_2$ ($z_0$ is overwritten in $s_3$). When the predicate $\text{PREREAD}_e(\mathcal{T})$ holds, then such states exist for all transactions in $\mathcal{T}$:

**Definition 3** *Let $\text{PREREAD}_e(T) \equiv \forall o \in \Sigma_T : \mathcal{RS}_e(o) \neq \emptyset$. Then $\text{PREREAD}_e(\mathcal{T}) \equiv \forall T \in \mathcal{T} : \text{PREREAD}_e(T)$.*

We say that a state $s$ is *complete* for $T$ in $e$ if every operation in $T$ can read from $s$. We write:

**Definition 4** $\text{COMPLETE}_{e,T}(s) \equiv s \in \bigcap_{o \in \Sigma_T} \mathcal{RS}_e(o)$.

Looking again at Figure 2, $s_2$ is a complete state for transaction $T_b$, as it is in the set of candidate read states of both $r_2(y,y_1)$ ($\{s_2\}$) and $r_3(z,z_0)$ ($\{s_0,s_1,s_2\}$). A complete state is not guaranteed to exist: no such state exists for $T_e$, as the sole candidate read states of $r_4$ and $r_5$ (respectively, $s_0$ and $s_3$) are distinct. As we will see in §4, complete states are key to determining whether transactions read from a consistent snapshot.

## 4 ISOLATION

Isolation guarantees specify the valid set of executions for a given set of transactions $\mathcal{T}$. We show that it is possible to formalize these guarantees solely in terms of each transaction's read and commit states, without relying on histories of low-level operations or on implementation details such as timestamps. The underlying reason is simple: ultimately, it is through the visible states produced during an execution that the storage system can "prove" to its users that a given isolation guarantee holds. Histories are just the mechanism that generates those probatory states; indeed, multiple histories can map to the same execution.

In a state-based model, isolation guarantees constrain each transaction $T \in \mathcal{T}$ in two ways. First, they limit which states, among those in the candidate read sets of the operations in $T$, are admissible. Second, they restrict which states can serve as parent states for $T$. We express these constraints by means of a *commit test*: for an execution $e$ of a set $\mathcal{T}$ of transactions to be valid under a given isolation level $\mathcal{I}$, each transaction $T$ in $e$ must satisfy the commit test $\text{CT}_\mathcal{I}(T,e)$ for $\mathcal{I}$.

**Definition 5** *Given a set of transactions $\mathcal{T}$ and their read states, a storage system satisfies an isolation level $\mathcal{I}$ iff $\exists e : \forall T \in \mathcal{T} : CT_\mathcal{I}(T,e)$.*

Table 1 summarizes the commit tests that define the isolation guarantees most commonly-used in research and industry: the ANSI SQL isolation levels (serializability, read committed, read uncommitted, and snapshot isolation) as well as parallel snapshot isolation [20, 53], strict serializability [47], and the recently proposed read atomic [13] isolation level. Though our state-based definitions make no reference to histories, we prove that they are equivalent to those in Adya's classic treatment. As the proofs follow a similar structure, we provide an informal proof sketch only for serializability and snapshot isolation, deferring a more complete and formal treatment to our extended technical report [22].

**Serializability** Serializability requires the values observed by the operations in each transaction $T$ to be consistent with those that would have been observed in a sequential execution. The commit test enforces this requirement through two complementary conditions on observable states. First, all of $T$'s operations must read from the same state $s$ (i.e., $s$ must be a complete state for $T$). Second, $s$ must be the parent state of $T$, i.e., the state that $T$ transitions from. These two conditions suffice to guarantee that $T$ will observe the effects of all transactions that committed before it. This definition is equivalent to Adya's cycle-based definition. Specifically, we prove that :

**Theorem 1** $\exists e : \forall T \in \mathcal{T} : CT_{SER}(T,e) \equiv \neg G1 \land \neg G2$.

Proof sketch. ($\exists e : \forall T \in \mathcal{T} : \text{CT}_{SER}(T,e) \Rightarrow \neg\text{G1} \land \neg\text{G2}$). By definition, $e$ is a totally-ordered execution where the parent state of every transaction $T$ is a complete state for $T$. Considering the order of transactions in $e$, we make three observations. First, all write-write edges in the DSG point in the same direction, as they map to state transitions in the totally-ordered execution $e$. Second, all write-read edges point in the same direction as write-write edges: given any transaction $T$, since all operations in $T$ read from $T$'s parent state, all write-read edges that end in $T$ must originate from a transaction that precedes $T$ in $e$'s total order. Finally, all read-write dependency edges point in the same direction as write-write and write-read edges: as all read operations in $T$ read from $T$'s parent state, the value they return cannot be later overwritten by a transaction $T'$ ordered before $T$ in $e$. Since all edges point in the same direction, no cycle can form in the DSG.

($\exists e : \forall T \in \mathcal{T} : \text{CT}_{SER}(T,e) \Leftarrow \neg\text{G1} \land \neg\text{G2}$). If no cycle exists in the DSG, we can construct an execution $e'$ such that the parent state $s_p$ of each transaction $T$ is a complete state for $T$. We construct $e'$ by topologically sorting the DSG (it is acyclic) and by applying every transaction in the resulting order. Thus, if a transaction $T'$ writes a value that $T$ subsequently reads (write-read edge), the state associated with $T'$ is guaranteed to precede $T$'s state in the execution $e'$. Moreover, as there are no backpointing read-write edges, no other

| Serializability ($\text{CT}_{SER}(T,e)$) | $\text{COMPLETE}_{e,T}(s_p)$ |
|---|---|
| Snapshot Isolation ($\text{CT}_{SI}(T,e)$) | $\exists s \in S_e . \text{COMPLETE}_{e,T}(s) \land \text{NO-CONF}_T(s)$ |
| Read Committed ($\text{CT}_{RC}(T,e)$) | $\text{PREREAD}_e(T)$ |
| Read Uncommitted ($\text{CT}_{RU}(T,e)$) | True |
| Parallel Snapshot Isolation ($\text{CT}_{PSI}(e,T)$) | $\text{PREREAD}_e(T) \land \forall T' \triangleright T : \forall o \in \Sigma_T : o.k \in \mathcal{W}_{T'} \Rightarrow s_{T'} \xrightarrow{*} sl_o$ |
| Strict Serializability ($\text{CT}_{SSER}(e,T)$) | $\text{COMPLETE}_{e,T}(s_p) \land \forall T' \in \mathcal{T} : T' <_s T \Rightarrow s_{T'} \xrightarrow{*} s_T$ |
| Read Atomic ($\text{CT}_{RA}(e,T)$) | $\forall r_1(k_1, v_1), r_2(k_2, v_2) \in \Sigma_T \land k_2 \in \mathcal{W}_{T_{sf_{r_1}}} \Rightarrow sf_{r_1} \xrightarrow{*} sf_{r_2}$ |

***Table 1: Commit Tests***

transaction in $e'$ will update an object read by $T$ between the state produced by $T'$ and $s_p$. $s_p$ is therefore a valid read state for every operation in $T$ and, consequently, a complete state for $T$. □

**Snapshot isolation (SI)** Like serializability, SI prevents transactions $T$ from seeing the effects of concurrently running transactions. The commit test enforces this requirement by having all operations in $T$ read from the same state $s$, produced by a transaction that precedes $T$ in the execution $e$. However, SI no longer insists on that state $s$ being $T$'s parent state $s_p$: other transactions, whose operations $T$ will not observe, may commit in between $s$ and $s_p$. The commit test only forbids $T$ from modifying any of the keys that changed value as the system's state progressed from $s$ to $s_p$. Denoting the set of keys in which $s$ and $s'$ differ as $\Delta(s,s')$, we express this as $\text{NO-CONF}_T(s) \equiv \Delta(s,s_p) \cap \mathcal{W}_T = \emptyset$. We prove that this definition is equivalent to Adya's:

**Theorem 2** $\exists e : \forall T \in \mathcal{T} : CT_{SI}(T,e) \equiv \neg G1 \land \neg G\text{-}SI.$

Proof sketch. ($\exists e : \forall T \in \mathcal{T} : \text{CT}_{SI}(T,e) \Leftarrow \neg\text{G1} \land \neg\text{G-SI}$). We construct a valid execution for any history satisfying $\neg\text{G1} \land \neg\text{G-SI}$ using the time-precedes partial order introduced by Adya. First, we topologically sort transactions according to their commit point, and apply them in the resulting order to generate an execution $e$. Next, we prove that every transaction $T$ satisfies the commit test: we first show that the state created by the last transaction $T_{rs}$ on which $T$ start-depends is a complete state. As $T$ start-depends on $T_{rs}$, it must also start-depend on all transactions that precede $T_{rs}$, since, by construction, these transactions have a commit timestamp smaller than $T_{rs}$. Moreover, as $T_{rs}$ is the last transaction that $T$ starts-depend on, all subsequent transactions will either be concurrent with $T$, or start-depend on $T$. Adya's ($\neg$G-SI) requirement (formally, that there cannot be a write-read /write-write edge without also a start dependency edge and there cannot be a cycle consisting of a single read-write edge) implies that $T$ can only read or overwrite a value written by a transaction $T'$ if $T$ start-depends on $T'$. Any such $T'$ must either be $T_{rs}$ or precede $T_{rs}$ in $e$. Similarly, if another transaction $T''$ overwrites a value that $T$ reads, $T$ cannot start-depend on $T''$ as it would otherwise create a cycle with a start-edge and a single read-write edge. $T''$ is therefore ordered after $T_{rs}$ in $e$. We conclude that $s_{T_{rs}}$ necessarily contains all the values that $T$ reads: it is a complete state. Next, we show that $\Delta(s_{T_{rs}}, s_T) = \emptyset$. By construction, $T$ cannot start-depend on any transaction $T'$ that follows $T_{rs}$ in the execution but precedes $T$. By G-SI, there cannot be a write-write dependency edge from $T'$ to $T$, and their write-sets must therefore be distinct. Consequently: $\Delta(s_{T_{rs}}, s_T) = \emptyset$.

($\exists e : \forall T \in \mathcal{T} : \text{CT}_{SI}(T,e) \Rightarrow \neg\text{G1} \land \neg\text{G-SI}$). We show that the serialization graph $SSG(H)$ corresponding to $e$ does not exhibit phenomena G1 or G-SI. Every transaction in $e$ reads from some previous state and commits in the total order defined by $e$. It follows that all write-write and write-read edges follow the total order introduced by $e$: there can be no cycle consisting of write-write/write-read dependencies. $\neg$G1 is thus satisfied. To show that $SSG(H)$ does not exhibit G-SI, we first select the start and commit point of each transaction. We assign commit points to transactions according to their order in $e$. We assign the start point of each transaction $T$ to be directly after the commit point of the first transaction $T_{rs}$ in $e$ whose generated state satisfies $\text{COMPLETE}_{e,T}(s) \land (\Delta(s,s_p) \cap \mathcal{W}_T = \emptyset)$. It follows that $T_{rs}$ (and all the transactions that precede it in $e$) start-precede $T$. Proving $\neg$G-SIa is then straightforward: any transaction $T'$ that $T$ write-read/write-write depends on precedes $T_{rs}$ in the execution, and consequently start-precedes $T$. Proving $\neg$G-SIb requires a little more care. By $\neg$G-SIa, there necessarily exists a corresponding start-depend edge for any write-read or write-write edge between two transactions $T$ and $T'$: if there exists a cycle with exactly one read-write edge in the $SSG(H)$, there must exist a cycle with exactly one read-write edge and only start-depend edges in $SSG(H)$. Assuming by contradiction that G-SIb holds and that there exists a cycle with one read-write edge and multiple start-depend edges (we reduce this cycle to a single start-depend edge as start-edges are transitive). Let $T$ read-write depend on $T'$: $s_{T'}$ is ordered after $s_{T_{rs}}$ in $e$ (otherwise $s_{T_{rs}}$ cannot be a valid read state for $T$). However, as previously mentioned, $T$ only has start-depend edges with transactions that precede $T_{rs}$ (included) in $e$. $T'$ thus does not start-depend on $T$, a contradiction. □

Unlike Adya's, however, the correctness of our state-based definition does not rely on using start and commit timestamps. This is a crucial difference. Including these low-level attributes in the definition has encouraged the development of variations of SI that differ in their use of timestamps, whose fundamental guarantees are, as a result, difficult to compare. In §5.2 we show that, when expressed in terms of application-observable states, several of these variations, thought to be distinct, are actually equivalent![4]

**Read committed** Read committed allows $T$ to see the effects of concurrent transactions, as long as they are committed. The commit test therefore no longer constrains all operations in $T$ to read from the *same* state; instead, it only requires each of them to read from a state that precedes $T$ in the execution $e$. We prove:

**Theorem 3** $\exists e : \forall T \in \mathcal{T} : CT_{RC}(T,e) \equiv \neg G1.$

[4] As proofs follow a similar structure, we defer all subsequent proofs to our technical report [22]

**Read uncommitted** Read uncommitted allows $T$ to see the effects of concurrent transactions, whether they have committed or not. The commit test reflects this permissiveness, to the point of allowing transactions to read arbitrary values. Still, we prove:

**Theorem 4** $\exists e : \forall T \in \mathcal{T} : CT_{RU}(T,e) \equiv \neg G0$.

The reason behind the laxity of the state-based definition is that isolation models in databases consider only committed transactions and are therefore unable to distinguish values produced by aborted transactions from those produced by future transactions. This distinction, however, is not lost in environments, such as transactional memory, where correctness depends on providing guarantees such as opacity [30] for all live transactions. We discuss this further in Section 7.

**Strict Serializability** Strict serializability guarantees that the real-time order of transactions will be reflected in the final history or execution. It can be expressed by adding the following condition to the serializability commit test: $\forall T' \in \mathcal{T} : T' <_s T \Rightarrow s_{T'} \xrightarrow{*} s_T$.

**Parallel Snapshot Isolation** Parallel snapshot isolation (PSI) was recently proposed by Sovran et al [53] to address SI's scalability issues in geo-replicated settings. Snapshot isolation requires transactions to read from a snapshot (a *complete state* in our parlance) that reflects a single commit ordering of transactions. The coordination implied by this requirement is expensive to carry out in a geo-replicated system and must be enforced even when transactions do not conflict. PSI aims to offer a scalable alternative by allowing distinct geo-replicated sites to commit transactions in different orders. The specification of PSI is given as an abstract specification code that an implementation must emulate. Specifically, a PSI execution must enforce three properties. First, *site snapshot read*: all operations read the most recent committed version at the transaction's origin site as of the time when the transaction began (P1). Second, *no write-write conflicts*: the write sets of each pair of somewhere-concurrent committed transactions must be disjoint (two transactions are somewhere-concurrent if they are concurrent on site($T_1$) or site($T_2$)) (P2). And finally, *commit causality across sites*: if a transaction $T_1$ commits at a site A before a transaction $T_2$ starts at site A, then $T_1$ cannot commit after $T_2$ at any site.

Our first step towards a state-based definition of PSI is to populate, using solely client-observable states, the *precede-set* of each transaction $T$, i.e., the set of transactions after which $T$ must be ordered. A transaction $T'$ is in $T$'s precede-set if (*i*) $T$ reads a value that $T'$ wrote; or (*ii*) $T$ writes an object modified by $T'$ and the execution orders $T'$ before $T$; or (*iii*) $T'$ precedes $T''$ and $T''$ precedes $T$. Formally: $\text{D-PREC}_e(\hat{T}) = \{T | \exists o \in \Sigma_{\hat{T}} : T = T_{sf_o}\} \cup \{T | s_T \xrightarrow{+} s_{\hat{T}} \wedge \mathcal{W}_{\hat{T}} \cap \mathcal{W}_T \neq \emptyset\}$. We write $T_i \blacktriangleright T_j$ if $T_i \in \text{D-PREC}_e(T_j)$ and $T_i \triangleright T_j$ if $T_i$ transitively precedes $T_j$. PSI guarantees that the state observed by a transaction $T$'s operation includes the effects of all transactions that precede it. We can express this requirement in PSI's commit test as follows:

**Definition 6** $CT_{PSI}(T,e) \equiv \text{PREREAD}_e(T) \wedge \forall T' \triangleright T : \forall o \in \Sigma_T : o.k \in \mathcal{W}_{T'} \Rightarrow s_{T'} \xrightarrow{*} sl_o$.

This client-centric definition of PSI makes immediately clear that the state which operations observe is not necessarily a complete state, and hence may not correspond to a snapshot of the database at a specific time. We prove the following theorem :

**Theorem 5** $\exists e : \forall T \in \mathcal{T} : CT_{PSI}(T,e) \equiv PSI$.

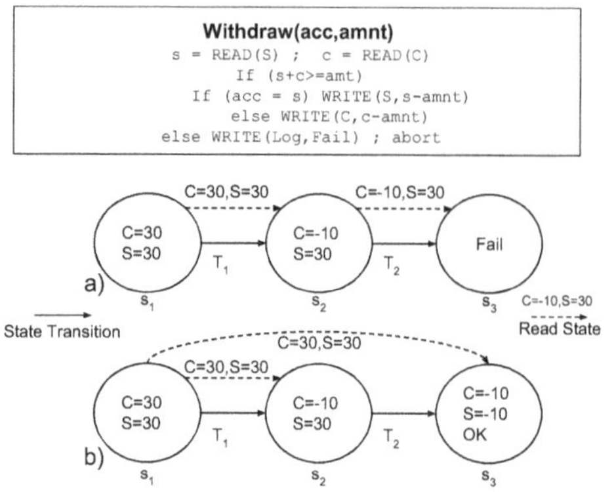


***Figure 3: Simple Banking Application. Alice and Bob share checking and savings accounts. Withdrawals are allowed as long as the sum of both account is greater than zero.***

**Read Atomic** Read atomic [13], like PSI, aims to be a scalable alternative to snapshot isolation. It preserves atomic visibility (transactions observe either all or none of a committed transaction's effects) but does not preclude write-write conflicts nor guarantees that transactions will read from a causally consistent prefix of the execution. These weaker guarantees allow for efficient implementations and nonetheless ensure *synchronization independence*: one client's transactions cannot cause another client's transactions to fail or stall. Read atomic can be expressed in our state-based model as follows:

**Definition 7** $CT_{RA}(T,e) \equiv \forall r_1(k_1,v_1), r_2(k_2,v_2) \in \Sigma_T \wedge k_2 \in \mathcal{W}_{T_{sf_{r_1}}} \Rightarrow sf_{r_1} \xrightarrow{*} sf_{r_2}$.

Intuitively, if an operation $o_1$ observes the writes of a transaction $T_i$'s, all subsequent operations that read a key included in $T_i$'s write set must read from a state that includes $T_i$'s effects. We prove the following theorem:

**Theorem 6** $\exists e : \forall T \in \mathcal{T} : CT_{RA}(T,e) \equiv RA$.

# 5 BENEFITS OF A STATE-BASED APPROACH

Specifying isolation using client-observable states rather than histories is not only equally expressive, but brings forth several benefits: it gives application developers a clearer intuition for the implications of choosing a given isolation level (§5.1), brings additional clarity to how different isolation levels relate (§5.2), and opens up opportunities for performance improvements in existing implementations (§5.3).

## 5.1 Minimizing the intuition gap

A state-based model makes it easier for application programmers to understand the anomalies allowed by weak isolation levels, as it precisely captures the *root cause* of these anomalies. Consider, for example, snapshot isolation: it allows for a non-serializable behavior called write-skew (see §1), illustrated in the simple banking example of Figure 3. Alice and Bob share checking (C) and savings (S) accounts, each holding \$30, the sum of which should never

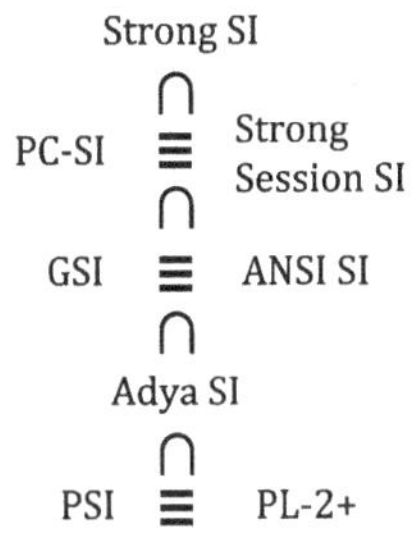


***Figure 4: Snapshot-based isolation guarantees hierarchy. (ANSI SI [15, 24], Adya SI [2], Strong SI [24], GSI [48], PSI [53], Strong Session SI [24], PL-2+ [3], PC-SI [24]).***

be negative. Before performing a withdrawal, they check that the total funds in their accounts allow for it. They then withdraw the amount from the specified account, using the other account to cover any overdraft. Suppose Alice and Bob try concurrently to withdraw \$40 from, respectively, their checking and savings account, and issue transactions $T_1$ and $T_2$. Figure 3(a) shows an execution under serializability. Because transactions read from their parent state (see Table 1), $T_2$ observes $T_1$'s withdrawal and, since the balance of Bob's accounts is below \$40, aborts. In contrast, consider the execution under snapshot isolation in Figure 3(b). As it is is legal for both $T_1$ and $T_2$ to read from a complete but stale state $s_1$, Alice and Bob can both find that the combined funds in the two accounts exceed \$40, and, unaware of each other, proceed to generate an execution whose final state $s_3$ is illegal. The state-based definitions of snapshot isolation and serializability make both the causes and the danger of write-skew immediately clear: to satisfy snapshot isolation, it suffices that both transactions read from the same complete state $s_1$, even though this behavior is clearly not serializable, as $s_1$ is not the parent state of $T_2$. The link is, arguably, less obvious with the history-based definition of snapshot isolation, which requires "disallowing all cycles consisting of write-write and write-read dependencies and a single anti-dependency".

## 5.2 Removing implementation artefacts

By cleanly separating high-level properties from low-level implementation details, a state-based model makes the plethora of isolation guarantees introduced in recent years easier to compare. We leverage this newfound clarity below to systematize snapshot-based guarantees, including ANSI SI [15], Adya SI [2], Weak SI [24], Strong SI [24], generalized snapshot isolation (GSI) [48], parallel snapshot isolation (PSI) [53], Strong Session SI [24], PL-2+ (Lazy Consistency) [3], Prefix-Consistent SI (PC-SI) [24]. We find that several of these isolation guarantees, previously thought to be distinct, are in fact *equivalent* from a client's perspective, and establish a clean *hierarchy* that encompasses them.

Snapshot-based isolation guarantees, broadly speaking, are defined as follows. A transaction is assigned both a start and a commit timestamp; the first determines the database snapshot from which the transaction can read (it includes all transactions with a smaller commit timestamp), while the second maintains the "first-committer-wins" rule: no conflicting transactions should write to the same objects. The details of these protocols, however, differ. Each strikes a different performance trade-off in how it assigns timestamps and computes snapshots that influences its high-level guarantee in ways that can only be understood by applications with in-depth knowledge of the internals of the systems. As a result, it is hard for application developers and researchers alike to compare and contrast them.

In contrast, formulating isolation in terms of client-observable states *forces* definitions that specify guarantees according to how they are *perceived by clients*. It then becomes straightforward to understand what guarantees are provided, and to observe their differences and similarities. Specifically, it clearly exposes the three dimensions along which snapshot-based guarantees differ: (*i*) *time* (whether timestamps are logical [2, 37, 53] or based on real-time [15, 24, 48]); (*ii*) *snapshot recency* (whether the computed snapshot contains *all* transactions that committed before the transaction start time) [2, 24] or can be stale [9, 24, 48, 53]; and *state completeness* (in our parlance, whether snapshots must correspond to a complete state [2, 15, 24, 48] or whether a causally consistent [4] snapshot suffices [3, 9, 37, 53]).

Grouping isolation guarantees in this way highlights a clean hierarchy between these definitions, and suggests that many of the newly proposed isolation levels proposed are in fact equivalent to prior guarantees. We summarize the different commit tests in Table 2 and the resulting hierarchy in Figure 4. As the existence of the hierarchy follows straightforwardly from the commit tests, we defer the proof of its soundness to our extended technical report [22], along with proofs of the corresponding equivalences.

At the top of the hierarchy is Strong SI [24]. It requires that a transaction $T$ observe the effects of all transactions that have committed (in real-time) before $T$ (in other words, read from the most recent database snapshot) and obtain a commit timestamp greater than any previously committed transaction. We express this (Table 2, first row) by requiring that the last state in the execution generated by a transaction that happens before $T$ in real time must be complete ($\forall T' <_s T : s_{T'} \xrightarrow{*} s$), and that the total order defined by the execution respects commit order ($\text{C-ORD}(T,T') \equiv T.commit < T'.commit$). We prove that this formulation is equivalent to its traditional implementation specification:

**Theorem 7** $\exists e : \forall T \in \mathcal{T} : CT_{StrongSI}(T,e) \equiv$ *Strong SI.*

Skipping for a moment one level in the hierarchy, we consider next ANSI SI [15]. ANSI SI weakens Strong SI's requirement that the snapshot from which $T$ reads include *all* transactions that precede $T$ in real-time (including those that access objects that $T$ does not access). This weakening, which improves scalability by avoiding the coordination needed to generate Strong SI's snapshot, can be expressed in our state-based approach by relaxing the requirement that the complete state be the most recent in real-time (Table 2, third line). An attractive consequence of this new formulation is that it clarifies the relationship between ANSI SI and *generalized snapshot isolation* [48], a refinement of ANSI SI for lazily replicated databases. We prove that these two decade-old guarantees are actually equivalent:

**Theorem 8** $\exists e : \forall T \in \mathcal{T} : CT_{ANSI\,SI}(T,e) \equiv$ *GSI* $\equiv$ *ANSI SI.*

This is not an isolated case: we find that the two less popular notions of isolation that occupy the level of the hierarchy between Strong SI and ANSI SI (Strong Session SI (SSessSI) [48] and Prefix-Consistent SI (PC-SI) [24]) are also equivalent These

| | |
|---|---|
| Strong SI ($\text{CT}_{Strong\ SI}(T,e)$) | $\text{C-ORD}(T_{sp},T) \land \exists s \in S_e : \text{COMPLETE}_{e,T}(s) \land \text{NO-CONF}_T(s) \land (T_s <_s T) \land (\forall T' <_s T : s_{T'} \xrightarrow{*} s)$ |
| Strong Session SI/PC-SI ($\text{CT}_{Session\ SI}(T,e)$) | $\text{C-ORD}(T_{sp},T) \land \exists s \in S_e : \text{COMPLETE}_{e,T}(s) \land \text{NO-CONF}_T(s) \land (T_s <_s T) \land (\forall T' \xrightarrow{se} T : s_{T'} \xrightarrow{*} s)$ |
| ANSI SI /GSI ($\text{CT}_{ANSI\ SI}(T,e)$) | $\text{C-ORD}(T_{sp},T) \land \exists s \in S_e : \text{COMPLETE}_{e,T}(s) \land \text{NO-CONF}_T(s) \land (T_s <_s T)$ |
| Adya SI ($\text{CT}_{SI}(T,e)$) | $\exists s \in S_e : \text{COMPLETE}_{e,T}(s) \land \text{NO-CONF}_T(s)$ |
| PSI/PL-2+ ($\text{CT}_{PSI}(T,e)$) | $\text{PREREAD}_e(T) \land \forall T' \rhd T : \text{CAUS-VIS}(e,T)$ |

***Table 2: Commit tests for snapshot-based protocols***

guarantees seek to prevent *transaction inversions* [24] (a client $c_1$ executes a transaction $T_1$ followed, in real-time by $T_2$ without $T_2$ observing the effects of $T_1$) that can arise when transactions read from a stale snapshot—but without requiring all transactions to read from the most recent snapshot. To this effect, they strike a balance between ANSI SI and Strong SI: they introduce the notion of *sessions* and require a transaction $T$ to read from a snapshot more recent than the commit timestamp of all transactions that precede $T$ in a session (formally: a session $se$ is a tuple $(T_{se}, \xrightarrow{se})$ where $\xrightarrow{se}$ is a total order over the transactions in $\mathcal{T}_{se}$ such that $T \xrightarrow{se} T' \Rightarrow T <_s T'$). Our model straightforwardly captures this definition (Table 2, second row) by requiring that the complete state from which a transaction reads follow the commit state of all transactions in a session. We prove the following theorem:

**Theorem 9** $\exists e : \forall t \in \mathcal{T} : CT_{Session\ SI}(t,e) \equiv SSessSI \equiv PC\text{-}SI.$

Though ANSI SI or Strong Session SI are both more scalable than Strong SI, their definitions still include several red flags for efficient large-scale implementations. First, they require a total order on transactions ($\text{C-ORD}(s,s_p)$), forcing developers to implement expensive coordination mechanisms, even as transactions may access different objects. Second, they limit a transaction $T$ to reading only from complete states that do not include transactions that committed in real time *after* $T$'s start timestamp. This implementation choice often forces transactions to read further in the past than necessary, making them more prone to write-write conflicts with concurrent transactions. Moreover, it prevents transactions from reading uncommitted operations, precluding efficient implementations for high-contention workloads [26, 60]. Adya's reformulation of SI [2] side-steps many of these baked-in implementation decisions by removing the dependence on real-time, instead allocating *logical* timestamps consistent with the transactions' observations. Our model can capture this distinction by simply removing the two aforementioned clauses from the commit test (Table 2, fourth row), allowing for maximum flexibility for how snapshot isolation can be implemented without affecting client-side guarantees.

The lowest level of the hierarchy covers snapshot-based isolation guarantees intended for large-scale geo-replicated systems. When transactions may be asynchronously replicated for performance and availability, it is challenging to require that transactions read a database snapshot that corresponds to a single moment in time (and hence read from a *complete state*) as it would require transactions to become visible atomically across all (possibly distant) datacenters. PSI [53] (introduced in §4) and PL-2+ [2, 3] consequently weaken Adya's SI to address these new challenges: PSI requires that transactions read from a committed snapshot but allows concurrent transactions to commit in a different order at different sites, while PL-2+ disallows cycles consisting of either write-write/write-read dependencies, or containing a single anti-dependency edge. Unlike what these widely different low-level definitions suggest, taking a client-centric view of these guarantees indicates that PSI and PL-2+ in fact weaken Adya's snapshot isolation in an identical fashion: they no longer require transactions to read from a complete state, and instead require that operations read from a (possibly different) state that includes the effects of all previously observed transactions. Our model cleanly captures the shared guarantee provided by PL-2+/PSI: that a transaction $T$ must observe the effects of all transactions that it is not concurrent with (Table 2, fifth line). We write: for every transaction $T'$ that a transaction $T$ depends on: $\forall o \in \Sigma_T : o.k \in \mathcal{W}_{T'} \Rightarrow s_{T'} \xrightarrow{*} sl_o \equiv \text{CAUS-VIS}(e,T)$. From this client-centric formulation, we prove the following theorem:

**Theorem 10** $\exists e : \forall T \in \mathcal{T} : CT_{PSI}(T,e) \equiv PSI \equiv PL\text{-}2+.$

## 5.3 Identifying performance opportunities

Beyond improving clients' understanding, defining isolation guarantees in terms of client-observable states helps prevent them from subjecting transactions to stronger requirements than what these guarantees require end-to-end. Indeed, by removing all implementation-specific details (timestamps, replicas) present in system-centric formulations, our model gives full flexibility to how these guarantees can be implemented. We illustrate this danger, and highlight the benefits of our approach using the specific example of PSI/PL-2+.

In its original specification, the definition of parallel snapshot isolation [53] requires datacenters to enforce snapshot isolation, even as it globally only offers (as we prove in Theorem 10) the guarantees of lazy consistency/PL-2+. This baked-in implementation decision makes the *very definition* of PSI unsuitable for large-scale partitioned datacenters as it makes the definition (and therefore any system that implements it) susceptible to slowdown cascades. Slowdown cascades (common in large-scale systems [5]) arise when a slow or failed node/partition delays operations that do not access that node itself, and have been identified by industry [5] as the primary barrier to adoption of stronger consistency guarantees. By enforcing SI on every site, the history-based definition of PSI creates a total commit order across all transactions within a datacenter, even as they may access different keys. Transactions thus become dependent on all previously committed transactions on that datacenter, and cannot be replicated to other sites until all these transactions have been applied. If a single partition is slow, all transactions that artificially depend on transactions on that node will be unnecessarily delayed, creating a cascading slowdown.

An approach based on client-observable states, in contrast, makes no such assumptions: the depend-set of a transaction is computed using client observations and read states only, and thus

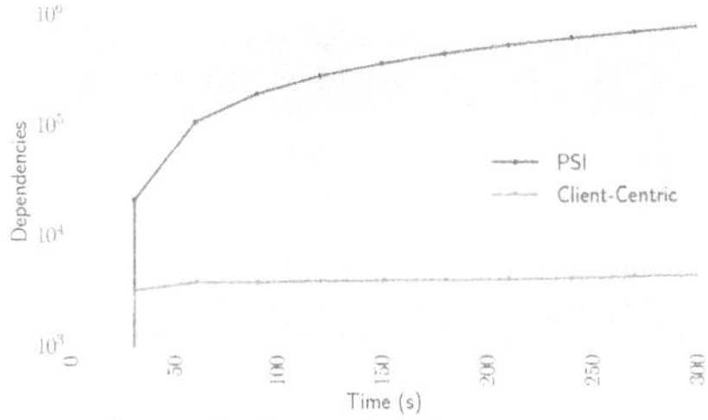


***Figure 5: Number of dependencies per transaction as a function of time. TARDiS [23] runs with three replicas on a shared local cluster (2.67GHz Intel Xeon CPU X5650, 48GB memory and 2Gbps network).***

consists exclusively of transactions that the application itself can *perceive* as ordered with respect to one another. Every dependency created stems from an actual *observation*: the number of dependencies that a client-centric definition creates is consequently minimal (and the fewer dependencies a system creates, the less likely it will be subject to slowdown cascades). To illustrate this potential benefit, we simulated the number of transactional dependencies created at each datacenter by the traditional definition of PSI as compared to the "true" dependencies generated by the proposed client-centric definition, using an asynchronously replicated transactional key-value store, TARDiS [23]. On a workload consisting of read-write transactions (three reads, three writes) accessing data uniformly over 10,000 objects (Figure 5), we found that a client-centric approach decreased dependencies, per transaction, by two orders of magnitude (175×), a reduction that can yield significant dividends in terms of scalability and robustness.

State-based specifications of isolation guarantees can also benefit performance, as they abstract away the details of specific mechanisms used to enforce isolation, and instead focus on how different flavors of isolation constrain permissible read states. A case-in-point is Ardekani et al.'s non-monotonic snapshot isolation (NMSI) [9]: NMSI logically moves snapshots forward in time to minimize the risk of seeing stale data (and consequent aborts due to write-write conflicts), without violating any consistency guarantees. This technique is premised on the observation that, given the values read by the client, the states at the earlier and later snapshot are indistinguishable.

## 6 RELATED WORK

Most past definitions of isolation and consistency [2, 9, 15–19, 27, 31, 47, 53, 55] refer to specific orderings of low-level operations and to system properties that cannot be easily observed or understood by applications. To better align these definitions with what clients perceive, recent work [10, 20, 36, 57] distinguishes between *concrete* executions (the nuts-and-bolts implementations details) and *abstract* executions (the system behaviour as perceived by the client). Attiya et al., for instance, introduce the notion of observable causal consistency [10], a refinement of causal consistency where causality can be inferred by client observations. Likewise, Cerone et al. [20, 21] introduce the dual notions of visibility and arbitration to define, axiomatically, a large number of existing isolation levels. The simplicity of their formulation, however, relies on restricting their model to consider only isolation levels that guarantee atomic visibility [13], which prevents them from expressing guarantees like read-committed, the default isolation level of most common database systems [39, 42, 45, 45, 46, 50, 51, 58], and the only supported level for some [45, 51][5]. Shapiro and Ardekani [52] adopt a similar approach to identify three orthogonal dimensions (total order, visibility and transaction composition) that they use to classify consistency and isolation guarantees. All continue, however, to characterize correctness by constraining the ordering of read and write operations and often let system specific details (e.g., system replicas) leak through definitions. Our model takes their approach a step further: it *directly defines* consistency and isolation in terms of the observable states that are routinely used by developers to express application invariants [6, 12, 23]. Finally, several practical systems have recognized the benefits of taking a client-centric approach to system specification and development. These systems target very different concerns, from file I/O [44] to cloud storage [38], and from Byzantine fault-tolerance [33] to efficient Paxos implementations [49]. In the specific context of databases and key-value stores, in addition to Ardekani et al.'s work [9], Mehdi et al. [37] recently proposed a client-centric implementation of causal consistency that is both scalable and resilient to slowdown cascades (§5.3).

## 7 CONCLUSION

We present a new way to reason about isolation based on application-observable states and prove it to be as expressive as prior approaches based on histories. We present evidence suggesting that this approach (*i*) maps more naturally to what applications can observe and illuminates the anomalies allowed by distinct isolation/consistency levels; (*ii*) makes it easy to compare isolation guarantees, leading us to prove that distinct, decade-old guarantees are in fact equivalent; and (*iii*) facilitates reasoning end-to-end about isolation guarantees, enabling new opportunities for performance optimization.

**Limitations** Nonetheless, our model currently has two main limitations, which we plan to address as future work. First, it does not constrain the behavior of ongoing transactions. It thus cannot express consistency models, like opacity [30] or virtual world consistency [32] designed to prevent STM transactions from accessing an invalid memory location. This limitation is consistent with the assumption, made in most isolation and consistency research, that applications never make externally visible decisions based on uncommitted data, so that their actions can be rolled back if the transaction aborts. Second, our model focuses on the traditional transactional/read/write model, predominant in database theory and modern distributed storage systems. To support semantically rich operations, abstract data types, and commutativity, we will start from Weikum et al's theory of multi-level serializability [59], which maps higher-level operations to reads and writes.

**Acknowledgements** We thank Peter Bailis, Phil Bernstein, Ittay Eyal, Idit Keidar, Fred Schneider, and Immanuel Trummer for their valuable feedback on earlier drafts of this work. This work was supported by the National Science Foundation under grants CNS-1409555 and CNS-1718709, and by a Google Faculty Research Award. Natacha Crooks was partially funded by a Google Fellowship in Distributed Computing.

[5] as of June 2017

## REFERENCES


[1] Facebook. http://www.facebook.com/.
[2] Adya, A. *Weak Consistency: A Generalized Theory and Optimistic Implementations for Distributed Transactions.* Ph.D., MIT, Cambridge, MA, USA, Mar. 1999. Also as Technical Report MIT/LCS/TR-786.
[3] Adya, A., and Liskov, B. Lazy consistency using loosely synchronized clocks. In *Proceedings of the Sixteenth Annual ACM Symposium on Principles of Distributed Computing* (New York, NY, USA, 1997), PODC '97, ACM, pp. 73–82.
[4] Ahamad, M., Neiger, G., Burns, J. E., Kohli, P., and Hutto, P. Causal memory: Definitions, implementation and programming. Tech. rep., Georgia Institute of Technology, 1994.
[5] Ajoux, P., Bronson, N., Kumar, S., Lloyd, W., and Veeraraghavan, K. Challenges to adopting stronger consistency at scale. In *Proceedings of the 15th USENIX Conference on Hot Topics in Operating Systems* (2015), HOTOS'15.
[6] Alvaro, P., Bailis, P., Conway, N., and Hellerstein, J. M. Consistency without borders. In *Proceedings of the 4th ACM Symposium on Cloud Computing* (2013), SOCC '13, pp. 23:1–23:10.
[7] Amazon elastic compute cloud. http://aws.amazon.com/ec2/.
[8] Apache. Cassandra. http://cassandra.apache.org/.
[9] Ardekani, M. S., Sutra, P., and Shapiro, M. Non-monotonic snapshot isolation: Scalable and strong consistency for geo-replicated transactional systems. In *Proceedings of the 32nd International Symposium on Reliable Distributed Systems* (2013), SRDS '13, pp. 163–172.
[10] Attiya, H., Ellen, F., and Morrison, A. Limitations of highly-available eventually-consistent data stores. In *Proceedings of the 2015 ACM Symposium on Principles of Distributed Computing* (2015), PODC '15, ACM, pp. 385–394.
[11] Bailis, P., Davidson, A., Fekete, A., Ghodsi, A., Hellerstein, J. M., and Stoica, I. Highly available transactions: Virtues and limitations. *PVLDB 7*, 3 (2013), 181–192.
[12] Bailis, P., Fekete, A., Franklin, M. J., Ghodsi, A., Hellerstein, J. M., and Stoica, I. Feral concurrency control: An empirical investigation of modern application integrity. In *Proceedings of the 2015 ACM SIGMOD International Conference on Management of Data* (2015), SIGMOD '15, pp. 1327–1342.
[13] Bailis, P., Fekete, A., Ghodsi, A., Hellerstein, J. M., and Stoica, I. Scalable atomic visibility with ramp transactions. *ACM Transactions on Database Systems 41*, 3 (July 2016), 15:1–15:45.
[14] Basho. Riak. http://basho.com/products/.
[15] Berenson, H., Bernstein, P., Gray, J., Melton, J., O'Neil, E., and O'Neil, P. A critique of ansi sql isolation levels. *SIGMOD Rec. 24*, 2 (May 1995), 1–10.
[16] Bernstein, P. A., and Goodman, N. Concurrency control in distributed database systems. *ACM Computing Survey 13*, 2 (June 1981), 185–221.
[17] Bernstein, P. A., and Goodman, N. Multiversion concurrency control;theory and algorithms. *ACM Transactions on Database Systems 8*, 4 (1983), 465–483.
[18] Bernstein, P. A., Hadzilacos, V., and Goodman, N. *Concurrency control and recovery in database systems.* 1987.
[19] Brzezinski, B., Sobaniec, C., and D., W. From session causality to causal consistency. In *Proceedings of the 12th Euromicro Conference on Parallel, Distributed and Network based Processing* (2004), PDP 2004.
[20] Cerone, A., Bernardi, G., and Gotsman, A. A framework for transactional consistency models with atomic visibility. In *26th International Conference on Concurrency Theory, CONCUR 2015,* (2015).
[21] Cerone, A., and Gotsman, A. Analysing snapshot isolation. In *Proceedings of the 2016 ACM Symposium on Principles of Distributed Computing* (2016), PODC '16, ACM, pp. 55–64.
[22] Crooks, N., Pu, Y., Alvisi, L., and Clement, A. Seeing is believing: A client-centric specification of database isolation. Tech. Rep. TR-17-06, Computer Science Department, UT Austin, May 2017.
[23] Crooks, N., Pu, Y., Estrada, N., Gupta, T., Alvisi, L., and Clement, A. Tardis: A branch-and-merge approach to weak consistency. In *Proceedings of the 2016 International Conference on Management of Data* (2016), SIGMOD '16, ACM, pp. 1615–1628.
[24] Daudjee, K., and Salem, K. Lazy database replication with snapshot isolation. In *Proceedings of the 32nd International Conference on Very Large Data Bases* (2006), VLDB '06, VLDB Endowment, pp. 715–726.
[25] Escriva, R., Wong, B., and Sirer, E. G. Warp: Lightweight multi-key transactions for key-value stores. *CoRR abs/1509.07815* (2015).
[26] Faleiro, J. M., Abadi, D., and Hellerstein, J. M. High performance transactions via early write visibility. *PVLDB 10*, 5 (2017), 613–624.
[27] Fekete, A., Liarokapis, D., O'Neil, E., O'Neil, P., and Shasha, D. Making snapshot isolation serializable. *ACM Transactions on Database Systems 30*, 2 (June 2005), 492–528.
[28] Google. Bigtable - massively scalable nosql. https://cloud.google.com/bigtable/.
[29] Google. Cloud sql - fully managed sql service. https://cloud.google.com/sql/.
[30] Guerraoui, R., and Kapalka, M. On the correctness of transactional memory. In *Proceedings of the 13th ACM SIGPLAN Symposium on Principles and Practice of Parallel Programming* (2008), PPoPP '08, ACM, pp. 175–184.
[31] Herlihy, M. P., and Wing, J. M. Linearizability: a correctness condition for concurrent objects. *ACM Transactions Programming Language Systems 12*, 3 (July 1990), 463–492.
[32] Imbs, D., and Raynal, M. Virtual world consistency: A condition for stm systems (with a versatile protocol with invisible read operations). *Theoretical Computer Science 444* (July 2012), 113–127.
[33] Kotla, R., Alvisi, L., Dahlin, M., Clement, A., and Wong, E. Zyzzyva: Speculative Byzantine Fault Tolerance. *ACM Transactions on Computer Systems 27*, 4 (Jan. 2010), 7:1–7:39.
[34] Kraska, T., Pang, G., Franklin, M. J., Madden, S., and Fekete, A. Mdcc: multi-data center consistency. In *Proceedings of the 8th ACM European Conference on Computer Systems* (2013), EuroSys '13, pp. 113–126.
[35] Kripke, S. A. Semantical considerations on modal logic. *Acta Philosophica Fennica 16*, 1963 (1963), 83–94.
[36] Mahajan, P., Alvisi, L., and Dahlin, M. Consistency, availability, convergence. Tech. Rep. TR-11-22, Computer Science Department, UT Austin, May 2011.
[37] Mehdi, A., Littley, C., Crooks, N., Alvisi, L., and Lloyd, W. I can't believe it's not causal. In *Proceedings of the 15th USENIX Symposium on Networked Systems Design and Implementation* (2017), NSDI '17.
[38] Mickens, J., Nightingale, E. B., Elson, J., Gehring, D., Fan, B., Kadav, A., Chidambaram, V., Khan, O., and Nareddy, K. Blizzard: Fast, Cloud-Scale Block Storage for Cloud-Oblivious Applications. In *Proceedings of the 11th USENIX Symposium on Networked Systems Design and Implementation* (2014), NSDI'14.
[39] Microsoft. Azure sql database. https://https://azure.microsoft.com/en-us/services/sql-database/?v=16.50.
[40] Microsoft. Azure storage - secure cloud storage. https://azure.microsoft.com/en-us/services/storage/.
[41] Microsoft. Documentdb - nosql service for json. https://azure.microsoft.com/en-us/services/documentdb/.
[42] Microsoft. SQL Server. https://https://www.microsoft.com/en-cy/sql-server/sql-server-2016.
[43] Mu, S., Cui, Y., Zhang, Y., Lloyd, W., and Li, J. Extracting more concurrency from distributed transactions. In *Proceedings of the 11th USENIX Conference on Operating Systems Design and Implementation* (Berkeley, CA, USA, 2014), OSDI'14, USENIX Association, pp. 479–494.
[44] Nightingale, E. B., Veeraraghavan, K., Chen, P. M., and Flinn, J. Rethink the Sync. *ACM Transactions on Computer Systems 26*, 3 (Sept. 2008), 6:1–6:26.
[45] Oracle. MySQL Cluster. https://www.mysql.com/products/cluster/.
[46] Oracle. Oracle 12c. https://docs.oracle.com/database/121/.
[47] Papadimitriou, C. H. The serializability of concurrent database updates. *J. ACM 26*, 4 (Oct. 1979), 631–653.
[48] Pedone, F., Zwaenepoel, W., and Elnikety, S. Database replication using generalized snapshot isolation. *24th IEEE Symposium on Reliable Distributed Systems* (2005), 73–84.
[49] Ports, D. R. K., Li, J., Liu, V., Sharma, N. K., and Krishnamurthy, A. Designing distributed systems using approximate synchrony in data center networks. In *Proceedings of the 12th USENIX Conference on Networked Systems Design and Implementation* (Berkeley, CA, USA, 2015), NSDI'15, pp. 43–57.
[50] Postgres. Postgresql. http://www.postgresql.org/.
[51] SAP. Hana. https://www.sap.com/products/hana.html.
[52] Shapiro, M., Ardekani, M. S., and Petri, G. Consistency in 3d (invited paper). In *27th International Conference on Concurrency Theory (CONCUR 2016)* (2016).
[53] Sovran, Y., Power, R., Aguilera, M. K., and Li, J. Transactional storage for geo-replicated systems. In *Proceedings of the 23rd ACM Symposium on Operating Systems Principles* (2011), SOSP '11, pp. 385–400.
[54] Su, C., Crooks, N., Ding, C., Alvisi, L., and Xie, C. Bringing modular concurrency control to the next level. In *Proceedings of the 2017 ACM International Conference on Management of Data* (2017), SIGMOD '17, pp. 283–297.
[55] Terry, D. B., Demers, A. J., Petersen, K., Spreitzer, M. J., Theimer, M. M., and Welch, B. B. Session guarantees for weakly consistent replicated data. In *Proceedings of the 3rd International Conference on on Parallel and Distributed Information Systems* (1994), PDIS '94, pp. 140–150.
[56] Twitter. Twitter. https://www.twitter.com/.
[57] Viotti, P., and Vukolić, M. Consistency in non-transactional distributed storage systems. *ACM Computing Survey 49*, 1 (June 2016), 19:1–19:34.
[58] Warszawski, T., and Bailis, P. Acidrain: Concurrency-related attacks on database-backed web applications. In *Proceedings of the 2017 ACM International Conference on Management of Data* (2017), SIGMOD '17, pp. 5–20.
[59] Weikum, G. Principles and realization strategies of multilevel transaction management. *ACM Transactions on Database Systems 16*, 1 (Mar. 1991), 132–180.
[60] Xie, C., Su, C., Littley, C., Alvisi, L., Kapritsos, M., and Wang, Y. High-performance acid via modular concurrency control. In *Proceedings of the 25th Symposium on Operating Systems Principles* (2015), SOSP '15, pp. 279–294.
[61] Zhang, I., Sharma, N. K., Szekeres, A., Krishnamurthy, A., and Ports, D. R. K. Building consistent transactions with inconsistent replication. In *Proceedings of the 25th Symposium on Operating Systems Principles* (2015), SOSP '15, pp. 263–278.

# Space Complexity of Fault-Tolerant Register Emulations

Gregory Chockler*
Department of Computer Science
Royal Holloway, University of London
Egham, United Kingdom TW20 0EX
Gregory.Chockler@rhul.ac.uk

Alexander Spiegelman†
Viterbi Department of Electrical Engineering
Technion, Haifa, Israel
sashas@tx.technion.ac.il

## ABSTRACT

Driven by the rising popularity of cloud storage, the costs associated with implementing reliable storage services from a collection of fault-prone servers have recently become an actively studied question. The well-known ABD result shows that an $f$-tolerant register can be emulated using a collection of $2f+1$ fault-prone servers each storing a single read-modify-write object, which is known to be optimal. In this paper we generalize this bound: we investigate the inherent space complexity of emulating reliable multi-writer registers as a function of the type of the base objects exposed by the underlying servers, the number of writers to the emulated register, the number of available servers, and the failure threshold.

We establish a sharp separation between registers, and both max-registers (the base object type assumed by ABD) and CAS in terms of the resources (i.e., the number of base objects of the respective types) required to support the emulation; we show that no such separation exists between max-registers and CAS. Our main technical contribution is lower and upper bounds on the resources required in case the underlying base objects are fault-prone read/write registers. We show that the number of required registers is directly proportional to the number of writers and inversely proportional to the number of servers.

## CCS CONCEPTS

• **Theory of computation** → **Distributed algorithms**;

## KEYWORDS

Faulty shared memory; reliable emulations; space complexity

*Gregory Chockler is supported in part by Royal Society International Exchanges and Coleman-Cohen Exchange Programme Grants.
†Alexander Spiegelman is grateful to the Azrieli Foundation for the award of an Azrieli Fellowship.


*PODC '17, July 25-27, 2017, Washington, DC, USA*

ACM ISBN 978-1-4503-4992-5/17/07...$15.00
https://doi.org/10.1145/3087801.3087824

**ACM Reference format:**
Gregory Chockler and Alexander Spiegelman. 2017. Space Complexity of Fault-Tolerant Register Emulations. In *Proceedings of PODC '17, Washington, DC, USA, July 25-27, 2017,* 10 pages.
https://doi.org/10.1145/3087801.3087824

## 1 INTRODUCTION

Reliable storage emulations seek to construct fault-tolerant shared objects, such as read/write registers, using a collection of *base objects* hosted on failure-prone servers. Such emulations are core enablers for many modern storage services and applications, including cloud-based online data stores [15, 26, 32–34] and Storage-as-a-Service offerings [17, 35, 38, 40].

Most existing storage emulation algorithms are constructed from storage services capable of supporting custom-built read-modify-write (RMW) primitives [3, 5, 16, 19, 19, 22, 23, 31, 36], and perhaps the most famous one is ABD [5]. This algorithm emulates an $f$-tolerant atomic wait-free register, accessed by an unbounded number of processes (readers and writers), on top of $2f+1$ servers, each of which stores a single RMW object. Since $f$-tolerant register emulation is impossible with less than $2f+1$ servers [8, 30], the ABD algorithm's space complexity is optimal.

However, support for atomic RMW is not always available: the operations exposed by network-attached disks are typically limited to basic reads and writes, and the interfaces exposed by cloud storage services sometimes augment this with simple conditional update primitives similar to Compare-and-Swap (CAS). A natural question that arises is therefore how the ABD results generalize when only weaker primitives (e.g., read/write registers) are available. More specifically, we are interested whether reliable storage emulations are possible with weaker primitives, and if so, what their space complexity is, and in particular, whether it depends on the number of writers and the number of servers.

To answer these questions, we consider a collection of $n$ fault-prone servers, each of which stores base objects supporting the given primitives. The failure granularity is servers, meaning that a server crash causes all base objects it stores to crash as well. We study three primitives: read/write register, max-register [4], and CAS. For each primitive, we are interested in the number of base objects required to emulate an $f$-tolerant register for $k$ writers using $n$ servers.

Table 1 summarizes our results. To strengthen our lower bounds, we prove them under weak liveness and safety guarantees, namely, *obstruction freedom* and *write-sequential safety (WS-Safety)*. The latter is a weak generalization of Lamport's notion of safety [29] to multi-writer registers, which we define

**Table 1: The number of base objects used by $f$-tolerant register emulations with $k$ writers and $n > 2f$ servers.**

| **Base object** | Lower bound (WS-Safe, obstruction-free) | Upper bound (WS-Regular, wait-free) |
|---|---|---|
| max-register | $2f+1$ | $2f+1$ |
| CAS | $2f+1$ | $2f+1$ |
| read/write register | $kf + \left\lceil \frac{k}{\frac{n-(f+1)}{f}} \right\rceil (f+1)$ | $kf + \left\lceil \frac{k}{\left\lfloor \frac{n-(f+1)}{f} \right\rfloor} \right\rceil (f+1)$ |

in Section 2. Since atomicity usually requires readers to write, which may induce a dependency on the number of readers, we consider regularity for our upper bound; we define in Section 2 *write-sequential regularity (WS-Regularity)*, which is a weaker form of multi-writer regularity defined in [36]. The lower bound of $n > 2f$ of servers required for $f$-tolerant register emulations [8, 30] can be easily generalized for WS-Safe obstruction-free emulations. Therefore, we assume that $n > 2f$ throughout the paper.

Interestingly, even though both read/write registers and max-registers have the lowest consensus number of 1 in Herlihy's hierarchy [24], we show that they are clearly separated with respect to their power to support a reliable multi-writer register in a space-efficient fashion. On the other hand, no such separation exists between CAS, which has an infinite consensus number, and max-register. As an aside, we note that this separation has implications for the standard shared memory model (without base object failures); for example, it implies that a $k$-writer max-register cannot be implemented from less than $k$ read/write registers (proven in Theorem 3.2) closing the gap between the known lower and upper bounds of $k-1$ [28] and $k$ [4] respectively.

*Results.* Despite the fact that the original ABD emulation [5] assumes a general RMW base object on every server, we observe that the code executed by each server in the multi-writer ABD protocol [23, 31, 36] can be encapsulated into the *write-max* (for handling update messages) and *read-max* (for handling read messages) primitives of max-register. Therefore, the upper bound of $n = 2f + 1$ applies to max-registers as well. In Appendix A we show how to emulate a max-register from a single CAS in a wait-free manner. Thus, the upper bound for max-register also applies to CAS.

Our main technical contribution is a lower bound on the number of read/write registers required to emulate an $f$-tolerant WS-Safe obstruction-free register for $k$ clients using $n$ servers. While the ABD [5] space complexity does not depend on the number of writers or the number of servers, we show in Section 3 (Theorem 3.1) that when servers support only read/write registers, the lower bound increases linearly with the number of writers and decreases (up to a certain point) with the number of available servers. In particular, our lower bound implies that at least $kf + f + 1$ registers are needed regardless of the number of available servers. We exploit asynchrony to construct a write-sequential failure-free run in which each write completes while leaving $f$ pending writes on base registers, forcing the next write to use a different set of registers, and so on.

In Section 4, we present a new upper bound construction that closely matches our lower bound (Theorem 4.1). Note that the two bounds are closely aligned, and in particular, coincide in the two important cases of $n = 2f + 1$ and $n \geq kf + f + 1$ where they are equal to $kf + k(f + 1)$ and $kf + f + 1$ respectively. An interesting open question is to close the remaining small gap.

Another open question is whether our lower bound is tight for stronger regularity definitions [36]. In the special case of $n = 2f + 1$ servers and $k$ writers, a matching upper bound of $(2f + 1)k$ registers can be achieved by simply having each server implement a single $k$-writer max-register from $k$ base registers [4]. The question of the general case of $n \geq 2f + 1$ remains open.

In the full paper [14], we prove the following three additional results implied by an extended variant of our main lower bound construction: (1) a lower bound of $k$ registers per server for $n = 2f + 1$ (Theorem 3.4); (2) a lower bound on the number of servers when the maximum number of registers stored on each server is bounded by a known constant (Theorem 3.5); and (3) impossibility of constructing fault-tolerant multi-writer register emulations adaptive to point contention [1, 7] (Theorem 3.6).

*Related work.* The space complexity of fault-tolerant register emulations has been explored in a number of prior works. Aguilera et al. [2] show that certain types of multi-writer registers cannot be reliably emulated from a fixed number of fault-prone ones if the number of writers is not a priori known. They however, do not provide precise bounds on the number of base registers as a function of the number of writers and servers, and the failure threshold as we do in this paper. The space complexity of reliable register emulations in terms of the amount of data stored on fault-prone RMW servers was studied in [13, 20], and more recently in [11, 12, 39]. Since we are only interested in the number of stored registers and not their sizes, these results are orthogonal to ours.

Basescu et al. [9] describe several fault-tolerant multi-writer register emulations from a collection of fault-prone read/write data stores. Their algorithms incorporate a garbage-collection mechanism that ensures that the storage cost is adaptive to the write concurrency, provided that the underlying servers can be accessed in a synchronous fashion. Our results show that asynchrony has a profound impact on storage consumption by exhibiting a *sequential* failure-free run where the number of registers that need to be stored grows linearly with the number of writers.

The proof of our main result (see Lemma 3.7) further extends the adversarial framework of [39] to exploit the notion of *register covering* (originally due to [10]) extended to fault-prone base registers as in [2]. Covering arguments have been successfully applied to proving numerous space lower bound results in the literature (see [6] for a survey) including the recent tight bounds for obstruction-free consensus [18, 21, 41].

# 2 PRELIMINARIES

## 2.1 Shared Objects

A *shared object* supports concurrent execution of *operations* performed by some set, $\mathbb{C} = \{c_1, c_2, \dots\}$, of client processes. Each operation has an *invocation* and *response*. An object *schedule* is a sequence of the operation invocations and their responses. An invoked operation is *complete* in a given schedule if the operation's response is also present in the schedule, and *pending* otherwise. For a schedule $\sigma$, $ops(\sigma)$ denotes the set of all operations that were invoked in $\sigma$, and $complete(\sigma)$ (resp., $pending(\sigma)$) denotes the subset of $ops(\sigma)$ consisting of all the complete (resp., pending) operations. Also, for a set $X$ of operations, we use $\sigma|X$ to denote the subsequence of $\sigma$ consisting of all the invocation and responses of the operations in $X$.

An operation *op precedes* an operation $op'$ in a schedule $\sigma$, denoted $op \prec_\sigma op'$, iff $op'$ is invoked after *op* responds in $\sigma$. Operations *op* and $op'$ are *concurrent* in $\sigma$, if neither one precedes the other. A schedule with no concurrent operations is *sequential*. Given a schedule $\sigma$, we use $\sigma|i$ to denote the subsequence of $\sigma$ consisting of all the actions executed by the client $c_i$. The schedule is *well-formed* if $\sigma|i$ is sequential for all $i > 0$. In the following, we will only consider well-formed schedules.

The object's *sequential specification* is a collection of the object's sequential schedules in which all operations are complete. For an object schedule $\sigma$, a *linearization* $L_\sigma$ of $\sigma$ is a sequential schedule consisting of all operations in $complete(\sigma)$ along with their responses and a subset of $pending(\sigma)$, each of which being assigned a matching response, so that $L_\sigma$ satisfies both the $\sigma$'s operation precedence relation ($\prec_\sigma$) and the object sequential specification.

*Consistency conditions* specify the shared object behaviour when accessed concurrently by the clients. They are expressed as a set of schedules satisfying a desired property. The basic consistency condition for shared objects of any type is *atomicity* [25] defined formally as follows:

*Definition 2.1 (Atomicity).* A set of schedules $C$ satisfies atomicity if for all schedules $\sigma \in C$, $\sigma$ has a linearization.

## 2.2 Object types

*Registers.* A *read/write register* object (or simply a *register*) supports two operations of the form *write*($v$), $v \in \mathbb{V}$, and *read*() returning *ack* and $v \in \mathbb{V}$ respectively where $\mathbb{V}$ is the register value domain. Its sequential specification consists of all sequential schedules in which every *read* returns the value written by the last preceding *write* or an initial value $v_0 \in \mathbb{V}$ if no such write exists.

A register is *multi-writer (MW)* (resp., *multi-reader (MR)*) if it can be written (resp., read) by an *unbounded* number of clients. A $k$-writer register, or simply, k-register, is a register that can be written by at most $k > 0$ distinct clients. A register is *single-writer (SW)* (resp., *single-reader (SR)*) if only one process can write (resp., read) the register. For a register schedule $\sigma$, we write $writes(\sigma)$ (resp., $reads(\sigma)$) to denote the sets of all write (resp., read) operations invoked in $\sigma$. We say that $\sigma$ is *write-sequential* if no two writes in $writes(\sigma)$ are concurrent.

Let $C$ be a set of register schedules. The following weaker consistency conditions will be considered for registers in addition to atomicity:

*Definition 2.2 (Write-Sequential Regularity (WS-Regularity)).* For all $\sigma \in C$, if $\sigma$ is write-sequential, then for each $rd \in reads(\sigma) \cap complete(\sigma)$ there is a linearization $L_{rd}$ of $\sigma|writes(\sigma) \cup \{rd\}$.

*Definition 2.3 (Write-Sequential Safety (WS-Safety)).* As WS-Regularity, but only required to hold for complete reads that are not concurrent with any writes.

*Max-registers.* Given an ordered set of values $\mathbb{V}$, a *max-register* [4] supports two operations: *write-max*($v$), $v \in \mathbb{V}$, that returns *ok*, and *read-max* that returns $v \in \mathbb{V}$. Its sequential specification consists of all sequential schedules in which every *read-max* returns the highest value written by a preceding *write-max*, or an initial value $v_0 \in \mathbb{V}$ if no such *write-max* exists.

*Compare-and-Swap (CAS).* A CAS object supports a single operation $C\&S(v, v')$, $v, v' \in \mathbb{V}$, and returns $v'' \in \mathbb{V}$ where $\mathbb{V}$ is a value domain. Its sequential specification consists of all sequential schedules in which every $C\&S(v, v')$ operation returns the current object value (which is initialized to $v_0$), and sets it to $v'$ if it equals $v$.

## 2.3 System Model

We consider an *asynchronous fault-prone shared memory system* [27] consisting of a set of shared *base* objects $\mathcal{B} = \{b_1, b_2, \dots\}$. The objects are accessed by a collection of clients in the set $\mathbb{C} = \{c_1, c_2, \dots\}$.

We consider a slight generalization of the model in [27] where the objects are mapped to a set $\mathcal{S} = \{s_1, s_2, \dots s_n\}$ of $n$ servers via a function $\delta$ from $\mathcal{B}$ to $\mathcal{S}$. For $B \subseteq \mathcal{B}$, we will write $\delta(B)$ to denote the *image* of $B$, i.e., $\delta(B) = \{\delta(b) : b \in B\}$. Conversely, for $S \subseteq \mathcal{S}$, we will write $\delta^{-1}(S)$ to denote the *pre-image* of $S$, i.e., $\delta^{-1}(S) = \{b : \delta(b) \in S\}$. Note that for all $B \subseteq \mathcal{B}$, $|\delta(B)| \leq |B|$, and conversely, for all $S \subseteq \mathcal{S}$, $|\delta^{-1}(S)| \geq |S|$. Both servers and clients can fail by crashing. A crash of a server causes all objects mapped to that server to instantaneously crash (i.e.,, stop responding to the client invocations)[1].

[1] Note that the original faulty shared model of [27] can be derived from our model by choosing $\delta$ to be an injective function.

*Emulation algorithms.* We study algorithms emulating a reliable k-register to a set of clients from a collection of fault-prone atomic base objects. Clients interact with the emulated register via *high-level* read and write operations. To distinguish the high-level emulated reads and writes from low-level base object invocations, we refer to the former as READ and WRITE. We say that high-level operations are *invoked* and *return* whereas low-level operations are *triggered* and *respond.* A high-level operation consists of a series of trigger and respond *actions* on base objects, starting with the operation's invocation and ending with its return. Since base objects are crash-prone, we assume that the clients can trigger several operations in a row without waiting for the previously triggered operations to respond.

An emulation algorithm $A$ defines the behaviour of clients as deterministic state machines where state transitions are associated with actions, such as trigger/response of low-level operations. A *configuration* is a mapping to states from system components, i.e., clients and base objects. An *initial configuration* is one where all components are in their initial states.

*Runs.* A *run* of $A$ is a (finite or infinite) sequence of alternating configurations and actions, beginning with some initial configuration, such that configuration transitions occur according to $A$. We use the notion of time $t$ during a run $r$ to refer to the configuration reached after the $t^{\text{th}}$ action in $r$. A *run fragment* is a contiguous sub-sequence of a run. A run is *write-only* if it has no invocations of the high-level READ operations. We say that a base object, client, or server is *faulty* in a run $r$ if it crashes at some time in $r$, and correct, otherwise.

*Fairness.* A run is *fair* if (1) for every low-level operation triggered by a correct client on a correct base object, there is eventually a matching response, and (2) every correct client gets infinitely many opportunities to both trigger a low-level operation and execute the return actions.

## 2.4 Properties of Emulation Algorithms

**Safety** The emulation algorithm safety will be expressed in terms of the write-sequential consistency conditions as given by Definitions 2.2 and 2.3. An emulation algorithm $A$ *satisfies* a consistency condition $C$ if for all runs $r$ of $A$, the subsequence of $r$ consisting of the invocations and responses of the high-level read and write operations is a schedule in $C$.

**Liveness** We consider the following liveness conditions that must be satisfied in fair runs of an emulation algorithm. A *wait-free* object is one that guarantees that every high-level operation invoked by a correct client eventually returns, regardless of the actions of other clients. An *obstruction-free* object guarantees that every high-level operation invoked by a correct client that is not concurrent to any other operation by a correct client eventually returns.

**Fault-Tolerance** The emulation algorithm is $f$-tolerant if it remains correct (in the sense of its safety and liveness properties) as long as at most $f$ servers crash for a fixed $f > 0$.

**Complexity measures** The *resource consumption* of an emulation algorithm $A$ in a (finite) run $r$ is the number of base objects used by $A$ in $r$. The *resource complexity* [27] of $A$ is the maximum resource consumption of $A$ in all its runs.

# 3 LOWER BOUNDS

We characterize the minimum resource complexity of the algorithms implementing an $f$-tolerant obstruction-free WS-Safe k-register as a function of the number $n$ of available servers. First, it is easy to see that if $n \leq 2f$, then no such algorithm can exist. This result is implied by an extended statement of Lemma 3.7 (proven in the full paper [14]), and can also be shown directly by a straightforward application of a partitioning argument as discussed in [8, 30]. For the case $n > 2f$, we prove the following main theorem:

THEOREM 3.1. *For all $k > 0$, $f > 0$, let $A$ be an $f$-tolerant algorithm emulating an obstruction-free WS-Safe k-register using a collection $\mathcal{S}$ of servers such that $n \geq 2f + 1$. Then, $A$ uses at least $kf + \left\lceil \frac{kf}{n-(f+1)} \right\rceil (f+1)$ base registers (i.e., $|\delta^{-1}(\mathcal{S})| \geq kf + \left\lceil \frac{kf}{n-(f+1)} \right\rceil (f+1)$).*

This result implies a new lower bound of $k$ registers on the resource complexity of emulating a single (i.e., non-fault-tolerant) max-register for $k$ writers that tightens the previously known lower bound of $k - 1$ [28]:

THEOREM 3.2 (RESOURCE COMPLEXITY OF $k$-WRITER MAX-REGISTER). *For all $k > 0$, any algorithm implementing a wait-free $k$-writer max-register from a collection of wait-free MWMR atomic base registers uses at least $k$ base registers.*

PROOF (SKETCH). Observe that an $f$-tolerant obstruction-free WS-Safe k-register emulation $A$ can be obtained (using an ABD-style algorithm) from $n = 2f+1$ servers each storing a single max-register object. It therefore, follows that $A$'s resource complexity using max-registers implemented from $< k$ registers will be $< (2f+1)k$ contradicting Theorem 3.1. The detailed proof appears in the full paper [14]. □

Since a $k$-writer max-register can be implemented from $k$ read/write registers [4], we have the following

COROLLARY 3.3. *$k$ wait-free multi-writer atomic registers are necessary and sufficient to implement a wait-free $k$-writer max-register in the standard shared memory model.*

The following lower bounds are proven in the full paper [14]:

THEOREM 3.4. *Let $n = 2f+1$. For all $k > 0$, $f > 0$, every $f$-tolerant algorithm emulating an obstruction-free WS-Safe $k$-register stores at least $k$ registers on each server in $\mathcal{S}$.*

THEOREM 3.5. *Let $m > 0$ be an upper bound on the number of registers mapped to each server in $\mathcal{S}$ (i.e., $\forall s \in \mathcal{S}, |\delta^{-1}(\{s\})| \leq m$). For all $f > 0$ and $k > 0$, every $f$-tolerant algorithm emulating an obstruction-free WS-Safe k-register from a collection $\mathcal{S}$ of servers such that $n > 2f + 1$ uses at least $\lceil kf/m \rceil + f + 1$ servers (i.e., $n \geq \lceil kf/m \rceil + f + 1$).*

THEOREM 3.6. *For any $f > 0$, there is no $f$-tolerant algorithm that emulates an WS-Safe obstruction-free k-register with resource complexity adaptive to point contention [1, 7].*

We now present the proof of our main result.

## 3.1 Proof of Theorem 3.1

*Overview.* Our proof exploits the fact that the environment is allowed to prevent a pending low-level write from taking effect for arbitrarily long [2]. As a result, a client executing a high-level WRITE operation cannot reliably store the requested value in a base register that has a pending write as this write may take effect at a later time thus erasing the stored value. At the same time, the client cannot wait for all base registers on which it triggers low-level operations to respond, since up to $f$ of them may reside on faulty servers. It therefore must be able to complete a high-level write without waiting for responses from up to $f$ registers. Consequently, the next high-level WRITE (by a different client) cannot reliably use these registers (as they might have outstanding low-level writes), and is therefore forced to use additional registers thus causing the total number of registers grow with each subsequent WRITE.

In our main lemma (Lemma 3.7), we formalize this intuition as follows: Starting from a run $r_0$ consisting of an initial configuration, we build a sequence of consecutive extensions $r_1, \ldots, r_k$ so that $r_i$ is obtained from $r_{i-1}$ by having a new client invoke a high-level WRITE $W_i$ of some (not previously used) value. We then let the environment behave in an adversarial fashion (Definition 3.10) by blocking the responses from the writes triggered on at most $f$ base registers as well as the prior pending low-level writes. In Lemma 3.13, we show that $W_i$ must terminate without waiting for these responses to arrive. Furthermore, in Lemma 3.14, we show that $W_i$ must invoke low-level writes on at least $2f + 1$ base registers (residing on $\geq 2f + 1$ different servers) that do not have any prior pending writes. This, combined with Lemma 3.13, implies that by the time $W_i$ completes, there are at least $f$ more registers on at least $f$ servers with pending writes after $W_i$ completes. Thus, by the time the $k$th high-level WRITE completes, the total number of covered registers is at least $kf$ (see Lemma 3.7(a)).

To obtain a stronger bound, our construction is parameterized by an *arbitrary* subset $F$ of servers such that $|F| = f+1$. We show that the extra storage available on these servers cannot in fact, be utilized by an emulation (see Lemma 3.7(b)) forcing it to use at least $kf$ registers on the remaining $\mathcal{S} \setminus F$ servers to accommodate the same number $k$ of writers. We use this result in the proof of Theorem 3.1, to show that the number of base registers required for the emulation is a function of $k$ and $n$.

*Detailed proof.* For any time $t$ (following the $t^{\text{th}}$ action) in a run $r$ of the emulation algorithm we define the following:

- *Covering write*: Let $w$ be a low-level write triggered on a base register $b$ at times $\leq t$. We will refer to $w$ as *covering at* $t$, and to $b$ as being *covered by* $w$ *at* $t$ if $w$ is pending at $t$.
- $C(t) \subseteq \mathbb{C}$: the set of all clients that have completed a high-level WRITE operation at times $\leq t$.
- $Cov(t) \subseteq \mathcal{B}$: the set of all base registers being covered by some low-level write at time $t$.
- $V(t) \subseteq \mathbb{V}$: the set of all values written by high-level WRITEs at times $\leq t$.

We first prove the following key lemma:

LEMMA 3.7. *For all $k > 0$, $f > 0$, let $A$ be an $f$-tolerant algorithm that emulates a WS-Safe obstruction-free k-register using a collection $\mathcal{S}$ of servers storing a collection $\mathcal{B}$ of wait-free MWMR atomic registers. Then, for every $F \subseteq S$ such that $|F| = f+1$, there exist $k+1$ failure-free runs $r_i$, $0 \leq i \leq k$, of $A$ such that (1) $r_0$ is a run consisting of an initial configuration and $t_0 = 0$ steps, and (2) for all $i \in [k]$, $r_i$ is a write-only sequential extension of $r_{i-1}$ ending at time $t_i > 0$ that consists of $i$ complete high-level* WRITE*s of $i$ distinct values $v_1, \ldots, v_i$ by $i$ distinct clients $c_1, \ldots, c_i$ such that:*

*a)* $|Cov(t_i)| \geq if$ *b)* $\delta(Cov(t_i)) \cap F = \emptyset$

Fix arbitrary $k > 0$, $f > 0$, and a set $F$ of servers such that $|F| = f+1$. We proceed by induction on $i$, $0 \leq i \leq k$. **Base:** Trivially holds for the run $r_0$ of $A$ consisting of $t_0 = 0$ steps. **Step:** Assume that $r_{i-1}$ exists for all $i \in [k-1]$. We show how $r_{i-1}$ can be extended up to time $t_i > t_{i-1}$ so that the lemma holds for the resulting run $r_i$. For the remainder of the Lemma 3.7's proof, we will limit our attention to the runs in which every low-level write operation is linearized simultaneously with its respond step. In particular, this implies that no low-level write $w$ that is covering some register $b$ at a time $t$ in $r$ will be observed by any low-level reads from $b$ as having taken effect until after $w$'s respond event occurs. Formally:

ASSUMPTION 1 (WRITE LINEARIZATION). *For every extension $r$ of $r_{i-1}$ and a base object $b \in \mathcal{B}$, let $L_{r|b}$ be a linearization of $r|b$. Then, $L_{r|b}$ does not include any low-level write operations in pending($r|b$), and for any two low-level writes $w_1, w_2 \in$ complete($r|b$) such that respond($w_1$) $\prec_{r|b}$ respond($w_2$), $w_1 \prec_{L_{r|b}} w_2$.*

Note that the above does not affect generality of our lower bound since the stipulated base register behaviour is allowed by atomicity, and therefore, must be tolerated by *every* emulation algorithm.

We proceed by introducing the following notation:

*Definition 3.8.* Let $r$ be an extension of $r_{i-1}$. For all times $t \geq t_{i-1}$ in $r$, let

(1) $Tr_i(t)$: the set of all base registers which have a low-level write triggered on between $t_{i-1}$ and $t$.
(2) $Rr_i(t) \subseteq Tr_i(t)$ be the set of all base registers which had a low-level write triggered on and responded (took effect) between $t_{i-1}$ and $t$.

(3) $Cov_i(t) = Cov(t) \setminus Cov(t_{i-1})$ be the set of all base registers that have been newly covered between $t_{i-1}$ and $t$. Note that $Cov_i(t) \subseteq Tr_i(t)$.
(4) $Q_i(t) \subseteq \mathcal{S}$ be the set of all servers such that $Q_i(t) = \delta(Cov_i(t)) \setminus F$ if $|\delta(Cov_i(t)) \setminus F| \leq f$, and $Q_i(t) = Q_i(t-1)$, otherwise. In other words, $Q_i(t)$ is the set of the first $f$ servers not in $F$ that have at least one register newly covered between $t_{i-1}$ and $t$.
(5) $F_i(t) \triangleq \{s \in F \mid \delta^{-1}(\{s\}) \cap Rr_i(t) \neq \emptyset\}$, i.e., $F_i(t)$ is the set of all servers in $F$ having a register that responded to a low-level write invoked after $t_{i-1}$.
(6) $M_i(t) \triangleq \delta(Cov_i(t)) \cap (F \setminus F_i(t))$, i.e., $M_i(t)$ is the set of all servers in $F$ with at least one register covered by a low-level write invoked after $t_{i-1}$ and without registers that have responded to the low-level writes invoked after $t_{i-1}$.
(7) $G_i(t) \subseteq \mathcal{S}$ be the set of all servers such that $G_i(t) = M_i(t)$ if $|Q_i(t)| < |F_i(t)|$, and $G_i(t) = \emptyset$, otherwise.

Below we will introduce the adversary $Ad_i$, which causes $A$ to gradually increase the number of base registers covered after $t_{i-1}$ by delaying the respond actions of some of the previously triggered low-level writes.

*Definition 3.9 (Blocked Writes).* Let $r$ be an extension of $r_{i-1}$. For all times $t \geq t_{i-1}$ in $r$, let BlockedWrites$_i(t)$ be the set of all low-level covering writes $w$ satisfying either one of the following two conditions:

(1) $w$ was triggered by a client in $C(t_{i-1})$, or
(2) $w$ was triggered on a base register in $\delta^{-1}(Q_i(t) \cup G_i(t))$.

We say that a pending low-level write $w$ is *blocked* in an extension $r$ of $r_{i-1}$ if there exists a time $t \geq t_{i-1}$ such that for all $t' > t$ in $r$, $w \in$ BlockedWrites$_i(t')$. The following definition specifies the set of the environment behaviours that are allowed by $Ad_i$ in all extensions of $r_{i-1}$:

*Definition 3.10 ($Ad_i$).* For an extension $r$ of $r_{i-1}$ we say that the environment *behaves like* $Ad_i$ after $r_{i-1}$ in $r$ if the following holds:

(1) There are no failures after time $t_{i-1}$ in $r$.
(2) For all $t \geq t_{i-1}$ in $r$, if a low-level write $w \in$ BlockedWrites$_i(t)$, then $w$ does not respond at $t$.
(3) If $r$ is infinite then:
   (a) Every pending low-level read or write that is not blocked in $r$ eventually responds.
   (b) Every trigger or return action that is ready to be executed at a client $c$ in $r$ is eventually executed.

For a finite extension $r$ of $r_{i-1}$, we will write $\langle r, Ad_i \rangle$ to denote the set of all extensions of $r$ in which the environment behaves like $Ad_i$ after $r_{i-1}$; and we will write $\langle r, Ad_i, t \rangle$ to denote the subset of $\langle r, Ad_i \rangle$ consisting of all runs having exactly $t$ steps. For $X \in \{Q_i, F_i, M_i\}$ and a run $r \in \langle r_{i-1}, Ad_i, t \rangle$, we say that $X$ is *stable* after $r$ if for all $t' \geq t$ for all extensions $r' \in \langle r, Ad_i, t' \rangle$, $X(t') = X(t)$.

The following lemma asserts several facts implied directly by Definitions 3.8 and 3.10. The proof is very technical and for space limitation appears in the full paper [14].

LEMMA 3.11. *For all $t \geq t_{i-1}$ and $r \in \langle r_{i-1}, Ad_i, t \rangle$, all of the following holds at time $t$ in $r$:*

*(1)* $Q_i(t) \subseteq \delta(Cov_i(t)) \setminus F$
*(2)* $Q_i(t) \subseteq Q_i(t+1)$
*(3)* $F_i(t) \subseteq F_i(t+1)$
*(4)* $|F_i(t)| - |Q_i(t)| \leq 1$
*(5)* $|Q_i(t)| \leq f$
*(6)* $|F_i(t)| \leq f + 1$
*(7)* $F_i(t) = F_i(t+1) \implies M_i(t) \subseteq M_i(t+1)$
*(8)* $|M_i(t)| \leq f + 1$
*(9)* $|\delta(Cov_i(t)) \setminus F| \geq f \implies |Q_i(t)| \geq f$
*(10)* $|\delta(Cov_i(t)) \setminus F| < f \implies \delta(Rr_i(t)) \setminus F = \emptyset$
*(11)* $(Q_i(t) \cup M_i(t)) \cap \delta^{-1}(Rr_i(t)) = \emptyset$

The following corollary follows immediately from the claims 2–3 and 5–8 of Lemma 3.11.

COROLLARY 3.12. *There exists a run $r \in \langle r_{i-1}, Ad_i \rangle$ such that $F_i$, $Q_i$, and $M_i$ are all stable after $r$.*

We first show that $r_{i-1}$ can be extended with a complete high-level WRITE $W_i$ of a value $v_i \notin V(t_{i-1})$ by a client $c_i \notin \{c_1, \ldots, c_{i-1}\}$ such that the environment behaves like $Ad_i$ until $W_i$ returns. Roughly, the reason for this is that $Ad_i$ guarantees that after $r_{i-1}$, $c_i$ would only miss responses from the writes invoked on at most $f$ servers (see Claim 1) as well as those that might have been invoked in $r_{i-1}$ by other clients $\{c_1, \ldots, c_{i-1}\}$, which $c_i$ is unaware of. As a result, the involved servers and clients would appear to $c_i$ as faulty after $r_{i-1}$, and therefore, to ensure obstruction freedom, it must complete $W_i$ without waiting for the outstanding writes to respond.

LEMMA 3.13. *Let $r \in \langle r_{i-1}, Ad_i \rangle$ be a run consisting of $r_{i-1}$ followed by a high-level* WRITE *invocation $W_i$ by client $c_i \notin C(t_{i-1})$. Then, there exists a run $r_r \in \langle r, Ad_i \rangle$ in which $W_i$ returns.*

By Corollary 3.12, there exists an extension $r' \in \langle r, Ad_i, t' \rangle$ where $t' > t_{i-1}$ such that $Q_i$, $F_i$, and $M_i$ are all stable after $r'$. If $W_i$ returns in $r'$, we are done. Otherwise, we will first bound the number of servers $|Q_i(t') \cup M_i(t')|$ controlled by $Ad_i$ as follows:

CLAIM 1. *Consider a time $t > t_{i-1}$, and a run $r \in \langle r_{i-1}, Ad_i, t \rangle$. If $M_i$ is stable after $r$, then $|Q_i(t) \cup M_i(t)| \leq f$.*

PROOF. By Lemma 3.11.5, $|Q_i(t)| \leq f$. Thus, if $M_i(t) = \emptyset$, then $|Q_i(t) \cup M_i(t)| \leq f$ as needed. Otherwise ($M_i(t) \neq \emptyset$), we show that $|F_i(t)| = |Q_i(t)| + 1$. Suppose to the contrary that $|F_i(t)| \neq |Q_i(t)| + 1$. Since by Lemma 3.11.4, $|F_i(t)| \leq |Q_i(t)| + 1$, the only possibility for $|F_i(t)| \neq |Q_i(t)| + 1$ is if $|F_i(t)| \leq |Q_i(t)|$. Thus, by Definition 3.8.7, $G_i(t) = \emptyset$, and hence, by Definition 3.9, no writes on the registers in $\delta^{-1}(M_i(t))$ are blocked. However, since $M_i(t) \neq \emptyset$, at least one register in $\delta^{-1}(M_i(t))$ must have an outstanding write. Therefore, by Definition 3.10.3(a), there exists time $t'$, and an extension $r' \in \langle r, Ad_i, t' \rangle$ such that one of the registers on some server $s \in M_i(t)$ responds at time $t'$. Thus, $s \in F_i(t')$, and therefore, $s \notin M_i(t')$. Hence, $M_i$ is not stable after $r$. A contradiction to the assumption.

# Brief Announcement: Readers of Wait-free Unbounded Registers Must Write

Eric Ruppert
York University,
Toronto, Canada

## ABSTRACT

Implementing stronger read/write registers from weaker ones is a classical problem in the theory of distributed computing. In some such implementations, implemented read operations have the desirable property of not having to write to the base registers used in the implementation. In other cases, it has been proved that implementations cannot have this property. Here, we describe a novel result of the latter type. Although a lock-free implementation of an unbounded register can be built where reads do not write, we show that in any *wait-free* implementation of unbounded registers from bounded registers, the implemented read operations must write to shared memory.

## 1 INTRODUCTION

Registers are the most basic building block of shared-memory systems. Researchers have specified many different types of registers with various characteristics.

- Single-writer (sw) registers can be written only by one process, whereas multi-writer (mw) registers can be written by every process.
- Similarly, a register may be single-reader (sr) or multi-reader (mr).
- A register may store a single bit, a fixed number of bits, or be unbounded, meaning that it can store a bit string of arbitrary length (or, equivalently, an arbitrary natural number).
- The three most prominent correctness properties used to specify the correct behaviour of a register when it is accessed by multiple processes are safety, regularity and linearizability [3].

Dozens of papers have appeared over the past three decades that describe how to build stronger types of registers in a system that provides weaker base registers. Chapters 11 to 13 of Raynal's textbook [4] give a good overview of many such constructions, together with references to even more. By combining these results, it can be shown that even the strongest type of register, an atomic mwmr unbounded register, has a wait-free implementation from registers of the weakest type, safe swsr single-bit registers.


*PODC '17, July 25–27, 2017, Washington, DC, USA*

ACM ISBN 978-1-4503-4992-5/17/07.
https://doi.org/http://dx.doi.org/10.1145/3087801.3087859

We use READ and WRITE to denote operations on the implemented registers and read and write to denote steps on the base registers used in the implementation. We use the notation read$(R) \to v$ to denote a step in which a process reads the base register $R$ and gets the result $v$.

Although unbounded registers are often discussed, the question of implementing them from bounded ones has not been explicitly addressed very often: constructions of unbounded registers typically assume that the base registers are also unbounded. However, a few of the constructions of large registers from single bits generalize easily to provide an implementation of an unbounded register too. For example, Kirousis, Kranakis and Vitányi [2] describe an implementation of an atomic swsr *bounded* register from safe swsr single-bit registers. The construction uses base registers divided into four 'tracks'. The writer writes its value in one of the tracks and the reader discovers the value of the implemented register by reading one of the tracks. The two processes coordinate with a kind of mutual exclusion algorithm that ensures they are never accessing the same track at the same time. (READS write to base registers as part of this coordination scheme.) This implementation can easily be adapted to yield a wait-free implementation of an *unbounded* register as follows. Each track becomes an infinite array of base registers, and any bit string to be written can be encoded by representing 0, 1 and an end of string marker as 00, 01 and 11. Once we have obtained a swsr unbounded register in this way, standard constructions yield wait-free mwmr unbounded registers (see [1, 4]).

Vidyasankar gave a wait-free implementation of an atomic swmr *bounded* register that can store $n$ possible values from atomic swmr single-bit registers [5]. It uses an array of $n$ bits. A WRITE$(v)$ operation writes a 1 in position $v$ and then 0's in positions $v-1, v-2, \ldots 1$. A READ reads the array from left to right until finding a 1, and then rereads that portion of the array from right to left, returning the index of the leftmost 1 seen. The exact same algorithm can be used to implement an *unbounded* swmr register, but it becomes lock-free instead of wait-free, since WRITES of larger and larger values can cause a READ to run forever. In this lock-free implementation, READ operations never write to the base registers.

It is a natural question to ask whether a construction like Vidyasankar's can be extended to obtain a wait-free implementation of an *unbounded* register in which the READ operations do not write to the base registers. Here, we show that although *lock-free* constructions of unbounded registers can have this desirable property, READS must write in *wait-free* implementations of unbounded registers, even if the implemented register is swsr.

Two results with a similar flavour have been proved before. READS must write to shared memory in any implementation of an atomic register from a finite number of regular registers [3], and in any implementation of atomic multi-reader registers from single-reader registers [1, Theorem 10.3].

## 2 PROOF THAT READS OF WAIT-FREE UNBOUNDED REGISTERS MUST WRITE

We first sketch the intuition behind the proof. To derive a contradiction, assume we have a wait-free implementation where READs do not write. Suppose a READ starts by reading register $R_1$. Since $R_1$ is bounded and the READ could return infinitely many different values, there must be executions of the READ that return infinitely many different results, but all start by reading some value $v_1$ in $R_1$. Thus, after reading $v_1$ in $R_1$, the READ must take at least one more step. Let $R_2$ be the register read in that next step. By a similar argument, for some $v_2$, there are infinitely many responses of the READ consistent with seeing $v_1$ in $R_1$ and then $v_2$ in $R_2$. By induction, there is a sequence of steps for the READ: read$(R_1) \rightarrow v_1$, read$(R_2) \rightarrow v_2$, ..., such that any prefix is the beginning of READ operations that return infinitely many different results. The next step of the proof is to stitch together a single *infinite* execution where a single READ performs this infinite sequence of reads, contradicting the assumption that the implementation is wait-free. This latter part of the proof is where the assumption that READs do not write is used.

THEOREM 2.1. *There is no wait-free implementation of an atomic swsr unbounded register from bounded atomic registers in which the reader does not perform any writes.*

PROOF. To derive a contradiction, assume there is a wait-free implementation of a swsr atomic unbounded register from bounded registers in which the reader performs no writes. For $i \geq 0$, let $\alpha_i$ be the finite execution where the writer performs the operations WRITE(1), WRITE(2), ..., WRITE($i$). Note that $\alpha_0$ is the empty execution. We prove the following claim by induction.

*Claim 1:* There is an infinite sequence of registers $R_1, R_2, R_3, \ldots$ and values $v_1, v_2, v_3, \ldots$ such that

(1) for all $j \geq 0$, there is an execution in which the first $j$ steps of the first READ are read$(R_1) \rightarrow v_1$, read$(R_2) \rightarrow v_2$, ..., read$(R_j) \rightarrow v_j$, and
(2) for all $j \geq 0$, there are infinitely many values of $i \in \mathbb{N}$ such that at the end of the execution $\alpha_i$, the values in $R_1, R_2, \ldots, R_j$ are $v_1, v_2, \ldots, v_j$, respectively.

*Proof of Claim 1:* We construct the two sequences inductively.

For $j = 0$, statement 1 is vacuous and all values of $i \in \mathbb{N}$ satisfy statement 2 vacuously.

Now, let $j \geq 1$ and assume that we have already constructed $R_1, R_2, \ldots, R_{j-1}$ and $v_1, v_2, \ldots, v_{j-1}$ to satisfy statements 1 and 2 for $j-1$. We construct $R_j$ and $v_j$ to satisfy the statements for $j$.

Let $S$ be the set of all $i$ such that at the end of $\alpha_i$, the values in $R_1, R_2, \ldots, R_{j-1}$ are $v_1, v_2, \ldots, v_{j-1}$, respectively. (Note that if $j = 1$, then $S = \mathbb{N}$.) For any $i \in S$, a READ executed by itself at the end of $\alpha_i$ will start with the steps read$(R_1) \rightarrow v_1$, read$(R_2) \rightarrow v_2$, ..., read$(R_{j-1}) \rightarrow v_{j-1}$. (This sequence of steps is what the READ algorithm specifies, according to induction hypothesis 1.) However, a READ after $\alpha_i$ must return a different result for each $i \in S$. By induction hypothesis 2, $|S| \geq 2$, so the READ cannot stop after performing this sequence of $j-1$ reads; it must perform at least one more read to determine what result it should return. Let $R_j$ be the register that the READ would read next.

Since $S$ is infinite and $R_j$ is a bounded register, there must be some value $v_j$ such that, for infinitely many values of $i$ in $S$, $R_j$ has the value $v_j$ at the end of $\alpha_i$. Let $S'$ be the (infinite) set of all such $i$'s. Since $S' \subseteq S$, the registers $R_1, R_2, \ldots, R_j$ have the values $v_1, v_2, \ldots, v_j$ at the end of $\alpha_i$ for all $i \in S'$. Thus, statement 2 is satisfied for $j$. Moreover, a READ executed at the end of $\alpha_i$ (for any $i \in S'$) satisfies statement 1 for $j$. This completes the proof of Claim 1.

*Claim 2:* There is an infinite sequence of finite executions $\beta_0, \beta_1, \ldots$ and an infinite sequence of non-negative integers $i(0), i(1), \ldots$ such that

(1) for all $j \geq 0$, the sequence of steps performed by the reader in $\beta_j$ is read$(R_1) \rightarrow v_1$, read$(R_2) \rightarrow v_2, \ldots$, read$(R_j) \rightarrow v_j$, and they are all steps of a single READ,
(2) for all $j \geq 0$, the writer performs exactly the steps of $\alpha_{i(j)}$ in $\beta_j$, and
(3) for all $j \geq 1$, $\beta_{j-1}$ is a strict prefix of $\beta_j$.

*Proof of Claim 2:* We use induction on $j$. For the base case, let $\beta_0$ be the execution containing no steps and $i(0) = 0$. For the inductive step, let $j \geq 1$ and assume we have constructed $\beta_{j-1}$ and $i(j-1)$ to satisfy the claim. We describe how to construct $\beta_j$ and $i(j)$.

By induction hypothesis 1, the reader performs $j-1$ steps of a single READ in $\beta_{j-1}$ and reads the values $v_1, \ldots, v_{j-1}$ in those steps. By Claim 1, there are infinitely many possible output values for the READ consistent with those results, so the READ must take at least one more step, in which it reads $R_j$. By Claim 1, there are infinitely many $\alpha_i$'s that would cause a subsequent READ to read $v_j$ from $R_j$. Choose $i(j)$ such that $i(j) > i(j-1)$ and $v_j$ is stored in $R_j$ at the end of $\alpha_{i(j)}$. Let $\beta_j$ be the execution

$$\beta_{j-1} \cdot \text{WRITE}(i(j-1)+1)) \cdot \text{WRITE}(i(j-1)+2) \cdots \text{WRITE}(i(j)) \cdot \text{read}(R_j) \rightarrow v_j.$$

It is easy to see that Claim 2 is satisfied, so this completes the proof of Claim 2.

Since, for all $j \geq 1$, $\beta_{j-1}$ is a strict prefix of $\beta_j$, the limit sequence $\beta$ of the $\beta_j$'s is a well-defined infinite sequence: the $k$th step in $\beta$ is simply the $k$th step of $\beta_k$. Since each $\beta_k$ is a legal execution of the algorithm and legal executions are limit-closed, $\beta$ is a legal execution of the algorithm in which a READ takes infinitely many steps without terminating. This contradicts the assumption that the implementation is wait-free. □

*Acknowledgement.* This research was funded by the Natural Sciences and Engineering Research Council of Canada.

## REFERENCES

[1] H. Attiya and J. Welch. *Distributed Computing: Fundamentals, Simulations and Advanced Topics, 2nd ed.* Wiley-Interscience, 2004.
[2] L. M. Kirousis, E. Kranakis, and P. M. B. Vitányi. Atomic multireader register. In *Proc. 2nd International Workshop on Distributed Algorithm*, pages 278–296, 1987.
[3] L. Lamport. On interprocess communication. *Distributed Computing*, 1(2):77–101, June 1986.
[4] M. Raynal. *Concurrent Programming: Algorithms, Principles and Foundations.* Springer, 2013.
[5] K. Vidyasankar. Converting Lamport's regular register to atomic register. *Inf. Process. Lett.*, 28:287–290, 1988.

# Brief Announcement: Fast Shared Counting using $O(n)$ Compare-and-Swap Registers

Pankaj Khanchandani
ETH Zurich
kpankaj@ethz.ch

Roger Wattenhofer
ETH Zurich
wattenhofer@ethz.ch

## ABSTRACT

We consider the problem of building a wait-free and linearizable counter using shared registers. The counter supports a read operation, which returns the value of the counter, and an increment operation, which increments the value of the counter and returns nothing. The shared registers support read, write and compare-and-swap instructions. We show that given $n$ processes and $O(n)$ shared registers, the increment operation is in $O(\log n)$ and read operation is in $O(1)$.

## CCS CONCEPTS

• **Theory of computation → Shared memory algorithms; Concurrent algorithms;**

## KEYWORDS

shared counter; wait-free; linearizable; compare-and-swap

## 1 INTRODUCTION

The compare-and-swap (CAS) instruction is widely available in commercial hardware and correspondingly used in software. It is therefore an incentive to design parallel algorithms with optimal time and space complexity using CAS instructions.

One of the basic problems in shared memory systems is to implement a linearizable and wait-free shared counter for $n$ processes. Jayanti et al. [5] showed that if the shared registers support only read and write instructions, then the read operation on a counter takes $\Omega(n)$ steps. An interesting question is how fast we can get with the shared counter operations using registers that support CAS instructions as well and what is the smallest number of registers required for the fastest algorithm. In this brief announcement, we show an implementation using $O(n)$ shared registers supporting CAS instructions where the increment operation takes $O(\log n)$ time and the read operation takes $O(1)$ time.

## 2 RELATED WORK

We consider the shared counter where the read operation returns the value of the counter where as the increment operation increments the counter and does not return anything. This is in contrast to the fetch-and-increment counter that increments the counter and returns the value prior to the increment. Ellen et al. [2] give an $O(\log n)$ implementation of fetch-and-increment counter using $O(n)$ load-link/store-conditional registers. It is possible to simulate $m$ load-link/store-conditional registers for $n$ processes using $O(n^2 + m)$ CAS registers so that the load-link and store-conditional operations are wait-free and take $O(1)$ steps [4]. Thus, we can implement an $O(\log n)$ fetch-and-increment counter and an $O(\log n)$ shared counter using $O(n^2)$ CAS registers. Regarding a lower bound on the time required, one can use the construction from Alistarh et al. [1] to show that the total number of steps required for a sequence of $\Theta(n)$ read and increment operations is $\Omega(n \log n)$. Thus, at least one of read or increment operation takes $\Omega(\log n)$ steps.

## 3 MODEL

The shared memory consists of registers. Each register $R$ supports the following operations: (i) `read`($R$), which returns the current value of register $R$, (ii) `write`($R, x$), which writes $x$ to $R$ and returns $\perp$, and (iii) `CAS`($R, v, v'$), which writes $v'$ to $R$ if and only if $R = v$ and returns whether $v'$ was written to $R$. The register $R$ allows concurrent operations from different processes.

We define the sequential counter object using the state set $\mathbb{N}_0$ and the following operations: (i) `get()`, which returns the current state $s \in \mathbb{N}_0$ without changing the next state, and (ii) `inc()`, which changes the next state to $s + 1$ and returns $\perp$. We give a wait-free and linearizable implementation [3] of the sequential counter for $n$ processes. We assume that $n = 2^x$ for an integer $x \geq 0$ and that the processes have ids $1, 2, \ldots, n$.

## 4 ALGORITHM

We denote the counter object with id $i$ by $C_i^k$, where $k$ is the number of concurrent `inc()` operations that the counter supports (no restriction on the number of concurrent `get()` operations). Algorithm 1 gives a recursive construction for $C_i^k$ using a register $R_i$ and two other counter objects that support $k/2$ concurrent `inc()` operations each. These are $C_{2i}^{k/2}$, called the *left child* and $C_{2i+1}^{k/2}$, called the *right child*.

The counter that supports all the $n$ processes is $C_1^n$. From Algorithm 1, the counter $C_1^n$ uses the register $R_1$ and the counters $C_2^{n/2}$ and $C_3^{n/2}$. Recursing further, we end up with a heap of $2n - 1$ registers $R_1, R_2, \ldots, R_{2n-1}$. The processes that access the counter $C_1^n$ have ids $1, 2, \ldots, n$. The sets $L$ and $H$ computed in Line 9 can be $\{1, 2, \ldots, n/2\}$ and $\{n/2+1, n/2+2, \ldots, n\}$, respectively. Thereafter, the range of process ids that access any counter $C_i^k$ is contiguous. Thus, the sets $L$ and $H$ can be computed by splitting the range in the middle. Figure 1 shows the construction for $n = 4$ for processes.


*PODC '17, July 25-27, 2017, Washington, DC, USA*

ACM ISBN 978-1-4503-4992-5/17/07
http://dx.doi.org/10.1145/3087801.3087841

```
1  C_i^k.get()
2      return read(R_i);
3  C_i^k.inc()
4      if k == 1 then
5          T ← read(R_i);
6          write(R_i, T + 1);
7          return ⊥;
8      else
9          Partition the id set of k processes that access this
           function into two equal sized sets, L and H;
10         Let p be the current process id;
11         if p ∈ L then
12             C_{2i}^{k/2}.inc();        // increment left child
13         else
14             C_{2i+1}^{k/2}.inc();      // increment right child
15     V ← read(R_i);
16     sum ← C_{2i}^{k/2}.get() + C_{2i+1}^{k/2}.get();
17     success ← CAS(R_i, V, sum);
18     if success ≠ true then
19         V ← read(R_i);
20         sum ← C_{2i}^{k/2}.get() + C_{2i+1}^{k/2}.get();
21         CAS(R_i, V, sum);
22     return ⊥;
```

**Algorithm 1:** The algorithm for inc() and read() operations on the counter $C_i^k$.

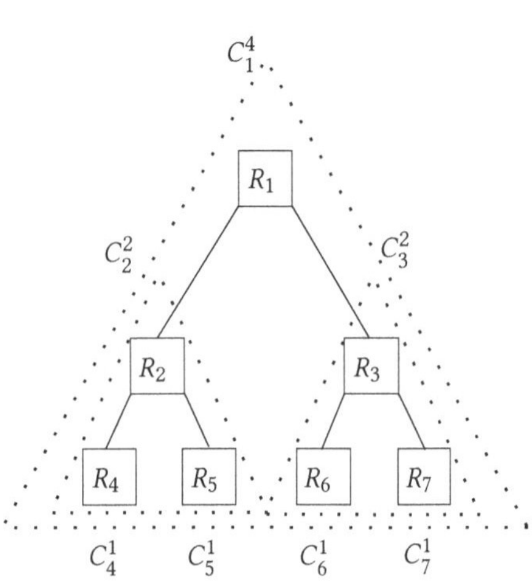


**Figure 1: The counter construction for $n = 4$ processes ($C_1^4$). It includes two counters that support two concurrent inc() operations each ($C_2^2$, $C_3^2$) and four single process counters ($C_4^1$, $C_5^1$, $C_6^1$, $C_7^1$).**

## 5 ANALYSIS

LEMMA 5.1. *Algorithm 1 is a linearizable implementation of shared counter $C_i^k$.*

PROOF. The claim is true for $k = 1$ because there is a single process that increments the register $R_i$ by one upon each inc() operation.

For $k > 1$, assume that the claim is true for $k/2$, i.e., both $C = C_{2i}^{k/2}$ and $C' = C_{2i+1}^{k/2}$ are linearizable counters. Then, we can consider the operations get() and inc() on both $C$ and $C'$ as atomic [3]. The value returned by a successive $C$.get() operation can only be larger as there can only be $C$.inc() operations in between. This is also true for $C'$.get(). Thus, the sum of $C$.get() and $C'$.get() and the value written to $R_i$ never decreases. Also, we can associate each distinct value $I$ written to $R_i$ with a unique pair of values $i$, $i'$ so that $I = i + i'$ and $i$, $i'$ are the values returned by $C$.get(), $C'$.get() respectively. We say that all the increment operations $C$.inc() and $C'$.inc() leading up to the value $i$ and $i'$ were *applied* to the register $R_i$.

Assume w.l.o.g that the process with id $p \in L$ and invokes $C$.inc(). To show linearizability, we have to show that $C$.inc() is applied when $C_i^k$.inc() returns (the linearization point being the point of application of $C$.inc()). Clearly, the operation is applied when either the CAS in Line 17 or Line 21 succeeds. So, we only need to check the case when both the CAS operations fail.

Assume that both the CAS operations fail. As the value of $R_i$ can only change by successful CAS operations and the CAS in Line 17 fails, a successful CAS operation by another process $q$ must have occurred between Lines 15 and 17. Process $q$ may or may not apply $C$.inc() from process $p$ depending on whether process $q$ calls $C$.get() before or after $p$ calls $C$.inc(). If it was after, then process $q$ applied $C$.inc() to $R_i$. If it was before, then $C$.inc() is not applied until the next successful CAS. But, as we know that the CAS in Line 21 also fails, a successful CAS from a process $q'$ must have occurred between Line 19 and Line 21. This CAS occurs on $R_i$ that is at least the value updated by CAS operation performed previously by process $q$. Thus, the *sum* calculated by $q'$ occurs after $C$.inc() from process $p$ and this is applied to $R_i$ by process $q'$. □

## 6 CONCLUSION

In this brief announcement, we gave an $O(\log n)$ time shared counter implementation using $O(n)$ space. This is both optimal in time and space. It is an interesting question to see if this technique can be applied to other problems such as fetch-and-increment counter using $O(n)$ space.

## REFERENCES


[1] Dan Alistarh, James Aspnes, Keren Censor-Hillel, Seth Gilbert, and Rachid Guerraoui. 2014. Tight Bounds for Asynchronous Renaming. *Journal of the ACM (JACM)* (2014).

[2] Faith Ellen and Philipp Woelfel. 2013. An Optimal Implementation of Fetch-and-Increment. In *27th International Symposium on Distributed Computing (DISC), Jerusalem, Israel.*

[3] Maurice P. Herlihy and Jeannette M. Wing. 1990. Linearizability: A Correctness Condition for Concurrent Objects. *ACM Transactions on Programming Languages and Systems (TOPLAS)* (1990).

[4] Prasad Jayanti and Srdjan Petrovic. 2005. Efficiently Implementing a Large Number of LL/SC Objects. In *9th International Conference on Principles of Distributed Systems (OPODIS), Pisa, Italy.*

[5] Prasad Jayanti, King Tan, and Sam Toueg. 2006. Time and Space Lower Bounds for Nonblocking Implementations. *SIAM Journal on Computing* (2006).

# Brief Announcement: Fence Insertion for Straight-line Programs is in P

Mohsen Lesani
University of California, Riverside
lesani@cs.ucr.edu

## ABSTRACT

Relaxed memory models reorder instructions in the interest of performance. However, reordering of instructions can jeopardize correctness and memory fences should be used to preserve specific orders. Programs that carry explicit fences are over-specified as they are tied to specific architectures and memory models and are hence unportable. On the other hand, once the program specifies the high-level required orders, optimizing compilers can allocate optimum memory fences for multiple architectures. However, the fence insertion problem for general programs is NP-hard. In this paper, we consider fence insertion for straight-line programs. We present a polynomial-time greedy algorithm via reduction to the chain multi-cut problem.

| $T_1$ | $T_2$ |
|---|---|
| 1: $write(l_1, 1)$ | 1: $write(l_2, 1)$ |
| 2: $x_1 = read(l_2)$ | 2: $x_2 = read(l_1)$ |
| $\{1 \rightarrow 2\}$ | $\{1 \rightarrow 2\}$ |

(a) Input Program

| $T_1$ | $T_2$ |
|---|---|
| 1: $write(l_1, 1)$ | 1: $write(l_2, 1)$ |
| $fence(w, r)$ | $fence(w, r)$ |
| 2: $x_1 = read(l_2)$ | 2: $x_2 = read(l_1)$ |

(b) Program with Fences

**Figure 1: Dekker**

## 1 INTRODUCTION

Compilers and processors reorder instructions to gain performance. However, preservation of the order of specific instructions is crucial to correctness. Hardware architectures provide memory fence instructions that preserve the relative order of specific instructions that come before and after them in the program. Synchronization programs have been traditionally written with explicit fence instructions for specific architectures. Such a program is an over-specification as it hard-codes the enforcement of the required orders for a particular architecture. Further, it is an under-specification as the required orders that are implicitly provided by the architecture are not explicitly documented. Thus, fences are an implementation mechanism for a high-level abstraction.

Many authors have presented approaches to insert fences that enforce sequential consistency, including Lee et al. [10], Fang et al. [7], and Alglave et al. [1]. Others have tried to infer the required orders including Kuperstein et al. [9], Meshman et al. [11] and Dan et al. [6]. We proposed [2] to capture the required orders as a relation on the operations of each thread. A compiler can translate these declared orders to optimum fence instructions. This approach separates what from how. The programs can be verified using architecture-independent and algorithm-level reasoning. The compiler can automatically translate the program to multiple target architectures.

Optimum fence insertion for general programs is NP-hard. The compiler of our previous work used an exponential-time algorithm to insert optimum fences. In this paper, we consider the basic straight-line class of programs. We present a polynomial-time fence insertion algorithm for this class. This opens the problem of whether there are optimum or approximation algorithms for fence insertion to programs with basic control structures.

As an example, consider the specification of the Dekker synchronization algorithm in Figure 1. Figure 1(a) shows the input program. Each thread first writes to a location and then reads from the location that the other thread writes to. It is crucial to the correctness of the algorithm that the write operation happens before the read operation in each thread. This ordering requirement is captured by a relation on the operations of each thread in Figure 1(a). The first operation should be ordered before the second operation. Figure 1(b) shows the allocated fences for the program in Figure 1(a). We denote the fence instruction that orders write instructions before read instructions as $fence(w,r)$. We use a similar notation for any pairs of $r$ or $w$.

As another example, consider Figure 2. The input program is depicted in Figure 2(a). It requires the order of two pairs of operations to be preserved: it requires the first operation to be ordered before the third operation and the second operation to be ordered before the fourth operation. On the order hand, it does not require the preservation of the order of other pairs of operations including the order of the first and second operations. Figure 2(b) shows a suboptimal fence insertion. This insertion is based on the heuristic of putting a fence right before the second operation of each pair of operations in the required order. Figure 2(c) shows the optimal fence insertion. A single fence after the second operation preserves the order of the two pairs of operations.

In this paper, we present an algorithm for optimal fence insertion for straight line programs and show that it runs in polynomial time.


*PODC'17, July 25-27, 2017, Washington, DC, USA*

ACM ISBN 978-1-4503-4992-5/17/07.
DOI: http://dx.doi.org/10.1145/3087801.3087849

```
1:   write(l1,1)
2:   write(l2,2)
3:   x1 = read(l3)
4:   x1 = read(l4)
{1 → 3,2 → 4}
```
(a) Input Program

```
1:   write(l1,1)
2:   write(l2,2)
     fence(w,r)
3:   x1 = read(l3)
     fence(w,r)
4:   x1 = read(l4)
```
(b) Suboptimal Fence Insertion

```
1:   write(l1,1)
2:   write(l2,2)
     fence(w,r)
3:   x1 = read(l3)
4:   x1 = read(l4)
```
(c) Optimal Fence Insertion

**Figure 2: Fence Insertion**

## 2 FENCE INSERTION PROBLEM

**Notation.** For a set $s$, let $|s|$ denote the size and $\mathbb{P}(s)$ denote the power set of $s$. Let $\langle e_1, .., e_n \rangle$ denote the tuple of elements $e_1$ to $e_n$. For a tuple $t$, let $|t|$ denote the length of $t$ and $t[i]$ denote the $i$-th element of $t$.

**Concurrent Program.** Let $D$ be a finite data domain, $L$ be a finite set of shared memory locations valued in $D$, and $X$ be a finite set of local variables valued in $D$. Let $O$ be the set of operations (1) $x = read(l)$, (2) $write(l,x)$ and (3) $write(l,d)$ where $x \in X$, $l \in L$ and $d \in D$. Intuitively, $x = read(l)$ denotes the read of the value of location $l$ into the variable $x$ and $write(l,d)$ and $write(l,x)$ denote the write of the value $d$ and the value of the variable $x$ into the location $l$ respectively. Let $\tau$ denote a function from $O$ to $\{r, w\}$ that maps operations to their types: $\tau(x = read(l)) = r$ $\tau(write(l,x)) = w$, and $\tau(write(l,d)) = w$ for every $x \in X$, $l \in L$, and $d \in D$. Similarly let $\ell$ denote the function from $O$ to $L$ that maps operations to the memory locations that they access.

A program $\pi$ is a pair $\langle p, \rightarrow \rangle$ such that $p$ is a tuple of operations over $O$ and $\rightarrow$ is an irreflexive subset of the increasing total order of numbers $\{1, .., |p|\}$. Intuitively, $p$ is the straight-line program of operations and the relation $\rightarrow$ is the set of pairs of operations that should preserve their order in $p$. A concurrent system is a tuple of programs.

**Fence Insertion Problem.** We now define the fence insertion problem. We present a definition and then revise it based on a decomposition.

Let $F$ be the set of the following fence types: $fence(r,r)$, $fence(r,w)$, $fence(w,r)$ and $fence(w,w)$. Intuitively, putting the fence $fence(r,w)$ between a *read* and a *write* operation prevents them from reordering. The effect of the other three fence operations is similar.

Intuitively, a fence insertion $f$ for a program $\langle p, \rightarrow \rangle$ specifies the set of fences whose addition to p ensures that the required order -¿ is preserved. A (multi-type) fence insertion $f$ for a program $\pi = \langle p, \rightarrow \rangle$ is a function from $\{1, .., |p|\}$ to $\mathbb{P}(F)$ such that for every $i$ and $j$ that $i \rightarrow j$, there exists $n$, $i \leq n < j$ such that $fence(\tau(p[i]), \tau(p[j])) \in f(n)$. For each $i \in \{1, .., |p|\}$, $f(i)$ specifies the set of fences that should be added between the $i$th and $(i+1)$-th operation of $p$.

For example, the fence insertion for the first thread of the Dekker example depicted in Figure 1(b) is $\{1 \mapsto \{fence(w,r)\}, 2 \mapsto \emptyset\}$. In other words, the fence $fence(w,r)$ should be put after the first operation and no fence is needed after the second operation. As another example, the fence insertion depicted in Figure 2(b) is $\{1 \mapsto \emptyset, 2 \mapsto \{fence(w,r)\}, 3 \mapsto \{fence(w,r)\}, 4 \mapsto \emptyset\}$. In other words, the fence $fence(w,r)$ should be put after the second and third operations and no fence is needed after the other operations.

The size of a fence insertion $f$ is the number of fences that it allocates. More precisely, the size of a fence insertion $f$ is $\Sigma_{i \in dom(f)} |f(i)|$. Given a program $\pi$, the fence insertion problem is to find the minimum-size fence insertion of $\pi$. Let $OptFI(\pi)$ denote the minimum-size fence insertion of $\pi$.

**Fence Instructions Independence.** We divide the required orders to four disjoint categories based on the fence types needed to preserve the order. For a program $\langle p, \rightarrow \rangle$, let $\rightarrow_{|wr}$ be the subset of $\rightarrow$ where the first operation is a write and the second operation is a read in $p$. More precisely, the order $\rightarrow_{|wr}$ is defined as the following relation $\{i \rightarrow_{|wr} j \mid i \rightarrow j \wedge \tau(p[i]) = w \wedge \tau(p[j]) = r\}$. The orders $\rightarrow_{|rr}$, $\rightarrow_{|rw}$ and $\rightarrow_{|ww}$ are similarly defined. Only the fence type $fence(w,r)$ can be used to preserve an order in the subset $\rightarrow_{|wr}$ and it cannot be used to preserve an order in any of the other three subsets. The following lemma states that (multi-type) fence insertion problem can be decomposed to four independent fence insertion problems for a single fence type.

LEMMA 2.1 (INDEPENDENCE OF FENCE TYPES). *For every program* $\langle p, \rightarrow \rangle$, $OptFI(\langle p, \rightarrow \rangle) = \lambda n, OptFI(\langle p, \rightarrow_{|rr} \rangle)(n) \cup OptFI(\langle p, \rightarrow_{|rw} \rangle)(n) \cup OptFI(\langle p, \rightarrow_{|wr} \rangle)(n) \cup OptFI(\langle p, \rightarrow_{|ww} \rangle)(n)$

The lemma is straightforward from the definition of the optimum fence insertion and the fact that each fence type can only preserve its corresponding order subset.

Note that in a memory model that implicitly provides a category of orders, no fence insertion is needed for that category. Equivalently, we can translate the allocated fences for that category to no operation. In addition, if a memory model provides the same fence instruction for two or more fence types, we merge the corresponding categories and consider the union of them as a category.

Based on the above lemma, we consider a single fence type $fence$ and the following definition of fence insertion in the rest of the paper.

*Definition 2.2 (Fence Insertion).* A fence insertion $f$ for a program $\pi = \langle p, \rightarrow \rangle$ is a subset $f$ of $\{1, .., |p|\}$ such that for every $i$ and $j$ that $i \rightarrow j$, there exists $n$, $i \leq n < j$ such that $n \in f$. Given a program $\pi$, the fence insertion problem *FenceIns* is to find the minimum-size fence insertion of $\pi$.

**Reduction of Fence Insertion to Multi-cut.** We reduce the fence insertion problem to the graph multi-cut problem. We first define the multi-cut problem.

*Definition 2.3 (Multi-cut).* Given a graph $G = \langle V, E \rangle$ with a set of of terminal node pairs $T \in \mathbb{P}(V \times V)$, a multi-cut is a set of edges

**Algorithm 1** Chain Multi-cut Greedy Algorithm

```
function CHAINMULTICUT(G⟨V, E⟩, T) where
V = {v_1, ..., v_n}, E = {{v_1, v_2}, ..., {v_{n-1}, v_n}},
T ∈ ℙ(V × V)

    T' ← {(v_i, v_j) | (⟨v_i, v_j⟩ ∈ T ∧ i < j) ∨
                        (⟨v_j, v_i⟩ ∈ T ∧ j < i)}
    T'' ← Sort pairs ⟨v_i, v_j⟩ ∈ T' by j

    E' ← ∅
    for each ⟨v_i, v_j⟩ ∈ T'' do
        if (∄{v_i', v_j'} ∈ E' : i ≤ i' ∧ j' ≤ j) then
            E' ← E' ∪ {{v_{j-1}, v_j}}

    return E'
```

$E' \subseteq E$ such that for every pair $\langle s, t \rangle \in T$, there is no path between $s$ and $t$ in $\langle V, E \setminus E' \rangle$. Given a graph $G$, the multi-cut problem *MultiCut* is to find the minimum-size multi-cut of $G$.

The fence insertion problem is reduced to the multi-cut problem.

LEMMA 2.4. *FenceIns* $\leq_p$ *MultiCut*

Given an instance $\langle p, \rightarrow \rangle$ of *FenceIns*, we construct an instance of *MultiCut* in polynomial time as follows. The graph is $G = \langle V, E \rangle$ where $V = \{1, .., |p|\}$ and $E = \{\{1, 2\}, ..., \{|p| - 1, |p|\}\}$ and the terminal node pairs $T = \rightarrow$. We define polynomial transformations from solutions of each instance to other. Given the solution $f$ for the *FenceIns* instance, the solution for *MultiCut* instance is $E' = \{\{i, i + 1\} \mid i \in f\}$. Given the solution $E' = \{\{i_1, i_1 + 1\}, ..., \{i_n, i_n + 1\}\}$ for *MultiCut*, the solution for the *FenceIns* instance is $f = \{i_1, ..., i_n\}$. It is straightforward to see the optimality of one solution from the the other.

## 3 CHAIN MULTI-CUT.

The multi-cut problem is known to be NP-Hard (even for trees) [3, 8]. But the graph constructed above is a chain, a restricted tree. In the following section, we describe a polynomial time algorithm for multi-cut of chains.

Algorithm 1 presents a greedy algorithm for the chain multi-cut problem. An instance of the problem is represented by the sequence of nodes $V = \{v_1, ..., v_n\}$, the edges $E = \{\{v_1, v_2\}, ..., \{v_{n-1}, v_n\}\}$ between the nodes and the set of terminal pair of nodes $T$. The algorithm first swaps the terminal pairs, if needed, to have the larger node of each pair as the second element. It then sorts the terminal pairs according to the *second* element. Then, the algorithm iterates over the sorted terminal pairs. It starts with an empty set of edges to cut $E'$. For each pair $\langle v_i, v_j \rangle$ of terminals, it adds the edge $\{v_{j-1}, v_j\}$ to the cut set $E'$ only if there is no edge in $E'$ that already cuts the path between $v_i$ and $v_j$.

The time complexity of the algorithm is dominated by the sort operation on the terminal pairs; thus, it is $O(n \cdot \log n)$. The optimality of the algorithm can be proved by the following pair of facts. First, the size of the minimum cut is at least the size of every disjoint set of paths between the terminals. Second, the pairs of terminals that lead to addition of an edge to the cut set during the iteration have disjoint paths.

Let us see why the second fact holds. Consider a pair of terminals $t_1$ with the path $p_1$ between them. Assume that iteration over $t_1$ leads to the addition of an edge to the cut set. The last edge of $p_1$ is added to the cut set. Let the pair of terminals $t_2$ with the path $p_2$ between them be the pair that leads to the addition of the next edge to the cut set. The algorithm adds an edge to the cut set only if there is no edge in the current cut set that is in the path between the current pair of terminals. The last edge of $p_1$ is in the cut set and yet the pair $t_2$ leads to the addition of a new edge. Hence, the last edge in $p_1$ is not in the path $p_2$. This means that either the last edge of $p_2$ is before the last edge of $p_1$ or the first edge of $p_2$ is after the last edge of $p_1$. As the pairs are iterated in the order of their last edge and the pair $t_1$ is iterated before $t_2$, the last edge of $p_2$ cannot be before the last edge of $p_1$ Hence, we have that the first edge of $p_2$ is after the last edge of $p_1$. Thus, the first edge of $p_2$ is after the last edge of $p_1$. This means that the path $p_1$ is disjoint from the path $p_2$. Similarly, by induction on the steps of iteration, it can be shown that the pairs that lead to addition of an edge to the cut set have disjoint paths.

## 4 GENERALIZATION

The graph multi-cut problem is known to be NP-hard (even for undirected trees) [3, 8]. However, in contrast to undirected trees, multi-cut for directed trees is in P [4]. The result is based on the total uni-modularity of the linear programming matrix for directed trees. For a survey of the complexity of multi-cut on different restricted graph types see [5]. Control flow graphs of programs are restricted graph types. If we consider only the if-then-else control structure, then the graph is a nested composition of diamonds and sequences. The question is whether our result can be extended to polynomial-time optimum or approximation algorithms for programs with basic control structures.

## REFERENCES


[1] Jade Alglave, Daniel Kroening, Vincent Nimal, and Daniel Poetzl. 2014. Don't sit on the fence: A static analysis approach to automatic fence insertion. In *CAV*. http://arxiv.org/abs/1312.1411

[2] John Bender, Mohsen Lesani, and Jens Palsberg. 2015. Declarative Fence Insertion. In *OOPSLA*.

[3] Julia Chuzhoy and Sanjeev Khanna. 2006. Hardness of Cut Problems in Directed Graphs. In *Proceedings of the Thirty-eighth Annual ACM Symposium on Theory of Computing (STOC '06)*. ACM, New York, NY, USA, 527–536.

[4] Marie-Christine Costa, Lucas LéTocart, and FréDéRic Roupin. 2003. A Greedy Algorithm for Multicut and Integral Multiflow in Rooted Trees. *Oper. Res. Lett.* 31, 1 (Jan. 2003), 21–27. https://doi.org/10.1016/S0167-6377(02)00184-0

[5] Marie-Christine Costa, Lucas Ltocart, and Frdric Roupin. 2005. Minimal multicut and maximal integer multiflow: A survey. *European Journal of Operational Research* 162, 1 (2005), 55 – 69.

[6] Andrei Marian Dan, Yuri Meshman, Martin Vechev, and Eran Yahav. 2013. *Predicate Abstraction for Relaxed Memory Models*. Springer Berlin Heidelberg, Berlin, Heidelberg, 84–104. https://doi.org/10.1007/978-3-642-38856-9_7

[7] Xing Fang, Jaejin Lee, and Samuel P. Midkiff. 2003. Automatic Fence Insertion for Shared Memory Multiprocessing. In *Proceedings of the 17th Annual International Conference on Supercomputing (ICS '03)*. ACM, New York, NY, USA, 285–294.

[8] N. Garg, V.V. Vazirani, and M. Yannakakis. 1997. Primal-dual approximation algorithms for integral flow and multicut in trees. *Algorithmica* 18, 1 (1997), 3–20. https://doi.org/10.1007/BF02523685

[9] Michael Kuperstein, Martin Vechev, and Eran Yahav. 2010. Automatic Inference of Memory Fences. In *Proceedings of the 2010 Conference on Formal Methods in Computer-Aided Design (FMCAD '10)*. FMCAD Inc, Austin, TX, 111–120.

[10] Jaejin Lee and David A. Padua. 2000. Hiding Relaxed Memory Consistency with Compilers. In *PACT*.

[11] Yuri Meshman, Andrei Dan, Martin Vechev, and Eran Yahav. *Synthesis of memory fences via refinement propagation*. Technical Report.

# LCL Problems on Grids*

Sebastian Brandt
ETH Zürich
sebastian.brandt@tik.ee.ethz.ch

Juho Hirvonen
IRIF, CNRS and University Paris Diderot
juho.hirvonen@aalto.fi

Janne H. Korhonen
Aalto University
janne.h.korhonen@aalto.fi

Tuomo Lempiäinen
Aalto University
tuomo.lempiainen@aalto.fi

Patric R. J. Östergård
Aalto University
patric.ostergard@aalto.fi

Christopher Purcell
Aalto University
christopher.purcell@aalto.fi

Joel Rybicki
University of Helsinki
joel.rybicki@helsinki.fi

Jukka Suomela
Aalto University
jukka.suomela@aalto.fi

Przemysław Uznański
ETH Zürich
przemyslaw.uznanski@inf.ethz.ch

## ABSTRACT

LCLs or locally checkable labelling problems (e.g. maximal independent set, maximal matching, and vertex colouring) in the LOCAL model of computation are very well-understood in cycles (toroidal 1-dimensional grids): every problem has a complexity of $O(1)$, $\Theta(\log^* n)$, or $\Theta(n)$, and the design of optimal algorithms can be fully automated.

This work develops the complexity theory of LCL problems for toroidal 2-dimensional grids. The complexity classes are the same as in the 1-dimensional case: $O(1)$, $\Theta(\log^* n)$, and $\Theta(n)$. However, given an LCL problem it is undecidable whether its complexity is $\Theta(\log^* n)$ or $\Theta(n)$ in 2-dimensional grids.

Nevertheless, if we correctly guess that the complexity of a problem is $\Theta(\log^* n)$, we can completely automate the design of optimal algorithms. For any problem we can find an algorithm that is of a normal form $A' \circ S_k$, where $A'$ is a finite function, $S_k$ is an algorithm for finding a maximal independent set in $k$th power of the grid, and $k$ is a constant.

Finally, partially with the help of automated design tools, we classify the complexity of several concrete LCL problems related to colourings and orientations.

*A full version of this paper [9] is available at https://arxiv.org/abs/1702.05456.


*PODC '17, July 25-27, 2017, Washington, DC, USA*

ACM ISBN 978-1-4503-4992-5/17/07...$15.00
https://doi.org/10.1145/3087801.3087833

## KEYWORDS

distributed algorithms; LOCAL model; LCL problems; computational complexity; algorithm synthesis; graph colouring

## 1 INTRODUCTION

### 1.1 Problem setting: LCL problems on grids

*Grids.* In this work, we study distributed algorithms in a setting where the underlying input graph is a grid. Specifically, we consider the complexity of locally checkable labelling problems, or LCL problems, in the standard LOCAL model of distributed complexity, and consider graphs that are toroidal two-dimensional $n \times n$ grids with a consistent orientation (see Figure 1). We focus on the two-dimensional case for concreteness, but most of our results generalise to $d$-dimensional grids of arbitrary dimensions.

Grids occupy a middle ground between the well-understood directed $n$-cycles [10, 32], where all solvable LCL problems are known to have deterministic time complexity either $O(1)$, $\Theta(\log^* n)$ or $\Theta(n)$, and the more complicated setting of general $n$-vertex graphs, where intermediate problems with time complexities such as $\Theta(\log n)$ are known to exist, even for bounded-degree graphs. Grid-like systems with local dynamics also occur frequently in the

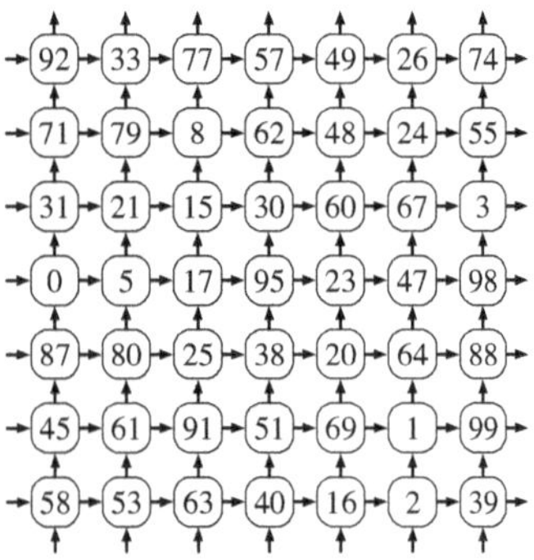


**Figure 1: A fragment of an oriented grid.**

study of real-world phenomena. However, grids have so far not been systematically studied from a distributed computing perspective.

LOCAL *model and* LCL *problems.* In the LOCAL model of distributed computing, nodes are labelled with unique numerical identifiers with $O(\log n)$ bits. A time-$t$ algorithm in this model is simply a mapping from radius-$t$ neighbourhoods to local outputs; equivalently, it can be interpreted as a message-passing algorithm in which the nodes exchange messages for $t$ synchronous rounds and then announce their local outputs.

LCL problems are graph problems for which the feasibility of a solution can be *verified* by checking the solution for each $O(1)$-radius neighbourhood; if all local neighbourhoods look valid, the solution is also globally valid. Examples of such problems include vertex colouring, edge colouring, maximal independent sets, and maximal matchings. We refer to Section 3 for precise definitions.

*Example: colouring the grid.* To illustrate the type of questions we are interested in this work, consider $k$-colouring on $n \times n$ grids. For $k = 2$, the problem is inherently global with complexity $\Theta(n)$, while colouring any graph of maximum degree $\Delta = 4$ with $\Delta + 1 = 5$ colours can be done in $O(\log^* n)$ rounds. But what about $k = 3$ and $k = 4$? In particular, does either of these have an intermediate (polylogarithmic) complexity, as is known to happen with $\Delta$-colouring on general bounded-degree graphs [10, 34]? We will see that neither 3-colouring nor 4-colouring is intermediate on grids: 3-colouring requires $\Theta(n)$ rounds, while 4-colouring can be solved in $O(\log^* n)$ rounds.

## 1.2 Results: classification and synthesis

*Classification.* Our first contribution is a complete *complexity classification* for LCL problems on grids in the case of deterministic algorithms. That is, we show that any LCL problem on $n \times n$ grids has one of the following time complexities, similarly to the case of cycles:

(a) $O(1)$ ("trivial" problem)
(b) $\Theta(\log^* n)$ ("local" problem)
(c) $\Theta(n)$ ("global" problem)

In particular, there are no problems of an intermediate complexity, such as $\Theta(\log n)$.

The separation between $O(1)$ and $\Omega(\log^* n)$ follows from the work of Naor and Stockmeyer [32] (see Appendix A of Chang and Pettie [11]), and obviously all problems can be solved in $O(n)$ rounds on $n \times n$ grids (assuming they can be solved at all). The interesting part is the separation between (b) and (c); here we extend the recent speed-up lemma of Chang et al. [10] to grids.

*Undecidability of classification.* It is known that the classification for LCL problems on cycles is decidable, that is, there is an algorithm that decides to which complexity class a given LCL problem belongs (see Section 4). We show that two-dimensional grids are fundamentally different from cycles in this regard: even if we have the promise that a given LCL problem has complexity of either $\Theta(\log^* n)$ or $\Theta(n)$, distinguishing between these cases is undecidable.

*Algorithm synthesis for $\Theta(\log^* n)$ problems.* The undecidability result would seem to suggest that automating the design of distributed algorithms on $n \times n$ grids is essentially impossible. Surprisingly, this is not the case: we develop a *synthesis algorithm* that, given a specification of an LCL problem $P$ with complexity $O(\log^* n)$, produces an asymptotically optimal algorithm for $P$ on grids. The caveat is that if the input problem $P$ is a global problem with complexity $\Theta(n)$, this algorithm cannot detect it and will never stop.

From a theory perspective, this means that for each LCL problem $P$ we will only need 1 bit of advice—whether $P$ is $O(\log^* n)$ or $\Theta(n)$—and then we can find an optimal algorithm for solving $P$: for $O(\log^* n)$ problems, we apply the synthesis algorithm, and for $\Theta(n)$ problems, brute force is optimal. From a practical perspective, we can use the synthesis algorithm as a one-sided oracle for understanding the complexity of LCL problems on grids: if the synthesis produces an output, we have an optimal algorithm, and if it does not, we can conjecture that the problem in question might be inherently global.

*Normal form for $\Theta(\log^* n)$ problems.* The algorithm synthesis is based on a result showing that every LCL problem $P$ with complexity $\Theta(\log^* n)$ on $n \times n$ grids has an algorithm of a specific *normal form*; see Figure 2. That is, there is an algorithm $A$ for $P$ that has the form $A = A' \circ S_k$ for some constant $k$, where

- $S_k$ is a problem-independent algorithm that finds a maximal independent set $I_k$ in the $k$th power of the $n \times n$ grid (we call these nodes "anchors"), and
- $A'$ is a problem-dependent algorithm with running time $O(k)$ that takes as an input only the set of anchors $I_k$ and the global orientation of the grid.

Note that here only the part of finding the set of anchors takes $\Theta(\log^* n)$ time, and all of the remaining parts can be done in $O(1)$ time. In particular, the only problem-dependent part besides the constant $k$ is the finite function defining the algorithm $A'$; thus, the algorithm synthesis becomes a matter of searching through the finite-size space of possible functions.

## 1.3 Results: upper and lower bounds for concrete LCL problems

Next, we turn our attention to concrete LCL problems. In particular, we are interested in problem families defined for a range of parameters, so that it makes sense to ask where exactly is the border between local and global problems:

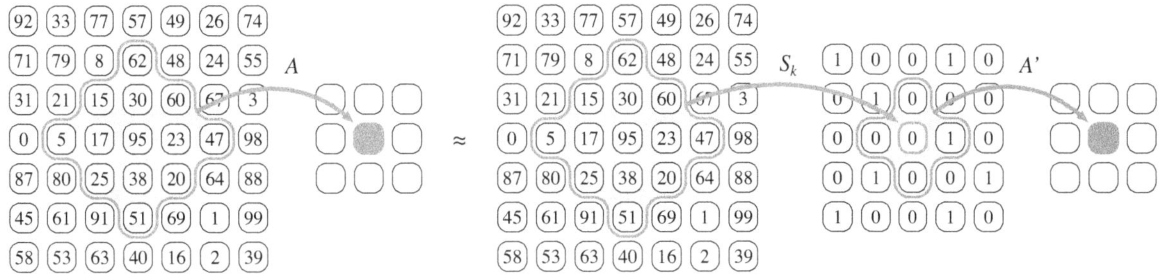

**Figure 2: Any sublinear-time algorithm $A$ can be normalised as $A' \circ S_k$, where $S_k$ is a problem-independent $O(\log^* n)$-time symmetry-breaking component and $A'$ is a problem-specific constant-time component.**

- *Vertex colouring.* The $k$-colouring problem is solvable in $O(\log^* n)$ rounds for $k \geq 4$ and global for $k \leq 3$.
- *Edge colouring.* The $k$-edge colouring problem is solvable in $O(\log^* n)$ rounds for $k \geq 5$ and global for $k \leq 4$.
- *Edge orientations.* For a set $X \subseteq \{0, 1, \ldots, 4\}$, an $X$-orientation is an orientation of the edges such that for each node $v \in V$ we have in-deg$(v) \in X$. The problem is trivial if $2 \in X$. We show that if $\{0, 1, 3\} \subseteq X$ or $\{1, 3, 4\} \subseteq X$, the problem is solvable in $O(\log^* n)$ rounds, and otherwise it is global.

The results on colourings can be generalised to $d$-dimensional grids. A 4-colouring can be found in time $\Theta(\log^* n)$ for any $d \geq 2$, while 3-colouring is global. In the case of edge colouring, we show that a $(2d + 1)$-colouring can be found in time $\Theta(\log^* n)$ for any $d \geq 1$, while $2d$-colouring is global. Both of the upper bounds hold even without any orientation or dimensional information, while both of the lower bounds hold even with full information.

We remark that the techniques used in the vertex colouring results have been discovered before in the context of *finitary colourings* of grids [25]; see Section 2 for more details.

## 2 RELATED WORK

LCL *problems on cycles.* As we noted before, two-dimensional grids can be seen as a generalisation of the widely studied setting of cycles; indeed, LCL problems were first studied on cycles in the distributed setting. Cole and Vishkin [14] showed that cycles can be 3-coloured in time $O(\log^* n)$, and Linial [30] showed that this is asymptotically optimal. This implies, via simple reductions, that many classical LCL problems, such as maximal independent set and maximal matching, also have a complexity of $\Theta(\log^* n)$ on cycles.

LCL *problems on graphs of bounded maximum degree.* Naor and Stockmeyer [32] showed that there exists a non-trivial LCL problem that can be solved in constant time: weak 2-colouring on graphs of odd degree. Many LCL problems are known to either have complexity $\Theta(\log^* n)$ [3, 5, 18, 33] or be global on graphs of bounded maximum degree. Until recently, no problems of an intermediate complexity were known. While Kuhn et al. [28] gave a lower bound of $\min\{\log \Delta / \log\log \Delta, \sqrt{\log n / \log\log n}\}$ for, among others, maximal independent set, this proof does not give an infinite family of graphs with a fixed maximum degree $\Delta$. Brandt et al. [8] showed that sinkless orientation and $\Delta$-colouring have randomised complexity $\Omega(\log\log n)$, and Chang et al. [10] proved that this implies a deterministic lower bound of $\Omega(\log n)$. These lower bounds provide the first examples of LCL problems with provably intermediate time complexity. Ghaffari and Su [22] proved a matching upper bound for sinkless orientation; no tight bounds are known for $\Delta$-colouring, but there is a polylogarithmic upper bound due to Panconesi and Srinivasan [34].

*Complexity theory of* LCL *problems.* LCL problems were formally introduced by Naor and Stockmeyer [32]. They showed that if there exists a constant-time algorithm for solving an LCL problem $P$, then there exists an order-invariant constant-time algorithm for $P$, such that the algorithm only uses the relative order of unique identifiers given to the nodes. Their argument works for any time $t = o(\log^* n)$: a time-$t$ distributed algorithm implies a constant-time order-invariant algorithm; hence there are no LCL problems with complexities strictly between $\omega(1)$ and $o(\log^* n)$.

Recently Chang et al. [10] showed that there are further gaps in the time complexities of LCL problems. They gave a speed-up lemma for simulating any deterministic $o(\log n)$-time algorithm in time $O(\log^* n)$ by computing new small and locally unique identifiers for the input graph. This implies that there are no LCL problems with deterministic complexity $\omega(\log^* n)$ and $o(\log n)$. They also show that the deterministic complexity of an LCL on instances of size $n$ is at most the randomised complexity on instances of size $2^{n^2}$. This implies a similar gap for randomised complexities between $\omega(\log^* n)$ and $o(\log\log n)$.

LCL *problems in restricted graph families.* It appears that the complexity of LCL problems specifically on grids has not been studied beyond the case of cycles. LCL problems have been, however, studied on other restricted graph classes, such as graphs of bounded independence [4, 21, 27, 40], bounded growth [39] and bounded diversity [6].

*Existence of algorithms and algorithm synthesis.* The notion of automatic synthesis of algorithms has been around for a long time; for example, already in the 1950s Church proposed the idea of synthesising circuits [12, 43]. Since then synthesis of distributed and parallel protocols has become a well-established research area in the formal methods community [1, 7, 13, 17, 29, 31, 37]. However, synthesis has received considerably less attention in the distributed computing community, even though they have been used to discover e.g. novel synchronisation algorithms [2, 7, 15] and local graph algorithms [24, 38].

The synthesis of optimal distributed algorithms in general is often computationally hard and even undecidable. In the context of the LOCAL model and LCL problems, Naor and Stockmeyer [32] show that simply deciding whether a given problem can be solved in constant time is undecidable; hence we cannot expect to completely automate the synthesis of asymptotically optimal distributed algorithms for LCL problems in general graphs. This result holds even if we study non-toroidal two-dimensional grids, but it does not hold in toroidal grids. In essence, in toroidal grids only trivial problems are solvable in constant time, and as we will see, the interesting case is the time complexity of $O(\log^* n)$.

*Other grid-like models.* While grids have not been studied from a distributed computing perspective, grid-like models with local dynamics have appeared in many different contexts:

- *Cellular automata* [20, 44, 47] have been studied both as a primitive computational model, and as a model for various complex systems and emergent phenomena, e.g. in ecology, sociology and physics [19, 26, 41].
- Various *tiling models* [23] have connections to computability questions, such as the abstract *Wang tilings* [45] and the variants of the *abstract Tile Assembly Model (aTAM)* [16, 35, 46, 48] for DNA self-assembly.

However, the prior work of this flavour is usually interested in understanding the dynamics of a specific fixed process, or what kind of global behaviours can arise from fixed number of local states—in particular, whether the system is computationally universal. Our distributed complexity perspective to grid-like systems seems mostly novel, and we expect it to have implications in other fields. Applying an existing result of distributed computing to tiling models has been previously demonstrated by Sterling [42], who makes use of a weak-colouring lower bound by Naor and Stockmeyer [32].

*Finitary colourings of grids.* Subsequently to the initial publication of this work, we have learned that the techniques in the $k$-colouring upper and lower bounds are essentially rediscoveries of prior work of Holroyd et al. [25] in the context of *finitary colourings of grids.* Very roughly speaking, this line of work concerns colouring the infinite $d$-dimensional grid $\mathbb{Z}^d$ using a specific type of random processes (*factors*) with an independent and identically distributed random variable for each node; more generally, one can consider *shifts of finite type,* which correspond to LCL problems. In particular, Holroyd et al. [25] study the *coding radius* of factors, which is analogous to the running time of a distributed algorithm, and prove a separation between 3-colouring and 4-colouring. However, despite the fact that techniques seem to translate between finitary colourings and distributed complexity, it remains unclear how to directly translate results from one setting to the other in a black-box manner; for instance, can we derive the lower bound for 3-colouring from the results of Holroyd et al. [25], and does our complexity classification imply answers to the open questions they pose?

# 3 PRELIMINARIES

LOCAL *model.* In the LOCAL model of distributed computing [30, 36], we have a computer network that is represented as a graph $G = (V, E)$; each node is a computer and each edge is a bidirectional communication link. The computers collaborate in order to solve a graph problem related to the structure of the graph $G$; note that here the same graph is both the topology of the computer network and the input graph.

Each node $v \in V$ is labelled with a unique identifier from the set $\{1, 2, \ldots, \mathrm{poly}(|V|)\}$. Each node has to produce its own part of the output: for example, if we are solving a graph colouring problem, each node has to output its own colour, and if our task is to find a maximal independent set $I$, each node has to output a binary label that indicates whether it is in set $I$. This can be extended in a straightforward manner to edge labellings.

All nodes run the same deterministic algorithm. Computation proceeds in synchronous rounds. In each round, all nodes in parallel send messages (of an arbitrary size) to their neighbours, then the messages are propagated along the edges to the recipients, then all nodes in parallel receive messages from each of their neighbours, and finally all nodes update their local state. The running time of an algorithm is the number of communication rounds until all nodes have stopped and announced their local outputs.

Note that in a time-$t$ algorithm, each node can gather its radius-$t$ neighbourhood and choose its local output based on this information. In essence, a time-$t$ algorithm in the LOCAL model is simply a mapping from radius-$t$ neighbourhoods to local outputs. Note that the neighbourhood contains not only the topology of the network but also the unique identifiers.

LCL *problems.* In distributed algorithms, the class of LCL problems [32] plays a role somewhat analogous to the class NP in centralised computing. Informally, problems in the class LCL are precisely those problems that can be solved in *constant time* with a *nondeterministic* algorithm in the LOCAL model: in LCL problems all nodes can nondeterministically guess the solution and then verify it by checking that the solution looks consistent in all local neighbourhoods. The key question is which of the LCL problems can be solved efficiently (e.g., in constant or near-constant time) with *deterministic* algorithms. (Cf.: which problems in NP are also in P.)

More precisely, let $P$ be a graph problem that associates with each unlabelled input graph $G = (V, E)$ a set of feasible node labellings $P(G)$; here each $f \in P(G)$ is a mapping $f\colon V \to X$ for some set of output labels $X$. We say that $P$ is an LCL problem if

(1) the set of local outputs $X$ is a finite set of size $|X| = O(1)$,
(2) there is a constant $r = O(1)$ such that for any candidate labelling $f\colon V \to X$ we have $f \in P(G)$ if and only if each radius-$r$ neighbourhood is compatible with some $g \in P(G)$.

Informally, for an LCL problem, a solution is feasible if it looks like a feasible solution in all local neighbourhoods. Examples of such problems include $k$-vertex colouring for $k = O(1)$, maximal independent sets, and minimal dominating sets. Again, we can extend the definitions in a natural manner to edge labellings; hence also $k$-edge colourings for $k = O(1)$, maximal matchings, and minimal edge dominating sets can be interpreted as LCL problems.

*Radius-1 LCL problems.* Above, parameter $r$ is called the *checkability radius* or simply *radius* of problem $P$. In bounded-degree graphs we can always define another LCL problem $P'$ with radius $r' = 1$ that is equivalent to $P$ in the following sense: $P'$ can be solved in time $t$ in the LOCAL model if and only if $P$ can be solved in time $t \pm O(1)$. In essence, the output labels in $P'$ are radius-$r$ neighbourhoods in $P$; given an algorithm for $P$ we can spend additional $r$ rounds to solve $P'$, and given an algorithm for $P'$, we can also directly solve $P$. Therefore we will often tacitly assume $r = 1$, with the understanding that this will only influence additive constants in the running time.

*Grid graphs.* Unless otherwise stated, we will study graphs that are 2-dimensional toroidal $n \times n$ square grids. Define $G_n = (V_n, E_n)$, where $V_n = \{(x, y) : 0 \leq x, y < n\}$. We will use the shorthand $u = (x_u, y_u)$ for the coordinates of each node $u \in V_n$. The nodes do not have access to these coordinates. Two nodes $u$ and $v$ are connected by an edge if and only if $|x_u - x_v| + |y_u - y_v| = 1$, where all coordinates are modulo $n$. All edges are oriented in a consistent manner towards the larger coordinate, and labelled so that each node knows which edge points "north" (increasing $y$ coordinate), "east" (increasing $x$ coordinate), "south", and "west". By definition the grid wraps around in both dimensions, forming a torus. We will use the shorthands $V = V(G)$ and $E = E(G)$ for the node and edge sets, respectively, of $G$. We will assume that all nodes are given the value of $n$ as input.

*On unsolvable problems.* Many LCL problems are unsolvable for some values of $n$. For example, there does not exist a 2-colouring if $n$ is odd, and many problems are ill-defined for e.g. $n = 1$. Throughout this text we will usually assume that $n$ is sufficiently large so that the problem that we consider is meaningful. Problems for which there are infinitely many values of $n$ for which a solution does not exist (e.g. 2-colouring) are regarded as global problems. Indeed, often the fact that solutions do not exist at all for some values of $n$ is a simple way of proving a lower bound of $\Omega(n)$, and such a bound holds even if we had a promise that $n$ is chosen so that a solution exists.

*Notation.* From now on, we write $G^{(k)}$ for the $k$th power of a graph $G$. That is, $V(G^{(k)}) = V(G)$ and

$$E(G^{(k)}) = \{\{u, v\} : \text{dist}_G(u, v) \leq k\}.$$

We denote the set $\{0, 1, \ldots, k-1\}$ by $[k]$.

## 4 WARM-UP: DIRECTED CYCLES

As a gentle introduction to our research questions, we will first have a look at LCL problems in directed cycles (i.e., 1-dimensional grids). This case is completely understood by prior work, but we will present it from a new perspective: in the 1-dimensional case, any LCL problem $P$ can be conveniently represented as a directed graph $H$. By studying elementary properties of graph $H$, we can directly deduce the computational complexity of problem $P$, and derive an asymptotically optimal algorithm for solving $P$—everything is decidable and algorithm synthesis is computationally tractable (see Figure 3).

We construct an *output neighbourhood graph* $H = (V, E)$ as follows. Problem $P$ can be interpreted as a set of feasible radius-$r$ local neighbourhoods $u_1 u_2 \ldots u_{2r+1} \in P$. For every such neighbourhood, we will have an edge $(u_1 u_2 \ldots u_{2r}, u_2 u_3 \ldots u_{2r+1}) \in E$ in graph $H$. For example, in the 3-colouring problem, the sequence "132" is a feasible neighbourhood, and hence we will have an edge $(13, 32)$ in the graph; here e.g. "13" corresponds to a node with output 3 that has a predecessor with output 1 (see Figure 3). The key observation is that walks in graph $H$ correspond to feasible output labellings in problem $P$.

Now we say that a node $u \in V$ is *flexible* if there exists an integer $k$ such that for all $k' \geq k$, there exists a walk in $G$ of length $k'$ that starts and ends at $u$. We call the smallest such $k$ the *flexibility* of $u$. It is clear that $u$ is flexible if and only if there are circuits $C, C'$ containing $u$ whose respective lengths are coprime.

Claim 4.1. *The complexity of $P$ is $O(1)$ if some node of $H$ has a self-loop; otherwise $\Theta(\log^* n)$ if some node of $H$ is flexible; and otherwise $\Theta(n)$.*

Proof. The case of $O(1)$ time is straightforward. Recall the result of Naor and Stockmeyer [32] that shows that unique identifiers do not help with $o(\log^* n)$-time algorithms; hence we have only trivial problems for which a constant labelling is a feasible.

Also the case of $\Theta(n)$ time is straightforward. There are only constantly many neighbourhoods, and hence some neighbourhood $u \in V$ has to be used $\Omega(n)$ times in the output. However, $u$ is not flexible, and hence the spacing between $u$-neighbourhoods requires global coordination. (For example, in 2-colouring the distance between any two occurrences of neighbourhood "12" has to be a multiple of 2.)

It remains to be shown that if $u$ is a flexible node with some minimum flexibility $k$, we can solve $P$ in time $O(\log^* n)$. Let $G$ be a cycle graph and let $G^{(k)}$ be the $k$th power of $G$. We can find a maximal independent set $I$ in $G^{(k)}$ in time $O(\log^* n)$. Let $v$ be a node in $I$, and let $v'$ be the next node in $I$ by the ordering of the nodes of $G$. Let the distance from $v$ to $v'$ in $G$ be $i$; we have $k+1 \leq i \leq 2k+1$. We label $v$ and $v'$ using the neighbourhood $u$, and fill in the gap between $v$ and $v'$ by following some circuit $C_i$ of length $i$ from $u$ back to $u$ in $H$. □

It would be tempting to try to generalise this result to the setting of 2-dimensional grids. Unfortunately, this is not possible; as we will see in Section 6, there does not exist an algorithm for finding the time complexity of a given LCL problem in 2-dimensional grids. Nevertheless, we can still prove that any LCL problem has a complexity of $O(1)$, $\Theta(\log^* n)$, or $\Theta(n)$ also in 2-dimensional grids. We will next prove the key ingredient: any $o(n)$-time algorithm can be turned into an $O(\log^* n)$-time algorithm that has a convenient structure.

## 5 SPEED-UP AND NORMAL FORM

In this section, we give the speed-up result underlying both the complexity classification of LCL problems and the synthesis. The following result is essentially a refined version of the speed-up lemma of Chang et al. [10] for two-dimensional oriented grids; the proof immediately yields the normal form algorithm for any LCL problem as discussed in Section 1.

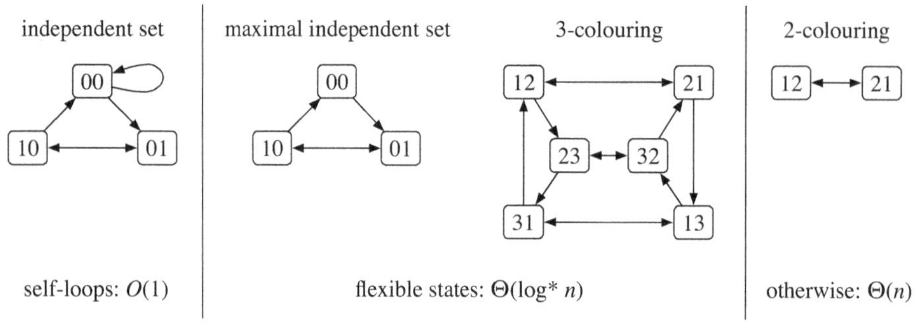


**Figure 3: LCL problems for cycles can be represented as directed graphs. Here we have four LCL problems with radius $r = 1$; each node corresponds to a sequence of $2r = 2$ output labels, and each edge corresponds to a sequence of $2r + 1 = 3$ output labels. We can read the time complexity of the LCL problem directly from the properties of the graph. For example, in the maximal independent set problem, state 00 is flexible, as we can find walks from 00 back to itself of lengths 3 and 5, and hence also of any length larger than 7.**

Theorem 5.1. *Given any* LCL *$P$ with an algorithm $A$ that solves $P$ in time $T(n) = o(n)$, there exists an algorithm $B$ that solves $P$ and has running time $O(\log^* n)$.*

Proof. Recall that w.l.o.g., we can assume that problem $P$ has checkability radius $r = 1$. Algorithm $B$ solves problem $P$ in an $n \times n$ grid $G$ as follows:

(1) Pick the smallest even $k \geq 4$ such that $T(k) < k/4 - 4$. Such a $k$ exists by assumption, and it is a constant that only depends on $T$.
(2) Find a maximal independent set $I$ in $G^{(k/2)}$. This can be done in time $O(\log^* n)$; the nodes of $I$ are called *anchors*.
(3) Simulate $A$ with *locally unique identifiers* from $[k^2]$ around each anchor in $I$.

Step (3) of the simulation proceeds as follows. First, $G$ is divided into a Voronoi tiling with respect to $I$, breaking ties arbitrarily—that is, we associate with each node $v \in I$ a Voronoi tile $T(v) = \{u \in V : v \text{ is the closest anchor to } u\}$; each node can compute which tile they belong to in constant time. Then, each node $v$ is assigned a *local coordinate* $c(v) = (x_v - x_{a(v)}, y_v - y_{a(v)})$, where $a(v)$ is the anchor of $v$'s tile. The local coordinates will be interpreted as locally unique identifiers.

There are no repeating identifiers within distance $k/2$ of any node: If two nodes $u$ and $v$ have the same coordinate, they are in different Voronoi tiles. Since the anchors are at distance at least $k/2$, and $u$ and $v$ are by assumption in the same relative positions with respect of their anchors, also $u$ and $v$ are at distance at least $k/2$.

Each Voronoi tile $T(v)$ holds nodes at distance at most $k/2 + 1$, since any node at distance $k/2 + 2$ from $v$ must have another anchor within distance $k/2$. We can calculate that the size of each tile is at most $|T(v)| \leq k^2$; hence we only need $k^2$ distinct locally unique identifiers.

Next we simulate $A$ on $G$, with a bit of cheating: we tell $A$ that we are actually solving $P$ for an instance of size $k \times k$; for each local neighbourhood of $G$, we feed it locally unique identifiers from $[k^2]$. Now $A$ has a running time $T(k) < k/4$, and hence it does not ever see repeating identifiers; it has to solve problem $P$ correctly in each local neighbourhood as this might be a legitimate instance of size $k \times k$. More precisely, if the local outputs of $A$ violated the constraints of the LCL problem $P$ for some local neighbourhoods, we could also construct a genuine instance $H$ of size $k \times k$ with globally unique identifiers, and $A$ would fail to solve $P$ in $H$. Hence the local outputs of $A$ have to constitute a globally feasible solution for $P$ also in $G$. □

# 6 UNDECIDABILITY OF CLASSIFICATION

In this section we show that in general deciding whether the running time of a given LCL problem is $\Theta(\log^* n)$ or $\Theta(n)$ is undecidable. We achieve this by defining, for each Turing machine $M$, an LCL problem $L_M$ such that $L_M$ can be solved in time $\Theta(\log^* n)$ if and only if $M$ halts, and in time $\Theta(n)$ otherwise.

Theorem 6.1. *The problem of deciding whether a given* LCL *can be solved in time $\Theta(\log^* n)$ or $\Theta(n)$ on grids is undecidable.*

It is good to compare this with the result of Naor and Stockmeyer [32]. They study grids with boundaries (non-toroidal grids; there are nodes of degrees 3 and 2). In such grids, deciding if an LCL can be solved in time $O(1)$ is already undecidable. In essence, for any Turing machine $M$ we can construct an LCL that specifies that in the lower-left corner of the grid we have to write out the complete execution history of $M$, and everything else can be padding. Now if and only if $M$ halts in some finite time $t$, then LCL can be solved in time $O(t) = O(1)$, as it suffices to check if we are within distance $\Theta(t)$ from the corner and otherwise we can just output padding.

In our case of toroidal grids, this no longer holds. It is trivial to decide if a given LCL can be solved in $O(1)$ time; only trivial problems in which a constant output is a feasible solution admit an $O(1)$-time solution in toroidal grids. For example, the problem constructed by Naor and Stockmeyer [32] is now trivial, as there are no corners, and we can always output padding.

We develop a different LCL problem $L_M$ that forces any efficient algorithm to *create corners.* The problem is defined so that the grid can be partitioned in "tiles" of arbitrary dimensions, but there are additional requirements:

(1) inside each tile we have to solve an inherently global problem, and

(2) in the "corner" of each tile we must output the complete execution table of $M$.

Now property (1) prevents efficient algorithms from producing an output that says that the entire grid consists of one tile. But as soon as the algorithm creates some tile boundaries, property (2) kicks in and makes sure that we can have finite tiles if and only if $M$ halts in finite time. Additional care is needed to make sure that the problem is solvable but global if $M$ does not halt, as we will discuss next.

LCL *problem* $L_M$ *in detail.* For each Turing machine $M$, we define $L_M$ as the disjoint union of two locally checkable labellings $P_1$ and $P_2$; to solve $L_M$, one has to solve either $P_1$ or $P_2$. The problem $P_1$ is defined to be 3-colouring in order to make sure that $L_M$ can always be solved in time $O(n)$, independent of $M$. On the other hand, 3-colouring requires time $\Omega(n)$. The problem $P_2$ is a problem that involves labelling the grid with the execution table of $M$, started on an empty tape. This problem is formulated so that it can be solved in time $O(\log^* n)$ if and only if $M$ halts on the empty tape.

Each node is labelled with the Turing machine $M$ and a *type*: each node is either an *anchor* or belongs either into one of the four *quadrants* NW, NE, SE, and SW, or one of the four *borders* N, S, E, and W. We overload the notation and define incidence operators as follows. For an arbitrary node $v = (x, y)$, define

$$\mathsf{NW}(v) = (x-1, y+1), \quad \mathsf{NE}(v) = (x+1, y+1),$$
$$\mathsf{SE}(v) = (x+1, y-1), \quad \mathsf{SW}(v) = (x-1, y-1),$$
$$\mathsf{N}(v) = (x, y+1), \quad \mathsf{S}(v) = (x, y-1),$$
$$\mathsf{E}(v) = (x+1, y), \quad \mathsf{W}(v) = (x-1, y).$$

We will use the types of the nodes to refer to the corresponding incidence operators. The idea of the type labels is that they can be followed to find an anchor.

Let $Q(u) \in \{\mathsf{NE}, \mathsf{SE}, \mathsf{SW}, \mathsf{NW}, \mathsf{N}, \mathsf{E}, \mathsf{S}, \mathsf{W}, \mathsf{A}\}$, denote the type of a node, and $x(u) \in \{0, 1\}$ a colouring. Define the diagonal neighbour $\mathrm{diag}(u)$ of node $u$ as the node reached by taking a step in direction $Q(u)$. For example, if $Q(u) = \mathsf{NW}$, then $\mathrm{diag}(u) = \mathsf{NW}(u)$. For completeness, define the diagonal of an anchor is the node itself.

We have the following local rules.

(1) If $Q(u) = \mathsf{NE}$, then $Q(\mathrm{diag}(u)) \in \{\mathsf{NE}, \mathsf{N}, \mathsf{E}, \mathsf{A}\}$.
(2) If $Q(u) = \mathsf{SE}$, then $Q(\mathrm{diag}(u)) \in \{\mathsf{SE}, \mathsf{S}, \mathsf{E}, \mathsf{A}\}$.
(3) If $Q(u) = \mathsf{SW}$, then $Q(\mathrm{diag}(u)) \in \{\mathsf{SW}, \mathsf{S}, \mathsf{W}, \mathsf{A}\}$.
(4) If $Q(u) = \mathsf{NW}$, then $Q(\mathrm{diag}(u)) \in \{\mathsf{NW}, \mathsf{N}, \mathsf{W}, \mathsf{A}\}$.

On the borders, we must have that $Q(\mathrm{diag}(u)) = Q(u)$, or that $Q(\mathrm{diag}(u)) = \mathsf{A}$. In addition, we require that the borders are surrounded with different labels. In particular we must have that

(1) If $Q(u) = \mathsf{N}$, then $Q(\mathsf{W}(u)) = \mathsf{NE}$ and $Q(\mathsf{E}(u)) = \mathsf{NW}$.
(2) If $Q(u) = \mathsf{S}$, then $Q(\mathsf{W}(u)) = \mathsf{SE}$ and $Q(\mathsf{E}(u)) = \mathsf{SW}$.
(3) If $Q(u) = \mathsf{E}$, then $Q(\mathsf{N}(u)) = \mathsf{SE}$ and $Q(\mathsf{S}(u)) = \mathsf{NE}$.
(4) If $Q(u) = \mathsf{W}$, then $Q(\mathsf{N}(u)) = \mathsf{SW}$ and $Q(\mathsf{S}(u)) = \mathsf{NW}$.

Finally for any anchor $v$, we require that $Q(\mathsf{N}(v)) = \mathsf{S}$, $Q(\mathsf{NW}(v)) = \mathsf{SE}$, $Q(\mathsf{E}(v)) = \mathsf{W}$, $Q(\mathsf{SE}(v)) = \mathsf{NW}$, $Q(\mathsf{S}(v)) = \mathsf{N}$, $Q(\mathsf{SW}(v)) = \mathsf{NE}$, $Q(\mathsf{W}(v)) = \mathsf{E}$, and $Q(\mathsf{NE}(v)) = \mathsf{SW}$.

In addition, the diagonals must be 2-coloured, that is, we require that if $Q(u) = Q(\mathrm{diag}(u))$, then $x(u) \neq x(\mathrm{diag}(u))$. This condition ensures that any fast solution cannot have large (e.g. linear-sized) contiguous fragments of nodes with the same type, and that anchor nodes must appear in the solution.

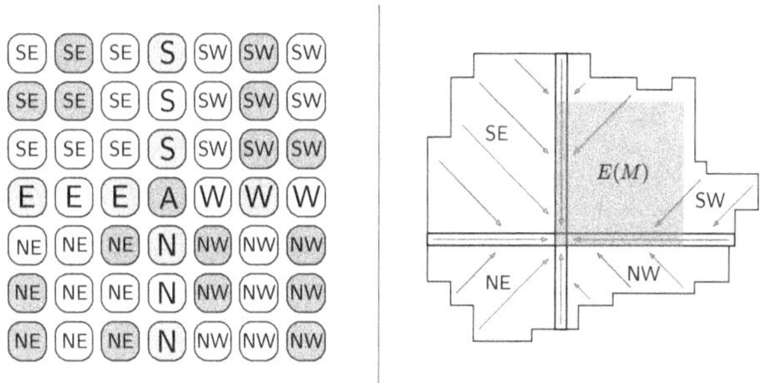


(a) (b)

**Figure 4: (a) The local rules for the labelling problem $P_2$: all nodes must have a type, indicated by the label, and their diagonal neighbours must have a type that is compatible. Every diagonal must be 2-coloured, that is, for every pair $u, v$ such that $u = \mathrm{diag}(v)$ and $Q(u) = Q(v)$ we must have that $x(u) \neq x(v)$. The anchor must be surrounded by the other labels. (b) The general structure of $O(\log^* n)$ time solution to $P_2$ if $M$ halts. The Voronoi tile of an anchor is split into four quadrants and four borders. Every diagonal can be followed to reach the anchor. An encoding of the execution table $E(M)$ starts from the anchor and is contained inside the Voronoi tile.**

Finally, we require that starting from each anchor, the grid is labelled with the encoding of the execution table of $M$ when started on an empty tape. This encoding is detailed in the following paragraph.

*Encoding the execution table of a Turing machine M.* Consider an anchor node $v$. We will translate the coordinate system of $G$ so that $v = (0, 0)$.

Assume that $M$ runs for $s$ steps on the empty tape. The encoding of the execution table $E(M)$ of $M$ consists of an $(s+1) \times r$ rectangular subgrid, where $r \leq s+1$, with the bottom left corner at the anchor $v$. Each row $j$ of $E(M)$ encodes the contents of the tape at the beginning of step $j$. Each column $i$ corresponds to a cell of the tape. Thus, each node $(i, j)$ is labelled with the contents of the cell $i$ before step $j$. In addition, one node on each row holds the machine head and the state of $M$. Each node $u$ on the left boundary of $E(M)$ must have $Q(u) = \mathsf{S}$, and each node $w$ on the bottom boundary must have $Q(w) = \mathsf{W}$.

On the first row each cell is empty and the anchor $v$ holds the machine head. Every $2 \times 2$ subgrid of $E(M)$ must be consistent with the transition rules of $M$. On the last row one of the nodes holds the machine head in a halting state. Each node may hold the encoding of at most one machine. Only nodes with labels $Q \in \{\mathsf{S}, \mathsf{W}, \mathsf{SW}\}$ may be labelled with an encoding of the Turing machine.

Note that since the labels contain no references to $s$ or the position of any node on $E(M)$, the encoding can be done using a constant number of labels.

*Local checkability of the encoding.* Since the nodes can detect if both $P_1$ and $P_2$ are used, we can look at the two cases separately. Clearly a 2-colouring is locally checkable. Now assume that the labelling $P_2$ is used.

The local rules related to the labelling $\ell$ are clearly locally checkable. The nodes can check that they agree on the identity of the Turing machine $M$. The Turing machine encoding is also locally checkable: every anchor and the nodes on the W border can check that the tape is initially empty. Between the rows, nodes can check that the encoding respects the transition rules of $M$. On the top and the right border of the tape nodes can check that the final state is a stopping state and that the encoding is complete.

*Solving $L_M$ in time $O(\log^* n)$ if $M$ halts.* Assume that $M$ halts in $s$ steps. $L_M$ can be solved in time $O(\log^* n)$ as follows.

(1) If $G$ has size $n < 2(s + 1)$, solve $P_1$ by brute force.
(2) Else, find a maximal independent set $I$ in $G^{(4(s+1))}$. This is the set of anchors.
(3) Construct the Voronoi tiling $T$ of the anchor set $I$, breaking ties in an arbitrary but consistent manner. The size of each tile is bounded by a constant. Inside each tile $T(v)$ with anchor $v = (x, v)$, label nodes according their position with respect to the anchor:

$$Q(u) = \begin{cases} \mathsf{NW}, \text{ if } x_u > x, y_u < y, \\ \mathsf{NE}, \text{ if } x_u < x, y_u < y, \\ \mathsf{SW}, \text{ if } x_u > x, y_u > y, \\ \mathsf{SE}, \text{ if } x_u < x, y_u > y. \end{cases} \tag{1}$$

Similarly, the borders are labelled as follows.

$$Q(u) = \begin{cases} \mathsf{N}, \text{ if } x_u = x, y_u < y, \\ \mathsf{S}, \text{ if } x_u = x, y_u > y, \\ \mathsf{E}, \text{ if } x_u < x, y_u = y, \\ \mathsf{W}, \text{ if } x_u > x, y_u = y. \end{cases} \tag{2}$$

From each anchor, start a labelling with the execution table of $M$ as described above. The distance of at least $4(s + 1)$ between anchors guarantees that each Voronoi tile can fit the execution table encoding inside it.

Everything is constant time, except finding the maximal independent set, which can be done in time $O(\log^* n)$.

*Solving $L_M$ requires time $\Omega(n)$ if $M$ does not halt.* Now assume that $M$ does not halt on the empty tape. Solving $P_1$ naturally requires $\Omega(n)$ time. There are two possibilities for the labelling $P_2$: either the labelling contains an anchor, or not.

First, assume that the labelling contains an anchor $v = (x, y)$. This means that around the anchor, the grid must be labelled with the execution table of $M$, starting with an empty tape. The nodes $(x, y + j)$, with $j > 0$, must be labelled with S and the contents of the first cell of $M$'s tape before time steps $j$. The nodes $(x + i, y)$, with $i > 0$, must be labelled with W and the initial, empty contents of $M$'s tape. Since $M$ does not halt on the empty tape, either some node detects and illegal transition in the encoding of the execution table, or the table wraps around the grid. Then there must be a node labelled with N or NW, and contents of $M$'s tape, a contradiction to the correctness of the output.

Now assume that there are no anchors. If there are no borders, then all nodes must be labelled with the same quadrant $Q \in \{\mathsf{NW}, \mathsf{NE}, \mathsf{SE}, \mathsf{SW}\}$, as otherwise there would a node with the wrong type of diagonal neighbour. Then we can find diagonals of length $\Omega(n)$ that must be 2-coloured, requiring time $\Omega(n)$. Now assume that there exists a node labelled with a border. Since there are no anchors, this node must have a diagonal labelled with the same border, until the border wraps around. The border has length $\Omega(n)$ and must again be 2-coloured, leading to a running time of $\Omega(n)$.

*Solving $L_M$ requires time $\Omega(\log^* n)$ if $M$ halts.* Finally, we note that solving $L_M$ requires time $\Omega(\log^* n)$, as it requires breaking symmetry between nodes.

We have shown that $L_M$ has an $O(\log^* n)$ time algorithm if and only if $M$ halts on an empty tape. This is known to be an undecidable problem, and therefore the problem of deciding whether an $O(\log^* n)$ time algorithm exists is in general also undecidable.

## 7 SYNTHESIS

At first, the undecidability result of Section 6 seems to suggest that there is little hope in automating algorithm design for LCL problems in grids. Indeed, given an LCL problem $P$, we cannot even tell if it can be solved in $O(\log^* n)$ time or if it is inherently global.

However, in a sense this is the *only* obstacle for automatic synthesis of optimal algorithms! Let us assume that we are given 1 bit of advice indicating whether $P$ is local (solvable in time $O(\log^* n)$) or global. We will now argue that this information is enough to automatically synthesise an asymptotically optimal algorithm for $P$.

If $P$ is global, then there is a trivial brute-force algorithm of time $O(n)$ that merely gathers the entire output at a single node and solves the problem globally.

If $P$ is local, we can first check whether it is trivial. If there is a constant label that can be used to fill the entire grid, then (and only then) the problem is solvable in time $O(1)$.

The remaining case is a local problem that cannot be solved in time $O(1)$. Now Theorem 5.1 and the classical result of Naor and Stockmeyer [32] imply that the only possibility is the complexity of $\Theta(\log^* n)$. Moreover, the proof of Theorem 5.1 suggests a convenient *normal form*: problem $P$ can be solved with an algorithm of the form $A' \circ S_k$ for some constant $k$, where

- $S_k$ finds a set of anchors $I$ that forms a maximal independent set in $G^{(k)}$,
- $A'$ is an algorithm with running time bounded by $O(k)$ that takes as an input only the set of anchors $I$ and the global orientation of the grid.

In the proof of Theorem 5.1, algorithm $A'$ first constructs Voronoi tiles, then assigns locally unique identifiers, and then simulates some $O(k)$-time algorithm $A$. But we do not need to worry about such details here; we can see this entire process as a black box $A'$ that simply takes the placement of anchors in the radius-$O(k)$ neighbourhood as input, and using only this information produces the final local output. In particular, $A'$ does not depend on the assignment of unique identifiers or on the value of $n$.

It follows that $A'$ is a *finite function*, mapping radius-$O(k)$ neighbourhoods in a $\{0, 1\}$-labelled grid to local outputs. There are only finitely many ways to assign $\{0, 1\}$ labels in a constant-sized fragment of the grid, and hence $A'$ can be conveniently represented as a finite lookup table.

The only missing piece is finding the value of $k$, and to do that, we can simply start with $k = 1$ and increment it until synthesis succeeds. (Note that if we were dealing with a global problem instead of a local problem this loop will never terminate.)

For each value of $k$, we proceed as follows. We pick sufficiently large values $r_1, r_2 = \Theta(k)$. Then we enumerate all possible ways in which the anchors may appear within a $r_1 \times r_2$ fragment of the grid; these are called *tiles*. We describe in the full version of the paper [9] a practical algorithm for such an enumeration. For example, for $k = 1$ we have the following $3 \times 2$ tiles; if we consider a maximal independent set in the grid, and pick a $3 \times 2$ window, we will see one of these configurations:

$$\boxed{\begin{matrix}00\\00\\10\end{matrix}}\ \boxed{\begin{matrix}00\\00\\01\end{matrix}}\ \boxed{\begin{matrix}00\\10\\00\end{matrix}}\ \boxed{\begin{matrix}00\\10\\01\end{matrix}}\ \boxed{\begin{matrix}00\\01\\00\end{matrix}}\ \boxed{\begin{matrix}00\\01\\10\end{matrix}}\ \boxed{\begin{matrix}10\\00\\00\end{matrix}}\ \boxed{\begin{matrix}10\\00\\10\end{matrix}}$$

$$\boxed{\begin{matrix}10\\00\\01\end{matrix}}\ \boxed{\begin{matrix}10\\01\\00\end{matrix}}\ \boxed{\begin{matrix}10\\01\\10\end{matrix}}\ \boxed{\begin{matrix}01\\00\\00\end{matrix}}\ \boxed{\begin{matrix}01\\00\\10\end{matrix}}\ \boxed{\begin{matrix}01\\00\\01\end{matrix}}\ \boxed{\begin{matrix}01\\10\\00\end{matrix}}\ \boxed{\begin{matrix}01\\10\\01\end{matrix}}$$

We will then construct a *neighbourhood graph* $H = (V_H, E_H)$, in which each node $u \in V_H$ corresponds to a $r_1 \times r_2$ tile, and each edge corresponds to a tile of dimensions $(r_1 + 1) \times r_2$ or $r_1 \times (r_2 + 1)$. For example, there is a $3 \times 3$ tile

$$\boxed{\begin{matrix}000\\010\\100\end{matrix}}$$

and hence in the neighbourhood graph of $3 \times 2$ tiles there is a directed *horizontal edge*

$$\left(\boxed{\begin{matrix}00\\01\\10\end{matrix}}, \boxed{\begin{matrix}00\\10\\00\end{matrix}}\right).$$

Similarly, we can identify directed vertical edges. Now $A'$ is simply a mapping from $V_H$ to local outputs; $A'(u)$ is what we output for a node whose local neighbourhood with respect to $I$ is equal to $u$. Furthermore, the constraints of the LCL problem $P$ (once sufficiently normalised) can be encoded as constraints related to horizontal and vertical edges. For example, in the 4-colouring problem, the constraint is simply that adjacent tiles have different labels.

Hence the task of synthesising algorithm $A'$ reduces to a combinatorial constraint satisfaction problem in which our task is to find a labelling of the nodes of graph $H$ that satisfies all constraints on the edges of the graph; if such an assignment does not exist, we simply repeat the process with a larger value of $k$ and larger tile dimensions.

We have successfully used this approach with many concrete LCL problems discussed in this work, and it works well in practice. As a concrete nontrivial example, consider the problem of 4-colouring 2-dimensional grids. Here it can be shown that no solution exists for $k = 1$ or $k = 2$, but synthesis succeeds with $k = 3$ for e.g. $7 \times 5$ tiles. While a priori it might seem that the number of tiles is impractical for such parameter values ($2^{7 \cdot 5}$ candidate tiles?), the key observation is that 1's are fairly sparse in any maximal independent set of $G^{(k)}$, and it turns out that we only need to consider 2079 tiles. Finding a proper 4-colouring of the neighbourhood graph can be done with modern SAT solvers in a matter of seconds.

## 8 UPPER AND LOWER BOUNDS FOR CONCRETE LCL PROBLEMS

We refer to the full version of the paper [9] for a complete characterisation of the complexity of vertex colouring and edge colouring in $d$-dimensional grids, and for a complete characterisation of bounded-indegree orientation problems on 2-dimensional grids.

## 9 DISCUSSION AND OPEN QUESTIONS

*Randomised complexity.* Chang et al. [10] showed that the randomised complexity of any LCL on instances of size $n$ is at least its deterministic complexity on instances of size $\sqrt{\log n}$. This, combined with our Theorem 5.1, implies that there are no LCL problems with randomised complexity between $\omega(\log^* n)$ and $o(\sqrt{\log n})$ on the grid. Whether problems with randomised complexity $O(\sqrt{\log n})$ exist is left as an open question.

*High-dimensional grids.* As mentioned in the beginning of the introduction, we can also consider the setting of $d$-dimensional (hypertoroidal oriented) grids with $n^d$ nodes. The complexity results extend to this setting: the classification theorem and the undecidability of classification hold for $d$-dimensional grids, and as noted before, the vertex and edge colouring results generalise. The techniques used in the synthesis algorithm also generalise to $d$-dimensional grids. However, we have not yet implemented the synthesis beyond $d = 2$, and we expect that the increased size of the search space may make the synthesis less feasible.

*Bounded growth graphs.* The proof of Theorem 5.1 intrinsically exploits the fact that the size of a neighbourhood $N_r(v)$ grows quadratically in $r$, and thus any algorithm with running time $T(n) = o(n)$ cannot see all $n^2$ nodes of the graph for large $n$. We show that this is not a phenomenon restricted to grids: for any class of graphs with limited neighbourhood growth rate, we get a large complexity gap. See the full version of the paper [9] for the precise statement and the proof.

*Sublinear problems on general graphs.* Finally, we use techniques inspired by grid graphs to expand our understanding of the complexity landscape of LCL problems on general bounded-degree graphs. Recall that in general we know that the lower end of the complexity landscape is sparse: for deterministic algorithms, there is nothing between the classes $O(1)$, $\Theta(\log^* n)$, and $\Theta(\log n)$. There are also obviously problems of complexity $\Theta(n)$, but the gap between $\Theta(\log n)$ and $\Theta(n)$ is largely unexplored. In the full version of the paper [9] we show how to engineer an LCL problem with a complexity of precisely $\Theta(\sqrt{n})$ in general bounded-degree graphs; subsequently, Chang and Pettie [11] have given a more general result showing that problems of complexity $\Theta(n^{1/k})$ exists for any integer $k \geq 2$ even when restricted to bounded-degree trees.

## ACKNOWLEDGMENTS

We would like to thank Orr Fischer for many discussions related to these research questions. This work was supported in part by the Academy of Finland, Grants 285721 and 289002.

## REFERENCES


[1] Paul C. Attie and E. Allen Emerson. 2001. Synthesis of concurrent programs for an atomic read/write model of computation. *ACM Trans. Program. Lang. Syst.* 23, 2 (2001), 187–242. https://doi.org/10.1145/383043.383044

[2] Yoah Bar-David and Gadi Taubenfeld. 2003. Automatic discovery of mutual exclusion algorithms. In *Proc. 17th International Conference on Distributed Computing (DISC 2003) (Lecture Notes in Computer Science)*, Vol. 2848. Springer, 136–150. https://doi.org/10.1007/978-3-540-39989-6_10

[3] Leonid Barenboim. 2015. Deterministic ($\Delta + 1$)-Coloring in Sublinear (in $\Delta$) Time in Static, Dynamic and Faulty Networks. In *Proc. 34th ACM Symposium on the Principles of Distributed Computing (PODC 2016)*. ACM, 345–354. https://doi.org/10.1145/2767386.2767410

[4] Leonid Barenboim and Michael Elkin. 2013. Distributed deterministic edge coloring using bounded neighborhood independence. *Distributed Computing* 26, 5 (2013), 273–287. https://doi.org/10.1007/s00446-012-0167-7

[5] Leonid Barenboim, Michael Elkin, and Fabian Kuhn. 2014. Distributed ($\Delta + 1$)-coloring in linear (in $\Delta$) time. *SIAM J. Comput.* 43, 1 (2014), 72–95. https://doi.org/10.1137/12088848X

[6] Leonid Barenboim, Michael Elkin, and Tzalik Maimon. 2016. Deterministic distributed ($\Delta + o(\Delta)$)-edge-coloring and vertex-coloring of graphs with bounded diversity. (2016). arXiv:1610.06759.

[7] Roderick Bloem, Nicolas Braud-Santoni, and Swen Jacobs. 2016. Synthesis of self-stabilising and Byzantine-resilient distributed systems. In *Proc. 28th International Conference on Computer Aided Verification (CAV 2016) (Lecture Notes in Computer Science)*, Vol. 9779. Springer, 157–176. https://doi.org/10.1007/978-3-319-41528-4_9

[8] Sebastian Brandt, Orr Fischer, Juho Hirvonen, Barbara Keller, Tuomo Lempiäinen, Joel Rybicki, Jukka Suomela, and Jara Uitto. 2016. A Lower Bound for the Distributed Lovász Local Lemma. In *Proc. 48th Annual Symposium on the Theory of Computing (STOC 2016)*. ACM, 479–488. https://doi.org/10.1145/2897518.2897570 arXiv:1511.00900.

[9] Sebastian Brandt, Juho Hirvonen, Janne H. Korhonen, Tuomo Lempiäinen, Patric R. J. Östergård, Christopher Purcell, Joel Rybicki, Jukka Suomela, and Przemysław Uznański. 2017. LCL problems on grids. (2017). arXiv:1702.05456.

[10] Yi-Jun Chang, Tsvi Kopelowitz, and Seth Pettie. 2016. An Exponential Separation Between Randomized and Deterministic Complexity in the LOCAL Model. In *Proc. 57th Annual IEEE Symposium on Foundations of Computer Science (FOCS 2016)*. IEEE, 615–624. arXiv:1602.08166.

[11] Yi-Jun Chang and Seth Pettie. 2017. A Time Hierarchy Theorem for the LOCAL Model. (2017). arXiv:1704.06297.

[12] Alonzo Church. 1957. Application of recursive arithmetic to the problem of circuit synthesis. In *Summaries of talks presented at the Summer Institute of Symbolic Logic*, Vol. 1. 3–50.

[13] Edmund M. Clarke and E. Allen Emerson. 1982. Design and synthesis of synchronization skeletons using branching time temporal logic. In *Proc. 3rd Workshop on Logic of Programs (LOP 1981) (Lecture Notes in Computer Science)*, Vol. 131. Springer, 52–71. https://doi.org/10.1007/BFb0025774

[14] Richard Cole and Uzi Vishkin. 1986. Deterministic coin tossing with applications to optimal parallel list ranking. *Information and Control* 70, 1 (1986), 32–53. https://doi.org/10.1016/S0019-9958(86)80023-7

[15] Danny Dolev, Keijo Heljanko, Matti Järvisalo, Janne H. Korhonen, Christoph Lenzen, Joel Rybicki, Jukka Suomela, and Siert Wieringa. 2016. Synchronous counting and computational algorithm design. *J. Comput. System Sci.* 82, 2 (2016), 310–332. https://doi.org/10.1016/j.jcss.2015.09.002

[16] David Doty. 2012. Theory of algorithmic self-assembly. *Commun. ACM* 55, 12 (2012), 78–88. https://doi.org/10.1145/2380656.2380675

[17] Bernd Finkbeiner and Sven Schewe. 2005. Uniform distributed synthesis. In *Proc. 20th Annual IEEE Symposium on Logic in Computer Science (LICS 2005)*. IEEE, 321–330. https://doi.org/10.1109/LICS.2005.53

[18] Pierre Fraigniaud, Marc Heinrich, and Adrian Kosowski. 2016. Local Conflict Coloring. In *Proc. 57th Annual IEEE Symposium on Foundations of Computer Science (FOCS 2016)*. IEEE, 625–634. https://doi.org/10.1109/FOCS.2016.73 arXiv:1511.01287.

[19] Niloy Ganguly, Biplab K. Sikdar, Andreas Deutsch, Geoffrey Canright, and P. Pal Chaudhuri. 2003. *A Survey on Cellular Automata*. Technical Report. Centre for High Performance Computing, Dresden University of Technology.

[20] Martin Gardner. 1970. The fantastic combinations of John Conway's new solitaire game 'life'. *Scientific American* 223, 4 (1970), 120–123.

[21] Beat Gfeller and Elias Vicari. 2007. A Randomized Distributed Algorithm for the Maximal Independent Set Problem in Growth-bounded Graphs. In *Proc. 26th Annual ACM Symposium on Principles of Distributed Computing (PODC 2007)*. ACM, New York, NY, USA, 53–60. https://doi.org/10.1145/1281100.1281111

[22] Mohsen Ghaffari and Hsin-Hao Su. 2017. Distributed Degree Splitting, Edge Coloring, and Orientations. In *Proc. 28th Annual ACM-SIAM Symposium on Discrete Algorithms (SODA 2017)*. Society for Industrial and Applied Mathematics, 2505–2523. https://doi.org/10.1137/1.9781611974782.166

[23] Branko Grünbaum and G. C. Shephard. 1987. *Tilings and Patterns*. W. H. Freeman and Company, New York, NY, USA.

[24] Juho Hirvonen, Joel Rybicki, Stefan Schmid, and Jukka Suomela. 2014. Large cuts with local algorithms on triangle-free graphs. (February 2014). arXiv:1402.2543.

[25] Alexander E. Holroyd, Oded Schramm, and David B. Wilson. 2014. Finitary Coloring. (2014). arXiv:1412.2725.

[26] Jarkko Kari. 2005. Theory of cellular automata: A survey. *Theoretical Computer Science* 334, 1 (2005), 3–33. https://doi.org/10.1016/j.tcs.2004.11.021

[27] Fabian Kuhn, Thomas Moscibroda, Tim Nieberg, and Roger Wattenhofer. 2005. Fast deterministic distributed maximal independent set computation on growth-bounded graphs. In *Proc. 19th International Symposium on Distributed Computing (DISC 2005) (Lecture Notes in Computer Science)*, Vol. 3724. Springer, 273–287. https://doi.org/10.1007/11561927_21

[28] Fabian Kuhn, Thomas Moscibroda, and Roger Wattenhofer. 2016. Local Computation: Lower and Upper Bounds. *J. ACM* 63, 2 (2016), 17:1–17:44. https://doi.org/10.1145/2742012 arXiv:1011.5470.

[29] Orna Kupferman and Moshe Y. Vardi. 2001. Synthesizing Distributed Systems. In *Proc. of the 16th Annual IEEE Symposium on Logic in Computer Science (LICS 2001)*. IEEE Computer Society, Washington, DC, USA, 389–398.

[30] Nathan Linial. 1992. Locality in distributed graph algorithms. *SIAM J. Comput.* 21, 1 (1992), 193–201. https://doi.org/10.1137/0221015

[31] Zohar Manna and Pierre Wolper. 1984. Synthesis of communicating processes from temporal logic specifications. *ACM Transactions on Programming Languages and Systems* 6, 1 (1984), 68–93.

[32] Moni Naor and Larry Stockmeyer. 1995. What can be computed locally? *SIAM J. Comput.* 24, 6 (1995), 1259–1277. https://doi.org/10.1137/S0097539793254571

[33] Alessandro Panconesi and Romeo Rizzi. 2001. Some simple distributed algorithms for sparse networks. *Distributed Computing* 14, 2 (2001), 97–100. https://doi.org/10.1007/PL00008932

[34] Alessandro Panconesi and Aravind Srinivasan. 1995. The local nature of $\Delta$-colouring and its algorithmic applications. *Combinatorica* 15, 2 (1995), 255–280. https://doi.org/10.1007/BF01200759

[35] Matthew J. Patitz. 2014. An introduction to tile-based self-assembly and a survey of recent results. *Natural Computing* 13, 2 (2014), 195–224. https://doi.org/10.1007/s11047-013-9379-4

[36] David Peleg. 2000. *Distributed Computing: A Locality-Sensitive Approach*. SIAM, Philadelphia.

[37] Amir Pnueli and Roni Rosner. 1990. Distributed reactive systems are hard to synthesize. In *Proc. 31st Annual Symposium on Foundations of Computer Science (FOCS 1990)*, Vol. 2. 746–757. https://doi.org/10.1109/FSCS.1990.89597

[38] Joel Rybicki and Jukka Suomela. 2015. Exact bounds for distributed graph colouring. In *Proc. 22nd International Symposium on Structural Information and Communication Complexity (SIROCCO 2015) (Lecture Notes in Computer Science)*, Vol. 9439. Springer, 44–60. https://doi.org/10.1007/978-3-319-25258-2 arXiv:1502.04963.

[39] Johannes Schneider, Michael Elkin, and Roger Wattenhofer. 2013. Symmetry breaking depending on the chromatic number or the neighborhood growth. *Theoretical Computer Science* 509 (2013), 40–50. https://doi.org/10.1016/j.tcs.2012.09.004

[40] Johannes Schneider and Roger Wattenhofer. 2010. An optimal maximal independent set algorithm for bounded-independence graphs. *Distributed Computing* 22, 5 (2010), 349–361. https://doi.org/10.1007/s00446-010-0097-1

[41] Alvy Ray Smith, III. 1976. Introduction to and survey of cellular automata or polyautomata theory. In *Automata, Language, Development*. North-Holland Publishing Co., 405–422.

[42] Aaron D. Sterling. 2008. A limit to the power of multiple nucleation in self-assembly. In *Proc. 22nd International Symposium on Distributed Computing (DISC 2008) (Lecture Notes in Computer Science)*, Vol. 5218. Springer, 451–465. https://doi.org/10.1007/978-3-540-87779-0_31 arXiv:0902.2422.

[43] Moshe Y. Vardi. 2008. From Church and prior to PSL. In *25 years of model checking (Lecture Notes in Computer Science)*, Vol. 5000. Springer, 150–171. https://doi.org/10.1007/978-3-540-69850-0_10

[44] John von Neumann. 1966. *Theory of Self-Reproducing Automata*. University of Illinois Press.

[45] Hao Wang. 1961. Proving theorems by pattern recognition – II. *Bell System Technical Journal* 40, 1 (1961), 1–41.

[46] Erik Winfree. 1998. *Algorithmic Self-Assembly of DNA*. Ph.D. Dissertation. California Institute of Technology. http://resolver.caltech.edu/CaltechETD:etd-05192003-110022

[47] Stephen Wolfram. 2002. *A New Kind of Science*. Wolfram Media.

[48] Damien Woods. 2015. Intrinsic universality and the computational power of self-assembly. *Philosophical Transactions of the Royal Society A* 373, 2046 (2015). https://doi.org/10.1098/rsta.2014.0214

# On The Multiparty Communication Complexity of Testing Triangle-Freeness

Orr Fischer
Computer Science Department,
Tel-Aviv University
orrfischer@mtau.ac.il

Shay Gershtein
Computer Science Department,
Tel-Aviv University
shaygl@tau.ac.il

Rotem Oshman
Computer Science Department,
Tel-Aviv University
roshman@tau.ac.il

## ABSTRACT

In this paper we initiate the study of property testing in multi-party communication complexity, focusing on testing triangle-freeness in graphs. We consider the *coordinator* model, where we have $k$ players receiving private inputs, and a coordinator who receives no input; the coordinator can communicate with all the players, but the players cannot communicate with each other. In this model, we ask: if an input graph is divided between the players, with each player receiving some of the edges, how many bits do the players and the coordinator need to exchange to determine if the graph is triangle-free, or *far* from triangle-free? We are especially interested in *simultaneous* communication protocols, where there is only one communication round.

For general communication protocols, we show that $\tilde{O}(k(nd)^{1/4}+k^2)$ bits are sufficient to test triangle-freeness in graphs of size $n$ with average degree $d$. We also give a simultaneous protocol using $\tilde{O}(k\sqrt{n})$ bits when $d = O(\sqrt{n})$ and $\tilde{O}(k(nd)^{1/3})$ when $d = \Omega(\sqrt{n})$. We show that for average degree $d = O(1)$, our simultaneous protocol is asymptotically optimal up to logarithmic factors. For higher degrees, we are not able to give lower bounds on testing triangle-freeness, but we give evidence that the problem is hard by showing that finding an edge that participates in a triangle is hard, even when promised that the graph is far from triangle-free.

## 1 INTRODUCTION

The field of property testing asks the following question: for a given property $P$, how hard is it to test whether an input *satisfies* $P$, or is $\epsilon$*-far from* $P$, in the sense that an $\epsilon$-fraction of its representation would need to be changed to obtain an object satisfying $P$? Property-testing has received extensive attention, including graph properties such as connectivity and bipartiteness [20], properties of Boolean functions (monotonicity, linearity, etc.), properties of distributions, and many others [15, 19, 32]. The usual model in which property-testing is studied is the *query* model, in which the tester cannot "see" the entire input, and accesses it by asking local queries, that is by only viewing a single entry in the object representation at a time. For example, for graphs represented by their adjacency matrix, the tester might ask whether a given edge is in the graph, or what is the degree of some vertex. The efficiency of a property tester is measured by the number of queries it needs to make. One can also distinguish between *oblivious* testers, which decide in advance on the set of queries, and *adaptive* testers, which decide on the next query after observing the answers to the previous queries. It is known that for many graph properties, one-sided oblivious testers are no more than quadratically more expensive than adaptive testers [22].

In this paper we study property testing from a different perspective, that of *communication complexity*. We focus on property testing for graphs, and we assume that the input graph is divided between several players, who must communicate in order to determine whether it satisfies the property or is far from satisfying it. Each player can operate on its own part of the input "for free", without needing to make queries; we charge only for the number of bits that the players exchange between them. This is on one hand easier than the query model, because players are not restricted to making local queries, and on the other hand harder, because the query model is centralized while here we are in a distributed setting. This leads us to questions such as: does the fact that players are not restricted to local queries make the problem easier, or even trivial? Which useful "building blocks" from the world of property testing can be implemented efficiently by multi-party protocols? Does *interaction* between the players help, or can we adopt the "oblivious approach" represented by *simultaneous* communication protocols?

Beyond the intrinsic interest of these questions, our work is motivated by two recent lines of research. First, [9, 18], study property testing in the CONGEST model, and show that many graph property-testing problems can be solved efficiently in the distributed setting. As pointed out in [18], existing techniques for proving lower bounds in the CONGEST model seem ill-suited to proving lower bounds for property testing. It seems that such lower bounds will require some advances on the communication complexity side, and in this paper we make initial steps in this direction. Second, recent work has shown that many *exact* problems are hard in the setting of multi-party communication complexity: Woodruff et al. [35] proved that for several natural graph properties, such as triangle-freeness, bipartiteness and connectivity, determining whether a graph satisfies the property essentially requires each player to send its entire input. We therefore ask whether weakening our requirements by turning to property testing can help.

In this paper we focus mostly on the specific graph property of *triangle-freeness*, an important property which has received a wealth of attention in the property testing literature. It is known that in dense graphs (average degree $\Theta(n)$) there is an *oblivious* tester for


*PODC '17, July 25-27, 2017, Washington, DC, USA*

ACM ISBN 978-1-4503-4992-5/17/07...$15.00
https://doi.org/10.1145/3087801.3087821

triangle-freeness which is asymptotically optimal in terms of the size of the graph (i.e., adaptivity does not help)[2, 17], and [3] also gives an oblivious tester for graphs with average degree $\Omega(\sqrt{n})$. The closest parallel to oblivious testers in the world of communication complexity is *simultaneous communication protocols*, where the players each send a single message to a referee, and the referee then outputs the answer. We devote special attention to the question of the simultaneous communication-complexity of testing triangle-freeness.

## 1.1 Our contributions

Our results are summarized in Table 1 below.

| | $d = \Theta(1)$ | $d = O(\sqrt{n})$ | $d = \Omega(\sqrt{n})$ |
|---|---|---|---|
| Unrestricted | $\tilde{O}(k\sqrt[4]{nd} + k^2)$ | | |
| Simultaneous | $\tilde{O}(k\sqrt{n})$, $\Omega(k\sqrt[6]{nd} + \sqrt[3]{nd})$ | | $\tilde{O}(k\sqrt[3]{nd})$ |
| "Extended one-way" | $\Omega(\sqrt[6]{nd})$ | | – |

**Table 1: Summary of our results for the various models of communication complexity and settings of the average degree *d*.**

*Basic building-blocks.* We show that many useful building-blocks from the property testing world can be implemented efficiently in the multi-player setting, allowing us to use existing property testers in our setting as well. For some primitives – e.g., sampling a random set of vertices – this is immediate. However, in some cases it is less obvious, especially when *edge duplication* is allowed (so that several players can receive the same edge from the input graph). We show that even with edge duplication the players can efficiently simulate a random walk, estimate the degree of a node, and implement other building blocks. For lack of space, this part of the paper is relegated to the appendix.

*Upper bounds on testing triangle-freeness.* For unrestricted communication protocols, we show that $\tilde{O}(k\sqrt[4]{nd} + k^2)$ bits are sufficient to test triangle-freeness, where $n$ is the size of the graph, $d$ is its average degree (which is not known in advance), and $k$ is the number of players. When interaction is not allowed (simultaneous protocols), we give a protocol that uses $\tilde{O}(k\sqrt{n})$ bits when $d = O(\sqrt{n})$, and another protocol using $\tilde{O}(k\sqrt[3]{nd})$ bits for the case $d = \Omega(\sqrt{n})$. We also combine these protocols into a single *degree-oblivious protocol*, which does not need to know the average degree in advance. (This is not as simple as might sound, since we are working with *simultaneous* protocols, where we cannot first estimate the degree and then use the appropriate protocol for it.)

*Lower bounds.* Our lower bounds are mostly restricted to simultaneous protocols, although we first prove lower bounds for one-way protocols for two or three players, and then then "lift" the results to simultaneous protocols for $k \geq 3$ players using the symmetrization technique [30].

We show that for average degree $d = O(1)$, $\Omega(k\sqrt{n})$ bits are required to simultaneously test triangle-freeness, matching our upper bound. For higher degrees, we are not able to give a lower bound on testing triangle-freeness, but we give evidence that the problem is hard: we show that it is hard to *find an edge that participates in a triangle*, even in graphs that are $\epsilon$-far from triangle free (for constant $\epsilon$), and where every edge participates in a triangle with (small) constant marginal probability.

## 2 RELATED WORK

Property testing is an important notion in many areas of theoretical computer science; see the surveys [15, 19, 32] for more background.

Triangle-freeness, the problem we consider in this paper, is one of the most extensively studied properties in the world of property testing; many different graph densities and restrictions have been investigated (e.g., [1, 2, 4, 21]). Of particular relevance to us is triangle-freeness in the *general model* of property testing, where the average degree of the graph is known in advance, but no other restrictions are imposed. For this model, [3] showed an upper bound of $\tilde{O}(\min\{\sqrt{nd}, n^{\frac{4}{3}}/d^{\frac{2}{3}}\})$ on testing triangle-freeness, and a lower bound of $\Omega(\max\{\sqrt{n}/d, \min\{d, n/d\}, \min\{\sqrt{d}, n^{2/3}\}n^{-o(1)}\})$, both for graphs with a average degree $d$ ranging from $\Omega(1)$ up to $n^{1-o(1)}$. For specific ranges of $d$, [31] and [23] improved these upper and lower bounds, by showing a $O(\max\{(nd)^{4/9}, n^{2/3}/d^{1/3}\})$ upper bound and a $\Omega(\min\{(nd)^{1/3}, n/d), n/d\})$ lower bound.

Our simultaneous protocols use ideas, and in one case an entire tester, from [3], but implementing them in our model presents different challenges and opportunities. (Our unrestricted-round protocol does not bear much similarity to existing testers.) As for lower bounds, we cannot use the techniques from [3] or other property-testing lower bounds, because they rely on the fact that the tester only has query access to the graph. For example, [3] uses the fact that a triangle-freeness tester with one-sided error must *find* a triangle before it can announce that the graph is far from triangle-free ([3] also gives a reduction lifting their results to two-sided error). In the communication complexity setting this is no longer true; there is no obvious reason why the players need to find a triangle in order to learn that the graph is not triangle-free.

*Property testing in other contexts.* Recently, property testing explored in distributed computing [6, 9, 18]. Among their other results, Censor-Hillel et al. [9] showed that triangle-freeness can be tested in $O(\frac{1}{\epsilon^2})$ rounds in the CONGEST model; expanding this,[18] showed that testing $H$-freeness for any 4 node graph $H$ can be done in $O(\frac{1}{\epsilon^2})$ rounds, and showed that their BFS and DFS approach fails for $K_5$ and $C_5$-freeness, respectively; [18] does not give a general lower bound. There has also been work on property testing in the streaming model [24]. The related problem of computing the exact or approximate number of triangles has also been studied in many contexts, including distributed computing [10, 12, 13, 27], sublinear-time algorithms (see [14] and the references therein), and streaming (e.g., [25]). Specifically, [25] shows a lower bound on the space complexity of approximating the number of triangles in the streaming model; we apply their reduction here to show the hardness of testing triangle-freeness, by reducing from a different variant of the problem they use.

*Communication complexity.* Multi-party number-in-hand communication complexity has received significant attention recently. In [35] it is shown that several graph problems, including exact triangle-detection, are hard in this model. Many other exact and approximation problems have also been studied, including [5, 7, 8,

28, 34, 36] and others. Unfortunately, it seems that canonical lower bounds and techniques in communication complexity cannot be leveraged to obtain property-testing lower bounds.

# 3 PRELIMINARIES

*Multi-player number-in-hand communication models.* In *number-in-hand* multi-party communication protocols, we have $k$ playerswith private inputs $X_1, \dots, X_k$. The players communicate with each other to accomplish some shared goal.

There are three popular models for how the players communicate: the *blackboard model*, where communication is by broadcast, and a message by any player is seen by everyone; the *message-passing model*, where every two players have a private communication channel and each message has a specific recipient; and the *coordinator model*, where we have a special player called the *coordinator*, and players can communicate back-and-forth with the coordinator but not directly with each other. More formally, a protocol for the coordinator model is divided into communication rounds: in each such round, the coordinator sends a message of arbitrary size to one of the players, who then responds back with a message. Eventually the coordinator outputs the answer.

The *communication complexity* of a protocol $\Pi$, denoted $CC(\Pi)$, is the maximum over inputs of the expected number of bits exchanged between the players and the coordinator in the protocol's run. For a problem $P$, we let $CC_{k,\delta}(P)$ denote the best communication complexity of any protocol that solves $P$ with worst-case error probability $\delta$ on any input.

In terms of communication complexity, the coordinator model is roughly equivalent to the message-passing model: any protocol for one model can be simulated in the other with a multiplicative overhead of $O(\log k)$ in the total communication cost.

For convenience, we assume that the players and the coordinator have access to *shared randomness* instead of private randomness; our protocols use shared randomness to simplify tasks like sampling a uniformly random vertex from the graph. For protocols that use more than one round, it is possible to get rid of this assumption and use private randomness instead, via Newman's Theorem [29], extended to multiple players. This costs at most additional $O(k \log n)$ bits.

*Simultaneous communication.* Of particular interest to us in this work are *simultaneous protocols*, which are, in a sense, the analog of oblivious property testers. This is the second primary model we investigate in addition to unrestricted communication. In a simultaneous protocol, there is only one communication round, where each player, after seeing its input, sends a *single message* to the coordinator (usually called the *referee* in this context). The coordinator then outputs the answer. Any oblivious graph property tester which uses only edge queries (which test whether a given edge is in the graph or not) can be implemented by a simultaneous protocol, but the converse is not necessarily true.

*Communication complexity of property testing in graphs.* we are given a graph $G = (V, E)$ on $n$ vertices, which is divided between the $k$ players, with each player $j$ receiving some subset $E_j \subseteq E$ of edges. More concretely, each player, $j$, receives the characteristic vector of $E_j$, where each entry corresponds to a single edge, such that if the bit is 1 then that edge exists in $E$, and if the bit is 0 it is unknown to the player whether it exists or not, as this entry might be 1 in the input of a different player. The logical OR of all inputs results in the characteristic vector of the graph edges, $E$. Note that there is no guarantee for any vertex for a single player to have all its adjacent edges in its input, as is the case in models like CONGEST. To make our results as broad as possible we follow the *general model* of property testing in graphs (see, e.g., [3]): we do not assume that the graph is regular or that there is an upper bound on the degree of individual nodes. As in [35], edges may be duplicated, that is, the sets $E_1, \dots, E_k$ are not necessarily disjoint.

The goal of a property tester for property $P$ is to distinguish the case where $G$ satisfies $P$ from the case where $G$ is $\epsilon$-far from satisfying $P$, that is, at least $\epsilon|E|$ edges would need to be added or removed from $G$ to obtain a graph satisfying $P$. An important parameter in our algorithms is the average degree, $d$, of the graph (also referred to as *density*); for our upper bounds, we do not assume that $d$ is known, but our lower bounds can assume that it is known to the protocol up to a tight multiplicative factor of $(1 \pm o(1))$. Moreover, as in [3], we focus on $d = \Omega(1)$ and $d \leq n^{1-\nu(n)}$, where $\nu(n) = o(1)$, since for graphs of average degree $d = \Theta(n)$ there is a known solution whose complexity is independent on $n$ in the property-testing query model and consequently in our model as well. The case of $d = o(1)$, although not principally different, is ignored for simplicity, as its extreme sparsity makes it of less interest than any degree which is $\Omega(1)$.

*Graph definitions and notation.* We let $\deg(v)$ denote the degree of a vertex $v$ in the input graph, and for a player $j \in [k]$, we denote by $d^j(v)$ the degree of $v$ in player $j$'s input (the subgraph $(V, E_j)$). We also let $\deg_S(v)$ denote the degree of vertex $v$ with respect to a subset $S \subseteq E$ of the graph edges.

We say that a pair of edges $\{\{u, v\}, \{v, w\}\} \subseteq E$ is a *triangle-vee* if $\{u, w\} \in E$, and in this case we call $v$ the *source* of the triangle-vee. We say that an edge $e \in E$ is a *triangle edge* if it participates in some triangle in the graph.

# 4 UPPER BOUNDS

## 4.1 Unrestricted Communication

The first protocol we present requires *interaction* between the players, and exploits the following advantage we have over the query model: suppose that the players have managed to find a set $S \subseteq E$ of edges that contains a "triangle-vee" — a pair of edges $\{u, v\}, \{v, w\} \in S$ such that $\{u, w\} \in E$ (but $\{u, w\}$ is not necessarily in $S$). Then even if $S$ is very large, the players can easily conclude that the graph contains a triangle: each player examines its own input and checks if it has an edge that closes a triangle together with some vee in $S$, and in the next round informs the other players. Thus, in our model, finding a triangle boils down to finding a triangle-vee. (In contrast, in the query model we would need to query $\{u, w\}$ for every 2-path $\{u, v\}, \{v, w\} \in S$, and this could be expensive if $S$ is large.) Notice that if $G$ is $\epsilon$-far from triangle-free, then it must contain at least $(\epsilon nd/3)$ pairwise disjoint triangles, each contributing three unique triangle-vees, hence the graph contains at least $\epsilon nd$ different triangle-vees.

Let us say that a vertex $v$ is *full* if it is the source of at least $\Omega(\epsilon \deg(v)/\log n)$ different triangle-vees. (Throughout this section, asymptotic notation is used for clarity, see full paper for concrete constants. [16]) If we can find a full vertex $v$, then we can use it to find a triangle-vee:

LEMMA 4.1. *If $v$ is a full vertex, then sampling each of its edges with probability $p_{d(v)} = \Theta(\sqrt{\log n/d(v)})$ will reveal a triangle-vee with constant probability.*

(This follows from the birthday paradox.) Note that $\deg(v)$ may be significantly higher than the average degree $d$ in the graph, so we cannot necessarily afford to sample each of $v$'s edges with probability $p_{d(v)}$; we need to find a *low-degree* vertex which is full. However, because there cannot be many nodes with "very high degree" ($\Omega(\sqrt{nd})$), this is not a major concern.

How can the players find a full vertex? A uniformly random vertex is not always likely to be full — there might be a small dense subgraph of relatively high-degree nodes which contains all the triangles. In order to target such dense subgraphs, we use *bucketing*: we partition the vertices into buckets, with each bucket $B_i$ containing the vertices with degrees in the range $[2^i, 2^{i+1})$[1]. By a pigeonhole argument, there is some bucket $B_i$ whose nodes are the sources of at least $\epsilon nd/\log n$ different triangle-vees. The size of $B_i$ cannot exceed $nd/2^i$, as each node in $B_i$ contributes at least $2^i$ edges, and the graph contains a total of $nd$ edges. Therefore, the average vertex in $B_i$ is the source of $\Omega(\epsilon 2^i/\log n)$ different triangle-vees, and since the degree in $B_i$ is bounded by $2^{i+1}$, this means the average vertex in $B_i$ is full. So if we sample a uniform vertex $v \in B_i$, and sample sufficiently many neighbors of $v$, according to Lemma 4.1 we stand a good chance of uncovering a triangle-vee, and the protocol will then identify a triangle in the next round. Of course, we cannot know in advance which bucket is full; we must try all the buckets.

It remains to describe, given $B_i$ is a full bucket, how we can sample a random vertex from it, that is, a random vertex with degree in the range $[2^i, 2^{i+1})$. We cannot do that, precisely, but we can come close. Because the edges are divided between the players, no single player initially knows the degree of any given vertex. However, by the pigeonhole principle, for each vertex $v$ there is some player that has at least $\deg(v)/k$ of $v$'s edges, and of course no player has more than $\deg(v)$ edges for $v$.

Let $\tilde{B}_i^j := \{v \in V \mid 2^i/k \le d^j(v) \le 2^{i+1}\}$ be the set of vertices that player $j$ can "reasonably suspect" belong to bucket $i$, where $d^j$ denotes the degree of vertex $v$ in the input of player $j$, and let $\tilde{B}_i := \bigcup_j \tilde{B}_j$. By the argument above, $B_i \subseteq \tilde{B}_i$. Also, $\tilde{B}_i \subseteq \bigcup_{i'=i-\log k}^{i+\log k} B_{i'}$, since the total degree of any vertex selected cannot exceed $k \cdot 2^{i+1}$ or be smaller than $2^i/k$. Therefore, sampling uniformly from $\tilde{B}_i$ is a good proxy for sampling from $B_i$, although we may also hit adjacent buckets. Nevertheless, since those adjacent buckets are roughly comparable to $B_i$ in size (up to a factor of $k$), a uniformly random sample will yield a vertex from $B_i$ with probability at least $\tilde{\Omega}(1/k)$, and $\tilde{\Theta}(k)$ samples yield a vertex from $B_i$ w.h.p.

To implement the sampling procedure we need two components: first, we need to be able to sample uniformly from $\tilde{B}_i$. The difficulty here is that each vertex $v \in \tilde{B}_i$ can be known to a different number of players — possibly only one player $j$ has $v \in \tilde{B}_i^j$, possibly all players do. If we try a naive approach, such as having each player $j$ post a random sample from $\tilde{B}_i^j$, then our sample will be biased in favor of vertices that belong to $\tilde{B}_i^j$ for many players $j$. Our solution is to impose a random order on the nodes in $\tilde{B}_i$ by publicly sampling a permutation $\pi$ on $V$ (this is done by interpreting the shared random bits as a random permutation), and we then choose the *smallest* node in $\tilde{B}_i$ with respect to $\pi$. This yields a uniformly random sample, unbiased by the number of players that know of a given node. We call this procedure TrySampleFromBucket($i$) (the code appears in full paper [16] ).

The second component verifies that a sampled node indeed belongs to $B_i$. We approximate the degree of the sampled node to within a constant, and discard vertices whose degree does not match bucket $B_i$ (we might falsely keep vertices from its two adjacent buckets, but this increases the sampled set by at most a small constant). We call this procedure ApproxDegree($v$).

The protocol for player $j$ is sketched in Algorithm 1. Here $N = \tilde{\Theta}(k)$ is the number of samples from $\tilde{B}_i$ required to produce a sample from $B_i$ with good probability. After the procedure described in Algorithm 1, the coordinator sends all the edges he received to all the players, and the players then check their own inputs for an edge that closes a triangle with some triangle-vee sent by the coordinator. With high probability, a triangle-vee *is* discovered, and the protocol ends in the next round.

**Algorithm 1** Code for player $j$

```
For each i = 0, ..., log n:
ℓ ← 0
Repeat until ℓ ≥ N:
    v ← TrySampleFromBucket(i)
    d̃(v) ← ApproxDegree(v)
    If d⁻(B_i)/√3 ≤ d̃(v) ≤ √3 d⁺(B_i):
        ℓ ← ℓ + 1
        Jointly generate a public random set S ⊆ V, where
each u ∈ S with iid probability p_d̃(v)
        Send E_j ∩ ({v} × S) to the coordinator
```

THEOREM 4.2. *The communication complexity in the model of unrestricted communication of triangle detection in graphs of average degree $d$, that are $\epsilon$-far from being triangle free, is $\tilde{O}(k \cdot \sqrt[4]{nd} + k^2)$.*

## 4.2 Simultaneous Protocols

In the simultaneous model, the players cannot interact with each other — they send only one message to the referee, and the referee then outputs the answer. This rules out our previous approach, as exposing a triangle-vee does not help us if the players cannot then check their inputs for an edge that completes the triangle. Indeed, the simultaneous model is closer to the query model in spirit. Accordingly, we will use the triangle-freeness testers of [3], but show that we can implement them more efficiently in our model. Moreover, we achieve roughly the same complexity without knowing the average degree in advance.

[1] We use in the appendix $[3^i, 3^{i+1})$ for technical reasons, although both are correct

We begin by describing how to adapt the testers of [3] to our model when the average degree is known. We then sketch the main ideas for dealing with an unknown degree; the details appear in the appendix.

*High-degree graphs.* For graphs with average degree $\Omega(\sqrt{n})$, the tester from [3] samples a uniformly random set $S \subseteq V$ of $\Theta(\sqrt[3]{n^2/d})$ vertices, queries all edges in $S^2$, and checks if the subgraph exposed contains a triangle. It is shown in [3] that if the graph is $\epsilon$-far from triangle-free, then the subgraph induced by $S$ will contain $\Theta(1)$ triangles in expectation, and the variance is small enough to ensure small error.

We can implement this tester easily, and in our model it is less expensive: instead of querying all pairs in $S^2$, the players simply send all the edges from $S^2$ in their input, paying only for edges that exist and not for edges that do not exist in the graph. The set $S$ is large enough that the number of edges in the subgraph does not deviate significantly from its expected value, $\Theta\left((nd)^{1/3}\right)$. In Section 5 we show that for average degree $\Theta(\sqrt{n})$ this is tight for 3 players.

*Low-degree graphs.* For density $d = o(\sqrt{n})$, the approach above no longer works, as the variance is too large. To illustrate this, consider a graph with $d$ vertices of degree $\Theta(n)$, which are the sources of $\Theta(nd)$ triangle-vees, and the remaining nodes are all of constant degree. If we sample vertices uniformly at random, we need to sample $\Theta(n/d)$ vertices in order to find one of the $d$ sources, hence we need at least $\Omega(n/d)$ to find a triangle. However, whereas in the query model we would need to make $\Theta(n^2/d^2)$ queries to learn the entire subgraph induced by the set we sampled, in our model we proceed as follows (using ideas from [3], which require adaptivity there, and deploying them in a different way): let $S$ be the set of $\Theta(n/d)$ uniformly-random vertices. We sample another set, $R$, of $\Theta(\sqrt{n})$ vertices, and we send all edges in $R \times (S \cup R)$. If indeed there is a small set of high-degree vertices participating in most of the triangles, then with good probability we will have one of them in $S$, and by the birthday paradox, one of its triangles will have its other two vertices in $R$. On the other hand, if the triangles are spread out "evenly", then the subgraph $R \times R$ will probably contain one. The expected size of $R \times (S \cup R)$ is $O(\sqrt{n})$, and we show that w.h.p. the total communication is $\tilde{O}(k\sqrt{n})$.

Note that both our solutions work for $d = \Theta(\sqrt{n})$, and for this density they are essentially the same: both sets, $S$ and $R$, are of size $\Theta(n/d) = \Theta(d) = \Theta\left((nd)^{1/3}\right)$, so for $d = \Theta(\sqrt{n})$ the second protocol is not very different from the first. We can also show that if edge duplication is not allowed, a factor of $k$ is saved in the communication complexity with high probability.

*A degree-oblivious protocol.*

Finally, let us give a high-level overview of how we combine the protocols above and modify them so that they can be used without advance knowledge of the degree. The challenge here is that no single player can get a good estimate of the degree from their input, and since the protocol is simultaneous, the players must decide what to do without consulting each other. The natural approach is to use $\log n$ exponentially-increasing "guesses" for the density, covering the range $[1, n]$, and try them all; however, if we do this we will incur a high cost for guesses that imply examining a larger sample than needed. We therefore take a more fine-grained approach.

Our first observation is that some players *can* make a reasonable estimate of the global density, although they do not *know* that they can. Let $\bar{d}^i$ denote the average degree in player $i$'s input $E_i$, and let us say that player $i$ is *relevant* if $\bar{d}^i \geq (\epsilon/(4k))d$. If we eliminate all the irrelevant players and their inputs, the graph still remains $(\epsilon/2)$-far from triangle-free, so we can afford to ignore the irrelevant players in our analysis — except for making sure that their messages are not too large.

Since players cannot know if they are relevant, all players assume that they are. Based on the degree $\bar{d}^i$ that player $i$ observes, it knows that *if* it is relevant, then the average degree in the graph is in the range $D_i = [\bar{d}^i, \Theta(k\bar{d}^i)]$. We fix in advance an exponential scale $\{2^j\}_{j=0}^{\log n}$ of guesses for the density, and execute in parallel $\log n$ instances of triangle-freeness protocols, one for each degree $2^j$. However, each player $i$ only participates in instances corresponding to density guesses that fall in $D_i$, and sends nothing for the other instances. For relevant players, we know that the true density falls in their range $D_i$, so they will participate in the "correct" instance. For irrelevant players, we do not care, and their message size is also not an issue: their density estimate is too low, and the communication complexity of each instance increases with the density it corresponds to.

If we are not careful, we may still incur a blow-up of $k^{1/3}$ in communication, as relevant players may use guesses lower than the true density by a factor of $k$, which increases the size of the sample beyond what is necessary. However, by carefully assigning each player $i$ a communication budget depending on $\bar{d}^i$, we can eliminate the blow-up, and match the degree-aware protocol up to polylogarithmic factors.

Theorem 4.3. *The simultaneous communication complexity of testing triangle-freeness in graphs of average degree $d$ is $\tilde{O}(k \max\left\{\sqrt{n}, (nd)^{1/3)}\right\})$, even if $d$ is not known to the players.*

# 5 LOWER BOUNDS

## 5.1 Testing Triangle-Freeness with $d = \Theta(1)$

For graphs of average degree $\Theta(1)$, we show that for a sufficiently small constant $\epsilon$, *one-sided* two-player protocols require $\Omega(\sqrt{n})$ communication to distinguish triangle-free graphs from graphs that are $\epsilon$-far from triangle-free. We use the same reduction used in [25] to show the hardness of approximating the number of triangles in the streaming model, but we reduce from a different variant of the Boolean Hypermatching problem [26, 33]. Using symmetrization, we then lift the bound to a lower bound of $\Omega(k\sqrt{n})$ for $k$-player simultaneous protocols. The details appear in the full version of the paper [16].

## 5.2 Finding a Triangle Edge in $\epsilon$-far from Triangle-Free Graphs

Our main result in this section is the following:

Theorem 5.1. *For any $d = O(\sqrt{n})$, let $T_{n,d}^{\epsilon}$ be the task of finding a triangle edge in graphs of size $n$ and average degree $d$ which are*

*$\epsilon$-far from triangle-free. Then for sufficiently small constant error probability $\delta$ we have:*

(1) *For $k > 3$ players:* $\mathrm{CC}^{sim}_{k,\delta}(T^{\epsilon}_{n,d}) = \Omega\left(k(nd)^{1/6}\right)$.

(2) *For 3 players:* $\mathrm{CC}^{sim}_{3,\delta}(T^{\epsilon}_{n,d}) = \Omega\left((nd)^{1/3}\right)$.

To show both results, we first prove them for average degree $d = \Theta(\sqrt{n})$, and then easily obtain the result for lower degrees by embedding a dense subgraph of degree $\Theta(\sqrt{n})$ in a larger graph with lower overall average degree and many isolated nodes. For lack of space, we describe here the lower bounds for graphs of average degree $\Theta(\sqrt{n})$, and defer the embedding into lower degree graphs to the full version of the paper.

To prove (1), we begin by proving that for graphs of average degree $\Theta(\sqrt{n})$, *three* players require $\Omega(n^{1/4})$ bits of communication to solve $T^{\epsilon}_{n,\sqrt{n}}$ in the *one-way* communication model, where Alice and Bob send messages to Charlie, and then Charlie outputs the answer. In fact, our lower bound is more general, and allows Alice and Bob to communicate back-and-forth for as many rounds as they like, with Charlie observing the transcript. We then "lift" the result to $k > 3$ players communicating simultaneously, using symmetrization [30].

To prove (2), we show directly that in the simultaneous communication model, three players require $\Omega(\sqrt{n})$ bits to solve $T^{\epsilon}_{n,d}$ in graphs of average degree $\Theta(\sqrt{n})$.

Our lower bounds actually bound the *distributional* hardness of the problems: we show an input distribution $\mu$ on which any protocol that has a small probability of error *on inputs drawn from* $\mu$ requires high communication. This is stronger than worst-case hardness, which would only assert that any protocol that has small error probability *on all inputs* requires high communication.

*The hard distribution.* We use a simple distribution $\mu$ to generate graphs that with high probability have average degree $\Theta(\sqrt{n})$ and are $\epsilon$-far from triangle-free: we let $G = (U \cup V_1 \cup V_2, \mathrm{E})$ be a tripartite graph, where $|U| = |V_1| = |V_2| = n$, and each edge of the tripartite graph is included in the edge set E iid with probability $\gamma/\sqrt{n}$, for a small constant $\gamma \in (0, 1)$. We give each player the edges on one side of the graph: Alice receives $\mathrm{E}_1 = \mathrm{E} \cap (U \times V_1)$, Bob receives $\mathrm{E}_2 = \mathrm{E} \cap (U \times V_2)$, and Charlie receives $\mathrm{E}_3 = \mathrm{E} \cap (V_1 \times V_2)$.

Clearly the distribution $\mu$ is not *guaranteed* to produce graphs with average degree $\Theta(\sqrt{n})$, or graphs that are $\epsilon$-far from triangle-free, but we show that it does so with constant probability:

LEMMA 5.2. *When $\gamma$ is sufficiently small, a graph sampled from $\mu$ is $O(1)$-far from triangle-free with probability at least $1/2$.*

Therefore, any protocol that succeeds with constant probability on graphs that have average degree $\Theta(\sqrt{n})$ and are $\epsilon$-far from triangle-free, must also succeed with (smaller) constant probability on $\mu$.

## 5.3 Information theory

Our lower bounds use information theory to argue that using a small number of communication bits, the players cannot convey much information about their inputs. For lack of space, we give here only the essential definitions and properties we need.

Let $(\mathbf{X}, \mathbf{Y}) \sim \mu$ be random variables. (For clarity, from now on we denote random variables with bold-face letters.) To measure the information we learned about $\mathbf{X}$ after observing $\mathbf{Y}$, we examine the difference between the *prior* distribution of $\mathbf{X}$, denoted $\mu(\mathbf{X})$, and the *posterior* distribution of $\mathbf{X}$ after seeing $\mathbf{Y} = y$, which we denote $\mu(\mathbf{X}|\mathbf{Y} = y)$. We use KL divergence to quantify this difference:

*Definition 5.3 (KL Divergence).* For distributions $\mu, \eta : \mathcal{X} \to [0, 1]$, the *KL divergence* between $\mu$ and $\eta$ is

$$\mathrm{D}(\mu \parallel \eta) := \sum_{x \in \mathcal{X}} \mu(x) \log(\mu(x)/\eta(x)).$$

We require the following property, which follows from the superadditivity of information [11]: if $(\mathbf{X}_1, \ldots, \mathbf{X}_n, \mathbf{Y}) \sim \mu$ are such that $\mathbf{X}_1, \ldots, \mathbf{X}_n$ are independent, and $\mathbf{Y}$ can be represented using $m$ bits (that is, its *entropy* is at most $m$), then

$$\mathop{\mathrm{E}}_{y \sim \mu(\mathbf{Y})}\left[\sum_{i=1}^{n} \mathrm{D}(\mu(\mathbf{X}_i|\mathbf{Y} = y) \parallel \mu(\mathbf{X}_i))\right] \le m.$$

We use superadditivity as follows: let $\{\mathbf{X}_e\}$ be a collection of indicators for the presence of edge $e$ in the input. In the input distribution $\mu$ defined above, the edges appear independently, so we can use superadditivity to argue that after observing the transcript $\Pi$ of the protocol, the *sum* of what we learn about each edge is at most $\mathrm{CC}(\Pi)$, the communication complexity of the protocol. In particular, if $\mathrm{CC}(\Pi)$ is small, then the average edge in the input has a *posterior probability* given the transcript that is close to its *prior probability* of appearing, $\gamma/\sqrt{n}$.

## 5.4 "Extended One-Way" 3-Player Protocols

Suppose we have a protocl $\Pi$ for three players, where Alice and Bob communicate back-and-forth for some number of rounds, and eventually Charlie, having observed the conversation between Alice and Bob, outputs an edge. If Charlie outputs an edge that is not in $\mathrm{E}_3$, this is an error, so let us assume for simplicity that he never does this (the full proof does not make this assumption).

Let $\pi$ be the distribution of $\Pi$'s transcripts on inputs drawn from $\mu$, and let $\mathbf{\Pi} \sim \pi$ be a random variable for $\Pi$'s transcript. Given a transcript $t$, let $\mu|t$ denote the conditional distribution of the input given $\mathbf{\Pi} = t$.

*Outline of the lower bound.* Intuitively, when Charlie outputs an edge $e = \{v_1, v_2\} \in \mathrm{E}_3$, he should *believe* that $e$ is part of a triangle, that is, he should "think" that there is a node $u \in U$ such that $\{u, v_1\} \in \mathrm{E}_1$ and $\{u, v_2\} \in \mathrm{E}_2$. We say that such an edge $e \in V_1 \times V_2$ is *covered*. Since Charlie cannot see $\mathrm{E}_1$ or $\mathrm{E}_2$, the set of covered edges is a function of the messages sent by Alice and Bob; we let $\mathrm{C}(t) \subseteq V_1 \times V_2$ denote the set of covered edges when $t$ is the transcript of Alice and Bob's communication. The edge output by Charlie should be an edge in $\mathrm{C}(t) \cap \mathrm{E}_3$, that is, an edge in Charlie's input that he believes is part of a triangle. The crux of our lower bound consists of showing that if Alice and Bob use only $O(n^{1/4})$ bits of communication, then typically we have $|\mathrm{C}(t)| = O(\sqrt{n})$; and since each edge in $\mathrm{C}(t)$ appears in $\mathrm{E}_3$ independently with probability $\gamma/\sqrt{n}$, the probability that $\mathrm{C}(t) \cap \mathrm{E}_3 \neq \emptyset$ is too small, leaving Charlie with no good edge to output.

*Covered edges.* We begin by formalizing what it means for Charlie to "believe" that edge $\{v_1, v_2\}$ is part of a triangle.

For $v_1 \in V_1, v_2 \in V_2$, let $\text{Vee}(\{v_1, v_2\})$ denote the event that there is a node $u \in U$ such that $\{u, v_1\} \in E_1$ and $\{u, v_2\} \in E_2$. We call $\{u, v_1\}, \{u, v_2\}$ a *vee supported on* $\{v_1, v_2\}$. Also, let $\text{Tri}(e)$ be the event that $e$ participates in a triangle; then $\text{Tri}(e) = (e \in E_3) \wedge \text{Vee}(e)$, that is, $e$ is in a triangle whenever it is in Charlie's input and there is a vee supported on it.

We formally capture Charlie's "belief" using the *posterior probability* that a vee exists, given the transcript that Charlie observed.

*Definition 5.4 (Covered edges).* We say that $e \in V_1 \times V_2$ is *covered* by transcript $t$ if $\Pr_{E\sim\mu|t}[\text{Vee}(e)] \geq 1/10$, and let $C(t)$ be the set of edges covered by $t$.

(The constant $1/10$ should, in general, depend on the error probability $\delta$ of the protocol, but here we use a specific value for clarity and assume that $\gamma$ and $\delta$ are small enough.)

Now let us show that with good probability Alice and Bob provide Charlie with $\Omega(\sqrt{n})$ covered edges: we show that whenever $|C(t)| < \alpha\sqrt{n}$ for an appropriately chosen constant $\alpha$, the protocol incurs a large probability of error.

Recall that that the inputs $E_1, E_2$ and $E_3$ to the three players are independent a-priori; by the properties of a communication protocol, they remain independent conditioned on the transcript, $\Pi = t$. Thus, each edge in $C(t)$ appears in $E_3$ iid with probability $\gamma/\sqrt{n}$. By Markov, whenever $|C(t)| < \alpha\sqrt{n}$, we have

$$\Pr_{E\sim\mu|t}[C(t) \cap E_3 \neq \emptyset] \leq (\gamma/\sqrt{n}) \cdot (\alpha\sqrt{n}) = \alpha\gamma.$$

This implies that

$$\Pr_{E\sim\mu}\left[C(t) \cap E_3 = \emptyset \,\middle|\, (|C(t)| < \alpha\sqrt{n})\right] \geq 1 - \alpha\gamma.$$

Since we assumed that Charlie always outputs an edge from his input, whenever $C(t) \cap E_3 = \emptyset$, Charlie outputs an edge that is not covered, $e \notin C(t)$. By definition, if $e \notin C(t)$,

$$\Pr_{E\sim\mu|t}[\text{Tri}(e)] \leq \Pr_{E\sim\mu|t}[\text{Vee}(e)] < 9/10,$$

and therefore,

$$\begin{aligned}
\delta &\geq \Pr_{\pi}[\Pi \text{ errs}] \\
&\geq \Pr_{t\sim\pi}[\Pi \text{ errs} \mid C(t) \cap E_3 = \emptyset] \cdot \Pr_{t\sim\pi}[C(t) \cap E_3 = \emptyset] \\
&\geq (1/10) \cdot \Pr_{t\sim\pi}[C(t) \cap E_3 = \emptyset] \\
&\geq (1/10) \Pr\left[C(t) \cap E_3 = \emptyset \,\middle|\, |C(t)| < \alpha\sqrt{n}\right] \cdot \Pr\left[|C(t)| < \alpha\sqrt{n}\right] \\
&\geq ((1 - \alpha\gamma)/10) \Pr\left[|C(t)| < \alpha\sqrt{n}\right].
\end{aligned}$$

Assuming that $1 - \alpha\gamma \geq 1/2$, we see that with probability at least $1 - 20\delta$ we have $|C(t)| \geq \alpha\sqrt{n}$. Next we show that this requires $\Omega(n^{1/4})$ bits of communication from Alice and Bob.

*The cost of covering $\Omega(\sqrt{n})$ edges.* Let us say that transcript $t$ is *good* if $|C(t)| \geq \alpha\sqrt{n}$. For simplicity, we assume that no transcript covers *more* than $\lceil\alpha\sqrt{n}\rceil$ edges (if it does, we remove some covered edges from $C(t)$ arbitrarily; this does not affect the math above).

What do Alice and Bob need to do to raise the posterior probability of $\text{Vee}(e)$? Since $\Pi$ is a communication protocol, and $E_1, E_2$ are independent a-priori, they remain independent given the transcript, that is, given $\Pi = t$ for any $t$. Therefore,

$$\begin{aligned}
\Pr_{E\sim\mu|t}[\text{Vee}(\{v_1, v_2\})] &\leq \sum_{u\in U} \Pr_{E\sim\mu|t}[\{u, v_1\} \in E_1 \wedge \{u, v_2\} \in E_2] \\
&\leq \sum_{u\in U} \left( \Pr_{E\sim\mu|t}[\{u, v_1\} \in E] \Pr_{E\sim\mu|t}[\{u, v_2\} \in E] \right). \qquad (1)
\end{aligned}$$

Now, let

$$\Delta_t(\{w_1, w_2\}) := \Pr_{E\sim\mu|t}[\{w_1, w_2\} \in E] - 2\gamma/\sqrt{n}$$

denote the *increase* from *twice* the prior probability that $\{w_1, w_2\} \in E$, which is $\gamma/\sqrt{n}$, to the posterior probability that $\{w_1, w_2\} \in E$ given $\Pi = 1$. (The reason we need to take twice the prior probability will be revealed shortly.) We can re-write (1) as

$$\begin{aligned}
&\Pr_{E\sim\mu|t}[\text{Vee}(\{v_1, v_2\})] \leq \\
&\leq \sum_{u\in U} \left[ (\Delta_t(\{u, v_1\}) + 2\gamma/\sqrt{n}) \cdot (\Delta_t(\{u, v_2\}) + 2\gamma/\sqrt{n}) \right].
\end{aligned}$$

Recall that if $t$ is good, then $\alpha\sqrt{n} \leq |C(t)| \leq \lceil\alpha\sqrt{n}\rceil$, and each edge $e \in C(t)$ has posterior probability of $\text{Vee}(e)$ at least $1/10$. Thus, for a good transcript $t$, summing over the edges in $C(t)$ and using Cauchy-Schwarz yields

$$\begin{aligned}
\left(1/10 - \gamma^2\right)\alpha\sqrt{n} &\leq \left( \sum_{e\in U\times(V_1\cup V_2)} \Delta_t(e) \right)^2 \\
&\quad + (2\gamma/\sqrt{n}) \cdot \lceil\alpha\sqrt{n}\rceil \left( \sum_{e\in U\times(V_1\cup V_2)} \Delta_t(e) \right) \\
&\leq 2\left( \sum_{e\in U\times(V_1\cup V_2)} \Delta_t(e) \right)^2.
\end{aligned}$$

(On the right-hand side we simplified the expression and added some edges that are not necessarily in $C(t)$.)

We see that if $t$ is a good transcript, then we must have

$$\sum_{e\in U\times(V_1\cup V_2)} \Delta_t(e) \geq \Omega(n^{1/4}). \qquad (2)$$

Using information theory, we can show that $\Omega(n^{1/4})$ bits of communication are required to achieve this with constant probability.

Let $X_e$ be an indicator for the event that edge $e$ is in the input, $e \in E$. Because the edges appear independently of each other, we can use the superadditivity of information to get:

$$CC(\Pi) \geq \sum_{e} \mathop{E}_{t\sim\pi}[D(\mu|t(X_e) \parallel \mu(X_e)]. \qquad (3)$$

In order to relate the KL divergence to $\Delta_t$, we prove the following lemma:

Lemma 5.5. *Let $p, q \in (0, 1)$, and let $D(p \parallel q)$ denote the KL divergence between* Bernoulli($p$) *and* Bernoulli($q$). *Then for any $q < 1/2$ we have $D(p \parallel q) \geq p - 2q$.*

(This relationship is, in general, *quadratic*: Pinsker's inequality asserts that $D(p \parallel q) \geq |p - q|$, and this is known to be tight in some cases. However, quadratic behavior occurs only when the prior $p$ is close to $1/2$; our lemma shows that for small priors the relationship is roughly linear.)

Plugging Lemma 5.5 into (3) yields $\mathrm{CC}(\Pi) \geq \sum_e \mathrm{E}_t [\Delta_t(e)]$. Together with (2) and the fact that the transcript must be good with probability at least $1 - 20\delta$, we see that $\Omega(n^{1/4})$ bits of communication are required.

For this particular input distribution, the lower bound is tight: suppose Alice and Bob choose in advance some vertex $u \in U$, and each of them sends Charlie $O(n^{1/4})$ nodes adjacent to $u$ in their input (with high probability, the degree of $u$ is $\Theta(\sqrt{n})$, so they have enough edges to send). This has the effect of covering $\Theta(\sqrt{n})$ edges in $V_1 \times V_2$ – for every combination $v_1, v_2$ of nodes sent by Alice and Bob respectively, the edge $\{v_1, v_2\}$ is covered. With good probability Charlie will find one of the covered edges in his input and he can then output it (and also the triangle containing it).

## 5.5 Simultaneous 3-Player Lower Bound

We now turn our attention to *simultaneous* protocols, where we have a referee who does not see any of the input; Alice, Bob and Charlie send messages to the referee, and the referee then outputs the answer. We assume for simplicity that the edge output is always from Charlie's side of the graph (this is not essential).

In our one-way lower bound we argued that Alice and Bob must provide Charlie with $\Omega(\sqrt{n})$ edges that "look like" there is a vee supported on them, so that w.h.p. Charlie will find one of those edges in his input. For simultaneous protocols, this is not enough: the referee does not see Charlie's input, and cannot know if a given edge is in $\mathbf{E}_3$ or not unless Charlie "tells him". Accordingly, we define the set $\mathrm{Rep}(t)$ of edges "reported by Charlie" to be the set of edges in $V_1 \times V_2$ with good posterior probability of being in $\mathbf{E}_3$ given $\Pi = t$. Moreover, because there is no interaction, the referee cannot look at the set of covered edges and *ask* Charlie which of them is in $\mathbf{E}_3$; Alice, Bob and Charlie need to provide the referee with sets $\mathrm{C}(t)$ and $\mathrm{Rep}(t)$ such that with high probability $\mathrm{C}(t) \cap \mathrm{Rep}(t) \neq \emptyset$, and the referee can then output an edge that has good probability of being in a triangle.

More formally, let $t = (m_1, m_2, m_3)$ be the transcript, where $m_1, m_2$ and $m_3$ are the messages of Alice, Bob and Charlie, respectively. We define

$$\mathrm{Rep}(t) = \left\{ e \in V_1 \times V_2 \mid \Pr_{\mathbf{E} \sim \mu | t} [\mathbf{X}_e = 1] \geq 1/10 \right\}.$$

In a simultaneous protocol, the messages sent by the players are independent of each other given the input. In our case, because the inputs are *also* independent of each other, the messages are independent even without conditioning on a particular input. We therefore abuse notation slightly by omitting parts of the transcript that are not relevant to the event at hand; we write $\mathrm{Rep}(m_1)$ for $\mathrm{Rep}(t)$ and $\mathrm{C}(m_1, m_2)$ for $\mathrm{C}(()\, t)$.

As we showed in the one-way case, whenever the edge output is not in $\mathrm{C}(m_1, m_2)$ we incur a large contribution to the error of the protocol. We can now show a similar claim for $\mathrm{Rep}(m_3)$ as well: if the referee outputs an edge with low posterior probability of being in the input, then the error probability is high. Combining, we get:

Lemma 5.6. *The probability that there exists an edge that is both reported by Charlie and covered by Alice and Bob is at least* $1 - 100\delta$.

*That is,*

$$\Pr_{(\mathbf{m}_1, \mathbf{m}_2, \mathbf{m}_3) \sim \pi} [\mathrm{Rep}(\mathbf{m}_3) \cap \mathrm{C}(\mathbf{m}_1, \mathbf{m}_2) \neq \emptyset] \geq 1 - 100\delta.$$

Because the inputs and messages are independent, for a fixed message $m_3$ of Bob, we get by union bound that

$$\Pr_{\mathbf{m}_1, \mathbf{m}_2 \sim \pi} [\mathrm{Rep}(m_3) \cap \mathrm{C}(\mathbf{m}_1, \mathbf{m}_2) \neq \emptyset] \leq \sum_{e \in \mathrm{Rep}(m_3)} \Pr_{\mathbf{m}_1, \mathbf{m}_2 \sim \pi} [e \in \mathrm{C}(\mathbf{m}_1, \mathbf{m}_2)]. \quad (4)$$

Let us define

$$\mathrm{Cov}(e) = \Pr_{\mathbf{m}_1, \mathbf{m}_2 \sim \pi} [e \in \mathrm{C}(\mathbf{m}_1, \mathbf{m}_2)].$$

Using this notation, the combination of Lemma 5.6 and (4) gives:

Corollary 5.7. $\mathrm{E}_{\mathbf{m}_3 \sim \pi} \left[ \sum_{e \in \mathrm{Rep}(\mathbf{m}_3)} \mathrm{Cov}(e) \right] \geq 1 - 100\delta.$

We show that if $\mathrm{CC}(\Pi) \leq \alpha\sqrt{n}$ where $\alpha$ is a sufficiently small constant, then this cannot be achieved, that is, the protocol cannot focus enough "cover probability" on the edges reported by Bob.

*Bob's "best strategy".* By definition, $\mathrm{Cov}(e)$ is a score measuring how likely Alice and Bob are to cover edge $e$. It depends on the protocol, but not on the specific input to Alice, Bob or Charlie. When Bob examines his input, he *knows* the score $\mathrm{Cov}(e)$ for each edge $e \in \mathbf{E}_3$. He cannot afford to report all the edges in $\mathbf{E}_3$, as this would require too much communication, so he must choose some subset to report. Intuitively, Bob's "best strategy" is to report those edges in $\mathbf{E}_3$ that have the highest $\mathrm{Cov}(e)$, as this maximizes the sum in Corollary 5.7 (i.e., it increases the probability that $\mathrm{C}(t) \cap \mathrm{Rep}(t) \neq \emptyset$, giving the referee a good edge to output).

Let us make this intuition a little more formal. Let $T \subseteq V_1 \times V_2$ be the set of $|T| = \Theta(n)$ edges with the highest $\mathrm{Cov}(e)$ scores in $V_1 \times V_2$. Bob can typically afford to report only $O(\sqrt{n})$ edges; this follows from the superadditivity of information and Lemma 5.5. In addition, each edge in $T$ only appears in Bob's input with probability $\gamma/\sqrt{n}$. Thus, if Bob reports all the edges in $T$ that appear in his input (the set $T \cap \mathbf{E}_3$), this consumes his entire communication budget. If Bob follows this strategy then each edge in $T$ is reported with probability nearly $\gamma/\sqrt{n}$: if it appears in Bob's input, it is reported – unless $T \cap \mathbf{E}_3$ is very large and Bob cannot afford to report all the edges in it, but this happens with very small probability. In the full version, we show that indeed reporting the edges in $T \cap \mathbf{E}_3$ is Bob's "best strategy", in the sense that

$$\mathrm{E}\left[ \sum_{e \in \mathrm{Rep}(\mathbf{E}_3)} \mathrm{Cov}(e) \right] \leq \Theta(1/\sqrt{n}) \cdot \sum_{e \in T} \mathrm{Cov}(e). \quad (5)$$

Therefore, it suffices to show that the protocol *for Alice and Bob* can achieve $\sum_{e \in T} \mathrm{Cov}(e) = \Omega(\sqrt{n})$ for a fixed set $T \subseteq V_1 \times V_2$ of $\Theta(n)$. If we can show this, then Corollary 5.7 does not hold, which is a contradiction.

*Bounding the cover scores.* Our goal now is to show that for any set $T$ of $\Theta(n)$ edges from $V_1 \times V_2$, we have $\sum_{e \in T} \mathrm{Cov}(e) = O(\sqrt{n})$.

Fix a set $T \subseteq V_1 \times V_2$ of $|T| = \xi n$ edges, where $\xi$ is constant. We first partition $T$ into subsets $T_1, T_2$, where, for some constant $\xi \in (0, 1)$, the set $T_1$ contains only edges $(u, v)$ such that $\deg_{T_1}(u) \leq$

$\xi\sqrt{n}$ and $T_2$ contains only edges $(u, v)$ such that $\deg_{T_2}(v) \leq \xi\sqrt{n}$. (Recall that $\deg_S(w)$ denotes the number of edges adjacent to $w$ in edge set $S$.)

To do this, we partition the nodes of $V_1, V_2$ into "low degree nodes", with degree at most $\sqrt{n}$ in $T$, and "high degree nodes", with degree more than $\sqrt{n}$ in $T$. All edges of $T$ that are adjacent to "low degree nodes" from $V_1$ go into $T_1$, and any remaining edges that are adjacent to "low degree nodes" from $V_2$ go into $V_2$. This leaves us with edges where both endpoints have high degree in $T$, more than $\sqrt{n}$. But since $|T| = O(n)$, there can be only $O(\sqrt{n})$ nodes with such high degree, so any such edge can go into either $T_1$ or $T_2$ arbitrarily.

We separately bound $\sum_{e\in T_1} \mathrm{Cov}(e)$ and $\sum_{e\in T_2} \mathrm{Cov}(e)$, and show that neither exceeds $O(\sqrt{n})$. This implies $\sum_{e\in T} \mathrm{Cov}(e) = O(\sqrt{n})$ as well. The proof is symmetric for the two sets, so we show here ony the lower bound for $T_1$.

To show that $\sum_{e\in T_1} \mathrm{Cov}(e) = O(\sqrt{n})$ we need to rule out the "quadratic effect" that we saw in the one-way protocol, where Alice and Bob each tell us about some number $t$ of edges in their input, and yet the sum of the cover probabilities reaches $t^2$. This would be catastrophic for us, because now Alice and Bob can afford to tell us about $\tilde{\Theta}(\sqrt{n})$ edges each, so if we use a naive analysis we might conclude that the sum of the cover probabilities can go as high as $O(n)$; to bound the sum at $O(\sqrt{n})$ we need to show that this cannot happen, and the key lies in the fact that we consider nodes with degree at most $\sqrt{n}$ in $T_1$. (The difference from the one-way case is that there we did not have a *fixed* set $T$ of $O(n)$ edges over which Alice and Bob tried to maximize the sum of the cover probabilities; and indeed, the optimal strategy for the one-way case produces a uniformly random set of edges with high cover probabilities, not a fixed set.)

Intuitively, suppose that $v_1 \in V_1$ has degree $O(\sqrt{n})$ in $T_1$, and let $S \in V_2$ be the neighbors of $v_1$ with respect to the edges in $T_1$. Because $|S| = \deg_{T_1}(v_1) = O(\sqrt{n})$, in expectation only $(\gamma/\sqrt{n}) \cdot O(\sqrt{n}) = O(1)$ edges connect $U$ and $S$. Thus, whatever effort Alice spends to tell the referree about edges in $U \times \{v_1\}$ is "multiplied" only by $O(1)$, even if Bob was able to tell us about *all* the edges in $U \times S$. We get that the sum of the cover probabilities is *linear* in Alice's communication budget, not quadratic.

We now make this intuition formal. Let $\mathrm{C}_e$ be an indicator for the event that $e \in \mathrm{C}(\mathbf{m}_1, \mathbf{m}_2)$. Then $\mathrm{Cov}(e) = \Pr_\mu[\mathrm{C}_e]$.

For fixed messages $m_1, m_2$ of Alice and Bob, if $e = (v_1, v_2) \in \mathrm{C}(m_1, m_2)$, then by definition of $\mathrm{C}(m_1, m_2)$ and by union bound,

$$\begin{aligned} 1/10 &\leq \Pr_{\mathrm{E}\sim\mu|m_1,m_2}[\exists u : (u, v_1) \in \mathrm{E}_1 \wedge (u, v_2) \in \mathrm{E}_2] \\ &\leq \sum_{u\in U} \Pr_{\mathrm{E}\sim\mu|m_1,m_2}[(u, v_1) \in \mathrm{E}_1 \wedge (u, v_2) \in \mathrm{E}_2]. \end{aligned}$$

Because $\mathrm{E}_1$ and $\mathrm{E}_2$ remain independent given $\mathbf{m}_1 = m_1, \mathbf{m}_2 = m_2$, we can re-write this as

$$\begin{aligned} 1/10 &\leq \sum_{u\in U}\left(\Pr_{\mathrm{E}\sim\mu|m_1}[(u, v_1) \in \mathrm{E}_1] \cdot \Pr_{\mathrm{E}\sim\mu|m_2}[(u, v_2) \in \mathrm{E}_2]\right) \\ &\leq \sum_{u\in U}\left((\Delta_{m_1}(u, v_1) + 2\gamma/\sqrt{n}) \Pr_{\mathrm{E}\sim\mu|m_2}[(u, v_2) \in \mathrm{E}_2]\right), \end{aligned}$$

where here, as in the previous section, we let

$$\Delta_{m_1}(u, v_1) = \Pr_{\mathrm{E}\sim\mu|m_1}[(u, v_1) \in \mathrm{E}_1] - 2\gamma/\sqrt{n}.$$

Consider first the edges in $T_1$. Let $M_2$ be the set of Bob's messages $m_2$ such that $(v_1, v_2) \in \mathrm{C}(m_1, m_2)$ (keeping $m_1$ fixed), and let $\pi_2(m_2)$ be the probability that Bob sends a specific message $m_2$. Multiplying both sides by $\pi_2(m_2)$ and summing over all $m_2 \in M_2$, we get

$$\begin{aligned} &\sum_{m_2\in M_2}\sum_{u\in U}\left(\pi_2(m_2) \Pr_{\mathrm{E}\sim\mu|m_2}[(u, v_2) \in \mathrm{E}_2] (\Delta_{m_1}(u, v_1) + 2\gamma/\sqrt{n})\right) \\ &\geq (1/10) \sum_{m_2\in M_2} \pi_2(m_2) = (1/10) \Pr_{\mu|m_1}\left[\mathrm{C}_{(v_1,v_2)}\right]. \end{aligned} \quad (6)$$

Notice that for any $u \in U$ and $m_1$,

$$\begin{aligned} &\sum_{m_2\in M_2}\left(\pi_2(m_2) \Pr_{\mathrm{E}\sim\mu|m_2}[(u, v_2) \in \mathrm{E}_2]\right) \\ &= \Pr_{\mathrm{E}\sim\mu|m_1}\left[(u, v_2) \in \mathrm{E}_2 \wedge \mathrm{C}_{(u,v_2)}\right] \\ &\leq \Pr_{\mathrm{E}\sim\mu}[(u, v_2) \in \mathrm{E}_2] = \gamma/\sqrt{n}. \end{aligned}$$

Plugging this into (6) yields

$$(\gamma/\sqrt{n}) \sum_{u\in U} (\Delta_{m_1}(u, v_1) + 2\gamma/\sqrt{n}) \geq (1/10) \Pr_{\mu|m_1}\left[\mathrm{C}_{(v_1,v_2)}\right].$$

Now, taking the expectation over all $m_1$, and summing across all $v_2$ such that $(v_1, v_2) \in T_1$ (while keeping $v_1$ fixed),

$$\begin{aligned} &\deg_{T_1}(v_1)(\gamma/\sqrt{n}) \mathop{\mathrm{E}}_{\mathbf{m}_1}\left[\sum_{u\in U}(\Delta_{\mathbf{m}_1}(u, v_1) + 2\gamma/\sqrt{n})\right] \\ &\geq (1/10) \sum_{v_2:(v_1,v_2)\in T_1} \mathop{\mathrm{E}}_{\mathbf{m}_1}\left[\Pr_{\mu|\mathbf{m}_1}\left[\mathrm{C}_{(v_1,v_2)}\right]\right] \\ &\geq (1/10) \sum_{v_2:(v_1,v_2)\in T_1} \mathrm{Cov}(v_1, v_2). \end{aligned}$$

Finally, summing over all $v_1 \in V_1$, and plugging in $\deg_{T_1}(v_1) \leq \xi\sqrt{n}$, we get

$$\begin{aligned} &\xi\gamma \sum_{v_1\in V_1} \mathop{\mathrm{E}}_{\mathbf{m}_1}\left[\sum_{v_1\in V_1}\sum_{u\in U} \Delta_{\mathbf{m}_1}(u, v_1) + 2\gamma/\sqrt{n}\right] \\ &= \xi\gamma\left(\mathop{\mathrm{E}}_{\mathbf{m}_1}\left[\sum_{v_1\in V_1}\sum_{u\in U} \Delta_{\mathbf{m}_1}(u, v_1)\right] + 2\gamma\sqrt{n}\right) \\ &\geq (1/10) \sum_{(v_1,v_2)\in T_1)} \mathrm{Cov}(v_1, v_2). \end{aligned}$$

As we saw previously, using Lemma 5.5 and the subadditivity of information we get that $\mathrm{E}_{\mathbf{m}_1}\left[\sum_{v_1\in V_1}\sum_{u\in U} \Delta_{\mathbf{m}_1}(u, v_1)\right] \leq \mathrm{CC}(\Pi) = O(\sqrt{n})$, so the left-hand side is bounded by $O(\sqrt{n})$, as desired: the sum of the cover scores of edges in $T_1$ cannot exceed $O(\sqrt{n})$.

## 5.6 Lifting 3-Player Lower Bounds to $k$ Players

To lift our lower bounds to $k > 3$ players we use *symmetrization*, a technique developed in [30] for embedding hard two-player problems in a multi player model. Here, we have a hard *3-player* problem, and we also work with a restricted communication pattern, either simultaneous or one-way; we adapt the technique from [30] to these changes, obtaining the following:

Theorem 5.8 (Informal). *Let $\mu$ be a 3-player input distribution, where each of the three players has the same marginal input distribution. Let $C$ be the one-way, $\delta$-error communication complexity of problem $P$ under $\mu$. Then there is a $k$-player input distribution $\eta$ such that the simultaneous $\delta$-error communication complexity of $P$ under $\eta$ is $\Omega(k \cdot C)$.*

Notice that we assumed that the problem was hard for 3-player *one-way* protocols, but the $k$-player lower bound we obtained was for *simultaneous* protocols. This behavior is inherent for a large number of players, $k = \Omega(n)$: a simultaneous $k$-player protocol can emulate a one-way protocol by having each of the $k$ players send their entire input to the referee with probability $\Theta(1/k)$, and otherwise send the message it would send under the one-way protocol. With good probability, the referee receives the input of at least one player, and it can then compute the output of the one-way protocol. When $k = \Omega(n)$, the overall cost of simulating a one-way protocol with communication cost $C$ is $O(n^2/k + k \cdot C) = O(k \cdot C)$, so Theorem 5.8 is tight in this sense. (For smaller $k$, it is possible that the result can be tightened.)

For *deterministic* and *symmetric* protocols we can do a little better: we show that if $P$ is hard for deterministic 3-player simultaneous protocols, then it is $k$ times harder for deterministic $k$-player simultaneous protocols.

# 6 CONCLUSIONS

We showed that in the setting of communication complexity, property testing can be significantly easier than exactly testing if the input satisfies the property: exactly determining if the input graph is triangle-free requires $\Omega(knd)$ bits in [35], but we showed that weakening the requirement to property-testing improves the complexity, and in fact even simultaneous communication protocols can do better than the best exact algorithm with unrestricted communication. Nevertheless, the problem does not appear to become completely trivial, as shown by our lower bounds for simultaneous and restricted one-way protocols.

*Acknowledgements.* We thank Noga Alon, Eldar Fischer and Dana Ron for fruitful discussions.

# REFERENCES


[1] Noga Alon. 2002. Testing Subgraphs in Large Graphs. *Random Struct. Algorithms* 21, 3-4 (Oct. 2002), 359–370.

[2] Noga Alon, Eldar Fischer, Michael Krivelevich, and Mario Szegedy. 2000. Efficient Testing of Large Graphs. *Combinatorica* 20, 4 (2000), 451–476.

[3] Noga Alon, Tali Kaufman, Michael Krivelevich, and Dana Ron. 2006. Testing Triangle-freeness in General Graphs. In *Proceedings of the Seventeenth Annual ACM-SIAM Symposium on Discrete Algorithms (SODA)*. 279–288.

[4] Noga Alon and Asaf Shapira. 2003. Testing Subgraphs in Directed Graphs. In *Proceedings of the Thirty-fifth Annual ACM Symposium on Theory of Computing (STOC '03)*. 700–709.

[5] Christos Boutsidis, David P. Woodruff, and Peilin Zhong. 2016. Optimal Principal Component Analysis in Distributed and Streaming Models. In *Proceedings of the 48th Annual ACM SIGACT Symposium on Theory of Computing, (STOC)*. 236–249.

[6] Zvika Brakerski and Boaz Patt-Shamir. 2011. Distributed Discovery of Large Near-Cliques. *Distributed Computing* 24, 2 (2011), 79–89.

[7] Mark Braverman, Faith Ellen, Rotem Oshman, Toniann Pitassi, and Vinod Vaikuntanathan. 2013. A Tight Bound for Set Disjointness in the Message-Passing Model. In *Proceedings of the 2013 IEEE 54th Annual Symposium on Foundations of Computer Science (FOCS)*. 668–677.

[8] Mark Braverman, Ankit Garg, Tengyu Ma, Huy L. Nguyen, and David P. Woodruff. 2016. Communication Lower Bounds for Statistical Estimation Problems via a Distributed Data Processing Inequality. In *Proceedings of the Forty-eighth Annual ACM Symposium on Theory of Computing (STOC)*. 1011–1020.

[9] Keren Censor-Hillel, Eldar Fischer, Gregory Schwartzman, and Yadu Vasudev. 2016. Fast Distributed Algorithms for Testing Graph Properties. In *Distributed Computing: 30th International Symposium (DISC)*. 43–56.

[10] Keren Censor-Hillel, Petteri Kaski, Janne H. Korhonen, Christoph Lenzen, Ami Paz, and Jukka Suomela. 2015. Algebraic Methods in the Congested Clique. In *Proceedings of the 2015 ACM Symposium on Principles of Distributed Computing (PODC '15)*. 143–152.

[11] Thomas M. Cover and Joy A. Thomas. 2006. *Elements of Information Theory (Wiley Series in Telecommunications and Signal Processing)*.

[12] Danny Dolev, Christoph Lenzen, and Shir Peled. 2012. "Tri, Tri Again": Finding Triangles and Small Subgraphs in a Distributed Setting. In *Proceedings of the 26th International Conference on Distributed Computing (DISC'12)*. 195–209.

[13] Andrew Drucker, Fabian Kuhn, and Rotem Oshman. 2014. On the Power of the Congested Clique Model. In *Proceedings of the 2014 ACM Symposium on Principles of Distributed Computing (PODC '14)*. 367–376.

[14] Talya Eden, Amit Levi, Dana Ron, and C. Seshadhri. 2015. Approximately Counting Triangles in Sublinear Time. In *IEEE 56th Annual Symposium on Foundations of Computer Science, (FOCS)*. 614–633.

[15] Eldar Fischer. 2001. The Art of Uninformed Decisions. *Bulletin of the EATCS* 75 (2001), 97.

[16] Orr Fischer, Shay Gershtein, and Rotem Oshman. 2017. On The Multiparty Communication Complexity of Testing Triangle-Freeness (Full Version). *CoRR* abs/1705.08438 (2017). http://arxiv.org/abs/1705.08438

[17] Jacob Fox. 2011. A New Proof of the Graph Removal Lemma. *Annals of Mathematics* (2011), 561–579.

[18] Pierre Fraigniaud, Ivan Rapaport, Ville Salo, and Ioan Todinca. 2016. Distributed Testing of Excluded Subgraphs. In *Distributed Computing - 30th International Symposium, (DISC)*. 342–356.

[19] Oded Goldreich. 1998. Combinatorial Property Testing – a Survey. *Randomization Methods in Algorithm Design* (1998), 45–60.

[20] Oded Goldreich, Shari Goldwasser, and Dana Ron. 1998. Property Testing and Its Connection to Learning and Approximation. *J. ACM* 45, 4 (1998), 653–750.

[21] Oded Goldreich and Dana Ron. 1997. Property Testing in Bounded Degree Graphs. In *Proceedings of the Twenty-ninth Annual ACM Symposium on Theory of Computing (STOC '97)*. 406–415.

[22] Oded Goldreich and Luca Trevisan. 2003. Three Theorems Regarding Testing Graph Properties. *Random Struct. Algorithms* 23, 1 (2003), 23–57.

[23] L. Gugelmann. 2006. Testing Trinagle-Freeness in General Graphs: Lower Bounds. Bachelor thesis, Dept. of Mathematics, ETH, Zurich. (2006).

[24] Zengfeng Huang and Pan Peng. 2016. Dynamic Graph Stream Algorithms in o(n) Space. In *43rd International Colloquium on Automata, Languages, and Programming (ICALP)*. 18:1–18:16.

[25] John Kallaugher and Eric Price. 2017. A Hybrid Sampling Scheme for Triangle Counting. In *Proceedings of the Twenty-Eighth Annual ACM-SIAM Symposium on Discrete Algorithms, SODA 2017*. 1778–1797.

[26] Iordanis Kerenidis and Ran Raz. 2006. The One-way Communication Complexity of the Boolean Hidden Matching Problem. *Electronic Colloquium on Computational Complexity (ECCC)* 13 (2006).

[27] François Le Gall. 2016. *Further Algebraic Algorithms in the Congested Clique Model and Applications to Graph-Theoretic Problems*. 57–70.

[28] Yi Li, Xiaoming Sun, Chengu Wang, and David P. Woodruff. 2014. *On the Communication Complexity of Linear Algebraic Problems in the Message Passing Model*. 499–513.

[29] Ilan Newman. 1991. Private vs. Common Random Bits in Communication Complexity. *Inf. Process. Lett.* 39, 2 (1991), 67–71.

[30] Jeff M. Phillips, Elad Verbin, and Qin Zhang. 2012. Lower Bounds for Number-in-hand Multiparty Communication Complexity, Made Easy. In *Proceedings of the Twenty-third Annual ACM-SIAM Symposium on Discrete Algorithms (SODA '12)*. 486–501.

[31] T. Rast. 2006. Testing Trinagle-Freeness in General Graphs: Upper Bounds. Bachelor thesis, Dept. of Mathematics, ETH, Zurich. (2006).

[32] Dana Ron. 2009. Algorithmic and Analysis Techniques in Property Testing. *Foundations and Trends in Theoretical Computer Science* 5, 2 (2009), 73–205.

[33] Elad Verbin and Wei Yu. 2011. The Streaming Complexity of Cycle Counting, Sorting by Reversals, and Other Problems. In *Proceedings of the Twenty-second Annual ACM-SIAM Symposium on Discrete Algorithms (SODA '11)*. 11–25.

[34] David P. Woodruff and Qin Zhang. 2012. Tight Bounds for Distributed Functional Monitoring. In *Proceedings of the Forty-fourth Annual ACM Symposium on Theory of Computing (STOC '12)*. 941–960.

[35] David P. Woodruff and Qin Zhang. 2013. When Distributed Computation Is Communication Expensive. In *Distributed Computing: 27th International Symposium, DISC 2013, Jerusalem, Israel, October 14-18, 2013. Proceedings*. 16–30.

[36] David P. Woodruff and Qin Zhang. 2014. An Optimal Lower Bound for Distinct Elements in the Message Passing Model. In *Proceedings of the Twenty-Fifth Annual ACM-SIAM Symposium on Discrete Algorithms (SODA)*. 718–733.

# What Can be Sampled Locally?

Weiming Feng
Nanjing University
fengwm@smail.nju.edu.cn

Yuxin Sun
Nanjing University
njuyuxin.sun@gmail.com

Yitong Yin
Nanjing University
yinyt@nju.edu.cn

## ABSTRACT

The local computation of Linial [FOCS'87] and Naor and Stockmeyer [STOC'93] concerns with the question of whether a locally definable distributed computing problem can be solved locally: more specifically, for a given local CSP (Constraint Satisfaction Problem) whether a CSP solution can be constructed by a distributed algorithm using local information. In this paper, we consider the problem of sampling a uniform CSP solution by distributed algorithms, and ask whether a locally definable joint distribution can be sampled from locally. More broadly, we consider sampling from Gibbs distributions induced by weighted local CSPs, especially the Markov random fields (MRFs), in the LOCAL model.

We give two Markov chain based distributed algorithms which we believe to represent two fundamental approaches for sampling from Gibbs distributions via distributed algorithms. The first algorithm generically parallelizes the single-site sequential Markov chain by updating in each step the variables from a random independent set in parallel, and achieves an $O(\Delta \log n)$ time upper bound in the LOCAL model, where $\Delta$ is the maximum degree, when the Dobrushin's condition for the Gibbs distribution is satisfied. The second algorithm is a novel parallel Markov chain which proposes to update all variables simultaneously yet still guarantees to converge correctly with no bias. It surprisingly parallelizes an intrinsically sequential process: stabilizing to a joint distribution with massive local dependencies, and may achieve an optimal $O(\log n)$ time upper bound independent of the maximum degree $\Delta$ under a stronger mixing condition.

We also show a strong $\Omega(\text{diam})$ lower bound for sampling: in particular for sampling independent set in graphs with maximum degree $\Delta \geq 6$. Independent sets are trivial to construct locally and the sampling lower bound holds even when every node is aware of the entire graph. This gives a strong separation between sampling and constructing locally checkable labelings.

## KEYWORDS

distributed sampling algorithms; local computation; LOCAL model; Gibbs sampling; Markov chain Monte Carlo

Research supported by the National Science Foundation of China under Grant No. 61672275 and No. 61272081. This work was done in part while Yitong Yin was visiting the Simons Institute for the Theory of Computing.

*PODC '17, July 25-27, 2017, Washington, DC, USA*

ACM ISBN 978-1-4503-4992-5/17/07...$15.00
http://dx.doi.org/10.1145/3087801.3087815

## 1 INTRODUCTION

*Local computation and the* LOCAL *model:* Locality of computation is a central theme in the theory of distributed computing. In the seminal works of Linial [39], and Naor and Stockmeyer [45], the locality of distributed computation and the locally definable distributed computing problems are respectively captured by the LOCAL model and the notion of *locally checkable labeling (LCL)* problems. In the LOCAL model [45, 48], a network of $n$ processors is represented as an undirected graph, where each vertex represents a processor and each edge represents a bidirectional communication channel. Computations and communications are organized in synchronized rounds. In each round, each processor may receive a message of arbitrary size from each of its neighbors, perform an arbitrary local computation with the information collected so far, and send a message of arbitrary size to each of its neighbors. The output value for each vertex in a $t$-round protocol is determined by the local information within the $t$-neighborhood of the vertex. The local computation tasks are usually formulated as *labeling* problems, such as the locally checkable labeling (LCL) problems introduced in [45], in which the distributed algorithm is asked to construct a feasible solution of a constraint satisfaction problem (CSP) defined by local constraints with constant diameter in the network. Many problems can be expressed in this way, including various vertex/edge colorings, or local optimizations such as maximal independent set (MIS) and maximal matching.

A classic question for local computation is whether a locally definable problem is locally computable. Mathematically, this asks whether a feasible solution for a given local CSP can be *constructed* using only local information. There is a substantial body of research works dedicated to this question [2–5, 9, 19, 20, 24–26, 29, 34–37, 39, 45, 50].

*The local sampling problem:* Given an LCL problem which defines a local CSP on the network, besides to construct a feasible solution of the local CSP, another interesting problem is to *sample* a *uniform* random feasible solution, e.g. to sample a uniform random proper coloring of the network $G$ with a given number of colors. More abstractly, given an instance of local CSP which, say, treats the vertices in the network $G(V, E)$ as variables, a joint distribution of uniform random feasible solution $\boldsymbol{X} = (X_v)_{v \in V}$ is accordingly defined by these local constraints. Our main question is *whether a locally definable joint distribution can be sampled from locally.*

Intuitively, sampling could be substantially more difficult than labeling, because to sample a feasible solution is at least as difficult as to construct one, and furthermore, the marginal distribution of each random variable $X_v$ in a jointly distributed feasible solution $\boldsymbol{X} = (X_v)_{v \in V}$ may already encapsulate certain amount of non-local information about the solution space. Retrieving such information about the solution space (as in sampling) instead of constructing one solution (as in labeling) by distributed algorithms is especially well motivated in the context of distributed machine learning [12, 13, 15, 27, 46, 53, 57–59], where the data (the description of the joint distribution) is usually distributed among a large number of servers.

Besides uniform distributions, it is also natural to consider sampling from general non-uniform distributions over the solution space, which are usually formulated as graphical models known as the weighted CSPs [7], also known as factor graphs [43]. In this model, a probability distribution called the *Gibbs distribution* is defined over the space $\Omega = [q]^V$ of configurations, in such a way that each constraint of the weighted CSP contributes a nonnegative factor in the probability measure of a configuration in $\Omega$.

We are particularly interested in a basic class of weighted local CSPs, namely the *Markov random fields (MRFs)*, where every local constraint (factor) is either a binary constraint over an edge or a unary constraint on a vertex. Specifically, given a graph $G(V, E)$ and a finite domain $[q] = \{1, 2, \ldots, q\}$, the probability measure $\mu(\sigma)$ of each configuration $\sigma \in [q]^V$ under the Gibbs distribution $\mu$ is defined to be proportional to the weight:

$$w(\sigma) := \prod_{e=uv\in E} A_e(\sigma_u, \sigma_v) \prod_{v\in V} b_v(\sigma_v), \tag{1}$$

where $\{A_e \in \mathbb{R}_{\geq 0}^{q\times q}\}_{e\in E}$ are non-negative $q \times q$ symmetric matrices and $\{b_v \in \mathbb{R}_{\geq 0}^{q}\}_{v\in V}$ are non-negative $q$-vectors, both specified by the instance of MRF. Examples of MRFs include combinatorial models such as independent set, vertex cover, graph coloring, and graph homomorphsm, or physical models such as hardcore gas model, Ising model, Potts model, and general spin systems. Due to Hammersley-Clifford's fundamental theorem of random fields, this model is universal for all the positive distributions $\mu$ defined over $\Omega = [q]^V$ satisfying the conditional independence (spatial Markovian) property.

## 1.1 Our results

We give two Markov chain based distributed algorithms for sampling. Given any $\epsilon > 0$, each algorithm returns a random output which is within total variation distance $\epsilon$ from the Gibbs distribution. Our expositions mainly focus on MRFs, although both algorithms can be extended straightforwardly to general weighted local CSPs.

Classic single-site Markov chain such as the Glauber dynamics converges to the Gibbs distribution $\boldsymbol{X} = (X_v)_{v\in V}$ by randomly updating one variable $X_v$ in each step according to its marginal distribution conditioning on the current values $X_u$ at its neighbors $u \sim v$. A generic approach for parallelizing a single-site sequential Markov chain is to update in each step the variables from an independent set in parallel. This natural idea has been considered in [27], also in a much broader context such as parallel job scheduling [42] or distributed Lovász local lemma [10, 44]. For sampling from locally defined joint distributions, it is especially suitable because of the *conditional independence* property of MRFs.

Our first algorithm, named *LubyGlauber*, naturally uses the "Luby step" in Luby's algorithm for maximal independent set (MIS) [1, 41] to sample random independent sets for parallelizing the Glauber dynamics. It is well known that the Glauber dynamics achieves the optimal mixing rate $\tau(\epsilon) = O\left(n \log\left(\frac{n}{\epsilon}\right)\right)$ under the *Dobrushin's condition* for the decay of correlation [14, 30]. By a standard coupling argument, we show that the *LubyGlauber* algorithm achieves a mixing rate $\tau(\epsilon) = O\left(\Delta \log\left(\frac{n}{\epsilon}\right)\right)$ under the same condition, where $\Delta$ is the maximum degree of the network. In particular, for uniformly sampling proper $q$-colorings, this implies:

Theorem 1.1. *If $q \geq \alpha\Delta$ for an arbitrary constant $\alpha > 2$, there is an algorithm which samples a uniform proper $q$-coloring within total variation distance $\epsilon > 0$ in $O\left(\Delta \log\left(\frac{n}{\epsilon}\right)\right)$ rounds of communications on any graph $G(V, E)$ with $n = |V|$ vertices and maximum degree $\Delta = \Delta(n)$.*

A fundamental limit of this natural approach is that it will perform poorly on general graphs with large chromatic number. The situation motivates us to ask following questions:

- Is it possible to update all variables in $\boldsymbol{X} = (X_v)_{v\in V}$ simultaneously and still converge to the correct stationary distribution $\mu$?
- More concretely, is it always possible to sample almost uniformly from proper $q$-colorings, for a $q = O(\Delta)$, on any graphs $G(V, E)$ with $n = |V|$ vertices and maximum degree $\Delta$, within $O(\log n)$ rounds of communications, especially when $\Delta = \Delta(n)$ is unbounded?

Surprisingly, the answers to both these questions are positive, and we give an algorithm, called the *LocalMetropolis* algorithm, achieving these goals. This algorithm is quite surprising, since it seems to fully parallelize a process which is intrinsically sequential due to the massive local dependencies, especially on graphs with unbounded maximum degree. The algorithm achieves this by proposing to update all variables independently and filtering the proposals properly to ensure it converges to the correct joint distribution. Our main discovery is that the filtering is *localizable* if the joint distribution is locally defined.

This algorithm is mixing at a better rate $O\left(\log\left(\frac{n}{\epsilon}\right)\right)$ under a stronger condition. For uniformly sampling proper $q$-colorings, this means we need a bigger number of colors $q$:

Theorem 1.2. *If $q \geq \alpha\Delta$ for an arbitrary constant $\alpha > 2 + \sqrt{2}$, there is an algorithm for sampling uniform proper $q$-coloring within total variation distance $\epsilon > 0$ in $O\left(\log\left(\frac{n}{\epsilon}\right)\right)$ rounds of communications on any graph $G(V, E)$ with $n = |V|$ vertices and maximum degree at most $\Delta = \Delta(n) \geq 9$.*

The analysis is due to a novel path-coupling argument. We also believe that the $2 + \sqrt{2}$ threshold is of certain significance to this chain as the Dobrushin's condition to the Glauber dynamics.

Neither of the algorithms abuses the power of the LOCAL model: each message is of $O(\log n)$ bits for a polynomial domain size $q = \text{poly}(n)$.

Due to the exponential correlation between variables in Gibbs distributions, the $O\left(\log\left(\frac{n}{\epsilon}\right)\right)$ time bound achieved in Theorem 1.2 is optimal.

It is a well known phenomenon that sampling may become computationally intractable when the model exhibits the non-uniqueness phase-transition property, e.g. independent sets in graphs of maximum degree bounded by a $\Delta \geq 6$ [22, 23, 51, 52]. For the same class of distributions, we show the following unconditional $\Omega(\text{diam})$ lower bound for sampling in the LOCAL model.

THEOREM 1.3. *For $\Delta \geq 6$, there exist infinitely many graphs $G(V,E)$ with maximum degree $\Delta$ and diameter* $\mathrm{diam}(G) = \widetilde{\Omega}(\sqrt{|V|})$ *such that any algorithm that samples uniform independent set in $G$ within sufficiently small constant total variation distance $\epsilon$ requires $\Omega(\mathrm{diam}(G))$ rounds of communications, even assuming the vertices $v \in V$ to be aware of $G$.*

The lower bound is proved by a now fairly well-understood reduction from maximum cut to sampling independent sets when $\Delta \geq 6$ [23, 51, 52]. Specifically, we show that when $\Delta \geq 6$ there are infinitely many graphs $G(V,E)$ such that if one can sample nearly uniform independent set in $G(V,E)$, then one can also sample almost uniform maximum cut in an even cycle of size $\widetilde{\Omega}(\sqrt{|V|})$, which is necessarily a global task because of the long-range correlation.

Theorem 1.3 strongly separates sampling from labeling problems for distributed computing:

- In the LOCAL model it is trivial to construct an independent set (because $\emptyset$ is an independent set). In contrast, Theorem 1.3 says that sampling a uniform independent set is very much a global task for graphs with maximum degree $\Delta \geq 6$.
- In the LOCAL model any labeling problem would be trivial once the network structure $G$ is known to each vertex. In contrast, the sampling lower bound in Theorem 1.3 still holds even when each vertex is aware of $G$. Unlike labeling whose hardness is due to the locality of information, for sampling the hardness is solely due to the locality of randomness.
- A very recent breakthrough of Ghaffari, Kuhn and Maus [25] shows that any labeling problem that can be solved sequentially with local information admits a $O(\mathrm{polylog}(n))$-round randomized protocol in the LOCAL model. In contrast, for sampling we have an $\Omega(\mathrm{diam})$ randomized lower bound for graphs with $\widetilde{\Omega}(\sqrt{n})$ diameter.

## 1.2 Related work

The topic of sequential MCMC (Markov chain Monte Carlo) sampling is extensively studied. The study of sampling proper $q$-colorings was initiated by the seminal works of Jerrum [32] and independently of Salas and Sokal [49]. So far the best rapid mixing condition for general bounded-degree graphs is $q \geq \frac{11}{6}\Delta$ due to Vigoda [55]. See [21] for an excellent survey.

The chromatic-scheduler-based parallelization of Glauber dynamics was studied in [27]. This parallel chain is in fact a special case of systematic scan for Glauber dynamics [16, 17, 30], in which the variables are updated according to a fixed order. Empirical studies showed that sometimes an *ad hoc* "Hogwild!" parallelization of sequential sampler might work well in practice [47] and the mixing results assuming bounded asynchrony were given in [12, 33].

In a very recent result [28], a sampling algorithm based on the Lovász local lemma is given. When sampling from the hardcore model with $\lambda < \frac{1}{2\sqrt{e}\Delta-1}$ on a graph of maximum degree $\Delta$, this sampling algorithm can be implemented in the LOCAL model which runs in $O(\log n)$ rounds.

A problem related to the local sampling is the *finitary coloring* [31], in which a random feasible solution from an arbitrary distribution instead of the Gibbs distribution is sampled locally. Therefore, the nature of this problem is still labeling rather than sampling.

Our algorithms are Markov chains which randomly walk over the solution space. A related notion is the *distributed random walks* [11], which walk over the network.

Our *LocalMetropolis* algorithm should be distinguished from the parallel Metropolis-Hastings algorithm [8] or the parallel tempering [54], in which the sampling algorithms makes $N$ proposals or runs $N$ copies of the system in parallel for a suitably large $N$, in order to improve the dynamic properties of the Monte Carlo simulation.

# 2 MODELS AND PRELIMINARIES

*The* LOCAL *model.* We assume Linial's LOCAL model [45, 48] for distributed computation, which is as described in Section 1. We further allow each node in the network $G(V,E)$ to be aware of upper bounds of $\Delta$ and $\log n$, where $n = |V|$ is the number of nodes. These informations are accessed only because the running time of the Monte Carlo algorithms may depend on them.

*Markov random field and local CSP.* The *Markov random field (MRF)*, or *spin system*, is a well studied stochastic model in probability theory and statistical physics. Given a graph $G(V,E)$ and a set of *spin states* $[q] = \{1, 2, \ldots, q\}$ for a finite $q \geq 2$, a *configuration* $\sigma \in [q]^V$ assigns each vertex one of the $q$ spin states. For each edge $e \in E$ there is a non-negative $q \times q$ symmetric matrix $A_e \in \mathbb{R}_{\geq 0}^{q\times q}$ associated with $e$, called the *edge activity*; and for each vertex $v \in V$ there is a non-negative $q$-dimensional vector $b_v \in \mathbb{R}_{\geq 0}^{q}$ associated with $v$, called the *vertex activity*. Then each configuration $\sigma \in [q]^V$ is assigned a weight $w(\sigma)$ which is as defined in (1). This gives rise to a natural probability distribution $\mu$, called the *Gibbs distribution*, over all configurations in the sample space $\Omega = [q]^V$ proportional to their weights, such that $\mu(\sigma) = w(\sigma)/Z$ for each $\sigma \in \Omega$, where $Z = \sum_{\sigma\in\Omega} w(\sigma)$ is the normalizing factor. A configuration $\sigma \in \Omega$ is *feasible* if $\mu(\sigma) > 0$.

Several natural joint distributions can be expressed as MRFs:

- **Independent sets / vertex covers:** When $q = 2$, set all $b_v = \begin{bmatrix}1\\1\end{bmatrix}$, and $A_e = \begin{bmatrix}1 & 1\\1 & 0\end{bmatrix}$. Then each feasible configuration indicates an independent set (or vertex cover, if the roles of 0 and 1 exchange) in $G$, and the Gibbs distribution $\mu$ is the uniform distribution over independent sets (or vertex covers) in $G$. When $b_v = \begin{bmatrix}1\\\lambda\end{bmatrix}$ for some parameter $\lambda > 0$, this is the *hardcore model* from statistical physics.
- **Colorings and list colorings:** When every matrix $A_e$ has $A_e(i,i) = 0$ and $A_e(i,j) = 1$ if $i \neq j$, and every $b_v$ is the all-1 vector, the Gibbs distribution $\mu$ becomes the uniform distribution over proper $q$-colorings of graph $G$. For *list colorings*, each vertex $v \in V$ can only use the colors from its list $L_v \subseteq [q]$ of available colors. Then we can let each $b_v$ be the indicator vector for the list $L_v$ and $A_e$'s are the same as for proper $q$-colorings, so that the Gibbs distribution is the uniform distribution over proper list colorings.

- **Physical models:** The proper $q$-coloring is a special case of the *Potts model* in statistical physics, in which each $A_e$ has $A_e(i,i) = \beta_e$ for some parameter $\beta_e > 0$ and $A_e(i,j) = 1$ if $i \neq j$. When further $q = 2$, the model becomes the *Ising model.*

The model of MRF can be further generalized to allow multivariate asymmetric constraints, by which gives us the *weighted CSPs*, also known as the *factor graphs*. In this model, we have a collection $C$ of *constraints* $c = (f_c, S_c)$ where each $f_c : [q]^{|S_c|} \to \mathbb{R}_{\geq 0}$ is a *constraint function* with *scope* $S_c \subseteq V$. Each configuration $\sigma \in [q]^V$ is assigned a weight: $w(\sigma) = \prod_{c=(f_c,S_c)\in C} f_c(\sigma|_{S_c})$, where $\sigma|_{S_c}$ represents the restriction of $\sigma$ on $S_c$. And the Gibbs distribution $\mu$ over all configurations in $\Omega = [q]^V$ is defined in the same way proportional to the weights. In particular, when $f_c$'s are Boolean-valued functions, the Gibbs distribution $\mu$ is the uniform distribution over CSP solutions.

A constraint $c = (f_c, S_c)$ is said to be *local* with respect to network $G$ if the diameter of the scope $S_c$ in network $G$ is bounded by a constant. Local CSPs are expressive, for example:

- **Dominating sets:** They can be expressed by having a "cover" constraint on each inclusive neighborhood $\Gamma^+(v)$ constraining that at least one vertex from $\Gamma^+(v)$ is chosen.
- **Maximal independent sets (MISs):** An MIS is a dominating independent set.

Clearly, the MRF is a special class of weighted local CSPs, defined by unary and binary symmetric local constraints with respect to $G$.

*Local Sampling.* The local sampling problem is defined as follows. Let $G(V,E)$ be a network. Given an MRF defined on $G$ (or more generally a weighted CSP that is local with respect to $G$), where the specifications of the local constraints are given as private inputs to the involved processors, for any $\epsilon > 0$ upon termination each processor $v \in V$ outputs a random variable $X_v$ such that the total variation distance between the distribution $\nu$ of the random vector $X = (X_v)_{v\in V}$ and the Gibbs distribution $\mu$ is bounded as $d_{\mathrm{TV}}(\mu,\nu) \leq \epsilon$, where the total variation distance between two distributions $\mu, \nu$ over $\Omega = [q]^V$ is defined as

$$d_{\mathrm{TV}}(\mu,\nu) = \sum_{\sigma\in\Omega} \frac{1}{2}|\mu(\sigma) - \nu(\sigma)| = \max_{A\subseteq\Omega} |\mu(A) - \nu(A)|.$$

*Mixing rate.* Our algorithms are given as Markov chains. Given an Markov chain $X^{(0)}, X^{(1)}, X^{(2)}, \ldots \in \Omega$ that is *irreducible* and *aperiodic*, for any $\sigma \in \Omega$ let $\pi_\sigma^{(t)}$ denote the distribution of $X^{(t)}$ conditioning on that $X^{(0)} = \sigma$. For $\epsilon > 0$, define *mixing rate* $\tau(\epsilon)$ as $\tau(\epsilon) = \max_{\sigma\in\Omega} \min\left\{t : d_{\mathrm{TV}}\left(\pi_\sigma^{(t)}, \pi\right) \leq \epsilon\right\}$, where $\pi$ is the *stationary distribution* for the chain. For formal definitions of these notions for Markov chain, we refer to a standard textbook of the subject [38]. Informally, irreducibility and aperiodicity guarantees that $X^{(t)}$ converges to the unique stationary distribution $\pi$ as $t \to \infty$, and the mixing rate $\tau(\epsilon)$ tells us how fast it converges.

*Notations.* Given a graph $G(V,E)$, we denote by $d_v = \deg(v)$ the degree of $v$ in $G$, $\Delta = \Delta_G$ the maximum degree of $G$, diam $=$ diam$(G)$ the diameter of $G$, and $\mathrm{dist}(u,v) = \mathrm{dist}_G(u,v)$ the shortest path distance between vertices $u$ and $v$ in $G$.

We also denote by $\Gamma(v) = \{u \mid uv \in E\}$ the neighborhood of $v$, and $\Gamma^+(v) = \Gamma(v) \cup \{v\}$ the inclusive neighborhood. Finally we write $B_r(v) = \{u \mid \mathrm{dist}(u,v) \leq r\}$ for the $r$-ball centered at $v$.

## 3 THE *LubyGlauber* ALGORITHM

In this section, we analyze a generic scheme for parallelizing Glauber dynamics, a classic sequential Markov chain for sampling from Gibbs distributions.

We assume a Markov random field (MRF) defined on the network $G(V,E)$, with edge activities $\boldsymbol{A} = \{A_e\}_{e\in E}$ and vertex activities $\boldsymbol{b} = \{b_v\}_{v\in V}$, which specifies a Gibbs distribution $\mu$ over $\Omega = [q]^V$. The *single-site heat-bath Glauber dynamics*, or simply the *Glauber dynamics*, is a well known Markov chain for sampling from the Gibbs distribution $\mu$. Starting from an arbitrary initial configuration $X \in [q]^V$, at each step a vertex $v \in V$ is sampled uniformly at random and the value of $X_v$ is resampled according to the marginal distribution induced by $\mu$ at vertex $v$ conditioning on the current spin states of $v$'s neighborhood.

Formally, supposed that $\sigma \in [q]^V$ is sampled from $\mu$, for any $v \in V$, $S \subseteq V$ and $\tau_S \in [q]^S$, the *marginal distribution* at vertex $v$ conditioning on $\tau_S$, denoted as $\mu_v(\cdot \mid \tau_S)$, is defined as $\mu_v(c \mid \tau_S) = \Pr[\sigma_v = c \mid \sigma_S = \tau_S]$ for any $c \in [q]$. In the Glauber dynamics, $X_v$ is resampled according to the marginal distribution $\mu_v(\cdot \mid X_{\Gamma(v)})$. Here $X_{\Gamma(v)}$ represents the current spin states of $v$'s neighborhood $\Gamma(v)$. For Markov random field, this marginal distribution can be computed as

$$\forall c \in [q], \quad \mu_v(c \mid X_{\Gamma(v)}) = \frac{b_v(c)\prod_{u\in\Gamma(v)} A_{uv}(c, X_u)}{\sum_{a\in[q]} b_v(a)\prod_{u\in\Gamma(v)} A_{uv}(a, X_u)}. \tag{2}$$

For example, when the MRF is the proper $q$-coloring, this is just the uniform distribution over available colors in $[q]$ which are not used by $v$'s neighbors. For the Glauber dynamics to work, it is common to assume that $\sum_{a\in[q]} b_v(a)\prod_{u\in\Gamma(v)} A_{uv}(a, X_u)$ is always positive, so that the marginal distributions are well-defined.[1]

A generic scheme for parallelizing the Glauber dynamics is that at each step, instead of updating one vertex, the chain updates a group of "non-interfering" vertices in parallel, as follows:

- independently sample a random independent set $I$ in $G$;
- for each $v \in I$, resample $X_v$ in parallel according to the marginal distribution $\mu_v(\cdot \mid X_{\Gamma(v)})$.

This can be seen as a relaxation of the chromatic-based scheduler [27] and systematic scans [16].

A convenient way for generating a random independent set in a distributed fashion is the "Luby step" in Luby's algorithm for distributed MIS [1, 41]: each vertex sample a uniform and independent ID from the interval $[0,1]$ (which can be discretized with $O(\log n)$ bits) and the vertices $v$ who are locally maximal among the inclusive neighborhood $\Gamma^+(v)$ are selected into the independent set $I$.

The resulting algorithm is called *LubyGlauber*, whose pseudocode is given in Algorithm 1.

According to the definition of marginal distribution (2), resampling $X_v$ can be done locally by exchanging neighbors' current spin

[1]This property holds automatically for feasible configurations $X$ with $\mu(X) > 0$, and is only needed when the Glauber dynamics is allowed to start from an infeasible configuration. For specific MRF, such as proper $q$-coloring, this property is guaranteed by the "uniqueness condition" $q \geq \Delta + 1$.

**Algorithm 1:** Pseudocode for vertex $v \in V$ in *LubyGlauber* algorithm

```
Input: Vertex v ∈ V receives {A_uv}_{u∈Γ(v)} and b_v as input.
initialize X_v to an arbitrary value in [q];
for t = 1 through T do
    sample a real β_v ∈ [0, 1] uniformly and independently;
    if β_v > max{β_u | u ∈ Γ(v)} then
        resample X_v according to marginal distribution
          μ_v(· | X_Γ(v));
return X_v;
```

states. After $T$ iterations, where $T$ is a threshold determined for specific Markov random field, the algorithm terminates and outputs the current $\boldsymbol{X} = (X_v)_{v\in V}$.

Remark. *The* LubyGlauber *algorithm can be straightforwardly extended to sample from weighted CSPs defined by local constraints $c = (f_c, S_c) \in C$, by simply overriding the definition of neighborhood as $\Gamma(v) := \{u \neq v \mid \exists c \in C, \{u, v\} \subseteq S_c\}$, thus $\Gamma(v)$ is the neighborhood of $v$ in the hypergraph where $S_c$'s are the hyperedges and now $I$ is the strongly independent set of this hypergraph.*

Let $\mu_{\mathrm{LG}}$ denote the distribution of $\boldsymbol{X}$ returned by the algorithm upon termination. As in the case of single-site Glauber dynamics, we assume that the marginal distribution (2) is always well-defined, and the single-site Glauber dynamics is irreducible among all feasible configurations. The following proposition is easy to obtain.

Proposition 3.1. *The Markov chain* LubyGlauber *is reversible and has stationary distribution $\mu$. Furthermore, under the above assumption, $d_{\mathrm{TV}}(\mu_{\mathrm{LG}}, \mu)$ converges to 0 as $T \to \infty$.*

We then apply a standard coupling argument from [17, 30] to analyze the mixing rate of the *LubyGlauber* chain. The following notions are essential to the mixing of Glauber dynamics.

*Definition 3.2 (influence matrix).* For $v \in V$ and $\sigma \in [q]^V$, we write $\mu_v^\sigma = \mu_v(\cdot \mid \sigma_{\Gamma(v)})$ for the marginal distribution of the value of $v$, for configurations sampled from $\mu$ conditioning on agreeing with $\sigma$ at all neighbors of $v$. For vertices $i, j \in V$, the *influence* of $j$ on $i$ is defined as

$$\rho_{i,j} := \max_{(\sigma,\tau)\in S_j} d_{\mathrm{TV}}(\mu_i^\sigma, \mu_i^\tau),$$

where $S_j$ denotes the set of all pairs of feasible configurations $\sigma, \tau \in [q]^V$ such that $\sigma$ and $\tau$ agree on all vertices except $j$. Let $R = (\rho_{i,j})_{i,j\in V}$ be the $n \times n$ *influence matrix.*

*Definition 3.3 (Dobrushin's condition).* Let $\boldsymbol{\alpha}$ be the *total influence* on a vertex, defined by $\boldsymbol{\alpha} := \max_{i\in V} \sum_{j\in V} \rho_{i,j}$. We say that the Dobrushin's condition is satisfied if $\boldsymbol{\alpha} < 1$.

It is a fundamental result that the Dobrushin's condition is sufficient for the rapid mixing of Glauber dynamics [14, 30, 49], with a mixing rate of $\tau(\epsilon) = O\left(\frac{n}{1-\boldsymbol{\alpha}} \log\left(\frac{n}{\epsilon}\right)\right)$. Here we show that the *LubyGlauber* chain is essentially a parallel speed up of the Glauber dynamics by a factor of $\Theta(\frac{n}{\Delta})$.

Theorem 3.4. *Under the same assumption as Proposition 3.1, if the total influence $\boldsymbol{\alpha} < 1$, then the mixing rate of the* LubyGlauber *chain is $\tau(\epsilon) = O\left(\frac{\Delta}{1-\boldsymbol{\alpha}} \log\left(\frac{n}{\epsilon}\right)\right)$.*

Remark. *In fact, Proposition 3.1 and Theorem 3.4 hold for a more general family of Markov chains, where the "Luby step" could be any subroutine which independently generates a random independent set $I$, as long as every vertex has positive probability to be selected into $I$. In general, the mixing rate in Theorem 3.4 is in fact $\tau(\epsilon) = O\left(\frac{1}{(1-\boldsymbol{\alpha})\gamma} \log\left(\frac{n}{\epsilon}\right)\right)$ where $\gamma$ is a lower bound for the probability $\Pr[v \in I]$ for all $v \in V$.*

For uniformly distributed proper $q$-coloring of graph $G$, it is well known that the Dobrushin's condition is satisfied when $q \geq 2\Delta + 1$ where $\Delta$ is the maximum degree of graph $G$.

We consider a more generalized problem, the list colorings, where each vertex $v \in V$ maintains a list $L_v \subseteq [q]$ of colors that it can use. The proper $q$-coloring is a special case of list coloring when everyone's list is precisely $[q]$. For each vertex $v \in V$, we denote by $q_v = |L_v|$ the size of $v$'s list, and $d_v = \deg(v)$ the degree of $v$. It is easy to verify that the total influence $\boldsymbol{\alpha}$ is now bounded as $\boldsymbol{\alpha} = \max_{i\in V} \sum_{j\in V} \rho_{i,j} = \max_{v\in V} \left\{\frac{d_v}{q_v - d_v}\right\}$.

Applying Theorem 3.4, we have the following corollary, which also implies Theorem 1.1.

Corollary 3.5. *If there is an arbitrary constant $\delta > 0$ such that $q_v \geq (2 + \delta)d_v$ for every vertex $v$, then the mixing rate of the* LubyGlauber *chain for sampling list coloring is $\tau(\epsilon) = O\left(\Delta \log\left(\frac{n}{\epsilon}\right)\right)$.*

## 4 THE *LocalMetropolis* ALGORITHM

In this section, we give an algorithm that may fully parallelize the sequential process under suitable mixing conditions, even on graphs with unbounded degree. The algorithm is inspired by the famous Metropolis-Hastings algorithm for MCMC, in which a random choice is *proposed* and then *filtered* to enforce the target stationary distribution. Our algorithm, called the *LocalMetropolis* algorithm, makes each vertex propose independently, and localizes the works of filtering to each edge.

We are given a Markov random field (MRF) defined on the network $G(V, E)$, with edge activities $\boldsymbol{A} = \{A_e\}_{e\in E}$ and vertex activities $\boldsymbol{b} = \{b_v\}_{v\in V}$, whose Gibbs distribution is $\mu$. Starting from an arbitrary configuration $X \in [q]^V$, in each iteration, the *LocalMetropolis* chain does the followings:

- **Propose:** Each vertex $v \in V$ independently proposes a spin state $\sigma_v \in [q]$ with probability proportional to $b_v(\sigma_v)$.
- **Local filter:** Each edge $e \in E$ flips a biased coin independently, with the probability of HEADS being
  $$\tilde{A}_e(\sigma_u, \sigma_v)\tilde{A}_e(X_u, \sigma_v)\tilde{A}_e(\sigma_u, X_v),$$
  where $\tilde{A}_e$ is the matrix obtained by normalizing $A_e$ as $\tilde{A}_e = A_e / \max_{i,j} A_e(i, j)$. We say that the edge *passes the check* if the outcome of coin flipping is HEADS.

  Then for each vertex $v \in V$, if all edges incident with $v$ passed their checks, $v$ accepts the proposal and updates the value as $X_v = \sigma_v$, otherwise $v$ leaves $X_v$ unchanged.

After $T$ iterations, where $T$ is a threshold determined for specific Markov random field, algorithm terminates and outputs the current

$X = (X_v)_{v \in V}$. The pseudocode for the *LocalMetropolis* algorithm is given in Algorithm 2.

**Algorithm 2:** Pseudocode for the *LocalMetropolis* algorithm

**Input:** Each vertex $v \in V$ receives $\{A_{uv}\}_{u \in \Gamma(v)}$ and $b_v$ as input.

each $v \in V$ initializes $X_v$ to an arbitrary value in $[q]$;<br>
**for** $t = 1$ *through* $T$ **do**<br>
  **foreach** $v \in V$ **do**<br>
    propose a random $\sigma_v \in [q]$ with probability $b_v(\sigma_v)/\sum_{c \in [q]} b_v(c)$;<br>
  **foreach** $e = (u, v) \in E$ **do**<br>
    pass the check independently with probability $\frac{A_e(\sigma_u, \sigma_v) A_e(X_u, \sigma_v) A_e(\sigma_u, X_v)}{(\max_{i,j \in [q]} A_e(i,j))^3}$;<br>
  **foreach** $v \in V$ **do**<br>
    **if** *all edges e incident with v pass the checks* **then**<br>
      $X_v \leftarrow \sigma_v$;<br>
each $v \in V$ **returns** $X_v$;

We remark that in each iteration, for each edge $e = uv$, the two endpoints $u$ and $v$ access the same random coin to determine whether $e$ passes the check in this iteration.

Remark. *The* LocalMetropolis *algorithm can be naturally extended to sample from weighted CSPs. The local filtering now occurs on each local constraint, such that a $k$-ary constraint $c = (f_c, S_c) \in C$ passes the check with the probability which is a product of $2^k - 1$ normalized factors $\tilde{f}_c(\tau)$ for the $\tau \in [q]^{S_c}$ obtained from $2^k - 1$ ways of mixing $\sigma_{S_c}$ with $X_{S_c}$ except the $X_{S_c}$ itself.*

Let $\mu_{\mathrm{LM}}$ denote the distribution of $X = (X_v)_{v \in V}$ returned by the *LocalMetropolis* algorithm after $T$ iterations. We need to ensure the chain is well behaved even when starting from infeasible configurations. Now we make the following assumption: for all $X \in [q]^V$ and $v \in V$,

$$\sum_{i \in [q]} b_v(i) \prod_{u \in \Gamma(v)} A_{uv}(i, X_u) \sum_{j \in [q]} b_u(j) A_{uv}(X_v, j) A_{uv}(i, j) > 0, \quad (3)$$

which is slightly stronger than the assumption made for the Glauber dynamics. As in the case of Glauber dynamics, the property is needed only when the chain is allowed to start from an infeasible configuration $X \in [q]^V$ with $\mu(X) = 0$. For specific MRF, such as graph colorings, the condition (3) is satisfied as long as $q \geq \Delta + 1$ and $q \geq 3$. As before, we further assume that the single-site Markov chain[2] is irreducible among feasible configurations.

Theorem 4.1. *The Markov chain* LocalMetropolis *is reversible and has stationary distribution $\mu$. Furthermore, under above assumptions, $d_{\mathrm{TV}}(\mu_{\mathrm{LM}}, \mu)$ converges to 0 as $T \to \infty$.*

Unlike the *LubyGlauber* chain, whose mixing rate is essentially due to the analysis of systematic scans. The mixing rate of *LocalMetropolis* chain is much more complicated to analyze. Here we analyze the mixing rate of the *LocalMetropolis* chain for proper $q$-colorings.

Given a graph $G(V, E)$, a $q$-coloring $\sigma \in [q]^V$ is proper if $\sigma_u \neq \sigma_v$ for all $uv \in E$. For this special MRF, the *LocalMetropolis* chain behaves simply as follows. Starting from an arbitrary coloring $X \in [q]^V$, not necessarily proper, in each step:

- each vertex $v$ proposes a uniform random color $c_v \in [q]$;
- each vertex $v$ accepts its proposal and updates $X_v$ to $c_v$ if for all neighbors $u \in \Gamma(v)$, $c_v \neq X_u$, $c_v \neq c_u$, and $X_v \neq c_u$.

Surprisingly, this natural parallel Markov chain has not been well studied before. It can be verified that when $q \geq \Delta + 2$, the condition (3) is satisfied and the single-site Glauber dynamics for proper $q$-coloring is irreducible, and hence the chain is mixing due to Theorem 4.1.

The following theorem states a condition in the form $q \geq \alpha\Delta$ for the logarithmic mixing rate even for unbounded $\Delta$ and $q$. This proves Theorem 1.2.

Theorem 4.2. *If $q \geq \alpha\Delta$ for a constant $\alpha > 2 + \sqrt{2}$, the mixing rate of the* LocalMetropolis *chain for proper $q$-coloring on graphs with maximum degree at most $\Delta = \Delta(n) \geq 9$ is $\tau(\epsilon) = O\left(\log\left(\frac{n}{\epsilon}\right)\right)$, where the constant factor in $O(\cdot)$ depends only on $\alpha$ but not on $\Delta$.*

This theorem is proved by path coupling, a powerful engineering tool for coupling Markov chains. A coupling of a Markov chain on space $\Omega$ is a Markov chain $(X, Y) \to (X', Y')$ on space $\Omega^2$ such that the transitions $X \to X'$ and $Y \to Y'$ individually follow the same transition rule as the original chain on $\Omega$. For path coupling, we can construct a coupled Markov chain $(X, Y) \to (X', Y')$ for $X, Y \in [q]^V$ which differ at only one vertex.

Lemma 4.3 (Bubley and Dyer [6]). *Given a pre-metric, which is a connected undirected graph on configuration space $\Omega$ with positive edge weight such that every edge is a shortest path, let $\Phi(X, Y)$ be the length of the shortest path between two configurations $X, Y \in \Omega$. Suppose that there is a coupling $(X, Y) \to (X', Y')$ of the Markov chain defined only for the pair $(X, Y)$ of configurations that are adjacent in the pre-metric, which satisfies that*

$$\mathbf{E}[\Phi(X', Y') \mid X, Y] \leq (1 - \delta)\Phi(X, Y),$$

*for some $0 < \delta < 1$. Then the mixing rate of the Markov chain is bounded by*

$$\tau(\epsilon) \leq \frac{\log(\mathrm{diam}(\Omega)/\epsilon)}{\delta},$$

*where $\mathrm{diam}(\Omega)$ denotes the diameter of $\Omega$ in the pre-metric.*

*An ideal coupling.* The $2 + \sqrt{2}$ threshold in Theorem 4.2 is due to an ideal coupling in the $\Delta$-regular tree. Let $\mathbb{T}_\Delta$ denote the infinite $\Delta$-regular tree rooted at $v_0$. We assume that the current pair of colorings $(X, Y)$ disagree only at the root $v_0$ and $X_u = Y_u \notin \{X_{v_0}, Y_{v_0}\}$ for all other vertices $u$ in $\mathbb{T}_\Delta$.

An ideal coupling can be constructed as follows in a breadth-first fashion: (1) the root $v_0$ proposes the same random color in both chains $X, Y$; (2) each child $u$ of the root proposes the same random color in both chains unless it proposed one of $\{X_{v_0}, Y_{v_0}\}$, in which case it switches the roles of the two colors $\{X_{v_0}, Y_{v_0}\}$ in the $Y$ chain; (3) for all other vertices $u$, it proposes the same random color in both chains unless its parent proposed different colors in the two

[2]For the MRFs, since the single-site Glauber dynamics has the same connectivity structure as the natural single-site version of Metropolis chain, we do not distinguish between them when referring to irreducibility.

chains, in which case $u$ switches the roles of $\{X_{v_0}, Y_{v_0}\}$ in the $Y$ chain. Now consider the root $v_0$. Since $v_0$ proposes the same color in two chains, the event $X'_{v_0} = Y'_{v_0}$ occurs if all edges incident with $v_0$ pass their checks, which means:

$$\Pr[X'_{v_0} = Y'_{v_0}] \geq \left(1 - \frac{\Delta}{q}\right)\left(1 - \frac{2}{q}\right)^{\Delta}.$$

For any non-root vertex $u$ in $\mathbb{T}_\Delta$ at distance $\ell$ from $v_0$, event $X'_u \neq Y'_u$ occurs only if all the vertices in the path from $v_0$ to $u$ except $v_0$ propose different colors and all edges incident with $u$ pass their checks. A simple calculation gives that:

$$\Pr[X'_u \neq Y'_u] \leq \frac{1}{q}\left(1 - \frac{2}{q}\right)^{\Delta-1}\left(\frac{2}{q}\right)^{\ell-1} = \frac{1}{2}\left(1 - \frac{2}{q}\right)^{\Delta-1}\left(\frac{2}{q}\right)^{\ell}.$$

The expected number of disagreeing vertices in $(X', Y')$ is then bounded as

$$\begin{aligned}
&\Pr[X'_{v_0} \neq Y'_{v_0}] + \sum_{\substack{u \in \mathbb{T}_\Delta \\ u \neq v_0}} \Pr[X'_u \neq Y'_u] \\
&\leq 1 - \left(1 - \frac{\Delta}{q}\right)\left(1 - \frac{2}{q}\right)^{\Delta} + \frac{1}{2}\left(1 - \frac{2}{q}\right)^{\Delta-1}\sum_{\ell=1}^{\infty}\Delta^{\ell}\left(\frac{2}{q}\right)^{\ell} \\
&= 1 - \left(1 - \frac{\Delta}{q}\right)\left(1 - \frac{2}{q}\right)^{\Delta} + \frac{\Delta}{q - 2\Delta}\left(1 - \frac{2}{q}\right)^{\Delta-1}.
\end{aligned}$$

The path coupling argument holds when this quantity is less than 1. For $q = \alpha^\star\Delta$ and $\Delta \to \infty$, this quantity becomes

$$1 - \mathrm{e}^{-2/\alpha^\star}\left(1 - \frac{1}{\alpha^\star} - \frac{1}{\alpha^\star - 2}\right),$$

which is less than 1 if $\alpha^\star > 2 + \sqrt{2}$.

For general graphs, it is easier to show the following weaker result by a simpler coupling.

THEOREM 4.4. *If $q \geq \alpha\Delta + 3$ for a constant $\alpha > \alpha^*$, where $\alpha^* \approx 3.634\ldots$ satisfies $\alpha^* = 2\mathrm{e}^{1/\alpha^*} + 1$, the mixing rate of the* LocalMetropolis *chain for proper $q$-coloring on graphs with maximum degree at most $\Delta = \Delta(n)$ is $\tau(\epsilon) = O\left(\log\left(\frac{n}{\epsilon}\right)\right)$, where the constant factor in $O(\cdot)$ depends only on $\alpha$ but not on $\Delta$.*

In the full version of the paper, Theorem 4.2 is proved by combining this weaker result with a mixing rate upper bound $\tau(\epsilon) = O\left(\log\left(\frac{n}{\epsilon}\right)\right)$ that holds for the regime $\alpha\Delta \leq q \leq 3.7\Delta + 3$ for an arbitrary constant $\alpha > 2 + \sqrt{2}$. The latter result is proved by a coupling which generalizes the above ideal coupling for the $\Delta$-regular tree to general graphs, whose analysis is very involved, which basically shows that the $\Delta$-regular tree represents the worst case for path coupling.

PROOF OF THEOREM 4.4. We use the following slightly modified pre-metric: A pair $(X, Y) \in \Omega = [q]^V$ is connected by an edge in the pre-metric if and only if $X$ and $Y$ differ at only one vertex, say $v$, and the edge-weight is given by $\deg(v)$. Based on this pre-metric, we introduce the following definition of distance. For any $X', Y' \in \Omega$, for $u \in V$, define $\phi_u(X', Y') = \deg(u)$ if $X'_u \neq Y'_u$ and $\phi_u(X', Y') = 0$ if otherwise; and for $S \subseteq V$, we define the distance between $X'$ and $Y'$ on $S$ as

$$\Phi_S(X', Y') := \sum_{u \in S: X'_u \neq Y'_u} \phi_u(X', Y').$$

And we denote $\Phi(X', Y') = \Phi_V(X', Y')$. Clearly, the diameter of $\Omega$ in distance $\Phi$ has $\mathrm{diam}(\Omega) \leq n\Delta$.

Let $X, Y \in [q]^V$ two $q$-colorings, not necessarily proper. Assume that $X$ and $Y$ disagree only at vertex $v_0 \in V$. The coupling rule is as follows:

- Each vertex $v \in V$ proposes the same random color in the two chains $X$ and $Y$. Then $(X', Y')$ is determined due to the transition rule of *LocalMetropolis* chain.

Unlike in the ideal coupling, in this simple coupling, within one step the disagreement at $v_0$ can only percolate to its neighbors but no further. Next we show the path coupling condition:

$$\mathbf{E}[\Phi(X', Y') \mid X, Y] \leq (1 - \delta)\Phi(X, Y) = (1 - \delta)\deg(v_0).$$

First, observe that if $v \notin \Gamma^+(v_0)$, where $v_0$ is the vertex at which $X$ and $Y$ disagree, then it always holds that $X'_v = Y'_v$, because all vertices except $v_0$ are colored the same in $X$ and $Y$ and will propose the same random color in the two chains due to the coupling. Therefore, it is sufficient to consider the difference between $X'$ and $Y'$ in $\Gamma^+(v_0)$ and we have

$$\Phi(X', Y') = \Phi_{\Gamma^+(v_0)}(X', Y').$$

For each $v$, let $c_v \in [q]$ be the uniform random color proposed independently by $v$, which is identical in both chains by the coupling. For the disagreeing vertex $v_0$, it holds that $X'_{v_0} = Y'_{v_0}$ if $v_0$ accepts the proposal in both chains, which occurs when $c_{v_0} \notin \{X_u, Y_u : u \in \Gamma(v_0)\}$ and $\forall u \in \Gamma(v_0), c_u \notin \{X_{v_0}, Y_{v_0}, c_{v_0}\}$. Since $X$ and $Y$ disagree only at $v_0$, we have

$$\Pr[X'_{v_0} = Y'_{v_0} \mid X, Y] \geq \left(1 - \frac{d_{v_0}}{q}\right)\left(1 - \frac{3}{q}\right)^{d_{v_0}}. \tag{4}$$

For each $u \in \Gamma(v_0)$, since $X_u = Y_u$, the event $X'_u \neq Y'_u$ occurs only when $c_u \in \{X_{v_0}, Y_{v_0}\}$ and $\forall w \in \Gamma(u), c_w \notin \{X_u, c_u\}$. Note that to guarantee $X'_u \neq Y'_u$ one must have $c_u \neq X_u$, thus

$$\forall u \in \Gamma(v_0): \quad \Pr[X'_u \neq Y'_u \mid X, Y] \leq \frac{2}{q}\left(1 - \frac{2}{q}\right)^{d_u}. \tag{5}$$

Combining (4) and (5) together and due to linearity of expectation, we have

$$\begin{aligned}
\mathbf{E}\left[\Phi(X', Y') \mid X, Y\right] &= \sum_{u \in V}\mathbf{E}\left[\phi_u(X', Y') \mid X, Y\right] \\
&= \sum_{u \in \Gamma^+(v_0)} d_u \Pr\left[X'_u \neq Y'_u \mid X, Y\right] \\
&\leq d_{v_0}\left[1 - \left(1 - \frac{d_{v_0}}{q}\right)\left(1 - \frac{3}{q}\right)^{d_{v_0}}\right] + \frac{2}{q}\sum_{u \in \Gamma(v_0)} d_u\left(1 - \frac{2}{q}\right)^{d_u} \\
&\leq d_{v_0}\left[1 - \left(1 - \frac{\Delta}{q}\right)\left(1 - \frac{3}{q}\right)^{\Delta} + \frac{2\Delta}{q}\left(1 - \frac{2}{q}\right)^{\Delta}\right].
\end{aligned}$$

where the last inequality holds when $q \geq 2\Delta$.

The path coupling condition is satisfied when

$$\left(1 - \frac{\Delta}{q}\right)\left(1 - \frac{3}{q}\right)^{\Delta} - \frac{2\Delta}{q}\left(1 - \frac{2}{q}\right)^{\Delta} \geq \delta. \tag{6}$$

For $q = \alpha^*\Delta$ and $\Delta \to \infty$, the LHS becomes

$$\left(1 - \frac{1}{\alpha^*}\right)\mathrm{e}^{-3/\alpha^*} - \frac{2}{\alpha}\mathrm{e}^{-2/\alpha^*},$$

which is 0 when $\alpha^*$ is the positive root of $\alpha^* = 2e^{1/\alpha^*} + 1$.

Furthermore, for $\Delta \geq 1$ and $q \geq \alpha\Delta + 3$, the LHS become:

$$\left(1-\frac{3}{q}\right)^{\Delta}\left[1-\frac{\Delta}{q}-\frac{2\Delta}{q}\left(1+\frac{1}{q-3}\right)^{\Delta}\right]$$
$$\geq \left(1-\frac{3}{\alpha\Delta+3}\right)^{\Delta}\left[1-\frac{1}{\alpha}-\frac{2}{\alpha}\left(1+\frac{1}{\alpha\Delta}\right)^{\Delta}\right]$$
$$\geq \frac{e^{-3/\alpha}}{\alpha}(\alpha - 2e^{1/\alpha} - 1),$$

which is a positive constant independent of $\Delta$ when $\alpha > \alpha^*$.

Therefore, when $\alpha > \alpha^*$, there is a constant $\delta > 0$ which depends only on $\alpha$, such that for all $\Delta \geq 1$ and $q \geq \alpha\Delta + 3$, the inequality (6) is satisfied, which by Lemma 4.3, gives us $\tau(\epsilon) = O\left(\log\left(\frac{n}{\epsilon}\right)\right)$. □

# 5 LOWER BOUNDS

In this section, we show lower bounds for local sampling. Let $G(V, E)$ be a network, and $\mathcal{I}$ an instance of MRF or weighted local CSP defined on graph $G$. For example, $\mathcal{I} = (G, [q], \boldsymbol{A}, \boldsymbol{b})$ for a MRF with edge activities $\boldsymbol{A} = \{A_e\}_{e\in E}$ and vertex activities $\boldsymbol{b} = \{b_v\}_{v\in V}$.

We assume that each vertex $v \in V$ may access to an independent random variable $\Psi_v$ as its source of randomness. Then a $t$-round protocol specifies a family of functions $\Pi_{v,\mathcal{I}}$, such that for each vertex $v \in V$, the output $X_v$ is produced as

$$X_v = \Pi_{v,\mathcal{I}}(\Psi_u, u \in B_t(v)),$$

where $B_t(v) = \{u \in V \mid \mathrm{dist}(u, v) \leq t\}$ represents the $t$-ball centered at $v$. Let $\mu_{\mathrm{out}}$ denote the distribution of the output random vector $\boldsymbol{X} = (X_v)_{v\in V}$. The goal is to have $d_{\mathrm{TV}}(\mu_{\mathrm{out}}, \mu) \leq \epsilon$, where $\mu = \mu_{\mathcal{I}}$ is the Gibbs distribution defined by the MRF instance $\mathcal{I}$.

Note that in above we allow the protocol $\Pi_{v,\mathcal{I}}$ executed at each vertex $v \in V$ to be aware of the instance $\mathcal{I}$ of the MRF. This is much stronger than the original LOCAL model. In fact, the only locality property we are using to prove our lower bounds is that for any $\boldsymbol{X} = (X_v)_{v\in V}$ returned by a $t$-round protocol:

$$\forall u, v \in V: \ dist(u, v) > 2t \implies X_u \text{ and } X_v \text{ are independent.} \quad (7)$$

The lower bounds implied by this property is due to the locality of randomness.

The following natural lower bound shows that the $O\left(\log\left(\frac{n}{\epsilon}\right)\right)$ upper bound in Theorem 1.2 is optimal.

THEOREM 5.1. *Let $q \geq 3$ be a constant and $\exp(-o(n)) < \epsilon < \frac{1}{3}$. Any $t$-round protocol that samples uniform proper $q$-coloring in a path within total variation distance $\epsilon$ must have $t = \Omega\left(\log\left(\frac{n}{\epsilon}\right)\right)$.*

This lower bound actually holds for all MRFs satisfying an exponential correlation property stated as follows: There exist constants $\delta, \eta > 0$ such that for a path $P$ of length $n$, for any non-adjacent vertices $x, u, v, y$ in the path from left to right, any spin states $\sigma_x, \sigma_y \in [q]$, there exist two spin states $\sigma_u, \sigma'_u \in [q]$ such that $\mu_u(\sigma_u \mid \sigma_x, \sigma_y) \geq \delta$, $\mu_u(\sigma'_u \mid \sigma_x, \sigma_y) \geq \delta$ and

$$d_{\mathrm{TV}}\left(\mu_v(\cdot \mid \sigma_u, \sigma_x, \sigma_y), \mu_v(\cdot \mid \sigma'_u, \sigma_x, \sigma_y)\right) \geq \eta^{\mathrm{dist}(u,v)}. \quad (8)$$

It can be verified by a simple recursion for marginal probabilities in paths [40] that this property is satisfied for uniform proper $q$-colorings in paths for any constant $q \geq 3$.

Next, we state a strong $\Omega(\mathrm{diam})$ lower bound for sampling with long-range correlations.

We consider the weighted independent sets of graphs, the *hardcore model*. Given a graph $G(V, E)$ and a *fugacity* parameter $\lambda > 0$, each configuration $\sigma$ in

$$\mathrm{IS}(G) = \left\{\sigma \in \{0, 1\}^V : \forall(u, v) \in E, \sigma_u\sigma_v = 0\right\}$$

indicates an independent set $I$ in $G$ and is assigned a weight $w(\sigma) = \lambda^{|I|}$. The Gibbs distribution $\mu = \mu_G$ is defined over all independent sets in $G$ proportional to their weights. As discussed in Section 2, the model is an MRF.

The hardcore model on graphs with maximum degree $\Delta$ undergoes a computational phase transition at the *uniqueness threshold* $\lambda_c(\Delta) = \frac{(\Delta-1)^{\Delta-1}}{(\Delta-2)^{\Delta}}$, such that sampling from the Gibbs distribution can be done in polynomial time in the *uniqueness regime* $\lambda < \lambda_c$ [18, 56] and is intractable unless NP=RP in the *non-uniqueness regime* $\lambda > \lambda_c$ [23, 51, 52]

The following theorem states an $\Omega(\mathrm{diam})$ lower bound for sampling from the hardcore model in the non-uniqueness regime. In particular when $\lambda = 1$ the model represents the uniform independent sets and the non-uniqueness $\lambda > \lambda_c(\Delta)$ holds when $\Delta \geq 6$, which gives us Theorem 1.3.

THEOREM 5.2. *Let $\Delta \geq 3$ and $\lambda > \lambda_c(\Delta)$. Let $\epsilon > 0$ be a sufficiently small constant. For all $N > 0$ there exists a graph $\mathcal{G}$ on $\Theta(N)$ vertices with maximum degree $\Delta$ and diameter $\mathrm{diam}(\mathcal{G}) = \widetilde{\Omega}(\sqrt{N})$ such that for the hardcore model on $\mathcal{G}$ with fugacity $\lambda$, any $t$-round protocol that samples within total variation distance $\epsilon$ from the Gibbs distribution $\mu = \mu_{\mathcal{G}}$ must have $t = \Omega(\mathrm{diam}(\mathcal{G}))$.*

We follow the approaches in [22, 23, 51, 52] for the computational phase transition. The network $\mathcal{G} = H^G$ is constructed by lifting a graph $H$ with a gadget $G$, such that sampling from the hardcore model on $H^G$ with $\lambda > \lambda_c(\Delta)$ effectively samples a maximum cut in $H$. We choose $H$ to be an even cycle, in which the maximum cut imposes a long-range correlation among vertices. And to sample with such a long-range correlation, the sampling algorithm must not be local.

Unlike the results of [22, 23, 51, 52] which are for computational complexity of approximate counting, here we prove unconditional lower bounds for sampling in the LOCAL model. Our lower bound is due to the long-range correlations in the random max-cut rather than the computational complexity of optimization. Technical-wise, this means that in addition to show that a max-cut in $H$ is sampled, we also need that the sampled max-cut is distributed almost uniformly.

*The random bipartite gadget.* We now describe the random bipartite graph gadget which is essential to the hardness of sampling. For positive integers $n, k$ and $\Delta$ where $n > 2k$, let $\mathcal{G}_n^k$ be the random bipartite (multi-)graph constructed as follows:

- Let $V^+$ and $V^-$ be two vertex sets with $|V^+| = |V^-| = n$, such that $V^\pm = U^\pm \uplus W^\pm$ where $|U^\pm| = n-k$ and $|W^\pm| = k$. Let $V = V^+ \cup V^-$ and $W = W^+ \cup W^-$. The vertices in $W$ are called "terminals".
- Uniformly and independently sample $\Delta - 1$ perfect matchings between $V^+$ and $V^-$ and then uniformly and independently sample a perfect matching between $U^+$ and $U^-$. The

union of all these matchings gives us the random bipartite (multi-)graph $\mathcal{G}_n^k$, in which every vertex in $U$ has degree $\Delta$ and every terminal in $W$ has degree $\Delta - 1$.

The *phase* of a configuration $\sigma \in \{0,1\}^V$, denoted as $Y(\sigma)$, is defined as

$$Y(\sigma) := \begin{cases} + & \text{if } \sum_{v \in V^+} \sigma_v > \sum_{v \in V^-} \sigma_v, \\ - & \text{if } \sum_{v \in V^+} \sigma_v < \sum_{v \in V^-} \sigma_v. \end{cases}$$

It is easy to see that $\mathcal{G}_n^k$ is an expander with high probability. And when $k = o(n)$, the sequence $\mathcal{G}_n^k$ of random graphs converge locally to the parity-labeled infinite $\Delta$-regular tree $\mathbb{T}_\Delta$, in the sense as defined in [52, Definitions 1.1 & 1.3]. The following proposition was proved in [52, Lemma 3.1 & Proposition 4.1].

Proposition 5.3 (Sly and Sun [52]). *If $\lambda > \lambda_c(\Delta) = \frac{(\Delta-1)^{\Delta-1}}{(\Delta-2)^\Delta}$ then there exist two constants $0 < q^- < q^+ < 1$ such that the followings hold. Let $Q_W^\pm$ denote the product measure on configurations in $\{0,1\}^W$ so that the spin states are i.i.d. Bernoulli with probability $q^\pm$ on $W^+$ and $q^\mp$ on $W^-$, that is:*

$$Q_W^\pm(\sigma_W) = \left(q^\pm\right)^{\sum_{w\in W^+}\sigma_w}\left(1-q^\pm\right)^{|W^+|-\sum_{w\in W^+}\sigma_w} \cdot \left(q^\mp\right)^{\sum_{w\in W^-}\sigma_w}\left(1-q^\mp\right)^{|W^-|-\sum_{w\in W^-}\sigma_w}.$$

*For any $\delta > 0$, there exists sufficiently large constant $N_0(\delta)$ such that for all $n > N_0(\delta)$ and $k = o(n)$ the followings hold altogether with positive probability for $G \sim \mathcal{G}_n^k$:*

- *(expander) $G$ is connected with $\mathrm{diam}(G) = O(\log n)$;*
- *(balanced phases) $\Pr_G[Y(\sigma) = \pm] \in [(1-\delta)/2, (1+\delta)/2]$;*
- *(phase-correlated almost independence) $\forall \tau_W \in \{0,1\}^W$, $\Pr_G[\sigma_W = \tau_W \mid Y(\sigma) = \pm] / Q_W^\pm(\tau_W) \in [1-\delta, 1+\delta]$;*

*where $\Pr_G$ is the probability law for $\sigma$ sampled from $\mu_G$.*

*By the probabilistic method, there exists a $G$ satisfying the above conditions.*

*Reduction from Max-Cut.* Let $H$ be a cycle with $m$ vertices where $m > 0$ is an even integer. Let $G \in \mathcal{G}_n^{2k}$, with $n = \Theta(m(\log m)^2)$ and $k = \Theta(m \log m) = o(n)$, be the graph that satisfies the conditions in Proposition 5.3.

- For each vertex $x \in H$ let $G_x$ be a copy of $G$. We denote by $W_x^\pm$ the respective set of $2k$ terminals in $G_x$. Let $\widehat{H}^G$ be the disconnected copies of the $G_x$, $x \in H$.
- For every edge $(x,y) \in H$, add $k$ edges between $W_x^+$ and $W_y^+$ and similarly add $k$ edges between $W_x^-$ and $W_y^-$. This can be done in such a way that the resulting (multi-)graph $H^G$ is $\Delta$-regular.

For each $x \in H$, we write $Y_x = Y_x(\sigma)$ for the phase of a configuration $\sigma$ on $G_x$. Let $\mathcal{Y} = (Y_x)_{x\in H} \in \{+,-\}^{V(H)}$. We also use $\Pr_{H^G}$ to represent the probability law for $\sigma$ sampled from $\mu_{H^G}$. Note that the cycle $H$ has precisely two maximum cuts. A key property for proving the lower bound is that in the non-uniqueness regime, sampling from the hardcore model on graph $H^G$ corresponds to sampling a maximum cut in $H$ almost uniformly, which is proved by applying a calculation in [51] with the improved gadget property Proposition 5.3.

Theorem 5.4. *Let $\lambda > \lambda_c(\Delta)$. Let $\mathcal{Y}_1, \mathcal{Y}_2 \in \{+,-\}^{V(H)}$ correspond respectively to the two maximum cuts in $H$. It holds that:*

$$\Pr_{H^G}[\mathcal{Y}(\sigma) = \mathcal{Y}_1] = \Pr_{H^G}[\mathcal{Y}(\sigma) = \mathcal{Y}_2] \ge \frac{1}{2} - o(1). \quad (9)$$

Theorem 5.2 can then be proved as follows. Let $N$ be sufficiently large. We choose an integer $n = \Theta\left(\sqrt{N}\log N\right)$ and an even integer $m = \Theta\left(\sqrt{N}/\log N\right)$ such that $m/2$ is odd. Let $G$ be a gadget satisfying Proposition 5.3, $H$ a cycle of length $m$, and $\mathcal{G} = H^G$ constructed as described earlier. Note that $\mathrm{diam}(\mathcal{G}) \ge \mathrm{diam}(H) \ge m/2$ and $|V(\mathcal{G})| = \Theta(N)$, therefore $\mathrm{diam}(\mathcal{G}) = \widetilde{\Omega}(\sqrt{N})$.

Let $\sigma'$ denote the output of a $t$-round protocol on network $\mathcal{G}$ with $t \le 0.49 \cdot \mathrm{diam}(\mathcal{G})$, whose distribution is denoted as $\mu_t$; and let $\sigma$ be sampled from the hardcore Gibbs distribution $\mu = \mu_{\mathcal{G}}$. By contradiction, we assume that $d_{\mathrm{TV}}(\mu_t, \mu) \le \epsilon$ for sufficiently small constant $\epsilon$.

Let $\mathcal{Y}', \mathcal{Y}'' \in \{+,-\}^{V(H)}$ denote the phases corresponding to the two maximum cuts in the cycle $H$. Therefore, by Theorem 5.4, we have

$$\Pr[\mathcal{Y}(\sigma) \in \{\mathcal{Y}', \mathcal{Y}''\}] \ge 1 - o(1).$$

We pick $u, v \in V(\mathcal{G})$ satisfying that $\mathrm{dist}_{\mathcal{G}}(u,v) = \mathrm{diam}(\mathcal{G})$. Since $\mathcal{G} = H^G$ is constructed by replacing each vertex $x$ in $H$ with $G_x$ which is an identical copy of $G$, it must hold that $u \in G_x, v \in G_y$ for some vertices $x, y$ in $H$ with $\mathrm{dist}_H(x,y) = m/2$. And since $m/2$ is odd, without loss of generality, we suppose that $Y'_x = +, Y'_y = -$ and $Y''_x = -, Y''_y = +$. Moreover, for all $u' \in G_x, v' \in G_y$, by the triangle inequality we have:

$$\mathrm{dist}_{\mathcal{G}}(u,u') + \mathrm{dist}_{\mathcal{G}}(u',v') + \mathrm{dist}_{\mathcal{G}}(v',v) \ge \mathrm{diam}(\mathcal{G}).$$

Due to Proposition 5.3, it holds that $\mathrm{diam}(G) = O(\log n)$, thus we have:

$$\mathrm{dist}_{\mathcal{G}}(u',v') \ge \mathrm{diam}(\mathcal{G}) - O(\log n) = (1-o(1))\mathrm{diam}(\mathcal{G}).$$

For the $\sigma'$ returned by a $t$-round protocol where $t \le 0.49 \cdot \mathrm{diam}(\mathcal{G})$, according to the property (7), the $\sigma'_{G_x}$ and $\sigma'_{G_y}$ are independent of each other, thus the phases of $G_x$ and $G_y$ on $\sigma'$ are independent of each other:

$$\Pr\left[Y_x(\sigma') = + \mid Y_y(\sigma') = -\right] = \Pr\left[Y_x(\sigma') = + \mid Y_y(\sigma') = +\right]. \quad (10)$$

On the other hand, since $d_{\mathrm{TV}}(\sigma', \sigma) \le \epsilon$, we have

$$\begin{aligned} &\Pr\left[Y_x(\sigma') = + \mid Y_y(\sigma') = -\right] \\ &= \frac{\Pr\left[Y_x(\sigma') = + \wedge Y_y(\sigma') = -\right]}{\Pr\left[Y_y(\sigma') = -\right]} \\ &\ge \frac{\Pr\left[Y_x(\sigma) = + \wedge Y_y(\sigma) = -\right] - \epsilon}{\Pr\left[Y_y(\sigma) = -\right] + \epsilon} \qquad (\text{by } d_{\mathrm{TV}}(\sigma', \sigma) \le \epsilon) \\ &\ge \frac{\Pr[\mathcal{Y}(\sigma) = \mathcal{Y}'] - \epsilon}{\Pr\left[Y_y(\sigma) = -\right] + \epsilon} \\ &\ge \frac{1/2 - o(1) - \epsilon}{\Pr[\mathcal{Y}(\sigma) \ne \mathcal{Y}''] + \epsilon} \ge \frac{1 - 2\epsilon - o(1)}{1 + 2\epsilon + o(1)}. \qquad (\text{by Theorem 5.4}) \end{aligned}$$

Similarly, we can show that

$$\Pr\left[Y_x(\sigma') = + \mid Y_y(\sigma') = +\right] \le \frac{2\epsilon + o(1)}{1 - 2\epsilon - o(1)}.$$

By taking $\epsilon$ to be a sufficiently small constant, we have

$$\Pr\left[Y_x(\sigma') = + \mid Y_y(\sigma') = +\right] < \Pr\left[Y_x(\sigma') = + \mid Y_y(\sigma') = -\right],$$

which contradicts the independence given in (10).

# 6 ACKNOWLEDGMENT

Yitong Yin wants to thank Daniel Štefankovič for the stimulating discussions in the beginning of this project. He also wants to thank Heng Guo, Tom Hayes, Eric Vigoda, and Chaodong Zheng for helpful discussions.

# REFERENCES


[1] Noga Alon, László Babai, and Alon Itai. 1986. A fast and simple randomized parallel algorithm for the maximal independent set problem. *Journal of Algorithms* 7, 4 (1986), 567–583.

[2] Baruch Awerbuch, Michael Luby, Andrew V Goldberg, and Serge A Plotkin. 1989. Network decomposition and locality in distributed computation. In *FOCS'89*.

[3] Leonid Barenboim. 2016. Deterministic (Δ+ 1)-coloring in sublinear (in Δ) time in static, dynamic, and faulty networks. *JACM* 63, 5 (2016), 47:1–47:22.

[4] Leonid Barenboim and Michael Elkin. 2011. Deterministic distributed vertex coloring in polylogarithmic time. *JACM* 58, 5 (2011), 23:1–23:25.

[5] Leonid Barenboim, Michael Elkin, Seth Pettie, and Johannes Schneider. 2016. The locality of distributed symmetry breaking. *JACM* 63, 3 (2016), 20:1–20:45.

[6] Russ Bubley and Martin Dyer. 1997. Path coupling: a technique for proving rapid mixing in Markov chains. In *FOCS'97*.

[7] Jin-Yi Cai, Xi Chen, and Pinyan Lu. 2016. Nonnegative weighted# CSP: an effective complexity dichotomy. *SICOMP* 45, 6 (2016), 2177–2198.

[8] Ben Calderhead. 2014. A general construction for parallelizing Metropolis-Hastings algorithms. *PNAS* 111, 49 (2014), 17408–17413.

[9] Yi-Jun Chang, Tsvi Kopelowitz, and Seth Pettie. 2016. An exponential separation between randomized and deterministic Complexity in the LOCAL Model. In *FOCS'16*.

[10] Kai-Min Chung, Seth Pettie, and Hsin-Hao Su. 2014. Distributed algorithms for the Lovász Local Lemma and graph coloring. In *PODC'14*.

[11] Atish Das Sarma, Danupon Nanongkai, Gopal Pandurangan, and Prasad Tetali. 2013. Distributed random walks. *JACM* 60, 1 (2013), 2:1–2:31.

[12] Christopher De Sa, Kunle Olukotun, and Christopher Ré. 2016. Ensuring rapid mixing and low bias for asynchronous Gibbs sampling. In *ICML'16*.

[13] Christopher De Sa, Ce Zhang, Kunle Olukotun, and Christopher Ré. 2015. Rapidly mixing Gibbs sampling for a class of factor graphs using hierarchy width. In *NIPS'15*.

[14] Roland L Dobrushin. 1970. Prescribing a system of random variables by conditional distributions. *Theory of Probability & Its Applications* 15, 3 (1970), 458–486.

[15] Finale Doshi-Velez, Shakir Mohamed, Zoubin Ghahramani, and David A Knowles. 2009. Large Scale Nonparametric Bayesian Inference: Data Parallelisation in the Indian Buffet Process. In *NIPS'09*.

[16] Martin Dyer, Leslie Ann Goldberg, and Mark Jerrum. 2006. Systematic scan for sampling colorings. *The Annals of Applied Probability* 16, 1 (2006), 185–230.

[17] Martin Dyer, Leslie Ann Goldberg, and Mark Jerrum. 2008. Dobrushin conditions and systematic scan. *Combinatorics, Probability & Computing* 17, 6 (2008), 761–779.

[18] Charilaos Efthymiou, Thomas P Hayes, Daniel Štefankovič, Eric Vigoda, and Yitong Yin. 2016. Convergence of MCMC and loopy BP in the tree uniqueness region for the hard-core model. In *FOCS'16*.

[19] Pierre Fraigniaud, Marc Heinrich, and Adrian Kosowski. 2016. Local conflict coloring. In *FOCS'16*.

[20] Pierre Fraigniaud, Amos Korman, and David Peleg. 2013. Towards a complexity theory for local distributed computing. *JACM* 60, 5 (2013), 35:1–35:26.

[21] Alan Frieze and Eric Vigoda. 2007. A Survey on the Use of Markov Chains to Randomly Sample Colourings. *Oxford Lecture Series in Mathematics and its Applications* 34 (2007), 53.

[22] Andreas Galanis, Daniel Štefankovič, and Eric Vigoda. 2015. Inapproximability for antiferromagnetic spin systems in the tree nonuniqueness region. *JACM* 62, 6 (2015), 50:1–50:60.

[23] Andreas Galanis, Daniel Štefankovič, and Eric Vigoda. 2016. Inapproximability of the partition function for the antiferromagnetic Ising and hard-core models. *Combinatorics, Probability and Computing* 25, 04 (2016), 500–559.

[24] Mohsen Ghaffari. 2016. An improved distributed algorithm for maximal independent set. In *SODA'16*.

[25] Mohsen Ghaffari, Fabian Kuhn, and Yannic Maus. 2017. On the complexity of local distributed graph problems. In *STOC'17*.

[26] Mohsen Ghaffari and Hsin-Hao Su. 2017. Distributed degree splitting, edge coloring, and orientations. In *SODA'17*.

[27] Joseph E Gonzalez, Yucheng Low, Arthur Gretton, and Carlos Guestrin. 2011. Parallel Gibbs sampling: from colored fields to thin junction trees. In *AISTATS'11*.

[28] Heng. Guo, Mark Jerrum, and Jingcheng Liu. 2017. Uniform Sampling through the Lovász Local Lemma. In *STOC'17*.

[29] David G Harris, Johannes Schneider, and Hsin-Hao Su. 2016. Distributed (Δ + 1)-coloring in sublogarithmic rounds. In *STOC'16*.

[30] Thomas P Hayes. 2006. A simple condition implying rapid mixing of single-site dynamics on spin systems. In *FOCS'06*.

[31] Alexander E Holroyd, Oded Schramm, and David B Wilson. 2014. Finitary coloring. *ArXiv e-prints* (2014). arXiv:1412.2725

[32] Mark Jerrum. 1995. A very simple algorithm for estimating the number of $k$-colorings of a low-degree graph. *Random Structures & Algorithms* 7, 2 (1995), 157–165.

[33] Matthew J Johnson, James Saunderson, and Alan S Willsky. 2013. Analyzing Hogwild parallel Gaussian Gibbs sampling. In *NIPS'13*.

[34] Fabian Kuhn, Thomas Moscibroda, and Roger Wattenhofer. 2004. What cannot be computed locally!. In *PODC'04*.

[35] Fabian Kuhn, Thomas Moscibroda, and Roger Wattenhofer. 2006. The price of being near-sighted. In *SODA'06*.

[36] Fabian Kuhn, Thomas Moscibroda, and Roger Wattenhofer. 2016. Local computation: Lower and upper bounds. *JACM* 63, 2 (2016), 17:1–17:44.

[37] Fabian Kuhn and Roger Wattenhofer. 2006. On the complexity of distributed graph coloring. In *PODC'06*.

[38] David Asher Levin, Yuval Peres, and Elizabeth Lee Wilmer. 2009. *Markov chains and mixing times*. American Mathematical Soc.

[39] Nathan Linial. 1987. Locality in distributed graph algorithms. In *FOCS'87*.

[40] Pinyan Lu and Yitong Yin. 2013. Improved FPTAS for multi-spin systems. In *RANDOM'13*.

[41] Michael Luby. 1986. A simple parallel algorithm for the maximal independent set problem. *SICOMP* 15, 4 (1986), 1036–1053.

[42] Dániel Marx. 2004. Graph colouring problems and their applications in scheduling. *Periodica Polytechnica Electrical Engineering* 48, 1-2 (2004), 11–16.

[43] Marc Mezard and Andrea Montanari. 2009. *Information, physics, and computation*. Oxford University Press.

[44] Robin A Moser and Gábor Tardos. 2010. A constructive proof of the general Lovász Local Lemma. *JACM* 57, 2 (2010), 11:1–11:15.

[45] Moni Naor and Larry Stockmeyer. 1993. What Can be Computed Locally?. In *STOC'93*.

[46] David Newman, Arthur Asuncion, Padhraic Smyth, and Max Welling. 2007. Distributed inference for latent Dirichlet allocation. In *NIPS'07*.

[47] Feng Niu, Benjamin Recht, Christopher Ré, and Stephen J Wright. 2011. Hogwild: A lock-free approach to parallelizing stochastic gradient descent. In *NIPS'11*.

[48] David Peleg. 2000. *Distributed computing: a locality-sensitive approach*. SIAM.

[49] Jesús Salas and Alan D Sokal. 1997. Absence of phase transition for antiferromagnetic Potts models via the Dobrushin uniqueness theorem. *Journal of Statistical Physics* 86, 3 (1997), 551–579.

[50] Atish Das Sarma, Stephan Holzer, Liah Kor, Amos Korman, Danupon Nanongkai, Gopal Pandurangan, David Peleg, and Roger Wattenhofer. 2012. Distributed verification and hardness of distributed approximation. *SICOMP* 41, 5 (2012), 1235–1265.

[51] Allan Sly. 2010. Computational transition at the uniqueness threshold. In *FOCS'10*.

[52] Allan Sly and Nike Sun. 2014. Counting in two-spin models on $d$-regular graphs. *The Annals of Probability* 42, 6 (2014), 2383–2416.

[53] Padhraic Smyth, Max Welling, and Arthur U Asuncion. 2009. Asynchronous distributed learning of topic models. In *NIPS'09*.

[54] Robert H Swendsen and Jian-Sheng Wang. 1986. Replica Monte Carlo simulation of spin-glasses. *Physical Review Letters* 57, 21 (1986), 2607.

[55] Eric Vigoda. 2000. Improved bounds for sampling colorings. *J. Math. Phys.* 41, 3 (2000), 1555–1569.

[56] Dror Weitz. 2006. Counting independent sets up to the tree threshold. In *STOC'06*.

[57] Minjie Xu, Balaji Lakshminarayanan, Yee Whye Teh, Jun Zhu, and Bo Zhang. 2014. Distributed Bayesian posterior sampling via moment sharing. In *NIPS'14*.

[58] Feng Yan, Ningyi Xu, and Yuan Qi. 2009. Parallel inference for latent Dirichlet allocation on graphics processing units. In *NIPS'09*.

[59] Yuan Yang, Jianfei Chen, and Jun Zhu. 2016. Distributing the stochastic gradient sampler for large-scale LDA. In *KDD'16*.

# Distributed MST and Routing in Almost Mixing Time

Mohsen Ghaffari
ETH Zurich, Switzerland
ghaffari@inf.ethz.ch

Fabian Kuhn
University of Freiburg, Germany
kuhn@cs.uni-freiburg.de

Hsin-Hao Su
MIT, USA
hsinhao@mit.edu

## ABSTRACT

We present a randomized distributed algorithm that computes a minimum spanning tree in $\tau_{\text{mix}}(G) \cdot 2^{O(\sqrt{\log n \log\log n})}$ rounds, in any $n$-node graph $G$ with mixing time $\tau_{\text{mix}}(G)$. This result provides a sub-polynomial complexity for a wide range of graphs of practical interest, and goes below the celebrated $\tilde{\Omega}(D + \sqrt{n})$ lower bound of Das Sarma et al. [STOC'11] which holds for some worst-case general graphs.

The core novelty in this result is a distributed method for *permutation routing*. In this problem, one is given a number of source-destination pairs, and we should deliver one packet from each source to its destination, all in parallel, in the shortest span of time possible. Our algorithm allows us to route and deliver all these packets in $\tau_{\text{mix}}(G) \cdot 2^{O(\sqrt{\log n \log\log n})}$ rounds, assuming that each node $v$ is the source or destination for at most $d_G(v)$ packets. The main technical ingredient in this routing result is a certain *hierarchical embedding of good-expansion random graphs* on the base graph, which we believe can be of interest well beyond this work.

## CCS CONCEPTS

• **Theory of computation → Distributed algorithms**;

## KEYWORDS

Distributed Graph Algorithms; CONGEST Model; Routing; Minimum Spanning Tree

## 1 INTRODUCTION & RELATED WORK

We present a distributed algorithm for computing a *minimum spanning tree* (MST) with a time complexity close to the network's *mixing time*. The core technical novelty in this result is the introduction of a certain hierarchical routing structure, which we believe will pave the road towards achieving a similar time complexity for a wider range of graph problems.

Throughout, we work with the standard CONGEST model of distributed computation: the network is abstracted as an $n$-node graph $G = (V, E)$. Initially each node knows only its own edges. Per synchronous round, each node can send an $O(\log n)$-bit message to each of its neighbors.


*PODC '17, July 25 27, 2017, Washington, DC, USA*

ACM ISBN 978-1-4503-4992-5/17/07...\$15.00
https://doi.org/10.1145/3087801.3087827

**Background**: The MST problem has played a central role in *distributed graph algorithms*, by providing a setup for developing new algorithmic or impossibility techniques, which were then extended to other problems. The work on distributed MST computations started with the seminal algorithm of Gallager, Humblet, and Spira [28], which has time complexity $O(n \log n)$ and which itself is a variant of the 1926 algorithm of Boruvka [58]. The time complexity was gradually improved [15, 27], eventually leading to the "*optimal*" algorithm of Awerbuch, which has time complexity $O(n)$ [7]. A round complexity of $O(n)$ was usually treated as optimal, because there are graphs of diameter $D = \Omega(n)$ on which one cannot do better (e.g., the $n$-node cycle).

Starting with the pioneering work of Garay, Kutten and Peleg [29, 44], the area took a turn, and moved towards seeking sublinear time algorithms, when this "excuse" of graphs with $D = \Omega(n)$ is ruled out. In particular, an $O(D + n^{0.61})$-round MST algorithm was presented in [29], which was subsequently improved in [44] to $O(D + \sqrt{n} \log^* n)$. This $\tilde{O}(D + \sqrt{n})$ time complexity turned out to be "optimal" for MST, and in fact for an extraordinarily wider range of problems, in the following sense: Peleg and Rubinovich [64] showed that there are graphs of diameter $D = O(\log n)$ on which $\Omega(\sqrt{n}/\log n)$ rounds are necessary for computing an MST. Subsequently, building on a construction of Elkin [23], Das Sarma et al. [17] showed that even approximating MST within any non-trivial factor requires $\Omega(D + \sqrt{n/\log n})$ time on some graphs with $D = O(\log n)$. They also showed that the same lower bound holds for several other fundamental problems, e.g., computing single-source shortest paths or an approximate minimum cut.

Faced with this seemingly omnipresent $\tilde{\Omega}(D + \sqrt{n})$ lower bound, there are two ways ahead. One is to take this lower bound as a last word and be contempt with the current $\tilde{O}(D + \sqrt{n})$ algorithm, because it is the best possible in some graphs. The other is to look for mathematically clean and practically relevant graph properties that allow one to go below the lower bound. This second approach has been pursued in three directions in the prior work:

- **Graphs with Small Constant Diameter:**
  Lotker et al. [51] showed an $O(\log n)$ round algorithm for diameter 2 graphs, and proved that for graphs of diameter 3 and 4, there are lower bounds of $\Omega(\sqrt[3]{n}/\sqrt{\log n})$ and $\Omega(\sqrt[4]{n}/\sqrt{\log n})$, respectively. Later, Lotker et al. [53] showed that in graphs with diameter $D = 1$–i.e., if the graph is a weighted complete graph, which is also known as the *congested clique* model–an MST can be computed in time $O(\log\log n)$. This complexity was improved recently by Hegeman et al. to $O(\log\log\log n)$ [36], and subsequently, by Ghaffari and Parter to $O(\log^* n)$ [33].
- **Graphs with Small MST Radius or Local Shortest-Path Diameter (SPD):**

Elkin [22] introduced the notion of MST radius, which roughly speaking is maximum radius each node needs to check to check whether any of its edges is in the MST. This is denoted by $\lambda(G, w)$ and it depends on both the topology and the weights. Elkin provided an algorithm with complexity $\tilde{O}(\lambda(G, w) + \sqrt{n})$. Khan and Pandurangan [41] introduced the notion of *local shortest path diameter* $L(G, w)$, which roughly speaking is the maximum number of hops of the minimum-weight path between each node and the other endpoint of its heaviest edge. Note that $L(G, w)$ dependends both on the topology and on the weights. The paper presented an $O(\log n)$ approximation algorithm for MST with time complexity $\tilde{O}(D + L(G, w))$.

- **Planar and Near-Planar Graphs:**
  Ghaffari and Haeupler [31] developed the general concept of *low-congestion shortcuts*, and applied it to obtain an MST algorithm with time complexity $\tilde{O}(D)$ in planar graphs. This was then extended by Haeupler, Izumi, and Zuzic [34, 35] to graphs with bounded genus or bounded tree-width.

**Our Contribution**: In this paper, we focus on graphs with good *expansion* properties. In particular, we analyze the round complexity of computing an MST and related problems as a function of the random walk mixing time $\tau_{\text{mix}}(G)$ of the network graph $G$. For a formal definition of $\tau_{\text{mix}}(G)$, we refer to Section 2. Our main result proves that an MST can be computed in almost the mixing time.

THEOREM 1.1. *There is a distributed, randomized Las Vegas algorithm that computes an MST in time* $\tau_{\text{mix}}(G) \cdot 2^{O(\sqrt{\log n \log\log n})}$ *in the* CONGEST *model, with high probability*[1].

We remark that while the $2^{O(\sqrt{\log n \log\log n})}$ term is more than any polylogarithmic function of $n$, it is a slowly growing function of $n$ and in particular substantially smaller than any fixed power of $n$. Theorem 1.1 in particular implies that in graphs with mixing time at most $2^{O(\sqrt{\log n \log\log n})}$ or conductance at lest $2^{-O(\sqrt{\log n \log\log n})}$, an MST can be computed in time $2^{O(\sqrt{\log n \log\log n})}$. This includes all graphs with maximum degree $2^{O(\sqrt{\log n \log\log n})}$ and edge or vertex expansion at least $2^{-O(\sqrt{\log n \log\log n})}$. Note that a wide range of the common (overlay) networks used in practical distributed applications fall in this category, see e.g. [4, 8, 45, 55, 60–62, 69].

By combining the above algorithm with techniques developed in [32, 57] and especially a method of [31], the same upper bound as in Theorem 1.1 can also be achieved for computing a $(1 + \varepsilon)$-approximate minimum cut.

At its heart, our MST algorithm is based on a new random-walk based distributed routing scheme to serve a large number of concurrent pair-wise routing requests. This routing scheme is then incorporated into an MST algorithm in the style of Boruvka's classic approach [58], with the help of a few additional algorithmic ingredients, to obtain the MST algorithm of Theorem 1.1. The routing scheme is the main technical contribution of the present paper.

THEOREM 1.2. *Consider a graph* $G = (V, E)$ *and a set of point-to-point routing requests, each given by the IDs of the corresponding source-destination pair. If each node of* $G$ *is the source and the destination of at most* $d_G(v) \cdot 2^{O(\sqrt{\log n \log\log n})}$ *messages, there is a randomized distributed algorithm that delivers all messages in time* $\tau_{\text{mix}}(G) \cdot 2^{O(\sqrt{\log n \log\log n})}$, *w.h.p.*

[1]As standard, *with high probability* (w.h.p.) indicates that an event has probability $1 - 1/n^c$ for a constant $c \geq 2$.

**Our Routing Method in a Nutshell**: A random walk starting from the packet source would be unlikely to get to the correct destination, unless it is very long, or we use a very large number of such walks. In our routing algorithm, we use random walks to construct a *hierarchical structure*, which roughly speaking recursively embeds good-expansion random graphs on the base graph. For the construction, we replace every node $v \in V$ by $d_G(v)$ virtual nodes so that overall, we have $2|E|$ virtual nodes. On the bottom level, we use parallel random walks of length $\tau_{\text{mix}}(G)$ to compute a low-congestion embedding of an approximate Erdős-Rényi random graph with average degree $O(\log n)$ among the virtual nodes. Because in the stationary distribution of a random walk on $G$, the probability of a node $v$ is proportional to its degree, we can run $O(\log n)$ random walks per virtual node with only a logarithmic slowdown compared to running a single random walk in the graph. On the second level, we partition the set of virtual nodes into $\alpha = 2^{O(\sqrt{\log n \log\log n})}$ parts and for each part, we compute a low-congestion embedding of another approximate Erdős-Rényi random graph on top of the bottom random graph. The time for computing such an embedding is $\alpha$ poly $\log n$. For each of the $\alpha$ parts, we proceed recursively, we divide the part into $\alpha$ smaller parts and embed a new random graph in each part. The construction has $O\left(\sqrt{\frac{\log n}{\log\log n}}\right)$ recursion levels and can be constructed in time $\alpha \operatorname{poly}\log n = 2^{O(\sqrt{\log n \log\log n})}$. As the random graph embedding on each recursion level adds a polylogarithmic stretch factor, the cost for routing a message is also $2^{O(\sqrt{\log n \log\log n})}$. The random graph embeddings guarantee that in parallel we can cope with up to $2^{O(\sqrt{\log n \log\log n})}$ messages per virtual node. By using a small number of shared random bits, which can be disseminated in $O(D \operatorname{poly}\log n)$ time, the position of a given node ID in the hierarchical partition can be determined by a globally known random hash function.

**A More Efficient Solution For Denser Routing Requests**: We also present more efficient routing algorithms for instances where the set of routing requests is larger. Due to the space limitations, the explanations of this part are deferred to the full version of the paper. Here, we simply overview the end-result:

We focus on routing instances where each node has to send one $O(\log n)$-bit message to each other node. Such a routing algorithm can be seen as emulating the *congested clique model* [53] on top of a general underlying graph. The congested clique model has recently received considerable attention [10, 11, 14, 20, 21, 30, 33, 36–39, 42, 50, 56, 63] and for general graphs, admitting a fast algorithm for the above *clique emulation problem* is considered as one of the desirable network 'axioms' in [5]. A simple cut-based argument shows that the clique emulation problem requires time at least $\Omega(n/h(G))$, where $h(G)$ is the edge expansion of $G$. We prove the following upper bound.

THEOREM 1.3. *There is a distributed algorithm that emulates the clique in a graph G, w.h.p., in* $O\Big(\frac{n}{h(G)}\cdot\Big(1+\frac{\Delta}{n}\cdot\frac{\Delta}{h(G)}\cdot\log n\Big)\cdot\log n\log^* n\Big)$ *rounds, where* $\Delta$ *denotes the maximum degree of G. Moreover, if* $h(G)=\Omega(\Delta)$ *and* $\Delta\geq n^{0.5+\varepsilon}$ *for constant* $\varepsilon>0$*, the bound can be improved to* $O\big(\frac{n}{h(G)}\cdot\log n\cdot\log^* n\big)$.

**Remark**: We note that as a simple corollary, this theorem yields an improvement of a recent result of Balliu et al. [9] about the time needed for emulating the clique in Erdős-Rényi [24] random graphs. From Theorem 1.3, we get that an Erdős-Rényi random graph $G_{n,p}$ above the connectivity threshold — i.e., where $p=\Omega(\frac{\log n}{n})$ — can emulate the clique in $O(1/p+\log n)$ rounds. This is because, by a simple calculation, we can see that in such graphs, with high probability, $h(G)=\Theta(np)$ and also $\Delta=\Theta(np)$. This $O(1/p+\log n)$-round emulation improves over the result of Balliu et al.[9], which emulates the clique in $O(\min\{1/p^2,np\})$ rounds assuming $p\geq\sqrt{\log n/n}$. Notice that $\Omega(1/p)$ is a clear lower bound as each node has degree $\Theta(np)$ and it should receive $n-1$ messages. Hence, this $O(1/p+\log n)$-round bound is nearly optimal.

## Other Related Work—the Centralized or Existential Analogues

We conclude the introduction by mentioning some other related work which concern the existential aspects of the routing problem that we consider, or the centralized algorithms for it. In the setting that we focus on in this paper, initially, the communication network $G$ is known only locally, i.e., each node knows only its neighbors. This is important for most of the plausible applications of our work. For instance, in overlay networks, the topology is usually dynamic and changes with time, and it is never fully known to one node, see e.g. [4, 43, 45, 60–62]. The variant of the routing problem where $G$ is globally known relates to some well-studied problems in the area of centralized computation, which we briefly review next.

**Multi-Commodity Flow with Short Paths**: If $G$ is known to a centralized computer, the seminal work of Leighton and Rao [48] can be used to route the packets: we formulate the problem as a *multi-commodity flow* instance with a unit flow demand per node pair, then do a randomized rounding on the flows to generate short paths, and finally schedules the packet routing of these paths using Lovasz Local Lemma. However, this method seems unlikely to lead to a fast distributed algorithm, the multi-commodity flow part itself needs a large polynomial centralized time complexity.

**Edge-Disjoint Paths in Expanders**: A problem that relates to the routing question is that of finding edge-disjoint paths in expanders, between given source-destination pairs. This problem began with the work of Peleg and Upfal[65], who showed a polynomial time algorithm for finding $n^{\varepsilon}$ paths, for a small constant $\varepsilon$. This problem has since receive extensive attention[12, 13, 25, 46, 47, 49]. This line of work was improved to optimality by [26], which finds $\Theta(\frac{n}{\log n})$ paths in a (large) polynomial time in regular-expanders with sufficiently large expansion. It does not seem likely to us that these computationally intensive centralized methods would yield a fast distributed routing algorithm.

## 2 PRELIMINARIES

**Mathematical notations**: Throughout the paper, we use $n$ to denote the number of nodes and $m$ to denote the number of edges of the network graph $G=(V,E)$. Further, we use $d_G(v)$ to denote the degree of some node $v\in V$, and $\Delta$ for the maximum degree of $G$. Moreover, given a nontrivial partition of $V$ to $S$ and $V\setminus S$, we use $e(S,V\setminus S)$ to denote the number of edges connecting $S$ and $V\setminus S$. The *edge expansion* $h(G)$ of a graph $G=(V,E)$ is defined as $h(G):=\min_{S\subseteq V,1\leq|S|\leq n/2}\frac{e(S,V\setminus S)}{|S|}$.

**Random Walks**: Our algorithms use random walks as a main tool. Note that random walks are by now quite a standard tool, used extensively throughout all branches of theory of computation, see, e.g.[1, 2, 6, 16, 18, 19, 54, 59, 67, 68, 70]. In order to guarantee that the resulting Markov chain is aperiodic, throughout the paper when referring to the random walk on a graph $G$, we implicitly assume the usual so-called lazy random walk: In every step, the walk remains at the current node with probability 1/2 and it transitions to a uniformly random neighbor otherwise. In case of multi-graphs, the transision is on a uniformly chosen random edge. The *stationary distribution* of such a random walk is proportional to the degree distribution, i.e., when performing enough steps of the random walk, the probability for ending in a node $v$ converges to $d_G(v)/2m$. We formally define the *mixing time* of the random walk as follows.

*Definition 2.1.* [Mixing Time] For $V=\{v_1,\ldots,v_n\}$ and a node $v\in V$, let $P_v^t=\big(P_v^t(v_1),\ldots,P_v^t(v_n)\big)$ be the probability distribution on the nodes after $t$ steps of a lazy random walk starting at $v$. We define the mixing time $\tau_{\text{mix}}(G)$ as the minimum $t$ such that for all $v,u\in V$, we have $\left|P_v^t(u)-\frac{d_G(v)}{2m}\right|\leq\frac{d_G(v)}{2mn}$. When the graph $G$ is clear from the context, we sometimes use $\tau_{\text{mix}}$ instead of $\tau_{\text{mix}}(G)$.

***Remark***. By running the walk for $O(\tau_{\text{mix}})$ steps, one can improve the deviation from the mixing time to $\left|P_v^{\tau_{\text{mix}}}(u)-\frac{d_G(v)}{2m}\right|\leq 1/n^c$ for an arbitrary constant $c>0$.

We sometimes need to perform random walks that have a uniform stationary distribution. By using standard ideas—see e.g., [6, 40]—we can "regularize" the graph to achieve this.

*Definition 2.2 (2Δ-Regular Random Walk).* Let $G=(V,E)$ be an $n$-node graph with maximum degree $\Delta$ and let $G'=(V,E')$ be the multi-graph that is obtained from $G$ by adding $\Delta-d_G(v)$ self-loops to each node $v$. A $2\Delta$*-regular random walk* on $G$ is defined as the usual lazy random walk on $G'$. We use $\overline{\tau}_{\text{mix}}(G)=\tau_{\text{mix}}(G')$ for the mixing time of the $2\Delta$-regular random walk on a graph $G$.

Hence, when running a $2\Delta$-regular random walk on $G$, in each step, the walk remains at the current node with probability $1-d(v)/2\Delta$ and otherwise, it transitions to each of the $d_G(v)$ neighbors with probability $1/\Delta$. In previous work, similar regularized random walks have also been called $\Delta$-lazy random walks [6] or max-degree random walks [40]. The following lemma uses Cheeger's theorem (see e.g. [54]) to upper bound the mixing time $\overline{\tau}_{\text{mix}}$ of a $2\Delta$-regular random on $G$ walk as a function of the edge expansion $h(G)$ of $G$.

LEMMA 2.3. *The mixing time* $\overline{\tau}_{\text{mix}}$ *of a* $2\Delta$*-regular random walk on a graph G is* $\overline{\tau}_{\text{mix}}\leq 8\cdot\frac{\Delta^2}{h^2(G)}\cdot\ln n$.

Proof of Lemma 2.3. The convergence of a random walk can expressed as a function the spectral properties of the stochastic random walk matrix and the most important connection to graph expansion is captured by Cheeger's inequality. For more details, we refer to [54], the following analysis is also based on [67]. The congergence of random walks to the stationary distribution can be upper bounded in the following way. For a node $v \in V$ and $V = \{v_1, \dots, v_n\}$, let $P_v^t = \left(P_v^t(v_1), \dots, P_v^t(v_n)\right)$ be the probability distribution on the nodes after $t$ steps of a *lazy random walk* on a graph $G$ starting at a node $v$ of $G$. In a lazy random walk, in each step, with probability 1/2, the walk stays at the same node and with probability 1/2 it moves on a uniformly random edge incident to the current node. Let $\pi = (\pi(w_1), \dots, \pi(w_n))$ denote the stationary distribution. For lazy random walks in a regular graph $G$, the stationary distribution is the uniform distribution and we have: $\left|P_v^t(w) - \pi(w)\right| \leq \left(1 - \frac{\phi^2(G)}{4}\right)^t$. Here, $\phi(G)$ denotes the *conductance* of a graph $G = (V, E)$, which is defined as follows:

$$\phi(G) := \min_{S \subseteq V : \mathrm{vol}(S) \leq m} \frac{e(S, V \setminus S)}{\mathrm{vol}(S)},$$

where for each $X \subseteq V$, we have $\mathrm{vol}(X) := \sum_{v \in X} d_G(v)$.

Note that the $2\Delta$-regular random walk can be seen as a lazy random walk on the $\Delta$-regular multi-graph $G' = (V, E')$ which is obtained from $G$ in the following way. To each node $v$ of degree $d_G(v)$, we add $\Delta - d_G(v)$ self loops. Taking a uniformly random edge with probability 1/2 now implies that each edge of $G$ incident to the current node is picked independently with probability $1/2\Delta$ and thus the lazy random walk on $G'$ is equivalent to the $2\Delta$-regular random walk on $G$. For the auxiliary multi-graph $G'$, we have $\phi(G') = h(G)/\Delta$. Therefore, after $t = \overline{\tau}_{\mathrm{mix}}(G) = 8\Delta^2 \ln n / h^2(G) = 8 \ln n / \phi^2(G)$ steps, we have

$$\left|P_v^t(w) - \frac{1}{n}\right| \leq \left(1 - \frac{\phi^2(G')}{4}\right)^{8 \ln n / \phi^2(G')} \leq e^{-2 \ln n} = \frac{1}{n^2}.$$

□

**Parallel Random Walks**: In all of our results, we run many random walks in parallel. We next discuss how we do this. We first prove a simple helper lemma. We comment that variants of these simple helper lemmas appear in prior work, see e.g. [18, 19].

Lemma 2.4. *Let $G = (V, E)$ be a n-graph and assume that we (synchronously) run at most $n^{O(1)}$ steps of a collection of independent, parallel random walks on $G$. If each node is starting node $v$ of at most $kd_G(v)$ random walks, w.h.p., after each parallel step, there are at most $O(kd_G(v) + \log n)$ random walks at each node $v \in V$.*

Proof of Lemma 2.4. The stationary distribution of a random walk on a graph $G$ is proportional to the degree distribution. Hence, if we start exactly $kd_G(v)$ random walks at every node $v$ of $G$, after every step, the expected number of random walks at every node $v$ is $kd_G(v)$. If at most $kd_G(v)$ random walks start at every node, at each time, the expected number of random walks at every node $v$ is upper bounded by $kd_G(v)$. Because the walks are run independently, the lemma follows from a standard Chernoff bound. □

When performing several random walks in parallel in a distributed way, we assume that in each round each node can send up to one random walk over each of its edges. If running several random walks in parallel such that each node is the starting node $v$ of $kd_G(v)$ random walks, in each parallel random walk step, each node has to forward around $k$ random walks over each of its edges. Simulating $T$ steps of all the random walks will therefore require at least around $kT$ rounds. The following lemma shows that even if all the random walks are run in an independent way, we can run them distributedly in a way that nearly matches this lower bound.

Lemma 2.5. *Let $G = (V, E)$ be an n-node graph and let $k \geq 1$ be a positive integer. Assume that we want to perform $T = n^{O(1)}$ steps of a collection of independent random walks in parallel. If each node $v \in V$ is the starting node $v$ of at most $kd_G(v)$ random walks, w.h.p., the $T$ steps of all the random walks can be performed in $O\left((k + \log n) \cdot T\right)$ rounds in a distributed way.*

Proof of Lemma 2.5. We perform all the walks synchronously, and we show that we can perform one step of all walks in parallel, in one phase, where each phase has $c(k+\log n)$ rounds for a sufficiently large constant $c > 0$. From Lemma 2.4 and a union bound over all the $T$ steps, we know that in each step, the number of walks in each node $v$ is at most $O(kd_G(v) + \log n)$, w.h.p. Each of these walks chooses each edge $e$ incident on $v$ with probability $1/2d_G(v)$. Hence, the number of walks that need to go through $e$ in one phase is upper bounded by $O(k + \log n)$ in expectation and by a standard Chernoff bound also w.h.p. Therefore, if choosing the constant $c$ sufficiently large, the number of walks that need to go through $e$ is less than the length of one phase, which means that the phase suffices for performing one step of all walks in parallel. □

The bound $O\left((k + \log n) \cdot T\right)$ in Lemma 2.5 is asymptotically optimal, matching the $kT$ lower bound, when $k = \Omega(\log n)$. However, when $k = o(\log n)$, the additive $\log n$ term becomes dominant and makes the bound sub-optimal. To overcome this issue, for some range of parameters, we will run the random walks in a carefully correlated fashion. The related details are deferred to the full version of the paper.

## 3 DISTRIBUTED PERMUTATION ROUTING IN ALMOST MIXING TIME

In this section, we explain our distributed algorithm for *permutation routing* and slightly more general routing instances. This algorithm constructs a certain *hierarchical routing structure*, which allows us to solve the following packet routing problem: given several packet routing requests, each specified by a *packet source* and the corresponding *packet destination*, and such that each node $v$ is the source or destination for at most $d_G(v)$ packets, we can route all these packets from their sources to their destinations in $\tau_{\mathrm{mix}} \cdot 2^{O(\sqrt{\log n \log \log n})}$ rounds.

The construction of this *hierarchical routing structure* and the general method for using it are explained in Section 3.1 and Section 3.2, respectively. In Section 4, we show the applications of this routing, by explaining a distributed algorithm for computing a minimum spanning tree in $\tau_{\mathrm{mix}} \cdot 2^{O(\sqrt{\log n \log \log n})}$ rounds.

## 3.1 The Routing Structure via Hierarchical Embedding of Random Graphs

Here, we explain the construction of our hierarchical routing structure. The two key aspects of this structure are: (1) it allows us to route many messages on this structure simultaneously and fast, (2) we can construct this structure fast.

*3.1.1 Embedding a Sparse Random Graph $G_0$ on $G$.* As a preparation step, which can be viewed the level zero of our hierarchical construction, we embed an Erdős-Rényi random graph $G_0$ on top of our base graph. After that, our construction will continue atop $G_0$. Working with the random graph $G_0$ simplifies some of our construction and analysis, in comparison to directly dealing with $G$, while as we will see, this transition has only a $\text{poly}\log n$ factor overhead in the round complexities.

Let $G = (V, E)$ be the base graph, and let $n = |V|$ and $m = |E|$. As we assume $G$ to be connected, we have $\log m = \Theta(\log n)$, and thus, we express all logarithmic terms as a function of $\log n$.

**The Level-Zero Random Graph $G_0$**: Graph $G_0$ has $2m$ nodes, where each node $v \in G$ simulates $d_G(v)$ many $G_0$-nodes. The construction of the random graph $G_0$ atop $G$ will be such that each communication round of $G_0$ can be implemented in $\text{poly}(\log n)$ rounds of $G$. The graph $G_0$ will be an Erdős-Rényi $G_0 = G(m, p)$ random graph, where $p = \frac{200 \log n}{m}$. To construct the overlay $G_0$, we select $mp = 100 \log n$ independent random outgoing neighbors for each node $v_0 \in G_0$, with a uniform distribution for each neighbor[2]. Then, we forget the direction of the edges.

The process of identifying the edges in $G_0$ is as follows. We start $200 \log n$ many independent random walks from each $G_0$-node. This is a total of $200 d_G(v) \log n$ random walks from each node $v \in G$. We run all these walks in parallel in $G$, each for $\tau_{\text{mix}}(G)$ steps. This can be done in $O(\tau_{\text{mix}} \text{poly}\log n)$ rounds, by Lemma 2.5. At the end, the tokens of each $G_0$-node $v_0$ are distributed (essentially) uniformly among the nodes of $G_0$. Thus, the tokens of node $v_0 \in G_0$ are in at least $100 \log n$ different $G_0$-nodes. These are the outgoing neighbors of $v_0$ in overlay $G_0$.

We then run the random walks in the reverse direction of their forward traversal, thus getting them back to their sources. Running the walks in reverse is possible because during the forward traversal, each node can remember in which direction it forwarded each random walk token. At the end, each $G_0$-node $v_0$ knows at least $100 \log n$ randomly selected other $G_0$-nodes. Node $v_0$ selects exactly $100 \log n$ of these, say at random, and considers them as its own out-neighbors in the graph $G_0$. Thus, each node $v_0$ knows its outgoing edges. By running the walks one more time in the forward direction, we can make all nodes $u_0 \in G_0$ also know their incoming edges. At this point, we forget the directions of the edges. These are the edges of $G_0$. Hence, we now have the random graph $G_0$ computed.

We can emulate a single communication round of $G_0$ in $\tau_{\text{mix}} \cdot \text{poly}(\log n)$ rounds of $G$, by re-running the exact random walks as above. That is, we can deliver one message from each $G_0$-node to each of its $G_0$-neighbors, using $\tau_{\text{mix}} \cdot \text{poly}(\log n)$ rounds of $G$.

[2]Note that the Erdős-Rényi model is usually described as connecting each node pair with probability $p$. For the range of $p$ in our discussion, this graph distribution is equivalent, modulo a negligible inverse-polynomially small probability, to the graph distribution resulting from randomly and uniformly picking $mp/2$ outgoing neighbors for each node.

*3.1.2 The Hierarchical Construction.* We now work on top of $G_0$. From here on, the construction of our hierarchical embedding is recursive. We start by explaining the first level; the other levels are repetitions of same method. Throughout, we have one main parameter $\beta$, and as we will see, setting $\beta = 2^{O(\sqrt{\log n \log\log n})}$ gives the best trade-off.

**First Level of the Recursion**: Partition the nodes of $G_0$ into $\beta$ disjoint sets $A_1, A_2, \ldots, A_\beta$ such that for each $i$, we have $|A_i| = \Theta(\frac{|G_0|}{\beta}) = \Theta(\frac{m}{\beta})$. We later discuss how this partitioning is done. For now, it is convenient to think that each $G_0$-node is put in one of these $\beta$ parts at random.

We generate a virtual random graph $G_1$ on the same vertex set as $G_0$. The graph $G_1$ is a disjoint union of $\beta$ random graphs, one for each $A_i$. That is, the graph $G_1$ has $\beta$ disconnected components, one for each set $A_i$. The connected component induced by the set $A_i$ is defined by having each node of $A_i$ pick $O(\log n)$ uniformly random neighbors from the same set $A_i$. The construction of $G_1$ will be such that one communication round of the graph $G_1$ can be emulated in $O(\log^2 n)$ communication rounds of graph $G_0$. In short terms, each round of $G_1$ embeds into $O(\log^2 n)$ rounds of $G_0$. After the construction, we will be able to think of $G_1$ as a collection of $\beta$ independent random graphs, one for each $A_i$, such that these $\beta$ random graphs can work effectively in parallel, modulo a multiplicative $O(\log^2 n)$ round complexity overhead.

To construct $G_1$, we start $O(\beta \log n)$ many $2\Delta$-regular random walks from each node $v \in G_0$, defined as in Definition 2.2. Each of these walk tokens carries the ID of node $v$ and also the number $i \in \{1, 2, \ldots, \beta\}$ for which $v \in A_i$. We run all the $O(m\beta \log n)$ random walks for $\tau_{\text{mix}}(G_0) = O(\log n)$ steps. As Lemma 2.5 shows, this can be performed in $O(\beta \log^2 n)$ rounds of $G_0$. We consider a random walk token *successful* if its starting point and end point are in the same set $A_i$. At the end, for each node $v$, there are $O(\beta \log n)$ tokens of $v \in A_i$ spread uniformly over the graph $G_0$. Since $|A_i| = \tilde{\Theta}(\frac{m}{\beta})$, w.h.p., $\Theta(\log n)$ of these random walk tokens of $v$ are successful, meaning that they ended in a node of $A_i$. Hence, $v$ has $\Theta(\log n)$ successful tokens, each of which gives $v$ one randomly sampled neighbor in $A_i$. We then run these random walks backwards, thus letting node $v$ know its $G_1$-neighbors. These successful walks, which are $O(\log n)$ many per node, can be re-run in $O(\log^2 n)$ rounds of $G_0$.

Lemma 3.1. *Each round of $G_1$ can be emulated in $O(\log^2 n)$ rounds of $G_0$.*

Proof of Lemma 3.1. The argument is essentially by invoking Lemma 2.5. Some care is needed because conditioning on the each random walk having a fixed source and destination can bias the distribution of the walks and conceivably increase the number of walks that need to go through one edge. However, this is not a real problem in our case. We can assume that the walks are run for a length more than a 2 factor of the mixing time. Then, given the source and destination, the walk can be viewed as going from the source to a random middle point, and then going from there to the destination, and each of these two parts clearly induces a distribution of tokens on edges similar to basic random walks, thus allowing us to repeat the arguments of Lemma 2.5. □

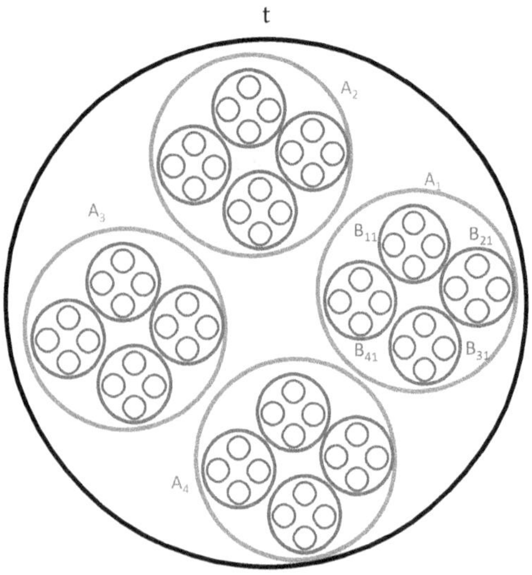


**Figure 1: An illustration of three levels of the hierarchical subsets. We have one random graph on each ball and random graphs of balls of each level can be implemented in $O(\log^2 n)$ rounds of one of the balls of the lower layer. Thus, for instance, we can run one round of graphs of $B_{11}$, $B_{21}$, $B_{31}$, and $B_{41}$ all in $O(\log^2 n)$ rounds of the graph of $A_1$.**

To conclude, using $O(\beta \log^2 n)$ rounds of $G_0$, we constructed the graph $G_1$, made of one random graph per set $A_i$. Moreover, each round of $G_1$ can be emulated in $O(\log^2 n)$ rounds of $G_0$. We are now ready to proceed to the next levels of our hierarchical embedding.

**Next Levels of the Recursion**: The next levels of the recursive hierarchical construction are similar. See Figure 1 for a pictorial illustration. In the second level, we partition each set $A_i$ into sets $B_{1i}, B_{2i}, B_{3i}, \ldots, B_{\beta i}$, of (almost) the same size. The exact partition will be discussed later. We then construct a random graph $G_2$ where each node of $B_{ji}$ is matched to $O(\log n)$ randomly chosen neighbors of $B_{ji}$, by running random walks as before, this time on $G_1$. This construction of $G_2$ takes $O(\beta \log^2 n)$ rounds of $G_1$, and thus $O(\beta \log^4 n)$ rounds of $G_0$. Moreover, the each round of the graph $G_2$ can be emulated in $O(\log^2 n)$ rounds of $G_1$.

Continuing $k$ levels of this recursive construction will produce graphs $G_0, G_1, \ldots, G_k$, where each graph is a structured random graph on some subsets, where each of these subsets is a refinement of those of the previous level. Since in each iteration, the size of each subset goes down by about a $\beta$ factor, we repeat this procedure for at most $k = O(\log_\beta m)$ iterations, until each subset has size at most $O(\log n)$. At that point, we just take the complete graph on each of those subsets as their "random" graph. The following lemma summarizes the complexity of this construction.

Lemma 3.2. *We can perform $k = \log n/\log \beta$ levels of this construction in $O(k\beta)(\log n)^{O(k)} = 2^{O(\sqrt{\log n \log\log n})}$ rounds of $G_0$. Moreover, each round of graph $G_i$ can be emulated in at most $(\log n)^{O(i)}$ rounds of graph $G_0$. This is at most $2^{O(\sqrt{\log n \log\log n})}$ rounds, even for the last level $k = \log n/\log \beta$.*

There are two aspects of the construction of our hierarchical embedding which remain to be discussed: (A) One aspect is how we partition the nodes, in different levels of recursion. In particular, this partition should be into parts of almost equal size, but also such that the source of each packet can know the part to which the corresponding destination belongs. (B) The other aspects is some *portals* that we add to the construction, which we use for moving the packets between different parts of the partition. We next explain these two aspects.

**Pseudo-Random Partitions, and the Hierarchical Labeling**: As we described above, we have $k$ iterative levels of partitioning, and as a result, each node $v \in G_0$ has a sequence of length $k = \log n/\log \beta$ of partition labels $(\ell_1, \ell_2, \ldots, \ell_k)$. Here, each partition label $\ell_p$ is a number in $\{1, 2, \ldots, \beta\}$, that indicates the subset that node $v$ chose in level $p$. Particularly, $\ell_1 = i$ means that $v \in A_i$; then $\ell_2 = j$ means that $v \in B_{ji}$, etc. It is intuitive to think of this partitioning as a $\beta$-ary tree with depth $k = \log_\beta \frac{m}{\log m}$. Then, the $p^{th}$ label $\ell_p$ indicates that in the $p^{th}$, node $v$ chose the branch of the parititon tree corresponding to the child number $\ell_p$.

We would like to have two properties about this partitioning: (P1) We want the partitioning to be nearly-uniform in all levels. More concretely, we want that for each label prefix $(\ell_1, \ell_2, \ldots, \ell_p)$ for $p \in [1, k]$, the number of nodes whose label starts with this prefix should be $\Theta(\frac{m}{\beta^p})$. In other words, at each level of the partitioning tree, the size of the subtrees rooted in the nodes of that level should be almost equal. (P2) We would like that each node $v$ can know the full label of each other node $u$.

Random partitioning gives (P1) but not (P2). More concretely, if we make each node $v$ put itself on a random one of the leaves of the $\beta$-ary tree of depth $k = \log_\beta \frac{m}{\log m}$, then with high probability, all the leaves would have $\Theta(\log m)$ nodes. Therefore, we would have the near-uniformity property of (P1). However, with such a fully random assignment, we will not have property (P2), meaning that a node $v$ would not know the partition label of another node $u$.

To overcome this problem and satisfy property (P2), instead of using fully random assignments, we use a pseudo-random partitioning. In particular, we use $\Theta(\log n)$-wise independent hash functions that map the set of IDs to the leaves of the $\beta$-ary tree of depth $k = \log_\beta \frac{m}{\log m}$. Here, $W$-wise independence for $W = \Theta(\log n)$ means that for any set of $W$ IDs, the probability that they are all mapped to one leaf is the same as in the fully random mapping, i.e., equal to $\frac{1}{(\beta^k)^W}$. It is known that to construct such a hash function, $\Theta(W \log n) = \Theta(\log n)$ bits of randomness suffice[3]. That is, one can use these $\Theta(\log^2 n)$ bits to pick a random hash function among $2^{\Theta(\log^2 n)}$ deterministic hash functions, in a way that ensures the desired $\Theta(\log n)$-wise independence. We make the leader of the network node pick $\Theta(\log^2 n)$ random bits, and then we deliver these bits to all nodes. Note that this can be done easily in $O(D \log n) = O(\tau_{\text{mix}} \log n)$ rounds of $G$. That allows nodes to compute these hash functions.

On the other hand, one can use extensions of the Chernoff bound to $\Theta(\log n)$-wise independent random variables[66] to conclude that when mapping $m$ nodes of $G_0$ using these $\Theta(\log n)$-wise independent hash functions, each leaf gets $\Theta(\log m)$ nodes, w.h.p. Hence, we have the near-uniformity described in property (P1).

**Adding Portals to the Hierarchical Construction**: During our routing, some of the packets will be kept and routed within the same branch of the partition, whereas others need to be hopped to the other branch. For instance, a packet residing in a node $s \in A_i$ may be destined for a node $t \in A_j \neq A_i$. In this case, we need to first deliver the packet to a node $t' \in A_i$ such that $t'$ has a $G_0$-neighbor $s'$ in the set $A_j$, and then to hop the packet from $t'$ to $s'$, and finally route it from $s'$ to $s$, recursively. In this case, we refer to $t'$ as the *portal of node $s \in A_i$ towards the set $A_j$*. We now describe how we augment our hierarchical routing structure with these portals.

We describe the process for the first level of the hierarchical construction. A similar procedure is used for the other levels. For the first level, we would like that for each $i, j \in \{1, 2, \dots, \beta\}$, each node $s \in A_i$ knows the label of a node $t' \in A_i$, such that $t'$ has a $G_0$-neighbor $s'$ in the set $A_j$. In this case, node $t'$ will be known as the *portal of node $s \in A_i$ to the set $A_j$*. Furthermore, we want an additional *uniformity property* for these portals, as follows. We would like that the portal of each node $s \in A_i$ towards set $A_j$ should be chosen uniformly at random among nodes of $A_i$ that have $G_0$-neighbors in $A_j$. The randomness in the choice of the portals $t'$ for different nodes $s \in A_i$ will be independent. The next lemma states that we can add these portals to our hierarchical embedding, within the promised round complexity.

LEMMA 3.3. *We can add the random portals to the hierarchical structure in $2^{O(\sqrt{\log n \log\log n})}$ rounds.*

PROOF OF LEMMA 3.3. This part of the construction will be in $\tilde{O}(\beta^2)$ rounds of $G_0$, where we spend $\tilde{\Theta}(\beta)$ rounds to identify the portals towards set $A_j$, for each $j \in \{1, 2, \dots, \beta\}$. Fix one $A_j$, we desribe how various sets $A_i$ can find their portals towards $A_j$ in $\Theta(\beta)$ rounds.

We start $\beta$ random walks from each node $s \in A_i$ and we run these random walks on $G_1[A_i]$ for $O(\log n)$ steps. We do this simultaneously for all $A_i$. This will take $O(\beta \log n)$ rounds of $G_1$, which means $O(\beta \log^3 n)$ rounds of $G_0$. At the end, random walks that are sitting on nodes that have a connection to $A_j$ are considered *successful*. Notice that since $G_0$ is a $G(m, p)$ random graph, there are $\Theta(m/\beta)^2 p = \Theta(m \log n/\beta^2)$ nodes of $A_i$ that have neighbors in $A_j$, that is, a $O(\log n/\beta)$ fraction of nodes of $A_i$. Hence, among the $\beta$ random walks of $s$, we expect $O(\log n)$ to be successful. That means, with high probability, $\Theta(\log n)$ of them are successful. We then run these successful random walks backwards towards their sources, thus letting each node $s$ know the label of a random portal towards $A_j$. This process takes $O(\beta \log n)$ rounds of $G_1$, and determines the portals towards one fixed $A_j$. Hence, performing this for all $j$ takes $O(\beta^2 \log n)$ rounds of $G_1$.

We will perform a similar construction for each level of the hierarchical structure. In level $k$, this portal construction takes $O(\beta^2 \log n)$ rounds of the graph $G_k$. Since $\beta = 2^{O(\sqrt{\log n \log\log n})}$ and as each round of $G_k$ is embedded in at most $2^{O(\sqrt{\log n \log\log n})}$ rounds of $G_0$, per level this is at most $2^{O(\sqrt{\log n \log\log n})}$ rounds of graph $G_0$. Moreover, even summed up over all the $k = O(\log n/\log \beta)$ levels, this is still $O(\log n/\log \beta) \cdot 2^{O(\sqrt{\log n \log\log n})} = 2^{O(\sqrt{\log n \log\log n})}$ rounds, for learning all the portals. □

## 3.2 Routing on the Hierarchical Structure

In this subsection, we explain how we use the described hierarchical structure to solve packet routing. Concretely, the problem we address is defined as follows: the input is a number of source-destination pairs $(s_i, t_i)$ where for each $i$ we should deliver one message from the source node $s_i \in G$ to the destination node $t_i \in G$. For each packet, the source $s_i$ knows the ID of the destination $t_i$. We are also given the promise that each node $v \in G$ is the source or destination in at most $d_G(v) \cdot O(\log n)$ packets. We explain a method that solves this problem in $\tau_{\text{mix}} \cdot 2^{O(\sqrt{\log n \log\log n})}$ rounds[3]. The method is recursive, with one level of recursion for each level of the hierarchical structure.

**A Preparation Step**: Before starting the recursion, we redistribute the packets uniformly and randomly on $G_0$. Make each packet take a regular walk of length $\tau_{\text{mix}}$ on $G$, starting from its source. At the end, if the packet ended up in a node $u \in G$, assign it to a random $G_0$-node $u_0$ simulated by $u$. By Lemma 2.5, all these walks can be performed in $O(\tau_{\text{mix}} \log^2 n)$ rounds. At the end, the packets are distributed uniformly among nodes of $G_0$, and there are $O(\log n)$ source tokens in each $G_0$-node, with high probability. From now on, we work with these randomly redistributed packets.

**The Recursion**: We now explain the recursion for the packet routing problem, corresponding to our hierarchical structure. We solve the problem of routing on an $m$-node random graph $G_0$ by two consecutive iterations of routing on random graphs with $\tilde{O}(m/\beta)$ nodes, and some smaller transitional steps between these two recursions.

Consider the first random graph $G_0$ as well as the sets $A_1, A_2, \dots, A_\beta$. For each packet with source and destination pair $(s_\ell, t_\ell)$, there are two cases: either (1) the source $s_\ell$ and destination $t_\ell$ are in the same set $A_i$, or (2) the source is in set $A_i$ and the destination is in a different set $A_j \neq A_i$. The former case can be directly solved as a problem of routing on the smaller graph $G_1[A_i]$, which has $\Theta(m/\beta)$ nodes, thus allowing recursion. The more interesting case is the latter. For the latter case, our approach is to first route the source token from $s_\ell$ to the portal node $t' \in A_i$ of $s_\ell$ towards $A_j$, which is adjacent to $A_j$ in graph $G_0$. This portal node $t'$ will be considered as the temporary destination while routing in $A_i$. Notice that node $s_\ell$ can know $j$ because node $s_\ell$ knows the hierarchical partition label of the destination $t_\ell$ of the packet, by applying the common random hash function to the ID of $t_\ell$, as described above. Since $s_\ell$ knows $j$, it can choose the portal $t'$ as the temporary destination of the packet, while routing in $A_i$. Once the packet arrives at the portal $t'$, we hop it over to a node $s' \in A_j$ that is $G_0$-neighbor of $t'$. Then, we route the packet from $s'$ to its destination $t_\ell$ in $A_j$. The first and last part in this method are essentially smaller instances of the same routing problem, respectively, on $G_1[A_i]$ and $G_1[A_j]$. Hence, to solve the routing on the random graph $G_0$ with $m$ nodes, we use two times of routing on each of disconnected random graphs of $G_1$ with $\Theta(m/\beta)$ nodes, as well as one time of hopping between the two sets. We next examine the round complexity of this recursion.

[3]Notice that the method can be easily extended to the case where each node is source or destination for up to $K = 2^{O(\sqrt{\log n \log\log n})}$ messages: randomly put each message in one of $K$ phases. This ensures that per phase, each node is source or destination for $O(\log n)$ pairs. Solve each phase using the algorithm claimed above. Overall this becomes $K \cdot 2^{O(\sqrt{\log n \log\log n})} = 2^{O(\sqrt{\log n \log\log n})}$ rounds.

Lemma 3.4. *The round complexity of the described hierarchical routing problem is $2^{O(\sqrt{\log n \log\log n})}$ rounds of $G_0$, which means $\tau_{\text{mix}} \cdot 2^{O(\sqrt{\log n \log\log n})}$ rounds of the base network $G$.*

Proof. Let us use $T(m)$ to denote the complexity of routing on $m$-node random graph $G_0$ with $O(\log n)$ tokens per node. We argue that $T(m) = 2T(\Theta(m/\beta)) \cdot O(\log^2 n) + O(\log n)$. Once that is established, given that $\beta = 2^{O(\sqrt{\log n \log\log n})}$ and $\log m = \Theta(\log n)$, we get $T(m) = 2^{O(\sqrt{\log n \log\log n})}$.

In the recursion $T(m) = 2T(\Theta(m/\beta)) \cdot O(\log^2 n) + O(\log n)$, the first term appears because of the following reason: to solve the $m$-node problem, we need to run two instances of $\Theta(m/\beta)$ node routing, one after the other. Moreover, these two subproblems are routing on $G_1[A_i]$ and $G_1[A_j]$, i.e., they are by communicating over graph $G_1$, which itself is embedded on $G_0$ with a emulation round complexity overhead of an $O(\log^2 n)$ factor. That is, each communication round of the graph $G_1$ can be emulated in $O(\log^2 n)$ communication rounds of the graph $G_0$.

We next explain the second term of the recursion. We particularly explain that we have enough capacity in $G_0$ to route the messages between different sets $A_i$ in just $O(\log n)$ rounds. Fix an arbitrary pair of subsets $A_i$ and $A_j$. Note that since $G_0$ is an Erdős-Rényi graph $G(m, p)$, the number of $G_0$-edges between $A_i$ and $A_j$ is $\Theta(m/\beta)^2 p = \Theta(m \log n/\beta^2)$. We note that this is under the assumption that $\beta \leq \sqrt{m}$, which is clearly satisfied for our choice of $\beta = 2^{O(\sqrt{\log n \log\log n})}$. On the other hand, since the source tokens are distributed uniformly and each node is destination for $O(\log n)$ tokens, the number of source tokens residing in $A_i$ destined for $A_j$ is $\Theta(m \log n/\beta) \cdot 1/\beta = \Theta(m \log n/\beta^2)$. Hence, the number of the edges between $A_i$ and $A_j$ in $G_0$ is, up to constant factor, equal to the number of the messages that should be passed from $A_i$ to $A_j$. This means hopping the messages from $A_i$ to $A_j$ can be done in $O(\log n)$ rounds, as we spread the messages in $A_i$ essentially uniformly over the endpoints of edges connecting to $A_j$, i.e., the portals. □

## 4 APPLICATIONS: MINIMUM SPANNING TREE AND MIN CUT

In this section, we explain our distributed MST algorithm. In any weighted graph $G = (V, E, W)$, this algorithm computes a minimum spanning tree in $\tau_{\text{mix}} \cdot 2^{O(\sqrt{\log n \log\log n})}$ rounds. The core novelty in this result the hierarchical routing method developed in the previous section. Here, we explain how to incorporate this hierarchical routing method in the standard approach of Boruvka[58] for computing a minimum spanning tree. This will require a few smaller new ideas, as we next explain.

The overall outline of our algorithm follows the classic approach of Boruvka[58] for computing an MST, which is also the base of most distributed MST algorithms [28, 29, 44, 52]. This approach has $O(\log n)$ iterations. The key ingredient for us is to implement each iteration in $2^{O(\sqrt{\log n \log\log n})}$ rounds, using our hierarchical routing scheme. Let us first briefly recall Boruvka's approach.

**Recalling Boruvka's Approach**: We start with an empty spanning forest $F = (V, \emptyset)$. In $O(\log n)$ iterations, we gradually add more and more edges to $F$, until it becomes a tree. Consider one iteration and the connected components of the current forest $F$. Assuming that all edge weights are distinct, it is well-known that the MST is unique, and moreover, for each component $C$ of $F$, the minimum weight edge that connects $C$ to $V \setminus C$ belongs to the MST. We can add all such edges to $F$. This is one iteration of Boruvka's approach. One can see that this reduces the number of components by (at least) a factor 2. Thus, after $\log n$ iterations, we have a tree.

**A Small Change in Boruvka's Approach**: To have efficient distributed implementation of each iteration, we make a minor change, as follows: per iteration, each component tosses a fair coin and decides randomly to be either a *head* component or a *tail* component, each with probability 1/2. Different components decide independently. We then add to the MST only minimum-weight outgoing edges that go from a tail component to a head component. It is easy to see that per iteration, the number of components goes down by a constant factor, in expectation. Hence, using Markov's inequality, we see that after $O(\log n)$ iterations, we reach a tree, w.h.p. Thus, even with this random merging, $O(\log n)$ iterations suffice. The additional nice property provided by these random coins is as follows: now, each new component is the result of a *star shaped* merge of old components, where tail components merge with a central head component. Thus, in terms of the number of components, each merge has diameter 2. This simplifies the distributed computation of new components and the related structures.

**Implementing Each Iteration of Boruvka using our Hierarchical Routing**: We now explain how in each iteration, we compute the minimum-weight outgoing edges of different components, in $\tau_{\text{mix}} \cdot 2^{O(\sqrt{\log n \log\log n})}$ rounds, and how we compute the identify the resulting merged components. Let $F$ be the current forest, at the beginning of the iteration. For each component $C$ of the forest $F$, we maintain a *virtual tree* $\mathcal{T}(C)$ spanning $C$. These *virtual trees* will be used for organizing the process of routing messages while computing the minimum weight edges. Particularly, we will preserve three key properties for these trees: (2) the depth of each virtual tree $\mathcal{T}(C)$ is at most $O(\log^2 n)$, (2) in each virtual tree $\mathcal{T}(C)$, each node $v \in G[C]$ has at most $d_G(v) \cdot O(\log n)$ edges, and (3) each virtual node knows its parent in the virtual tree $\mathcal{T}(C)$.

We explain in the proof of Lemma 4.1 how to preserve these properties throughout the iterations. Let us discuss how we use these trees. To compute the minimum weight outgoing edge of each component $C$, we use a simple minimum computation upcast on the virtual tree $\mathcal{T}(C)$ of the component, as follows: we start with the bottom level of $\mathcal{T}(C)$ and each node sends to its $\mathcal{T}(C)$-parent its minimum-weight edge going out of $C$. This is done in $\tau_{\text{mix}} \cdot 2^{O(\sqrt{\log n \log\log n})}$ rounds, by invoking the hierarchical routing scheme described in the previous section. We can invoke the routing scheme because of two reasons: (1) each node $v$ in $\mathcal{T}(C)$ has degree at most $d_G(v) \cdot O(\log n)$, which means each node is the source or destination of at most $d_G(v) \cdot O(\log n)$ messages, and (2) each node knows its parent, which is the destination of its packet.

We repeat this procedure once for each level of $\mathcal{T}(C)$, and thus $O(\log^2 n)$ times in total. Each time, when a node receives some outgoing edges from its virtual tree children, and possibly having some of its own, it only remembers the outgoing edge with the smallest weight, and forwards this minimum to its own $\mathcal{T}(C)$-parent in the next upcast step. Since the virtual tree has depth $O(\log^2 n)$, after $O(\log^2 n)$ upcast steps, the root of the virtual tree gets the minimum weight outgoing edge of component $C$. Then, by reversing the direction of these communications, we can deliver this minimum weight outgoing edge $e^*$ to all nodes of the component, within the same round complexity. This particularly informs the node at the endpoint of this chosen minimum weight outgoing edge $e^*$ that edge $e^*$ should be added to the MST. The next lemma shows that we can maintain these virtual trees throughout the merges.

LEMMA 4.1. *Throughout the iterations, using* $\tau_{\text{mix}} \cdot 2^{O(\sqrt{\log n \log\log n})}$ *rounds of computation per iteration, we can preserve the three key properties of virtual trees: (1) the depth of each virtual tree* $\mathcal{T}(C)$ *is at most* $O(\log^2 n)$*, (2) in each virtual tree* $\mathcal{T}(C)$*, each node* $v \in G[C]$ *has at most* $d_G(v) \cdot O(\log n)$ *edges, and (3) each node knows its parent in the virtual tree.*

PROOF OF LEMMA 4.1. Initially, when each $F$-component is just a singleton node, the related virtual tree is also simply that singleton node. What we need to explain is how maintain the virtual tree, when some components of $F$ merge. That is, how to construct the virtual tree of a new component resulting from the merge of a number of $F$-components $C_0, C_1, \ldots, C_k$ merge, where $C_0$ is the component of the merge, who had a head coin toss, and $C_1$ to $C_k$ are the tail components of the merge. This construction/maintenance is done in a manner that provides the above three properties.

We merge the their virtual trees of $\mathcal{T}(C_0), \mathcal{T}(C_1), \ldots, \mathcal{T}(C_k)$, as follows: For each $i \in [1, k]$, let $e_i$ be the minimum weight outgoing edge connecting $C_i$ to $C_0$, which is to be added to $F$, and let node $v_i \in C_0$ be the physical endpoint of $e_i$ in $C_0$. Let $v_i' \in \mathcal{T}(C_i)$ be the virtual node corresponding to $v_i$. We then define $v_i'$ as the virtual parent of the root of $\mathcal{T}(C_i)$. For each node $v_i \in C_0$, this adds at most $d_G(v)$ new incoming virtual edges for $v_i$. Hence, over the $O(\log n)$ iterations of Burovka's approach, the number of virtual edges incoming to $v_i$ is at most $d_G(v) \cdot O(\log n)$, as desired.

This step may increase the depth of the virtual tree. We now start a sort of a balancing process, where we redefine the parents of these virtual nodes $v_i'$, and consequently their new parents, in a way that allows us to bound the depth of the virutal tree.

This process of finding new parents will be done by walking up the virtual tree of $\mathcal{T}(C_0)$, starting from nodes $v_i'$, which are the virtual nodes corresponding to the $C_0$ endpoints of recently added $F$-edges. We start from the bottom level of $\mathcal{T}(C_0)$ and move up in a synchronous manner, each time going one level higher in $\mathcal{T}(C_0)$. During this process, we try to redefine the parents of $v_i'$ in a way that they induce a shallow tree, similar to a balanced binary tree.

Concretely, the process is as follows: we create one token at each virtual node $v_i'$. Then, we upcast these tokens from the deepest level of $\mathcal{T}(C_0)$ towards its root. Whenever two or more tokens arrive (simultaneously) at a node $v \in \mathcal{T}(C_0)$, we essentially merge them. Then, we create a new token at this merge point, and we upcast only this new token towards the root of $\mathcal{T}(C_0)$.

The merge process has some steps, as follows. Suppose two or more tokens arrived at $v \in \mathcal{T}(C_0)$. For each of these tokens, if the token's creation point was a child $u$ of $v$, we do not do anything and just keep $v$ as the parent of $u$ in the virtual tree. Otherwise, we create a new virtual edge, which connects the creation point $w$ of the token to a child $u$ of $v$, where $u$ is the child through which the token arrived at $v$. Then, node $u$ is the new parent of node $w$. Node $v$ still remains as the parent of $u$. Notice that in this case, node $u$ was not one of the places were two or more tokens merged, and hence, we have increased the in-degree of $u$ by at most 1. On the other hand, the in-degree of node $v$ does not change. Now, node $v$ creates a new token, and sends it upwards in $\mathcal{T}(C_0)$, effectively searching for a new parent for itself.

Throughout this balancing process, each node's in-degree grows by an additive one. This is in addition to the at most $d_G(v)$ in-edges added at the beginning to each node $v$, which correspond to the just merged $F$-edges. Hence, over all the $O(\log n)$ iterations of Boruvka, the in-degree of each node $v$ is at most $d_G(v) \cdot O(\log n)$.

We now discuss the depth. In each iteration of Boruvka's approach, when we do the virtual tree maintenance described above, each virtual node's distance from its root increases by at most an additive $O(\log n)$. Hence, overall the distance from the root remains bounded to $O(\log^2 n)$. The $O(\log n)$ increase is because the addition to the distance from the root is exactly the depth in the newly defined part of the $\mathcal{T}(C_0)$, from $v_i'$ to the root. This part has depth $O(\log n)$, because it is a tree where in each root-leaf path, each other node has at least 2 children. □

By incorporating this method into the framework of [31, Section 5], essentially in a black-box manner, we can compute a $(1+\varepsilon)$ approximation of the min-cut, for any constant $\varepsilon > 0$, in $\tau_{\text{mix}} \cdot 2^{O(\sqrt{\log n \log\log n})}$ rounds. We defer the details to the full version.

## REFERENCES


[1] David Aldous and Jim Fill. 2002. Reversible Markov chains and random walks on graphs. (2002).

[2] Noga Alon, Chen Avin, Michal Koucký, Gady Kozma, Zvi Lotker, and Mark R Tuttle. 2011. Many random walks are faster than one. *Combinatorics, Probability and Computing* 20, 04 (2011), 481–502.

[3] Noga Alon and Joel H Spencer. 2004. *The probabilistic method.* John Wiley & Sons.

[4] John Augustine, Gopal Pandurangan, Peter Robinson, Scott Roche, and Eli Upfal. 2015. Enabling Robust and Efficient Distributed Computation in Dynamic Peer-to-Peer Networks. In *Foundations of Computer Science (FOCS), 2015 IEEE 56th Annual Symposium on.* IEEE, 350–369.

[5] Chen Avin, Michael Borokhovich, Zvi Lotker, and David Peleg. 2014. Distributed computing on core-periphery networks: Axiom-based design. In *International Colloquium on Automata, Languages, and Programming.* Springer, 399–410.

[6] Chen Avin, Michal Koucký, and Zvi Lotker. 2008. How to explore a fast-changing world (cover time of a simple random walk on evolving graphs). In *International Colloquium on Automata, Languages, and Programming.* Springer, 121–132.

[7] B. Awerbuch. 1987. Optimal distributed algorithms for minimum-weight spanning tree, counting, leader election and related problems. In *Proc. of the 19th Symposium on Theory of Computing (STOC).* 230–240.

[8] Baruch Awerbuch and Christian Scheideler. 2004. The hyperring: a low-congestion deterministic data structure for distributed environments. In *Proceedings of the fifteenth annual ACM-SIAM symposium on Discrete algorithms.* Society for Industrial and Applied Mathematics, 318–327.

[9] Alkida Balliu, Pierre Fraigniaud, Zvi Lotker, and Dennis Olivetti. 2016. Sparsifying congested cliques and core-periphery networks. In *International Colloquium on Structural Information and Communication Complexity.* Springer, 307–322.

[10] Florent Becker, Antonio Fernandez Anta, Ivan Rapaport, and Eric Reémila. 2015. Brief Announcement: A Hierarchy of Congested Clique Models, from Broadcast to Unicast. In *the Proc. of the Int'l Symp. on Princ. of Dist. Comp. (PODC) (PODC '15).* ACM, 167–169.

[11] Andrew Berns, James Hegeman, and Sriram V Pemmaraju. 2012. Super-fast distributed algorithms for metric facility location. In *Automata, Languages, and Programming.* Springer, 428–439.

[12] AZ Broder, AM Frieze, and E Upfal. 1997. Existence and construction of edge low congestion paths on expander graphs. In *Proc. of the Symp. on Theory of Comp. (STOC).* 531–539.

[13] Andrei Z Broder, Alan M Frieze, and Eli Upfal. 1994. Existence and construction of edge-disjoint paths on expander graphs. *SIAM J. Comput.* 23, 5 (1994), 976–989.

[14] Keren Censor-Hillel, Petteri Kaski, Janne H. Korhonen, Christoph Lenzen, Ami Paz, and Jukka Suomela. 2015. Algebraic Methods in the Congested Clique. In *the Proc. of the Int'l Symp. on Princ. of Dist. Comp. (PODC).* ACM, 143–152.

[15] F Chin and HF Ting. 1985. An almost linear time and $O$(nlogn+ e) messages distributed algorithm for minimum-weight spanning trees. In *Proc. of the Symp. on Found. of Comp. Sci. (FOCS).* 257–266.

[16] Colin Cooper, Alan Frieze, and Tomasz Radzik. 2009. Multiple random walks in random regular graphs. *SIAM J. on Discrete Math.* 23, 4 (2009), 1738–1761.

[17] Atish Das Sarma, Stephan Holzer, Liah Kor, Amos Korman, Danupon Nanongkai, Gopal Pandurangan, David Peleg, and Roger Wattenhofer. 2011. Distributed Verification and Hardness of Distributed Approximation. In *Proc. of the Symp. on Theory of Comp. (STOC).* 363–372.

[18] Atish Das Sarma, Danupon Nanongkai, and Gopal Pandurangan. 2009. Fast distributed random walks. In *Proceedings of the 28th ACM symposium on Principles of distributed computing.* ACM, 161–170.

[19] Atish Das Sarma, Danupon Nanongkai, Gopal Pandurangan, and Prasad Tetali. 2010. Efficient Distributed Random Walks with Applications. In *the Proc. of the Int'l Symp. on Princ. of Dist. Comp. (PODC).* 201–210.

[20] Danny Dolev, Christoph Lenzen, and Shir Peled. 2012. âĂIJTri, Tri AgainâĂİ: Finding Triangles and Small Subgraphs in a Distributed Setting. In *Distributed Computing.* Springer, 195–209.

[21] Andrew Drucker, Fabian Kuhn, and Rotem Oshman. 2014. On the Power of the Congested Clique Model. In *the Proc. of the Int'l Symp. on Princ. of Dist. Comp. (PODC).* ACM, 367–376.

[22] Michael Elkin. 2004. A faster distributed protocol for constructing a minimum spanning tree. In *Pro. of ACM-SIAM Symp. on Disc. Alg. (SODA).* 359–368.

[23] Michael Elkin. 2004. Unconditional Lower Bounds on the Time-approximation Tradeoffs for the Distributed Minimum Spanning Tree Problem. In *Proc. of the Symp. on Theory of Comp. (STOC).* 331–340.

[24] Pául Erdos. 1942. On an elementary proof of some asymptotic formulas in the theory of partitions. *Annals of Mathematics* (1942), 437–450.

[25] Alan M Frieze. 1998. Disjoint paths in expander graphs via random walks: A short survey. In *Rand. and Approx. Techniques in Comp. Sci.* Springer, 1–14.

[26] Alan M Frieze. 2001. Edge-disjoint paths in expander graphs. *SIAM J. on Computing* 30, 6 (2001), 1790–1801.

[27] Eli Gafni. 1985. Improvements in the time complexity of two message-optimal election algorithms. In *the Proc. of the Int'l Symp. on Princ. of Dist. Comp. (PODC).* ACM, 175–185.

[28] Robert G. Gallager, Pierre A. Humblet, and Philip M. Spira. 1983. A distributed algorithm for minimum-weight spanning trees. *ACM Trans. on Programming Languages and systems (TOPLAS)* 5, 1 (1983), 66–77.

[29] J. Garay, S. Kutten, and D. Peleg. 1998. A sub-linear time distributed algorithm for minimum-weight spanning trees. *SIAM J. Comput.* 27 (1998), 302–316.

[30] Mohsen Ghaffari. 2016. An Improved Distributed Algorithm for Maximal Independent Set. In *Pro. of ACM-SIAM Symp. on Disc. Alg. (SODA).*

[31] Mohsen Ghaffari and Bernhard Haeupler. 2016. Distributed Algorithms for Planar Networks II: Low-Congestion Shortcuts, MST, and Min-Cut. In *Pro. of ACM-SIAM Symp. on Disc. Alg. (SODA).*

[32] M. Ghaffari and F. Kuhn. 2013. Distributed Minimum Cut Approximation. In *Proc. of the Int'l Symp. on Dist. Comp. (DISC).* 1–15.

[33] Mohsen Ghaffari and Merav Parter. 2016. MST in Log-Star Rounds of Congested Clique. In *the Proc. of the Int'l Symp. on Princ. of Dist. Comp. (PODC).* 19–28.

[34] Bernhard Haeupler, Taisuke Izumi, and Goran Zuzic. 2016. Low-congestion shortcuts without embedding. In *Proceedings of the 2016 ACM Symposium on Principles of Distributed Computing.* ACM, 451–460.

[35] Bernhard Haeupler, Taisuke Izumi, and Goran Zuzic. 2016. Near-Optimal Low-Congestion Shortcuts on Bounded Parameter Graphs. In *International Symposium on Distributed Computing.* Springer, 158–172.

[36] James W. Hegeman, Gopal Pandurangan, Sriram V. Pemmaraju, Vivek B. Sardeshmukh, and Michele Scquizzato. 2015. Toward Optimal Bounds in the Congested Clique: Graph Connectivity and MST. In *the Proc. of the Int'l Symp. on Princ. of Dist. Comp. (PODC).* ACM, 91–100.

[37] James W Hegeman and Sriram V Pemmaraju. 2014. Lessons from the congested clique applied to MapReduce. In *the Proceedings of the International Colloquium on Structural Information and Communication Complexity.* Springer, 149–164.

[38] James W Hegeman, Sriram V Pemmaraju, and Vivek B Sardeshmukh. 2014. Near-constant-time distributed algorithms on a congested clique. In *Distributed Computing.* Springer, 514–530.

[39] Monika Henzinger, Sebastian Krinninger, and Danupon Nanongkai. 2016. A deterministic almost-tight distributed algorithm for approximating single-source shortest paths. In *Proceedings of the 48th Annual ACM SIGACT Symposium on Theory of Computing.* ACM, 489–498.

[40] Mark Jerrum and Alistair Sinclair. 1989. Approximating the permanent. *SIAM journal on computing* 18, 6 (1989), 1149–1178.

[41] Maleq Khan and Gopal Pandurangan. 2008. A fast distributed approximation algorithm for minimum spanning trees. *Distributed Comp.* 20, 6 (2008), 391–402.

[42] Janne H Korhonen. 2016. Deterministic MST Sparsification in the Congested Clique. *arXiv preprint arXiv:1605.02022* (2016).

[43] Fabian Kuhn, Stefan Schmid, and Roger Wattenhofer. 2010. Towards worst-case churn resistant peer-to-peer systems. *Distributed Comp.* 22, 4 (2010), 249–267.

[44] Shay Kutten and David Peleg. 1995. Fast Distributed Construction of K-dominating Sets and Applications. In *the Proc. of the Int'l Symp. on Princ. of Dist. Comp. (PODC).* 238–251.

[45] Ching Law and Kai-Yeung Siu. 2003. Distributed construction of random expander networks. In *INFOCOM 2003. Twenty-Second Annual Joint Conference of the IEEE Computer and Communications. IEEE Societies*, Vol. 3. IEEE, 2133–2143.

[46] FT Leighton and Satish Rao. 1996. Circuit switching: a multicommodity ow based approach,". In *Proc. of a Workshop on Randomized Parallel Comp.*

[47] Tom Leighton, Chi-Jen Lu, Satish Rao, and Aravind Srinivasan. 2001. New algorithmic aspects of the Local Lemma with applications to routing and partitioning. *SIAM J. Comput.* 31, 2 (2001), 626–641.

[48] Tom Leighton and Satish Rao. 1999. Multicommodity max-flow min-cut theorems and their use in designing approximation algorithms. *Journal of the ACM (JACM)* 46, 6 (1999), 787–832.

[49] Tom Leighton, Satish Rao, and Aravind Srinivasan. 1998. Multicommodity flow and circuit switching. In *System Sciences, 1998., Proceedings of the Thirty-First Hawaii International Conference on*, Vol. 7. IEEE, 459–465.

[50] Christoph Lenzen. 2013. Optimal Deterministic Routing and Sorting on the Congested Clique. In *the Proc. of the Int'l Symp. on Princ. of Dist. Comp. (PODC).* 42–50.

[51] Zvi Lotker, Boaz Patt-Shamir, and David Peleg. 2001. Distributed MST for constant diameter graphs. In *Proceedings of the twentieth annual ACM symposium on Principles of distributed computing.* ACM, 63–71.

[52] Zvi Lotker, Boaz Patt-Shamir, and David Peleg. 2006. Distributed MST for constant diameter graphs. *Distributed Computing* 18, 6 (2006), 453–460.

[53] Zvi Lotker, Elan Pavlov, Boaz Patt-Shamir, and David Peleg. 2003. MST construction in O(log $log n$) communication rounds. In *the Proceedings of the Symposium on Parallel Algorithms and Architectures.* ACM, 94–100.

[54] László Lovász. 1993. Random walks on graphs: A survey. *Combinatorics, Paul erdos is eighty* 2, 1 (1993), 1–46.

[55] Peter Mahlmann and Christian Schindelhauer. 2005. Peer-to-peer networks based on random transformations of connected regular undirected graphs. In *the Proceedings of the Symposium on Parallel Algorithms and Architectures.* 155–164.

[56] Danupon Nanongkai. 2014. Distributed Approximation Algorithms for Weighted Shortest Paths. In *Proc. of the Symp. on Theory of Comp. (STOC).*

[57] D. Nanongkai and H.-H. Su. 2014. Almost-Tight Distributed Minimum Cut Algorithms. In *Proc. of the Int'l Symp. on Dist. Comp. (DISC).* 439–453.

[58] Jaroslav Nešetřil, Eva Milková, and Helena Nešetřilová. 2001. Otakar Boruvka on minimum spanning tree problem translation of both the 1926 papers, comments, history. *Discrete Mathematics* 233, 1 (2001), 3–36.

[59] Lawrence Page, Sergey Brin, Rajeev Motwani, and Terry Winograd. 1999. The PageRank citation ranking: bringing order to the web. (1999).

[60] Gopal Pandurangan, Peter Robinson, and Amitabh Trehan. 2014. DEX: self-healing expanders. In *Parallel and Distributed Processing Symposium, 2014 IEEE 28th International.* IEEE, 702–711.

[61] Gopal Pandurangan and Amitabh Trehan. 2011. Xheal: localized self-healing using expanders. In *the Proc. of the Int'l Symp. on Princ. of Dist. Comp. (PODC).* ACM, 301–310.

[62] Gopal Peer-to-Peer Networks Pandurangan, Prabhakar Raghavan, Eli Upfal, et al. 2003. Building low-diameter peer-to-peer networks. *Selected Areas in Communications, IEEE Journal on* 21, 6 (2003), 995–1002.

[63] Boaz Patt-Shamir and Marat Teplitsky. 2011. The round complexity of distributed sorting. In *the Proc. of the Int'l Symp. on Princ. of Dist. Comp. (PODC).* 249–256.

[64] D. Peleg and V. Rubinovich. 2001. A near-tight lower bound on the time complexity of distributed MST construction. *SIAM J. Comput.* 30, 5 (2001), 1427–1442.

[65] David Peleg and Eli Upfal. 1989. Constructing disjoint paths on expander graphs. *Combinatorica* 9, 3 (1989), 289–313.

[66] Jeanette P Schmidt, Alan Siegel, and Aravind Srinivasan. 1995. Chernoff-Hoeffding bounds for applications with limited independence. *SIAM Journal on Discrete Mathematics* 8, 2 (1995), 223–250.

[67] Daniel A. Spielman. 2015. Spectral Graph Theory : Random Walks on Graphs. lecture notes. (2015). http://www.cs.yale.edu/homes/spielman/561/2012/lect10-12.pdf.

[68] Frank Spitzer. 2013. *Principles of random walk.* Vol. 34. Springer Science & Business Media.

[69] Ion Stoica, Robert Morris, David Karger, M Frans Kaashoek, and Hari Balakrishnan. 2001. Chord: A scalable peer-to-peer lookup service for internet applications. *ACM SIGCOMM Computer Communication Review* 31, 4 (2001), 149–160.

[70] G Weiss. 2005. Aspects and Applications of the Random Walk (Random Materials & Processes S.). (2005).

# Distributed MIS via All-to-All Communication

Mohsen Ghaffari
ETH Zurich, Switzerland
ghaffari@inf.ethz.ch

## ABSTRACT

Computing a Maximal Independent Set (MIS) is a central problem in distributed graph algorithms. This paper presents an improved randomized distributed algorithm for computing an MIS in an all-to-all communication distributed model, known as the *congested clique* model, defined as follows: Given a graph $G = (V, E)$, initially each node knows only its neighbors. Communication happens in synchronous rounds over a complete graph, and per round each node can send $O(\log n)$ bits to each other node.

We present a randomized algorithm that computes an MIS in $\tilde{O}(\log \Delta/\sqrt{\log n} + 1) \le \tilde{O}(\sqrt{\log \Delta})$ rounds of congested clique, with high probability. Here $\Delta$ denotes the maximum degree in the graph. This improves quadratically on the $O(\log \Delta)$ algorithm of [Ghaffari, SODA'16]. The core technical novelty in this result is a certain *local sparsification* technique for MIS, which we believe to be of independent interest.

## CCS CONCEPTS

• **Theory of computation → Distributed algorithms**;

## KEYWORDS

Distributed Graph Algorithms; Maximal Independent Set (MIS); Congested Clique

## 1 INTRODUCTION & RELATED WORK

Maximal Independent Set (MIS) is a central problem in the area of *distributed graph algorithms*, and it has been studied extensively since the 1980s. In this paper, we present an improved randomized distributed MIS algorithm for distributed settings where the communication is all-to-all. Let us first overview the models.

**The Three Models of Distributed Graph Algorithms**: There are three standard synchronous message passing models of distributed computation:

(1) The CONGEST model [36]: The network is abstracted as an $n$-node graph $G = (V, E)$. There is one processor per node of the graph, which initially knows only the edges incident on that node. Per round each processor/node can send one $B$-bit message to each of its neighbors, where typically one assumes $B = O(\log n)$.
(2) The LOCAL model [27, 36]: This is the same as the CONGEST model, except the relaxation that the message sizes are not bounded.
(3) The CONGESTED-CLIQUE model [29, 30]: This is the same as the CONGEST model, except the relaxation that the communication is *all-to-all*, and per round, each node can send $B = O(\log n)$ bits to each other node.

In all three of the models, the solution is output in a distributed format, which means that each node should know its own part of the output, e.g., whether it is in the computed maximal independent set or not. It should be noted that the third model is much younger, and its study started with the work of [29, 30]. However, nowadays, there are a wide range of settings where all-to-all communication is available to the distributed system, which makes the CONGESTED-CLIQUE model far more relevant. As such, this model has attracted a vast amount of attention over the past few years, see e.g. [6–9, 11–13, 15–19, 22, 25, 32, 35].

### 1.1 Related Work

**Algorithms in LOCAL and CONGEST models**: In 1986, Luby[31] and Alon, Babai, and Itai[3] presented randomized algorithms that compute an MIS in $O(\log n)$ rounds of the CONGEST model, with high probability[1]. Due to well-known reductions[28], these algorithm directly lead to $O(\log n)$ round algorithms for a few other classic problems, including maximal matching, $(\Delta + 1)$-vertex coloring, and $(2\Delta - 1)$-edge coloring, where $\Delta$ denotes the graph's maximum degree.

Recently, faster MIS algorithms were presented for graphs with small maximum degree: Barenboim et al.[5] gave an $O(\log^2 \Delta) + 2^{O(\sqrt{\log \log n})}$ round algorithm, and Ghaffari[13] improved the bound to $O(\log \Delta) + 2^{O(\sqrt{\log \log n})}$. However, it should be noted that these algorithms work in the LOCAL model and use large messages.

**Lower Bounds in LOCAL and CONGEST models**: The following lower bounds hold even in the stronger LOCAL model. Linial[27] showed that $\Omega(\log^* n)$ rounds are necessary for computing an MIS, even on a cycle graph. Kuhn et al. [23, 24] showed that any algorithm for MIS needs $\Omega(\min\{\frac{\log \Delta}{\log \log \Delta}, \sqrt{\frac{\log n}{\log \log n}}\})$ rounds.

**Algorithms in the CONGESTED-CLIQUE model**: Clearly, the $O(\log n)$ round MIS algorithms of [3, 31] work in the CONGESTED-CLIQUE model as well. But ideally we would like to see much faster algorithms in CONGESTED-CLIQUE.

Particularly, since there is no locality limitation here, the aforementioned lower bounds do not apply. Moreover, no other lower bound is known. Because of that, there has been a general question lurking around in the area for a while:

[1] As standard, "*with high probability*" indicates probability at least $1 - 1/n^c$, for a desirably large constant $c \ge 2$.


*PODC '17, July 25 27, 2017, Washington, DC, USA*

ACM ISBN 978-1-4503-4992-5/17/07...$15.00
https://doi.org/10.1145/3087801.3087830

> *Can we solve any of the classic local problems — MIS, maximal matching, $(\Delta + 1)$-vertex-coloring, or $(2\Delta - 1)$-edge-coloring — much faster in the* CONGESTED-CLIQUE *model. In particular, can we go below the respective locality-based lower bounds?*

An improved $O(\log \Delta)$ round MIS algorithm in CONGESTED-CLIQUE follows from [13]. By standard reductions (with minor modifications) [28], this round complexity also extends to the other three problems. This $O(\log \Delta)$ upper bound avoids the $\Omega(\log^* n)$ lower bound, but in the worst case it is still $O(\log n)$. It also does not go below the $\Omega(\min\{\frac{\log \Delta}{\log\log \Delta}, \sqrt{\frac{\log n}{\log\log n}}\})$ bound.

**Some other related work**: It is worth noting that there are few work in the CONGESTED-CLIQUE model, which do not address MIS or the other three problems mentioned above, but provide solutions for some weaker forms of the problems. In particular, Berns et al.[7] presented an algorithm with expected round complexity of $O(\log\log n)$ for computing a 2-ruling set, and Hegeman et al.[18] extended this to an expected $O(\log\log\log n)$-round algorithm for 3-ruling set. A $k$-ruling set is an independent set $S$ in which any node of the graph has some $S$-node within its distance $k$. Finally, Hegeman and Pemmaraju[17] presented an algorithm with expected round complexity $O(\log\log\log n)$ for $O(\Delta)$-vertex-coloring. All of these are significantly more relaxed problems than MIS, and to the best of our understanding, none of the methods seem to imply anything for MIS (in general graphs). Moreover, the fact that the provided complexity guarantees hold only in expectation makes these results even less related to our problem.

## 1.2 Our Result and Approach

Theorem 1.1. *There is a randomized distributed algorithm that computes a maximal independent set in $O(\frac{\log \Delta \cdot \log\log \Delta}{\sqrt{\log n}} + \log\log \Delta)$ rounds of the congested clique model, with high probability.*

This improves over the $O(\log \Delta)$ round MIS algorithm of [13] roughly quadratically, and exponentially if $\Delta \leq 2^{\sqrt{\log n}}$. Connecting back to the question stated above, this round complexity provides the first positive answer for it, by going below the aforementioned $\Omega(\min\{\frac{\log \Delta}{\log\log \Delta}, \sqrt{\frac{\log n}{\log\log n}}\})$ lower bound of [24].

**Our Approach in a Nutshell**: Here, we provide a brief intuition of our approach. For simplicity, we discuss only an $\tilde{O}(\sqrt{\log n})$-round algorithm for computing an MIS in the congested clique model.

The starting point in our approach is an algorithm of [13], which computes an MIS in $O(\log n)$ rounds of the CONGEST model (with some additional nice properties). We are now working in a more powerful model, the congested clique model, which allows all-to-all communications. Thus, wishfully thinking, we may hope to simulate the algorithm much faster in this model. In particular, an ideal case would be if we can simulate each $r = O(\sqrt{\log n})$ rounds of the algorithm, much faster in the CONGESTED-CLIQUE model, say in merely $O(\log\log n)$ rounds. Then, we would get an $O(\sqrt{\log n} \cdot \log\log n)$ round MIS algorithm.

Towards that hope, let us recall a well-known *locality* property of distributed models, as observed by Linial[27, 28]: In any $r$-round algorithm in the CONGEST model, each node $v$ can learn at most the information known at the beginning to the nodes within its $r$-hop neighborhood, that is, the topology induced by the $r$-hop neighborhood of $v$ and the bits of randomness in those nodes. This simple property has been used extensively by the lower bounds, and also by some algorithmic results, for instance by Parnas and Ron [34] and the follow up work to transform distributed graph algorithms into *sublinear centralized algorithms* or *local computation algorithms* as introduced by Alon et al. [4] and Rubinfeld et al. [38].

Having this property in mind, if we could somehow make each node $v$ learn its $r$-hop neighborhood fast, afterward node $v$ would be able to simulate the $r$-round algorithm locally and compute its own output. However, that is not so feasible! This neighborhood can be quite large, e.g., it can include even up to $O(n^2)$ edges. Thus, learning the $r$-hop neighborhood is hopeless.

So what do we do? In a rough sense, we design a certain *local graph sparsification* method, coupled with a new $O(\log n)$-round MIS algorithm in the CONGEST model — which builds on the algorithm of [13] — such that the following holds: We can make each node $v$ simulate $r = O(\sqrt{\log n})$ rounds of the latter algorithm if it knows its $r$-hop neighborhood in a locally sparse graph $G_*$ generated by the *local sparsification* procedure. The sparsification is such that, this whole $r$-neighborhood is small has size at most $n^\delta$ for a desirably small constant $\delta > 0$. In particular, the maximum degree in $G_*$ is bounded to $2^{O(\sqrt{\log n})}$. Designing these two coupled algorithms, the sparsification and the corresponding MIS algorithm, is the core technical novelty of this paper.

We also explain a simple approach which allows each node to learn its $r$-hop neighborhood in a locally-sparse graph $G_*$, with sufficient sparsity, in only $O(\log r)$ rounds of the congested clique model. In short, the method works by making each node learn its 2-hop neighborhood in $O(1)$ rounds, and then applying this procedure recursively on the $G_*^{2^i}$ powers of the base graph $G_*$.

Putting the above pieces together, we can simulate each $r = O(\sqrt{\log n})$ rounds of the new CONGEST-model MIS algorithm in $\log r = O(\log\log n)$ rounds of CONGESTED-CLIQUE, hence leading to a $O(\sqrt{\log n} \cdot \log\log n)$ round MIS algorithm in this model.

We believe that the particular *local sparsification* methodology set forth here, where the sparsification is coupled with a corresponding algorithm for the graph problem at hand and can be used to simulate the algorithm more efficiently, can be of interest beyond this work. Intuitively, one may be able to design similar procedures for some of the other local problems. Furthermore, it is conceivable that such a *local sparsification* method may lead to more efficient *local computation algorithms* [4, 38] in high-degree graphs, a subarea which remains relatively open.

# 2 MIS IN $\tilde{O}(\sqrt{\text{LOG}\,\Delta})$ ROUNDS OF CONGESTED CLIQUE

In this section, we present our randomized distributed algorithm that proves Theorem 1.1. In particular, it computes an MIS in $\tilde{O}(\sqrt{\log \Delta})$ rounds of the congested clique model.

See Section 1.2 for a high-level explanation of the approach. As mentioned there, the starting point in our approach is the MIS algorithm of [13]. We will modify this algorithm, in a series of steps, such that at the end, we have a CONGEST-model algorithm coupled with a *local sparsification* procedure, with the following crucial property: the CONGEST-model MIS algorithm can be simulated much faster in the CONGESTED-CLIQUE model by (iterations of) each node learning its neighborhood in a certain locally sparse graph generated by the sparsification.

In particular, we present an $O(\log \Delta)$ round algorithm in the CONGEST model that computes a nearly-maximal independent set $S$, with high probability, in the sense that, after removing the $S$-nodes and their neighbors from the graph, the remaining graph has no more than $O(n)$ edges. This is formalized in Lemma 2.11. We will refer to this still as an MIS algorithm because running it for $O(\log n)$ rounds would indeed generate a maximal independent set, with high probability. However, instead of doing it that way, after the first $O(\log \Delta)$ rounds, we will use standard techniques of the congested clique to solve the remaining graph — i.e., decide about nodes that remain undecided — in $O(1)$ rounds. This will add some nodes to $S$ to ensure that it is a maximal independent set. In the following, the core of our discussion is the $O(\log \Delta)$ round algorithm in the CONGEST model and its simulation in $\tilde{O}(\sqrt{\log \Delta})$ rounds of congested clique.

Since the final CONGEST-model MIS algorithm and its sparsification may seem somewhat unintuitive at a first glance, we present the algorithm in a number of gradual steps. Interestingly, as we will point out, each of the intermediate algorithms has some nice properties, making it interesting on its own. Indeed, the intermediate MIS algorithm and analysis that we present in Section 2.2 can be viewed as improving on [1, 39], as we shall clarify.

## 2.1 A Brief Recap on the MIS Algorithm of [13]

We start with a brief review of the MIS algorithm of [13]:

**The MIS Algorithm of [13]**: In each round, each node $v$ gets *marked* with probability $p_t(v)$. If $v$ is marked and none of its neighbors is marked, then $v$ joins the MIS and gets removed along with its neighbors. The marking probabilities are set as follows: Initially $p_0(v) = 1/2$, and

$$p_{t+1}(v) = \begin{cases} p_t(v)/2, & \text{if } d_t(v) = \sum_{u \in N(v)} p_t(u) \geq 2 \\ \min\{2p_t(v), 1/2\}, & \text{if } d_t(v) = \sum_{u \in N(v)} p_t(u) < 2. \end{cases}$$

Despite its extreme simplicity, this algorithm is in a sense *too dynamic/active* for our purposes of fast simulation in the congested clique. To predict whether $p_t(v)$ should increase or decrease in one round, we need to compute $d_t(v) = \sum_{u \in N(v)} p_t(u)$, which itself means we should know the state (e.g. marking probability) of all the neighbors in that round. That requires receiving the values from all the neighbors. Moreover, it in turn essentially requires knowing the state of all 2-hop neighborhood nodes in round $t-1$, and so on. Keeping track of this rapidly growing topology would require a message size larger than what the congested clique model admits.

## 2.2 Intermediate Algorithm (1): The Beeping MIS Algorithm

### Intuition

One observation is that, per round of the above algorithm, each node $u$ needs to send its $p_t(u)$ value to each of its neighbors. This seems inefficient, given that the objective is to just distinguish whether $d_t(v) = \sum_{u \in N(v)} p_t(u)$ is large or small. We can even allow some slack in distinguishing these two situations.

We would like to have a much simpler way to distinguish these two possibilities. Particularly, we wish to have much less communication. We use a simple observation: A good indicator of whether $d_t(v)$ is large or not is whether there is a marked node in $N_t(v)$ or not. If $d_t(v)$ is larger than some constant, there is a constant probability that there is at least one marked neighbor, and if $d_t(v)$ is smaller than some other constant, the chances of having a marked neighbor are less than a constant. Hence, we can intuitively take the existence of a marked neighbor as an indicator signal for whether $d_t(v)$ is large or not, and use it to change $p_t(v)$ accordingly. An important property of this method, which we will formalize and leverage later on, is that when $d_t(v)$ is small, the set of "important" neighbors is locally spare. We will see later that this small $d_t(v)$ is the key regime of interest during the execution. To put the property in different words, we can say that per round only a small number of neighbors have a chance to mark themselves, and knowing these potential marks suffices for simulating the algorithm.

### The Algorithm

We present the algorithm in the terminology of the (full-duplex) *beeping* model, which is a very basic distributed model. See [10] for one of the early works introducing (the half-duplex) variant of this model. In the full-duplex beeping model, per round each node either *beeps* or listens, and each node can distinguish only whether zero or at least one of its neighbors is beeping. A node cannot distinguish the number of beeping neighbors, if there is at least one. This model and its close variants are known to capture a wide range of wireless networks [1, 10, 14] and biological networks — see e.g., [2] and the follow up theoretical work[1, 33, 39].

The algorithm is a simple and natural dynamic. It is essentially the same algorithm as [39], and also somewhat close to the algorithms presented in [13]. Our novelty here is in the analysis.

**The Beeping MIS Algorithm**: The algorithm works in iterations, each made of two rounds:

(R1) In the first round of iteration $t$, each node $v$ *beeps* with probability $p_t(v)$ and remains silent otherwise. Initially $p_1(v) = 1/2$. If $v$ beeps and all its neighbors are silent, then $v$ joins the MIS. Node $v$ updates its beeping probability for the next iteration as follows:

$$p_{t+1}(v) = \begin{cases} p_t(v)/2, & \text{if some neighbor of } v \text{ beeps,} \\ \min\{2p_t(v), \frac{1}{2}\}, & \text{otherwise.} \end{cases}$$

(R2) In the second round of iteration $t$, all nodes in the MIS beep. If a non-MIS node hears a beep, it learns that it has an MIS neighbor. MIS nodes and their neighbors get removed from the problem, for the next iterations.

### The Analysis

In Theorem 2.1 we show that after $O(\log \Delta + \log 1/\varepsilon)$ rounds of this algorithm, each node is removed with probability at least $1 - \varepsilon$. This can be viewed as an improvement/refinement of the analysis of

Scott, Jeavons, and Xu[39], which proved an $O(\log n)$ global round complexity, with high probability[2].

To analyze the algorithm, we focus on an arbitrary node $v$. Suppose that $\deg(v)$ denotes the degree of node $v$ at the beginning of the algorithm. We prove that:

THEOREM 2.1. *For each node $v$, during $T = C(\log\deg(v)+\log 1/\varepsilon)$ rounds, where $C$ is a large enough constant, with probability at least $1-\varepsilon$, either node $v$ or a neighbor of $v$ is added to MIS. Furthermore, this guarantee holds independent of the randomness outside 2-hop neighborhood of $v$.*

This theorem implies that the expected time for removal of each node $v$ is at most $O(\log\deg(v))$, and perhaps more importantly, we have an *exponential* decay of the probability of remaining after that point. Thus, after $O(\log\Delta)$ rounds, the probability of node $v$ remaining is at most $\varepsilon = 1/\operatorname{poly}(\Delta)$. This, in addition to the stated independence property, allows us to prove that after $O(\log\Delta)$ rounds, the graph is shattered, the remaining components are "small", and at most $O(n)$ edges remain. See Lemma 2.11 for the formal statement.

For the analysis, we focus on the first rounds of the iterations; the second rounds are the basic clean up steps for removing MIS nodes and their neighbors. In fact, ignoring those second rounds per iteration, and with a slight abuse of terminology, in the sequel, we use *rounds* to refer to the first rounds of the corresponding iterations.

We start with some notations. Define $d_t(v) = \sum_{u\in N(v)} p_t(v)$. We call a node $v$ in iteration $t$ *heavy*, *moderate*, and *light* if we have $d_t(v) > 10$, $0.01 \le d_t(v) \le 10$, and $d_t(v) < 0.01$, respectively. Also we define $d'_t(v)$ to be the summation of the beeping probabilities over non-heavy neighbors of $v$, that is, $d'_t(v) = \sum_{u\in N(v),\, d_t(u)\le 10} p_t(u)$. We also define two types of golden rounds:

**Golden Type-1 Round**: $p_t(v) = 1/2$ and $d_t(v) \le 0.02$, or

**Golden Type-2 Round**: $d_t(v) > 0.01$ and $d'_t(v) \ge 0.01 d_t(v)$.

One can see with simple calculations that in each golden round, node $v$ gets removed with at least a positive constant probability. This is because of node $v$ joining MIS, or a neighbor joining MIS, in type-1 and type-2 golden rounds, respectively. This statement is captured by the following lemma, the proof of which is left as a simple exercise.

LEMMA 2.2. *In each golden round, node $v$ gets removed with at least a constant probability $\gamma > 0$.*

As the core of the analysis, we prove Lemma 2.3, stated below. This lemma shows that during the first $T$ rounds, with probability at least $1-\varepsilon/2$, there are at least $0.05T$ golden rounds for $v$. Having this, we can conclude that the probability of $v$ remaining after all these golden rounds is at most $\varepsilon/2 + (1-\gamma)^{0.05T} < \varepsilon/2 + \varepsilon/2 = \varepsilon$, where the inequality holds by choosing a large enough constant $C$ in the definition of $T$. Thus, to prove Theorem 2.1, it suffices to prove the following key lemma.

LEMMA 2.3. *For each node $v$, during $T = C(\log\deg(v) + \log 1/\varepsilon)$ rounds, where $C$ is a large enough constant, with probability at least $1-\varepsilon/2$, there are at least $0.05T$ golden rounds.*

To prove Lemma 2.3, we first present two simple helper lemmas, Lemma 2.4 and Lemma 2.5, which intuitively state that the system is far more likely to move in the desirable direction. Let us say we have a *wrong move* if one of the following two holds: (1) $d_t(v) \le 0.02$ and $p_{t+1}(v) = p_t(v)/2$, or (2) $d_t(v) > 0.01$ and $d'_t(v) < 0.01 d_t(v)$ but $d_{t+1}(v) > 0.6 d_t(v)$. In the following two lemmas, we show that the probability of a wrong move is at most 0.02. Then, we use these two lemmas to prove Lemma 2.3.

LEMMA 2.4. *If $d_t(v) \le 0.02$, then with probability at least 0.98, we have $p_{t+1}(v) = \min\{2p_t(v), \frac{1}{2}\}$.*

PROOF OF LEMMA 2.4. Suppose that $d_t(v) \le 0.02$. If no neighbor of $v$ beeps, then $p_{t+1}(v) = \min\{2p_t(v), \frac{1}{2}\}$. The probability that no neighbor of $v$ beeps is

$$\prod_{u\in N(v)} (1-p_t(u)) \ge 4^{-\sum_{u\in N(v)} p_t(u)} = 4^{-d_t(v)} \ge 0.98.$$

□

LEMMA 2.5. *If $d_t(v) > 0.01$ and $d'_t(v) < 0.01 d_t(v)$, with probability 0.98, we have $d_{t+1}(v) \le 0.6 d_t(v)$.*

PROOF OF LEMMA 2.5. Suppose that $d_t(v) > 0.01$ and $d'_t(v) < 0.01 d_t(v)$. Hence, a 0.99 fraction of $d_t(v)$ is contributed by heavy neighbors of $v$. Let us call a heavy neighbor $u$ bad if it has no beeping neighbor and thus sets $p_{t+1}(u) = \min\{2p_t(u), \frac{1}{2}\}$. We would like to upper bound $d_{t+1}(v)$. The contributions to $d_{t+1}(v)$ comes from three sources: (1) bad heavy neighbors, which will at most double their probability (2) good heavy neighbors, which will halve their probability, (3) non-heavy neighbors, which will at most double their probability. The contribution of the last two categories to $d_{t+1}(v)$ is at most $0.5d_t(v) + 0.02d_t(v) = 0.52d_t(v)$, and this holds deterministically. What is crucial to analyze is the contribution of the first group, that is, bad heavy neighbors. For each heavy neighbor $u$ of $v$, the probability that $u$ is bad—that is, the probability that no neighbor of $u$ beeps—is

$$\prod_{w\in N(v)} (1-p_t(w)) < e^{-\sum_{w\in N(u)} p_t(u)}$$

$$= e^{-d_t(v)} < e^{-10} < 0.0001.$$

Thus, by linearity of the expectation, the expected contribution of bad heavy neighbors to $d_{t+1}(v)$ is at most $0.0002d_t(v)$, as each at most doubles its probability. By Markov's inequality, the probability that this contribution is more than $0.01d_t(v)$ is at most 0.02. In other words, with probability at least 0.98, the contribution is no more than $0.01d_t(v)$. Therefore, considering all the three categories, with probability at least 0.98, we have $d_{t+1}(v) \le (0.52 + 0.01)\cdot d_t(v) < 0.6d_t(v)$. □

Now that we are equipped with these two helper lemmas, we go back to proving Lemma 2.3.

[2]We emphasize that the algorithm that we discuss works in the full-duplex variant of the beeping model, where each node $v$ can detect whether any of its neighbors are beeping or not, even if $v$ is beeping at the same time. We refer the interested reader to a recent work of Holzer and Lynch [20, 21], which discusses a beeping MIS algorithm in the half-duplex model—where only a listening node can detect whether any of its neighbors are beeping or not. Their analysis gives the guarantee that each node decides after $O((\log\Delta + \log 1/\varepsilon)\log 1/\varepsilon)$ rounds with probability at least $1-\varepsilon$.

Proof of Lemma 2.3. By Lemma 2.4 and Lemma 2.5, the probability of a wrong move is at most 0.02. Each wrong move depends only on the randomness of the its own round. Thus, the events of wrong moves in different rounds are independent. Therefore, using a Chernoff bound, we can infer that over $T = C(\log \deg(v) + \log 1/\varepsilon)$ rounds, with probability at least $1 - \varepsilon/2$, we have at most $0.04T$ wrong moves. In the rest of this proof, we assume that the number of wrong moves is no more than $0.04T$. The $\varepsilon/2$ probability of the incorrectness of this assumption is handled via a union bound.

Let $g_1$ and $g_2$ be the number of golden rounds of type-1 and type-2, respectively. Also, let $h$ be the number of rounds in which $d_t(v) > 0.02$. We show that, assuming at most $0.04T$ wrong moves, $g_2 < 0.05T$ implies $h < 0.27T$, which in turn implies $g_1 > 0.05T$, hence proving the lemma.

**Small $g_2$ implies small $h$**: Suppose that $g_2 \le 0.05T$. Consider rounds in which $d_t(v) \ge 0.01$. Divide these rounds into two categories: (A1) those in which $d'_t(v) \ge 0.01 d_t(v)$ and (A2) those in which $d'_t(v) < 0.01 d_t(v)$. Note that the (A1) rounds are the same as golden type-2 rounds. In each (A1) round or an (A2) round with a wrong move, $d_t(v)$ increases by at most a 2 factor. There are at most $0.09T$ rounds such rounds, because $g_2 \le 0.05T$ and the number of wrong moves are upper bounded to $0.04T$. In each (A2) round without a wrong move, $d_t$ decreases by a 0.6 factor. Each 2 factor increase cancels the effect of at most two rounds with 0.6 factor decrease, because $(0.6)^2 < 1/2$. Thus, there are at most $0.18T$ rounds in (A2) without a wrong move. Therefore, in total, we have at most $0.27T$ rounds in which $d_t(v) > 0.02$. That is, $h < 0.27T$.

**Small $h$ implies large $g_1$**: Assume that $h < 0.27T$, which means that in at least $0.73T$ rounds, we have $d_t(v) \le 0.02$. In each of these rounds, if we have a wrong move, $p_{t+1}(v) = p_t(v)/2$, and otherwise, $p_{t+1}(v) = \min\{2p_t(v), \frac{1}{2}\}$. Thus, overall, we have at most $0.31T$ rounds in which $p_{t+1}(v) = p_t(v)/2$. This includes the at most $0.27T$ rounds in which $d_t(v) > 0.01$. Now, every round of halving $p_t(v)$ cancels the effect of at most one round of doubling $p_t(v)$. Since we start with $p_1(v) = 1/2$, we can conclude that there are at least $(1 - 2 \times 0.31)T$ rounds in which $p_1(v) = 1/2$. That is, there are at least $0.38T$ such rounds. Among these, at most $h < 0.27T$ can be rounds in which $d_t(v) > 0.02$. Therefore, there are at least $(0.38 - 0.27)T > 0.05T$ rounds in which $p_t(v) = 1/2$ and $d_t(v) \le 0.02$. These are golden rounds of type-1 by definition. Hence, $g_1 \ge 0.05T$. □

## 2.3 Intermediate Algorithm (2): The Sparsified Beeping MIS Algorithm

### Intuition

In the algorithm presented in the previous subsection, there is a clear difference between the amount of beeps in neighborhoods with small $d_t(v)$ and those with large $d_t(v)$. The former are good, because in a rough sense, the communications in those neighborhoods are *sparse*. On the other hand, the latter might be problematic, unless we do something about them. Here we explain intuitively what we want to do about each branch of this dichotomous situation. We then formalize this intuition in the algorithm and its analysis. We imagine that we divide the rounds of the algorithm into phases, each having $R = \sqrt{\delta \log n}/10$ rounds for a desirably small constant $\delta > 0$.

**Sparsely Marked Neighborhoods**: Consider one phase made of $R = \sqrt{\delta \log n}$ rounds, starting at a round $t_0$. Imagine a node $v$ that has a small $d_{t_0}(v) \le L$ for $L = 2^{\sqrt{\delta \log n}/5}$. In each round $t$ of this phase, each neighbor $u$ gets marked with probability $p_t(v) \le \min\{1/2, 2^R p_{t_0}(u)\}$. This is because, per round their marking probability at most doubles. Hence, if at the beginning of the phase, for each round $t$ in this phase, we *sample* the node $u$ with probability $\min\{1/2, 2^R p_{t_0}(u)\}$, the set of sampled neighbors stochastically dominates the set of the nodes that will be actually marked. That is—in a sense to be formalized—the sampled set contains all the marked nodes, though potentially also much more other nodes.

On the positive side, this sampled set has size at most at most $2^{3\sqrt{\delta \log n}/10}$. Thus, if we locally gather these sampled sets, and then carefully work through the simulation of the markings only among these sampled nodes, we will be able to simulate the marking process in these neighborhoods with small $d_t(v)$. Since the sampled set has size at most $2^{3\sqrt{\delta \log n}/10}$, gathering the local topology induced by sampled nodes is essentially similar to learning the local topology in a graph with maximum degree $2^{3\sqrt{\delta \log n}/10}$. As we see later, this level of sparsity is sufficient for us.

**Stabilizing Super-Heavy Neighborhoods**: But what do we do about nodes with large $d_t(v)$? For these, the set of marked neighbors per round can be quite large. Let us call a node $v$ *super-heavy* in a phase if in the first round $t$ of that phase, we have $d_t(v) = \sum_{u \in N(v)} p_t(u) \ge L$ for $L = 2^{\sqrt{\delta \log n}/5}$. We argue that for each such super-heavy node $v$, to determine the behavior of $v$, we do not really need to simulate the markings of the neighbors of $v$ within this phase — instead we can just assume that $v$ always has beeping neighbors.

During the $R = \sqrt{\delta \log n}/10$ rounds of this phase, some of neighbors of $v$ might get removed because of joining the MIS or having a neighbor join. But let us ignore that possibility for the moment. Then, per round $d_t(v)$ shrinks at most by a 2 factor, which means throughout the whole period, $d_t(v) \ge 2^{\sqrt{\delta \log n}/10} \gg \Theta(\log n)$. Hence, indeed in each of those rounds at least one neighbor of $v$ is marked, w.h.p. Thus, $v$ practically has no chance of entering the MIS during this phase.

For each node $v$ that is super-heavy in a given phase, we will hedge our bets and assume that $v$ will see marked neighbors in all rounds of this phase. Because of that, $v$ has a perfectly predictable change in its $p_t(v)$. Namely, $p_t(v)$ decreases by a 2 factor in each round of this phase. This means we do not need to really simulate the effect of markings of the neighbors of $v$ to compute its $p_t(v)$ throughout the phase. Recall that the above ignores the possibility of many neighbors of $v$ getting kicked out during the phase, which could imply that $v$ has rounds with no marked neighbor. We will show later in the analysis that ignoring this possibility does not slow us down significantly.

## The Algorithm

We now present the sparsified variant of the algorithm. The concrete advantage of this sparsified algorithm will become clear later when we simulate it quickly in the congested clique model.

**The Sparsified MIS Algorithm**: The algorithm works in phases, each made of $P = \sqrt{\delta \log n}/10$ iterations and one additional round. At the beginning each phase, before the iterations, we have one round where each node sends its $p_t(v)$ to its neighbors. Then, node $v$ sets $d_t(v) = \sum_{u \in N(v)} p_t(u)$ and if $d_t(v) \geq 2^{\sqrt{\delta \log n}/5}$, we call node $v$ *super-heavy* throughout this phase. The algorithm then proceeds in iterations, each having two rounds, as follows:

(R1) In the first round of iteration $t$, each node $v$ *beeps* with probability $p_t(v)$ and remains silent otherwise. As before, initially $p_1(v) = 1/2$. Now a node $v$ joins MIS if three conditions are satisfied: (A) $v$ is not super-heavy, (B) $v$ beeps, and (C) all its neighbors are silent. Node $v$ updates its beeping probability for the next iteration as follows:

$$p_{t+1}(v) = \begin{cases} p_t(v)/2, & \text{if node } v \text{ is super-heavy, or if} \\ & \text{at least one neighbor beeped} \\ \min\{2p_t(v), \frac{1}{2}\}, & \text{otherwise.} \end{cases}$$

(R2) In the second round of iteration $t$, all nodes in the MIS beep. If a non-MIS node hears a beep, it learns that it has an MIS neighbor. MIS nodes and their neighbors get removed from the problem, for the next iterations.

## The Analysis

Again, the analysis will focus only on the first rounds of the iterations, and will ignore the second rounds which are there for basic clean up operations. With a slight abuse of terminology, in the sequel, we use *rounds* to refer to the first rounds of the corresponding iterations.

THEOREM 2.6. *For each node $v$, during $T = C(\log \deg(v) + \log 1/\varepsilon)$ rounds, where $C$ is a large enough constant, with probability at least $1 - \varepsilon$, either node $v$ or a neighbor of $v$ is added to MIS. Furthermore, this guarantee holds independent of the randomness outside 2-hop neighborhood of $v$.*

We start with redefining some notations. We use the notation $v \in \mathrm{SH}_t$ to indicate that node $v$ is *super-heavy*, that is, it had $d_{t'}(v) \geq 2^{\sqrt{\delta \log n}/5}$ at the first round $t'$ of the corresponding phase. We call a node $v$ in round $t$ *heavy* if either $v \in \mathrm{SH}_t$ or $d_t(v) > 10$. Define $d'_t(v)$ to be the summation of the beeping probabilities over non-heavy neighbors of $v$ in round $t$, that is,

$$d'_t(v) = \sum_{u \in N(v),\, u \notin \mathrm{SH}_t,\, d_t(u) \leq 10} p_t(u).$$

Golden rounds are redefined as follows:

**Golden Type-1 Round**: $p_t(v) = 1/2, v \notin \mathrm{SH}_t, \& \, d_t(v) \leq 0.02$,

**Golden Type-2 Round**: $d_t(v) > 0.01$ and $d'_t(v) \geq 0.01 d_t(v)$.

One can see that these new definitions give us the property that, in the new algorithm, node $v$ gets removed with at least a constant probability per golden round.

LEMMA 2.7. *In each golden round, node $v$ gets removed with at least a constant probability $\gamma > 0$.*

As before, the heart of the argument is to prove that there are many golden rounds for node $v$, which we show in Lemma 2.8. Then, Theorem 2.6 follows directly from Lemma 2.8 and Lemma 2.7.

LEMMA 2.8. *For each node $v$, during $T = C(\log \deg(v) + \log 1/\varepsilon)$ rounds, where $C$ is a large enough constant, with probability at least $1 - \varepsilon/2$, there are at least $0.05T$ golden rounds.*

To prove Lemma 2.8, as before, we have two helper lemmas, Lemma 2.9 and Lemma 2.9, which show that the system is more likely to move in the desired direction. In other words, they show that some *wrong moves* have small probability. Though, the statements are slightly different.

LEMMA 2.9. *If $d_t(v) \leq 0.02$ and $v \notin \mathrm{SH}_t$, then with probability at least $0.98$, we have $p_{t+1}(v) = \min\{2p_t(v), \frac{1}{2}\}$.*

PROOF. Suppose that $d_t(v) \leq 0.01$ and $v \notin \mathrm{SH}_t$. If no neighbor of $v$ beeps, then $p_{t+1}(v) = \min\{2p_t(v), \frac{1}{2}\}$. The probability of that is $\prod_{u \in N(v)} (1 - p_t(u)) \geq 4^{-\sum_{u \in N(v)} p_t(u)} \geq 0.98$. □

LEMMA 2.10. *If $d_t(v) > 0.01$ and $d'_t(v) < 0.01 d_t(v)$, then with probability at least $0.98$, we have $d_{t+1}(v) \leq 0.6 d_t(v)$.*

PROOF. Suppose that $d_t(v) > 0.01$ and $d'_t(v) < 0.01 d_t(v)$. Hence, a 0.99 fraction of $d_t(v)$ is contributed by heavy neighbors of $v$. Notice that now a node $u$ is heavy either because $u \in \mathrm{SH}_t$ or because $d_t(u) > 10$. The first category will reduce their $p_t(u)$ by a 1/2 factor, as the algorithm indicates. The behavior of the second category is as analyzed before, they are more likely to reduce their $p_t(u)$ by a 1/2 factor, but they also have a small chance of not doing that, and instead, even raising it up by to a 2 factor. The worst case of the increase in $d_{t+1}(v)$ would be if all heavy neighbors actually are in the second category, in which case the analysis follows the exact proof of Lemma 2.5, concluding that with probability at least 0.98, we have $d_{t+1}(v) < 0.6 d_t(v)$. □

Now that we are equipped with these two helper lemmas, we go back to proving Lemma 2.8.

PROOF OF LEMMA 2.8. First note that by Lemma 2.4 and Lemma 2.5, the probability of a wrong move is at most 0.02. Each wrong move depends only on the randomness of the corresponding round. Thus, the events of wrong moves in different rounds are independent. Therefore, using a Chernoff bound, we can infer that over $T = C(\log \deg(v) + \log 1/\varepsilon)$ rounds, with probability at least $1 - \varepsilon/2$, we have at most $0.04T$ wrong moves. In the rest of this proof, we assume that the number of wrong moves is no more than $0.04T$. The $\varepsilon/2$ probability of the incorrectness of the assumption is taken into account later via a union bound.

Let $g_1$ and $g_2$ be the number of golden rounds of type-1 and type-2, respectively. Also, let $h$ be the number of rounds in which $d_t(v) > 0.02$ or $v \in \mathrm{SH}_t$. We show that, assuming at most $0.04T$

wrong moves, $g_2 < 0.05T$ implies $h < 0.27T$, which in turn implies $g_1 > 0.05T$.

**Small $g_2$ implies small $h$:** Suppose that $g_2 \leq 0.05T$. We prove that, assuming at most $0.04T$ wrong moves, this implies $h < 0.27T$. Notice that $h$ counts the number of rounds in which $v \in \mathsf{SH}_t$ or $d_t(v) > 0.01$. Let us first examine super-heavy rounds. For each phase in which $v$ is super-heavy, if there is at least one round during the phase in which $d_t(v) \leq 0.02$, call that phase a *drop* phase. Notice that in a drop phase, at the beginning of the phase, we have $d_t(v) \geq 2^{\sqrt{\delta \log n}/5}$ and at the end of the phase, we have $d_t(v) \leq 0.02 \cdot 2^{\sqrt{\delta \log n}/10} \ll 2^{\sqrt{\delta \log n}/10}$. Hence, the phase observes a significant drop — at least a $2^{\sqrt{\delta \log n}/10}$ factor — in the value of $d_t(v)$. Amortized, this is even stronger than a 1/2 factor decrease per each round of the phase. For the sake of our bookkeeping in the next paragraph, we bundle all these rounds together and simply imagine that each round of a drop phase gives a 1/2 factor decrease in $d_t(v)$.

Aside from the rounds of drop phases, what remains in the count $h$ are rounds which have $d_t(v) > 0.02$ (which may be in super-heavy phases or not). We consider two (slightly broader) classes of rounds, as before: (A1) rounds in which $d_t(v) > 0.01$ and $d'_t(v) \geq 0.01 d_t(v)$ and (A2) rounds in which rounds in which $d_t(v) > 0.01$ and $d'_t(v) < 0.01 d_t(v)$. Note that the (A1) rounds are the same as golden type-2 rounds and their count is $g_2$. In each (A1) round or an (A2) round with a wrong move, $d_t(v)$ increases by at most a 2 factor. There are at most $0.09T$ rounds such rounds. In each (A2) round without a wrong move, $d_t(v)$ decreases by a 0.6 factor. In each round in a drop phase, $d_t(v)$ decreases by a $1/2 < 0.6$ factor. Each 2 factor increase cancels the effect of at most two rounds with a 0.6 factor decrease, because $(0.6)^2 < 1/2$. Thus, there are at most $0.18T$ rounds in (A2) without a wrong move or in drop phases. Therefore, in total, we have at most $0.27T$ rounds in which $v \in \mathsf{SH}_t$ or $d_t(v) > 0.01$. That is, $h < 0.27T$.

**Small $h$ implies large $g_1$:** Assume that $h < 0.27T$. This implies that in at least $0.73T$ rounds, we have $d_t(v) \leq 0.02$ and $v \notin \mathsf{SH}_t$. In each of these rounds, if we have a wrong move, $p_{t+1}(v) = p_t(v)/2$, and otherwise, $p_{t+1}(v) = \min\{2p_t(v), \frac{1}{2}\}$. Thus, overall, we have at most $0.31T$ rounds in which $p_{t+1}(v) = p_t(v)/2$. This includes the at most $0.27T$ rounds in which $d_t(v) > 0.02$ or $v \in \mathsf{SH}_t$. Now, every round of halving $p_t(v)$ cancels the effect of at most one round of doubling $p_t(v)$. Since we start with $p_1(v) = 1/2$, we can conclude that there are at least $(1 - 2 \times 0.31)T$ rounds in which $p_t(v) = 1/2$. That is, there are at least $0.38T$ such rounds. Among these, at most $h < 0.27T$ can be rounds in which $d_t(v) > 0.02$ or $v \in \mathsf{SH}_t$. Therefore, there are at least $(0.38 - 0.27)T > 0.05T$ rounds in which we have the following three properties: $p_t(v) = 1/2$, $v \notin \mathsf{SH}_t$, and $d_t(v) \leq 0.02$. These are golden rounds of type-1 by definition. Hence, $g_1 \geq 0.05T$. □

LEMMA 2.11. *The graph remaining after $\Theta(\log \Delta)$ rounds of the sparsified MIS algorithm has at most $O(n)$ edges, w.h.p.*

PROOF. As can be inferred from Theorem 2.6, after $\Theta(\log \Delta)$ rounds, each vertex remains with probability at most $1/\Delta^{50}$. If $\Delta \geq n^{0.1}$, w.h.p., no edge remains. Suppose $\Delta \leq n^{0.1}$. Then, we expect at most $\frac{n\Delta}{\Delta^{50}} \ll n$ remaining edges. Whether a node $v$ remains is independent of the randomness outside its 2-hop neighborhood. Thus, each edge's event of remaining depends on no more than $2\Delta^5 \leq n^{0.6}$ edges. By applying the extension of the Chernoff bound to settings with bounded dependency[37], we get that, w.h.p., at most $O(n)$ edges remain. □

## 2.4 Simulation in Congested Clique

We now describe our distributed algorithm that computes an MIS in $\tilde{O}(\sqrt{\log \Delta})$ rounds of congested clique, thus proving Theorem 1.1.

Overall, the algorithm has two parts. The first part is the main ingredient, the second is a simple and standard clean up step. In the first part, we simulate $O(\log \Delta)$ rounds of the sparsified variant of the beeping-based MIS algorithm, presented in Section 2.3, but much faster, in just $\tilde{O}(\sqrt{\log \Delta})$ rounds of congested clique. The first part may leave a small graph, which as proven by Lemma 2.11 can have at most $O(n)$ edges, with high probability. In the second part, we explain how to solve this remaining graph in $O(1)$ additional rounds of the congested clique.

### The First Part of the Congested Clique Algo.

As outlined above, the heart of the algorithm is the first part, that is, faster simulation of the sparsified algorithm in the congested clique. Recall that the sparsified algorithm is made of phases, each having $\sqrt{\delta \log n}/10$ rounds. We explain how to simulate each of these phases in merely $O(\log \log \Delta)$ rounds of the congested clique. Thus, overall, simulating $O(\log \Delta)$ rounds of the sparsified algorithm takes $O(\frac{\log \Delta \cdot \log \log \Delta}{\sqrt{\delta \log n}})$ rounds in the congested clique model. We next explain how the simulation of each phase works.

Before that, we remark that in this subsection, without loss of generality, we will assume that $\log \log \Delta = \Theta(\log \log n)$. This is without loss of generality, because in the complementary case, there is a simpler variant of our approach that solves the problem in $O(\log \log \Delta)$ rounds of the congested clique, see Lemma 2.15.

**Simulating One Phase in $\Theta(\log \log n) = O(\log \log \Delta)$ Rounds:** The first round of the phase, which is simply exchanging the initial values of $p_t(v)$, can be performed in one round. We explain how to simulate the rest of the phase, which is made of $\frac{\sqrt{\delta \log n}}{10}$ iterations, in $O(\log \log \Delta)$ rounds. At the end of the simulation, we want each node $v$ to know two things about its configuration at the end of the phase: (1) whether $v$ is in the MIS or not, (2) the value of $p_t(v)$ for the last round of the phase. Given this, in one additional round, we can remove the MIS nodes and those adjacent to them, and then proceed to simulating the next iteration.

We now discuss how we simulate the iterations. Since we are dealing with randomized algorithms, it is crucial to be formal what a simulation means. We disentangle the randomness from the simulation, as follows: note that the only randomized step in the algorithm is deciding whether to beep or not, with probability $p_t(v)$ for beeping. We imagine that for this, node $v$ has a random variable $r_t(v)$ chosen uniformly at random from $[0, 1]$, with $\Theta(\log \Delta)$ bits of precision. Then, if $r_t(v) \leq p_t(v)$, node $v$ beeps, and otherwise, it remains silent. To separate the randomness from the simulation, we imagine that each node $v$ draws all of its random values $r_t(v)$ for all rounds $t$ of this phase at the beginning of the phase. Having fixed these values, we are left with simulating a deterministic procedure.

First, notice that the simulation for the super-heavy nodes is straightforward. For each super-heavy node $v$, its $p_t(v)$ will decrease by a 2 factor in each round. Let each super-heavy node locally calculate its $p_t(v)$ for the rounds of this phase, and then determine whether it beeps or not in each round, according to these calculated probabilities $p_t(v)$ and its random values $r_t(v)$ by checking whether $r_t(v) \leq p_t(v)$ or not. These outcomes of these decisions can be represented in a binary string of $\sqrt{\delta \log n}/10$ bits, one bit per round. We call this the *beep vector* of node $v$ for this phase. We use one round to have super-heavy nodes send their *beep vectors* to all their neighbors.

What remains is simulating other nodes, who are not super heavy and thus at the beginning of the phase have $d_t(v) \leq 2^{\sqrt{\delta \log n}/5}$. Consider the following subset $S$ of vertices. Let $t_0$ be the first round the phase. Include each node $v$ in $S$ if there is at least one round $t$ of this phase for which $r_t(v) \leq 2^{\sqrt{\delta \log n}/10} p_{t_0}(v)$. Notice that if $v \notin S$, then $v$ does not beep during this phase. However, the converse is not true and it is possible that $v$ is included in the set but does not beep in this phase. Therefore, $S$ is a super-set of nodes that beep during this phase. In particular, $S$ includes all nodes that join the MIS, but most likely also many other nodes.

The set $S$ has one extremely useful property: with high probability, the subgraph $G[S]$ induced by $S$ is locally sparse and in particular, it has a small maximum degree.

Lemma 2.12. *W.h.p., each node $s \in S$ has no more than $2^{1+\sqrt{\delta \log n}/2}$ neighbors in $S$.*

We decorate the vertices of $G[S]$ with some additional information, and call the resulting decorated graph $G_*[S]$. For each node $v \in S$, in $G_*[S]$, we record two additional items of information, besides the edges of $v$: (1) the bit-wise OR of the beep vectors that $v$ received from its super-heavy neighbors, and (2) the values of $r_t(v)$ for all the rounds of this phase. Notice that overall this is no more than $O(\log^2 n)$ bits of information per node. It is convenient to imagine that these bits are appended to the ID of the vertices, and we now have a graph $G_*[S]$ with IDs of size $O(\log^2 n)$ bits. The next lemma shows that once a node $s \in S$ learns a small neighborhood around itself in $G_* S$, it can simulate its behavior in this phase locally. The proof appears in Lemma 2.13.

Lemma 2.13. *If each node $s \in S$ learns its $\sqrt{\delta \log n}/10$-hop neighborhood in $G_*[S]$, then node $s$ can simulate its behavior in this phase locally. In particular, node $s$ learn two things: (1) whether $s$ joined the MIS in this phase or not, (2) the value of $p_t(s)$ at the end of the phase.*

Proof of Lemma 2.13. The proof is by a simple induction. We argue that for any $k$, the behavior of each node $v \in S$ in the first $k$ rounds of the phase can be determined from its $k$-hop neighborhood in $G_*[S]$. The base of the induction where $k = 0$ is trivial. To know the behavior of node $v$ in the first $k+1$ rounds, we need to know two things: (1) the behavior of node $v$ in the first $k$ rounds, and (2) for each neighbor $u$ of $v$ in $G$, whether $u$ beeps in the $(k+1)^{th}$ of the phase or not. The latter can be divided into three categories: (A) if $u$ is super-heavy, then node $v$ already has the beeping vector of $u$ and thus it knows whether $u$ beeps in the $(k+1)^{th}$ round or it. (B) if $u$ is not super-heavy and $u \notin S$, then $u$ clearly does not beep in any round of the phase and thus also not in the $(k+1)^{th}$ round of the phase. (C) if $u \in S$, then whether $u$ beeps or not in the $(k+1)^{th}$ round can be determined by knowing the behavior of $u$ in the first $k$ rounds, which dictates $p_t(u)$ in that round, and $r_t(u)$. The latter is in the decoration of $u$, and the former can be learned from the $k$-hop neighborhood of $u$ in $G_*[S]$, by the induction assumption. Hence, by knowing the $k+1$-hop neighborhood of $v$ in $G_*[S]$, node $v$ can determine its behavior in the first $k+1$ rounds. □

Lemma 2.14. *There is an $O(\log \log n)$ round algorithm that allows each node $s \in S$ to learns its $\sqrt{\delta \log n}/10$-hop neighborhood in $G_*[S]$.*

We have been informed that the simple *graph exponentiation* idea that we use for proving this lemma has been used before, and in this regard, one can view as reproving a brief announcement result of Lenzen and Wattenhofer [26]. Regardless, to be self-contained, we include a proof here, especially as it is short and simple.

Proof Lemma 2.14. First notice that the size of the neighborhood to be learned by each node is at most

$$\left(2^{1+\sqrt{\delta \log n}/2} \cdot \log^2 n\right)^{2\sqrt{\delta \log n}/10} \ll n^{\delta/5}.$$

Let $H$ be an arbitrary $n$-node graph with maximum degree at most $n^{\delta/4}$ and suppose that each node $v$ knows its neighbors, i.e. the edges incident on it. We first explain how in $O(1)$ rounds, we can make each node $v$ know all the edges incident on its neighbors. This will in particular all the node to know $H^2$, the graph where there is an edge between each two nodes with distance at most 2.

The procedure on $H$ is as follows: each vertex $v$ with degree $deg(v)$ prepares $deg^2(v)$ packets, each describing one of its edges, and to be sent to one of its neighbors. Thus, each vertex $v$ is the source of $(deg(v))^2 \leq n^{\delta/2}$ packets. Moreover, each node $v$ is the destination for at most $n$ packets, as node $v$ has at most $deg(v) \leq n^{\delta/4}$ neighbors and $v$ is the destination for $deg(u) \leq n^{\delta/4}$ packets beginning at each neighbor $u$ of $v$. Thus, each node is the source or destination for at most $n^{\delta/2}$ packets. We apply Lenzen's routing method[25] to deliver all these packets from their sources to their destinations in just $O(1)$ round of the congested clique.

We apply the above procedure recursively on graphs $G_*[S]$, $G_*^2[S]$, $G_*^4[S]$, $G_*^8[S]$ ..., $G_*^\kappa[S]$, where $\kappa$ is the least power of 2 no less than $\sqrt{\delta \log n}/10$. The procedure is applicable as the maximum degree in each of these graphs is at most $(2^{1+\sqrt{\delta \log n}/2} \cdot \log^2 n)^\kappa \leq n^{\delta/4}$. At the end, each node learns its $\sqrt{\delta \log n}/10$-neighborhood in $G_*[S]$. Moreover, this whole scheme takes $O(\log \kappa) = O(\log \log n)$ rounds, that is, $O(1)$ rounds for each recursive application. □

## The Second Part of the Congested Clique Algo.

After simulating $O(\log \Delta)$ rounds of the CONGEST-model algorithm, which computes a nearly-maximal independent set $S$, a number of nodes may remain. Let $B$ be these remaining nodes. The set $B$ is the set of all nodes who have no neighbor in the computed nearly-maximal independent set independent set $S$. Note that each node has probability at most $1/\Delta^{10}$ to be in $B$. As Lemma 2.11 proves, the subgraph induced by $B$ has at most $O(n)$ edges. This remaining graph $G[B]$ can be handled easily, via a standard idea in the congested clique. In particular, we make each node in $B$ send its $G[B]$ edges to the leader node (which can be elected in $O(1)$ round). This can be done in $O(1)$ rounds, using Lenzen's routing method[25]. At the end, the leader computes an MIS $S_B$ of $G[B]$ and informs those MIS nodes. Then, the overall MIS is $S \cup S_B$.

## 2.5 Faster MIS in Low-Degree Graphs

LEMMA 2.15. *Suppose that $\Delta \leq 2^{c\sqrt{\delta \log n}}$ for a sufficiently small constant c. Then, there is a distributed algorithm that computes an MIS in merely $O(\log \log \Delta)$ rounds of the congested clique.*

PROOF SKETCH. Each node can learn its $O(\log \Delta)$-hop neighborhood in $G$ via Lemma 2.14 in $O(\log \log \Delta)$ rounds. This is possible because the related $O(\log \Delta)$ neighborhood has size at most $n^{\delta}$. Then, the nodes can simulate $O(\log \Delta)$ rounds of the MIS algorithm of [13] locally. The remaining graph would have $O(n)$ edges and could be solved using $O(1)$ rounds as explained in the second part of the algorithm. □

**Acknowledgment**: I am grateful to Merav Parter. Our discussions about her recent work with Keren Censor-Hillel and Gregory Schwartzman[9] — which presents an $O(\log \Delta \log n)$ round congested clique derandomization of the $O(\log \Delta)$ round MIS algorithm of [13] — reignited my interest in looking for a sublogarithmic MIS algorithm in the congested clique model. I am also thankful to Stephan Holzer and Nancy Lynch. Our discussions about their (half-duplex) beeping model MIS algorithm [20] and its *local complexity* guarantees made me try to find a (tighter) characterization of the *local complexity* of the beeping MIS algorithm of [39], as discussed in Section 2.2. Though, at the time, I did not expect that this improvement and more generally a beeping MIS algorithm could be useful as an intermediate step towards a faster congested clique algorithm; in fact, even in hindsight, I find this extraordinary. I am also thankful for the valuable feedback and comments by the anonymous reviewers of PODC17.

## REFERENCES


[1] Yehuda Afek, Noga Alon, Ziv Bar-Joseph, Alejandro Cornejo, Bernhard Haeupler, and Fabian Kuhn. 2013. Beeping a maximal independent set. *Distributed computing* 26, 4 (2013), 195–208.

[2] Yehuda Afek, Noga Alon, Omer Barad, Eran Hornstein, Naama Barkai, and Ziv Bar-Joseph. 2011. A biological solution to a fundamental distributed computing problem. *science* 331, 6014 (2011), 183–185.

[3] Noga Alon, László Babai, and Alon Itai. 1986. A fast and simple randomized parallel algorithm for the maximal independent set problem. *Journal of algorithms* 7, 4 (1986), 567–583.

[4] Noga Alon, Ronitt Rubinfeld, Shai Vardi, and Ning Xie. 2012. Space-efficient local computation algorithms. In *Pro. of ACM-SIAM Symp. on Disc. Alg. (SODA)*. 1132–1139.

[5] Leonid Barenboim, Michael Elkin, Seth Pettie, and Johannes Schneider. 2012, also coRR abs/1202.1983v3. The locality of distributed symmetry breaking. In *Foundations of Computer Science (FOCS) 2012*. IEEE, 321–330.

[6] Florent Becker, Antonio Fernandez Anta, Ivan Rapaport, and Eric Reémila. 2015. Brief Announcement: A Hierarchy of Congested Clique Models, from Broadcast to Unicast. In *the Proc. of the Int'l Symp. on Princ. of Dist. Comp. (PODC)*. ACM, 167–169.

[7] Andrew Berns, James Hegeman, and Sriram V Pemmaraju. 2012. Super-fast distributed algorithms for metric facility location. In *the Pro. of the Int'l Colloquium on Automata, Languages and Programming (ICALP)*. 428–439.

[8] Keren Censor-Hillel, Petteri Kaski, Janne H. Korhonen, Christoph Lenzen, Ami Paz, and Jukka Suomela. 2015. Algebraic Methods in the Congested Clique. In *the Proc. of the Int'l Symp. on Princ. of Dist. Comp. (PODC)*. ACM, 143–152.

[9] Keren Censor-Hillel, Merav Parter, and Gregory Schwartzman. 2016. Derandomizing Local Distributed Algorithms under Bandwidth Restrictions. *arXiv preprint arXiv:1608.01689* (2016).

[10] Alejandro Cornejo and Fabian Kuhn. 2010. Deploying wireless networks with beeps. In *International Symposium on Distributed Computing*. Springer, 148–162.

[11] Danny Dolev, Christoph Lenzen, and Shir Peled. 2012. âĂIJTri, Tri AgainâĂİ: Finding Triangles and Small Subgraphs in a Distributed Setting. In *Distributed Computing*. Springer, 195–209.

[12] Andrew Drucker, Fabian Kuhn, and Rotem Oshman. 2014. On the Power of the Congested Clique Model. In *the Proc. of the Int'l Symp. on Princ. of Dist. Comp. (PODC)*. ACM, 367–376.

[13] Mohsen Ghaffari. 2016. An Improved Distributed Algorithm for Maximal Independent Set. In *Pro. of ACM-SIAM Symp. on Disc. Alg. (SODA)*.

[14] Mohsen Ghaffari and Bernhard Haeupler. 2013. Near optimal leader election in multi-hop radio networks. In *Pro. of ACM-SIAM Symp. on Disc. Alg. (SODA)*. 748–766.

[15] Mohsen Ghaffari and Merav Parter. 2016. MST in Log-Star Rounds of Congested Clique. In *the Proc. of the Int'l Symp. on Princ. of Dist. Comp. (PODC)*.

[16] James W. Hegeman, Gopal Pandurangan, Sriram V. Pemmaraju, Vivek B. Sardeshmukh, and Michele Scquizzato. 2015. Toward Optimal Bounds in the Congested Clique: Graph Connectivity and MST. In *the Proc. of the Int'l Symp. on Princ. of Dist. Comp. (PODC)*. ACM, 91–100.

[17] James W Hegeman and Sriram V Pemmaraju. 2014. Lessons from the congested clique applied to MapReduce. In *the Proceedings of the International Colloquium on Structural Information and Communication Complexity*. Springer, 149–164.

[18] James W Hegeman, Sriram V Pemmaraju, and Vivek B Sardeshmukh. 2014. Near-constant-time distributed algorithms on a congested clique. In *Proc. of the Int'l Symp. on Dist. Comp. (DISC)*. Springer, 514–530.

[19] Monika Henzinger, Sebastian Krinninger, and Danupon Nanongkai. 2016. A deterministic almost-tight distributed algorithm for approximating single-source shortest paths. In *Proceedings of the 48th Annual ACM SIGACT Symposium on Theory of Computing*. ACM, 489–498.

[20] Stephan Holzer and Nancy Lynch. 2016. Brief Announcement - Beeping a Maximal Independent Set Fast. In *Proc. of the Int'l Symp. on Dist. Comp. (DISC)*.

[21] Stephan Holzer and Nancy Lynch. April, 2017. Beeping a Maximal Independent Set Fast. *preprint arXiv:1704.07133* (April, 2017).

[22] Janne H Korhonen. 2016. Deterministic MST Sparsification in the Congested Clique. *arXiv preprint arXiv:1605.02022* (2016).

[23] Fabian Kuhn, Thomas Moscibroda, and Rogert Wattenhofer. 2004. What Cannot Be Computed Locally!. In *the Proc. of the Int'l Symp. on Princ. of Dist. Comp. (PODC)*. 300–309.

[24] Fabian Kuhn, Thomas Moscibroda, and Roger Wattenhofer. 2016. Local Computation: Lower and Upper Bounds. *J. ACM* 63, 2, Article 17 (March 2016), 44 pages.

[25] Christoph Lenzen. 2013. Optimal Deterministic Routing and Sorting on the Congested Clique. In *the Proc. of the Int'l Symp. on Princ. of Dist. Comp. (PODC)*. 42–50.

[26] Christoph Lenzen and Roger Wattenhofer. 2010. Brief Announcement: Exponential Speed-up of Local Algorithms Using Non-local Communication. In *the Proc. of the Int'l Symp. on Princ. of Dist. Comp. (PODC)*. ACM, New York, NY, USA, 295–296.

[27] Nathan Linial. 1987. Distributive graph algorithms Global solutions from local data. In *Proc. of the Symp. on Found. of Comp. Sci. (FOCS)*. IEEE, 331–335.

[28] Nathan Linial. 1992. Locality in distributed graph algorithms. *SIAM J. Comput.* 21, 1 (1992), 193–201.

[29] Zvi Lotker, Boaz Patt-Shamir, Elan Pavlov, and David Peleg. 2005. Minimum-weight spanning tree construction in O(log log **n**) communication rounds. *SIAM J. Comput.* 35, 1 (2005), 120–131.

[30] Zvi Lotker, Elan Pavlov, Boaz Patt-Shamir, and David Peleg. 2003. MST construction in O(log log **n**) communication rounds. In *the Proceedings of the Symposium on Parallel Algorithms and Architectures*. ACM, 94–100.

[31] Michael Luby. 1985. A simple parallel algorithm for the maximal independent set problem. In *Proc. of the Symp. on Theory of Comp. (STOC)*. 1–10.

[32] Danupon Nanongkai. 2014. Distributed Approximation Algorithms for Weighted Shortest Paths. In *Proc. of the Symp. on Theory of Comp. (STOC)*.

[33] Saket Navlakha and Ziv Bar-Joseph. 2015. Distributed information processing in biological and computational systems. *Commun. ACM* 58, 1 (2015), 94–102.

[34] Michal Parnas and Dana Ron. 2007. Approximating the minimum vertex cover in sublinear time and a connection to distributed algorithms. *Theoretical Computer Science* 381, 1 (2007), 183–196.

[35] Boaz Patt-Shamir and Marat Teplitsky. 2011. The round complexity of distributed sorting. In *the Proc. of the Int'l Symp. on Princ. of Dist. Comp. (PODC)*. 249–256.

[36] David Peleg. 2000. *Distributed Computing: A Locality-sensitive Approach*. Society for Industrial and Applied Mathematics, Philadelphia, PA, USA.

[37] Sriram V. Pemmaraju. 2001. Equitable Colorings Extend Chernoff-Hoeffding Bounds. In *Pro. of ACM-SIAM Symp. on Disc. Alg. (SODA)*. 924–925.

[38] R. Rubinfeld, G. Tamir, S. Vardi, and N. Xie. 2011. Fast Local Computation Algorithms. In *Proc. 2nd Symp. on Innovations in Computer Science (ICS)*. 223–238.

[39] Alex Scott, Peter Jeavons, and Lei Xu. 2013. Feedback from nature: an optimal distributed algorithm for maximal independent set selection. In *the Proc. of the Int'l Symp. on Princ. of Dist. Comp. (PODC)*. 147–156.

# Brief Announcement: Optimal Address-Oblivious Epidemic Dissemination

Hugues Mercier
Schools of Computer Science and Mathematics
Université de Neuchâtel
Neuchâtel, Switzerland
hugues.mercier@unine.ch

Laurent Hayez
Schools of Computer Science and Mathematics
Université de Neuchâtel
Neuchâtel, Switzerland
laurent.hayez@unine.ch

Miguel Matos
Instituto Superior Técnico
Universidade de Lisboa
INESC-ID
Lisboa, Portugal
miguel.matos@inesc-id.pt

## ABSTRACT

We consider the problem of reliable gossip/epidemic dissemination in a network of $n$ processes using push and pull algorithms. We generalize the random phone call model so that processes can refuse to push a rumor or answer pull requests. With this relaxation, we show that it is possible to disseminate a rumor to all processes with high probability using $\Theta(\ln n)$ rounds of communication and only $n + O(\frac{n}{\ln n})$ messages, both of which are optimal and achievable with push-pull and pull-only algorithms. Our algorithms are strikingly simple, address-oblivious and thus fully distributed. This contradicts a well-known result of Karp et al. [3] stating that any address-oblivious algorithm requires $\Omega(n \ln \ln n)$ messages.

We also develop precise estimates of the number of rounds required in the push and pull phases of our algorithms to guarantee dissemination to all processes with a certain probability. For the push phase, we focus on a practical infect upon contagion approach that balances the load evenly across all processes. As an example, our push-pull algorithm requires 17 rounds to disseminate a rumor to all processes with probability $1 - 10^{-100}$ in a network of one million processes with a communication overhead of only 0.4%.

## 1 INTRODUCTION

Since the proposal to update replicated databases [2], gossip algorithms have been used to address a wide variety of problems. The randomness inherent to the selection of the communication peers makes gossip algorithms particularly robust to all kinds of failures such as message loss and process failures, which tend to be the norm rather than the exception in large systems. Their appeal also stems from their simplicity and highly distributed nature.

***Push algorithms.*** The simplest epidemic dissemination algorithms are push-based, where processes that know the rumor propagate it to other processes. Consider the following "infect forever" push algorithm. The algorithm starts with a single process knowing a rumor, and at every round, every informed process pushes the rumor to a process chosen uniformly and independently at random. There are other flavors of push algorithms such as an "infect upon contagion" approach [4] where a process propagates the rumor immediately after it is received regardless of previous receptions. Unfortunately, push algorithms must transmit $\Theta(n \ln n)$ messages if every process is to learn a rumor with high probability[1].

***Pull algorithms.*** Instead of pushing a rumor, a different strategy is for an uninformed process to ask an interlocutor chosen at random to convey the rumor if it is already in its possession. Pulling algorithms are advantageous when rumors are frequently created because pull requests will more often than not reach processes with new rumors to share. However, pull requests in systems without activity result in useless traffic.

***Push-pull algorithms and the random phone call model.*** The idea to push and pull rumors simultaneously was first considered by Demers et al. [2], and further studied by Karp et al. [3] who considered the following random phone call model. At each round, each process randomly chooses an interlocutor and calls it. If, say, Alice calls Bob, once the communication is established, Alice pushes the rumor to Bob if she has it, and pulls the rumor from Bob if he has it. Establishing communication (the phone call itself) is free, and only messages that include the rumor are counted. Using the random phone call model, Karp et al. [3] presented a push-pull algorithm that transmits a rumor to every process with high probability using $O(\ln n)$ rounds of communication and $O(n \ln \ln n)$ messages.

### 1.1 Our contributions

***Generalized random phone call model.*** In the original random phone call model, rumors are transmitted in both directions whenever both players on the line have the rumor. We remove this restriction and generalize the model: at each communication round, each process calls between 0 and $f_{\text{in}}$ processes uniformly at random to request a rumor, calls between 0 and $f_{\text{out}}$ processes uniformly at random to push a rumor, and has the option not to answer pull requests. We assume, like for the original model, that establishing the communication is free, and we only count the number of messages that contain the rumor. We also assume that there is a counter attached to the rumor keeping track of the number of dissemination rounds since its creation, that processes can reply to pull requests in the same round, that the rounds are synchronous, and that processes have a complete view of the system.

***Breaking the lower bounds from [3].*** In their seminal work, the authors define the model such that processes do not have to share the rumor once the communication is established. They state


*PODC'17, July 25-27, 2017, Washington, DC, USA*
 978-1-4503-4992-5/17/07...$15.00
DOI: http://dx.doi.org/10.1145/3087801.3087862

[1]With high probability (w.h.p) means with probability at least $1 - O(n^{-c})$ for a constant $c > 0$.

that any algorithm in the random phone call model running in $O(\ln n)$ rounds with communication peers chosen uniformly at random requires $\omega(n)$ messages, and that any address-oblivious algorithm needs $\Omega(n \ln \ln n)$ messages to disseminate a rumor. Address-obliviousness means that the decisions taken locally by each process are oblivious to the address of the other processes. However, in the proofs of their lower bounds it is implicitly assumed that processes always pull and push the rumor once the connection is established, which, it turns out, is not optimal and allows us to break both lower bounds.

***Optimal algorithms with $O(\ln n)$ rounds and $O(n)$ messages.*** If we discount the cost of establishing the communication (the phone call), it is natural to let processes choose whether or not to call, and whether or not to reply when called. This generalization makes a huge difference: we present a pull-only algorithm and a push-pull algorithm that disseminate a rumor to all processes with high probability in $O(\ln n)$ rounds of communication using only $O(n)$ messages. The idea is simple: we do not push old rumors because doing so results in a large communication overhead.

Our pull-only algorithm obviously never pushes rumors: uninformed processes attempt to pull the rumor from $f_{\text{in}}$ processes per round until they receive it, and informed processes always reply to pull requests. Our infect-forever-push-pull algorithm first pushes the rumor during $r_{\text{push}}$ rounds, stopping when at least $\frac{n}{\ln n}$ processes are informed with high probability. During this push phase, informed processes push the rumor to $f_{\text{out}}$ processes at every round in an infect forever fashion. Uninformed processes send pull requests during the push phase, but informed processes do not reply to them. After $r_{\text{push}}$ rounds, informed processes stop pushing the rumor and a pull-only phase is executed for $r_{\text{pull}}$ rounds until all processes have received the rumor with high probability. Informed processes always reply to pull requests during this pull phase.

Both our pull and push-pull algorithms are optimal for the generalized phone call model. Their message complexity is optimal, their bit complexity is optimal, and we prove that their round complexity is also optimal by showing that pushing and pulling at the same time using potentially complex rules is not necessary: any algorithm in the generalized random phone call model requires $\Omega(\log_{\max(f_{\text{in}}, f_{\text{out}})+1} n)$ rounds of communication to disseminate a rumor with high probability.

***Toward practical implementations.*** We derive precise analytic and numerical bounds on the number of rounds required for the push and pull phases of our algorithms. For the push phase, we focus on the infect upon contagion model for which, in round $r$, processes transmit all the rumors received in round $r-1$ even when they are not received for the first time. This model is of particular interest to us because it spreads the load uniformly across all processes as opposed to infect forever algorithms, while having the same asymptotic behavior. It is thus well-suited for practical implementations, especially if the payload (rumor) is large. Our infect-upon-contagion-push-pull algorithm shares the optimal properties of the infect-forever-push-pull algorithm. Furthermore, by adjusting the number of messages transmitted during the last round of the push phase, we can decrease the number of messages to $n + O(\frac{n}{\ln n})$ even when $f_{\text{out}} \in O(\ln n)$.

## 2 ANALYSIS OF THE INFECT UPON CONTAGION PUSH MODEL

We model the infect upon contagion push model as an occupancy problem where messages are abstracted as balls, and processes play the role of bins. Let $X_r$ be the number of bins that receive at least one ball during round $r$. We show that $\mathbb{E}[X_{r+1}] = \mathbb{E}[\varphi(X_r)] \leq \psi(r+1)$, where $\psi(r+1) \triangleq \varphi(\psi(r)) = n\left(1 - \left(1 - \frac{1}{n}\right)^{f_{\text{out}} \cdot \psi(r)}\right)$ and $\varphi(x) \triangleq n\left(1 - \left(1 - \frac{1}{n}\right)^{f_{\text{out}} \cdot x}\right)$. We lower bound the function $\psi(r)$ by a logistic equation. It is easy to see that $\psi(r)$ converges to a limit $\gamma$ because it is monotonically increasing and bounded above by $n$. A solution for $\gamma$ is given by Corless et al. [1] with the principal branch of the Lambert-$W$ function: $\gamma = n\frac{f_{\text{out}} + W(-f_{\text{out}} e^{-f_{\text{out}}})}{f_{\text{out}}}$.

LEMMA 2.1. *Let $X(r) = \frac{\gamma f_{\text{out}}^r}{\gamma + f_{\text{out}}^r - 1}$. If $f_{out} \geq 2$, then $\psi(r) \geq X(r)$ for every $r \in \mathbb{N}$.*

We observed that the logistic equation $X(r)$ closely approximates $\psi(r)$ and the estimation $\hat{\mathbb{E}}[X_r]$ of $\mathbb{E}[X_r]$ obtained with numerical simulations, but it is not a true lower bound for $\mathbb{E}[X_r]$ because $\mathbb{E}[X_r]$ is slightly lower than $\psi(r)$. However, $\psi(r)$ and $\hat{\mathbb{E}}[X_r]$ are always almost superposed and we conjecture that $\psi(r) - \mathbb{E}[X_r] \leq 1$ when $n \geq 3$ and $f_{\text{out}} \geq 2$. This is more than sufficient to use $X(r)$ to accurately bound the number of rounds of the push phase of our algorithms when implemented in large-scale systems. This is a significant improvement over the bounds of [4], which are only discussed asymptotically for $f_{\text{out}} \in \Omega\left(\frac{\ln n}{\ln \ln n}\right)$. For instance, for $n = 10^4$ and $p_e = 10^{-15}$, the bounds from [4] require $f_{\text{out}} = 23$ and $r = 50$ (i.e., $\approx$ 10 million balls), whereas our bounds require $r = 41$ with $f_{\text{out}} = 2$, or $r = 10$ with $f_{\text{out}} = \lfloor \ln n \rfloor = 14$ (i.e., $\approx$ 500000 balls).

## 3 PULL ALGORITHMS

Besides the seminal work of Demers et al. [2] and Karp et al. [3], there are few results on pull-only algorithms. Our first conclusion is that pulling and pushing have the same asymptotic round complexity, which is implicit in [3]. On expectation, pulling is always at least as good as pushing, although the higher variance of pull at the early stage of the dissemination makes pulling less efficient when the rumor is new. However, the behavior reverses and then more: pulling is much more efficient than pushing when the rumor is old. The second albeit trivial conclusion is that $O(n)$ messages are sufficient to disseminate a rumor with high probability when the fan-in is constant.

Let $u_r$ be the number of uninformed processes after round $r$. We show that if we start the pull phase with $u_0 = n - \frac{n}{\ln n}$ uninformed processes, then $\mathbb{E}[u_r] \geq n \cdot \left(1 - \frac{1}{\ln n}\right)^{(f_{\text{in}}+1)^r}$, and $\mathbb{E}[u_r] \geq n^{-c}$ if $r \leq \log_{f_{\text{in}}+1}(c+1) + \log_{f_{\text{in}}+1} \ln n - \log_{f_{\text{in}}+1} \ln \frac{\ln n}{\ln n - 1}$. The distribution of $u_r$ is very closely concentrated around the mean, thus we can derive precise estimates of the number of pull rounds for practitioners. This is useful for the pull phase of our push-pull algorithms.

LEMMA 3.1. *Let $u_r$ be the number of informed processes at round $r$, let $1 \leq f_{out} = f_{in} \leq n-1$, and let $n \geq 4$.*

$$\mathbb{E}_{pull}[u_{r+1} | u_r] \leq \mathbb{E}_{push}[u_{r+1} | u_r] \quad (1)$$

*where $\mathbb{E}_{pull}[u_{r+1}|u_r]$ and $\mathbb{E}_{push}[u_{r+1}|u_r]$ are the expected values of the number of uninformed processes at round $r+1$ given $u_r$ uninformed processes at round $r$ for the pull and push version, respectively.*

LEMMA 3.2. *The number of pull rounds required to inform all processes with high probability starting from $\frac{n}{\ln n}$ informed processes is in $\Theta(\log_{f_{in}+1} \ln n)$.*

THEOREM 3.3. *Our pull-only algorithm disseminates a rumor to all processes with high probability in $\Theta(\log_{f_{in}+1} n)$ rounds of communication, which is optimal for the generalized random phone call model.*

THEOREM 3.4. *If $f_{in} \in O(1)$, then the total number of messages (replies to pull requests) required by the pull algorithm is in $\Theta(n)$.*

# 4 PUSH-PULL ALGORITHMS

We now discuss our push-pull algorithms. We push when the rumor is young, then pull when the rumor is old. Processes do not reply to pull requests if the rumor is new, nor do they push the rumor if it is old.

LEMMA 4.1. *$\Theta(\frac{n}{\ln n})$ messages transmitted uniformly at random are necessary and sufficient to inform at least $\frac{n}{\ln n}$ processes with high probability. More precisely, if $m \geq \frac{n}{\ln n} + \frac{n}{\ln^2 n}$ messages are transmitted uniformly at random, then the probability of informing less than $\frac{n}{\ln n}$ processes is at most*

$$2e^{-\frac{\left(1-\frac{1}{\ln n}-\left(1-\frac{1}{n}\right)^m\right)^2\left(n-\frac{1}{2}\right)}{1-\left(1-\frac{1}{n}\right)^{2m}}}. \qquad (2)$$

THEOREM 4.2. *If $f_{in} \in O(1)$ and $f_{out} \in O(\ln n)$, our push-pull algorithm can disseminate a rumor to all processes with high probability using $\Theta(n)$ messages. The algorithm requires $\log_{f_{out}+1} n + O(\ln \ln n)$ rounds using an infect forever push phase, and $\log_{f_{out}} n + O(\ln \ln n)$ rounds with the infect upon contagion push strategy when $f_{out} \geq 2$. If $f_{out} \in O(1)$ and $f_{in} = 1$, both algorithms require $n + O\left(\frac{n}{\ln n}\right)$ messages.*

THEOREM 4.3. *Let $f = \max(f_{in}, f_{out})$. Any protocol in the generalized random phone call model requires $\Omega(\log_{f+1} n)$ rounds of communication to disseminate a rumor to all processes with high probability.*

We now illustrate the performance of our infect-upon-contagion-push-pull algorithm. First, using the tools of Section 2 and Lemma 4.1, we calculate the number of push rounds required to inform at least $\frac{n}{\ln n}$ processes with a chosen probability of imperfect dissemination. The threshold is very sharp for networks with a few hundred processes or more: there is a $r'$ such that the probability of informing $\frac{n}{\ln n}$ processes goes from $\approx 0$ in round $r'-1$ to $\approx 1$ in round $r'$. In practice this phase transition is the sweet spot to switch from the push phase to the pull phase. We then calculate the number of rounds of the pull phase using the tools of Section 3.

The communication overhead is in $O\left(f_{\text{out}} \cdot \frac{n}{\ln n}\right)$, and the transition phase is such that with a logarithmic fan-out, we sometimes go from slightly less than $\frac{n}{\ln n}$ informed processes in round $r_{\text{push}}-1$ to almost $n$ informed processes in round $r_{\text{push}}$. In these situations, we can decrease the number of overhead messages by transmitting each message in round $r_{\text{push}}$ with a scaling probability $p_{\text{scale}}$ such that the number of informed processes after round $r_{\text{push}}$ is above but close to $\frac{n}{\ln n}$ with high probability. This ensures that the communication overhead is in $O\left(\frac{n}{\ln n}\right)$ even with a logarithmic fan-out. We can easily calculate $p_{\text{scale}}$ with Eq. (2) and the machinery of Section 2.

Figure 1 shows the communication overhead for varying system sizes, $f_{\text{out}}$ and $f_{\text{in}}$ for a probability of error of $p_e = 10^{-15}$. The $f_{\text{out}} = \lfloor \ln n \rfloor$ $f_{\text{in}} = 1$ configuration is of particular interest in practice because it provides sublogarithmic latency with a negligible communication and process overhead. More precisely, for systems with between ten thousand and one million processes, the algorithm requires between 13 and 15 rounds, a fan-out of size 9 to 13, and when scaling the last push round the communication overhead varies between 1.2% for ten thousand processes and 0.3% for one million processes. The $10^{-15}$ probability of imperfect dissemination is on par with the failure probability of modern hardware. If this is still insufficient, we can decrease the probability of imperfect dissemination to $10^{-100}$ by reducing the scaling of the last push round, which slightly increases the communication overhead (to 2.6% for ten thousand processes and 0.4% for one million processes), and pulling for two to three additional rounds.

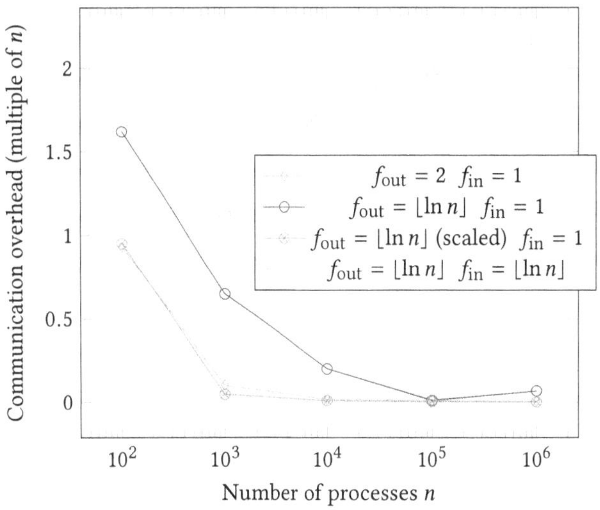


**Figure 1: Communication overhead of the infect-upon-contagion-push-pull algorithm for $p_e = 10^{-15}$ and different $f_{\text{in}}$, $f_{\text{out}}$ and network size $n$. Each data point is the average over 10 simulations. The simulations labeled (scaled) scale the last push round.**

# REFERENCES

[1] Robert M Corless, Gaston H Gonnet, David EG Hare, David J Jeffrey, and Donald E Knuth. 1996. On the Lambert W function. *Advances in Computational mathematics* 5, 1 (1996), 329–359.

[2] Alan Demers, Dan Greene, Carl Hauser, Wes Irish, John Larson, Scott Shenker, Howard Sturgis, Dan Swinehart, and Doug Terry. 1987. Epidemic Algorithms for Replicated Database Maintenance. In *Proceedings of the Sixth Annual ACM Symposium on Principles of Distributed Computing (PODC '87)*. ACM, New York, NY, USA, 1–12. https://doi.org/10.1145/41840.41841

[3] Richard M. Karp, Christian Schindelhauer, Scott Shenker, and Berthold Vöcking. 2000. Randomized Rumor Spreading. In *41st Annual Symposium on Foundations of Computer Science, FOCS 2000, 12-14 November 2000, Redondo Beach, California, USA*. IEEE Computer Society, 565–574. https://doi.org/10.1109/SFCS.2000.892324

[4] Boris Koldehofe. 2004. Simple gossiping with balls and bins. *Stud. Inform. Univ.* 3, 1 (2004), 43–60.

# Blockchains and the Future of Distributed Computing

Maurice Herlihy
Brown University
Computer Science Department
Providence, Rhode Island
maurice.herlihy@gmail.com

## ABSTRACT

There has been a recent explosion of interest in blockchain-based distributed ledger systems such as Bitcoin, Ethereum, and many others. Much of this work originated outside the distributed computing community, but the questions raised, such as consensus, replication, fault-tolerance, privacy, and security, and so on, are all issues familiar to our community.

This talk surveys the theory and practice of blockchain-based distributed systems from the point of view of classical distributed computing, along with reckless speculation about promising future research directions for our community.


*PODC'17, July 24-27, 2017, Washington, DC, USA.*

ACM ISBN 978-1-4503-4992-5/17/07
DOI: http://dx.doi.org/10.1145/3087801.3087873

## BIOGRAPHY

Maurice Herlihy has an A.B. in Mathematics from Harvard University, and a Ph.D. in Computer Science from M.I.T. He has served on the faculty of Carnegie Mellon University and the staff of DEC Cambridge Research Lab. He is the recipient of the 2003 Dijkstra Prize in Distributed Computing, the 2004 Gödel Prize in theoretical computer science, the 2008 ISCA influential paper award, the 2012 Edsger W. Dijkstra Prize, the 2013 Wallace McDowell award, and the 2017 Brown University Research Innovation Award. He received a 2012 Fulbright Distinguished Chair in the Natural Sciences and Engineering Lecturing Fellowship, and he is fellow of the ACM, a fellow of the National Academy of Inventors, the National Academy of Engineering, and the National Academy of Arts and Sciences.

# A Simple Deterministic Distributed MST Algorithm, with Near-Optimal Time and Message Complexities

Michael Elkin*
Department of Computer Science, Ben-Gurion University of the Negev
Beer-Sheva, Israel
elkinm@cs.bgu.ac.il

## ABSTRACT

Distributed *minimum spanning tree* (MST) problem is one of the most central and fundamental problems in distributed graph algorithms. Kutten and Peleg [KP98] devised an algorithm with running time $O(D + \sqrt{n} \cdot \log^* n)$, where $D$ is the hop-diameter of the input $n$-vertex $m$-edge graph, and with message complexity $O(m + n^{3/2})$. Peleg and Rubinovich [PR99] showed that the running time of the algorithm of [KP98] is essentially tight, and asked if one can achieve near-optimal running time *together with near-optimal message complexity.*

In a recent breakthrough, Pandurangan et al. [PRS16] answered this question in the affirmative, and devised a *randomized* algorithm with time $\tilde{O}(D + \sqrt{n})$ and message complexity $\tilde{O}(m)$. They asked if such a simultaneous time- and message-optimality can be achieved by a *deterministic* algorithm.

In this paper, building upon the work of [PRS16], we answer this question in the affirmative, and devise a *deterministic* algorithm that computes MST in time $O((D + \sqrt{n}) \cdot \log n)$, using $O(m \cdot \log n + n \log n \cdot \log^* n)$ messages. The polylogarithmic factors in the time and message complexities of our algorithm are significantly smaller than the respective factors in the result of [PRS16]. Also, our algorithm and its analysis are very *simple* and self-contained, as opposed to rather complicated previous sublinear-time algorithms [GKP98, KP98, Elk04b, PRS16].

## CCS CONCEPTS

• **Theory of computation → Shortest paths; Distributed algorithms;**

**ACM Reference format:**
Michael Elkin. 2017. A Simple Deterministic Distributed MST Algorithm, with Near-Optimal Time and Message Complexities. In *Proceedings of PODC'17, July 25-27, 2017, Washington, DC, USA*, , 7 pages.
DOI: http://dx.doi.org/10.1145/3087801.3087823

*This research was supported by the ISF grant No. (724/15).


*PODC'17, July 25-27, 2017, Washington, DC, USA*

DOI: http://dx.doi.org/10.1145/3087801.3087823

## 1 INTRODUCTION

### 1.1 Background and New Results

Distributed *minimum-weight spanning tree* (henceforth, MST) problem is one of the most fundamental and extensively studied problems in distributed graph algorithms [GHS83, CT85, Gaf85, Awe87, SB95, GKP98, KP98, PR99, Elk04a, Elk04b, FM04, KP08, KKP11, KKT15, PRS16, MK17]. The seminal work of Gallager et al. [GHS83] gave an algorithm with running time $O(n \log n)$ and message complexity $O(m + n \log n)$ for the problem, where $n = |V|$ and $m = |E|$ are the number of vertices and edges of the input graph $G = (V, E)$, respectively. The time complexity was then improved to $O(n)$ [CT85, Gaf85, Awe87, FM04], while still retaining the bound of $O(m + n \log n)$ on the number of messages.

Kutten and Peleg [KP98], improving a previous result by Garay et al. [GKP98], devised an algorithm with running time $O(D + \sqrt{n} \cdot \log^* n)$, where $D$ is the hop-diameter (equivalently, unweighted diameter) of $G$, albeit with message complexity $O(m + n^{3/2})$. Peleg and Rubinovich [PR99] showed a lower bound of $\tilde{\Omega}(\sqrt{n})$ for the problem,[1] even when $D = O(\log n)$. In the open problems section of their groundbreaking paper they raised the question of devising a nearly time- and message-optimal algorithm:

"*Another research direction is to try to reduce the* communication *complexity of nearly time optimal algorithm of [KP98] from* $O(|E| + n^{3/2})$ *towards the lower bound of* $O(|E| + n \log n)$."

In a recent breakthrough, Pandurangan et al. [PRS16] devised a randomized algorithm with time complexity $\tilde{O}(D + \sqrt{n})$ and message complexity $\tilde{O}(m)$. In the Conclusion section of their paper they write:

"*An intriguing open question is whether randomization is necessary to simultaneously achieve time and message optimality.*"

In this paper we answer this question, and devise a *deterministic* algorithm with running time $O((D + \sqrt{n}) \cdot \log n)$, and message complexity $O(|E| \cdot \log n + n \log n \cdot \log^* n)$. In addition to being deterministic, our algorithm is also drastically simpler than that of [PRS16].[2] Also, the polylogarithmic factors in the time and message complexities of our algorithm are significantly smaller than the respective factors in [PRS16]. (Pandurangan et al. [PRS16] do not specify explicitly these factors. However, since they are using an algorithm for constructing neighborhood covers from [Elk04b],

[1] $\tilde{O}$, $\tilde{\Omega}$ and $\tilde{\Theta}$ notations hide factors polylogarithmic in $n$.
[2] Though we stress that it heavily builds upon several crucial ideas from [PRS16]; see more details below.

and the latter algorithm has running time $O(D\log^3 n)$ and message complexity $O(m \cdot \log^2 n)$, these factors are definitely incurred by the algorithm of [PRS16]. Also, it is apparent from their analysis that the $\sqrt{n}$ term in their time complexity is multiplied by at least $\log^2 n$.)

We also generalize our result to the $CONGEST(b\log n)$ model, for any positive integer parameter $b$. In this model the bandwidth of every edge is $b$ edge weights and/or vertex identities. (See Section 2 for a formal definition.) We show that our algorithm can be implemented in $O((D + \sqrt{\frac{n}{b}}) \cdot \log n)$ time, using $O(|E| + n\log n \cdot \log^* n)$ messages.

The lower bound for the time required to compute MST in the $CONGEST(b\log n)$ model is $\Omega(D + \sqrt{\frac{n}{b\log n}})$ [Elk04a, PR99], i.e., our upper bound is $\Theta(\log n)$-off the lower bound in the first term and $\Theta(\log^{3/2} n)$-off in the second term, for all values of $b$. (In particular, this is also the gap in the standard $CONGEST$ model, i.e., when $b = 1$.)

The lower bound on message complexity, due to Awerbuch et al. [AGPV90], is $\Omega(|E|)$. The lower bound of [AGPV90] applies to deterministic algorithms, and also even to randomized comparison-based algorithms. It also applies to randomized not comparison-based ones, as long as they apply to the so-called *clean network model*. In the latter model, at the beginning of the computation every vertex $v$ knows only its own identity number. On the other hand, if a vertex knows also (at the beginning of the computation) identities of all its neighbors, then a not comparison-based randomized algorithm of King et al. [KKT15] achieves message complexity of $\tilde{O}(n)$ (though their time complexity is not sublinear in $n$).

Our algorithm is deterministic, comparison-based, and applies to the clean network model. (Any one of these three properties makes the lower bound of [AGPV90] applicable.) Hence its message complexity is $O(|E|\log n + n\log n \cdot \log^* n)$ is optimal up to a $\log n$ factor in the first term, and a $\log n \cdot \log^* n$ factor in the second.

## 1.2 Technical Overview

The sublinear-time MST algorithm of [KP98, GKP98] consists of two phases. In the first phase one constructs an *MST forest*, i.e., a collection of vertex-disjoint subtrees of the same fixed MST, that cover all vertices of the input graph $G = (V, E)$. These subtrees are called *fragments*. Moreover, each of these fragments in the algorithm of [KP98] has diameter $O(\sqrt{n})$, and there are $O(\sqrt{n})$ such fragments in the forest. The computation of this MST forest requires $\tilde{O}(\sqrt{n})$ time: it is done by an ingenious variant of Boruvka's algorithm.

At this stage there are only $O(\sqrt{n})$ MST edges missing. These are computed by a procedure, called Pipeline-MST [GKP98]. In this procedure one uses an auxiliary BFS tree $\tau$ of the input graph $G$. All candidate edges (i.e., crossing between different fragments) are pipelined towards the root $rt$ of $\tau$, but the key to efficiency is that every intermediate vertex $v$ of $\tau$ filters out all candidate edges $e$ that are discovered to be heaviest in some cycle. This (second) phase of the algorithm of [KP98] is responsible for its large message complexity, and it also involves heavy local computations.

The recent nearly message-optimal algorithm of [PRS16] also consists of two phases, where the first phase is the same as in the algorithm of [KP98]. However, on the second phase, the algorithm of [PRS16] employs a different strategy than that of [KP98]. Rather than using a communication-heavy Pipeline-MST procedure, they continue merging fragments via a Boruvka-type algorithm.

The problem with merging large-diameter fragments via Boruvka's algorithm is that a naive implementation of this merging requires time proportional to the diameter of these fragments. When $D = O(\sqrt{n})$, Pandurangan et al. [PRS16] overcome this problem by maintaining two MST forests at all times: one is the *base forest* $\mathcal{F}$ (and its fragments are referred to as *base fragments*), which was computed at the first phase of the algorithm. Recall that $\mathcal{F}$ consists of $O(\sqrt{n})$ fragments of size $O(\sqrt{n})$ each. (For a pair of parameters $\alpha, \beta$, an $(\alpha, \beta)$-*MST forest* is an MST forest with at most $\alpha$ fragments, each of diameter at most $\beta$. The base forest is an $(O(\sqrt{n}), O(\sqrt{n}))$-MST forest.)

The second MST forest $\hat{\mathcal{F}}$ that the algorithm of [PRS16] maintains is obtained by merging some of the base fragments into fragments of $\hat{\mathcal{F}}$ via Boruvka's algorithm. To compute the *minimum weight outgoing edge* (henceforth, MWOE) of a fragment $\hat{F} \in \hat{\mathcal{F}}$, the algorithm computes in each base fragment $F \in \mathcal{F}$ a minimum-weight edge $e_F$ crossing between $V(F)$ and $V \setminus V(\hat{F})$, where $F \subseteq \hat{F}$, and $\hat{F} \in \hat{\mathcal{F}}$. Then the algorithm upcasts these edges $e_F$ to the root $rt$ of the auxiliary BFS tree $\tau$. The root $rt$ uses this information to compute the MWOE $e_{\hat{F}}$ of every fragment $\hat{F} \in \hat{\mathcal{F}}$, and then to compute a new MST forest $\hat{\mathcal{F}}'$. The fragments of the latter forest are obtained by merging some of the fragments of $\hat{\mathcal{F}}$, via Boruvka's algorithm.

When $D \leq \sqrt{n}$, the procedure described above is both time- and message-efficient. However, generally, its message complexity is $\tilde{\Theta}(D\sqrt{n} + n)$, and this is super-linear for $D = \omega(\sqrt{n})$. To resolve this issue, [PRS16] employ hierarchies of sparse neighborhood covers [ABCP93, Coh93, Elk04b], and use them to build what they call "communication-efficient fragments and paths" within large-diameter fragments. This results in a sophisticated and complicated algorithm, with an elaborate analysis, which incurs quite a few polylogarithmic factors in both time and message complexities, and requires storing certain non-trivial local data structures in every vertex. Moreover, since there are currently no known *deterministic* distributed time- and message-efficient algorithms for constructing neighborhood covers, the algorithm of [PRS16] resorts to using a *randomized* algorithm of [Elk04b]. As a result, the solution of [PRS16] becomes randomized as well.

In this paper we propose a different, and a much simpler solution, for the situation when $D \geq \sqrt{n}$. Instead of constructing an $(O(\sqrt{n}), O(\sqrt{n}))$-MST forest $\mathcal{F}$ as a base forest, we construct an $(O(n/D), O(D))$-MST forest. By slightly generalizing and refining the analysis of [KP98, Len16, PRS16], we show that this can be done in $O(D \cdot \log^* n)$ time, and with $O(|E| \cdot \log D + n \cdot \log D \cdot \log^* n)$ messages. By doing so we spend more time on the first phase than the algorithms of [KP98, PRS16]; this is however still well within our desired time bounds.

Then we use the algorithm of [PRS16] on top of this base forest, as opposed to using it on top of an $(O(\sqrt{n}), O(\sqrt{n}))$-MST forest. (Recall that, as was argued above, the latter would have not been message-efficient.) Now computing a minimum-weight edge $e_F$ crossing between the vertex set $V(F)$ of a base fragment $F$ and

$V \setminus V(\hat{F})$, where $\hat{F} \in \hat{\mathcal{F}}$ is the fragment that contains $F$, can be done in $O(D + n/D) = O(D)$ time. Even more importantly, upcasting all these edges $e_F$ to the root $rt$ of the auxiliary tree $\tau$ requires now just $O(D \cdot n/D) = O(n)$ messages. As a result, the entire message complexity of our algorithm is near-linear.

As opposed to previous solutions, our entire algorithm and its analysis are ultimately very simple. In fact, we essentially provide all the details (including those which originate from previous work) in this extended abstract.

### 1.3 Related Work

Singh and Bernstein [SB95] devised an MST algorithm with near-optimal message complexity, and with running time $O((\Delta + Diam(MST)) \cdot \log n)$, where $\Delta$ is the maximum degree of the input graph $G = (V, E, \omega)$, [3] and $Diam(MST)$ is the hop-diameter of the computed MST of $G$. The latter parameter is always greater or equal to $D = Diam(G)$, but for many instances it is smaller than $n$.

The current author [Elk04b] devised an MST algorithm with running time $\tilde{O}(\mu(G,\omega) + \sqrt{n})$, where $\mu(G,\omega)$ is a parameter which is never greater than $D$, and for many instances it is much smaller than $D$. There is also a lower bound of $\Omega(\mu(G,\omega)) + \tilde{\Omega}(\sqrt{n})$ for the MST computation on an input graph $(G,\omega)$ [Elk04b]. Albeit, the algorithm of [Elk04b] does not detect termination (unless it is given an estimate of $\mu(G,\omega)$ as a part of the input).

Khan and Pandurangan [KP08] devised an $O(\log n)$-approximate MST algorithm with running time $\tilde{O}(D + L(G,\omega))$, where $L(G,\omega)$ is yet another parameter, called *local shortest path diameter*. It may be smaller or larger than $D$.

Lower bounds on the time required to compute an approximate MST were shown in [Elk04a, SHK+12, EKNP14]. In particular, [EKNP14] showed such lower bounds even when quantum distributed communication is allowed. Lower bounds for MST on graphs with constant hop-diameter $D$ were shown in [LPP06, Elk04a]. MST on graphs with $D = 1$ (the *Congested Clique* model) was studied in [LPPP05, HPP+15, GP16]. In particular, [HPP+15] devised a message-optimal and time-efficient MST algorithm for this model.

Mahreghi and King [MK17] devised randomized, not comparison-based MST algorithm with running time $\tilde{O}(Diam(MST))$, and with $\tilde{O}(n)$ messages. (This algorithm assumes that at the beginning of the computation, every vertex knows the identities of all its neighbors, i.e., the so-called $KT_1$ model.)

Efficient MST algorithms for planar graphs, and more generally, graphs of bounded genus, were given in [GH16, HIZ16].

## 2 PRELIMINARIES

We consider the synchronous *CONGEST* model of distributed communication. Every vertex $v$ of an input graph $G = (V, E)$ hosts a processor, and these processors communicate with one another via $O(\log n)$-size messages in synchronous rounds. All edge weights are assumed to be at most polynomial in $n$, or alternatively, the message size can be restricted to $O(1)$ edge weights or/and identity numbers. In a more general $CONGEST(b \log n)$ model, for a parameter $b \geq 1$, on every round every vertex is allowed to send messages of size $O(b \log n)$ bits, or alternatively, $O(b)$ edge weights and/or vertex identities via every edge incident on it.

We assume that $G$ is a connected graph, i.e., $|E| \geq n - 1$.

At the beginning of the communication every vertex $v$ knows its own unique identity number, denoted $Id(v)$. The *running time* of an algorithm in this model is the worst-case number of rounds that it runs. The *message complexity* of an algorithm is the worst-case overall number of messages sent throughout an execution of the algorithm. At the end of an execution, every vertex $v$ is required to know which among the edges incident on it belong to the MST.

We assume that the MST is unique. This assumption is without loss of generality, see, e.g., [Pel00], Ch. 5. A connected subtree of the unique MST is called an *MST fragment*, or simply a *fragment*.

We say that a collection $\{F_1, F_2, \ldots, F_h\}$, for some positive integer $h$, is an *MST forest*, if for each $i \in [h]$, $F_i$ is an MST fragment, these fragments are vertex-disjoint, and $\bigcup_{i=1}^{h} V(F_i) = V$. For a pair of positive parameters $\alpha$ and $\beta$, we say that an MST forest $\mathcal{F}$ is an $(\alpha,\beta)$-*MST-forest*, if it contains at most $\alpha$ fragments, each with strong diameter at most $\beta$. (*Strong diameter* of a subgraph $F$ is the maximum distance in $F$ between a pair of vertices $u, v \in V(F)$.) A *diameter* of an MST forest $\mathcal{F}$ is the maximum diameter of one of its fragments.

We say that an MST forest $\mathcal{F}'$ *coarsens* MST forest $\mathcal{F}$, if for every fragment $F \in \mathcal{F}$, there exists a fragment $F' \in \mathcal{F}'$ that contains it, i.e., $V(F) \subseteq V(F')$ (and, as a result, also $E(F) \subseteq E(F')$, because $F$ and $F'$ are subtrees of the same spanning tree).

Boruvka's algorithm starts from a collection of MST fragments. On each phase it computes the MWOE of every fragment, and computes the fragments' graph, whose vertices are the fragments, and edges are the MWOEs. It then merges each connected component of the fragments' graph into a greater fragment, and obtains an MST forest with fewer fragments. In fact, the number of fragments decreases at least by a factor of 2, and so the number of phases is $O(\log n)$. See [Pel00], Ch. 5, for further details.

For a rooted tree $T$ and a non-root vertex $v$ in $T$, we denote by $\pi_T(v)$ the *parent* of $v$ in $T$. For a vertex $v$, we denote by $Id(v)$ the identity of the vertex $v$. For each fragment $F$, there is a designated root vertex $rt_F$, and the identity $Id(F)$ of $F$ is set to be the identity $Id(rt_F)$ of the root $rt_F$.

## 3 THE ALGORITHM AND ITS ANALYSIS

Based on [GKP98, KP98] (see also [PRS16], Algorithm 1, called Controlled-GHS, and Lemma 1, and Lenzen's lecture notes [Len16], the chapter about MST, Lemmas 6.15-6.17), we show in Section 4 that for any positive parameter $k$, an $(n/k, O(k))$-MST forest $\mathcal{F} = \mathcal{F}_0$ can be computed in $O(k \cdot \log^* n)$ time, and using $O(|E| \log k + n \log k \cdot \log^* n)$ messages. [4] We refer to $\mathcal{F}_0$ as the *base* MST forest, and call its fragments *base fragments*.

The algorithm starts with constructing an auxiliary BFS tree $\tau$ for the entire graph $G$ rooted at a root vertex $rt$. This step requires $O(D)$ time and $O(|E|)$ messages.

[3] $\omega : E \rightarrow \mathrm{R}^+$ is a weight function on edges of $G$.

[4] In fact, Lemma 6.17 of [Len16] applies this only for $k \leq \sqrt{n}$, but inspecting its proof reveals that it holds for larger values of $k$ as well. The message complexity of this procedure is not analyzed in [KP98, Len16], while its analysis in [PRS16] provides a slightly weaker bound. For the sake of completeness, we provide a self-contained proof of this result in Section 4.

Every base fragment $F$ has its designated root vertex $r_F$. We need every vertex $v$ of $\tau$ to be able to route messages from the root $rt$ of $\tau$ to each of the roots $r_F$ of base fragments $F \in \mathcal{F}$, which belong to the subtree $\tau_v$ of $\tau$ rooted at $v$. For this end, we compute intervals $I_v$ for each vertex $v \in V(\tau)$, such that for every pair $u, v$ of vertices in $V$, their intervals are either disjoint (if they belong to different branches of $\tau$), or nested if the vertex with a larger interval is an ancestor in $\tau$ of the vertex with a smaller interval. Given these intervals, when a vertex $v$ needs to route a message to a root $r_F$ of a base fragment $F$ which belongs to $V(\tau_v)$, it finds a child $u$ of $v$ whose interval $I(u)$ contains $I(r_F)$, and sends the message to this child.

To compute the intervals, we first conduct a convergecast in $\tau$. As a result of this convergecast, every vertex $v$ knows the size $|V(\tau_v)|$ of its subtree. Then the root $rt$ of $\tau$ assigns itself the interval $I(rt) = [1,n]$, $n = |V(\tau)| = |V|$, and assigns its children $u_1, \ldots, u_d$, for $d = deg(rt)$, disjoint intervals $I(u_1), \ldots, I(u_d) \subseteq I(rt)$, with $|I(u_i)| = |V(\tau_{u_i})|$, for every $i \in [d]$. (This is possible because $\sum_{i=1}^{d} |V(\tau_{u_i})| = n - 1 = |I(rt)| - 1$. Observe also that $rt$ can learn $|V(\tau_{u_i})|$, for all $i \in [d]$, within one round.) Next, each of the children $u_i$ assigns (in parallel) disjoint intervals to their children, etc. Finally, at the end of this process, we conduct a pipelined convergecast during which the root $rt$ learns the $|\mathcal{F}|$ intervals of all the base fragments.

The entire process of computing the intervals requires $O(D)$ time and $O(n)$ messages, while the final pipelined convergecast requires $O(D + |\mathcal{F}|) = O(D + n/k)$ time, and $O(D \cdot n/k)$ messages.

Consider first the case $D \le \sqrt{n}$. We set $k = \sqrt{n}$. Suppose we have already conducted $j$ phases of the Boruvka's algorithm, starting from $\mathcal{F}_0$, and obtained a coarsening forest $\mathcal{F}_j$, for some $j = 0, 1, 2, \ldots$, of $\mathcal{F}$. We now show how to implement the next phase of Boruvka's algorithm, and to construct a coarsening MST forest $\mathcal{F}_{j+1}$ of $\mathcal{F}_j$ (and, consequently, of $\mathcal{F}$ too).

We assume that every vertex $v$ knows the identities of both the base fragment $F_v$ and the fragment $\hat{F}_v$ of $\mathcal{F}_j$ that it belongs to. Also, for every neighbor $u$ of $v$, we assume that $v$ knows the identities of $F_u$ and $\hat{F}_u$. We also assume that the root $rt$ knows the identities of all base fragments, and at the beginning of phase $j$, $j = 0, 1, \ldots$, it knows the identities of all fragments of $\mathcal{F}_j$, and for each base fragment $F \in \mathcal{F}$, the root knows the identity of the fragment $\hat{F} \in \mathcal{F}_j$ that coarsens it. This is argued by induction on $j$.

To guarantee that the induction base $j = 0$ holds, after the base MST forest is constructed, every vertex $v$ updates its neighbors with the identity of $F_v$. This requires $O(1)$ time and $O(|E|)$ messages. Also, an upcast of $|\mathcal{F}_0| \le n/k$ identities of base fragments is conducted over the BFS tree $\tau$ at this stage. This step requires $O(D + n/k)$ time, and $O(D \cdot n/k)$ messages.

In every base fragment $F \in \mathcal{F}_0$ we compute (in parallel in all base fragments) the edge $e = (u, v)$ of minimum weight that crosses between $u \in V(F)$ and $v \in V \setminus V(\hat{F})$, where $\hat{F} \in \mathcal{F}_j$ is the fragment that coarsens the base fragment $F$. This computation requires $O(k) = O(\sqrt{n})$ time, and $O(n)$ messages.

Once this is done, we upcast all these $O(n/k) = O(\sqrt{n})$ pieces of information over the auxiliary BFS tree $\tau$ to the root vertex $rt$ of $\tau$. This is done via a pipelined convergecast procedure, in which every intermediate vertex $u$ of $\tau$ forwards to his parent $\pi_\tau(u)$ in $\tau$ only the lightest edge for each fragment $\hat{F} \in \mathcal{F}_j$, among edges that were initially stored at one of the vertices $z$ of the subtree $\tau_u$ of $\tau$, rooted at $u$. This step requires $O(D + |\mathcal{F}_j|)$ time, and $O(D \cdot |\mathcal{F}_j|)$ messages. (See [Pel00], ch. 3.)

The root $rt$ locally computes the MWOE $e_{\hat{F}}$ for every fragment $\hat{F} \in \mathcal{F}_j$. It then locally computes the fragments' graph whose vertices are fragments of $\mathcal{F}_j$, and edges are the MWOEs, and computes the MST forest $\mathcal{F}_{j+1}$. Specifically, for every base fragment $F \in \mathcal{F}$, the root knew the identity of a fragment $\hat{F} \in \mathcal{F}_j$ that coarsens it. As a result of the computation that $rt$ conducts, it now knows the identity of a fragment $\hat{F}' \in \mathcal{F}_{j+1}$ that coarsens $\hat{F}$. (Consequently, the fragment $\hat{F}'$ also coarsens the base fragment $F$.) The root $rt$ then sends $|\mathcal{F}|$ messages over $\tau$, each message is of the form $(F, \hat{F}')$, where $F \in \mathcal{F}$, $\hat{F}' \in \mathcal{F}_{j+1}$, $\hat{F}'$ coarsens $F$. Each such a message $(F, \hat{F}')$ has the destination interval $I(rt_F)$ attached to it, and it is routed along the unique $rt - rt_F$ path in $\tau$. The root $rt_F$ of the base fragment $F$ receives this message, and writes down to itself that it belongs to $\hat{F}'$. This (pipelined) downcast requires $O(D + |\mathcal{F}|) = O(D + n/k)$ time, and $O(D \cdot |\mathcal{F}|) = O(D \cdot n/k)$ messages. (This is because every one of the $|\mathcal{F}|$ messages is routed to its destination along a path with at most $D$ edges.)

Next, every root vertex $r_F$ of a base fragment $F \in \mathcal{F}$ broadcasts the identity $Id(\hat{F}')$ of their new $(j+1)$st level fragment $\hat{F}' \in \mathcal{F}_{j+1}$ to all vertices of $F$. This requires $O(k)$ time and $O(n)$ messages. Finally, every vertex $v$ updates its neighbors in $G$ with its new $(j+1)$st level's fragment identity. This requires $O(1)$ time, and $O(|E|)$ messages. This completes the description of a single phase of Boruvka's algorithm.

To analyze the running time and message complexity, observe that for every $j = 0, 1, 2, \ldots$ we have $|\mathcal{F}_{j+1}| \le (1/2) \cdot |\mathcal{F}_j|$, and so the number of phases $\ell$ is $O(\log n)$ phases. Since $D \le \sqrt{n} = k$, the overall time is

$$
\begin{aligned}
&O(D + n/k) + O(k \cdot \log^* n) + O((D + k + |\mathcal{F}|) \cdot \log n) \\
&= O((D + k + n/k) \cdot \log n) \;=\; O(\sqrt{n} \cdot \log n).
\end{aligned}
$$

Similarly, the message complexity is $O(|E| \log n + n \log n \cdot \log^* n)$ for constructing $\mathcal{F}$, $O(D \cdot n/k + n)$ for computing the intervals, and $O(D \cdot n/k + |E| + n)$ on each consequent phase. As $D \le k$, the overall message complexity is $O(|E| \log n + n \log n \cdot \log^* n)$.

For $D > \sqrt{n}$, we compute the $(n/k, O(k))$-MST forest $\mathcal{F} = \mathcal{F}_0$ with parameter $k = D$ in $O(D \cdot \log^* n)$ time, and $O(|E| \log n + n \log n \cdot \log^* n)$ messages. From this point on, the algorithm is identical to the one that we have just described. For every $j = 0, 1, 2, \ldots$, the $j$th phase of it requires $O(D + k + |\mathcal{F}|) = O(D + k + n/k) = O(D)$ time, i.e., all phases altogether require $O(D \log n)$ time.

The number of messages is $O(|E| + n + D \cdot |\mathcal{F}|)$ on every phase, i.e., $O((|E| + n) \cdot \log n)$ messages in all the $\ell$ phases. Hence the total message complexity is $O(|E| \log n + n \log n \cdot \log^* n)$.

We summarize this result below.

Theorem 3.1. *The deterministic algorithm that was described above computes the minimum spanning tree in the CONGEST model, in $O((D + \sqrt{n}) \cdot \log n)$ time, using $O(|E| \log n + n \log n \cdot \log^* n)$ messages.*

Next, we extend the algorithm to the *CONGEST*$(b \log n)$ model, for a positive integer parameter $b$. We first discuss the case of small diameter, i.e., $D \le \sqrt{\frac{n}{b}}$, and then proceed to discussing the complementary case.

In the small-diameter regime, we set $k = \sqrt{\frac{n}{b}}$, i.e., $D \le k$. We construct an $(n/k, O(k))$-MST forest $\mathcal{F}_0$ in $O(k \log^* n)$ time, using $O(|E| \log n + n \log n \cdot \log^* n)$ messages. The upcast of $|\mathcal{F}_0| \le n/k$ identities of base fragments requires $O(D + \frac{n}{k \cdot b})$ time and $O(D \cdot n/k)$ messages. Now consider the $j$th phase of the algorithm, for some $j = 0, 1, 2, \ldots$. Computing minimum weight crossing edges in parallel in all base fragments $\{e = (u,v) \mid u \in V(F), v \in V \setminus V(\hat{F}), F \in \mathcal{F}, \hat{F} \in \mathcal{F}_j\}$ requires $O(k)$ time and $O(n)$ messages. Pipelined convergecast of $|\mathcal{F}_j|$ items requires $O(D + \frac{|\mathcal{F}_j|}{b})$ time and $O(D \cdot |\mathcal{F}_j|)$ messages. The pipelined downcast of $|\mathcal{F}| \le n/k$ messages requires $O(D + |\mathcal{F}|/b) = O(D + \frac{n}{kb}) = O(D + \sqrt{n/b})$ time, and $O(D \cdot |\mathcal{F}|) = O(D \cdot n/k)$ messages. (Note that this downcast sends each message only along its own root-destination path, rather than broadcasting it to the entire graph.) Updating neighbors with new fragments' identities requires $O(1)$ time and $O(|E|)$ messages. The overall running time of the $\ell$ phases is

$$O\left(D + \frac{n}{k \cdot b}\right) + O(k \log n + D \log n + |\mathcal{F}| \cdot \log n)$$
$$= O\left(\left(D + k + \frac{n}{k \cdot b}\right) \cdot \log n\right)$$
$$= O\left(\sqrt{\frac{n}{b}} \cdot \log n\right).$$

This is also the upper bound on the total running time. The overall number of messages used in the $\ell$ phases is $O((D \cdot n/k + n + |E|) \log n) = O(|E| \cdot \log n)$. Hence the total message complexity is $O(|E| \log n + n \log n \cdot \log^* n)$.

In the large-diameter regime, i.e., when $D > \sqrt{\frac{n}{b}}$, we set $k = D$. Constructing $\mathcal{F} = \mathcal{F}_0$ requires $O(D \log^* n)$ time and $O(|E| \log n + n \log n \cdot \log^* n)$ messages. Computing minimum weight crossing edges in all base fragments in parallel requires (on each phase) $O(D)$ time and $O(n)$ messages. Other than that on phase $j$, for $j = 0, 1, \ldots, \ell - 1$, we have time $O(D + \frac{|\mathcal{F}|}{b})$ time and $O(D \cdot |\mathcal{F}|)$ messages. Overall, this sums up to

$$O((D + |\mathcal{F}|/b) \cdot \log n) = O\left(\left(D + \frac{n}{Db}\right) \cdot \log n\right) = O(D \log n)$$

time, and $O((D \cdot n/k + n + |E|) \cdot \log n) = O(|E| \cdot \log n)$ messages. Hence the total running time of the entire algorithm in this case is $O(D \log n)$, and its message complexity is $O(|E| \log n + n \log n \cdot \log^* n)$.

THEOREM 3.2. *For any $b \ge 1$, the deterministic algorithm that was described above computes the minimum spanning tree in CONGEST$(b \log n)$ model, in $O((D + \sqrt{n/b}) \cdot \log n)$ time, using $O(|E| \log n + n \log n \cdot \log^* n)$ messages.*

# 4 CONSTRUCTING AN MST FOREST

For the sake of completeness, we next describe the algorithm (due to [GKP98, KP98, Len16]) for constructing an $(n/k, O(k))$-MST forest, for an integer parameter $k \le n/10$. (The constant 10 is quite arbitrary.) Our version of the algorithm is slightly more general than that in [Len16], and our bounds on its time and message complexities are slightly better than the respective bounds in [PRS16].

The algorithm runs for $t = \lceil \log k \rceil$ phases. At the beginning of a phase $i = 0, 1, 2, \ldots, t-1$, the algorithm has already computed $(n/2^{i-1}, 6 \cdot 2^i)$-MST forest $\mathcal{F}_i$. The induction base $i = 0$ holds for the MST forest of singletons. We next describe a single phase of the algorithm, and show that the resulting collection $\mathcal{F}_{i+1}$ is an $(n/2^i, 6 \cdot 2^{i+1})$-MST forest.

At the beginning of a phase $i$, every fragment $F \in \mathcal{F}_i$ with diameter at most $2^i$ computes the edge $e_F = MWOE(F)$. We denote the set of fragments $\mathcal{F}_i'$. This step requires $O(2^i)$ time and $O(n)$ messages. (Also, at the beginning of each phase, every vertex updates its neighbors with the identity of its fragment. This requires $O(1)$ time and $O(|E|)$ messages.) Then, for every $e_F = (u,v)$, $u \in V(F)$, $v \in V \setminus V(F)$, a message is sent over $e_F$, and the receiver $v$ writes down $u$ as a "foreign-fragment" child of itself. (In the special case when $(u,v) = MWOE(F_u) = MWOE(F_v)$, with $u \in V(F_u)$, $v \in V(F_v)$, the endpoint belonging to a higher-identity fragment becomes the parent of the other endpoint.)

This defines a *candidate fragment graph* $\mathcal{G}_i' = (\mathcal{F}_i', \mathcal{E}_i)$, whose vertices are the fragments of $\mathcal{F}_i'$, and edges are the *MWOE* edges of these fragments. We then compute a maximal matching (henceforth, MM) $M$ in $\mathcal{G}_i'$. (We will soon elaborate on this.) For every pair $(F, F') \in M$, the two fragments merge into a single fragment, along the *MWOE* edge that connects them. Every fragment $F'' \in \mathcal{F}_i' \setminus \mathcal{F}_i'(M)$ is necessarily connected via its $MWOE(F'') = e''$ to either a matched fragment $F \in \mathcal{F}_i'(M)$, or to a fragment $F \in \mathcal{F}_i \setminus \mathcal{F}_i'$ of diameter larger than $2^i$. In either case, it now merges with $F$ along the edge $e''$. Except for the procedure that computes an MM, this completes the description of the algorithm. The MST forest $\mathcal{F}_{i+1}$ consists now of the resulting merged fragments, and of those fragments of $\mathcal{F}_i \setminus \mathcal{F}_i'$ that did not participate in the merging process described above. (These are the fragments $F$ with diameter $Diam(F) > 2^i$, and such that no unmatched fragment $F' \in \mathcal{F}_i'$ has its *MWOE* $(u,v)$ with an endpoint in $F$.)

**Remark**: The next two lemmas and their proofs are closely related to that of Lemmas 6.15 and 6.17 in [Len16].

LEMMA 4.1. *$Diam(\mathcal{F}_{i+1}) \le 6 \cdot 2^{i+1}$.*

PROOF. Each new fragment $\hat{F} \in \mathcal{F}_{i+1}$ can be viewed as a subtree of diameter at most 3 in the fragment graph $\mathcal{G}_i = (\mathcal{F}_i, \mathcal{E}_i)$, whose edge set $\mathcal{E}_i$ is the set of all the *MWOE*s of fragments of $\mathcal{F}_i$. Moreover, at most one of the fragments in this subtree may have diameter greater than $2^i$. (But, by induction hypothesis, its diameter is, nevertheless, at most $6 \cdot 2^i$.) Hence the diameter of $\hat{F}$ in $G$ is at most $6 \cdot 2^i + 3 \cdot 2^i + 3 \le 12 \cdot 2^i = 6 \cdot 2^{i+1}$. ∎

LEMMA 4.2. *For $i = 0, 1, \ldots, t-2$, each fragment $\hat{F} \in \mathcal{F}_{i+1}$ contains at least $2^i$ vertices.*

PROOF. The proof is by induction on $i$. The base $i = 0$ holds, as every fragment of $\hat{F}_1$ contains at least one vertex.

By induction hypothesis, every fragment $F \in \mathcal{F}_i$ contains at least $2^{i-1}$ vertices. Consider a fragment $F \in \mathcal{F}_i$ with $|F| < 2^i$. Then $Diam(F) < 2^i$ too, and hence $F \in \mathcal{F}_i'$. Thus $F$ merges with at least one other fragment $F'$ of $\mathcal{F}_i$. (As $|F| < 2^i \le n$, $F$ has outgoing edges, and thus has an *MWOE*.) Since, by induction hypothesis, $|F|, |F'| \ge 2^{i-1}$, it follows that the merged fragment has size at least $2^i$. ∎

Hence $|\mathcal{F}_i| \leq n/2^{i-1}$. By substituting $i = t - 1 = \lceil \log k \rceil - 1$, we get $|\mathcal{F}_{t-1}| = O(n/k)$, and $Diam(F_{t-1}) = O(k)$. By rescaling (setting $k' = c \cdot k$, for an appropriate constant $c$), we obtain the desired $(n/k, O(k))$-MST forest.

Next, we sketch the procedure that computes an MM in the forest $\mathcal{G}'_i = (\mathcal{F}_i', \mathcal{E}'_i)$, and analyze its time and message complexities. Recall that, by Lemma 4.1, each fragment $F \in \mathcal{F}_i'$ has diameter $O(2^i)$.

The first step is to simulate Cole-Vishkin's 3-vertex-coloring algorithm [CV86] in $\mathcal{G}'_i$. For this end, on every step every internal fragment $F \in \mathcal{F}_i'$ needs to send a message with its current color to its children in $\mathcal{G}'_i$. (Initial colors are set as fragments' identities.) This is implemented in $O(2^i)$ time, using $O(n)$ messages, in a straightforward manner. Since there are $\log^* n + O(1)$ such steps, overall this computation requires $O(2^i \cdot \log^* n)$ time and $O(n \cdot \log^* n)$ messages.

Given a 3-vertex-coloring of $\mathcal{G}'_i$, there are 3 steps. On each step $j \in \{1, 2, 3\}$, fragments $F'$ of color $j$ that have at least one of their children $F''$ unmatched, insert an edge $(F', F'')$ connecting them to such an unmatched child into the matching, and update their parents $F$ that they became matched. The second step involves a convergecast in the parent fragment $F$, during which the root of $F$ learns if it still has an unmatched child. Also, every internal vertex $v \in F$ learns if one of its descendents leads to an unmatched child of $F$ or not.

This entire part of the algorithm can also be implemented in $O(2^i)$ time and $O(n)$ messages, in a straightforward manner. Hence the entire computation of MM on phase $i$ of the algorithm requires $O(2^i \cdot \log^* n)$ time, and $O(n \cdot \log^* n)$ messages. Thus, the total running time of phase $i$ is $O(2^i \cdot \log^* n)$, and the number of messages is $O(|E| + n \cdot \log^* n)$. Summing up over all the $\lceil \log k \rceil$ phases, we obtain running time $O(\log^* n \sum_{i=0}^{\lceil \log k \rceil} 2^i) = O(k \cdot \log^* n)$, and message complexity $O(|E| \cdot \log k + n \log k \cdot \log^* n)$.

We summarize this section in the following theorem.

THEOREM 4.3. *For an integer parameter $k \leq n/10$, the deterministic algorithm described above computes an $(n/k, O(k))$-MST forest in time $O(k \cdot \log^* n)$, using $O(|E| \cdot \log k + n \cdot \log k \cdot \log^* n)$ messages.*

## REFERENCES


[ABCP93] Baruch Awerbuch, Bonnie Berger, Lenore Cowen, and David Peleg. Near-linear cost sequential and distribured constructions of sparse neighborhood covers. In *34th Annual Symposium on Foundations of Computer Science, Palo Alto, California, USA, 3-5 November 1993*, pages 638–647, 1993.

[AGPV90] Baruch Awerbuch, Oded Goldreich, David Peleg, and Ronen Vainish. A trade-off between information and communication in broadcast protocols. *J. ACM*, 37(2):238–256, 1990.

[Awe87] Baruch Awerbuch. Optimal distributed algorithms for minimum weight spanning tree, counting, leader election and related problems (detailed summary). In *Proceedings of the 19th Annual ACM Symposium on Theory of Computing, 1987, New York, New York, USA*, pages 230–240, 1987.

[Coh93] Edith Cohen. Fast algorithms for constructing t-spanners and paths with stretch t. In *34th Annual Symposium on Foundations of Computer Science, Palo Alto, California, USA, 3-5 November 1993*, pages 648–658, 1993.

[CT85] Francis Y. L. Chin and H. F. Ting. An almost linear time and o(n log n + e) messages distributed algorithm for minimum-weight spanning trees. In *26th Annual Symposium on Foundations of Computer Science, Portland, Oregon, USA, 21-23 October 1985*, pages 257–266, 1985.

[CV86] Richard Cole and Uzi Vishkin. Deterministic coin tossing with applications to optimal parallel list ranking. *Information and Control*, 70(1):32–53, 1986.

[EKNP14] Michael Elkin, Hartmut Klauck, Danupon Nanongkai, and Gopal Pandurangan. Can quantum communication speed up distributed computation? In *ACM Symposium on Principles of Distributed Computing, PODC '14, Paris, France, July 15-18, 2014*, pages 166–175, 2014.

[Elk04a] M. Elkin. An unconditional lower bound on the time-approximation tradeoff of the minimum spanning tree problem. In *Proc. of the 36th ACM Symp. on Theory of Comput. (STOC 2004)*, pages 331–340, 2004.

[Elk04b] Michael Elkin. A faster distributed protocol for constructing a minimum spanning tree. In *Proceedings of the Fifteenth Annual ACM-SIAM Symposium on Discrete Algorithms, SODA 2004, New Orleans, Louisiana, USA, January 11-14, 2004*, pages 359–368, 2004.

[FM04] Michalis Faloutsos and Mart Molle. A linear-time optimal-message distributed algorithm for minimum spanning trees. *Distributed Computing*, 17(2):151–170, 2004.

[Gaf85] Eli Gafni. Improvements in the time complexity of two message-optimal election algorithms. In *Proceedings of the Fourth Annual ACM Symposium on Principles of Distributed Computing, Minaki, Ontario, Canada, August 5-7, 1985*, pages 175–185, 1985.

[GH16] Mohsen Ghaffari and Bernhard Haeupler. Distributed algorithms for planar networks II: low-congestion shortcuts, mst, and min-cut. In *Proceedings of the Twenty-Seventh Annual ACM-SIAM Symposium on Discrete Algorithms, SODA 2016, Arlington, VA, USA, January 10-12, 2016*, pages 202–219, 2016.

[GHS83] Robert G. Gallager, Pierre A. Humblet, and Philip M. Spira. A distributed algorithm for minimum-weight spanning trees. *ACM Trans. Program. Lang. Syst.*, 5(1):66–77, 1983.

[GKP98] Juan A. Garay, Shay Kutten, and David Peleg. A sublinear time distributed algorithm for minimum-weight spanning trees. *SIAM J. Comput.*, 27(1):302–316, 1998.

[GP16] Mohsen Ghaffari and Merav Parter. MST in log-star rounds of congested clique. In *Proceedings of the 2016 ACM Symposium on Principles of Distributed Computing, PODC 2016, Chicago, IL, USA, July 25-28, 2016*, pages 19–28, 2016.

[HIZ16] Bernhard Haeupler, Taisuke Izumi, and Goran Zuzic. Low-congestion shortcuts without embedding. In *Proceedings of the 2016 ACM Symposium on Principles of Distributed Computing, PODC 2016, Chicago, IL, USA, July 25-28, 2016*, pages 451–460, 2016.

[HPP+15] James W. Hegeman, Gopal Pandurangan, Sriram V. Pemmaraju, Vivek B. Sardeshmukh, and Michele Scquizzato. Toward optimal bounds in the congested clique: Graph connectivity and mst. In *Proceedings of the 2015 ACM Symposium on Principles of Distributed Computing, PODC 2015, San Sebastian, Spain*, pages 91–100, 2015.

[KKP11] Liah Kor, Amos Korman, and David Peleg. Tight bounds for distributed MST verification. In *28th International Symposium on Theoretical Aspects of Computer Science, STACS 2011, March 10-12, 2011, Dortmund, Germany*, pages 69–80, 2011.

[KKT15] Valerie King, Shay Kutten, and Mikkel Thorup. Construction and impromptu repair of an MST in a distributed network with o(m) communication. In *Proceedings of the 2015 ACM Symposium on Principles of Distributed Computing, PODC 2015, Donostia-San Sebastián, Spain, July 21 - 23, 2015*, pages 71–80, 2015.

[KP98] Shay Kutten and David Peleg. Fast distributed construction of small $k$-dominating sets and applications. *J. Algorithms*, 28(1):40–66, 1998.

[KP08] Maleq Khan and Gopal Pandurangan. A fast distributed approximation algorithm for minimum spanning trees. *Distributed Computing*, 20(6):391–402, 2008.

[Len16] C. Lenzen. Lecture notes on theory of distributed systems. https:/www.mpi-inf.mpg.de/fileadmin/inf/d1/teaching/winter15/tods/ToDS.pdf, 2016.

[LPP06] Zvi Lotker, Boaz Patt-Shamir, and David Peleg. Distributed MST for constant diameter graphs. *Distributed Computing*, 18(6):453–460, 2006.

[LPPP05] Zvi Lotker, Boaz Patt-Shamir, Elan Pavlov, and David Peleg. Minimum-weight spanning tree construction in $O(\log \log n)$ communication rounds. *SIAM J. Comput.*, 35(1):120–131, 2005.

[MK17] Ali Mashreghi and Valerie King. Time-communication trade-offs for minimum spanning tree construction. In *Proceedings of the 18th International Conference on Distributed Computing and Networking, Hyderabad, India, January 5-7, 2017*, page 8, 2017.

[Pel00] D. Peleg. *Distributed Computing: A Locality-Sensitive Approach.* SIAM, 2000.

[PR99] D. Peleg and V. Rubinovich. A near-tight lower bound on the time complexity of distributed mst construction. In *Proc. 40th IEEE Symp. on Foundations of Computer Science*, pages 253–261, 1999.

[PRS16] Gopal Pandurangan, Peter Robinson, and Michele Scquizzato. A time- and message-optimal distributed algorithm for minimum spanning trees. *CoRR, accepted to STOC'17*, abs/1607.06883, 2016.

[SB95] Gurdip Singh and Arthur J. Bernstein. A highly asynchronous minimum spanning tree protocol. *Distributed Computing*, 8(3):151–161, 1995.

[SHK+12] Atish Das Sarma, Stephan Holzer, Liah Kor, Amos Korman, Danupon Nanongkai, Gopal Pandurangan, David Peleg, and Roger Wattenhofer. Distributed verification and hardness of distributed approximation. *SIAM J. Comput.*, 41(5):1235–1265, 2012.

# Distributed Approximation of Maximum Independent Set and Maximum Matching*

Reuven Bar-Yehuda
Technion, Department of Computer Science
reuven@cs.technion.ac.il

Keren Censor-Hillel
Technion, Department of Computer Science
ckeren@cs.technion.ac.il

Mohsen Ghaffari
ETH Zurich
ghaffari@mit.edu

Gregory Schwartzman
Technion, Department of Computer Science
gregory.schwartzman@gmail.com

## ABSTRACT

We present a simple distributed $\Delta$-approximation algorithm for maximum weight independent set (MaxIS) in the CONGEST model which completes in $O(\texttt{MIS}(G) \cdot \log W)$ rounds, where $\Delta$ is the maximum degree, $\texttt{MIS}(G)$ is the number of rounds needed to compute a maximal independent set (MIS) on $G$, and $W$ is the maximum weight of a node. Plugging in the best known algorithm for MIS gives a randomized solution in $O(\log n \log W)$ rounds, where $n$ is the number of nodes. We also present a deterministic $O(\Delta + \log^* n)$-round algorithm based on coloring.

We then show how to use our MaxIS approximation algorithms to compute a 2-approximation for maximum weight matching without incurring any additional round penalty in the CONGEST model. We use a known reduction for simulating algorithms on the line graph while incurring congestion, but we show our algorithm is part of a broad family of *local aggregation algorithms* for which we describe a mechanism that allows the simulation to run in the CONGEST model without an additional overhead.

Next, we show that for maximum weight matching, relaxing the approximation factor to $(2 + \varepsilon)$ allows us to devise a distributed algorithm requiring $O(\frac{\log \Delta}{\log \log \Delta})$ rounds for any constant $\varepsilon > 0$. For the unweighted case, we can even obtain a $(1 + \varepsilon)$-approximation in this number of rounds. These algorithms are the first to achieve the provably optimal round complexity with respect to dependency on $\Delta$.

**ACM Reference format:**
Reuven Bar-Yehuda, Keren Censor-Hillel, Mohsen Ghaffari, and Gregory Schwartzman. 2017. Distributed Approximation of Maximum Independent Set and Maximum Matching. In *Proceedings of PODC '17, Washington, DC, USA, July 25-27, 2017,* 10 pages.
https://doi.org/http://dx.doi.org/10.1145/3087801.3087806

*Supported in part by the Israel Science Foundation (grant 1696/14).


*PODC '17, July 25-27, 2017, Washington, DC, USA*

ACM ISBN 978-1-4503-4992-5/17/07...$15.00
https://doi.org/http://dx.doi.org/10.1145/3087801.3087806

## 1 INTRODUCTION

We address the fundamental problems of approximating the maximum independent set and the maximum matching of a graph in the classic distributed CONGEST model [39]. In this model, the $n$ nodes of the graph communicate in synchronous rounds, by sending one $O(\log n)$-bit message per round along links of the graph. Table 1 summarizes our contributions. Below, we elaborate on our results, the challenges, and how we overcome them.

| Problem | Approx. | Prev. Results | Our Results | notes |
|---|---|---|---|---|
| MaxIS \| MWM | $\Delta \mid 2$ | – | $O(\texttt{MIS}(G) \log W)$ | rand. |
| MaxIS \| MWM | $\Delta \mid 2$ | – | $O(\Delta + \log^* n)$ | det. |
| MWM | $2 + \varepsilon$ | $O(\log n)$ | $O(\log \Delta / \log \log \Delta)$ | rand. |
| MCM | $1 + \varepsilon$ | $O(\log n)$ | $O(\log \Delta / \log \log \Delta)$ | rand. |

**Table 1: Summary of results for the CONGEST model. Here $n$ denotes the number of nodes, $\Delta$ is their maximum degree, and $W$ is the maximum weight.**

### 1.1 Our Results, Part I: Better Approximations

*$\Delta$-approximation algorithms for maximum weight independent set.* We present a simple distributed $\Delta$-approximation algorithm for maximum weight independent set (MaxIS), where $\Delta$ is the maximum degree, which completes in $O(\texttt{MIS}(G) \cdot \log W)$ rounds, where $\texttt{MIS}(G)$ is the number of rounds needed to compute a maximal independent set (MIS) on $G$, and $W$ is the maximum weight of a node. As standard, we assume that $W$ is at most polynomial in $n$, so that the weight of each edge can be described in one message. Our algorithm adapts the *local ratio* technique [7] for maximization problems [4] to the distributed setting in a novel, yet simple, manner. Roughly speaking, in the simplest form of this technique, one repeatedly picks a node $v$ and reduces its weight from every $u \in N(v)$, where $N(v)$ is the set of neighbors of $v$. Every neighbor $u \in N(v)$ whose weight becomes less than or equal to zero is removed from the graph, while $v$ is added to a stack. We repeat this process with the induced graph until no nodes remain. We then begin popping nodes from the stack, adding them to the independent set if they have no neighbors in the set. This yields a $\Delta$-approximation.

The challenge in translating this framework to the distributed setting is that if we allow all nodes to perform weight reductions simultaneously, then the above does not hold. For example, consider a star graph where the weight of the center is larger than the weight of any of its neighbors but smaller than their sum. After a single iteration the weights of all the nodes become negative, and no node gets selected. However, we show that if we first compute an independent set and then go on to perform weight reductions we achieve a $\Delta$-approximation factor, while allowing using the power of parallelism. At each iteration we find an MIS, and the nodes chosen to the MIS perform weight reductions. This process is repeated until no nodes with positive weight remain. Nodes are then added to the independent set in reverse order of removal while maintaining the independence constraints. To analyze the running time, our main technique is to group the nodes into $\log W$ *layers* based on their weight. At each iteration, all of the nodes from the topmost layer move to lower layers.

This results in a round complexity of $O(\mathtt{MIS}(G) \cdot \log W)$ in the CONGEST model. Our algorithm is deterministic apart from using a black-box algorithm to find an MIS at each iteration. Whether our algorithm is randomized or deterministic depends on the MIS algorithm it uses as a black-box.

We also present a deterministic coloring-based algorithm running in $O(\Delta + \log^* n)$ rounds. Here we first color the graph using $\Delta + 1$ colors, and then use each color group as an independent set to perform weight reductions as in the previous algorithm.

*2-approximation algorithms for maximum weighted matching.* We use a known reduction to simulate algorithms on the line graph [29], our MaxIS $\Delta$-approximation algorithm gives a 2-approximation for maximum weight matching. Simulating an execution on the line graph in a naive fashion results in a $O(\Delta)$ multiplicative overhead in the CONGEST model. We show our algorithm is part of a broad family of *local aggregation* algorithms for which we describe a mechanism which allows the simulation to run in the CONGEST model without added overhead.

Our deterministic coloring-based algorithm has a favorable running time compared to the algorithm presented in [17] with parameters that result in a 2-approximation. Our randomized algorithm improves upon the $(2 + \epsilon)$-approximation factor of [33]. Using the maximal matching algorithm of [10] on the original graph as an MIS algorithm on the line graph we get a running time of $O((\log \Delta + \log^4 \log n) \cdot \log W)$ [1], with high probability, for the LOCAL model, and using Luby's classical MIS algorithm[36], we get an $O(\log n \cdot \log W)$ algorithm[2] for the CONGEST model. For constant values of $W$, this is $O(\log n)$ rounds.

## 1.2 Our Results, Part II: Faster Approximations

*Approximations with Optimal Time-Complexity:* We provide two approximations algorithms for maximum matching that achieve the optimal round complexity of $O(\log \Delta / \log \log \Delta)$: The first achieves a $(2 + \epsilon)$-approximation of maximum weight matching, and the second a $(1 + \epsilon)$-approximation of maximum cardinality matching, for any constant $\varepsilon > 0$.

These two algorithms improve upon the $O(\log n)$-round algorithms of Lotker et al.[34] for the same problems and same approximation guarantees. Furthermore, these two algorithms are the first constant-approximation algorithms that achieve an optimal round complexity, matching the $\Omega(\log \Delta / \log \log \Delta)$ lower bound of Kuhn et al. [30]. We note that this lower bound holds for any constant approximation, and so long as $\log \Delta \leq \sqrt{\log n}$.

*Method Outline.* A key ingredient in both of the above fast algorithms is an improvement of the *nearly-maximal independent set* algorithm of Ghaffari [20]. A nearly-maximal independent set is an independent set for which each node in the graph is in the set or has a neighbor in the set with probability at least $1 - \delta$ for a small $\delta$. The main result of [20] is a maximal independent set algorithm with round complexity of $O(\log \Delta) + 2^{O(\sqrt{\log \log n})}$. The central building block in that result was finding a nearly-maximal independent set in $O(\log \Delta)$ rounds. Here, we provide an improved nearly-maximal independent set algorithm with a round complexity of $O(\log \Delta / \log \log \Delta)$. This algorithm builds upon the techniques of [20], but with some crucial modifications. The modification is partially inspired by the ideas of the recent vertex-cover approximation algorithm of Bar-Yehuda et al. [6], of balancing two types of progresses. While this improvement does not allow us to improve upon Ghaffari's MIS algorithm, it helps us in obtaining our fast maximum matching approximation algorithms, as we discuss next.

For the $(2 + \epsilon)$-approximation, this improved nearly-maximal independent set algorithm is essentially enough. We run it on the line graph of the network graph, and argue that it gives an $(2 + \epsilon)$-approximation of the maximum unweighted matching. To argue that the algorithm works in the CONGEST model, even when run on the line graph of the network graph, we use the property that this nearly-maximal independent set algorithm is a local aggregation algorithm. Then, we extend this approximation algorithm to the *weighted* case, using techniques of [34, 35].

For the unweighted $(1 + \epsilon)$-approximation, our goal is to use the general framework of Hopcroft and Karp [26], in which we repeatedly search for short non-intersecting augmenting paths and augment the matching with them, hence improving its size. However, in our setting, this does not work as is and poses significant challenges. One key challenge is that, to have the desired approximation factor, we need a much stronger near-maximality guarantee. It does not suffice to have a low probability for each short augmenting path to remain; we need to show that each node has a low probability of having a remaining augmenting path. To overcome the obstacles, first we show how to find a nearly-maximal matching in low-rank hypergraphs and how to modify the algorithm for obtaining the $(1 + \epsilon)$-approximation guarantee in the LOCAL model.

Making the algorithm suitable for the CONGEST model is even more demanding, in part because here we cannot explicitly work with the structure of the intersections between short augmenting paths; instead, we need to have a new variant of the near-maximal independent set algorithm that works *on the fly*. At a high level, we first address bipartite graphs, and show how to find a nearly-maximal independent set of short augmenting paths in them. Since the augmenting paths are not known explicitly, an interesting aspect here will be a variant of the dynamic probability adjustments in the algorithm of[20]. Now, various nodes of a path might decide differently regarding whether to raise or lower its probability. However, we will prove that still the net effect provides a sufficient move in the right direction. We complete by generalizing this from bipartite graphs to all graphs, using an idea of Lotker et al. [34],

[1] Note that $\Delta$ and $n$ are the parameters of the original graph and not the line graph.
[2] Here the MIS algorithm is executed on the line graph, so we get $O(\mathtt{MIS}(G)) = O(\log n^2) = O(\log n)$.

which essentially transforms the problem into randomly chosen bipartite subgraphs of it.

## 1.3 Related Work

The maximum independent set problem is known to be NP-hard, as it is complementary to the maximum clique problem, which is one of Karp's 21 NP-hard problems [28]. In the sequential setting, an excellent summary of the known results is given by [3], which we overview in what follows. For general graphs, the best known algorithm achieves a $O(n \log^2 \log n/\log^3 n)$-approximation factor [18]. Assuming $NP \nsubseteq ZPP$, [25] shows that no $(n^{1-\epsilon})$-approximation exists for every constant $\epsilon > 0$.

When the degree is bounded by $\Delta$, a simple $(\Delta+2)/3$-approximation is achieved by greedily adding the node with minimal degree to the independent set and removing its neighbors [23]. The best known approximation factor is $O(\Delta \log\log \Delta/\log \Delta)$ [1, 21, 22, 24, 27]. Conditioned on the Unique Games Conjecture, there exist a $\Omega(\Delta/\log^2 \Delta)$-approximation bound [2], where $\Delta$ is constant or some mildly increasing function of $n$. Assuming $P \neq NP$, a bound of $\Omega(\Delta/\log^4 \Delta)$ is given in [12].

As for the distributed case, [14, 31] give a lower bound of $\Omega(\log^* n)$ rounds for any deterministic algorithm approximating MaxIS, while [14] provide randomized and deterministic approximations for planar graphs. In [11], an $O(1/\epsilon)$-round LOCAL randomized algorithm for $O(n^\epsilon)$-approximation is presented for the unweighted case, along with a matching lower bound.

Maximum matching is a classical optimization problem, for which the first polynomial time algorithm was given by Edmonds [15, 16] for both the weighted and unweighted case. In the distributed setting, the first algorithm for computing an approximate maximum matching was given in [40], where a 5-approximation factor is achieved w.h.p for general graphs, in $O(\log^2 n)$ rounds. In [35] a randomized $(4+\epsilon)$-approximation for the weighted case is given, running in $O(\log n)$ rounds for constant $\epsilon > 0$. This was later improved in [33] to achieve a $(2+\epsilon)$-approximation in $O(\log \epsilon^{-1} \log n)$ rounds. In [17] a deterministic $(1+\epsilon)$-approximation is given, in $\Delta^{O(1/\epsilon)} + O(1/(\epsilon^2)) \cdot \log^* n$ rounds for the unweighted case, and $\log(\min\{1/w_{min}, n/\epsilon\})^{O(1/\epsilon)} \cdot (\Delta^{O(1/\epsilon)} + \log^* n)$ rounds for the weighted case, where the edge weights are in $[w_{min}, 1]$. In [13] a deterministic $(1+\epsilon)$-approximation is given, which finishes after $O(\log^{D(1/\epsilon)} n)$ rounds, where $D(1/\varepsilon)$ is some function of $1/\varepsilon$. Due to [30], every algorithm achieving a constant approximation for the problem requires $\Omega(\min\{\log \Delta/\log\log \Delta, \sqrt{\log n/\log\log n}\})$ rounds.

The first distributed algorithm that uses the local ratio technique is due to [38]. The local ratio technique was also used in [6] to compute a distributed $(2+\epsilon)$-approximation for weighted vertex cover. In [37], a similar technique of weight grouping is used in the primal-dual framework for scheduling.

# 2 MAXIS APPROXIMATION

We begin, in Subsection 2.1, by showing the idea behind the use of local ratio for approximating MaxIS. This is done by presenting a sequential meta-algorithm and analyzing its correctness. Then, in Subsection 2.2, we show how to implement this algorithm in the CONGEST model, and prove the claimed round complexity.

## 2.1 Sequential MaxIS approximation via local ratio

Here we provide a sequential $\Delta$-approximation meta-algorithm to be used as the base for our distributed algorithm. The correctness of the algorithm is proved using the local ratio technique for maximization problems [4]. We assume a given weighted graph $G = (V, w, E)$, where $w : V \rightarrow \mathbb{R}_+$ is an assignment of weights for the nodes and the degree of each node is bounded by $\Delta$. A simple $\Delta$-approximation local ratio algorithm exists for the problem [5]. We rely on the following local ratio theorem for maximization problems [5, Theorem 9] in our proof.

Theorem 2.1. *Let $C$ be a set of feasibility constraints on vectors in $\mathbb{R}^n$. Let $w, w_1, w_2 \in \mathbb{R}^n$ be vectors such that $w = w_1 + w_2$. Let $x \in \mathbb{R}^n$ be a feasible solution (with respect to $C$) that is $r$-approximate with respect to $w_1$ and with respect to $w_2$. Then $x$ is $r$-approximate with respect to $w$ as well.*

In our case the vector $w$ is the weight vector representing the weight function of $G(V, w, E)$, $x$ is a binary vector indicating which nodes are chosen to the solution and the set of constraints $C$, is the set of independence constraints. We call the graph with weight vector $w_1$ the *reduced graph* and the graph with weight vector $w_2$ the *residual graph*.

As standard practice with the local ratio technique, the splitting of the weight vector into $w_1, w_2$ is done such that any $r$-approximate solution to the reduced graph can be easily transformed into an $r$-approximate solution to the residual graph, while keeping it an $r$-approximate solution for the reduced graph. This allows us to apply weight reductions iteratively, solving each subproblem while maintaining the constraints. It is important to note that the theorem also holds if the weights in the reduced graph take negative values.

For the specific problem of MaxIS, we note that picking some node $v \in V$ and reducing the weight of $v$ from every $u \in N(v)$ splits the weight vector $w$ into two vectors, $w_1$ and $w_2$. Where $w_2(v) = w(v)$ for every $u \in N(v)$ and zero for every other node, and $w_1 = w - w_2$. Note that any $\Delta$-approximate solution for the reduced graph can be easily turned into a $\Delta$-approximate solution for the residual graph. This is done by making sure that at least some $u \in N(v)$ is in the solution: If this is not the case, we can always add one $u \in N(v)$ to the solution without violating the independence constraints. This only increases the value of our solution, making it $\Delta$-approximate for both the residual and the reduced graphs.

The above solution is sequential by nature. Implementing it directly in the distributed setting will require $O(n)$ rounds. We notice that if two nodes are in different neighborhoods of the graph then this process can be performed by both of them simultaneously without affecting each other. This observation forms the base for our distributed implementation.

We expand this idea by taking any independent set $U \subseteq V$ and for every $v \in U$ reducing the weight of $v$ from every $u \in N(v)$ in parallel. Next, solve the problem for the reduced graph. If for some $v \in U$, every $u \in N(v)$ is not in the solution for the reduced graph, we add $v$ to the solution for the reduced graph. This yields a $\Delta$-approximate solution for the problem. For the sake of simplicity let $V = [n]$. Let $w_2$ be the weight vector of the residual graph after performing weight reductions as described above for some independent set $U \subseteq V$. By definition $w_2[v] = \sum_{u \in U \cap N(v)} w[u]$. The weight of the reduced graph is given by $w_1 = w - w_2$. Let $x \in \{0,1\}^n$ be some $\Delta$-approximate solution for the reduced graph. The cost of the solution $x$ is $\sum_v w[v]x[v]$. Let $x' \in \{0,1\}^n$ be defined as follows:

$$x'[u] = \begin{cases} 1 & u \in U \wedge \forall v \in N(u), x[v] = 0 \\ x[u] & \text{otherwise} \end{cases} \tag{1}$$

We prove the following lemma.

Lemma 2.2. *$x'$ is a $\Delta$-approximate solution for both the reduced graph and the residual graph.*

Proof. We note that $w_2[u] = w[u]$ for every $u \in U$. Thus, $w_1[u] = 0$ for every $u \in U$. We do not incur any additional cost for the reduced graph because $x'$ is created by adding nodes from $U$ to $x$. Because $x$ is $\Delta$-approximate for the reduced graph, so is $x'$.

For the residual graph, only nodes in $\cup_{u \in U} N(u)$ have non zero weights. Let $x^* \in \{0,1\}^n$ be an optimal solution for the residual graph. We can bound from above the weight of $x^*$ by summing over the weights of $N(u)$ for every $u \in U$ where $x^*[u] = 1$, taking into account that for any neighborhood $N(u)$, at most $|N(v)| - 1$ nodes can be selected to a solution due to the independence constraints. We get the following upper bound for the weight $x^*$:

$$\sum_{v \in V} w_2[v]x^*[v] = \sum_{v \in V} \sum_{u \in U \cap N(v)} w_2[u]x^*[u] = \sum_{u \in U} \sum_{v \in N(u)} w_2[u]x^*[u]$$
$$\leq \sum_{u \in U} w_2[u] \cdot (|N(u)| - 1) = \sum_{u \in U} w_2[u] \cdot deg(u) \leq \Delta \sum_{u \in U} w_2[u].$$

On the other hand, $x'$ is selected such that for each $u \in U$ at least one $v \in N(u)$ is in $x'$ for any $u \in U$. Thus, $x' \cdot w_2 = \sum_{u \in U} \sum_{v \in N(u)} w_2[u] \cdot x'[u] \geq \sum_{u \in U} w_2[u]$, which means that $x'$ is at least a $\Delta$-approximation for $x^*$ on the residual graph, and the proof is complete. □

*Overview of Algorithm 1:* Using Lemma 2.2 we construct a meta-algorithm that at each iteration picks an independent set $U \subseteq V$, reduces the weights of the elements in $U$ from their neighborhood and calls itself recursively with the reduced weights. This implicitly splits the graph into the reduced graph and the residual graph. A recursive call returns a $\Delta$-approximate solution for the reduced graph which is turned into a $\Delta$-approximate solution for both graphs by adding all nodes in the independent set that do not have neighbors in the returned solution. According to the local ratio theorem the final solution is a $\Delta$-approximation. Currently we are only interested in the correctness of the algorithm, thus it does not matter how the set $U$ is picked. The recursive step of Algorithm 1 returns a $\Delta$-approximate solution for the reduced graph which is then turned into a $\Delta$-approximate solution for the residual graph. Correctness follows from Lemma 2.2 combined with a simple inductive argument. In the next section we implement this algorithm in a distributed setting.

## 2.2 Distributed MaxIS approximation via local ratio

In this section we implement Algorithm 1 in the distributed setting. We present an algorithm which iteratively finds independent sets and finishes after $\log W$ iterations. This yields a $\Delta$-approximation

**Algorithm 1:** SeqLR($V, E, w$) - Sequential LR algorithm for maximum independent set

```
if V = ∅ then
    Return ∅
foreach v ∈ V do
    if w(v) ≤ 0 then
        V = V \ {v}
        E = E \ {(v, u) | u ∈ V}
Let U ⊆ V be an independent set
Let w1 = w
foreach u ∈ U do
    foreach v ∈ N(u) do
        w1(v) = w(v) − w(u)
R = SeqLR(V, E, w1)
U = U \ ⋃_{v∈R} N(v)
Return R ∪ U
```

in $O(\texttt{MIS}(G) \log W)$ rounds, where $\texttt{MIS}(G)$ is the running time of a black-box MIS algorithm used. The algorithm that wraps the MIS procedure is deterministic, while the MIS procedure may be random. If the MIS procedure is random and finishes after $T$ rounds w.h.p then our algorithm requires $O(T \log W)$ rounds w.h.p. This holds for the CONGEST model.

From now on we assume that all node weights are integers in $[W]$. The sequential meta algorithm can be implemented distributedly, by having each node in the set perform weight reductions independently of other nodes. The key questions left open in the transition to the distributed setting is how to select our independent set at each iteration and how many rounds we need. Iteratively running the MIS procedure and performing weight reductions does not guarantee anything with regard to the number of nodes removed at each iteration or to the amount of weight reduced.

*Overview of the distributed algorithm.* The algorithm works by dividing the nodes into *layers* according to their weights. The $i$-th layer is given by $L_i = \{v \mid 2^{i-1} < w(v) \leq 2^i\}$. During the algorithm each node keeps track of the weights (and layers) of neighboring nodes and updates are sent regarding weight changes and node removals. We divide the algorithm into two stages: the *removal stage* and the *addition stage*.

In the removal stage we find an independent set in the graph and perform weight reductions exactly as in the sequential meta algorithm. When finding the MIS, nodes in higher layers are prioritized over nodes in lower layers. A node cannot start running the MIS algorithm as long as it has a neighbor in a higher level. The most important thing to note here is that nodes in the topmost level never need to wait. A node who is selected to the MIS during the removal stage is a *candidate node.* A node whose weight becomes zero or negative without being added to the MIS is said to be a *removed node.* Removed nodes output `NotInIS` and finish, while candidate nodes continue to the addition stage. Both candidate and removed nodes are deleted from the neighborhood of their neighbors.

In the addition stage, a candidate node $v$ remains only with neighbors with higher weights. We say these nodes have *precedence* over the node $v$. A node $v$ may add itself to the solution only if it has no neighboring nodes which have precedence over it. After a

**Algorithm 2:** A distributed Δ-approximation for weighted MaxIS, code for node $v$

```
//w(v) is the initial weight of v, w_v(v) changes during the run
  of the algorithm
w_v(v) = w(v)
ℓ_v(v) = ⌈log w_v⌉
status = waiting
while true do
    foreach reduce(x) received from u ∈ N(v) do
        w_v(v) = w_v(v) − x
        N(v) = N(v) \ {u}
        if w_v(v) ≤ 0 then
            Send removed(v) to all neighbors
            return NotInIS
    foreach removed(u) received from N(v) do
        N(v) = N(v) \ {u}
    ℓ_v(v) = ⌈log w_v(v)⌉
    Send weightUpdate(v, w_v(v)) to all neighbors
    foreach weightUpdate(u, w') received from N(v) do
        w_v(u) = w'
        ℓ_v(u) = ⌈log w_v(u)⌉
    if status = waiting then
        if ∀u ∈ N(v), ℓ_v(u) ≤ ℓ_v(v) then
            status(v) = ready
            while ∃u ∈ N(v), ℓ_v(u) = ℓ_v(v) and
              status(u) ≠ ready do
                Continue
            v starts running MIS algorithm
        if v in MIS then
            Send reduce(w_v(v)) to all neighbors
            w_v(v) = 0
            status = candidate
        else
            status = waiting
    else if status = candidate then
        if N(v) = ∅ then
            Send addedToIS(v) to all neighbors
            Return InIS
        if addedToIS(u) received from N(v) then
            Send removed(v) to all neighbors
            Return NotInIS
```

node is added to the solution, all of its neighbors become removed. This corresponds line 13 in the sequential meta algorithm.

The correctness of the distributed algorithm follows directly from the correctness of the sequential meta algorithm. We are only left to bound the number of rounds. Let us consider the communication cost of the removal stage. We define the topmost layer to be $L_{top} = L_j$ where $j = arg\,max_i\, L_i \neq \emptyset$. Note that nodes in $L_{top}$ never wait to run the MIS, and that after the MIS finishes for $L_{top}$, the weight of every $v \in L_{top}$ is reduced by at least a factor of two, emptying that layer. This can repeat at most $\log W$ times.

We assume a black-box MIS algorithm that finishes after $\mathtt{MIS}(G)$ rounds with probability at least $1 - p$.

Lemma 2.3. *With probability at least* $1 - p$, $L_{top} = \emptyset$ *after* $\mathtt{MIS}(G)$ *rounds.*

Proof. Let $G'$ be the graph induced by $L_{top}$. By the code, nodes in $L_{top}$ need not wait to run an MIS algorithm and as long as a node is not in $L_{top}$ it does not participate in an MIS algorithm. With probability at least $1-p$ an MIS is selected for $G'$ after $\mathtt{MIS}(G)$ rounds. All nodes selected to the MIS have their weights reduced to zero. Every other node $v$ has at least one neighbor in the MIS, whose weight, by our definition of layers, is at least half of the weight of $v$. Thus the weight of every node $v \in L_{top}$ is halved, emptying the layer. □

We now arrive at the main theorem for this section.

Theorem 2.4. *The distributed MaxIS approximation algorithm (Algorithm 2) finishes within* $O(\mathtt{MIS}(G) \cdot \log W)$ *rounds with probability at least* $1 - p \log W$ *in the* CONGEST *model.* [3]

Proof. Applying a union bound over all layers, gives that all layers are empty after at most $\mathtt{MIS}(G) \cdot \log W$ iterations with probability at least $1 - p \log W$, by Lemma 2.3. We require $p = o(1/\log W)$. This bounds the communication cost for the removal stage.

Denote by $C_i$ the set of candidate nodes from level $L_i$. These nodes are at level $L_i$ when they are set to be candidate nodes. Nodes in $C_i$ wait for neighbors with higher precedence to decided whether they enter the solution. We note that nodes in $C_0$ do not have any neighbors with higher precedence. After nodes in $C_0$ have decided, the nodes in $C_1$ do not have to wait and so on. Thus, all candidate nodes make a decision after at most $\log W$ rounds. This bounds the communication cost for the addition stage. □

## 2.3 Deterministic coloring-based approximation algorithm

In this section we present a simple coloring-based Δ-approximation algorithm for MaxIS. The advantage of this approach is that we have no dependence on $W$, yielding a deterministic algorithm running in $O(\Delta + \log^* n)$ rounds in the CONGEST model.

In the algorithm (pseudocode in Algorithm 3), instead of partitioning the nodes based on weights, they are partitioned based on colors, where colors with larger index have priority. This will result in a runtime independent of the maximum weight. Nodes perform weight reductions if their color is a local maxima. As in the previous section we have two stages: *removal* and *addition*, and three types of node states: *removed*, *candidate* and *precedent*. After one iteration all nodes of the top color are either candidate or removed nodes. Thus after $\Delta + 1$ iterations all nodes are either candidate or removed nodes. Thus, the removal stage finishes in $O(\Delta)$ rounds.

As in Algorithm 2, after the removal stage all candidate nodes only have nodes who have precedence over them as their neighbors.

[3]The MIS algorithm is always executed on the entire graph $G$. Thus, its success probability does not change as we move between levels.

A node adds itself to the independent set if it has no neighbors with precedence over it, in which case all of its neighbors become removed. We again note that candidate nodes of the smallest color have no neighbors and are added to the solution. Thus, the removal stages finishes in $O(\Delta)$ rounds.

**Algorithm 3:** Coloring-based distributed $\Delta$-approximation for weighted MaxIS, code for node $v$

```
Run a Δ + 1 coloring algorithm
Let c : v → [Δ + 1] be a coloring for the nodes
w(v) = w_v
foreach reduce(w') received from u ∈ N(v) do
    w(v) = w(v) − w'
    N(v) = N(v) \ {u}
    if w(v) ≤ 0 then
        Send removed(v) to all neighbors
        return NotInIS
foreach removed(u) received from N(v) do
    N(v) = N(v) \ {u}
if N(v) = ∅ then
    Send addedToIS(v) to all neighbors
    Return InIS
if addedToIS(u) received from N(v) then
    Send removed(v) to all neighbors
    Return NotInIS
if ∀u ∈ N(v) \ {v} it holds that c(v) > c(u) then
    foreach u ∈ N(v) do
        Send reduce(w(v))
    w(v) = 0
```

Algorithm 3 is a distributed implementation of Algorithm 1, where the independent set is selected via its color at each iteration. The correctness of the algorithm follows from the correctness of Algorithm 1. The number of rounds of Algorithm 3 is $O(\Delta + \log^* n)$ by using a deterministic distributed coloring algorithm of $O(\Delta + \log^* n)$ rounds [8, 9].[4] The $\log^* n$ factor cannot be improved upon due to a lower bound by Linial [32].

## 2.4 Distributed 2-approximation for maximum weighted matching

From the results in the previous section we can now derive local 2-approximation algorithms for maximum matching. Let $G$ be a graph with weighted nodes, and let $L(G)$ be the line graph of $G$. It is well known that a maximum independent set in $L(G)$ corresponds to a maximum matching in $G$. An algorithm is executed on the line graph by assigning each edge in $G$ to have its computation simulated by one of its endpoints [29]. We show that running our local ratio based approximation algorithms on $L(G)$ yields a 2-approximate maximum matching in $G$. The main challenge is how to handle congestion, since nodes in $G$ may need to simulate many edges, thus may have to send many messages in a naive simulation [5].

Recall Algorithm 1, the sequential $\Delta$-approximation meta-algorithm. The approximation factor was proved in Lemma 2.2 to be $\Delta$. Specifically, the following equation provided an upper bound for the weight of an optimal solution $x^*$. Where $U$ is some MIS in $L(G)$.

$$\sum_{u \in U} \sum_{v \in N(u)} w[u]x^*[u] \leq \sum_{u \in U} w[u] \cdot (|N(u)| - 1)$$
$$= \sum_{u \in U} w[u] \cdot deg(u) \leq \Delta \sum_{u \in U} w[u].$$

The above bound uses the fact that for any node $u \in U$, at most $|N(u)| - 1$ nodes in $N(v)$ can be selected for the solution due to independence constraints. But in $L(G)$ the largest independent set in the neighborhood of some node in $L(G)$ is at most 2, yielding the following upper bound: $\sum_{u \in U} \sum_{v \in N(u)} w[u]x^*[u] \leq \sum_{u \in U} 2w[u]$. We conclude that the algorithms presented in the previous sections provide 2-approximation for maximum matching when executed on $G(L)$.

As for the communication complexity, the line graph has at most $n\Delta$ nodes and degree bounded by $2\Delta - 2$. Thus, simulating our algorithms on $L(G)$ in the LOCAL model does not incur any additional asymptotic cost. However, in a naive implementation in the CONGEST model, we pay an $O(\Delta)$ multiplicative penalty due to congestion. This can be avoided with some modifications to our algorithms, as explained next.

For $e = (v, u)$ that is simulated by $v$, we call $v$ its *primary* node and $u$ its *secondary* node. We define a family of algorithms called *local aggregation algorithms* and show that these algorithms can be augmented to not incur any additional communication penalty when executed on the line graph relative to their performance on the original graph in the CONGEST model. We begin with some definitions.

*Definition 2.5.* We say that $f : \Sigma^n \to \Sigma$ is *order invariant*, if for any set of inputs $\{x_i\}_{i=1}^n$, and any permutation $\pi$, it holds that $f(x_1, ..., x_n) = f(x_{\pi(1)}, ..., x_{\pi(n)})$.

For the sake of simplicity, if $f$ is order invariant we write $f(x_1, ..., x_n)$ as $f(\{x_i\})$. We may also give a partial parameter set to our function, in which case we assume all remaining inputs to the function are the empty character $\epsilon \in \Sigma$. Formally, for $X' = \{x_i\}_{i=1}^k$, denote $f(X') = f(x_1, ..., x_k, \epsilon, ..., \epsilon)$.

*Definition 2.6.* We say that a function $f : \Sigma^n \to \Sigma$ is an *aggregate function* if it is order invariant and there exists a function $\phi : \Sigma^2 \to \Sigma$ such that for any set of inputs $X = \{x_i\}^k$, and any disjoint partition of the inputs into $X_1, X_2$ it holds that $f(X) = \phi(f(X_1), f(X_2))$. The function $\phi$ is called the *joining function*.

OBSERVATION 2.7. *It is easy to see that Boolean "and" and "or" functions are aggregate functions.*

Let *Alg* be some algorithm for the CONGEST model. Let $D_{v,i}$ be the local data stored by $v$ during the round $i$ of the algorithm

[4] [19] gives a faster coloring but is in LOCAL and in any case we need to pay for the number of colors as well.

[5] What follows is equivalent to iteratively running a maximal matching on weight groups in $G$ and performing local ratio steps on the edges of the matching. We go to $L(G)$ in order to demonstrate how a wide class of algorithms can be executed on the line graph while avoiding congestion.

at. Let $D_{N(v),i} = \{D_{u,i} \mid u \in N(v)\}$ be the data of $v$'s immediate neighborhood.

*Definition 2.8.* We call *Alg* a *local aggregation algorithm* if it only accesses $D_{N(v),i}$ using aggregate functions where $|\Sigma| = O(\log n)$ and $|D_{v,i}| = O(\log n)$ for every $v \in V, i \in [t]$.

We prove the following theorems:

THEOREM 2.9. *If Alg is a local aggregation algorithm running in the* CONGEST *model in $O(t)$ rounds, it can be executed on the line graph in $O(t)$ rounds.*

PROOF. *Alg* is executed on the primary node, and we maintain the invariant that $D_{v,i}$ is always present in both the primary and secondary nodes. Every time *Alg* needs to execute a function $f$, both the primary and secondary nodes already have the data of all of their neighbors. Each node calculates $f$ on the data of its neighbors, the secondary node sends this calculation to the primary which in turn executes the joining function yielding the desired result. Afterwards the new node data is sent to the secondary node.

No communication is needed to access the data of the neighbors, as a neighbor of $e$ must share a node with it, which contains its data. There is no congestion when sending the value of $f$ or the new data to the secondary node. Thus, the number of rounds is $O(t)$. □

THEOREM 2.10. *Algorithm 2 is a local aggregation algorithm.*

PROOF. Let us explicitly define $D_{v,i}$. Each node knows its weight, status and degree. Formally, $D_{v,i} = \{w_i(v), status_v, deg_i(v)\}$. The algorithm uses "and" and "or" Boolean functions, which by Observation 2.7, are aggregate functions. Each node also needs to update its weight at each iteration. The weight update function can be written as $f_w(w_v, \{w_u \mid u \in N(v)\}) = w_v - \sum w_u$, which is of course an aggregate function. □

This exact same technique can be applied to Algorithm 3, giving the main result for this section:

THEOREM 2.11. *There exist a randomized 2-approximation algorithm for maximum weighted matching in the* CONGEST *model running in $O(\mathsf{MIS}(G) \cdot \log W)$ rounds, and a deterministic 2-approximation algorithm for maximum weighted matching in the* CONGEST *model running in $O(\Delta + \log^* n)$ rounds.*

# 3 TIME-OPTIMAL APPROXIMATIONS OF MAXIMUM MATCHING

Here, we provide our $O(\frac{\log \Delta}{\log \log \Delta})$-round algorithms for $(2+\varepsilon)$-approximation of maximum weighted matching and a sketch of a $(1+\varepsilon)$-approximation of maximum unweighted matching. As stated before, these are the first to obtain the provably optimal round complexity, matching the $\Omega(\frac{\log \Delta}{\log \log \Delta})$ lower bound of [30], which holds for *any* constant approximation.

## 3.1 A fast $(2+\varepsilon)$-approximation of maximum weighted matching

We first present a simple $O(\frac{\log \Delta}{\log \log \Delta})$-round $(2+\varepsilon)$ approximation for maximum unweighted matching. We then explain how this approximation extends to the weighted setting via known methods.

To get a $(2+\varepsilon)$-approximation, we gradually find large matchings and remove them from along with the other edges that are incident on them. At the end, we show that the remaining graph has only a small matching left, hence allowing us to prove an approximation guarantee.

The key algorithmic component in our approach is an adaptation of the algorithm of Ghaffari [20]. Ghaffari presented an MIS algorithm, which if executed on a graph $H$ with maximum degree $\Delta$ for $O(\log \Delta + \log 1/\delta)$ rounds, computes an independent set IS of nodes of $H$, with the following probabilistic near-maximality guarantee: each node of $H$ is either in IS or has a neighbor in it, with probability at least $1-\delta$. We will be applying a similar method on the line graph of our original graph, hence choosing a nearly-maximal independent set of edges. However, this running time is not quite fast enough for our target complexity.

We first explain relatively simple changes in the algorithm and its analysis that improve the complexity to $O(\frac{\log \Delta}{\log \log \Delta})$, for any constant $\varepsilon > 0$. We then explain how that leads to an $O(\frac{\log \Delta}{\log \log \Delta})$-round $(2+\varepsilon)$-approximation for maximum unweighted matching.

> *The Modified Nearly-Maximal Independent Set Algorithm.* In each iteration $t$, each node $v$ has a probability $p_t(v)$ for trying to join the independent set IS. Initially $p_0(v) = 1/K$, for a parameter $K$ to be fixed later. The total sum of the probabilities of neighbors of $v$ is called its *effective-degree* $d_t(v)$, i.e., $d_t(v) = \sum_{u \in N(v)} p_t(u)$. The probabilities change over time as follows:
>
> $$p_{t+1}(v) = \begin{cases} p_t(v)/K, & \text{if } d_t(v) \geq 2 \\ \min\{Kp_t(v), 1/K\}, & \text{if } d_t(v) < 2. \end{cases}$$
>
> The probabilities are used as follows: In each iteration, node $v$ gets *marked* with probability $p_t(v)$ and if no neighbor of $v$ is marked, $v$ joins IS and gets removed along with its neighbors.

THEOREM 3.1. *For each node $v$, the probability that by the end of round $\beta(\log \Delta/\log K + K^2 \log 1/\delta) = O(\frac{\log \Delta}{\log \log \Delta})$, for a large enough constant $\beta$, node $v$ is not in* IS *and does not have a neighbor in* IS *is at most $\delta$. Furthermore, this holds even if coin tosses outside $N_2^+(v)$ are determined adversarially.*

Let us say that a node $u$ is *low-degree* if $d_t(u) < 2$, and *high-degree* otherwise. We define two types of *golden rounds* for a node $v$: (1) rounds in which $d_t(v) < 2$ and $p_t(v) = 1/K$, (2) rounds in which $d_v(t) \geq 1$ and at least $d_t(v)/(2K^2)$ of $d_t(v)$ is contributed by low-degree neighbors.

LEMMA 3.2. *By the end of round $\beta(\log \Delta/\log K + K^2 \log 1/\delta)$, either $v$ has joined* IS*, or has a neighbor in* IS*, or at least one of its golden round counts reached $\frac{\beta}{13}(\log \Delta/\log K + K^2 \log 1/\delta)$.*

PROOF. Let $T = \beta(\log \Delta/\log K + K^2 \log 1/\delta)$ for a sufficiently large constant $\beta$. We focus only on the first $T$ rounds. Let $g_1$ and $g_2$ respectively be the number of golden rounds of types 1 and 2 for $v$, during this period. We assume that by the end of round $T$, node $v$ is not removed and $g_1 \leq T/13$, and we conclude that $g_2 \geq T/13$.

Let $h$ be the number of rounds during which $d_t(v) \geq 2$. Notice that the changes in $p_t(v)$ are governed by the condition $d_t(v) \geq 2$

and the rounds with $d_t(v) \geq 2$ are exactly the ones in which $p_t(v)$ decreases by a $K$ factor. Since the number of $K$-factor increases in $p_t(v)$ can be at most equal to its number of $K$-factor decreases, there are at least $T - 2h$ rounds in which $p_t(v) = 1/K$. Out of these rounds, at most $h$ rounds can have $d_t(v) \geq 2$. Hence, $g_1 \geq T - 3h$. The assumption $g_1 \leq T/13$ gives that $h \geq 4T/13$. Let us now consider the changes in the effective-degree $d_t(v)$ of $v$ over time. If $d_t(v) \geq 1$ and this is not a golden round of type-2, then we have

$$d_{t+1}(v) \leq K\frac{1}{2K^2}d_t(v) + \frac{1}{K}(1 - \frac{1}{2K^2})d_t(v) < \frac{3}{2K}d_t(v).$$

There are $g_2$ golden rounds of type-2. Except for these, whenever $d_t(v) \geq 1$, the effective-degree $d_t(v)$ shrinks by at least a $\frac{3}{2K}$ factor. In these exception cases, it increases by at most a $K$ factor. Each of these exception rounds cancels the effect of no more than 2 shrinkage rounds, as $(\frac{3}{2K})^2 \cdot K \ll 1$. Thus, ignoring the total of at most $3g_2$ rounds lost due to type-2 golden rounds and their cancellation effects, every other round with $d_t(v) \geq 2$ pushes the effective-degree down by a $\frac{3}{2K}$ factor. This cannot happen more than $\log_{\frac{2K}{3}} \Delta$ times as that would lead the effective degree to exit the $d_t(v) \geq 2$ region. Hence, the number of rounds in which $d_t(v) \geq 2$ is at most $\frac{\log \Delta}{\log \frac{2K}{3}} + 3g_2$. That is, $h \leq \frac{\log \Delta}{\log \frac{2K}{3}} + 3g_2$. Since $h \geq 4T/13$, and because $T = \beta(\log \Delta/\log K + K^2 \log 1/\delta)$ for a sufficiently large constant $\beta$, we get that $g_2 > T/13$. □

Lemma 3.3. *In each type-1 golden round, with probability at least $\Theta(1/K)$, $v$ joins the IS. Moreover, in each type-2 golden round, with probability at least $\Theta(1/K^2)$, a neighbor of $v$ joins the IS. Hence, the probability that by the end of round $\beta(\log \Delta/\log K + K^2 \log 1/\delta)$, node $v$ has not joined the IS and does not have a neighbor in it is at most $\delta$. These statements hold even if the coin tosses outside $N_2^+(v)$ are determined adversarially.*

Proof. In each golden type-1 round, we have $d_t(v) < 2$ and $p_t(v) = 1/K$. The latter means that node $v$ gets marked with probability $1/K$, and the former means that the probability that none of the neighbors of $v$ is marked is at least $\prod_{u \in N_t(v)}(1 - p_t(u)) \geq 4^{-\sum_{u \in N_t(v)} p_t(u)} = 4^{-d_t(v)} \geq 1/16$. Hence, in each golden type-1 round, node $v$ joins the IS with probability at least $1/(16K)$.

In each golden type-2 rounds, we have $d_v(t) \geq 1$ and at least $d_t(v)/(2K^2)$ of $d_t(v)$ is contributed by low-degree neighbors. Suppose we examine the set $L_t(v)$ of low-degree neighbors of $v$ one by one and check whether they are marked or not. We stop when we reach the first marked node. The probability that we find at least one marked node is at least $1 - \prod_{u \in L_t(v)}(1 - p_t(u)) \geq 1 - e^{-\sum_{u \in L_t(v)} p_t(u)} \geq 1 - e^{-d_t(v)/(2K^2)} \geq 1 - e^{-1/2K^2} \geq 1/4K^2$, given that $(2K^2) \geq 1$. Now that we have found the first marked light neighbor $u$, the probability that no neighbor $w$ of $u$ is marked is at least $\prod_{w \in N_t(u)}(1 - p_t(w)) \geq 4^{-\sum_{w \in N_t(u)} p_t(w)} = 4^{-d_t(u)} \geq 1/16$. Therefore, overall, the probability that node $v$ gets removed in a type-2 golden round is at least $\frac{1}{64K^2}$.

Now notice that these events are independent in different rounds. Hence, the probability that node $v$ does not get removed after $\Theta(K^2 \log 1/\delta)$ golden rounds is at most $(1 - \frac{1}{64K^2})^{\Theta(K^2 \log 1/\delta)} \leq \delta$. Furthermore, in the above arguments, we only relied on the randomness in the nodes that are at most within 2 hops of $v$. Hence, the guarantee is independent of the randomness outside the 2-neighborhood of $v$. □

Proof of 3.1. By 3.2, within the first $\beta(\log \Delta/\log K + K^2 \log 1/\delta)$ round, each node $v$ is either already removed (by joining or having a neighbor in the IS) or one of its golden round counts reaches at least $\beta(\log \Delta/\log K + K^2 \log 1/\delta)/13$. As 3.3 shows, in each golden round, node $v$ gets removed with probability at least $\Theta(1/K^2)$. Hence, given a large enough constant $\beta$, the probability that node $v$ remains through $\beta(K^2 \log 1/\delta)/13$ golden rounds is at most $\delta$. □

Theorem 3.4. *There is a distributed algorithm in the* CONGEST *model that computes a $(2+\varepsilon)$-approximation of maximum unweighted matching in $O(\frac{\log \Delta}{\log \log \Delta})$ rounds, for any constant $\varepsilon > 0$, whp.*

Proof. The algorithm executes the nearly-maximal independent set algorithm explained above on the line-graph. This finds a nearly-maximal set of independent edges, i.e., edges which do not share an endpoint, or in other words, a nearly-maximal matching. The fact that the algorithm can be run on the line-graph in the CONGEST model follows from 2.4, since it is easy to see that this is a local aggregation algorithm. The round complexity of $O(\frac{\log \Delta}{\log \log \Delta})$ follows from the $O(\log \Delta/\log K + K^2 \log 1/\delta)$ bound of 3.1, by setting $K = \Theta(\log^{0.1} \Delta)$ and $\delta = 2^{-\log^{0.7} \Delta}$. Let us now examine the approximation factor. Each edge of the optimal matching has probability at most $\delta$ of becoming unlucky and not being in our found matching and not having any adjacent edge in it either. These are the edges that remain after all iterations of the nearly-maximal independent set algorithm. Thus, we expect at most $\delta \ll \varepsilon$ fraction of the edges of the optimal matching to become unlucky. The number also has an exponential concentration around this mean[6]. Ignoring these $\varepsilon|OPT|$ unlucky edges of the optimal matching, among the rest of the edges, each edge of the found matching can be blamed for removing at most 2 edges of the optimal matching. So the found matching is a $(2 + \varepsilon)$-approximation. □

*Extension to the Weighted Case via Methods of Lotker et al.* Above, we explain an $O(\log \Delta/\log \log \Delta)$-round algorithm for $(2+\varepsilon)$-approximation of maximum unweighted matching. This can be extended to the weighted case via known methods, while preserving the asymptotic complexity, as follows: First, we sketch a method of Lotker et al.[35] which allows one to turn a $(2 + \varepsilon)$-approximation for the unweighted case to an $O(1)$-approximation for the weighted case. Classify the weights of edges into powers of a large constant $\beta$, i.e., by defining weight buckets of the form $[\beta^i, \beta^{i+1}]$. In each of these big-buckets, partition the weight range further into $O(\log_{1+\varepsilon} \beta)$ *small-buckets* in powers of $1 + \varepsilon$. Run the following procedure in all big-buckets in parallel: Starting from the edges of the highest weight small-bucket in this big-bucket, find a $(2 + \varepsilon)$-approximation of the matching in that small-bucket using the unweighted matching algorithm, remove all their incident edges in that big-bucket, and move to the next biggest small-bucket. After $O(\log_{1+\varepsilon} \beta)$ iterations of going through all the small-buckets, for each big-bucket, we have found a matching that is a $2 + O(\varepsilon)$ approximation of the

[6] This concentration is due to the fact that the dependencies are local and each edge's event of being unlucky depends on only at most $\Delta$ other edges. However, one can obtain a better success probability. See ?? for an algorithm which provides a stronger concentration, giving a $(2 + \varepsilon)$-approximation with probability $1 - e^{-\Omega(-|OPT|)}$.

maximum weight matching among all the edges with weight in this big-bucket. However, altogether, this is not a matching as a node might have a "matching"-edge incident on it in each of the big-buckets. Keep each of these chosen edges only if it has the highest weight among the chosen edges incident on it. Lotker et al.[35] showed that this produces an $O(1)$-approximation of the maximum weight matching.

This $O(1)$-approximation can be turned into a $(2+\varepsilon)$-approximation. Lotker et al. [34, Section 4] present a method that via $O(1/\varepsilon)$ black-box usages of an $O(1)$-approximation Maximum Weight Matching algorithm $\mathcal{A}$, produces a $(2+\varepsilon)$-approximation of the maximum weight matching. We here provide only a brief and intuitive sketch. The method is iterative, each iteration is as follows. Let $M$ be the current matching. We look only at weighted augmenting paths of $M$ with length at most 3. We define an auxiliary weight for each unmatched edge $e$, which is equal to the overall weight-gain that would be obtained by adding $e$ to the matching and instead erasing the matching $M$ edges incident on endpoints of $e$ (if there are any). Note that this auxiliary weight can be computed easily in $O(1)$ rounds. Then, we use algorithm $\mathcal{A}$ to find a matching which has an auxiliary weight at most an $O(1)$ factor smaller than the maximum weight matching, according to the auxiliary weights. Then we augment $M$ with all these found matching edges, erasing the previously matching edges incident on their endpoints. We are then ready for the next iteration. As Lotker et al. show, after $O(1/\varepsilon)$ iterations, the matching at hand is a $(2+\varepsilon)$-approximation of the maximum weight matching.

## 3.2 A fast $(1+\varepsilon)$-approximation of maximum cardinality matching

We now discuss our $O(\log\Delta/\log\log\Delta)$-round algorithm for $(1+\varepsilon)$-approximation of maximum unweighted matching. Since the algorithm and its analysis are somewhat lengthy and technical, we can present only a bird's-eye view of them. We first discuss the algorithm for the LOCAL model, and then briefly discuss some of the ideas we use for extending it to the CONGEST model.

We follow a classical approach of Hopcroft and Karp[26]. Given a matching $M$, an augmenting path $P$ with respect to $M$ is a path that starts with an unmatched vertex, and alternates between non-matching and matching edges, and ends in an unmatched vertex. Flipping an augmenting path $P$ means removing $P \cap M$ edges from $M$ and replacing them with edges of $P \setminus M$. The approximation algorithm based on the method of Hopcroft and Karp[26] works as follows: For each $\ell = 1$ to $O(1/\varepsilon)$, find a *maximal set of vertex-disjoint augmenting paths of length* $\ell$, and flip all of them.

The analysis of [26] shows that this finds a $(1+\varepsilon)$-approximation of maximum matching. Hence, all that we need to do is to find a maximal set of vertex-disjoint augmenting paths of length $\ell$. This problem can be formulated as a maximal independent set problem in a virtual graph, called the *conflict graph*: put one vertex for each augmenting path of length $\ell$, and connect two vertices if their corresponding paths intersect. Each communication round on the conflict graph can be simulated in $O(\ell) = O(1)$ rounds in the network in the LOCAL model. Thus, if we could find an MIS in $O(\log\Delta/\log\log\Delta)$ rounds, we would be done. However, we only know how to compute a nearly-maximal independent set in this number of rounds.

When applied in this context, the guarantee that our nearly-maximal independent set algorithm provides is that each augmenting path of length $\ell$ has only a small $\delta$ probability of remaining (without any intersecting $\ell$-length augmenting path in the computed nearly-maximal set). However, this notion of near-maximality is not strong enough for us to be able to say that we still get a good approximation. For instance, one natural idea would be to simply discard the remaining augmenting paths (and thus also their vertices). However, this is not possible because with the current notion of near-maximality, each node may have a high probability of having at least one of the augmenting paths going through it remain. Notice that there are up to $\Delta^\ell$ such paths and we cannot afford to use a union bound over them.

In a nutshell, our approach is to provide a much tighter analysis of (a simple variation of) the algorithm, by leveraging the fact that the paths are short, having length $O(1/\varepsilon)$. This tighter analysis allows us to say that if we run the algorithm for slightly more time, larger by an $O(1/\varepsilon^2)$ factor, then the probability of each node having a remaining augmenting path will be small enough to allow us to discard such nodes. This tighter analysis is presented in a more general framework, which may be of independent interest. It concerns computing a nearly-maximal matching in a low-rank hypergraph, where each hyperedge contains a small number of vertices. The relation is that we can think of each augmenting path as one hyperedge, on the same set of vertices. These hyperedges would have rank $O(1/\varepsilon)$, and a matching of hyperedges — that is, a set of hyperedges that do not share a vertex — would be the a set of vertex-disjoint paths.

The above sketches our algorithm in the LOCAL model. Making this algorithm work in the CONGEST model brings in a range of new challenges. For instance, we cannot build the conflict graph explicitly and hence, the above algorithm does not work as is. We use a number of ideas, in order to extend the algorithm to the CONGEST model, which are described in the full version.

One of the key ideas, which we find particularly interesting and may prove useful beyond our work, is a decentralized manner of performing the increase or decreases of the marking probabilities in the nearly-maximal independent set algorithm (as discussed in the previous subsection). Notice that now each augmenting path has a probability, which we would like to increase or decrease. Roughly speaking, we define an attenuation parameter $\alpha_t(v)$ for each node $v$ and we let the marking probability of each augmenting path be the multiplication of the attenuations of its vertices. Each node will decide on its own whether to increase or decrease its attentuation. Of course it is possible that some nodes of the path raise their attenuation and some lower it. However, we prove that in a long enough span of time and by choosing the increase or decrease parameters right, the net effect will still be in the correct direction, allowing us to mimic the analysis of the ideal LOCAL model algorithm, and thus prove the approximation guarantee.

# 4 DISCUSSION

This papers gives distributed approximation algorithms for maximum independent set and maximum matching in CONGEST. We obtain a $\Delta$-approximation for the former using local-ratio techniques, and deduce a 2-approximation for the latter by defining local aggregation algorithms and showing that they allow simulation on the line graph in the restricted CONGEST model, despite the need to simulate many nodes.

We then provide fast approximations that relax either the approximation factor to $2 + \varepsilon$ or the setting to an unweighted case, but have the optimal round complexity of $O(\log \Delta / \log \log \Delta)$.

One intriguing open question is whether this fast running time can also be obtained for the problem of finding a maximal independent set. Notice that by the algorithm we describe in 3.1, we can compute an almost maximal independent set in $O(\log \Delta / \log \log \Delta)$ rounds. Particularly, this is an independent set where the probability of each node remaining (without being, or having a neighbor, in the independent set) is at most $2^{-\log^{1-\gamma} \Delta}$, for any desirably small constant $\gamma > 0$. However, to be able to extend this to a maximal independent set, we would need this failure probability to be at most $2^{-\Theta(\log \Delta)}$. Furthermore, given our algorithm and the lower bound of Kuhn et al. [30], we now know that this is the complexity of finding a constant approximation for maximum matching. Similarly, by Bar-Yehuda et al. [6], we also know that this is the complexity of finding a constant approximation for the vertex-cover problem. However, for the problem of finding a maximal independent set, there remains a $\log \log \Delta$ gap between the lower bound of [30] and the algorithm of Ghaffari [20].

## REFERENCES


[1] Noga Alon and Nabil Kahale. 1998. Approximating the independence number via the$\vartheta$-function. *Mathematical Programming* 80, 3 (1998), 253–264.

[2] Per Austrin, Subhash Khot, and Muli Safra. 2009. Inapproximability of vertex cover and independent set in bounded degree graphs. In *Computational Complexity, 2009. CCC'09. 24th Annual IEEE Conference on*. IEEE, 74–80.

[3] Nikhil Bansal. 2015. Approximating independent sets in sparse graphs. In *Proceedings of the Twenty-Sixth Annual ACM-SIAM Symposium on Discrete Algorithms*. SIAM, 1–8.

[4] Amotz Bar-Noy, Reuven Bar-Yehuda, Ari Freund, Joseph Naor, and Baruch Schieber. 2001. A unified approach to approximating resource allocation and scheduling. *Journal of the ACM (JACM)* 48, 5 (2001), 1069–1090.

[5] Reuven Bar-Yehuda, Keren Bendel, Ari Freund, and Dror Rawitz. 2004. Local ratio: A unified framework for approximation algorithms. in memoriam: Shimon even 1935-2004. *ACM Computing Surveys (CSUR)* 36, 4 (2004), 422–463.

[6] Reuven Bar-Yehuda, Keren Censor-Hillel, and Gregory Schwartzman. To Appear 2016. A Distributed $(2 + \epsilon)$-Approximation for Vertex Cover in $O(\log \Delta/\epsilon \log \log \Delta)$ Rounds. In *Proceedings of the 2016 ACM Symposium on Principles of Distributed Computing, PODC 2016, Chicago, IL, USA, July 25-28, 2016*. https://doi.org/10.1145/2933057.2933086

[7] Reuven Bar-Yehuda and Shimon Even. 1985. A local-ratio theorem for approximating the weighted vertex cover problem. *North-Holland Mathematics Studies* 109 (1985), 27–45.

[8] Leonid Barenboim. 2015. Deterministic $(\Delta + 1)$-Coloring in Sublinear (in $\Delta$) Time in Static, Dynamic and Faulty Networks. In *Proceedings of the 2015 ACM Symposium on Principles of Distributed Computing, PODC 2015, Donostia-San Sebastián, Spain, July 21 - 23, 2015*, Chryssis Georgiou and Paul G. Spirakis (Eds.). ACM, 345–354. https://doi.org/10.1145/2767386.2767410

[9] Leonid Barenboim, Michael Elkin, and Fabian Kuhn. 2014. Distributed (Delta+1)-Coloring in Linear (in Delta) Time. *SIAM J. Comput.* 43, 1 (2014), 72–95. https://doi.org/10.1137/12088848X

[10] Leonid Barenboim, Michael Elkin, Seth Pettie, and Johannes Schneider. 2016. The Locality of Distributed Symmetry Breaking. *J. ACM* 63, 3 (2016), 20:1–20:45. https://doi.org/10.1145/2903137

[11] Marijke HL Bodlaender, Magnús M Halldórsson, Christian Konrad, and Fabian Kuhn. To Appear 2016. Brief Announcement: Local Independent Set Approximation. In *Proceedings of the 2016 ACM Symposium on Principles of Distributed Computing, PODC 2016, Chicago, IL, USA, July 25-28, 2016*.

[12] Siu On Chan. 2013. Approximation resistance from pairwise independent subgroups. In *Proceedings of the forty-fifth annual ACM symposium on Theory of computing*. ACM, 447–456.

[13] Andrzej Czygrinow and Michal Hanckowiak. 2003. Distributed Algorithm for Better Approximation of the Maximum Matching. In *Computing and Combinatorics, 9th Annual International Conference, COCOON 2003, Big Sky, MT, USA, July 25-28, 2003, Proceedings*. 242–251. https://doi.org/10.1007/3-540-45071-8_26

[14] Andrzej Czygrinow, Michal Hańćkowiak, and Wojciech Wawrzyniak. 2008. Fast distributed approximations in planar graphs. In *Distributed Computing*. Springer, 78–92.

[15] Jack Edmonds. 1965. Maximum matching and a polyhedron with 0, l-vertices. *J. Res. Nat. Bur. Standards B* 69, 1965 (1965), 125–130.

[16] Jack Edmonds. 1965. Paths, trees, and flowers. *Canadian Journal of mathematics* 17, 3 (1965), 449–467.

[17] Guy Even, Moti Medina, and Dana Ron. 2015. Distributed maximum matching in bounded degree graphs. In *Proceedings of the 2015 International Conference on Distributed Computing and Networking*. ACM, 18.

[18] Uriel Feige. 2004. Approximating maximum clique by removing subgraphs. *SIAM Journal on Discrete Mathematics* 18, 2 (2004), 219–225.

[19] Pierre Fraigniaud, Marc Heinrich, and Adrian Kosowski. 2015. Local Conflict Coloring. *arXiv preprint arXiv:1511.01287* (2015).

[20] Mohsen Ghaffari. 2016. An Improved Distributed Algorithm for Maximal Independent Set. In *Proceedings of the Twenty-Seventh Annual ACM-SIAM Symposium on Discrete Algorithms (SODA '16)*. SIAM, 270–277. http://dl.acm.org/citation.cfm?id=2884435.2884455

[21] Magnús M Halldórsson. 1998. Approximations of independent sets in graphs. In *Approximation algorithms for combinatiorial optimization*. Springer, 1–13.

[22] Magnús M Halldórsson. 2000. Approximations of weighted independent set and hereditary subset problems. *Journal of Graph Algorithms and Applications* 4, 1 (2000), 1–16.

[23] Magnús M Halldórsson and Jaikumar Radhakrishnan. 1997. Greed is good: Approximating independent sets in sparse and bounded-degree graphs. *Algorithmica* 18, 1 (1997), 145–163.

[24] Eran Halperin. 2002. Improved approximation algorithms for the vertex cover problem in graphs and hypergraphs. *SIAM J. Comput.* 31, 5 (2002), 1608–1623.

[25] Johan Håstad. 1996. Clique is hard to approximate within $n^{1-\epsilon}$. In *Foundations of Computer Science, 1996. Proceedings., 37th Annual Symposium on*. IEEE, 627–636.

[26] John E Hopcroft and Richard M Karp. 1973. An $n^{5/2}$ algorithm for maximum matchings in bipartite graphs. *SIAM Journal on computing* 2, 4 (1973), 225–231.

[27] David Karger, Rajeev Motwani, and Madhu Sudan. 1998. Approximate graph coloring by semidefinite programming. *Journal of the ACM (JACM)* 45, 2 (1998), 246–265.

[28] Richard M. Karp. 1972. Reducibility Among Combinatorial Problems. In *Proceedings of a symposium on the Complexity of Computer Computations, held March 20-22, 1972, at the IBM Thomas J. Watson Research Center, Yorktown Heights, New York*. 85–103. http://www.cs.berkeley.edu/~luca/cs172/karp.pdf

[29] Fabian Kuhn. 2005. *The price of locality*. Diss., Eidgenössische Technische Hochschule ETH Zürich, Nr. 16213, 2005.

[30] Fabian Kuhn, Thomas Moscibroda, and Roger Wattenhofer. 2006. The price of being near-sighted. In *Proceedings of the seventeenth annual ACM-SIAM symposium on Discrete algorithm*. Society for Industrial and Applied Mathematics, 980–989.

[31] Christoph Lenzen and Roger Wattenhofer. 2008. Leveraging Linial's locality limit. In *Distributed Computing*. Springer, 394–407.

[32] Nathan Linial. 1987. Distributive Graph Algorithms Global Solutions from Local Data. In *Proceedings of the 28th Annual Symposium on Foundations of Computer Science (SFCS '87)*. IEEE Computer Society, Washington, DC, USA, 331–335. https://doi.org/10.1109/SFCS.1987.20

[33] Zvi Lotker, Boaz Patt-Shamir, and Seth Pettie. 2008. Improved distributed approximate matching. In *Proceedings of the twentieth annual symposium on Parallelism in algorithms and architectures*. ACM, 129–136.

[34] Zvi Lotker, Boaz Patt-Shamir, and Seth Pettie. 2015. Improved distributed approximate matching. *Journal of the ACM (JACM)* 62, 5 (2015).

[35] Zvi Lotker, Boaz Patt-Shamir, and Adi Rosén. 2009. Distributed approximate matching. *SIAM J. Comput.* 39, 2 (2009), 445–460.

[36] Michael Luby. 1986. A simple parallel algorithm for the maximal independent set problem. *SIAM journal on computing* 15, 4 (1986), 1036–1053.

[37] Alessandro Panconesi and Mauro Sozio. 2008. Fast distributed scheduling via primal-dual. In *Proceedings of the twentieth annual symposium on Parallelism in algorithms and architectures*. ACM, 229–235.

[38] Boaz Patt-Shamir, Dror Rawitz, and Gabriel Scalosub. 2008. Distributed approximation of cellular coverage. In *Principles of Distributed Systems*. Springer, 331–345.

[39] David Peleg. 2000. *Distributed Computing: A Locality-sensitive Approach*. Society for Industrial and Applied Mathematics, Philadelphia, PA, USA.

[40] Mirjam Wattenhofer and Roger Wattenhofer. 2004. *Distributed weighted matching*. Springer.

# Deterministic Distributed ($\Delta + o(\Delta)$)-Edge-Coloring, and Vertex-Coloring of Graphs with Bounded Diversity

Leonid Beranboim
The Open University of Israel
Raananna, Israel
leonidb@openu.ac.il

Michael Elkin
Ben-Gurion University of the Negev
Beer Sheva, Israel
elkinm@cs.bgu.ac.il

Tzalik Maimon
The Open University of Israel
Raananna, Israel
tzali.tm@gmail.com

## ABSTRACT

In the distributed message-passing setting a communication network is represented by a graph whose vertices represent processors that perform local computations and communicate over the edges of the graph. In the distributed *edge-coloring* problem the processors are required to assign colors to edges, such that all edges incident on the same vertex are assigned distinct colors. The previously-known deterministic algorithms for edge-coloring employed at least $(2\Delta - 1)$ colors, even though any graph admits an edge-coloring with $\Delta + 1$ colors [36]. Moreover, the previously-known deterministic algorithms that employed at most $O(\Delta)$ colors required superlogarithmic time [3, 6, 7, 17]. In the current paper we devise deterministic edge-coloring algorithms that employ only $\Delta + o(\Delta)$ colors, for a very wide family of graphs. Specifically, as long as the arboricity $a$ of the graph is $a = O(\Delta^{1-\epsilon})$, for a constant $\epsilon > 0$, our algorithm computes such a coloring within *polylogarithmic* deterministic time.

We also devise significantly improved deterministic edge-coloring algorithms for *general graphs* for a very wide range of parameters. Specifically, for any value $\kappa$ in the range $[4\Delta, 2^{o(\log \Delta)} \cdot \Delta]$, our $\kappa$-edge-coloring algorithm has smaller running time than the best previously-known $\kappa$-edge-coloring algorithms. Our algorithms are actually much more general, since edge-coloring is equivalent to *vertex-coloring of line graphs*. Our method is applicable to vertex-coloring of the family of graphs with *bounded diversity* that contains line graphs, line graphs of hypergraphs, and many other graphs. We significantly improve upon previous vertex-coloring of such graphs, and as an implication also obtain the improved edge-coloring algorithms for general graphs.

Our results are obtained using a novel technique that connects vertices or edges in a certain way that reduces clique size. The resulting structures, which we call *connectors*, can be colored more efficiently than the original graph. Moreover, the color classes constitute simpler subgraphs that can be colored even more efficiently using appropriate connectors. We introduce several types of connectors that are useful for various scenarios. We believe that this technique is of independent interest.

## CCS CONCEPTS

• **Mathematics of computing → Graph coloring**; • **Theory of computation → Graph algorithms analysis**;

## KEYWORDS

Distributed Coloring; Clique Decomposition; Network Partition

**ACM Reference format:**
Leonid Beranboim, Michael Elkin, and Tzalik Maimon. 2017. Deterministic Distributed ($\Delta + o(\Delta)$)-Edge-Coloring, and Vertex-Coloring of Graphs with Bounded Diversity. In *Proceedings of PODC '17, Washington, DC, USA, July 25-27, 2017,* 10 pages.
https://doi.org/10.1145/3087801.3087812

## 1 INTRODUCTION

### 1.1 Distributed Synchronous Message Passing Model

In the synchronous message passing model a communication network is represented by an $n$-vertex graph $G = (V, E)$ of maximum degree $\Delta = \Delta(G)$. Each vertex in the graph has its own processing power and local memory. The vertices communicate via message passing over the edges of the graph. Computation proceeds in discrete rounds of local computations and exchange of messages. A single round is required for a message to traverse an edge. The running time is the number of synchronized rounds until all vertices terminate. Generally, local computation is unrestricted. Vertices have distinct IDs of size $O(\log n)$.

### 1.2 Coloring Problems

The *vertex-coloring* and *edge-coloring* problems are among the most fundamental problems in distributed computing. These problems are significant in communication networks since appropriate labeling of stations, antennas and clients using a small number of colors is important for various network tasks. For example, channel allocation, scheduling, and work-load balancing can benefit considerably from a good coloring. In particular, edge-coloring is useful in open shop scheduling and scheduling production processes [37], path coloring in fiber-optic communication [15], and link-scheduling in sensor networks [19]. The less colors one uses, the smaller cost one pays for performing a task. On the other hand, restricting the number of colors makes a problem more difficult.

In 1987 Linial devised a deterministic algorithm for vertex coloring and edge-coloring using quite a large number of colors, but with extremely good running time. Specifically, Linial obtained $O(\Delta^2)$-coloring that requires just $O(\log^* n)$ rounds. Roughly in the same

* This research has been supported by ISF grant No. 724/15 and by the Open University of Israel research fund.

*PODC '17, July 25-27, 2017, Washington, DC, USA*

ACM ISBN 978-1-4503-4992-5/17/07...$15.00
https://doi.org/10.1145/3087801.3087812

time Cole and Vishkin [12] and Goldberg et al. [21] devised deterministic algorithms for vertex-coloring of oriented paths and oriented trees with just 3 colors. Since then these problems have been very intensively studied, resulting in a continuous progress both in general graphs and specific graph families. Recent results make it possible to color vertices and edges of general graphs using $\Delta^{1+\epsilon}$-colors in deterministic polylogarithmic time [6, 7]. However, when a smaller number of colors is used, the current results of distributed algorithms are far from being satisfactory. In particular, no deterministic polylogarithmic algorithms for $(\Delta + 1)$-vertex-coloring or $(2\Delta - 1)$-edge-coloring are known. The situation with edge coloring is even worse, in the sense that although any graph can be edge-colored using at most $(\Delta + 1)$ colors [36], no efficient deterministic $(\Delta + o(\Delta))$-edge-coloring algorithms is known in the distributed setting. (However, there are very efficient randomized algorithms for $\Delta(1 + \epsilon)$-edge-coloring, for any constant $\epsilon > 0$, that are applicable whenever $\Delta$ is sufficiently large [14, 16, 22].)

In this paper we address the problem of edge-coloring with significantly less than $2\Delta - 1$ colors for a very wide family of graphs. Specifically, we obtain a deterministic algorithm that employs $\Delta + o(\Delta)$ colors for graphs with *arboricity*[1] $a = o(\Delta)$. Bounded arboricity graphs include planar graphs, graphs of bounded treewidth, graphs that exclude any fixed minor, and many other graphs. Unless the arboricity is very close to the maximum degree, the running time of our algorithm is *polylogarithmic* in $n$.

Our results are actually more general than that. For general graphs (with unbounded arboricity), for any positive integer $x \in o(\log \Delta)$, we compute a $(2^{x+1}\Delta)$-edge-coloring within $\tilde{O}(x \cdot \Delta^{\frac{1}{2x+2}} + \log^* n)$ time.[2] This improves almost quadratically upon the state-of-the-art for the entire range of $x \in o(\log \Delta)$ (cf. Table 1). This table compares our new algorithms with the best previously-known ones. The latter are obtained by plugging in the state-of-the-art $(\Delta + 1)$-vertex-coloring algorithm [17] in the algorithm of [7]. Our results address an open question raised in a PODC 2011 paper [7] by the first-named and second-named authors of the current paper.

In addition to these results, we obtain even more general ones, that apply to *vertex-coloring* of a wide family of graphs. In particular, this family includes line-graphs. (Recall that an edge coloring of a graph is a vertex coloring of its line graph.) However, line graphs are just an example of a more general family of graphs, namely *graphs with bounded diversity*. Roughly speaking, we define *vertex diversity* of a vertex $v$ in a graph $G$ as the number of maximal cliques to which $v$ belongs. [3] The diversity of a graph, which is denoted as $D = D(G)$, is the maximal vertex diversity among all the vertices of the graph. Clearly, line graphs have diversity 2. Indeed, each vertex of a line graph corresponds to an edge in the original graph. Each endpoint of this edge corresponds to a clique in the line graphs. Since an edge has two endpoints, the diversity of any line graph is at most 2. More generally, for any positive constant $c$, the diversity of the line graph of a $c$-uniform hypergraph is $c$. Given a graph of diversity $D$ and maximal clique size $S$, we obtain a $(D^{x+1}S)$-coloring within $\tilde{O}(x \cdot \sqrt{DS^{1/(x+1)}} + \log^* n)$ time, for any positive integer $x \in o(\log S)$. The best previous results that apply to this family of graphs are the results for graphs with *bounded neighborhood independence* [7]. (The latter family generalizes graphs with bounded diversity, thus the results of [7] apply to graphs of bounded diversity as well.) Our new results compare favorably on this family of graphs. (Cf. Table 2.) Although not as general, the family of graphs with bounded diversity is still an important graph family that captures many characteristics of graphs with bounded neighborhood independence, but has some specific helpful properties that we use to obtain our improved results.

### 1.3 Clique Decomposition as a New Approach

In this paper we show a new approach for solving coloring problems. In this approach we think of a clique as the "worst enemy" of coloring. Note that in general there are graphs that contain no large clique, but still have large chromatic number. In particular, triangle-free graphs may have arbitrarily large chromatic number [31]. However, in the family of graphs with bounded diversity $D$ and maximal clique size $S$, the chromatic number is at most $D(S-1)+1$, and thus, graphs with smaller cliques are better for coloring. Our goal is then breaking down these cliques by removing edges within them, thus breaking the cliques to smaller components. We refer to the new structure we obtain as a *connector*. Roughly speaking, a connector $G'$ of $G$ is a graph which is highly instrumental to coloring $G$, but which is easier to color than $G$, i.e., it has smaller maximum clique size, or smaller maximum degree, or smaller arboricity. We then color the connector, and make sure that when we return the edges that were removed, the coloring remains proper. We then take this one step further by using the same concept recursively to obtain a better running time at the expense of using more colors. This technique not only allows us to obtain better results than any previously known ones, but it is also easier to implement. We note that in general, identifying all maximal cliques is a computationally intractable problem. (Though, in the current distributed setting, a vertex can identify all maximal cliques it belongs to within a single round). However, in various graph families, such as line graphs (that are provided with their original graphs), a consistent identification of cliques is not hard, even in the centralized setting. (Note that in the distributed setting we have no limitations on local computation performed by the vertices, and as a result, clique identification is generally easier in the distributed setting than in the centralized one.)

Connectors turn out to be extremely useful in various scenarios. They allow us to compute *clique-decompositions*, in which the graph is partitioned into a bounded number of subgraphs in which the maximal cliques are significantly smaller than in the original graph. Together with the bound on diversity, this fact allows us to color these subgraphs efficiently in parallel, and obtain a proper *vertex-coloring* for the entire input graph. Another type of connectors is very useful for an *edge-coloring*. In this case it is used for computing

[1] The *arboricity* of a graph is the minimum number of forests into which its edge set can be decomposed. The arboricity is always smaller than or equal to the maximum degree of the graph.

[2] The $\tilde{O}$-notation supresses polylogarithmic factors. We note however, that whenever we write $\tilde{O}(f(\Delta) + \log^* n)$, the actual running time is $\tilde{O}(f(\Delta)) + O(\log^* n)$. We use the former notation for brevity.

[3] A clique $Q$ is *maximal* in $G$ if there is no other clique in $G$ that strictly contains $Q$'s vertices. The number of cliques is counted with respect to a consistent clique identification whenever the family of graphs in hand allows this. Otherwise, each vertex identifies all maximal cliques it belongs to, which results in a consistent identification. In both cases, the cliques that a vertex belongs to contain all its neighbors. For example, in line graphs, each clique corresponds to a vertex of the original graph, and the clique vertices correspond to the edges incident on that vertex of the original graph. See Section 2 for a formal definition.

**Table 1: Edge coloring of general graphs.**

| Our Results | | Previous Results ([7] + [17]) | |
|---|---|---|---|
| Number of colors | Running time | Number of colors | Running time |
| $4\Delta$ | $\tilde{O}(\Delta^{1/4}) + O(\log^* n)$ | $(4+\epsilon)\Delta$ | $O(\Delta^{1/3} + \log^* n)$ |
| $8\Delta$ | $\tilde{O}(\Delta^{1/6}) + O(\log^* n)$ | $(8+\epsilon)\Delta$ | $O(\Delta^{1/4} + \log^* n)$ |
| $16\Delta$ | $\tilde{O}(\Delta^{1/8}) + O(\log^* n)$ | $(16+\epsilon)\Delta$ | $O(\Delta^{1/5} + \log^* n)$ |
| $2^x\Delta$ | $\tilde{O}(x \cdot \Delta^{\frac{1}{2x}}) + O(\log^* n)$ | $(2^x+\epsilon)\Delta$ | $\tilde{O}(x \cdot \Delta^{\frac{1}{x+1}} + \log^* n)$ |

**Table 2: A Vertex-coloring of graphs with bounded diversity $D$ and maximal clique size $S \leq \Delta + 1$.**

| Our Results | | Previous Results ([7] + [17]) | |
|---|---|---|---|
| Number of colors | Running time | Number of colors | Running time |
| $D^2S$ | $\tilde{O}(\sqrt{D}S^{1/4}) + O(\log^* n)$ | $(D^2+\epsilon)\Delta$ | $O(D^2 \cdot \Delta^{1/3} + \log^* n)$ |
| $D^3S$ | $\tilde{O}(\sqrt{D}S^{1/6}) + O(\log^* n)$ | $(D^3+\epsilon)\Delta$ | $O(D^3 \cdot \Delta^{1/4} + \log^* n)$ |
| $D^4S$ | $\tilde{O}(\sqrt{D}S^{1/8}) + O(\log^* n)$ | $(D^4+\epsilon)\Delta$ | $O(D^4 \cdot \Delta^{1/5} + \log^* n)$ |
| $D^{x+1}S$ | $\tilde{O}(x \cdot \sqrt{D}S^{1/(2x+2)}) + O(\log^* n)$ | $(D^{x+1}+\epsilon)\Delta$ | $\tilde{O}(xD^x \cdot \Delta^{\frac{1}{x+2}} + \log^* n)$ |

a different kind of decomposition, in which subgraphs have *stars* of bounded size. These star-decompositions turn out to be very useful for an edge-coloring. Yet another type of connectors allows us to compute a decomposition in which the subgraphs have both bounded arboricity and bounded degree. This allows us to bound the number of colors further, and obtain an ultimate edge-coloring with $\Delta + o(\Delta)$ colors of graphs with arboricity bounded away from $\Delta$.

### 1.4 Related Work

Panconesi and Rizzi [33] devised a deterministic edge-coloring algorithm for general graphs with $(2\Delta - 1)$ colors that requires $O(\Delta + \log^* n)$ time. This result was recently improved in [3, 17], that obtained a $(2\Delta - 1)$-edge-coloring within $\tilde{O}(\sqrt{\Delta} + \log^* n)$ time. Efficient deterministic edge-coloring algorithms that employ $O(\Delta)$ colors and $\Delta^{1+\epsilon}$ colors were devised in [7]. Czygrinow et al. devised a deterministic $O(\Delta \log n)$-edge-coloring algorithm with $O(\log^4 n)$ time [13]. In parallel to our work and independently of us, Ghaffari and Su obtained a $(2 + \epsilon)\Delta$-edge-coloring in deterministic time $O(\log^{11} n/\epsilon^3)$ [20]. Randomized edge-coloring was studied in [14, 16, 22]. For graphs with arboricity $a$, the algorithm of [4] computes a $(2\Delta - 1)$-edge-coloring within $O(a + \log n)$ time. For the family of graphs with $a = O(\Delta^{1-\epsilon})$, for a constant $\epsilon > 0$, a $(\Delta + 1)$-vertex-coloring algorithm with deterministic polylogarithmic time was devised in [6]. The latter result, however, does not imply edge-coloring algorithms in polylogarithmic time, since the arboricity of line graphs is $\Theta(\Delta)$. Moreover, if the algorithm of [6] is used for edge-coloring via vertex-coloring of line graphs, the number of colors is at least $2\Delta - 1$.

Edge coloring was also extensively studied in the PRAM model [18, 23, 25, 29, 38]. There are known PRAM NC deterministic algorithms for $(\Delta + o(\Delta))$-edge-coloring [11, 32], obtained by derandomizing Karloff-Shmoys' randomized algorithm [25]. Zhou and Nishizeki [38] also devised a deterministic PRAM NC $O(\max\{\Delta, a^2\})$ edge-coloring of graphs with constant arboricity $a$. However, these algorithms [11, 25, 32, 38] heavily rely on assumptions of the PRAM model, i.e., that processors can efficiently fetch information concerning any edge or vertex in the graph. Hence these algorithms appear to be inapplicable to the distributed setting.

## 2 CLIQUE DECOMPOSITION

In this section we devise an algorithm that partitions an input graph into subgraphs in a way that reduces maximum clique size. Specifically, each clique in each subgraph is smaller by a factor of $k > 1$, where $k$ is a parameter, than a maximum-size clique in the original graph. We begin with a formal definition of diversity.

*Definition 2.1.* Suppose that we are given a graph $G = (V, E)$, and a set of cliques $Q = \{Q_1, Q_2, ..., Q_z\}$, each of which is a maximal clique in $G$. Moreover, each edge of $E$ belongs to at least one clique in $Q$. (I.e., for each $v \in V$, the union of cliques that contain $v$ contains also all neighbors of $v$.) Such a clique set will be referred to as *clique cover*. Then the *diversity* of $G$ with respect to $Q$, denoted $D_Q = D_Q(G)$, is the maximum number of cliques in $Q$ that a vertex $v \in V$ belongs to. The *diversity* of $G$, denoted $D(G)$, is given by $D(G) = \min\{D_Q(G) \mid Q \text{ is a clique cover of } G\}$.

In a line graph $\tilde{G} = (\tilde{V}, \tilde{E})$ of a graph (or, more generally, a hypergraph), $G = (V, E)$, $E = \tilde{V}$, the set $Q$ of cliques is given by $Q = \cup\{Q_v \mid v \in V\}$, where $Q_v \subseteq \tilde{V} = E$ is the set of vertices of $\tilde{G}$ corresponding to (hyper)edges of $G$ that contain the vertex $v$. In general graphs, $Q_v$ is the set of all maximal cliques containing the vertex $v$. Next, we define clique-decompositions.

*Definition 2.2.* For parameters $p, q > 0$, a *$(p, q)$-clique- decomposition* of a graph $G = (V, E)$ is a vertex partition $U_1, U_2, \ldots, U_p$ of $V$, such that the maximum size of a clique in $G(U_i)$ is at most $q$, for all $i \in [p]$. A *clique master* is a unique vertex of a clique which has the highest ID in the clique.

It is possible that a master of a clique belongs to another clique and may even be its master as well. Also, non-masters of certain cliques may be masters in other cliques they belong to.

We construct clique-decompositions using the following structure, which we call a *connector*. A connector is constructed as follows. Given a graph $G$ and an integer parameter $t > 1$, we start by constructing a clique cover $\mathcal{Q}$ and selecting a master in each clique $Q \in \mathcal{Q}$. Clique identification and master selection is performed in $O(1)$ rounds in the distributed setting, since each clique has diameter 1. Each such a master is responsible for the computation in its clique. Let us denote the size of a clique $Q$ by $S(Q)$. Each clique $Q$ of $\mathcal{Q}$ partitions its vertex set into disjoint subsets $Q_1, Q_2, \ldots, Q_{\hat{k}}$ of size $t$ each, except for the last set $Q_{\hat{k}}$ that can be smaller. Thus, we get $\hat{k} = \lceil S(Q)/t \rceil$ subsets for each clique $Q$. Denote $k = \max\{\lceil S(Q)/t \rceil \mid Q \in \mathcal{Q}\}$. Let $E' = \{(u,v) \in E \mid u, v \in Q_i$, for some clique $Q \in \mathcal{Q}$ and some $i \in [k]\}$ denote the set of edges connecting vertices from the same part $Q_i$ of a maximal clique $Q \in \mathcal{Q}$. Let $G' = (V, E')$ be the graph with the original vertex set, and edge set $E'$. The graph $G'$ will be referred to as *connector*. Let $\mathcal{Q}' = \cup_{Q \in \mathcal{Q}}\{Q_1, Q_2, \ldots, Q_{\hat{k}}\}$, where $Q_1, Q_2, \ldots, Q_{\hat{k}}$ are the cliques obtained from the clique $Q$ by partitioning it into subcliques. It is easy to verify that $\mathcal{Q}'$ is a clique cover of $G'$. (See Figure 1). Note that $D(G') \leq D_{\mathcal{Q}'}(G') \leq D = D_{\mathcal{Q}}(G)$. Indeed, for each $v \in V$, each clique $Q_i$ in $\mathcal{Q}'$ that contains $v$ corresponds to a distinct clique from $\mathcal{Q}$. Next, we analyze the maximum degree of $G'$.

Lemma 2.3. *The maximum degree $\Delta' = \Delta(G')$ of $G'$ is at most $D \cdot (t-1)$.*

Proof. By definition of diversity, for a vertex $v \in V$, the vertex $v$ belongs to at most $D = D_{\mathcal{Q}}(G)$ maximal cliques in $\mathcal{Q}$. By construction of $G'$ and $\mathcal{Q}'$, the vertex $v$ belongs also to at most $D$ maximal cliques from $\mathcal{Q}'$. Each such a clique has size at most $t$, and their union contains all neighbors of $v$ in $G'$. Thus, $v$ has at most $D \cdot (t-1)$ neighbors in $G'$. □

Now we can color $G'$ using the algorithm [17]. We obtain a coloring $\varphi$ within running time $O(\sqrt{\Delta'}\log^{2.5}\Delta' + \log^* n)$. The number of colors of $\varphi$ is $\Delta' + 1 \leq D(G)(t-1)+1$. We denote the right-hand-side by $\gamma$.

We consider the original graph $G$ with the above coloring $\varphi$ of the vertices of $G$. Denote by $G_i$, $1 \leq i \leq \gamma$, the subgraphs induced by the subset of all vertices with the same color $i$, $1 \leq i \leq \gamma$. Even though $\varphi$ is a proper coloring of $G'$, it is not necessarily a proper coloring of $G$. However, the following holds.

Lemma 2.4. *The maximum degree $\Delta(G_i)$ of $G_i$ for each $1 \leq i \leq \gamma$, is at most $(k-1)D_{\mathcal{Q}}(G)$.*

Proof. For a vertex $v \in V$, the vertex $v$ belongs to at most $D$ maximal cliques. In each such clique $Q$, there could be at most $k-1$ neighbors with the same color as $v$. (Recall that the vertex set of $Q$ is partitioned into subsets $Q_1, Q_2, \ldots, Q_k$. Each such subset is a clique in $G'$, and therefore all the vertices of $Q_j$, $1 \leq j \leq k$, have distinct colors. Thus, $v$ has at most $k-1$ neighbors in $Q$ with the same color as that of $v$.) Hence, $v$ has at most $(k-1)D$ neighbors in $G$ with the same color as that of $v$. □

Let $\mathcal{Q}_i = \{Q \mid Q$ is a maximal clique in $G_i$ and $Q \in \mathcal{Q}_v, \mathcal{Q}_v \subseteq \mathcal{Q}, v \in V\}$ denote the clique cover in $G_i$ constructed by our algorithm. Then the following hold.

Lemma 2.5. *For each vertex $v$ of $G_i$, $i \in [\gamma]$, it holds that:*
*(i) The size of all cliques of $\mathcal{Q}_i$ that $v$ belongs to is at most $k$.*
*(ii) The diversity of $v$ with respect to $G_i$ and $\mathcal{Q}_i$ is at most $D = D_{\mathcal{Q}}(G)$, i.e., $D_{\mathcal{Q}_i}(G_i) \leq D$.*

Proof. We begin by proving part (i) of the lemma. Denote by $Q'$ a clique that $v$ belongs to in the clique cover $\mathcal{Q}_i$. By construction of $G_i$ and $\mathcal{Q}_i$, there exists a clique $\hat{Q} \in \mathcal{Q}$ such that $Q' \subseteq \hat{Q}$. In the clique $\hat{Q}$ the vertex $v$ can have at most $k-1$ neighbors with the same $\varphi$-color. Thus, in $Q'$ there could be at most $k-1$ neighbors for $v$.

Now we prove part (ii) of the lemma. Let us assume for contradiction that there is a vertex $v$ in $G_i$ with diversity with respect to $\mathcal{Q}_i$ greater than $D$. Since each clique in $\mathcal{Q}_i$ is a subgraph of a clique in $\mathcal{Q}$, there must be two distinct maximal cliques $Q_1, Q_2$ (of $\mathcal{Q}_i$) which $v$ belongs to that are contained in the same maximal clique $\hat{Q}$ in $\mathcal{Q}$. (This is because the number of maximal cliques in $\mathcal{Q}$ that contain $v$ is smaller than that in $\mathcal{Q}_i$, according to our assumption.) Since $G_i$ is a vertex-induced subgraph of $G$, if two vertices with the color $i$ are connected by an edge in $G$, then they are connected by an edge in $G_i$. Let $u$ and $w$ be vertices of $Q_1$ and $Q_2$, respectively. Both $u$ and $w$ belong to $\hat{Q}$. Hence the edge $(u, w)$ belongs to $E(G)$, and thus also belongs to $E(G_i)$. Hence a set of vertices containing $Q_1 \cup Q_2$ is fully connected and belongs to $\mathcal{Q}_i$, contradicting the maximality of $Q_1$ and $Q_2$. Thus the diversity of each $v \in G_i$ is at most $D$. By definition, the diversity of $G_i$ with respect to $\mathcal{Q}_i$ is the maximal diversity with respect to $\mathcal{Q}_i$ of its vertices, that is, at most $D$. □

Recall that $\gamma = (t-1) \cdot D + 1$. By Lemmas 2.3 and 2.5, for any integer $t > 1$, we can compute $(\gamma, k)$-clique-decomposition $V_1, V_2, \ldots, V_\gamma$ of $G$. Recall that $k = \lceil S/t \rceil \leq S/t + 1$, where $S = \max\{S(Q) \mid Q \in \mathcal{Q}\}$. In other words, for any integer $t > 1$, we obtain a $(t \cdot D, S/t + 1)$-clique-decomposition. Now the maximal cliques in the subgraphs $G_1, G_2, \ldots, G_\gamma$ are smaller than maximal cliques in $G$. Also, the diversities $D_1, D_2, \ldots, D_\gamma$ of $G_1, G_2, \ldots, G_\gamma$, respectively, with respect to their respective clique covers $\mathcal{Q}_1, \mathcal{Q}_2, \ldots, \mathcal{Q}_\gamma$, are all at most $D$. We recursively apply our method to obtain yet smaller cliques at the expense of increasing the number of subgraphs. Once we obtain subgraphs with sufficiently small clique size, we can color them directly. We will determine the parameter $t$ and the number of recursion levels $x$ in Section 3.

Now we are ready to describe our coloring algorithm using clique-decomposition. (See Algorithm 1, called CD-Coloring.) The algorithm accepts as input a graph $G$, the diversity $D = D_{\mathcal{Q}}(G)$, the size $S$ of the maximal clique of $G$, the parameter $t$ of the connector to be constructed, and the number of recursion levels $x$. The algorithm starts by computing a connector in line 1. Then the connector is colored with $\gamma$ colors in line 3. These color classes induce $\gamma$ subgraphs. The algorithm is invoked recursively in parallel on all these subgraphs in line 7. The recursion terminates in lines 9 - 13, where the subgraphs are colored directly. The colorings of the recursion levels are combined in line 15. Once the algorithm terminates, we have a proper coloring of the entire input graph. This completes the description of the algorithm. See the pseudo-code below.

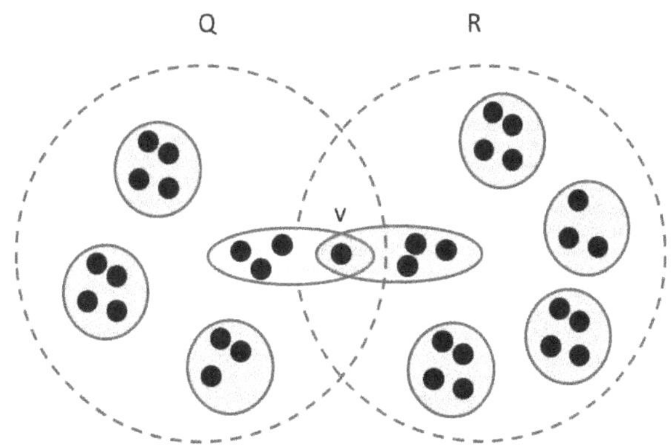


**Figure 1: A connector with $t = 4$ of a pair of cliques $Q, R$ that share a vertex $v$.**

**Algorithm 1** CD-Coloring($G, D, S, t, x$)

1: $G'$ := compute the connector of $G$ with the parameter $t$.
2: $\Delta' := D(t-1)$ /* $\Delta'$ is the maximum degree of $G'$ by Lemma 2.3*/
3: $\varphi$ := color $G'$ with $\gamma = \Delta' + 1$ colors. /* using [17] */
4: Denote by $G_i, 1 \le i \le \gamma$, the subgraphs induced by color classes of $\varphi$.
5: **if** $x > 1$ **then**
6:   **for** each $G_i$ in parallel **do**
7:     $\psi$ := CD-Coloring($G_i, D, \lceil S/t \rceil, t, x-1$) /* cliques' size decreases by a factor of $t$ */
8:   **end for**
9: **else**
10:   /* $x = 1$ */
11:   **for** each $G_i$ in parallel **do**
12:     $\psi$ := color $G_i$ with $D \cdot (\lceil S/t \rceil - 1) + 1$ colors. /* using [17] */
    /* Note that $D \cdot (\lceil S/t \rceil - 1) + 1 \ge \Delta(G_i) + 1$. So this number of colors is sufficient. */.
13:   **end for**
14: **end if**
15: **return** $\langle \varphi, \psi \rangle$

Denote by $S$ the size of a maximal clique in the original input graph $G$, and by $S_i$ the size of a maximal clique in a subgraph $G_i$, for all $i \in [\gamma]$. We recursively apply our method on $G_i, i \in [\gamma]$, in parallel. (See line 7 of Algorithm 1.) That is, we compute $(t \cdot D, S_i/t + 1)$-clique-decomposition in each $G_i$. In other words, this is a $(t \cdot D, (S/t)/t + 1/t + 1)$-clique-decomposition of each $G_i$, $1 \le i \le t \cdot D$. (Recall that the diversity of $G_i$ is not greater than the diversity of $G$.) Thus, the overall number of subsets is $(t \cdot D)^2$. Hence, after two recursion levels we obtain $((t \cdot D)^2, S/(t^2) + 1/t + 1)$-clique-decomposition of the original graph $G$. After three recursion levels we obtain $((t \cdot D)^3, S/(t^3) + 1/t^2 + 1/t + 1)$-clique-decomposition. In general, after $x$ recursion levels, $x = 1, 2, \ldots$, we obtain $((t \cdot D)^x, S/(t^x) + 1/t^{x-1} + 1/t^{x-2} + \cdots + 1/t + 1)$-clique-decomposition. Since $t \ge 2$, we have a geometric sequence $1/t^{x-1} + 1/t^{x-2} + \cdots + 1/t + 1 \le 2$, and thus we obtain $((t \cdot D)^x, S/t^x + 2)$-clique-decomposition of $G$. Since the maximum degree of each connector is $(t-1) \cdot D$, by Lemma 2.3, the coloring of the connectors in each recursion level requires $\tilde{O}(\sqrt{D \cdot t} + \log^* n)$ time. Since there are $x$ recursion levels, we obtain the following lemma.

LEMMA 2.6. *We compute $((t \cdot D)^x, S/(t^x) + 2)$-clique-decomposition of $G$ in time $\tilde{O}(x \cdot (\sqrt{D \cdot t} + \log^* n))$.*

In the end of the $x$ recursion levels, we obtain $(t \cdot D)^x$ subgraphs. We color these subgraphs as follows. Let us denote the degree of a subgraph $G_i$, $1 \le i \le (t \cdot D(G))^x$, by $\Delta_i$. Recall that $\Delta_i$ is at most the product of the diversity $D(G_i) \le D$ with respect to the clique cover we have constructed for $G_i$ by the maximum clique size in $G_i$. The latter is at most $S/(t^x) + 2$. Hence, $\Delta_i$ is at most $O(D(G) \cdot S/(t^x))$.

Now we use the algorithm of [17] again on each $G_i$ in parallel. (See line 12 of Algorithm 1.) We obtain a $(\Delta_i + 1)$-coloring within $\tilde{O}(\sqrt{\Delta_i} + \log^* n) = \tilde{O}(\sqrt{D(G)S/(t^x)} + \log^* n)$ time. Let us denote the obtained coloring by $\psi$. At the final stage, each vertex $v \in V$ colors itself with $\langle i, \psi(v) \rangle$, where $i$, $1 \le i \le (t \cdot D)^x$, is the index of the subgraph $G_i$ that $v$ belongs to (in the end of $x$ recursion levels). In the next lemmas we prove the correctness and analyze the running-time of Procedure CD-Color.

LEMMA 2.7. *The resulting coloring is proper.*

PROOF. Let $u, v$ be adjacent vertices in $G$. If they belong to different subsets $G_i, G_j, i \ne j$, then $\langle i, \psi(u) \rangle \ne \langle j, \psi(v) \rangle$, and we are done. Otherwise, there is an index $j$, such that $v, u \in G_j$. Hence, in the last stage of the algorithm, they obtain different colors $\psi$, and thus $\psi(u) \ne \psi(v)$. Hence, $\langle j, \psi(v) \rangle \ne \langle j, \psi(u) \rangle$. □

LEMMA 2.8. *The resulting coloring employs $O((t \cdot D)^x \cdot (S/(t^x) + 2) \cdot D)$ colors.*

PROOF. The number of subgraphs in the last stage is $(t \cdot D)^x$. The maximal clique size in each subgraph is at most $S/t^x + 2$. Hence each vertex has at most $S/t^x + 1$ neighbors of the same clique. Thus, the maximum degree in each subgraph is at most $(S/(t^x) + 1) \cdot D$. Therefore, the coloring $\psi$ (of the last stage) employs at most $(S/(t^x) + 1) \cdot D + 1$ colors. The overall number of colors is $O((t \cdot D)^x \cdot (S/(t^x) + 2) \cdot D)$. □

LEMMA 2.9. *The running time of* CD-Coloring *is $\tilde{O}(x \cdot (\sqrt{D \cdot t} + \log^* n) + \sqrt{D \cdot S/t^x} + \log^* n)$.*

Proof. By Lemma 2.6, computing the decomposition requires $\tilde{O}(x \cdot (\sqrt{D \cdot t} + \log^* n))$ time. The maximal clique size of the decomposition is $k \leq S/(t^x) + 2$. This means that each vertex $v$ of $G_i$ has degree of at most $D \cdot (S/t^x + 1)$. By [17], the running time of the final stage of the algorithm is $\tilde{O}(\sqrt{D \cdot S/t^x} + \log^* n)$. □

## 3 CHOOSING $X$ AND $T$

Lemmas 2.8 and 2.9 are optimized by selecting $t = S^{1/(x+1)}$. The $\tilde{O}(x \log^* n)$ factor can be eliminated (as described below), and only a single factor of $O(\log^* n)$ will remain.

The $\tilde{O}(x \log^* n)$ factor corresponds to invoking a proper $O(\Delta^2)$-coloring algorithm $x$ times. (Later these coloring are used for computing $O(\Delta)$-colorings.) Instead of performing $x$ executions, we can compute a proper $O(\Delta^2)$-coloring once in the beginning using the algorithm of Linial [30], and then employ these colors instead of IDs. Moreover, whenever distinct IDs are required for subgraphs of maximum degree $\Delta'$, we can compute a $O(\Delta'^2)$-coloring of these subgraphs from an $O(\Delta^2)$-coloring of the input graph within $\log^* \Delta - \log^* \Delta' = O(1)$ time. (See [5] for an analogous argument.) Consequently, each additional $\log^* n$ term is replaced by a $\log^* \Delta' - \log^* \Delta'' = O(1)$ term, where $\Delta'$ is the degree of the previously computed subgraph, and $\Delta''$ is the degree of the currently computed subgraph (which is a subgraph of the former). Hence, the overall running time of these invocations is $O(\log^* n)$.

Note that for sufficiently large $S$, the expression $S/t^x = S/(S^{(x/(x+1))}) = S^{1/(x+1)}$ is super-constant for all $1 \leq x \leq o(\log S)$. In this range, for $S$ larger than some sufficiently large fixed constant, it holds that $S/t^x + 2 = (1 + 2t^x/S) \cdot S/t^x \leq (1 + \mu)S/t^x$, for an arbitrarily small constant $\mu > 0$. We note that actually $\mu = o(1)$, for superconstant $S$. (If $S$ is a constant, we directly obtain a $(D(S-1)+1)$-coloring in $\tilde{O}(\sqrt{D} + \log^* n)$ time.) Hence, we obtain the following theorem.

Theorem 3.1. *For all integers $1 \leq x \leq o(\log S)$, we compute a $((1+\mu) \cdot D^{x+1}S)$-coloring within $\tilde{O}(x \cdot \sqrt{D \cdot S^{1/(x+1)}} + \log^* n)$ running time.*

We refine the analysis and improve upon Theorem 3.1. This is summarized below in Theorem 3.2.

Theorem 3.2. *We compute a $(D^{x+1}S)$-coloring, in $\tilde{O}(x \cdot (\sqrt{D \cdot t} + \log^* n) + \sqrt{D \cdot S/t^x} + \log^* n)$ time.*

Proof. In the first stage, we choose $x = 1$ and $t = \lfloor \sqrt{S} \rfloor$. We construct the connector accordingly. Now each vertex has $D \cdot (t-1)$ neighbors in the connector. We color the connector using [17] with $D \cdot (t-1) + 1$ colors. Denote this coloring $\varphi$. Each color class of $\varphi$ induces a subgraph with cliques of maximum size $k = \lceil S/t \rceil$. Each vertex in each subgraph belongs to at most $D$ cliques, and therefore the maximum degree in each subgraph is $D \cdot (k-1)$. Now we color each subgraph, using [17] again, with $D \cdot (k-1) + 1$ colors. Denote this coloring by $\psi$. The combination of the two colorings $\langle \varphi, \psi \rangle$ is a proper coloring of the entire graph. The overall number of colors (for $D \geq 2$ and $S$ larger than some constant) is

$$\begin{aligned}
& D \cdot (t-1) + 1) \cdot (D \cdot (k-1) + 1) \\
= \;& D^2 tk - Dt(D-1) - Dk(D-1) + (D-1)^2 \\
\leq \;& D^2 S + D^2 \lfloor \sqrt{S} \rfloor - Dt(D-1) - Dk(D-1) + (D-1)^2 \\
= \;& D^2 S + D^2 \lfloor \sqrt{S} \rfloor - D(D-1)(t+k) + (D-1)^2 \\
\leq \;& D^2 S + D^2 \lfloor \sqrt{S} \rfloor - (D^2 - D)(2 \lfloor \sqrt{S} \rfloor - 1) \\
\leq \;& D^2 S + D^2 \lfloor \sqrt{S} \rfloor - D^2 2 \lfloor \sqrt{S} \rfloor + D^2 + 2D \lfloor \sqrt{S} \rfloor - D \\
= \;& D^2 S - D^2 \lfloor \sqrt{S} \rfloor + D^2 + 2D \lfloor \sqrt{S} \rfloor - D \\
\leq \;& D^2 S + 2.
\end{aligned}$$

Since $DS$ is larger than the maximum degree of the graph, we can apply the basic reduction for 2 rounds, and obtain a $D^2S$-coloring. Recall that the basic color reduction computes a $(\Delta + 1)$-coloring from a $(\Delta + r)$-coloring within $r - 1$ rounds, for any integer $r > 1$. This is achieved by iterating over the color classes $\Delta + 1, \Delta + r - 1, \ldots, \Delta + 2$, and for each color class, selecting in parallel proper colors from $[\Delta + 1]$.

Denote the resulting algorithm $\mathcal{A}_1$. Next, we describe how to obtain an algorithm $\mathcal{A}_{i+1}$ from $\mathcal{A}_i$ for $i = 1, 2, \ldots$, where $\mathcal{A}_i$ is an algorithm that computes a $(D^{i+1}S)$-coloring. We choose $x = i + 1$, $t = \lfloor S^{1/(i+1)} \rfloor$. Algorithm $\mathcal{A}_{i+1}$ starts by constructing a connector (with the parameter $t$) of the input graph $G$. Next, the algorithm computes a coloring $\hat{\varphi}$ of the connector using $D(t-1) + 1$ colors. Each subgraph induced by a color class of $\hat{\varphi}$ contains cliques of maximum size $k = \lceil S/t \rceil$. Then the algorithm computes coloring $\hat{\psi}$ of subgraphs induced by color classes of $\hat{\varphi}$, using $\mathcal{A}_i$. The number of colors in each such coloring is $D^{i+1}k$. The overall number of colors is at most

$$\begin{aligned}
& (D(t-1) + 1)(D^{i+1}k) \\
\leq \;& (D(t-1) + 1)(D^{i+1}(S/t + 1)) \\
= \;& D^{i+2}S + D^{i+2}t - D^{i+2}(S/t) - D^{i+2} + D^{i+1}(S/t) + D^{i+1} \\
\leq \;& D^{i+2}S + D^{i+2}t - (D-1)D^{i+1}(S/t) \\
\leq \;& D^{i+2}S.
\end{aligned}$$

The last inequality holds for any $S$ larger than some constant since $(D-1)(S/t) > Dt$, because $t = \lfloor S^{1/(i+1)} \rfloor$ and $i \geq 2$.

Now we analyze the running time of the algorithm for some chosen number of iterations. Specifically, we analyze the running time of $\mathcal{A}_i$ for all $i = 1, 2, \ldots$. The running time of $\mathcal{A}_1$ is the time of coloring the connector and then coloring each color class in the resulting coloring. Coloring the connector requires $\tilde{O}(\sqrt{D(t-1)} + \log^* n) = \tilde{O}(\sqrt{Dt} + \log^* n)$ rounds by [17]. Coloring the subgraphs induced by different color classes requires $\tilde{O}(\sqrt{D(\lceil S/t \rceil - 1)} + \log^* n) = \tilde{O}(\sqrt{D \cdot S/t} + \log^* n)$ time by [17]. Thus, $\mathcal{A}_1$ has running time $\tilde{O}(\sqrt{Dt} + \sqrt{D \cdot S/t} + \log^* n)$.

Next, we analyze the running time of the algorithm $\mathcal{A}_{i+1}$ for coloring $G$. We assume inductively that $\mathcal{A}_i$ runs on any subgraph $G'$ of $G$ within time $T_i = \tilde{O}(i \cdot (\sqrt{D \cdot t} + \log^* n) + \sqrt{D \cdot S'/t^i} + \log^* n)$, where $S'$ is the maximal clique size in $G'$. We prove that the running time of $\mathcal{A}_{i+1}$ executed on $G$ is $\tilde{O}(\sqrt{D \cdot t} + \log^* n) + T_i$. Denote by $S = S_G$ the maximal clique size in $G$. In $\mathcal{A}_{i+1}$, it holds that $t = \left\lfloor S^{1/(i+2)} \right\rfloor$. Algorithm $\mathcal{A}_{i+1}$ starts by using [17] to color the connector within time $\tilde{O}(\sqrt{Dt} + \log^* n)$. The maximal clique size in the subgraphs induced by color classes of the resulting coloring is at most $k = \lceil S/t \rceil$. Hence, for each such subgraph $G'$, it holds that $S' \leq \lceil S/t \rceil$. Consequently, the algorithm $\mathcal{A}_i$ colors each subgraph inuced by a color class within time $T_i = \tilde{O}(i \cdot (\sqrt{D \cdot t} + \log^* n) + \sqrt{D \cdot S'/t^i} + \log^* n) = \tilde{O}(i \cdot (\sqrt{D \cdot t} + \log^* n) + \sqrt{D \cdot S/t^{i+1}} + \log^* n)$. The overall running time of $\mathcal{A}_{i+1}$ executed on $G$ is $\tilde{O}(\sqrt{Dt} + \log^* n) + T_i = \tilde{O}((i+1) \cdot (\sqrt{D \cdot t} + \log^* n) + \sqrt{D \cdot S/t^{i+1}} + \log^* n)$. □

We note that for a special case of line-graphs it holds that $D(G) = 2$. Indeed, let $e_{(u,v)}$ be a vertex in a line-graph that corresponds to an edge $(u, v)$ of the original graph. Then $e_{(u,v)}$ can belong to at most 2 maximal cliques in $Q$ corresponding to edges that contain $u$ and edges that contain $v$ in the original graph. In addition, as we have explained, the term of $O(\log^* n)$ can appear exactly once in the running time, if we invoke only once the algorithm of Linial [30], and then employ proper $O(\Delta^2)$-colorings instead of an $n$-coloring. Hence, by setting $t = S^{1/x+1}$ in Theorem 3.2, we obtain the following result.

Theorem 3.3. *(i) For any positive integer $x \in o(\log S)$, we compute a $(D^{x+1}S)$-coloring of graphs with diversity $D$ within $\tilde{O}(x \cdot \sqrt{D \cdot S^{1/(x+1)}} + \log^* n)$ time.*
*(ii)For any positive integer $x \in o(\log \Delta)$, we compute a $(2^{x+1}\Delta)$-edge-coloring in $\tilde{O}(x \cdot \Delta^{\frac{1}{2x+2}} + \log^* n)$ time.*

We now analyze the results for specific values of $x$. For $x = 1$ we obtain an $(S \cdot D^2)$-coloring within $\tilde{O}(\sqrt{D \cdot S^{\frac{1}{2}}} + \log^* n)$ time. For $x = 2$ we obtain an $(S \cdot D^3)$-coloring within $\tilde{O}(\sqrt{D \cdot S^{\frac{1}{3}}} + \log^* n)$ time. For $x = 3$ we obtain an $(S \cdot D^4)$-coloring within $\tilde{O}(\sqrt{D \cdot S^{\frac{1}{4}}} + \log^* n)$ time, and so forth.

We now take a second look at the above results in the case of line graphs. For $x = 1$ we obtain a $4\Delta$-coloring within $\tilde{O}(\sqrt[4]{\Delta} + \log^* n)$ time. For $x = 2$ we obtain a $8\Delta$-coloring within $\tilde{O}(\sqrt[6]{\Delta} + \log^* n)$ time. For $x = 3$ we obtain a $16\Delta$-coloring within $\tilde{O}(\sqrt[8]{\Delta} + \log^* n)$ time, etc.

Another interesting corollary for line graphs is the following. Since we aim at poly-logarithmic time, we set $x = \log S/(\epsilon \log \log S)$, for some $\epsilon > 0$. By Theorem 3.3, this results in $(S \cdot 2^{\log S/(\epsilon \log \log S)+1}) = 2S^{1+1/(\epsilon \log \log S)}$ colors. The running time we achieve is

$$\tilde{O}(\log S/(\epsilon \log \log S) \cdot \sqrt{2 \cdot S^{1/((\log S/(\epsilon \log \log S))+1)}} + \log^* n)$$

$$\leq \tilde{O}((\log S)^{1+\frac{\epsilon}{2}} + \log^* n).$$

Note that for a line graph, $(\Delta + 1)/2 \leq S \leq \Delta + 1$.

## 4 EDGE COLORING USING STAR-PARTITION

If we would use the above algorithm for coloring edges we would need to simulate the line graph of the given graph and invoke on it the above algorithm. This simulation requires some local computation and resources. In this section we show a different technique that does not require this simulation. We do this by introducing a different type of connectors.

Given a graph $G = (V, E)$, an edge subset $\hat{E} \subsetneq E$ is a *star* if there is vertex $u \in V$ that is shared by all edges in $\hat{E}$. The vertex $u$ is the *center* of the star. The partition we present in this section decomposes the given graph $G$ into subgraphs with smaller *stars*. This time we partition the edge set rather than the vertex set. For parameters $p, q > 0$, a *$(p, q)$-star-partition* of a graph $G = (V, E)$ is an edge partition $E_1, E_2, \ldots, E_p$ of $E$, such that the maximum size of a star in $E_i$ is at most $q$, for all $i \in [p]$.

We construct this decomposition in the following way. For some integer $t > 1$, each vertex $v$ in $G$ groups its edges into subsets, each of which is of size at most $t$. Each vertex $v \in V$ defines virtual vertices $v_1, v_2, ..., v_k$, a vertex for each such subset. These vertices are simulated locally by $v$. We obtain at most $k = \lceil \Delta/t \rceil$ virtual vertices for each original vertex. We define the *edge-connector* as $G' = (V', E')$, where $V'$ is the set of all virtual vertices, and $E'$ consists of all edges in $E$, but an edge $e'$ of $E'$ replaces the original vertices of its endpoints with the corresponding vertices from $V'$. More precisely, each vertex $v$ enumerates the edges adjacent on it using the set $\{1, 2, .., \Delta\}$, such that each edge of $v$ is assigned a distinct number. Now, each edge $(u, v)$ holds two numbers $l(u), l(v)$. For each such edge in $E$, the set $E'$ contains an edge $(u_i, v_j)$, where $i = \lceil l(u)/t \rceil$ and $j = \lceil l(v)/t \rceil$.

Note that the maximum degree of the edge-connector is at most $t$. We employ the edge-connector as follows. In the first stage, we edge-color the connector using [17]. We obtain $(2t-1)$-edge-coloring $\varphi$ of the connector within $\tilde{O}(\sqrt{t} + \log^* n)$ time.

In the second stage we group edges from $G$ that have the same $\varphi$ color into subsets $\hat{E}_1, \hat{E}_2, \ldots, \hat{E}_{2t-1}$. Since each vertex $v$ of $G$ has $k$ virtual vertices, and each such virtual vertex has all its edges colored with distinct colors, the number of edges of the same color adjacent on $v$ is at most $k$. Hence, the maximum degree of each $G(\hat{E}_i)$, $i \in [2t-1]$, is $k = \lceil \Delta/t \rceil$. Now we color these subgraphs in parallel using [17]. We obtain a $(2k-1)$-edge-coloring $\psi$ in each subgraph within $\tilde{O}(\sqrt{k} + \log^* n)$ time.

Each edge has now a color which is a combination of two colors. The overall number of colors is $(2t-1) \cdot (2k-1)$. The overall running time of the two stages is $\tilde{O}(\sqrt{t} + \sqrt{k} + \log^* n)$. We note that $(2t-1) \cdot (2k-1) = 4t \cdot \lceil \Delta/t \rceil - 2\lceil \Delta/t \rceil - 2t + 1 \leq 4\Delta + 2t - 2\Delta/t + 1$. Let us choose $t = \left\lfloor \sqrt{\Delta} \right\rfloor$. We get $4\Delta + 2t - 2\Delta/t + 1 \leq 4\Delta + 1$. Within an additional round the number of colors can be reduced to $4\Delta$. This gives us a $4\Delta$-coloring algorithm with $\tilde{O}(\Delta^{\frac{1}{4}} + \log^* n)$ time.

As in the case of clique-decomposition we can compute star-partition recursively on each of the subgraphs. To this end, we set $t = \Delta^{1/(x+1)}$, for a positive integer $x$. As usual, $x$ denotes the number of recursion levels. In each level we compute star-partition of the subgraphs. This increases the number of subgraphs and reduces the maximum size of stars in each subgraph. Once the size of all stars becomes sufficiently small, we color the subgraphs directly using [17]. This scheme is the same as that of Theorem 3.3, and thus we obtain the following result.

Theorem 4.1. *For $x = 1, 2, \ldots$, we compute a $(2^{x+1}\Delta)$-edge-coloring within $\tilde{O}(x \cdot \Delta^{\frac{1}{2x+2}} + \log^* n)$ time. Moreover, this computation does not require maintaining the line graph by the original graph.*

# 5 EDGE-COLORING WITH $\Delta + o(\Delta)$ COLORS OF BOUNDED ARBORICITY GRAPHS

An $H$-partition with degree $d$ of a graph $G = (V, E)$ is a partition of $V$ into $\ell$ subsets $H_1, H_2, ..., H_\ell$, such that the number of neighbors of each $v \in H_i$, $i = 1, 2, ..., \ell$, in $\cup_{j=i}^{\ell} H_j$ is at most $d$. Given a graph $G$ with arboricity $a = a(G)$, an $H$-partition with degree $d = (2 + \epsilon)a$, for any constant $\epsilon > 0$, can be constructed in $O(\log n)$ time [4]. Using this partition we obtain a $(\Delta + O(a))$-edge-coloring of $G$ within $O(a \log n)$ time. This is achieved using the following auxiliary algorithm.

Suppose that we are given a graph $G = (V = A \cup B, E)$, in which $A \cap B = \emptyset$. Suppose that the maximum degree of $G(A)$ is at most $d$, and that for each vertex $v \in A$, the number of neighbors of $v$ in $A \cup B$ is also bounded by $d$. Moreover, the graph $G(A)$ already has a proper edge-coloring $\varphi_A$ using $O(d)$ colors, and the graph $G(B)$ already has a proper edge-coloring $\varphi_B$ using $\Delta + O(d)$ colors. Next we devise an algorithm that extends the colorings $\varphi_A$ and $\varphi_B$ into a unified coloring $\varphi$ of all the edges of $G$, including those that cross between $A$ and $B$. The number of employed colors is $\Delta + O(d)$, and the running time is $O(d)$.

This algorithm proceeds as follows. Each vertex in $A$ labels its edges which cross to $B$ using unique labels from $\{1, 2, \ldots, d\}$. Now we perform $d$ rounds. In each round $i$, $1 \leq i \leq d$, all edges with label $i$ become active. (Recall that each such edge has endpoints in $A$ and $B$.) Denote by $E_i''$ such active edges of round $i$. For each edge $e \in E_i''$, its endpoint $v$ in $B$ collects the colors from all the edges incident to $e$. Then, the endpoint $v$ finds a new color available for $e$. Since $e$ has at most $d - 1 + \Delta - 1$ neighboring edges, there must be an available color within a palette of size $\Delta + d - 1$. Moreover, if a vertex $v$ in $B$ is shared by several crossing edges, it is still able to assign them colors in the same round, one after another. Indeed, the endpoints in $A$ of these crossing edges are not shared by multiple edges of $E_i''$. (Otherwise, a vertex in $A$ would have assigned the same label to some of its edges. However, it has assigned unique labels.) Hence, all color assignments made by vertices in the same round are performed on sets of edges, such that no endpoint belongs to multiple sets. Therefore, any assignment of distinct available colors by $v$ to its edge set of label $i$ results in a proper coloring. Overall, there are $d$ such rounds until the algorithm terminates. Then, the entire graph $G$ is properly colored using $\Delta + O(d)$ colors. This discussion is summarized in Lemma 5.1. We use this lemma to prove Theorem 5.2 below.

LEMMA 5.1. *Suppose that we are given a graph $G = (V = A \cup B, E)$, $A \cap B = \emptyset$, and the degrees of vertices of $A$ in $G$ are at most $d$. Moreover, the graph $G(A)$ already has a proper edge-coloring $\varphi_A$ using $O(d)$ colors and the graph $G(B)$ already has a proper edge-coloring $\varphi_B$ using $\Delta + O(d)$ colors. Then a proper edge-coloring $\varphi$ of $G$ using $\Delta + O(d)$ colors can be computed in $O(d)$ time. This coloring $\varphi$ extends $\varphi_A$ and $\varphi_B$. Moreover, if $\varphi_A$ employs at most $2d - 1$ colors, then $\varphi$ employs at most $\Delta + d - 1$ colors.*

THEOREM 5.2. *A $(\Delta + O(a))$-edge-coloring of $G$ can be computed in $O(a \log n)$ time.*

PROOF. Compute an $H$-partition of $G$ using [4] in $O(\log n)$ time. Note that the maximum degree of each $H$-set is $O(a)$, and the number of $H$-sets is $\ell = O(\log n)$. Compute an $O(a)$-edge-coloring of the $H$-sets in parallel. Since each $H$-set has maximum degree $O(a)$, this is computed within $\tilde{O}(\sqrt{a} + \log^* n)$ using the algorithm presented in the current article in Section 4. (Actually, this step can be performed much faster at the expense of increasing the constant hidden by the $O$-notation in the number of colors $O(a)$. See Theorem 4.1.) Now we go over the sets from $H_\ell$ back to $H_1$. In each stage we color the edges that cross between $H_i$ and $H_{i+1} \cup \ldots \cup H_\ell$, using Lemma 5.1. (It holds that $A = H_i$, $B = H_{i+1} \cup, \ldots, \cup H_\ell$, $d = O(a)$.) This requires overall of $\Delta + O(a)$ colors. The running time of each stage is $O(a)$, and there are total of $O(\log n)$ such stages. This results in a $(\Delta + O(a))$-edge-coloring of $G$ within $O(a \log n)$ time. □

Note that if the number of $H$-sets $\ell$ in the $H$-partition is smaller than $\log n$, then the running time of the $(\Delta + O(a))$-edge-coloring algorithm also decreases to $O(a \cdot \ell)$. Note also that the constant hidden by the $O$-notation in the number of colors is the maximum number of neighbors of a vertex of an $H$-set $H_i, i \in [\ell]$, in $H_i \cup H_{i+1} \cup \ldots \cup H_\ell$.

Next we demonstrate how to improve the running time using a yet another kind of connectors. To this end, we first need an acyclic orientation of the edge set of $G$ with bounded out-degree. As shown in [4], it is achieved by orienting edges that cross between different $H$-sets towards the sets with greater indices, and edges of the same $H$-set towards the endpoints with greater IDs. This results in an acyclic orientation with out-degree $d = (2 + \epsilon)a$. Now we construct the following *orientation-connector*. Each vertex $v \in V$ defines $k = \lceil \sqrt{\Delta} \rceil$ virtual vertices $v_1, v_2, ..., v_k$. Then it groups its incoming edges into $k$ subsets of size at most $\Delta/k$ edges each. Each edge of the $i$th subset, $i \in [k]$, is connected to $v_i$ (and oriented towards $v_i$). The vertex $v$ also groups its outgoing edges into $\lceil \sqrt{d} \rceil$ subsets of size at most $\sqrt{d}$ edges each. Each edge of the $i$-th subset, $i \in \lceil \sqrt{d} \rceil$, is connected to $v_i$ (and oriented outwards of $v_i$). (See Figure 2).

The above connector has arboricity at most $\sqrt{d}$, since the out-degree is bounded by $\sqrt{d} = O(\sqrt{a})$, and the orientation is acyclic. Moreover, its maximum degree is at most $\sqrt{\Delta} + O(\sqrt{a})$. Therefore, using Theorem 5.2, we obtain a $(\sqrt{\Delta} + O(\sqrt{a}))$-coloring $\varphi$ of the connector within $O(\sqrt{a} \log n)$ time. For each $i \in [\sqrt{\Delta} + O(\sqrt{a})]$, let $\hat{E}_i \subseteq E$ be the set of edges colored by $\varphi$-color $i$. Then every vertex in $G(\hat{E}_i)$ has at most $k = \lceil \sqrt{\Delta} \rceil$ incoming edges and $O(\sqrt{d}) = O(\sqrt{a})$ outgoing edges. (This is because there are $k$ virtual vertices per original vertex, all incoming edges of a virtual vertex are of distinct colors, all outgoing edges of a virtual vertex are of distinct colors, and only $O(\sqrt{d}) = O(\sqrt{a})$ virtual vertices have outgoing edges.) Thus, the maximum degree of $G(\hat{E}_i)$ is $\lceil \sqrt{\Delta} \rceil + O(\sqrt{a})$, and its arboricity is $O(\sqrt{a})$. This allows us to color all subgraphs $\{G(\hat{E}_i) \mid i \in [\sqrt{\Delta} + O(\sqrt{a})]\}$, in parallel using Theorem 5.2. We obtain an edge-coloring $\psi$ in each subgraph that employs $\lceil \sqrt{\Delta} \rceil + O(\sqrt{a})$ colors per subgraph. The running time of this step is $O(\sqrt{a} \log n)$ as well. To summarize, we obtained a proper edge coloring $\langle \varphi, \psi \rangle$ of the entire input graph. The number of colors is $(\sqrt{\Delta} + O(\sqrt{a})) \cdot (\lceil \sqrt{\Delta} \rceil + O(\sqrt{a})) = \Delta + O(\sqrt{\Delta \cdot a}) + O(a)$. This directly implies the following.

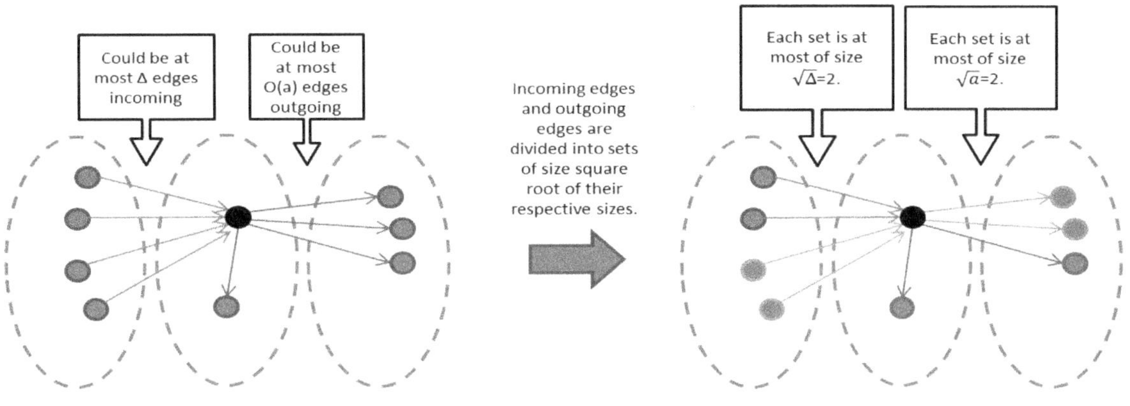


**Figure 2: Orientation-connector**

THEOREM 5.3. *For graphs with $a(G) = o(\Delta)$, we compute a $(\Delta + o(\Delta))$-coloring within $O(\sqrt{a}\log n)$ time.*

Next, we improve our result further. Let $q \geq (2+\epsilon)$ be a positive parameter, for some arbitrarily small constant $\epsilon > 0$. Let $\hat{a} = q \cdot a$. We compute an $H$-partition with out-degree $\hat{a}$ in $O(\frac{\log n}{\log q})$ time [4]. Next we describe an algorithm for computing a $(\Delta^{1/x} + 2\hat{a}^{1/x} + 1)(\Delta^{1/x} + \hat{a}^{1/x} + 3)^{x-1}$-edge-coloring in $O(a^{1/x} \cdot (x + \frac{\log n}{\log q}))$ time, for any positive integer parameter $x$. The algorithm starts by defining $\delta = \lfloor \Delta^{1-1/x} \rfloor$ virtual vertices $v_1, v_2, ..., v_\delta$ and $\hat{\alpha} = \lfloor \hat{a}^{1-1/x} \rfloor$ virtual vertices $v'_1, v'_2, ..., v'_{\hat{\alpha}}$ per each original vertex $v$ of $G$. Then, incoming edges of $v$ are grouped into subsets of size at most $\lceil \Delta^{1/x} \rceil + 1$ each, and connected to $v_1, v_2, ..., v_\delta$, oriented towards the virtual vertices. Specifically, this grouping is such that incoming edges from neighbors from the same $H$-set are grouped into subsets of size at most $\lceil \hat{a}^{1/x} \rceil + 1$ each, and connected to $v_1, v_2, ..., v_{\hat{\alpha}}$. In addition, outgoing edges of $v$ are grouped into subsets of size at most $\lceil \hat{a}^{1/x} \rceil + 1$ each, and connected to $v'_1, v'_2, ..., v'_{\hat{\alpha}}$, oriented outwards from the virtual vertices. Note that the resulting orientation-connector is a bipartite graph. Indeed, for any $v, u \in V(G)$ and any indices $i, j$, the vertices $v_i$ and $u_j$ are not connected by an edge, and neither are $v'_i$ and $u'_j$. Thus, all virtual vertices of the form $v_i$ are on one side in the bipartite graph, while all virtual vertices of the form $v'_i$ are on the other, for all indices $i$. Note that all vertices on one side have degree at most $\lceil \Delta^{1/x} \rceil + 1$, and all vertices on the other side have degree at most $\lceil \hat{a}^{1/x} \rceil + 1$. Therefore, this orientation-connector can be colored with at most $\Delta^{1/x} + \hat{a}^{1/x} + 3$ colors within $O(\hat{a}^{1/x})$ time (See Lemma 5.1.) Denote this coloring by $\varphi$.

The edge-coloring $\varphi$ constitutes a partition of the original graph $G$ into $\Delta^{1/x} + \hat{a}^{1/x} + 3$ color classes. The subgraph of $G$ induced by each color class has maximum in-degree at most $\delta = \Delta^{1-1/x}$, and maximum out-degree at most $\hat{\alpha} = \hat{a}^{1-1/x}$. Moreover, the $H$-partition restricted to each subgraph has the property that the number of neighbors of a vertex of some $H_j$, $j \in [\ell]$, within the $H$-sets $H_j \cup H_{j+1} \cup ... \cup H_\ell$ is at most $\hat{a}^{1-1/x} + 1$. By repeating the same procedure again in each subgraph in parallel, we obtain $\Delta^{1/x} + \hat{a}^{1/x} + 3$ colors within each subgraph in time $O(\hat{a}^{1/x})$. The overall number of colors is now $(\Delta^{1/x} + \hat{a}^{1/x} + 3)^2$. The subgraph of $G$ induced by each color class has maximum in-degree at most $\Delta^{1-2/x}$, and maximum out-degree at most $\hat{a}^{1-2/x}$. Overall, if we perform $x-1$ such stages, we obtain a $(\Delta^{1/x} + \hat{a}^{1/x} + 3)^{x-1}$-coloring, such that each color class induces a subgraph $G_i$, $1 \leq i \leq (\Delta^{1/x} + \hat{a}^{1/x} + 3)^{x-1}$, of $G$ with maximum in-degree at most $\Delta^{1/x}$, and maximum out-degree at most $\hat{a}^{1/x}$.

The vertex set of each such a subgraph $G_i$ is partitioned according to the partition of these vertices in the original $H$-partition of $G$, into subsets $H^i_1, H^i_2, ..., H^i_\ell$. Observe that the maximum degree of each $G_i$ is at most $\Delta^{1/x} + \hat{a}^{1/x}$, and the number of neighbors of a vertex of $H^i_j, j \in [\ell]$, within the $H$-sets $H^i_j \cup H^i_{j+1} \cup ... \cup H^i_\ell$ is at most $\hat{a}^{1/x} + 2$. (Note that initially this number of neighbors is $\hat{a}$, in the next iteration it is $\hat{a}^{1-1/x} + 1$, in the following one it is $\hat{a}^{1-2/x} + \frac{1}{\hat{a}^{1/x}} + 1$, and so on. We end up with $\hat{a}^{1/x} + \frac{1}{\hat{a}^{1-1/x}} + \frac{1}{\hat{a}^{1-2/x}} + ... + 1 < \hat{a}^{1/x} + 2$ neighbors.) All these subgraphs $G_i$ can be colored in parallel using $\Delta^{1/x} + 2\hat{a}^{1/x} + 1$ colors per subgraph within $O(\hat{a}^{1/x} \cdot \frac{\log n}{\log q})$ time, by Theorem 5.2. (Note that the $H$-partition that we use contains $\ell = O(\frac{\log n}{\log q})$ $H$-sets.) We use disjoint palettes for distinct subgraphs $G_i$. This results in a proper edge coloring of the entire input graph. To summarize, we obtained the following result.

THEOREM 5.4. *For any $q \geq (2+\epsilon)$, $\hat{a} = q \cdot a$, and $x = 1, 2, ...,$ we obtain a $(\Delta^{1/x} + 2\hat{a}^{1/x} + 1)(\Delta^{1/x} + \hat{a}^{1/x} + 3)^{x-1}$-edge-coloring within $O(\hat{a}^{1/x}(x + \frac{\log n}{\log q}))$ time.*

Next, we analyze how large the arboricity of a graph can be to still allow for $\Delta + o(\Delta)$ colors in polylogarithmic time. Since $\hat{a}^{1/x}(\Delta^{1/x} + \hat{a}^{1/x} + 3)^{x-1} = o(\Delta)$ whenever $\hat{a} = o(\Delta)$ and $x = o(\log \Delta)$, it is sufficient to perform this analysis for the expression $(\Delta^{1/x} + \hat{a}^{1/x} + 3)^x$. We set $x = \frac{\log \hat{a}}{c \log\log \hat{a}}$, for a (possibly large) constant $c > 0$. Hence $\hat{a}^{1/x} = \log^c \hat{a}$. Let $\eta > 0$ be a parameter. Suppose that we have

$$\Delta^{1/x} \geq \frac{x}{\eta}(\hat{a}^{1/x} + 3). \quad (1)$$

Then the number of colors is $(\Delta^{1/x} + \hat{a}^{1/x} + 3)^x = \Delta(1 + \frac{\hat{a}^{1/x}+3}{\Delta^{1/x}})^x \leq \Delta(1+\eta/x)^x \leq \Delta \cdot e^{\eta} \leq \Delta(1+2\eta)$, for a sufficiently small $\eta > 0$. The condition (1) is equivalent to

$$\Delta \geq \frac{x^x}{\eta^x}(\hat{a}^{1/x} + 3)^x \tag{2}$$

Observe that $\hat{a}^{1/x} = \log^c \hat{a} \geq 3$, for $\hat{a} \geq 2^{3^{1/c}}$. Set $q = 2 + \epsilon'$, for some constant $\epsilon' > 0$. (Recall that $\hat{a} = q \cdot a$.) Hence $\hat{a}^{1/x} \geq 3$, for $(2+\epsilon)a \geq 2^{3^{1/c}}$. We have $2^{3^{1/c}} \leq 2 + O(1/c)$, and so by selecting a sufficiently large constant $c$, we can ensure that $\hat{a}^{1/x} + 3 \leq 2\hat{a}^{1/x}$.

Then $\Delta \geq \hat{a}^{1+1/c+\frac{\log(2/\eta)}{c \log\log \hat{a}}}$ implies (2) and (1). If $a > \Delta^{\frac{1}{4\log\log\Delta}}$, then we set $\eta = O(1/\log\Delta)$, and obtain a $\Delta(1 + O(\frac{1}{\log\Delta}))$-edge-coloring, assuming $\Delta \geq a^{1+O(1/c)}$. The running time is $O(x \cdot a^{1/x} + a^{1/x}\log n) = O(\log^c a \log n)$. If $a < \Delta^{\frac{1}{4\log\log\Delta}}$, then we set $x = \log\hat{a} = \log(aq)$. Here we do not set $q = 2 + \epsilon'$, but rather use a larger value, $q = \frac{1}{a} \cdot 2^{\frac{\log\Delta}{\log\log\Delta + \log\frac{1}{\eta} + 1}}$, and $\eta = \frac{1}{\log\Delta}$. Note that $q \geq 3$ in this range of parameters. The running time becomes $O(\log\hat{a} + \frac{\log n}{\log q}) = O(\log a + \log q + \frac{\log n}{\log q})$
$= O(\frac{\log\Delta}{\log\log\Delta} + \frac{\log n}{\log\Delta/(2\log\log\Delta) - \log a})$. This expression is always $O(\log n)$, and it is $o(\log n)$ whenever $\Delta = \omega(1)$. The number of colors is again $\Delta(1 + O(\frac{1}{\log\Delta}))$.

Corollary 5.5. *Whenever $a < \Delta^{\frac{1}{4\log\log\Delta}}$, a variant of our algorithm computes a $\Delta(1 + O(\frac{1}{\log\Delta})) = \Delta(1 + o(1))$-edge-coloring in $O(\log n)$ time. Moreover, the time is $o(\log n)$ whenever $\Delta = \omega(1)$. For larger arboricity, for any arbitrarily large positive parameter $c > 0$, a variant of our algorithm computes a $\Delta(1 + O(\frac{1}{\log\Delta}))$-edge-coloring in time $O(\log^c a \log n)$, assuming $\Delta \geq a^{1+O(1/c)}$.*

In other words, the larger the gap between the maximum degree $\Delta$ and the arboricity $a$, the faster is our algorithm. Moreover, the algorithm runs in polylogarithmic time whenever the gap is at least polynomial, i.e., $\Delta \geq a^{1+\epsilon}$, for some constant $\epsilon > 0$.

**Acknowledgements**

The authors are grateful to Alessandro Panconesi for fruitful discussions.

## REFERENCES


[1] N. Alon, L. Babai, and A. Itai. A fast and simple randomized parallel algorithm for the maximal independent set problem. *J. of Algorithms*, 7(4):567–583, 1986.

[2] B. Awerbuch, A. V. Goldberg, M. Luby, and S. Plotkin. Network decomposition and locality in distributed computation. In *Proc. of the 30th Annual Symposium on Foundations of Computer Science*, pages 364–369, 1989.

[3] L. Barenboim. Deterministic $(\Delta + 1)$-Coloring in Sublinear (in $\Delta$) Time in Static, Dynamic and Faulty Networks. In *Proc of the 34th ACM Symp. on Principles of Distributed Computing*, pages 345-354, 2015.

[4] L. Barenboim, and M. Elkin. Sublogarithmic distributed MIS algorithm for sparse graphs using Nash-Williams decomposition. In *Proc. of the 27th ACM Symp. on Principles of Distributed Computing*, pages 25–34, 2008.

[5] L. Barenboim, and M. Elkin. Distributed $(\Delta + 1)$-coloring in linear (in $\Delta$) time. In *Proc. of the 41th ACM Symp. on Theory of Computing*, pages 111-120, 2009.

[6] L. Barenboim, and M. Elkin. Deterministic distributed vertex coloring in polylogarithmic time. In *Proc. 29th ACM Symp. on Principles of Distributed Computing*, pages 410-419, 2010.

[7] L. Barenboim, and M. Elkin. Distributed deterministic edge coloring using bounded neighborhood independence. In *Proc. of the 30th ACM Symp. on Principles of Distributed Computing*, pages 129 - 138, 2011.

[8] L. Barenboim, and M. Elkin. *Distributed Graph Coloring: Fundamentals and Recent Developments.* Morgan-Claypool Synthesis Lectures on Distributed Computing Theory, 2013.

[9] L. Barenboim, M. Elkin, and F. Kuhn. Distributed (Delta+1)-Coloring in Linear (in Delta) Time. *SIAM Journal on Computing*, 43(1): 72-95, 2014.

[10] L. Barenboim, M. Elkin, S. Pettie, and J. Schneider. The locality of distributed symmetry breaking. In *Proc. of the 53rd Annual Symposium on Foundations of Computer Science*, pages 321-330, 2012.

[11] B. Berger, and J. Rompel. Simulating $(\log cn)$-wise independence in NC. *Journal of the ACM*, 38(4), pages 1026-1046. 1991.

[12] R. Cole, and U. Vishkin. Deterministic coin tossing with applications to optimal parallel list ranking. *Information and Control*, 70(1):32–53, 1986.

[13] A. Czygrinow, M. Hanckowiak, and M. Karonski. Distributed O(Delta logn)-edge-coloring algorithm. In *Proc. of the 9th Annual European Symposium on Algorithms*, pages 345–355, 2001.

[14] D. Dubhashi, D. Grable, and A. Panconesi. Nearly-optimal distributed edge-colouring via the nibble method. *Theoretical Computer Science, a special issue for the best papers of ESA95*, 203(2):225–251, 1998.

[15] T. Erlebach, and K. Jansen. The complexity of path coloring and call scheduling. *Theoretical Computer Science*, 255 (1-2), pages 33-50, 2001.

[16] M. Elkin, S. Pettie, and H. Su. $(2\Delta - 1)$-Edge-Coloring is Much Easier than Maximal Matching in the Distributed Setting. In *Proc. of the 26th ACM-SIAM Symp. on Discrete Algorithms*, pages 355-370, 2015.

[17] P. Fraigniaud, M. Heinrich, and A. Kosowski. Local Conflict Coloring. http://arxiv.org/abs/1511.01287. To appear in FOCS 2016.

[18] M. Fürer, and B. Raghavachari. Parallel edge coloring approximation. *Parallel processing letters*, 6(3), pages 321-329, 1996.

[19] S. Gandham, M. Dawande, and R. Prakash. Link scheduling in sensor networks: distributed edge coloring revisited. In *Proc. of IEEE 24th Annual Joint Conference of the IEEE Computer and Communications Societies*, pp. 2492-2501, 2005.

[20] M. Ghaffari and H. Su. Distributed Degree Splitting, Edge Coloring, and Orientations. https://arxiv.org/abs/1608.03220. To appear in SODA 2016.

[21] A. Goldberg, S. Plotkin, and G. Shannon. Parallel symmetry-breaking in sparse graphs. *SIAM Journal on Discrete Mathematics*, 1(4):434–446, 1988.

[22] D. Grable, and A. Panconesi. Nearly optimal distributed edge colouring in O(log log n) rounds. *Random Structures and Algorithms*, 10(3): 385-405, 1997.

[23] Y. Han, W. Liang, and X. Shen. Very fast parallel algorithms for approximate edge coloring. *Discrete applied mathematics*, 108(3), 227-238, 2001.

[24] M. Hanckowiak, M. Karonski, and A. Panconesi. On the distributed complexity of computing maximal matchings. *SIAM Journal on Discrete Mathematics*, 15(1):41–57, 2001.

[25] H. Karloff, and D. Shmoys. Efficient parallel algorithms for edge coloring problems. *Journal of Algorithms*, 8(1), pages 39-52, 1987.

[26] A. Korman, J. Sereni, and L. Viennot. Toward more localized local algorithms: removing assumptions concerning global knowledge. In *Proc. of the 30th ACM Symp. on Principles of Distributed Computing*, pages 49-58, 2011.

[27] F. Kuhn. Weak graph colorings: distributed algorithms and applications. In *Proc. of the 21st ACM Symposium on Parallel Algorithms and Architectures*, pages 138–144, 2009.

[28] F. Kuhn, and R. Wattenhofer. On the complexity of distributed graph coloring. In *Proc. 25th ACM Symp. on Principles of Distributed Computing*, pages 7–15, 2006.

[29] W. Liang, X. Shen, and Q .Hu. Parallel Algorithms for the Edge-Coloring and Edge-Coloring Update Problems. *Journal of Parallel and Distributed Computing*, 32(1), Pages 66-73, 1996.

[30] N. Linial. Distributive graph algorithms: Global solutions from local data In *Proc. of the 28th Annual Symp. on Foundation of Computer Science*, pp. 331–335, 1987.

[31] J. Mycielski. Sur le coloriage des graphes. *Colloq. Math.* 3, pages 161-162, 1955.

[32] R. Motwani, J. Naor, and M. Naor. The probabilistic method yields deterministic parallel algorithms. *J. of Computer and System Sciences*, 49(3), 478-516, 1994.

[33] A. Panconesi, and R. Rizzi. Some simple distributed algorithms for sparse networks. *Distributed Computing*, 14(2):97–100, 2001.

[34] A. Panconesi, and A. Srinivasan. Randomized Distributed Edge Coloring via an Extension of the Chernoff-Hoeffding Bounds. *SIAM Journal on Computing*, 26(2):350-368, 1997.

[35] D. Peleg. *Distributed Computing: A Locality-Sensitive Approach.* SIAM, 2000.

[36] V. Vizing. On an estimate of the chromatic class of a p-graph. *Metody Diskret. Analiz*, 3: 25-30, 1964.

[37] D. Williamson, L. Hall, J. Hoogeveen, C. Hurkens, J. Lenstra, S. Sevast'janov, and D. Shmoys. Short shop schedules. *Operations Research*, 45 (2), pp. 288-294, 1997.

[38] X. Zhou, and T. Nishizeki. Edge-coloring and f-coloring for various classes of graphs. *Journal of Graph Algorithms and Applications*, 3(1), 1-18. 1998.

# Optimal Distance Labeling Schemes for Trees

Ofer Freedman
University of Haifa, Israel

Paweł Gawrychowski
University of Haifa, Israel

Patrick K. Nicholson
Bell Labs, Dublin, Ireland

Oren Weimann
University of Haifa, Israel

## ABSTRACT

Labeling schemes seek to assign a short label to each node in a network, so that a function on two nodes (such as distance or adjacency) can be computed by examining their labels alone. For the particular case of trees, following a long line of research, optimal bounds (up to low order terms) were recently obtained for adjacency labeling [FOCS '15], nearest common ancestor labeling [SODA '14], and ancestry labeling [SICOMP '06]. In this paper we obtain optimal bounds for distance labeling. We present labels of size $1/4\log^2 n + o(\log^2 n)$, matching (up to low order terms) the recent $1/4\log^2 n - O(\log n)$ lower bound [ICALP '16].

Prior to our work, all distance labeling schemes for trees could be reinterpreted as *universal trees*. A tree $T$ is said to be universal if any tree on $n$ nodes can be found as a subtree of $T$. A universal tree with $|T|$ nodes implies a distance labeling scheme with label size $\log|T|$. In 1981, Chung et al. proved that any distance labeling scheme based on universal trees requires labels of size $1/2\log^2 n - \log n \cdot \log\log n + O(\log n)$. Our scheme is the first to break this lower bound, showing a separation between distance labeling and universal trees.

The $\Theta(\log^2 n)$ barrier for distance labeling in trees has led researchers to consider distances bounded by $k$. The size of such labels was shown to be $\log n + O(k\sqrt{\log n})$ in [WADS '01], and then improved to $\log n + O(k^2\log(k\log n))$ in [SODA '03] and finally to $\log n + O(k\log(k\log(n/k)))$ in [PODC '07]. We show how to construct labels whose size is the minimum between $\log n + O(k\log((\log n)/k))$ and $O(\log n \cdot \log(k/\log n))$. We complement this with almost tight lower bounds of $\log n + \Omega(k\log(\log n/(k\log k)))$ and $\Omega(\log n \cdot \log(k/\log n))$. Finally, we consider $(1+\varepsilon)$-approximate distances. We show that the recent labeling scheme of [ICALP '16] can be easily modified to obtain an $O(\log(1/\varepsilon)\cdot\log n)$ upper bound and we prove a matching $\Omega(\log(1/\varepsilon)\cdot\log n)$ lower bound.

## CCS CONCEPTS

• **Mathematics of computing → Trees**; • **Theory of computation → Distributed algorithms**;

OF, PG and OW were supported in part by Israel Science Foundation grant 794/13.

*PODC '17, July 25-27, 2017, Washington, DC, USA*

ACM ISBN 978-1-4503-4992-5/17/07...$15.00
http://dx.doi.org/10.1145/3087801.3087804

## KEYWORDS

labeling scheme; universal tree

## 1 INTRODUCTION

Labeling schemes seek to assign a short label to each vertex in a network, so that a function on two nodes (such as distance or adjacency) can be computed by examining their labels alone. This is particularly desirable in distributed settings, where nodes are often processed using only some locally stored data. Recently, with the rise in popularity of distributed computing platforms such as Spark and Hadoop, labeling schemes have found renewed interest. Indeed, the goal of minimizing the size of the maximal label has been the subject of a great deal of recent research [1, 5–10, 15, 16, 25]. For the particular case of trees, the functions that have been studied are distance [5, 8, 19, 20, 24], adjacency [6, 11, 12], nearest common ancestor [9, 15], and ancestry [1, 16] (a recent survey of these results can be found here [26]). Tree labeling schemes have recently found new uses in large scale graph processing. For example, distance oracles for general graphs use distance labelings for spanning trees rooted at judiciously chosen vertices [2–4].

*Universal trees.* A particularly clean way of looking at labeling schemes is through *universal graphs*. A graph $G$ is said to be *universal* for a given family of graphs, if every graph in the family is an induced subgraph of $G$. Similarly, a tree $T$ is said to be universal for *all* trees on $n$ nodes if any tree on $n$ nodes can be found as a subtree of $T$. For *adjacency labeling in graphs*, Kannan et al. [22] observed that if a family of graphs has a universal graph with $|G|$ vertices then it has an adjacency labeling scheme with label size $\log|G|$, and vice versa. For *distance labeling in trees*, until the present work, this statement was only known to be true in one direction. Namely, a universal tree $T$ of all trees on $n$ nodes implies a distance labeling scheme with label size $\log|T|$. We prove that the converse is in fact not true.

The use of universal trees is powerful, but it is limited. Already 50 years ago, Goldberg and Livshits [21] showed how to construct a universal tree $T$ that is of size $|T| = n^{(\log n - 2\log\log n + O(1))/2}$ which was shown by Chung et al. [13] to be the smallest possible up to the $O(1)$ error term. This shows the first limitation of using universal trees for distance labeling: there is a lower bound of $\log|T| = 1/2\log^2 n - \log n \cdot \log\log n + O(\log n)$ on the label size. The second limitation is the query time. The universal tree construction of Goldberg and Livshits was given before labeling schemes were ever invented. Of course, one could naively use their universal tree $T$ for distance labeling of an arbitrary tree on $n$ nodes by finding its isomorphic subtree in $T$ and assigning labels which are just the IDs of the nodes in $T$. However, such a non-algorithmic labeling would require prohibitive query time and space since $T$ needs to be computed. This latter limitation was overcome by algorithmic labeling schemes achieving logarithmic query time: An upper bound of $O(\log^2 n)$ bits on the label size was first shown by Peleg [24] and a lower bound of $1/8 \log^2 n - O(\log n)$ bits was shown by Gavoille et al. [20]. Very recently, Alstrup et al. [8] improved the lower bound to $1/4 \log^2 n - O(\log n)$ and observed that the upper bound can be improved to $1/2 \log^2 n + O(\log n)$ with a somewhat straightforward use of a nearest common ancestor labeling scheme.

All the above labeling schemes can be reinterpreted as building a universal tree, and are therefore subject to the $1/2 \log^2 n - \log n \cdot \log\log n + O(\log n)$ lower bound of Chung et al. In other words, the scheme of Alstrup et al. is optimal (up to low order terms) amongst all schemes that translate to universal trees. To see why the scheme of Alstrup et al. indeed translates to a universal tree, we show in Section 3.5 that their scheme can be casted as a level-ancestor scheme and we show in Section 3.4 that every level-ancestor scheme translates to a universal tree.

We give the first distance labeling scheme that does not translate to a universal tree. This enables us to circumvent the Chung et al. [13] lower bound for labels based on universal trees and to match the general lower bound of Alstrup et al. [8]. Namely, in Section 3 we prove the following:

THEOREM 1.1. *There is a scheme for tree distance labeling with* $1/4 \log^2 n + o(\log^2 n)$ *bit labels and constant query time.*

The above theorem means that universal trees capture more than is required for distance labeling. To illustrate this, we need to describe the related problem of level-ancestor labelings.

*Labeling schemes for level-ancestor.* In this problem, we are given a rooted tree and seek to assign labels so that we can compute (the label of) any $k$-th ancestor of a node from its label alone. Notice that here a query receives a single label and a value $k$, and that all labels must be distinct (no scheme which uses the same label twice can be correct).

It is not hard to see that labels supporting level-ancestor queries can be used to answer distance queries. Thus, any lower bound for tree distance labeling immediately applies to level-ancestor labeling, but the converse is not true. Nevertheless, it turns out that all previous distance labeling schemes are also level-ancestor schemes. Like the labeling scheme of Alstrup et al. [8], our scheme is also based on a *heavy path decomposition* of the tree, which can be seen as a way of transforming an arbitrary tree into an edge-weighted tree of logarithmic depth. However, while the labels in [8] store the weights of every edge on the path to the root (thus allowing for level-ancestor queries), we show that it is possible to carefully distribute the bits between the labels so that the distance can be computed given any pair of labels, yet a single label is not enough to extract the level-ancestors.

We determine this separation between tree distance labeling and level-ancestor labeling by proving that labeling for distances is roughly half as expensive as labeling for level-ancestors:

THEOREM 1.2. *Any scheme for level-ancestor labeling must use at least* $1/2 \log^2 n - \log n \log\log n$ *bits for the maximum length label.*

We prove the above theorem in Section 3.4 by showing that, as opposed to distance labeling, no level-ancestor labeling scheme can do better than the one based on universal trees. Namely, we prove that any level-ancestor labeling scheme with labels of length $L$ implies a universal rooted tree of size $O(2^L)$, and then invoke the known lower bound for universal trees [13, 21]. In particular, it means that for level-ancestor queries, the scheme of Alstrup et al. [8] is optimal (after some modifications described in Section 3.5).

*Labeling schemes for bounded distances.* The $\Theta(\log^2 n)$ barrier on distance labeling in trees has initiated a line of research that improves the label size when the distances are bounded: In *$k$-distance labeling*, we are given the labels of $u$ and $v$ and need to decide if the length of the $u$-to-$v$ path is at most $k$, and if so return it. For $k = 1$, this is exactly adjacency labeling, which was recently shown by Alstrup et al. [6] to require only $\log n + O(1)$ bits. For $k \geq 2$, this was first considered by Kaplan and Milo [23] who showed how to construct labels of length $\log n + O(k\sqrt{\log n})$. The query time was not explicitly specified in their implementation, but appears to be $O(k)$. A shorter label of $\log n + O(k^2 \log(k \log n))$ bits was then given by Alstrup, Bille, and Rauhe [5] who also proved that any scheme for $k \geq 2$ (i.e., any scheme that is able to answer "ancestor or sibling" queries) requires $\log n + \Omega(\log\log n)$ bits. Hence the $O(\log\log n)$ addend cannot be avoided, but it remained unclear what should be the exact dependency on $k$ nor the query time (Alstrup, Bille, and Rauhe considered constant $k$ in which case their bounds are tight and their $O(k^2)$ query time is constant). The labeling scheme of Alstrup, Bille, and Rauhe was then improved by Gavoille and Labourel [19] who presented a bound of $\log n + O(k \log(k \log(n/k)))$ bits and $O(k)$ query time.

In Section 4 we show how to construct a labeling scheme with improved label size and constant query time, and prove an almost matching lower bound. Formally, we prove:

THEOREM 1.3. *For* $k < \log n$*, there is a $k$-distance labeling scheme with labels of length* $\log n + O(k \log((\log n)/k))$ *bits, and any such scheme requires* $\log n + \Omega(k \log(\log n/(k \log k)))$ *bits.*
*For* $k \geq \log n$*, there is a $k$-distance labeling scheme with labels of length* $O(\log n \cdot \log(k/\log n))$ *bits, and any such scheme requires* $\Omega(\log n \cdot \log(k/\log n))$ *bits. In both cases, the query time is constant.*

For the upper bound, our starting point is the scheme of Alstrup, Bille, and Rauhe [5]. We observe that, instead of storing the same information for each of the nearest $k$ heavy paths above a node, it is possible to store all information for the topmost of these heavy paths and less information for all the rest. To improve the query time, we show that only a subtle change is needed in the definition of the so-called significant preorder numbers. The new definition retains all the nice properties of the previous while being much easier to operate on. Our constant query time assumes the standard word-RAM model with word size $\Omega(\log n)$.

For the lower bounds we take two different approaches. For $k < \log n$, we show how to construct a family of trees such that, in any $k$-distance labeling scheme, different trees can share some labels but every tree has to introduce many additional unique labels. For $k \geq \log n$, we use the clever lower bound technique from (unbounded) distance labelings, that was introduced by Gavoille et al. [20] and refined by Alstrup et al. [8]. It is based on constructing a *weighted* almost complete binary tree, where all the leaves are at the same distance from the root. After arguing that the labels of nodes in such a tree must be long, the weights are removed by subdividing edges while not increasing the size of the tree by too much. We show that only a small tweak is required to this known lower bound for distance labeling in order to get a lower bound for $k$-distance labeling.

*Labeling schemes for approximate distances.* Finally, we consider $(1+\varepsilon)$*-approximate distance labeling*, where given the labels of $u$ and $v$ we need to output a value that is at least $\mathsf{d}(u,v)$ and at most $(1+\varepsilon)\cdot\mathsf{d}(u,v)$. For the case $\varepsilon = 1/\log n$, Gavoille et al. [18] proved a tight bound of $\Theta(\log(1/\varepsilon)\cdot\log n)$. Very recently, Alstrup et al. [8] considered the general trade-off and designed, for any constant $\varepsilon \le 1$, an $O(\log n)$ bit labeling scheme. We show that their solution can be easily made to produce labels of size $O(\log(1/\varepsilon)\cdot\log n)$ and that this is the best possible:

Theorem 1.4. *For any $\varepsilon \le 1$, there is a $(1+\varepsilon)$-approximate distance labeling scheme with labels of length $O(\log(1/\varepsilon)\cdot\log n)$ bits, and any such scheme requires $\Omega(\log(1/\varepsilon)\cdot\log n)$ bits.*

The proof of Theorem 1.4 appears in the full version of this paper [17]. The lower bound is obtained by reducing exact distance labeling to $(1+\varepsilon)$-approximate distance labeling. This is achieved by appropriately stretching the lengths of the edges in the lower bound instances of Gavoille et al. [20]. For the upper bound, we slightly modify the scheme of Alstrup et al. [8], which originally stored a sequence of integers using simple unary encoding. Such an encoding requires $O(1/\varepsilon\cdot\log n)$ bits. We show that with a more complicated binary encoding we can obtain a scheme with $O(\log(1/\varepsilon)\cdot\log n)$ bits and a constant query time.

We conclude this section with the following table summarizing our contribution.

| Label type | | Upper bound | Lower bound |
|---|---|---|---|
| Exact | | $1/4\log^2 n + o(\log^2 n)$ | $1/4\log^2 n - O(\log n)$ [8] |
| Approximate | | $O(\log(1/\varepsilon)\cdot\log n)$ | $\Omega(\log(1/\varepsilon)\cdot\log n)$ |
| $k$-distance | $k \ge \log n$ | $O(\log n\cdot\log\frac{k}{\log n})$ | $\Omega(\log n\cdot\log\frac{k}{\log n})$ |
| | $k < \log n$ | $\log n + O(k\log\frac{\log n}{k})$ | $\log n + \Omega(k\log\frac{\log n}{k\log k})$ [1] |

[1] This lower bound only holds for $k = o(\frac{\log n}{\log\log n})$.

## 2 PRELIMINARIES

We consider a rooted tree $T$, or we arbitrarily root it. We denote the root by $\mathsf{root}(T)$, and the distance between node $v$ to $\mathsf{root}(T)$ by $\mathsf{root\text{-}dist}(v)$. We denote the subtree rooted at $u$ as $T_u$, and the number of nodes of $T$ by $|T|$, or simply $n$ if $T$ is known from the context. For two nodes $u, v$, we denote their distance by $\mathsf{d}(u,v)$, their nearest common ancestor by $\mathsf{NCA}(u,v)$. First, observe that:

$$\mathsf{d}(u,v) = \mathsf{root\text{-}dist}(u) + \mathsf{root\text{-}dist}(v) - 2\cdot\mathsf{root\text{-}dist}(\mathsf{NCA}(u,v)).$$

This means that a labeling scheme for $\mathsf{root\text{-}dist}(\mathsf{NCA}(u,v))$ that assumes $u \ne v$ can actually be used for $\mathsf{d}(u,v)$ queries with only $O(\log n)$ additional bits to the label size (the additional bits are simply the distance to the root). Next, observe that although our input tree is unweighted (i.e., all edges have weight 1), if our distance labeling scheme can handle edges-weights in $\{0,1\}$ then we can assume the input tree is binary and that the queries are on leaves only. This can be achieved by connecting every internal node $u$ to a leaf node $u_\ell$ with an edge of weight 0, and then standardly binarizing the tree (by inserting $O(n)$ intermediate nodes with edge-weights 0 connecting them).

*Heavy path decompositions.* We apply a variant of heavy path decompositions [28]. We start at the root of the tree $T$ and repeatedly descend from the current node to its (unique) child whose subtree is of size at least $|T|/2$ as long as possible, that is, we terminate when there is no such child. Note that this is different than the more common versions in which we descend from the current node $u$ to its child $v$ with the largest subtree until (depending on the version) we reach a leaf or $|T_v| < |T_u|/2$. This gives us a *heavy path* $P$ starting at $\mathsf{root}(T)$ and many subtrees hanging off the heavy path. We call the edges of $P$ *heavy*, and all other edges outgoing from the nodes of $P$ *light*. The construction is then applied recursively to all subtrees hanging off the heavy path. In the end, each node $u \in T$ has at most one heavy child, denoted $\mathsf{heavy}(u)$, so we obtain a decomposition of $T$ into disjoint heavy paths (some of which consist of a single node). The light depth of a node $u \in T$, denoted $\mathsf{lightdepth}(u)$, is the number of light edges on the path from $u$ to the root and is at most $\log n$ [27]. We order the children of every node $u$ so that $\mathsf{heavy}(u)$ is the rightmost child and assign preorder numbers $\mathsf{pre}(u)$ to every node $u$. Then, for any node $v \in T_u$, we have that $\mathsf{pre}(v) \in [\mathsf{pre}(u), \mathsf{pre}(u) + |T_u|)$.

*The collapsed tree.* Given the heavy path decomposition of a *binary* tree $T$, we define its *collapsed tree*, denoted $C(T)$, whose nodes correspond to heavy paths in $T$. The heavy path starting at $\mathsf{root}(T)$ corresponds to the root of the collapsed tree. Every light edge hanging off this heavy path corresponds to an edge outgoing from the root of $C(T)$, and so on. The children of every node in $C(T)$ are ordered according to the top-to-bottom order on the hanging subtrees (i.e, if two subtrees connect to the same heavy path $P$ then the one connecting at a lower depth is to the left of the other). Since $T$ is binary, ties can only happen at the last node of the heavy path $P$, in which case we set the right subtree to be the subtree of maximum size, and call the light edge branching to the right subtree the *exceptional* edge associated with heavy path $P$. See Figure 1 (right). Note that the height of the collapsed tree is at most $\log n$.

Every heavy path $P$ in $T$ is associated with a node $u'$ in $C(T)$ and every node $u \in P$ is said to be *associated* with $u'$. We refer to the node $u \in P$ closest to the root of $T$ as the *head* of $P$ and denote it as $\mathsf{head}(P)$ or $\mathsf{head}(u')$. We use $\mathsf{lightdepth}(u,v)$ to denote $\mathsf{lightdepth}(\mathsf{NCA}(u,v))$. Finally, we say that $u$ *dominates* $v$ if the inorder number of $u$'s associated node in $C(T)$ is smaller than that of $v$'s. Observe that (1) If the $\mathsf{NCA}(u,v)$-to-$u$ path in $T$ starts with a light edge and the $\mathsf{NCA}(u,v)$-to-$v$ path starts with a heavy edge then $u$ dominates $v$, and (2) If both these paths start with a light edge then the dominated vertex is the one whose path starts with the exceptional edge.

*Labeling schemes for NCA.* A nearest common ancestor scheme assigns a unique label to every node, so that given the labels of nodes $u, v$ we can return the label of $\mathsf{NCA}(u,v)$. Alstrup et al. [9] design such a scheme with labels of length $O(\log n)$ bits. They use a heavy path decomposition that slightly differs from ours, but it can be easily verified that the following lemma still holds:

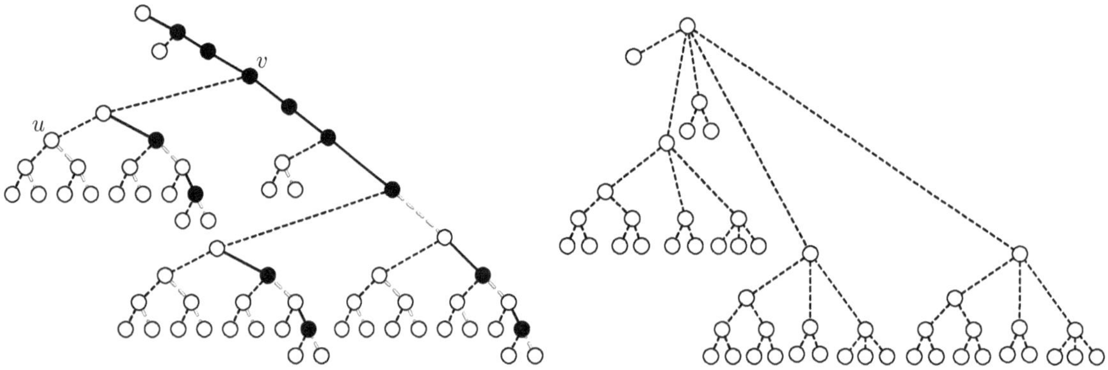


**Figure 1: On the left, a heavy path decomposition of a binary tree $T$. Light nodes are white, and heavy nodes are black. The heavy edges are solid, the light edges are dashed, and the exceptional edges are dashed and hollowed. On the right, the collapsed tree $C(T)$.**

Lemma 2.1 ([8, 9]). *There is an* NCA *labeling scheme with label size $O(\log n)$ bits, which given the labels of $u$ and $v$ returns the label of* $\mathsf{NCA}(u, v)$ *as well as* $\mathsf{lightdepth}(u, v)$ *in constant time.*

*Encoding integers.* To store a single integer $x$, we use Elias $\delta$ codes [14] that require $\log x + O(\log \log x)$ bits. This encoding is *self-delimiting*, meaning we can concatenate multiple variable-length values into a single label in a way that each individual value can be decoded later. To store a monotone sequence of integers we use the following lemma. The proof appears in the full version [17].

Lemma 2.2. *A monotone sequence of $s$ integers in $[0, M]$ can be encoded with $O(s \cdot \max\{1, \log \frac{M}{s}\})$ bits, so that we can:*

*(1) extract the $k^{th}$ number in the sequence,*
*(2) find the position of the successor of a given integer in the sequence,*
*(3) given the representation of two sequences, find the longest common suffix of two specified prefixes.*

*The first operation takes constant time, and the second and third take constant time if both $s$ and $M$ are $O(\log n)$.*

*$(h, M)$-trees.* To obtain a lower bound for distance labeling, Gavoille et al. [20] consider a family of rooted binary trees called $(h, M)$-trees. The trees are weighted and the weight of every edge is in $[0, M]$. For $h = 0$ the tree is a single node. For $h \geq 1$, the tree consists of a root connected to its single child with an edge of length $M - x$ for some $x \in [0, M)$, and the child is connected to two (possibly different) $(h - 1, M)$-trees with edges of length $x$. A lower bound for tree distance labeling is implied by the following lemma:

Lemma 2.3 ([20]). *For $h \geq 1$ and $M \geq 2$, any scheme for distance labeling in $(h, M)$-trees requires labels of at least $h/2 \cdot \log M$ bits, even if we only query leaves.*

# 3 DISTANCE LABELING

In this section we prove Theorem 1.1. In Section 3.1 we review the labeling scheme framework of the existing solutions (in a slightly different way), and in Section 3.2 we describe our improved solution and its analysis.

## 3.1 Distance Arrays

We now review the general framework for distance labeling. For each node $u \in T$, consider the set of light edges $\ell_1(u), \ldots, \ell_k(u)$ along the root-to-$u$ path. For any light edge $e$ in the collapsed tree $C(T)$ branching from $u'$ to its child $v'$ let $\mathsf{d}(e) = \mathsf{d}(\mathsf{head}(u'), \mathsf{head}(v'))$. That is, the distance along the heavy path represented by $u'$ to the endpoint where the light edge branches and to its other end. Let $D(u)$ denote the list $[\mathsf{d}(\ell_1(u)), \ldots, \mathsf{d}(\ell_k(u))]$, which we call the *distance array* of $u$. The next lemma shows that designing an efficient distance labeling scheme boils down to efficiently encoding distance arrays.

Lemma 3.1. *If we can access the elements of the distance arrays $D(u)$ and $D(v)$ then with additional $O(\log n)$ bits we can compute* $\mathsf{d}(u, v)$.

Proof. We first describe the additional $O(\log n)$ bits. They are composed of:

(1) $\mathsf{root\text{-}dist}(u)$,
(2) the NCA label of $u$ generated by Lemma 2.1,
(3) the inorder number of the node $u'$ corresponding to $u$ in $C(T)$ (so that given $u, v \in T$ we can determine which node dominates the other).

Now, suppose that $u$ is associated with $u' \in C(T)$ and $v$ with $v' \in C(T)$. We use (2) to determine $j = \mathsf{lightdepth}(u, v) + 1$. We assume that the inorder number of $u'$ is smaller than that of $v'$ (using (3) we can verify this and swap $u$ with $v$ otherwise). Thus, $u$ dominates $v$, which implies that $\mathsf{root\text{-}dist}(\mathsf{NCA}(u, v)) = \sum_{i=1}^{j} \mathsf{d}(\ell_i(u)) - 1$. Recall from Section 2 that $\mathsf{root\text{-}dist}(\mathsf{NCA}(u, v))$ together with $\mathsf{root\text{-}dist}(u)$ and $\mathsf{root\text{-}dist}(v)$ suffice to compute $\mathsf{d}(u, v)$. □

## 3.2 Modified Distance Arrays

The main challenge remaining, is how to efficiently encode $D(u)$ for an arbitrary node $u$. This can clearly be done using $\Theta(\log^2 n)$ bits. By using properties of the heavy path decomposition, Alstrup et al. [8] gave a more precise bound of: $\sum_{i=1}^{k} \log \mathsf{d}(\ell_i(u)) = \sum_{i=1}^{\log n} \log(n/2^i) = 1/2 \log^2 n + O(\log n)$. In their description, sums of the suffixes of $D(u)$ are stored instead of $D(u)$ itself, but this is essentially the same. Furthermore, distance arrays must be made self-delimiting by adding an additional $O(\log n \log\log n)$ bits, so we get an overall space bound of $1/2\log^2 n + O(\log n \log\log n)$.

In this section, we present an improved method and analysis for encoding the distance arrays. We show that our encoding uses less space, but in the process we lose the ability to compute the sum $\sum_{i=1}^{j} \mathrm{d}(\ell_i(u))$, which is used to answer the query. However, in Section 3.3 we show that in fact a query can still be answered by adding only a small amount of auxiliary information. Our *modified distance array* $\hat{D}(u)$ will have the following key property, which is weaker than that of the original distance array:

PROPERTY 3.2. *Given the modified distance arrays* $\hat{D}(u)$ *and* $\hat{D}(v)$ *for leaves* $u, v \in T$ *such that* $u$ *dominates* $v$, *we can compute the value* $\mathrm{d}(\ell_j(u))$ *where* $j = \mathrm{lightdepth}(u, v) + 1$.

At a high level, the main idea behind the modified distance array is that, to reduce the number of bits stored for each distance $\mathrm{d}(\ell_1(u)), \ldots, \mathrm{d}(\ell_k(u))$ at node $u$, we potentially push some of the bits to labels of nodes dominated by $u$. This is acceptable if our goal is to satisfy Property 3.2 since we need only compute $\mathrm{d}(\ell_i(u))$ if the other queried node $v$ is dominated by $u$. An important observation for the analysis later is that if $\ell_i(u)$ is *exceptional*, we need not store $\mathrm{d}(\ell_i(u))$ at all in order to satisfy Property 3.2. The modified distance array consists of two parts:

(1) a list of *truncated distances* $\hat{\mathrm{d}}(\ell_1(u)), \ldots, \hat{\mathrm{d}}(\ell_k(u))$;
(2) a list of *accumulators* $\mathrm{a}(\ell_1(u)), \ldots, \mathrm{a}(\ell_k(u))$.

Accumulator $\mathrm{a}(\ell_i(u))$ will potentially (but not necessarily) store some of the bits of the distances $\mathrm{d}(\ell_i(v))$ where $v$ is a node that dominates $u$, and $i = \mathrm{lightdepth}(u, v) + 1$.

The construction of the labels is recursive: Consider the heavy path $P$ extending from the root of $T$. Let $n_1, \ldots, n_{m+1}$ be the sizes of the subtrees $T_1, \ldots, T_{m+1}$ hanging from $P$ via light edges $e_1, \ldots, e_{m+1}$, where $e_{m+1}$ is the *exceptional* edge. The edges $e_1, \ldots, e_{m+1}$ are ordered according to their left-to-right order in the collapsed tree, and we use $w_1, \ldots, w_m$ to denote the nodes in $P$ from which $e_1, \ldots, e_m$ branch ($e_{m+1}$ also branches from $w_m$). See Figure 2. We use $n'_1, \ldots, n'_m$ to denote the sizes of the subtrees $T'_1, \ldots, T'_m$ rooted at nodes $w_1, \ldots, w_m$. For consistency, $n'_{m+1}$ denotes the size of $T'_{m+1} = T_{m+1}$. Note that, for an arbitrary node $u \in T_i$ we have that $\ell_1(u) = e_i$.

For an arbitrary node $u \in T_i$ where $i \in [1, m]$, we assume that we have some encoding of its modified distance array excluding the encoding of $\mathrm{d}(e_i) = \mathrm{d}(\ell_1(u))$ using $(\log^2 n_i + \log n_i \log q)/4$ bits, where $q$ is a parameter to be fixed later. We call this encoding the *recursive problem*, and the problem of encoding $\mathrm{d}(\ell_1(u))$ the *top-level problem*. Recall that if $i = m + 1$ (i.e., $u \in T_{m+1}$) we need not encode the distance $\mathrm{d}(e_{m+1})$, since that edge is *exceptional*.

We analyze the space of the top-level problem for $T'_i$ for $i = m, m-1, \ldots, 1$ (i.e., from bottom to top), bounding the overall label size in terms of $n'_i$. The goal of each iteration is to produce labels for $T'_i$ of size $(\log^2 n'_i + \log n'_i \log q)/4$. Consider the labels generated in the recursive problem for nodes in $T_i$ and in the previous iteration for $T'_{i+1}$ (or, if $i = m$, in the recursive problem for $T_{m+1}$). The following two lemmas show how many bits we can spend to generate the labels for nodes in $T'_i$. Note that these lemmas ignore the cost of making the encoding self-delimiting, as well the fact

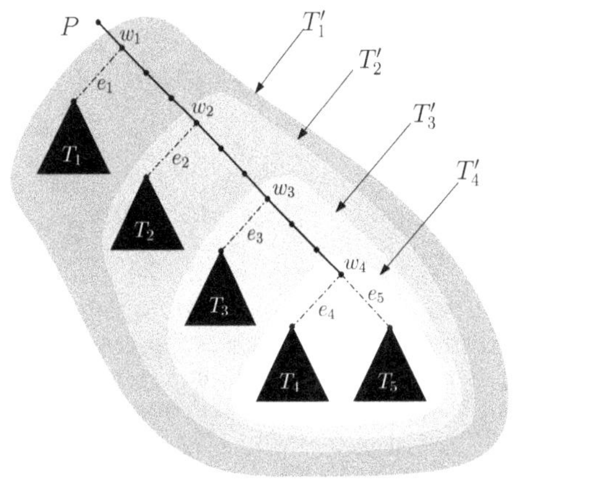


**Figure 2: A heavy path $P$ and the subtrees $T_1, \ldots, T_{m+1}$ and $T'_1, \ldots, T'_m$. The edge $e_5$ is exceptional.**

that we must take the ceiling of the bound because we cannot store a fraction of a bit. We handle these issues later.

LEMMA 3.3 (SLACK LEMMA). *Assume that the recursive problem for nodes in* $T_i$ *can be solved by storing an encoding of size* $(\log^2 n_i + \log n_i \log q)/4$ *bits for some parameter* $q$. *If* $n_i = p \cdot n'_i$ *and* $p \geq 1/q$ *then we can spend additional* $1/2\log(1/p)\log n'_i$ *bits on the top-level problem for nodes in* $T_i$ *to obtain an encoding of size* $(\log^2 n'_i + \log n'_i \log q)/4$ *bits.*

PROOF. To prove the lemma it is enough to calculate the difference between the size of the final encoding and the encoding for the recursive problem:

$$= (\log^2 n'_i + \log q \log n'_i)/4 - (\log^2(p \cdot n'_i) + \log q \log(p \cdot n'_i))/4$$
$$= (\log^2 n'_i + \log q \log n'_i - (\log p + \log n'_i)^2 - \log q \log p - \log q \log n'_i)/4$$
$$= (-\log^2 p - 2\log p \log n'_i - \log q \log p)/4$$
$$= (2\log(1/p)\log n'_i + \log q \log(1/p) - \log^2(1/p))/4$$
$$= (2\log(1/p)\log n'_i + \log(1/p)(\log q - \log(1/p)))/4$$
$$\geq 1/2\log(1/p)\log n'_i.$$

□

Additionally, we have the following:

LEMMA 3.4 (THIN LEMMA). *Assume that the recursive problem for nodes in* $T_i$ *can be solved by storing an encoding of size* $(\log^2 n_i + \log n_i \log q)/4$ *bits for some parameter* $q \geq 2$. *If* $n_i = p \cdot n'_i$ *and* $p \leq 1/2^8$ *then we can spend additional* $2\log n'_i$ *bits on the top-level problem for nodes in* $T_i$ *to obtain an encoding of size* $(\log^2 n'_i + \log n'_i \log q)/4$ *bits.*

PROOF. Similarly as in the proof of Lemma 3.3, we calculate the difference:

$$= (\log^2 n'_i + \log q \log n'_i)/4 - (\log^2(p \cdot n'_i) - \log q \log(p \cdot n'_i))/4$$
$$= (2\log(1/p)\log n'_i + \log(1/p)(\log q - \log(1/p)))/4.$$

Now, assuming that $2\log n'_i$ is larger than the difference and using that $p \geq 1/n'_i$ we obtain:

$$2\log n'_i > 1/2\log(1/p)\log n'_i + 1/4\log(1/p)\log q - 1/4\log^2(1/p)$$

$$\geq 1/2\log(1/p)\log n'_i - 1/4\log^2(1/p)$$
$$\geq 1/2\log(1/p)\log n'_i - 1/4\log(1/p)\log n'_i$$
$$= 1/4\log(1/p)\log n'_i$$

so, after dividing by $\log n'_i$, $8 > \log(1/p)$ and $p > 1/2^8$. Hence for $p \leq 1/2^8$ we can indeed use $2\log n'_i$ additional bits. □

We call $T_i$ *thin* if $n_i \leq n'_i/2^8$, and *fat* otherwise. We observe that, by the definition of the heavy path decomposition, $\log n \leq \log(2n'_i) \leq 2\log n'_i$. Thus, an immediate consequence of Lemma 3.4 is that if $T_i$ is thin, then we can afford to store $\mathrm{d}(e_i)$ explicitly as $\hat{\mathrm{d}}(e_i)$, without having to push any bits to the accumulators of nodes in $T_{i+1}, \ldots, T_{m+1}$. However, if $T_i$ is fat, Lemma 3.3 indicates that we do not have enough *slack* to store all the bits of $\mathrm{d}(e_i)$. Instead, we store as many bits as the slack allows (rounding up to the nearest bit) in the labels of nodes $u$ in $T_i$. We then append all the remaining bits to the accumulators $\mathrm{a}(\ell_i(v))$ of all nodes $v \in \bigcup_{j=i+1}^{m+1} T_j$ (i.e., nodes dominated by $u$).

Because $T_i$ is fat, by the slack lemma for nodes in $T_i$ we have slack $1/2\log(n'_i/n_i)\log n'_i$ (the assumption that $T_i$ is fat allows us to adjust the constant $q$). On the other hand, using the same calculations as in the slack lemma, the nodes in $T'_{i+1}$ have slack $1/2\log(n'_i/n'_{i+1})\log n'_i$: note that the size of $T'_{i+1}$ is larger than $n'_i/2^8$ by the properties of the heavy path decomposition, as either $i < m$ and $n'_{i+1} \geq n/2$, or $i = m$ and then $n_{i+1} \geq n_i$ so $n'_{i+1} \geq n/4 - 1/2$. Since $n'_i > n_i + n'_{i+1}$, we have that the sum $1/2(\log(n'_i/n_i) + \log(n'_i/n'_{i+1}))\log n'_i$ can be lower bounded by the minimum of $1/2(\log(1+x) + \log(1+x^{-1}))\log n_i$ for $x \in (0, \infty)$. Thus, the slack is at least $\log n'_i$ bits in total. However, the distance $d(\ell(u)_1)$ occupies $\log n$ bits, rather than $\log n'_i$. As before, we can use the properties of the heavy path decomposition to bound $\log n \leq \log(2n'_i) = 1 + \log n'_i$. Thus, $\mathrm{d}(\ell_1(u))$ occupies one extra bit more than we have accounted for with the slack. We store this extra bit in the truncated distance $\hat{\mathrm{d}}(\ell_1(u))$. Therefore, the truncated distance $\hat{\mathrm{d}}(\ell_1(u))$ consists of the most significant $\lceil 1/2\log(n'_i/n_i)\log n'_i\rceil + 1$ bits of $\mathrm{d}(\ell_i(u))$. The remaining least significant $\lfloor 1/2\log(n'_i/n'_{i+1})\log n'_i\rfloor$ bits are concatenated to the accumulators of the nodes dominated by $u$ in $T_{i+1}, \ldots, T_{m+1}$.

For each entry in the modified distance array for a node $u$, we are pushing at most two extra bits beyond those accounted for in the slack lemma. Thus, this works out to an additional $O(\log n)$ bits in total, per label. We make both parts of the modified distance array (the accumulators and truncated distances) self-delimiting, and also record, for each truncated distance, the number of bits pushed to the accumulators of dominated nodes. Overall, we end up with the following:

Lemma 3.5. *The modified distance array $\hat{D}(u)$ occupies at most $1/4\log^2 n + O(\log n \log\log n)$ bits.*

It remains to show that these modified distance arrays satisfy Property 3.2. To see this, consider the modified distance array for $u$ and $v$, where $j = \mathsf{lightdepth}(u, v) + 1$, and $u$ dominates $v$. We have stored the number of bits that were pushed to the accumulator $\mathrm{a}(\ell_j(v))$ explicitly. The starting position of this contiguous range of bits can be found by noticing that the accumulator $\mathrm{a}(\ell_j(u))$ is a suffix of $\mathrm{a}(\ell_j(v))$, since all nodes that dominate $u$ also dominate $v$. Hence, knowing the length of the accumulator $\mathrm{a}(\ell_j(u))$ allows us to determine the starting position and, together with the explicitly stored number of pushed bits, recover the bits themselves. By combining them with $\hat{\mathrm{d}}(\ell_j(u))$ we can reconstruct $\mathrm{d}(\ell_j(u))$.

We have therefore satisfied Property 3.2. It remains to show why this is enough for a distance query. In Section 3.3 we show that it is, with only additional lower order terms to the label size.

## 3.3 Wrapping Up the Proof of Theorem 1.1

In order to prove Theorem 1.1 we need to show how to answer a distance query without inflating the space of Lemma 3.5 by more than lower order terms.

Let $u$ be some node contained in the heavy path mapped to $u' \in C(T)$, and consider the path from $u'$ to the root of $C(T)$. We partition this path into $B = \sqrt{\log n}$ *fragments*. The first fragment is the prefix starting at the root, denoted $f_0(u)$, and terminating at the first node $f_1(u)$ such that the subtree rooted at $\mathsf{head}(f_1(u))$ has size at most $n/2^B$. The $i$-th fragment is defined recursively from $f_{i-1}(u)$, ending at a node $f_i(u)$ such that the subtree rooted at $\mathsf{head}(f_i(u))$ has size at most $n/2^{iB}$, for $i \in [1, h]$, where $h = O(\sqrt{\log n})$. We explicitly store the distances $\mathrm{d}(f_i(u), \mathsf{root}(T))$ for each $i \in [1, h]$ as the *fragment distance array* $F(u)$.

Next, consider a light edge $e$ in $C(T)$ that branches from the heavy path corresponding to $u'$ to the heavy path corresponding to $v'$. Recall that, in bounding the number of bits for the modified distance arrays, we used the fact that if the subtree rooted at $\mathsf{head}(u')$ has size $n$, then the distance, $r = \mathrm{d}(\mathsf{head}(u'), \mathsf{head}(v'))$, associated with the light edge $e$ is bounded by $n$. Instead of recording this distance $r$, for each node $u$ that stores $r$ we instead record the distance $r' = \mathrm{d}(\mathsf{head}(f_j(u)), \mathsf{head}(v'))$, where $j$ is the largest index such that the subtree rooted at $\mathsf{head}(f_j(u))$ contains node $\mathsf{head}(v')$.

Obviously, $r'$ requires more bits to store than $r$, $O(\sqrt{\log n})$ additional bits to be precise. However, since there are at most $\log n$ truncated distances in $\hat{D}(u)$, we can afford to inflate each of these by $O(\sqrt{\log n})$ bits. This only increases the lower order space term to $O(\log^{1.5} n)$ bits. Furthermore, for each truncated distance, we can also afford to store the corresponding index $j$ from the fragment array using $O(\log n \log\log n)$ extra bits. Thus, since Property 3.2 still holds after expanding the truncated distances, we can now recover $r'$ and read $\mathrm{d}(f_j(u), \mathsf{root}(T))$ from $F(u)$. These two values sum to $\mathrm{d}(\mathsf{head}(u'), \mathsf{root}(T))$, which is exactly what we wanted to compute with distance arrays.

The proof of Theorem 1.1 follows from the above $1/4\log^2 n + o(\log^2 n)$-bit labeling scheme and the fact that we only need to label leaves and can assume $T$ is binary (see Section 2).

## 3.4 Lower Bound for Level-Ancestor Labeling

In this section we prove Theorem 1.2. The main idea of the proof is to show a lower bound for *parent labeling*, where the goal is to assign a distinct label to every $u \in T$ so that given the label of $u$ we can return the label of its parent (or a special value $\perp$ denoting that $u = \mathsf{root}(T)$). This is clearly a special case of the level-ancestor problem. The lower bound is obtained by showing a correspondence between the parent labeling and the following *universal tree* problem: what is the size of the smallest rooted tree

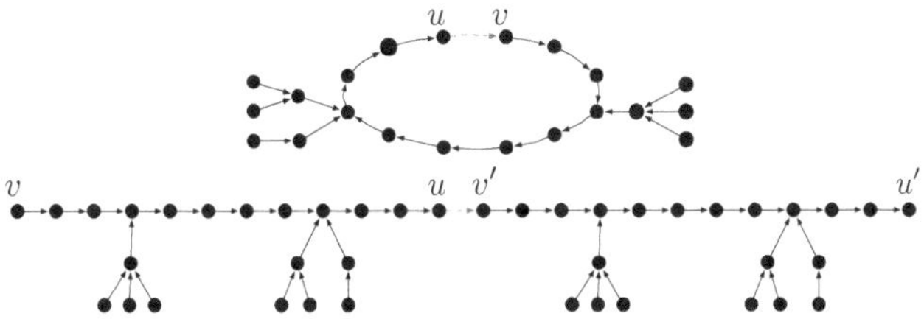


**Figure 3: Converting a weakly connected component to a rooted tree $G'$ by duplicating the path at the dashed line.**

containing any rooted tree on $n$ nodes as a subtree? The connection between these two problems is captured by the following lemma.

LEMMA 3.6. *If there exists a parent labeling scheme on trees of size $n$ that produces labels of size at most $S(n)$, then there exists a universal rooted tree containing all rooted trees on up to $n$ nodes as subtrees of size $O(2^{S(n)})$.*

PROOF. The proof is by construction. Let $V$ be the set of all possible labels generated by the labeling scheme, and $E$ be the directed edges between these labels defined as follows: if, a label $u$ is assigned to a node of some tree, and $v \neq \perp$ is the label returned by the scheme for $u$, then $(u, v)$ belongs to $E$. Note that $v$ is determined solely from the bits of $u$, hence the graph $G = (V, E)$ consists of one or more directed cycles. See Figure 3 (left) for an example of such a graph. It is clear that $G$ must contain any tree $T$ on up to $n$ nodes as a subgraph, since the labeling scheme works for all trees on $n$ nodes or less. $G$ is not necessarily a tree itself, but we now describe a general procedure that converts $G$ into a new graph $G' = (V', E')$ that itself is a rooted tree, and is such that that $|V'| \leq 2|V| + 1$.

Each weakly connected component of $G$ is either already a tree, or contains a cycle. In the latter case, we arbitrarily remove an edge $(u, v)$ from the cycle (in the figure the chosen edge is intersected by the dashed line). After deleting $(u, v)$ we duplicate the entire weakly connected component, and add a new edge $(u, v')$ where $v'$ is the duplicate of $v$. After doing this for each weakly connected component, we have increased the number of vertices to at most $2|V|$, and the resultant graph $G'$ is a forest of rooted trees. We add a single global root to make $G'$ a rooted tree. The total number of nodes in $G'$ is hence at most $2|V| + 1$.

Since $G$ was a universal graph for rooted trees on $n$ nodes, any rooted tree not containing the deleted edge clearly appears as a subgraph in $G'$. Moreover, for any rooted tree $T$ containing $(u, v)$, there exists some subpath of the cycle in $G$ which was in $T$. Since we duplicated each node in the cycle, it is clear that any such subpath also exists in $G'$ (together with any trees rooted at nodes in the subpath), thus, $T$ appears as a subtree in $G'$.

The final detail is to consider the maximum length label output by the labeling scheme, which consists of $S(n)$ bits. Hence, there are at most $2^{S(n)}$ nodes in $G$ and therefore at most $O(2^{S(n)})$ nodes in $G'$. □

Equipped with the previous lemma, we immediately get a lower bound on $S(n)$, provided we have a lower bound on the number of nodes in such a rooted universal tree. Goldberg and Lifschitz [21] have proved very accurate bounds on the number of nodes in such rooted universal trees (see [13] for the bound as we state it):

LEMMA 3.7 ([13, 21]). *The smallest rooted tree containing all rooted trees on up to $n$ nodes as subtrees has size $n^{(\log n - 2\log\log n + O(1))/2}$.*

By combining Lemmas 3.6 and 3.7, we obtain Theorem 1.2.

## 3.5 Effective Level-Ancestor Scheme

While Alstrup et al. [8] describe their scheme in terms of labeling for distance queries, in fact it is not difficult to tweak it to obtain a scheme for level-ancestor queries. We describe the necessary modifications to obtain a scheme for parent queries. This immediately implies a scheme for level-ancestor queries by repeatedly moving to the parent as long as necessary.

The labeling consists of three parts. For a node $u$ on a heavy path $P$ we store:

(1) $\mathrm{d}(u, \mathrm{root}(T))$,
(2) the $O(\log n)$ label generated by Lemma 2.1 applied on $\mathrm{head}(P)$,
(3) the array $D(u)$ and, additionally, $\mathrm{d}(u, \mathrm{head}(P))$. (This is differently phrased but essentially equivalent to what the original labeling stores.)

The labels in the NCA scheme are required to be distinct, so the labels of nodes belonging to different heavy paths are distinct. For two nodes on the same heavy path, storing $\mathrm{d}(u, \mathrm{head}(P))$ explicitly ensures that their labels are not the same. Each label consists of $1/2 \log^2 n + O(\log n)$ bits, because of the bound on the encoding of $D(u)$. We need to argue that given the label of $u \neq \perp$ we can construct the label of its parent.

The NCA labeling scheme from Lemma 2.1 has the property that the label of every node $u$ is a concatenation of heavy and light labels $h_0\ell_1h_1\ell_2 \cdots \ell_kh_k$. These labels uniquely determine the path from the root to $u$: $h_0$ encodes how far along the heavy path starting at the root we should continue. Then, either $k = 0$ and $u$ in fact lies on the heavy path starting at the root, or $\ell_1$ encodes which light edge outgoing from the current node should be followed. Finally, $h_1\ell_2 \cdots \ell_kh_k$ recursively encodes the remaining part of the path to $u$ in the subtree hanging off the heavy path starting at the root. It is not necessarily true that given the NCA label of a node $u$ we can determine the NCA label of its parent. However, by truncating the NCA label of $u$ we can construct the NCA label of the parent of $\mathrm{head}(P)$.

Given the label of $u$, we construct the label of its parent $u'$ as follows. $\mathrm{d}(u, \mathrm{root}(T))$ needs to be decreased by 1. Then we inspect $\mathrm{d}(u, \mathrm{head}(P))$. If $u \neq \mathrm{head}(P)$, we decrease $\mathrm{d}(u, \mathrm{head}(P))$ by 1 and are done. Otherwise, we use the NCA label of $u$ to determine the label of its parent as explained above. Let $P'$ be the heavy path of $u'$. The last element of the array $D$ is $\mathrm{d}(u, \mathrm{head}(P'))$, so by subtracting 1 we obtain $\mathrm{d}(u', \mathrm{head}(P'))$. Finally, we remove the last element of $D$.

## 4 K-DISTANCE LABELING

Recall that in $k$-distance labeling, given the labels of $u$ and $v$ we need to decide if the length of the $u$-to-$v$ path is at most $k$, and if so return it. In this section we prove Theorem 1.3.

## 4.1 Lower Bound for Small $k$

We define a family of trees and show that labeling the leaves of all trees in that family for $k$-distance queries requires $\log n + \Omega(k \cdot \log \frac{\log n}{k \log k})$ bits.

An $\vec{x}$-regular tree, where $\vec{x} = (x_1, \cdots, x_k) \in \mathbb{N}^k$, is a rooted tree of height $k$ where all depth-$i$ nodes have the same degree $x_{i+1}$. An $(\vec{x}, h, d)$-regular tree, where $(x_1, \cdots, x_k) = \vec{x} \in [h]^k$, is a $\vec{y}$-regular tree with $\vec{y} = (d^{x_1}, d^{h-x_1}, d^{x_2}, d^{h-x_2}, \cdots, d^{x_k}, d^{h-x_k})$. The total number of leaves in such a tree is $d^{k \cdot h}$. See Figure 4 for an example.

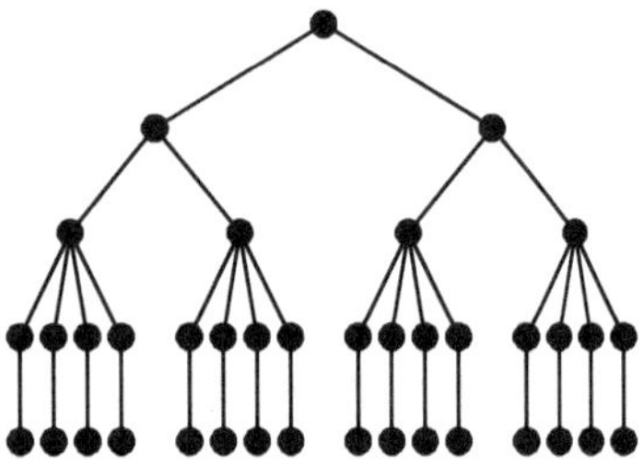

**Figure 4: $(\vec{x}, d, h)$-regular tree with $\vec{x} = (1, 2)$ and $d = h = 2$.**

We consider $(\vec{x}, h, d)$-regular trees for some parameters $h$ and $d$ to be chosen later. Consider a labeling scheme that assigns a label to every leaf of such a tree for $2k$-distance queries. The following lemma shows that a $(\vec{x}, h, d)$-regular tree and a $(\vec{y}, h, d)$-regular tree cannot share many identical labels. More formally, let $\text{common}(\vec{x}, \vec{y})$ denote the maximum number of labels that can be used in both trees. The following is an upper bound on the sum of $\text{common}(\vec{x}, \vec{y})$.

Lemma 4.1. $\sum_{\vec{x}, \vec{y} \in [h]^k} \text{common}(\vec{x}, \vec{y}) \le \left(h \cdot d^h \left(1 + \frac{2}{d-1}\right)\right)^k$.

Proof. We first prove that

$$\text{common}(\vec{x}, \vec{y}) \le \prod_{i=1}^{k} d^{\min\{x_i, y_i\}} d^{h-\max\{x_i, y_i\}}.$$

By asking all $2k$-distance queries between a specified subset $S$ of leaves of the $(\vec{x}, h, d)$-regular tree we can recover the shape of the subtree induced by $S$. Hence, if two trees share $\text{common}(\vec{x}, \vec{y})$ labels, then they must have a common isomorphic subtree on $\text{common}(\vec{x}, \vec{y})$ leaves. To bound the maximum number of leaves in such a subtree, observe that the degree of a node at depth $2i - 2$ is at most $\min\{d^{x_i}, d^{y_i}\}$, and the degree of a node at depth $2i - 1$ is at most $\min\{d^{h-x_i}, d^{h-y_i}\}$. The maximum number of shared labels is hence the product of all these quantities over $i = 1, \ldots, k$. We conclude that that $\text{common}(\vec{x}, \vec{y}) \le \prod_{i=1}^{k} d^{\min\{x_i, y_i\}} d^{h-\max\{x_i, y_i\}}$. It then follows that

$$\begin{aligned}
\sum_{\vec{x}, \vec{y} \in [h]^k} \text{common}(\vec{x}, \vec{y}) &= \sum_{\vec{x}, \vec{y} \in [h]^k} \prod_{i=1}^{k} d^{\min\{x_i, y_i\}} d^{h-\max\{x_i, y_i\}} \\
&= \prod_{i=1}^{k} \sum_{1 \le x, y \le h} d^{\min\{x, y\}} d^{h-\max\{x, y\}} \\
&= \prod_{i=1}^{k} (h \cdot d^h + 2 \sum_{x<y} d^x d^{h-y}) \\
&= \prod_{i=1}^{k} (h \cdot d^h + 2 \sum_{x=1}^{h-1} d^x \sum_{y=0}^{h-x-1} d^y) \\
&= \prod_{i=1}^{k} (h \cdot d^h + 2 \sum_{x=1}^{h-1} d^x \frac{d^{h-x} - 1}{d - 1}) \\
&\le \prod_{i=1}^{k} (h \cdot d^h + 2 \cdot h \frac{d^h}{d-1}) \\
&= \left(h \cdot d^h \left(1 + \frac{2}{d-1}\right)\right)^k. \qquad \square
\end{aligned}$$

Since the total number of leaves in the $(\vec{x}, h, d)$-regular trees family is $d^{k \cdot h} \cdot h^k$, the number of distinct labels required to label them is thus at least

$$\begin{aligned}
d^{k \cdot h} \cdot h^k - \sum_{\vec{x} < \vec{y}} \text{common}(\vec{x}, \vec{y}) &= d^{k \cdot h} \cdot h^k - \frac{1}{2} \sum_{\vec{x} \ne \vec{y}} \text{common}(\vec{x}, \vec{y}) \\
&= \frac{3}{2} \cdot d^{k \cdot h} \cdot h^k - \frac{1}{2} \sum_{\vec{x}, \vec{y} \in [h]^k} \text{common}(\vec{x}, \vec{y}).
\end{aligned}$$

Now we set $d = 2k+1$, and since $(1+\frac{1}{k}) \le e^{\frac{1}{k}}$ we have from Lemma 4.1 that $\sum_{\vec{x}, \vec{y}} \text{common}(\vec{x}, \vec{y}) \le e \cdot d^{k \cdot h} \cdot h^k$, so the number of unique labels is at least: $(3/2 - e/2) \cdot d^{k \cdot h} \cdot h^k > 0.1 \cdot d^{k \cdot h} \cdot h^k$. Setting $n = d^{k \cdot h}$ this becomes $0.1 \cdot h^k \cdot n$, making the number of required bits at least

$$\begin{aligned}
\log n + k \log h - O(1) &= \log n + k \log \frac{\log n}{k \log d} - O(1) \\
&= \log n + \Omega(k \cdot \log \frac{\log n}{k \log k}).
\end{aligned}$$

Note that the above calculation assumes $d^k \le n$.

## 4.2 Lower Bound for Large $k$

The lower bound from Section 4.1 is not meaningful for large values of $k \in [\log n, n]$. In this section we show that the lower bound of Gavoille et al. [20] for general distance queries, can be translated into a lower bound of $\Omega(\log n \cdot \log(k/\log n))$ for $k$-distance queries.

The lower bound uses the family of $(h, M)$-trees (see Section 2). Recall that every edge of an $(h, M)$-tree has a weight from $[0, M]$. It is easy to verify that the number of nodes in such a tree is $3 \cdot 2^h - 2$, hence the distance between any two leaves is no more than $2hM$.

If $M \le k/(2h)$ then, because the distance between any two leaves in the tree is at most $2hM \le k$, any labeling of the leaves for $k$-distance can be used for general distance labeling. By Lemma 2.3, such a labeling scheme would require labels of at least $h/2 \cdot \log M$ bits. We set $h = \log \sqrt{n/3}$ and $M = \min\{k/2h, 2^h\}$. Then, by subdividing the edges of an $(h, M)$-tree we obtain an unweighted tree on at most $n$ nodes. Labeling the leaves of such a tree for $k$-distance can be used for general distance labeling of the $(h, M)$-tree, so we obtain the following lower bounds:

(1) if $\frac{k}{2h} \le 2^h$, the number of required bits is $\frac{h}{2} \cdot \log \frac{k}{2h} = \Omega(\log n \cdot \log \frac{k}{\log n})$;
(2) if $\frac{k}{2h} > 2^h$, the number of required bits is $\frac{h}{2} \cdot h = \Omega(\log^2 n)$, so $\Omega(\log n \cdot \log \frac{k}{\log n})$ for $k \le n$.

## 4.3 Upper Bound

In this section we present our improved upper bound for $k$-distance labeling. We build upon the ideas of Alstrup, Bille, and Rauhe [5], who presented an $\log n + O(k^2 \log(k \log n))$-bits labeling scheme. As a preliminary step, we will show an $O(\log k \cdot \log n)$ bits scheme for $k \geq \log n$, and then move to the more complicated $\log n + O(k \log(\log n/k))$ bits scheme for $k < \log n$.

Consider the heavy path decomposition of $T$. We define the *light range* of $u$, denoted $\mathsf{L}_u$, to contain the preorder number of all nodes in $T_u$ if $u$ has no heavy child, and all nodes in $T_u \setminus T_{\mathsf{heavy}(u)}$ otherwise. We say that $v$ is a *significant ancestor* of $u$ if $\mathsf{pre}(u) \in \mathsf{L}_v$. For example, in Figure 1 $v$ is a significant ancestor of $u$ since the light range of $v$ is $\mathsf{L}_v = [5, 23)$. The number of significant ancestors of $u$ is equal to $\mathsf{lightdepth}(u) = O(\log n)$. The nearest common significant ancestor of $u$ and $v$, denoted $\mathsf{NCSA}(u, v)$, is $w$ such that $\mathsf{pre}(w)$ is as large as possible and $w$ is a significant ancestor of both $u$ and $v$. In other words, $w$ is the first significant ancestor on the path from $u$ to the root, which is also a significant ancestor of $v$. The heavy path $P$ such that $\mathsf{head}(P)$ is a child of $\mathsf{NCSA}(u, v)$ is called the nearest common heavy path of $u$ and $v$ and denoted $\mathsf{NCH}(u, v)$. When there is no common significant ancestor for $u$ and $v$ we set $\mathsf{NCSA}(u, v)$ to nil and $\mathsf{NCH}(u, v)$ to be the heavy path starting at the root.

Let the significant ancestors of $u$ and $v$ on $\mathsf{NCH}(u,v)$ be $u'$ and $v'$, respectively. Then $\mathsf{d}(u, v) = \mathsf{d}(u, u') + \mathsf{d}(u', v') + \mathsf{d}(v, v')$. Computing $\mathsf{d}(u, v)$ consists of two steps:

(1) identifying $\mathsf{NCH}(u, v)$, $u'$ and $v'$, and computing $\mathsf{d}(u, u')$ and $\mathsf{d}(v, v')$,
(2) computing $\mathsf{d}(u', v')$.

We describe these steps separately, and then describe how to implement them in constant time.

*Identifying* $\mathsf{NCH}(u, v)$. For an integer range $A = [a, b] \subset [1, n]$ we define its identifier $\mathsf{id}(A)$ by considering a binary trie representing all words of length $\lceil \log n \rceil$. The label of a node $u$ in the trie is the concatenation of the labels of the edges on the path from the root to $u$. Every integer $x \in [1, n]$ corresponds to a leaf $u$ in the trie, such that the label of $u$ is the binary expansion of $x$. Then, $\mathsf{NCA}(a, b)$ is the nearest common ancestor of the leaves corresponding to $a$ and $b$ in the trie, $\mathsf{height}(A)$ is the height of the subtree rooted at $\mathsf{NCA}(a, b)$, and finally $\mathsf{id}(A)$ is the label of $\mathsf{NCA}(a, b)$.

Observation 4.2. *For any range $A$:*

*(1) $\mathsf{id}(A)$ can be computed given $\mathsf{height}(A)$ and any $x \in A$,*
*(2) $A \cap B = \emptyset \implies \mathsf{id}(B) \neq \mathsf{id}(A)$.*

Alstrup, Bille, and Rauhe [5] use the notion of *significant preorder numbers*. We replace it with our notion of range identifier, that has very similar properties, yet is somewhat easier to operate on (and hence we are able to achieve a better query time). For any node $u \in T$, let $\mathsf{id}(u) = (\mathsf{id}(\mathsf{L}_u), \mathsf{lightdepth}(u))$.

Lemma 4.3. *For any nodes $u, v \in T$, if $u \neq v$ then $\mathsf{id}(u) \neq \mathsf{id}(v)$.*

Proof. If $\mathsf{lightdepth}(u) \neq \mathsf{lightdepth}(v)$ then we are done. Otherwise, $\mathsf{L}_v$ and $\mathsf{L}_u$ are disjoint, so by Observation 4.2.2 $\mathsf{id}(\mathsf{L}_v) \neq \mathsf{id}(\mathsf{L}_u)$ and we are also done. □

Consider a node $u \in T$ and let $u = u_0, u_1, u_2, \ldots$ be all of its significant ancestors in the order in which they appear on the path from $u$ to $\mathsf{root}(T)$. Let $u_r$ be the last of these ancestors such that $\mathsf{d}(u, u_r) \leq k$. We call $u_r$ the top significant ancestor of $u$. The label of $u$ consists of $\mathsf{pre}(u)$, $\mathsf{lightdepth}(u)$, and an encoding of $\mathsf{height}(\mathsf{L}_{u_i})$ for every $i = 0, 1, \ldots, r$. By Observation 4.2.1 this is enough to compute $\mathsf{id}(u_i)$ for every $i = 0, 1, \ldots, r$. Consequently, given the labels of $u$ and $v$, we can either detect that the distance from $u$ or $v$ to $\mathsf{NCA}(u, v)$ exceeds $k$, or calculate $\mathsf{lightdepth}(\mathsf{NCSA}(u, v))$.

To encode $\mathsf{height}(\mathsf{L}_{v_i})$ for every $i = 0, 1, \ldots, r$, we observe that $\mathsf{L}_{v_i} \subsetneq \mathsf{L}_{v_{i+1}}$ and that $r \leq \min\{\log n, k\}$. Hence, we need to encode a non-decreasing sequence of $\min\{\log n, k\}$ numbers from $[0, \log n]$. By Lemma 2.2, for $k < \log n$ this can be done using $O(k \log(\log n/k))$ bits and for $k \geq \log n$ using $O(\log n)$ bits, and allows us to calculate $\mathsf{lightdepth}(\mathsf{NCSA}(u, v))$ or detect that $\mathsf{d}(u, v) > k$.

We encode in the label of $u$ the distance from $u$ to $u_i$ for every $i = 0, 1, \ldots, r-1$. Because $0 = d(u, u_0) < d(u, u_1) < \cdots < d(u, u_{r-1}) \leq k$ we need to encode an increasing sequence of $\min\{\log n, k\}$ numbers from the range $[0, k]$. By Lemma 2.2, if $k < \log n$ this can be done using $O(k)$ bits and if $k \geq \log n$ using $O(\log n \cdot \log(k/\log n))$ bits. Then, after having found $\mathsf{lightdepth}(\mathsf{NCSA}(u, v))$ we can compute $\mathsf{d}(u, u')$ and $\mathsf{d}(v, v')$.

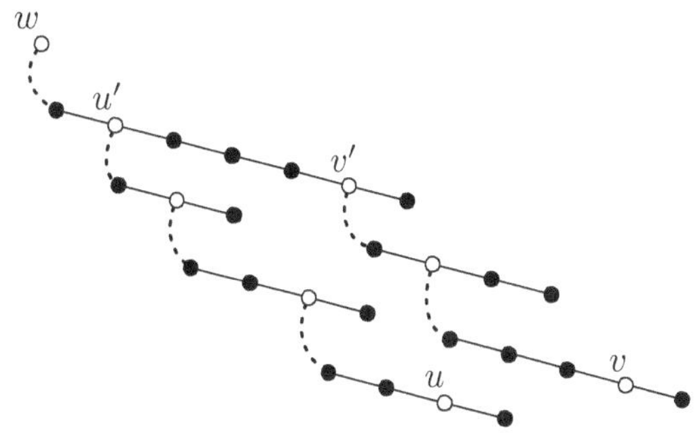


**Figure 5: $w$ = NCSA($u, v$), $u'$ and $v'$ are the significant ancestors of $u$ and $v$ on NCH($u, v$), respectively. Significant ancestors are white, heavy edges are solid, and light edges are dashed.**

*Computing* $\mathsf{d}(u', v')$. Recall that $u'$ and $v'$ are the significants ancestors on the $\mathsf{NCH}(u, v)$ of $u$ and $v$, respectively. We want to compute $\mathsf{d}(u', v')$. If $u'$ is not the top significant ancestor of $u$ and $v'$ is not the top significant ancestor of $v'$ then from the distances encoded in the labels of $u$ and $v$ we can retrieve $\mathsf{d}(u', \mathsf{NCSA}(u, v))$ and $\mathsf{d}(v', \mathsf{NCSA}(u, v))$, and return their absolute difference as $\mathsf{d}(u', v')$. Now consider the case that $u'$ is the top significant ancestor of $u$, but $v'$ is not the top significant ancestor of $v$. To deal with this case, the label of $u$ should also encode the distance $\alpha$ from $u'$ to the head of it's heavy path. This distance might be very large (even up to $n$), so we cap it at $2k + 1$ to use only $O(\log k)$ bits. Since $v'$ is not the top significant ancestor of $v$, we can retrieve $\beta = \mathsf{d}(v', \mathsf{NCSA}(u, v))$ as in the previous case. We know that $\beta \leq k$ because otherwise $v'$ would be the top significant ancestor of $v$. Recall that $\mathsf{d}(u', v')$ is equal to the absolute difference between $\mathsf{d}(u', \mathsf{NCSA}(u, v))$ and

$d(v', NCSA(u, v))$. If $\alpha = 2k + 1$ then this value must exceed $k$, so we terminate. Otherwise, we return $|\alpha - \beta|$.

The remaining and most complicated case is when $u'$ is the top significant ancestor of $u$ and $v'$ is the top significant ancestor of $v'$. If $k > \log n$, the solution is simple, as we can afford to store the distance from the top significant ancestor to the head of its heavy path for every node (i.e., $d(u, u_{r+1})$) using $O(\log n)$ bits. The rest of this section is dedicated for solving $k \leq \log n$.

To make the further exposition more concise, we define the 2-approximation of an integer $x$, denoted $\lfloor x \rfloor_2$, as the largest power of 2 not exceeding $x$. That is, $\lfloor x \rfloor_2 = 2^{\lfloor \log x \rfloor}$. Clearly, 2-approximation is monotone, meaning that $x \leq y$ implies $\lfloor x \rfloor_2 \leq \lfloor y \rfloor_2$, and furthermore $\lfloor x \rfloor_2 < \lfloor 2x \rfloor_2$.

LEMMA 4.4. *Let $A, B, C$ be three open intervals such that $A \cap B = \emptyset$ and $A, B \subseteq C$. Then $\lfloor |C| \rfloor_2 \neq \lfloor |A| \rfloor_2$ or $\lfloor |C| \rfloor_2 \neq \lfloor |B| \rfloor_2$.*

PROOF. Assume that $|B| \leq |A|$. Then $2|B| \leq |A| + |B| \leq |C|$ and by the properties of 2-approximation $\lfloor |B| \rfloor_2 < \lfloor |C| \rfloor_2$, so $\lfloor |B| \rfloor_2 \neq \lfloor |C| \rfloor_2$. Symmetrically, if $|A| \leq |B|$ then $\lfloor |A| \rfloor_2 \neq \lfloor |C| \rfloor_2$. □

The following lemma captures the essence of the $k$-distance scheme of Alstrup, Bille, and Rauhe [5], while being optimized so that we can obtain our improvement.

LEMMA 4.5. *Consider an increasing sequence of integers $a_1 < a_2 < \ldots < a_s$. Given $a_i < a_j$, $i' = i \bmod k$, $j' = j \bmod k$, and $\lfloor a_{i+t} - a_i \rfloor_2$ and $\lfloor a_j - a_{j-t} \rfloor_2$ for every $t = 1, 2, \ldots, k$ we can calculate $j - i$ or determine that $j - i > k$ in constant time.*

PROOF. We start by setting $t = j' - i'$. Now either $t = j - i$ or $j - i \geq k + t$. Hence, we only need to distinguish between these two cases.

Consider three intervals $(a_i, a_{i+t})$, $(a_{j-t}, a_j)$ and $(a_i, a_j)$. If $t = j - i$ then these three intervals are equal and so are $\lfloor a_{i+t} - a_i \rfloor_2$, $\lfloor a_j - a_{j-t} \rfloor_2$ and $\lfloor a_j - a_i \rfloor_2$. Otherwise $j - i \geq k + t > 2t$, so $(a_i, a_{i+t})$ and $(a_{j-t}, a_j)$ are two disjoint intervals contained in $(a_i, a_j)$. Hence by Lemma 4.4 either $\lfloor a_{i+t} - a_i \rfloor_2 \neq \lfloor a_j - a_i \rfloor_2$ or $\lfloor a_j - a_{j-t} \rfloor_2 \neq \lfloor a_j - a_i \rfloor_2$. Therefore after retrieving $\lfloor a_{i+t} - a_i \rfloor_2$ and $\lfloor a_j - a_{j-t} \rfloor_2$ and calculating $\lfloor a_j - a_i \rfloor_2$ we can distinguish between the two cases and either return $j - i$ or report that $j - i > k$. Notice that $\lfloor a_j - a_i \rfloor_2$ can be calculated in constant time using standard word-RAM operations. □

We need to show that, for every heavy path, we store enough information for applying Lemma 4.5. Consider a heavy path $u_1 - u_2 - \ldots - u_s$, where $u_1$ is the head. By the properties of the heavy path decomposition, $\text{id}(L_{u_1}) < \text{id}(L_{u_2}) < \ldots < \text{id}(L_{u_s})$. The label of every $u \in T$ such that $u_i$ is the top significant ancestor of $u$ encodes the following: (1) $\text{id}(L_{u_i})$, (2) $i \bmod k$, and (3) $\lfloor \text{id}(L_{u_{i+t}}) - \text{id}(L_{u_i}) \rfloor_2$ and $\lfloor \text{id}(L_{u_i}) - \text{id}(L_{u_{i-t}}) \rfloor_2$ for every $t = 1, 2, \ldots, k$.

To encode $\text{id}(L_{u_i})$, we store $\text{height}(L_{u_i})$ using $O(\log \log n)$ bits. Encoding $\lfloor \text{id}(L_{u_{i+t}}) - \text{id}(L_{u_i}) \rfloor_2$ and $\lfloor \text{id}(L_{u_i}) - \text{id}(L_{u_{i-t}}) \rfloor_2$ for every $t = 1, 2, \ldots, k$ reduces to encoding two non-decreasing sequences of $k$ integers from $[0, \log n]$. By Lemma 2.2, such a sequence can be stored using $O(k \log \frac{\log n}{k})$ bits. Finally, $i \bmod k$ is encoded using $O(\log k)$ bits. Notice that both $O(\log \log n)$ and $O(\log k)$ are absorbed by $O(k \log \frac{\log n}{k})$.

To conclude, given the labels of $u$ and $v$, whose significant ancestors $u'$ and $v'$ are on $\text{NCH}(u, v) = u_1 - u_2 - \ldots - u_s$ and are both the top significant ancestors, we can now calculate $d(u', v')$ or detect that it exceeds $k$ by retrieving the necessary information from the labels of $u$ and $v$ and then applying Lemma 4.5. Finally, in the full version we show that queries can be supported in constant time.

## REFERENCES


[1] Serge Abiteboul, Stephen Alstrup, Haim Kaplan, Tova Milo, and Theis Rauhe. 2006. Compact Labeling Scheme for Ancestor Queries. *SIAM J. Comput.* 35, 6 (2006), 1295–1309.

[2] Deepak Ajwani, Ulrich Meyer, and David Veith. 2015. An I/O-efficient Distance Oracle for Evolving Real-World Graphs. In *17th ALENEX.* 159–172. https://doi.org/10.1137/1.9781611973754.14

[3] Takuya Akiba, Yoichi Iwata, and Yuichi Yoshida. 2013. Fast exact shortest-path distance queries on large networks by pruned landmark labeling. In *32nd SIGMOD.* 349–360. https://doi.org/10.1145/2463676.2465315

[4] Takuya Akiba, Christian Sommer, and Ken-ichi Kawarabayashi. 2012. Shortest-path queries for complex networks: exploiting low tree-width outside the core. In *15th EDBT.* 144–155. https://doi.org/10.1145/2247596.2247614

[5] Stephen Alstrup, Philip Bille, and Theis Rauhe. 2005. Labeling schemes for small distances in trees. *SIAM Journal on Discrete Mathematics* 19, 2 (2005), 448–462.

[6] Stephen Alstrup, Søren Dahlgaard, and Mathias Bæk Tejs Knudsen. 2015. Optimal induced universal graphs and adjacency labeling for trees. In *56th FOCS.* 1311–1326.

[7] Stephen Alstrup, Cyril Gavoille, Esben Bistrup Halvorsen, and Holger Petersen. 2016. Simpler, faster and shorter labels for distances in graphs. In *27th SODA.* 338–350.

[8] Stephen Alstrup, Inge Li Gørtz, Esben Bistrup Halvorsen, and Ely Porat. 2016. Distance labeling schemes for trees. In *43rd ICALP.* 132:1–132:16.

[9] Stephen Alstrup, Esben Bistrup Halvorsen, and Kasper Green Larsen. 2014. Near-optimal labeling schemes for nearest common ancestors. In *25th SODA.* 972–982.

[10] Stephen Alstrup, Haim Kaplan, Mikkel Thorup, and Uri Zwick. 2015. Adjacency labeling schemes and induced-universal graphs. In *47th STOC.* 625–634.

[11] Stephen Alstrup and Theis Rauhe. 2002. Small induced-universal graphs and compact implicit graph representations. In *43rd FOCS.* 53–62.

[12] Nicolas Bonichon, Cyril Gavoille, and Arnaud Labourel. 2007. Short labels by traversal and jumping. *Electronic Notes in Discrete Mathematics* 28 (2007), 153–160.

[13] FRK Chung, RL Graham, and D Coppersmith. 1981. On trees containing all small trees. *The Theory and Applications of Graphs* (1981), 265–272.

[14] Peter Elias. 1975. Universal codeword sets and representations of the integers. *IEEE transactions on information theory* 21, 2 (1975), 194–203.

[15] Johannes Fischer. 2009. Short labels for lowest common ancestors in trees. In *17th ESA.* 752–763.

[16] Pierre Fraigniaud and Amos Korman. 2010. Compact ancestry labeling schemes for xml trees. In *21st SODA.* 458–466.

[17] O. Freedman, P. Gawrychowski, P.K. Nicholson, and O. Weimann. 2017. Optimal Distance Labeling Schemes for Trees. *Arxiv 1608.00212* (2017).

[18] Cyril Gavoille, Michal Katz, Nir A. Katz, Christophe Paul, and David Peleg. 2001. Approximate Distance Labeling Schemes. In *9th ESA.* 476–487.

[19] Cyril Gavoille and Arnaud Labourel. 2007. Distributed relationship schemes for trees. In *18th ISAAC.* 728–738. Announced at PODC'07.

[20] Cyril Gavoille, David Peleg, Stéphane Pérennes, and Ran Raz. 2004. Distance labeling in graphs. *Journal of Algorithms* 53, 1 (2004), 85–112. A preliminary version in *12th SODA*, 2001.

[21] MK Gol'dberg and EM Livshits. 1968. On minimal universal trees. *Mathematical Notes of the Academy of Sciences of the USSR* 4, 3 (1968), 713–717.

[22] Sampath Kannan, Moni Naor, and Steven Rudich. 1992. Implicit Representation of Graphs. *SIAM Journal on Discrete Mathematics* 5, 4 (1992), 596–603.

[23] Haim Kaplan and Tova Milo. 2001. Short and simple labels for small distances and other functions. In *7th WADS.* 246–257.

[24] David Peleg. 2000. Proximity-preserving labeling schemes. *Journal of Graph Theory* 33, 3 (2000), 167–176.

[25] Casper Petersen, Noy Rotbart, Jakob Grue Simonsen, and Christian Wulff-Nilsen. 2016. Near-optimal adjacency labeling scheme for power-law graphs. In *43rd ICALP.* 133:1–133:15.

[26] Noy Galil Rotbart. 2016. *New Ideas on Labeling Schemes.* Ph.D. Dissertation. University of Copenhagen.

[27] Daniel D Sleator and Robert Endre Tarjan. 1983. A data structure for dynamic trees. *Journal of computer and system sciences* 26, 3 (1983), 362–391.

[28] Mikkel Thorup and Uri Zwick. 2001. Compact routing schemes. In *13th SPAA.* 1–10.

# Brief Announcement: How Large is your Graph?

Varun Kanade
University of Oxford
The Alan Turing Institute
varunk@cs.ox.ac.uk

Frederik Mallmann-Trenn
École normale supérieure
Simon Fraser University
frederik.mallmann-trenn@ens.fr

Victor Verdugo
École normale supérieure
Universidad de Chile
vverdugo@dii.uchile.cl

## ABSTRACT

We consider the problem of estimating the graph size, where one is given only local access to the graph. We formally define a query model in which one starts with a *seed* node and is allowed to make queries about neighbours of nodes that have already been seen. In the case of undirected graphs, an estimator of Katzir *et al.* (2014) based on a sample from the stationary distribution $\pi$ uses $O\left(\frac{1}{\|\pi\|_2} + d_{\text{avg}}\right)$ queries; we prove that this is tight. In addition, we establish this as a lower bound even when the algorithm is allowed to crawl the graph arbitrarily; the results of Katzir *et al.* give an upper bound that is worse by a multiplicative factor $t_{\text{mix}} \cdot \log(n)$.

## CCS CONCEPTS

• **Mathematics of computing** → *Probabilistic algorithms*;

## KEYWORDS

Estimation; Random Walks; Social Networks

**ACM Reference format:**
Varun Kanade, Frederik Mallmann-Trenn, and Victor Verdugo. 2017. Brief Announcement: How Large is your Graph?. In *Proceedings of PODC '17, Washington, DC, USA, July 25-27, 2017,* 3 pages.
https://doi.org/10.1145/3087801.3087855

## 1 INTRODUCTION

Networks contain a wealth of information and studying properties of networks may yield important insights. However, most networks of interest are very large and ordinary users may have rather restricted access to them. One of most basic questions about networks is the number of nodes contained in them. For example, the number of pages on the world wide web (WWW) is estimated to be just shy of 50 billion at the time of writing.[1] Facebook currently reports having about one and three quarter billion users;[2] Twitter reports having about 300 million active users. It is undesirable to rely on a small number of sources for such information. At times we might be interested in more specific graphs for which there is no public information available at all. Is there a way to estimate the total number of nodes using rather limited access to these graphs?

[1] www.worldwidewebsize.com
[2] Here, billion refers to one thousand million, not a million million.


ACM ISBN 978-1-4503-4992-5/17/07.
https://doi.org/10.1145/3087801.3087855

Our model is motivated by the kind of access ordinary users may have to graphs of interest. For example, most social network companies provide some sort of an application programming interface (API). In the case of the world wide web, one option is to simply crawl. The graph query access models we use are formally defined in Section 1.3. In this work we consider query models inspired in four different network models such Facebook, the world wide web, the *fan network* and Twitter.

While memory and computational requirements do act as constraints when dealing with large graphs, possibly the most important one is the rate limits set on queries made using the API. Even when crawling the web, there is the risk of simply being blocked if large volumes of requests are sent to the same server. Thus, the most scarce resource in this instance is the number of queries made about the graph. Our query model counts these costs strictly—essentially every time a new node is discovered, its degree is revealed at unit cost and a unit cost is incurred for every neighbour requested.

### 1.1 Related Work

There is a large body of literature on estimating statistical properties of graphs, reflecting the relevance of and interest in studying complex networks. Much of this work is in the more applied literature and in particular, we were unable to pin down a precisely defined query model. The work most closely related to ours is that of Katzir *et al.* [9]. They consider a model where a random sample drawn from the stationary distribution of the random walk is available. If the random walk mixes rapidly and a suitable bound on the mixing time is known, this can be simulated in the models we consider. They show that $O\left(\frac{1}{\|\pi\|_2} + d_{\text{avg}}\right)$ queries suffice, where $\pi$ is the stationary distribution and $d_{\text{avg}}$ is the average degree. We show that this is tight when given access to a sample from the stationary distribution. When only neighbour queries are allowed, we show that this bound is tight up to a multiplicative factor of the mixing time and other polylogarithmic factors.

In more recent work, Hardiman and Katzir give another estimator based on counting shared neighbours [8]. They give a slightly better bound on the number of nodes sampled than the earlier work of Katzir *et al.* [9]. However, it is unclear that this can be implemented efficiently in the query model in our paper. Cooper *et al.* [4] obtain estimators for the number of edges, triangles and nodes. The estimators are based on random walks over the graph, but in particular, for estimating the number of nodes, the transition probabilities are not inversely proportional to the degree. Musco *et al.* [12] develop a distributed collision based approach where several random walks traverse the graph and counts the number of collisions with other random walks. Dasgupta *et al.* [6] provide an estimator of the average degree that uses $O(\log U \log\log U)$ samples, where $U$ is an upper bound on the maximum degree. Somewhat surprisingly, this seems to be an easier task than estimating the number of nodes. We refer to the full version for a more extensive literature review for other settings like dynamic graphs [3], directed graphs [10, 11, 13], property testing [1, 5, 7] and support size estimation of a distribution [14, 15].

## 1.2 Our contributions

Firstly, our contribution is to express the problem of estimating graph properties formally. As discussed in the introduction, networks of interest vary significantly in terms of what access might be easily available to an ordinary user. Keeping in mind the examples of Facebook, the web, the fan-network and Twitter, we introduce different types of oracles that provide access to the graph.

The focus of this work is on estimating the number of nodes. For any $\varepsilon > 0$ and $\delta > 0$, we say that an algorithm (with access to a query oracle) provides an $\varepsilon$-accurate estimate of the number of nodes, if with probability at least $1 - \delta$ it outputs $\widehat{n}$, such that $|n - \widehat{n}| \leq \varepsilon n$. The main quantity to be optimised is the number of oracle queries, though all algorithms considered in this paper are also computationally highly efficient. Throughout we will assume that $\varepsilon$ and $\delta$ are constants and the use of $O(\cdot)$ and $\Omega(\cdot)$ notation in this paper hides all dependence on $\varepsilon$ and $\delta$.

**Undirected Graphs.** Katzir *et al.* [9] implicitly assume the ability to sample from the stationary distribution. They show that in this setting $O\left(\frac{1}{\|\pi\|_2} + d_{\text{avg}}\right)$ samples from the stationary distribution $\pi$ suffice, where $d_{\text{avg}}$ is the average degree. If the graph is connected and a suitable bound on the mixing time exists which is known to the algorithm, $O(t_{\text{mix}} \log n)$ queries suffice to draw one node from a distribution that is close (up to inverse polynomial factors in variation distance) to the stationary distribution using only neighbour queries. This gives an upper bound of $O\left(t_{\text{mix}} \cdot \log n \cdot \left(\frac{1}{\|\pi\|_2} + d_{\text{avg}}\right)\right)$ queries with a neighbour query oracle (??). In terms of lower bounds, we establish that:

- (Theorem 2.1) Any algorithm that has access to random samples from the *stationary distribution* $\pi$ and outputs a 0.1-accurate estimate of the number of nodes with probability at least 0.99, requires $\Omega\left(\frac{1}{\|\pi\|_2} + d_{\text{avg}}\right)$ samples.
- (Theorem 2.2) Any algorithm that has access to neighbour queries and outputs a 0.1-accurate estimate of the number of nodes with probability at least 0.99, requires $\Omega\left(\frac{1}{\|\pi\|_2} + d_{\text{avg}}\right)$ queries.

We remark that there is a gap between the upper bound and lower bound when considering an oracle with neighbour access. A question left open by our work is whether the multiplicative factor of $t_{\text{mix}} \log(n)$ is required, or whether a more efficient estimator can be designed. We refer the full version of this article for our results about the query models involving directed graphs.

## 1.3 Query Model

In this section, we formally define the query model that allows us to access the graph. Due to space constraints we only include the oracle model $O$ that allows us to handle undirected networks such as Facebook.

The oracle makes use of labelling functions[3] ; for some space $L$, a labelling function $\ell : V \to L$ is an injection and we allow $\ell$ to be defined dynamically. The labelling function we use throughout the paper is the *consecutive labelling function.* In this case, the label set is $L = \mathbb{N}$. If $S$ denotes all the vertices labelled by the oracle so far, for a new vertex $v \notin S$ picked by the oracle, the label is assigned as follows: if $S = \emptyset$, $\ell(v) = 1$, else $\ell(v) = \max\{\ell(u) \mid u \in S\} + 1$.

Any algorithm with access to this oracle can essentially make two types of queries, (i) init, and (ii) $(l, i)$ for undirected graphs. For the init, the oracle initialises a set $S := \{v\}$, where $v$ is chosen to be an arbitrary node in the graph, and $O$ responds with $(\ell(v), \deg(v))$ for some $v \in V$. For a query of type $(l, i)$, if there is $v \in S$ such that $\ell(v) = l$ and $i \leq \deg(v)$, then $O$ returns $(\ell(u), \deg(u))$, where $u$ is the $i^{th}$ element in the adjacency list of $v$. The oracle updates $S \leftarrow S \cup \{u\}$. Otherwise it returns null.

Finally, we consider the *stationary query oracle,* $O^{\pi}$, which when queried returns $(\ell(v), \deg(v))$, where $v \sim \pi$; $\pi$ is the stationary distribution.

# 2 UNDIRECTED GRAPHS

As mentioned before, we show that the upper bounds obtained by Katzir *et al.* [9] are essentially tight, up to a factor of the mixing time and polylogarithmic terms in $n$. This suggests that rapid mixing is a critical condition for being able to estimate the size of the graph. We begin by discussing very simple examples which show that this is indeed the case.

*Some Simple Observations.* First we construct two simple graphs, one having twice as many nodes as the other. No algorithm can distinguish between these two graphs with probability greater than 3/4 (say) unless $\Omega(m)$ queries to the oracle $O$ are made. The graphs are shown in Figure 1. The first graph is simply $G_{n,p}$ with each node being connected to an additional node with degree 1. The second graph is identical, except that for one randomly chosen node, instead of this additional edge to a degree 1 node, it is connected to a copy of $G_{n,p}$. Suppose $p > \log(n)/n$ so that the graphs are connected with high probability and that $m = \Theta(n^2 p)$.

We don't provide a formal proof here, which can be given along the lines of the proof of Theorem 2.1. We outline a sketch here. Assuming the oracle $O$ returns some $v \in V$ in the part that is $G_{n,p}$ with an additional edge coming out of each node, how long will it take before we discover the edge to the copy of $G_{n,p}$, if it exists? Since we made no assumption on the order in which neighbours are stored in an adjacency list, we have to query at least a constant fraction of neighbours of a given node to discover, with constant probability, the edge that leads out of the $G_{n,p}$. However, most of these will just lead us to a single vertex. Thus, unless we explore at least a constant fraction of the edges of a constant fraction of the vertices, we don't stand a significant chance of finding the edge that leads to the copy of the $G_{n,p}$. Thus, $\Omega(m)$ queries to the oracle are required.

Clearly, if we're in the second case, that is the graph with an additional copy of $G_{n,p}$ connected to the earlier one by a single

[3]We do assume that there is unit cost in sending the label of a node to the algorithm, thus implicitly we may think of every label having a bit-representation that is logarithmic in the size of the graph. However, the bit-length of the label reveals minimal information, which we assume that the algorithm has access to anyway.

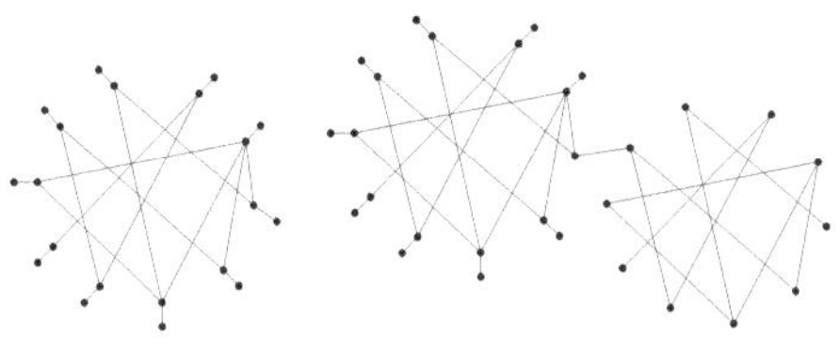

**Figure 1: Example showing that $\Omega(m)$ samples might be required if no assumption like rapid mixing is made.**

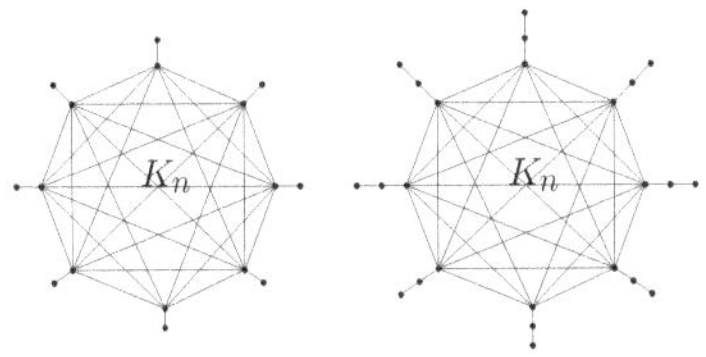


**Figure 2: The *sun* graph and the *bright sun*.**

edge, a random walk on this graph does not mix rapidly. What this example shows is that if one wishes to do asymptotically better than breadth-first search, one needs additional assumptions on the graph, such as rapid mixing.

## 2.1 Lower Bound Stationary Query Model

We show that for any undirected, connected graph $G = (V, E)$, there exists an undirected, connected graph $\widetilde{G}$, such that any algorithm which has access to either the oracle $O^{\pi}(G)$ or $O^{\pi}(\widetilde{G})$, cannot distinguish between the two with significant probability without making a large number of queries. Thus, it cannot output an estimate $\widehat{n}$ satisfying $|\widehat{n} - |V|| < |V|/2$ with probability 2/3. The proof of the following theorem can be found in the full version.

THEOREM 2.1. *Given an undirected, connected graph $G = (V, E)$, there exist graphs $\widetilde{G}$, $\bar{G}$ with $2|V|$ nodes and a constant $p < 1$, such that any algorithm that is given access to one of three oracles $O^{\pi}(G)$, $O^{\pi}(\widetilde{G})$ and $O^{\pi}(\bar{G})$, chosen with equal probability, requires $\Omega\left(\frac{1}{\|\pi_G\|_2} + d_{\text{avg}}(G)\right)$ queries to distinguish between them with probability at least $p$. As a consequence, any algorithm that outputs $\widehat{n}$, such that $|\widehat{n} - n^*| < n^*/2$ requires at least $\Omega\left(\frac{1}{\|\pi_G\|_2} + d_{\text{avg}}(G)\right)$ queries, where $n^* = n$ if the graph is $G$ and $n^* = 2n$ if the graph is either $\widetilde{G}$ or $\bar{G}$.*

## 2.2 Lower Bound Neighbour Query Model

We show that with access to the oracle $O$, any algorithm that predicts the number of nodes in a graph $G$ to within a small constant fraction requires $\Omega\left(\frac{1}{\|\pi_G\|_2} + d_{\text{avg}}\right)$ queries. For proving the lower bounds we use graphs generated according to the *configuration model* [2]. A vector $\mathbf{d} = (d_1, d_2, \ldots, d_n)$ is said to be *graphical* if there exists an undirected graph on $n$ nodes such that vertex $i \in [n]$ has degree $d_i$. We briefly describe here how graphs are generated in the configuration model:

(1) Create disjoint sets $W_i$, for $i \in \{1, \ldots n\}$, with $|W_i| = d_i$. The elements of $W_i$ are called *stubs*.
(2) Create a uniform random maximum matching in the set $\bigcup_{i=1}^{n} W_i$ (note that $\sum_{i=1}^{n} d_i$ must be even since $\mathbf{d}$ is graphical).
(3) For a stub edge $\{x, y\}$ in the matching, such that $x \in W_i$ and $y \in W_j$, the edge $\{i, j\}$ is added to the graph.

The above procedure creates a graph where vertex $i$ has degree exactly $d_i$, possibly with multi-edges. This procedure does not necessarily produce a uniform distribution over graphs having degree sequence $\mathbf{d}$. We use $G \sim \mathcal{G}(\mathbf{d})$ to denote that a graph $G$ was generated in the configuration model with degree sequence $\mathbf{d}$. The proof of the following theorem can be found in the full version.

THEOREM 2.2. *Let $\mathbf{d} = (d_1, \ldots, d_n)$ be a graphical vector satisfying $\min_i d_i \geq 3$. Then there exists a graphical*

$$\widetilde{\mathbf{d}} = (\widetilde{d}_1, \ldots, \widetilde{d}_n, \widetilde{d}_{n+1}, \ldots, \widetilde{d}_{2n})$$

*with $\min_i \widetilde{d}_i \geq 3$, such that for $G \sim \mathcal{G}(\mathbf{d})$ and $\widetilde{G} \sim \mathcal{G}(\widetilde{\mathbf{d}})$, there exists $c > 0$, such that any algorithm with access to one of two oracles $O(G)$ or $O(\widetilde{G})$ chosen equal probability, cannot distinguish between the two with probability greater than $1 - c$ unless it makes $\Omega\left(\frac{1}{\|\pi_G\|_2} + d_{\text{avg}}(G)\right)$ queries to the oracle.*

## REFERENCES


[1] Michael A. Bender and Data Ron. 2002. Testing properties of directed graphs: Acyclicity and connectivity. *Random Structures and Algorithms* 20, 2 (2002), 184–205.
[2] Béla Bollobás. 1980. A Probabilistic Proof of an Asymptotic Formula for the Number of Labelled Regular Graphs. *European Journal of Combinatorics* 1, 4 (1980), 311 - 316. https://doi.org/10.1016/S0195-6698(80)80030-8
[3] Colin Cooper and Alan Frieze. 2002. Crawling on web graphs. In *Proceedings of the thiry-fourth annual ACM symposium on Theory of computing*. ACM, 419–427.
[4] Colin Cooper, Tomasz Radzik, and Yiannis Siantos. 2012. Estimating network parameters using random walks. In *Computational Aspects of Social Networks, 4th International Conference on*. 33–40.
[5] Artur Czumaj, Pan Peng, and Christian Sohler. 2016. Relating Two Property Testing MOdels for Bounded Degree Directed Graphs. In *Proceedings of the ACM Symposium on the Theory of Computing (STOC)*.
[6] Anirban Dasgupta, Ravi Kumar, and Tamás Sarlós. 2014. On estimating the average degree. In *Proceedings of the 23rd international conference on World Wide Web*. ACM, 795–806. https://doi.org/10.1145/2566486.2568019
[7] Oded Goldreich. 2010. Introduction to Testing Graph Properties. Survey article available at http://www.wisdom.weizmann.ac.il/~oded/COL/tgp-intro.pdf. (2010).
[8] Liran Katzir and Stephen J. Hardiman. 2015. Estimating Clustering Coefficients and Size of Social Networks via Random Walk. *ACM Transactions on the Web* 9, 4, Article 19 (2015), 20 pages.
[9] Liran Katzir, Edo Liberty, Oren Somekh, and Ioana A. Cosma. 2014. Estimating Sizes of Social Networks via Biased Sampling. *Internet Mathematics* 10, 3-4 (2014), 335–359. https://doi.org/10.1080/15427951.2013.862883
[10] Donald E. Knuth. 1975. Estimating the efficiency of backtrack programs. *Mathematics of computation* 29, 129 (1975), 122–136.
[11] Alberto Marchetti-Spaccamela. 1988. On the estimate of the size of a directed graph. In *International Workshop on Graph-Theoretic Concepts in Computer Science*. Springer, 317–326.
[12] Cameron Musco, Hsin-Hao Su, and Nancy A. Lynch. 2016. Ant-Inspired Density Estimation via Random Walks: Extended Abstract. In *Proceedings of the 2016 ACM Symposium on Principles of Distributed Computing, PODC 2016, Chicago, IL, USA, July 25-28, 2016*. 469–478.
[13] Leonard Pitt. 1987. A note on extending Knuth's tree estimator to directed acyclic graphs. *Information processing letters* 24, 3 (1987), 203–206.
[14] Gregory Valiant and Paul Valiant. 2011. Estimating the unseen: an n/log(n)-sample estimator for entropy and support size, shown optimal via new CLTs. In *Proceedings of the forty-third annual ACM symposium on Theory of computing*. ACM, 685–694.
[15] Gregory Valiant and Paul Valiant. 2013. Estimating the unseen: improved estimators for entropy and other properties. In *Advances in Neural Information Processing Systems*. 2157–2165.

# Brief Announcement: Distributed Approximation for Tree Augmentation*

Keren Censor-Hillel
Technion, Department of Computer Science
Haifa, Israel
ckeren@cs.technion.ac.il

Michal Dory
Technion, Department of Computer Science
Haifa, Israel
smichald@cs.technion.ac.il

## ABSTRACT

A minimum spanning tree (MST) is an essential structure for distributed algorithms, since it is a low-cost connected subgraph which provides an efficient way to communicate in a network. However, trees cannot survive even one link failure. In this paper, we study the Tree Augmentation Problem (TAP), for which the input is a graph $G$ and a spanning tree $T$ of $G$ and the goal is to augment $T$ with a minimum (or minimum weight) set of edges $Aug$ from $G$, such that $T \cup Aug$ remains connected after a failure of any single link.

Being central tasks for network design, TAP and additional connectivity augmentation problems have been well studied in the sequential setting. However, despite the distributed nature of these problems, they have not been studied in the distributed setting. We address this fundamental topic and provide a study of distributed TAP. In the full version of this paper, we present distributed 2-approximation algorithms for TAP, both for the unweighted and weighted versions, which have a time complexity of $O(h)$ rounds, where $h$ is the height of $T$. We also present a distributed 4-approximation for unweighted TAP that has a time complexity of $O(\sqrt{n}\log^* n+D)$ rounds for a graph $G$ with $n$ vertices and diameter $D$, which is an improvement for large values of $h$. We complement our algorithms with lower bounds and some applications to related problems.

## CCS CONCEPTS

• **Mathematics of computing → Graph algorithms**;

## KEYWORDS

approximation algorithms; distributed network design; connectivity augmentation

## 1 BACKGROUND

Highly connected spanning subgraphs are crucial components of network design, since they are resistant to failures. Thus, a central question is how to increase the connectivity of a given subgraph by adding to it a minimum size (or a minimum weight) set of edges, in order to improve the network reliability while paying a minimal cost. Such problems are called *connectivity augmentation* problems, and have been widely studied in the sequential setting [6–8, 12, 14–18, 21, 28]. However, due to the distributed nature of networks, it is necessary to have distributed algorithms for connectivity augmentation problems.

The fundamental problem of finding a minimum spanning tree (MST) is an example of a connectivity augmentation problem, and has been thoroughly studied by the distributed computing community [2, 4, 5, 9, 10, 20, 23]. However, a spanning tree cannot survive even one link failure. In order to guarantee more reliable backbones, it is vital to find subgraphs with higher connectivity. Since increasing connectivity typically comes at a certain price, if we are already given a subgraph with some connectivity guarantee then we would naturally like to augment it with additional edges of minimum number or weight, rather than to compute a well-connected low-cost subgraph from scratch. A prime example for such a task is the *Tree Augmentation Problem* (TAP), in which the input is a graph $G$ with $n$ vertices and $m$ edges, and a spanning tree $T$ of $G$, and the goal is to add to $T$ a minimum size (or a minimum weight) set of edges $Aug$ from $G$, such that $T \cup Aug$ remains connected after a failure of any single link. In other words, $T \cup Aug$ is 2-edge-connected, where a graph $G$ is *$k$-edge-connected* if it remains connected after the removal of any $k-1$ edges.

We provide a first step in a study of distributed connectivity augmentation. In the full version of this paper, we present distributed approximation algorithms for TAP in the CONGEST model, for both the unweighted and weighted variants of the problem, and complement our results with lower bounds.

## 2 OUR CONTRIBUTIONS

### 2.1 Unweighted TAP

A natural approach for constructing a distributed algorithm for unweighted TAP is to simulate the sequential 2-approximation algorithm of Khuller and Thurimella [16]. In their algorithm, they first convert the input graph $G$ into a modified graph $G'$, as follows. The graph $G'$ includes all the edges of $T$, and all the non-tree edges in $G$ that are between an ancestor to its descendant in $T$. Any other non-tree edge $\{u, v\}$ is replaced by two edges $\{t, u\}, \{t, v\}$ where $t$ is the lowest common ancestor (LCA) of $u$ and $v$ in $T$. Then, they find a directed MST in $G'$, which induces a corresponding augmentation in $G$.

This approach imposes two difficulties in the distributed setting. The first is that we cannot simply modify the input graph, because it is the graph that represents the underlying distributed network, whose topology is given and not under our control. The second

*Supported in part by the Israel Science Foundation (grant 1696/14).


*PODC '17, July 25–27, 2017, Washington, DC, USA*

ACM ISBN 978-1-4503-4992-5/17/07.
https://doi.org/10.1145/3087801.3087842

obstacle is in the directed MST procedure. Finding a directed MST efficiently in the distributed setting seems to be difficult, with the currently best known complexity of $O(n^2)$ [13].

We overcome the above using two key ingredients. First, we bring in to our construction the tool of computing lowest common ancestors (LCAs). We show that building $G'$ and simulating a distributed computation over it can be done by an efficient computation of LCAs, and we achieve the latter by leveraging the *labeling scheme* for LCAs presented in [1].

Second, we replace the expensive directed MST construction by a completely different procedure, as follows. We show that the simple structure of $G'$ allows us to find an optimal augmentation in $G'$ efficiently by scanning the input tree $T$ from the leaves to the root. Each vertex sends to its parent information about edges that may be relevant to the augmentation since they cover many edges of the tree, and the vertices use the LCA labels in order to decide which edges to add to the augmentation. While a direct implementation of this would result in much information that is sent through the tree, we show that at most two edges need to actually be sent by each vertex. Then, applying the labeling scheme and scanning the tree $T$ result in a time complexity of $O(h)$ rounds where $h$ is the height of $T$.

Finally, we prove that an optimal augmentation in $G'$ gives a 2-approximation augmentation for $G$, which gives our first main result.

Theorem 2.1. *There is a distributed 2-approximation algorithm to the unweighted TAP problem that runs in $O(h)$ rounds.*

## 2.2 Weighted TAP

Once the edges have weights, we cannot argue anymore that the two edges per vertex that are sent in the algorithm for the unweighted case are guaranteed to be sufficient. This is because of the tension between light edges that cover only few edges and heavier edges that cover many edges, whose resolution might not be possible to obtain at the current vertex. In other words, the challenge is that now sending information about two edges from each vertex to its parent is not enough in order to decide which edges to add to the augmentation. The number of edges that may be relevant for the augmentation could be much larger and vertices cannot decide locally which edges are relevant without feedback from their ancestors in the tree.

Nevertheless, we show how to overcome this by introducing a technique of having each vertex send to its parent edges with altered weights. The trick here is to modify the weight that is sent for an edge, in a way that captures the cost for covering each edge of the tree. This allows focusing on a smaller number of edges that may be relevant for the augmentation. Using standard pipelining, this gives a time complexity of $O(h)$ rounds for the weighted case as well, summarized as follows.

Theorem 2.2. *There is a distributed 2-approximation algorithm to the weighted TAP problem that runs in $O(h)$ rounds.*

## 2.3 Faster unweighted TAP

The time complexity of both of our aforementioned algorithms is linear in the height $h$ of the tree $T$. However, $h$ may be large, even if the diameter of $G$ is small. To address such cases, we suggest another algorithm for unweighted TAP that has a significantly smaller round complexity for large values of $h$. This comes at the price of a slight increase in the approximation ratio, from 2 to 4. The key ingredient of the algorithm is breaking the tree $T$ into fragments and applying our 2-approximation for unweighted TAP algorithm on each fragment separately, as well as on the tree of fragments. With a subtle case-analysis, we show that this approach gives a 4-approximation to unweighted TAP in a time complexity of $O(\sqrt{n}\log^* n + D)$ rounds, where $D$ is the diameter of $G$.

Theorem 2.3. *There is a distributed 4-approximation algorithm to the unweighted TAP problem that runs in $O(\sqrt{n}\log^* n + D)$ rounds.*

## 2.4 Lower Bounds and Additional Applications

We complement our algorithms by presenting lower bounds for TAP. We first show that TAP is a global problem which requires $\Omega(D)$ rounds, implying that if $h = O(D)$ then our algorithms are optimal up to a constant factor. We also consider the case of $h = \omega(D)$, for which we show a family of graphs based on the construction in [26], for which $\Omega(h)$ rounds are needed in order to approximate weighted TAP, where $h = O(\sqrt{n})$.

Finally, we conclude by presenting several applications for related problems. We show that our algorithms give efficient approximation algorithms for the minimum weight 2-edge-connected spanning subgraph problem. We also show that our algorithm for weighted TAP can be used in order to increase the connectivity of any spanning subgraph $H$ of $G$ from 1 to 2. In addition, we show that our unweighted TAP algorithm can be used in order to verify if a graph $G$ is 2-edge-connected in $O(D)$ rounds.

# 3 RELATED WORK

Connectivity augmentation problems are well studied in the sequential context. They were first studied by Eswaran and Tarjan [6], who showed a polynomial time algorithm for increasing the connectivity of an unweighted graph to 2, when an edge between any two vertices can be added to the augmentation. They also showed that the weighted version of the problem is NP-hard. Since many types of augmentation problems are NP-hard, including TAP for both the weighted and the unweighted cases, approximation algorithms for them have been studied. The first 2-approximation algorithm for weighted TAP was given by Frederickson and Jaja [8], and has time complexity of $O(n^2)$. This was later simplified by Khuller and Thurimella [16], which compute a directed MST in a related directed graph $G'$, in order to approximate TAP in $G$. Their algorithm works in $O(m + n \log n)$ time. Other 2-approximation algorithms for weighted TAP are the primal-dual algorithm of Goemans et al. [12], and the iterative rounding algorithm of Jain [14]. These are LP-based algorithms that solve general network design problems, in which the goal is to find a minimum-cost subgraph having at least a specified number of edges in each cut. Recently, a new algorithm achieved a 1.5-approximation for unweighted TAP [18]. Achiveing an approximation for the weighted case which is smaller than 2 is still an open problem. A survey about approximation algorithms for connectivity problems can be found in [15].

In the distributed setting, the problem of finding an MST, that is, finding a minimum weight subgraph with connectivity 1, is well studied. The first distributed algorithm for this problem is the GHS algorithm that works in $O(n \log n)$ time [9]. Following algorithms improved the time complexity to $O(\sqrt{n} \log^* n + D)$ for a graph with $n$ vertices and diameter $D$ [10, 20].

There are several distributed algorithms for additional related problems. The most related to our work are the distributed approximation algorithms for finding a minimum weight 2-edge-connected spanning subgraph (2-ECSS) of Krumke et al. [19]. Their approach is to start by finding a specific spanning tree and then augment it to a 2-edge-connected graph. In the unweighted case, they augment a DFS tree following the sequential algorithm of Khuller and Vishkin [17], which results in a $\frac{3}{2}$-approximation algorithm for 2-ECSS that takes $O(n)$ rounds. In the weighted case they augment an MST and suggest a general 2-approximation algorithm for weighted TAP that takes $O(n \log n)$ rounds. This results in a 3-approximation algorithm to 2-ECSS that takes $O(n \log n)$ rounds. Our algorithms for TAP imply faster solutions for 2-ECSS as well.

Another related problem is the construction of fault-tolerant tree structures. Distributed algorithms for constructing fault tolerant BFS and MST structures are given in [11], producing sparse subgraphs of the input graph $G$ that contain a BFS (or an MST) of $G \setminus \{e\}$ for each edge $e$, for the purpose of maintaining the functionality of a BFS (or an MST), even when an edge fails. Note that TAP is different from these problems in several aspects. First, we augment a specific spanning tree $T$ rather then build the whole structure from scratch. In addition, since we need to preserve only connectivity when an edge fails and not the functionality of a BFS tree, optimal solutions for TAP may be much sparser.

There are distributed algorithms that find the 2-edge-connected and 3-edge-connected components of a connected graph [24, 25], distributed algorithms that decompose a graph with large connectivity into many disjoint trees, while almost preserving the total connectivity through the trees [3], and an algorithm that finds a sparse $k$-edge-connected subgraph [27].

## 4 DISCUSSION

In this paper, we discuss distributed algorithms for TAP. Many intriguing problems remain open: Can we develop an efficient distributed algorithm for TAP with a better approximation ratio, as in the centralized setting [18]? Can we construct algorithms with a better time complexity? Otherwise, can we prove stronger lower bounds?

Additional open problems are designing efficient distributed algorithms for many related tasks. Such tasks include augmentation for increasing the edge connectivity from $k$ to $k + 1$ or to some function $f(k)$, as well as augmentation for increasing the vertex connectivity.

## REFERENCES


[1] Stephen Alstrup, Cyril Gavoille, Haim Kaplan, and Theis Rauhe. 2004. Nearest common ancestors: A survey and a new algorithm for a distributed environment. *Theory of Computing Systems* 37, 3 (2004), 441–456.

[2] Baruch Awerbuch. 1987. Optimal distributed algorithms for minimum weight spanning tree, counting, leader election, and related problems. In *Proceedings of the nineteenth annual ACM symposium on Theory of computing*. ACM, 230–240.

[3] Keren Censor-Hillel, Mohsen Ghaffari, and Fabian Kuhn. 2014. Distributed connectivity decomposition. In *Proceedings of the 2014 ACM symposium on Principles of distributed computing*. ACM, 156–165.

[4] Michael Elkin. 2006. A faster distributed protocol for constructing a minimum spanning tree. *J. Comput. System Sci.* 72, 8 (2006), 1282–1308.

[5] Michael Elkin. 2006. An unconditional lower bound on the time-approximation trade-off for the distributed minimum spanning tree problem. *SIAM J. Comput.* 36, 2 (2006), 433–456.

[6] Kapali P Eswaran and R Endre Tarjan. 1976. Augmentation problems. *SIAM J. Comput.* 5, 4 (1976), 653–665.

[7] András Frank. 1992. Augmenting graphs to meet edge-connectivity requirements. *SIAM Journal on Discrete Mathematics* 5, 1 (1992), 25–53.

[8] Greg N Frederickson and Joseph Ja'Ja'. 1981. Approximation algorithms for several graph augmentation problems. *SIAM J. Comput.* 10, 2 (1981), 270–283.

[9] Robert G. Gallager, Pierre A. Humblet, and Philip M. Spira. 1983. A distributed algorithm for minimum-weight spanning trees. *ACM Transactions on Programming Languages and systems (TOPLAS)* 5, 1 (1983), 66–77.

[10] Juan A Garay, Shay Kutten, and David Peleg. 1998. A sublinear time distributed algorithm for minimum-weight spanning trees. *SIAM J. Comput.* 27, 1 (1998), 302–316.

[11] Mohsen Ghaffari and Merav Parter. 2016. Near-Optimal Distributed Algorithms for Fault-Tolerant Tree Structures. In *Proceedings of the 28th ACM Symposium on Parallelism in Algorithms and Architectures*. ACM, 387–396.

[12] Michel X Goemans, Andrew V Goldberg, Serge A Plotkin, David B Shmoys, Eva Tardos, and David P Williamson. 1994. Improved Approximation Algorithms for Network Design Problems.. In *SODA*, Vol. 94. 223–232.

[13] Pierre Humblet et al. 1983. A distributed algorithm for minimum weight directed spanning trees. *Communications, IEEE Transactions on* 31, 6 (1983), 756–762.

[14] Kamal Jain. 2001. A factor 2 approximation algorithm for the generalized Steiner network problem. *Combinatorica* 21, 1 (2001), 39–60.

[15] Samir Khuller. 1996. Approximation algorithms for finding highly connected subgraphs. In *Approximation algorithms for NP-hard problems*. PWS Publishing Co., 236–265.

[16] Samir Khuller and Ramakrishna Thurimella. 1993. Approximation algorithms for graph augmentation. *Journal of Algorithms* 14, 2 (1993), 214–225.

[17] Samir Khuller and Uzi Vishkin. 1994. Biconnectivity approximations and graph carvings. *Journal of the ACM (JACM)* 41, 2 (1994), 214–235.

[18] Guy Kortsarz and Zeev Nutov. 2016. A simplified 1.5-approximation algorithm for augmenting edge-connectivity of a graph from 1 to 2. *ACM Transactions on Algorithms (TALG)* 12, 2 (2016), 23.

[19] Sven O Krumke, Peter Merz, Tim Nonner, and Katharina Rupp. 2007. Distributed approximation algorithms for finding 2-edge-connected subgraphs. In *Principles of Distributed Systems*. Springer, 159–173.

[20] Shay Kutten and David Peleg. 1995. Fast distributed construction of k-dominating sets and applications. In *Proceedings of the fourteenth annual ACM symposium on Principles of distributed computing*. ACM, 238–251.

[21] Dalit Naor, Dan Gusfield, and Charles Martel. 1997. A fast algorithm for optimally increasing the edge connectivity. *SIAM J. Comput.* 26, 4 (1997), 1139–1165.

[22] David Peleg. 2000. *Distributed Computing: A Locality-Sensitive Approach*. SIAM.

[23] David Peleg and Vitaly Rubinovich. 2000. A near-tight lower bound on the time complexity of distributed minimum-weight spanning tree construction. *SIAM J. Comput.* 30, 5 (2000), 1427–1442.

[24] David Pritchard. 2005. *Robust network computation*. Master's thesis. MIT.

[25] David Pritchard and Ramakrishna Thurimella. 2011. Fast computation of small cuts via cycle space sampling. *ACM Transactions on Algorithms (TALG)* 7, 4 (2011), 46.

[26] Atish Das Sarma, Stephan Holzer, Liah Kor, Amos Korman, Danupon Nanongkai, Gopal Pandurangan, David Peleg, and Roger Wattenhofer. 2012. Distributed verification and hardness of distributed approximation. *SIAM J. Comput.* 41, 5 (2012), 1235–1265.

[27] Ramakrishna Thurimella. 1995. Sub-linear distributed algorithms for sparse certificates and biconnected components. In *Proceedings of the fourteenth annual ACM symposium on Principles of distributed computing*. ACM, 28–37.

[28] Toshimasa Watanabe and Akira Nakamura. 1987. Edge-connectivity augmentation problems. *J. Comput. System Sci.* 35, 1 (1987), 96–144.

# Brief Announcement: Leader Election in SINR Model with Arbitrary Power Control

Magnús M. Halldórsson*
ICE-TCS, Reykjavik University
101 Reykjavik
Iceland
mmh@ru.is

Stephan Holzer†
TDS Group, MIT
77 Massachusetts Ave
Cambridge, MA
holzer@mit.edu

Evangelia Anna Markatou‡
TDS Group, MIT
77 Massachusetts Ave
Cambridge, MA
markatou@mit.edu

## ABSTRACT

In this article, we study the leader election problem in the Signal-to-Interference-plus-Noise-Ratio (SINR) model where nodes can adjust their transmission power. We show that in this setting it is possible to solve the leader election problem in two communication rounds, with high probability. Previously, it was known that $\Omega(\log n)$ rounds were sufficient and necessary when using uniform power, where $n$ is the number of nodes in the network.

We then examine how much power control is needed to achieve fast leader election. We show that any 2-round leader election algorithm in the SINR model running correctly w.h.p. requires a power range $2^{\Omega(n)}$ even when $n$ is known. We match this with an algorithm that uses power range $2^{\tilde{\Theta}(n)}$, when $n$ is known and $2^{\tilde{O}(n^{1.5})}$ when $n$ is not known. We also explore tradeoffs between time and power used, and show that to elect a leader in $t$ rounds, a power range $exp(n^{1/\Theta(t)})$ is sufficient and necessary.

## CCS CONCEPTS

•**Networks** → **Network algorithms;** •**Theory of computation** → **Distributed algorithms;**

## KEYWORDS

SINR; leader election; power control; capture effect

**ACM Reference format:**
Magnús M. Halldórsson, Stephan Holzer, and Evangelia Anna Markatou. 2017. Brief Announcement: Leader Election in SINR Model with Arbitrary Power Control. In *Proceedings of PODC'17, July 25-27, 2017, Washington, DC, USA,* 3 pages.
DOI: http://dx.doi.org/10.1145/3087801.3087851

## 1 INTRODUCTION

In this article we explore what can be accomplished in an SINR network by utilizing *power control*, the ability of nodes to transmit with variable transmission power, and the *capture effect*, a property of SINR networks, where a transmission can be successful while other transmissions within the communication range occur in the same round.

We study the leader election problem as our vehicle to explore this frontier. Leader election, the problem of electing a *unique leader* node among the nodes in a network, is one of the oldest and most studied problems in distributed computing. It is the ultimate way of breaking symmetry within radio networks in an initially unknown system, and is frequently used as a preliminary step in more complex communication tasks.

The best solution known for this problem in an SINR network has $O(\log n)$ runtime with high probability (w.h.p.) using uniform transmission power [1]. In the classical radio network model, the leader election problem requires $\Theta(\log^2 n)$ rounds w.h.p. [2]. Fineman et al. [1] prove a $\Omega(\log n)$ lower bound for the leader election problem in the SINR model using uniform power and suggest that it may be possible to develop algorithms with faster runtimes using power control.

Indeed, by using power control we are able to improve on the $\Omega(\log n)$ previous bound and achieve an $O(1)$ algorithm for leader election.

## 2 MODEL AND PROBLEM STATEMENT

Let $V$ be a set of $n$ nodes, deployed in a single-hop network, that represent wireless devices. Every node can communicate with any other node using transmission power $P$, in absence of interference from other nodes. Time is divided into synchronous rounds. In each round, a node $v$ can either transmit a message of size $O(\log n)$ with some power $P_v$, or listen. Node $v \in V$ can receive a message transmitted by node $u \in V$, iff $v$ is listening and

$$SINR(u, v, I) = \frac{\frac{P_u}{d(u,v)^\alpha}}{N + \sum_{w \in I} \frac{P_w}{d(w,v)^\alpha}} \geq \beta, \qquad (1)$$

where $I$ is the set of other nodes $\notin \{u, v\}$ that transmit simultaneously.

Here, $P_u \in \mathbb{R}_{\geq 1}$ is the transmission power of node $u$, $d(u, v)$ is the distance between nodes $v$ and $u$, $\alpha$ is the path-loss exponent, $N$ is the non-zero ambient noise, and $\beta$ is a hardware-dependent minimum SINR threshold required for a successful message reception. Our algorithms work for any $\beta > 0$, and the lower bounds require $\beta \geq 2$.

We denote by $R$ the ratio of the longest to shortest distance between any two nodes in the network. We assume that the shortest distance between two nodes in the network is 1. Similar to [1], we

*Supported by grants 152679-05 and 174484-05 from the Icelandic Research Fund.
†Supported by grant AFOSR FA9550-13-1-0042.
‡Supported by grants NSF CCF-1461559 and NSF CCF-0939370


ACM ISBN 978-1-4503-4992-5/17/07.
DOI: http://dx.doi.org/10.1145/3087801.3087851

assume that $R$ is bounded by a polynomial in $n$, $R \leq n^c$, for some $c \in \mathbb{N}$. Let $\gamma$ be a constant such that $\gamma \geq (c\alpha + 2)\log \beta$. We assume that the nodes know or can infer (an upper bound on) $\gamma$.

The $\tilde{O}$-notation omits logarithmic factors. All logs are base 2. We consider that an event happens with high probability (w.h.p.) if it happens with probability greater than $1 - 1/n$.

Problem 1 (Leader Election Problem). *Given $n$ nodes in a network, elect exactly one node (called the leader), with all nodes knowing whether or not they were elected to be the leader.*

# 3 2-ROUND LEADER ELECTION

## 3.1 The Essence of Our Algorithm

Below we present a high level description of the key ideas behind our algorithm.

1. **Geometric random variable**: The nodes use a geometric random variable $k$ to count the tails flipped in a sequence of coin flips before the first heads is flipped. This geometric random variable allows some nodes to approximate $n$ with no prior knowledge of the instance. More specifically, at least one and at most $16 \log n$ nodes flip a coin more than $\log n - \log\log n - 3$ times.
2. **Random** *IDs*: Each node chooses an *ID* (identification number) randomly using $k$. The geometric random variable $k$ ensures that exactly one node $v$ holds the maximum *ID*, which allows node $v$ to break the symmetry of the network and stand out as the leader.
3. **Feedback**: In order to inform all nodes of the leader node $v$, we split the set of nodes $V$ into listeners and competitors. The competitors compete for the leader position during the first round. The listeners inform the competitors of the winner during the second round. Both rounds use the same protocol with different message contents.
4. **The loudest node wins:** Each broadcasting node $v$ determines its transmission power by evaluating power function $f(ID_v) = P \cdot ID_v^{\gamma ID_v}$ using its identification number, $ID_v$. Transmission power function $f$ ensures that all listening nodes receive a message exactly from the node with the largest *ID*, as long as that *ID* is unique.

In summary, a *geometric random variable* allows the nodes to approximate $n$ with no prior knowledge of the instance, *random IDs* ensure that the node $v$ with the maximum *ID* stands out, *arbitrary transmission power* allows node $v$ to inform the other nodes it is the leader, and *feedback* makes sure that all nodes know who the leader node is.

## 3.2 Leader Election Algorithm

The algorithm proceeds as follows. Initially, each node $v$ flips a coin (a Bernoulli random variable) to determine its *role*: a *competitor* if heads are flipped, and a *listener* if tails. It then computes a geometric random variable (r.v.) $k_v$, which counts the tails flipped in a sequence of coin flips before the first heads is flipped. The ID of the node, $ID_v$, is an integer selected uniformly at random from the range $[J, 2 \cdot J]$, where $J = g(k_v) := 2^{k_v} k_v^4$. Finally, the power $P_v$ that $v$ uses for broadcast is given by $f(ID_v) := P \cdot ID_v^{\gamma ID_v}$, where $P$ is the minimum power needed to reach all nodes in the network (overcoming the ambient noise).

During round 1, competitors transmit their ID using the assigned power $P_v$, which is to be received by the listeners. In round 2, the roles are reversed, as the listeners report back the ID of the purported leader that they received.

## 3.3 Analysis

We proceed by showing that the highest power used by a competitor is sufficient to overpower all the other competitors, ensuring that this competitor is heard by all the listeners. Identical arguments hold for the reporting back in round 2.

To this end, we first show that there is a competitor whose geometric r.v. is nearly $\log n$, and at most a polylogarithmic number of competitors have that large value.

Lemma 3.1. *Let $k_1 := \log n - \log\log n - 3$. For at least one and at most $O(\log n)$ competitors $v$ it holds that $k_v \geq k_1$ with probability greater than $1 - \frac{1}{6n}$.*

We then show that all the $O(\log n)$ IDs at the high end of the spectrum are unique, i.e., selected by a single node.

Lemma 3.2. *A single competitor receives the highest ID with probability greater than $1 - \frac{1}{20n}$, given that at least one node calculated $k_v \geq k_1$.*

The difference in power used by nodes with different ID ensures that the competitor with highest ID will overpower all the other competitors and be heard by all the listeners.

Lemma 3.3. *The competitor $v$ with the highest $ID_v$ is received by all the listeners, if $ID_v \geq g(k_1)$.*

Using the above lemmas, we can prove Theorem 3.4.

Theorem 3.4. *The 2-round leader election algorithm terminates with all nodes agreeing on a common leader, with probability at least $1 - \frac{1}{2n}$.*

**Remark** Radios operate in *full-duplex* when they can transmit and receive simultaneously (effectively by subtracting their transmitted signal from the received one). This is a powerful assumption since full-duplex is hard to implement but the technology has been progressing in recent years. With full-duplex, a single round suffices for the leader election algorithm. Namely, our arguments apply unchanged to the success of reception by the other competitors.

# 4 RANGE OF POWER NEEDED FOR A 2-ROUND LEADER ELECTION

Power control is the essential property that allows our algorithms to work. That begs the question *how much* power control is needed?

We say that an algorithm uses a *power range X* if the powers assigned fall in the range $[P, \ldots, X \cdot P]$. The basic question is then how does the power range need to grow as a function of $n$ for leader election to work correctly.

## 4.1 Upper Bound

If the power range is bounded, we may assume that the nodes know the upper bound of the range, $P_{max}$. Thus, the algorithm would automatically truncate the power assigned to be at most $P_{max}$. Using this observation, we prove the following theorem.

THEOREM 4.1. *Our 2-round leader election algorithm can work correctly with a power range of* $2^{\tilde{O}(n^{1.5})}$, *with probability greater than* $1 - \frac{1}{n}$.

If nodes know $n$, we can work with a smaller power range as follows: We can first sample the nodes with probability $\Theta(\log n/n)$, and have each selected node select ID uniformly at random from the range $[J, 2J]$, where $J = n \log^2 n$. The power used is $f(ID_v)$ as before, and the arguments are otherwise the same. This results in a power range of $2^{\tilde{\Theta}(n)}$.

PROPOSITION 4.2. *When nodes know* $n$, *a power range of* $2^{\tilde{O}(n)}$ *suffices.*

## 4.2 Lower Bound

We show that an exponential-size power range is actually necessary for any leader election protocol running in (at most) two rounds. We prove the following theorem assuming that the nodes are in a uniform metric space, and dividing the available range of power into subranges, each within factor 2. We then calculate the minimum power range needed such that the highest subrange used is used by exactly one node.

THEOREM 4.3. *Any 2-round leader election algorithm in the SINR model running correctly w.h.p. requires a power range* $2^{\Omega(n)}$. *This holds even if the nodes know* $n$, *the number of nodes in the network, and the nodes are located in a uniform metric (where all distances are equal).*

Observe that for the case of known $n$, we obtain an essentially tight bound of $2^{\tilde{\Theta}(n)}$ on the needed power range.

# 5 TRADING TIME FOR POWER

In this section, we explore how much the power range can be reduced by increasing the round complexity. We present a multi-round protocol that requires limited power range and derive a lower bound on the power range required by any $t$-round leader election algorithm, for $t \geq 2$.

## 5.1 Multi-Round Protocol

When a smaller power range is available, we can give a protocol that uses a larger number of rounds.

Our multi-round algorithm simply repeats the 2-round algorithm $t$ times, for a given number $t \geq 1$, but using a slower-growing power function. Namely, we change the ID-selection function to $g_t(k) = 2^k k^{3t+1}$, and the power function to $f_k(ID_v) = P \cdot ID_v^{\gamma(ID_v)^{1/t}}$. After each repetition, each competitor $v$ updates its $leader_v$ value to the largest among those heard so far.

To argue correctness, we first observe that it suffices to succeed in one of the round-pairs.

OBSERVATION 1. *If, in some round-pair, all receivers hear from a particular node* $v$, *and the senders all get informed of* $v$ *as a leader, then the algorithm successfully terminates with* $v$ *as leader.*

We then prove a counterpart of Lemma 3.2.

LEMMA 5.1. *With probability at least* $1/(2n^{1/t})$, *a single node received a higher ID in a given round than all the others.*

Correctness now follows from the above observations.

THEOREM 5.2. *For each* $t \geq 1$, *there is a* $2t$*-round algorithm that elects a leader with probability at least* $1 - 1/n$.

## 5.2 Lower Bound

Using Theorem 4.3 and assuming that the nodes are in a uniform metric space, we prove a lower bound for multi-round protocols.

THEOREM 5.3. *Any* $t$*-round leader election algorithm in the SINR model running correctly w.h.p. requires a power range* $2^{\Omega(\sqrt[t-1]{n})}$, $t \geq 2$. *This holds even if the nodes know* $n$, *the number of nodes in the network, and the nodes are located in a uniform metric (where all distances are equal).*

# 6 CONCLUSIONS AND ACKNOWLEDGMENTS

We have shown that power control can yield the ultimate speedup for leader election in the SINR model. This is thanks to the capture effect, which is the crucial property in which SINR differs from graphs-based models.

It would be exciting to see these techniques applied more widely. Multi-hop settings and more restricted power ranges are natural directions to examine, as well as problems beyond leader election. In general, the value of power control and the capture effect is still not fully understood.

We would like to thank Hsin-Hao Su, Nancy Lynch, Evangelos Markatos and Catherine Chronaki for the helpful comments and discussions.

## REFERENCES

[1] Jeremy T Fineman, Seth Gilbert, Fabian Kuhn, and Calvin Newport. Contention resolution on a fading channel. In *Proceedings of the 2016 ACM Symposium on Principles of Distributed Computing*, pages 155–164. ACM, 2016.

[2] Calvin C. Newport. Radio network lower bounds made easy. *CoRR*, abs/1405.7300, 2014.

# Brief Announcement: Symmetry Breaking in the CONGEST Model: Time- and Message-Efficient Algorithms for Ruling Sets

Shreyas Pai
Department of Computer Science
The University of Iowa
Iowa City, IA 52240-1419
shreyas-pai@uiowa.edu

Gopal Pandurangan*
Department of Computer Science
University of Houston
Houston, TX 77204
gopalpandurangan@gmail.com

Sriram V. Pemmaraju†
Department of Computer Science
The University of Iowa
Iowa City, IA 52240-1419
sriram-pemmaraju@uiowa.edu

Talal Riaz
Department of Computer Science
The University of Iowa
Iowa City, IA 52240-1419
talal-riaz@uiowa.edu

Peter Robinson
Department of Computer Science
Royal Holloway, University of London
peter.robinson@rhul.ac.uk

## ABSTRACT

We study local symmetry breaking problems in the CONGEST model, focusing on ruling set problems, which generalize the fundamental Maximal Independent Set (MIS) problem. Our work is motivated by the following central question: can we break the long-standing $\Theta(\log n)$ time-complexity barrier and the $\Theta(m)$ message-complexity barrier in the CONGEST model for MIS or closely-related symmetry breaking problems?

This paper presents progress towards this question for the distributed ruling set problem in the CONGEST model. A *β-ruling set* is an independent set such that every node in the graph is at most $\beta$ hops from a node in the independent set. We present the following results:

*Time Complexity:* We show that we can break the $O(\log n)$ "barrier" for 2- and 3-ruling sets. We compute 3-ruling sets in $O\left(\frac{\log n}{\log \log n}\right)$ rounds with high probability (whp). More generally we show that 2-ruling sets can be computed in $O\left(\log \Delta \cdot (\log n)^{1/2+\varepsilon} + \frac{\log n}{\log \log n}\right)$ rounds for any $\varepsilon > 0$, which is $o(\log n)$ for a wide range of $\Delta$ values (e.g., $\Delta = 2^{(\log n)^{1/2-\varepsilon}}$). These are the first 2- and 3-ruling set algorithms to improve over the $O(\log n)$-round complexity of Luby's algorithm in the CONGEST model.

*Message Complexity:* We show an $\Omega(n^2)$ lower bound on the message complexity of computing an MIS (i.e., 1-ruling set) which holds also for randomized algorithms and present a contrast to this by showing a randomized algorithm for 2-ruling sets that, whp, uses only $O(n \log^2 n)$ messages and runs in $O(\Delta \log n)$ rounds. This is the first message-efficient algorithm known for ruling sets, which has message complexity nearly linear in $n$ (which is optimal up to a polylogarithmic factor).

Our results are a step toward understanding the time and message complexity of symmetry breaking problems in the CONGEST model.

## CCS CONCEPTS

• **Theory of computation → Distributed algorithms**;

## KEYWORDS

Congest model; Local model; Maximal independent set; Message complexity; Round complexity; Ruling sets; Symmetry breaking

## 1 INTRODUCTION

The *maximal independent set (MIS)* problem is one of the fundamental problems in distributed computing because it is a simple and elegant abstraction of "local symmetry breaking," an issue that arises repeatedly in many distributed computing problems. About 30 years ago Alon, Babai, and Itai [1] and Luby [9] presented a randomized algorithm for MIS, running on $n$-node graphs in $O(\log n)$ rounds with high probability (whp)[1]. Since then the MIS problem has been studied extensively and recently, there has been some exciting progress in designing faster MIS algorithms. For $n$-node graphs with maximum degree $\Delta$, Ghaffari [5] presented an MIS algorithm running in $O(\log \Delta) + 2^{O(\sqrt{\log \log n})}$ rounds, improving over the algorithm of Barenboim et al. [3] that runs in $O(\log^2 \Delta) + 2^{O(\sqrt{\log \log n})}$ rounds. Ghaffari's MIS algorithm is the first MIS algorithm to improve over the round complexity of Luby's algorithm when $\Delta = 2^{o(\log n)}$ and $\Delta$ is bounded below by $\Omega(\log n)$.[2]

While the results of Ghaffari and Barenboim et al. constitute a significant improvement in our understanding of the round complexity of the MIS problem, it should be noted that both of these

*Supported, in part, by NSF grants CCF-1527867, CCF-1540512, and IIS-1633720.
†Suported in part by NSF grant CCF-1318166.


*PODC '17, July 25-27, 2017, Washington, DC, USA*

ACM ISBN 978-1-4503-4992-5/17/07.
https://doi.org/10.1145/3087801.3087865

[1] Throughout, we use "with high probability (whp)" to mean with probability at least $1 - 1/n^c$, for some $c \geqslant 1$.

[2] For $\Delta = o(\log n)$, the deterministic MIS algorithm of Barenboim, Elkin, and Kuhn [2] that runs $O(\Delta + \log^* n)$ rounds is faster than Luby's algorithm.

results are in the LOCAL model. The LOCAL model [11] is a synchronous, message-passing model of distributed computing in which *messages can be arbitrarily large.* Luby's algorithm, on the other hand, is in the CONGEST model [11] and uses small messages, i.e., messages that are $O(\log n)$ bits or $O(1)$ words in size. In fact, to date, *Luby's algorithm is the fastest known MIS algorithm in the* CONGEST *model*; this is the case even when $\Delta$ is between $\Omega(\log n)$ and $2^{o(\log n)}$.

The focus of previous results on the MIS problem has been on the time (round) complexity. *Message complexity,* on the other hand, has been largely ignored in the context of local symmetry breaking problems such as MIS and ruling sets. For a graph with $m$ edges, Luby's algorithm uses $O(m)$ messages in the CONGEST model and until now there has been no MIS or ruling set algorithm that uses $o(m)$ messages. We note that the ruling set algorithm of Goldberg et al. [6] which can be implemented in the CONGEST model [7] also takes at least $\Omega(m)$ messages.

The focus of this paper is symmetry breaking problems in the CONGEST model and the specific question that motivates our work is whether we can go beyond Luby's algorithm in the CONGEST model for MIS or any closely-related symmetry breaking problems such as *ruling sets.* In particular, *can we break the $\Theta(\log n)$ time complexity barrier and the $\Theta(m)$ message complexity barrier, in the* CONGEST *model for MIS and ruling sets?*

We present two sets of results, one set focusing on time (round) complexity and the other on message complexity.

1. *Time complexity:* (cf. Section 2) We first show that 2-ruling sets can be computed in $O\left(\log \Delta \cdot (\log n)^{1/2+\varepsilon} + \frac{\log n}{\log\log n}\right)$ rounds whp in the CONGEST model for $n$-node graphs with maximum degree $\Delta$ and for any $\varepsilon > 0$. This is the first algorithm to improve over Luby's algorithm, by running in $o(\log n)$ rounds in the CONGEST model, for a wide range of values of $\Delta$. Specifically our algorithm runs in $o(\log n)$ rounds for $\Delta$ bounded above by $2^{(\log n)^{1/2-\varepsilon}}$ for any value of $\varepsilon > 0$. Using this 2-ruling set algorithm as a subroutine, we show how to compute 3-ruling sets (for any graph) in $O\left(\frac{\log n}{\log\log n}\right)$ rounds whp in the CONGEST model. We also present a simple 5-ruling set algorithm based on Ghaffari's MIS algorithm that runs in $O(\sqrt{\log n})$ rounds in the CONGEST model.
2. *Message complexity:* (cf. Section 3) We show that $\Omega(n^2)$ is a fundamental lower bound for computing an MIS (i.e., 1-ruling set) by showing that there exists graphs (with $m = \Theta(n^2)$ edges) where any distributed MIS algorithm needs $\Omega(n^2)$ messages. In contrast, we show that 2-ruling sets can be computed using significantly smaller message complexity. In particular, we present a randomized 2-ruling set algorithm that, whp, uses $O(n \log^2 n)$ messages and runs in $O(\Delta \log n)$ rounds. This is the first $o(m)$-message algorithm known for ruling sets, which takes near-linear (in $n$) message complexity. This message bound is tight up to a polylogarithmic factor, since we show that any $O(1)$-ruling set (randomized) algorithm that succeeds with probability $1 - o(1)$ requires $\Omega(n)$ messages in the worst case. We also present a simple 2-ruling set algorithm that uses $O(n^{1.5} \log n)$ messages, but runs faster — in $O(\log n)$ rounds.

Throughout this work, we assume the standard CONGEST model [11]. For complete details of the results briefly announced here, we refer the reader to the full version of the paper [10].

## 2 TIME-EFFICIENT RULING SET ALGORITHMS

The main result of this section is a 2-ruling set algorithm in the CONGEST model that runs in $O\left(\log \Delta \cdot (\log n)^{1/2+\varepsilon} + \frac{\log n}{\log\log n}\right)$ rounds whp, for any constant $\varepsilon > 0$, on $n$-node graphs with maximum degree $\Delta$. An implication of this result is that for graphs with $\Delta = 2^{O((\log n)^{1/2-\varepsilon})}$ for any $\varepsilon > 0$, we can compute a 2-ruling set in $O\left(\frac{\log n}{\log\log n}\right)$ rounds in the CONGEST model. A second implication is that using this 2-ruling set algorithm as a subroutine, we can compute a 3-ruling set for *any* graph in $O\left(\frac{\log n}{\log\log n}\right)$ rounds whp in the CONGEST model. These are the first sublogarithmic-round CONGEST model algorithms for 2-ruling sets (for a wide range of $\Delta$) and 3-ruling sets. Combining some of the techniques used in these algorithms with the first phase of Ghaffari's MIS algorithm [5], we also show that a 5-ruling set can be computed in $O(\sqrt{\log n})$ rounds whp in the CONGEST model.

**The 2-ruling Set Algorithm.** Our 2-ruling set algorithm takes as input an $n$-node graph with maximum degree $\Delta \leqslant 2^{\sqrt{\log n}}$, along with a parameter $\varepsilon > 0$. For $\Delta > 2^{\sqrt{\log n}}$, we simply execute Luby's MIS algorithm to solve the problem. The algorithm consists of $\lceil \log \Delta \rceil$ *scales* and in scale $t$, $1 \leqslant t \leqslant \lceil \log \Delta \rceil$, nodes with degrees at most $\Delta_t := \Delta/2^{t-1}$ are processed. Each scale consists of $\Theta(\log^{1/2+\varepsilon} n)$ *iterations.* In an iteration $i$, in scale $t$, each undecided node independently joins a set $M_{i,t}$ with probability $1/(\Delta_t \cdot \log^\varepsilon n)$. Neighbors of nodes in $M_{i,t}$, that are themselves not in $M_{i,t}$, are set aside and placed in a set $W_{i,t}$. The nodes in $M_{i,t} \cup W_{i,t}$ have decided their fate and we continue to process the undecided nodes. At the end of all the iterations in a scale $t$, any undecided node that still has $\Delta_t/2$ or more undecided neighbors is placed in a "bad" set $B_t$ for that scale, thus effectively deciding the fate of all nodes with degree at least $\Delta_t/2$. We now process the set of scale-$t$ "bad" nodes, $B_t$, by simply running a greedy 2-ruling set algorithm on $B_t$. We also need to process the sets $M_{i,t}$ and for that we rely on a greedy 1-ruling set algorithm (i.e., a greedy MIS algorithm). Note that the $M_{i,t}$'s are all disconnected from each other since the $W_{i,t}$'s act as "buffers" around the $M_{i,t}$'s. Thus after all the scales are completed, we can compute an MIS on all of the $M_{i,t}$'s in parallel. Since each node in $W_{i,t}$ has a neighbor in $M_{i,t}$, this will guarantee that every node in $W_{i,t}$ has an independent set node at most 2 hops away. In the following algorithm we use $deg_S(v)$ to denote the degree of a vertex $v$ in the $G[S]$, the graph induced by $S$.

The overall round complexity of this algorithm critically depends on the greedy 2-ruling set algorithm terminating quickly on each $B_t$ and the greedy 1-ruling set algorithm terminating quickly on each $M_{i,t}$.

THEOREM 2.1. *Algorithm 2-RULINGSET computes a 2-ruling set in the* CONGEST *model in* $O\left(\log \Delta \cdot (\log n)^{1/2+\varepsilon} + \frac{\log n}{\varepsilon \log\log n}\right)$ *rounds, whp.*

**The 3-ruling Set Algorithm** This 2-ruling set algorithm can be used to obtain a 3-ruling set algorithm running in $O\left(\frac{\log n}{\log\log n}\right)$ rounds for *any* graph in the CONGEST model. The 3-ruling set algorithm starts by using the simple, randomized subroutine called

SPARSIFY [4, 8] to construct in, say $O((\log n)^{2/3})$ rounds, a set $S$ such that (i) $\Delta(G[S]) = 2^{O((\log n)^{1/3})}$ whp and (ii) every node is in $S$ or has a neighbor in $S$. Using Algorithm 2-RULING SET on $G[S]$ yields the following corollary.

COROLLARY 2.2. *It is possible to compute a 3-ruling set in* $O\left(\frac{\log n}{\log\log n}\right)$ *rounds whp in the* CONGEST *model.*

If we relax the problem a bit further and settle for a 5-ruling set, we can improve the round complexity even further. In the long version of the paper we present a 5-ruling set algorithm that runs in $O(\sqrt{\log n})$ rounds in the CONGEST model. This algorithm critically uses the first phase of Ghaffari's MIS algorithm [5] and certain independence properties of the nodes that remain undecided after the execution of this phase.

## 3 MESSAGE COMPLEXITY BOUNDS

In this section, we present a randomized distributed algorithm for computing a 2-ruling set in the CONGEST model that takes $O(n \log^2 n)$ messages and $O(\Delta \log n)$ rounds whp, where $n$ is the number of nodes and $\Delta$ is the maximum node degree. The algorithm does not require any global knowledge, including knowledge of $n$ or $\Delta$. We show in Theorem 3.2 that the algorithm is essentially message-optimal (up to a polylog($n$) factor). This is the first message-efficient algorithm known for 2-ruling set, i.e., it takes $o(m)$ messages, where $m$ is the number of edges in the graph.[3]

The algorithm is inspired by Luby's algorithm for MIS [9]; however, there are crucial differences. (Note that Luby's algorithm sends $\Theta(m)$ messages.) Given a ruling set $R$, we classify nodes in $V$ into three categories: CATEGORY-1: nodes that belong to the ruling set $R$; CATEGORY-2: nodes that have a neighbor in $R$; and CATEGORY-3: the rest of the nodes, i.e., nodes that have a neighbor in CATEGORY-2.

At the beginning of the algorithm, each node is UNDECIDED, i.e., its category is not set and upon termination, each node knows its category.

Let us describe one iteration of the algorithm from the perspective of an arbitrary node $v$. Each undecided node $v$ marks itself with probably $1/2d(v)$. If $v$ is marked it samples a set of $\Theta(\log(d(v))$ random neighbours and checks whether any of them belong to CATEGORY-2 — we call this the *checking sampling step.* If so, then $v$ becomes a CATEGORY-3 node and is done (i.e., it will never broadcast again, but will continue to answer checking sampling queries, if any, from its neighbors). Otherwise, $v$ performs the *broadcast step*, i.e., it communicates with all its neighbors and checks if there is a marked neighbor that is of equal or higher degree, and if so, it unmarks itself; else it enters the ruling set and becomes a CATEGORY-1 node. Then node $v$ informs all its neighbors about its CATEGORY-1 status causing them to become CATEGORY-2 nodes (if they are not already) and they are done.

A node that does not hear from any of its neighbors knows that it is not a neighbor of any CATEGORY-1 node. Note that CATEGORY-2 and CATEGORY-3 nodes do not initiate messages, which is important for keeping the message complexity low. Another main idea in reducing messages is the random sampling check of a few neighbors to see whether any of them are CATEGORY-2. Although some nodes might send $O(d(v))$ messages, we show that most nodes send (and receive) only $O(\log n)$ messages in an amortized sense. Nodes that remain undecided at the end of one iteration continue to the next iteration. It is easy to implement each iteration in a constant number of rounds.

THEOREM 3.1. *The algorithm* `2-rulingset-msg` *computes a 2-ruling set using* $O(n \log^2 n)$ *messages and terminates in* $O(\Delta \log n)$ *rounds with high probability.*

In the next theorem we point out that the bound of Theorem 3.1 is tight up to logarithmic factors.

THEOREM 3.2. *Any* $O(1)$*-ruling set algorithm that succeeds with probability* $1 - o(1)$ *sends* $\Omega(n)$ *messages in the worst case. This is true even if nodes have prior knowledge of the network size* $n$.

Finally, we show a clear separation between the message complexity of computing an $t$-ruling set ($t > 1$) and a maximal independent set (i.e., 1-ruling set) by proving an unconditional $\Omega(n^2)$ lower bound for the latter.

THEOREM 3.3. *Any maximal independent set algorithm that succeeds with probability* $1 - \epsilon$ *on connected networks, where* $0 \leqslant \epsilon < \frac{1}{2}$ *is a constant, must send* $\Omega(n^2)$ *messages in the worst case. This is true even if nodes have prior knowledge of the network size* $n$.

[3] In the full paper [10] we present a simpler algorithm for 2-ruling set that, whp, takes $O(n^{1.5} \log n)$ messages and runs in $O(\log n)$ rounds.

## REFERENCES

[1] Noga Alon, László Babai, and Alon Itai. 1986. A Fast and Simple Randomized Parallel Algorithm for the Maximal Independent Set Problem. *J. Algorithms* 7, 4 (1986), 567–583.
[2] Leonid Barenboim, Michael Elkin, and Fabian Kuhn. 2014. Distributed ($\Delta$ + 1)-Coloring in Linear (in $\Delta$) Time. *SIAM J. Comput.* 43, 1 (2014), 72–95.
[3] Leonid Barenboim, Michael Elkin, Seth Pettie, and Johannes Schneider. 2016. The Locality of Distributed Symmetry Breaking. *J. ACM* 63, 3, Article 20 (June 2016), 45 pages.
[4] Tushar Bisht, Kishore Kothapalli, and Sriram Pemmaraju. 2014. Brief Announcement: Super-fast T-ruling Sets. In *Proceedings of the 2014 ACM Symposium on Principles of Distributed Computing (PODC '14)*. ACM, New York, NY, USA, 379–381.
[5] Mohsen Ghaffari. 2016. An Improved Distributed Algorithm for Maximal Independent Set. In *Proceedings of the Twenty-Seventh Annual ACM-SIAM Symposium on Discrete Algorithms, SODA 2016, Arlington, VA, USA, January 10-12, 2016.* 270–277.
[6] A. Goldberg, S. Plotkin, and G. Shannon. 1989. Parallel Symmetry breaking in sparse graphs. *SIAM J. Discrete Math.* 1 (1989), 434–446.
[7] Monika Henzinger, Sebastian Krinninger, and Danupon Nanongkai. 2016. A deterministic almost-tight distributed algorithm for approximating single-source shortest paths. In *Proceedings of the 48th Annual ACM SIGACT Symposium on Theory of Computing, STOC 2016, Cambridge, MA, USA, June 18-21, 2016.* 489–498.
[8] Kishore Kothapalli and Sriram V. Pemmaraju. 2012. Super-Fast 3-Ruling Sets. In *FSTTCS*. 136–147.
[9] M. Luby. 1986. A Simple Parallel Algorithm for the Maximal Independent Set. *SIAM J. Comput.* 15 (1986), 1036–1053.
[10] Shreyas Pai, Gopal Pandurangan, Sriram V. Pemmaraju, Talal Riaz, and Peter Robinson. 2017. Symmetry Breaking in the Congest Model: Time- and Message-Efficient Algorithms for Ruling Sets. *ArXiv e-prints* (May 2017). arXiv:1705.07861
[11] David Peleg. 2000. *Distributed computing: a locality-sensitive approach.* Society for Industrial and Applied Mathematics.

# Recoverable Mutual Exclusion in Sub-logarithmic Time

Wojciech Golab*
Department of Electrical and Computer Engineering
University of Waterloo, Canada
wgolab@uwaterloo.ca

Danny Hendler†
Department of Computer Science
Ben-Gurion University, Israel
hendlerd@cs.bgu.ac.il

## ABSTRACT

Recoverable mutual exclusion (RME) is a variation on the classic mutual exclusion (ME) problem that allows processes to crash and recover. The time complexity of RME algorithms is quantified in the same way as for ME, namely by counting remote memory references – expensive memory operations that traverse the processor-to-memory interconnect. Prior work on the RME problem established an upper bound of $O(\log N)$ RMRs in an asynchronous shared memory model with $N$ processes that communicate using atomic read and write operations, prompting the question whether sub-logarithmic RMR complexity is attainable using common read-modify-write primitives. We answer this question positively in the cache-coherent model by presenting an RME algorithm that incurs $O(\log N/\log\log N)$ RMRs and uses read, write, Fetch-And-Store, and Compare-And-Swap instructions. We also present an $O(1)$ RMRs algorithm that relies on double-word Compare-And-Swap and a double-word variation of Fetch-And-Store. Both algorithms are inspired by Mellor-Crummey and Scott's queue lock.

## CCS CONCEPTS

• **Theory of computation** → **Shared memory algorithms**; • **Software and its engineering** → *Mutual exclusion*; • **Computer systems organization** → Reliability;

## KEYWORDS

Mutual exclusion; recovery; fault tolerance; concurrency; shared memory; multi-core algorithms; non-volatile main memory; persistent data structures.

## 1 INTRODUCTION

The traditional coupling of volatile main memory with non-volatile secondary storage in computer architectures has led to a separation of program state into operational data stored using in-memory data structures, and recovery data stored using sequential on-disk structures such as transaction logs. In the event of a system-wide failure, such as a power outage, the in-memory data structures are lost and must be reconstructed entirely from the recovery data, making the software system temporarily unavailable. As a result, the design of in-memory data structures emphasizes disposable constructs optimized for parallelism, in contrast to the structures that hold recovery data, which cannot be discarded upon a failure and which benefit less from parallelism since their performance is limited by the secondary storage.

Recent developments in non-volatile main memory (NVRAM) media foreshadow the eventual convergence of primary and secondary storage into a single layer in the memory hierarchy that combines the performance benefits of conventional main memory with the durability of secondary storage. Traditional log-based recovery techniques can be applied correctly in such systems but fail to take full advantage of the parallelism enabled by allowing processing cores to access recovery data directly using memory operations rather than slow block transfers from secondary storage. As a result, harnessing the performance benefits of NVRAM-based platforms requires a careful rethinking of recovery mechanisms.

This paper focuses specifically on recoverable lock-based data structures, in which synchronization is achieved using mutual exclusion [10]. The abstract problem of implementing locks that tolerate crash-recovery failures was formalized recently by Golab and Ramaraju as Recoverable Mutual Exclusion (RME) [16]. In short, RME is a generalization of the standard mutual exclusion problem (ME) whereby a process that crashes while accessing (i.e., acquiring, releasing, or holding) a lock is resurrected eventually and allowed to execute recovery actions. This abstraction captures both individual process failures and system-wide failures, such as due to power outages. In contrast, the ME problem assumes that a process never fails while accessing a lock, as otherwise a conventional lock becomes vulnerable to starvation.

RME is, informally speaking, a harder problem than conventional ME because the solution must deal simultaneously with both concurrency and failures. However, no formal proof of this point has been published, and indeed little is known about the RME problem as compared to ME, which has been studied thoroughly [2, 30]. Recent work on ME established tight bounds on time complexity, which in this context is quantified by counting *remote memory references* (RMRs) – expensive memory operations that cause traffic on the interconnect joining processors with memory. For the class of algorithms that use only reads, writes and comparison primitives (e.g., CAS), the tight bound for acquiring and releasing an $N$-process mutex lock once is $\Theta(\log N)$ RMRs in the worst case [4, 32]. The same bound applies for RME [16]. For the class of algorithms that use additional primitives such as Fetch-And-Store, ME is solvable

*Wojciech Golab is supported in part by the Natural Sciences and Engineering Research Council (NSERC) of Canada, Discovery Grants Program, and by a Google Faculty Research Award.
†Danny Hendler is supported in part by the Israel Science Foundation (grant 1749/14).


*PODC '17, July 25-27, 2017, Washington, DC, USA*

ACM ISBN 978-1-4503-4992-5/17/07...$15.00
http://dx.doi.org/10.1145/3087801.3087819

in only $O(1)$ RMRs but initial attempts to establish the same upper bound for RME were unsuccessful, with all known solutions incurring $\Omega(\log N)$ RMRs in the worst case [16]. This points to the difficulty of using read-modify-write primitives in a crash recovery model, where failures can annihilate the response of a memory operation (e.g., the value fetched by a Fetch-And-Store) before it can be written to shared memory. Thus, a recovering process is unable to determine this response directly using its private state, or even decide whether the read-modify-write primitive was executed at all.

The technical contribution of this paper is a pair of upper bounds on the RMR complexity of the RME problem that improve upon prior results. First, we prove an $O(1)$ bound in both the cache-coherent and distributed shared memory models using double-word Compare-And-Swap and a double-word variant of Fetch-And-Store (Section 3). This matches the RMR complexity of solving ME using reads, writes, and common single-word read-modify-primitives. Second, we establish an $O(\log N/\log\log N)$ bound in the cache-coherent model using common single-word primitives, and thus prove a time complexity separation versus the class of algorithms that use only single-word reads, writes and comparison-primitives (Sections 4–5). These are the first sub-logarithmic upper bounds on worst-case RMR complexity for the RME problem, ignoring trivial solutions that assume queue operations are supported directly in hardware.

## 2 MODEL

Our model follows [16]. We consider $N$ asynchronous unreliable processes, labeled $p_1, p_2, \ldots, p_N$, that communicate by accessing variables in shared memory. These processes compete for an exclusive lock (mutex), which protects a shared resource, by following the execution path illustrated in Figure 1. In the *non-critical section* (NCS), processes do not access the lock or the shared resource. In the *recovery protocol*, denoted **Recover**, a process cleans up the internal structure of the lock, if needed, following a crash failure. In the *entry protocol*, denoted **Enter**, a process attempts to acquire the lock and waits for the lock to become available. The entry protocol is sometimes modeled as a bounded section of code called the *doorway*, which determines the order in which processes access the shared resource, followed by the *waiting room*, where processes wait for their turn. Access to the shared resource is confined to the *critical section* (CS). In the *exit protocol*, denoted **Exit**, a process releases the lock and makes the shared resource available to others.

**loop forever**
- Non-Critical Section (NCS)
- **Recover**
- **Enter** { Doorway / Waiting Room }
- Critical Section (CS)
- **Exit**

**Figure 1: Execution path of a process participating in RME.**

Correctness properties for mutex algorithms are expressed in reference to *histories* that record the actions of processes as they execute the pseudo-code in Figure 1. Formally, a history $H$ is a sequence of *steps* that come in two varieties: *ordinary steps* and *crash steps*. An ordinary step is a shared memory operation combined with bounded local computation such as arithmetic operations, accessing one or more private variables,[1] and advancing the program counter. A crash step denotes a process failure that resets the private variables of a process to their initial values, including the program counter, which is reset to the non-critical section (top of the loop in Figure 1). The next step a process takes after a crash step is either another crash step, or the first step of **Recover**. A process is said to *recover* following a crash step by executing the first step of **Recover**. A *passage* is a sequence of steps taken by a process from when it begins **Recover** to when it completes **Exit**, or crashes, whichever occurs first. A process is *in cleanup* if it is executing **Recover** following a passage that ended with a crash step. A passage is called *failure-free* if it does not end with a crash step. A *super-passage* is a maximal non-empty sequence of consecutive passages executed by the same process where (only) the last passage in the sequence is failure-free.

Process failures may influence the time complexity of a passage through a recoverable mutex algorithm. We formalize the notion of potential influence by reasoning precisely about interleaving among passages. We say that two passages *interfere* if their super-passages are concurrent, meaning that neither super-passage ends before the other begins. We call a passage *cleanup-concurrent* if it begins in cleanup, or if the passage interferes with some passage that begins in cleanup.

The set of histories generated by a mutex algorithm is prefix-closed. Given a history $H$ and a process $p_i$, we say that $p_i$ is *active in* $H$ if it takes at least one step in $H$. A history $H$ is *fair* if it is finite, or if it is infinite and every active process either executes infinitely many steps or stops taking steps after completing a failure-free passage. We assume that the critical section is bounded.

The fundamental correctness properties of RME algorithms are defined as follows:

**Mutual Exclusion (ME):** For any finite history $H$, at most one process is in the CS at the end of $H$.

**Starvation Freedom (SF):** For any infinite fair history $H$, if a process $p_i$ leaves the NCS in some step of $H$ then eventually $p_i$ itself enters the CS, or else there are infinitely many crash steps in $H$.

**Terminating Exit (TE):** For any infinite fair history $H$, if a process $p_i$ begins executing the exit protocol then it eventually returns to the NCS or crashes.

**Bounded Recovery (BR):** For any infinite history $H$, any execution of **Recover** by a process $p_i$ completes in a bounded number of $p_i$'s steps unless $p_i$'s passage is cleanup-concurrent.

**Critical Section Re-entry (CSR):** For any history $H$ and for any process $p_i$, if $p_i$ crashes inside the CS then no other process may enter the CS before $p_i$ re-enters the CS after its own crash failure.

The time complexity of RME algorithms is defined as the number of *remote memory references* (RMRs) executed by a process per passage. An RMR is any memory operation that traverses the

[1] In this paper a "private" variable is accessed by only one process and stored in a volatile CPU register. Variables with local (e.g., function) scope are private.

processor-to-memory interconnect, and its precise definition depends on the shared memory hardware architecture. In this paper we consider both the cache-coherent (CC) and distributed shared memory (DSM) models [2]. In the CC model, we (conservatively) count each shared memory operation as an RMR with the exception of an *in-cache* read, which occurs when a process $p_i$ reads a variable $v$ that it has already read in an earlier step, following which step no process has accessed $v$ except by a read operation. In the DSM model, each shared variable is local to exactly one process, which is determined statically at initialization. A mutex algorithm is called *local spin* if its worst-case RMR complexity per passage is bounded.

The use of volatile caches in the CC model complicates access to non-volatile main memory. Shared memory operations must be combined with explicit cache line flushes or write-backs, for example using Intel's clflush or clwb instructions, to ensure that their effects are persistent. The interleaving of such instructions with shared memory operations is outside the scope of this paper.

## 3 AN $O(1)$ RMRS ALGORITHM

The RME problem can be solved easily in $O(1)$ RMRs per passage in the CC and DSM models if sufficiently powerful primitives are available. In particular, if a queue of process IDs can be implemented with fundamental operations incurring $O(1)$ RMRs then a queue-based lock can be constructed as described in [14]. However, such a queue is itself difficult to implement, and hardware transactional memory [20] does not solve the problem fully since memory transactions are not guaranteed to complete in a bounded number of RMRs under contention. The RME algorithm presented in this section relies instead on double-word atomic read-modify-write instructions. The design is inspired by Mellor-Crummey and Scott's queue lock (MCS lock) [27], whose pseudo-code is included for completeness in Figure 2. [2]

The MCS lock maintains a linked list of *QNode* structures that determines the order of entry into the CS. Each QNode contains a link *next* to the successor, as well as a spin variable *locked* that is used to transfer ownership of the CS from a predecessor to a successor. The QNode of process $p_i$ is denoted by $q_i$. In total, two memory operations are required to append a QNode in the entry protocol: (a) The tail of the list is updated using an atomic Fetch-And-Store (FAS) operation at line 2, which returns a reference to the predecessor's QNode or $\perp$ if the list was empty. This reference is stored in a private variable *prev*. (b) The predecessor's *next* pointer is updated, if required, at line 5.

The exit protocol similarly uses multiple memory operations to delete a QNode from the linked list: (c) If no successor is identified by reading $q_i.next$ at line 7, then a Compare-And-Swap (CAS) operation is executed at line 8 to swing the tail pointer $T$ from the caller's QNode back to $\perp$. A successful CAS removes the QNode explicitly from the linked list. (d) A failed CAS implies the arrival of a successor whose QNode is determined by busy-waiting on the predecessor's *next* pointer at line 10. (e) Finally, the successor is notified by resetting its *locked* variable at line 11, which marks the successor's QNode as the new head node of the linked list while preserving the *next* pointer from the (former) predecessor's QNode.

[2] The notation & in the pseudo-code means "address of", as in C/C++.

**Define** QNode: struct { *next*: **ref to** QNode, *locked*: **Boolean** }

**Shared variables:**

- $T$: **ref to** QNode, **init** $\perp$
- $q_i$: **ref to** QNode structure **init** $\langle \perp, \textbf{false} \rangle$ and local to process $p_i$ in DSM model

**Private variables:**

- *prev*: **ref to** QNode, uninitialized

```
Procedure Enter ( )
1  qi.next := ⊥
   // insert QNode into linked list
2  prev := FAS(&T, qi)
   // check for predecessor
3  if prev ≠ ⊥ then
       // link with predecessor
4      qi.locked := true
5      prev.next := qi
       // wait for predecessor to release lock
6      await qi.locked ≠ true
```

```
Procedure Exit ( )
   // check for successor
7  if qi.next = ⊥ then
       // no known successor, try to unlink from T
8      if CAS(&T, qi, ⊥) = true then
           // no successor, lock idle
9          return
       // wait for successor to link with pi
10     await qi.next ≠ ⊥
   // transfer lock ownership to successor
11 qi.next.locked := false
```

**Figure 2: Mellor-Crummey and Scott's queue lock for process $p_i$.**

Figure 3 illustrates a possible configuration of the QNode structures in an execution of the MCS algorithm where processes arrive in the following order: $p_1, p_2, p_3, p_4$. Process $p_1$ has already returned to the NCS with $q_1.locked$ = **false**, and $q_1.next = q_2$ implies that $p_1$ passed the CS to $p_2$ at line 11 rather than by unlinking itself at line 8. In other words, $p_2$ appended its QNode at line 2 before $p_1$ executed the CAS instruction in **Exit**. Accordingly, process $p_2$ is currently in the CS with $q_2.locked$ = **false** and $prev = q_1$. Process $p_3$ is the successor of $p_2$ with $prev = q_2$. Process $p_4$ is the successor of $p_3$, and has not yet linked with $p_3$ at line 5 of **Enter**, which is why $q_3.next = \perp$. Similarly, $q_4.next = \perp$ since $p_4$ does not yet have a successor. The *prev* pointers are stored in private variables and do not appear in the QNode structures.

The non-atomic collection of atomic memory operations used in the entrance and exit protocols makes it difficult to recover the MCS lock following a crash failure as a process $p_i$ cannot determine

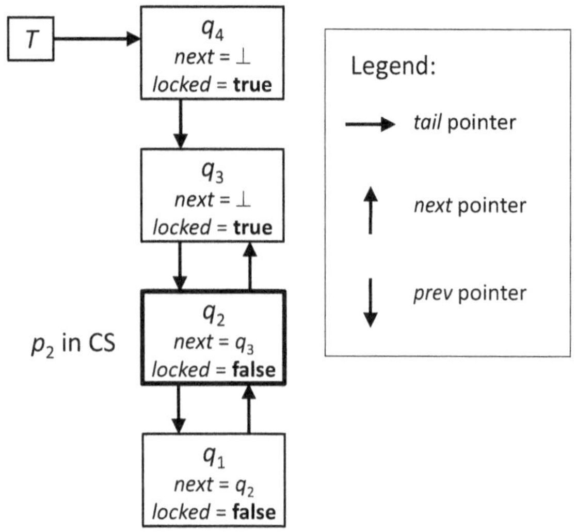


**Figure 3: Example configuration of QNode structures in an execution of the MCS algorithm for processes $p_1, p_2, p_3, p_4$.**

only from its private state whether a failure occurred immediately before the FAS at line 2, in which case $p_i$ must attempt to append its QNode again using FAS, versus immediately after, in which case the QNode is already in the linked list and $p_i$ must not append it again. The exit protocol suffers from a similar problem around the CAS instruction at line 8, whose response is needed to determine whether $p_i$'s QNode is still in the linked list. A scan of the linked list from the tail to find $p_i$'s QNode is not helpful since it requires following the predecessor pointers, which are never written to main memory. For example, in Figure 3 the QNodes $q_3$ and $q_4$ become disconnected following a failure of process $p_4$, making a scan of the linked list from the tail infeasible. Even if a *prev* field was added to the QNode as a shared variable, a failure between the FAS instruction and the write operation on this new field could lead to breaks in the linked list, making a complete traversal infeasible even in the absence of concurrent updates to the list.

Aside from the problematic FAS instruction, the MCS algorithm contains several write operations that cannot be repeated safely after a failure: one in the entry protocol at line 5, where predecessor's *next* pointer is written, and the other in the exit protocol at line 11, where the successor's *locked* variable is set to **false** after the successor's QNode is determined at line 10. Failures around such write operations also complicate recovery, although they are arguably easier to deal with compared to the FAS instruction since there is no danger of a lost return value.

We derive a recoverable mutex from MCS by leveraging double-word atomic read-modify-write instructions, whose greater power makes it possible to determine their outcome (or lack thereof) following a crash failure. First, the FAS in the entry protocol is replaced with a Fetch-And-Store-And-Store (FASAS). FASAS takes two memory locations, $M1$ and $M2$, as arguments, as well as a value $V$, and has the following effect: it copies the value at $M1$ to $M2$, and then stores $V$ at $M1$. Thus, FASAS is the atomic composition of FAS and a write of the response to memory. Second, the CAS in the exit

**Define** QNode: struct { *prev*: **ref to** QNode, *next*: **ref to** QNode, *linked*: **Boolean** }

**Shared variables:**

- $T$: **ref to** QNode, **init** $\bot$
- $q_i$: **ref to** QNode structure of process $p_i$ **init** $\langle q_i, \bot, \textbf{false}\rangle$ and local to process $p_i$ in DSM model

**Private variables:**

- *prev*: **ref to** QNode or $\bot$, uninitialized

```
Procedure Recover ( )
  // empty, recovery actions integrated into Enter
```

```
Procedure Enter ( )
  prev := qi.prev
  // check whether previous passage was failure-free
  if prev = qi then
  |   qi.next := ⊥
  |   qi.linked := false
  |   // insert QNode into linked list
  |   FASAS(&T, &(qi.prev), qi)
  |   prev := qi.prev
  // check for predecessor
  if prev ≠ ⊥ then
  |   // link with predecessor
  |   DCAS(&(prev.next), &(qi.linked), ⊥, false, qi, true)
  |   // wait for predecessor to release lock
  |   await qi.prev = ⊥
```

```
Procedure Exit ( )
  // try to unlink from T
  if DCAS(&T, &(qi.prev), qi, ⊥, ⊥, qi) = false then
  |   // wait for successor to link with pi
  |   await qi.next ≠ ⊥
  |   // transfer lock ownership to successor
  |   FASAS(&(qi.next.prev), &(qi.prev), ⊥)
```

**Figure 4: $O(1)$-RMRs recoverable mutex for process $p_i$.**

protocol is replaced by a double-word Compare-And-Swap (DCAS), which swaps values into two memory locations provided that their prior values both match the comparison arguments.[3] These instructions, when used correctly, resolve the technicalities surrounding recovery around line 2 or line 8 of MCS. They can also replace the writes at line 5 and line 11 to ensure that the *next* and *locked* fields are updated at most once irrespective of failures.

Our MCS-based RME algorithm is presented in Figure 4. Like MCS, our recoverable lock incurs $O(1)$ RMRs per passage in the worst case in both the CC and DSM models, and is *context-free*, meaning that neither the number of processes nor their identities

[3]In the cache-coherent model, the FASAS and DCAS instructions must write the updated values of both memory locations atomically to non-volatile memory.

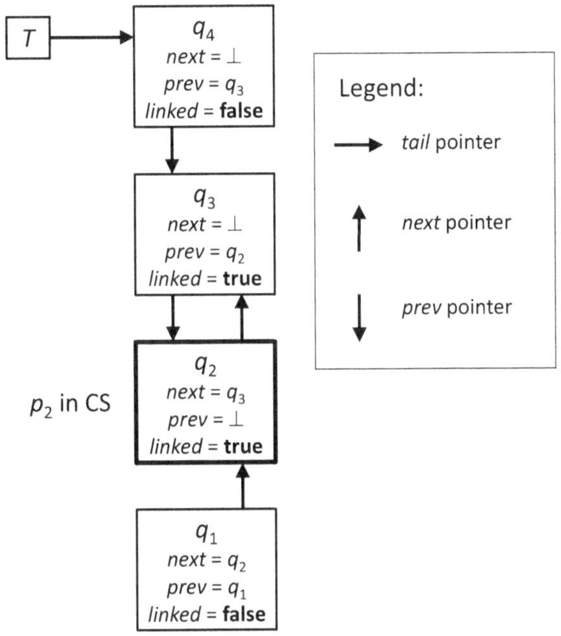


**Figure 5: Example configuration of QNode structures in an execution of the recoverable mutex for processes** $p_1, p_2, p_3, p_4$.

need to be known in advance. The doorway comprises the bounded code at lines 12–16 of the entry protocol, and the recovery protocol is empty since all recovery actions are folded into the entry and exit protocols. In the absence of failures, process $p_i$ reads the initial value $q_i$ from $q_i.prev$ at line 12 and proceeds to reinitialize $q_i$ at lines 14–15. The FASAS at line 16 atomically swings the tail pointer $T$ to $p_i$'s QNode $q_i$ and saves the previous value to $q_i.prev$, which establishes a link from $q_i$ to the predecessor's QNode (if any). Next, $p_i$ inspects $q_i.prev$ at line 17 to determine whether it is the head of the queue. A value of ⊥ indicates that $q_i$ is the head element, in which case $p_i$ proceeds directly to the CS. Any other value indicates that $q_i$ is not the head and that $p_i$ must create a link from the predecessor's QNode to $q_i$ and then wait. To create such a link, $p_i$ updates the predecessor's *next* field at line 19 using DCAS, which also sets $q_i.linked$ = **true**. At line 20, $p_i$ waits for the predecessor to release the CS by overwriting $q_i.prev$ with ⊥. The exit protocol then attempts to atomically swing the tail pointer from $q_i$ back to ⊥, and reset $q_i.prev$ back to $q_i$ using a DCAS at line 21. If the DCAS is unsuccessful, $p_i$ waits at line 22 for the successor to write $q_i.next$, then executes FASAS at line 23, resetting the successor's *prev* pointer to ⊥ and its own *prev* pointer to $q_i$. Thus, the successor is unblocked atomically with the deletion of $q_i$ from the linked list.

Figure 5 illustrates a possible configuration of the QNode structures in an execution of the recoverable mutex where processes arrive in the following order: $p_1, p_2, p_3, p_4$. Process $p_1$ has already returned to the NCS with $q_1.prev = q_1$, and $q_1.next = q_2$ implies that $p_1$ passed the CS to $p_2$ at line 23 rather than by unlinking itself at line 21. In other words, $p_2$ appended itself at line 16 before $p_1$ executed the DCAS instruction in **Exit**. Accordingly, process $p_2$ is currently in the CS with $q_2.prev$ = ⊥. Process $p_3$ is the successor of $p_2$ with $q_3.prev = q_2$ and $q_3.linked$ = **true**, reflecting the fact that $q_2.next = q_3$. Process $p_4$ has not yet linked with $p_3$ at line 19 of **Enter**, which is why $q_3.next$ = ⊥ and $q_4.linked$ = **false**. Similarly, $q_4.next$ = ⊥ since $p_4$ does not yet have a successor. The *prev* pointers are stored in the QNode structures alongside the *next* pointers to facilitate recovery.

The execution path on recovery from a crash failure is based on the following invariant: $q_i.prev$ points to $q_i$ if $q_i$ is not in the linked list, points to the predecessor's QNode if $q_i$ is in the linked list but not the head element, and equals ⊥ if $q_i$ is the head node. Thus, the doorway is executed only if $q_i.prev = q_i$ (line 13), and the remainder of the entry protocol is executed only if $q_i.prev \neq \perp$ (line 18). Recovery from a failure in the critical section with $q_i.prev = \perp$ bypasses the entry protocol entirely after line 12, and so $p_i$ is able to re-enter the CS in a bounded number of its own steps. The use of DCAS at line 19 ensures that the *next* pointer is written at most once per super-passage.

In the context of Figure 5, failures are dealt with as follows. If $p_1$ fails and then takes another step then it begins a new passage on recovery. If $p_2$ fails then it bypasses **Enter** via lines 13 and 18 because $q_2.prev$ = ⊥, and so $p_2$ re-enters the CS. If $p_3$ fails then it repeats the DCAS instruction at line 19 of **Enter** assuming that $q_3.prev = q_2$ continues to hold, and this DCAS fails because $q_3.linked$ = **true**, forcing $p_3$ to wait for the CS at line 20. Alternatively, if $p_2$ leaves the CS concurrently with $p_3$'s recovery then it is possible that $p_3$ executes **Enter** with $q_3.prev$ = ⊥ as a result of $p_2$ executing line 23, in which case $p_3$ proceeds to the CS. If $p_4$ fails then it proceeds to the DCAS instruction at line 19 of **Enter** assuming that $q_4.prev = q_3$ continues to hold, and this DCAS succeeds because $q_3.next$ = ⊥ and $q_4.linked$ = **false**. Alternatively, if $p_3$ enters and then leaves the CS concurrently with $p_4$'s recovery then it is possible that $p_4$ executes **Enter** with $q_4.prev$ = ⊥, in which case $p_4$ proceeds to the CS.

THEOREM 3.1. *The algorithm satisfies ME, SF, BR, CSR, and TE. Furthermore, its worst-case RMR complexity per passage is* $O(1)$ *in the CC and DSM models.*

The ME and SF properties were verified successfully for $N = 3$ using a PlusCal [24] translation of the algorithm and the TLC model checker [25].

## 4 A $K$-PORT EXTENDED MCS LOCK

In this section, we present a *k-port extended MCS lock object* for the cache-coherent (CC) model. As the name implies, this is an extension of the MCS lock, enabling concurrent access by up to $k$ processes out of the $N$ processes in the system. Implementation correctness relies on the *sequential port access* assumption: there are no two concurrent passages on any port. The salient feature of the extended MCS lock is that a process incurs $O(1)$ RMRs per passage unless recovering from a failure that occurred outside the non-critical section (NCS) and critical section (CS), and $O(k)$ RMRs in the worst case. This property is necessary for the algorithm to function correctly as a building block of our $O(\log N/\log\log N)$ RMRs recoverable mutex, which is presented later on in Section 5. In comparison, Golab and Ramaraju's transformation [16, Section 4.2] applied to MCS achieves the same worst-case complexity but guarantees $O(1)$ RMRs only when a passage is not *cleanup-concurrent*, which is insufficient for our purposes as it allows the failure of one process to inflate the RMR complexity for another process.

The extended MCS lock uses a modified QNode structure (see Figure 6). The fields *locked* and *next* are defined as in MCS (see Section 3). The field *prev* identifies the predecessor, and may hold a special value FAIL when the owner of the QNode is recovering from a failure. The field *nextStep* is new, and holds a pseudo-code line number that identifies the next step to be performed by the process in the entry or exit protocol. It may also assume a special value *inCS*, signifying that the process finished the **Enter** procedure and has not begun executing **Exit**. The *nextStep* field is updated in these parts of the pseudo-code in order to announce the intention of taking the step. Updates of this field are not shown in the pseudo-code for presentation simplicity, and occur in every execution of **Enter** and **Exit**, except when a portion of **Exit** is executed at line 54 or line 58 of **Recover**. Nevertheless, upon recovery, there remains uncertainly regarding whether the fault occurred before or after the indicated step. The other new field is *fin*, which specifies whether the passage that used this QNode record completed the exit protocol successfully (see line 39). We assume that a QNode is never reused following the completion of a failure-free passage, which makes it possible to read *fin* = **true** in a QNode whose process has returned to the NCS or even started a new passage. In addition to QNode structures, the extended MCS lock uses a *tail* variable analogous to $T$ in MCS (Figure 2), which points to the QNode of the last process in the waiting queue, or **null** if the queue is empty. Finally, an auxiliary recoverable lock, denoted *rLock*, is used to protect the most sensitive part of the recovery protocol (lines 74–96 in Figure 8). This lock is implemented using a $k$-process instance of the $O(\log N)$ RMRs RME algorithm by Golab and Ramaraju [16, Section 3.2].

The **Enter** procedure (lines 24–31 in Figure 6) receives two parameters: a port number *pNum* and a reference *myNode* to a QNode record, which is allocated newly for each passage except in some recovery situations. The executing process $p$ first initializes the *myNode* record and then stores a reference to it in the *pNum*'th entry of the *nodes* array (lines 24–25). At line 26, $p$ links itself to the queue by swapping *myNode* into *tail*. It then stores *tail*'s previous value to *myNode.prev* at line 27. Process $p$ then checks at line 28 whether or not it has a predecessor. If not, it proceeds immediately to the CS. Otherwise, it prepares for waiting (line 29), links to its predecessor by writing a reference to *myNode* in the *next* field of its predecessor record (line 30), and then waits to be signalled (line 31). Upon being signalled, $p$ proceeds to the CS.

The **Exit** procedure (lines 32–39) receives the port number as its single parameter and uses it to extract the port's QNode record from the *nodes* array (line 32). Then, process $p$ checks whether the *next* field of its record was set by a successor process (line 33). If unset, $p$ attempts to CAS *tail* back to **null** in line 34, which will succeed only if $p$ has no successor. If the CAS is successful, $p$ returns to the NCS after setting the *fin* flag of *myNode* (line 39), which signifies that the passage that used this record has terminated. If the CAS fails, then there is a successor, so $p$ awaits for it to link to *myNode* (line 35) and, once it does, signals it (line 36) and returns to the NCS.

Finally, if the *next* field is found to have been set at line 33, $p$ signals its successor at line 38 and returns to the NCS.

The **Recover** procedure (lines 40–65) receives the port number as its single parameter. If this is the first passage on this port or the previous passage was completed (line 41), then there is no need for recovery. In this case, the procedure simply returns and the process continues to execute the entry protocol (line 42). Otherwise, recovery proceeds according to the step a process was about to perform upon failure. If the failure occurred at a point when the FAS at line 26 may have been performed but the *prev* field of the port's record was not updated (line 43), then $p$ checks *prev* and, if it observes a $\perp$ value, determines whether a reference to its QNode from the last passage is visible to anyone by calling the helper function **IsLinkedTo** (line 44), which we describe shortly. If the QNode is not visible, then $p$ repeats the entry protocol using the same QNode (line 45). Otherwise, if *prev* does not point to a QNode (line 46) then $p$ announces that it is about to repair the queue structure by writing *prev* = FAIL (line 47) and then performs repairs by calling helper procedure **RecoverSwap** (line 48), which we describe shortly. Finally, if *prev* does point to a QNode then there is no need to repair the queue, but a failure may have occurred inside **RecoverSwap** while $p$ was holding *rLock*. In this case $p$ makes one passage through *rLock* to recover it (line 50). Execution then continues in the middle of the entry protocol (line 51).

If the failure occurred when the process was about to perform the CAS of line 34 (line 52), then the following cases exist: 1) if *tail* still stores a reference to the *myNode* record (line 53), then the failure occurred *before* the CAS executed and so recovery is done by executing lines 34–39 of **Exit** (line 54), which repeats the CAS; 2) If *tail* equals **null**, then it must be that the CAS was performed successfully, and so execution simply continues with the entry protocol (lines 55–56); 3) otherwise, other processes linked to the queue either before or after the failure and the only way to tell how to proceed is to check whether *myNode* has a successor by calling the **IsLinkedTo** function (line 57). If *myNode* has a successor, then recovery is done by executing lines 35–39 of the **Exit** procedure (line 58), otherwise it must be that the CAS was successfully executed and the process proceeds to the entry section (line 59). If the failure occurred in the **Exit** procedure not when about to perform the CAS of line 34 (line 62), then recovery is done by completing the execution of the **Exit** procedure and then continuing to the **Enter** procedure (line 63). If a failure other than a swap failure occurred in the **Enter** procedure, recovery is done by resuming **Enter** starting from *nextStep* (line 65).

The **IsLinkedTo** function, presented in Figure 7 (lines 66–72), checks whether the QNode record associated with port *pNum* is referenced. It does so by reading the current value of *tail* (line 67) and the current values of the records used by all other ports (lines 68–69). For any such record, the function waits for the *prev* field to be updated to a non-$\perp$ value (line 71). If either *tail* or any of these records holds a reference to *pNum*'s record, **IsLinkedTo** returns **true**, otherwise it returns **false**.

Procedure **RecoverSwap**, presented in Figure 8 (lines 73–96), is invoked by processes that incur *swap failures*, that is, they fail just before or after they perform the FAS of line 26. It is challenging to recover from such failures, because failing processes must be able

**Define** QNode: struct { *locked*: **Boolean**, *prev,next*: **ref to** QNode, *nextStep*: **int**, fin: **Boolean** }

**Shared variables:**

- *nodes*: **array** [0..*k*-1] **of ref to** QNode **init null**
- *tail*: **ref to** QNode **init null**
- *rLock*: *k*-process recoverable lock [16, Sec. 3.2]

**Private variables:**

- *myNode, prev*: **ref to** QNode **init null**

**Procedure Enter (int *pNum*, ref to QNode *myNode*)**

```
24 myNode.next := null, myNode.prev := ⊥, myNode.fin := false
25 nodes[pNum] := myNode
   // insert QNode into linked list
26 prev := FAS (&tail, myNode)
27 myNode.prev := prev
   // check for predecessor
28 if prev ≠ null then
      // link with predecessor
29    myNode.locked := true
30    prev.next := myNode
      // wait for predecessor to release lock
31    await myNode.locked := false
```

**Procedure Exit (int *pNum*)**

```
32 myNode := nodes[pNum]
   // check for successor
33 if myNode.next = null then
      // no known successor, try to unlink from tail
34    if CAS (&tail, myNode, null) = false then
         // wait for successor to link with p_i
35       await myNode.next ≠ null
         // transfer lock ownership to successor
36       myNode.next.locked := false
37 else
      // transfer lock ownership to successor
38    myNode.next.locked := false
   // record successful completion of exit protocol
39 myNode.fin := true
```

**Procedure Recover (int *pNum*)**

```
40 myNode := nodes[pNum]
41 if myNode = null ∨ myNode.fin then
      // easy case: no failure or failure in NCS
42    continue to Enter(pNum, new QNode)
43 else if myNode.nextStep ∈ {26, 27} then
      // swap failure
44    if myNode.prev = ⊥ ∧ ¬IsLinkedTo(pNum) then
         // not in the queue, nothing to recover
45       continue to Enter(pNum, myNode)
46    else if myNode.prev ∈ {⊥, FAIL} then
         // in the queue, must repair queue structure
47       myNode.prev := FAIL
48       call RecoverSwap(pNum)
49    else
         // recover the auxiliary lock in case a
            failure occurred inside RecoverSwap
50       rLock.Recover(), rLock.Enter(), rLock.Exit()
      // recovery complete, proceed to waiting room
51    continue to Enter(pNum, myNode) at line 28
52 else if myNode.nextStep = 34 then
      // failure in exit protocol
53    if tail = myNode then
         // still at the tail, attempt CAS again
54       execute lines 34-39 of Exit(pNum)
55    else if tail = null then
         // no longer in the queue
56       continue to Enter(pNum, new QNode)
57    else if IsLinkedTo(pNum) then
         // in the queue but not at the tail, wait
            for successor and transfer lock ownership
58       execute lines 35-39 of Exit(pNum)
      // recovery complete
59    continue to Enter(pNum, new QNode)
60 else if myNode.nextStep = inCS then
      // critical section re-entry
61    skip Enter and continue to critical section
62 else if myNode.nextStep ∈ Exit then
      // benign failure in exit protocol
63    complete Exit from line myNode.nextStep and continue to
      Enter(pNum, new QNode)
64 else if myNode.nextStep ∈ Enter then
      // benign failure in entry protocol
65    continue to Enter(pNum, myNode) at line myNode.nextStep
```

**Figure 6: Entry, exit and recovery protocol of *k*-Port Extended MCS Algorithm for process $p_i$, entering via port $pNum \in 0..k\text{-}1$.**

to distinguish between a scenario where their swap operation failed without changing *tail* (we call this an *invisible swap failure*) and another scenario where the failure occurred after the swap took place, but before the *prev* field was updated in line 27 (we call this a *visible swap failure*). When the swap failure is invisible, the process must retry its swap, whereas in case of a visible swap failure it

**Private variables:**

- *lTail*: **ref to** QNode
- *lnodes* **array** [0..*k*-1] **of ref to** QNode **init null**

**Function IsLinkedTo (int *pNum*)**

```
66 myNode := nodes[pNum]
   // save tail pointer
67 lTail := tail
   // inspect the latest QNode of every other process
68 for i := 0 to k-1, i ≠ pNum do
69     lnodes[i] := nodes[i]
       // determine prev pointer if QNode exists
70     if lnodes[i] ≠ null then
71         await lnodes[i].prev ≠ ⊥
   // decide whether my QNode is referenced by the
      tail pointer or by another QNode's prev pointer
72 return myNode ∈ {lTail} ∪
   {lnodes[j].prev | 0 ≤ j < k ∧ lnodes[j] ≠ null}
```

**Figure 7: Helper function IsLinkedTo of the Extended MCS Algorithm.**

**Private variables:**

- *myNode, cur, prv*: **ref to** QNode
- *R*: binary relation, initially empty

**Procedure RecoverSwap (int *pNum*)**

```
73 myNode := nodes[pNum]
   // acquire auxiliary lock
74 rLock.Recover(), rLock.Enter()
75 R := ∅
   // inspect the tail pointer and the latest QNode
      of every other processes
76 for i := 0 to k-1 do
77     if i ≠ pNum then
           // inspect the next QNode
78         cur := nodes[i]
79     else
           // inspect the tail pointer
80         cur := tail
81         R := R ∪ (tail, TAIL)
       // trace prev pointers from QNode
82     while cur ≠ null do
83         await cur.prev ≠ ⊥
84         prv := cur.prev
85         if prv ∉ {null, FAIL} ∧ ¬prv.fin then
86             R := R ∪ (prv, cur)
87             cur := prv
88         else
89             break
90 derive maximal fragments from R:
   (n_{1,1} → ··· → n_{1,l_1}), ..., (n_{j,1} → ..., n_{j,l_j})
91 let f ∈ {1, ..., j} be myNode's fragment number
92 if f > 1 then
       // link my QNode to previous fragment
93     myNode.prev := n_{f-1, l_{f-1}}
94 else
       // my QNode is at the head of the queue
95     myNode.prev := null
96 rLock.Exit()
```

**Figure 8: Helper procedure RecoverSwap of the Extended MCS Algorithm.**

may need to find an appropriate predecessor and link to it. The difficulty is compounded further by the fact that multiple processes may be recovering simultaneously and that new passages may start on other ports.

Figure 9 depicts a configuration that may arise from multiple swap failures. In this scenario, the processes using $q_1$-$q_6$ underwent a swap failure: processes using $q_1$,$q_2$,$q_4$,$q_5$ underwent an invisible swap failure and those using $q_3$,$q_6$ underwent a visible swap failure. As a result, the queue is split into several *fragments* of QNode records, each ordered according to the reverse of the *prev* references (which equals the order determined by the eventual values of the *next* references): $(s_0, s_1, r_1)$, $(q_3, s_2, r_2)$, and $(q_6, s_3, r_3)$. By invoking **IsLinkedTo**, the processes using $q_1$,$q_2$,$q_4$,$q_5$ are able to determine that their records are not linked to (i.e., do not belong to any fragment) and so they must retry the swap. Each of the processes using $q_3$,$q_6$, on the other hand, will be able to determine in turn that its swap was performed and then, by invoking **RecoverSwap**, to compute which fragments exist, and to reconnect the queue structure. We differentiate between several types of fragments. The fragment containing records reachable from *tail* is the *tail fragment.* At most a single fragment may be *non-failed,* that is, containing only records associated with passages that already executed lines 26–27. All other fragments (if any) are *middle fragments.*

We proceed to describe the **RecoverSwap** procedure, which receives the port number as its parameter (line 73). It starts by capturing the *rLock* recoverable lock (line 74), which simplifies recovery by ensuring mutual exclusion among processes attempting to reconnect the queue structure. Next, in the loop of lines 76–89, for each port, the *prev* references are traced back starting from the port's record (if any) until a **null** or a FAIL reference value is encountered. The references starting from *tail* are also traced back, in iteration *pNum* of the loop. If the *prev* field is yet to be updated, *p* awaits for this to occur at line 83. Tracing stops if the *prev* field is **null**, equals FAIL, or is a reference to a record whose passage was completed (line 85). All these predecessor-successor pairs are added to a set *R* (line 86). All pairs added to *R* consist of two record references, with the single exception of the record referenced from the *tail* variable, which is designated as a special TAIL relation (line 81). The reasons for this are twofold. First, this facilitates identifying the tail fragment. Second, whereas non-tail fragments always consist of at least two records, the tail fragment may consist of the single record referenced by *tail.* Based on *R*, process *p* may

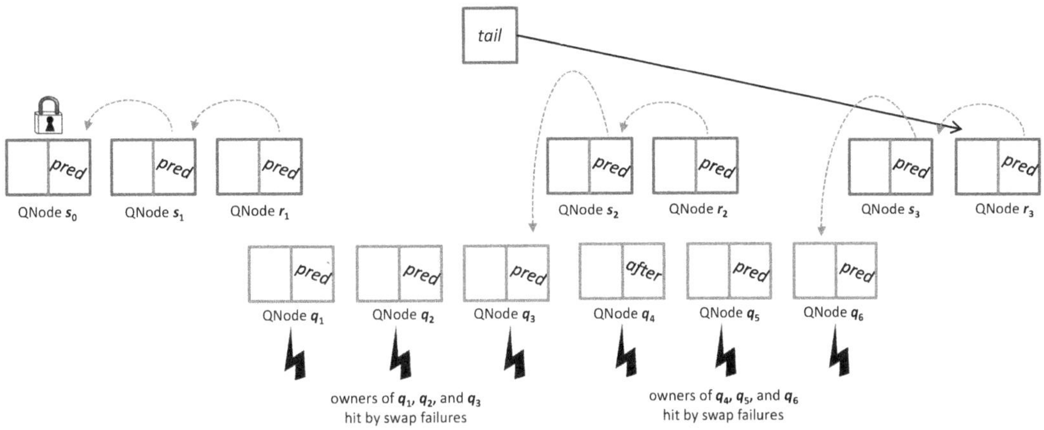


**Figure 9: Queue fragments after multiple swap failures. Dashed arrows represent *prev* references. QNode records $q_6, s_3, r_3$ constitute a tail-fragment, $q_3, s_2, r_2$ constitute a middle-fragment, and $s_0, s_1, r_1$ constitute a non-failed fragment.**

compute maximal queue-fragments and determine their types – tail-fragment, middle-fragment, or non-failed fragment (line 90). Fragments $1, \ldots, j$ are indexed such that if there is a non-failed fragment then it is indexed as 1, and the tail fragment is indexed as last (fragment $j$). The computation of maximal fragments is relatively straightforward. Due to lack of space, its pseudo-code is omitted. We note that new records may be associated with some of the ports throughout the execution of **RecoverSwap** but this does not compromise the correctness of the RME algorithm and, moreover, only $O(k)$ distinct records are accessed throughout a single execution of **RecoverSwap**.

If *myNode* is not part of the first fragment, then $p$ "glues" its fragment to the predecessor fragment, which is either a middle fragment or the non-failed fragment (if there is one). Process $p$ does this by updating its *prev* field to link to the last record of the predecessor fragment (line 92), and then releases *rLock* (line 96). Otherwise, *myNode is* part of the first fragment, implying that there is no non-failed fragment (which may happen if the first visible swap failure occurred when the queue was empty). In this case, $p$ updates its *prev* reference to **null** (line 95), effectively making its fragment the new single non-failed fragment, and then releases *rLock* at line 96. In both cases, after **RecoverSwap** returns, execution resumes from line 28 of the **Enter** procedure (line 51).

The correctness properties of the algorithm are captured in Theorem 4.1. The RMR complexity bound does not apply in the DSM model due to the busy-wait loops at line 71 and line 83.

THEOREM 4.1. *The $k$-port extended MCS lock satisfies ME, SF, TE, BR, and CSR. The RMR complexity in the CC model is $O(1)$ for a passage that does not begin in cleanup, and $O(k)$ for any other passage.*

## 5 $O(\text{LOG } N/\text{LOG LOG } N)$ RMRS ALGORITHM

Let $k = \lceil \log N/\log\log N \rceil$. We obtain an $O(k)$ RMRs upper bound in the CC model by using the $k$-port extended MCS lock from Section 4 in an arbitration tree of degree $k$. The height of such a tree with $N$ leaves is $\Theta(k)$. Each node in the tree contains its own instance of the $k$-port lock. To enter the CS, a process $p$ must complete the recovery and entry protocol of every $k$-port lock instance on the path from its designated leaf node to the root node. When climbing to a node from its $i$'th child, $p$ uses the $i$'th port. Similarly, to exit the CS, a process must complete the exit protocol of every $k$-port lock instance on this path in the reverse order. All recovery actions are performed in the recovery protocol of the $k$-port algorithm, and for that reason the arbitration tree does not require a separate recovery protocol. The following theorem follows from Theorem 4.1, the fact that both the degree and the height of the tree used by the algorithm is $O(\log N/\log\log N)$, as well as the observation that each extended MCS lock instance is accessed correctly by at most $k$ processes at a time.

THEOREM 5.1. *The arbitration tree algorithm satisfies ME, SF, TE, BR, and CSR. Its RMR complexity in the CC model is $O(\log N/\log\log N)$.*

## 6 RELATED WORK

Mutual exclusion (ME) is one of the oldest topics in distributed computing [2, 30]. Recent work on this topic has focused on *local spin* algorithms, which guarantee bounded RMR complexity per passage by busy-waiting only on locally accessible shared variables. Local spinning bounds the communication overhead associated with synchronization and contributes to scalability [3, 9]. For the class of $N$-process algorithms that use reads, writes and comparison primitives (defined in [2]), the tight bound on worst-case RMRs is $\Theta(\log N)$. Yang and Anderson [32] proved the upper bound in the CC and DSM models using an arbitration tree modeled after Kessels [21]. Attiya, Hendler, and Woelfel [4] later proved the matching lower bound, building on a series of earlier results [1, 8, 11, 15]. Sub-logarithmic RMR complexity is attainable on expectation using randomization [5, 12, 13, 19], and $O(1)$ RMR complexity is attainable deterministically if additional atomic primitives are available, such as Fetch-And-Store or Fetch-And-Add [3, 17, 26, 27].

Solutions to the ME problem generally assume reliable processes since synchronization is achieved by busy-waiting, although variations of the problem are solvable in some failure models. Lamport and Taubenfeld define several such models for algorithms based on single-writer registers, assuming that failures affect the values of such shared variables in specific ways [23, 31]. Lamport's Bakery algorithm [22] tolerates crash failures provided that any registers owned by the failed process are reset to zero [22]. Bohannon et al. instead consider a failure model in which process crashes are permanent and do not affect the values of shared variables, which complicates recovery [6, 7]. Their solutions rely on operating system support for failure detection and assume for simplicity that recovery is performed in a dedicated process that is itself reliable. Michael and Kim's fault-tolerant mutex lock similarly relies on failure detection but does not require a dedicated recovery process [28]. Instead, a process that is waiting to acquire a lock may "usurp" the lock if it determines that the previous lock holder has crashed permanently.

Recoverable mutual exclusion (RME), which is the problem solved in this paper, was formalized recently by Golab and Ramaraju [16]. RME does not rely on a dedicated recovery process or on failure detection, but assumes that processes recover eventually from crashes outside of the non-critical section. Two of Golab and Ramaraju's RME solutions are local-spin in both the CC and DSM models, and both incur $\Omega(\log N)$ RMRs per passage in the worst case. Ramaraju's earlier RME algorithm incurs $\Theta(N)$ RMRs in the worst case and relies on the Fetch-And-Store-And-Store (FASAS) instruction described in Section 3 [29].

The FASAS and DCAS instructions used by our algorithm in Section 3 are not supported by mainstream multiprocessors, and we are not aware of any RMR-efficient software implementations. Non-blocking DCAS implementations from commonly supported primitives have been studied previously in the conventional asynchronous model with crash failures (e.g., [18]).

## 7 CONCLUSION

In this paper, we presented RMR-efficient solutions to the recoverable mutual exclusion (RME) problem, and answered positively one of the questions posed recently by Golab and Ramaraju [16]: "Can this problem be solved using $o(\log N)$ RMRs per passage in the worst case using commonly supported primitives?" Our upper bound of $O(\log N/\log\log N)$ RMRs holds in the CC model, and establishes a complexity separation for RME between the class of algorithms that use reads, writes, and single-word comparison primitives versus those that additionally use unconditional single-word primitives such as Fetch-And-Store. This observation complements the known RMR complexity separation for conventional mutual exclusion (ME). Our results raise two follow-up questions: First, what is the tight bound for the worst-case RMR complexity of solving RME using commonly supported single-word primitives? Second, is this tight bound the same in the CC and DSM models, or is one model inherently more powerful than the other for solving RME?

## REFERENCES


[1] J. Anderson and Y.-J. Kim. An improved lower bound for the time complexity of mutual exclusion. *Distributed Computing*, 15(4):221–253, 2002.

[2] J. Anderson, Y.-J. Kim, and T. Herman. Shared-memory mutual exclusion: Major research trends since 1986. *Distributed Computing*, 16(2-3):75–110, 2003.

[3] T. Anderson. The performance of spin lock alternatives for shared-memory multiprocessors. *IEEE Transactions on Parallel and Distributed Systems*, 1(1):6–16, 1990.

[4] H. Attiya, D. Hendler, and P. Woelfel. Tight RMR lower bounds for mutual exclusion and other problems. In *Proc. of the 40th ACM Symposium on Theory of Computing (STOC)*, pages 217–226, 2008.

[5] M. A. Bender and S. Gilbert. Mutual Exclusion with $O(\log^2 \log n)$ Amortized Work. In *Proc. of the 52nd Symposium on Foundations of Computer Science (FOCS)*, pages 728–737, 2011.

[6] P. Bohannon, D. F. Lieuwen, and A. Silberschatz. Recovering scalable spin locks. In *Proc. of the 8th IEEE Symposium on Parallel and Distributed Processing (SPDP)*, pages 314–322, 1996.

[7] P. Bohannon, D. F. Lieuwen, A. Silberschatz, S. Sudarshan, and J. Gava. Recoverable user-level mutual exclusion. In *Proc. of the 7th IEEE Symposium on Parallel and Distributed Processing (SPDP)*, pages 293–301, 1995.

[8] R. Cypher. The communication requirements of mutual exclusion. In *Proc. of the 7th ACM Symposium on Parallel Algorithms and Architectures (SPAA)*, pages 147–156, 1995.

[9] T. David, R. Guerraoui, and V. Trigonakis. Everything you always wanted to know about synchronization but were afraid to ask. In *Proc. of the 24th ACM SIGOPS Symposium on Operating Systems Principles (SOSP)*, pages 33–48, 2013.

[10] E. W. Dijkstra. Solution of a problem in concurrent programming control. *Communications of the ACM*, 8(9):569, 1965.

[11] R. Fan and N. Lynch. An $\Omega(n \log n)$ lower bound on the cost of mutual exclusion. In *Proc. of the 25th ACM Symposium on Principles of Distributed Computing (PODC)*, pages 275–284, 2006.

[12] G. Giakkoupis and P. Woelfel. A tight RMR lower bound for randomized mutual exclusion. In *Proc. of the 44th Symposium on Theory of Computing (STOC)*, pages 983–1002, 2012.

[13] G. Giakkoupis and P. Woelfel. Randomized mutual exclusion with constant amortized RMR complexity on the DSM. In *Proc. of the 55th Symposium on Foundations of Computer Science (FOCS)*, pages 504–513, 2014.

[14] W. Golab. Deconstructing queue-based mutual exclusion Hewlett-Packard Labs Technical Report HPL-2012-100.

[15] W. Golab, V. Hadzilacos, D. Hendler, and P. Woelfel. RMR-efficient implementations of comparison primitives using read and write operations. *Distributed Computing*, 25(2):109–162, 2012.

[16] W. Golab, and A. Ramaraju. Recoverable mutual exclusion. In *Proc. of the 35th Annual ACM Symposium on Principles of Distributed Computing (PODC)*, pages 65–74, 2016.

[17] G. Graunke and S. Thakkar. Synchronization algorithms for shared-memory multiprocessors. *IEEE Computer*, 23(6):60–69, 1990.

[18] T. L. Harris, K. Fraser, and I. A. Pratt. A practical multi-word compare-and-swap operation. In *Proc. of the 16th International Conference on Distributed Computing (DISC)*, pages 265–279, 2002.

[19] D. Hendler and P. Woelfel. Randomized mutual exclusion with sub-logarithmic RMR-complexity. *Distributed Computing*, 24(1):3–19, 2011.

[20] M. Herlihy and E. Moss. Transactional Memory: Architectural Support for Lock-Free Data Structures. In *Proc. of the 20th ACM/IEEE International Symposium on Computer Architecture (ISCA)*, pages 289–300, 1993.

[21] J. Kessels. Arbitration without common modifiable variables. *Acta Informatica*, 17:135–141, 1982.

[22] L. Lamport. A new solution of Dijkstra's concurrent programming problem. *Communications of the ACM*, 17(8):453–455, 1974.

[23] L. Lamport. The mutual exclusion problem: part II – statement and solutions. *Journal of the ACM*, 33(2):327–348, 1986.

[24] L. Lamport. The PlusCal algorithm language. In *Proc. of the 6th International Colloquium on Theoretical Aspects of Computing (ICTAC)*, pages 36–60, 2009.

[25] L. Lamport. Specifying systems: the TLA+ language and tools for hardware and software engineers. Addison-Wesley, 2002.

[26] P. Magnusson, A. Landin, and E. Hagersten. Queue locks on cache coherent multiprocessors. In *Proc. of the 8th International Parallel Processing Symposium (IPPS)*, pages 165–171, 1994.

[27] J. Mellor-Crummey and M. Scott. Algorithms for scalable synchronization on shared-memory multiprocessors. *ACM Transactions on Computer Systems*, 9(1):21–65, 1991.

[28] M. Michael and Y. Kim. Fault tolerant mutual exclusion locks for shared memory systems. US Patent 7,493,618, 2009.

[29] A. Ramaraju. RGLock: Recoverable mutual exclusion for non-volatile main memory systems. Master's thesis, University of Waterloo, 2015. https://uwspace.uwaterloo.ca/handle/10012/9473.

[30] M. Raynal. *Algorithms for Mutual Exclusion*. MIT Press, 1986.

[31] G. Taubenfeld. *Synchronization Algorithms and Concurrent Programming*. Prentice Hall, 2006.

[32] J.-H. Yang and J. Anderson. A fast, scalable mutual exclusion algorithm. *Distributed Computing*, 9(1):51–60, 1995.

# Randomized Abortable Mutual Exclusion with Constant Amortized RMR Complexity on the CC Model

George Giakkoupis
INRIA, Rennes
France
george.giakkoupis@inria.fr

Philipp Woelfel
University of Calgary
Canada
woelfel@ucalgary.ca

## ABSTRACT

We present an abortable mutual exclusion algorithm for the cache-coherent (CC) model with atomic registers and CAS objects. The algorithm has constant expected amortized RMR complexity in the oblivious adversary model and is deterministically deadlock-free. This is the first abortable mutual exclusion algorithm that achieves $o(\log n/\log\log n)$ RMR complexity.

## KEYWORDS

Mutual exclusion; RMR complexity; shared memory; oblivious adversary; CC model

## 1 INTRODUCTION

*Mutual exclusion*, introduced by Dijkstra [17], is one of the best studied problems in concurrent computing. A mutual exclusion object (or *lock*) allows processes to coordinate their access to a shared resource by serializing the execution of a piece of code, called the *critical section*. Each process obtains a lock through an *entry section*, but at any time at most one process can own the lock. A process that owns the lock executes the critical section, and to release the lock it executes an *exit section*. Raynal devoted a textbook [35] to mutual exclusion research up to the mid 80s, and a survey by Anderson, Kim, and Herman [5] covers the research between 1986 and 2003.

Early mutual exclusion algorithms did not take into account the gap between high processor speeds and the low speed and bandwidth of the processor-memory interconnect [13]. In *distributed shared memory (DSM)* systems, each shared variable is permanently locally accessible to a single processor and remote to all other processors. In *cache-coherent (CC)* systems, each processor keeps local copies of shared variables in its cache; the consistency of copies in different caches is maintained by a *coherence protocol*. Memory accesses that cannot be resolved locally and have to traverse the processor-to-memory interconnect are called *remote memory references* (RMRs). RMRs are orders of magnitude slower than local memory accesses. Hence, the performance of many algorithms for shared memory multiprocessor systems depends critically on the number of RMRs they incur [6, 33]. Recent research has almost entirely used the RMR complexity as a metric for the performance of mutual exclusion algorithms [3, 4, 6, 9, 12, 14, 15, 20, 21, 25–32, 34]. Tradeoffs between RMRs and fence operations have also been studied more recently [8, 10, 11].

However, even RMR-efficient mutual exclusion locks do not meet a critical demand of many systems [36]. Specifically, the locks employed in database and real-time systems must support a "timeout" capability that allows a process waiting too long for the lock, to abort its attempt. In database systems, such as Oracle's Parallel Server and IBM's DB2, the ability of a thread to abort lock attempts serves the dual purpose of recovering from a transaction deadlock and tolerating preemption of the thread that holds the lock [36]. In real time systems, the abort capability can be used to avoid overshooting a deadline. Locks that allow a process to abort its attempt to enter the critical section, and return to the remainder section within a finite number of their own steps, are called *abortable* locks.

*Randomization* can be used to improve the efficiency of mutual exclusion algorithms. For the analysis of randomized algorithms, the order in which processes take steps is determined by an *adversary*. Among the most common adversary models are the *strong adaptive adversary*, where scheduling decisions can depend on all past events including local coin flips, and the *oblivious adversary*, where scheduling decisions are independent of random decisions made by processes (i.e., the adversary fixes the schedule in advance).

Unless mentioned otherwise, the results discussed below hold for the CC and the DSM models with atomic registers and CAS objects, and $n$ is the number of processes. The deterministic RMR complexity of mutual exclusion is $\Theta(\log n)$ RMRs per passage through the critical section [9, 37]. Jayanti showed that this RMR complexity can even be achieved for abortable mutual exclusion [27]. Randomization can only slightly improve RMR complexity in the strong adaptive adversary model. Giakkoupis and Woelfel [20] showed that any mutual exclusion algorithm in this model has expected RMR complexity $\Omega(\log n/\log\log n)$, matching an upper bound by Hendler and Woelfel [26].

Recently, researchers have increasingly focused on devising efficient randomized algorithms for the weaker, oblivious adversary model, e.g., for test-and-set [2, 19] or consensus [7] implemented from registers. Bender and Gilbert devised a randomized mutual exclusion algorithm using atomic registers and CAS objects, which achieves $O(\log^2 \log n)$ expected amortized RMR complexity against the oblivious adversary in the CC model [12]. The algorithm is Monte Carlo in the sense that it provides only probabilistic progress guarantees. A deterministically deadlock-free algorithm with constant expected amortized RMR complexity in the DSM model with


*PODC'17, July 25-27, 2017, Washington, DC, USA.*

ACM ISBN 978-1-4503-4992-5/17/07...$15.00.
https://doi.org/10.1145/3087801.3087837

atomic registers was presented by Giakkoupis and Woelfel [21]. But this algorithm is not RMR efficient for the CC model.

None of the randomized algorithms above are abortable or can easily be made so. A much more complicated randomized abortable mutual exclusion algorithm was devised by Pareek and Woelfel [34], and has expected RMR complexity $O(\log n/\log\log n)$ for an adversary that is slightly weaker than the strong adaptive adversary.

In this paper we present an abortable mutual exclusion algorithm with $O(1)$ expected amortized RMR complexity on the CC model with atomic registers and CAS objects, against a natural adversary model that is stronger than the oblivious adversary. The algorithm is deterministically deadlock-free. It is the first mutual exclusion algorithm that achieves optimal amortized RMR complexity in this model, and also the first one that combines abortability with an RMR complexity of $o(\log n/\log\log n)$.

Note that due to the constant-RMR implementations of linearizable CAS objects from registers [22], all deterministic mutual exclusion algorithms as well as some of the randomized ones, need only registers. But these simulations do not in general preserve the randomized RMR complexity of algorithms [16, 24]. The algorithm by Bender and Gilbert for the oblivious adversary model [12] needs atomic[1] CAS objects, and it is not clear whether they can be replaced by linearizable constant RMR implementations.

## 1.1 Model and Problem Statement

Let $\mathbb{N}$ denote the set of positive integers, $\mathbb{N}_0 = \mathbb{N} \cup \{0\}$, $\mathcal{P} = \{1, \ldots, n\}$, and $\mathcal{P}_0 = \mathcal{P} \cup \{0\}$. We consider the standard cache-coherent (CC) model, where a set of $n$ processes with unique IDs in $\mathcal{P}$ communicate by executing atomic operations on shared registers and CAS objects. A *compare-and-swap (CAS)* object $C$ supports the operations $C$.`read()`, which returns the value of $C$, and $C$.`CAS`$(old, new)$, which writes $new$ into $C$ if $C = old$, and otherwise does not change $C$. A `CAS()` operation returns a Boolean value indicating whether it successfully changed the value. Processes are equipped with local caches for read operations on registers, and a cache protocol ensures coherency. A *remote memory reference (RMR)* is a shared memory access of a register that cannot be resolved locally (i.e., a cache miss). Each write of a register, and all operations on CAS objects are considered cache misses, and thus each of them incurs an RMR (even though some systems also provide write caches). A read by process $p$ on a register $R$ only incurs an RMR if $p$ never read $R$ before, or if some process wrote to it since $p$ read or wrote it last. Note that this implies that $p$ obtains a cache copy of a register $R$ by writing to it, which is generally the case for write-through caches. Our RMR complexity analysis does not require this behaviour; it suffices if only a read of $R$ yields a cache copy. In fact, since we assume an adversary that can distinguish between cache hits and cache misses (as explained later), the fact that additional cache copies can be obtained by writing leads to significant complications in the algorithm design and analysis.

A (non-abortable) mutual exclusion algorithm supports the methods `lock()` and `release()`. Once the `lock()` method terminates, the process is in the critical section. At the end of the critical section, the process calls `release()`, and it enters the remainder section when that call terminates. The safety property *mutual exclusion* requires that no two processes are in the critical section at the same time. In an *abortable* mutual exclusion algorithm, a process may receive a signal to abort at any point during its `lock()` method call. When that happens, the `lock()` method call must terminate within a finite number of the calling process' steps, and upon termination the process enters either the critical section or the remainder section. (Which one it is can be indicated by the return value of the `lock()` method, but for readability reasons we use **goto** statements in our code.)

[1]With atomic we mean that each operation is executed instantaneously.

The standard progress condition for mutual exclusion is *deadlock-freedom*. This means that as long as there is a pending `lock()` method call, one such call will terminate, provided all processes that have pending `lock()` or `release()` method calls continue to take steps. For an abortable mutual exclusion algorithm it is also required that the `release()` method is wait-free, i.e., any process can finish it within a finite number of its own steps.

We consider an adversary that is obtained by restricting the strong adaptive adversary and is significantly stronger than the oblivious adversary. In particular correlations between whether past steps were RMRs and the future schedule are allowed; more precisely, we assume that the adversary knows for each completed operation whether or not it incurred an RMR. Moreover, at any time the adversary knows the state of each CAS object, and for any process poised to execute an operation on a CAS object, it knows the type and parameters of that operation. Finally, it also knows for each process if it is poised to enter the critical section or the remainder section in its next step, or if it is busy-waiting (see lines 3, 18, 21 and 33 in the pseudocode at the end of this article).

## 1.2 Result

The properties of our mutual exclusion algorithm are summarized in the next theorem.

THEOREM 1.1. *There is a randomized abortable mutual exclusion algorithm for the CC model with atomic registers and CAS objects, which has constant expected amortized RMR complexity against the oblivious adversary.*

We designed our algorithm in such a way, that atomic CAS objects can be replaced by linearizable ones; the amortized RMR complexity of the mutual exclusion algorithm then becomes asymptotically the same as that of operations on the CAS objects. However, abortability of our algorithm is only preserved if operations on the CAS objects are abortable. It is not hard to see [18] that such randomized CAS implementations with expected amortized constant RMR complexity on the CC model can be obtained from registers by combining existing randomized test-and-set algorithms [2, 19] with an abortable version of the algorithm in [22] (see Section 3.2 for more details).

In Section 2 we describe the main ideas of our algorithm, and then give a detailed line by line description. Our RMR complexity analysis and correctness proofs are involved, and will be made available in the arXiv.org e-Print archive.

The version of the algorithm described in Section 2 uses unbounded sequence numbers and an unbounded number of registers. In Section 3.1 we sketch how the number and size of all base objects can be bounded using techniques for bounded tagging [1] (more details can be found in the full version of the paper). In Section 3.2

we give more details on how atomic CAS objects in our algorithm can be replaced by atomic registers without increasing the amortized RMR complexity, but sacrificing a wait-free abort path for a randomized wait-free one.

## 2 ALGORITHM

### 2.1 Main Ideas

The pseudocode for our algorithm can be found at the end of this article (after the references). We assume that an adversary may send an abort signal at any point in time while $p$ is not idle, by setting $p$'s local variable *abort_sig* to `True`.

We first describe the high level idea of the algorithm, assuming no aborts. Later we discuss how we deal with aborts. Some of the variables in the pseudocode are indexed by $\alpha$. We will explain the purpose of this index later, and for now we will omit $\alpha$ from the corresponding variable names.

In order to avoid busy waiting on CAS objects, we use registers that change their value to signal waiting processes that CAS objects have been updated. For example after a process changes the value of the CAS object $S$ from $(\cdot, locked)$ to $(\cdot, unlocked)$ in line 57, it writes to $S'$ in line 58 to signal that it has changed $S$. Processes waiting for $S$ to become $(\cdot, unlocked)$, busy wait by reading $S'$ instead of $S$ (in lines 3, 21 and 33). Similarly, registers $B'[p]$ and $A'[p]$ are used for signaling, and to avoid busy waiting on CAS objects $B[p][0]$ and $A[p]$, respectively.

The critical section is protected by CAS object $S$. When some process is critical (meaning it is in the critical section), the value of $S$ is $(i, locked)$ (where $i$ is a sequence number), and otherwise it is $(i, unlocked)$. A naive way to implement that would be as follows: To capture the lock, a process $p$ waits until the value of $S$ is $(\cdot, unlocked)$, and then tries to change it to $(\cdot, locked)$ with a `CAS()` operation (similar to lines 21–23). But then for each successful `CAS()` operation on $S$ we may have up to $n-1$ failed ones, yielding a forbiddingly large RMR complexity.

The idea is now that before processes start waiting for $S$ to become $(\cdot, unlocked)$, they get a chance to contact each other and join forces (i.e., share work). To do that, each process $p$ uses a *backpack*, represented by CAS object $B[p][1]$. Initially, the process sets the CAS object to an integer (which is a unique sequence number), meaning the backpack is *open*. We then use a randomized mechanism that gives other processes a chance to discover $p$, i.e., see that $p$ is participating and has an open backpack. A process $b$ that discovers $p$ tries to write its own ID and a sequence number into $B[p][1]$ using a `CAS()` operation (line 16). If that succeeds, $b$ can simply start waiting (in the repeat-until loop in lines 17–20), and let $p$ do the work.

After each attempt to enter the critical section via "winning" $S$, process $p$ checks its backpack $B[p][1]$, and adds the process it found there, if any, to its local set *bpack* (see method `closeBackpacks()`). Once process $p$ is critical, it adds all processes collected in *bpack* during its earlier attempts to win $S$, to a multiset $Q$ (line 53). All accesses to $Q$ will be protected by the critical section, so a sequential data structure (such as a linked list) can be used to implement $Q$. Then $p$ removes a process $q$ from $Q$ (if $Q$ is not empty) and tries to *promote* $q$, meaning that it calls a method `promote()` which is used to signal $q$ that it is $q$'s turn to become critical. The promotion mechanism requires some handshaking between $p$ and $q$, because $q$ may have decided to abort, and then $p$ and $q$ need to agree whether $q$ enters the remainder or the critical section. If the promotion fails (i.e., $q$ enters the remainder section), then $p$ repeats this procedure by removing another process from $Q$, provided $Q \neq \emptyset$ (lines 54–56).

For this approach to work we need to deal with two issues: First, we need a way for processes to discover each other. Second, once a process $b$ discovers a process $p$, $p$ may finish its `lock()` and `release()` methods before $b$ can join $p$'s backpack. (Process $p$ has to *close* its backpack before entering the remainder section, by changing the value of $B[p][1]$ to *closed*, so that $b$ does not join the backpack and then deadlocks, waiting to be signaled by $p$.) Thus, $b$ may waste an RMR by its `CAS()` operation in a failed attempt to join $p$'s backpack. We have to make sure that this does not happen too often. In particular, at least a constant fraction of such backpack join attempts need to succeed in expectation. We now show how to deal with those issues.

To allow processes to discover each other, we use a register $Z$. Before each attempt to lock $S$, a process $b$ first flips a random coin, and based on the outcome either it writes to $Z$ a pair consisting of its ID and a sequence number, or it reads $Z$ (lines 12–15). In the latter case, if $p$ finds the ID and sequence number of a process, it tries to join that process' backpack as described earlier (line 16). The idea is that if two processes consecutively access $Z$, and the first one writes to $Z$ while the second one reads $Z$ (which happens with probability 1/4), then the second one will discover the first one, and may later be able to enter the first one's backpack.

We now show how to deal with the second issue, which is to ensure that a process $b$, which discovered a process $p$, gets a chance of entering $p$'s backpack before $p$ closes it. Recall that eventually, processes that do not manage to enter a backpack, have to wait for $S$ to become unlocked and try to lock $S$ themselves (lines 21–23). Suppose $S$ is locked, and let $p^*$ be the process that locked $S$. While $p^*$ is critical, it will try and select a random process $r^*$ (and some other processes) among all of those that participated in the discovery phase (how this is done will be explained shortly). Process $p^*$ will then allow $r^*$ to go through the critical section before $S$ gets unlocked, by adding it to the multiset $Q$ (as described earlier). This has the effect that all processes waiting for $S$ to become unlocked keep waiting and will not close their backpacks until the randomly chosen process $r^*$ has taken sufficiently many steps. As a result, a constant fraction of all processes will make equally many steps as $r^*$ (because the adversary does not know who $r^*$ is), and that will suffice for each of them to join the backpack of their discovered process, if any.

To find a random process $r^*$ we borrow a technique from [21]. We use a shared array $R[1 \ldots \ell+1]$, where $\ell = \lceil \log n \rceil$, and each array entry is initially $(0,0)$. At the beginning of an attempt to capture the lock, a process writes a pair consisting of its ID and sequence number to $R[\lambda]$, where $\lambda \in \{1, \ldots, \ell\}$ is chosen according to a truncated geometric distribution, satisfying $\lambda = i$ with probability $\Theta(1/2^i)$ (lines 10–11). After locking $S$, process $p^*$ scans this array from left to right (ignoring $R[1]$ for reasons explained later) until it finds the first index $i$ such that $R[i] = (0,0)$ or $R[i]$ was last written by $p^*$. While scanning, it adds each process found (other than itself) to $Q$, and erases each scanned register on $R[]$. Let $K$ be the set of processes that write to $R[]$ before the point $t$ when $p^*$ begins scanning $R[]$, and let $\kappa = \lceil \log |K| \rceil$. Assume that $K$ is at least as large as some predefined large enough constant (otherwise it suffices that only $p^*$ enters the critical section). Then with constant probability all of the following happen: $\kappa > 1$, all registers $R[1], \ldots, R[\kappa]$ were written to, exactly one process in $K$ wrote to $R[\kappa]$, and $p^*$ only wrote to $R[1]$. Suppose this "good event" happens. Since $p^*$ ignores $R[1]$ when scanning, possible writes by $p^*$ do not interfere with those of other processes. Then the process $r^*$ that wrote to $R[\kappa]$ is (roughly) uniformly distributed over $K \setminus \{p^*\}$. As a result, in expectation $\Omega(|K|)$ processes will manage to join backpacks of other processes while $S$ is locked. Note that this is just a simplified description of the core insight; the intricate analysis considers a possibly larger set of writes, depending on the execution.

However, processes that write to $R[]$ after $p^*$ finished scanning the array, and before $S$ gets unlocked again, may not have a chance of joining a backpack. To deal with this issue we use instead two registers, $Z_0$ and $Z_1$, and two arrays, $R_0[]$ and $R_1[]$. In each attempt, a process chooses one of the two "sides" (0 or 1) uniformly at random. Moreover, which of the two arrays $R_0[]$ and $R_1[]$ is being scanned when a process wins $S$, alternates with each such win of $S$. More precisely, the sequence number stored with $S$ gets incremented every time $S$ gets locked, and when it is $i$, array $R_{i \bmod 2}[]$ is scanned. As a result, all processes that write to $R_{i \bmod 2}[]$ while $S \in \{(i-1, \mathit{locked}), (i-1, \mathit{unlocked})\}$ get a chance of joining some other process' backpack after reading $Z_{i \bmod 2}$. Since a process chooses at random one of the two sides, it makes the right choice with probability 1/2. Then in expectation a constant fraction of the processes that write to $Z_\alpha$, $\alpha \in \{0, 1\}$, will be able to join a backpack, and then later get added to multiset $Q$ by the backpack owner.

Processes that neither manage to join any backpack nor lock $S$, will simply restart the procedure. Before a process $p$ does that, it has to check whether its backpack $B[p][1]$ is occupied. If so, it has to move that backpacked process into a local variable *bpack*, in order to make room in its backpack for the next attempt (see method `closeBackpacks()`).

Next we describe how our algorithm accommodates process aborts. Suppose that a process $p$ receives an abort signal while it is executing its `lock()` method. This means that its flag *abort_sig* will be set. When that happens, the process will not busy wait in any `await()` statement, or the repeat-until loop in lines 17–20. Within a finite number of steps it will either enter the critical section in one of lines 32 and 35, or it will begin another iteration of the while-loop in lines 2–35, and then call `abort()` in line 4. In the simplest case, $p$ has no process in its backpack set *bpack*. Then $p$ can go to the remainder section, but as explained above, handshaking is necessary to synchronize with a potential process in the critical section that may be trying to promote $p$. The handshaking mechanism is implemented in method `giveUp()`. Note that if $p$ calls `abort()` in line 4 in the first iteration of its while-loop, then it cannot have joined any other process's backpack, so no `giveUp()` call is necessary. If $p$ calls `abort()` in the second or later iteration of the while-loop, then it calls `giveUp()` in line 34 before its `abort()` call.

As a result of the handshaking mechanism in `giveUp()`, $p$ may either enter the remainder section, or get promoted in the critical section without any further waiting. In the former case, and if $p$ has some processes in its backpack set *bpack* when it aborts (which it finds via a `closeBackpacks()` call in line 34), it has to make sure that those processes do not deadlock, because they are waiting under the assumption that they will eventually be added to the multiset $Q$ and then get promoted. Since we can only allow non-concurrent access to $Q$, an aborting process cannot add the elements of its backpack to $Q$. Therefore (see the while-loop in `abort()`) $p$ removes an arbitrary process $r$ from *bpack*, and tries to hand over to it the set of remaining processes in *bpack*, by writing that set to CAS object $B[r][0]$, by using a `CAS()` operation. It then signals $r$, using variable $B'[r]$, that $B[r][0]$ has changed. If that `CAS()` succeeds, process $r$ will find out (because while in a backpack, it also spins on $B'[r]$ in line 18), and it will learn that it has been removed from $p$'s backpack. When that happens, $r$ will continue trying to capture the lock itself. But while waiting, $r$ may have also aborted. If it did so, it would have closed $B[r][0]$, and $p$ would not have managed to hand over its backpack (i.e., the corresponding `CAS()` would have failed). Therefore, $p$ has to repeat the procedure of removing processes from its backpack and trying to hand over the backpack to them, until this succeeds, or until its backpack is empty.

One issue to be careful about is to avoid cyclic backpack relationships. Let $b \leftarrow p$ denote that process $b$ is in process $p$'s backpack (at a fixed point in time). If the binary relation $\leftarrow$ is cyclic at any point, then processes deadlock, because each process that is part of the cycle will not make progress until its carrier (the process whose backpack it is in) passes through the critical section. This affects some implementation decisions, as discussed below.

## 2.2 Implementation

We first give a description of the helper method `closeBackpacks()`. As explained above, during its attempt to enter the critical section a process' backpack may be joined by other processes. The shared CAS objects $B[p][j]$, $j \in \{0, 1\}$, represent backpacks which are empty if their value is $p$'s current sequence number $c$, and closed (i.e., cannot be joined by other processes) if their value is *closed*. Otherwise, each of those objects may store a set of pairs consisting of a process ID and a sequence number. The purpose of method `closeBackpacks()` is to transfer the contents of those sets to $p$'s local variable *bpack* and to close the shared backpacks. To do that, a process simply first tries to change the value of each CAS object $B[p][j]$ from $c$ to *closed* using a `CAS()` operation in line 37. If that `CAS()` succeeds, then the backpack was empty. Otherwise, the backpack contains a set of process ID, sequence number pairs. Process $p$ reads that set in line 38, and then performs another `CAS()` on $B[p][j]$ to close the backpack, using the value just read as the first argument. This guarantees that the `CAS()` succeeds. Finally, $p$ adds the set it found to the set stored in local variable *bpack*.

We now discuss the `lock()` method. In line 1, process $p$ sets *abort_sig* to `False` (so that abort signals can be received) and its set *bpack* to $\emptyset$, because it has no processes backpacked. It then begins attempts of entering the critical section in an infinite while-loop (that begins in line 2), until it either enters the critical section in one of lines 32 and 35 or calls `abort()` in line 4. Before each attempt, in line 3 the process reads $S$, and waits until the value of $S'$ is at least as large as the first component of $S$ (or the abort-signal is received). Our code guarantees that $S' = i - 1$ as long as $S = (i, locked)$. Hence, line 3 guarantees, that a process does not proceed unless $S = (\cdot, unlocked)$. This prevents a process from making multiple attempts while it cannot "win" $S$ anyway.

With each attempt, process $p$ increments a sequence number stored in the first component of the pair in $A[p]$ (line 5), and then it changes the second component of that pair from *done* to *want* to indicate that it is making an attempt to capture the lock (line 6). In line 7, process $p$ makes sure that $B'[p] =$ `False`. This allows other processes to signal $p$ that $B[p][0]$ has changed by writing `True` to $B'[p]$. In line 8 process $p$ opens its shared backpacks $B[p][0]$ and $B[p][1]$ by changing them from *closed* to $c$, where $c$ is $p$'s current sequence number. Then, in lines 9–15 the process makes all its random decisions: It first chooses a "side" $\alpha \in \{0, 1\}$ and writes to $R_\alpha[\lambda]$, where $\lambda$ is a truncated geometric distribution. Then it chooses $\beta \in \{0, 1\}$ at random, and if $\beta = 1$ process $p$ writes to $Z_\alpha$, otherwise $p$ reads a pair $(carrier, carrier\_seq)$ from $Z_\alpha$. In the latter case, $p$ tries to join the backpack of process *carrier* by executing a `CAS()` operation on $B[carrier][1]$ in line 16. If that is successful, process $p$ repeats the loop in lines 17–20 until it received the abort signal, or until it gets notified that it has been promoted or that some aborting process has given $p$ its backpack by writing it to $B[p][0]$. The signal for promotion is received on $A'[p]$; specifically, a process trying to promote $p$ writes a pair consisting of its own ID and $p$'s sequence number to $A'[p]$. Hence, $p$ breaks out of the repeat-until loop (and any `await()` statement) if $A'[p] = (\cdot, c)$. Similarly, a process $b$ that aborts, and wants to hand its backpack over to $p$, changes the value of $B[p][0]$ to $b$'s backpack contents, and then signals $p$ by writing `True` to $B'[p]$. This allows $p$ to break out of its `await()` statement in line 18. After that $p$ resets $B'[p]$ in line 19, and then checks in line 20 if $B[p][0]$ has indeed received a backpack. If not, it starts another iteration of the repeat-until loop.

The reason why the second check of $B[p][0]$ is necessary, is rather subtle: An aborting process $b$ may successfully write its backpack contents to $B[p][0]$ (see line 62), but then fall asleep just before being able to write `True` to $B'[p]$ (in line 64). Now $p$ may abort and call `lock()` again. Then $p$'s execution may again reach the `await()` statement in line 18, and then $b$ wakes up and signals $p$ that it transferred $b$'s backpack to $B[p][0]$, even though $B[p][0]$ is still empty. As a result, $p$ breaks out of the `await()` statement. But we cannot allow $p$ to continue, because it is still in a backpack, and starting another attempt to win the lock might lead to a situation where the backpack relation $\leftarrow$ is cyclic. (E.g., the carrier of $p$ might get an opportunity to join $p$'s backpack.)

Now suppose $p$ does not manage to join a backpack, or it finishes the repeat-until loop. Then, in line 21 it first reads $S$, and, provided it does not receive the abort signal, waits until $S'$ is at least as large as the sequence number, $i$, stored in $S$, or until $A'[p] = (\cdot, c)$. If $A'[p] = (\cdot, c)$, then $p$ has been promoted, so it proceeds directly to call `giveUp()` in line 34. The handshaking mechanism in that method will ensure that the `giveUp()` call returns `False`, so $p$ enters the critical section. If, on the other hand, $p$ finishes the `await()` statement in line 21 because $abort\_sig =$ `True`, and if $S' < i$ when $p$ executes line 22, then $p$ will also call `giveUp()` in line 34. In this case, it may still get promoted into the critical section via the hand shaking mechanism in method `giveUp()` in line 34. That call returns `False` if $p$ got promoted, and `True` otherwise. In the latter case, $p$ calls `closeBackpacks()` to move processes from its shared backpack variables $B[p][j]$, $j \in \{0, 1\}$, to its local *bpack* set, and then starts another iteration of the while-loop, where it will call `abort()` in line 4.

Now suppose that $p$ breaks out of the `await()` statement in line 21 because $S' \geq i$. Then it is ensured that at some point after reading $S$, the value of $S$ was $(i, unlocked)$ (because $i$ is only written to $S'$ after a process changes $S$ from $(i, locked)$ to $(i, unlocked)$, in lines 57–58). Therefore, $p$ now makes an attempt to lock $S$ in line 23.

First suppose that this attempt fails. Then in line 33 $p$ waits until $S'$ has become larger than $i$ (or until $A[p] = (c, critical)$ or $abort\_sig =$ `True`). Once $S'$ is larger than $i$, it is ensured that $S$ has been unlocked again. The fact that $p$ waits twice, once in line 21 and once in line 33 ensures that $p$ does not finish line 33 before $S$ has been at least once unlocked, then locked, and unlocked again. As a result $p$ will wait long enough for a process that may have discovered $p$ on $Z_\alpha$ to get a fair chance to join $p$'s backpack. After waiting, $p$ calls `giveUp()` in line 34. As described earlier, if $p$ gets promoted, it enters the critical section, and otherwise it calls `closeBackpacks()` and starts another attempt by repeating the while-loop.

We now consider the case in which $p$ manages to lock $S$ by changing its value from $(i, unlocked)$ to $(i + 1, locked)$ in line 23. Then in lines 24–26, $p$ changes its status $A[p]$ to $(c, critical)$, writes its current sequence number $c$ to $X[p]$, and increments $i$. Updating $A[p]$ indicates that $p$ is now poised to enter the critical section, and updating $X[p]$ indicates that $p$ cannot be promoted anymore. The increment of $i$ ensures that $i$ reflects the value of the first component of $S$.

In the for-loop in lines 27–32, $p$ scans through $R_{i \bmod 2}[]$ as described earlier (ignoring $R_{i \bmod 2}[1]$), until it finds the first entry with a *terminal value*, (0,0) or $(p, \cdot)$. Each non-terminal value $(r, d)$ process $p$ finds in an array entry $R[j]$ gets added to $Q$, and each non-(0,0) array entry $R[j]$ is reset to $(0, 0)$. Once the first terminal value (0,0) or $(p, \cdot)$ is found, $p$ enters the critical section in line 32. (Since $R[\ell + 1]$ is never written, its value remains $(0, 0)$, and thus $p$ will eventually executed line 32.)

In the `release()` method, process $p$ first changes its status from $(c, critical)$ to $(c, done)$ in line 51. After that, it calls method `closeBackpacks()` in line 52, where it moves all processes found in its shared backpack variables $B[p][j]$, $j \in \{0, 1\}$, to the local set *bpack*. Then, in line 53, $p$ adds the elements of that set to $Q$. In each iteration of the while-loop in lines 54–56, process $p$ removes a pair $(r, d)$ from $Q$, and then tries to call promote $r$ by calling `promote(`$r, d$`)`. If that call returns `True`, then $p$ successfully promoted $r$, and can enter the remainder section. Otherwise, it keeps attempting to promote processes until one promotion succeeds or $Q = \emptyset$. If $Q$ becomes empty, then there are no more processes that can be promoted into the critical section. In this case, $p$ unlocks $S$ in line 57, and signals in line 58 that it has done so by writing to $S'$. Finally, $p$ enters the remainder section.

We now describe methods `giveUp()` and `promote(`$r, d$`)`. A process calls `giveUp()` when it wants to terminate its current attempt to win the lock at the end of the while-loop of `lock()` (line 34). A process calls `promote(r, d)` to promote process $r$ into the critical section, after it found the pair $(r, d)$ in $Q$. Both methods are wait-free and guarantee that if a `promote(r, d)` call returns `True`, then and only then $r$'s call of `giveUp()` while $r$ has a sequence number of $d$ returns `False`.

In method `giveUp()`, process $p$ first writes its current sequence number to $X[p]$, and then reads $A'[p]$ into a pair $(proc, seq)$ (lines 40–41). If $seq$ matches $p$'s current sequence number, then process $proc$ is trying to promote $p$. In that case, in lines 43–44 process $p$ writes to $Y[proc]$ to indicate that it has received the promotion signal, and tries to changes $A[p]$ from $(c, want)$ to $(c, critical)$. In either case, in line 45, $p$ executes $A[p]$.CAS($(c, want), (c, done)$), and its `giveUp()` call returns the return value of that CAS. If the `CAS()` fails, then either $p$'s `CAS()` in the previous line succeeded, or process $proc$ successfully promoted $p$ by changing $A[p]$ (in line 49). Otherwise, $p$ will not get promoted, and thus successfully gave up on its attempt to enter the critical section.

In method `promote(r, d)` the calling process, $p$, first writes `False` to $Y[p]$, and then signals $r$ by writing $(p, d)$ to $A'[r]$ (lines 46–47). In line 48, process $p$ checks if $X[r][d] =$ `False`; if yes, then $r$ has not called `giveUp()` yet, so $p$ knows that when $r$ calls `giveUp()`, $r$ will receive the signal on $A'[r]$ in time, and get promoted. Otherwise, $p$ tries to change $A[r]$ from $(d, want)$ to $(d, critical)$ using a CAS. If that `CAS()` succeeds, then again $r$ is promoted in time (and $r$ will find out when its `CAS()` in line 45 fails). Because of that CAS, the check of $X[r][d]$ in line 48 is not necessary for correctness. But our analysis requires that the adversary does not learn the identity of $r$ before process $r$ has proceeded far enough in its current attempt of getting the lock (i.e., it must have at least tried to enter a backpack in line 16, if it chose $\beta = 0$ in line 12). Due to our assumption that a `CAS()` reveals information to the adversary, we cannot execute this `CAS()` too early; the check in line 48 ensures that $r$ has already called `giveUp()` when the `CAS()` in line 49 gets performed. If the return value of that `CAS()` is `True`, then $p$ successfully promoted $r$. Otherwise, $p$ needs to check $Y[p]$ to determine if the promotion was successful. If $Y[p] =$ `True`, then $r$ wrote to line 43 after $p$ reset $Y$ in line 46. Then and only then $r$ got promoted due to its own successful `CAS()` in line 44.

We finally describe the `abort()` method that process $p$ may call in line 4 after it received the abort signal during its `lock()` method. By the time $p$ calls this method after having executed an earlier iteration of the while-loop in method `lock()`, processes may have joined its backpack and thus may have been stored in $B[p][0]$ or $B[p][1]$. At the end of such a while-loop iteration $p$ has called `closeBackpacks()` (in line 34) and thus collected the set of all those processes into its local variable $bpack$. Processes in that set may now be waiting to get promoted by $p$, so in its `abort()` method, $p$ tries to hand its backpack over to some other process. To do so in the while-loop in lines 60–64, it first removes a pair $(r, d)$ from $bpack$ and tries to change $B[r][0]$ to $bpack$ using a CAS. It keeps repeating this, as long the `CAS()` fails and as long as $bpack \neq \emptyset$. (If such a `CAS()` fails, then this means that $r$ has already aborted itself, and thus is not waiting to be promoted by $p$ anymore.) If $bpack$ becomes empty, then $p$ can enter the critical section, because no process is waiting in $p$'s backpack anymore. Otherwise, in one of the while-loop iterations $p$ successfully hands its backpack over to some process $r$. It can then reset $bpack$ to $\emptyset$, and signal $r$ by writing `True` to $B'[r]$. This enables $r$ to break out of the repeat-until loop (lines 17–20) in `lock()`, and thus continue attempting to capture the lock itself instead of waiting to be promoted by $p$.

# 3 EXTENSIONS

## 3.1 Bounding Space

Our algorithm uses an unbounded array $X$ as well as base objects of unbounded size, because they store unbounded sequence numbers. The size as well as the number of base objects can be bounded without affecting the amortized RMR complexity. Below we will sketch the main idea.

First note, that, except for array $X$, our algorithm uses only polynomially many CAS objects and registers. Array $X$ is only unbounded, because we need for each process $p$ and each sequence number $c$ used by $p$ an array entry $X[p][c]$. Thus, if the number of sequence numbers can be bounded by a polynomial in $n$, then we also need only polynomially many base objects, each storing $O(\log n)$-bit values.

The idea is now that we use multiple abortable lock objects, as the one we described in earlier sections, but where sequence numbers are bounded by some threshold $K$, which is polynomial in $n$. The "current" lock object is stored in a register $ptr$.

In the entry section, a process now calls `lock()` on the current lock object pointed to by $ptr$. Once a process runs out of sequence numbers, it sets a flag associated with the current lock object, and the next process winning that lock changes $ptr$ so that it points to a new lock object. Other processes have to monitor $ptr$ and switch to the new lock object, if they see that $ptr$ has changed. Our algorithm guarantees that in an interval in which a process increases its sequence number twice, at least one process wins the lock. As a result, a process will not increase its sequence number more than once after $ptr$ has changed.

To bound the number of lock objects used, we can then use a *taggable register* introduced by Aghazadeh and Woelfel [1]. Such an object stores a pointer to objects from some bounded object pool $B$. In our case, $B$ will consist of abortable lock objects with bounded sequence numbers, and the taggable register will store the pointer $ptr$ to the "current" lock object. The main point of the taggable register abstraction is that it allows a process to find at any point a "free" lock object $L \in B$, which may not be accessed by any other process anymore. (The exact semantics of taggable register objects is involved; see [1] for a complete description.) Thus, a process that wants to swing the pointer $ptr$ to a new object $L$, can first find a free one, $L'$, reinitialize it, and then change the pointer to $ptr$. Reinitializing $L'$ can be done while no process is accessing $L'$, and thus while $p$ has exclusive access to it. As a result, assuming that each single lock object can be used for sufficiently many `lock()` calls in total, the work for resetting a `lock()` object can be amortized over the total number of those `lock()` calls. This way, the amortized RMR complexity only increases by a constant factor.

The implementations of taggable registers from atomic registers presented in [1] are wait-free and have constant step complexity, and thus do not affect the asymptotic RMR complexity. For our purpose, the total space requirements are polynomial in $n$, and registers of logarithmic size suffice as base objects.

### 3.2 Avoiding Compare-and-Swap

As discussed earlier, there are linearizable, deterministic implementations of CAS objects from atomic registers with constant RMR complexity in the worst-case [22]. However, those implementations are not abortable, and thus cannot be used in our mutual exclusion algorithm without sacrificing abortability. The construction in [22] uses the constant RMR implementation of a test-and-set object from registers in [23], and then implements a CAS object from test-and-set. This construction can easily be made abortable on the CC model if abortable test-and-set object are available, maintaining constant RMR complexity [18]. On the other hand, it seems the test-and-set algorithm of [23] cannot be made abortable without sacrificing constant RMR complexity [18]. However, the randomized test-and-set algorithms in [2, 19] have expected constant amortized step complexity against an oblivious adversary. Thus, combining those test-and-set algorithms with a straight-forward abortable version of the CAS construction from test-and-set in [22], yields an abortable CAS implementation from registers with constant amortized RMR complexity, where the after abort path is randomized wait-free.

Note that our algorithm allows the adversary to know at any point the values of all CAS objects, and whether a process is poised to perform a CAS operation, and if so, the parameters of that operation. Hence, using implemented CAS operations does not increase the power of the adversary. Thus, we can safely use CAS implementations as described above in our mutual exclusion algorithm, sacrificing the wait-freedom in the abort path for randomized wait-freedom, but maintaining expected constant amortized RMR complexity.

## REFERENCES


[1] Zahra Aghazadeh and Philipp Woelfel. Upper bounds for boundless tagging with bounded objects. In *Proceedings of the 30th International Symposium on Distributed Computing (DISC)*, pages 442–457, 2016.

[2] Dan Alistarh and James Aspnes. Sub-logarithmic test-and-set against a weak adversary. In *Proceedings of the 25th International Symposium on Distributed Computing (DISC)*, pages 97–109, 2011.

[3] James Anderson and Yong-Jik Kim. Adaptive mutual exclusion with local spinning. In *Proceedings of the 14th International Symposium on Distributed Computing (DISC)*, pages 29–43, 2000.

[4] James Anderson and Yong-Jik Kim. An improved lower bound for the time complexity of mutual exclusion. *Distributed Computing*, 15:221–253, 2002.

[5] James Anderson, Yong-Jik Kim, and Ted Herman. Shared-memory mutual exclusion: Major research trends since 1986. *Distributed Computing*, 16:75–110, 2003.

[6] Thomas Anderson. The performance of spin lock alternatives for shared-memory multiprocessors. *IEEE Transactions on Parallel and Distributed Systems*, 1:6–16, 1990.

[7] James Aspnes. Faster randomized consensus with an oblivious adversary. In *Proceedings of the 31st SIGACT-SIGOPS Symposium on Principles of Distributed Computing (PODC)*, pages 1–8, 2012.

[8] Hagit Attiya, Danny Hendler, and Smadar Levy. An $O(1)$-barriers optimal RMRs mutual exclusion algorithm. In *Proceedings of the 31st SIGACT-SIGOPS Symposium on Principles of Distributed Computing (PODC)*, pages 220–229, 2013.

[9] Hagit Attiya, Danny Hendler, and Philipp Woelfel. Tight RMR lower bounds for mutual exclusion and other problems. In *Proceedings of the 40th Annual ACM Symposium on Theory of Computing (STOC)*, pages 217–226, 2008.

[10] Hagit Attiya, Danny Hendler, and Philipp Woelfel. Trading fences with rmrs and separating memory models. In *Proceedings of the 34th SIGACT-SIGOPS Symposium on Principles of Distributed Computing (PODC)*, pages 173–182, 2015.

[11] Ohad Ben-Baruch and Danny Hendler. The price of being adaptive. In *Proceedings of the 34th SIGACT-SIGOPS Symposium on Principles of Distributed Computing (PODC)*, pages 183–192, 2015.

[12] Michael Bender and Seth Gilbert. Mutual exclusion with $O(\log^2 \log n)$ amortized work. In *Proceedings of the 52nd Annual IEEE Symposium on Foundations of Computer Science (FOCS)*, pages 728–737, 2011.

[13] David E. Culler, Jaswinder Pal Singh, and Anoop Gupta. *Parallel Computer Architecture: A Hardware/Software Approach*. Morgan Kaufmann, August 1998.

[14] Robert Danek and Wojciech Golab. Closing the complexity gap between FCFS mutual exclusion and mutual exclusion. *Distributed Computing*, 23(2):87–111, 2010.

[15] Robert Danek and Hyonho Lee. Brief announcement: Local-spin algorithms for abortable mutual exclusion and related problems. In *Proceedings of the 22nd International Symposium on Distributed Computing (DISC)*, pages 512–513, 2008.

[16] Oksana Denysyuk and Philipp Woelfel. Are shared objects composable under an oblivious adversary? In *Proceedings of the 35th SIGACT-SIGOPS Symposium on Principles of Distributed Computing (PODC)*, pages 335–344, 2016.

[17] Edsger Dijkstra. Solution of a problem in concurrent programming control. *Communications of the ACM*, 8:569, 1965.

[18] Aryaz Eghbali and Philipp Woelfel. Personal communication, 2017.

[19] George Giakkoupis and Philipp Woelfel. On the time and space complexity of randomized test-and-set. In *Proceedings of the 31st SIGACT-SIGOPS Symposium on Principles of Distributed Computing (PODC)*, pages 19–28, 2012.

[20] George Giakkoupis and Philipp Woelfel. A tight RMR lower bound for randomized mutual exclusion. In *Proceedings of the 44th Annual ACM Symposium on Theory of Computing (STOC)*, pages 983–1002, 2012.

[21] George Giakkoupis and Philipp Woelfel. Randomized mutual exclusion with constant amortized RMR complexity on the DSM. In *Proceedings of the 55th Annual IEEE Symposium on Foundations of Computer Science (FOCS)*, pages 504–513, 2014.

[22] Wojciech Golab, Vassos Hadzilacos, Danny Hendler, and Philipp Woelfel. RMR-efficient implementations of comparison primitives using read and write operations. *Distributed Computing*, 25(2):109–162, 2012.

[23] Wojciech Golab, Danny Hendler, and Philipp Woelfel. An $O(1)$ RMRs leader election algorithm. *SIAM Journal on Computing*, 39(7):2726–2760, 2010.

[24] Wojciech Golab, Lisa Higham, and Philipp Woelfel. Linearizable implementations do not suffice for randomized distributed computation. In *Proceedings of the 43rd Annual ACM Symposium on Theory of Computing (STOC)*, pages 373–382, 2011.

[25] Danny Hendler and Philipp Woelfel. Adaptive randomized mutual exclusion in sub-logarithmic expected time. In *Proceedings of the 29th SIGACT-SIGOPS Symposium on Principles of Distributed Computing (PODC)*, pages 141–150, 2010.

[26] Danny Hendler and Philipp Woelfel. Randomized mutual exclusion with sub-logarithmic RMR-complexity. *Distributed Computing*, 24(1):3–19, 2011.

[27] Prasad Jayanti. Adaptive and efficient abortable mutual exclusion. In *Proceedings of the 22nd SIGACT-SIGOPS Symposium on Principles of Distributed Computing (PODC)*, pages 295–304, 2003.

[28] Prasad Jayanti, Srdjan Petrovic, and Neha Narula. Read/write based fast-path transformation for FCFS mutual exclusion. In *31st Conference on Current Trends in Theory and Practice of Informatics (SOFSEM)*, pages 209–218, 2005.

[29] Yong-Jik Kim and James Anderson. A time complexity bound for adaptive mutual exclusion. In *Proceedings of the 15th International Symposium on Distributed Computing (DISC)*, pages 1–15, 2001.

[30] Yong-Jik Kim and James Anderson. Nonatomic mutual exclusion with local spinning. *Distributed Computing*, 19(1):19–61, 2006.

[31] Hyonho Lee. Transformations of mutual exclusion algorithms from the cache-coherent model to the distributed shared memory model. In *Proceedings of the 25th International Conference on Distributed Computing Systems (ICDCS)*, pages 261–270, 2005.

[32] Hyonho Lee. Fast local-spin abortable mutual exclusion with bounded space. In *Proceedings of 14th International Conference On Principles Of DIstributed Systems (OPODIS)*, pages 364–379, 2010.

[33] John M. Mellor-Crummey and Michael L. Scott. Algorithms for scalable synchronization on shared-memory multiprocessors. *ACM Transactions on Computer Systems*, 9(1):21–65, 1991.

[34] Abhijeet Pareek and Philipp Woelfel. RMR-efficient randomized abortable mutual exclusion. In *Proceedings of the 26th International Symposium on Distributed Computing (DISC)*, pages 267–281, 2012.

[35] Michel Raynal. *Algorithms for Mutual Exclusion*. MIT Press, 1986.

[36] Michael L. Scott. Non-blocking timeout in scalable queue-based spin locks. In *Proceedings of the 21st SIGACT-SIGOPS Symposium on Principles of Distributed Computing (PODC)*, pages 31-40, 2002.

[37] Jae-Heon Yang and James Anderson. A fast, scalable mutual exclusion algorithm. *Distributed Computing*, 9(1):51–60, 1995.

**Class** CCLock

```
shared:
  // ℓ := ⌈log n⌉
  Register R_s[1...ℓ+1], for s ∈ {0,1}; init (0,0)                // Stores values in 𝒫_0 × ℕ_0
  Register Z_s, for s ∈ {0,1}; init (1,0)                        // Stores values in 𝒫 × ℕ_0
  Compare-and-Swap S; init (0, unlocked)                         // Stores a pair in ℕ_0 × {locked, unlocked}
  Compare-and-Swap A[1...n]; init (0, done)                      // Stores pairs in ℕ_0 × {want, critical, done}
  Compare-and-Swap B[1...n][0...1]; init closed                  // Stores values in ℕ ∪ {closed} ∪ 2^(𝒫×ℕ)
  Sequential Multiset Q; init ∅                                  // Stores pairs in 𝒫 × ℕ
  Register S'; init 0                                            // Stores values in ℕ_0
  Register A'[1...n]; init (0,0)                                 // Stores values in 𝒫_0 × ℕ_0
  Register B'[1...n], Y[1...n], X[1...n][1...∞]; init False      // Stores Boolean values
// All other variables are local and their scope spans the entire class
// abort_sig is a local Boolean; it becomes True when an abort signal is received
```

**Method** lock()

```
abort_sig := False; bpack := ∅
while True do
    (i,·) := S; await(S' ≥ i or abort_sig)
    if abort_sig then abort()
    (c,·) := A[id()]; c := c + 1
    A[id()].CAS((c − 1, done), (c, want))
    B'[id()] := False
    foreach i ∈ {0,1} do B[id()][i].CAS(closed, c)
    Choose α ∈ {0,1} uniformly at random
    Choose λ ∈ {1,...,ℓ} s.t. Pr(λ = j) = 2^(−j) if 1 ≤ j < ℓ, and Pr(λ = ℓ) = 2^(−ℓ+1)
    R_α[λ] := (id(), c)
    Choose β ∈ {0,1} uniformly at random
    if β = 1 then Z_α := (id(), c)
    else
        (carrier, carrier_seq) := Z_α
        if B[carrier][1].CAS(carrier_seq, {(id(), c)}) then
            repeat
                await(A'[id()] = (·,c) or B'[id()] or abort_sig)
                B'[id()] := False
            until A'[id()] = (·,c) or B[id()][0] ≠ c or abort_sig
    (i,·) := S; await(S' ≥ i or A'[id()] = (·,c) or abort_sig)
    if S' ≥ i then
        if S.CAS((i, unlocked), (i + 1, locked)) then
            A[id()].CAS((c, want), (c, critical))
            X[id()][c] := True
            i := i + 1
            for j = 2,...,ℓ + 1 do
                (r,d) := R_{i mod 2}[j]
                if (r,d) ≠ (0,0) then R_{i mod 2}[j] := (0,0)
                if (r,d) ≠ (0,0) and r ≠ id() then
                    Q := Q ∪ {(r,d)}
                else goto critical section
        await(S' ≥ i + 1 or A'[id()] = (·,c) or abort_sig)
    if giveUp() then closeBackpacks()
    else goto critical section
```

**Method** closeBackpacks()

```
foreach i ∈ {0, 1} do
    if B[id()][i].CAS(c,closed) = False then
        tmp := B[id()][i]
        B[id()][i].CAS(tmp, closed); bpack := bpack ∪ tmp
```

**Method** giveUp()

```
X[id()][c] := True
(proc, seq) := A′[id()]
if seq = c then
    Y[proc] := True
    A[id()].CAS((c, want), (c, critical))
return A[id()].CAS((c, want), (c, done))
```

**Method** promote(r, d)

```
Y[id()] := False
A′[r] := (id(), d)
if X[r][d] = False then return True
if A[r].CAS((d, want), (d, critical)) then return True
return Y[id()]
```

**Method** release()

```
A[id()].CAS((c, critical), (c, done))
closeBackpacks()
Q := Q ∪ bpack; bpack := ∅
while Q ≠ ∅ do
    Remove an arbitrary pair (r, d) from Q
    if promote(r, d) then goto remainder section
(i, ·) := S; S.CAS((i, locked),(i, unlocked))
S′ := i
goto remainder section
```

**Method** abort()

```
while bpack ≠ ∅ do
    Remove an arbitrary pair (r, d) from bpack
    if B[r][0].CAS(d, bpack) then
        bpack := ∅
        B′[r] := True
goto remainder section
```

# Transactional Lock Elision Meets Combining

Alex Kogan
alex.kogan@oracle.com
Oracle Labs
Burlington, MA, USA

Yossi Lev
yossi.lev@oracle.com
Oracle Labs
Burlington, MA, USA

## ABSTRACT

Flat combining (FC) and transactional lock elision (TLE) are two techniques that facilitate efficient multi-thread access to a sequentially implemented data structure protected by a lock. FC allows threads to delegate their operations to another (combiner) thread, and benefit from executing multiple operations by that thread under the lock through combining and elimination optimizations tailored to the specific data structure. TLE employs hardware transactional memory (HTM) that allows multiple threads to apply their operations concurrently as long as they do not conflict. This paper explores how these two radically different techniques can complement one another, and introduces the HTM-assisted Combining Framework (HCF). HCF leverages HTM to allow multiple combiners to run concurrently with each other, as well as with other, non-combiner threads. This makes HCF a good fit for data structures and workloads in which some operations may conflict with each other while others may run concurrently without conflicts. HCF achieves all that with changes to the sequential code similar to those required by TLE and FC, and in particular, without requiring the programmer to reason about concurrency.

## KEYWORDS

hardware transactional memory; lock elision; flat combining; elimination; concurrent data structures

## 1 INTRODUCTION

Flat combining (FC) [11] and transactional lock elision (TLE) [5] are two synchronization techniques that, given a sequentially implemented data structure and a lock, enable efficient application of concurrent operations to the data structure.

FC allows threads to delegate their operations to another thread, a *combiner*, which applies those operations while holding the lock. The key benefit of having a combiner to run operations on behalf of other threads is the ability to combine and eliminate multiple delegated operations with each other, thus reducing the total work under the lock. The code to combine and eliminate operations varies between one data structure to another. Thus, FC relies on exploiting data structure specific semantics to achieve better performance when multiple concurrent operations are applied to the data structure by the same thread. Furthermore, even when combining and elimination is not applicable, applying multiple operations by the same thread also often results in a more cache-friendly execution. FC is compelling because it relieves programmers from the need to reason about concurrency: as long as they provide a sequential code to efficiently combine and/or eliminate multiple operations together, a multi-thread execution can provide a significant performance benefit despite the fact that all operations are executed under a single lock [9, 11].

TLE also introduces parallelism to lock-based sequential code; it achieves that by using hardware transactional memory (HTM), a feature introduced in recent multicore processors that allows running multiple critical sections speculatively in parallel. With TLE, operations are *logically* sequentialized by a critical section's lock, but in practice they can run in parallel as long as they do not conflict on accesses to shared locations. If the speculative execution fails (perhaps after multiple trials), TLE reverts to execute the critical section under the lock.

TLE can be used to introduce concurrency between operations of a sequential data structure, and provides excellent scalability when the operations rarely conflict [15]. Unfortunately, it performs poorly in the presence of conflicts (even between a small faction of operations), which lead to lock acquisitions, as no operation can run using a hardware transaction while the lock is being held [1, 4, 7, 15]. Unlike FC, TLE does not delegate operations to other threads, and does not benefit from data structure specific optimizations that can make the execution of multiple operations under the lock more efficient.

In this paper we explore how these two techniques can complement each other. Consider, for example, a priority queue with two operations: Insert and RemoveMin. Depending on the underlying data structure (e.g., if a priority queue is based on a skip list), Insert operations may be able to run concurrently using hardware transactions, as they would access a disjoint set of memory locations. RemoveMin operations, however, will always conflict with each other, as they are all required to remove the same element from the queue. Using TLE to execute priority queue operations will therefore result in frequent failures to the lock when a few threads try to execute RemoveMin operations concurrently. At the same time, although RemoveMin operations can easily be combined together, Insert operations generally cannot, undermining the efficiency of FC in this case. Moreover, FC does not allow those Insert operations to proceed in parallel with combining of RemoveMin operations. Note that a simple idea of applying TLE and then combining operations that fail to the lock would not address this issue either. This is because the combined RemoveMin operations would run while holding the lock, blocking all other operations, including Insert operations that do not conflict and could run in parallel.


*PODC '17, July 25-27, 2017, Washington, DC, USA*

ACM ISBN 978-1-4503-4992-5/17/07...$15.00
https://doi.org/http://dx.doi.org/10.1145/3087801.3087838

The key contribution of this paper is the introduction of a novel approach that achieves "the best of both words" by using HTM to combine and run multiple delegated operations together while still allowing other operations to run concurrently with them. We implement this approach using *HTM-assisted Combining Framework* (HCF), a new framework that provides the following benefits:

- Works with sequential code of a data structure.
- Supports delegation, i.e., a thread can run operations on behalf of other threads.
- Delegated operations can be applied concurrently with other, non-delegated operations that are run by their respective threads.
- Allows concurrent execution of different subsets of delegated operations.
- Allows taking advantage of data structure specific knowledge by using:
  - Combining and elimination of multiple delegated operations, resulting in a shorter total execution time.
  - Using operation specific policies to decide, at run time, whether (or when) an operation should be delegated.

To elaborate on those points, HCF does not require a thread to decide upfront whether to delegate an operation or execute it by its own. A thread can start by trying to execute an operation speculatively just like with TLE, and only after a certain number of failures make it available for other threads to execute it on its behalf. Furthermore, using HTM, multiple threads can run their own operations concurrently with multiple combining threads, each applying a separate set of delegated operations.

Note that HCF is not intended to improve over FC or TLE when one of those is beneficial on its own, i.e., where operations cannot execute in parallel on HTM due to conflicts, but may combine and/or eliminate one another (the case where FC may perform well), or where all operations can run in parallel using HTM (the case where TLE is beneficial). Rather, HCF is aimed for data structures and workloads that fall in between these two cases, where *some* of the operations can run efficiently in parallel, and other cannot, but may benefit from combining. Later in the paper we describe a few examples for such data structures and workloads, and show how they benefit from the properties of HCF.

# 2 THE HCF FRAMEWORK

## 2.1 Overview

HCF executes operations of a sequentially implemented data structure protected by a lock. An execution of an operation invoked by a thread $T$, denoted as the operation's *owner*, goes through at most four phases until completion:

(1) `TryPrivate`: the owner tries, perhaps several times, to execute the operation using a hardware (HW) transaction.
(2) `TryVisible`: the owner *announces* its operation by adding it to a *publication array*, a container holding operations that are visible to other threads, and then tries, perhaps serval times, to execute them using HW transactions.
(3) `TryCombining`: a thread selects a subset of the announced operations, including its own, and executes them using one or more HW transactions. In this phase we can benefit from data structure semantics to combine and/or eliminate multiple operations, as well as to adjust the number of operations executed by a single HW transaction.
(4) `CombineUnderLock`: the combiner acquires the data structure lock and executes, without using HW transactions, the operations that were selected but not completed in the `TryCombining` phase.

An operation returns once one of these phases is completed successfully, as demonstrated below:

```
Execute(Op) {
  // Choose the publication array Op is associated with
  Pa = choosePubArr(Op);
  if (!TryPrivate(Op,Pa) &&
      !TryVisible(Op,Pa) &&
      !TryCombining(Op,Pa)) {
        CombineUnderLock(Op, Pa);
  }
  return Op.retVal;
}
```

As suggested by the pseudocode, there could be multiple publication arrays, while each operation may reside in only one of them at any given time. Supporting multiple publication arrays, and configuring how HCF handles operations using each of those arrays (e.g., how many HTM attempts are made in each of the first three phases) is a key to customizing HCF for each particular operation. Going back to the priority queue mentioned in the Introduction, RemoveMin operations can use a separate publication array from Insert operations. This way, we can configure HCF to skip HTM attempts in the first two phases for (highly contended) RemoveMin operations and go directly to the combining phases (`TryCombining` and `CombineUnderLock`), after announcing the operation in `TryVisible`. On the other hand, Insert operations (using a separate publication array) can be handled differently, with HTM attempts in all of the first three phases.

Critically, the configuration of HCF, including the number of publication arrays and the assignment of operations to these arrays, cannot affect the correctness, but only the performance. In particular, each operation is guaranteed to execute exactly once. (Note that once an operation is announced, it may be applied in either the `TryVisible` phase by its owner, or in the `TryCombining` or `CombineUnderLock` phases by its owner or by a combiner.) Using HW transactions (in configurations that enable them) is crucial for providing this guarantee. We elaborate on this point in the following sections.

## 2.2 Algorithmic Details

Like with FC, each operation is associated with an *operation descriptor* that contains input arguments required for the sequential execution of the operation and a field to store the operation result (when applicable). In addition, the descriptor includes a `status` field that is used to synchronize between the different phases, and holds one of the following values: `UnAnnounced`, `Announced`, `BeingHelped`, or `Done`. The field is initialized to `UnAnnounced` when an operation is invoked.

The operation descriptor also specifies three *sequential* methods: runSeq, shouldHelp and runMulti. The runSeq method is used for running the operation's sequential code. The shouldHelp method is used by a combiner to select a subset of (announced) operations from a publication array (to execute in the TryCombining and CombineUnderLock phases). The runMulti method is used to combine and eliminate multiple operations with one another, and then apply the combined operation(s) on the data structure. The runSeq and runMulti can be sequential simply because they are always executed either while holding the data structure lock, or using a HW transaction. On the other hand, allowing the shouldHelp to be sequential requires some additional care, for which we use an additional *selection lock*, as we later describe when presenting the pseudo code of the HCF framework. All the three methods are independent of the operation descriptor usage by the HCF algorithm to synchronize between the different phases, and in particular, do not change the status field.

runSeq is the only method that the programer is *required* to provide (which can be just a wrapper around a sequential implementation of the operation); the framework provides multiple default implementations for shouldHelp and runMulti. For example, one default implementation for shouldHelp returns **true** for every invocation, causing the combiner to choose all announced operations in the publication array, while another variant returns **false** , causing the combiner to apply only its own operation without helping others. The former is useful when all operations in a particular publication array can be easily combined, while the latter when combining is not applicable and we rather run each operation by its own. Similarly, the framework provides a runMulti implementation that simply runs the chosen operations, without combining them, by invoking runSeq for each. The user can override those default implementations and provide variants tailored for a specific data structure, e.g., shouldHelp that selects only operations that can be combined with each other, and runMulti that combines and runs them as a single operation. Yet, even the default generic implementations can be useful, e.g., when used with publication arrays that only hold operations that cannot benefit from combining (e.g., Insert operations in the priority queue example).

We now describe the main functions for each of the algorithm phases mentioned in Section 2.1; the pseudo-code is shown in Figure 1. We note that the **HTMClause-onAbort** syntax used in Figure 1 is merely a convenient shortcut for the standard syntax of

```
if (begin hardware transaction) {
   transaction code;
   commit;
} else { abort handling code; }
```

In addition, we use an auxiliary function chooseOpsToHelp (omitted for brevity) that selects operations to help from a publication array by invoking shouldHelp for each announced operation, as we describe later.

The TryPrivate function, implementing the corresponding TryPrivate phase, acts on an operation that is still in its UnAnnounced state, and simply tries to apply it using a HW transaction, up to TryPrivateTrials times. Like with TLE, each HW transaction subscribes to the data structure's lock L, and aborts if it is acquired (Line 5). If the operation was not completed by TryPrivate, we move to the TryVisible phase, implemented by the corresponding TryVisible function. The latter begins by setting the operation descriptor status to Announced, and then adds it to the publication array Pa (Line 14).[1] It then continues to try applying the operation using a HW transaction, up to TryVisibleTrials times, similar to the TryPrivate function. In this case, however, because the operation is now visible to a combiner thread, some care must be taken to guarantee that the operation is not applied twice — once by the owner and once by a combiner thread.

The approach we take is as follows. First, we check that the status of our operation remains Announced when starting a HW transaction (Line 18). Second, we disallow applying our operation while another (combining) thread is selecting operations it will help to, so we will not apply an operation that is selected by that thread. This is achieved by checking the selection lock (Line 19) when starting a HW transaction; this lock is held throughout the selection process as described below. Finally, we remove the announced operation from the publication array *in the same transaction* that has applied this operation (Line 22). This is done to avoid the race between the owner of the operation and a combiner thread that starts selection of operations after the owner has applied its operation and before it has removed that operation from the publication array.

If the transaction aborts and the operation is no longer in the Announced state, then a combiner is responsible for applying this operation. Thus, the owner waits for the combiner to complete the operation by spinning on the status field, waiting for it to be changed to Done (Line 27).

Next, if the operation did not complete in the TryVisible phase (and was not chosen to be applied by a combiner), its owner thread $T$ moves on to the TryCombining phase implemented by the corresponding TryCombining function. There, it tries to become a combiner for the operations in Pa. It does so by acquiring the selection lock of the Pa that ensures that it is the only thread that selects operations from that Pa. Before $T$ continues with the selection of operations from Pa, though, it has to check that while competing for the selection lock, its own operation was not selected (and, perhaps, applied) by another thread that acquired the selection lock before $T$. If $T$'s operation was selected, $T$ immediately releases the selection lock and waits for the status of its operation to become Done (cf. Line 40). Otherwise, it is guaranteed that $T$'s operation status remains Announced, because no other thread can choose $T$'s operation that resides in Pa while $T$ is holding Pa's selection lock. At that point, $T$ calls the auxiliary chooseOpsToHelp method to choose the subset of operations from Pa to apply (Line 43). chooseOpsToHelp (not shown for brevity) scans the publication array, calling shouldHelp for every announced operation it finds there (except for $T$'s operation, which is chosen by default). If an operation is chosen (i.e., the corresponding call to shouldHelp returns **true** or it is $T$'s operation), its status is changed by chooseOpsToHelp to BeingHelped, it is removed from the publication array, and is added to the set returned by chooseOpsToHelp.

Note that when scanning a publication array, chooseOpsToHelp does not need to see a consistent snapshot. In fact, new operations can be added to the array while the combiner scans it, but they

[1] In our implementation we simply use an array with a slot per thread, but other dynamic schemes are possible.

```
1  TryPrivate(OpDesc Op, OpArr Pa) {
2    numFailures = 0;
3    while (numFailures < TryPrivateTrials) {
4      HTMClause {
5        if (L.isLocked()) abortHT;
6        Op.runSeq();
7        return true;
8      } onAbort { numFailures++; }
9    }
10   return false;
11 }

12 TryVisible(OpDesc Op, OpArr Pa) {
13   op.Status = Announced;
14   Pa.add(Op);
15   numFailures = 0;
16   while (numFailures < TryVisibleTrials) {
17     HTMClause {
18       if (L.isLocked() || Op.status != Announced ||
19         Pa.selectionL.isLocked()) abortHT;
20       Op.runSeq();
21       // remove Op from Pa as part of the HW Tx
22       Pa.remove(Op);
23       return true;
24     } onAbort {
25       if (Op.status != Announced) {
26         // a combiner helped or is helping us
27         while (Op.status == BeingHelped) yield();
28         return true;
29       }
30       numFailures++;
31     }
32   }
33   return false;
34 }

35 TryCombining(OpDesc Op, OpArr Pa) {
36   Pa.selectionL.lock();
37   if (Op.status != Announced) {
38     // someone picked our op in the meanwhile
39     Pa.selectionL.unlock()
40     while (Op.status == BeingHelped) yield();
41     return true;
42   }
43   opsToHelp = Op.chooseOpsToHelp(Pa);
44   Pa.selectionL.unlock();
45   numFailures = 0;
46   while (numFailures < TryCombiningTrials) {
47     HTMClause {
48       if (L.isLocked()) abortHT;
49       opsHelped = Op.runMulti(opsToHelp);
50     } onAbort { numFailures++; continue; }
51     // signal threads whose operations are done
52     updateOpsStatus(opsHelped,Done);
53     opsToHelp.remove(opsHelped);
54     if (opsToHelp.empty()) return true;
55   }
56   return false;
57 }

58 CombineUnderLock(OpDesc Op, OpArr Pa) {
59   L.lock();
60   while (!opsToHelp.empty()) {
61     opsHelped = Op.runMulti(opsToHelp)
62     updateOpsStatus(opsHelped,Done);
63     opsToHelp.remove(opsHelped);
64   }
65   L.unlock();
66 }
```

**Figure 1: HCF framework functions. Code in HTMClause executes in a hardware transaction; if aborted, control is transferred to the onAbort clause. A `return` statement inside HTMClause commits the transaction before returning from a function.**

cannot be removed (by their owners) since $T$ is holding the Pa's selection lock. This allows an efficient selection process without atomic operations.

Once `chooseOpsToHelp` returns the set of selected operation descriptors, stored in `opsToHelp`, The `TryCombining` function repeatedly calls `runMulti` to apply some (or all) of the selected operations. Recall that `runMulti` is a sequential function and assumes that it runs in isolation, and therefore it must be called from within a hardware transaction (or under a lock). If a call to `runMulti` completes successfully within a hardware transaction, the `status` field of operations applied by that `runMulti` call is set to `Done` (Line 52), signaling the owners of those operations that the operations have been completed. After that, these operations are removed from the `opsToHelp` set (Line 53). We invoke `runMulti` multiple times to allow an implementation that applies only some of the selected operations in each invocation, making them more likely to complete in a single hardware transaction.

The `TryCombining` function completes if either it successfully applied all selected operations, or if all budgeted (`TryCombiningTrials`) HW transactions failed while trying to apply them. In the former case, `opsToHelp` is empty, and `TryCombining` returns true (Line 54). Otherwise, $T$ moves on to the `CombineUnderLock` phase, implemented by the corresponding `CombineUnderLock` function. The latter acquires the data structure lock `L` (Line 59), and applies the rest of the operations in `opsToHelp` by repeatedly calling `runMulti`. This is similar to the `TryCombining` function, except that now `runMulti` is called outside of a hardware transaction. Once `opsToHelp` is empty (that is, all selected operations were applied successfully), the `CombineUnderLock` function releases `L` (Line 65) and completes.

## 2.3 Correctness

Here we outline the main claims showing that using HCF with a sequential implementation of a data structure results in a correct, linearizable concurrent implementation of the data structure.

First, if an operation is applied to a data structure via the HCF framework, then it is done by either calling the `runSeq` or the `runMulti` method (that may call the `runSeq` method for that operation, or apply that operation as a part of another, combined operation). In any case, this is done either while holding the data structure lock, or inside a hardware transaction. Thus, since no hardware transaction can access the data structure while the lock is held, the operation seems to take effect atomically, either when the transaction commits or when the lock is released.

Second, we note that every operation always takes effect between the operation's invocation and response. This is trivial if the operation is applied by its owner. When the operation is applied by a combiner, the combiner learns about it only after the operation has been invoked (and announced by its owner). Along with that, the combiner changes the status of the operation to Done only after the operation takes effect. The owner of the operation returns a response only after it learns that the operation's status was changed to Done. Thus, even when the operation is applied by a combiner, the response is returned only after the operation takes effect.

Next, we claim that an operation is never applied more than once by the HCF framework. Recall that each announced operation has exactly one descriptor, and it is associated with exactly one publication array. Thus, it is sufficient to show that for any pair of Op and Pa, no series of invocations of the HCF methods can result in multiple applications of Op. To this end, consider the first invocation of runSeq (or runMulti) with Op that completed successfully (i.e, it was executed by a committed hardware transaction, or while holding the lock L). If that invocation was done by the TryPrivate function, then Op is not yet stored in the Pa at this point, and thus could not be executed by any other thread running as a combiner. Furthermore, TryPrivate returns **true** in this case. Thus, no other HCF function is called for Op, so Op was applied exactly once.

If the first successful invocation was done by the TryVisible function, then we know that: a) The operation descriptor status field had the Announced value when the operation took effect. b) A combiner has not been executing chooseOpsToHelp. c) The operation descriptor was removed from Pa as part of the transaction that applied Op. The fact that the status of the operation was still Announced when it was applied implies that a combiner thread in the TryCombining function has yet changed its status to BeingHelped. The fact that no combiner has been executing chooseOpsToHelp means that no other thread was reading the publication array during the execution of Op. The fact that we successfully removed the descriptor from Pa in the hardware transaction implies that any subsequent traversal of the publication array in chooseOpsToHelp will not find Op, and thus no combiner will try to apply Op again. Thus, the operation Op is applied exactly once (by its owner). The TryVisible function then returns **true**, and thus no additional attempts to execute Op are done.

Similarly, the TryCombining function only executes Op if it first changes its status to BeingHelped, which can only happen if the descriptor is still in the publication array when it calls chooseOpsToHelp. Thus, if Op was applied by the TryCombining function, it must be in a BeingHelped state, and hence can no longer be applied by the TryVisible function. Furthermore, upon selection of Op in chooseOpsToHelp, TryCombining removes it from Pa so no other combiner could select (and apply) it as well. We note that unlike the TryPrivate and TryVisible functions, TryCombining may return **false** even if Op was successfully completed; however, because the descriptor of Op in that case is no longer in the opsToHelp array, combineUnderLock will not execute Op again.

Finally, the CombineUnderLock function runs after acquiring L. This disallows the owner of Op (as well as any other thread) to make any progress until L is released or Op is completed (unless the owner of Op happens to be the combiner). Once the combiner applies Op in CombineUnderLock, it changes its status to Done. Since the owner of Op checks the status of Op in a HW transaction in TryVisible and after acquiring the selection lock in TryCombining, it will not attempt to apply Op again.

**Progress properties:** Unlike the original FC algorithm [11], not all usage patterns of the HCF framework result in a starvation free algorithm. In particular, because we may have multiple publication arrays, an unfair lock L may have a combiner thread executing CombineUnderLock on one array starve another combiner thread running on a different array. Since a descriptor only resides in one of the arrays, this may cause an operation to be starved if L is unfair.

If L and selection locks guarantee starvation freedom, however, a concurrent implementation of a data structure that uses the HCF framework will also be starvation free, that is, each operation will eventually complete as long as a thread that is holding a lock keeps taking steps and eventually releases it. To see why, note that with starvation free locks, any thread that calls TryCombining(Op,Pa) will eventually complete Op. This is because it will either discover that Op was applied by another combiner or it will select Op in chooseOpsToHelp (chooseOpsToHelp always selects at least the operation of the thread that executes it). In the latter case, HCF guarantees that the combiner returns only after applying all operations it has selected by chooseOpsToHelp, including Op. The only case in which the owner of an incomplete operation may be prevented from reaching the TryCombining function is if it spins indefinitely in the loop at Line 27. However, as just discussed, an operation in a BeingHelped state will be helped by the combiner thread that transitioned it to that state, and that combiner must eventually complete this operation given that the locks are starvation free.

## 2.4 Framework Customization

HCF supports two mechanisms in order to allow parallel combining. First, we can use one publication array for all operations and have chooseOpsToHelp to choose only operations that would easily combine with the operation of the thread that called it. For instance, in the case of a set based on a binary search tree, one can choose to combine only operations on the same key or on keys in the same (left or right) subtree of the tree. Another mechanism is having multiple publication arrays with separate combiners that always select all operations announced in the respective array. Such approach is appealing when it is known a-priori which operations are expected to conflict with each other, e.g., operations on different ends of a double-ended queue. Note that in this case, we do not need to allow multiple combiners for the same publication array. In fact, we have created a specialized version of our framework for this case. There we let the combiner to hold the selection lock of the publication array for the whole duration of its execution (rather than just for the selection process). This prevents any operation in the TryVisible phase from running when there is an active combiner for the same publication array (and thus avoids conflicts between those operations with the combiner). At the same time, it avoids the need to use an extra state (BeingHelped) and thus simplifies the implementation of this variant of the framework.

We note that those two mechanisms are not mutually exclusive. That is, we may configure HCF to use several publication arrays with `chooseOpsToHelp` that chooses a subset of operations to be combined, or we can use one publication array and have the combiner thread hold the selection lock until it is done. The latter case provides a form of contention control (since selected operations cannot run concurrently with the combiner), which in some sense is similar to the idea of using an auxiliary lock in TLE [1]. The contention control in HCF is more efficient, though, since by running multiple operations by the same combiner thread we reduce the contention on the selection (i.e., auxiliary) lock. Besides, by allowing the combiner to run several operations in the same hardware transaction, the overhead of starting and committing transactions is amortized.

The flexibility of HCF allows straightforward implementation of other synchronization techniques on top of it. For instance, TLE is achieved when the number of HTM attempts in the second and third phases are set to 0, while `chooseOpsToHelp` returns only the operation of the combiner (which then applies it under the lock). The functionality of FC is achieved when the number of HTM attempts in all the first three phases is set to 0, while `chooseOpsToHelp` returns all announced operations.

In general, HCF allows customization not only for a particular data structure, but also divergent customizations for different operations of the same data structure. Moreover, because the number of publication arrays used as well as the way operations are assigned to the arrays is the issue of performance, not correctness, the customization may be dynamic — we can begin with a certain number of publication arrays and the way operations are assigned to them, and change that on-the-fly to better fit the given workload. It is fair to assume that no single configuration of HCF fits all data structures and workloads, calling for an adaptive runtime mechanism to tune the HCF performance. Exploring such a mechanism is left for future work.

# 3 PERFORMANCE EVALUATION

## 3.1 HCF vs. FC and TLE

We start by a qualitative comparison of HCF to the original FC technique [11]. Concurrent threads make most use of HTM when they do not conflict with each other; when data conflicts are frequent, time spent on futile HTM attempts is wasted. As a result, one should not expect HCF always to be the winner when the contention is high, e.g., when experimenting with a stack or when a priority queue is used in a workload composed solely of RemoveMin operations.

We expect the benefit of HCF over FC, however, to be evident when a data structure does allow at least some amount of parallelism. The HCF algorithm is designed to exploit this parallelism in multiple dimensions. First, it allows threads to access the shared data structure concurrently without any help from a combiner. Second, even when a thread fails to complete its operation on its own and decides to become a combiner, it allows other threads, i.e., other combiners and non-combiners, to proceed concurrently. As a result, HCF is likely to provide substantial benefit over FC in a wide range of data structures and workloads, e.g., in hash tables, search trees, skip lists, etc.

When comparing HCF to TLE [5], we note that differences in performance results are likely to arise only in workloads that involve contention. Otherwise, when threads apply their operations with one (or a few) HTM attempt(s), the techniques are similar and expected to deliver the same performance. Under contention, however, HCF has a few important advantages over TLE. First, it enables combining and elimination, potentially reducing the total amount of work required to apply contended operations. Second, HCF provides better control of the level of allowed parallelism between threads applying contending operations. In particular, while TLE allows either all threads to run in parallel or only one thread (that holds the lock) to run [5], HCF can gradually reduce the level of parallelism by having one combiner help some operations (whose owners are not allowed to run concurrently with it), while other threads can still run their operations concurrently. Finally, HCF reduces contention on the global lock that protects the access to the shared data structure. This is because the largest number of threads competing over this lock is equal to the number of combiners in HCF as opposed to the total number of threads in TLE. Thus, while the actual benefit of HCF over TLE depends on the number of combiners and the potential for the combining and elimination optimizations, we expect this benefit to increase with the contention level, leading to better scalability for HCF.

## 3.2 Experimental Setup

We implemented the HCF framework in C++, using templates for customizing the framework for different data structures and synchronization techniques, as we describe in the following sections.

All experiments were run on an Oracle Server X5-2 (dual socket, each socket featuring an Intel Xeon E5-2699 v3 processor with 18 hyper-threaded cores per socket) running at 2.3GHz and operated by Ubuntu 16.04. In order to reduce the effect of non-uniform memory access (NUMA) on the results, we used only one socket in this machine. We experimented with both sockets as well, and observed the performance of all algorithms being harmed by inter-socket communication when threads were running on both sockets, consistent with observations made in [2]. The relative performance, however, has not changed from the one observed when only one socket was used; we show a representative example of this behavior in one of the charts below. To eliminate the impact of non-deterministic thread placement and thread migration, all threads were pinned to cores s.t. thread $i$ and $i + X$ were sharing the same core (where X=18 is the number of cores per socket).

In each experiment, threads accessed the data structure concurrently and independently, applying operations selected uniformly and randomly from the given workload distribution. We report the average total throughput based on five runs per each configuration. We note that the standard deviation of those results is small, in the order of a few percents or less from the mean for the vast majority of the results and up to 9.5% in the worst case (21.1% in the runs that use both sockets).

## 3.3 Hash Table

We have implemented a simple sequential hash table data structure which contains a preset number of buckets. Each bucket is a singly linked list of key-value pairs whose key hashes into the bucket. In

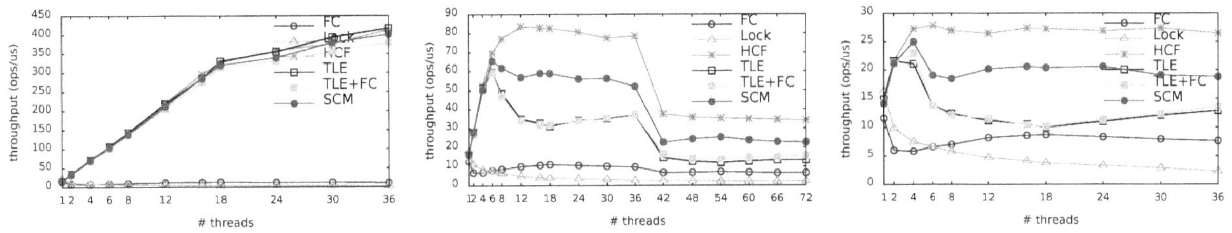


(a) 100% Find (b) 80% Find (c) 40% Find

**Figure 2: Throughput results (hash table).**

addition, in order to support efficient iteration over key-value pairs stored in the table, we also maintain a doubly linked list of those pairs (which we call a table list). Thus, the Insert operation on the table locates the bucket into which the given key should be inserted by hashing the key, and scans the list of elements in the bucket (which is expected to be very short). If the key is already there, it completes by updating the value. Otherwise, it allocates a new node, initializes it with the given key and value, and inserts that node into the head of the bucket list as well as into the head of the table list. The hash table also supports Find and Remove operations with usual semantics, except that Remove also removes the given key from the table list.

Given this sequential implementation, we note that for any reasonable table capacity, Find and Remove operations are unlikely to conflict when run concurrently as hardware transactions. This is despite the fact that Remove modifies the table list, as it removes the key from a random location in the list, without scanning the list or reading its head pointer. Insert operations, on the other hand, are expected to experience contention as they all insert into the head of the table list. The different nature of the data structure operations makes it fit naturally in the gap between TLE and FC that HCF is designed to address: having all operations run using TLE is not likely to perform well because Insert operations will tend to acquire the lock (after a few attempts on HTM), blocking Remove and Find operations that could otherwise run in parallel; on the other hand, using FC will have *all* operations execute while holding the lock, waisting potential parallelism between the Find and Remove operations.

HCF allowed to customize the hash table implementation as follows. We used one publication array for Find and Remove operations and configured their respective operation descriptors to operate like in TLE, that is, skipping HTM attempts in `TryVisible` and `TryCombining` and going directly to the `CombineUnderLock` phase if HTM attempts in the `TryPrivate` phase fail. For Insert operations, we used another publication array and configured its operation descriptor to exploit all four phases, with the `chooseOps-ToHelp` function that selects all announced operations in the array and combines them into one operation on the hash table. To this end, we added a (sequential) Insert-n operation to the hash table that allows insertion of multiple key-value pairs. The advantage of this operation over simply invoking Insert $n$ times is in its ability to chain new key-value pairs that can be inserted into the table list with just one modification of the `head` pointer.

In the hash table experiment, we set the key range and the number of buckets to 16K and prefill the table to the half of that range. We compared the following alternatives:

**HCF:** the HCF-based implementation described above,
**Lock:** simply uses a lock for every operation,
**TLE:** implements TLE over that lock,
**FC:** implements flat combining, in which Insert operations are combined using the same Insert-n operation described above while announced Find and Remove operations are applied sequentially afterwards,
**SCM:** uses TLE with an auxiliary lock for conflicting transactions [1],
**TLE+FC:** employs a naive combination of TLE and FC, where a thread tries to apply an operation using HTM (as in TLE), and if fails, proceeds (as in FC) by announcing its operation and trying to become a combiner under the lock (and then using the same Insert-n operation for Insert operations).

All versions that use HW transactions (HCF, TLE, SCM and TLE+FC) were given the same total budget of (ten) HTM attempts. For the HCF operation descriptor configuration that uses HW transactions in all the first three phases (e.g., for Insert operations), we set `TryPrivateTrials`, `TryVisibleTrials` and `TryCombiningTrials` to 2, 3 and 5, respectively. We found experimentally that this setup works reasonably well across a wide range of data structures and workloads. Thus, we opted to use it in all experiments where operation descriptors are configured to try HW transactions in all first three phases of HCF.

Figure 2 shows results for three workloads where 40, 80 and 100% of the operations are Find, respectively, while the rest of the operations in each workload are split evenly between Insert and Remove. Note that Figure 2 (b) presents data with 72 threads, i.e., collected on both sockets of the machine. This is a representative example that shows how NUMA effects harm the performance of all algorithms. Since interesting observations happen when those NUMA effects do not present, the focus of our analysis is on the results achieved on a single socket.

As Figure 2 (a) shows, when the workload does not include any updates, HCF scales similarly to TLE (as well as SCM and TLE+FC), exhibiting no overhead comparing to those alternatives. This is not surprising, as most operations complete on HTM, without acquiring the lock. The difference in scaling for all these variants after 18 threads can be attributed to the enabled hyper-threading. Along

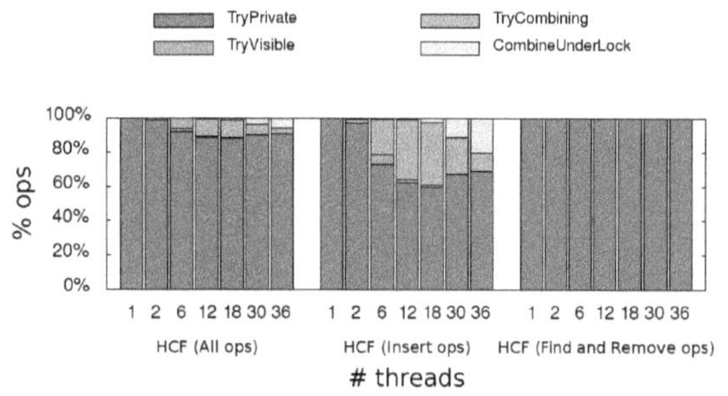


**Figure 3: Percentage of operations completed in each phase in HCF (hash table with 40% Find).**

with that, Lock and FC show no scalability as they execute all operations under the lock.

When workloads include updates (cf. Figures 2 (b) and (c)), the HCF variant peaks with higher throughput and, perhaps more importantly, preserves this throughput as the number of threads increases (modulo the effects of cross-socket communication when going beyond a single socket). This is in contrast to all other variants that employ HTM in which conflicts between Insert operations increase the rate of lock acquisitions; we provide data on lock acquisition rates below.

In general, the gap between HCF and other alternatives grows with the number of update operations. This is because more operations fail to complete on HTM due to increased number of conflicts between Insert operations. Instead of acquiring the lock and blocking all other operations, however, HCF allows more parallelism by attempting to combine those operations using HTM. Also, we note that TLE+FC performs almost identically to TLE, providing very little benefit and in particular, performing substantially worse than HCF. As we show below, this is in part because TLE+FC, in contrast to HCF, combines only a few operations in practice.

In the rest of this section, we present and discuss some additional performance data that shed some light on where the advantage of HCF over its alternatives comes from. As an example, we focus on the workload presented in Figure 2 (c), i.e., 40% Find operations. Figure 3 shows the percentage of operations completed in each of the four phases of HCF, for all operations as well as when considering Insert operations separately from Find and Remove operations. As Figure 3 shows, these two classes of operations perform differently indeed. While Find and Remove operations do not suffer from conflicts and manage to succeed on HTM even when the number of threads grows, Insert operations experience conflicts causing them to combine on HTM (in phase 3) and at times combine under lock (in phase 4). Yet, the majority of combined Insert operations are applied using HTM, which does not block Find and Remove operations. This leads to a low portion of total operations applied under lock, as shown in the left part of Figure 3.

Figure 4 (a) shows the percentage of lock acquisitions from the total number of operations for all variants. We note that lower lock acquisition rates do not necessarily translate to better performance, as the amount of time spent under lock is different between various algorithms. This is especially true for algorithms that employ combining (such as HCF, FC and TLE+FC). Yet, this data helps to explain some of the throughout results in Figure 2. In particular, the rate of lock acquisitions for TLE, TLE+FC and SCM increases after 4–6 threads, causing their throughput to drop (as shown in Figures 2 (b) and (c)). In general, though, TLE (and SCM) experience relatively low rate of failures to the lock. Thus, relatively few threads reach the combining phase in TLE+FC, and when they do, they start combining right after announcing their respective operations. In practice, as we show below, this causes TLE+FC to miss the benefits of combining, which explains why TLE+FC performs very similarly to TLE in Figure 2. At the same time, the design of HCF facilitates combining by allowing threads to announce their operations way before they actually abandon their attempts on HTM.

Figure 4 (b) shows the *combing degree*, that is the average number of operations that are executed by a combiner, for all variants that employ combining. Note that for HCF, the combining degree is calculated only for Insert operations, since Find and Remove operations do not employ combining. As expected, the combining degree of FC is similar to the number of threads. The degree of HCF is smaller than that of FC since HCF applies combining only for (conflicting) Insert operations (rather than all operations as FC does) at the time other threads can run other, non-conflicting operations. More importantly, though, the degree of HCF grows linearly with the number of threads. This shows that HCF succeeds to group and combine several pending (Insert) operations, ripping the benefit of combining, but only where it is indeed profitable (i.e., for Insert operations that conflict with each other). At the same time, the combining degree of TLE+FC does not change much with the number of threads and remains very close to 1.

Finally, Figure 4 (c) shows statistics on the rate of L1 Data cache misses for all considered variants, collected using the `perf` tool. As expected, FC exhibits the lowest rate of cache misses, since it allows one thread to apply all pending operations. Notably, HCF follows very closely since, as we have seen above, it manages to combine effectively conflicting (Insert) operations, enjoying the reduction in the cache miss rate yielded by combining. TLE exhibits the worse performance in terms of the cache miss rate, since conflicting operations are retried, causing repeated cache misses (which in turn cause repeated conflicts). TLE+FC produces less cache misses compared to TLE, but only slightly since, as we have seen above, the combining degree of the former is very small.

In summary, the hash table experiments show one of the main benefits of HCF, which is enabling operation specific policies. That is, conflict-free operations are executed in TLE-like fashion, enjoying the very low rate of failures to the lock. At the same time, conflicting operations employ combining (following attempts on HTM), ripping the benefits typical to FC but without compromising the parallelism of other, non-conflicting operations.

## 3.4 AVL Tree-based Set

The hash table example demonstrates how well HCF deals with data structures that have different types of operations: ones that rarely conflict with each other and work well with TLE, and others that often conflict, and are better fitted to the FC technique. In this section, we focus on data structures where any of their operations *may* experience contention, depending on the actual workload. Unlike the case of the hash table, here the programmer cannot

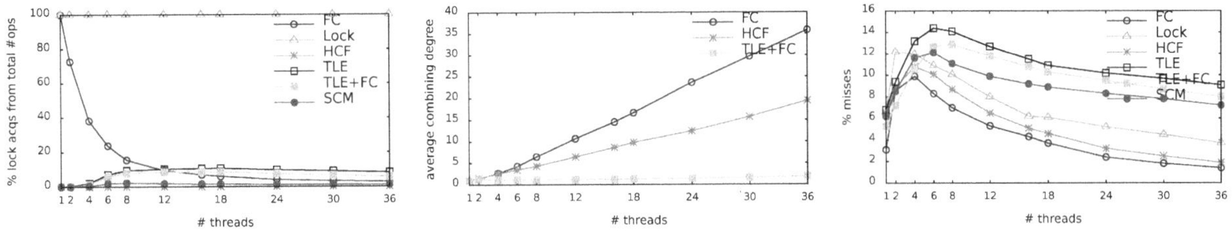


(a) % lock acquisitions (b) Combining degree (c) L1 Data cache miss rate

**Figure 4: Performance statistics (hash table with 40% Find).**

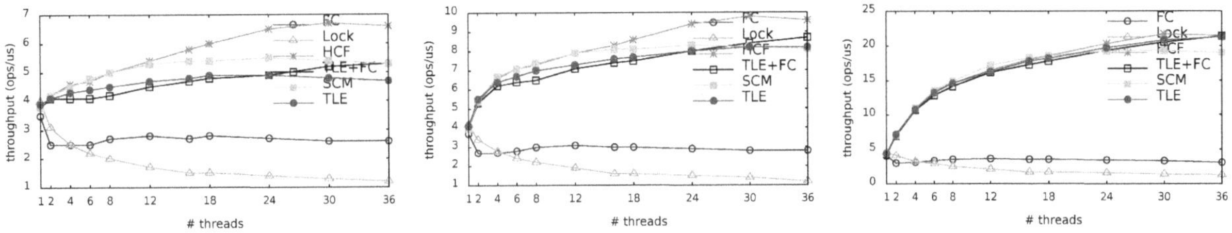


(a) 0% Find (b) 40% Find (c) 80% Find

**Figure 5: Throughput results (set).**

know upfront which (or whether) operations will contend, and has to rely on the ability of HCF to *dynamically* select conflicting operations, and apply them together (perhaps using combining and elimination) while letting operations that do not conflict to run in parallel. We demonstrate the importance of this dynamic selection feature in HCF using experiments with an AVL tree-based set.

The AVL tree data structure is known to scale well under TLE when keys stored in the tree are accessed uniformly at random [2]. In addition, in the case of a uniform workload, when the tree is accessed through the set interface (with Find, Insert and Remove operations), the combining and elimination are known to be unprofitable [11]. However, an interesting question to consider is whether these two facts hold under skewed, non-uniform workloads.

To address this question, we used the HCF framework with the following customization. We used one publication array for all operations, for which a combiner was configured to select only pending (announced) operations on keys falling in the same (left or right) subtree (of the root) as its own operation. To this end, we modified a sequential AVL tree implementation through a few trivial changes to maintain a look-aside variable that holds the root's key; this variable is used by a custom `shouldHelp` function. In a custom version of `runMulti`, the selected operations are then sorted by their key and operation type, and applied to the tree after operations on the same key are combined and eliminated according to the semantics of the set interface (e.g., out of two or more Insert operations on the same key that does not present in the set, only the first one takes effect, while all others return with an indication that the key is already in the set).

Figure 5 shows throughput results for the AVL tree-based set experiment. There, a tree is initialized to hold half the key range of [0..1023] and threads access keys according to a Zipfian distribution with the skew parameter $\theta = 0.9$. ($\theta$ is a parameter of the distribution in the range [0..1), where a higher number gives a higher probability to the lower part of the key range, thus producing more skewed distribution). We compare the HCF variant to Lock, TLE, SCM, FC and TLE+FC, where the latter two use the same function to apply multiple operations as HCF (albeit on all announced operations).

Figures 5 (a), (b) and (c) show results for the case where 0%, 40% and 80% of operations are Find, respectively, while the rest of the operations are split evenly between Insert and Remove. As expected, we see the advantage of HCF over other alternatives growing with the increase in the number of update operations (and thus conflicts between hardware transactions). This is because when the conflict rate is high, more operations need to announce and become (or get helped by) a combiner, providing more benefit to the combining and elimination optimizations. Those operations would normally require a lock in TLE or SCM, blocking all other threads and thus leading to sub-par performance of those variants compared to HCF. In general, the correlation between the rate of conflicts and the advantage of HCF was notable when we experimented with different key ranges and/or different $\theta$ parameters of the Zipfian distribution.

Other performance statistics, such as the combining degree of various variants and L1 Data cache miss rates, exhibit similar patterns and lead to similar conclusions as in the case of hash table. We also note that we experimented with other HCF-based variants, e.g., one that does not use combining and elimination optimizations (but rather a combiner applies all announced operations one after another) and another that uses two publication arrays, one for each of the two subtrees under the root. All alternative variants performed closely to, but worse than, the HCF variant shown in the figures. This underlines the importance of two features of HCF, namely allowing a combiner to run concurrently with other operations (in this case, operations on another subtree, or operations on the same subtree that were not selected by the combiner) and supporting efficient application of multiple operations through combining and elimination.

# 4 RELATED WORK

The FC technique uses one global lock to protect the access to a shared data structure [11]. This key feature is what makes designing concurrent data structures that use FC trivial, and works well when the data structure has one or a few contention points. In fact, as Hendler et al. show in [11], and as demonstrated by a revised combining technique in [9], combining-bases stacks and queues perform much better than other, blocking or non-blocking alternatives. However, the use of a single lock can harm scalability when the data structure allows concurrent access.

Several papers have considered extending the FC technique to support multiple combiners. Hendler et al. [12] present the design of concurrent synchronous queues using a parallel flat combining algorithm. The idea is to split dynamically the publication array into chunks, where each chunk can be processed in parallel by a different combiner. Each combiner matches pending requests in its chunk, and uses an additional single-combiner synchronous queue to store an overflow of operations of the same type that did not have a matching pair. Budovsky attempts to use multiple combiners when designing skip-lists-based sets [3]. His idea is to divide the skip-list statically into multiple non-intersecting regions, where requests belonging to each region are managed by a different combiner. The margins of each region are identified by specially marked nodes of the skip-list; these nodes are assumed to be immutable. Unlike HCF (and the original FC technique), however, both these approaches are tailored to very specific data structures. Moreover, they seem to perform well only when operations of the data structure can eliminate each other [3, 12].

More recent work by Drachsler-Cohen and Petrank [8] considers applying combining to lazy linked lists [10], where threads traverse list nodes in a lock-free fashion, and acquire a per-node lock if they need to update that node. The idea in [8] is to modify locks used to protect list nodes so that a thread acquiring the lock may combine its operation with those of other threads waiting for the same lock. This technique inherently relies on the existence of a scalable concurrent implementation that uses locks, and thus is not intended for sequentially implemented data structures.

The TLE technique [5] (or, more precisely, the closely related SLE technique [14]) was introduced more than fifteen years ago, but it became practically useful only recently with the availability of commercial architectures featuring HTM. TLE was shown to scale nearly linearly when concurrently running threads do not conflict, but its performance deteriorates substantially when such conflicts do occur or when capacity limits are reached [1, 7, 13, 15]. Several recent papers suggest ways to enhance TLE to cope better with these limitations. Afek et al. [1], for instance, propose to use an auxiliary lock to synchronize between threads that fail to commit their respective HW transactions due to contention. Diegues et al. [6] introduce core locks, which synchronize between threads running on the same core when transactions fail due to capacity limits. To the best of our knowledge, however, none of the previous work in the context of TLE considers combining operations of concurrent threads.

# 5 CONCLUSIONS

In this paper, we explored how one can effectively combine advantages of the pessimistic FC technique [11] and the optimistic HTM-based TLE approach [5] into a novel synchronization framework called HCF. In particular, we discussed how the FC technique can leverage HTM to allow parallel execution of operations on sequential data structures that are protected by a global lock, while still enjoying the benefit of elimination and combining that FC provides. Using multiple examples, we demonstrated that HCF can significantly outperform TLE, FC and other related alternatives on a variety of workloads.

# ACKNOWLEDGMENTS

We would like to thank Tim Harris, Erez Petrank and anonymous reviewers for insightful comments and excellent suggestions to improve the presentation of the material in the paper.

# REFERENCES

[1] Yehuda Afek, Amir Levy, and Adam Morrison. 2014. Software-improved hardware lock elision. In *Proceedings of ACM PODC*. 212–221.

[2] Trevor Brown, Alex Kogan, Yossi Lev, and Victor Luchangco. 2016. Investigating the Performance of Hardware Transactions on a Multi-Socket Machine. In *Proceedings of ACM SPAA*. 121–132.

[3] Vladimir Budovsky. 2010. *Combining Techniques Application for Tree Search Structures*. Master's thesis. Tel Aviv University.

[4] Dave Dice, Alex Kogan, Yossi Lev, Timothy Merrifield, and Mark Moir. 2014. Adaptive integration of hardware and software lock elision techniques. In *Proceedings of the ACM Symposium on Parallelism in Algorithms and Architectures (SPAA)*. 188–197.

[5] Dave Dice, Yossi Lev, Mark Moir, and Daniel Nussbaum. 2009. Early experience with a commercial hardware transactional memory implementation. In *Proceedings of ASPLOS*. 157–168.

[6] Nuno Diegues, Paolo Romano, and Stoyan Garbatov. 2015. Seer: Probabilistic Scheduling for Hardware Transactional Memory. In *Proceedings of the ACM Symposium on Parallelism in Algorithms and Architectures (SPAA)*. 224–233.

[7] Nuno Diegues, Paolo Romano, and Luís Rodrigues. 2014. Virtues and Limitations of Commodity Hardware Transactional Memory. In *Proceedings of the International Conference on Parallel Architectures and Compilation (PACT)*. 3–14.

[8] Dana Drachsler-Cohen and Erez Petrank. 2014. LCD: Local Combining on Demand. In *Proceedings of OPODIS*. 355–371.

[9] Panagiota Fatourou and Nikolaos D. Kallimanis. 2012. Revisiting the Combining Synchronization Technique. In *Proceedings of ACM PPOPP*. 257–266.

[10] Steve Heller, Maurice Herlihy, Victor Luchangco, Mark Moir, William N. Scherer, and Nir Shavit. 2005. A Lazy Concurrent List-based Set Algorithm. In *Proceedings of the Int. Conference on Principles of Distributed Systems (OPODIS)*. 3–16.

[11] Danny Hendler, Itai Incze, Nir Shavit, and Moran Tzafrir. 2010. Flat Combining and the Synchronization-parallelism Tradeoff. In *Proceedings of the ACM Symposium on Parallelism in Algorithms and Architectures (SPAA)*. 355–364.

[12] Danny Hendler, Itai Incze, Nir Shavit, and Moran Tzafrir. 2010. Scalable Flat-Combining Based Synchronous Queues. In *Proceedings of DISC*. 79–93.

[13] Takuya Nakaike, Rei Odaira, Matthew Gaudet, Maged Michael, and Hisanobu Tomari. 2015. Quantitative Comparison of Hardware Transactional Memory for Blue Gene/Q, zEnterprise EC12, Intel Core, and POWER8. In *Proceedings of the International Symposium on Computer Architecture (ISCA)*. 144–157.

[14] Ravi Rajwar and James R. Goodman. 2001. Speculative Lock Elision: Enabling Highly Concurrent Multithreaded Execution. In *Proceedings of the ACM/IEEE International Symposium on Microarchitecture (Micro)*. 294–305.

[15] Richard M. Yoo, Christopher J. Hughes, Konrad Lai, and Ravi Rajwar. 2013. Performance evaluation of Intel® transactional synchronization extensions for high-performance computing. In *International Conference for High Performance Computing, Networking, Storage and Analysis (SC)*. Article 19.

# On Using Time Without Clocks via Zigzag Causality

Asa Dan
Technion
asa.dan.2@gmail.com

Rajit Manohar
Yale University
rajit.manohar@yale.edu

Yoram Moses
Technion
moses@ee.technion.ac.il

## ABSTRACT

Even in the absence of clocks, time bounds on the duration of actions enable the use of time for distributed coordination. This paper initiates an investigation of coordination in such a setting. A new communication structure called a *zigzag pattern* is introduced, and shown to guarantee bounds on the relative timing of events in this clockless model. Indeed, zigzag patterns are shown to be necessary and sufficient for establishing that events occur in a manner that satisfies prescribed bounds. We capture when a process can know that an appropriate zigzag pattern exists, and use this to provide necessary and sufficient conditions for timed coordination of events using a full-information protocol in the clockless model.

## KEYWORDS

coordination; time; clocks; temporal ordering; time bounds

## 1 INTRODUCTION

Coordination is a fundamental task in distributed systems. The order in which events take place, and often also the relative timing of the events, can be of primary concern in many applications. Timing of actions can be useful, for example, when we wish to dispatch trains in a manner that ensures proper use of critical single-lane sections of the track, or schedule plane takeoffs to alleviate unnecessary congestion at the destination airports.

In asynchronous systems, processes have no access to clocks. Furthermore, they have no timing information except for what they can obtain based on the happens-before relation of [22]. In such systems, only the ordering of events can be determined, and not their relative timing. Using accurate clocks, it is possible to orchestrate much more finely-tuned temporal patterns of events at the different sites than in the asynchronous setting. Moreover, this can often be achieved using significantly less communication [5, 23]. Of course, clocks are not always available, and when they are, maintaining clocks accurate and in synchrony may be non-trivial. But even when processes do not have access to clocks, bounds on the timing of communication and of actions are routinely monitored, and system designers can often have access to reliable timing information [14].

This paper initiates an investigation of the use of time for distributed coordination when processes do not have clocks, but do have bounds on the duration of events and of communication. We call this the *bounded communication model without clocks* (or the "clockless model" for short), and denote it by bcm. It is not *a priori* obvious that the clockless model is any more powerful than the asynchronous model. We will show that it is. Throughout the text we will use notation borrowed from [31] that states timed precedence between events. We write $e \xrightarrow{x} e'$ to state that the event $e$ takes place at least $x$ time units before $e'$ does.[1] In an asynchronous system, only the relative ordering of events can be coordinated, and not their timing. Thus, for example, the only way to ensure that an action $\underline{b}$ is performed by process $B$ no more than 10000 time steps before $\underline{a}$ is performed by process $A$ (in our notation, this is denoted by $\underline{a} \xrightarrow{-10000} \underline{b}$) is by having $B$ perform $\underline{b}$ *after* $\underline{a}$. This is far from optimal, of course, as $\underline{b}$ could be performed way before $\underline{a}$. Similarly, the only way that $B$ can be sure to act before $A$ does, is if $\underline{a}$ cooperates, and waits until a message chain from $B$ informs it that $\underline{b}$ has been performed. As we shall see, in the clockless model it is possible to allow $B$ (or $A$) to act much earlier. In this paper, we will focus on two basic coordination problems in which $B$ should act in a manner that is causally and temporally related to $A$'s action, without requiring $A$ to adjust its own decision to act, and often without requiring any communication between the two.

*Definition 1.1 (Timed Coordination).* Given processes $A$, $B$ and $C$, suppose that $A$ performs the action $\underline{a}$ when it receives a "go" message from $C$. Moreover, assume that $C$'s decision to send this message is spontaneous. We define two coordination problems:

**Early**$\langle \underline{b} \xrightarrow{x} \underline{a} \rangle$, in which $B$ should perform $\underline{b}$ at least $x$ time units before $\underline{a}$ is performed; and

**Late**$\langle \underline{a} \xrightarrow{x} \underline{b} \rangle$, in which similarly $B$ should perform $\underline{b}$ at least $x$ time units after $\underline{a}$ is performed.

In both cases, $\underline{b}$ should be performed in a run only if $\underline{a}$ is performed.

In each of these coordination problems, $A$ acts unconditionally when it receives $C$'s message. Process $B$ needs to perform $\underline{b}$ only if it can do so in a manner that conforms to the stated bounds.

Suppose that we wish to ensure that $\underline{a} \xrightarrow{0} \underline{b}$, i.e., that $\underline{a}$ occurs no later than $\underline{b}$. We can of course ensure this by creating a message chain from $A$ to $B$, which starts at or after the occurrence of $\underline{a}$. Once the final message in this chain is received, $\underline{b}$ can safely be performed. In an asynchronous system, such a message chain

[1] As discussed in [31], although $e \xrightarrow{x} e'$ states a lower bound of $x$ on the time difference between the events (i.e., $t_{e'} \geq t_e + x$), the same notation can also be used to state upper bounds. Since $t_{e'} \leq t_e + y$ is equivalent to $t_e \geq t_{e'} - y$, we can capture an upper bound of $y$ on how much later $e'$ occurs by writing $e \xrightarrow{-y} e'$.

This research was supported in part by a Ruch grant from the Jacobs Institute at Cornell Tech, and by a grant from the United States-Israel Binational Science Foundation (BSF), Jerusalem, Israel, and the United States National Science Foundation (NSF) under grant CCF 1617945. Yoram Moses is the Israel Pollak academic chair at the Technion.

*PODC'17, July 25-27, 2017, Washington, DC, USA*

978-1-4503-4992-5/17/07...$15.00
DOI: http://dx.doi.org/10.1145/3087801.3087839

would be necessary. Is it possible to ensure in our model that $\underline{a}$ happens before $\underline{b}$ without creating a message chain from $A$ to $B$?

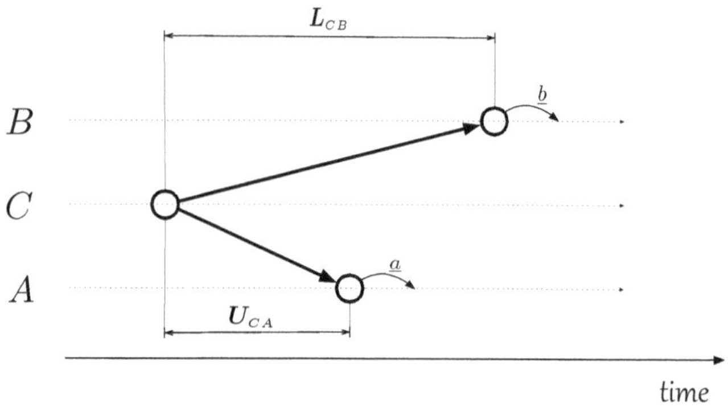


**Figure 1: Coordination without direct communication**

Let us return to the question of ensuring that $\underline{a} \xrightarrow{x} \underline{b}$ for a general value of $x$, and consider the example depicted in Figure 1. Here process $C$ simultaneously sends messages to $A$ and $B$. Let us denote by $U_{CA}$ the upper bound on message transmission times for the channel $CA$, and by $L_{CB}$ the lower bound for $CB$. It is easy to check that if $L_{CB} \geq U_{CA} + x$ then $B$ is guaranteed to receive $C$'s message no less than $x$ time units after $A$ receives it. In that case, as $A$ is assumed to perform $\underline{a}$ upon receiving $C$'s message, it is possible to ensure that $\underline{b}$ happens at least $x$ time units later than $\underline{a}$, by having $B$ perform $\underline{b}$ upon receiving $C$'s message. Notice that this guarantees a (timed) causal connection between actions at $A$ and at $B$ even without any communication between $A$ and $B$.

Clearly, the analysis underlying the example of Figure 1 remains valid if we replace each of the direct messages from $C$ to $A$ and $B$ by a message chain, and replace the condition $L_{CB} \geq U_{CA} + x$ by a requirement that the sum of lower bounds along the chain from $C$ to $B$ exceeds $x$ plus the sum of upper bounds along the chain from $C$ to $A$. We remark that, in a precise sense, the asynchronous solution (for a simple happened-before requirement) is an instance of Figure 1 in which $C = A$, and $L_{CB} > 0 = U_{CA}$.

Note that if $L_{CB} < U_{CA} + x$ then, by waiting for more than $\delta = U_{CA} - L_{CB} + x$ time units before performing $\underline{b}$, process $B$ would also ensure that $\underline{a}$ takes place $x$ time units before $\underline{b}$ does. But we are assuming that $B$ ***has no clock or timer*** that it can use to measure the passage of $\delta$ time steps. It can only use bounds on communication or internal actions to estimate the passage of time. We remark that in current-day technology, clocks and timers are often available. A vast portion of computer chip come with built-in clocks, and highly accurate clock synchronization algorithms are by now standard [18]. But this does not cover all distributed systems of interest. Indeed, it is becoming popular to consider biological systems such as the brain or human body as instances of distributed systems. There, no explicit clock can be found, although timing appears to play a role [6, 20]. Another setting that fits the bcm model is that of asynchronous (or self-timed) VLSI circuits, where there is no clock but there are bounds on data transfer along wires and on delays of gates [32].

A natural question at this point is whether the pattern depicted in Figure 1 is typical for coordinating actions based on transmission bounds. In other words, is this essentially the only way in which $B$ can guarantee that $\underline{a}$ will be performed (sufficiently long) before $\underline{b}$ in the clockless model? Interestingly, the answer is No. Consider the scenario depicted in Figure 2a. In this case $E$ sends a message to $B$ and to $D$, while $C$ sends a message to $D$ and to $A$. Moreover, $D$ receives $C$'s message before it receives $E$'s message. Finally, $A$ performs $\underline{a}$ upon receiving $C$'s message, and $B$ performs $\underline{b}$ when it receives the message that $E$ sends. As depicted in Figure 2a, denote the sending times of $C$ and $E$'s messages by $t_c$ and $t_e$. Moreover, let $t_a$ and $t_d$ be the times at which $A$ and $D$ receive $C$'s message, and let $t_b$ the time at which $B$ receives $E$'s message. Clearly, $\underline{b}$ is performed no earlier than time $t_e + L_{EB}$, yielding inequality (i) below. Similarly, the action $\underline{a}$ is performed no later than time $t_c + U_{CA}$, yielding inequality (iv). However, the fact that $E$'s message to $D$ arrives after $C$'s message arrives implies that $t_e$ can not be pushed "too far" back relative to $t_c$. After all, the message along $ED$ took no more than $U_{ED}$ time units (inequality (ii)), and the one along $CD$ took no less than $L_{CD}$ (inequality (iii)). Altogether, we have:

$$\begin{array}{llll} \text{(i)} & t_b & \geq & t_e + L_{EB}, \\ \text{(ii)} & t_e & > & t_d - U_{ED}, \\ \text{(iii)} & t_d & \geq & t_c + L_{CD}, \text{ and} \\ \text{(iv)} & t_c & \geq & t_a - U_{CA}. \end{array}$$

By substitution, we have that $t_b > t_a - U_{CA} + L_{CD} - U_{ED} + L_{EB}$. Thus, $t_b > t_a + x$ is guaranteed in this case if

$$-U_{CA} + L_{CD} - U_{ED} + L_{EB} \geq x. \quad (1)$$

The reader may correctly suspect at this point that the zigzag pattern of Figure 2a can be extended by adding an arbitrary finite number of additional zigs and zags. Indeed, in that case a more elaborate condition in the style of Equation (1), based on a longer derivation, will ensure that $\underline{a}$ happens more than $x$ time units before $\underline{b}$. The first result of our analysis is a proof that this is tight. We will show that, in a precise sense, the existence of an appropriate zigzag pattern is a necessary condition for $B$'s performing the action $\underline{b}$ in Late$\langle \underline{a} \xrightarrow{x} \underline{b} \rangle$ or Early$\langle \underline{b} \xrightarrow{x} \underline{a} \rangle$.

Since a zigzag pattern is necessary, we have by the *Knowledge of Preconditions principle* of [30] that $B$ must *know* that a zigzag pattern exists when it performs $\underline{b}$. Interestingly, even if the processes follow a full-information protocol,[2] the mere existence of a zigzag pattern is not sufficient to enable process $B$ to correctly coordinate its action. In a run containing the pattern of Figure 2a, for example, if $B$ receives no messages from $D$, then $B$ would not be able to detect the existence of the zigzag pattern, because in the eyes of $B$ it may be possible that $C$ will send its messages only in the far future.

There are, of course, cases in which $B$ can detect that an appropriate zigzag pattern exists. In such a case, $B$ can decide to perform its action $\underline{b}$ and be sure that $\underline{a}$ happens before $\underline{b}$. Consider Figure 2b. Suppose that the bounds satisfy the condition of Equation (1). Moreover, let's assume that every message contains a header specifying who its intended recipients are. Once $B$ receives $E$'s message (with an indication that it was also sent to $D$), and receives a message from $D$ (denoted by a dashed line in Figure 2b) indicating that $D$

[2] A *full-information protocol (fip)* is one in which every message sent encodes the sender's complete history up to the point at which it is sent.

(a) Zigzag-based happens-before (b) Zigzag-based coordination

**Figure 2: A zigzag communication pattern**

heard from $C$ before $D$ heard from $E$, then $B$ can perform $\underline{b}$ and be guaranteed to satsify $\mathsf{Late}\langle \underline{a} \xrightarrow{x} \underline{b}\rangle$. This is an instance of a *visible zigzag* pattern, which is a zigzag pattern that is extended by an appropriate set of message chains. Our analysis will identify particular visible zigzag patterns as necessary and sufficient for $B$'s action in instances of $\mathsf{Early}\langle \underline{b} \xrightarrow{x} \underline{a}\rangle$ or $\mathsf{Late}\langle \underline{a} \xrightarrow{x} \underline{b}\rangle$.

This paper is organized as follows: Section 2 introduces the bounded communication model, protocols, and standard aspects of causality. It also presents two ways of describing a point on a local timeline: Since processes do not have access to clocks, one way is in terms of the local state that the process is in, and another way is as the point at which a message chain arrives from a point of the first type. Section 3 introduces zigzag patterns and shows that they are necessary and sufficient for guaranteeing a precedence relation. In Section 4 the notion of a visible zigzag pattern is introduced, and it is shown to be necessary and sufficient for optimal behavior in a coordination task. Section 5 sketches the two variants of bounds graphs used in our technical analysis, and sketches the ideas underlying the proofs of our main theorems. Finally, Section 6 provides a discussion of our results, their implications, and direction for future work. Detailed proofs of our theorems and claims appear in [9].

## 1.1 Related Work

Lamport's seminal work [22] on the ordering of events in asynchronous systems introduced the happened before relation, and initiated an orderly account of the role of causality in the ordering of events. Roughly speaking, his work shows that the only way to implement instances of $\mathsf{Late}\langle \underline{a} \xrightarrow{0} \underline{b}\rangle$ in an asynchronous setting is by constructing a message chain from $A$ to $B$. Using the terminology of [22], one can consider the *causal past* of an event in an asynchronous setting to be the set of events from which it has received a message chain. In our analysis, this set also plays an important role. However, the bounds provide partial information on the timing of events in the past, and, moreover, the past guarantees the occurrence of events that are not seen by the process (i.e., they do not have explicit message chains to the process).

Clocks are very useful tools for coordinating actions in distributed systems (see, e.g., [8, 10, 17, 19, 26–28]). There is a vast literature on real-time systems and on time in multi-agent systems (see, e.g., [21]). Clock synchronization based on bounds on message transmission times was studied extensively in the 70's and 80's [1, 11, 12, 16, 24, 25, 33, 35]; see [34] for an early survey.

One important aspect that our work shares with the clock synchronization literature is the fact that bounds on the duration of events or on transmission times play an important role. Indeed, some of our technical analysis is based on bounds graphs that are strongly inspired by [33] and [31]. In particular, the notion of timed precedence we use comes from [31]. Our study diverges from the existing literature in the fact that no clocks or timers whatsoever are assumed, and the only timing information comes from the observed events and the guaranteed bounds.

An early suggestion to use knowledge to study time and coordination appeared in [29]. Knowledge theory has been used to investigate the protocols and communication patterns that can solve coordination problems in systems with global clocks or accurate timers in [2–5, 15]. In such settings, these works provide tools for a wide variety of coordination tasks.

# 2 MODEL AND PRELIMINARY DEFINITIONS

## 2.1 The Bounded Communication Model

We focus on a simple setting of a communication network $\mathsf{Net} = (\mathsf{Procs}, \mathsf{Chans})$ modeled by a directed graph whose nodes are the processes $\mathsf{Procs} = \{1, \ldots, n\}$ and whose edges are the communication channels among them. We identify time with the natural numbers, $\mathbb{N}$, where a single time step should be thought of as the minimal relevant unit of time. There are lower and upper bounds on message transmission times per channel, specified by a pair of functions $L, U\colon \mathsf{Chans} \to \mathbb{N}$, that satisfy $1 \le L_{ij} \le U_{ij} < \infty$ for all $(i, j) \in \mathsf{Chans}$.

Paths in Net are specified by sequences of process names. We denote a singleton sequence $[i]$ simply by $i$, and the concatenation of sequences $p$ and $q$ by $p \cdot q$. We define the composition of two sequences $p = [i_1, \ldots, i_k, j]$ and $q = [j, h_1, \ldots, h_m]$ in which the last element of $p$ coincides with the first element of $q$ by $p \odot q \triangleq [i_1, \ldots, i_k, j, h_1, \ldots, h_m]$. We extend the notation of upper and lower bounds on message transmission times to paths $p = [i_1, \ldots, i_d]$ in the network graph by defining

$$L(p) \triangleq \sum_{i_k=1}^{d-1} L_{i_k i_{k+1}} \quad \text{and} \quad U(p) \triangleq \sum_{i_k=1}^{d-1} U_{i_k i_{k+1}}.$$

For ease of exposition, actions are assumed to be instantaneous.[3] A global state (or a snapshot of the system) will have the form $g = (\ell_e, \ell_1, \ldots, \ell_n)$, consisting of a state $\ell_e$ for the environment $e$, and one local state $\ell_i$ for every process $i \in$ Procs. A tuple $\gamma = ((\mathsf{Net}, \boldsymbol{L}, \boldsymbol{U}), \mathcal{G}_0)$ whose first component is a time-bounded network as described above, and $\mathcal{G}_0$ is a set of possible initial global states, is called the ***context*** in which a protocol operates.

A run $r$ is an infinite sequence of global states. Thus, $r(m)$ is a global state for every $m \in \mathbb{N}$. We denote by $r_i(m)$ process $i$'s local state in $r(m)$. Processes can perform (application-dependent) local actions and send messages along their outgoing edges. For simplicity, we will assume that the local state of a process consists of an initial state followed by the sequence of events (local actions, message sends and message receives) that the process has observed.

The bounds on message delivery are enforced by assuming the existence of a scheduler, which we call the *environment*. The environment's local state contains the current contents of all channels in Chans, and for every message in a channel it also records the time at which the message was sent. At any point in time, the environment can deliver messages to each of the processes. It can nondeterministically choose whether or not to deliver a message $\mu$ in a channel $(i, j) \in$ Chans at time $t$ if the sending time $t_\mu$ of $\mu$ satisfies $\boldsymbol{L}_{ij} \le t - t_\mu < \boldsymbol{U}_{ij}$. The environment ***must*** deliver $\mu$ to $j$ at time $t$ if $t - t_\mu = \boldsymbol{U}_{ij}$. We remark that if a message $\mu$ is delivered to $i$ at time $t$ in the run $r$, then $i$'s local state at time $t$, $r_i(t)$, will record the fact that $i$ received $\mu$.

We assume a set $\mathbb{E}$ of ***external*** messages, where the environment may nondeterministically choose at any point ($t > 0$) whether to deliver messages from $\mathbb{E}$ to an arbitrary process. Such delivery is spontaneous, and is independent of other (past or present) events in the run. For simplicity we assume that a particular external message of $\mathbb{E}$ can be delivered to at most one process in a given run. Since processes in the bcm model have no clocks, we assume that their actions are event based. A process is scheduled to move only when it receives messages (either external or internal).[4] It can then perform a finite sequence of actions.

Recall that we assumed in Definition 1.1 that $C$'s decision to send a "go" message in an instance of Early$\langle \underline{b} \xrightarrow{x} \underline{a} \rangle$ or Late$\langle \underline{a} \xrightarrow{x} \underline{b} \rangle$ is spontaneous. Formally, we will assume that there is a message $\mu_{go} \in \mathbb{E}$ such that $C$ will send the "go" message to $A$ when it receives $\mu_{go}$.

Processes follow a protocol $\mathsf{P} = (\mathsf{P}_1, \ldots, \mathsf{P}_n)$, where $\mathsf{P}_i$, process $i$'s protocol, is a deterministic function of $i$'s local state. A specific class of protocols we use in this paper are what we call ***flooding full-information protocols*** (FFIP). An FFIP is a protocol in which each process that receives a message immediately sends a message, containing its entire local state, to all of its neighbors. In a precise sense, FFIP's are general protocols for bcm: Just as with standard full-information protocols in the synchronous model (see, e.g., [7]), it is possible to simulate any given protocol in the bcm model by one that communicates according to the FFIP.

[3]Our analysis will apply even in the case in which actions extend over time. Such an action will be modeled as a special channel from the process to itself, with lower and upper bounds for the channel. The invocation and completion of the action would each be instantaneous events.

[4]In particular, processes do not spontaneously perform actions at time 0.

Given a protocol P and a bounded context $\gamma = ((\mathsf{Net}, \boldsymbol{L}, \boldsymbol{U}), \mathcal{G}_0)$, we denote by $\mathcal{R} = \mathcal{R}(\mathsf{P}, \gamma)$ the set of runs of P in context $\gamma$. We call it the system representing P in $\gamma$. A run $r$ belongs to $\mathcal{R}$ exactly if (1) $r(0) \in \mathcal{G}_0$, and (2) for all $m > 0$, $r(m)$ is obtained from $r(m-1)$ following the rules described above. A more formal definition appears in [9]. Henceforth, whenever a system is mentioned, it is assumed to have this form. We say that a given protocol P ***implements*** Early$\langle \underline{b} \xrightarrow{x} \underline{a} \rangle$ (resp. Late$\langle \underline{a} \xrightarrow{x} \underline{b} \rangle$) if in all runs $r \in \mathcal{R}(\mathsf{P}, \gamma)$ process $A$ performs $\underline{a}$ when it receives the "go" message, and process $B$ performs $\underline{b}$ in $r$ only if $\underline{a}$ is performed in $r$, and only at a time that is consistent with the specification of Early$\langle \underline{b} \xrightarrow{x} \underline{a} \rangle$ (resp. the specification of Late$\langle \underline{a} \xrightarrow{x} \underline{b} \rangle$).

## 2.2 Reasoning about bcm Systems

In the coordination problems Early$\langle \underline{b} \xrightarrow{x} \underline{a} \rangle$ and Late$\langle \underline{a} \xrightarrow{x} \underline{b} \rangle$ specified in Definition 1.1, process $B$ needs to decide whether and when to perform a particular action $\underline{b}$. In particular, it needs to estimate the relative time difference between points on different processes' timelines: It's current point, and the point at which $A$ performs $\underline{a}$. Because processes have no clocks, formally defining points on a timeline is somewhat subtle. Rather than distinguishing the points along the timeline of a given process according to the times at which they arise, to which processes have no access, one useful way is to identify a local point with the local state of the process. We call a pair $\sigma = (i, \ell)$ consisting of a process name and a local state for this process a *basic node*. In order to emphasize its site $i$, we sometimes call such a node an ***i-node***. We say that a basic node $\boldsymbol{\sigma} = (i, \ell)$ ***appears in r*** if $r_i(m) = \ell$ holds for some time $m$.

While the local state of a process in the FFIP protocol does not repeat twice in non-contiguous intervals of the same run, a local state can remain constant along some time interval. During such an interval the process cannot observe the passage of time; it observes only the state transitions. For a basic node $\sigma = (i, \ell)$ that appears in a run $r$, we define $\mathbf{time}_r(\boldsymbol{\sigma})$ to be the minimal $m$ such that $r_i(m) = \ell$. This allows us to treat a basic node as specifying a particular (externally observable) time in the run.[5] While a run $r$ can be uniquely determined by the set of its basic nodes and their respective times, different runs can possess the same set of basic nodes, and differ in their timing.

For a given site $i$, an $i$-node $\sigma'$ is called a *successor* of another $i$-node $\sigma$ in $r$ if $\mathsf{time}_r(\sigma) < \mathsf{time}_r(\sigma')$ and there is no $i$-node $\sigma''$ such that $\mathsf{time}_r(\sigma) < \mathsf{time}_r(\sigma'') < \mathsf{time}_r(\sigma')$. If $\sigma'$ is the successor of $\sigma$, then we call $\sigma$ the *predecessor* of $\sigma'$.

*Definition 2.1.* Given a run $r$, we define Lamport's *happens-before* relation among basic nodes that appear in $r$, denoted by $\boldsymbol{\sigma' \rightsquigarrow_r \sigma}$, to be the minimal transitive relation that satisfies (i) Locality: If both $\sigma'$ and $\sigma$ are $i$-nodes and $\mathsf{time}_r(\sigma') \le \mathsf{time}_r(\sigma)$, then $\sigma' \rightsquigarrow_r \sigma$, and (ii) if a message is sent in the run $r$ at $\sigma'$ and delivered to $\sigma$, then $\sigma' \rightsquigarrow_r \sigma$. We say that $\sigma'$ is ***in the past of σ*** in $r$ if $\sigma' \rightsquigarrow_r \sigma$, and we define $\mathbf{past}(\boldsymbol{r}, \boldsymbol{\sigma}) \triangleq \{\sigma' : \sigma' \rightsquigarrow_r \sigma\}$.[6]

[5]Since processes act in an event-driven fashion, the time at which $i$ acts in $r$ when in local state $\ell$ is precisely $\mathsf{time}_r(\sigma)$.

[6] The $\rightsquigarrow_r$ condition is defined w.r.t. a specific run $r$. However, since we restrict attention to full-information protocols, the run does not play an essential role. This is because if $\sigma \rightsquigarrow_r \sigma'$ holds, then $\sigma \rightsquigarrow_{r'} \sigma'$ holds for every run $r'$ in which both nodes appear.

*General Nodes.* We view a process as having access to its local state, and hence to its current basic node, at any point. Indeed, since processes are assumed to be following a full-information protocol, it also has access to all the basic nodes that appear in its past. But the points with which $B$ should coordinate its action (the points where $A$ performs $\underline{a}$) are often not in its past. So $B$ is aware neither of the real time at which they occur, nor of the basic nodes, since it cannot identify their local states. Recall, however, that processes are assumed to follow an FFIP protocol, in which whenever a process receives a message, it broadcasts (its local state) to all of its neighbors. So if $\sigma' \in \mathsf{past}(r, \sigma)$ and $\sigma'$ is not an initial node (i.e. not a node from time 0), then there are typically many message chains starting at $\sigma'$. Along these message chains appear new nodes, and it is with such nodes that it may need to coordinate, and about whose timing we need to reason. We now define the class of general nodes, which can be defined as being at the end of a path in the network from a given basic node. We proceed as follows.

*Definition 2.2.* Let $\sigma$ be a basic $i$-node, and $p$ be a path in Net that begins at $i$, then $\langle\sigma, p\rangle$ is a (general) node that describes the basic node that will receive the message chain that goes along $p$ starting at $\sigma$. We say that $\boldsymbol{\theta = \langle\sigma, p\rangle}$ ***appears in*** a run $\boldsymbol{r}$ if both $\sigma$ appears in $r$, and $p$ is a path in Net (so that there is a message chain in $r$ that leaves $\sigma$ and goes along $p$).

Note that if $p$ is a singleton (i.e. $p = [i]$) and $\sigma$ is an $i$-node, then $\theta = \langle\sigma, p\rangle$ denotes $\sigma$ itself. However, if $p$ is not a singleton, then $\theta$ corresponds to a basic node whose identity depends on the run in question. The correspondence is defined as follows.

*Definition 2.3.* Let $\theta = \langle\sigma, p\rangle$ be a node that appears in the run $r \in \mathcal{R}$. The basic node that corresponds to $\theta$ in $r$, $\mathtt{basic}(\theta, r)$, is defined inductively as follows:

(a) If $\theta = \langle\sigma, j\rangle$ (so $p$ is a singleton), then $\mathtt{basic}(\theta, r) = \sigma$. Otherwise,

(b) Let $p = p' \cdot j$ be a non-singleton, and let $\mathtt{basic}(\langle\sigma, p'\rangle, r) = \sigma'$. If the message sent in $r$ from $\sigma'$ to process $j$ is delivered at $\sigma''$, then $\mathtt{basic}(\langle\sigma, p\rangle, r) = \sigma''$.

General nodes will inherit properties from their corresponding basic nodes. Thus, we define $\mathsf{time}_r(\theta) \triangleq \mathsf{time}_r(\mathtt{basic}(\theta, r))$, we write $\theta \rightsquigarrow_r \theta'$ iff $\mathtt{basic}(\theta, r) \rightsquigarrow_r \mathtt{basic}(\theta', r)$, and call $\theta$ an $i$-node if $\mathtt{basic}(\theta, r)$ is an $i$-node. For a $j$-node $\theta = \langle\sigma, p\rangle$ of $r$ and a path $q$ in Net, where $q$ begins at process $j$, it will be convenient to write $\theta \odot q$ as shorthand for the node $\langle\sigma, p \odot q\rangle$.

Clearly, a node $\theta' = \langle\sigma', p'\rangle$ can appear in a run $r$ only if $\sigma'$ appears in $r$. However, if $\sigma$ appears in $r$ and $\sigma' \not\rightsquigarrow_r \sigma$, then $\sigma$ might not be able to distinguish whether $\theta' = \langle\sigma', p'\rangle$ indeed appears in the current run. We shall say that a general node $\theta' = \langle\sigma', p'\rangle$ is $\boldsymbol{\sigma}$***-recognized*** iff $\sigma' \rightsquigarrow_r \sigma$ and either (i) $p'$ is a singleton, or otherwise (ii) $\langle\sigma', p''\rangle \not\rightsquigarrow_r \sigma$ for every non singleton prefix $p''$ of $p'$. Note that in an FFIP protocol, $\sigma$ actually "knows" that every $\sigma$-recognized node appears in the run. Moreover, such nodes have a unique representation using $\sigma$-recognized nodes. More formally, in a given run $r$, if node $\theta$ can be represented in the form $\langle\sigma', p'\rangle$ where $\sigma' \rightsquigarrow_r \sigma$, then there is a unique $\sigma$-recognized node $\sigma''$ and path $p''$ such that $\theta = \langle\sigma'', p''\rangle$. Intuitively, in the eyes of $\sigma$, every node has a well-defined "$\sigma$-recognized" representation.

# 3 ZIGZAG PATTERNS AND TIMED PRECEDENCE

We adapt the notion of timed precedence from [31] to nodes in our setting. Formally, given a run $r \in \mathcal{R}$, we say that a run $\boldsymbol{r}$ ***satisfies*** $\theta \xrightarrow{x} \theta'$, and write $(R, r) \models \theta \xrightarrow{x} \theta'$, iff both (i) the nodes $\theta$ and $\theta'$ appear in $r$, and (ii) $\mathsf{time}_r(\theta) + x \leq \mathsf{time}_r(\theta')$. (While the system $\mathcal{R}$ does not play a role in this definition, it is included here because it will play a role in our later analysis.)

Our discussion in Section 1 shows that communication as in Figure 1 ensures that $\underline{a} \xrightarrow{L_{CB}-U_{CA}} \underline{b}$, and similarly that a pattern as in Figure 2a ensures a precedence as captured in Equation (1). We now define general zigzag patterns and relate them to timed precedence. The basic building block is a *two-legged fork* (see Figure 3):

*Definition 3.1.* A **two-legged fork** in $r$ is a triple $F = \langle\theta_0, \theta_1, \theta_2\rangle$ of nodes of $r$, such that $\theta_1 = \theta_0 \odot p_1$ and $\theta_2 = \theta_0 \odot p_2$, for process sequences $p_1$ and $p_2$. We denote $\mathsf{base}(F) = \theta_0$, $\mathsf{head}(F) = \theta_1$, and $\mathsf{tail}(F) = \theta_2$.

In a two-legged fork, there are direct message chains (possibly empty) from the base node to the head and to the tail of the fork. Figure 1 is an example of a two-legged fork in which the message chains consist of single messages, while Figure 3 depicts one with longer paths from the base node to head and tail nodes.

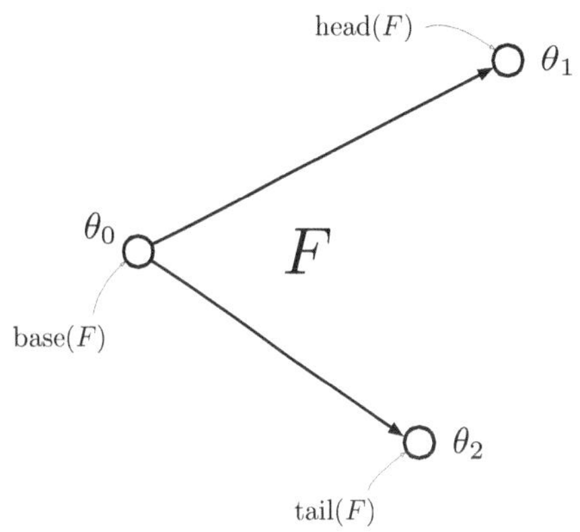


**Figure 3: A two-legged fork** $F = \langle\theta_0, \theta_1, \theta_2\rangle$**.**

Let $\theta$ be an $i$-node, and let $F = \langle\theta, \theta \odot p_1, \theta \odot p_2\rangle$ be a two-legged fork in $r$. We define the ***weight*** of $F$ to be

$$\mathsf{wt}(F) \triangleq L(p_1) - U(p_2).$$

In Figure 1, for example, $\mathsf{wt}(F) = L_{CB} - U_{CA}$. The existence of a two-legged fork $F$ in $r$ with tail $\theta_1$ and head $\theta_2$ implies that $(R, r) \models \theta_1 \xrightarrow{\mathsf{wt}(F)} \theta_2$.

A Zigzag pattern is made of a sequence of suitably composed two-legged forks. Roughly speaking, the head of each fork should be on the same timeline as, but appear no later than, the tail of the next fork in the sequence. If they coincide at the same basic node the forks are called *joined*. Otherwise, the tail will be at least one time unit later than the preceding head. More formally, we define

*Definition 3.2.* A ***zigzag pattern*** from node $\theta$ to $\theta'$ in the run $r$ is a sequence $Z = (F_1, \ldots, F_c)$ of two-legged forks in $r$, with $c \geq 1$, such that $\mathsf{tail}(F_1) = \theta$ and $\mathsf{head}(F_c) = \theta'$. Moreover, if $c > 1$ then for every $k = 1, \ldots, c-1$ there is a process $j$ such that both $\mathsf{head}(F_k)$ and $\mathsf{tail}(F_{k+1})$ correspond to $j$-nodes, and $\mathsf{time}_r(\mathsf{head}(F_k)) \leq \mathsf{time}_r(\mathsf{tail}(F_{k+1}))$.

Figure 2a depicts a zigzag pattern consisting of $c = 2$ forks, which are not joined, since the head of the lower fork and the tail of the upper one correspond to distinct nodes on $D$'s timeline.

The notion of weight extends to zigzag patterns. Consider a zigzag pattern $Z = (F_1, \ldots, F_c)$, and denote by $S(Z)$ the number of forks $F_k \in Z$ that are not joined to their successor (i.e., $\mathsf{head}(F_k)$ strictly precedes $\mathsf{tail}(F_{k+1})$). The ***weight*** of $Z$ is defined by

$$\mathsf{wt}(Z) \triangleq \sum_{k=1}^{c} \mathsf{wt}(F_k) + S(Z).$$

We can thus justify the claim that zigzag patterns are sufficient for establishing timed precedence in bcm systems:

Theorem 3.3 (Zigzag Sufficiency). *Let $Z$ be a zigzag pattern from node $\theta_1$ to $\theta_2$ in the run $r \in \mathcal{R}$. Then $(R, r) \models \theta_1 \xrightarrow{\mathsf{wt}(Z)} \theta_2$.*

The intuition is that each fork implies a timed precedence between its tail and its head, and the concatenation of forks in the zigzag pattern introduce a simple timed precedence between the head of one fork and the tail of its successor. Recall that, by assumption, if the successive forks are not joined, then they are separated by at least one time unit.

What is perhaps more instructive than Theorem 3.3 is that, in a precise sense, the only way to guarantee a timed precedence relation is via a zigzag pattern of this type. More formally, we say that a system $\mathcal{R}$ ***supports*** the statement $\theta_1 \xrightarrow{x} \theta_2$ if, for all $r \in \mathcal{R}$, if one of the nodes $\theta_1$ or $\theta_2$ appears in $r$, then both nodes appear in $r$, and $(\mathcal{R}, r) \models \theta_1 \xrightarrow{x} \theta_2$. We can show:

Theorem 3.4 (Zigzag Necessity). *Suppose that $\mathcal{R}$ supports $\theta_1 \xrightarrow{x} \theta_2$. Moreover, assume that $\theta_1$ and $\theta_2$ both appear in a run $r \in \mathcal{R}$, with $\mathsf{time}_r(\theta_1) > 0$ and $\mathsf{time}_r(\theta_2) > 0$. Then there is a zigzag pattern $Z$ in $r$ from $\theta_1$ to $\theta_2$ with $\mathsf{wt}(Z) \geq x$.*

Suppose that a protocol guarantees a particular time precedence constraint among a given pair of actions. Then it must ensure the existence of an appropriate zigzag pattern in the run. We remark that the requirement that $\mathsf{time}_r(\theta_2) > 0$ in the theorem ensures that the node $\theta_2$ is not an initial node. In our model, protocols cannot perform actions at initial nodes, and precedence among initial nodes can be obtained without the existence of zigzags.

# 4 USING ZIGZAG CAUSALITY FOR COORDINATION

Theorems 3.3 and 3.4 show that zigzag patterns are necessary and sufficient for ensuring that a precedence relation between two nodes holds. It follows, for example, that $B$ can act in an instance of $\mathsf{Early}\langle \underline{b} \xrightarrow{x} \underline{a} \rangle$ only at a node that is the tail of a zigzag pattern of weight $x$ whose head is the node at which A performs $\underline{a}$. (Similarly, the roles of head and tail need to be reversed for an instance of $\mathsf{Late}\langle \underline{a} \xrightarrow{x} \underline{b} \rangle$.) However, as discussed in the introduction, it is not guaranteed that a node at either end of the zigzag pattern is able to detect the existence of the pattern, and such endpoint node might not know that the necessary precedence condition holds.

We will show that in order to act in one of the two coordination tasks we are considering, $B$ must know that $\theta_1 \xrightarrow{x} \theta_2$ holds, for the two nodes at which $A$ and $B$ act. Next, we will characterize the communication patterns that give rise to such knowledge of a timed precedence, and thus are necessary for coordinating $A$ and $B$'s actions. We start by defining an appropriate notion of knowledge for the bcm model, which will allow us to formulate and prove these results.

## 4.1 Reasoning About Coordination

Our focus is on coordinating actions at different sites in a manner that satisfies temporal constraints. We use the notion of knowledge of [13] to reason about what a process knows about the relevant aspects of the timing of events. We now describe just enough of the logical framework to support our analysis.

Two runs $r, r' \in \mathcal{R}$ are said to be ***indistinguishable*** at the basic node $\sigma$, which we denote by $r \sim_\sigma r'$, if $\sigma$ appears both in $r$ and in $r'$. Intuitively, if $\sigma = (i, \ell)$ appears in both runs, then when $i$'s local state is $\ell$, it cannot distinguish whether the run is $r$ or $r'$. Knowledge is the dual of indistinguishability. I.e., a fact is known at a node if it is true of all indistinguishable runs. In particular, in this paper, we focus on knowledge of precedence statements at basic nodes. We write $(\mathcal{R}, r) \models K_\sigma(\theta_1 \xrightarrow{x} \theta_2)$ to state that in the run $r \in \mathcal{R}$ the precedence statement is known at the basic node $\sigma$. It is formally defined as follows:[7]

$$(\mathcal{R}, r) \models K_\sigma(\theta_1 \xrightarrow{x} \theta_2) \quad \text{iff} \quad (\mathcal{R}, r') \models \theta_1 \xrightarrow{x} \theta_2 \text{ holds for all } r' \in \mathcal{R} \text{ such that } r \sim_\sigma r'.$$

When performing the action $\underline{b}$ in solving a coordination problem such as $\mathsf{Early}\langle \underline{b} \xrightarrow{x} \underline{a} \rangle$ or $\mathsf{Late}\langle \underline{a} \xrightarrow{x} \underline{b} \rangle$, process $B$ must know that its current basic node satisfies the required precedence condition with respect to the node $\theta'$ at which $A$ performs its action $\underline{a}$. This is formalized as follows.

Theorem 4.1. *Suppose that $C$ sends $A$ a "go" message at basic node $\sigma_C$ in run $r \in \mathcal{R} = \mathcal{R}(\mathsf{P}, \gamma)$, and that $B$ performs $\underline{b}$ at node $\sigma$ in $r$. If $\mathsf{P}$ implements $\mathsf{Late}\langle \underline{a} \xrightarrow{x} \underline{b} \rangle$ then $(\mathcal{R}, r) \models K_\sigma(\sigma_C \cdot A \xrightarrow{x} \sigma)$. Similarly, $(\mathcal{R}, r) \models K_\sigma(\sigma \xrightarrow{x} \sigma_C A)$ if $\mathsf{P}$ implements $\mathsf{Early}\langle \underline{b} \xrightarrow{x} \underline{a} \rangle$.*

By Theorem 4.1, $B$ cannot perform $\underline{b}$ in a protocol solving one of the coordination tasks of Definition 1.1 unless it knows that it is at a node satisfying an appropriate temporal precedence to the one at which $A$ performs $\underline{a}$. Since such knowledge is also a sufficient condition for $B$'s action, we can obtain an optimal solution for the coordination tasks by characterizing when the corresponding knowledge statements hold. So, an optimal protocol for $B$ when performing the coordination tasks of Definition 1.1, is:

[7] It will suffice to define knowledge at basic nodes, here, since our analysis does not concern knowledge about what is known at other nodes. For a more general treatment, it is possible to define $(\mathcal{R}, r) \models K_\theta p$ to hold precisely if $(\mathcal{R}, r) \models K_\sigma p$ holds at $\sigma = \mathtt{basic}(\theta, r)$.

Protocol 4.2. *In local state $\ell$, denoting $\sigma \triangleq (B,\ell)$: If B has not performed $\underline{b}$ yet, and C sends a "go" message at a basic node $\sigma_C \rightsquigarrow_r \sigma$, then:*

- *For* $\mathsf{Late}\langle \underline{a} \xrightarrow{x} \underline{b}\rangle$*: If* $(\mathcal{R},r) \models K_\sigma(\sigma_C \cdot A \xrightarrow{x} \sigma)$*, then perform* $\underline{b}$*.*
- *For* $\mathsf{Early}\langle \underline{b} \xrightarrow{x} \underline{a}\rangle$*: If* $(\mathcal{R},r) \models K_\sigma(\sigma \xrightarrow{x} \sigma_C \cdot A)$*, then perform* $\underline{b}$*.*

This description of the optimal protocols is made in terms of $B$'s knowledge about timed precedence between nodes. Our goal is to translate this into a more concrete description, in terms of the communication pattern that is recorded in $B$'s local state. We will do so at once for both problems by solving a more general problem. I.e., we will characterize the communication patterns that determine when $(\mathcal{R},r) \models K_\sigma(\theta_1 \xrightarrow{x} \theta_2)$ holds, for general nodes $\theta_1$ and $\theta_2$.

It can be shown (and will follow from our results) that in order to know that $\theta_1 \xrightarrow{x} \theta_2$, a node $\sigma$ must know that a zigzag pattern of weight at least $x$ connects these two nodes. In contrast to the case of message chains in asynchronous systems, information does not flow along a zigzag pattern. Indeed, it does not pass from the tail of a fork to its head, or vice-versa. The shape and existence of a zigzag pattern depends on whether or not the head of one fork occurs before the tail of its successor (e.g., at node $D$ in Figure 2a). Thus, roughly speaking, the only way in which $\sigma$ can observe that a zigzag pattern exists is by being informed of the ordering among adjacent forks. Moreover, if $\sigma$ does not belong to the top fork in the pattern, then it must also be informed of the existence of this fork. We thus define:

*Definition 4.3 (Visible Zigzag).* Let $\sigma$ be a node of run $r \in \mathcal{R}$, and let $Z = (F_1,\ldots,F_c)$ be a zigzag pattern in $r$. Then $Z$ is called ***σ-visible in r*** if both (i) $\mathsf{head}(F_k) \rightsquigarrow_r \sigma$ for all $1 \le k \le c-1$, and (ii) $\mathsf{base}(F_c) = \langle \sigma', p'\rangle$ for a node $\sigma' \rightsquigarrow_r \sigma$.

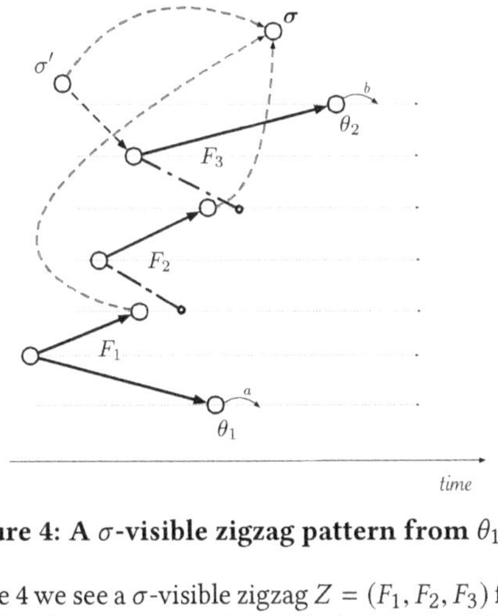


**Figure 4: A $\sigma$-visible zigzag pattern from $\theta_1$ to $\theta_2$**

In Figure 4 we see a $\sigma$-visible zigzag $Z = (F_1,F_2,F_3)$ from $\theta_1$ to $\theta_2$. Note that $\mathsf{head}(F_1) \rightsquigarrow_r \sigma$ and $\mathsf{head}(F_2) \rightsquigarrow_r \sigma$, and so $\sigma$ knows that $\mathsf{tail}(F_2)$ doesn't appear before $\mathsf{head}(F_1)$, and $\mathsf{tail}(F_3)$ doesn't appear before $\mathsf{head}(F_2)$. We remark that the definition of a $\sigma$-visible zigzag does not require a path from the base of other forks to $\sigma$, because for all forks except the top one, there is a path consisting of a message from the base to the head and, by condition (i), a path from the fork's head to $\sigma$. We can now show:

Theorem 4.4 (Visible Zigzag Theorem). *Let $\mathcal{R} = \mathcal{R}(\mathsf{P},\gamma)$ and suppose that* P *is an* FFIP*. Moreover, let $\sigma$ be a basic node of $r \in \mathcal{R}$, and let $\theta_1$ and $\theta_2$ be $\sigma$-recognized nodes in $r$, such that both $\mathsf{time}_r(\theta_1) > 0$ and $\mathsf{time}_r(\theta_2) > 0$. Then $(\mathcal{R},r) \models K_\sigma(\theta_1 \xrightarrow{x} \theta_2)$ iff there exists a $\sigma$-visible zigzag pattern $Z$ from $\theta_1$ to $\theta_2$ in $r$ with $\mathsf{wt}(Z) \ge x$.*

The Visible Zigzag Theorem provides a precise characterization of the pattern of communication that is necessary and sufficient for knowledge at $\sigma$ of precedence among timepoints at distinct sites of the system. This is a fundamental aspect of information flow in bcm systems. The fact that a $\sigma$-visible pattern is sufficient for such knowledge appears reasonable given our analysis so far. The main technical challenge is to prove the converse: that such a pattern is also necessary.

We can now rephrase the optimal protocol defined before (Protocol 4.2), in terms of concrete communication patterns:

Protocol 4.5. *In local state $\ell$, denoting $\sigma \triangleq (B,\ell)$: If B has not performed $\underline{b}$ yet, and C sends a "go" message at a basic node $\sigma_C \rightsquigarrow_r \sigma$, then:*

- *For* $\mathsf{Late}\langle \underline{a} \xrightarrow{x} \underline{b}\rangle$*: If there is a $\sigma$-visible zigzag pattern $Z$ in $r$ from $\sigma_C \cdot A$ to $\sigma$ with $\mathsf{wt}(Z) \ge x$, then perform $\underline{b}$.*
- *For* $\mathsf{Early}\langle \underline{b} \xrightarrow{x} \underline{a}\rangle$*: If there is a $\sigma$-visible zigzag pattern $Z$ in $r$ from $\sigma$ to $\sigma_C \cdot A$ with $\mathsf{wt}(Z) \ge x$, then perform $\underline{b}$.*

The visible zigzag patterns of Protocol 4.5 are instances of Figure 4, in which one of the endpoints of the pattern is $\sigma$ in itself. The pattern for $\mathsf{Late}\langle \underline{a} \xrightarrow{x} \underline{b}\rangle$ is illustrated in Figure 5. Note that there is no need for a separate message chain from $\mathsf{base}(F_c)$ to $\sigma$ in this pattern, because $\mathsf{base}(F_c) \rightsquigarrow_r \sigma = \mathsf{head}(F_c)$ holds for the two-legged fork $F_c$, and so condition (ii) of Definition 4.3 is trivially guaranteed. In the pattern for the case of $\mathsf{Early}\langle \underline{b} \xrightarrow{x} \underline{a}\rangle$ we have that $\sigma = \mathsf{tail}(F_1) = \theta_1$. It contains all of the message chains depicted in Figure 4.

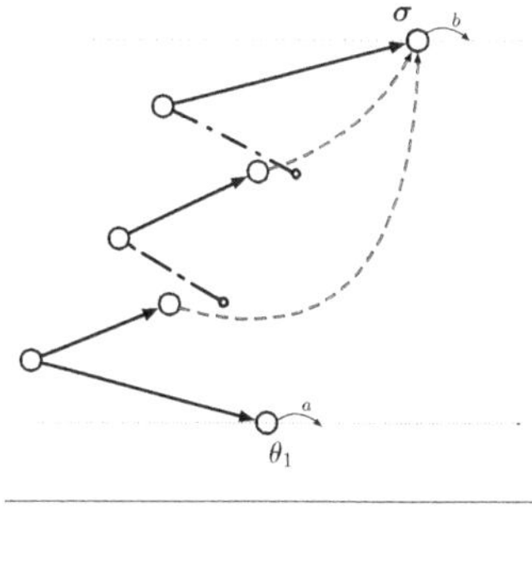


**Figure 5: A visible zigzag pattern for $\mathsf{Late}\langle \underline{a} \xrightarrow{x} \underline{b}\rangle$**

While the conditions described above for the optimal protocol are more figurative (communication patterns), there are actually simple algorithms to check for their truth (using a structure that is described next), but this is beyond the scope of this paper.

## 5 HIGHLIGHTS OF THE ANALYSIS

In this section we survey the general approach used for proving our main results. Of course, the essence of the analysis has to do with extracting knowledge about timing from the actual communication in a run, given the *a priori* bounds on message transmission times. This has been considered in the literature, for example, in the work on clock synchronization [1, 11, 12, 16, 24, 25, 31, 33, 35].

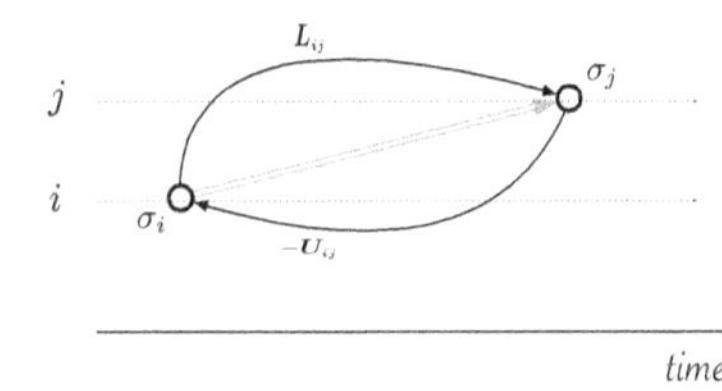


**Figure 6: The bound edges created by a direct message**

Inspired by [31, 33], we use a weighted graph to capture the timing guarantees provided by the system, and to reason about time differences between local timepoints in a given run $r$.

*Definition 5.1.* Given a run $r \in \mathcal{R}$, the ***basic bounds graph for r*** is a graph $G_B(r) = (V_B, E_B, w)$, where $V_B$ are the basic nodes that appear in $r$. The edges of $E_B$ are defined as follows: (a) If $\sigma$ and $\sigma'$ are $i$-nodes (for the same process $i$) and $\sigma'$ is the successor of $\sigma$, then $(\sigma, \sigma') \in E_B$, and $w(\sigma, \sigma') = 1$. (b) If some message sent at an $i$-node $\sigma_i$ in $r$ is received at a $j$-node $\sigma_j$, then both $(\sigma_i, \sigma_j) \in E_B$ and $(\sigma_j, \sigma_i) \in E_B$, with $w(\sigma_i, \sigma_j) = L_{ij}$ and $w(\sigma_j, \sigma_i) = -U_{ij}$.

The basic bounds graph captures timed precedence information about the temporal relation among basic nodes: (a) is justified by the fact that successive nodes are at least one time step apart, while (b) embodies the upper and lower bounds on message transmission times. Figure 6 illustrates the edges of $G_B$ that are induced according to case (b) by a single message delivery. It is straightforward to check (see, e.g., [31]) that

Lemma 5.2. *Let $p$ be a path connecting nodes $\sigma$ and $\sigma'$ in $G_B(r)$. If $w(p) = x$, then $(\mathcal{R}, r) \models \sigma \xrightarrow{x} \sigma'$.*

Figure 7 highlights a path in the bounds graph that captures the timing guarantees implied by the zigzag pattern of Figure 2a via Lemma 5.2.

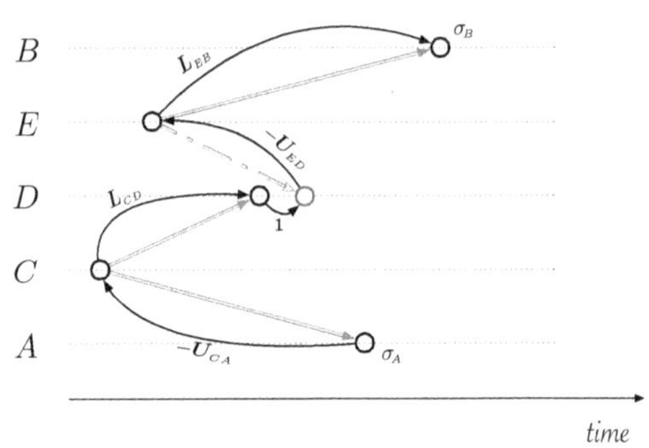


**Figure 7: A path in the bounds graph justifying Equation (1)**

In addition to imposing a precedence constraint, a path in $G_B(r)$ induces a zigzag pattern in the run $r$. More precisely:

Lemma 5.3. *If $p$ is a path connecting nodes $\sigma$ and $\sigma'$ in $G_B(r)$, then there exists a zigzag pattern $Z$ in $r$, from $\sigma$ to $\sigma'$, with $\mathrm{wt}(Z) = \mathrm{wt}(p)$.*

The faint lines in Figure 7 show the zigzag communication pattern underlying the path in $G_B(r)$, which is depicted by the solid lines.

We now give a sketch for the proof of Theorem 3.4. Assume that $\mathcal{R}$ supports $\sigma_1 \xrightarrow{x} \sigma_2$, for two basic nodes $\sigma_1$ and $\sigma_2$ that appear in $r$. By Lemma 5.2, each path between $\sigma_1$ and $\sigma_2$ in $G_B(r)$ defines a constraint on the difference of their times. I.e., if $p$ is a path between $\sigma_1$ and $\sigma_2$, then $(\mathcal{R}, r) \models \sigma_1 \xrightarrow{\mathrm{wt}(p)} \sigma_2$. The longer the path is, the stronger the constraint. Thus, we are interested in finding the longest path from $\sigma_1$ to $\sigma_2$.

Assume that $p$ is the longest path (between $\sigma_1$ and $\sigma_2$). Our main claim is that there exists a run $r' \in \mathcal{R}$ such that $G_B(r) = G_B(r')$, both $\sigma_1$ and $\sigma_2$ appear in $r'$, and $\mathrm{time}_{r'}(\sigma_2) = \mathrm{time}_{r'}(\sigma_1) + \mathrm{wt}(p)$. This means that the constraint dictated by the longest path $p$ is tight (a similar argument appears in [33]). By definition of *supports*, we obtain that $\mathrm{time}_{r'}(\sigma_2) \geq \mathrm{time}_{r'}(\sigma_1) + x$ and so $\mathrm{wt}(p) \geq x$. By Lemma 5.3 there exists in $r$ a zigzag pattern $Z$ from $\sigma_1$ to $\sigma_2$, with $\mathrm{wt}(Z) = \mathrm{wt}(p) \geq x$, just as stated in Theorem 3.4.

But what if $G_B(r)$ does not contain a path from $\sigma_1$ to $\sigma_2$? In such case we can show that there is a run $r'' \in \mathcal{R}$ containing $\sigma_2$, in which $\sigma_1$ doesn't appear. This contradicts the assumption that $\mathcal{R}$ supports $\sigma_1 \xrightarrow{x} \sigma_2$, since by definition of *supports* $\sigma_1$ and $\sigma_2$ must either both appear in $r''$, or neither should appear.

The proof shows that, for every node $\sigma_2$ in $G_B(r)$, there is a single run, $r'$, in which, intuitively, every node of $G_B(r)$ is "delayed" as much as possible, relative to $\mathrm{time}_{r'}(\sigma_2)$. In other words, for every node $\sigma'$ that has a path to $\sigma_2$ in $G_B(r)$ we will have that $\mathrm{time}_{r'}(\sigma_2) = \mathrm{time}_{r'}(\sigma') + \mathrm{wt}(p')$, where $p'$ is the longest path from $\sigma'$ to $\sigma_2$. Moreover, every node that doesn't have a path to $\sigma_2$ will not appear in $r'$. This proves Theorem 3.4.

### 5.1 The Extended Bounds Graph

The proof of Theorem 4.4 is similar in its nature to the proof of Theorem 3.4, but is much more complex. While Theorem 3.4 states the existence of a zigzag pattern following a general run property (*supports*), Theorem 4.4 deals with the knowledge of a specific node. In the previous proof we used $G_B(r)$. Essentially everything that can be deduced about the timing of events in a run $r$ based on the combined information in all processes' histories is captured by $G_B(r)$. Figure 7, for example, presents a path in the bounds graph that justifies the analysis leading to Equation (1). However, $G_B(r)$ is defined by the entire run, and a process at a given basic node $\sigma = \langle i, \ell \rangle$ observes only a portion of this information that is generated by the nodes in $\mathrm{past}(r, \sigma)$, which we denote by $G_B(r, \sigma)$. This subgraph of $G_B(r)$ does not completely capture the timing information available to $\sigma$, however. For example, assume that an $i$-node $\sigma_i$ and a $j$-node $\sigma_j$ are both in $\mathrm{past}(r, \sigma)$, and assume that a message sent at $\sigma_i$ to process $j$ isn't received at any node in $\mathrm{past}(r, \sigma)$. We know that the node at which this message will be received, i.e. $\langle \sigma_i, [i, j] \rangle$, must appear in $G_B(r)$ later than $\sigma_j$. We also have that $\mathrm{time}_r(\sigma_i) + U_{ij} \geq \mathrm{time}_r(\langle \sigma_i, [i, j] \rangle)$ by definition of $U_{ij}$. Combining this with the requirement that $\text{time}_r(\langle\sigma_i, [i,j]\rangle) \geq \text{time}_r(\sigma_j) + 1$ we have that $\text{time}_r(\sigma_i) - \text{time}_r(\sigma_j) \geq 1 - U_{ij}$, and thus $(\mathcal{R}, r) \models \sigma_j \xrightarrow{1-U_{ij}} \sigma_i$. In our setting processes follow an FFIP, and so the contents of past$(r,\sigma)$ depend only on $\sigma$ and not on $r$. So this precedence holds for any run $r'$ containing $\sigma$. Such a run satisfies $r' \sim_\sigma r$, and we thus obtain that $(\mathcal{R}, r) \models K_\sigma(\sigma_j \xrightarrow{1-U_{ij}} \sigma_i)$. This time precedence does not correspond to a path in $G_B(r,\sigma)$, and so $G_B(r,\sigma)$ misses important information.

In order to fully capture the information available to a node $\sigma$ based on its partial view of the run, we define an extended bounds graph based on the nodes of past$(r,\sigma)$, to which we add $n$ auxiliary nodes $\{\psi_1, \ldots, \psi_n\}$, one per process timeline. Intuitively, each node $\psi_j$ represents the earliest among the nodes on $j$'s timeline that are beyond view (intuitively "over the horizon") for $\sigma$. Messages that are sent to process $j$ and not received at nodes from past$(r,\sigma)$, will be received at $\psi_j$ or later. This extended graph is denoted by $\boldsymbol{G_E(r,\sigma)}$. Three sets of edges $E'$, $E''$ and $E'''$ are added to the induced subgraph $G_B(r,\sigma)$ of $G_B(r)$ to obtain the extended graph: (a) $E'$ consists of edges $(\sigma_i, \psi_i)$ from the latest $i$-node in past$(r,\sigma)$ to $i$'s auxiliary node, with weight $w(\sigma_i, \psi_i) = 1$; (b) if a message was sent from an $i$-node $\sigma_i$ in past$(r,\sigma)$ to process $j$ and not delivered to a node in past$(r,\sigma)$, then an edge $(\psi_j, \sigma_i)$ is added to $E''$ with weight $-U_{ij}$ as in the basic bounds graph. Finally, (c) the set $E'''$ consists of edges $(\psi_j, \psi_i)$ with weight $-U_{ij}$ that are added for every channel $(i,j) \in$ Chans. (Intuitively, these edges are justified by the fact that the processes follow an FFIP, and so when a message will be delivered at a node beyond the view of $\sigma$, it will be sent to all neighbors in the Net graph.) Figure 8 illustrates the extended bounds graph $G_E(r,\sigma)$, for an $i$-node $\sigma$. The underlying network includes three processes, $i$, $j$ and $k$, and communication channels (in both directions) between processes $j$ and $i$, and between processes $i$ and $k$. The figure highlights the four types of edges that appear in $G_E(r,\sigma)$. The shaded area depicts the past$(r,\sigma)$ region. On the right are the auxiliary nodes $\psi_i$, $\psi_j$ and $\psi_k$, one per process. Note that the bound edges to and from auxiliary nodes handle upper bounds only.

Now, the graph $G_E(r,\sigma)$ plays a similar role in the proof of Theorem 4.4 to the role of $G_B(r)$ in the proof of Theorem 3.4. Indeed, $G_E(r,\sigma)$ exhibits similar (albeit more complex) features to those of $G_B(r)$. For example, any path in $G_E(r,\sigma)$ whose endpoints are both basic nodes from past$(r,\sigma)$ (and not auxiliary nodes), still defines a constraint between its endpoints (in any run $r' \sim_\sigma r$). It also defines a $\sigma$-visible zigzag in $r$ with the same weight. Note the small differences: (1) The constraint here holds in any run $r' \sim_\sigma r$ (as for any such run, $G_E(r,\sigma) = G_E(r',\sigma)$), instead of any run $r'$ with the same complete bounds graph (i.e $G_B(r') = G_B(r)$), and (2) the zigzag pattern is a *$\sigma$-visible* zigzag. Paths that start at, or end in, auxiliary nodes also exhibit important features, which are essential for the proof. The full details are beyond the scope of our presentation here and are available in [9].

Crucially, the extended bounds graph, $G_E(r,\sigma)$, can be used to construct valid runs of $\mathcal{R}$ with desirable properties. This is based on a careful assignment of times to nodes of $G_E(r,\sigma)$, in the following manner:

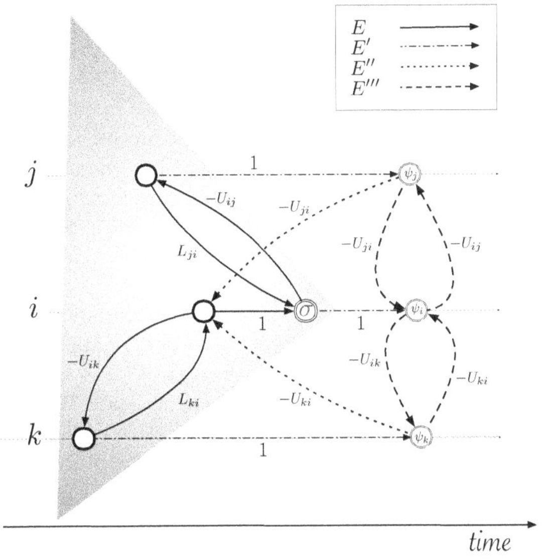


**Figure 8: An illustration of the extended bounds graph** $G_E(r,\sigma)$

*Definition 5.4.* Let $\sigma$ be a basic node appearing in $r \in \mathcal{R}$. A valid timing function for $G_E(r,\sigma) = (V_E, E_E, w)$ is a function $T : V_E \to \mathbb{N}$, such that $T(\theta_1) + w(\theta_1, \theta_2) \leq T(\theta_2)$ holds for each $(\theta_1, \theta_2) \in E_E$.

Based on a valid timing function $T$ for $G_E(r,\sigma) = (V_E, E_E, w)$, we can define a run $r' \sim_\sigma r$ of $\mathcal{R}$ in which the nodes of past$(r,\sigma)$ appear at the prescribed times, and all the other nodes appear no earlier than the time of the auxiliary node $\psi_j$ that belongs to their timeline $j$. This result is achieved by the fact that the bounds associated with auxiliary nodes make sure that nodes outside past$(r,\sigma)$ won't appear too early relative to nodes from past$(r,\sigma)$. (That, in turn, could force a message sent outside past$(r,\sigma)$ to be received inside past$(r,\sigma)$, which would modify $\sigma$'s past and cause $r' \not\sim_\sigma r$).

## 6 DISCUSSION

The principles underlying coordination in purely asynchronous systems are by now fairly well understood, based on [22] and the four decades since it was published. Message chains play a central role in determining the ordering of events and coordinating their timing. More recently, the study of coordination in systems with global clocks was initiated by [5]. The current paper considers yet another timing model, the bcm model, in which there are no built-in timers and clock. Nevertheless, timing information can be gleaned from observed events, because there are upper and lower bounds on the message transmission times among processes. A direct use of bounds in such a model is the one illustrated in Figure 1: Given two message chains that start from the same point, if the sum of lower bounds on one is greater than the sum of upper bounds on the other, then the first message chain is guaranteed to end later than the second one. Indeed, the bounds can be used to provide a quantitative estimate of the time difference between these two events. We introduced the notion of a zigzag message pattern and showed that it provides another way to deduce the time precedence between events. The existence of an appropriate zigzag pattern was shown to be necessary and sufficient for the message pattern of an execution of the system to ensure that a given timed precedence among events is satisfied.

Interestingly, whereas it is possible to ensure that the existence of a message chain will be observed by the process receiving the chain's final message, this is not the case with general zigzag patterns. Information about the pattern's existence is distributed among the processes. In order to use a zigzag pattern in coordination, it is necessary for its relevant endpoints to obtain information about the order in which pivotal intermediate messages were delivered. Only then can a process know that the pattern exists, and hence to know that the precedence that the zigzag pattern implies is satisfied. Our analysis provides a characterization of when a precedence statement is known by a process at a given local state. This requires a *visible zigzag*, consisting of an appropriate zigzag pattern, as well as message chains informing the node about the pivotal parts of the zigzag pattern. A corollary of this is a characterization of patterns that allow coordinating actions according to Early and Late specifications.

The main mathematical structures underlying our analysis are the basic bounds graph and the extended bounds graphs presented in Section 5. In these, the start and end points of events are nodes, and the bounds are represented by weighted edges among these nodes. While the basic bounds graph has appeared in the analysis of clock synchronization (see, e.g., [33], in which it is used to capture synchronization even in the presence of clock drift), the extended bounds graph seems to be novel. It allows an analysis of the timing information at a node based on its subjective view of the computation. Events in its direct causal past, as well as the fact that events do not appear there, provide information on the timing and ordering of events.

As remarked in the Introduction, the bcm model can easily be adapted to capture bounds on the duration of other events as well. A natural setting that fits the bcm model is that of asynchronous, or self-timed, VLSI circuits, which are circuits that operate without clocks. In such settings, time bounds are often used to coordinate actions and ensure correctness of the computation. The typical way to do so is by using a simple fork as in Figure 1. Such forks are also the basis for correct operation in synchronous circuits, where extreme care is taken to ensure that clock inputs to different flip-flops are arranged to have very similar delays from a common source for the implementation of sequencing [36]. To the best of our knowledge, it is an open problem whether zigzag causality and our characterization of solutions to the Early and Late coordination problems may facilitate the design of new circuits.

## REFERENCES


[1] H. Attiya, A. Herzberg, and S. Rajsbaum. Optimal clock synchronization under different delay assumptions. *SIAM J. Comput.*, 25, February 1996.

[2] I. Ben-Zvi and Y. Moses. On interactive knowledge with bounded communication. *Journal of Applied Non-Classical Logics*, 21(3-4):323–354, 2011.

[3] I. Ben-Zvi and Y. Moses. Agent-time epistemics and coordination. In *Indian Conference on Logic and Its Applications*, pages 97–108. Springer, 2013.

[4] I. Ben-Zvi and Y. Moses. The shape of reactive coordination tasks. In *Proceedings of the 14th Conference on Theoretical Aspects of Rationality and Knowledge (TARK 2013), Chennai, India, January 7-9, 2013*, 2013.

[5] I. Ben-Zvi and Y. Moses. Beyond Lamport's *happened-before*: On time bounds and the ordering of events in distributed systems. *J. ACM*, 61(2):13:1–13:26, 2014.

[6] G.-q. Bi and M.-m. Poo. Synaptic modifications in cultured hippocampal neurons: dependence on spike timing, synaptic strength, and postsynaptic cell type. *Journal of neuroscience*, 18(24):10464–10472, 1998.

[7] B. A. Coan. A communication-efficient canonical form for fault-tolerant distributed protocols. In *Proceedings of the fifth annual ACM symposium on Principles of distributed computing*, pages 63–72. ACM, 1986.

[8] J. C. Corbett, J. Dean, M. Epstein, A. Fikes, C. Frost, J. Furman, S. Ghemawat, A. Gubarev, C. Heiser, P. Hochschild, et al. Spanner: Google's globally distributed database. *ACM Transactions on Computer Systems (TOCS)*, 31(3):8, 2013.

[9] A. Dan, R. Manohar, and Y. Moses. On using time without clocks via zigzag causality. arXiv.org article, http://arxiv.org/abs/1705.08627, 2017.

[10] B. Dickerson. Time in the power industry: how and why we use it. Arbiter Systems, technical report, http://www.arbiter.com/ftp/datasheets/TimeInThePowerIndustry.pdf, 2010.

[11] D. Dolev, J. Y. Halpern, B. B. Simons, and H. R. Strong. A new look at fault-tolerant network routing. *Information and Computation*, 72(3):180–196, 1987.

[12] D. Dolev, J. Y. Halpern, and H. R. Strong. On the possibility and impossibility of achieving clock synchronization. *Journal of Computer and System Sciences*, 32(2):230–250, 1986.

[13] R. Fagin, J. Y. Halpern, Y. Moses, and M. Y. Vardi. *Reasoning about Knowledge*. MIT Press, Cambridge, Mass., 2003.

[14] P. Giusto, G. Martin, and E. Harcourt. Reliable estimation of execution time of embedded software. In *Proceedings of the conference on Design, automation and test in Europe*, pages 580–589. IEEE Press, 2001.

[15] Y. A. Gonczarowski and Y. Moses. Timely common knowledge. In *Proceedings of the 14th Conference on Theoretical Aspects of Rationality and Knowledge (TARK 2013), Chennai, India, January 7-9, 2013*, 2013.

[16] J. Y. Halpern, N. Megiddo, and A. Munshi. Optimal precision in the presence of uncertainty. *Journal of Complexity*, 1:170–196, 1985.

[17] K. Harris. An application of IEEE 1588 to industrial automation. In *International IEEE Symposium on Precision Clock Synchronization for Measurement Control and Communication (ISPCS)*, 2008.

[18] IEEE TC 9. 1588 IEEE Standard for a Precision Clock Synchronization Protocol for Networked Measurement and Control Systems Version 2. *IEEE*, 2008.

[19] ITU-T G.8271/Y.1366. Time and phase synchronization aspects of packet networks. *ITU-T*, 2012.

[20] M. Konishi. Centrally synthesized maps of sensory space. *Trends in Neurosciences*, 9:163–168, 1986.

[21] H. Kopetz. *Real-time systems: design principles for distributed embedded applications*. Springer Science & Business Media, 2011.

[22] L. Lamport. Time, clocks, and the ordering of events in a distributed system. *Communications of the ACM*, 21(7):558–565, 1978.

[23] L. Lamport. Using time instead of timeout for fault-tolerant distributed systems. *ACM Trans. Program. Lang. Syst.*, 6(2):254–280, 1984.

[24] L. Lamport and P. M. Melliar-Smith. Synchronizing clocks in the presence of faults. *Journal of the ACM*, 32(1):52–78, 1985.

[25] J. Lundelius and N. Lynch. An upper and lower bound for clock synchronization. *Information and control*, 62(2-3):190–204, 1984.

[26] N. A. Lynch and N. Shavit. Timing-based mutual exclusion. In *Proceedings of the Real-Time Systems Symposium - 1992, Phoenix, Arizona, USA, December 1992*, pages 2–11, 1992.

[27] P. Moreira, J. Serrano, T. Wlostowski, P. Loschmidt, and G. Gaderer. White rabbit: Sub-nanosecond timing distribution over ethernet. In *Precision Clock Synchronization for Measurement, Control and Communication, 2009. ISPCS 2009. International Symposium on*, pages 1–5. IEEE, 2009.

[28] A. Morrison and Y. Afek. Temporally bounding TSO for fence-free asymmetric synchronization. In *Proceedings of the Twentieth International Conference on Architectural Support for Programming Languages and Operating Systems, ASPLOS '15, Istanbul, Turkey, March 14-18, 2015*, pages 45–58, 2015.

[29] Y. Moses. Knowledge and communication (a tutorial). In Y. Moses, editor, *Theoretical Aspects of Reasoning about Knowledge: Proc. Fourth Conference*, pages 1–14. Morgan Kaufmann, San Francisco, Calif., 1992.

[30] Y. Moses. Relating knowledge and coordinated action: The knowledge of preconditions principle. In *Proceedings Fifteenth Conference on Theoretical Aspects of Rationality and Knowledge, TARK 2015, Carnegie Mellon University, Pittsburgh, USA, June 4-6, 2015.*, pages 231–245, 2015.

[31] Y. Moses and B. Bloom. Knowledge, timed precedence and clocks. In *Proc. 13th ACM Symp. on Principles of Distributed Computing*, pages 294–303, 1994.

[32] C. J. Myers. *Asynchronous circuit design*. John Wiley & Sons, 2004.

[33] B. Patt-Shamir and S. Rajsbaum. A theory of clock synchronization (extended abstract). In *STOC '94: Proceedings of the twenty-sixth annual ACM symposium on Theory of computing*, pages 810–819, New York, NY, USA, 1994. ACM.

[34] B. Simons. An overview of clock synchronization. In *Fault-Tolerant Distributed Computing*, pages 84–96. Springer, 1990.

[35] T. K. Srikanth and S. Toueg. Optimal clock synchronization. In *Proc. 4th ACM Symp. on Principles of Distributed Computing*, pages 71–86, 1985.

[36] N. Weste and D. Harris. *CMOS VLSI Design: A Circuits and Systems Perspective (4th Edition)*. Pearson, 2010.

# Brief Announcement: Proust: A Design Space for Highly-Concurrent Transactional Data Structures

Thomas Dickerson
Brown University
thomas_dickerson@brown.edu

Paul Gazzillo
Yale University
paul.gazzillo@yale.edu

Maurice Herlihy
Brown University
maurice_herlihy@brown.edu

Eric Koskinen
Yale University
eric.koskinen@yale.edu

## ABSTRACT

Most STM systems are poorly equipped to support libraries of concurrent data structures. One reason is that they typically detect conflicts by tracking transactions' *read sets* and *write sets*, an approach that often leads to false conflicts. A second is that existing data structures and libraries often need to be rewritten from scratch to support transactional conflict detection and rollback. This brief announcement introduces *Proust*, a framework for the design and implementation of transactional data structures. Proust is designed to maximize reuse of existing well-engineered libraries by providing transactional "wrappers" to make existing thread-safe concurrent data structures transactional. Proustian objects are also integrated with an underlying STM system, allowing them to take advantage of well-engineered STM conflict detection mechanisms. Proust generalizes and unifies prior approaches such as boosting and predication.

## 1 INTRODUCTION

Software Transactional Memory (STM) has become a popular alternative to conventional synchronization models, both as programming language libraries [7, 10, 15, 18] and as stand-alone systems [1, 3, 8, 13, 16, 17]. STM systems structure code as a sequence of *transactions*, blocks that are executed *atomically*, meaning that steps of concurrent transactions do not appear to interleave.

Most STM systems, however, are not well-equipped to support libraries of concurrent data structures. One limitation is that STM systems typically detect conflicts by tracking transactions' *read sets* and *write sets*, an approach that often leads to false conflicts, when operations that could have correctly executed concurrently are deemed to conflict, causing unnecessary rollbacks and serialization. Instead, it would be preferable to exploit data type semantics to enhance concurrency by recognizing when operations do not interfere at the semantic level, even if they might interfere at some lower level.

A second limitation is that existing thread-safe libraries and data structures must typically be rewritten from scratch to accommodate idiosyncrasies of the underlying STM system. The prospect of discarding so much carefully engineered concurrent software is unappealing. Instead, it would be preferable to provide a pathway for porting at least some existing thread-safe concurrent data structures and algorithms into STM systems.

We are not the first to identify these limitations. *Transactional boosting* [12] describes a methodology for constructing a transactional "wrapper" for prior thread-safe concurrent data structures. A boosting wrapper requires identifying which operations commute, as well as providing operation inverses. Boosting is a stand-alone process, not integrated with an STM. *Transactional predication* [2] describes a way to leverage standard STM functionality to encompass highly-concurrent sets and maps. Predication, however, does not appear to extend beyond sets and maps, and does not provide an explicit path to migrate legacy data structures and libraries. *Software transactional objects* [14] (STO) is an STM design that provides built-in primitives to track conflicts among arbitrary operations, not just read-write conflicts. It does not provide a migration path for legacy libraries.

This brief announcement introduces *Proust*[1], a framework which generalizes key insights from transactional boosting and predication. Proust is designed to ease reuse of existing well-engineered libraries in two ways. First, Proust is a methodology for the design and implementation of transactional "wrappers" that transform existing libraries of thread-safe concurrent data structures into transactional data structures so as to minimize false data conflicts. Unlike predication, Proust supports objects of arbitrary abstract type, not just sets and maps. Second, unlike boosting, Proustian objects are integrated with an underlying STM system, allowing them to take advantage of well-engineered STM conflict detection mechanisms.

Two key elements are necessary to wrap an existing non-transactional concurrent data structure into an STM-compatible object. First, as with boosting, it is necessary to characterize the commutativity relationships between the various operations on that data structure. For example, in a map, queries and updates to non-intersecting key ranges commute. Sometimes, this determination

Supported in part by NSF CCF Awards #1421126 and #003991.

*PODC '17, July 25-27, 2017, Washington, DC, USA*

ACM ISBN 978-1-4503-4992-5/17/07...$15.00
https://doi.org/10.1145/3087801.3087866

[1]This name is a portmanteau of *predication* and *boosting*, both influential prior works. The name is also an *hommage* to Marcel Proust, an author famous for his exploration of the complexities of memory.

can be performed automatically by reduction to SMT[2] solvers. Moreover, in most cases these relationships can be conservatively approximated with traditional two-phase locks, without much loss in expressivity.

Second, the wrapper must provide an *update strategy*, either by providing an inverse for each operation, or a *shadow copy*[3] functionality. Inverses and shadow copies correspond to alternative update strategies, as discussed in Section 2.

This paper makes several contributions. First, techniques for transforming black-box highly-concurrent linearizable data structures into transactional objects with minimal false conflicts, generalizing key insights of boosting and predication. Second, the concept of a *conflict abstraction* that translates an abstract data type's semantic notions of conflict into concrete forms that can be efficiently managed by a generic software transactional memory run-time. Third, systematic guidelines for choosing a transactional API for an underlying thread-safe data structure. Effectively, the transactional API must choose between *optimistic* or *pessimistic* conflict resolution, and *eager* or *lazy* update strategies (Section 2).

In addition to these conceptual contributions, we also developed the ScalaProust prototype implementation, built on top of ScalaSTM. It shows scalability matching existing specialized approaches, but with a much wider range of applicability (Section 3).

## 2 OVERVIEW

**The Proust Design Space** The Proust methodology, like Boosting, Predication, and optimistic transactional boosting (OTB) [2, 11, 12] is based on the principles that (1) synchronization conflicts should be defined over an object's abstract (not concrete) state, and (2) the abstract state can be mapped to an underlying STM mechanism by proper synchronization and an ability to roll back changes.

By the Proust *design space*, we mean the following several implementation choices. Concurrency control can be optimistic (as in Predication, OTB) or pessimistic (as in Boosting). The base data structure can be modified *eagerly* as the transaction executes, or *lazily* postponed to commit time. Each prior work cited commits to one fixed choice from each category, while Proust provides a unifying structure allowing choices to be mixed and matched.

**The Proust Methodology** Proust detects and resolves synchronization conflicts through *conflict abstractions*, which are (roughly speaking) maps carrying abstract states to concurrency control primitives provided by an underlying STM. At the concrete end, programmers are responsible for providing a *lock allocator policy* (LAP), which allocates concurrency control primitives as needed. The LAP is either optimistic or pessimistic. A pessimistic LAP allocates standard re-entrant read-write locks, while an optimistic LAP returns an object, which maps `lock` invocations to operations on standard STM memory locations, allowing the STM to detect and manage synchronization conflicts.

Programmers also choose whether wrapped objects are modified lazily or eagerly. A lazy strategy requires the ability to construct a shadow copy, while an eager strategy requires each operation to have a declared inverse, registered as a rollback handler by the abstract lock. If shadow copy functionality is provided, each operation on the wrapped object is forwarded through a *replay log*. The replay log computes the result of the operation at execution time using the shadow copy, and registers a handler to reapply the operation to the wrapped object.

[2]n.b. "Satisfiability modulo theories", **not** "Software Transactional Memory"

[3]A shadow copy essentially provides copy-on-write semantics. The most effective way to provide this functionality is type-dependent.

**Proust Design Space**

| Conflict Resolution \ Update Strategy | Eager | Lazy |
|---|---|---|
| Optimistic | - STM and inverses<br>- Eager/Eager<br>- Trivial<br>- Predication* | - STM and replay<br>- Full (prefer Lazy)<br>- Moderate<br>- OTB* |
| Pessimistic | - Locks and inverses<br>- Full<br>- Difficult<br>- Boosting | |

**STM Conflict Detection**

| R/W Conflicts \ W/W Conflicts | Eager | Lazy |
|---|---|---|
| Lazy | SwissTM/CCSTM | TL2 |
| Eager | TinySTM | |

**Figure 1: Design spaces for STMs and STM-integrated data structures. The top table outlines the Proust design space, listing for each how the transactional API is implemented, its compatibility with the STM strategies below, the difficulty of correctly synchronizing an AbstractLock implementation with the underlying STM, and the most conceptually similar prior work. The bottom table maps conflict detection strategies to popular STMs as outlined by Dragojevic, et al [6].**

There are many considerations in making these choices, depending on the data structure's operations, or the strengths and weaknesses of the underlying STM system (Figure 1).

Not all combinations make sense. For example, the empty quarter in Figure 1 reflects an impractical combination of choices. Some combinations are more complicated. For example, the eager-optimistic combination satisfies *opacity* [9] only under STMs that provide eager detection of both read-write and write-write conflicts. Here, Proust differs from Predication. While both are eager, Predication delegates state modifications to the underlying STM, instead of using the STM only for synchronization. Some second-order considerations include the degree to which the STM's contention management is exposed and can be coupled with traditional pessimistic locks, and the memory overhead of allocating shadow copies on target systems.

## 3 EVALUATION

We evaluated several of our map implementations for ScalaProust with a benchmarking setup similar to that used by Bronson, et al. for predication [2]. For each experiment, running on an Amazon

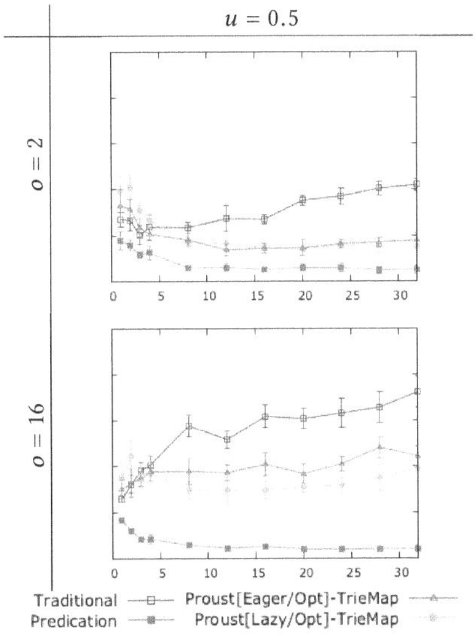


**Figure 2: Time to process $10^6$ operations on concurrent maps, using a 32-core Amazon EC2 `m4.10xlarge` instance, as the number of threads increases. Each chart is the result for a particular fraction of writes and operations per transaction. For each chart, the x-axis is the number of threads from 0 to 32 and the y-axis is the average time in milliseconds from 0 to 250.**

EC2 `m4.10xlarge` instance[4], we performed $10^6$ randomly selected operations on a shared map, split across $t$ threads, with $o$ operations per transaction. A $u$ fraction of the operations were writes (evenly split between `put` and `remove`), and the remaining $(1-u)$ were `get`. We varied $1 \leq t \leq 32$, $1 \leq o \leq 256$, and $u \in \{0, 0.25, 0.5, 0.75, 1\}$.

The experimental results depicted in Figure 2 display the effects of several competing trends. Initial results show that, as expected, Proust's performance on map operations parallelizes better than the traditional STM approach, though not as well as the highly engineered predication approach.

The full version of this paper also demonstrates the expressivity of Proust by walking through the implementation of a wrapper for a concurrent priority queue providing an efficient shadow copy operation [4].

## 4 CONCLUSIONS

We believe that the Proust methodology serves a useful niche in the transactional data structures ecosystem. Like Boosting, we offer sufficient expressivity to wrap arbitrary data structures, but with reduced design complexity (constraints are expressed as commutativity of updates to abstract state elements, rather than as pairwise commutativity rules between operations). Furthermore, our well-characterized design-space permits the use of different synchronization and update strategies to selectively optimize the performance of wrapped data structures for different STMs and different expected work-loads.

The full version of this paper further elaborates on a number of topics treated only briefly here, including techniques for implementing shadow copies, a formalization of conflict abstraction, opacity correctness arguments for Proustian objects, and an example wrapper for concurrent priority queues. [5]

[4] https://aws.amazon.com/blogs/aws/the-new-m4-instance-type-bonus-price-reduction-on-m3-c4/

## REFERENCES


[1] A.-R. Adl-Tabatabai, C. Kozyrakis, and B. Saha. Transactional programming in a multi-core environment. In K. A. Yelick and J. M. Mellor-Crummey, editors, *PPoPP*, page 272. ACM, 2007.

[2] N. G. Bronson, J. Casper, H. Chafi, and K. Olukotun. Transactional predication: High-performance concurrent sets and maps for stm. In *Proceedings of the 29th ACM SIGACT-SIGOPS Symposium on Principles of Distributed Computing*, PODC '10, pages 6–15, New York, NY, USA, 2010. ACM.

[3] L. Dalessandro, M. F. Spear, and M. L. Scott. Norec: streamlining stm by abolishing ownership records. In *Proceedings of the 15th ACM SIGPLAN Symposium on Principles and Practice of Parallel Programming*, PPoPP '10, pages 67–78, New York, NY, USA, 2010. ACM.

[4] T. D. Dickerson. Fast snapshottable concurrent braun heaps. *arXiv preprint arXiv:1705.06271*, 2017.

[5] T. D. Dickerson, P. Gazzillo, E. Koskinen, and M. Herlihy. Proust: A design space for highly-concurrent transactional data structures. *arXiv preprint arXiv:1702.04866*, 2017.

[6] A. Dragojević, R. Guerraoui, and M. Kapalka. Stretching transactional memory. In *ACM sigplan notices*, volume 44, pages 155–165. ACM, 2009.

[7] D. Goodman, B. Khan, S. Khan, M. Luján, and I. Watson. Software transactional memories for scala. *Journal of Parallel and Distributed Computing*, 73(2):150 – 163, 2013.

[8] J. E. Gottschlich, M. Vachharajani, and J. G. Siek. An efficient software transactional memory using commit-time invalidation. In *Proceedings of the International Symposium on Code Generation and Optimization (CGO)*, April 2010.

[9] R. Guerraoui and M. Kapalka. On the correctness of transactional memory. In *Proceedings of the 13th ACM SIGPLAN Symposium on Principles and practice of parallel programming (PPoPP'08)*, pages 175–184, New York, NY, USA, 2008. ACM.

[10] T. Harris, S. Marlow, S. L. P. Jones, and M. Herlihy. Composable memory transactions. *Commun. ACM*, 51(8):91–100, 2008.

[11] A. Hassan, R. Palmieri, and B. Ravindran. Optimistic transactional boosting. In *Proceedings of the 19th ACM SIGPLAN Symposium on Principles and Practice of Parallel Programming*, PPoPP '14, pages 387–388, New York, NY, USA, 2014. ACM.

[12] M. Herlihy and E. Koskinen. Transactional boosting: a methodology for highly-concurrent transactional objects. In *Proceedings of the 13th ACM SIGPLAN Symposium on Principles and practice of parallel programming*, PPoPP '08, pages 207–216, New York, NY, USA, 2008. ACM.

[13] M. Herlihy, V. Luchangco, M. Moir, and I. William N. Scherer. Software transactional memory for dynamic-sized data structures. In *Proceedings of the symposium on principles of distributed computing*, pages 92–101, New York, NY, USA, 2003. ACM.

[14] N. Herman, J. P. Inala, Y. Huang, L. Tsai, E. Kohler, B. Liskov, and L. Shrira. Type-aware transactions for faster concurrent code. In *Proceedings of the Eleventh European Conference on Computer Systems*, EuroSys '16, pages 31:1–31:16, New York, NY, USA, 2016. ACM.

[15] Intel Corporation. Intel C++ STM Compiler, Prototype Edition. Web. Retrieved from http://software.intel.com/en-us/articles/intel-c-stm-compiler-prototype-edition/, 20 November 2011.

[16] V. J. Marathe and M. Moir. Toward high performance nonblocking software transactional memory. In *PPoPP '08: Proceedings of the 13th ACM SIGPLAN Symposium on Principles and practice of parallel programming*, pages 227–236, New York, NY, USA, 2008. ACM.

[17] T. Riegel, C. Fetzer, and P. Felber. Time-based transactional memory with scalable time bases. In *Proceedings of the nineteenth annual ACM symposium on Parallel algorithms and architectures*, SPAA '07, pages 221–228, New York, NY, USA, 2007. ACM.

[18] The Deuce STM Group. Deuce stm - java software transactional memory. web. Retrieved from http://www.deucestm.org/documentation, 20 November 2011.

# Brief Announcement: Gossiping with Latencies*

Seth Gilbert
National University of Singapore
seth.gilbert@comp.nus.edu.sg

Peter Robinson
Royal Holloway, University of London
peter.robinson@rhul.ac.uk

Suman Sourav†‡
National University of Singapore
sourav@comp.nus.edu.sg

## ABSTRACT

Consider the classical problem of information dissemination: one (or more) nodes in a network have some information that they want to distribute to the remainder of the network. In this paper, we study the cost of information dissemination in networks where edges have latencies, i.e., sending a message from one node to another takes some amount of time. We first generalize the idea of conductance to weighted graphs, defining $\phi_*$ to be the "weighted conductance" and $\ell_*$ to be the "critical latency." One goal of this paper is to argue that $\phi_*$ characterizes the connectivity of a weighted graph with latencies in much the same way that conductance characterizes the connectivity of unweighted graphs. We give near tight lower and upper bounds on the problem of information dissemination. Specifically, we show that in a graph with (weighted) diameter $D$ (with latencies as weights), maximum degree $\Delta$, weighted conductance $\phi_*$ and critical latency $\ell_*$, any information dissemination algorithm requires at least $\Omega(\min(D + \Delta, \ell_*/\phi_*))$ time. We then give nearly matching algorithms, showing that information dissemination can be solved in $O(\min((D + \Delta) \log^3 n), (\ell_*/\phi_*) \log(n))$ time.

## KEYWORDS

Information Dissemination; Gossip; Latencies; Weighted Conductance; Critical latency; Weighted Spanner; Guessing Game

## 1 INTRODUCTION

Consider the problem of disseminating information in a large-scale distributed system: nodes in the network have information that they want to share/aggregate/reconcile with others. The fundamental problem of information dissemination has been widely studied under various names, e.g., rumor spreading ([5]), global broadcast ([10]), and information spreading ([3]).

**Model.** We model the network as a connected, undirected graph $G = (V, E)$ with $n = |V|$ nodes. Nodes know the identities of their neighbors and a polynomial upper bound on $n$. Communication is synchronous and occurs bidirectionally over the graph edges. Each edge has an integer *latency* that captures how long communication takes. Latencies occur in the communication channel and not on the nodes. Nodes do not know the weighted diameter $D$ (with latencies as weights) or the maximum latency $\ell_{\max}$.[1] In each round, each node sends a message to a neighbor and (automatically) receives a response. For edge latency $\ell$, the round-trip exchange takes time $\ell$.

**Results.** Our goal in this paper is to determine how long it takes to disseminate information in a graph with latencies. Clearly the running time will depend on the (weighted) diameter $D$ of the graph. Typically, the time also depends on how well connected the graph is, and this is normally captured by the conductance $\phi$. Unfortunately, conductance is no longer a good indicator of connectivity in a graph with latencies, as slow edges (edges with large latency) are much worse than fast edges.

We begin by generalizing the idea of conductance, defining $\phi_*$ to be the weighted conductance of a graph with latencies. At the same time, we define the critical latency $\ell_*$, which specifies the latency at which the graph is connected with that conductance. A core goal of this paper is to argue that weighted conductance is a good way to capture the connectivity of weighted graphs with latencies by showing nearly tight (within poly-logarithmic factors) lower and upper bounds on the time to disseminate information.

For a graph $G$, with diameter $D$, maximum degree $\Delta$, weighted conductance $\phi_*$, and critical latency $\ell_*$, we show that any information dissemination algorithm requires $\Omega(\min(D+\Delta, \ell_*/\phi_*))$ rounds. That is, in the worst case it may take time $D + \Delta$ to distribute information. However, if the graph is well connected, then we may do better and the time is characterized by the weighted conductance. We show that this lower bound holds even in various special cases, e.g., for graphs with small diameter, or with small max-degree, etc.

The main technique we use is a reduction to a simpler combinatorial guessing game. (See [15] for a demonstration of how other variants of guessing games can be used to prove lower bounds for radio networks.) We first show that the guessing game itself takes a large number of rounds. Then we reduce the problem of solving the game to that of solving information dissemination via a simulation.

We then show nearly matching upper bounds, i.e., algorithms for solving information dissemination. In this regard, we differentiate our model into two cases. For the case where nodes are not aware of the adjacent edge latencies, we show that the classical push-pull random phone call algorithm [12] in which each node initiates a connection with a randomly chosen neighbor in each round, completes in time $O((\ell_*/\phi_*) \log(n))$.

For the case where nodes do know the latencies of the incident edges, we obtain nearly tight bounds that are independent of $\Delta$ and $\phi_*$: we give a $O(D \log^3 n)$-time algorithm (which is within polylogarithmic factors of the trivial $\Omega(D)$ lower bound). The key idea of the algorithm is to build a (weighted) spanner (similar to that in [1]). This spanner is then used to distribute the information.

*A full version of the paper is available in [9]. Authors are listed alphabetically.
†This author is the corresponding author.
‡Supported by Singapore MOE grant (MOE2014-T2-1-157).


*PODC '17, July 25-27, 2017, Washington, DC, USA*

ACM ISBN 978-1-4503-4992-5/17/07
https://doi.org/10.1145/3087801.3087846

[1] In real world settings, nodes are often aware of their neighbors. However, due to fluctuations in network quality (and hence latency), a node cannot necessarily predict the latency of a connection.

We observe that we can discover the latencies of the "important" adjacent edges in $\tilde{O}(D+\Delta)$ time.[2] Hence, we can always solve the information dissemination in $O(\min((D+\Delta)\log^3 n), (\ell_*/\phi_*)\log(n))$ time, matching the lower bounds up to polylogarithmic factors.

**Prior work.** The classic model for studying information dissemination is the *random phone call model*, introduced by [6]: in each round, each node communicates with a single randomly selected neighbor; if it knows the rumor, then it "pushes" the information to its neighbor; if it does not know the rumor, then it "pulls" it from its neighbor (see, e.g.,[7],[13], [8]). In a seminal paper, Karp et al.[12] show that a rumor can be disseminated in a complete graph in $O(\log n)$ rounds with $O(n \log\log n)$ message complexity. When the graph is not a clique, the performance of the classical push-pull protocol, wherein a node exchanges information with a random neighbor in each round, typically depends on the topology of the graph, specifically, how well connected the graph is. An exciting sequence of papers (see [4, 5, 8, 14] and references therein) eventually showed that rumor spreading in this manner takes time $O((\log n)/\phi)$, where $\phi$ is the conductance of the graph.

The question that remained open was whether a more careful choice of neighbors would lead to faster information dissemination. In a breakthrough result, Censor-Hillel et al. [2] gave a randomized algorithm for solving information dissemination in any (unweighted) graph in time $O(D_{hop} + \text{polylog} n)$, where $D_{hop}$ is the graph diameter. Haeupler [10] then showed how local broadcast could be achieved in $O(\log^2 n)$ time using a deterministic algorithm.

The conclusion, then, is that in an unweighted graph (with unit latency edges), information dissemination can be achieved in time $O(\min(D + \text{polylog} n)$ or in time $O((\log n)/\phi))$.

## 2 WEIGHTED CONDUCTANCE

For a given graph $G = (V, E)$, and for a set of edges $S \subseteq E$, we define $E_\ell(S)$ as the subset of edges of $S$ that have latency $\leqslant \ell$. For a set of nodes $U \subseteq V$, we define $E_\ell(U, V \setminus U)$ as the subset of edges across the cut $(U, V\setminus U)$ with latency $\leqslant \ell$, and we define the volume $\text{Vol}(U) = \sum_{v\in U} deg_v$, where $deg_v$ refers to the degree of node $v$.

We first define the weighted conductance of a cut for a given latency $\ell$, and then define the weight-$\ell$ conductance as the minimum weighted conductance across all cuts.

*Definition 2.1 (Weight-$\ell$ Conductance).* Consider a graph $G = (V, E)$. For any subset of nodes $U \subseteq V$ and integer $\ell$, we define

$$\phi_\ell(U) = \frac{|E_\ell(U, V \setminus U)|}{\min\{\text{Vol}(U), \text{Vol}(V \setminus U)\}}.$$

The *weight-$\ell$ conductance* is given by $\phi_\ell(G) = \min_{U\subseteq V} \phi_\ell(U)$.

Thus, for $G$, we have the set $\Phi(G) = \{\phi_1(G), \ldots, \phi_{\ell_{\max}}(G)\}$.

*Definition 2.2 (Weighted Conductance : $\phi_*(G)$).*

$$\phi_*(G) = \underset{\phi_\ell(G)\in\Phi(G)}{\arg\max} \frac{\phi_\ell(G)}{\ell}. \tag{1}$$

We call $\ell_*$ the *critical latency* for $G$ if $\ell_* = \ell$ and $\phi_*(G) = \phi_\ell(G)$.

We simply write $\phi_*$ (or $\phi_\ell$ ) instead of $\phi_*(G)$ (or $\phi_\ell(G)$) when graph $G$ is clear from the context. If all edges have latency 1, then $\phi_*$ is exactly equal to the classical graph conductance [11].

[2]The notation $\tilde{O}$ hides polylogarithmic factors, which arise due to unknown $D$ and $\Delta$.

## 3 LOWER BOUNDS

We define a guessing game played by Alice against an oracle. Conceptually, the game is played on a bipartite graph with $2m$ nodes. Let $A$ and $B$ be two disjoint sets of $m$ integers, i.e., the left and right nodes in the bipartite graph. The winning condition of the game depends on a predicate $P$, which returns a subset of edges from $A \times B$. For example, $P = \text{Random}_p$ contains elements chosen from of $A \times B$ with probability $p$.

**The Guessing Game.** or Guessing$(2m, P)$ begins when Alice receives two disjoint sets $A$ and $B$. The oracle chooses a *target set* $T_1 \subseteq A \times B$ returned by the predicate. Alice's goal is to eliminate all the elements in the target set. In each round $r \geqslant 1$, Alice submits a set $X_r \subseteq A{\times}B$ of size at most $2m$ as her *round r guesses* to the oracle. The oracle replies by revealing the items she guessed correctly, i.e., $X_r \cap T_r$. The oracle then computes the *round $r+1$ target set $T_{r+1}$* by removing the items that Alice hit, i.e., all the items in $T_r$ that have the same $B$-component as an item in $X_r \cap T_r$. This concludes round $r$ and the next round begins.

The game is solved in the first round $r'$, where Alice's guesses result in an empty target set; at this point, the oracle answers `halt`. Alice's aim is to minimize the number of rounds until the target set becomes empty. We say that a *protocol* $\Pi$ *solves* Guessing$(2m, P)$ *with probability* $1-\epsilon$ *in r rounds*, if $\Pi$ always terminates within $r$ rounds, and $T_{r+1} = \emptyset$ with probability $\geqslant 1-\epsilon$, for any target set $T$. In this case, we call $\Pi$ an *$\epsilon$-error protocol.*

Based on the guessing game, we define a *guessing game gadget* ($G(2m, lo, hi, P)$ or $G^{\text{sym}}(2m, 1, h, P)$) embedded as a subgraph in an $n$-node distributed network. The parameters here, refer to the size of the gadget (i.e. $2m$), the low latency value $lo$, the high latency value $hi$, and the predicate $P$ respectively. We show our lower bounds using variants of this guessing game gadget. Refer to [9] regarding the details of how exactly the gadget is created and used for subsequent proofs.

LEMMA 3.1 (GOSSIP PROTOCOL SIMULATION). *Suppose that there is a $t$-round $\epsilon$-error algorithm $\mathcal{A}$ that solves local broadcast on a given $n$-node network $H$ that contains $G(2m, 1, h, P)$ or $G^{\text{sym}}(2m, 1, h, P)$ such that the cross edges of the gadget form a cut of $H$, for $h \geqslant t$, $n \geqslant 2m$, and a predicate $P$. Then there is an $\epsilon$-error protocol $\Pi$ for* Guessing$(2m, P)$ *that terminates in $\leqslant t$ rounds.*

### 3.1 Lower Bounds for the Guessing Game

The following lemma is instrumental for showing the $\Omega(\Delta)$ lower bound of Theorem 3.4, which holds when there are no other assumptions on the weighted conductance of the graph.

LEMMA 3.2. *Let* Guessing$(2m, |T| = 1)$ *be a guessing game where the target set is a single pair chosen uniformly at random from $A \times B$. If protocol $\Pi$ is an $\epsilon$-error protocol for* Guessing$(2m, |T| = 1)$ *where $\epsilon < 1$, then the number of rounds until $\Pi$ terminates is at least $\Omega(m)$.*

The next lemma bounds the number of guesses required when the target set is less restricted and its edges form a random subset of the cross edges between $A \times B$. This will allow us to derive a lower bound on the local broadcast time complexity in terms of the weighted conductance in Theorem 3.5.

LEMMA 3.3. *For the guessing game input sets $A$ and $B$, let* $\text{Random}_p$ *be the predicate that defines a target set $T$ by adding each element of*

*$A \times B$ to $T$ with probability $p$, for $p \geqslant \Omega(1/m)$. Then, any protocol that solves* Guessing$(2m, \text{Random}_p)$ *requires $\Omega(1/p)$ rounds in expectation. Alternatively, if Alice uses the protocol where she submits $2m$ guesses in each round by choosing, for each $a \in A$, an element $b' \in B$ uniformly at random, and, for each $b \in B$, an $a' \in A$ uniformly at random, then $\Omega(\log m/p)$ rounds are required in expectation.*

## 3.2 Information Dissemination Lower Bounds

In this section we show three different lower bounds. Together, these show what properties cause poor performance in information dissemination protocols: in some graphs, high degree is the cause of poor performance (Theorem 3.4); in other graphs, poor connectivity (i.e., small $\phi_*$) is the cause of poor performance (Theorem 3.5). And finally, we give a family of graphs where we can see the trade-off between $D$, $\Delta$, and $\phi_*$ (Theorem 3.6). We begin with a result showing that $\Omega(\Delta)$ is a lower bound:

THEOREM 3.4. *For any $\Delta \in [\omega(1), \lfloor \frac{n}{2} \rfloor]$, there is an $n$-node network having weighted diameter of $O(1)$, constant (non-weighted) conductance, and max. node degree $\Theta(\Delta)$, where any algorithm requires $\Omega(\Delta)$ rounds to solve local broadcast with constant probability.*

We next show that every local broadcast algorithm requires time at least $\Omega(1/\phi_* + \ell_*)$. We prove the following result by constructing a network that corresponds to the bipartite guessing game graph with a target set where each edge is fast with probability $\phi_*$. That way, we obtain a network with weighted conductance $\Theta(\phi_*)$, hop diameter $O(1)$, and a weighted diameter of $O(\ell_*)$. The guessing game lower bound of Theorem 3.3 tells us that the cost of information dissemination still depends on $\phi_*$.

THEOREM 3.5. *For any $\ell \in [1, n]$ and $\phi_\ell$ where $\Omega(\log(n)/n) \leqslant \phi_\ell \leqslant 1/2$, there is a $2n$ node network that has a weighted diameter $O(\ell)$ (whp), and weighted conductance $\Theta(\phi_\ell)$ (whp), such that any gossip algorithm requires $\Omega((1/\phi_\ell) + \ell)$ rounds for solving local broadcast. Also, solving local broadcast using push-pull requires $\Omega((\log n/\phi_\ell) + \ell)$ rounds.*

Finally, we give a family of graphs that illustrate the trade-off among the parameters. Intuitively, when the edge latencies are larger, it makes sense to search for the best possible path and the lower bound is $\Omega(D + \Delta)$; when the edge latencies are smaller, then we can simply rely on connectivity and the lower bound is $\Omega(\ell/\phi_\ell)$.

THEOREM 3.6. *For a given $\alpha \in [\Omega(1/n), O(1)]$ and any integer $\ell \in [1, O(n^2\alpha^2)]$, there is a class of networks of $2n$ nodes, weighted conductance $\phi_* = \phi_\ell = \Theta(\alpha)$, maximum degree $\Delta = \Theta(\alpha n)$, and weighted diameter $D = \Theta(1/\phi_\ell)$, such that any gossip algorithm that solves broadcast with at least constant probability, requires $\Omega(\min\{\Delta + D, (\ell/\phi_\ell)\})$ rounds.*

# 4 DISSEMINATION ALGORITHMS

In this section, we give two algorithms that match the lower bounds from the preceding section. Combined, these two algorithms yield the following theorem:

THEOREM 4.1. *There exists a randomized gossip algorithm that solves all-to-all information dissemination in $O(\min((D+\Delta)\log^3 n), (\ell_*/\phi_*)\log(n))$ time when nodes do not know the latency of its adjacent edges and in $O(\min(D\log^3 n, (\ell_*/\phi_*)\log(n)))$ time otherwise.*

## 4.1 Push-Pull

First, we observe that the push-pull gossip protocol solves broadcast quickly when the graph is well-connected:

THEOREM 4.2. *The push-pull protocol achieves broadcast whp in $O((\ell_* \log n)/\phi_*)$ rounds in a network $G$, where $\phi_*$ is the weighted conductance of $G$ and $\ell_*$ is the corresponding critical latency.*

## 4.2 Spanner Algorithm

Our algorithm leverages the spanner construction of Baswana and Sen [1] to obtain a sparse communication network. A subgraph $S$ of a graph $G$ is called an $\alpha$-spanner if any two nodes $u, v$ with distance $\ell$ in $G$ have distance at most $\alpha\ell$ in $S$.

The first step of the spanner algorithm requires each node to know the latencies of its adjacent edges. In this regard, we show that a node can discover the edge latencies of all the edges that it might require to achieve optimal information dissemination, in $O((D + \Delta)\log^3 n)$ by a guess-and-double strategy.

We show how to construct an $O(\log n)$-spanner and then orient the graph such that each node has small $O(\log n)$ out-degree.[3] Finally, use simple round-robin flooding on the resulting structure, yielding the following result:

LEMMA 4.3. *There is an $O(D\log^3 n)$ time algorithm $\mathcal{A}$ in the gossip model that yields an $O(\log n)$-spanner that has $O(n \log n)$ edges (whp). Moreover, $\mathcal{A}$ also computes an orientation of the edges that guarantees that each node has an out-degree of $O(\log n)$ (whp).*

THEOREM 4.4. *For a graph $G$ with diameter $D$, there exists an algorithm that takes $O(D\log^3 n)$ time for solving all-to-all information dissemination whp when nodes are aware of adjacent edge latencies.*

# REFERENCES


[1] S. Baswana and S. Sen. 2007. A simple and linear time randomized algorithm for computing sparse spanners in weighted graphs. *Random Structures and Algorithms* 30, 4 (2007), 532–563. https://doi.org/10.1002/rsa.20130

[2] K. Censor-Hillel, B. Haeupler, J. Kelner, and P. Maymounkov. Global Computation in a Poorly Connected World: Fast Rumor Spreading with No Dependence on Conductance *(STOC '12)*. ACM, NY, USA, 961–970.

[3] K. Censor-Hillel and H. Shachnai. 2011. Fast Information Spreading in Graphs with Large Weak Conductance *(SODA '11)*. SIAM, 440–448.

[4] F. Chierichetti, S. Lattanzi, and A. Panconesi. 2010. Almost Tight Bounds for Rumour Spreading with Conductance *(STOC '10)*. ACM, NY, USA, 399–408.

[5] F. Chierichetti, S. Lattanzi, and A. Panconesi. 2010. Rumour Spreading and Graph Conductance *(SODA '10)*. SIAM, PA, USA, 1657–1663.

[6] A. Demers, D. Greene, C. Hauser, W. Irish, J. Larson, S. Shenker, H. Sturgis, D. Swinehart, and D. Terry. 1987. Epidemic Algorithms for Replicated Database Maintenance *(PODC '87)*. ACM, 1–12. https://doi.org/10.1145/41840.41841

[7] U. Feige, D. Peleg, P. Raghavan, and E. Upfal. 1990. Randomized broadcast in networks. In *Algorithms*. Lecture Notes in Computer Science, Vol. 450. 128–137.

[8] G. Giakkoupis. 2011. Tight bounds for rumor spreading in graphs of a given conductance *(STACS '11)*. 57–68.

[9] S. Gilbert, P. Robinson, and S. Sourav. 2016. Gossiping with Latencies. *CoRR* abs/1611.06343 (2016). http://arxiv.org/abs/1611.06343

[10] B. Haeupler. 2013. Simple, Fast and Deterministic Gossip and Rumor Spreading *(SODA '13)*. SIAM, 705–716.

[11] M. Jerrum and A. Sinclair. Conductance and the Rapid Mixing Property for Markov Chains: The Approximation of Permanent Resolved *(STOC '88)*.

[12] R. Karp, C. Schindelhauer, S. Shenker, and B. Vocking. 2000. Randomized rumor spreading *(FOCS '00)*. 565–574.

[13] D. Kempe, J. Kleinberg, and A. Demers. 2001. Spatial Gossip and Resource Location Protocols *(STOC '01)*. ACM, NY, USA, 163–172.

[14] D. Mosk-Aoyama and D. Shah. 2006. Computing Separable Functions via Gossip *(PODC '06)*. ACM, NY, USA, 113–122. https://doi.org/10.1145/1146381.1146401

[15] C. Newport. Radio Network Lower Bounds Made Easy *(DISC '14)*. 258–272.


[3] E.g., in a star graph it is impossible to guarantee small degree in an undirected sense.

# Brief Announcement: A Probabilistic Performance Model and Tuning Framework for Eventually Consistent Distributed Storage Systems

Shankha Chatterjee
Department of Electrical and Computer Engineering
University of Waterloo, Canada
sschatte@uwaterloo.ca

Wojciech Golab*
Department of Electrical and Computer Engineering
University of Waterloo, Canada
wgolab@uwaterloo.ca

## ABSTRACT

Replication protocols in distributed storage systems are fundamentally constrained by the finite propagation speed of information, which necessitates trade-offs among performance metrics even in the absence of failures. We make two contributions toward a clearer understanding of such trade-offs. First, we introduce a probabilistic model of eventual consistency that captures precisely the relationship between the workload, the network latency, and the consistency observed by clients. Second, we propose a technique for adaptive tuning of the consistency-latency trade-off that is based partly on measurement and partly on mathematical modeling. Experiments demonstrate that our probabilistic model predicts the behavior of a practical storage system accurately for low levels of throughput, and that our tuning framework provides superior convergence compared to a state-of-the-art solution.

## CCS CONCEPTS

• **Information systems** → **Key-value stores**; *Database performance evaluation*;

## KEYWORDS

Distributed storage; data consistency; performance modeling.

## 1 INTRODUCTION

Distributed storage systems form the backbone of essential online services including web search, e-mail, social networking, and shopping. The replication protocols that protect such systems from permanent data loss are fundamentally constrained by the finite propagation speed of information, which necessitates trade-offs among performance metrics even in the absence of failures. In particular, any storage system that is replicated across data centers in different geographies may either guarantee that clients always see fresh data, or guarantee that operation latencies are small relative to the inter-data-center latencies, but not both. This leads to a difficult choice for application developers – bite the bullet and pay the high latency cost of strong consistency, optimize the system for low latency at the risk of exposing inconsistent data to applications and their users, or strike a compromise.

Responding to a real world need for reasoning precisely about performance trade-offs in distributed storage systems, we aim in this paper to develop a deeper understanding of the consistency-latency trade-off in quorum-replicated distributed storage systems. First, we present a probabilistic model of consistency under latency-optimized settings that captures precisely the relationship between the workload (characterized by the arrival rates of read and write operations), the environment (characterized by the network latency), and consistency. The model predicts the probability of inconsistency to within 0.001 of the value calculated using a stochastic simulation of our storage system abstraction, and to within 0.1 (in the low throughput case) of the value calculated by measuring consistency in a practical cloud storage system (Cassandra [3]). Our second contribution is a technique for adaptive tuning of the consistency-latency trade-off that is based partly on consistency measurement and partly on mathematical modeling. Microbenchmark experiments using a practical cloud storage system show that, compared to a state-of-the-art solution [5], our framework achieves superior convergence by extracting deeper insight from the consistency measurements.

## 2 BACKGROUND AND DEFINITIONS

We model a distributed storage system abstractly as a collection of processes $p_1, p_2, ..., p_n$ that communicate by exchanging messages. Since we are interested in the consistency-latency trade-off in the absence of failures, we assume that both the processes and the network are reliable. Each process has access to a global clock that is used to resolve the order of concurrent writes. The processes simulate a collection of shared read/write register objects, each identified by a unique *key*. Any process may read or write any key, and stores the values of a subset of the keys. The value for a given key is stored at $N$ particular processes out of $n$, called the *replicas* of that key, and is updated in response to write operations using a quorum-based replication protocol. For each key, a replica stores a pair of the form $(t, v)$ where $t$ is a timestamp and $v$ is the value of the key, initially $(0, \perp)$. Such a pair at process $p_i$ is denoted by $k_i$. The timestamp $t$ reflects the time when $v$ was written, and is obtained from a global clock that returns a distinct value each time it is read.

*Author supported in part by the Natural Sciences and Engineering Research Council (NSERC) of Canada, Discovery Grants Program, and by a Google Faculty Research Award.


*PODC '17, July 25-27, 2017, Washington, DC, USA*

ACM ISBN 978-1-4503-4992-5/17/07.
https://doi.org/http://dx.doi.org/10.1145/3087801.3087850

The protocol for Read and Write operations supports *tunable consistency* in the following sense: the number of replicas accessed by a read, as well as the number of replicas that must be updated during a write, are determined by per-operation parameters $R$ and $W$, respectively ($1 \leq R, W \leq N$). A Read of key $k$ pulls timestamp-value pairs from $R$ replicas and returns the value with the highest timestamp. A Write of value $v$ to key $k$ generates a new timestamp $t$, pushes $(t, v)$ to all replicas, and returns when $W$ replicas have replied. Upon receiving such a tuple $(t, v)$ for key $k$, a process overwrites the local timestamp-value pair $k_i = (t', v')$ for $k$ if $t > t'$, and leaves $k_i$ unchanged otherwise.

A *history* of the distributed storage system is a sequence of *steps*, representing the invocations and responses of the procedures Read and Write. The abstract system defined above guarantees Lamport's regularity property [4] in all histories when configured in so-called "strong consistency" mode, meaning that $R + W > N$ (e.g., $R = W = \lceil (N + 1)/2 \rceil$). If $R + W \leq N$ then the partial quorums accessed by reads and writes are not guaranteed to overlap, and yet a large subset of operations in a given history $H$ may satisfy regularity by chance, especially when the mean operation inter-arrival time exceeds the network latency. The degree of consistency in such histories can be quantified precisely by calculating the proportion of values (read or written) that participate in consistency anomalies, following the methodology of Golab, Li and Shah [1]. The severity of the anomaly arising due to the interaction of operations on key $k$ that access value $v$ with other operations on key $k$ in an execution history $H$ is denoted by the *score function* $\chi(H, k, v)$. Roughly speaking, this function quantifies the staleness (relative to the latest value) of the values returned by reads. A history $H$ is regular if and only if $\chi(H, k, v) = 0$ for all $k$ and $v$.

# 3 PROBABILISTIC MODEL

In this section we model mathematically the behavior of the abstract storage system presented in Section 2 in response to a stochastic workload comprising a mixture of read and write operations. The analysis assumes failure-free execution with the weakest possible consistency settings, namely $R = W = 1$, and aims to determine how frequently consistency anomalies arise in this setting. In particular, given an infinite history $H$ of the storage system, we wish to compute for a given key $k$ and value $v$ the probability that $v$ participates in a consistency anomaly with respect to $k$, meaning that $\chi(H, k, v) > 0$.

We make the following assumptions to simplify the analysis: network delays between processes are uniform and symmetric with a one-way delay of $L$, processing delays are zero (meaningful when processing delays are small relative to the operation inter-arrival time and network delay), and each key is fully replicated (i.e., the replication factor $N$ equals the number of processes $n$). The workload comprises a mixture of read and write operations arriving according to a Poisson process with rate $\lambda$. For each operation, an independent and uniformly random choice determines the operation type (i.e., read vs. write) and the process at which the operation is invoked. A read is selected with fixed probability $\rho$, $0 < \rho < 1$, and each server receives $1/n$ of the operations on expectation. We denote the read rate by $\lambda_r = \rho\lambda$ and the write rate by $\lambda_w = (1 - \rho)\lambda$. We assume without loss of generality that all operations are applied to a single key $k$ (since regularity is analyzed independently for each key) whose value is initialized to zero, and that the values written to this key are consecutive integers starting with one. The initial value is established by the first operation in $H$, which is a WriteOp$(k, 0)$.

THEOREM 3.1. *For any infinite history $H$ of the system, and for any value $v \in \mathbb{Z}^{>0}$ written to the key $k$ in $H$:*

$$P(\chi(H,k,v)=0)$$

$$= \left[\left(\frac{\lambda_w}{\lambda_r + \lambda_w}\right) + \left(\frac{\lambda_r}{\lambda_r + \lambda_w}\right) e^{-(\lambda_r/n+\lambda_w/n)L}\right]^{n-1} \times$$

$$\left[\left(\frac{\lambda_w}{\lambda_w + \lambda_r\left(\frac{n-1}{n}\right)}\right) + \left(\frac{\lambda_r\left(\frac{n-1}{n}\right)}{\lambda_w + \lambda_r\left(\frac{n-1}{n}\right)}\right) e^{-(\lambda_w+\lambda_r(\frac{n-1}{n}))L}\right]$$

We validate the above formula using an event-driven simulator as well as by comparing to consistency measurements obtained using a real storage system (Apache Cassandra 2.2.7) deployed in Amazon's Elastic Compute Cloud (EC2) across three geographical regions, with an average one-way inter-data-center network delay of 83ms. The results are presented graphically in Figure 1 for a variety of $\rho$ and $\lambda$ parameter values. Simulated and measured data represent the average of three runs, and error bars are shown representing the minimum and maximum measurement. The proportion of positive scores calculated using simulation matches the predicted probability of a positive score to within 0.001 in all twelve cases. Consistency measurements are within 0.1 of the predicted values when $\lambda \leq 100$. Measurements deviate substantially from the predictions at higher rates of throughput ($\lambda \geq 1000$), which is when processing delays become non-negligible relative to operation inter-arrival times.

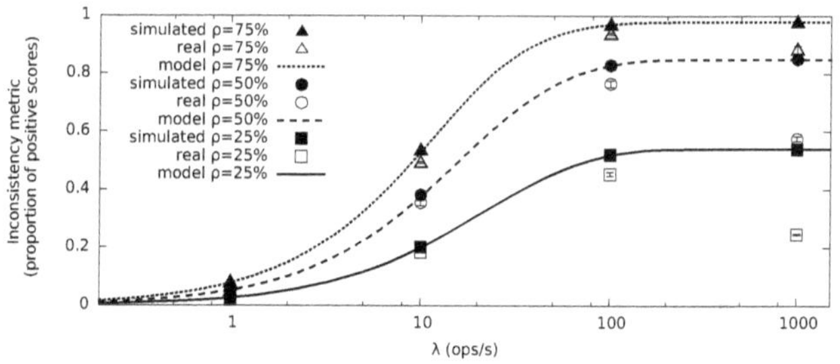


**Figure 1: Comparison of predicted proportion of a positive scores ("model"), simulated proportion of positive scores ("simulated"), and measured proportion of positive scores ("real") with $N = n = 3$ and $L = 83$ms for various $\lambda$.**

Theorem 3.1 allows us to study the asymptotic behavior of the abstract storage system with respect to consistency for extreme values of the parameters. For example, the formula implies that consistency anomalies disappear entirely as the network delay $L$ tends to zero or the operation rate $\lambda$ tends to zero:

$$\lim_{\lambda \to 0} P(\chi(H,k,v)=0) = \lim_{L \to 0} P(\chi(H,k,v)=0) = 1$$

On the other hand, as $L$ or $\lambda$ tends to infinity the formula predicts an upper limit on inconsistency that is determined by the read proportion $\rho$:

$$\lim_{\lambda \to \infty} P(\chi(H, k, v) = 0) = \lim_{L \to \infty} P(\chi(H, k, v) = 0) = \frac{(1 - \rho)^n}{1 - \rho/n}$$

Our probabilistic model correctly predicts some of the behaviors observed previously in an experimental study of eventual consistency in Cassandra [2]. Notably, it predicts that the frequency of consistency anomalies tends to zero as the throughput is decreased, or as the number of keys increases while throughput is kept constant, which reduces the throughput per key. It also predicts that at constant throughput, the frequency of consistency anomalies increases with the read proportion $\rho$ as well as with the replication factor.

# 4 CONSISTENCY-LATENCY TUNING

Figure 1 demonstrates that in a real world storage system, consistency deteriorates initially as $\lambda$ increases, and then tends to improve again as operation latencies become comparable to operation interarrival times, suggesting that consistency can be controlled directly by tuning the operation latency. In this section we outline a framework that achieves such a trade-off by slowing down operations using artificial delays, where the length of the delay is determined partly by measurement and partly by mathematical modeling.

Our tuning framework, called SPECSHIFT, is a control loop that measures consistency, compares the consistency metric against a target, and adjusts the delay duration accordingly to either increase or decrease the consistency metric. The delay is injected at the beginning of each read and at the end of each write. The duration of the delay is fixed in each iteration, and is adjusted between iterations by analyzing the distribution of the scores $\chi(H, k, v)$. Letting $d$ denote the delay duration in the previous iteration, the adjustment works by first transforming the history $H$ to a history $H'$ by shifting the start times of all reads by $+d$, and the finish times of all writes by $-d$. Intuitively, this transformation "undoes" the effect of the artificial delay on both latency and consistency. Next, the distribution of $\chi(H', k, v)$ scores is analyzed to determine the smallest delay $d'$ that reduces the proportion of positive scores to the desired target level, and no further. The analysis is based on the principle that a delay of $d'$ time units reduces all $\chi(H', k, v)$ scores in the interval $[0, d']$ to zero and decreases the remaining scores by $d'$. This property follows from the definition of the score function, as well as the assumption that delays do not affect the arrival rate of operations or read/write mixture. Given the target proportion of positive scores, the optimal $d'$ is computed by inverting the cumulative distribution function corresponding to the distribution of scores.

We evaluate SPECSHIFT by comparing its convergence against the PCAP multiplicative control loop [5], as well as a binary search for the optimal AD over the constrained range $[0, 100]$. The experiment is orchestrated in EC2 similarly to the consistency measurements presented in Section 3. Figure 2 illustrates the behavior of each tuning technique with the termination condition defined as convergence to a proportion of positive scores within 0.005 of the target proportion (denoted by a solid horizontal line). Each iteration lasts 30 seconds and sustains a throughput of 6000 operations/s, with a read proportion of 0.8. Two runs are presented with different initial delay durations and target proportions. The upper plot uses a target proportion (0.05) and initial delay of zero, leading to a positive adjustment in the artificial delay. The lower plot uses a higher target proportion (0.20) and initial delay of 70ms, leading to a negative delay adjustment.

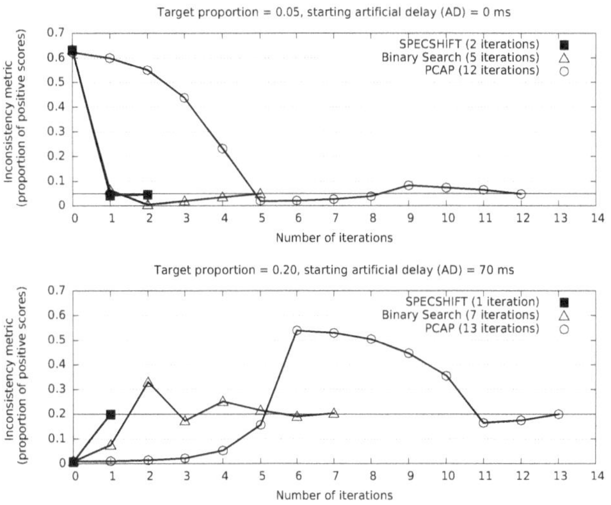


**Figure 2: Comparing the convergence of SPECSHIFT against PCAP and binary search.**

PCAP operates by starting with a unit step size and doubling it at each iteration until the control loop overshoots or undershoots, at which point the direction of the steps is reversed and the step size is reset to unity. This technique is prone to oscillations and requires 12-13 iterations to converge in the two runs shown. The binary search over the interval $[0, 100]$ converges in 5-7 iterations, which is roughly twice as fast as PCAP. In general, the number of iterations required is at most logarithmic in the length of the search interval, assuming that the workload, as well as network and processing delays, do not change. SPECSHIFT exhibits the best convergence of the three techniques, and reaches the termination condition in 1-2 iterations. Moreover, the predictions at each iteration in the upper plot are progressively closer to the target. SPECSHIFT converges rapidly and steadily by analyzing the severity of consistency anomalies, whereas the other two techniques ignore the special structure of the tuning problem and merely evaluate whether the measured consistency metric value is above or below the given target.

# REFERENCES

[1] W. Golab, X. Li, and M. A. Shah. Analyzing consistency properties for fun and profit. In *Proc. of the 30th ACM Symposium on Principles of Distributed Computing (PODC)*, pages 197–206, June 2011.

[2] W. Golab, M. R. Rahman, A. AuYoung, K. Keeton, and I. Gupta. Client-centric benchmarking of eventual consistency for cloud storage systems. In *Proc. of the 34th International Conference on Distributed Computing Systems (ICDCS)*, pages 493–502, 2014.

[3] A. Lakshman and P. Malik. Cassandra: A decentralized structured storage system. *SIGOPS Oper. Syst. Rev.*, 44(2):35–40, Apr. 2010.

[4] L. Lamport. On interprocess communication, Part I: Basic formalism and Part II: Algorithms. *Distributed Computing*, 1(2):77–101, June 1986.

[5] M. R. Rahman, L. Tseng, S. Nguyen, I. Gupta, and N. H. Vaidya. Characterizing and adapting the consistency-latency tradeoff in distributed key-value stores. *ACM Transactions on Autonomous and Adaptive Systems*, 11(4), 2017.

# Effectiveness of Delaying Timestamp Computation

Sandeep S. Kulkarni
Michigan State University
Department of Computer Science and Engineering
428 S. Shaw Lane
East Lansing, MI 48824
sandeep@cse.msu.edu

Nitin H. Vaidya
University of Illinois at Urbana-Champaign
Department of Electrical and Computer Engineering
1308 W Main St
Urbana, IL 61801
nhv@illinois.edu

## ABSTRACT

Practical algorithms for determining causality by assigning timestamps to events have focused on *online* algorithms, where a permanent timestamp is assigned to an event as soon as it is created. We address the problem of reducing size of the timestamp by utilizing the underlying topology (which is often not fully connected since not all processes talk to each other) and deferring the assignment of a timestamp to an event for a suitably chosen period of time after the event occurs. Specifically, we focus on inline timestamps, which are a generalization of offline timestamps that are assigned after the computation terminates. We show that for a graph with vertex cover $\mathcal{VC}$, it is possible to assign inline timestamps which contains only $2|\mathcal{VC}|+2$ elements. In particular, for a system with $n$ processes and $K$ events per process, the size of a timestamp for any event is at most $\log_2 n + (2|\mathcal{VC}|+1)\log_2(K+1))$ bits. By contrast, if online timestamps are desired, then even for a star network, vector timestamp of length $n$ (for the case of integer elements) or $n-1$ (for the case of real-valued elements) is required. Moreover, in addition to being efficient, the inline timestamps developed can be used to solve typical problems such as predicate detection, replay, recovery that are solved with vector clocks.

## 1 INTRODUCTION

The paper considers an asynchronous system consisting of $n$ processes that communicate over message-passing channels. The message-passing channels form a communication network, which may or may not be completely connected. One of the important problems in such distributed systems is detection of causality among events, as defined by the happened-before relation $\rightarrow$ [14]. (As defined in [14], event $A$ happened-before event $B$ iff either (1) $A$ and $B$ are events on the same process and $A$ occurred before $B$, (2) $A$ is a send event and $B$ is a corresponding receive event, or (3) there is an event $C$ such that $A$ happened-before $C$ and $C$ happened before $B$.) Such causality detection is important for debugging, monitoring, and other applications. Vector clocks are often used to track causality. An important challenge in detecting causality using vector clocks is that for a system with $n$ processes, without any additional assumptions, the minimum vector length necessary is $n$.

Much of the existing work on practical algorithms for assigning timestamps, which capture the causality relation (e.g., [7, 16]), inherently requires that timestamp of an event is assigned as soon as that event is created. We denote these algorithms as *online* algorithms. In particular, in vector clock algorithms, each event $e$ is assigned a timestamp $vc_e$ which is a vector consisting of integer elements. Furthermore, to determine causality, these timestamps are compared by pairwise element comparison, such that (i) $vc_e \leq vc_f$ iff for each $k$, $vc_e[k] \leq vc_f[k]$, and (ii) $vc_e < vc_f$ iff $vc_e \leq vc_f \wedge vc_e \neq vc_f$. We refer to this $<$ operator as the *standard vector clock comparison*.

The goal of this paper is to identify an efficient timestamp design by relaxing the assumptions that (1) a permanent timestamp is assigned as soon as an event is created, and (2) timestamps are compared using the standard vector clock comparison. Relaxing the first assumption, we let the timestamp of an event to be either $\perp$, or a permanent value that will not change subsequently. When an event occurs, it may possibly be assigned value $\perp$, which is eventually changed to its permanent value. We refer to such timestamps as *inline timestamps*. Given two events $e$ and $f$ with timestamps $timestamp_e \neq \perp$ and $timestamp_f \neq \perp$, respectively, we will specify a suitable $<$ operator on the timestamps such that $e \rightarrow f$ iff $timestamp_e < timestamp_f$. Observe that *Online* and *Offline* timestamps can be viewed as two extreme instantiations of the inline timestamps. In particular, for *offline timestamps*, each event's timestamp remains $\perp$ until the execution terminates; only after the execution terminates, each event is assigned a timestamp.

Compared with offline timestamps, inline timestamps provide a significant advantage provided the the inline timestamp is made permanent *quickly*. For example, in an application such as rollback recovery, we can use inline timestamps by simply ignoring events whose timestamps is not finalized. This would cause the *recovery line* to be somewhat earlier than that achievable by online timestamps. However, as long as the timestamps become finalized quickly, this change would be negligible. By contrast, offline timestamps cannot be used for such recovery as they are not available until the system terminates.

In this work, we focus on reducing the size of timestamps by exploiting the knowledge of the underlying communication topology. Specifically, we make the following contributions.

(1) We show that online vector timestamps do not benefit from the knowledge of the communication topology. That is, if we require that the *standard vector clock comparison* be used to compare timestamps, then efficient timestamps cannot be obtained even for specific known topology. In


*PODC'17, July 25-27, 2017, Washington, DC, USA*

978-1-4503-4992-5/17/07...$15.00
DOI: http://dx.doi.org/10.1145/3087801.3087818

particular, we show that for a *star* network, any online algorithm that uses *standard vector clock comparison* must use clocks of length $n$ if the vector elements are restricted to be integers. The vector length can be reduced slightly to $n-1$ if we permit vector elements to be real numbers. On the other hand, the inline timstamps only require 4 integer elements in the star graph, but use a new $<$ operator. Thus, our results show that requiring online timestamps with the standard vector clock comparison operator is too restrictive, and prevents us from exploiting the underlying communication topology.

(2) The above results for vectors clocks motivate the use of alternative timestamp algorithms. It turns out that there indeed exists a simple timestamp scheme that can reduce the timestamp size by exploiting the knowledge of the communication graph. In particular, for a communication graph with a vertex cover $\mathcal{VC}$, we present an inline algorithm that assigns timestamps containing $2|\mathcal{VC}|+2$ integer elements. In a system of $n$ processes, provided that at most $K$ events occur at each of these processes, $2|\mathcal{VC}|+1$ of the timestamp elements are of size at most $\log_2(K+1)$ bits, and the remaining element is of size $\log_2 n$ bits. Thus, if $|\mathcal{VC}| < \frac{n}{2} - 1$, the above inline timestamp would have a smaller size that the standard vector clock.

**Organization of the paper.** In Section 2, we identify lower bounds associated with online timestamps. In Section 3, we discuss our algorithm for inline timestamps in star network. Section 4 generalizes this solution to arbitrary graphs. Section 5 discusses related work. Finally, we discuss applications of our work in Section 6 and conclude in Section 7. Feasibility of using inline timestamps to solve problems such as predicate detection and replay/recovery is discussed in [23].

## 2 ONLINE VECTOR TIMESTAMPS

In this section, we consider the benefits of knowing the communication network on the minimum size necessary for vector timestamps (i.e., using the standard vector clock comparison). It is known that vector clocks of length $n$ suffice in any network. The results presented here are negative in that in most networks, no significant reduction can be achieved even with the knowledge of the communication topology. This motivates the work presented later on *inline algorithms*, which can be significantly more efficient.

Lemma 2.1. *Suppose that an* online *algorithm for the star graph assigns distinct* **real-valued** *vector timestamps to distinct events such that, for any two events $e$ and $f$, $e \rightarrow f$ if and only if $timestamp_e < timestamp_f$, where* $<$ is standard vector clock comparison. *Then the vector length must be at least $n-1$.*

Proof. The proof is trivial for $n \leq 2$. Now assume that $n \geq 3$. The proof is by contradiction. Suppose that a given online algorithm assigns vector timestamps of length $s \leq n-2$.

Let $e^j_q$ denote the $q$-th event at process $p_j$. Consider an execution that includes a send event $e^i_1$ at radial process $p_i$, $1 \leq i \leq n-1$, where the radial process $p_i$ sends a message to the central process $p_0$. These $n-1$ send events are concurrent with each other. At process $p_0$, there are $n-1$ *receive* events corresponding to the above *send* events at the other processes. The execution contains no other events.

Note that $timestamp_{e^j_q}$ denotes the vector timestamp of length $s$ assigned to event $e^j_q$ by the online algorithm. Create a set $S$ of processes as follows: for each $l$, $0 \leq l < s$, add to $S$ any one radial process $p_j$ such that $timestamp_{e^j_1}[l] = \max_{1\leq i<n} timestamp_{e^i_1}[l]$. Note that $timestamp_{e^i_1}[l]$ is the $l$-th element of vector $timestamp_{e^i_1}$. Clearly, $|S| \leq s \leq n-2$. Consider a radial process $p_k \notin S$ (note that $p_k \neq p_0$). Such a process $p_k$ must exist since $|S| \leq n-2$, and there are $n-1$ radial processes.

Suppose that the message sent by process $p_k$ at event $e^k_1$ reaches process $p_0$ after all the other messages, including messages from all the processes in $S$, reach process $p_0$. That is, $e^0_{n-1}$ is the receive event for the message sent by process $p_k$. By the time event $e^0_{n-1}$ occurs, (online) timestamps must have been assigned to all the other events in this execution. This scenario is possible because the message delays can be arbitrary, and an online algorithm assigns timestamps to the events when they occur.

Now consider event $e^0_{n-2}$. By event $e^0_{n-2}$, except for the message sent by process $p_k$, all the other messages, including messages sent by all the processes in $S$, are received by process $p_0$.

Define vector $E$ such that $E[l] = \max_{1\leq i<n} timestamp_{e^i_1}[l]$, $0 \leq l < s$. By definition of $S$, we also have that $E[l] = \max_{p_i \in S} timestamp_{e^i_1}[l]$, $0 \leq l < s$. The above assumption about the order of message delivery implies that $E \leq timestamp_{e^0_{n-2}}$. Also, since $p_k \notin S$, we have that $timestamp_{e^k_1} \leq E$. The above two inequalities together imply that $timestamp_{e^k_1} \leq timestamp_{e^0_{n-2}}$.

Since $e^k_1 \neq e^0_{n-2}$, their timestamps must be distinct too. Therefore, $timestamp_{e^k_1} < timestamp_{e^0_{n-2}}$, which, in turn, implies that $e^k_1 \rightarrow e^0_{n-2}$. However, $e^k_1$ and $e^0_{n-2}$ are concurrent, leading to a contradiction. □

Lemma 2.2. *Suppose that an* online *algorithm for the star graph $\mathcal{G}$ assigns distinct* **integer-valued** *vector timestamps to distinct events such that, for any two events $e$ and $f$, $e \rightarrow f$ if and only if $timestamp_e < timestamp_f$, where $<$ is* standard vector clock comparison. *Then the vector length must be at least $n$.*

Proof. Without loss of generality, let us assume that all vector elements of a vector timestamp must be non-negative integers. The proof of the lower bound is trivial for $n = 1$. Now assume that $n \geq 2$. The proof is by contradiction. Suppose that the vector length is $s \leq n-1$.

Consider an execution that includes a send event $e^i_1$ at process $p_i$, $1 \leq i \leq n-1$, where the radial process $p_i$ sends a message to the central process $p_0$. Let $M$ be the largest value of any of the $s$ elements of the timestamps of any of these $n-1$ send events. Suppose that process $p_0$ initially performs $P$ computation events. Assume that there are no other events; thus, process $p_0$ does not send any messages. Thus, the timestamps of the send events at the radial processes cannot depend on $P$, the number of computation events at $p_0$. Thus, we can assume that $P = (M+2)n$. Since these $(M+2)n$ computation events occur at $p_0$ before it receives any messages, the timestamps for these events are computed before $p_0$ learns timestamps of any send events at the other processes.

Since the timestamp elements are constrained to be non-negative integers, one of the elements of the timestamp of the last of these computation events at $p_0$, namely $e^0_P$, must be $> M$. Recall that $P = (M+2)n$.

Consider set $W$ that contains event $e^0_P$ and $e^i_1$, $0 < i < n$. Thus, $W$ contains $n$ events, with one event at each of the $n$ processes. Create a set $S$ of processes as follows: for each $l$, $0 \le l < s$, add to $S$ any one process $p_j$ such that the $l$-th element of the timestamp of its event in $W$ is the largest among the $l$-th elements of the timestamps of all the events in $W$. Clearly, $p_0 \in S$ and $|S| \le s \le n-1$. Consider a radial process $p_k \notin S$ (note that $p_k \ne p_0$). Such a process $p_k$ must exist since $|S| \le n-1$, $p_0 \in S$, and there are $n-1$ radial processes.

Suppose that the message sent by process $p_k$ at event $e^k_1$ reaches process $p_0$ after all the other messages, including messages from the *radial* processes in $S$, reach process $p_0$. Let $e = e^0_{P+n-2}$. By event $e$ at $p_0$, except for the message sent by process $p_k$, all the other messages, including messages sent by all the radial processes in $S$, are received by process $p_0$.

Rest of the proof of this lemma is similar to the proof of Lemma 2.1. In particular, define vector $E$ such that $E[l] = \max_{0 \le i < n} timestamp_{e^i_1}[l]$, $0 \le l < s$. By definition of $W$, we also have that $E[l] = \max_{p_i \in W} timestamp_{e^i_1}[l]$, $0 \le l < s$.

The above assumption about the order of message delivery implies that

$$E \le timestamp_{e^0_{P+n-2}}.$$

Also, since $p_k \notin W$, we have that $timestamp_{e^k_1} \le E$. This implies that $timestamp_{e^k_1} \le timestamp_{e^0_{P+n-2}}$.

Since $e^k_1 \ne e^0_{P+n-2}$, their timestamps must be distinct too. This implies that $timestamp_{e^k_1} < timestamp_{e^0_{P+n-2}}$, which, in turn, implies that $e^k_1 \to e^0_{P+n-2}$. However, $e^k_1$ and $e^0_{P+n-2}$ are concurrent events, leading to a contradiction.

□

Lemma 2.3. *Suppose that the communication $\mathcal{G}$ graph has vertex connectivity $\ge 2$. For this graph, an* online *algorithm assigns distinct vector timestamps to distinct events such that, for any two events $e$ and $f$, $e \to f$ if and only if $timestamp_e < timestamp_f$. Then the vector length must be $\ge n$.*

Proof. Recall that $\mathcal{G}$ is the communication graph formed by the $n$ processes.

This proof is analogous to the proof of Lemma 2.1. The proof is trivial for $n \le 2$.

Now assume that $n \ge 3$. The proof is by contradiction. Suppose that the vector length is $s \le n-1$.

Consider an execution in which, initially, each process $p_i$, $0 \le i < n$, sends a message to each of its neighbors in the communication graph. Subsequently, whenever a message is received from any neighbor, a process forwards the message to all its other neighbors. Thus, essentially, the messages are being flooded throughout the network (the execution is infinite, although we will only focus on a finite subset of the events).

Create a set $S$ of processes as follows: for each $l$, $0 \le l < s$, add to $S$ any one process $p_j$ such that $timestamp_{e^j_1}[l] = \max_{0 \le i < n} timestamp_{e^i_1}[l]$. Clearly, $|S| \le s \le n-1$. Consider a process $p_k \notin S$. Such a process $p_k$ must exist since $|S| \le n-1$.

Suppose that all the communication channels between $p_k$ and its neighbors are very slow, but each of the remaining communication channels has a delay upper bounded by some constant $\delta > 0$. For convenience of discussion, let us ignore local computation delay between the receipt of a message at a process and its forwarding to the neighbors. Let $D$ be defined as the maximum over the diameters of all the subgraphs of $\mathcal{G}$ containing $n-1$ vertices. Let the delay on all communication channels of $p_k$ be $> 2\delta D$. Because the network's vertex connectivity is $\ge 2$, within duration $\delta D$, $n-1$ processes, except $p_k$, will have received messages initiated by those $n-1$ processes (i.e., all messages except the message initiated by $p_k$).

Define vector $E$ such that $E[l] = \max_{0 \le i < n} timestamp_{e^i_1}[l]$, $0 \le l < s$. By definition of $S$, we also have that $E[l] = \max_{p_i \in S} timestamp_{e^i_1}[l]$, $0 \le l < s$.

Consider any process $p_i \ne p_k$. Let $e$ be the earliest receive event at $p_i$ such that by event $e$ (i.e., including event $e$), $p_i$ has received the messages initiated by all processes except $p_k$. Due to the definition of $D$ and $\delta$, event $e$ occurs at $p_i$ by time $\delta D$. Since by event $e$, $p_i$ has received the messages initiated by all other processes except $p_k$, and $p_k \notin S$, we have

$$E \le timestamp_e.$$

Also, since $p_k \notin S$, we have

$$timestamp_{e^k_1} \le E.$$

The above two inequalities together imply that $timestamp_{e^k_1} \le timestamp_e$.

Since $e^k_1$ and $e$ occur on different processes, $e^k_1 \ne e$, and their timestamps must be distinct too. Thus, $timestamp_{e^k_1} < timestamp_e$, which, in turn, implies that $e^k_1 \to e$. However, $e^k_1$ and $e$ are concurrent events, because $e^k_1$ is the first event at $p_k$, there are no messages received by $p_k$ before $2\delta D$, and similarly, no process receives messages from $p_k$ during $2\delta D$. This results in a contradiction.

□

For any graph, upper bound of $n$ is obtained by using the standard vector clock algorithm for $n$ processes [8, 15]. Thus, the bound $n$ is tight for communication graphs with vertex connectivity $\ge 2$.

Lemma 2.4. *Suppose that the communication graph has vertex connectivity $= 1$. Define $X$ to be the set of processes such that no process in set $X$ by itself forms a vertex cut of size 1. For this graph, an* online *algorithm assigns distinct vector timestamps to distinct events such that, for any two events $e$ and $f$, $e \to f$ if and only if $timestamp_e < timestamp_f$. Then the vector length must be at least $|X|$.*

Proof. Recall that $\mathcal{G}$ is the communication graph formed by the $n$ processes.

This proof is analogous to the proof of Lemma 2.3. The proof is trivial for $|X| = 1$.

Now assume that $|X| \ge 2$. The proof is by contradiction. Suppose that the vector length is $s \le |X| - 1$.

Consider an execution in which, initially, each process $p_i \in X$ sends a message to each of its neighbors in the communication graph. Subsequently, whenever a message is received from any neighbor, a process forwards the message to all its other neighbors. Thus, essentially, the messages initiated by processes in $X$ are being flooded throughout the network (the execution is infinite, although we will only focus on a finite subset of the events).

Create a set $S$ of processes as follows: for each $l$, $0 \leq l < s$, add to $S$ any one process $p_j \in X$ such that $timestamp_{e_1^j}[l] = \max_{p_i \in X} timestamp_{e_1^i}[l]$. Clearly, $|S| \leq s \leq |X| - 1$. Consider a process $p_k \in X$ such that $p_k \notin S$. Such a process $p_k$ must exist since $|S| \leq |X| - 1$.

Suppose that all the communication channels between $p_k$ and its neighbors are very slow, but each of the remaining communication channels has a delay upper bounded by some constant $\delta > 0$. For convenience of discussion, let us ignore local computation delay between the receipt of a message at a process and its forwarding to the neighbors. Let $D$ be defined as the maximum over the diameters of all the subgraphs of $\mathcal{G}$ containing all vertices except any one vertex in $X$ (there are $|X|$ such subgraphs). By definition of $X$, removing any one process in $X$ from the graph $\mathcal{G}$ will not partition the subgraph. Let the delay on all communication channels of $p_k$ be $> 2\delta D$. Within duration $\delta D$, all $n - 1$ processes, except $p_k$, will have received the messages initiated by the $|X| - 1$ processes in $X - \{p_k\}$.

Define vector $E$ such that $E[l] = \max_{p_i \in X} timestamp_{e_1^i}[l]$, $0 \leq l < s$. By definition of $S$, we also have that $E[l] = \max_{p_i \in S} timestamp_{e_1^i}[l]$, $0 \leq l < s$.

Consider any process $p_i \in X$ such that $p_i \neq p_k$. Let $e$ be the earliest receive event at $p_i$ such that by event $e$ (i.e., including event $e$), $p_i$ has received the messages initiated by all processes except $p_k$. Due to the definition of $D$ and $\delta$, event $e$ occurs at $p_i$ by time $\delta D$. Since by event $e$, $p_i$ has received the messages initiated by all other processes except $p_k$, and $p_k \notin S$, we have

$$E \leq timestamp_e.$$

Also, since $p_k \notin S$, we have

$$timestamp_{e_1^k} \leq E.$$

The above two inequalities together imply that $timestamp_{e_1^k} \leq timestamp_e$.

Since $e_1^k$ and $e$ occur on different processes, $e_1^k \neq e$, and their timestamps must be distinct too. Therefore, $timestamp_{e_1^k} < timestamp_e$, which, in turn, implies that $e_1^k \rightarrow e$. However, $e_1^k$ and $e$ are concurrent events, because $e_1^k$ is the first event at $p_k$, there are no messages received by $p_k$ before $2\delta D$, and similarly, no process receives messages from $p_k$ during $2\delta D$. This results in a contradiction.

Observe that for star graph, vertex connectivity is 1, and $X$ consists of all the radial processes. Thus, $|X| = n - 1$.

For a communication graph with vertex connectivity 1, an upper bound of $n - 1$ (not necessarily tight) is obtained by assigning the role of $p_0$ in the star graph to any one process that forms a cut of the communication graph, and then using the vector timestamping algorithm presented below for the star graph. In general, there is a gap between the above upper bound of $n - 1$ and lower bound of $|X|$. It is presently unknown whether $|X|$ is a tight bound for online algorithms that assign vector timestamps.

□

## 3 ILLUSTRATING INLINE ALGORITHM: CASE STUDY WITH STAR NETWORK

Before presenting the inline algorithm for general network topologies, we illustrate it in the special case of a *star* network. The generalized algorithm is presented in Section 4. A star network consists of one *central* process, say $C$, and $n - 1$ *radial* processes. Each radial process can communicate directly only with process $C$. The key idea behind the inline algorithm is that for any two events $e$ and $f$ at *different* radial processes such that $e \rightarrow f$, there must exist an event $g$ at $C$ such that $e \rightarrow g \rightarrow f$. This observation is used to reduce the timestamps for events at radial processes, essentially by using appropriate events at $C$ as proxies for the events at radial processes. The generalized algorithm in Section 4 extends this observation to a vertex cover of the communication graph (observe that the center process by itself is a vertex cover of the star graph).

### 3.1 Timestamping Algorithm

Instead of describing the algorithm for the star graph operationally (i.e., what occurs when events take place), we first describe it in a declarative manner. The algorithm assigns timestamp of event $e$ on process $j$ as $timestamp_e = \langle id_e, ctr_e, pre_e, post_e \rangle$, defined as follows:

- $id_e = j$, the process where event $e$ occurred.
- $ctr_e$ (denoting 'counter'): If event $e$ is $x^{th}$ event on process $j$ then $ctr_e = x$. For the first event at any process, $ctr$ is 1.
- $pre_e = \max\ (ctr_f \mid f$ is an event at $C$ such that $e = f$ or $f \rightarrow e)$ ).

  For convenience, we adopt the convention that maximum of an empty set is 0.

Finally, we define $post_e$ for event $e$. $post$ is defined only for events at radial processes.

- $post_e = \min\ (ctr_f \mid f$ is an event at $C$ such that $e \rightarrow f)$ ).

  For convenience, we adopt the convention that minimum of an empty set is $\infty$ (this may seem counter-intuitive, but the benefit of the convention should become clearer later).

Observe that for an event $e$ at $C$, $pre_e = ctr_e$ (and $post_e$ is not defined for events at $C$). When $post_e$ in the timestamp of event $e$ is $\infty$, we sometimes write $timestamp_e = \perp$ for brevity. Since $post_e$ is not defined for events on C, if $e$ is an event on C, $timestamp_e$ will never be equal to $\perp$. ($\perp$ should be interpreted here as "unknown").

### 3.2 Operational Description

Since the above algorithm is given in a declarative fashion as opposed to operational manner, next, we identify how and when these timestamps can be determined. Please refer Figure 1.

At each process $j$, $ctr_j$ and $pre_j$ are initialized to 0. In our pseudocode in Figure 1, $a, b, c = p, q, r$ is equivalent to $a = p;\ b = q; c = r$.

**Rules for assigning** $ctr_e$: For any event $e$, $ctr_e$ is just the index of the event at process $j$. The index of first event at

**If** $e$ **is a local or send event at radial process** $j$
  $ctr_j = ctr_j + 1$ ($ctr_j$ initialized to 0)
  $ctr_e, pre_e, post_e = ctr_j, pre_j, \infty$
  If $e$ corresponds to sending of message $m$,
    include $\langle ctr_e, pre_e \rangle$ with message $m$.

**If** $e$ **corresponds to receiving** $m\langle ctr_m, pre_m \rangle$ **at radial process** $j$
  $ctr_j = ctr_j + 1$
  $pre_j = max(pre_j, pre_m)$

**If** $e$ **is a local or send event at** $C$
  $ctr_C = ctr_C + 1$
  $ctr_e, pre_e = ctr_C, ctr_C$
  If $e$ corresponds to sending of message $m$,
    include $\langle ctr_e, pre_e \rangle$ with message $m$.

**If** $e$ **corresponds to receiving** $m\langle ctr_m, pre_m \rangle$ **at C**
  $ctr_C = ctr_C + 1$
  $ctr_e, pre_e = ctr_C, ctr_C$
  Send control message with $\langle ctr_m, ctr_C \rangle$ to $j$
  // This message can be piggybacked with a future message to $j$

**Upon Receiving control message** $\langle a, b \rangle$ **at radial process** $j$
  For each event $e$ on process $j$ such that $ctr_e \leq a$
    $post_e = min(post_e, b)$

**Figure 1: Algorithm for Star Network**

$j$ is 1. $ctr_j$ is used as a counter at process $j$ to determine $ctr_e$.

**Rules for assigning** $pre_e$: For an event $e$ on the central process, $pre_e = ctr_e$. This follows from the definition of $pre$.

Each radial process $j$ maintains a variable $pre_j$ that keeps track of the maximum value of $pre_e$ for any event $e$ created on process $j$. Initially, $pre_j = 0$. Local events and send events at process $j$ leave $pre_j$ unchanged. For a new send/local event $e$, $pre_e = pre_j$. When sending a message $m$, the tuple $\langle ctr_e, pre_e \rangle$ is included with $m$.

Now consider a receive event $e$ at radial process $j$. Let the message received at $e$ be $m$. Let the tuple piggybacked on $m$ be $\langle ctr_m, pre_m \rangle$. When $m$ is received, process $j$ sets $pre_e$ and $pre_j$ to equal $max(pre_j, ctr_m)$. Observe that $ctr_m$ equals the index of the send event corresponding to $m$ – the send event must necessarily have occurred at $C$, since the message is received at a radial process in the star graph.

**Rules for assigning** $post_e$: For an event $e$ at $C$, $post_e$ is not defined. For event $e$ on a radial process $j$, $post_e$ is defined when a message is sent by $j$ at or after $e$ and is received by $C$. Until this point, $timestamp_e$ is equal to $\perp$. Recall that we treat $timestamp_e$ as $\perp$ while $post_e$ remains $\infty$.

There are several approaches for defining $post_e$. One approach is as follows: Upon receiving a message $m$ from a radial process $j$ with timestamp $\langle ctr_m, pre_m \rangle$, $C$ sends a *control message* that contains $\langle ctr_m, ctr_f \rangle$, where $f$ is the corresponding receive event. If this *control channel* is FIFO then $j$ can update *post* entry for any event that corresponds to sending of $m$ and any previous events for which the *post* field is still $\infty$. Specifically, let $e$ be any event on process $j$ such that $post_e$ is not yet defined and either $e = send(m)$ or $f$ happened before sending of $send(m)$. Upon receiving the control message for message $m$, process $j$ marks $post_e$ to be $ctr_f$.

We note that there are several possible approaches for computing the *post* field in events on radial process. The above discussion relies on *FIFO control channels* so that the radial process learns about receive events on $C$ in order. The application messages still could be delivered in any order. In an implementation, instead of separate control messages, this information could be piggybacked to any future messages as well. However, the piggybacking approach may potentially delay assignment of permanent timestamp assignment to events on radial processes. It is easy to simulate a FIFO channel for the control messages that are piggybacked on the application messages, even if the application messages themselves are not necessarily delivered to the processes in a FIFO order.

Figure 1 summarizes how the above rules can be implemented in an operational manner. Each process $j$ maintains $ctr_j$ and $pre_j$, initialized to 0. The *id* in the timestamp corresponds to the process where the event occurred. The pseudo-code assumes that the control messages are sent on separate control channels that are FIFO.

## 3.3 Correctness Property

If $timestamp_e \neq \perp$ and $timestamp_f \neq \perp$ (i.e., $post_e$ and $post_f$ are finalized) then they can be used to deduce causality information, as specified by Theorem 3.1.

THEOREM 3.1. *For any two events, e and f, if $timestamp_e \neq \perp$ and $timestamp_f \neq \perp$ then e happened before f iff $timestamp_e < timestamp_f$, where*

$$timestamp_e < timestamp_f$$

*iff*

$$\begin{cases} pre_e < pre_f & if\ id_e = C\ and\ id_f = C \\ pre_e \leq pre_f & if\ id_e = C\ and\ id_f \neq C \\ post_e \leq pre_f & if\ id_e \neq C\ and\ id_f \neq id_e \\ ctr_e < ctr_f & if\ id_e \neq C\ and\ id_f = id_e \end{cases}$$

PROOF. We sketch the proof from the four cases in the comparison relation above.

$id_e = id_f = C$: In this case $pre_e = ctr_e$ captures the sequence number for event $e$. Hence, $e$ happened before $f$ iff $pre_e < pre_f$.

$id_e = C$ **and** $id_f \neq id_e$: By definition of $pre_f$, event $x$ on C happened before $f$ iff $ctr_x \leq pre_f$. Also, for event $x$ on $C$, $ctr_x = pre_x$. Hence, if $e$ is on $C$ and $f$ is on a radial process then $e$ happened before $f$ iff $pre_e \leq pre_f$.

$id_e \neq C$ **and** $id_f \neq id_e$: First consider the case where $f$ is on $C$. In this case, $ctr_f = pre_f$. And, by definition of *post*, if $x$ is an event on $C$ then $post_e \leq pre_x$. Hence, $e$ happened before $f$ iff $post_e \leq pre_f$.

Next, we consider the case where $f$ is outside $C$. Since the graph is a star network and $e$ and $f$ are outside $C$, $e$ happened before $f$ is true iff there exists an event $x$ on $C$ such that $e$ happened before $x$ and $x$ happened before $e$. If $x$ is on C then from above discussion $e$ happened before $x$ iff $post_e \leq pre_x$. Also, from the second case, $x$ happened before $f$ iff $pre_x \leq pre_f$. Thus, $e$ happened before $f$ iff $post_e \leq pre_f$.

$id_e = C$ **and** $id_f = id_e$: In this case, by definition of *ctr*, it follows that $e$ happened before $f$ iff $ctr_e < ctr_f$.

□

# 4 GENERALIZATION TO ALL COMMUNICATION GRAPHS

While the discussion in Section 3 focuses on the star graphs, we can extend it to other (static) graphs by identifying the role played by the central process. The key property of interest of the central process was that every message was either sent to it or from it. We use this observation to extend the algorithm in Section 3 for arbitrary topology.

Instead of having just one central process $C$, we use the vertex cover associated with the given communication graph. Let $\mathcal{VC}$ be the vertex cover associated with the given communication graph. In other words, every message is either sent from some process in $\mathcal{VC}$ or to some process in $\mathcal{VC}$ (or possibly both).

Before we explain our algorithm, we identify the two extremes: When $\mathcal{VC}$ consists of just one process; this corresponds to a star graph, and the algorithm in Section 3 can be applied here. On the other extreme, when $\mathcal{VC}$ contains all the processes, one can use the traditional vector clocks.

Our algorithm combines both these extremes. Specifically, processes in $\mathcal{VC}$ maintain a vector clock among themselves. These entries play the same role as *pre* in the algorithm in Section 3. Nodes outside $\mathcal{VC}$ maintain entries similar to that of *pre* and *post*. However, instead of just maintaining it for one process, they have to maintain it for every process in $\mathcal{VC}$. In other words, *pre* and *post* become vectors with one entry per process in $\mathcal{VC}$. We use *mpre* and *mpost* to denote these vectors. Specifically, let $e$ be an event on process $j$ (either in $\mathcal{VC}$ or outside $\mathcal{VC}$) and $c$ be a process in $\mathcal{VC}$. We define

- $id_e = j$, i.e., the process where $j$ occurred.
- If $e$ is $x^{th}$ event on process $j$ then $mctr_e = x$.
- $mpre_e[c] = max(\{mctr_f | f$ is an event on process $c$ such that $e = f$ or $f \rightarrow e\})$

Recall our convention that *maximum* of an empty set is 0, and *minimum* of an empty set is $\infty$. Finally, we define *mpost* only for events $e$ that occur on processes outside $\mathcal{VC}$, where

- $mpost_e[c] = min(\ \{\ mctr_f \mid f$ is an event at process c such that there exists a message $m$ such that
  $m$ is sent from $j$ to $c$,
  ($e = send(m)$ or $e \rightarrow send(m)$) and
  $f = receive(m)$ or $receive(m) \rightarrow f$)
  $\})$

**Remark.** Let $e$ be an event at process $j \notin \mathcal{VC}$. Observe that if there is no channel between $c \in \mathcal{VC}$ and $j$ then $timestamp_e[c]$ is always $\infty$. Only when there is a channel between $c$ and $j$, but for an event $e$ at $j$, we have $post_e[c] = \infty$, then we treat the $timestamp_e$ as being $\perp$ (here $\perp$ should be interpreted as "unknown").

## 4.1 Illustration of our Timestamping Algorithm

Figure 2 provides an illustration of our algorithm for the case where the vertex cover is $p_0$ and $p_1$, process $p_2$ is connected to $p_1$ and process $p_3$ is connected to $p_0$. For brevity, we omit the *id* from the timestamps. In this figure, processes $p_0$ and $p_1$ are in $\mathcal{VC}$. Hence, the timestamp at these processes show the values of *mctr* and *mpre*. For instance, for event $e$ at $p_0$, $mctr_e = 4$ and $mpre = (4, 1)$. For events at processes outside $\mathcal{VC}$, *mctr*, *mpre* and *mpost* are shown. For instance, for event $h$, $mctr_h = 1$, $mpre_h = (0, 1)$ and $mpost_h = (4, \infty)$.

Computation of *mctr* is straightforward since it simply is incremented by 1 every time. For sake of illustration, consider event $g$. Computation of $mpre_g$ is based on events on $p_0$ and $p_1$ that happened before $g$. There is no such event on $p_0$ and there is only one event on $p_1$ (with *mctr* value 1). Hence, $mpre_g$ is set to $(0, 1)$. Next, consider computation of $mpost_g$: $mpost_g[0]$ is set when a message is sent by $p_3$ is received at $p_0$. When such a message is received, the corresponding event has *mctr* set to 4. Hence, $mpost_g[0]$ is set to 4. Since there is no link between $p_3$ and $p_1$, $mpost_g[1]$ will always be $\infty$.

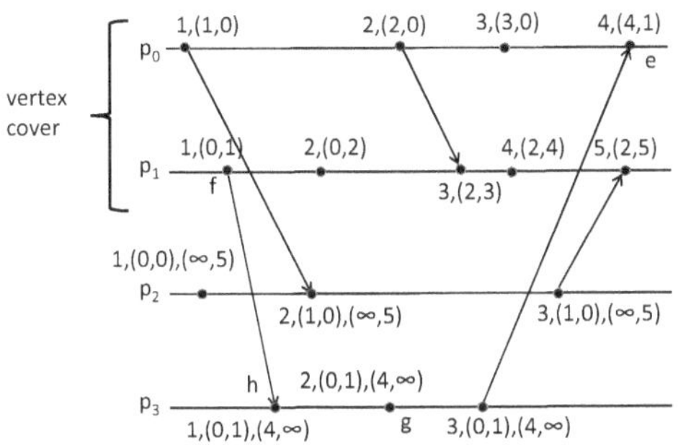


**Figure 2: Illustration of Our Algorithm**

## 4.2 Proof of Correctness

To show that the definitions of *mpre* and *mpost* suffice to capture causality between two events $e$ and $f$, we need to identify how to compare their timestamps. Since these inline timestamps combine the ideas from vector clocks (for processes in $\mathcal{VC}$) and the ideas from the clock for star network (for processes outside $\mathcal{VC}$), the comparison also focuses on whether events are from $\mathcal{VC}$ or outsides $\mathcal{VC}$.

Recall that the standard vector clock comparison to compare two vectors is to compare the corresponding elements. Time. Also, $mpre_e < mpre_f$ iff $mpre_e \leq mpre_f \wedge mpre_e \neq mpre_f$. Using this comparison, we formalize our correctness requirement in Theorem 4.1:

Theorem 4.1. *For any two events, $e$ and $f$, if $timestamp_e \neq \perp$ and $timestamp_f \neq \perp$ then $e \longrightarrow f$ iff $timestamp_e < timestamp_f$, where*
*$timestamp_e < timestamp_f$ iff*

$$\begin{cases} mpre_e < mpre_f & \text{if } id_e \in \mathcal{VC} \text{ and } id_f \in \mathcal{VC} \\ mpre_e \leq mpre_f & \text{if } id_e \in \mathcal{VC} \text{ and } id_f \notin \mathcal{VC} \\ \exists c \in \mathcal{VC} :: mpost_e[c] \leq mpre_f[c] & \text{if } id_e \notin \mathcal{VC} \text{ and } id_f \neq id_e \\ mctr_e < mctr_f & \text{if } id_e \notin \mathcal{VC} \text{ and } id_f = id_e \end{cases}$$

Proof. We sketch the proof based on the four cases in comparison of timestamps. In this discussion, let $c$ be a process in $\mathcal{VC}$.

$id_e \in \mathcal{VC}$ **and** $id_f \in \mathcal{VC}$: Observe that *mpre* essentially creates the vector clock among processes in $\mathcal{VC}$. Hence, $e \longrightarrow f$ iff $mpre_e < mpre_f$.

$id_e \in \mathcal{VC}$ **and** $id_f \notin \mathcal{VC}$: By definition of $mpre_f$, given an event $x$ on a process in $\mathcal{VC}$, $x$ happened before $f$ iff $mctr_x \leq mpre_f[c]$. Also, for event $x$ on $c$, $mctr_x = mpre_x[c]$. Hence, if $e$ is on $\mathcal{VC}$ and $f$ on a process outside $\mathcal{VC}$ then $e$ happened before $f$ iff $mpre_e \leq mpre_f$.

$id_e \notin \mathcal{VC}$ **and** $id_f \neq id_e$: Since $\mathcal{VC}$ is a vertex cover, if $id_f \neq id_e$ then $e$ happened before $f$ iff there exists an event $x$ on a process, say $c$ in $\mathcal{VC}$ and a message $m$ from $id_e$ to $c$ such that (1) $c = send(m)$ or $e$ happened before $send(m)$, (2) $x = receive(m)$ or $receive(m)$ happened before $x$ and (3) either $f = x$ or $x$ happened before $f$. Regarding the first condition, $e$ happened before $x$ iff $mpost_e[c] \leq mpre_x[c] = mctr_x$. Regarding the second condition, ($x = f$ or $x$ happened before $f$) iff $mpre_x \leq mpre_f$. Thus, $e$ happened before $f$ iff $\exists c$ such that $mpost_e[c] \leq mpre[c]$.

$id_e \notin \mathcal{VC}$ **and** $id_f = id_e$: In this case, by definition of *mctr*, it follows that $e$ happened before $f$ iff $mctr_e < mctr_f$.

□

Theorem 4.2. *For any event $e$, $|timestamp_e| \leq 2|\mathcal{VC}| + 2$*

Proof. This follows from the fact that *mpre* and *mpost* each contain at most $|\mathcal{VC}|$ elements. Additionally, *id* and *mctr* each require one element. □

Theorem 4.3. *Given a system with $n$ processes where each process has (at most) $K$ events, for any event $e$, $timestamp_e$ requires at most $(2|\mathcal{VC}| + 1)\log(K + 1) + \log n$ bits.*

Proof. This follows from the fact that *ctr*, each entry in *mpre* and each entry in *mpost* requires $\leq \log(K + 1)$ bits each, and *id* requires $\log n$ bits.

□

## 4.3 Lower Bounds for Offline Timestamps

In Section 2, we showed that for online timestamps, with standard vector clock comparison, size of the clock was either $n$ or $n - 1$ depending upon whether we permit real-valued timestamps or only integer-valued timestamps. In Section 3, we presented an algorithm for the star graph that had 4 entries in every timestamp. In this section, we consider the minimum size for such timestamps. This lower bound also applies to offline timestamps.

Theorem 4.4. *Given a star graph consisting of 4 processes, there does not exist an offline algorithm that assigns each event $e$ in every execuction a vector $vc_e$ of size 2 such that*

$$e \longrightarrow f$$

*iff*

$$vc_e < vc_f, \text{ where } < \text{ denotes the standard vector clock comparison}$$

Proof. The proof is presented in [23]. □

Based on the results in this section, we find that inline timestamps provide a significant reduction compared to the size of online timestamps. Also, for the star graph, the size of the inline vector timestamps is within 1 of feasible lower bound. An open question in this context is whether the size of vector timestamps can be reduced to 3 elements.

## 5 RELATED WORK AND DISCUSSION

Closest to our work is (i) a timestamp algorithm for *synchronous messages* by Garg et al. [10, 11], (ii) timestamps used in causal shared memory, particularly, *SwiftCloud* [25] and *Lazy Replication* [13], and (iii) a hierarchical cluster timestamping scheme [24]. We will discuss the prior work below.

**Timestamps in message-passing systems:** The concept of vector clock or vector timestamp was introduced by Mattern [15] and Fidge [8]. Charron-Bost [2] showed that there exist communication patterns that require vector timestamp length equal to the number of processes. Schwarz and Mattern [19] provided a relationship between the size of the vector timestamps and the dimension of the partial order specified by happened-before. Garg et al. [9] also demonstrated analogous bounds on the size of vector timestamps using the notion of event *chains*. Singhal and Kshemkalyani [21] proposed a strategy for reducing the communication overhead of maintaining vector timestamps. Rodrigues and Veríssimo [18] focus on providing causal delivery in arbitrary network with the help of causal separators. In particular, similar to the vertex cover used in our work, they utilize the common nodes used in the routes of different messages to assign timestamps. However, since they only need to focus on causal delivery of messages, they do not need to timestamp all events in the system. Shen et al. [20] encode of a vector clock of length $n$ using a single integer that has powers of $n$ distinct prime numbers as factors. Torres-Rojas and Ahmad propose constant size logical clocks that trade-off clock size with the accuracy with which happened-before relation is captured [22]. Meldal et al. [17] propose a scheme that helps determine causality between two messages *sent to the same process*. Because their timestamps do not need to capture the happened-before relation between *all events*, the timestamps can be smaller. Some of the algorithms by Meldal et al. [17] exploit information about the paths over which messages may be propagated.

**Synchronous messages [10, 11]:** For synchronous messages, the sender process, after sending a message, must *wait* until it receives an acknowledgement from the receiver process, as illustrated in Figure 3. This constraint is exploited in [10, 11] to design small timestamps. In particular, if the communication network formed by the processes is decomposed into, say, $d$ components that are either *triangles* or *stars*, then the timestamps contain $d+4$ integer elements. Due to the synchronous nature of communication, messages within each component are totally ordered. The timestamps in [10, 11] exploit this total ordering, such that the $j$-th element of a vector included in the timestamp for an event represents the number of messages within the $j$-th component (of the decomposition) that happened before the given event.

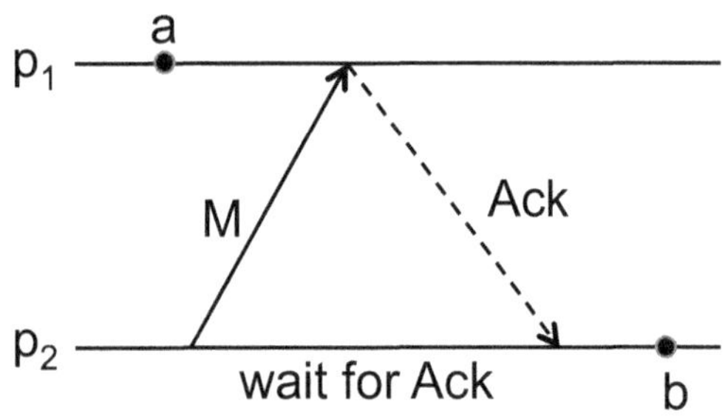


**Figure 3: Synchronous message**

Our timestamping algorithm does *not* constrain the messages to be synchronous. Our approach has some similarities to [10, 11] and also some key differences. In our case, the timestamp contains $2|\mathcal{VC}|+2$ integer elements, where $\mathcal{VC}$ is a vertex cover of the communication network formed by the processes. Thus, the timestamps contain more elements because we allow the flexibility of using asynchronous messages. A consequence of allowing asynchronous messages is that the *mpost* field becomes permanent only after the process communicates (and hears from) every process in $\mathcal{VC}$ to which it is connected. Given a vertex cover $\mathcal{VC}$, the network can be decomposed into $|\mathcal{VC}|$ stars. However, our algorithm does not utilize the decomposition as such (but instead uses the knowledge of a cover set $\mathcal{VC}$). On the other hand, the algorithm in [10, 11] explicitly uses the decomposition into triangle and stars.

The *mpost* field in our timestamp for events outside $\mathcal{VC}$ includes an index for the receive event of one message sent to each of the processes in the vertex cover. Thus, the *mpost* field includes $|\mathcal{VC}|$ elements. On the other hand, the timestamps in [10, 11] include just 1 index that has functionality analogous to one of the elements in our *mpost* field. This index in the timestamp in [10, 11] counts messages in a component of the edge decomposition, whereas in our case, the index counts number of events at a process. These distinctions are caused by the restriction of synchronous messages in [10, 11], and allowance for asynchronous messages in our scheme.

**Causal memory [1, 13, 25]:** The purpose of the timestamps used in the work on causal memory is to ensure causal consistency. There are close similarities between our timestamps and comparable objects maintained in some causal memory schemes [1, 13, 25].

In *Lazy Replication* [13], a client-server architecture is used to implement causally consistent shared memory. Each server maintains a copy of the shared memory. Each client sends its updates and queries to one of the servers. A server that receives an update from one of the clients then propagates the update to the other servers. Each server maintains a vector clock: the $i$-th entry of the vector at the $j$-server essentially counts the number of updates propagated to the $j$-th server by the $i$-th server. Each client also maintains a similar vector: the $i$-th element of the client's vector counts the number of updates propagated by the $i$-th server on which the client's state depends. Additionally, when a client sends its update to the $j$-th server, the $j$-th element of the client's vector is updated to the index of the client's update at the $j$-th server. The client may potentially send the same update to multiple servers, say, $j$-th and $k$-th servers; in this case, the $j$-th and $k$-th elements of the client's vector will be updated to the indices of the client's updates at the respective servers. Finally, a server cannot process an update or a query from a client until the server's vector clock is $\geq$ the vector at the client. The $\geq$ operator here performs an element wise comparison of the vector elements: vector $v \geq w$ only if each element of $v$ is $\geq$ the corresponding element of vector $w$.

The mechanism used in *SwiftCloud* [25] is motivated by *Lazy Replication* [13], and has close similarities to the vectors in [13]. In *SwiftCloud*, if a client sends its update to multiple servers, then the indices returned by the servers are *merged* into the dependency vector maintained by the client (optionally, some of the returned indices may not be merged). Importantly, a server can only respond to future requests from the client provided that the server's vector covers the client's dependency vector. *Swiftcloud* uses objects with elements comparable to *pre* and *post* in our timestamps, but relies on the assumption that the servers are completely connected.

Beyond some small differences in how the timestamp comparison is performed, the other difference between shared memory schemes above and our solution is that the above schemes rely on a set of *servers* through which the processes interact with each other.

Thus, the communication network in their case is equivalent to a clique of servers to which the clients are connected. The size of the timestamps is a function of the number of servers. On the other hand, we allow arbitrary communication networks, with the size of the timestamps being a function of a *vertex cover* for the communication network. The vertex cover is not necessarily completely connected. Secondly, dependencies introduced through *events* happening at the servers (e.g., receipt of an update from a client) in the shared memory systems are not necessarily *true* dependencies. For instance, suppose that process $p_0$ propagates update to variable $x$ to replica R, then process $p_1$ propagates update to variable $y$ to replica R, and finally process $p_2$ reads updated value of $y$ from replica R. In the shared memory dependency tracking schemes above, the update of $x$ by $p_0$ would be treated as having happened-before the read by $p_2$. In reality, there is no such causal dependency. But the dependency is introduced artificially as a cost of reducing the timestamp size. On the other hand, in the message-passing context, if the communication network reflects the communication channels used by the processes, then no such artificial dependencies will arise. However, in the message-passing case as well, we can introduce artificial dependencies by disallowing the use of certain communication channels in order to decrease the vertex cover size. This is illustrated below through the example in Figure 4.

In [1], authors maintain a dotted vector $(d, v)$ where $v$ is a version vector and $d$ is a *dot* that has $O(1)$ size, and the value of $d$ is utilized in evaluating causality relation in $O(1)$ time. However, to capture causality, they need to maintain several version vectors to capture possible concurrent operations by multiple clients. In our work, one such vector is maintained by processes in $\mathcal{VC}$, the vertex cover and two vectors by processes outside $\mathcal{VC}$.

The size of the timestamps in above causal memory schemes is a function of the number of servers (that are completely connected to each other). On the other hand, we allow arbitrary communication networks, with the size of the timestamps depending on *vertex cover* size for the communication network. This enable alternative implementations. For instance, consider a client-server architecture, wherein a large number of clients may interact with a large number of servers. Due to the dense communication (or interconnection) pattern in this case, the cover size will be large, resulting in large timestamps. An alternative is illustrated in Figure 4, where the solid edges represent an abstract communication network. A *client* or a *server* may communicate with multiple *sequencers*. By design, the *sequencers* form a cover of this network. When the number of servers is much larger than the number of sequencers, this approach can result in a much smaller vertex cover. In Figure 4, all communication must go through the sequencers, and the *inline* timestamp size is proportional to number of sequencers. However, routing all server communication via sequencers can be expensive, since the sequencers will have to handle a large volume of data. A simple optimization can mitigate this shortcoming. For example, as shown by a dashed arrow in Figure 4, server $R_1$ may send message contents (data) *directly* to server $R_2$, but server $R_2$ will need to wait to receive *metadata*, in the form of timestamp information, via sequencer $S_1$ (as shown by a dotted arrow in the figure). Thus, while the sequencers must still handle small messages to help determine inline timestamps, bulk of the traffic can travel between the servers directly (or similarly between servers and clients). A similar optimization was suggested previously for *totally-ordered multicast* using a sequencer [4]. This optimization, in conjunction with our scheme, provides a trade-off between timestamp size and the delay incurred in routing metadata through sequencers.

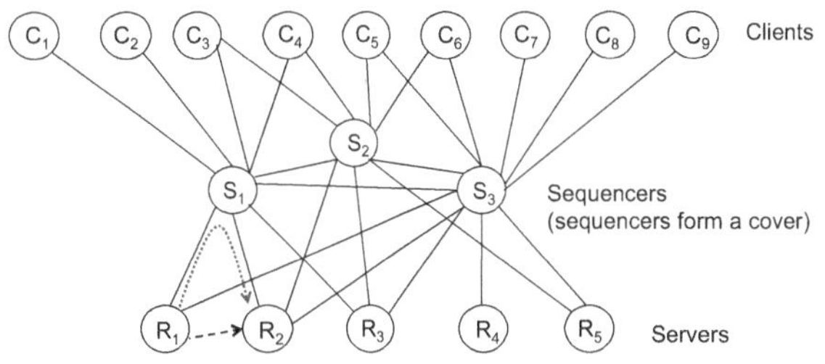


**Figure 4: Alternate architecture**

**Exploiting Physical Time:** In [12], authors have focused on a weaker version of causality that only focuses on causal relation introduced in the recent past and assume that events that occurred beyond a window of $\epsilon$, a configurable parameter, are already reflected. In [5, 6], authors utilize physical time to ensure that servers in a data center are aware of updates on other servers on the same replica. In our work, we assume that the system is asynchronous and do not utilize synchrony assumptions associated with physical time. Also, in [5, 6], it is possible that a version is not visible to a client even though no dependency exists.

**Cluster timestamps:** Ward and Taylor [24] describe an improvement over the strategy previously proposed by Summers, which divides the processes into clusters. They maintain short timestamps (proportional to cluster size) for events that occur *inside* the cluster, and longer timestamps (vectors with length equal to total number of processes) for "cluster-receive" events. In [24], the "cluster-receive" events are assigned long timestamps; such long timestamps are not necessary in our case.

# 6 APPLICATIONS

Inline timestmaps considered in this paper are useful for solving typical problems in distributed systems for which vector clocks are used. Examples of such applications include predicate detection [3], checkpointing and recovery, detection of concurrent updates, and so on. Unlike offline timestmaps that defer assignment of timestamps until the computation is complete, inline timestamps assign timestamps after the process has completed round trip communication with all processes in $\mathcal{VC}$ to which it is connected.

The basic idea to apply inline timestamps is to consider a cut of the system that removes all events $e$ such that $timestamp_e = \perp$. When we remove event $e$, we must also remove event $f$ such that $e$ happened before $f$ to ensure that the cut is consistent. Once such events are removed, we have a consistent cut of the system where all timestamps are finalized and, hence, we can utilize them in the same way as we can use online timestamps. The only difference is that the analysis will focus on an earlier cut of the system. For example, predicate detection would only be feasible by considering the events in this cut. However, as timestamps get finalized the cut in which predicates can be detected will grow. Thus, if the predicate of interest becomes true, it would be detected eventually. Additional details of these applications are available in [23].

## 7 CONCLUSION AND FUTURE WORK

In this paper, we focused on the following problem: If we delay assigning the timestamp to an event, then is it possible to reduce the size of the timestamps necessary to deduce causality? Another related question is: Is this delay necessary to achieve the desired reduction in the size of timestamps? With this motivation, we introduced the notion of *Inline* timestamps that delay assignment of timestamps to events. They generalize *Online* timestamps that require that this delay be 0 and *Offline* timestamps that allow this delay to be $\infty$. In our work, we consider the case where we have a vertex cover $\mathcal{VC}$ such that any message is sent either from a process in $\mathcal{VC}$ or to a process in $\mathcal{VC}$. The timestamps at processes in $\mathcal{VC}$ are finalized immediately. Moreover, the timestamps at other processes are finalized after they communicate with all processes in $\mathcal{VC}$ to which they are connected. Thus, introducing a delay in finalizing timestamps can reduce the size of the timestamp substantially. Specifically, we show that it is possible to assign timestamps with $2|\mathcal{VC}| + 2$ entries for *Inline* timestamps. By contrast, timestamps of size $n$ (for integer valued timestamps) or $n - 1$ (for real valued timestamps) are necessary even for a star graph. We demonstrate this by generalizing the result by Charron-Bost [2] for the case of star graphs when *Online* timestamps are required. By contrast, for star graph where $|\mathcal{VC}| = 1$, *Inline* timestamps of size 4 suffice for any number of processes.

Although there is a delay in assigning timestamps, these timestamps can be used in many applications that utilize vector clocks. This is due to the fact that in long running applications, we anticipate that the timestamps for most events would already be finalized; only timestamps of recent events are expected to change. We can focus on solving the problem at hand by only considering events whose timestamps are finalized. In [23], we have shown how the timestamps proposed in this work can be used to perform predicate detection or rollback recovery.

*Acknowledgements:* Kulkarni is supported in part by NSF CNS 1329807, NSF CNS 1318678, and XPS 1533802. Vaidya is supported in part by NSF 1409416 and Toyota InfoTechnology Center USA. Any opinions, findings, and conclusions or recommendations expressed here are those of the authors and do not necessarily reflect the views of the funding agencies or the U.S. government.

The authors thank Vijay Garg, Ajay Kshemkalyani and Jennifer Welch for their feedback. We thank Marek Zawirski for answering questions about SwiftCloud [25].

## REFERENCES

[1] Paulo Sérgio Almeida, Carlos Baquero, Ricardo Gonçalves, Nuno Preguiça, and Victor Fonte. 2014. *Scalable and Accurate Causality Tracking for Eventually Consistent Stores.* Springer Berlin Heidelberg, Berlin, Heidelberg, 67–81. DOI: http://dx.doi.org/10.1007/978-3-662-43352-2_6

[2] Bernadette Charron-Bost. 1991. Concerning the Size of Logical Clocks in Distributed Systems. *Inf. Process. Lett.* 39, 1 (1991), 11–16. DOI: http://dx.doi.org/10.1016/0020-0190(91)90055-M

[3] Himanshu Chauhan, Vijay K. Garg, Aravind Natarajan, and Neeraj Mittal. 2013. A Distributed Abstraction Algorithm for Online Predicate Detection. In *IEEE 32nd Symposium on Reliable Distributed Systems, SRDS 2013, Braga, Portugal, 1-3 October 2013.* IEEE Computer Society, 101–110. DOI: http://dx.doi.org/10.1109/SRDS.2013.19

[4] George Coulouris, Jean Dollimore, Tim Kindberg, and Gordon Blair. 2011. *Distributed Systems: Concepts and Design* (5th ed.). Addison-Wesley Publishing Company, USA.

[5] Jiaqing Du, Sameh Elnikety, Amitabha Roy, and Willy Zwaenepoel. 2013. Orbe: Scalable Causal Consistency Using Dependency Matrices and Physical Clocks. In *Proceedings of the 4th Annual Symposium on Cloud Computing (SOCC '13).* ACM, New York, NY, USA, Article 11, 14 pages. DOI: http://dx.doi.org/10.1145/2523616.2523628

[6] Jiaqing Du, Călin Iorgulescu, Amitabha Roy, and Willy Zwaenepoel. 2014. Gentlerain: Cheap and scalable causal consistency with physical clocks. In *Proceedings of the ACM Symposium on Cloud Computing.* ACM, 1–13.

[7] C. J. Fidge. 1989. Partial Orders for Parallel Debugging. *Proceedings of the ACM SIGPLAN/SIGOPS Workshop on Parallel and Distributed Debugging, published in ACM SIGPLAN Notices* 24, 1 (Jan. 1989), 183–194.

[8] Colin J. Fidge. 1991. Logical Time in Distributed Computing Systems. *IEEE Computer* 24, 8 (1991), 28–33. DOI: http://dx.doi.org/10.1109/2.84874

[9] Vijay K. Garg and Chakarat Skawratananond. 2001. String realizers of posets with applications to distributed computing. In *Proceedings of the Twentieth Annual ACM Symposium on Principles of Distributed Computing, PODC 2001, Newport, Rhode Island, USA, August 26-29, 2001.* 72–80. DOI: http://dx.doi.org/10.1145/383962.383988

[10] Vijay K. Garg and Chakarat Skawratananond. 2002. Timestamping Messages in Synchronous Computations. In *ICDCS.* 552–559. DOI: http://dx.doi.org/10.1109/ICDCS.2002.1022305

[11] Vijay K. Garg, Chakarat Skawratananond, and Neeraj Mittal. 2007. Timestamping messages and events in a distributed system using synchronous communication. *Distributed Computing* 19, 5-6 (2007), 387–402. DOI: http://dx.doi.org/10.1007/s00446-006-0018-5

[12] Sandeep S Kulkarni, Murat Demirbas, Deepak Madappa, Bharadwaj Avva, and Marcelo Leone. 2014. Logical physical clocks. In *International Conference on Principles of Distributed Systems.* Springer, 17–32.

[13] Rivka Ladin, Barbara Liskov, Liuba Shrira, and Sanjay Ghemawat. 1992. Providing High Availability Using Lazy Replication. *ACM Trans. Comput. Syst.* 10, 4 (1992), 360–391. DOI: http://dx.doi.org/10.1145/138873.138877

[14] Leslie Lamport. 1978. Time, Clocks, and the Ordering of Events in a Distributed System. *Commun. ACM* 21, 7 (1978), 558–565.

[15] Friedemann Mattern. 1988. Virtual Time and Global States of Distributed Systems. In *Parallel and Distributed Algorithms.* North-Holland, 215–226.

[16] F. Mattern. 1989. Virtual time and global states of distributed systems. In *Parallel and Distributed Algorithms: Proc. of the International Workshop on Parallel and Distributed Algorithms.* Elsevier Science Publishers B.V. (North-Holland), 215–226.

[17] Sigurd Meldal, Sriram Sankar, and James Vera. 1991. Exploiting Locality in Maintaining Potential Causality. In *Proceedings of the Tenth Annual ACM Symposium on Principles of Distributed Computing, Montreal, Quebec, Canada, August 19-21, 1991.* 231–239. DOI: http://dx.doi.org/10.1145/112600.112620

[18] Luís E. T. Rodrigues and Paulo Veríssimo. 1995. Causal Separators for Large-Scale Multicast Communication. In *ICDCS.*

[19] Reinhard Schwarz and Friedemann Mattern. 1994. Detecting Causal Relationships in Distributed Computations: In Search of the Holy Grail. *Distributed Computing* 7, 3 (1994), 149–174. DOI: http://dx.doi.org/10.1007/BF02277859

[20] Min Shen, Ajay D. Kshemkalyani, and Ashfaq A. Khokhar. 2013. Detecting Unstable Conjunctive Locality-Aware Predicates in Large-Scale Systems. In *IEEE 12th International Symposium on Parallel and Distributed Computing, ISPDC 2013, Bucharest, Romania, June 27-30, 2013.* 127–134. DOI: http://dx.doi.org/10.1109/ISPDC.2013.25

[21] Mukesh Singhal and Ajay D. Kshemkalyani. 1992. An Efficient Implementation of Vector Clocks. *Inf. Process. Lett.* 43, 1 (1992), 47–52. DOI: http://dx.doi.org/10.1016/0020-0190(92)90028-T

[22] Francisco J. Torres-Rojas and Mustaque Ahamad. 1999. Plausible Clocks: Constant Size Logical Clocks for Distributed Systems. *Distrib. Comput.* 12, 4 (Sept. 1999), 179–195. DOI: http://dx.doi.org/10.1007/s004460050065

[23] Nitin H. Vaidya and Sandeep S. Kulkarni. 2016. Efficient Timestamps for Capturing Causality. *CoRR* abs/1606.05962 (2016). http://arxiv.org/abs/1606.05962

[24] Paul A. S. Ward and David J. Taylor. 2001. Self-Organizing Hierarchical Cluster Timestamps. In *Proceedings of the 7th International Euro-Par Conference Manchester on Parallel Processing (Euro-Par '01).* Springer-Verlag, London, UK, UK, 46–56. http://dl.acm.org/citation.cfm?id=646666.699445

[25] M. Zawirski, N. Preguica, S. Duarte, A. Bieniusa, V. Balegas, and M. Shapiro. 2015. Write Fast, Read in the Past: Causal Consistency for Client-Side Applications. In *ACM Middleware, Vancouver.* https://pages.lip6.fr/Marc.Shapiro/papers/write-fast-read-past-middleware-2015.pdf

# Symmetry Breaking with Noisy Processes

Seth Gilbert
National University of Singapore
seth.gilbert@comp.nus.edu.sg

Calvin Newport
Georgetown University
cnewport@cs.georgetown.edu

## ABSTRACT

Biology and computer science intersect at the problem of symmetry breaking, which is relevant in both fields. Accordingly, in recent years, distributed algorithm theorists have studied symmetry breaking problems in models inspired by biology to help provide insight into the capabilities and constraints of this natural process. A potential shortcoming of these models, however, is that they execute distributed algorithms precisely as specified. In nature, where computation is often implemented by messy analog systems, this precision cannot necessarily be guaranteed. Motivated by this observation, in this paper we present a general method for injecting "computational noise" into any distributed system model that describes processes as interacting state machines. Our method captures noise as a force that can cause state machines to transition to the wrong state. We combine this formalization of noise with the beeping models that have been a popular target of recent work on bio-inspired symmetry breaking. We produce new upper and lower bounds for both single hop and multihop models—studying leader election in the former and the maximal independent set problem in the latter. These bounds introduce new techniques for achieving robustness to noise, and identify some fundamental limits in this pursuit. We argue that both our general approach and specific results can help advance the productive relationship between biology and algorithm theory.

## KEYWORDS

noisy computation; beeping; biological distributed computing; leader election; MIS

## 1 INTRODUCTION

Symmetry breaking is fundamental in the study of distributed algorithms, where it acts as a core primitive for network graph algorithms and contention resolution strategies. Symmetry breaking is also fundamental in biology. To quote a recent survey of this topic by biologists Rong Li and Bruce Bowerman [11]: "Symmetry breaking, which may occur at multiple levels...is a prevalent process in biology, because organismal survival depends critically on well-defined structures and patterns at both microscopic and macroscopic scales, [and these structures and patterns] are consequences of broken symmetry."

This research was support by NSF grant CCF 1649484 and Singapore MOE grant MOE2014-T2-1-157.

*PODC '17, July 25-27, 2017, Washington, DC, USA*

ACM ISBN 978-1-4503-4992-5/17/07...$15.00
https://doi.org/10.1145/3087801.3087814

This overlap creates an opportunity for algorithm theorists to translate techniques from computer science to biology to better understand symmetry breaking in the latter setting. Indeed, in recent years, the growing *biological distributed algorithm* (BDA) community (c.f., [1]) has pursued this opportunity by studying several basic symmetry breaking tasks in biology motivated models; e.g., [2–5, 7–10, 13, 16, 17].

A potential shortcoming of this existing work is the *precision* of its models, which execute the relevant distributed algorithms precisely as specified. This assumption makes sense in the world of digital computer processors, but is less well motivated in the world of biological computation where processes are inherently noisy. The "state" of a digital computational process is typically defined by bits stored in discrete memory. A processor executing a command updates this state in a predictable manner. In a biological computational process such as a cell, by contrast, the "state" might instead capture a combination of multiple analog quantities, e.g., relative enzyme concentrations or cell membrane potentials. These quantities are subject to numerous sources of noise from the internal and external environment [14], and cannot always be expected to transition precisely or predictably in response to stimuli.

It follows that a fuller understanding of symmetry breaking algorithms in biological systems will require models that include bounded amounts of noise capable of causing processes to deviate from their specified control logic. This paper introduces and motivates a new formal approach for introducing this *computational noise* into most existing distributed computation models. We then revisit some of the core symmetry breaking problems and models cited above in the context of this new computational noise formalism—producing new upper and lower bounds that provide new insight into the capabilities and constraints of this fundamental problem in the fundamentally noisy reality of nature.

*Modeling Computational Noise.* Distributed systems are traditionally modeled as a collection of interacting state machines corresponding to computational processes. In this paper, we model computational noise in such settings as a force that can cause a state machine to transition to the wrong state—thus deviating from the control logic encapsulated by its transition function.

Our formal model for this type of computational noise (detailed in Section 2) requires that a state machine designer now define two things: (1) a state machine; and (2) an embedding of the state machine states in an underlying *configuration space*. The latter is a bounded metric space where each point in the space can be interpreted as a vector of values describing a possible *configuration* of the real world system the state machine abstracts. For example, consider a state machine that describes the computational logic of a cell attempting to break symmetry with its neighbors. The cell might represent its "state" with different concentrations of a small collection of relevant enzymes. A configuration of this system is a vector describing the concentration of these enzymes at the moment. Each state in the state machine can be understood as corresponding to a region in this configuration space.

Describing computation with both a high-level state machine and corresponding low-level configuration space enables a natural definition of noise: after each transition of the state machine, bounded random noise can be added to the values of the underlying configuration vector. If this new vector falls in the region of a different state, then the state machine will erroneously shift into this new state. The state machine designer, therefore, must take care in defining a state embedding, as the size and/or proximity of state regions in this space affect the possible impacts of noise. Notice, this noise formalism can be applied to any distributed system model that represents processes as interacting state machines, regardless of the details of how the machines are scheduled or interact.

*Comparison of Computational Noise to Other Fault Models.* This general approach to modeling computational noise describes something fundamentally different than most traditional work on distributed fault tolerance. These traditional models assume a bounded fraction of the processes in the system suffer from a catastrophic fault (e.g., they crash or begin behaving arbitrarily), while the remainder of the processes execute their logic perfectly and can work together to compensate for these failures. In the noisy computation model studied here, by contrast, every process can suffer from faults, but these faults are less catastrophic. The question is not how non-faulty nodes can compensate for extremely faulty nodes, but is instead how a collection of mildly faulty nodes can still work together to produce a non-faulty result.[1]

A potentially interesting connection is to error-correcting codes. For example, one could treat the state of a probabilistically corrupted state machines as a coded message subjected to noise—allowing for the application of information theory techniques to *decode* the proper system state. This approach might seem to require the presence of an uncorrupted central decoder (while in our model, the only computational entities are the noisy processes themselves). From another perspective, error-correcting codes might yield efficient mappings of states to the low-level configuration space. (For the problems considered in this paper, such techniques did not seem to provide a benefit.) We believe that the connection to error-correcting codes both supports our choice of model and leaves open the potential for exciting future work.

*Results.* In this paper, after defining our new noise formalism, we study upper and lower bounds for single and multihop leader election in synchronous beeping models in the presence of noise.

We start, in Section 3, by formally defining the beeping state machine models. Next, in Section 4, we introduce the first problem of interest: leader election in a single-hop beeping network. We begin by describing and analyzing a new leader election algorithm (state machine definition) that elects a single leader with probability $1 - \epsilon$ in $O((1/\epsilon)\log^3(1/\epsilon) + \log n)$ rounds (in expectation) when run in a network of $n$ nodes (where $n$ is unknown in advance). This algorithm uses the simplest possible configuration space in our model: a 1-dimensional configuration space (i.e., we embed the states in a configuration space described by only a single analog value). Critically, we show the algorithm tolerates the maximum possible amount of computational noise.

By contrast, in the synchronous beeping model *without* noise, the best known leader election algorithm is much faster, requiring only $O(\log(n + (1/\epsilon))\log(1/\epsilon))$ rounds [9]. It is possible, therefore, that the use of a more complex configuration space (i.e., more values in each configuration vector), or smarter algorithmic logic, might generate a significantly faster result. We answer this question negatively by proving that every leader election algorithm requires at least $\Omega(\sqrt{1/\epsilon} + \log n)$ rounds in the presence of maximum noise, regardless of the complexity of its underlying configuration space.

In Section 5, we turn our attention to leader election in multihop beeping networks, which we define as the maximal independent set (MIS) problem. We note that this problem has been particularly relevant to the BDA community since the 2011 publication of a paper in the journal *Science* claiming that pre-cursor cells in fruit fly development are likely selected by a biological process that implements an MIS beep algorithm [4].

In Section 5, we describe and analyze the first known distributed MIS algorithms that can tolerate significant amounts of computational noise. In particular, we study the problem under two assumptions about the transition probabilities of the underlying state machines: (1) the *strong* model in which state machine transition probabilities can be an arbitrary function of the error bound $\epsilon$; and (2) the *weak* model in which the probabilities must be constant (our single hop results assume the weak model). In both models, we describe novel MIS algorithms that build an MIS with local success probability $1 - \epsilon$, and terminate with high probability in time that ranges from $\tilde{O}((1/\epsilon))$ to $\tilde{O}((1/\epsilon)^3)$ rounds as we increase the bound on the amount of possible noise from small to large values (where $\tilde{O}$ omits polylogarithmic terms in $1/\epsilon$ and $n$).

For both algorithms, the maximum tolerated noise is a constant value that is independent of the network size and error bound, but less than what our single hop leader election solution tolerates. In more detail, our single hop solution works for the maximum amount of noise allowed by our noise model. Our MIS solutions, by contrast, have fixed bounds on the noise they can tolerate that are slightly less (by a small constant fraction) than this maximum.

One interesting question is the impact of dimension on the robustness of algorithms. Our MIS algorithms embed their states in a 1-dimensional configuration space. This leaves open the possibility that increasing the dimensions of the configuration space might yield more noise robustness. We validate this possibility by describing and analyzing an embedding of the strong model MIS algorithm into a 2-dimensional configuration space that increases its noise robustness as compared to 1 dimension.

*Related Work.* We study randomized single hop leader election in a synchronous beeping model with computational noise. In the absence of noise, the best known leader election algorithms in this setting require $O(\log((1/\epsilon) + n)\log(1/\epsilon))$ rounds to solve the problem with probability $1 - \epsilon$ in networks of size $n$; e.g., [9]. It is also shown in [9], that any solution with error bound $\epsilon$ needs at least $\log(1/\epsilon)$ states in its state machine representation assuming (as we do in this paper) only constant transition probabilities.

We also study the MIS problem in multihop beeping networks. Motivated by the original paper connecting MIS to biology [4], the algorithm in [2] builds an MIS with beeps in $O(\log^2 n)$ rounds without transmitter collision detection, and the algorithm in [13]

[1]There are also key differences with respect to self-stabilization. In the study of self-stabilizing system, *every* process might suffer from a one-time state corruption, but they are then provided perfect computation moving forward to compensate for this one-time corruption. In our model, the corruptions are bounded, but potentially occur after every round.

build an MIS in $O(\log n)$ rounds with collision detection. These existing results are more efficient than our noise robust results, but they depend on state machine logic that executes precisely, and use a state count that grows in the network size. The algorithm in [2], for example, leverages a synchronized global schedule of $\Omega(\log n)$ broadcast probabilities.

Finally, we note that computational noise for state machines has a philosophical (though not technical) connection to the well-studied subject of computational noise in the context of circuit gates, introduced by Von Neumann [15], and subsequently widely explored for the past 60 years.

## 2 COMPUTATIONAL NOISE

A core objective of this paper is to propose a useful approach for formalizing noise in the computation of distributed state machines. Here, we detail the notion of noise summarized in the introduction.

*Configuration Spaces.* A state machine abstracts computation that takes place in an underlying concrete *system*. At any given step of computation, the system's state can be described by a *configuration*: a collection of relevant system values. In a digital system, a configuration describes the discrete state of the relevant memory. In a biological system, a configuration is more likely to describe a collection of analog values relevant to the computation; e.g., the concentration of key enzymes in the cellular fluid or the membrane potential. For a given system, we call the space of all possible configurations the *configuration space* of the system. In a biological system, as noted, each configuration can be represented as a vector of bounded real values. The configuration space of such a system can be understood as a bounded multidimensional metric space. An execution of an abstract state machine has a corresponding representation as a series of configurations in an underlying configuration space. As we detail below, our approach to modeling noise applies bounded perturbations to the values in the underlying configuration, and then determines if this perturbed configuration shifts the abstract state machine into a new state.

*Noise Aware State Machines.* Our approach to computational noise requires a state machine designer to specify the corresponding configuration space for the system the machine abstracts, and provide an embedding of the machine's states into this space. We call the combination of a state machine and the corresponding configuration space embedding a *noise aware* state machine.

In more detail, to simplify the definition of a noise aware machine, in this paper we restrict the possible configuration spaces to be closed Euclidean *d-balls* of fixed radius $1/2$, for dimensions $d = 1, 2, 3, \ldots$. Recall, a $d$-ball of radius $1/2$ consisting of all $d$-dimensional points within distance $1/2$ of a fixed point (assumed to be the origin $(0, 0, \ldots, 0)$ in this paper). This decision fixes the metric space to be Euclidean and scales all configuration values to the range $(-1/2, 1/2)$. A 1-ball of radius $1/2$, for example, is a 1-dimensional line of length 1, a 2-ball is a circle with radius $1/2$, a 3-ball is a sphere with radius $1/2$, and so on. The only choice for the state machine designer in fixing the underlying configuration space is to indicate the number of dimensions.

Once the state machine designer has fixed the number of dimensions of the underlying configuration space, the next step is to provide a *state embedding*, which is a partition of the configuration space into contiguous *regions*, and a bijection from these regions to the state machine states.

*Noise Bounds and State Shifts.* We parameterize each execution of our noise model with a *noise bound*, which we denote with a non-negative real number $\gamma$. We apply noise after *every* noise aware state machine transition as follows.

For each region, the designer specifies a "center," e.g., the geometric center of the region. In this paper, we will always use the geometric center. Let $p_q$ be the center of the region corresponding to state $q$ in the noise aware machine's configuration space. Think of $p_q$ as the target configuration the system attempts to transform into upon shifting into abstract state $q$.

Assume the state machine transitions into some state $q$ according to its transition function. We probabilistically perturb this point by sampling a *new* point $p'_q$ from the ball of all points within distance $\gamma$ of $p_q$; e.g., the points in closed ball $B_\gamma[p_q]$. If $p'_q$ is in a region that corresponds to some different state $r \neq q$, then we conclude the state machine transition by having the machine *shift* erroneously into state $r$.[2] There are many different sampling distributions that might be used to select $p'_q$. For simplicity, we assume the new point is sampled uniformly from all points in $B_\gamma[p_q]$ that are within the $d$-ball.[3] Notice that this approach to noise is independent from the specifics of how the state machines are scheduled and interact, and therefore can be combined with any distributed state machine model.

*Robustness Metric.* Our new model of computational noise requires a new performance property to quantify the ability of a *distributed algorithm* (e.g., a collection of noise aware state machines) to solve a problem in the presence of such errors. Here, we focus on *robustness*. In more detail, when we say a distributed algorithm is a $\Gamma$-*robust* solution to a problem, for some real value $\Gamma \geq 0$, we mean that it solves this problem when combined with our definition of noise and any noise bound $\gamma$, such that $0 \leq \gamma \leq \Gamma$. That is, $\Gamma$ provides an upper bound on the maximum noise bound for which the algorithm still works. The choice of the specific noise bound $\gamma$, $0 \leq \gamma \leq \Gamma$, used in a given execution is made arbitrarily. State machines are not provided advance knowledge of this choice.

*Final States.* Some types of problems feature a terminal final decision that once made cannot be changed. For example, in the leader election problems studied in this paper we fix a decision to become a leader as a one-time, irrevocable commitment. We capture this behavior in our noise model by allowing problem definitions that exempt specially designated *final* states from the impact of noise. These states do not need to be included in the configuration space embedding, and once a machine transitions into a final state it never leaves. We emphasize that these final states are an abstraction that capture a significant phase shift in the underlying system that once triggered cannot be undone. The number of such states that are allowed (if any), and the behavior of machines in these states, are considered part of a problem definition.

[2]There are, of course, many interesting alternate approaches to adding noise. Here, it seems natural that the next transition depends only on your current state, e.g., the choice of a center. Other approaches might not identify the center of a configuration, but imagine more of a random walk on the configuration space.

[3]For configuration topologies that are more complicated than balls, a different distribution may make more sense, e.g., when many nearby points may not be in the configuration space.

*Discussion.* This approach to noise provides interesting design options to the state machine designer. For example, the designer might decide to allocate an important state to a region that takes up a large fraction of the configuration space—minimizing the chance that noise induces a transition error when the machine enters this state. And the relative location of states' regions in the configuration space is also an important design decision.

Here we have fixed a particular shape of configuration space (i.e., a $d$-ball). However, we do not believe that the specific choice is that important. We are not studying a specific biological system, but instead the general dynamics of systems in which abstract states are embedded into regions of finite configuration spaces and subject to noise. We expect that roughly similar results will hold for a variety of related (finite) configuration topologies.

One parameter that may matter is the dimensionality of the space. In some cases, it does seem that higher dimension allows for more robustness—though this is not always clearly the case. Here, we treat the dimensionality of the space as specified by the algorithm designer, in the sense that it is a "minimum requirement" of the system in order to use the algorithm.

# 3 THE BEEPING MODEL

Our definition of noisy computation can apply to many different models of distributed computation. It only requires that the computational processes are modeled as state machines. In this paper, we focus on the impact of noise on the well-studied *synchronous beeping model*. This model assumes a collection of probabilistic state machines (also called *nodes* in the following) that proceed in synchronized rounds. The machines communicate with their neighbors with a simple *beep* primitive. A key property is that channels are shared: a given receiver can only distinguish between *no beeps* and *one or more beeps* from its neighbors. We also assume the channels are half-duplex: a transmitting machine cannot determine if neighbors are transmitting concurrently. We consider both *single hop* topologies, where all machines are neighbors, and *multihop topologies*, where the neighbor relations are described by a connected graph with a unique machine corresponding to each vertex. A notable aspect of this model is that the state machine design does not depend on the network size (which we indicate as $n$). The state machine is fixed in advance and then $n$ copies are connected and executed in a network for some arbitrary size $n \geq 1$.

*Formal Definition.* Formally, a computational process (equiv., node) is a state machine defined by a 7-tuple $(Q, F, b, \delta_\perp, \delta_\top, \delta_b, q_0)$, where $Q$ is the finite set of states, $F \subseteq Q$ are the final states (note: the necessity and behavior of final states is part of a problem definition). The element $b : Q \to \{0, 1, \frac{1}{2}\}$ is the *beeping function* where $b(q)$, for $q \in Q$, is the probability that the machine beeps when starting a round in state $q$. The elements $\delta_\perp$, $\delta_\top$, and $\delta_b$ are transitions functions that map each state in $Q$ to a probability distribution defined over $Q$, where $\delta_\perp$ describes the transition that occurs when the machine receives and detects no beeps, $\delta_\top$ describes the transition when the machine receives and detects beeps, and $\delta_b$ describes the transition when the machine beeps. Notice, unless otherwise stated (e.g., in Section 5.1), the probability distributions returned by these functions are restricted to map each state to either 0, 1, or $\frac{1}{2}$. More precise probabilities can be simulated at the expense of more states. Finally, $q_0 \in Q$ is the machine's *start state*.

The model proceeds in synchronous rounds, $r = 1, 2, 3....$ At the beginning of each round, each node $i$ beeps with probability $b(q_i)$, where $q_i$ is the state of node $i$'s machine at the beginning of the round. Each such node $i$ then selects its next state from the distribution returned by $\delta_\perp(q_i)$, $\delta_\top(q_i)$, or $\delta_b(q_i)$, where the choice of which transition function depends on whether or not $i$ beeped, and if it did not, whether or not it detected a beep. By convention, we assume that states in $F$ are terminal (that is, once in a state in $F$ a node never transitions away), though we leave the details of these states to the relevant problem definition.

# 4 LEADER ELECTION

We consider the problem of *leader election* in a single hop network. We describe a noise aware state machine embedded in a 1 dimensional configuration space, and show it solves the problem in time polynomial in $1/\epsilon$ (for error bound $\epsilon$) for any amount of noise. We then prove that a polynomial bound in $1/\epsilon$ is necessary to tolerate large amounts of noise, regardless of the number of dimensions in the configuration space.

*The Leader Election Problem.* A solution to leader election must include two terminal final states *leader* and *notleader*. Once a machine transitions into one of these states it never again beeps or leaves the state—its decision is final. We say a state machine (equiv. algorithm) *solves* leader election with error bound $\epsilon$ if it guarantees the following two properties when run in any size network: (1) *liveness:* with probability 1, every machine eventually enters the *leader* or *notleader* final state, and with probability at least $1 - \epsilon$ there is at least one leader; and (2) *safety*: with probability at least $1 - \epsilon$, there is never more than one leader. We emphasize that each computational process is running a copy of the same state machine. This machine can be defined with respect to $\epsilon$, but it must solve leader election no matter how many machines we connect in our network. This formalizes the idea that the algorithm does not know $n$ and there are no unique ids.

## 4.1 Leader Election Upper Bound

We begin by describing a noise aware algorithm that solves leader election for the maximum allowable amount of noise: $\gamma = 1$ (our noise model behaves the same for all $\gamma \geq 1$).[4] In the absence of noise, our leader election solution leverages a standard knock-out strategy. Every node starts *active*. In each round, each active node beeps with probability $1/2$. If a node chooses to receive and it detects a beep, it becomes *inactive* by transitioning to the terminal *notleader* state. If a node remains active long enough—which we define to be at least $k = c \log(1/\epsilon)$ rounds (for a constant $c \geq 1$ we fix in the analysis)—then it elects itself leader by transitioning to the *leader* state.

To tolerate noise, we embed the *gateway* state (which is connected to the *leader* final state) into a configuration space region small enough that nodes are unlikely to be pushed into it by noise, but not so small that it takes nodes a long time to reach it in the presence of large noise. The trickiest part of the analysis is dealing with moderate amounts of noise: we treat the final active node in this case as executing a random walk biased toward the gateway.

[4]For any $\gamma \geq 1$, our noise model selects a perturbed point uniformly from all points in the configuration space. Therefore, there is no reason to consider any noise bounds $\gamma > 1$.

*State Machine Definition.* To capture this logic in a state machine, we define $k$ step states, $s_1, s_2, ..., s_k$. Each machine starts in state $s_1$ and advances one state in each round. After state $s_k$, the machine moves to a special *gateway* state $g$. In any of these states, if a node decides to listen and detects a beep, it moves to the *nonleader* state. In state $s_1$, if a node decides to listen and detects silence, it moves to state $s_2$; otherwise, if it decides to beep, then it remains in state $s_1$. For all other step states $s_i$, where $i > 1$, it always moves to the next state $s_{i+1}$ (or to $g$ if $i = k$), whether it decides to listen and detects silence, or if it decides to beep. In state $g$, if a machine decides to listen and detects silence, it transitions to *leader*. (The extra restriction on $s_1$ is due to the possibility of noise and will be discussed in the analysis.) This state machine is described more formally in Figure 1.

*State Embedding.* We now define an embedding our state machine states into a 1-dimensional configuration space (e.g., a line of length 1). As required by the problem definition, we exempt the final *leader* and *notleader* from this embedding. For the remaining states in $Q' = Q \setminus F$ we must describe, for each state's region, its location and size in the configuration space. We arrange the state regions in the following order in left-to-right fashion starting from the left endpoint of the line: $s_1, s_2, ..., s_k, q$. In terms of region size, the region for each step state (e.g., $s_1, s_2, ..., s_k$) is the same width, that we label $w_s$. The region for $g$ is a smaller width that we label $w_g$. We define these two widths relative to each other as follows: $w_g = \frac{\epsilon}{c' \log(1/\epsilon)} \cdot w_s$, for a constant $c' \geq 1$ that we fix in the analysis. Because the region widths must sum to 1, it follows that: $kw_s + w_g = 1 \Rightarrow kw_s + \frac{\epsilon}{c' \log(1/\epsilon)} w_s = 1 \Rightarrow w_s = \frac{1}{k + \frac{\epsilon}{c' \log(1/\epsilon)}}$. In other words, each step state takes up slightly less than $1/k$ of the space, where the gap shrinks along with $\epsilon$. The width $w_g$ is then another factor of $(\epsilon)/(c' \log(1/\epsilon))$ smaller than this step width.

*Analysis.* We now analyze the leader election algorithm. We begin by proving that silence is unlikely until the number of active nodes is significantly reduced:

LEMMA 4.1. *Let $t_q$ be the first quiet round, i.e., a round in which no node broadcast. Then with probability at most $\epsilon/2$, there are at most $6 \log 1/\epsilon$ nodes that remain active at the end of round $t_q - 1$.*

PROOF. Since $t_q$ is the first quiet round, there are no transitions to the leader state before $t_q$: every node is either active (in a step state or the gateway state) or passive (in the not-leader state).

Consider a round in which there are $n_j$ nodes active. In this case, the probability of a silent round is $1/2^{n_j}$. If the round is not silent, then every node that listens becomes inactive, and only the broadcasting nodes remain active. The expected number of broadcasting nodes is $n_j/2$, and so by Markov's Inequality, the probability that $\geq 3n_j/4$ nodes remain active is $\leq 2/3$.

We label the states of our system as follows, fixing a constant $\alpha \geq 1$ to be determined later. We say that the system is in state $c_j$ when there are $< (4/3)^j \alpha \log 1/\epsilon$ active nodes, and $\geq (4/3)^{j-1} \alpha \log 1/\epsilon$ active nodes. The system begins in some state $c_\ell$ where $\ell \leq 4 \log n$. When the system reaches state $c_1$ (or below), there are fewer than $(4/3)\alpha \log 1/\epsilon$ nodes remaining active.

When the system is in state $c_j$ at the beginning of some round, then there are three possible outcomes at the end of the round: the system remains in state $c_j$, the system advances to state $c_{j-1}$ with probability at least $1/3$, or a silent round occurs (and our analysis ends) with probability no more than $p_j = (1/2)^{(4/3)^j \alpha \log 1/\epsilon}$.

We want to determine the probability that the system reaches state $c_1$ (or below) before a silent round occurs. In state $c_j$, the probability of a silent round before transitioning to $c_{j-1}$ is $\leq (p_j/(1/3 + p_j) \leq 3p_j$. Thus starting in some state $c_\ell$ where $\leq 4 \log n$, we see by a union bound that the probability of entering a silent round before entering state $c_1$ is at most $3 \sum_{i=1}^{4 \log n} p_i$.

With some algebra, we can show that $3 \sum_{i=10}^{4 \log n} p_i \leq 6\epsilon^{(4/3)\alpha}$. For $j \leq 9$, we note that $p_j \leq p_1$, and so $3 \sum_{i=1}^{9} p_i \leq 9p_1 \leq 27(1/2)^{(4/3)\alpha \log 1/\epsilon} \leq 27\epsilon^{(4/3)\alpha}$.

Thus, in total, the probability of a silent round occurring before the number of active nodes drops below $(4/3)\alpha \log 1/\epsilon$ is at most $33\epsilon^{(4/3)\alpha}$. Choosing $\alpha = 6$, and assuming $\epsilon \leq 1/2$, we conclude that with probability at most $(33/128)\epsilon \leq \epsilon/2$, there are at most $6 \log 1/\epsilon$ nodes that remain active at the end of round $t_q - 1$. □

We now divide the remainder of this section into two parts, depending on the value of $\gamma$.

Assume $\gamma \leq w_s/2$, i.e., noise cannot perturn a node out of a step state. In this case, we combine the fact that not too many nodes survive state $s_1$ (see Lemma 4.1), with the fact that enough nodes are knocked out during the remaining step states to show that it is unlikely to elect two leaders.

LEMMA 4.2. *If $\gamma \leq w_s/2$, then with probability $\epsilon$, no more than one node enters the leader state.*

PROOF. Since the noise $\gamma \leq w_s/2$, we know that a node in a step state transitions exactly according to the transition rule until reaching the gateway state $g$.

First, we know that with probability at least $1 - \epsilon/2$, at most $6 \log 1/\epsilon$ nodes enter state $s_2$, according to Lemma 4.1. Before entering the leader state, each of these (at most) $6 \log 1/\epsilon$ nodes must survive for $k - 1$ rounds, as they transiton through the remaining $k - 1$ step states.

Next, we consider the probability that more than one node survives the subsequent step states. (Recall that a node can not be moved out of a step state by noise because $\gamma \leq w_s/2$.)

The probability that any pair of nodes survives $r$ rounds of step states is at most $1/2^r$, and so setting $r = 10 \log 1/\epsilon$, and taking a union bound over all possible pairs of the $6 \log 1/epsilon$ actives nodes, we bound the probability that any pair of active nodes arrive in step state $s_k$ by $\epsilon/2$. Fixing the number of step states $k = 11 \log 1/\epsilon$ (and fixing the constant $c = 10$, we see that the probability that any pair survives $k - 1$ step states is $\leq \epsilon/2$. Via a union bound with the result from Lemma 4.1, we conclude that with probability at least $(1 - \epsilon)$, there is no more than one leader. □

We next consider the case where $\gamma > w_s/2$. Here, we cannot depend on the step states, as noise may cause the nodes to skip steps. Instead, we rely on the noise itself, along with the fact that state $g$ is small, to prevent electing more than one leader.

LEMMA 4.3. *Assume $\gamma > w_s/2$. Then with probability at least $1 - \epsilon$, only one node enters the leader state.*

PROOF. Notice that before the first silent round $t_q$, no node can enter the leader state (by the transition rule for the gateway state

| **Single Hop Leader Election State Machine** | |
|---|---|
| $Q = \{s_1, s_2, ..., s_k, g, leader, notleader\}$ | $\delta_\top(q) = notleader$, for all $q \in Q \setminus F$ |
| $F = \{leader, notleader\}$ | $\delta_b(s_1) = s_1$ and $\delta_b(g) = g$ |
| $q_0 = s_1$ | $\delta_b(s_i) = \delta_\perp(s_i) = s_{i+1}$, for $1 < i < k$ |
| $b(q) = \begin{cases} \frac{1}{2}, \text{if } q \in Q \setminus F \\ 0, \text{if } q \in F \end{cases}$ | $\delta_b(s_k) = \delta_\perp(s_k) = g$ |
| $\delta_\perp(s_1) = s_2$ and $\delta_\perp(g) = leader$ | $\delta_\perp(q) = \delta_\top(q) = \delta_b(q) = q$, for $q \in F$ |

**Figure 1: The state machine specification for the single hop leader election algorithm.**

$g$). By Lemma 4.1, we know that with probability at least $(1 - \epsilon/2)$, at most $6 \log 1/\epsilon$ nodes remain active at the end of round $t_q - 1$.

Consider a node $u$ that is active at the end of round $t$ for $t \geq t_q - 1$. At the end of round $t$, node $u$ transitions into either a step state or the gateway state $g$, and then is perturbed by noise. Due to noise and the fact that the state $g$ is small, the gateway is hard to hit.

That is, the noise ensures that the probability of ending the round in state $g$ is at most $w_g/(2\gamma)$ (whether or not $u$ intended to transition to $g$). Since $\gamma > w_s/2$ and $w_g = 2\frac{\epsilon}{c' \log(1/\epsilon)} \cdot w_s$, we conclude that node $u$ ends round $t$ in state $g$ with probability at most $\frac{w_g}{w_s} \leq 2\frac{\epsilon}{c' \log(1/\epsilon)}$.

Of note, we observe via a union bound that with probability at least $1-(12/c')\epsilon$, the at most $6 \log 1/\epsilon$ nodes active at the beginning of round $t_q$ are all in step states, i.e., not in state $g$.

Starting in round $t_q$, there are two processes occurring: the set of active nodes is reduced via knockouts, and nodes attempt to get to state $g$. We bound the probability that any of the active nodes are in state $g$, as long as there are at least two active nodes.

We say that in round $t \geq t_q$, the system is in state $c_j$ if: (i) No node has ended the round in state $g$ in rounds after $t_q - 1$ and prior to $t$; and (ii) At the beginning of round $t$, there are $> (3/4)^j (6 \log 1/\epsilon)$ active nodes and $\leq (3/4)^{j-1} (6 \log 1/\epsilon)$ active nodes. Notice that in state $c_j$, there are three possibilities for the next round: (i) a node ends the round in state $g$, (ii) the system remains in state $c_j$, or (iii) the system enters state $c_{j+1}$. By a union bound, the probability of any node ending the round in state $g$ is at most $(3/4)^{j-1}(12/c')\epsilon$.

We also observe that, as long as there are $\geq 2$ active nodes, the system moves from state $c_j$ to state $c_{j+1}$ with probability at least 1/3: if there are $n_j$ active nodes, the expected number of nodes to broadcast (and remain active) is $n_j/2$; so by Markov's Inequality, the probability that more than $(3/4)n_j$ remain active is $< 2/3$.

Thus, in state $c_j$, the probability of ending the round in state $g$ before entering state $c_{j+1}$ is at most $(3/4)^{j-1}(12/c')\epsilon/(1/3 + (3/4)^{j-1}(12/c')\epsilon) \leq (3/4)^{j-1}(36/c')\epsilon$.

We now taking a union bound to bound the probability that any active node enters state $g$ while there is more than 1 active node: $\sum_{j=1}^{\infty}(3/4)^{j-1}(36/c')\epsilon \leq (144/c')\epsilon$ . We combine this, via a union bound, with the probability that any of the nodes begin $t_q$ in state $g$, calculated above to be $(12/c')\epsilon$ to show that the probability of more than one node entering state $g$ is at most $(156/c')\epsilon$. Choose $c' = 312$, this is no greater than $\epsilon/2$.

We conclude the main result by combining this via a union bound with Lemma 4.1. □

Together, Lemma 4.2 and Lemma 4.3 show that with probability at least $(1 - \epsilon)$, the algorithm selects only one leader.

*Performance.* We now analyze the expected running time of the leader election algorithm. For small amounts of noise it is straightforward to establish efficient election:

Lemma 4.4. *If $\gamma \leq w_s/2$, then the expected time for electing a leader is $O(\log n/\epsilon + (1/\epsilon)\log(1/\epsilon))$.*

On the other hand, when the noise is large, i.e., $\gamma > w_s/2$, it can perturb a node from one step state to another. We view this node as performing a random walk on the step steps, biased "to the right," until it gets sufficiently close to the gateway state: at which point it has a chance to enter the state and become leader.

We focus on the case where there is only one node remaining active, which is reached, in expectation, in $O(\log n)$ rounds. We can view this node as performing a random walk on the step states until it gets sufficiently close to the gateway state. It then gets a chance to enter the gateway state and become the leader.

Consider some node $u$ that is active, and assume all the remaining nodes are inactive starting in some round $t_0$. Assume node $u$ is in step state $s_j$ at the beginning of time $t_0$. Effectively, node $u$'s behavior over the following rounds is a random walk among the step states: in each round, node $u$ moves to the next step state, and then move forward or backward according to noise $\gamma > w_s$.

We now define a *boundary* state, i.e., a state from which node $u$ can reach the gateway state with sufficient probability. Let step state $s_r$ be the smallest step state such that $center(s_{r+1}) + \gamma \geq end(g)$, i.e., $s_{r+1}$ is the smallest step state where the noise adjustment (to the right) entirely encompasses state $g$. If $r$ is undefined, then we define $r = k$.

Let $s_\ell$ be the largest step state such that $center(s_{\ell+1}) - \gamma \leq start(g)$), i.e., $s_{\ell+1}$ is the largest step state where the noise adjustment (to the left) entirely encompasses state $g$. If $\ell$ is undefined and $\gamma \geq (1.5)w_s$, then define $\ell = 1$; otherwise, it remains undefined.

We define the step states $\geq s_r$ and $\leq s_\ell$ (if $\ell$ is defined) to be the boundary states. Note if $\gamma \geq (1.5)w_s$, we always define $s_1$ as a boundary state.

Our goal is to show that the expected time for $u$ to arrive in in a boundary state or to reach $g$ is $O(\log 1/\epsilon)$. At that point, then in the next step node $u$ will have a reasonable probability of ending up in state $g$, and subsequently of becoming the leader.

Lemma 4.5. *Assume node $u$ is the only active node and is in one of the non-boundary step states in round $t_0$ and assume $\gamma > w_s/2$. Then the expected number of rounds to reach a boundary state or $g$ is $2k = O(\log(1/\epsilon))$.*

Proof (sketch). We begin by defining a random walk on the step states with variable size. We consider the model where noise can *wrap* around one end of the space to the other, and consider the alternate process in which in every step, if node $u$ begins in state $s_j$, then it moves uniformly at random to a state in the range $[s_{j-d}, s_{j+d+1}]$. Notice that this overestimates the probability of moving to state $s_{j-d}$, and underestimates the probability of moving to state $s_{j+d+2}$. Thus this this random walks moves "to the right" no faster than the original state machine process.

Let $h(j)$ be the expected number of steps for node $u$, starting in state $j$, to reach a boundary state or $g$. For all non-boundary states $s_j$, the behavior of the random walk is captured by this recurrence: $h(j) = 1 + \sum_{i=-d}^{d+1} \frac{1}{2d+2} h(j+i)$ .

Solving this recurrence, we observe that $h(j) \leq 2(k-j)$. From this we conclude that the expected number of steps to reach a state $\geq k$ or $\leq \ell$ is at most $2k = O(\log(1/\epsilon)$. □

At this point, we can conclude the analysis, examining the expected number of times we have to execute the random walk before entering the gateway state and become the leader.

Lemma 4.6. *Assume $\gamma > w_s/2$. Then the expected number of rounds before there is a leader is $O(\log n + (1/\epsilon)\log^3 1/\epsilon)$.*

Proof. First, as before, we observe that within (expected) $O(\log n)$ rounds, there is at most 1 active node (because the expected number of rounds for 1/2 the nodes to become inactive is 1).

Next, by Lemma 4.5 and Markov's Inequality, with probability at least 1/2, node $u$ ends a round in a boundary state within $O(\log(1/\epsilon))$ rounds.

At this point, by the definition of a boundary state, with probability at least 1/2, in the following round node $u$ will transition to a state from which the noise completely covers the gateway state $g$. (The only case where the probability is $< 1$ is when the boundary state is $s_1$.)

Thus, the probability that node $u$ ends the next round in the gateway state is: $(1/2)(w_g/2\gamma) = (1/2)\left(\frac{\epsilon}{c'\log(1/\epsilon)}\right)(w_s/2\gamma)$.

Since $w_s > 1/(c\log(1/\epsilon)+1)$, this yields a probability of at least $p = (\epsilon/(2(c+1)c')(1/\log^2(1/\epsilon)$ that node $u$ ends in state $g$.

If it fails, the process repeats itself, beginning with the random walk. Thus, in expectation, it takes $O((1/\epsilon)\log^2(1/\epsilon)$ retries to enter state $g$. Since each retry takes $O(\log 1/\epsilon)$ tie (in expectation), we conclude that the total running time, in expectation, is $O(\log n + (1/\epsilon)\log^3(1/\epsilon)$ □

At this point, we can conclude the analysis:

Theorem 4.7. *Our noise aware leader election algorithm is a 1-robust solution to leader election with error bound $\epsilon$ and a 1-dimensional configuration space. When run in a network of size n it terminates in $O((1/\epsilon)\log^3(1/\epsilon) + \log(n/\epsilon))$ rounds in expectation.*

## 4.2 Leader Election Lower Bound

Here we prove for every 1-robust noise aware leader election algorithm with error bound $\epsilon$, the expected number of rounds until termination is in $\Omega(\sqrt{1/\epsilon}+\log n)$. This lower bound holds regardless of the number of dimensions in the underlying metric space.

*The Necessity of $\Omega(\log n)$ Rounds.* We first show that for a fixed $\epsilon < 1/2$ the expected rounds until termination is in $\Omega(\log n)$. This argument follows from a straightforward symmetry breaking argument applied to the case of no noise $\gamma = 0$. Nodes in our beeping model are anonymous (i.e., identical state machine definitions), and there are only (at most) two fair coin flips possible in each round to help break symmetry: whether or not the node beeps, and the choice of the next state. We can, therefore, think of the randomness used by each node as a sequence of bits generated with independent uniform randomness. Each round, each node consumes at most two of these bits. For a collection of $n$ nodes, it is likely that every node has some *partner* in the system that shares the same bits in the first $\approx \log n$ positions of their sequences.

Lemma 4.8. *With probability at least 1/2, for every possible binary string of length $\log(n)/2$, at least two nodes share this pattern at the beginning of their random bit sequences.*

From this we conclude that no algorithm can move a node into the leader position too quickly, as its partner would follow.

Theorem 4.9. *Fix a noise aware state machine that solves leader election with some error bound $\epsilon < 1/2$ and configuration space dimension $d \geq 1$. Let $f_\epsilon(n)$ be the expected termination time in a network of size n with $\gamma = 0$. It follows that $f_\epsilon(n) \in \Omega(\log n)$.*

*The Necessity of $\Omega(\sqrt{1/\epsilon})$ Rounds.* We now prove the necessity of $\Omega(\sqrt{1/\epsilon})$ rounds. Whereas our above argument for the necessity of $\log n$ rounds ignored noise, this lower bound depends on the necessity for the algorithm to handle the maximum amount of noise (e.g., 1-robustness).

Our below bounds holds for every number of configuration space dimensions and all possible embeddings. To do so, we ignore the details of the embeddings and focus instead on the total volume of the configuration space dedicated to states that can act as a *gateway* to the final states. In a system with $\gamma = 1$, after every transition, a new configuration is chosen uniformly from *all* points in the configuration space. Therefore, the fraction of the space volume dedicated to a given state type directly specifies the probability of shifting into a state of that type.

If the algorithm terminates in fewer than $\Omega(\sqrt{1/\epsilon})$ rounds, even when one node is running all by itself, then it means that there are gateway states with volume at least $\Omega(\sqrt{\epsilon})$ in which a node elects itself leader. However, in that case, if there are two nodes in the network, then with probability at least $\Omega(\sqrt{\epsilon}^2) = \Omega(\epsilon)$, they both elect themselves leader, violating correctness. We thus conclude:

Theorem 4.10. *Fix a 1-robust noise aware state machine that solves leader election with some error bound $\epsilon < 1$ and configuration space dimension $d \geq 1$. Let $f(\epsilon)$ be the maximum expected termination time of this machine in networks of size no more than $O(1/\epsilon)$ and $\gamma = 1$. It follows that $f(\epsilon) \in \Omega(\sqrt{1/\epsilon})$.*

# 5 MAXIMAL INDEPENDENT SET

We now tackle a more complex problem: building a *maximal independent set* (MIS) in a multihop beeping network. We seek the first known solutions to this problem that tolerate computational noise. As mentioned in the introduction, we think the MIS problem is a particularly good fit for such an investigation because it has been conjectured that key biological processes approximate a beeping MIS algorithm [4]. It is therefore important to understand how to solve this process in a noisy environment.

Recall that by default the beeping model defined in Section 3 restricts probabilistic transitions to use constant probabilities. Some of the results in this section will consider a variation of this model in which transition probabilities can be any function of the error bound $\epsilon$ (but are still independent of the network size $n$). We call this variation the *strong* model. We begin by studying the problem in the strong model with a 1-dimensional configuration space. We describe a noise aware algorithm that provides a $(1/6)$-robust solution to the MIS problem. This noise bound is large and independent of the network size and error bound. It is still, however, smaller than the maximum bound of 1 tolerated by our single hop leader election algorithm—reflecting the added difficulty of multiple hops. We then provide and analyze a new state embedding for this algorithm in a 2-*dimensional* configuration space. We show this new embedding increases the maximum noise bound. Our goal with this analysis is not to maximize this improvement, but is instead to provide evidence that increasing configuration complexity can yield improved results in some settings. The key strategy to tolerate noise in both algorithms is to solve the MIS problem using only a handful of states (a result perhaps of standalone interest): allowing us to embed each state in a large noise-robust region.

We then turn our attention to the original (standard) beeping model, and describe and analyze a new noise aware MIS algorithm that provides a $(1/10)$-robust solution to the problem using only constant transition probabilities and a 1-dimensional configuration space. This algorithm simulates finer-grained transitions from the strong model using multiple states. This increased state count increases the impact of noise. Borrowing analytical techniques from our preceding study of leader election, we prove our transition simulations still work sufficiently well even as noise causes transition errors on the underlying states.

Our algorithm's time complexity increases from $\tilde{O}((1/\epsilon))$ to $\tilde{O}((1/\epsilon)^3)$ as $\gamma$ increases from 0 to the relevant noise upper bound (where $\tilde{O}$ suppresses polylogarithmic factors). This is slower than the best known results for no noise, which tend to be polylogarithmic in $(1/\epsilon)$ and $n$, but are arguably within the general range of what is considered pragmatic for biological settings.[5]

*The MIS Problem.* Given a connected graph $G = (V, E)$, a maximal independent set (MIS) of $G$ is a subset of nodes $M \subseteq V$ that satisfies the following two properties: (1) *maximality:* every node in $V$ is in $M$ or neighbors a node in $M$; and (2) *independence:* no two nodes in $M$ are neighbors. For a given $u \in V$, we say that $u$ *locally satisfies* the MIS properties (with respect to $M$), if either: (1) $u$ is in $M$ and no neighbor is in $M$; *or* (2) $u$ is not in $M$ and at least one neighbor of $u$ is in $M$.

Here we define what it means to build an MIS with state machines in our multihop beeping model. In more detail, a state machine definition that solves the MIS problem must have a single terminal final *MIS* state. Entering this state indicates that the machine has joined the MIS. We assume that when a node $u$ a enters the *MIS* state at the end of some round $r$, all neighbors of $u$ receive a special signal that deactivates them at the beginning of round $r+1$.[6] We say a network of such state machines is *terminated* if every machine is either in the *MIS* final state or can never enter the *MIS* final state on any possible extension of the current execution. We say a machine *solves* the MIS problem with a given error bound $\epsilon$, if it guarantees the following two properties when run in a connected multihop network of any size $n$: (1) *liveness*: with probability 1, the network eventually terminates; and (2) *safety:* consider the network after termination and let $M$ be the set of nodes in the MIS; for each machine $A$, with probability at least $1-\epsilon$, $A$ locally satisfies the MIS properties with respect to $M$. To achieve a global error probability $\epsilon_g$ that the *entire* network satisfies the MIS property, it is sufficient to set $\epsilon \leq \epsilon_g/n$ and apply a union bound.

*Bounded Polynomial Independence.* Our algorithms require a restriction on the graph topology that generalizes many standard assumptions used in the study of graph algorithms: *bounded polynomial independence.* (This is an important class of graphs, particularly for wireless networks and other networks where MIS is a useful building block, see, e.g., [6, 12].) Let $G = (V, E)$ be the network topology. This assumption requires that there is some polynomial $f$, such that for every $u \in V$ and hop count $h \geq 1$, the independence number of $u$'s $h$-hop neighborhood in $G$ is upper bounded by $f(h)$. This $f(h)$ function shows up in our time complexity analysis. It is important to emphasize that $f$'s order is constant with respect to $h$.

## 5.1 A $(1/6)$-Robust MIS Algorithm for the Strong Model and 1 Dimension

We describe an algorithm that works properly in a strong version of our model that allows small transition probabilities and a noise bound $\gamma \leq 1/6$. It requires a 1-dimensional configuration space.

*Algorithm Description.* The machine consists of a *waiting, gateway, dominating,* and *MIS* state. We sometimes use the abbreviations W, G, D, and M, respectively, for these states. Each machine starts in the waiting state. In the waiting state, the machine always receives. If it hears silence it moves to the gateway state otherwise it stays in the waiting state. In the gateway state, a machine beeps with probability $1/2$. If a machine in this state receives and hears a beep, it returns to the waiting state. If a machine in this state beeps it stays in the gateway state. If a machine receives and hears silence, it moves to the dominating state. In the *dominating* state, a machine beeps with probability 1 in every round. In this state, the machine will transition to the MIS final state with probability $p_M = \epsilon/(\alpha \log(1/\epsilon))$, for some constant $\alpha \geq 1$ that we fix in the analysis. Otherwise, it loops in the dominating state. (Notice: it is this single transition that we leverage the strong model assumption that we will subsequently remove.) For completeness, we provide the state machine definition below. When we omit a probability when specifying a transition function, assume the probability of the transition is 1 (e.g., $\delta(a) = b$ means that when the machine is in state $a$ and function $\delta$ is relevant it transitions to $b$ with probability 1). We omit some transitions that can never occur.

| **MIS in Strong Model** | |
|---|---|
| $Q = \{W, G, D, M\}$ | $\delta_\perp(W) = G$ and $\delta_\perp(G) = D$ |
| $F = \{M\}$ | $\delta_\top(W) = W$ and $\delta_\top(G) = W$ |
| $q_0 = W$ | $\delta_b(G) = G$ |
| $b(q) = \begin{cases} 0, \text{if } q = W \\ \frac{1}{2}, \text{if } q = G \\ 1, \text{if } q = D \end{cases}$ | $\delta_b(D) = \begin{cases} M, \text{with prob. } p_M \\ D, \text{with prob. } 1-p_M \end{cases}$ |

[5]A general principle for symmetry breaking is that polylogarithmic in the relevant parameters is the goal for digital computers, polynomial is the goal for biological settings, and super-polynomial is too inefficient for all settings.

[6]A similar behavior can be obtained by assuming instead that the final MIS state always beeps. This variation of the final state assumptions, however, requires a slightly more involved construction of state $D$ (see the below algorithm description) that now has nodes in this state occasionally listen and allow themselves to be knocked out if they hear a beep. The main idea is to make this check slightly less likely than transitioning to the MIS final state, so that by the time a node in $D$ makes this check, there is likely a nearby node in the MIS and it is okay for it to be knocked back into state $W$, where it will remain suppressed. We omit a treatment of this variation for the sake of concision.

*Noise Embedding.* For our noise embedding, we partition 1-ball into three equal size regions of length 1/3: one for each of the three non-final states, $W$, $G$, and $D$.

*Analysis.* We analyze the MIS algorithm described above under the assumption that $\gamma \leq 1/6$. This bound is small enough that noise does not impact the machine's execution; when we remove the strong model assumption, our embedded state count will increase from 3 to $\log(1/\epsilon)$, leading to more difficulties due to noise. Our goal is to to prove the following theorem:

THEOREM 5.1. *Our noise aware MIS algorithm is a (1/6)-robust solution to the MIS problem with error bound $\epsilon$ and a 1-dimensional configuration space in the strong model when run in a network topology that satisfies bounded polynomial independence for polynomial $f$. The algorithm terminates in $O\left(f(\log n)((1/\epsilon)\log(1/\epsilon)\log n + \log^2 n)\right)$ rounds, with high probability in $n$.*

The full analysis is deferred to the full version of the paper. We begin by showing that once a node makes it into state $D$, then pretty soon, it or its neighbor makes it into $M$ with high probability. This is true because a node in $D$ will remain in $D$ until either it transitions to $M$ (with probability $p_M$ in each round), or a neighbor transitions into $M$, deactivating $u$.

LEMMA 5.2. *If some node $u$ is in state $D$ in round $r$, then within $O(\log n/p_M)$ rounds a node in $N^+(u)$ enters state $M$, with high probability in $n$.*

We then show a key property, that within $\log n$ hops of any node $u$, there most be a neighborhood that is well-suited for nodes to make it to state $D$—at which point Lemma 5.2 can apply to ensure someone makes it to $M$ after not too many additional rounds.

LEMMA 5.3. *Fix some node $u$ with no neighbor in $M$ and fix a round $r > 1$. With constant probability, within the round range $r$ to $r + \log n$, a node $v$ within $\log n$ hops of $u$ will be in state $D$.*

PROOF. Fix some node $u$ and round $r$ as specified, anda ssume that every node within $\log n$ hops of $u$ begins $r$ in $M$, $W$, or $G$.

The first step concerns the nodes that begin $r$ in state $G$. We want to find one such node $v$, within $\log n$ hops of $u$, that is *popular*, which we define to mean: for every $w \in N_g(v)$: $|N_g(w)| \leq 2|N_g(v)|$, where $N_g$ is the neighbor function that only considers nodes that are in state $G$ at the beginning of round $r$.

To begin this search we need to start with a *source* node in $N^+(u)$ that is in state $G$. If $u$ is in $G$, we use $u$ as the source. If $u$ is not in $G$ then it must have at least one neighbor in $G$. To see why this is true, first note that if $u$ is not in $G$, and it has no neighbor in $M$ (as we assumed), then it must be in $D$ or $W$ at the beginning of $r$. We know $u$ is not in $D$ because we assumed no nearby node is in $D$. If $u$ is in $W$ at the beginning of $r$, however, then it must have heard a beep in $r - 1$ (since $r > 1$). Because we assumed no nodes in $D$ nearby, then this beep must have come from a neighbor $\hat{u}$ in state $G$. We have, therefore, identified a source node $u_0 \in N^+(u)$.

Our search for a popular node proceeds as follows. First we consider $u_0$. If $u_0$ is popular, then are done. If $u_0$ is not popular, then by the definition of this property, there must exist a neighbor $u_1 \in N_g(u_0)$ such that $|N_g(u_1)| > 2|N_g(u_0)|$. Let us move our consideration then to $u_1$. We can now repeat the process. If $u_1$ is popular, we are done. Otherwise, there must be a neighbor $u_2 \in N_g(u_1)$ such that $|N_g(u_2)| > 2|N_g(u_1)| > 2|N(u_0)|$. Notice, because the neighborhood size at least doubles in each iteration of this search, we cannot get to $u_{\log n}$, as this node would, by transitivity, have a neighborhood size more than a factor of $n$ larger than $N_g(u_0)$—which is impossible given the network only has $n$ total nodes. Therefore, we will find a popular node $v$ that is in $G$ at the beginning of round $r$ and that is within $\log n$ hops of $u$.

The second part of our argument considers the next $\log n$ rounds that unfold. We will argue that within these rounds, with constant probability, one of the neighbors of $v$ enters state $D$. To make this argument, fix $\Delta = |N_g(v)|$ to be the number of neighbors of $v$ in state $G$. Notice that because $v$ is popular, each of the nodes in $N_g(v)$ has at most $2\Delta$ neighbors.

Consider the probability that a node $w \in N_g(v)$ makes a *beep run* in which: (1) $w$ beeps for $\log\Delta$ consecutive rounds; (2) every neighbor of $w$ in state $G$ receives in at least one of these rounds and is therefore knocked back to $W$; (3) every other node $w' \in N_g(v)$ receives in at least one of these rounds; and (4) at the end of these rounds of consecutive beeps $w$ receives, hears silence, and therefore enters state $D$. (Notice, if behavior 2 holds, then when $w$ receives at the end of its beep run, all of its neighbors that could beep are in $W$ so we know it will receive nothing and move on to $D$.) Notice that the event that a beep run occurs for a node $w$ is disjoint for the event of a beep run for any other nodes in $N_g(v)$, since condition (3) of a beep run requires every other node in $N_g(v)$ to receive at least once—i.e., not to be on a beep run.

The probability of that a node $w$ is on a beep run is at least:

$$\begin{aligned} &\geq (1/2)^{\log\Delta}(1/2)(1-(1/2)^{\log\Delta})^{3\Delta} \\ &\geq (1/\Delta)(1/2)(1/4)^{(1/2)^{\log\Delta}\cdot 3\Delta} = \Omega(1/\Delta), \end{aligned}$$

where in the first equation: $(1/2)^{\log\Delta}$ is the probability that $w$ beeps for $\log\Delta$ rounds in a row, $(1/2)$ is the probability that $w$ receives in the round after this run, and $1-(1/2)^{\log\Delta}$ is the probability that a given neighbor of $w$ or $v$ does *not* beep in all $\log\Delta$ rounds of the run. (The $3\Delta$ comes from summing the at most $2\Delta$ neighbors of $w$ and the $\Delta$ neighbors of $v$ in $G$.)

We have, therefore, identified $\Delta$ nodes that each join $D$ with probability $\Omega(1/\Delta)$. Furthermore, the join events for these nodes are disjoint, as you cannot have more than one node in $N_g(v)$ make a successful beep runs. Therefore, the probability that one node in $N_g(v)$ makes a successful beep run is simply the sum of disjoint events, i.e., $\sum_{i=1}^{\Delta}\Omega(1/\Delta) = \Theta(1)$. That is, with constant probability, at least one node in $N_g(v)$ goes on a beep run. Finally, to achieve the stated time complexity, we note that $\Delta < n$ and therefore the $\log\Delta$ rounds required for a run is less than $\log n$. □

Combining this lemma with the bounded independence property guarantees the performance property of Theorem 5.1. The safety property follows by bounding the probability that multiple neighboring nodes make the same transition into the MIS in the same round. (See the full version for more details.)

## 5.2 A $((\sqrt{2}\cdot 4)^{-1})$-Robust Algorithm for the Strong Model and 2 Dimensions

The (1/6)-robust MIS algorithm described above assumed a 1-dimensional configuration space. We show in the full version that increasing configuration space dimensions can improve robustness.

The MIS state machine we are studying includes three non-final states. For our analysis to hold, it is necessary that noise can never induce a transition error. For a 1-dimensional configuration space, the best we could do was divide the 1-ball (which is a line of length 1) into three regions of length $1/3$, and so the largest noise bound we could tolerate was $1/6$.

Here we describe an embedding of our three states into a 2-ball with radius $1/2$, i.e., a circle with this radius, such that the distance from the center of each region to its boundary is strictly greater than $1/6$. In particular, consider a circle of radius $\alpha = \frac{1}{\sqrt{2}\cdot 4}$ centered at point $(\alpha, \alpha)$ with radius $\alpha$. This circle, which we will call the *safe circle*, is entirely contained within the first quadrant of the configuration space, and we can similarly fit a safe circle in the other three quadrants without overlap.

This then implies that we can tolerate noise $\gamma \leq \alpha$ without transition errors, and hence the previously described state machine works correctly with improved robustness.

## 5.3 A $(1/10)$-Robust MIS Algorithm for the Standard Model and 1 Dimension

We now modify our strong model MIS algorithm to work for constant probability transitions. These modifications decrease our noise bound slightly to $(1/10)$. At the same time, they also add more than $\log(1/\epsilon)$ states to the machine definition—ensuring that our analysis will have to cope with state shifts due to computational noise. The main sacrifice we make in shifting from the strong to standard model is in the time complexity required as $\gamma$ approaches its maximum values. As mentioned above, the key strategy in these modifications is implementing a noise robust simulation of smaller transition probabilities.

*State Machine Modifications.* In the original algorithm we have a state $D$ that transitions to $M$ with probability $p_M$, and loops to $D$ with probability $1 - p_M$. Machines in state $D$ always beep. Here we approximate this behavior using only transition probabilities in $\{0, 1/2, 1\}$. To do so, we replace $D$ with $q+2$ states where $q = \lceil 1/p_M \rceil$. In the following we call these collections of states the *simulated D* states. We label these states: $b1, b2, s_1, s_2, ..., s_q$. We define all states to always beep: therefore, $\delta_b$ is the only relevant transition function. We define $\delta_b(b1) = \delta_b(b2) = s_1$. For $k < q$, we define $\delta_b(s_k) = s_{k+1}$ with probability $1/2$ and $\delta_b(s_k) = s_1$ with probability $1/2$. We define $\delta_b(s_q) = s_1$ with probability $1/2$, and $\delta_b(s_q) = M$ with probability $1/2$. Finally, we update the transition $\delta_\perp(G) = D$ (with probability 1) from the original machine to now specify $\delta_\perp(G) = s_1$. (This is the only transition into $D$ from outside $D$ in the original machine, so it is the only such transition we have to update now that we have replaced $D$ with our collection of simulated $S$ states.)

*Noise Embedding Modifications.* In the original embedding, state $D$ took up a $1/3$ fraction of the line describing the 1-dimensional configuration space. We now expand this to a $6/10$ fraction to contain the simulated $D$ states. The $W$ and $G$ states now each take up a $2/10$ fraction of the space. We order the simulated $D$ states in their region as follows (in clockwise order): $b1, s_1, s_2, ..., s_q, b2$. The $b1$ and $b2$ each get a $2/10$ fraction of the space. We divide the middle $2/10$ fraction among the *step* states $s_1, s_2, ..., s_q$. We assign metric space to these steps in the same general manner as with the step states for single hop leader election studied earlier in this paper. That is, the steps $s_1$ to $s_{q-1}$ each get the same width $w_s$, while the *gateway* step $s_q$ gets width $w_g = p_M \cdot w_s$.

*Analysis.* Our goal is to prove the following result:

Theorem 5.4. *Our modified noise aware MIS algorithm is a $(1/10)$-robust solution to the MIS problem with error bound $\epsilon$ and a 1-dimensional configuration space in the standard model when run in a network topology that satisfies bounded polynomial independence for polynomial $f$. With high probability in $n$, the algorithm terminates in a time that grows from $O\left(f(\log n)[(1/\epsilon)\log n \log^2(1/\epsilon) + \log^2 n]\right)$ to $O\left(f(\log n)[(1/\epsilon^3)\log n \log^5(1/\epsilon) + \log^2 n]\right)$, as $\gamma$ increases from 0 to $1/10$.*

We must prove two things about our simulation of the original $D$. First, we must show that in any given round, the probability that a node $u$ in the simulated $D$ transitions to $M$ is upper bounded by $p_M$. Second, we must show that once a node is in the $D$ simulation, it will either be deactivated or transition to $M$. This latter step is captured by the following lemma:

Lemma 5.5. *Fix some node $u$ that enters the simulated $D$ states. Let $T$ be the number of rounds for a node in $N^+(u)$ to subsequently enter $M$, with high probability in $n$. The value of $T$ grows from $O((\log n \log(1/\epsilon))/p_M)$ to $O((\log n \log^2(1/\epsilon))/p_M^3)$ as $\gamma$ grows from 0 to $1/10$.*

The full analysis and proof details are deferred to the full version.

## REFERENCES


[1] 2015. The 3rd Annual Workshop on Biological Distributed Algorithms. Online at: http://www.snl.salk.edu/~navlakha/BDA2015/. (2015).

[2] Yehuda Afek, Noga Alon, Ziv Bar-Joseph, Alejandro Cornejo, Bernhard Haeupler, and Fabian Kuhn. 2011. Beeping a Maximal Independent Set. In *Proceedings of the Symposium on Distributed Computing (DISC)*.

[3] Yehuda Afek, Noga Alon, Ziv Bar-Joseph, Alejandro Cornejo, Bernhard Haeupler, and Fabian Kuhn. 2013. Beeping a maximal independent set. *Distributed Computing* 26, 4 (2013), 195–208.

[4] Yehuda Afek, Noga Alon, Omer Barad, Eran Hornstein, Naama Barkai, and Ziv Bar-Joseph. 2011. A Biological Solution to a Fundamental Distributed Computing Problem. *Science* 331, 6014 (2011), 183–185.

[5] Alejandro Cornejo and Fabian Kuhn. 2010. Deploying Wireless Networks with Beeps. In *Proceedings of the Symposium on Distributed Computing (DISC)*.

[6] Sebastian Daum, Mohsen Ghaffari, Seth Gilbert, Fabian Kuhn, and Calvin C. Newport. 2013. Maximal independent sets in multichannel radio networks. In *Symposium on Principles of Distributed Computing (PODC)*. 335–344.

[7] Yuval Emek and Roger Wattenhofer. 2013. Stone Age Distributed Computing. In *Proceedings of the Symposium on Principles of Distributed Computing (PODC)*.

[8] Klaus-Tycho Förster, Jochen Seidel, and Roger Wattenhofer. 2014. Deterministic Leader Election in Multi-hop Beeping Networks - (Extended Abstract). In *Proceedings of the Symposium on Distributed Computing (DISC)*.

[9] Seth Gilbert and Calvin Newport. 2015. The Computational Power of Beeps. In *Proceedings of the Symposium on Distributed Computing (DISC)*.

[10] Peter Jeavons, Alex Scott, and Lei Xu. 2016. Feedback from nature: simple randomised distributed algorithms for maximal independent set selection and greedy colouring. *Distributed Computing* 29, 5 (2016), 377–393.

[11] Rong Li and Bruce Bowerman. 2010. Symmetry breaking in biology. *Cold Spring Harbor perspectives in biology* 2, 3 (2010), a003475.

[12] Johannes Schneider and Roger Wattenhofer. 2010. An optimal maximal independent set algorithm for bounded-independence graphs. *Distributed Computing* 22, 5-6 (2010), 349–361.

[13] Alex Scott, Peter Jeavons, and Lei Xu. 2013. Feedback from nature: an optimal distributed algorithm for maximal independent set selection. In *Proceedings of the Symposium on Principles of Distributed Computing (PODC)*.

[14] Emily Singer. 2014. Inside the Din, Cells Fight Noise with Noise. *Quanta Magazine* (May 2014). Available Online: http://www.scientificamerican.com/article/cells-in-living-things-fight-noise-with-noise/.

[15] John Von Neumann. 1956. Probabilistic Logics and the Synthesis of Reliable Organisms from Unreliable Components. *Automata studies* 34 (1956), 43–98.

[16] Lei Xu and Peter Jeavons. 2015. Patterns from nature: Distributed greedy colouring with simple messages and minimal graph knowledge. *Information Sciences* 316 (2015), 550–566.

[17] Lei Xu and Peter Jeavons. 2015. Simple Algorithms for Distributed Leader Election in Anonymous Synchronous Rings and Complete Networks Inspired by Neural Development in Fruit Flies. *International journal of neural systems* 25, 07 (2015), 1550025.

# The Power of Choice in Priority Scheduling

Dan Alistarh
IST Austria & ETH Zurich
dan.alistarh@inf.ethz.ch

Justin Kopinsky
MIT
jkopin@mit.edu

Jerry Li
MIT
jerryzli@mit.edu

Giorgi Nadiradze
ETH Zurich
giorgi.nadiradze@inf.ethz.ch

## ABSTRACT

Consider the following random process: we are given $n$ queues, into which elements of increasing labels are inserted uniformly at random. To remove an element, we pick two queues at random, and remove the element of lower label (higher priority) among the two. The *cost* of a removal is the *rank* of the label removed, among labels still present in any of the queues, that is, the distance from the optimal choice at each step. Variants of this strategy are prevalent in state-of-the-art concurrent priority queue implementations. Nonetheless, it is not known whether such implementations provide any rank guarantees, even in a sequential model.

We answer this question, showing that this strategy provides surprisingly strong guarantees: Although the single-choice process, where we always insert and remove from a single randomly chosen queue, has degrading cost, going to infinity as we increase the number of steps, in the two choice process, the expected rank of a removed element is $O(n)$ while the expected worst-case cost is $O(n \log n)$. These bounds are tight, and hold irrespective of the number of steps for which we run the process. The argument is based on a new technical connection between "heavily loaded" balls-into-bins processes and priority scheduling. Our analytic results inspire a new concurrent priority queue implementation, which improves upon the state of the art in terms of practical performance.

## 1 INTRODUCTION

The last two decades have seen tremendous progress in the area of concurrent data structures, to the point where scalable versions of many classic data structures are now known, including lists [15], skip-lists [12, 17, 20], hash-tables [18, 24], or search trees [1, 8, 22]. In this context, significant research attention has been given to concurrent *producer-consumer* data structures, such as queues, stacks, or priority queues, which are critical in concurrent systems. On the one hand, several elegant designs, e.g. [10, 11, 26, 27], have pushed these data structures to the limits of scalability on current processor architectures. On the other, impossibility results [2, 9] show that such data structures providing strong ordering semantics also have inherent sequential bottlenecks which limit their scalability.

A popular approach for circumventing these impossibility results is to *relax* data structure semantics [33]. The first instance of this strategy is probably the relaxed PRAM priority queue structure of Karp and Zhang [19], designed for efficient parallel execution of branch-and-bound programs. A flurry of subsequent work, e.g. [3, 5, 14, 23, 28, 31, 32, 34, 36], has shown that relaxed semantics can yield extremely good practical results, and that it can be very useful in the context of higher-level constructs, such as concurrent graph algorithms [28].[1]

Notably, the current state-of-the-art concurrent priority queue is obtained by the following *MultiQueue* strategy [13, 31]. We start from $n$ queues, each protected by a lock. To *insert* an element, a processor picks one of the $n$ queues uniformly at random, locks it, and inserts into it. To *remove* an element, the processor picks *two queues* uniformly at random, and removes the element of *higher priority* among their two top elements, after locking the corresponding queue. Extensive testing [13, 31] has shown that this natural strategy can provide state-of-the-art throughput, and that the average number of priority inversions is relatively low. Further variants of this strategy have been used to implement general priority schedulers [28] and relaxed concurrent queues [14].

Despite their significant practical success, randomized relaxed concurrent data structures still lack a theoretical foundation: it is not known whether distributed strategies such as the MultiQueue can provide any *guarantees* in terms of their inversion cost, or whether their performance can still be improved.

**Contribution.** In this paper, we take a first step towards addressing this challenge. We focus on the analysis of the following sequential process, inspired by the MultiQueue strategy: we are given $n$ queues, into which a large number of consecutively labeled elements are inserted initially, uniformly at random. To remove an element, we pick two queues at random, and remove the element of lower label on top of either queue. We are interested in the *cost* of removals, defined as the *rank* of the removed label among labels still present in any of the queues, i.e., the "linear distance" from the optimal choice at each step, which would be the top element among all queues.

Our main technical contribution is showing that this process provides surprisingly strong rank guarantees: for any time $t \geq 0$ in the execution of the process, the expected rank of an element removed at time $t$ is $O(n)$, while the expected worst-case rank


*PODC '17, July 25-27, 2017, Washington, DC, USA*

ACM ISBN 978-1-4503-4992-5/17/07...$15.00
https://doi.org/10.1145/3087801.3087810

[1] In practice, it is often possible to offset the cost of *priority inversions* by performing *additional work*. For instance, in Dijkstra's single-source shortest-paths algorithm, priority inversions can be offset by nodes being relaxed multiple times.

removed at a step is $O(n \log n)$. These bounds are asymptotically tight, and hold for arbitrarily large $t$. Our analysis generalizes to a $(1 + \beta)$ extension of the process, where the algorithm deletes from the higher priority among two random queues with probability $0 < \beta \leq 1$, and from a single randomly chosen queue with probability $(1 - \beta)$. It also extends to show that the process is *robust to bias* in the insertion distribution towards some bins by a constant factor $\gamma \in (0, 1)$. By contrast, we show that the strategy which always removes from *a single* randomly chosen queue *diverges*, in the sense that its average rank guarantee evolves as $\Omega\left(\sqrt{tn \log n}\right)$, for time $t \geq n \log n$. The $(1 + \beta)$ strategy can be extended to an efficient implementation, which improves upon the state-of-the-art in terms of practical performance.

**Technical Overview.** A tempting first approach at analysis is to reduce to classic "power of two choices" random processes, e.g. [4, 29], in which balls are always inserted into the least loaded of two randomly chosen bins. A simple reduction between these two processes exists for the case where labels are inserted into the queues in *round-robin* fashion. However, this reduction breaks if elements are inserted uniformly at random, as is the case in real systems. Another important difference from the classic process is that elements are *labelled*, and so the state of the system at a given step is highly correlated with previous steps. For instance, given a queue $Q$ whose top element has label $\ell$, if we wish to characterize the probability that the next label on top of $Q$ is a specific value $\ell' > \ell$, we need to know whether the history of elements examined by the algorithm (in other queues) contains element $\ell'$. Such correlations make a standard step-by-step analysis extremely challenging.

We circumvent these issues by relating the original labelled process to a continuous *exponential process*, which reduces correlations by replacing integer labels with real-valued labels. In this process, on every "insertion," we insert a new label whose value equals that of the latest inserted label in that bin (or 0 for the first insertion), plus *an exponential random variable* of mean $n$. Intuitively, we wish to simulate the integer label insertion process with the same mean $n$, while removing correlations but using continuous label values to prevent label clashes and reduce correlations. Once this insertion process has ended, we replace each (real-valued) label with its *rank* among all (real-valued) labels.

We relate these two processes by the following key claim: *the rank distributions for the original process and for the exponential process are identical.* More precisely, for any queue $i$ and rank $j$, the event that, after insertion, the label with rank $j$ is located in queue $i$ has the same probability in the original process and in the exponential process (and all such events are independent in both processes).

Given this fact, we can couple the two processes as follows. We first couple the insertion steps such that each bin contains the same sequence of ranks in both processes. We then couple the removal steps so that they make exactly the same sequence of random choices. Under this coupling, the two processes will pay the same rank cost. Thus, it will suffice to characterize the rank cost of the exponential process under our removal scheme.

This is achieved via two steps. The first is a potential argument which carefully characterizes the average value of labels on top of the queues, and the maximum deviation from the average by a queue, at any time $t > 0$. This part of the proof is technical, and slightly generalizes upon an analytic approach developed for weighted balls-into-bins processes by Peres, Talwar and Wieder [29]. Specifically, if we let $x_i(t)$ be the difference between the label on top of queue $i$ at time $t$ and the mean top label across all queues, then the *total potential* of the system at time $t$ is defined as $\sum_{i=1}^{n} [\exp(\alpha x_i(t)/n) + \exp(-\alpha x_i(t)/n)]$, with $\alpha < 1$ constant.

The key claim in the argument is showing that the expected value of this potential is bounded by $O(n)$ for any step $t$. This is done by a careful technical analysis of the expected change in potential at a step, which proves that the potential has supermartingale-like behavior: that is, it tends to decrease in expectation once it surpasses the $O(n)$ threshold. It is interesting to note that neither of the two exponential factors in the definition of the potential satisfies this bounded increase property in isolation, yet their sum can be bounded in this way.

The $O(n)$ bound on the total potential provides a strong handle on the maximum deviation from the mean in the exponential process. The last step of our argument builds on this characterization to show that, since label values cannot stray too far either above or below the mean, the *ranks* of these values among all values on top of queues cannot be too large. In particular, the average rank of elements on top of queues must be $O(n)$, and the maximum rank is $O(n \log n)$. The rank equivalence theorem implies our main claim.

The analytic framework we sketched above is quite general. It can be extended to showing that this implementation strategy is robust to insertion bias, i.e. that it guarantees similar rank bounds even if the insertion process is biased (within some constant $\gamma \ll 1$) towards some of the bins. Further, it also applies to the $(1 + \beta)$ variant of the process, where each removal considers two randomly chosen queues with probability $\beta < 1$, and a single queue otherwise. Formally, the expected cost at a step becomes $O(n/\beta^2)$, and the expected maximum cost at a step is $O(n \log n/\beta)$.

**Applications.** The process considered above is sequential, and has FIFO semantics, since we are inserting labels in strictly increasing order, and assumes that all labels are inserted initially. We discuss sufficient conditions for extending the analysis to concurrent and general priority insertions. To validate the practicality of our results, we implemented a variant of the $(1 + \beta)$ priority queue in C++. Empirical results, given in Section 5, show that it improves upon the state-of-the-art implementation of Rihani et al. [31] by 20% in terms of throughput, while providing similar rank guarantees. Moreover, when used in Dijkstra's algorithm, $(1+\beta)$ priority queue reduces running time by 10% over the original MultiQueue, and by 40% over a deterministic implementation [36]. This suggests that the decrease in rank guarantees is well compensated by improved scalability.

## 2 RELATED WORK

The first instance of a distributed data structure implementation using a similar approach to the one we consider is probably the parallel branch-and-bound framework by Karp and Zhang [19]. In their construction, each processor is assigned a queue, and elements are inserted randomly into one of the queues. Each processor removes from its own queue. This critically relies on the synchronicity of

PRAM processors to achieve bounds on average rank and maximum rank difference. It is easy to see that processor delays can cause the rank difference to become unbounded. Quantitative relaxations of concurrent data structures have been previously formalized by Henzinger et al. [16], but only for *deterministic* relaxations.

**The MultiQueue.** The strategy we consider is based on the MultiQueue data structure of Rihani et al. [31]. They start from $n$ sequential priority queues, each of which is protected by a lock. To *insert* an element, each processor repeatedly picks a queue at random, and tries to lock it. When successful, the processor inserts the element into the queue, and unlocks it. Otherwise, the process re-tries with a new randomly chosen lock.

To *delete* an element, the algorithm samples two queues uniformly, and reads the top element from both. It then locks the queue whose top element had higher priority, removes that element, and returns it. If the algorithm failed to obtain the lock on the chosen queue, then it restarts the whole process. (They also consider variations of this strategy, which are essentially equivalent from the point of view of the sequential version.)

In the paper, the authors show via a basic balls-into-bins argument that, initially, before any elements are removed, the expected rank cost is $O(n)$, and the max cost is $O(n \log n)$ with high probability. Our argument applies to a sequential version of the concurrent process described above. Our analysis is significantly more general than theirs, since it applies to any time in the execution of the process. Variants of this approach have also been considered in other contexts, for instance for relaxed queues [14] and priority schedulers [28]. Designing efficient concurrent priority queues is a very active research area, see e.g. [3, 5, 34, 36] for recent examples, and [3] for a survey.

**Balls-into-bins Processes.** In the classic two-choice balanced allocation process, at each step, one new ball is to be inserted into one of $n$ bins; the ball is inserted into the less loaded among two random choices [4, 25]. In this setting, it is known that the most loaded bin is at most $O(\log \log n)$ above the average. The literature studying extensions of this process is extremely vast; we direct the reader to [30] for a survey. Considerable effort has been dedicated to understanding guarantees in the "heavily-loaded" case, where the number of insertion steps is unbounded [6, 29], and in the "weighted" case, in which ball weights come from a probability distribution [7, 35]. In a tour-de-force, Peres, Talwar, and Wieder [29] gave a potential argument characterizing a general form of the heavily-loaded, weighted process on some graphs. The second step in our proof, which characterizes the deviation of weights from the mean in the exponential process, builds on their approach. Specifically, we use a similar potential function, and the parts of the analysis are similar. However, we generalize their approach to the case of biased insert distributions, and our argument diverges in a few technical points: in particular, the potential analysis under unbalanced conditions is different. The first and third steps of our argument are new, as we consider a more complex *labelled* allocation process.

# 3 PROCESS DEFINITION

We are given with $n$ priority queues, labeled $1, \ldots, n$, into which a large, potentially infinite number $M \gg n$ of labelled balls is inserted. To insert, we choose queue $i$ with probability $\pi_i \in (0, 1)$, and insert into that queue. We assume that $\sum_{i=1}^{n} \pi_i = 1$, and that the bias is bounded, i.e. there exists a constant $\gamma \in (0, 1)$ such that, for any queue $i$, $1-\gamma \leq \frac{1}{n\pi_i} \leq 1+\gamma$. To remove, with probability $0 < \beta \leq 1$, we pick two queues u.a.r., and remove the element of minimum label among the two choices, and with probability $(1 - \beta)$ remove from a random queue. We call such a process a $(1 + \beta)$-sequential process. We omit $\beta$ when unimportant or clear from context.

At any point in the execution, we define the *rank* of any element to be the number of elements currently in the system which have lower label than it (including itself), so the minimal rank is 1. Our goal is to show that the ranks of the elements returned by the random process are small, throughout the entire execution. We will restrict our attention to executions which never inspect empty queues, and no priority inversions on inserts are visible to the removal process. Formally:

*Definition 3.1.* An execution of the sequential process is *prefixed* if except with negligible probability (i.e. probability less than $n^{-\omega(1)}$), the sequential process never inspects an empty queue in a remove, and no remove sees an insert with lower priority than one that is inserted later in the same queue.

There are many natural types of executions which are prefixed. For instance, a common strategy in practice is to insert a large enough "buffer" of elements initially, so as to minimize the likelihood of examining empty queues. More formally, since in each iteration we touch a queue with probability at most $\frac{2}{n} + O(\frac{1}{n^2})$ and only remove one element at a time, by Bernstein's inequality, any execution of length $T$ whose first $T/2 + \sqrt{n \cdot \omega(\log n)}$ operations are inserts, and which contains no inserts after this time, or which only inserts larger labels after this point, will be prefixed.

For the rest of the paper, we will tacitly assume that no remove inspects any empty queue in the sequential process, and that no priority inversions are visible to the removal process, and condition on the event that this does not happen. By Markov's inequality, as long as we only consider prefixed executions, then for any sequence of operations of length poly$(n)$, this will change the max rank or average rank of the operations by at most a subconstant factor.

# 4 ANALYSIS OF THE SEQUENTIAL PROCESS

The goal of this section is to prove the following theorem, whose proof follows by combining Corollary 4.14 and Corollary 4.19.

THEOREM 4.1. *Fix a bias bound $\gamma \ll 1$. In any prefixed $(1 + \beta)$ sequential process, with $\beta = \Omega(\gamma)$ and $M \geq n$, the following holds: for any time $t > 0$, the max rank of any element on top of a queue at time $t$ is at most $O(\frac{1}{\beta}(n \log n + n \log \frac{1}{\beta}))$, and the average rank at time $t$ is at most $O(n/\beta^2)$.*

**The Exponential Process.** For the purposes of analysis, it is useful to consider an alternative process, which we will call the *exponential process*, in which each bin independently generates real-valued labels by starting from 0, and adding an exponentially-distributed random variable with parameter $\lambda_i = 1/\pi_i$ to its previous label. More precisely, if $w_i(t)$ is the label present on top of bin $i$ at time $t$, then the value of the next label is $w_i(t + 1) = w_i(t) + \exp(1/\pi_i)$. Once we have enqueued all the items we wanted to enqueue, we proceed to remove items by the two-choice rule: we always pick the element of minimum rank (label value) among two random choices. At any step, and for any $v \in \mathbb{R}$, we define rank($v$) to be the number of elements currently in the system with label at most $v$. At each step, we pay a cost equal to the rank of the element we just removed.

**Proof Strategy.** The argument proceeds in three steps. First, we show that, after all insertion steps have been performed, the rank distribution of the exponential process is *the same* as the rank distribution of the original process (Section 4.1). With this in place, we will perform the following coupling between the two processes:

Given an arbitrary number $M$ of balls to be inserted into the $n$ bins, we first generate $M$ total weights across the $n$ queues in the exponential process, so that each bin has exactly the same number of elements in both processes. We then replace each (real-valued) generated weight with its *rank* among all weights in the system. As we will see, for any rank $j$ and queue $i$, the probability that the ball with rank $j$ is in bin $i$ is exactly the same as in the simple process, where queue $i$ has probability of insertion $\pi_i$. More precisely, if we fix an increasing sequence of ranks $r_1, r_2, \ldots$, the probability that bin $i$ contains this exact sequence of ranks is the same across the two processes. Hence, we can couple the two processes to generate the same sequence of ranks in each bin.

For the removal step, we couple the two processes such that, in every step, they generate exactly the same $\beta$ values and random choice indices. Since the ranks are the same, and the choices are the same, the two processes will remove from exactly the same bins at each step, and will pay the same rank cost in every step.

Hence, it will suffice to bound the expected rank cost paid at a step in the exponential process. Since this is difficult to do directly, we will first aim to characterize the *concentration* of the difference between the weight (value) on top of each bin and the average weight on top of bins, via a potential argument (Section 4.2). This will show that relatively few values can stray far from the mean. In turn, this will imply a bound on the average rank removed (Section 4.4). In the following, we use the terms "queue" and "bin" interchangeably.

## 4.1 Equivalence between Rank Distributions

Let $\pi_i$ be the probability that a ball is inserted into bin $i$. This section will be dedicated to showing that the distribution of ranks in the exponential process where bin $i$ gets weights exponentially distributed with mean $1/\pi_i$ is identical to the distribution of labels in the original process, where the $i$th bin is chosen for insertion with probability $\pi_i$.

THEOREM 4.2. *Let $I_{j \leftarrow i}$ be the event that the label with rank $i$ is located in bin $j$, in either process. Let $\Pr_e[I_{j \leftarrow i}]$ be its probability in the exponential process, and $\Pr_o[I_{j \leftarrow i}]$ be its probability in the original process. Then for both processes $I_{j \leftarrow i}$ is independent from $I_{j' \leftarrow i'}$ for all $i \neq i'$ and*

$$\Pr_e[I_{j \leftarrow i}] = \Pr_o[I_{j \leftarrow i}] = \pi_j.$$

PROOF. That $\Pr_o[I_{j \leftarrow i}] = \pi_j$ and that $I_{j \leftarrow i}, I_{j' \leftarrow i'}$ are independent for $i \neq i'$ in the original process both follow immediately by the construction of the sequential process.

We now require some notation. Let $\ell(i)$ be the label with rank $i$ in the exponential process, and let $b(i)$ be the bin containing $\ell(i)$.

We will employ the following *memoryless* property of exponential random variables:

FACT 1. *Let $X \sim \text{Exp}(r)$. Then, for all $s, t \geq 0$, we have* $\Pr[X > s + t] = \Pr[X > s] \Pr[X > t]$.

Fix an arbitrary $i \geq 1$, and let $L = \ell(i-1)$ be the label of the $(i-1)$th element. For each bin $i$, we isolate the two consecutive weights between which $L$ can be ordered. More precisely, for each bin $1 \leq j \leq n$, denote the smallest label *larger* than $L$ in bin $j$ by $\ell_{j,>L}$ and let the largest label in $B_j$ *smaller* than $L$ be $\ell_{j,<L}$. By construction of the exponential process, $\ell_{j,>L} = \ell_{j,<L} + X_j$ where $X_j$ is an exponentially distributed random variable with mean $1/\pi_j$. Furthermore, by assumption we have that $\ell_{j,>L} > L$, so $X_j > L - \ell_{j,<L}$. Then by memoryless-ness, $\forall s \geq 0$,

$$\begin{aligned}\Pr[\ell_{j,>L} > \ell_{j,<L} + s | \ell_{j,>L} > L] &= \Pr[X_j > s | X_j > (L - \ell_{j,<L})] \\ &= \Pr[X_j > s - (L - \ell_{j,<L}].\end{aligned}$$

Let $\Delta_j = \ell_{j,>L} - L$, observing by the above that $\Delta_j$ is distributed exponentially with mean $1/\pi_j$. Furthermore, since the $X_j$ are independent, the $\Delta_j$ are independent as well. Consider the event that $\ell_{j,>L}$ is the smallest label larger than $L$ in the system; that is $\ell(i) = \ell_{j,>L}$ and $b(i) = j$. This occurs if $\Delta_j < \Delta'_j$ for all $j' \neq j$, i.e. if $\Delta_j$ is the smallest such value among all bins. In turn, this occurs with probability

$$\begin{aligned}&\int_0^\infty \Pr[\Delta_j = t] \Pi_{k \neq j} \Pr[\Delta_k > t] dt = \\ &= \int_0^\infty \pi_j \exp\left(-t\pi_j\right) \Pi_{k \neq j} \exp\left(-t\pi_k\right) dt = \\ &= \pi_j \int_0^\infty \exp\left(-t \sum_{k=1}^n \pi_k\right) dt = \pi_j.\end{aligned}$$

□

## 4.2 Analysis of the Exponential Process

In the previous section, we have shown that the rank distributions are the same at the end of the insert process. The coupling described in Section 4, by which we inspect the same queues in each removal steps, implies that two processes will produce the same cost in terms of average rank removed. Hence, we focus on bounding the *rank* of the labels removed from the exponential process at each step $t$. Our strategy will be to first bound the deviation of the *weight* (top label) on top of each queue from the average, at every step $t$, and then re-interpret the deviation in terms of *rank cost.*

**Notation.** From this point on, we will assume for simplicity that, at the beginning of each step, queues are always ranked in *increasing order of their top label.* If $p_i$ is the probability that we pick the $i$th ranked bin for a removal, and $\beta$ is the two-choice probability, then it is easy to see that the $(1 + \beta)$ process guarantees that

$$p_i = (1-\beta)\frac{1}{n} + \beta\left[\frac{2}{n}\left(1 - \frac{i-1}{n}\right) - \frac{1}{n^2}\right].$$

Further, notice that, for any $1 \leq m \leq n$, we have, ignoring a negligible $O(1/n^2)$ factor, that

$$\sum_{i=1}^m p_i \simeq \frac{m}{n}\left(1 + \beta - \frac{m}{n}\beta\right).$$

For any bin $j$ and time $t$, let $w_j(t)$ be the label on top of bin $j$ at time $t$, and let $x_j(t) = w_j(t)/n$ be the normalized label. Let $\mu(t) = \sum_{j=1}^{n} x_j(t)/n$ be the average normalized label at time $t$ over the bins. Let $y_i(t) = x_i(t) - \mu(t)$, and let $\alpha < 1$ be a parameter we will fix later. Define

$$\Phi(t) = \sum_{j=1}^{n} \exp(\alpha y_i(t)), \text{ and } \Psi(t) = \sum_{j=1}^{n} \exp(-\alpha y_i(t)).$$

Finally, define the potential function

$$\Gamma(t) = \Phi(t) + \Psi(t).$$

**Parameters and Constants.** Define $\epsilon = \frac{\beta}{16}$. Recall that the parameter $\gamma > 0$ is such that, for every $1 \le i \le n$, $\frac{1}{n\pi_i} \in [1-\gamma, 1+\gamma]$. Next, let $c \ge 2$ be a constant, and $\delta$ be a parameter such that

$$1 + \delta = \frac{1 + \gamma + c\alpha(1+\gamma)^2}{1 - \gamma - c\alpha(1+\gamma)^2}. \tag{1}$$

In the following, we assume that the parameters $\alpha$, $\beta$, and $\gamma$ satisfy the inequality

$$\frac{\beta}{16} = \epsilon \ge \delta. \tag{2}$$

We assume that the insertion bias $\gamma \le 1/2$ is small, and hence this is satisfied by setting $\beta = \Omega(\gamma)$ and $\alpha = \Theta(\beta)$.
The rest of this section is dedicated to the proof of this following claim. Due to space constraints, we present a detailed sketch of this argument, and leave the complete proof to the full version of our paper.

THEOREM 4.3. *Let $\vec{p} = (p_1, p_2, \ldots, p_n)$ be the vector of probabilities, sorted in increasing order. Let $\epsilon = \beta/16$, and $c \ge 2$ be a small constant. Let $\alpha, \beta, \gamma, \delta$ be parameters as given above, such that $\epsilon \ge \delta$. Then there exists a constant $C(\epsilon) = \text{poly}(\frac{1}{\epsilon})$ such that, for any time $t \ge 0$, we have $\mathbb{E}[\Gamma(t)] \le C(\epsilon)n$.*

**Potential Argument Overview.** The argument proceeds as follows. We will begin by bounding the change of each potential function $\Psi$ and $\Phi$, at each queue in a step (Lemmas 4.4 and 4.5). We then use these bounds to show that, if not too many queues have weights above or below the mean ($y_{n/4} \le 0$ and $y_{3n/4} \ge 0$), then $\Phi$ and $\Psi$ respectively decrease in expectation (Lemmas 4.6 and 4.7). Unfortunately, this does not necessarily hold in general configurations. However, we are able to show the following claim: if the configuration is unbalanced (e.g. $y_{n/4} > 0$ ) and $\Phi$ does not decrease in expectation at a step, then either the symmetric potential $\Psi$ is large, and will decrease on average, or the global potential function $\Gamma$ must be in $O(n)$ (Lemma 4.8). We will prove a similar claim for $\Psi$. Putting everything together, we get that the global potential function $\Gamma$ always decreases in expectation once it exceeds the $O(n)$ threshold, which implies Theorem 4.3.

**Potential Change at Each Step.** We begin by analyzing the expected change in potential for each queue from step to step. We first look at the change in the weight vector $\vec{y} = (y_1, y_2, \ldots, y_n)$. (Recall that we always re-order the queues in increasing order of weight at the beginning of each step.) Below, let $\kappa_j$ be the cost increase if the bin of rank $j$ is chosen, which is an exponential random variable with mean $1/\pi_j$. We have that, for every rank $i$,

$$y_i(t+1) = \begin{cases} y_i(t) + \kappa_i(1 - 1/n), & \text{with probability } p_i; \text{ and} \\ y_i(t) - \frac{\kappa_j}{n}, & \text{if some other bin } j \neq i \text{ is chosen.} \end{cases}$$

**The Change in $\Phi$ at a Step.** We prove the following bound on the expected increase in $\Phi$ at a step.

LEMMA 4.4. *For any time $t$, we have that*

$$\mathbb{E}[\Delta\Phi \mid y(t)] \le \sum_{i=1}^{n} \hat{\alpha}\left((1+\delta)p_i - \frac{1}{n}\right)\exp(\alpha y_i(t)).$$

PROOF. Let $\Phi_i(t) = \exp(\alpha y_i(t))$. We have two cases. If the bin is chosen for removal, then the change is:

$$\begin{aligned} \Delta\Phi_i &:= \Phi_i(t+1) - \Phi_i(t) = \\ &= \exp\left(\frac{\alpha}{n}\left(y_i(t) + \kappa_i\left(1 - \frac{1}{n}\right)\right)\right) - \exp\left(\frac{\alpha}{n}y_i(t)\right) = \\ &= \exp\left(\frac{\alpha}{n}y_i(t)\right)\left(\exp\left(\frac{\alpha}{n}\kappa_i\left(1 - \frac{1}{n}\right)\right) - 1\right). \end{aligned}$$

Taking expectations with respect to the random choices made on insertion, that is, the value of $\kappa_j$, we have

$$\mathop{\mathbb{E}}_i\left[\exp\left(\kappa_i\frac{\alpha}{n}\left(1 - \frac{1}{n}\right)\right)\right] \overset{(a)}{=} \frac{\pi_i}{\pi_i - \left(\frac{\alpha}{n}(1 - \frac{1}{n})\right)} = \frac{1}{1 - \frac{\alpha}{\pi_i n}\left(1 - \frac{1}{n}\right)} \overset{(b)}{\le} 1 + \frac{\alpha}{\pi_i n}\left(1 - \frac{1}{n}\right) + c\left(\frac{\alpha}{\pi_i n}\left(1 - \frac{1}{n}\right)\right)^2,$$

for some constant $c > 1$. Step (a) follows from the observation that the expectation we wish to compute is the moment-generating function of the exponential distribution at $\frac{\alpha}{n}(1 - \frac{1}{n})$, while (b) follows from the Taylor expansion. (We slightly abused notation in step (a) by denoting with $\pi_i$ the insert probability for the $i$th ranked queue, according to the ranking in this step.)
The second step if if some other bin $j \neq i$ is chosen for removal, then the change is:

$$\begin{aligned} \Delta\Phi_i &= \exp\left(\frac{\alpha}{n}(y_i(t) - \kappa_j\frac{1}{n})\right) - \exp\left(\frac{\alpha}{n}y_i(t)\right) = \\ &= \exp\left(\frac{\alpha}{n}y_i(t)\right)\left(\exp\left(-\frac{\alpha\kappa_j}{n^2}\right) - 1\right). \end{aligned}$$

Again taking expectations with respect to the random choices made on insertion, i.e. the value of $\kappa_j$, we have

$$\mathop{\mathbb{E}}_i\left[\exp\left(-\kappa_j\frac{\alpha}{n^2}\right)\right] = \frac{\pi_j}{\pi_j + \frac{\alpha}{n^2}} = \frac{1}{1 + \frac{\alpha}{\pi_j n^2}} \le 1 - \frac{\alpha}{\pi_j n^2} + \left(\frac{\alpha}{\pi_j n^2}\right)^2 - \ldots \le 1 - \frac{\alpha}{\pi_j n^2} + \left(\frac{\alpha}{\pi_j n^2}\right)^2.$$

Therefore, we have that

$$\mathbb{E}[\Delta\Phi_i]/\Phi_i(t) \leq \left(1 + \frac{\alpha}{\pi_i n}\left(1-\frac{1}{n}\right) + c\left(\frac{\alpha}{\pi_i n}\left(1-\frac{1}{n}\right)\right)^2\right)p_i + \sum_{j\neq i}\left(1 - \frac{\alpha}{\pi_j n^2} + \left(\frac{\alpha}{\pi_j n^2}\right)^2\right)p_j - 1 \leq$$

$$\left(\frac{\alpha}{\pi_i n} + c\left(\frac{\alpha}{\pi_i n}\right)^2\right)p_i - \sum_{j=1}^{n}\left(\frac{\alpha}{\pi_j n^2} - c\left(\frac{\alpha}{\pi_j n^2}\right)^2\right)p_j \leq$$

$$\left(1+\gamma+c\alpha(1+\gamma)^2\right)\alpha p_i - \frac{\alpha}{n}\sum_{j=1}^{n}\left(1-\gamma-c\alpha(1+\gamma)^2\right)p_j.$$

If we denote for convenience

$$\hat{\alpha} = \alpha\left(1-\gamma-c\alpha(1+\gamma)^2\right),$$

and recall that

$$\delta := \frac{1+\gamma+c\alpha(1+\gamma)^2}{1-\gamma-c\alpha(1+\gamma)^2} - 1,$$

then we can rewrite this as

$$\mathbb{E}[\Delta\Phi \mid y(t)] \leq \sum_{i=1}^{n}\hat{\alpha}\left(p_i(1+\delta) - \frac{1}{n}\right)\Phi_i(t).$$

□

**The Change in $\Psi$.** Using a symmetric argument, we can prove the following about the expected change in $\Psi$.

Lemma 4.5. *For any time t,*

$$\mathbb{E}[\Delta\Psi \mid y(t)] \leq \sum_{i=1}^{n}\hat{\alpha}\left((1+\delta)\frac{1}{n} - p_i\right)\exp(-\alpha y_i(t)).$$

**Bounds under Balanced Conditions.** Let us briefly stop to examine the bounds in the above Lemmas. The terms $\left(p_i(1+\delta) - \frac{1}{n}\right)$ are *decreasing* in $i$, and in fact become *negative* as $i$ increases. (The exact index where this occurs is controlled by $\beta$ and $\delta$.) The $\exp(\alpha y_i(t))$ terms are *increasing* in $i$. Bins whose weight is *below* the mean (i.e., $y_i(t) \leq 0$) have a negligible effect on $\Phi$, since each of their contributions is at most 1. At the same time, notice that the contribution of bins of large index $i$ will be negative. Hence, we can show that, if at least $n/4$ bins have weights below average, then the value of $\Phi$ tends to *decrease* on average.

Lemma 4.6. *If $y_{n/4} \leq 0$, then we have that*

$$\mathbb{E}[\Phi(t+1) \mid y(t)] \leq \left(1 - \frac{\hat{\alpha}\epsilon}{3n}\right)\Phi(t) + 1.$$

A similar claim holds for $\Psi$, under the condition that there are at least $n/4$ bins with weight *larger* than average.

Lemma 4.7. *If $y_{3n/4} \geq 0$, then we have that*

$$\mathbb{E}[\Psi(t+1) \mid y(t)] \leq \left(1 - \tfrac{\hat{\alpha}\epsilon}{3n}\right)\Psi + 1.$$

**Bounds under Unbalanced Conditions.** We now analyze unbalanced configurations, where there are either many bins whose weights are above average (e.g., $y_{n/4} > 0$), or below average ($y_{3n/4} < 0$). The rationale we used to bound each potential function independently no longer applies. In particular, as shown in [29], we can have unbalanced settings where for example $\Phi$ does not decrease in expectation. However, we can show that, one of two things must hold: either the other potential $\Psi$ is *larger* and *does decrease* in expectation, or the global potential $\Gamma$ is in $O(n)$.

Lemma 4.8. *Given $\epsilon$ as above, assume that $y_{n/4}(t) > 0$, and $\mathbb{E}[\Delta\Phi] \geq -\frac{\epsilon\hat{\alpha}}{3n}\Phi(t)$. Then either $\Phi < \frac{\epsilon}{4}\Psi$ or $\Gamma = O(n)$.*

Proof. Fix $\lambda = 2/3 - 1/54$ for the rest of the proof. We can split the inequality in Lemma 4.4 as follows:

$$\mathbb{E}[\Delta\Phi \mid y(t)] \leq \sum_{i=1}^{\lambda n}\hat{\alpha}\left((1+\delta)p_i - \frac{1}{n}\right)\exp(\alpha y_i(t)) + \tag{3}$$

$$\sum_{i=\lambda n+1}^{n}\hat{\alpha}\left((1+\delta)p_i - \frac{1}{n}\right)\exp(\alpha y_i(t)). \tag{4}$$

We bound each term separately. Since the probability terms are non-increasing and the exponential terms are non-decreasing, the first term is maximized when all $p_i$ terms are equal. Since these probabilities are at most 1, we have

$$\sum_{i=1}^{\lambda n}\hat{\alpha}\left((1+\delta)p_i - \frac{1}{n}\right)\exp(\alpha y_i(t)) \leq \frac{\hat{\alpha}}{n}\left((1+\delta)\frac{1}{\lambda} - 1\right)\Phi_{\leq\lambda n}. \tag{5}$$

The second term is maximized by noticing that the $p_i$ factors are non-increasing, and are thus dominated by their value at $\lambda n$. Noticing that we carefully picked $\lambda$ such that

$$p_{\lambda n} \leq \frac{1}{n} - \frac{4\epsilon}{n},$$

we obtain, using the assumed inequality $\delta \leq \epsilon$, that

$$\sum_{i=\lambda n+1}^{n}\hat{\alpha}\left((1+\delta)p_i - \frac{1}{n}\right)\exp(\alpha y_i(t)) \leq \tag{6}$$

$$\hat{\alpha}(\delta - 4\epsilon)\frac{\Phi_{>\lambda n}}{n} \leq -\frac{3\epsilon\hat{\alpha}}{n}\Phi_{>\lambda n}. \tag{7}$$

By the case assumption, we know that $\mathbb{E}[\Delta\Phi \mid y(t)] \geq -\frac{\hat{\alpha}\epsilon}{3n}\Phi(t)$. Combining the bounds yields:

$$\frac{\hat{\alpha}}{n}\left((1+\delta)\frac{1}{\lambda} - 1\right)\Phi_{\leq\lambda n} - \frac{3\epsilon\hat{\alpha}}{n}\Phi_{>\lambda n} \geq -\frac{\hat{\alpha}\epsilon}{3n}\Phi(t).$$

Substituting $\Phi_{>\lambda n} = \Phi - \Phi_{\leq\lambda n}$ yields:

$$(3\epsilon - \epsilon/3)\Phi \leq \left((1+\delta)\frac{1}{\lambda} - 1 + 3\epsilon\right)\Phi_{\leq\lambda n}.$$

For simplicity, we fix $C(\epsilon) = \frac{(1+\delta)\frac{1}{\lambda}-1+3\epsilon}{3\epsilon-\epsilon/3} = O\left(\frac{1}{\epsilon}\right)$, to obtain

$$\Phi \leq C(\epsilon)\Phi_{\leq\lambda n}. \tag{8}$$

Let $B = \sum_{y_i>0} y_i$. Since we are normalizing by the mean, it also holds that $B = \sum_{y_i<0}(-y_i)$. Notice that

$$\Phi_{\leq\lambda n} \overset{y_i\,\text{incr.}}{\leq} \lambda n\exp(\alpha y_{\lambda n}) \overset{y_i\,\text{incr.}}{\leq} \lambda n\exp\left(\frac{\alpha B}{(1-\lambda)n}\right). \tag{9}$$

We put inequalities (8) and (9) together and get

$$\Phi(t) \leq \lambda n C(\epsilon)\exp\left(\tfrac{\alpha B}{(1-\lambda)n}\right), \tag{10}$$

Let us now lower bound the value of $\Psi$ under these conditions. Since $y_{n/4} > 0$, all the costs below average must be in the first quarter of $y$. We can apply Jensen's inequality to the first $n/4$ terms of $\Psi$ to get that

$$\Psi \geq \sum_{i=1}^{n/4} \exp(-\alpha y_i) \geq \frac{n}{4} \exp\left(-\alpha \frac{\sum_{i=1}^{n/4} y_i}{n/4}\right).$$

We now split the sum $\sum_{i=1}^{n/4} y_i$ into its positive part and its negative part. We know that the negative part is summing up to exactly $-B$, as it contains all the negative $y_i$'s and the total sum is 0. The positive part can be of size at most $B/4$, since it is maximized when there are exactly $n-1$ positive costs and they are all equal. Hence the sum of the first $n/4$ elements is at least $-3B/4$, which implies that the following bound holds:

$$\Psi \geq \frac{n}{4} \exp\left(-\alpha \frac{-3B/4}{n/4}\right) \geq \frac{n}{4} \exp\left(\alpha \frac{3B}{n}\right). \tag{11}$$

If $\Phi < \frac{\epsilon}{4}\Psi$, then there is nothing to prove. Otherwise, if $\Phi \geq \frac{\epsilon}{4}\Psi$, we get from (11) and (10) that

$$\frac{\epsilon}{4}\frac{n}{4} \exp\left(\alpha \frac{3B}{n}\right) \leq \frac{\epsilon}{4}\Psi \leq \Phi(t) \leq \lambda n C(\epsilon) \exp\left(\frac{\alpha B}{(1-\lambda)n}\right),$$

Therefore, we get that:

$$\exp\left(\alpha \frac{B}{n}\left(3 - \frac{1}{1-\lambda}\right)\right) \leq \frac{4\lambda}{\epsilon} C(\epsilon) = O\left(\frac{1}{\epsilon^2}\right).$$

Using the mundane fact that $3 - \frac{1}{1-\lambda} = 3/19$, we get that

$$\exp\left(\frac{\alpha B}{n}\right) \leq O\left(\frac{1}{\epsilon^{14}}\right). \tag{12}$$

To conclude, notice that (12) implies we can upper bound $\Gamma$ in this case as:

$$\Gamma = \Phi + \Psi \leq \frac{4+\epsilon}{\epsilon}\Phi \leq \frac{4+\epsilon}{\epsilon}\lambda n C(\epsilon) \exp\left(\frac{\alpha B}{(1-\lambda)n}\right) \leq$$
$$O\left(\frac{1}{\epsilon^{14/(1-\lambda)}}\right) \frac{4+\epsilon}{\epsilon} C(\epsilon)\lambda n = O(\text{poly}\left(\frac{1}{\epsilon}\right) n).$$

□

We can prove a symmetric claim for $\Psi$ by a slightly different argument.

Lemma 4.9. *Given $\epsilon$ as above, assume that $y_{\frac{3n}{4}} < 0$, and that $\mathbb{E}[\Delta\Psi] \geq -\frac{\hat{\alpha}\epsilon}{3n}\Psi$. Then either $\Psi < \frac{\epsilon}{4}\Phi$ or $\Gamma = O(n)$.*

**Endgame.** We now finally have the required machinery to prove that $\Gamma$ satisfies a supermartingale property:

Lemma 4.10. *There exists a constant $\epsilon$ such that*

$$\mathbb{E}[\Gamma(t+1)|y(t)] \leq \left(1 - \frac{\hat{\alpha}\epsilon}{4n}\right)\Gamma(t) + C,$$

*where $C$ is a constant in $O\left(\text{poly}\left(\frac{1}{\epsilon}\right)\right)$.*

Proof. **Case 1:** If $y_{n/4} \leq 0$ and $y_{3n/4} \geq 0$, then the property follows by putting together Lemmas 4.6 and 4.7.

**Case 2:** If $y_{3n/4} \geq y_{n/4} \geq 0$. This means that the weight vector is unbalanced, in particular that there are few bins of low cost, and many bins of high cost. However, we can show that the expected decrease in $\Psi$ can compensate this decrease, and the inequality still holds. Notice that Lemmas 4.4 and 4.5 imply that $\mathbb{E}[\Delta\Phi] \leq \frac{\hat{\alpha}\delta}{n}\Phi(t)$ and $\mathbb{E}[\Delta\Psi] \leq \frac{\hat{\alpha}\delta}{n}\Psi(t)$, respectively.

If $\mathbb{E}[\Delta\Phi] \leq -\frac{\epsilon\hat{\alpha}}{4n}\Phi(t)$, then the claim follows by putting this bound together with Lemma 4.7. Otherwise, if $\mathbb{E}[\Delta\Phi] \geq -\frac{\epsilon\hat{\alpha}}{4n}\Phi(t)$, we obtain from Lemma 4.8 that either $\Phi < \frac{\epsilon}{4}\Psi$ or $\Gamma = O(n)$. In the first sub-case, we have that

$$\mathbb{E}[\Delta\Gamma] = \mathbb{E}[\Delta\Phi] + \mathbb{E}[\Delta\Psi] \leq$$
$$\frac{\hat{\alpha}\delta}{n}\Phi(t) + 1 - \frac{\hat{\alpha}\epsilon}{3n}\Psi(t) \leq \quad -\frac{\hat{\alpha}\epsilon}{3n}\Psi(t) + 1 + \frac{\epsilon\delta\hat{\alpha}}{4n}\Psi(t) \leq$$
$$-\frac{\hat{\alpha}\epsilon}{3n}\left(1 - \frac{3\delta}{4}\right)\Psi(t) + 1 \leq \quad -\frac{\hat{\alpha}}{3n}\frac{1-\frac{3\delta}{4}}{1+\frac{\epsilon}{4}}\Gamma(t) \leq -\frac{\hat{\alpha}}{4n}\Gamma(t),$$

as claimed.

In the second sub-case, we know that $\Gamma \leq Cn$, for some constant $C$. Hence, we can get that

$$\mathbb{E}[\Delta\Gamma] = \mathbb{E}[\Delta\Phi] + \mathbb{E}[\Delta\Psi] \overset{(a)}{\leq} \frac{\hat{\alpha}\delta}{n}\Gamma \overset{\Gamma=O(n)}{\leq} 2C\hat{\alpha},$$

where in step (a) we used the upper bounds in Lemmas 4.4 and 4.5, respectively. On the other hand,

$$C - \frac{\hat{\alpha}\epsilon}{4n}\Gamma(t) \geq C - \frac{\hat{\alpha}\epsilon}{4n}Cn = C\left(1 - \frac{\hat{\alpha}\epsilon}{4}\right) \geq 3C\hat{\alpha} \geq \mathbb{E}[\Delta\Gamma].$$

**Case 3:** If $y_{n/4} \leq y_{3n/4} < 0$. This case is symmetric to the one above. □

The intuition behind the above bound is that $\Gamma$ will always tend to decrease once it surpasses the $\Theta(n)$ threshold. This implies a bound on the expected value of $\Gamma$, which completes the proof of Theorem 4.3.

Lemma 4.11. *For any $t \geq 0$, $\mathbb{E}[\Gamma(t)] \leq \frac{4C}{\hat{\alpha}\epsilon}n$.*

Proof. By induction. This holds for $t = 0$ by a direct computation: see Lemma 4.10 for the argument. Then, we have

$$\mathbb{E}[\Gamma(t+1)] = \mathbb{E}[\mathbb{E}[\Gamma(t+1)|\Gamma(t)]] \leq \mathbb{E}\left[\left(1 - \frac{\hat{\alpha}\epsilon}{4n}\right)\Gamma(t) + C\right] \leq$$
$$\leq \frac{4C}{\hat{\alpha}\epsilon}n\left(1 - \frac{\hat{\alpha}\epsilon}{4n}\right) + C \leq \frac{4C}{\hat{\alpha}\epsilon}n.$$

□

## 4.3 Guarantees on Max Rank

We can use the characterization of the exponential process to prove the following:

Lemma 4.12. *If $w_{\max}(t)$ is the maximum bin weight at time $t$ and $w_{\min}(t)$ is the minimum, then*

$$\mathbb{E}[w_{\max}(t) - w_{\min}(t)] = O\left(\frac{1}{\alpha}n(\log n + \log C)\right). \tag{13}$$

Proof. Let $x_{\max}(t) = w_{\max}(t)/n$ and $x_{\min}(t) = w_{\min}(t)/n$. By definition, we have $\exp(\alpha(x_{\max}(t) - \mu(t))) \leq \Gamma(t)$ and $\exp(\alpha(\mu(t) - x_{\min}(t))) \leq \Gamma(t)$. Therefore $\alpha(x_{\max}(t) - x_{\min}(t)) \leq 2\log\Gamma(t)$. Thus, we have

$$\mathbb{E}[\alpha(x_{\max}(t) - x_{\min}(t))] \leq 2\,\mathbb{E}[\log\Gamma(t)] \overset{(a)}{\leq}$$
$$2\log(\mathbb{E}[\Gamma(t)]) \overset{(b)}{=} O(\log n + \log C),$$

where (a) follows from Jensen's inequality and (b) follows from Theorem 4.3. Simplifying yields the desired claim. □

This implies the following theorem:

Theorem 4.13. *For all $t \geq 0$, we have*

$$\mathbb{E}[\max \text{rank}(t)] = O\left(\frac{1}{\alpha}n(\log n + \log C)\right).$$

By plugging in constants as in (1) and (2), we get:

Corollary 4.14. *For all $t \geq 0$, and any $\beta = \Omega(\gamma)$, we have* $\mathbb{E}[\max \text{rank}(t)] = O\left(\frac{1}{\beta}n(\log n + \log 1/\beta)\right)$.

## 4.4 Guarantees on Average Rank

We now focus on at the rank cost paid in a step by the algorithm. Let $A = \log C/\alpha$. For real values $s \geq 0$, we "stripe" the bins according to their top value, denoting by $b_{>s}(t)$ the number of bins with $w_j(t) \geq (s+A)n + \mu$ at time $t$, and let $b_{<-s}(t)$ be the number of bins with $w_j(t) \leq \mu - (s+A)n$ at time $t$. For any bin $j$ and interval $I$, we also let $\ell_{j,I}(t)$ be the number of elements in $j$ at time $t$ with label in $I$. Finally, let $p_{j,\mu}$ denote the PDF of $w_j(t)$ given $\mu_t$.

We discuss the proof strategy at a high level here. First, we use the bounds on $\Gamma$ to obtain the following bounds on the quantities defined previously:

Lemma 4.15. *For any time $t$, we have that $\mathbb{E}[b_{>s}] \leq n\exp(-\alpha s)$ and that $\mathbb{E}[b_{<-s}] \leq n\exp(-\alpha s)$.*

Proof. Recall that $\Phi(t) = \sum_{i=1}^n \exp(\alpha(x_i(t) - \mu))$ and that $\mathbb{E}[\Phi(t)] \leq Cn$. By linearity of expectation, we have

$$\mathbb{E}[\Phi(t)] \geq \mathbb{E}[b_{>s}\exp(\alpha(s+A))] = C\exp(\alpha s)\cdot\mathbb{E}[b_{>s}],$$

which implies the claim. The converse claim follows from the bound on $\Psi(t)$. □

This lemma gives us strong bounds on the tail behavior of the $w_j$. We show that this implies a bound on the average rank. We will need the following technical result.

Lemma 4.16. *For any interval $I = [a, b]$ which may depend on $\mu$, we have $\mathbb{E}[\text{rank}(b) - \text{rank}(a)|\mu] \leq n(b - a + 1)$.*

We then show a bound on the rank of $\mu$:

Lemma 4.17. *For all $t$, we have $E[\text{rank}(\mu(t))] \leq O\left((A + 1/\alpha^2)n\right)$.*

The proof of this lemma works as follows. We divide up the interval $(-\infty, \mu]$ into infinitely many intervals of constant length. We will count the number of $w_j(t)$ within each interval separately. Within each such interval, we can give a crude upper bound the number of weights that could have ever been in that interval at any point in the execution. We then use Lemma 4.15 to show that at the current time in the execution, the number of bins with elements in each interval decays exponentially as we take intervals which are further and further away from $\mu$. Summing these values up gives the desired bound. Finally, this implies:

Theorem 4.18. *For all $t$, we have*

$$\mathbb{E}\left[\frac{1}{n}\sum_{i=1}^n \text{rank}_j(t)\right] = O\left(A + \frac{1}{\alpha^2}\right)n.$$

Proof. By Lemma 4.17 and Lemma 4.16, we have that

$$\begin{aligned}\mathbb{E}[\text{rank}_j(t)|w_j(t) \leq \mu(t) + An] &\leq O\left((A + 1/\alpha^2)n\right) + (A+1)n \\ &= O\left((A + 1/\alpha^2)n\right).\end{aligned}$$

Thus, we have

$$\begin{aligned}
&\mathbb{E}\left[\sum_{i=1}^n \text{rank}_j(t)\right] \\
&= \mathbb{E}\left[\sum_{w_j(t)\leq\mu+An} \mathbb{E}[\text{rank}_j(t)|\mu] + \sum_{w_j(t)>\mu+An} \mathbb{E}[\text{rank}_j(t)|\mu]\right] \\
&= \mathbb{E}\left[\sum_{w_j(t)\leq\mu+An} \mathbb{E}[\text{rank}_j(t)|\mu] + \right. \\
&\qquad \left.\sum_{j=1}^n \sum_{w_j(t)>\mu+An} \mathbb{E}[\text{rank}_j(\mu + An) + \ell_{j,(\mu,w_j(t))}|\mu, w_j(t)]\right] \\
&\overset{(a)}{\leq} O\left(\left(A + \frac{1}{\alpha^2}\right)n^2\right) + \sum_{j=1}^n \mathbb{E}\left[\sum_{w_j(t)>\mu+An} \mathbb{E}[\ell_{j,(\mu,w_j(t))}|\mu, w_j(t)]\right] \\
&\overset{(b)}{\leq} O\left(\left(A + \frac{1}{\alpha^2}\right)n^2\right) + \sum_{j=1}^n \mathbb{E}\left[\sum_{w_j(t)>\mu+An} (w_j(t) - \mu + 1)\right] \\
&= O\left(\left(A + \frac{1}{\alpha^2}\right)n^2\right) + \\
&\qquad \sum_{j=1}^n \sum_{k=0}^\infty \mathbb{E}\left[\sum_{w_j(t)\in[\mu+(A+k)n, \mu+(A+k+1)n]} (w_j(t) - \mu + 1)\right] \\
&\leq O\left(\left(A + \frac{1}{\alpha^2}\right)n^2\right) + n\sum_{k=0}^\infty (A + k + 2)n\,\mathbb{E}[b_{>k}] \\
&\overset{(c)}{\leq} O\left(\left(A + \frac{1}{\alpha^2}\right)n^2\right) + O\left(\frac{1}{\alpha^2}n^2\right).
\end{aligned}$$

where (a) follows by Lemma 4.17, (b) follows by Lemma 4.16, and (c) follows from Lemma 4.15. Thus

$$\mathbb{E}\left[\frac{1}{n}\sum_{i=1}^n \text{rank}_j(t)\right] = O\left(A + \frac{1}{\alpha^2}\right)n$$

as claimed. □

We now show how these imply bounds for our removal processes. The actual rank choice at time $t$ is always better than a uniform choice in expectation, since it uses power of two choices. If we consider an $(1+\beta)$ process, where we only do two choices with probability $\beta = \Omega(\gamma)$, we obtain the following, by setting parameters as in (1) and (2) :

Corollary 4.19. *For all $t$, if we let $\beta = \Omega(\gamma)$, and we let $r(t)$ denote the rank of the removed element at time $t$, then*

$$\mathbb{E}[r(t)] = O\left(\left(\frac{\log C}{\alpha} + \frac{1}{\alpha^2}\right)n\right) = O\left(\frac{n}{\beta^2}\right).$$

## 5 EXPERIMENTAL RESULTS

**Setup and Methodology.** We implemented a $(1+\beta)$ priority queue based on the MultiQueue implementation from the priority queue benchmark framework of [13]. We implement the variant where, before removal, we check that the value of the minimal element we are removing is the same as the value read before the comparison. We benchmarked it against the original MultiQueue ($\beta = 1$) and the Linden-Jonsson [23] skiplist-based implementation. The MultiQueue uses efficient sequential priority queues from the boost library. Tests were performed on a recent Intel(R) Xeon(R) CPU E7-8890 (Haswell architecture), with 18 hardware threads, each running at 2.5GHz. The tests for mean rank returned use coherent timestamps to record the times when elements are returned at each thread. We use these in a post-processing step to count rank inversions. This methodology might not be 100% accurate, since the use of timestamps might change the schedule; however, we believe results should be reasonably close to the true values.

For the throughput experiments, we consider executions consisting of alternating insert and deleteMin operations, for 10 seconds. Experiment outputs are averaged over 10 trials. Removals on empty queues do not count towards throughput. Since we are interested in the regime where queues are never empty, we insert 10 million elements initially. Threads are pinned to cores, and memory allocation is affinitized. The single-source shortest paths benchmark is a version of Dijkstra's algorithm, running on a weighted, directed California road network graph [21].

**Results.** Figure 1(a) illustrates the throughput differential between the various implementations, As previously stated, the MultiQueue variants are superior to other implementations (except at very low thread counts). Of note, the variants with $\beta < 1$ improve on the standard implementation by up to 20%. Since throughput figures are not conclusive in isolation, we also benchmarked the average rank cost in Figure 1(b). (The y axis is logarithmic.) Note that the increase in average cost due to the further $\beta$ relaxation is relatively limited. Results are conformant with our analysis for $\beta \geq 0.5$. The apparent inflection point at around $\beta = 0.5$ could be explained by the $\epsilon \geq \delta$ bias assumptions breaking down after this point, or by non-trivial correlations in the actual execution which mean that our analysis no longer applies.

Finally, Figure 1(c) gives a running times for a single-source shortest path benchmark, using a parallel version of Dijkstra's algorithm. We note that the relaxed versions with $\beta < 1$ can be superior in terms of running time to the version with $\beta = 1$, by up to 10%. The version with $\beta = 0$ (not shown) is the fastest at low thread counts, but then loses performance at thread counts $\geq 8$, probably because of excessive relaxation.

## 6 DISCUSSION AND FUTURE WORK

We have provided tight rank guarantees for a practically-inspired randomized priority scheduling process. Moreover, we showed that this strategy is robust in terms of its bias and randomness requirements. Intuitively, our results show that, given biased random insertions into the queues, the preference towards lower ranks provided by the two-choice process is enough to give strong linear bounds on the average rank removed. We extended our analysis to a practical algorithm which improves on the state-of-the-art MultiQueues in Section 5.

**Tightness.** The bounds we provide for the two-choice process are asymptotically tight. To see that the $O(n)$ bound is tight, it suffices to notice that, even in a best-case scenario, the rank of the $k$th least expensive queue is at least $k$. Hence, the process has to have expected rank cost $\Omega(n)$. The tightness argument for $\Theta(n \log n)$ expected worst-case cost is more complex. In particular, it is known [29, Example 2] that the gap between the most loaded and average bin load in a weighted balls-into-bins process with weights coming from an exponential distribution of mean 1 is $\Theta(\log n)$ in expectation. That is, there exists a queue $j$ from which we have removed $\Theta(\log n)$ fewer times than the average. We can extend the argument in Section 4.4 to prove that there exist $\Theta(n)$ queues which have $\Theta(\log n)$ elements of higher label than the top element of queue $j$. This implies that the *rank cost* of queue $j$ is $\Theta(n \log n)$, as claimed. We conjecture that the dependency in $\beta$ for the expected rank bound on the $(1 + \beta)$ process can be improved to *linear*.

**Relation to Concurrent Processes.** An important question is whether we can show that the practical *concurrent* implementations provide similar bounds. This claim holds if we assume that, in the concurrent implementation, the steps comparing the two top elements of the randomly chosen queues and removing the better top element are all performed *atomically*, e.g. through hardware transactional memory. In this case, we can show that the probability distributions of ranks returned by the concurrent and sequential processes are identical, and hence our guarantees apply.

This property does not appear to hold in general for fine-grained lock-based or lock-free implementations. In particular, due to complex correlations implied by concurrent execution, our bounds might not hold for some locking strategies for subtle reasons, and it appears highly non-trivial to rigorously extend them to any particular fine-grained strategy.

In future work, we plan to examine whether variants this process can precisely model fine-grained lock-based or lock-free implementations, which would allow our bounds to be extended without additional assumptions. Our experimental results suggest that existing implementations do satisfy strong rank guarantees.

An extremely intriguing question regards the impact of using such relaxed priority queue structures in the context of existing parallel algorithms, e.g. for shortest-paths computation. In particular, it would be interesting to bound the amount of extra work caused by relaxation versus the benefits of parallelism.

Another interesting question in terms of future work is whether our results can also be extended to processes on *graphs*. More precisely, imagine we are given a strongly connected, undirected graph with $n$ vertices. In every removal step, we pick a random edge, remove the higher priority label among its endpoints, and pay the rank of this label among all labels. It is not hard to see that our analytic framework generalizes to graph families with good expansion.

## 7 ACKNOWLEDGMENTS

We would like to thank James Aspnes, Thomas Sauerwald, Nir Shavit, Milan Vojnovic, and Udi Wieder for useful discussions. Dan Alistarh and Giorgi Nadiradze were supported by the Swiss National Fund Ambizione Project PZ00P2 161375. Justin Kopinsky was supported by the NSF under grants IIS-1447786 and CCF-1563880. Jerry Li was supported by NSF CAREER Award CCF-1453261, a Google Faculty Research Award, and an NSF Fellowship.

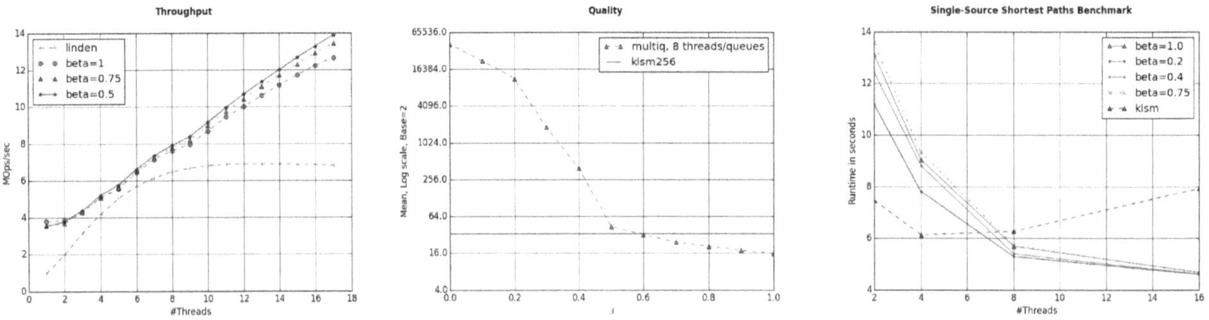


(a) Throughput comparison versus the original MultiQueues and the Linden-Jonsson implementation. Higher is better.

(b) Mean rank returned (log scale) for the $(1+\beta)$ priority queue, for various values of $\beta$ on 8 queues and 8 threads. Lower is better.

(c) Mean rank returned (log scale) for the $(1+\beta)$ priority queue, for various values of $\beta$ on 8 queues and 8 threads. Lower is better.

# REFERENCES


[1] Yehuda Afek, Haim Kaplan, Boris Korenfeld, Adam Morrison, and Robert E. Tarjan. Cbtree: A practical concurrent self-adjusting search tree. In *Proceedings of the 26th International Conference on Distributed Computing*, DISC'12, pages 1–15, Berlin, Heidelberg, 2012. Springer-Verlag.

[2] Dan Alistarh, James Aspnes, Keren Censor-Hillel, Seth Gilbert, and Rachid Guerraoui. Tight bounds for asynchronous renaming. *J. ACM*, 61(3):18:1–18:51, June 2014.

[3] Dan Alistarh, Justin Kopinsky, Jerry Li, and Nir Shavit. The spraylist: A scalable relaxed priority queue. In *20th ACM SIGPLAN Symposium on Principles and Practice of Parallel Programming*, PPoPP 2015, San Francisco, CA, USA, 2015. ACM.

[4] Yossi Azar, Andrei Z Broder, Anna R Karlin, and Eli Upfal. Balanced allocations. *SIAM journal on computing*, 29(1):180–200, 1999.

[5] Dmitry Basin, Rui Fan, Idit Keidar, Ofer Kiselov, and Dmitri Perelman. CafÉ: Scalable task pools with adjustable fairness and contention. In *Proceedings of the 25th International Conference on Distributed Computing*, DISC'11, pages 475–488, Berlin, Heidelberg, 2011. Springer-Verlag.

[6] Petra Berenbrink, Artur Czumaj, Angelika Steger, and Berthold Vöcking. Balanced allocations: The heavily loaded case. In *Proceedings of the Thirty-second Annual ACM Symposium on Theory of Computing*, STOC '00, pages 745–754, New York, NY, USA, 2000. ACM.

[7] Petra Berenbrink, Tom Friedetzky, Zengjian Hu, and Russell Martin. On weighted balls-into-bins games. *Theor. Comput. Sci.*, 409(3):511–520, December 2008.

[8] Trevor Brown, Faith Ellen, and Eric Ruppert. A general technique for non-blocking trees. *SIGPLAN Not.*, 49(8):329–342, February 2014.

[9] Faith Ellen, Danny Hendler, and Nir Shavit. On the inherent sequentiality of concurrent objects. *SIAM J. Comput.*, 41(3):519–536, 2012.

[10] Panagiota Fatourou and Nikolaos D. Kallimanis. Revisiting the combining synchronization technique. *SIGPLAN Not.*, 47(8):257–266, February 2012.

[11] Panagiota Fatourou and Nikolaos D. Kallimanis. Highly-efficient wait-free synchronization. *Theory Comput. Syst.*, 55(3):475–520, 2014.

[12] Mikhail Fomitchev and Eric Ruppert. Lock-free linked lists and skip lists. In *Proceedings of the 23rd annual ACM symposium on Principles of Distributed Computing (PODC' 04)*, pages 50–59, New York, NY, USA, 2004. ACM Press.

[13] Jakob Gruber, Jesper Larsson Träff, and Martin Wimmer. Brief announcement: Benchmarking concurrent priority queues. In *Proceedings of the 28th ACM Symposium on Parallelism in Algorithms and Architectures*, SPAA '16, pages 361–362, New York, NY, USA, 2016. ACM.

[14] Andreas Haas, Michael Lippautz, Thomas A. Henzinger, Hannes Payer, Ana Sokolova, Christoph M. Kirsch, and Ali Sezgin. Distributed queues in shared memory: multicore performance and scalability through quantitative relaxation. In *Computing Frontiers Conference, CF'13, Ischia, Italy, May 14 - 16, 2013*, pages 17:1–17:9, 2013.

[15] Tim L. Harris. A pragmatic implementation of non-blocking linked-lists. In *Proceedings of the International Conference on Distributed Computing (DISC)*, pages 300–314, 2001.

[16] Thomas A. Henzinger, Christoph M. Kirsch, Hannes Payer, Ali Sezgin, and Ana Sokolova. Quantitative relaxation of concurrent data structures. *SIGPLAN Not.*, 48(1):317–328, January 2013.

[17] Maurice Herlihy, Yossi Lev, Victor Luchangco, and Nir Shavit. A simple optimistic skiplist algorithm. In *Proceedings of the 14th international conference on Structural information and communication complexity*, SIROCCO'07, pages 124–138, Berlin, Heidelberg, 2007. Springer-Verlag. http://dl.acm.org/citation.cfm?id=1760631.1760646.

[18] Maurice Herlihy, Nir Shavit, and Moran Tzafrir. Hopscotch hashing. In *Proceedings of the 22nd international symposium on Distributed Computing*, DISC '08, pages 350–364, Berlin, Heidelberg, 2008. Springer-Verlag. http://dl.acm.org/citation.cfm?id=1432316.

[19] R. M. Karp and Y. Zhang. Parallel algorithms for backtrack search and branch-and-bound. *Journal of the ACM*, 40(3):765–789, 1993.

[20] Doug Lea, 2007. http://java.sun.com/javase/6/docs/api/java/util/concurrent/ConcurrentSkipListMap.html.

[21] Jure Leskovec and Andrej Krevl. SNAP Datasets: Stanford large network dataset collection. http://snap.stanford.edu/data, June 2014.

[22] Justin J Levandoski, David B Lomet, and Sudipta Sengupta. The bw-tree: A b-tree for new hardware platforms. In *Data Engineering (ICDE), 2013 IEEE 29th International Conference on*, pages 302–313. IEEE, 2013.

[23] Jonatan Lindén and Bengt Jonsson. A skiplist-based concurrent priority queue with minimal memory contention. In *International Conference On Principles Of Distributed Systems*, pages 206–220. Springer, 2013.

[24] Maged M Michael. High performance dynamic lock-free hash tables and list-based sets. In *Proceedings of the fourteenth annual ACM symposium on Parallel algorithms and architectures*, pages 73–82. ACM, 2002.

[25] Michael Mitzenmacher. The power of two choices in randomized load balancing. *IEEE Transactions on Parallel and Distributed Systems*, 12(10):1094–1104, 2001.

[26] Adam Morrison. Scaling synchronization in multicore programs. *Commun. ACM*, 59(11):44–51, October 2016.

[27] Adam Morrison and Yehuda Afek. Fast concurrent queues for x86 processors. *SIGPLAN Not.*, 48(8):103–112, February 2013.

[28] Donald Nguyen, Andrew Lenharth, and Keshav Pingali. A lightweight infrastructure for graph analytics. In *Proceedings of the Twenty-Fourth ACM Symposium on Operating Systems Principles*, SOSP '13, pages 456–471, New York, NY, USA, 2013. ACM.

[29] Yuval Peres, Kunal Talwar, and Udi Wieder. Graphical balanced allocations and the 1 + beta-choice process. *Random Struct. Algorithms*, 47(4):760–775, December 2015.

[30] Andrea W Richa, M Mitzenmacher, and R Sitaraman. The power of two random choices: A survey of techniques and results. *Combinatorial Optimization*, 9:255–304, 2001.

[31] Hamza Rihani, Peter Sanders, and Roman Dementiev. Brief announcement: Multiqueues: Simple relaxed concurrent priority queues. In *Proceedings of the 27th ACM Symposium on Parallelism in Algorithms and Architectures*, SPAA '15, pages 80–82, New York, NY, USA, 2015. ACM.

[32] P. Sanders. Randomized priority queues for fast parallel access. *Journal Parallel and Distributed Computing, Special Issue on Parallel and Distributed Data Structures*, 49:86–97, 1998.

[33] Nir Shavit. Data structures in the multicore age. *Commun. ACM*, 54(3):76–84, 2011.

[34] Nir Shavit and Itay Lotan. Skiplist-based concurrent priority queues. In *Parallel and Distributed Processing Symposium, 2000. IPDPS 2000. Proceedings. 14th International*, pages 263–268. IEEE, 2000.

[35] Kunal Talwar and Udi Wieder. Balanced allocations: The weighted case. In *Proceedings of the Thirty-ninth Annual ACM Symposium on Theory of Computing*, STOC '07, pages 256–265, New York, NY, USA, 2007. ACM.

[36] Martin Wimmer, Jakob Gruber, Jesper Larsson Träff, and Philippas Tsigas. The lock-free k-lsm relaxed priority queue. In *ACM SIGPLAN Notices*, volume 50, pages 277–278. ACM, 2015.

# A Template for Implementing Fast Lock-free Trees Using HTM

Trevor Brown
Technion, Israel
me@tbrown.pro

## ABSTRACT

Algorithms that use hardware transactional memory (HTM) must provide a software-only fallback path to guarantee progress. The design of the fallback path can have a profound impact on performance. If the fallback path is allowed to run concurrently with hardware transactions, then hardware transactions must be instrumented, adding significant overhead. Otherwise, hardware transactions must wait for any processes on the fallback path, causing concurrency bottlenecks, or move to the fallback path. We introduce an approach that combines the best of both worlds. The key idea is to use three execution paths: an HTM fast path, an HTM middle path, and a software fallback path, such that the middle path can run concurrently with each of the other two. The fast path and fallback path do *not* run concurrently, so the fast path incurs no instrumentation overhead. Furthermore, fast path transactions can move to the middle path instead of waiting or moving to the software path. We demonstrate our approach by producing an accelerated version of the tree update template of Brown et al., which can be used to implement fast lock-free data structures based on down-trees. We used the accelerated template to implement two lock-free trees: a binary search tree (BST), and an $(a,b)$-tree (a generalization of a B-tree). Experiments show that, with 72 concurrent processes, our accelerated $(a,b)$-tree performs between 4.0x and 4.2x as many operations per second as an implementation obtained using the original tree update template.

## 1 INTRODUCTION

Concurrent data structures are crucial building blocks in multi-threaded software. There are many concurrent data structures implemented using locks, but locks can be inefficient, and are not fault tolerant (since a process that crashes while holding a lock can prevent all other processes from making progress). Thus, it is often preferable to use hardware synchronization primitives like compare-and-swap (CAS) instead of locks. This enables the development of *lock-free* (or *non-blocking*) data structures, which guarantee that at least one process will always continue to make progress, even if some processes crash. However, it is notoriously difficult to implement lock-free data structures from CAS, and this has inhibited the development of advanced lock-free data structures.

One way of simplifying this task is to use a higher level synchronization primitive that can atomically access multiple locations. For example, consider a $k$-word compare-and-swap ($k$-CAS), which atomically: reads $k$ locations, checks if they contain $k$ expected values, and, if so, writes $k$ new values. $k$-CAS is highly expressive, and it can be used in a straightforward way to implement *any* atomic operation. Moreover, it can be implemented from CAS and registers [16]. However, since $k$-CAS is so expressive, it is difficult to implement efficiently.

Brown et al. [6] developed a set of new primitives called LLX and SCX that are less expressive than $k$-CAS, but can still be used in a natural way to implement many advanced data structures. These primitives can be implemented much more efficiently than $k$-CAS. At a high level, LLX returns a snapshot of a node in a data structure, and after performing LLXs on one or more nodes, one can perform an SCX to atomically: change a field of one of these nodes, and *finalize* a subset of them, *only if* none of these nodes have changed since the process performed LLXs on them. Finalizing a node prevents any further changes to it, which is useful to stop processes from erroneously modifying deleted parts of the data structure. In a subsequent paper, Brown et al. used LLX and SCX to design a *tree update template* that can be followed to produce lock-free implementations of down-trees (trees in which all nodes except the root have in-degree one) with any kinds of update operations [7]. They demonstrated the use of the template by implementing a chromatic tree, which is an advanced variant of a red-black tree (a type of balanced binary search tree) that offers better scalability. The template has also been used to implement many other advanced data structures, including lists, relaxed AVL trees, relaxed $(a,b)$-trees, relaxed $b$-slack trees and weak AVL trees [5, 7, 17]. Some of these data structures are highly efficient, and would be well suited for inclusion in data structure libraries.

In this work, we study how the new hardware transactional memory (HTM) capabilities found in recent processors (e.g., by Intel and IBM) can be used to produce significantly faster implementations of the tree update template. By accelerating the tree update template, we also provide a way to accelerate all of the data structures that have been implemented with it. Since library data structures are reused many times, even minor performance improvements confer a large benefit.

HTM allows a programmer to run blocks of code in transactions, which either commit and take effect atomically, or abort and have no effect on shared memory. Although transactional memory was originally intended to *simplify* concurrent programming, researchers have since realized that HTM can also be used effectively to *improve the performance of existing concurrent code* [21, 22, 28]: Hardware transactions typically have very little overhead, so they can often be

This work was performed while Trevor Brown was a student at the University of Toronto. Funding was provided by the Natural Sciences and Engineering Research Council of Canada. I would also like thank my supervisor Faith Ellen for her helpful comments on this work, and to Oracle Labs for providing access to the 72-thread Intel machine used in my experiments.

*PODC '17, July 25-27, 2017, Washington, DC, USA*

ACM ISBN 978-1-4503-4992-5/17/07...$15.00
http://dx.doi.org/10.1145/3087801.3087834

used to replace other, more expensive synchronization mechanisms. For example, instead of performing a sequence of CAS primitives, it may be faster to perform reads, if-statements and writes inside a transaction. Note that this represents a *non-standard use of HTM*: we are *not* interested in its ease of use, but, rather, in its ability to reduce synchronization costs.

Although hardware transactions are fast, it is surprisingly difficult to obtain the full performance benefit of HTM. Here, we consider Intel's HTM, which is a *best-effort* implementation. This means it offers *no guarantee* that transactions will ever commit. Even in a single threaded system, a transaction can repeatedly abort because of internal buffer overflows, page faults, interrupts, and many other events. So, to guarantee progress, any code that uses HTM must also provide a *software fallback path* to be executed if a transaction fails. The design of the fallback path profoundly impacts the performance of HTM-based algorithms.

**Allowing concurrency between two paths.** Consider an operation $O$ that is implemented using the tree update template. One natural way to use HTM to accelerate $O$ is to use the original operation as a fallback path, and then obtain an HTM-based fast path by wrapping $O$ in a transaction, and performing optimizations to improve performance [21]. We call this the **2-path concurrent** algorithm (*2-path con*). Since the fast path is just an optimized version of the fallback path, transactions on the fast path and fallback path can safely run concurrently. If a transaction aborts, it can either be retried on the fast path, or be executed on the fallback path. Unfortunately, supporting concurrency between the fast path and fallback path can add significant overhead on the fast path.

The first source of overhead is *instrumentation* on the fast path that manipulates the *meta-data* used by the fallback path to synchronize processes. For example, lock-free algorithms often create a *descriptor* for each update operation (so that processes can determine how to help one another make progress), and store pointers to these descriptors in Data-records, where they act as locks. The fast path must also manipulate these descriptors and pointers so that the fallback path can detect changes made by the fast path.

The second source of overhead comes from constraints imposed by algorithmic assumptions made on the fallback path. The tree update template implementation in [7] assumes that only child pointers can change, and all other fields of nodes, such as keys and values, are never changed. Changes to these other *immutable* fields must be made by replacing a node with a new copy that reflects the desired change. Because of this assumption on the fallback path, transactions on the fast path *cannot* directly change any field of a node other than its child pointers. This is because the fallback path has no mechanism to detect such a change (and may, for example, erroneously delete a node that is concurrently being modified by the fast path). Thus, just like the fallback path, the fast path must replace a node with a new copy to change one of its immutable fields, which can be much less efficient than changing the field directly.

**Disallowing concurrency between two paths.** To avoid the overheads described above, concurrency is often *disallowed* between the fast path and fallback path. The simplest example of this approach is a technique called **transactional lock elision** (TLE) [25, 26]. TLE is used to implement an operation by wrapping its sequential code in a transaction, and falling back to acquire a global lock after a certain number of transactional attempts. At the beginning of each transaction, a process reads the state of the global lock and aborts the transaction if the lock is held (to prevent inconsistencies that might arise because the fallback path is not atomic). Once a process begins executing on the fallback path, all concurrent transactions abort, and processes wait until the fallback path is empty before retrying their transactions.

If transactions never abort, then *TLE represents the best performance we can hope to achieve*, because the fallback path introduces almost no overhead and synchronization is performed entirely by hardware. Note, however, that TLE is not lock-free. Additionally, in workloads where operations periodically run on the fallback path, performance can be very poor.

As a toy example, consider a TLE implementation of a binary search tree, with a workload consisting of insertions, deletions and *range queries*. A range query returns all of the keys in a range $[lo, hi)$. Range queries access many memory locations, and cause frequent transactional aborts due to internal processor buffer overflows (capacity limits). Thus, range queries periodically run on the fallback path, where they can lead to numerous performance problems. Since the fallback path is sequential, range queries (or any other long-running operations) cause a severe *concurrency bottleneck*, because they prevent transactions from running on the fast path while they slowly complete, serially.

One way to mitigate this bottleneck is to replace the sequential fallback path in TLE with a lock-free algorithm, and replace the global lock with a fetch-and-increment object $F$ that counts how many operations are running on the fallback path. Instead of aborting if the lock is held, transactions on the fast path abort if $F$ is non-zero. We call this the **2-path non-concurrent** algorithm (*2-path* $\overline{con}$). In this algorithm, if transactions on the fast path retry only a few times before moving to the fallback path, or do not wait between retries for the fallback path to become empty, then the lemming effect [13] can occur. (The lemming effect occurs when processes on the fast path rapidly fail and move to the fallback path, simply because other processes are on the fallback path.) This can cause the algorithm to run only as fast as the (much slower) fallback path. However, if transactions avoid the lemming effect by retrying many times before moving to the fallback path, and waiting between retries for the fallback path to become empty, then processes can spend most of their time *waiting*.

**The problem with two paths.** In this paper, we study two different types of workloads: **light workloads**, in which transactions rarely run on the fallback path, and **heavy workloads**, in which transactions more frequently run on the fallback path. In light workloads, algorithms that allow concurrency between paths perform very poorly (due to high overhead) in comparison to algorithms that disallow concurrency. However, in heavy workloads, algorithms that disallow concurrency perform very poorly (since transactions on the fallback path prevent transactions from running on the fast path) in comparison to algorithms that allow concurrency between paths. Consequently, all two path algorithms have workloads that yield poor performance. Our experiments confirm this, showing surprisingly poor performance for two path algorithms in many cases.

**Using three paths.** We introduce a technique that simultaneously achieves high performance for both light and heavy workloads by

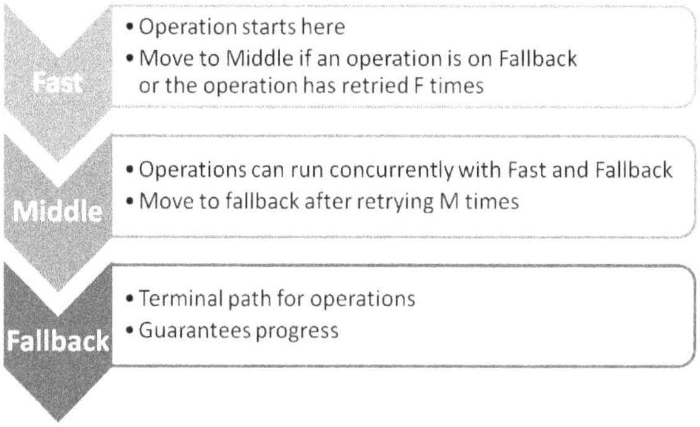


**Figure 1: Overview of the 3-path algorithm.**

using three paths: an HTM fast path, an HTM middle path and a non-transactional fallback path. (See Figure 1.) Each operation begins on the fast path, and moves to the middle path after it retries $F$ times. An operation on the middle path moves to the fallback path after retrying $M$ times on the middle path. The fast path does not manipulate any synchronization meta-data used by the fallback path, so operations on the fast path and fallback path cannot run concurrently. Thus, whenever an operation is on the fallback path, all operations on the fast path move to the middle path. The middle path manipulates the synchronization meta-data used by the fallback path, so operations on the middle path and fallback path can run concurrently. Operations on the middle path can also run concurrently with operations on the fast path (since conflicts are resolved by the HTM system). We call this the **3-path** algorithm (*3-path*).

We briefly discuss why this approach avoids the performance problems described above. Since transactions on the fast path do not run concurrently with transactions on the fallback path, transactions on the fast path run with *no instrumentation overhead.* When a transaction is on the fallback path, transactions can freely execute on the middle path, *without waiting*. The *lemming effect* does not occur, since transactions do not have to move to the fallback path simply because a transaction is on the fallback path. Furthermore, we enable a high degree of concurrency, because the fast and middle paths can run concurrently, and the middle and fallback paths can run concurrently.

We performed experiments to evaluate our new template algorithms by comparing them with the original template algorithm. In order to compare the different template algorithms, we used each algorithm to implement two data structures: a binary search tree (BST) and a relaxed $(a,b)$-tree. We then ran microbenchmarks to compare the performance (operations per second) of the different implementations in both light and heavy workloads. The results show that our new template algorithms offer significant performance improvements. For example, on an Intel system with 72 concurrent processes, our best implementation of the relaxed $(a,b)$-tree outperformed the implementation using the original template algorithm by an average of 410% over all workloads.

**Contributions**

- We present four accelerated implementations of the tree update template of Brown et al. that explore the design space for HTM-based implementations: *2-path con*, *TLE*, *2-path* $\overline{con}$, and *3-path*.
- We highlight the importance of studying both light and heavy workloads in the HTM setting. Each serves a distinct role in evaluating algorithms: light workloads demonstrate the potential of HTM to improve performance by reducing overhead, and heavy workloads capture the performance impact of interactions between different execution paths.
- We demonstrate the effectiveness of our approach by accelerating two different lock-free data structures: an unbalanced BST, and a relaxed $(a,b)$-tree. Experimental results show a significant performance advantage for our accelerated implementations.

The remainder of the paper is structured as follows. The model is introduced in Section 2. Section 3 describes LLX and SCX, and the tree update template. In Section 4, we describe our four accelerated template implementations, and argue correctness and progress. Experimental results are presented in Section 5. Related work is surveyed in Section 7. Section 6 describes an optimization to two of our accelerated template implementations. Finally, we conclude in Section 8.

## 2 MODEL

We consider an asynchronous shared memory system with $n$ processes, and Intel's implementation of HTM. Arbitrary blocks of code can be executed as transactions, which either commit (and appear to take place instantaneously) or abort (and have no effect on the contents of shared memory). A transaction is started by invoking *txBegin*, is committed by invoking *txEnd*, and can be aborted by invoking *txAbort*. Intel's implementation of HTM is best-effort, which means that the system can force transactions to abort at any time, and no transactions are ever guaranteed to commit. Each time a transaction aborts, the hardware provides a reason why the abort occurred. Two reasons are of particular interest. *Conflict* aborts occur when two processes contend on the same cache-line. Since a cache-line contains multiple machine words, *conflict* aborts can occur even if two processes never contend on the same memory location. *Capacity* aborts occur when a transaction exhausts some shared resource within the HTM system. Intuitively, this occurs when a transaction accesses too many memory locations. (In reality, *capacity* aborts also occur for a variety of complex reasons that make it difficult to predict when they will occur.)

## 3 BACKGROUND

**The LLX and SCX primitives.** The load-link extended (LLX) and store-conditional extended (SCX) primitives are multi-word generalizations of the well-known load-link (LL) and store-conditional (SC), and they have been implemented from single-word CAS [6]. LLX and SCX operate on Data-records, each of which consists of a fixed number of mutable fields (which can change), and a fixed number of immutable fields (which cannot).

LLX($r$) attempts to take a snapshot of the mutable fields of a Data-record $r$. If it is concurrent with an SCX involving $r$, it may return FAIL, instead. Individual fields of a Data-record can also be read directly. An SCX($V$, $R$, $fld$, $new$) takes as its arguments a sequence $V$ of Data-records, a subsequence $R$ of $V$, a pointer $fld$ to a mutable field of one Data-record in $V$, and a new value $new$ for that field. The SCX tries to atomically store the value $new$ in

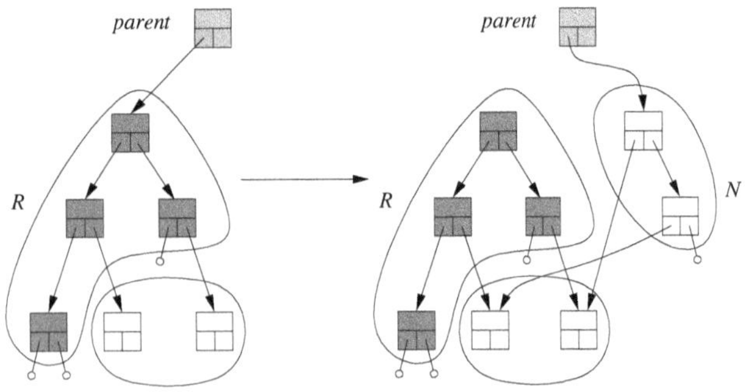


**Figure 2: Example of the tree update template.**

the field that *fld* points to and *finalize* each Data-record in $R$. Once a Data-record is finalized, its mutable fields cannot be changed by any subsequent SCX, and any LLX of the Data-record will return FINALIZED instead of a snapshot.

Before a process $p$ invokes SCX, it must perform an LLX($r$) on each Data-record $r$ in $V$. For each $r \in V$, the last LLX($r$) performed by $p$ prior to the SCX is said to be *linked* to the SCX, and this linked LLX must return a snapshot of $r$ (not FAIL or FINALIZED). An SCX($V, R, fld, new$) by a process modifies the data structure and returns TRUE (in which case we say it *succeeds*) only if no Data-record $r$ in $V$ has changed since its linked LLX($r$); otherwise the SCX fails and returns FALSE. Although LLX and SCX can fail, their failures are limited in such a way that they can be used to build data structures with lock-free progress. See [6] for a more formal specification.

We briefly describe the implementation of SCX. Each Data-record is augmented with two fields: *marked* and *info*. Each SCX($V$, $R$, $fld$, $new$) starts by creating an SCX-record $D$, which contains all of the information necessary to perform the SCX, and then completes the SCX by invoking a function called HELP, and passing $D$ as its argument. Invocations of SCX synchronize with one another by taking a special kind of lock on each Data-record in $V$. These locks grant exclusive access to an SCX *operation*, rather than to a *process*. An SCX $S$ locks a Data-record $u$ by using CAS to store a pointer to its SCX-record in *u.info*. Suppose $S$ successfully locks all Data-records in its $V$ sequence. Then, $S$ finalizes each Data-record $u \in R$ by setting *u.marked* := TRUE, and releases its locks on all *other* Data-records (leaving finalized Data-records permanently locked). Whenever a process encounters a (non-finalized) node locked for $S$, it invokes HELP($D$) to help $S$ complete and release its locks.

Observe that SCX can only change a single value in a Data-record (and finalize a sequence of Data-records) atomically. Thus, to implement an *operation* that changes multiple fields, one must create *new* Data-records that contain the desired changes, and use SCX to change *one* pointer to replace the old Data-records.

**The tree update template.** The tree update template implements lock-free updates that atomically replace an old connected subgraph $R$ of a down-tree by a new connected subgraph $N$ (as shown in Figure 2). Such an update can implement any change to the tree, such as an insertion into a BST or a rotation in a balanced tree. The old subgraph includes all nodes with a field to be modified. The new subgraph may have pointers to nodes in the old tree. Since every node in a down-tree has indegree one, the update can be performed by changing a single child pointer of some node *parent*. However, problems could arise if a concurrent operation changes the part of the tree being updated. For example, nodes in the old subgraph, or even *parent*, could be removed from the tree before *parent*'s child pointer is changed. The template takes care of the process coordination required to prevent such problems.

Each tree node is represented by a Data-record with a fixed number of child pointers as its mutable fields. Each child pointer either points to a Data-record or contains NIL (denoted by –∘ in our figures). Any other data in the node is stored in immutable fields. Thus, if an update must change some of this data, it makes a new copy of the node with the updated data. There is a Data-record *entry* which acts as the entry point to the data structure and is never deleted.

At a high level, an update that follows the template proceeds in two phases: the *search phase* and the *update phase*. In the search phase, the update searches for a location where it should occur. Then, in the update phase, the update performs LLXs on a connected subgraph of nodes in the tree, including *parent* and the set $R$ of nodes to be removed from the tree. Next, it decides whether the tree should be modified, and, if so, creates a new subgraph of nodes and performs an SCX that atomically changes a child pointer, as shown in Figure 2, and finalizes any nodes in $R$. See [7] for further details.

# 4 ACCELERATED TEMPLATE IMPLEMENTATIONS

**HTM-based** LLX **and** SCX**.** In the following, we use $\text{SCX}_O$ and $\text{LLX}_O$ to refer to the original lock-free implementation of LLX and SCX. We give an implementation of SCX that uses an HTM-based fast path called $\text{SCX}_{HTM}$, and $\text{SCX}_O$ as its fallback path. Hardware transactions are instrumented so they can run concurrently with processes executing $\text{SCX}_O$. This algorithm guarantees lock-freedom and achieves a high degree of concurrency. Pseudocode appears in Figure 3. At a high level, an $\text{SCX}_{HTM}$ by a process $p$ starts a transaction, then attempts to perform a highly optimized version of $\text{SCX}_O$. Each time a transaction executed by $p$ aborts, control jumps to the onAbort label, at the beginning of the SCX procedure. If a process *explicitly* aborts a transaction at line 19, then SCX returns FALSE at line 4. Each process has a budget *AttemptLimit* that specifies how many times it will attempt hardware transactions before it will fall back to executing $\text{SCX}_O$.

In $\text{SCX}_O$, SCX-records are used (1) to facilitate helping, and (2) to lock Data-records and detect changes to them. In particular, $\text{SCX}_O$ guarantees the following property. **P1**: between any two changes to (the user-defined fields of) a Data-record $u$, a new SCX-record pointer is stored in *u.info*. However, $\text{SCX}_{HTM}$ does not create SCX-records. In a transactional setting, helping causes unnecessary aborts, since executing a transaction that performs the same work as a running transaction will cause at least one (and probably both) to abort. Helping in transactions is also *not necessary* to guarantee progress, since progress is guaranteed by the fallback path. So, to preserve property P1, we give each process $p$ a *tagged sequence number* $tseq_p$ that contains the process name, a sequence number, and a *tag* bit. The *tag* bit is the least significant bit. On modern systems where pointers are word aligned, the least significant bit in a pointer is always zero. Thus, the tag bit allows a process

```
1  Private variable for process p: attempts_p, tagseq_p

2  SCX(V, R, fld, new) by process p
3  onAbort:                              ▷ jump here on transaction abort
4      if we jumped here after an explicit abort then return FALSE
5      if attempts_p < AttemptLimit then
6          attempts_p := attempts_p + 1
7          retval := SCX_HTM(V, R, fld, new) ▷ Fast
8      else
9          retval := SCX_O(V, R, fld, new) ▷ Fallback
10     if retval then attempts_p := 0
11     return retval
```

```
12 SCX_HTM(V, R, fld, new) by process p
13     Let infoFields be a pointer to a table in p's private memory containing,
           for each r in V, the value of r.info read by p's last LLX(r)
14     Let old be the value for fld returned by p's last LLX(r)
15     Begin hardware transaction
16     tagseq_p := tagseq_p + 2^⌈log n⌉
17     for each r ∈ V do
18         Let rinfo be the pointer indexed by r in infoFields
19         if r.info ≠ rinfo then Abort hardware transaction (explicitly)
20     for each r ∈ V do r.info := tagseq_p
21     for each r ∈ R do r.marked := TRUE
22     write new to the field pointed to by fld
23     Commit hardware transaction
24     return TRUE
```

**Figure 3: HTM-based implementation of SCX.**

to distinguish between a tagged sequence number and a pointer. In $SCX_{HTM}$, instead of having $p$ create a new SCX-record and store pointers to it in Data-records to lock them, $p$ increments its sequence number in $tseq_p$ and stores $tseq_p$ in Data-records. Since no writes performed by a transaction $T$ can be seen until it commits, it never actually needs to hold any locks. Thus, every value of $tseq_p$ stored in a Data-record represents an unlocked value, and writing $tseq_p$ represents $p$ locking and immediately unlocking a node.

After storing $tseq_p$ in each $r \in V$, $SCX_{HTM}$ finalizes each $r \in R$ by setting *r.marked* := TRUE (mimicking the behaviour of $SCX_O$). Then, it stores *new* in the field pointed to by $fld$, and commits. Note that eliminating the creation of SCX-records on the fast path also eliminates the need to *reclaim* any created SCX-records, which further reduces overhead.

The $SCX_{HTM}$ algorithm also necessitates a small change to $LLX_O$, to handle tagged sequence numbers. An invocation of $LLX_O(r)$ reads a pointer *rinfo* to an SCX-record, follows *rinfo* to read one of its fields, and uses the value it reads to determine whether $r$ is locked. However, *rinfo* may now contains a tagged sequence number, instead of a pointer to an SCX-record. So, in our modified algorithm, which we call $LLX_{HTM}$, before a process tries to follow *rinfo*, it first checks whether *rinfo* is a tagged sequence number, and, if so, behaves as if $r$ is unlocked.

**Correctness and progress.** Due to a lack of space, we omit the full proof of correctness and progress for our HTM-based implementation of LLX and SCX, and give a brief sketch, instead. The high-level idea is to show that one can start with $LLX_O$ and $SCX_O$, and obtain our HTM-based implementation by applying a sequence of transformations. Intuitively, these transformations preserve the semantics of SCX and maintain backwards compatibility with $SCX_O$ so that the transformed versions can be run concurrently with invocations of $SCX_O$. More formally, for each execution of a transformed algorithm, there is an execution of the original algorithm in which: the same operations are performed, they are linearized in the same order, and they return the same results. After arguing correctness and progress for each transformation, the proof of correctness and progress for the HTM-based implementation of LLX and SCX follows immediately from the original proof for $LLX_O$ and $SCX_O$.

**The *2-path con* algorithm.** We now use our HTM-based LLX and SCX to obtain an HTM-based implementation of a template operation $O$. The fallback path for $O$ is simply a lock-free implementation of $O$ using $LLX_O$ and $SCX_O$. The fast path for $O$ starts a transaction, then performs the same code as the fallback path, except that it uses the HTM-based LLX and SCX. Since the *entire operation* is performed inside a transaction, we can optimize the invocations of $SCX_{HTM}$ that are performed by $O$ as follows. Lines 15 and 23 can be eliminated, since $SCX_{HTM}$ is already running inside a large transaction. Additionally, lines 17-19 can be eliminated, since the transaction will abort due to a data conflict if *r.info* changes after it is read in the (preceding) linked invocation of LLX($r$), and before the transaction commits. The proof of correctness and progress for *2-path con* follows immediately from the proof of the original template and the proof of the HTM-based LLX and SCX implementation.

Note that it is not necessary to perform the entire operation in a single transaction. In Section 6, we describe a modification that allows a read-only *searching* prefix of the operation to be performed before the transaction begins.

**The *TLE* algorithm.** To obtain a TLE implementation of an operation $O$, we simply take *sequential code* for $O$ and wrap it in a transaction on the fast path. The fallback path acquires and releases a global lock instead of starting and committing a transaction, but otherwise executes the same code as the fast path. To prevent the fast path and fallback path from running concurrently, transactions on the fast path start by reading the lock state and aborting if it is held. An operation attempts to run on the fast path up to *AttemptLimit* times (waiting for the lock to be free before each attempt) before resorting to the fallback path. The correctness of TLE is trivial. Note, however, that TLE only satisfies deadlock-freedom (not lock-freedom).

**The *2-path $\overline{con}$* algorithm.** We can improve concurrency on the fallback path and guarantee lock-freedom by using a lock-free algorithm on the fallback path, and a global fetch-and-increment object $F$ instead of a global lock. Consider an operation $O$ implemented with the tree update template. We describe a *2-path $\overline{con}$* implementation of $O$. The fallback path increments $F$, then executes the lock-free tree update template implementation of $O$, and finally decrements $F$. The fast path executes *sequential code* for $O$ in a transaction. To prevent the fast path and fallback path from running concurrently, transactions on the fast path start by reading $F$ and aborting if it is nonzero. An operation attempts to run on the fast path up to *AttemptLimit* times (waiting for $F$ to become zero before each attempt) before resorting to the fallback path.

Recall that operations implemented using the tree update template can only change a single pointer atomically (and can perform multiple changes atomically only by creating a connected set of new nodes that reflect the desired changes). Thus, each operation on the fallback path simply creates new nodes and changes a single pointer (and assumes that all other operations also behave this way). However, since the fast path and fallback path do not run concurrently, the fallback path does *not* impose this requirement on the fast path. Consequently, the fast path can make (multiple) direct changes to nodes. Unfortunately, as we described above, this algorithm can still suffer from concurrency bottlenecks.

**The *3-path* algorithm.** One can think of the *3-path* algorithm as a kind of hybrid between the *2-path con* and *2-path* $\overline{con}$ algorithms that obtains their benefits while avoiding their downsides. Consider an operation $O$ implemented with the tree update template. We describe a 3-path implementation of $O$. As in *2-path* $\overline{con}$, there is a global fetch-and-increment object $F$, and the fast path executes *seqeuential code* for $O$ in a transaction. The middle path and fallback path behave like the fast path and fallback path in the *2-path con* algorithm, respectively. Each time an operation begins (resp., stops) executing on the fallback path, it increments (resp., decrements) $F$. (If the scalability of fetch-and-increment is of concern, then a *scalable non-zero indicator* object [15] can be used, instead.) This prevents the fast and fallback paths from running concurrently. As we described above, operations begin on the fast path, and move to the middle path after *FastLimit* attempts, or if they see $F \neq 0$. Operations move from the middle path to the fallback path after *MiddleLimit* attempts. Note that an operation never waits for the fallback path to become empty—it simply moves to the middle path.

Since the fast path and fallback path do not run concurrently, the fallback path does not impose any overhead on the fast path, except checking if $F = 0$ (offering low overhead for light workloads). Additionally, when there are operations running on the fallback path, hardware transactions can continue to run on the middle path (offering high concurrency for heavy workloads).

**Correctness and progress for *3-path*.** The correctness argument is straightforward. The goal is to prove that all template operations are linearizable, regardless of which path they execute on. Recall that the fallback path and middle path behave like the fast path and fallback path in *2-path con*. It follows that, if there are no operations on the fast path, then the correctness of operations on the middle path and fallback path is immediate from the correctness of *2-path con*. Of course, whenever there is an operation executing on the fallback path, no operation can run on the fast path. Since operations on the fast path and middle path run in transactions, they are atomic, and any conflicts between the fast path and middle path are handled automatically by the HTM system. Therefore, template operations are linearizable.

The progress argument for *3-path* relies on three assumptions.

**A1.** The sequential code for an operation executed on the fast path must terminate after a finite number of steps if it is run on a static tree (which does not change during the operation).

**A2.** In an operation executed on the middle path or fallback path, the search phase must terminate after a finite number of steps if it is run on a static tree.

**A3.** In an operation executed on the middle path or fallback path, the update phase can modify only a finite number of nodes.

We give a simple proof that *3-path* satisfies lock-freedom. To obtain a contradiction, suppose there is an execution in which after some time $t$, some process takes infinitely many steps, but no operation terminates. Thus, the tree does not change after $t$. We first argue that no process takes infinitely many steps in a transaction $T$. If $T$ occurs on the fast path, then A1 guarantees it will terminate. If $T$ occurs on the middle path, then A2 and A3 guarantee that it will terminate. Therefore, eventually, processes only take steps on the fallback path. Progress then follows from the fact that the original tree update template implementation (our fallback path) is lock-free.

# 5 EXPERIMENTS

We used two different Intel systems for our experiments: a dual-socket 12-core E7-4830 v3 with hyperthreading for a total of 48 hardware threads (running Ubuntu 14.04LTS), and a dual-socket 18-core E5-2699 v3 with hyperthreading for a total of 72 hardware threads (running Ubuntu 15.04). Each machine had 128GB of RAM. We used the scalable thread-caching allocator (tcmalloc) from the Google perftools library. All code was compiled on GCC 4.8+ with arguments `-std=c++0x -O2 -mcx16`. (Using the higher optimization level `-O3` did not significantly improve performance for any algorithm, and decreased performance for some algorithms.) On both machines, we *pinned* threads such that we saturate one socket before scheduling any threads on the other.

**Data structures implemented with the template.** We used two data structures to study the performance of our accelerated template implementations: an unbalanced BST, and a relaxed $(a,b)$-tree. The BST is similar to the chromatic tree in [7], but with no rebalancing. The relaxed $(a,b)$-tree is a concurrency-friendly generalization of a B-tree that is based on the work of Jacobson and Larsen [18]. Nodes contain up to $b$ keys, and, when there are no ongoing updates, they contain at least $a$ keys (where $b \geq 2a-1$). In our experiments, we fix $a = 6$ and $b = 16$. With $b = 16$, each node occupies four consecutive cache lines. Since $b \geq 2a - 1$, with $b = 16$, we must have $a \leq 8$. We chose to make $a$ slightly smaller than 8 in order to exploit a performance tradeoff: a smaller minimum degree may slightly increase depth, but decreases the number of rebalancing steps that are needed to maintain balance.

**Template implementations studied.** We implemented each of data structures with four different template implementations: *3-path*, *2-path con*, *TLE* and the original template implementation, which we call *Non-HTM*. (*2-path* $\overline{con}$ is omitted, since it performed similarly to TLE, and cluttered the graphs.) The *2-path con* and *TLE* implementations perform up to 20 attempts on the fast path before resorting to the fallback path. *3-path* performs up to 10 attempts (each) on the fast path and middle path. We implemented memory reclamation using DEBRA [4], an epoch based reclamation scheme.

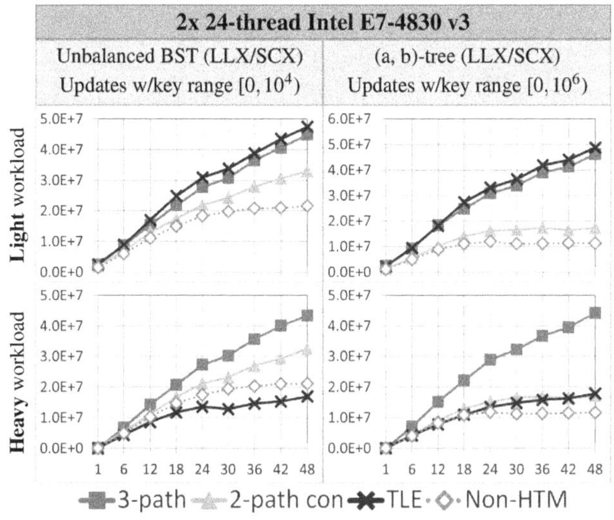


**Figure 4: Results (48-thread system) showing throughput (operations per second) versus the number of concurrent processes.**

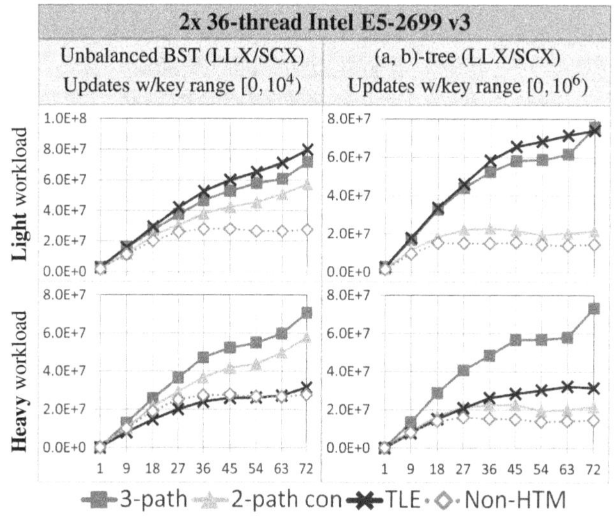


**Figure 5: Results (72 thread system) showing throughput (operations per second) versus the number of concurrent processes.**

## 5.1 Light vs. Heavy workloads

**Methodology.** We study two workloads: in **light**, $n$ processes perform updates (50% insertion and 50% deletion), and in **heavy**, $n-1$ processes perform updates, and one thread performs 100% range queries (RQs). For each workload and data structure implementation, and a variety of thread counts, we perform a set of five randomized trials. In each trial, $n$ processes perform either updates or RQs (as appropriate for the workload) for one second, and counted the number of completed operations. Updates are performed on keys drawn uniformly randomly from a fixed key range $[0, K)$. RQs are performed on ranges $[lo, lo+s)$ where $lo$ is uniformly random in $[0, K)$ and $s$ is chosen, according to a probability distribution described below, from $[1, 1000]$ for the BST and $[1, 10000]$ for the $(a, b)$-tree. (We found that nodes in the $(a, b)$-tree contained approximately 10 keys, on average, so the respective maximum values of $s$ for the BST and $(a, b)$-tree resulted in range queries returning keys from approximately the same number of nodes in both data structures.) To ensure that we are measuring steady-state performance, at the start of each trial, the data structure is prefilled by having threads perform 50% insertions and 50% deletions on uniform keys until the data structure contains approximately half of the keys in $[0, K)$.

We verified the correctness of each data structure after each trial by computing *key-sum hashes*. Each thread maintains the sum of all keys it successfully inserts, minus the sum of all keys it successfully deletes. At the end of the trial, the total of these sums over all threads must match the sum of keys in the tree.

**Probability distribution of $s$.** We chose the probability distribution of $s$ to produce many small RQs, and a smaller number of very large ones. To achieve this, we chose $s$ to be $\lfloor x^2 S \rfloor + 1$, where $x$ is a uniform real number in $[0, 1)$, and $S = 1000$ for the BST and $S = 10000$ for the $(a, b)$-tree. By squaring $x$, we bias the uniform distribution towards zero, creating a larger number of small RQs.

**Results.** We briefly discuss the results from the 48 thread machine, which appear in Figure 4. The BST and the relaxed $(a, b)$-tree behave fairly similarly. Since the $(a, b)$-tree has large nodes, it benefits much more from a low-overhead fast path (in *TLE* or *3-path*) which can avoid creating new nodes during updates. In the light workloads, *3-path* performs significantly better than *2-path con* (which has more overhead) and approximately as well as *TLE*. On average, the *3-path* algorithms completed 2.1x as many operations as their *non-HTM* counterparts (and with 48 concurrent processes, this increases to 3.0x, on average). In the heavy workloads, *3-path* significantly outperforms *TLE* (completing 2.0x as many operations, on average), which suffers from *excessive waiting*. Interestingly, *3-path* is also significantly faster than *2-path con* in the heavy workloads. This is because, even though RQs are always being performed, some RQs can succeed on the fast path, so many update operations can still run on the fast path in *3-path*, where they incur much less overhead (than they would in *2-path con*).

Results from the 72-thread machine appear in Figure 5. There, *3-path* shows an even larger performance advantage over *Non-HTM*.

## 5.2 Code path usage and abort rates

To gain further insight into the behaviour of our accelerated template implementations, we gathered some additional metrics about the experiments described above. Here, we only describe results from the 48-thread Intel machine. (Results from the 72-thread Intel machine were similar.)

**Operations completed on each path.** We started by measuring how often operations completed successfully on each execution path. This revealed that operations almost always completed on the fast path. Broadly, over all thread counts, the minimum number of operations completed on the fast path in any trial was 86%, and the average over all trials was 97%.

In each trial that we performed with 48 concurrent threads, at least 96% of operations completed on the fast path, *even in the workloads with RQs*. Recall that RQs are the operations most likely to run on the fallback path, and they are only performed by a single thread, so they

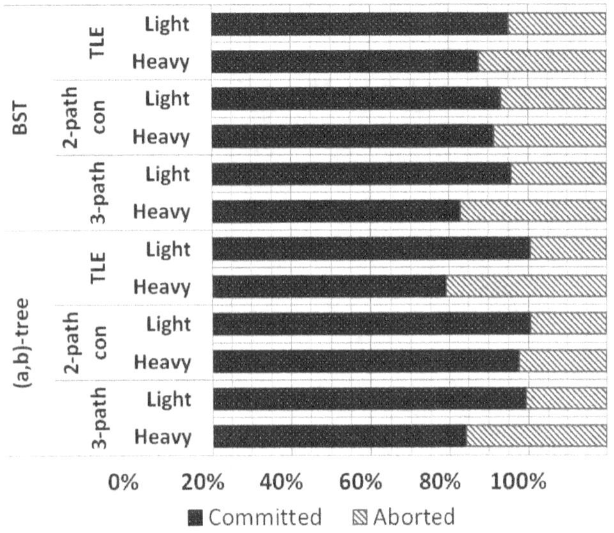


**Figure 6: Summary of how many transactions commit vs. how many abort in our experiments on the 48-thread Intel machine.**

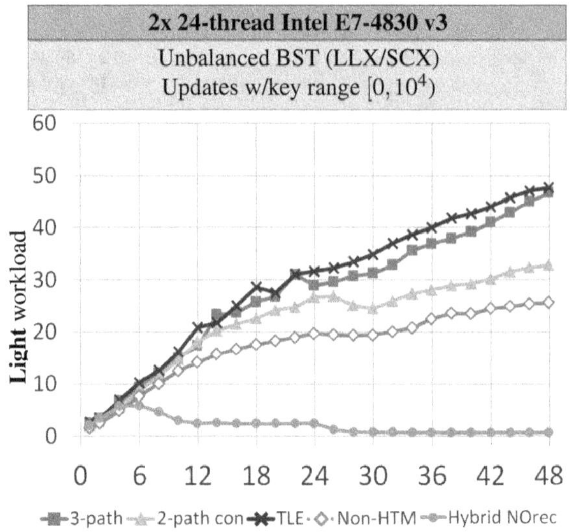


**Figure 7: Results showing throughput (operations per second) versus number of processes for an unbalanced BST implemented with different tree update template algorithms, and with the hybrid TM algorithm *Hybrid NOrec*.**

make up a relatively small fraction of the total operations performed in a trial. In fact, our measurements showed that the number of operations which completed on the fallback path was never more than a fraction of one percent in our trials with 48 concurrent threads.

In light of this, it might be somewhat surprising that the performance of TLE was so much worse in heavy workloads than light ones. However, the cost of serializing threads is high, and this cost is compounded by the fact that the operations which complete on the fallback path are often long-running. Of course, in workloads where more operations run on the fallback path, the advantage of improving concurrency between paths would be even greater.

**Commit/abort rates.** We also measured how many transactions committed and how many aborted, on each execution path, in each of our trials. Figure 6 summarizes the average commit/abort rates for each data structure, template implementation and workload. Since nearly all operations completed on the fast path, we decided not to distinguish between the commit/abort rate on the fast path and the commit/abort rate on the middle path.

## 5.3 Comparing with hybrid transactional memory

*Hybrid transactional memory* (hybrid TM) combines hardware and software transactions to hide the limitations of HTM and guarantee progress. This offers an alternative way of using HTM to implement concurrent data structures. Note, however, that state of the art hybrid TMs use locks. So, **they cannot be used to implement lock-free data structures.** Regardless, to get an idea of how such implementations would perform, relative to our accelerated template implementations, we implemented the unbalanced BST using Hybrid NOrec, which is arguably the fastest hybrid TM implementation with readily available code [27].

If we were to use a precompiled library implementation of Hybrid NOrec, then the unbalanced BST algorithm would have to perform a library function call for *each read and write to shared memory*, which would incur significant overhead. So, we directly compiled the code for Hybrid NOrec into the code for the BST, allowing the compiler to inline the Hybrid NOrec functions for reading and writing from shared memory into our BST code, eliminating this overhead. Of course, if one intended to use hybrid TM in practice (and not in a research prototype), one would use a precompiled library, with all of the requisite overhead. Thus, the following results are quite charitable towards hybrid TMs.

We implemented the BST using Hybrid NOrec by wrapping sequential code for the BST operations in transactions, and manually replacing each read from (resp., write to) shared memory with a read (resp., write) operation provided by Hybrid NOrec. Figure 7 compares the performance of the resulting implementation to the other BST implementations discussed in Section 5.

The BST implemented with Hybrid NOrec performs relatively well with up to six processes. However, beyond six processes, it experiences severe negative scaling. The negative scaling occurs because Hybrid NOrec increments a global counter in each updating transaction (i.e., each transaction that performs at least one write). This global contention hotspot in updating transactions causes many transactions to abort, simply because they contend on the global counter (and not because they conflict on any data in the tree). However, even without this bottleneck, Hybrid NOrec would still perform poorly in heavy workloads, since it incurs very high instrumentation overhead for software transactions (which must acquire locks, perform repeated validation of read-sets, maintain numerous auxiliary data structures for read-sets and write-sets, and so on). Note that this problem is not unique to Hybrid NOrec, as every hybrid TM must use a software TM as its fallback path in order to guarantee progress. In contrast, in our template implementations, the software-only fallback path is a fast lock-free algorithm.

# 6 MODIFICATIONS FOR PERFORMING SEARCHES OUTSIDE OF TRANSACTIONS

In this section, we describe how the *3-path* implementations of the unbalanced BST and relaxed $(a,b)$-tree can be modified so that each operation attempt on the fast path or middle path performs its search phase *before* starting a transaction (and only performs its update phase in a transaction). (The same technique also applies to the *2-path con* implementations.) First, note that the lock-free search procedure for each of these data structures is actually a standard, sequential search procedure. Consequently, a simple sequential search procedure will return the correct result, regardless of whether it is performed inside a transaction. (Generally, whenever we produce a *3-path* implementation starting from a lock-free fallback path, we will have access to a correct non-transactional search procedure.)

The difficulty is that, when an operation starts a transaction and performs its update phase, it may be working on a part of the tree that was deleted by another operation. One can imagine an operation $O_d$ that deletes an entire subtree, and an operation $O_i$ that inserts a node into that subtree. If the search phase of $O_i$ is performed, then $O_d$ is performed, then the update phase of $O_i$ is performed, then $O_i$ may erroneously insert a node into the deleted subtree.

We fix this problem as follows. Whenever an operation $O$ on the fast path or middle path removes a node from the tree, it sets a *marked* bit in the node (just like operations on the fallback path do). Whenever $O$ first accesses a node $u$ in its transaction, it checks whether $u$ has its *marked* bit set, and, if so, aborts immediately. This way, $O$'s transaction will commit only if every node that it accessed is in the tree.

We found that this modification yielded small performance improvements (on the order of 5-10%) in our experiments. The reason this improves performance is that fewer memory locations are tracked by the HTM system, which results in fewer capacity aborts. We briefly discuss why the performance benefit is small in our experiments. The relaxed $(a,b)$-tree has a very small height, because it is balanced, and its nodes contain many keys. The BST also has a fairly small height (although it is considerably taller than the relaxed $(a,b)$-tree), because processes in our experiments perform insertions and deletions on uniformly random keys, which leads to trees of logarithmic height with high probability. So, in each case, the sequence of nodes visited by searches is relatively small, and is fairly unlikely to cause capacity aborts.

The performance benefit associated with this modification will be greater for data structures, operations or workloads in which an operation's search phase will access a large number of nodes. Additionally, IBM's HTM implementation in their POWER8 processors is far more prone to capacity aborts than Intel's implementation, since a transaction *will* abort if it accesses more than 64 different cache lines [24]. (In contrast, in Intel's implementation, a transaction can potentially commit after accessing tens of thousands of cache lines.) Thus, this modification could lead to significantly better performance on POWER8 processors.

# 7 RELATED WORK

Hybrid TMs share some similarities to our work, since they all feature multiple execution paths. The first hybrid TM algorithms allowed HTM and STM transactions to run concurrently [10, 19]. Hybrid NOrec [9] and Reduced hardware NOrec [23] are hybrid TMs that both use global locks on the fallback path, eliminating any concurrency. We discuss two additional hybrid TMs, Phased TM [20] (PhTM) and Invyswell [8], in more detail.

PhTM alternates between five *phases*: HTM-only, STM-only, concurrent HTM/STM, and two global locking phases. Roughly speaking, PhTM's HTM-only phase corresponds to our uninstrumented fast path, and its concurrent HTM/STM phase corresponds to our middle HTM and fallback paths. However, their STM-only phase (which allows no concurrent hardware transactions) and global locking phases (which allow no concurrency) have no analogue in our approach. In heavy workloads, PhTM must oscillate between its HTM-only and concurrent HTM/STM phases to maximize the performance benefit it gets from HTM. When changing phases, PhTM typically waits until all in-progress transactions complete before allowing transactions to begin in the new mode. Thus, after a phase change has begun, and before the next phase has begun, there is a window during which new transactions must wait (reducing performance). One can also think of our three path approach as proceeding in two phases: one with concurrent fast/middle transactions and one with concurrent middle/fallback transactions. However, in our approach, "phase changes" do not introduce any waiting, and there is always concurrency between two execution paths.

Invyswell is closest to our three path approach. At a high level, it features an HTM middle path and STM slow path that can run concurrently (sometimes), and an HTM fast path that can run concurrently with the middle path (sometimes) but not the slow path, and two global locking fallback paths (that prevent any concurrency). Invyswell is more complicated than our approach, and has numerous restrictions on when transactions can run concurrently. Our three path methodology does not have these restrictions. The HTM fast path also uses an optimization called lazy subscription. It has been shown that lazy subscription can cause opacity to be violated, which can lead to data corruption or program crashes [11].

Hybrid TM is very general, and it pays for its generality with high overhead. Consequently, data structure designers can extract far better performance for library code by using more specialized techniques. Additionally, we stress that state of the art hybrid TMs use locks, so they cannot be used to produce lock-free data structures.

Different options for concurrency have recently begun to be explored in the context of TLE. Refined TLE [12] and Amalgamated TLE [1] both improve the concurrency of TLE when a process is on the fallback path by allowing HTM transactions to run concurrently with a *single process* on the fallback path. Both of these approaches still serialize processes on the fallback path. They also use locks, so they cannot be used to produce lock-free data structures.

Timnat, Herlihy and Petrank [28] proposed using a strong synchronization primitive called *multiword compare-and-swap* ($k$-CAS) to obtain fast HTM algorithms. They showed how to take an algorithm implemented using $k$-CAS and produce a two-path implementation that allows concurrency between the fast and fallback paths. One of their approaches used a lock-free implementation of $k$-CAS on the fallback path, and an HTM-based implementation of $k$-CAS on the fast path. They also experimented with two-path implementations that do not allow concurrency between paths, and found that allowing concurrency between the fast path and fallback path introduced significant overhead. Makreshanski, Levandoski and Stutsman [22] also independently proposed using HTM-based $k$-CAS in the context of databases.

Liu, Zhou and Spear [21] proposed a methodology for accelerating concurrent data structures using HTM, and demonstrated it on several lock-free data structures. Their methodology uses an HTM-based fast path and a non-transactional fallback path. The fast path implementation of an operation is obtained by encapsulating part (or all) of the operation in a transaction, and then applying sequential optimizations to the transactional code to improve performance. Since the optimizations do not change the code's logic, the resulting fast path implements the same logic as the fallback path, so both paths can run concurrently. Consequently, the fallback path imposes overhead on the fast path.

Some of the optimizations presented in that paper are similar to some optimizations in our HTM-based implementation of LLX and SCX. For instance, when they applied their methodology to the lock-free unbalanced BST of Ellen et al. [14], they observed that helping can be avoided on the fast path, and that the descriptors which are normally created to facilitate helping can be replaced by a small number of statically allocated descriptors. However, they did not give details on exactly how these optimizations work, and did not give correctness arguments for them. In contrast, our optimizations are applied to a more complex algorithm, and are proved correct.

Multiversion concurrency control (MVCC) is another way to implement range queries efficiently [2, 3]. At a high level, it involves maintaining multiple copies of data to allow read-only transactions to see a consistent view of memory and serialize even in the presence of concurrent modifications. However, our approach could also be applied to operations that *modify* a range of keys, so it is more general than MVCC.

# 8 CONCLUDING REMARKS

In this work, we explored the design space for HTM-based implementations of the tree update template of Brown et al. and presented four accelerated implementations. We discussed performance issues affecting HTM-based algorithms with two execution paths, and developed an approach that avoids them by using three paths. We used our template implementations to accelerate two different lock-free data structures, and performed experiments that showed significant performance improvements over several different workloads. This makes our implementations an attractive option for producing fast concurrent data structures for inclusion in libraries, where performance is critical.

# REFERENCES


[1] Y. Afek, A. Matveev, O. R. Moll, and N. Shavit. Amalgamated lock-elision. In *Distributed Computing: 29th International Symposium, DISC 2015, Tokyo, Japan, October 7-9, 2015, Proceedings*, pages 309–324. Springer Berlin Heidelberg, Berlin, Heidelberg, 2015.

[2] H. Attiya and E. Hillel. A single-version stm that is multi-versioned permissive. *Theory of Computing Systems*, 51(4):425–446, 2012.

[3] P. A. Bernstein and N. Goodman. Multiversion concurrency control-theory and algorithms. *ACM Transactions on Database Systems (TODS)*, 8(4):465–483, 1983.

[4] T. Brown. Reclaiming memory for lock-free data structures: There has to be a better way. In *Proceedings of the 2015 ACM Symposium on Principles of Distributed Computing*, PODC '15, pages 261–270, 2015.

[5] T. Brown. *Techniques for Constructing Efficient Data Structures*. PhD thesis, University of Toronto, 2017.

[6] T. Brown, F. Ellen, and E. Ruppert. Pragmatic primitives for non-blocking data structures. In *Proceedings of the 2013 ACM Symposium on Principles of Distributed Computing*, PODC '13, pages 13–22, 2013.

[7] T. Brown, F. Ellen, and E. Ruppert. A general technique for non-blocking trees. In *Proceedings of the 19th ACM SIGPLAN Symposium on Principles and Practice of Parallel Programming*, PPoPP '14, pages 329–342, 2014.

[8] I. Calciu, J. Gottschlich, T. Shpeisman, G. Pokam, and M. Herlihy. Invyswell: a hybrid transactional memory for haswell's restricted transactional memory. In *Proceedings of the 23rd international conference on Parallel architectures and compilation*, pages 187–200. ACM, 2014.

[9] L. Dalessandro, F. Carouge, S. White, Y. Lev, M. Moir, M. L. Scott, and M. F. Spear. Hybrid norec: A case study in the effectiveness of best effort hardware transactional memory. In *Proceedings of the Sixteenth International Conference on Architectural Support for Programming Languages and Operating Systems*, ASPLOS XVI, pages 39–52, New York, NY, USA, 2011. ACM.

[10] P. Damron, A. Fedorova, Y. Lev, V. Luchangco, M. Moir, and D. Nussbaum. Hybrid transactional memory. In *Proceedings of the 12th International Conference on Architectural Support for Programming Languages and Operating Systems*, ASPLOS XII, pages 336–346, New York, NY, USA, 2006. ACM.

[11] D. Dice, T. Harris, A. Kogan, Y. Lev, and M. Moir. Pitfalls of lazy subscription. In *Proceedings of the 6th Workshop on the Theory of Transactional Memory, Paris, France*, 2014.

[12] D. Dice, A. Kogan, and Y. Lev. Refined transactional lock elision. In *Proceedings of the 21st ACM SIGPLAN Symposium on Principles and Practice of Parallel Programming*, PPoPP '16, pages 19:1–19:12, New York, NY, USA, 2016. ACM.

[13] D. Dice, Y. Lev, M. Moir, and D. Nussbaum. Early experience with a commercial hardware transactional memory implementation. In *Proceedings of the 14th Int. Conf. on Architectural Support for Programming Languages and Operating Systems*, ASPLOS XIV, pages 157–168, New York, NY, USA, 2009.

[14] F. Ellen, P. Fatourou, E. Ruppert, and F. van Breugel. Non-blocking binary search trees. In *Proceedings of the 29th ACM SIGACT-SIGOPS Symposium on Principles of Distributed Computing*, PODC '10, pages 131–140, 2010. Full version available as Technical Report CSE-2010-04, York University.

[15] F. Ellen, Y. Lev, V. Luchangco, and M. Moir. Snzi: Scalable nonzero indicators. In *Proceedings of the twenty-sixth annual ACM symposium on Principles of distributed computing*, pages 13–22. ACM, 2007.

[16] T. L. Harris, K. Fraser, and I. A. Pratt. A practical multi-word compare-and-swap operation. In *Proceedings of the 16th International Conference on Distributed Computing*, DISC '02, pages 265–279, 2002.

[17] M. He and M. Li. Deletion without rebalancing in non-blocking binary search trees. In *Proceedings of the 20th International Conference on Principles of Distributed Systems*, 2016.

[18] L. Jacobsen and K. S. Larsen. Variants of (a, b)-trees with relaxed balance. *Int. J. Found. Comput. Sci.*, 12(4):455–478, 2001.

[19] S. Kumar, M. Chu, C. J. Hughes, P. Kundu, and A. Nguyen. Hybrid transactional memory. In *Proceedings of the Eleventh ACM SIGPLAN Symposium on Principles and Practice of Parallel Programming*, PPoPP '06, pages 209–220, New York, NY, USA, 2006. ACM.

[20] Y. Lev, M. Moir, and D. Nussbaum. Phtm: Phased transactional memory. In *Workshop on Transactional Computing (Transact)*, 2007.

[21] Y. Liu, T. Zhou, and M. Spear. Transactional acceleration of concurrent data structures. In *Proc. of 27th ACM Sym. on Parallelism in Algorithms and Arch.*, SPAA '15, pages 244–253, New York, NY, USA, 2015. ACM.

[22] D. Makreshanski, J. Levandoski, and R. Stutsman. To lock, swap, or elide: on the interplay of hardware transactional memory and lock-free indexing. *Proceedings of the VLDB Endowment*, 8(11):1298–1309, 2015.

[23] A. Matveev and N. Shavit. Reduced hardware norec: A safe and scalable hybrid transactional memory. In *Proceedings of the Twentieth International Conference on Architectural Support for Programming Languages and Operating Systems*, ASPLOS '15, pages 59–71, New York, NY, USA, 2015. ACM.

[24] A. T. Nguyen. *Investigation of Hardware Transactional Memory*. PhD thesis, Massachusetts Institute of Technology, 2015.

[25] R. Rajwar and J. R. Goodman. Speculative lock elision: Enabling highly concurrent multithreaded execution. In *Proceedings of the 34th annual ACM/IEEE international symposium on Microarchitecture*, pages 294–305. IEEE Computer Society, 2001.

[26] R. Rajwar and J. R. Goodman. Transactional lock-free execution of lock-based programs. In *Proceedings of the 10th International Conference on Architectural Support for Programming Languages and Operating Systems*, ASPLOS X, pages 5–17, New York, NY, USA, 2002. ACM.

[27] T. Riegel, P. Marlier, M. Nowack, P. Felber, and C. Fetzer. Optimizing hybrid transactional memory: The importance of nonspeculative operations. In *Proceedings of the 23rd ACM Symposium on Parallelism in Algorithms and Architectures*, pages 53–64. ACM, 2011.

[28] S. Timnat, M. Herlihy, and E. Petrank. A practical transactional memory interface. In *Euro-Par 2015: Parallel Processing*, pages 387–401. Springer, 2015.

# Adding Concurrency to Smart Contracts

Thomas Dickerson
Brown University
thomas_dickerson@brown.edu

Paul Gazzillo
Yale University
paul.gazzillo@yale.edu

Maurice Herlihy
Brown University
maurice_herlihy@brown.edu

Eric Koskinen
Yale University
eric.koskinen@yale.edu

## ABSTRACT

Modern cryptocurrency systems, such as Ethereum, permit complex financial transactions through scripts called *smart contracts*. These smart contracts are executed many, many times, always without real concurrency. First, all smart contracts are serially executed by *miners* before appending them to the blockchain. Later, those contracts are serially re-executed by *validators* to verify that the smart contracts were executed correctly by miners.

Serial execution limits system throughput and fails to exploit today's concurrent multicore and cluster architectures. Nevertheless, serial execution appears to be required: contracts share state, and contract programming languages have a serial semantics.

This paper presents a novel way to permit miners and validators to execute smart contracts in parallel, based on techniques adapted from software transactional memory. Miners execute smart contracts speculatively in parallel, allowing non-conflicting contracts to proceed concurrently, and "discovering" a serializable concurrent schedule for a block's transactions, This schedule is captured and encoded as a deterministic *fork-join* program used by validators to re-execute the miner's parallel schedule deterministically but concurrently.

Smart contract benchmarks run on a JVM with ScalaSTM show that a speedup of 1.33x can be obtained for miners and 1.69x for validators with just three concurrent threads.

## 1 INTRODUCTION

Cryptocurrencies such as Bitcoin [20] or Ethereum [8] are very much in the news. Each is an instance of a *distributed ledger*: a publicly-readable tamper-proof record of a sequence of events. Simplifying somewhat, early distributed ledgers, such as Bitcoin's, work like this: *clients* send *transactions*[1] to *miners*, who package the transactions into *blocks*. Miners repeatedly *propose* new blocks to be applied to the ledger, and follow a global consensus protocol to agree on which blocks are chosen. Each block contains a cryptographic hash of the previous block, making it difficult to tamper with the ledger. The resulting distributed data structure, called a *blockchain*, defines the sequence of transactions that constitutes the distributed ledger[2].

Modern blockchain systems often interpose an additional software layer between clients and the blockchain. Client requests are directed to scripts, called *smart contracts*, that perform the logic needed to provide a complex service, such as managing state, enforcing governance, or checking credentials. Smart contracts can take many forms, but here we will use (a simplified form of) the Ethereum model [8].

A smart contract resembles an object in a programming language. It manages long-lived *state*, which is encoded in the blockchain. The state is manipulated by a set of *functions*, analogous to *methods* in many programming languages. Functions can be called either directly by clients or indirectly by other smart contracts. Smart contract languages are typically Turing-complete. To ensure that function calls terminate, the client is charged for each computational step in a function call. If the charge exceeds what the client is willing to pay, the computation is terminated and rolled back.

When and where is smart contract code executed? There are two distinct circumstances. Each smart contract is first executed by one or more *miners*, nodes that repeatedly propose new blocks to append to the blockchain. When a miner creates a block, it selects a sequence of user requests and executes the associated smart contract code for each Ethereum transaction in sequence, transforming the old contract state into a new state. It then records both the sequence of transactions and the new state in the block, and proposes it for inclusion in the blockchain.

Later, when the block has been appended to the blockchain, each smart contract is repeatedly re-executed by *validators*: nodes that reconstruct (and check) the current blockchain state. As a validator acquires each successive block, it replays each of the transactions' contract codes to check that the block's initial and final states match. Each miner validates blocks proposed by other miners, and older block are validated by newly-joined miners, or by clients querying the contract state. Code executions for validation vastly exceed code executions for mining.

[1] Following blockchain terminology, a transaction is a payment or set of payments, not an atomic unit of synchronization as in databases or transactional memory.
[2] This description omits many important issues, such as incentives, forking, and fork resolution.

Supported in part by NSF CCF Awards #1421126 and #003991.

*PODC '17, July 25-27, 2017, Washington, DC, USA*

ACM ISBN 978-1-4503-4992-5/17/07...$15.00
https://doi.org/10.1145/3087801.3087835

Existing smart contract designs limit throughput because they admit no concurrency. When a miner creates a block, it assembles a sequence of transactions, and computes a tentative new state by executing those transactions' smart contracts serially, in the order they occur in the block. A miner cannot simply execute these contracts in parallel, because they may perform conflicting accesses to shared data, and an arbitrary interleaving could produce an inconsistent final state. For Bitcoin transactions, it is easy to tell in advance when two transaction conflict, because input and output data are statically declared. For smart contracts, by contrast, it is impossible to tell in advance whether two contract executions will conflict, because the contract language is Turing-complete.

Miners are rewarded for each block they successfully append to the blockchain, so they have a strong incentive to increase throughput by parallelizing smart contract executions. We propose to allow miners to execute contract codes in parallel by adapting techniques from Software Transactional Memory (STM) [12]: treating each invocation as a speculative atomic action. Data conflicts, detected at run-time, are resolved by delaying or rolling back some conflicting invocations. Treating smart contract invocations as speculative atomic actions dynamically "discovers" a *serializable* concurrent schedule, producing the same final state as a serial schedule where the contract functions were executed in some one-at-a-time order.

But what about later validators? Existing STM systems are *non-deterministic*: if a later validator simply mimics the miner by re-running the same mix of speculative transactions, it may produce a different serialization order and a different final state, causing validation to fail incorrectly. Treating contract invocations as speculative transactions improves miners' throughput, but fails to support deterministic re-execution as required by validators.

Notice, however, that the miner has already "discovered" a serializable concurrent schedule for those transactions. We propose a novel scheme where the miner records that successful schedule, along with the final state, allowing later validators to replay that same schedule in a concurrent but deterministic way. Deterministic replay avoids many of the the miner's original synchronization costs, such as conflict detection and roll-back. Over time, parallel validation would be a significant benefit because validators perform the vast majority of contract executions. Naturally, the validator must be able to check that the proposed schedule really is serializable.

This paper makes the following contributions.

- A way for miners to speculatively execute smart contracts in parallel. We adapt techniques from *transactional boosting* [11] to permit non-conflicting smart contracts to execute concurrently.
- A way for miners to capture the resulting parallel execution in the form of a *fork-join* [1] schedule to be executed by validators, deterministically, verifiably, and in parallel.
- A prototype implementation, built on the Java virtual machine and ScalaSTM [21]. An evaluation using smart contract examples drawn from the Solidity documentation yields an overall speedup of 1.33x for miners, and 1.69x for validators with three concurrent threads of execution.

```
1  contract Ballot {
2    mapping(address => Voter) public voters;
3    // more state definitions
4    function vote(uint proposal) {
5      Voter sender = voters[msg.sender];
6      if (sender.voted)
7        throw;
8      sender.voted = true;
9      sender.vote = proposal;
10     proposals[proposal].voteCount += sender.weight;
11   }
12   // more operation definitions
13 }
```

**Figure 1: Part of the Ballot contract**

## 2 BLOCKCHAINS AND SMART CONTRACTS

In Bitcoin and similar systems, transactions typically have a simple structure, distributing the balances from a set of input accounts to a set of newly-created output accounts. In Blockchains such as Ethereum, however, each block also includes an explicit *state* capturing the cumulative effect of transactions in prior blocks. A Transaction is expressed as executable code, often called a *smart contract*, that modifies that state. Ethereum blocks thus contain both transactions' smart contracts and the final state produced by executing those contacts.

The contracts themselves are stored in the blockchain as byte-code instructions for the Ethereum virtual machine (EVM). Several higher-level languages exist for writing smart contracts. Here, we describe smart contracts as expressed in the Solidity language [22].

Listing 1 is part of the source code for an example smart contract that implements a ballot box [23]. The owner initializes the contract with a list of proposals and gives the right to vote to a set of Ethereum addresses. Voters cast their votes for a particular proposal, which they may do only once. Alternatively, voters may delegate their vote. The contract keyword declares the smart contract (Line 1).

The contract's persistent state is recorded in *state variables*. For Ballot, the persistent state includes fields of scalar type such as the owner (omitted for lack of space). State variables such as voters (declared on Line 2) can also use the built-in Solidity type mapping which, in this case, associates each voter's address with a Voter data structure (declaration omitted for brevity). The keys in this mapping are of built-in type address, which uniquely identifies Ethereum accounts (clients or other contracts). These state variables are the persistent state of the contract.

Line 4 declares contract *function*, vote, to cast a vote for the given proposal. Within a function there are transient *memory* and *stack* areas such as sender. The function vote first recovers the Voter data from the contract's state by indexing into the voters mapping using the sender's address msg.sender. The msg variable is a global variable containing data about the contract's current invocation. Next, the sender.vote flag is checked to prevent multiple votes. Note that sequential execution is critical: if this code were naïvely run in parallel, it would be vulnerable to a race condition permitting double voting. Ethereum contract functions can be aborted at any time via **throw**, as seen here when a voter is detected attempting to vote twice. The **throw** statement causes the contract's transient state and tentative storage changes to be discarded. Finally, this Ballot contract also provides functions to register voters, delegate one's vote, and compute the winning proposal. The complete Ballot example is available elsewhere[3].

**Execution Model: Miners and Validators.** When a miner prepares a block for inclusion in the blockchain, it starts with the ledger state as of the chain's most recent block. The miner selects a sequence of new transactions, records them in the new block, and executes them, one at a time, to compute the new block's state. The miner then participates in a consensus protocol to decide whether this new block will be appended to the blockchain.

To ensure that each transaction terminates in a reasonable number of steps, each call to contract bytecode comes with an explicit limit on the number of virtual machine steps that a call can take. (In Ethereum, these steps are measured in "gas" and clients pay a fee to the miner that successfully appends that transaction's block to the blockchain.)

After a block has been successfully appended to the blockchain, that block's transactions are sequentially re-executed *by every node in the network* to check that the block's state transition was computed honestly and correctly. (Smart contract transactions are deterministic, so each re-execution yields the same results as the original.) These *validator* nodes do not receive fees for re-execution.

To summarize, a transaction is executed in two contexts: once by miners before attempting to append a block to the blockchain, and many times afterward by validators checking that each block in the blockchain is honest. In both contexts, each block's transactions are executed sequentially in block order.

## 3 SPECULATIVE SMART CONTRACTS

This section discusses how miners can execute contract codes concurrently. Concurrency for validators is addressed in the next section.

Smart contract semantics is *sequential*: each miner has a single thread of control that executes one EVM instruction at a time. The miner executes each of the block's contracts in sequence. One contract can call another contract's functions, causing control to pass from the first contract code to the second, and back again. (Indeed, misuse of this control structure has been the source of well-known security breaches [6].) Clearly, even sequential smart contracts must be written with care, and introducing explicit concurrency to contract programming languages would only make the situation worse. We conclude that concurrent smart contract executions must be *serializable*: indistinguishable, except for execution time, from a sequential execution.

There are several obstacles to running contracts in parallel. First, smart contract codes read and modify shared storage, so it is essential to ensure that concurrent contract code executions do not result in inconsistent storage states. Second, smart contract languages are Turing-complete, and therefore it is impossible in general to determine statically whether contracts have data conflicts.

We propose that miners execute contract codes as *speculative actions*. A miner schedules multiple concurrent contracts to run in parallel. Contracts' data structures are instrumented to detect synchronization conflicts at run-time, in much the same way as mechanisms like transactional boosting [11]. If one speculative contract execution conflicts with another, the conflict is resolved either by delaying one contract until the other completes, or by rolling back and restarting one of the conflicting executions. When a speculative action completes successfully, it is said to *commit*, and otherwise it *aborts*.

**Storage Operations.** We assume that, as in Solidity, state variables are restricted to predefined types such as scalars, structures, enumerations, arrays, and mappings. A *storage operation* is a primitive operation on a state variable. For example, binding a key to a value in a mapping, or reading from a variable or an array are storage operations. Two storage operations *commute* if executing them in either order yields the same result values and the same storage state. For example, in the address-to-Voter Ballot mapping in Listing 1, binding Alice's address to a vote of 42 commutes with binding Bob's address to a vote of 17, but does not commute when deleting Alice's vote. An *inverse* for a storage operation is another operation that undoes its effects. For example, the inverse of assigning to a variable is restoring its prior value, and the inverse of adding a new key-value pair to a mapping is to remove that binding, and so on. The virtual machine system can provide all storage operations with inverses.

The virtual machine is in charge of managing concurrency for state variables such as mappings and arrays. Speculation is controlled by two run-time mechanisms, invisible to the programmer, and managed by the virtual machine: *abstract locks*, and *inverse logs*.

Each storage operation has an associated abstract lock. The rule for assigning abstract locks to operations is simple: if two storage operations map to distinct abstract locks, then they must commute. Before a thread can execute a storage operation, it must acquire the associated abstract lock. The thread is delayed while that lock is held by another thread[4]. Once the lock is acquired, the thread records an *inverse operation* in a log, and proceeds with the operation.

If the action commits, its abstract locks are released and its log is discarded. If the action aborts, the inverse log is replayed, most recent operation first, to undo the effects of that speculative action. When the replay is complete, the action's abstract locks are released.

The advantage of combining abstract locks with inverse logs is that the virtual machine can support very fine-grained concurrency. A more traditional implementation of speculative actions might associate locks with memory regions such as cache lines or pages, and keep track of old and versions of those regions for recovery. Such a coarse-grained approach could lead to many false conflicts, where operations that commute in a semantic sense are treated as conflicting because they access overlapping memory regions. In the next section, we will see how to use abstract locks to speed up verifiers.

[3] http://solidity.readthedocs.io/en/develop/solidity-by-example.html

[4] For ease of exposition, abstract locks are mutually exclusive, although it is not hard to accommodate shared and exclusive modes.

When one smart contract calls another, the run-time system creates a *nested* speculative action, which can commit or abort independently of its parent. A nested speculative action inherits the abstract locks held by its parent, and it creates its own inverse log. If the nested action commits, any abstract locks it acquired are passed to its parent, and its inverse log is appended to its parent's log. If the nested action aborts, its inverse log is replayed to undo its effects, and any abstract locks it acquired are released. Aborting a child action does not abort the parent, but a child action's effects become permanent only when the parent commits. The abstract locking mechanism also detects and resolves deadlocks, which are expected to be rare.

The scheme described here is *eager*, acquiring locks, applying operations, and recording inverses. An alternative *lazy* implementation could buffer changes to a contract's storage, applying them only on commit.

A miner's incentive to perform speculative concurrent execution is the possibility of increased throughput, and hence a competitive advantage against other miners. Of course, the miner undertakes a risk that synchronization conflicts among contracts will cause some contracts to be rolled back and re-executed, possibly delaying block construction, and forcing the miner to re-execute code not compensated by client fees. Nevertheless, the experimental results reported below suggest that even a small degree of concurrent speculative execution pays off, even in the face of moderate data conflicts.

## 4 CONCURRENT VALIDATION

The speculative techniques proposed above for miners are no help for validators. Here is the problem: miners use speculation to discover a concurrent schedule for a block's transactions, a schedule equivalent to some sequential schedule, except faster. That schedule is constructed non-deterministically, depending on the order in which threads acquired abstract locks. To check that the block's miner was honest, validators need to reconstruct the same (or an equivalent) schedule chosen by the miner.

Validators need a way to deterministically reproduce the miner's concurrent schedule. To this end, we extend abstract locks to track dependencies, that is, who passed which abstract locks to whom. Each speculative lock includes a *use counter* that keeps track of the number of times it has been released by a committing action during the construction of the current block. When a miner starts a block, it sets these counters to zero.

When a speculative action commits, it increments the counters for each of the locks it holds, and then it registers a *lock profile* with the VM recording the abstract locks and their counter values.

When all the actions have committed, it is possible to reconstruct their common schedule by comparing their lock profiles. For example, consider three committed speculative actions, $A$, $B$, and $C$. If $A$ and $B$ have no abstract locks in common, they can run concurrently. If an abstract lock has counter value 1 in $A$'s profile and 2 in $C$'s profile, then $C$ must be scheduled after $A$.

A miner includes these profiles in the blockchain along with usual information. From this profile information, validators can construct a *fork-join* program that deterministically reproduces the

**Algorithm 1** MINEINPARALLEL($T$) - Mine in parallel

**Require:** A set of contract transactions $T$
**Ensure:** A serial order $S$ of transactions and a happens-before graph $H$ of the locking schedule

**function** MINEINPARALLEL($B$)
  Initialize log $L$ for recording locking operations
  Execute all transactions $t \in T$ in parallel, recording locking activity in $L$
  Generate happens-before graph $H$ from $L$
  Create the serial ordering $S$ via a topological sort of $H$
  **return** $(S, H)$
**end function**

**Algorithm 2** CONSTRUCTVALIDATOR($S, H$) - Construct a parallel validator

**Require:** The serial ordering $S$ and happens-before graph $H$ from the miner
**Ensure:** A set of fork-join tasks ensuring parallel execution according to the happens-before graph

**function** CONSTRUCTVALIDATOR($B$)
  Initialize a mapping $F$ from each transaction $t$ to its fork-join task $f$
  Create the happens-after graph $H'$ by reversing the edges of $H$
  **for all** $t \in S$ **do**
    $B \leftarrow$ all transactions $u \in H'$ that happen immediately before $t$, i.e., its outedges
    Create a fork-join task $f$ for $t$ that first joins with all tasks in $B$, i.e.,
    $f \leftarrow$ **for** ($b$ in $B$) { $F$.get($b$).join() } execute($t$)
    Save the new fork-join task in $F$, i.e., $F$.put($t, f$)
  **end for**
  **return** the value set of $F$, the fork-join tasks
**end function**

miner's original, speculative schedule. Algorithm 1 provides a high-level sketch of the operation of the miner. By logging the locking schedule during parallel execution, the miner generates a happens-before graph of transactions according to the order in which they acquire locks and commit. A valid serial history is produced from a topological sort of this graph. Algorithm 2 constructs the validator by scanning through the list of actions as they appear in the serial history. A fork-join task is created for each action and stored for lookup by its identifier. Each task will first lookup and join any tasks that must precede it according to the locking schedule before executing the action itself.

The resulting fork-join program is not speculative, nor does it require inter-thread synchronization other than forks and joins. The validator is not required to match the miner's level of parallelism: using a work-stealing scheduler [1], the validator can exploit whatever degree of parallelism it has available. The validator does not need abstract locks, dynamic conflict detection, or the ability to roll back speculative actions, because the fork-join structure ensures that conflicting actions never execute concurrently.

To check that the miner's proposed schedule is correct, the validator's virtual machine records a trace of the abstract locks each thread would have acquired, had it been executing speculatively. This trace is thread-local, requiring no expensive inter-thread synchronization. At the end of the execution, the validator's VM compares the traces it generated with the lock profiles provided by the miner. If they differ, the block is rejected.

What is a miner's incentive to publish a block's fork-join schedule? A miner who publishes an incorrect schedule will be detected and its block rejected, but a miner might publish a correct sequential schedule equivalent to, but less parallel than the schedule it discovered. Such a tactic seems ill-advised, however, because that block may be competing with other blocks produced at the same time, and the miner will be rewarded only if the other miners choose to build on that block. Publishing a block with a parallel valiation schedule makes the block more attractive for validation by other miners. Because fork-join schedules are published in the blockchain, their degree of parallelism is easily evaluated.

## 5 CORRECTNESS

Concurrent calls to smart contract functions might leave persistent storage in an inconsistent state not possible after a serial execution. Instead, we must show that every concurrent execution permitted by our proposal is equivalent to some sequential execution. Because miners are free to choose the order in which contracts appear in a block, any sequential execution will do.

Our argument builds on prior proofs that transactional boosting is serializable [11, 16, 17]. A given execution of a contract's function involves a sequence of storage operations on persistent objects. (The Ethereum gas restriction ensures this sequence is finite.) Recall that if two storage operations map to distinct abstract locks, then they commute. If another thread executes another sequence of operations, and there are two operations that do not commute, then both threads will try to acquire the same lock, and one will be delayed until the other completes. (Deadlocks are detected and resolved by aborting one execution.) As proved elsewhere [11, 16, 17], the result is a serializable execution[5].

We cannot guarantee that the schedule published by the miner is the same one that it executed, but we can guarantee the two are equivalent to a common sequential history. Validators replay the concurrent schedule published by the miner, and will detect if the schedule produces a final state different from the one recorded in the block, or if the schedule has a data race (an unsynchronized concurrent access).

## 6 IMPLEMENTATION

Because the EVM is not multithreaded, our prototype uses the Java Virtual Machine (JVM). Speculative actions are executed by the Scala Software Transactional Memory Library (ScalaSTM [21]).

Examples of smart contracts were translated from Solidity into Scala, then modified to use the concurrency libraries. Each function from the Solidity contract is turned into a speculative transaction by wrapping its contents with a ScalaSTM atomic section. Solidity mapping objects are implemented as boosted hashtables, where key values are used to index abstract locks. Additionally, solidity `struct` types were translated into immutable case classes. Methods take a `msg` field to emulate Solidity contracts' global state, which includes details of the transaction, addresses of participants, and so on. Scalar fields are implemented as a single a boosted mapping.

The Solidity **throw** operation, which explicitly rolls back a contract execution, is emulated by throwing a Java runtime exception caught by the miner.

In our prototype, abstract locks are implemented via interfaces exported by ScalaSTM, relying on ScalaSTM's native deadlock detection and resolution mechanisms.

[5] Because speculative executions take place entirely within a virtual machine, opacity [10] is not an issue.

### 6.1 Miners and Validators

Miners manage concurrency using Java's `ExecutorService`. This class provides a pool of threads and runs a collection of `callable` objects in parallel. A block of transactions in Ethereum is implemented as a set of `callable` objects passed to the thread pool. To generate locking profiles from the parallel execution, we instrument smart contracts to log when atomic sections start and end, as well as calls to boosted operations. From the log, we can encode the locking schedule as a happens-before graph for the validator. The validator transforms this happens-before graph into a fork-join program. Each transaction from the block is a fork-join task that first joins with all tasks according to its in-edges on the happens-before graph.

## 7 EXPERIMENTAL EVALUATION

Our goal is to improve throughput for miners and validators by allowing unrelated contracts to execute in parallel. To evaluate this approach, we created a series of benchmarks for sample contracts that vary the number of transactions and their degree of conflict. These benchmarks are conservative, operating on only one or a few contracts at a time and permitting higher degrees of data conflict than one would expect in practice.

Our experiments are designed to answer two questions. (1) For a given amount of data conflict, how does speedup change over increasing transactions? We expect to see more speedup as the number of transactions increases, limited by the number of cores available on the underlying hardware. (2) How does the speedup change as data conflict increases? For low data conflict, we expect our parallel miner to perform better than serial. But as data conflict increases, we expect a drop-off in speedup, limited by core availability.

### 7.1 Benchmarks

There are four benchmarks, one for each of the example contracts we implemented, Ballot, SimpleAuction, and EtherDoc, as well as the Mixed benchmark containing transactions from all other contracts. For each benchmark, our implementation is evaluated on blocks containing between 10 and 400 transactions with 15% data conflict, as well as blocks containing 200 transactions with data conflict percentages ranging from 0% to 100% data conflict. The data conflict percentage is defined to be the percentage of transactions that contend with at least one other transaction for shared data. As we will see, the impact of data conflict on speedup depends on the contract implementation.

These benchmarks are conservative. For all benchmarks besides Mixed, the entire block operates on the same contract, calling only one or two methods. In reality, mined blocks contained transactions on unrelated contracts and accounts. While the theoretical maximum number of transactions per block is currently around 200 transactions[6], we test a wide range from 10 to 400. This maximum increases and decreases over time, as determined by miner preference [9]. In practice, the number of transactions can be far fewer per block, e.g., when there are costly transactions. For testing speedup over number of transactions, we fix the data conflict rate at 15%, though we expect that blocks in practice rarely have very much internal data conflict. While we did not measure data conflict in the existing blockchain, our approach implemented in EVM could be used to collect such data on an existing blockchain. For testing speedup as data conflict increases, we fix the number of transactions per block to 200, the current theoretical maximum.

**Ballot.** This contract is an example voting application from the Solidity documentation [23] and is described in Section 2. For all benchmarks, the contract is put into an initial state where voters are already registered. All block transactions for this benchmark are requests to vote on the same proposal. To add data conflict, some voters attempt to double-vote, creating two transactions that contend for the same voter data. 100% data conflict occurs when all voters attempt to vote twice.

**SimpleAuction.** This contract, also from the Solidity documentation [23] implements an auction. There is a single owner who initiates the auction, while any participant can place bids with the `bid()` method. A mapping tracks how much money needs to be returned to which bidder once the auction is over. Bidders can then `withdraw()` their money. For the benchmarks, the contract state is initialized by several bidders entering a bid. The block consists of transactions that withdraw these bids. Data conflict is added by including new bidders who call `bidPlusOne()` to read and increase the highest bid. The rate of data conflict depends on how many bidders are bidding at the same time, thus accessing the same highest bidder. 100% data conflict happens when all transactions are `bidPlusOne()` bids.

**EtherDoc.** EtherDoc[7] is a "Proof of Existence" decentralized application (DAPP) that tracks per-document metadata including hashcode and owner. It permits new document creation, metadata retrieval, and ownership transfer. For the benchmarks, the contract is initialized with a number of documents and owners. Transactions consist of owners checking the existence of the document by hashcode. Data conflict is added by including transactions that transfer ownership to the contract creator. As with SimpleAuction, all contending transactions touch the same shared data, so we expect a faster drop-off in speedup with increased data conflict than Ballot. 100% data conflict happens when all transactions are transfers.

**Mixed.** This benchmark combines transactions on the above smart contracts in equal proportions, and data conflict is added the same way in equal proportions from their corresponding benchmarks.

[6] A transaction costs 21,000 gas plus the gas for the computation [25]. The gas limit on block 3,110,235 (latest as of writing) was 4,005,875, a maximum close to 200.

[7] https://github.com/maran/notareth

## 7.2 Results

We ran our experiments on a 4-core 3.07GHz Intel Xeon W3550 with 12 GB of memory running Ubuntu 16. All of our experiments run on the Java Virtual Machine (JVM) with JIT compilation disabled. Parallel mining and validation are run with a fixed pool of three threads, leaving one core available for garbage collection and other system processes/threads.

For each benchmark, blocks were generated for each combination of the number of transactions and data conflict percentage. Each block is run on the parallel miner, the validator, and a serial miner that runs the block without parallelization. The serial results serve as the baseline for computing speedup. The running time is collected five times and the mean and standard deviation are measured. All runs are given three warm-up runs per collection.

Figure 2 shows the speedup of the parallel miner and validator relative to the serial miner for all. (The running times with mean and standard deviation can be found in Appendix A.) The left charts plot the speedup over the number of transactions in the block at a fixed data conflict percentage of 15%. The speedup for all benchmarks follows roughly the same pattern. For low numbers of transactions, there is no speedup and even some slowdown. This is likely due to data conflict as well as the overhead of multithreading. For over around 50 transactions, there is a speedup that increases to about 2x, in line with expectations from a thread pool of size three. EtherDoc is an exception, seeing less than 1.5x speedup. The validator generally has a higher speedup than the parallel miner. This is because the parallel miner has done the hard work of finding data conflict and produced a locking schedule for the validator to follow.

The right-hand charts of Figure 2 plot the speedup as the data conflict percentage increases for fixed blocks of 200 transactions. As data conflict increases, the miner's speedup reduces from 2x to close to serial as many transactions touch shared data. The validator also starts at around 2x with no data conflict, but goes down to about 1.5x, again benefiting from the work of the parallel miner.

Ballot's parallel mining hovers around 1.5x speedup, suffering little from the extra data conflict. Data conflict in SimpleAuction and EtherDoc, however, has an expectedly higher impact, because each contending transaction touches the same data. The Mixed benchmark provides a more realistic view of a block by combining transactions from unrelated contracts. Even though EtherDoc reduces parallelism under high data conflict, when mixed with other transactions, the parallel miner can still gain a substantial speedup.

The average of speedups of all benchmarks is 1.33x for the parallel miner and 1.69x for the validator. Table 1 shows the average speedups for each benchmark.

## 7.3 Discussion

These results show that speculative concurrent execution speeds up mining when threads are occupied and the data conflict rate is not too high. Data conflicts among transactions in the same block is likely to be infrequent over the long term. (Miners could also choose transactions so as to reduce the likelihood of conflict, say by including only those contracts that operate on disjoint data sets.) Due to limited hardware, our experiments used only three concurrent threads, but even this modest level of concurrency showed a

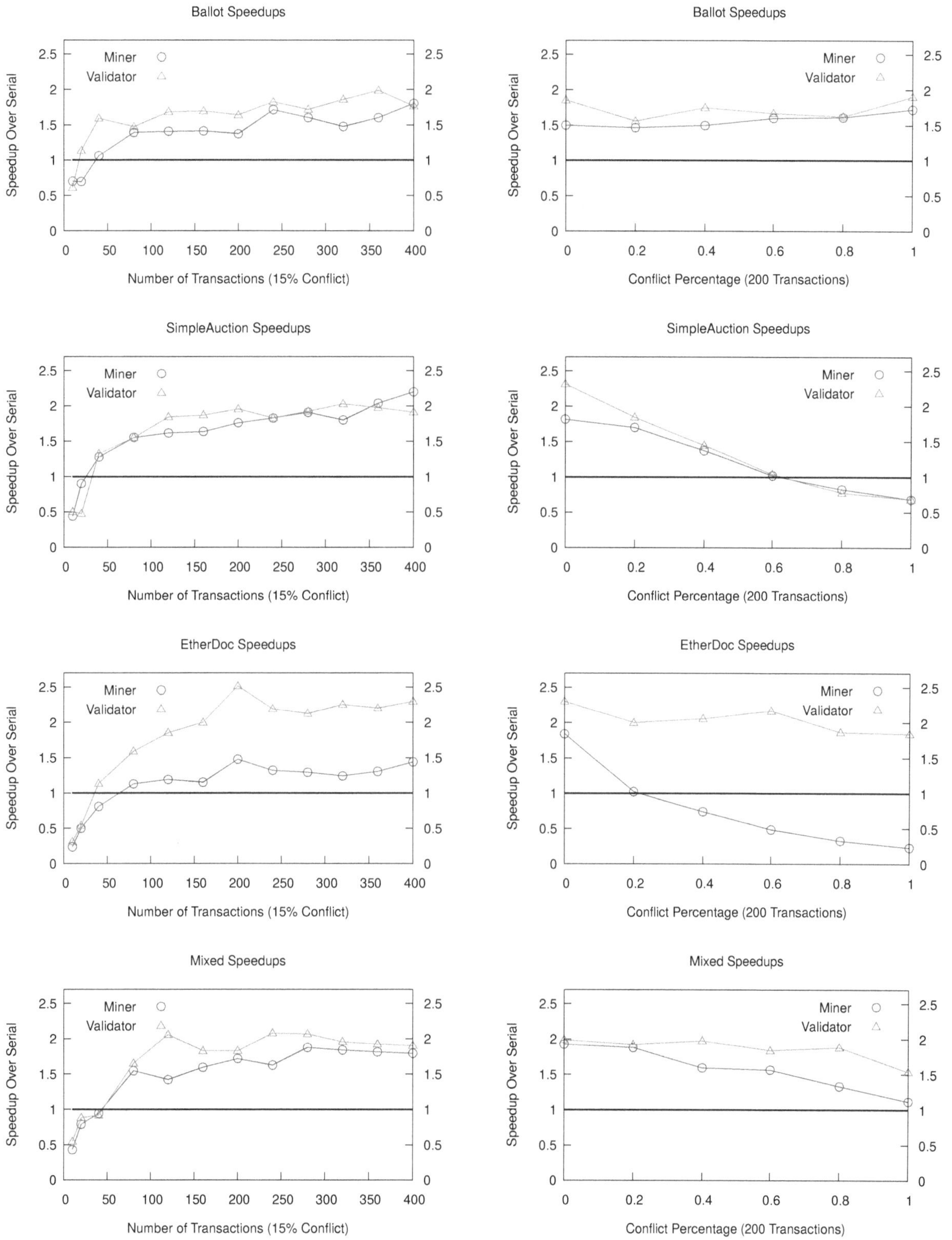


**Figure 2: The speedup of the miner and validator versus serial mining for each benchmark. The left charts are the speedup as block size increases, while the right are the speedup as data conflict increases.**

| | SimpleAuction | | Ballot | | EtherDoc | | Mixed | |
|---|---|---|---|---|---|---|---|---|
| | Conflict | BlockSize | Conflict | BlockSize | Conflict | BlockSize | Conflict | BlockSize |
| **Miner** | 1.23x | 1.58x | 1.57x | 1.35x | 0.78x | 1.09x | 1.57x | 1.45x |
| **Validator** | 1.35x | 1.60x | 1.73x | 1.58x | 2.04x | 1.75x | 1.86x | 1.64x |

**Table 1: The average speedups for each benchmark.**

benefit. Concurrent hardware has proved effective for speeding up solutions to proof-of-work puzzles, and now similar investments could speed up smart contract execution and validation.

Concurrent smart contract execution speeds up miners by enabling them to construct blocks faster before appending them to the chain. But in permissionless blockchains, the bulk of miner time is spent computing proof-of-work for the block after construction. Concurrent smart contracts, however, still provide a big win for validators. Validators spend much time executing transactions, while validating the proof-of-work by miners is fast. Ethereum is transitioning to proof-of-stake to reduce the computational burden imposed by proof-of-work. Additionally, permissioned blockchains eschew proof-of-work, so concurrent smart contract execution provides even more of a boost to throughput to these blockchains.

## 8 RELATED WORK

The notion of smart contracts can be traced back to an article by Nick Szabo in 1997 [24]. Bitcoin [20] includes a scripting language whose expressive power was limited to protect against nonterminating scripts. Ethereum [8] is perhaps the most widely used smart contract platform, employing a combination of a Turing-complete virtual machine protected from non-termination by charging clients for contract running times. Solidity [22] is the most popular programming language for programming the Ethereum virtual machine.

Luu *et al.* [18] identify a number of security vulnerabilities and pitfalls in the Ethereum smart contract model. Luu *et al.* [19] also identify perverse incentives that cause rational miners sometimes to accept unvalidated blocks. Delmolino *et al.* [7] document common programming errors observed in smart contracts. The Hawk [15] smart contract system is designed to protect the privacy of participants.

As noted, many of the speculative mechanisms introduced here were adapted from *transactional boosting* [11], a technique for transforming thread-safe linearizable objects into highly-concurrent transactional objects. Boosting was originally developed to enhance the concurrency provided by software transactional memory systems [12] by exploiting type-specific information. Other techniques that exploit type-specific properties to enhance concurrency in STMs include *transactional predication* [3] and *software transactional objects* [13].

There are other techniques for deterministically reproducing a prior concurrent execution. See Bocchino *et al.* [2] for a survey.

Cachin et al. discuss non-deterministic execution of smart contracts in the context of BFT-based permissioned blockchains [4].

## 9 CONCLUSION

We have shown that one can exploit multi-core architectures to increase smart contract processing throughput for both miners and validators. First, miners execute a block's contracts speculatively and in parallel, resulting in lower latency whenever the block's contracts lack data conflicts. Miners are incentivized to include in each block an encoding of the serializable parallel schedule that produced that block. Validators convert that schedule into a deterministic, parallel fork-join program that allows them to validate the block in parallel. Even with only three threads, a prototype implementation yields overall speedups of 1.33x for miners and 1.69x for validators on representative smart contracts.

Although our discussion has focused on "permisionless" systems where anyone can participate, the mechanisms proposed here would also be useful for "permissioned" systems, such as Hyperledger [14], where participants are controlled by an authority such as an organization or consortium. For example, in a permissioned blockchain based on Practical Byzantine Fault-Tolerance (PBF) [5], the leader might use speculative execution to discover a concurrent schedule for a block, while particpants in the PBFT protocol would use the concurrent schedule to validate the block before voting.

Future work includes adding support for multithreading to the Ethereum virtual machine, in much the same way as today's Java virtual machines. Our proposal for miners only is compatible with current smart contract systems such as Ethereum, but our overall proposal is not, because it requires including scheduling metadata in blocks and incentivizing miners to publish their parallel schedules. It may well be compatible with a future "soft fork" (backward compatible change), a subject for future research.

In addition to a multithreaded VM, we see room for advancement in programming language support for smart contracts. Designing a language that lends itself to finer-grained concurrency will increase the success of speculative execution thereby increasing throughput. It would also be useful for the language to provide better control of concurrency, helping the smart contract developer maximize throughput while avoiding concurrency pitfalls.

## REFERENCES


[1] R. D. Blumofe, C. F. Joerg, B. C. Kuszmaul, C. E. Leiserson, K. H. Randall, and Y. Zhou. Cilk: An efficient multithreaded runtime system. In *Proceedings of the Fifth ACM SIGPLAN Symposium on Principles and Practice of Parallel Programming*, PPOPP '95, pages 207–216, New York, NY, USA, 1995. ACM.

[2] R. L. Bocchino, Jr., V. S. Adve, S. V. Adve, and M. Snir. Parallel programming must be deterministic by default. In *Proceedings of the First USENIX Conference on Hot Topics in Parallelism*, HotPar'09, pages 4–4, Berkeley, CA, USA, 2009. USENIX Association.

[3] N. G. Bronson, J. Casper, H. Chafi, and K. Olukotun. Transactional predication: High-performance concurrent sets and maps for stm. In *Proceedings of the 29th ACM SIGACT-SIGOPS Symposium on Principles of Distributed Computing*, PODC '10, pages 6–15, New York, NY, USA, 2010. ACM.

[4] C. Cachin, S. Schubert, and M. Vukolic. Non-Determinism in Byzantine Fault-Tolerant Replication. In P. Fatourou, E. Jiménez, and F. Pedone, editors, *20th International Conference on Principles of Distributed Systems (OPODIS 2016)*, volume 70 of *Leibniz International Proceedings in Informatics (LIPIcs)*, pages 24:1–24:16, Dagstuhl, Germany, 2017. Schloss Dagstuhl–Leibniz-Zentrum fuer Informatik.

[5] M. Castro and B. Liskov. Practical byzantine fault tolerance. In *Proceedings of the Third Symposium on Operating Systems Design and Implementation*, OSDI '99, pages 173–186, Berkeley, CA, USA, 1999. USENIX Association.

[6] DAO. Thedao smart contract. Retrieved 8 February 2017.

[7] K. Delmolino, M. Arnett, A. Kosba, A. Miller, and E. Shi. *Step by Step Towards Creating a Safe Smart Contract: Lessons and Insights from a Cryptocurrency Lab*, pages 79–94. Springer Berlin Heidelberg, Berlin, Heidelberg, 2016.

[8] Ethereum. https://github.com/ethereum/.

[9] Ethereum design Rationale. http://github.com/ethereum/wiki/wiki/Design-Rationale#gas-and-fees.

[10] R. Guerraoui and M. Kapalka. On the correctness of transactional memory. In *Proceedings of the 13th ACM SIGPLAN Symposium on Principles and practice of parallel programming (PPoPP'08)*, pages 175–184, New York, NY, USA, 2008. ACM.

[11] M. Herlihy and E. Koskinen. Transactional boosting: A methodology for highly-concurrent transactional objects. In *Proceedings of the 13th ACM SIGPLAN Symposium on Principles and Practice of Parallel Programming*, PPoPP '08, pages 207–216, New York, NY, USA, 2008. ACM.

[12] M. Herlihy, V. Luchangco, M. Moir, and W. N. Scherer, III. Software transactional memory for dynamic-sized data structures. In *Proceedings of the twenty-second annual symposium on Principles of distributed computing*, PODC '03, pages 92–101, New York, NY, USA, 2003. ACM.

[13] N. Herman, J. P. Inala, Y. Huang, L. Tsai, E. Kohler, B. Liskov, and L. Shrira. Type-aware transactions for faster concurrent code. In *Proceedings of the Eleventh European Conference on Computer Systems*, EuroSys '16, pages 31:1–31:16, New York, NY, USA, 2016. ACM.

[14] Hyperledger white paper. http://www.the-blockchain.com/docs/Hyperledger%20Whitepaper.pdf.

[15] A. E. Kosba, A. Miller, E. Shi, Z. Wen, and C. Papamanthou. Hawk: The blockchain model of cryptography and privacy-preserving smart contracts. In *IEEE Symposium on Security and Privacy*, 2015.

[16] E. Koskinen and M. J. Parkinson. The push/pull model of transactions. In *Proceedings of the 36th ACM SIGPLAN Conference on Programming Language Design and Implementation (PLDI'15), Portland, OR, USA*. ACM, 2015.

[17] E. Koskinen, M. J. Parkinson, and M. Herlihy. Coarse-grained transactions. In *Proceedings of the 37th ACM SIGPLAN-SIGACT Symposium on Principles of Programming Languages (POPL'10)*, pages 19–30. ACM, 2010.

[18] L. Luu, D. Chu, H. Olickel, P. Saxena, and A. Hobor. Making smart contracts smarter. In *Proceedings of the 2016 ACM SIGSAC Conference on Computer and Communications Security, Vienna, Austria, October 24-28, 2016*, pages 254–269, 2016.

[19] L. Luu, J. Teutsch, R. Kulkarni, and P. Saxena. Demystifying incentives in the consensus computer. In *Proceedings of the 22Nd ACM SIGSAC Conference on Computer and Communications Security*, CCS '15, pages 706–719, New York, NY, USA, 2015. ACM.

[20] S. Nakamoto. Bitcoin: A peer-to-peer electronic cash system. May 2009.

[21] Scala STM Expert Group. Scalastm. web. Retrieved from http://nbronson.github.com/scala-stm/, 20 November 2011.

[22] Solidity documentation. http://solidity.readthedocs.io/en/latest/index.html.

[23] Solidity documentation: Solidity by example. http://solidity.readthedocs.io/en/develop/solidity-by-example.html.

[24] N. Szabo. Formalizing and securing relationships on public networks. *First Monday*, 2(9), 1997.

[25] G. Wood. Ethereum: A secure decentralised generalised transaction ledger.

# A MEAN AND STANDARD DEVIATION OF BENCHMARK RUNNING TIMES

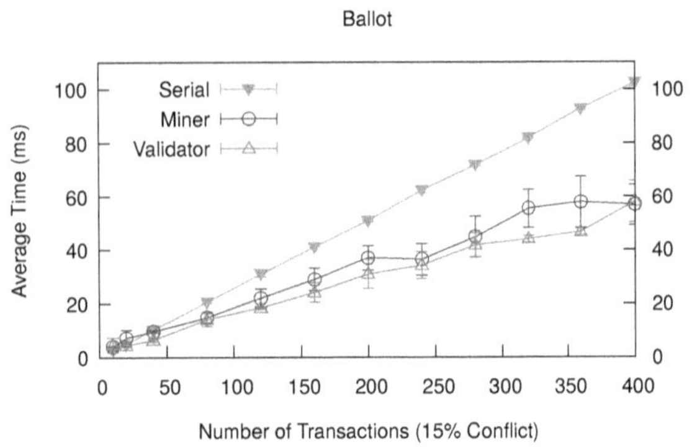


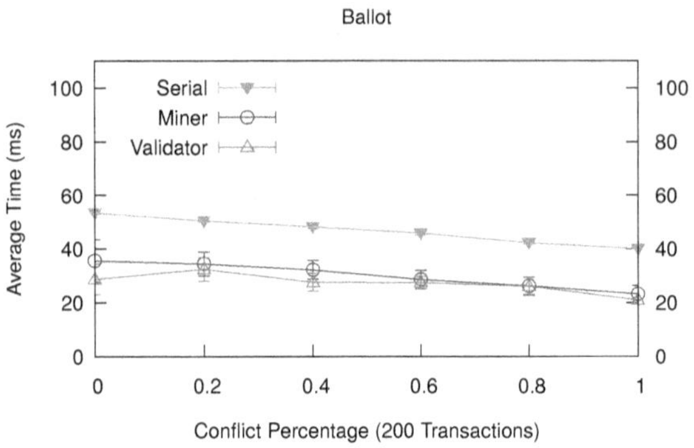


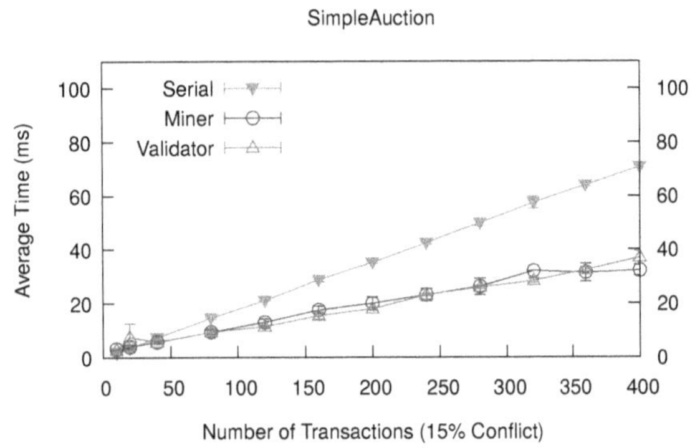


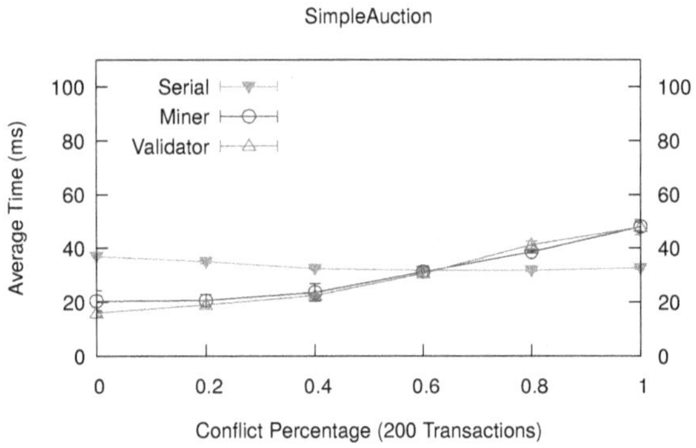


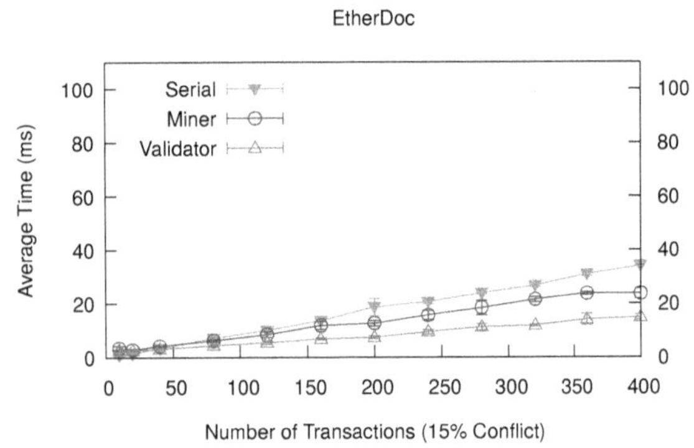


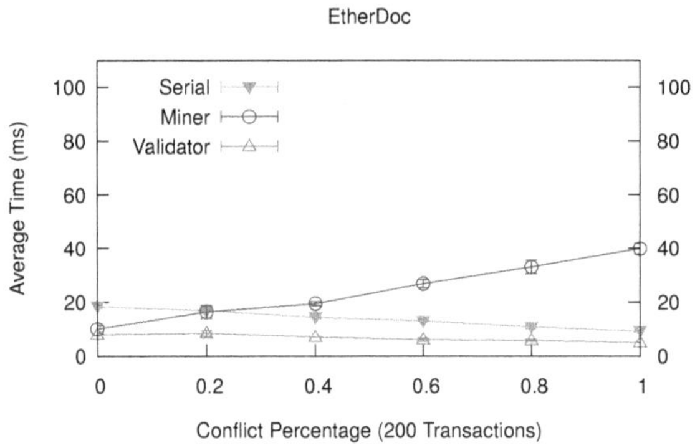


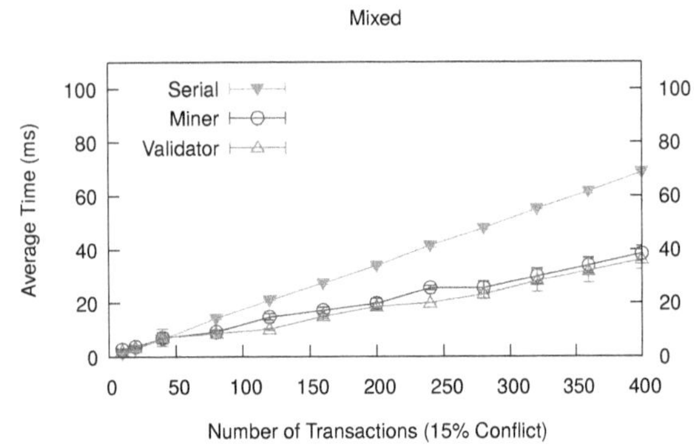


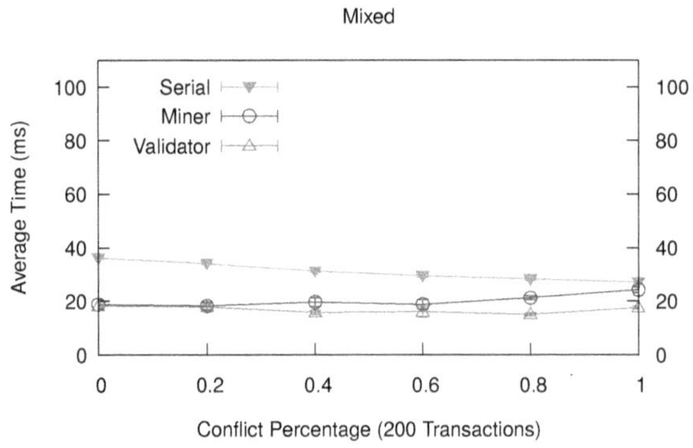

# Verifiable Outsourced Computation: A Survey

Rosario Gennaro
The City College of New York

## ABSTRACT

I will review recent (and not so recent) research on the topic of Verifiable Outsourced Computation. The problem of verifying the correctness of computations done by untrusted parties was a driving motivation behind some of the most celebrated results in Complexity Theory in the 90s, from Interactive Proofs to the PCP Theorem. More recently this problem has received renewed attention from more applied corners of Computer Science, due to the rise of the Cloud Computing paradigm, where data and computation is outsourced to external providers who may not be necessarily trusted. Current research is focused on making some of those old theoretical results applicable in practice, a task that ultimately will require both theoretical and more applied systems breakthroughs.


*PODC '17, July 25-27, 2017, Washington, DC, USA*

ACM ISBN 978-1-4503-4992-5/17/07.
http://dx.doi.org/10.1145/3087801.3087872

## Author Keywords

Zero-Knowledge Protocols; Verifiable Computation; Cloud Computing

## BIOGRAPHY

Rosario Gennaro received his Ph.D. in 1996 from the Massachusetts Institute of Technology under the supervision of Prof. Silvio Micali. He then joined the Network Security Department at the IBM T.J.Watson Research Center. In 2012 he moved to the City University of New York, where he directs the Center for Algorithms, a research center focused on practice driven Theoretical Computer Science, with a focus on cryptography and network security and quantum computing.

# FruitChains: A Fair Blockchain

Rafael Pass
CornellTech
New York, NY
rafael@cs.cornell.edu

Elaine Shi
Cornell
Ithaca, NY
elaine@cs.cornell.edu

## ABSTRACT

Nakamoto's famous *blockchain* protocol enables achieving consensus in a so-called *permissionless setting*—anyone can join (or leave) the protocol execution, and the protocol instructions do not depend on the identities of the players. His ingenious protocol prevents "sybil attacks" (where an adversary spawns any number of new players) by relying on *computational puzzles* (a.k.a. "moderately hard functions") introduced by Dwork and Naor (Crypto'92). Recent work by Garay et al (EuroCrypt'15) and Pass et al (manuscript, 2016) demonstrate that this protocol provably achieves *consistency* and *liveness* assuming a) honest players control a majority of the computational power in the network, b) the puzzle-hardness is appropriately set as a function of the maximum network delay and the total computational power of the network, and c) the computational puzzle is modeled as a random oracle. Assuming honest participation, however, is a strong assumption, especially in a setting where honest players are expected to perform a lot of work (to solve the computational puzzles). In Nakamoto's Bitcoin application of the blockchain protocol, players are *incentivized* to solve these puzzles by receiving rewards for every "block" (of transactions) they contribute to the blockchain. An elegant work by Eyal and Sirer (FinancialCrypt'14), strengthening and formalizing an earlier attack discussed on the Bitcoin forum, demonstrates that a *coalition* controlling even a minority fraction of the computational power in the network can gain (close to) 2 times its "fair share" of the rewards (and transaction fees) by deviating from the protocol instructions. In contrast, in a *fair* protocol, one would expect that players controlling a $\phi$ fraction of the computational resources to reap a $\phi$ fraction of the rewards.

We present a new blockchain protocol—the FruitChain protocol—which satisfies the same consistency and liveness properties as Nakamoto's protocol (assuming an honest majority of the computing power), and additionally is *$\delta$-approximately fair*: with overwhelming probability, any honest set of players controlling a $\phi$ fraction of computational power is guaranteed to get at least a fraction $(1-\delta)\phi$ of the blocks (and thus rewards) in *any* $\Omega(\frac{\kappa}{\delta})$ length segment of the chain (where $\kappa$ is the security parameter). Consequently, if this blockchain protocol is used as the ledger underlying a cryptocurrency system, where rewards and transaction fees are *evenly distributed* among the miners of blocks in a length $\kappa$ segment of the chain, no coalition controlling less than a majority of the computing power can gain more than a factor $(1+3\delta)$ by deviating from the protocol (i.e., honest participation is an *$\frac{n}{2}$-coalition-safe $3\delta$-Nash equilibrium*). Finally, the FruitChain protocol enables decreasing the *variance* of mining rewards and as such significantly lessens (or even obliterates) the need for mining pools.

## CCS CONCEPTS

• **Security and privacy → Distributed systems security**;

## KEYWORDS

Distributed consensus; blockchains; fairness; Nash equilibrium

## 1 INTRODUCTION

Distributed systems have been historically analyzed in a *closed* setting—a.k.a. the *permissioned setting*—in which the number of participants in the system, as well as their identities, are common knowledge. In 2008, Nakamoto [16] proposed his celebrated "blockchain protocol" which attempts to achieve consensus in a *permissionless* setting: anyone can join (or leave) the protocol execution (without getting permission from a centralized or distributed authority), and the protocol instructions do not depend on the identities of the players. The core blockchain protocol (a.k.a. "Nakamoto consensus", or the "Bare-bones blockchain protocol"), roughly speaking, is a method for maintaining a *public*, *immutable* and *ordered* ledger of records (for instance, in the Bitcoin application, these records are simply transactions); that is, records can be added to the *end* of the ledger at any time (but only to the end of it); additionally, we are guaranteed that records previously added cannot be removed or reordered and that all honest users have a *consistent view* of the ledger—we refer to this as *consistency*. Additionally, the protocol should satify a *liveness* property: transactions submitted by an honest user get incorporated into the ledger sufficiently fast.

The key challenge with the permissionless setting is that an attacker can trivially mount a so-called "sybil attack"—it simply spawns lots of players (that it controls) and can thus easily ensure that it controls a majority of all the players. Indeed, Barak et al [3] proved that this is a fundamental problem with the permissionless model. Nakamoto blockchain protocol overcomes this issue by relying on "computational puzzles"—a.k.a. *moderately hard functions* or *proofs of work*—put forth by Dwork and Naor [6]: roughly speaking, the participants are required to solve the computational puzzle of some well-defined diffulty in order to confirm transactions—this is referred to as *mining*. Next, rather than attempting to provide robustness whenever the majority of the participants are honest (since participants can be easily spawned in the permissionless setting), Nakamoto's goal was to provide robustness of the protocol under the assumption that a *majority of the computing power* is held


ACM ISBN 978-1-4503-4992-5/17/07...$15.00
https://doi.org/10.1145/3087801.3087809

by honest participants. Indeed, recent works by Garay et al. [8] and Pass et al. [18] formally proved that Nakamoto's blockchain protocol satisfies the above-mentioned consistency and liveness under different network assumptions, as long as the puzzle difficulty (referred to as the *mining hardness*) is apporpriately set as a function of the maxiumum delay in the network.

Nakamoto's blockchain represents an exciting breakthrough: it demonstrated that distributed consensus is possible on an Internet scale. The above analyses, however, assume that a majority of the computing power is controlled by honest players, and that honest players correctly execute the protocol. Assuming such honest participation is a strong assumption, especially in a setting where honest players are expected to perform a lot of work (to solve the computational puzzles)—why would we expect players to want to participate if it is costly! (This can be formalized in the Game-Theory with Costly computation framework of Halpern and Pass [9]). In Nakamoto's ingenious Bitcoin application of the blockchain protocol, players are thus *incentivized* to solve these puzzles by receiving, so-called, *block rewards* for every "blocks" (of transactions) they contribute to the blockchain; additionally, the miners also receive *transaction fees* for all the transactions that are confirmed in the block. The hope is that these reward mechanism (block rewards and transaction fees) properly incentivize honest participation. Unfortunately, as shown by several recent work, this is not the case:

- *Selfish mining undermines incentive compatibility.* Nakamoto's blockchain suffers from a so-called *selfish-mining* attack, where even a minority coalition that controls network delivery can manage to reap close to twice its fair share of block rewards [4, 7, 15, 17, 21] — in particular, if the adversary wields close to a half of the computational power, it can reap almost all of the rewards, thus denying honest players of (almost) any reward! (More specifically, whenever the adversary mines a new block, it simply *withholds it* (not sharing it with the honest players), and only releases it when some honest player mines a new block—if the adversary controls the network it can ensure that all honest players receive the adversarial block before the block mined by the honest players, and as such, it effectively "erases" the honest player's block replacing it with its own block.) This selfish mining attack was first observed in discussions on the Bitcoin forum [15]; the first analytical study provided by Eyal and Sirer [7], and subsequently improved by Sapirshtein et al. [21] and Nayak et al. [17].
- *Transaction fees exacerbate instability.* Due to Bitcoin's particular coin minting schedule, the block reward is scheduled to decrease over time and miners are expected to obtain rewards increasingly more from transaction fees. A recent work by Carlsten et al. [4] (concurrent to ours) demonstrates that the situation gets even worse once we take into account the transaction fees: as a simplest example, if a block contains transactions with large fees, miners will be incentivized to create a "fork" and attempt to confirm the transaction themselves.
- *Mining pools harm decentralization.* Finally, to maintain consistency of the blockchain, the puzzle difficulty is (and by the analysis of [18] need to be set) so that the whole world combined mines a block (i.e., solves a computational puzzle) roughly every 10 minutes. Consequently, an individual "solo miner" with state-of-the-art equiment must wait on average, roughly, 2 years before it gets any rewards [2]. This has led to the formation of "mining pools" where miners are coordinated by a pool operator and share the rewards to reduce the variance of their gains. In essence, the decentralized nature of the blockchain is lost.

## 1.1 Our Results

In this work, we introduce a notion of fairness for blockchain protocols: Roughly speaking, we say that a blockchain protocol that is *fair* if honest players that wield $\phi$ fraction of the computational resources will reap at least $\phi$ fraction of the blocks in any sufficiently long window of the chain. (This notion of fairness can be viewed as a strengthen form of the notion of "ideal chain quality" considered, but not acheived, in [8, 18]) More precisely, we say that a blockchain protocol is *$\delta$-approximately fair* w.r.t. $\rho$ attackers if, with overwhelming probability, any $\phi$ fraction coalition of *honest* users is guaranteed to get at least a $(1-\delta)\phi$ fraction of the blocks in every sufficiently long window of the chain, even in the presence of an adversary controlling up to a $\rho$ fraction of the computing power. Our main theorem shows how to acheive a blockchain which satisfies the same consistency and liveness properties as Nakamoto's one, as well as fairness:

THEOREM 1.1 (INFORMALLY STATED). *Let $\rho < \frac{1}{2}$ be a constant. Then, for every constant $\delta > 0$, there exists a blockchain protocol that satisfies consistency, liveness and $\delta$-approximate fairness.*

Note that approximate fairness directly implies that an attacker cannot get "much" more than its fair share of the block rewards (and thus it disincentivizes selfish mining). But the instability issue with transaction fees still remains, and so does the mining pool issue. We finally demonstrate that our protocol provides a solution to both these issues as well:

- Regarding transaction fees: we suggest a method for spreading out the transaction fees of a block over the miners of a *sequence* of blocks preceeding it. As we show, any fair blockchain protocol can be used to disincentivize deviation even in the presence of transaction fee under this new reward rule. More precisely, we show that no coalition controlling less than a majority of the computing power can gain more than a factor $(1+3\delta)$ of the block rewards and transaction fees by deviating from the protocol—that is, honest participation is an *$\frac{n}{2}$-coalition-safe $3\delta$-Nash equilibrium.*
- Regarding mining pools, we demonstrate that the block (i.e., fruit) mining difficulty in our protocol can be made almost arbitrarily small, and as a consequence, miners can get paid much more often. Indeed, experimental results implenting our new blockchain [1] show that with Bitcoin current block size of 1MB, by sacrificing 8% to 10% of the block to new meta data, we can ensure that miners get paid 1000x more often (and thus on average, roughly, twice per day). Consequently, there is no longer a need for pooled mining.

## 1.2 Protocol Overview

To explain our protocol, let us first recall Nakamoto's blockchain protocol as we will make use of it.

*Nakamoto's protocol in a nutshell.* Roughly speaking, players "confirm" records/transactions by "mining blocks of transactions" through solving some computational puzzle that is a function of the transactions and the history so far. More precisely, each participant maintains its own local "chain" of "blocks" of records —called the *blockchain*. Each block consists of a triple $(h_{-1}, \eta, \mathsf{m})$ where $h_{-1}$ is a pointer to the previous block in chain, m is the record component of the block, and $\eta$ is a "proof-of-work"—a solution to a computational puzzle that is derived from the pair $(h_{-1}, \mathsf{m})$. The proof of work can be thought of as a "key-less digital signature" on the whole blockchain up until this point.

Concretely, Nakamoto's protocol is parametrized by a parameter $p$—which we refer to as the *mining hardness parameter*, and a proof-of-work is deemed valid if $\eta$ is a string such that $\mathsf{H}(h_{-1}, \eta, \mathsf{m}) < D_p$, where H is a hash function (modeled as a random oracle) and $D_p$ is set so that the probability that an input satisfies the relation is less than $p$. At any point of the protocol execution, each participant attempts to increase the length of its own chain by "mining" for a new block: upon receiving some record m, it picks a random $\eta$ and checks whether $\eta$ is a valid proof of work w.r.t. m and $h_{-1}$, where $h_{-1}$ is a pointer to the last block of its current chain; if so, it extends is own local chain and broadcast it to the all the other participants. Whenever a participant receives a chain that is longer than its own local chain, it replaces its own chain with the longer one.

*The* FruitChain *protocol.* Roughly speaking, our FruitChain protocol will be running an instance of Nakamoto's blockchain protocol, but instead of directly storing the records m inside the blockchain, the records are put inside "fruits" denoted $f$; these fruits themselves require solving some proof of work, with a *different hardness parameter* $p_f$; additionally, we require the fruits to "hang" from a block in the chain which is not too "far" from the block which records the fruit—more specifically, the fruit needs to "point" to an earlier block in the chain which is not too far from the block containing it (and thus, the fruit could not have been mined "too" long ago)—we refer to such a fruit as being *recent*. In this new protocol, the fruits play the roles of "blocks"—i.e., *"orange is the new block"*[1]—and chain quality is thus defined in terms of fruits.

In each round, honest players simultaneously mine for a fruit and a block (for Nakamoto's blockchain) by making one invocation of the hash function—this follows the 2-for-1 trick of [8] where, say, the prefix of the output of $H$ determines whether fruit mining is successful, and the suffix is used to determine whether block mining is successful. Whenever a player successfully mines a fruit it broadcasts it to all other players; fruits that have not yet been recorded in the blockchain (and are still recent) are stored in a buffer and all honest players next attempt to add them to the blockchain.

Intuitively, the reason why "selfish mining" fails is that even if an adversary tries to "erase" some block mined by an honest player (which contains some honest fruits), by the chain growth and chain quality properties of the underlying blockchain, eventually an honest player will mine a new block which is stable and this honest player will include the fruits in it—in fact, the time before such an "honest block" arrives is short enough for the fruit to still be "recent" at the time of the honest block arriving.

Intuitively, the reason why we require fruits to be recent is to prevent a different kind of attack: without it, an attacker could *withhold fruits*, and suddenly release lots of them at the same time, thereby creating an very high fraction of adversarial fruits in some segment of the (fruit) chain. By requiring the fruits to be recent, we prevent the adversary from squirreling away (too many of) its fruits: since the underlying blockchain has a guaranteed liveness, we can upperbound the extra amount of time the attacker can withhold fruits and thus upperbound the number of extra fruits it can release in any window.

## 1.3 Related Work

*Comparison with GHOST, the Inclusive Blockchain, and [8].* Although our approach of including fruits in a main blockchain take inspiration from to the earlier elegant works on GHOST [22] and inclusive blockchains [14], we stress that these earlier works do not attain our goals of providing a provably secure, fair blockchain. GHOST [22] is a mechanism such that forking blocks not on the main chain will affect the chain selection rule— however, as the subsequent work by Kiayias and Panagiotakos [12] shows, GHOST actually worsens "chain quality" (i.e., the fraction of honest blocks in the chain) whereas our goal is to improve chain quality and fairness. The inclusive blockchain work proposes to maintain a direct acyclic graph rather than a chain, such that forking subtrees may be included in the linearized transaction log — despite the superficial resemblance at first sight, the mechanisms employed by the inclusive blockchain is actually quit different from how we include fruits in the main blockchain.

As mentionned above, our protocol borrows the 2-for-1 trick from the work Garay et al [8] which also relied on a separate "mining process" to acheive a different goal (namely, to implement a broadcast channel from a blockchain).

*Subsequent works.* In both Nakamoto's blockchain and ours, the time needed to confirm transactions grows with the *worst-case upper-bound* on the network delay [18, 20]. In contrast, in a *responsive* protocol, we require the confirmation time to only be a function of the *actual* network delay, which may be a lot smaller than the worst-case one. In a companion paper called *hybrid consensus* [20], we show how to combine any blockchain protocol with classical asynchronous consensus to improve the latency of the blockchain protocol and achieve responsiveness. Roughly speaking, hybrid consensus makes use of a blockchain to elect a committee—more specifically, the miners of blocks in a sufficiently long segment of the chain are elected as the committee—and then this committee executes the classical consensus protocol. The chain quality of the blockchain determines the fraction of honest players in the committee: if we employ Nakamoto's blockchain, we would need to require that $\frac{3}{4}$ of the computing power is controlled by honest player to ensure a chain quality of $\frac{2}{3}$ and thus a fraction $\frac{2}{3}$ honest committee members (which is required by the consensus protocol). In contrast, by relying on our new FruitChain protocol, it suffices to assume that $\frac{2}{3}$ of the computing power is controlled by honest players. We highlight that, as shown in [20], achieving a responsive protocol

[1] We thank Hugo Krawczyk for this phrase!

also *requires* assuming that $\frac{2}{3}$ of the computing is held by honest parties, and as such relying on our FruitChain protocol enables achieving an *optimal resilience* for low-latency blockchains.

Besides hybrid consensus, other subsequent works have also employed ideas from FruitChain to achieve incentive compatibility in blockchain style protocols. Notably, recent provably secure proof-of-stake protocols, including Snow White [5] and Ouroboros [13], argue that the idea from FruitChain is applicable to non-proof-of-work blockchains as well.

*Other related works.* Kiayias et al. [10] model Bitcoin mining as a game, where nodes decide on which blocks to extend and whether to release a mined block. They show that for small players controlling less than $\frac{1}{3}$ of the resources, following Bitcoin's protocol specification is a Nash equilibrium. Their results, however, only apply to a rather constrained idealistic model where all honest miners can communicate with 0 latency, and the adversary cannot perform form any network level attacks (such as rushing). As we mentionned in the introduction, in our model where the adversary can control the delivery of messages, the bitcoin protocol is not incentive compatible even for players controlling less than a $\frac{1}{3}$ of the computational resources—there is a selfish mining attack which enables an attacker to gain $\frac{1}{2}$ of the block rewards.

# 2 PRELIMINARIES AND DEFINITIONS

## 2.1 Protocol Execution Model and Notations

A protocol refers to an algorithm for a set of interactive Turing Machines (also called nodes) to interact with each other. The execution of a protocol $\Pi$ that is directed by an environment $Z(1^\kappa)$ (where $\kappa$ is a security parameter), which activates a number of parties $1, 2, \ldots, n$ as either "honest" or corrupted parties. Honest parties would faithfully follow the protocol's prescription, whereas corrupt parties are controlled by an adversary $A$ which reads all their inputs/message and sets their outputs/messages to be sent.

The environment $Z$ is a terminology often used in protocol composition in the cryptography literature — one can regard the environment $Z$ a catch-all term that encompasses everything that lives outside the "box" defined by the protocol. For example, as mentioned later, part of the environment $Z$'s job is to provide inputs to honest nodes and receive outputs from them. This models the fact that the inputs to the protocol may originate from external applications and the protocol's outputs can be consumed by external applications where any external application or other protocols running in the system are viewed as part of $Z$.

- A protocol's execution proceeds in *rounds* that model atomic time steps. At the beginning of every round, honest nodes receive inputs from an environment $Z$; at the end of every round, honest nodes send outputs to the environment $Z$.
- $A$ is responsible for delivering all messages sent by parties (honest or corrupted) to *all* other parties. $A$ cannot modify the content of messages broadcast by honest players, *but it may delay or reorder the delivery of a message* as long as it eventually delivers all messages. (Later, we shall consider restrictions on the delivery time.) The identity of the sender is not known to the recipient.[2]
- At any point, $Z$ can *corrupt* an honest party $j$ which means that $A$ gets access to its local state and subsequently, $A$ controls party $j$. (In particular, this means we consider a model with "erasures"; random coin tosses that are no longer stored in the local state of $j$ are not visible to $A$.)[3]
- At any point, $Z$ can *uncorrupt* a corrupted player $j$, which means that $A$ no longer controls $j$. A player that becomes uncorrupt is treated in the same way as a newly spawning player, i.e., the player's internal state is re-initialized and then the player starts executing the honest protocol no longer controlled by $A$.

*Notations for randomized execution.* A protocol's execution is randomized, where the randomness comes from honest players as well as the adversary denoted $A$ that controls all corrupt nodes, and the environment $Z$ that sends inputs to honest nodes during the protocol execution. We use the notation $\mathsf{view} \xleftarrow{\$} \mathsf{EXEC}^{\Pi}(A, Z, \kappa)$ to denote a randomly sampled execution trace, and $|\mathsf{view}|$ denotes the number of rounds in the execution trace view. More specifically, view is a random variable denoting the joint view of all parties (i.e., all their inputs, random coins and messages received, including those from the random oracle) in the above execution; note that this joint view fully determines the execution.

*Constraints on $(A, Z)$.* The environment $Z$ and the adversary $A$ must respect certain constraints. We say that a p.p.t. pair $(A, Z)$ is *$(n, \rho, \Delta)$-respecting* w.r.t. $\Pi$, iff for every $\kappa \in N$, every view view in the support of $\mathsf{EXEC}^{\Pi}(A, Z, \kappa)$, the following holds:

(1) $Z$ activates $n$ parties in view;
(2) For any message broadcast by an honest player at any time $t$ in view, any player that is honest at time $t + \Delta$ or later must have received the message (including those that might have newly spawned). As long as this $\Delta$ contraint is respected, $A$ is allowed to delay or reorder honest players' messages arbitrarily.
(3) at any round $r$ in view, $A$ controls at most $\rho \cdot n$ parties; and

Let $\Gamma(\cdot, \cdot, \cdot)$ be a boolean predicate. We say that a p.p.t. pair $(A, Z)$ is *$\Gamma$-compliant* w.r.t. protocol $\pi$ iff

- $(A, Z)$ is $(n, \rho, \Delta)$-respecting w.r.t. $\pi$; and
- $\Gamma(n, \rho, \Delta) = 1$.

In other words $\Gamma$ is a predicate that places constraints on additional constraints on the parameter $(n, \rho, \Delta)$ that $(A, Z)$ must respect. When the context is clear, we often say that $(A, Z)$ is $\Gamma$-compliant while omitting to specify w.r.t. which protocol.

## 2.2 Conventions

*Variables that are functions of the security parameter.* Unless otherwise noted, by default we assume that all variables are a function of the security parameter $\kappa$. If any variable is not a function of $\kappa$, we shall explicitly note that the variable is a *constant*. Variables may also be functions of each other as defined later by relations

[2]We could also consider a seemingly weaker model where messages sent by corrupted parties need not be delivered to all honest players. We can easily convert the weaker model to the stronger model by having honest parties "gossip" all messages they receive.

[3]Our proof actually extends also to the model "without erasures".

that $(A, Z)$ must additionally satisfy for our blockchain protocol to be secure.

For two variables that by default are functions of $\kappa$, we say that $\mathsf{var}_1 < \mathsf{var}_2$ iff for every $\kappa \in \mathbb{N}$, $\mathsf{var}_1(\kappa) < \mathsf{var}_2(\kappa)$. Similarly, if we say that var is positive, we mean that $\mathsf{var}(\kappa)$ is positive for any $\kappa \in \mathbb{N}$.

*Other conventions.* Throughout this paper, whenever we refer to p.p.t. machines, we mean that the machine is *non-uniform* probabilistic polynomial-time.

## 2.3 Blockchain Protocols

In this section, we recall the abstract model for blockchain protocols from [18] and a provide a description of Nakamoto's original blockchain protocol which we will heavily make use of.

In a blockchain protocol $\Pi$, nodes receive input records from an environment $Z$, and nodes interact with each other to agree on a linearly ordered log of transactions in a way that achieves consistency and liveness.

*Inputs and outputs of a blockchain protocol.* At the beginning of each time step, the environment $Z$ inputs a record m to each honest player. At the end of each time step, each honest player outputs a chain to the environment $Z$, where chain denotes an ordered sequence of records (also referred to as blocks). Each record (or block) may in turn contain an ordered sequence of transactions. Henceforth we use the notation

$$\text{output of node } i \text{ in round } t: \ \ \mathsf{chain}_i^t(\mathsf{view})$$

to denote the output of node $i$ in round $t$ to $Z$ in a given execution trace view.

*Modeling proofs-of-work.* To model Nakamoto's blockchain protocol, we need to extend the protocol execution model with a random oracle. In an execution with security parameter $\kappa$, we assume all parties have access to a random function $H : \{0,1\}^* \to \{0,1\}^\kappa$ which they can access through two oracles: $\mathsf{H}(x)$ simply outputs $H(x)$ and $\mathsf{H.ver}(x, y)$ output 1 iff $H(x) = y$ and 0 otherwise. In any round $r$, the players (as well as $A$) may make *any* number of queries to H.ver. On the other hand, in each round $r$, honest players can make only a *single* query to H, and an adversary $A$ controlling $q$ parties, can make $q$ *sequential* queries to H. (This modeling is meant to capture the assumption that we only "charge" for the effort of finding a solution to a "proof of work" [6], but checking the validity of a solution is cheap. We discuss this further after introducing Nakamoto's protocol.) We emphasize that the environment $Z$ does not get direct access to the random oracle (but can instruct $A$ to make queries).

## 2.4 Nakamoto's Blockchain Protocol

We describe Nakamoto's protocol [16] referred to as $\Pi_{\mathrm{nak}}(p)$. $\Pi_{\mathrm{nak}}(p)$ takes in a puzzle difficulty parameter $p$ that denotes the probability that each player mines a block in a single round.

*Protocol overview.* In $\Pi_{\mathrm{nak}}$, each honest node maintains an internal state *chain* at any point of time. Each *chain*$[i]$ is referred to as a (mined) block and is of the format $chain[i] := (h_{-1}, \eta, \mathsf{m}, h)$, containing the hash of the previous block denoted $h_{-1}$, a nonce $\eta$, a record m, and a hash $h$ [4] Let chain := extract(*chain*) be the sequence of records contained in the sequence of blocks *chain*. chain is the version that honest nodes output to the environment.

The $\Pi_{\mathrm{nak}}$ works as follows:

- Nodes that are newly spawned or that have been become uncorrupt start with initial chain containing only a special genesis block: $chain := (0, 0, \perp, \mathsf{H}(0, 0, \perp))$.
- In every round: a node reads all incoming messages (delivered by $A$). If any incoming message $chain'$ is a valid sequence of blocks that is longer than its local state *chain*, replace *chain* by $chain'$. We define what it means for a chain to be valid later. Checking the validity of $chain'$ can be done using only H.ver queries.
- Read an input record m from the environment $Z$. Now parse $\mathsf{chain}[-1] := (\_, \_, \_, h_{-1})$, pick a random nonce $\eta \in \{0,1\}^\kappa$, and issue query $h = \mathsf{H}(h_{-1}, \eta, \mathsf{m})$. If $h < D_p$, then append the *newly mined* block $(h_{-1}, \eta, b, h)$ to *chain* and broadcasts the updated *chain*. More specifically, $D_p = p(\kappa) \cdot 2^\kappa$ such that for all $(h, \mathsf{m})$, $\Pr_\eta[\mathsf{H}(h, \eta, \mathsf{m}) < D_p] = p$. In other words, $D_p$ is appropriately parameterized such that the probability that any player mines a block in a round is $p$.
- Output chain := extract(*chain*) to the environment $Z$. Note that the notation chain extracts only the sequence of records from *chain* removing all other metadata that are not needed by external applications.

*Valid chain.* We say a block $chain[i] = (h_{-1}, \eta, \mathsf{m}, h)$ is *valid with respect to (a predecessor block)* $chain[i-1] = (h'_{-1}, n', m', h')$ if two conditions hold: $h_{-1} = h'$, $h = \mathsf{H}(h_{-1}, \eta, \mathsf{m})$, and $h < D_p$. A chain of blocks *chain* is *valid* if a) $chain[0] = (0, 0, \perp, \mathsf{H}(0, 0, \perp))$ is the genesis block, and b) for all $i \in [\ell]$, $chain[i]$ is valid with respect to $chain[i-1]$.

*Remark: on our use of the random oracle.* Recall that in our model, we restrict players to a single evaluation query H per round, but allow them any number of verification queries H.ver in the same round. We do this to model the fact that checking the validity of mined blocks is "cheap" whereas the mining process is expensive. (To enable this, we have included a pointer $h$ to the current record in every mined block in the description of Nakamoto).

In practice, the cost of evaluating a hash function (which is used to instantiate the random oracle) is the same as verifying its outputs, but our modeling attempts to capture the phenomena that a miner typically use various heuristics (such as black lists of IP addresses that have sent invalid blocks) and different hardware to check the validity of a mined block versus to mine a new block.

## 2.5 Security of Blockchain Protocols

We recall the security properties of blockchains from [18], which in turn are based on earlier definitions from [8, 11] For our purposes, we slightly generalize the properties from [18] (see below for a discussion of this generalization), but point out that our generalized definitions suffice for all known applications of them; see [18] for more discussion (and historical remarks) on these definitions.

[4] In reality (as well as in the description in the introduction), $h$ is not included in the block (as it can be easily determined from the remaining elements); we include it to ensure that we can verify validity of a block using only H.ver.

*Negligible functions.* A function $\epsilon(\cdot)$ is said to be *negligible* if for every polynomial $p(\cdot)$, there exists some $\kappa_0$ such that $\epsilon(\kappa) \leq \frac{1}{p(\kappa)}$ for all $\kappa \geq \kappa_0$.

We now define three useful properties, referred to as chain growth, chain quality, and consistency respectively. Note that all properties are defined over honest nodes' outputs to the environment that are visible at the abstraction level (rather than over nodes' internal states *chain*).

*2.5.1 Chain Growth.* The first desideratum is that the chain grows proportionally with the number of time steps. Let,

$$\text{min-chain-increase}_{t,t'}(\text{view}) = \min_{i,j} |\text{chain}_j^{t+t'}(\text{view})| - |\text{chain}_i^t(\text{view})|$$

$$\text{max-chain-increase}_{t,t'}(\text{view}) = \max_{i,j} |\text{chain}_j^{t+t'}(\text{view})| - |\text{chain}_i^t(\text{view})|$$

where we quantify over nodes $i, j$ such that $i$ is honest at round $t$ and $j$ is honest at round $t + t'$ in view.

Let $\text{growth}^{t_0,t_1}(\text{view}, \Delta, T) = 1$ iff the following properties hold:

- **(consistent length)** for all time steps $t \leq |\text{view}| - \Delta$, $t + \Delta \leq t' \leq |\text{view}|$, for every two players $i, j$ such that in view $i$ is honest at $t$ and $j$ is honest at $t'$, we have that $|\text{chain}_j^{t'}(\text{view})| \geq |\text{chain}_i^t(\text{view})|$
- **(chain growth lower bound)** for every time step $t \leq |\text{view}| - t_0$, we have $\text{min-chain-increase}_{t,t_0}(\text{view}) \geq T$.
- **(chain growth upper bound)** for every time step $t \leq |\text{view}| - t_1$, we have $\text{max-chain-increase}_{t,t_1}(\text{view}) \leq T$.

In other words, $\text{growth}^{t_0,t_1}$ is a predicate which tests that a) honest parties have chains of roughly the same length, and b) during any $t_0$ time steps in the execution, all honest parties' chains increase by at least $T$, and c) during any $t_1$ time steps in the execution, honest parties' chains increase by at most $T$.

*Definition 2.1 (Chain growth).* A blockchain protocol $\Pi$ satisfies $(T_0, g_0, g_1)$-chain growth in $\Gamma$-environments, if for all $\Gamma$-compliant p.p.t. pair $(A, Z)$, there exists some negligible function negl such that for every $\kappa \in \mathbb{N}$, $T \geq T_0$, $t_0 \geq \frac{T}{g_0}$ and $t_1 \leq \frac{T}{g_1}$,

$$\Pr\left[\text{view} \leftarrow \text{EXEC}^{\Pi}(A, Z, \kappa) : \text{growth}^{t_0,t_1}(\text{view}, \Delta, \kappa) = 1\right] \geq 1 - \text{negl}(\kappa)$$

*2.5.2 Chain Quality.* The second desideratum is that the number of blocks contributed by the adversary is not too large.

Given a chain, we say that a block $B := \text{chain}[j]$ is honest w.r.t. view and prefix $\text{chain}[: j']$ where $j' < j$ if in view there exists some node $i$ honest at some time $t \leq |\text{view}|$, such that 1) $\text{chain}[: j'] \prec \text{chain}_i^t(\text{view})$ where $\prec$ denotes "is a prefix of" and 2) $Z$ input $B$ to node $i$ at time $t$. Informally, for an honest node's chain denoted chain, a block $B := \text{chain}[j]$ is honest w.r.t. a prefix $\text{chain}[: j']$ where $j' < j$, if earlier there is some honest node who received $B$ as input when its local chain contains the prefix $\text{chain}[: j']$.

Let $\text{quality}^T(\text{view}, \mu) = 1$ iff for every time $t$ and every player $i$ such that $i$ is honest at $t$ in view, among any consecutive sequence of $T$ blocks $\text{chain}[j+1..j+T] \subseteq \text{chain}_i^t(\text{view})$, the fraction of blocks that are honest w.r.t. view and $\text{chain}[: j]$ is at least $\mu$.

*Definition 2.2 (Chain quality).* A blockchain protocol $\Pi$ satisfies *$(T_0, \mu)$−chain quality*, in $\Gamma$-environments if for all $\Gamma$-compliant p.p.t. pair $(A, Z)$, there exists some negligible function negl such that for every $\kappa \in \mathbb{N}$ and every $T \geq T_0$ the following holds:

$$\Pr\left[\text{view} \leftarrow \text{EXEC}^{\Pi}(A, Z, \kappa) : \text{quality}^T(\text{view}, \mu) = 1\right] \geq 1 - \text{negl}(\kappa)$$

*2.5.3 Consistency.* Roughly speaking, consistency stipulates common prefix and future self-consistency. Common prefix requires that all honest nodes' chains, except for roughly $O(\kappa)$ number of trailing blocks that have not stabilized, must all agree. Future self-consistency requires that an honest node's present chain, except for roughly $O(\kappa)$ number of trailing blocks that have not stabilized, should persist into its own future. These properties can be unified in the following formal definition (which additionally requires that at any time, two honest nodes' chains must be of similar length).

Let $\text{consistent}^T(\text{view}) = 1$ iff for all times $t \leq t'$, and all players $i, j$ (potentially the same) such that $i$ is honest at $t$ and $j$ is honest at $t'$ in view, we have that the prefixes of $\text{chain}_i^t(\text{view})$ and $\text{chain}_j^{t'}(\text{view})$ consisting of the first $\ell = |\text{chain}_i^t(\text{view})| - T$ records are identical — this also implies that the following must be true: $\text{chain}_j^{t'}(\text{view}) > \ell$, i.e., $\text{chain}_j^{t'}(\text{view})$ cannot be too much shorter than $\text{chain}_i^t(\text{view})$ given that $t' \geq t$.

*Definition 2.3 (Consistency).* A blockchain protocol $\Pi$ satisfies *$T_0$-consistency*, in $\Gamma$-environments if for all $\Gamma$-compliant p.p.t. pair $(A, Z)$, there exists some negligible function negl such that for every $\kappa \in \mathbb{N}$ and every $T \geq T_0$ the following holds:

$$\Pr\left[\text{view} \leftarrow \text{EXEC}^{\Pi}(A, Z, \kappa) : \text{consistent}^T(\text{view}) = 1\right] \geq 1 - \text{negl}(\kappa)$$

Note that a direct consequence of consistency is that at any time, the chain *lengths* of any two honest players can differ by at most $T$ (except with negligible probability).

## 2.6 Security of Nakamoto's Blockchain

The results from [18] (and as we shall shortly see, also ours) are parametrized by the following quantities (which are defined for some fixed mining hardness function $p(\cdot)$; recall that Nakamoto's protocol is parametrized a *single* hardness parameter $p$):

- let $\alpha := 1 - (1-p)^{(1-\rho)n}$. That is, $\alpha$ is the probability that *some* honest player succeeds in mining a block in a round;
- let $\beta := \rho n p$. That is $\beta$ is the expected number blocks that an attacker can mine in a round.
- let $\gamma := \frac{\alpha}{1+\Delta\alpha}$. $\gamma$ is a "discounted" version of $\alpha$ which takes into account the fact that messages sent by honest parties can be delayed by $\Delta$ rounds and this may lead to honest players "redoing work"; $\gamma$ corresponds to their "effective" mining power.

In essence, the quantities capture the per round expected "chain length increase" by the honest parties and the adversary; the reason that $\alpha, \beta$ are defined differently is that we assume that the adversary can sequentialize its queries in a round, whereas honest players make a single parallel query (they each act independently), and thus even if they manage to mine several blocks, the longest chain held by honest players can increase by at most 1. Note, however, that when $p$ is small (in comparison to $1/n$), which is case for the Bitcoin protocol, $\alpha$ is well approximated by $(1-\rho)np$ and thus $\frac{\alpha}{\beta} \approx \frac{1-\rho}{\rho}$, so this difference is minor; additionally, when $p$ is small, $\gamma \approx \alpha$ and thus $\frac{\gamma}{\beta} \approx \frac{1-\rho}{\rho}$.

*Compliant executions for Nakamoto's blockchain.* We now specify the compliance predicate $\Gamma^p_{\text{nak}}(\cdot,\cdot,\cdot)$ for the Nakamoto blockchain. We say that $\Gamma^p_{\text{nak}}(\cdot,\cdot,\cdot) = 1$ iff there is a constant $\lambda > 1$ such that

$$\alpha(1 - 2(\Delta + 1)\alpha) \geq \lambda\beta$$

where $\alpha$ and $\beta$ are functions of the parameters $n, \rho, \Delta$ and $\kappa$ as defined above.

*Formal guarantees of Nakamoto's blockchain.* The following theorem was proven in [18].

Theorem 2.4 (Security of Nakamoto [18]). *For any constant $\delta > 0$, any $0 < p < 1$, any superlogarithmic function $T_0 = \omega(\log \kappa)$ Nakamoto's blockchain protocol $\Pi_{\text{nak}}(p)$ satisfies the following properties in $\Gamma^p_{\text{nak}}$-environments:*

- *$T_0$-consistency;*
- *chain growth rate $(T_0, g_0, g_1)$ where $g_0 = (1-\delta)\gamma$, $g_1 = (1+\delta)np$*
- *chain quality $(T_0, \mu)$ where $\mu = 1 - (1+\delta)\frac{\beta}{\gamma}$*

Remark 2.5 (Blockchain quality and consistency). *The consistency property proven in [18] is actually a bit stronger than stated. Not only it shows that players agree on the* records *contained in their blockchains, but also that the actual* blockchains *agree except for potentially the last $\kappa$ blocks. We refer to this property as* blockchain consistency, *and will rely on it in the sequel.*

*Additionally, the chain quality property is also stronger in that not only the records of honest blocks are contributed by honest players, but also the actual blocks are mined by honest players. We refer to this property as* blockchain quality, *and will rely on it in the sequel.*

*2.6.1 Liveness.* The liveness property from [18] (which generalized the one from [8]), stipulates that from any given round $r$, if a sufficiently long period of time $t$ elapses—we refer to this time as the *wait-time* of the blockchain—*every* honest player will have a record m sufficiently "deep" in their chain (technically, $\kappa$ blocks from the end of the chain), where m was provided as an input to some honest player between rounds $r$ and $r + t$[5] More precisely, let live(view, $t$) = 1 iff for any $t$ consecutive rounds $r, \ldots, r+t$ in view there exists some round $r'$ s.t. $r \leq r' \leq r+t$ and player $i$ such that in view, 1) $i$ is honest at $r'$, 2) $i$ received a record m as input at round $r'$, and 3) for every player $j$ that is honest at $r+t$ in view, $\mathsf{m} \in \mathsf{chain}_j^{r+t}(\mathsf{view})[:-\kappa]$.

*Definition 2.6.* We say that blockchain ($\Pi$, chain) satisfies *liveness with wait-time $w$* in $\Gamma$-environments if for all $\Gamma$-compliant p.p.t. pair $(A, Z)$, there exists a negligible function $\epsilon$ in the security parameter $\kappa \in \mathbb{N}$, such that

$$\Pr\left[\mathsf{view} \leftarrow \mathsf{EXEC}^{\Pi}(A, Z, \kappa) : \mathsf{live}(\mathsf{view}, w) = 1\right] \geq 1 - \epsilon(\kappa)$$

The following theorem was shown in the prior work [18].

Theorem 2.7 ([18]). *For any boolean predicate $\Gamma(\cdot,\cdot,\cdot)$, let $\Pi$ be a blockchain protocol satisfying chain growth $(T_0, g_0, g_1)$, chain quality $(T_0, \mu)$ and $T_0$-chain consistency in $\Gamma$-environments where $\mu$ and $g_0$ are strictly positive, and $T_0$ is sublinear.*[6] *Then, $\Pi$ satisfies liveness with wait-time $w = (1+\delta)\frac{\kappa}{g_0}$ against in $\Gamma$-environments*

As a direct corollary of 2.7 and 2.4, we get:

Corollary 2.8 ([18]). *For any constant $\delta > 0$, and any $0 < p < 1$, $\Pi_{\text{nak}}(p)$ satisfies liveness with wait-time*

$$w = (1+\delta)\frac{\kappa}{\gamma}$$

*in $\Gamma^p_{\text{nak}}$-environments.*

# 3 DEFINING FAIRNESS

We turn to defining our notion of fairness. Roughly speaking, a blockchain protocol is *$\delta$-approximately fair* w.r.t. $\rho$ attackers if, with overwhelming probability, any honest subset controlling $\phi$ fraction of the compute power is guaranteed to get at least a $(1-\delta)\phi$ fraction of the blocks in every sufficiently long window, even in the presence of an adversary controlling a $\rho$ fraction of the computation power. Note that this condition trivially implies $(1-\delta)(1-\rho)$ chain quality (by considering $\phi = 1 - \rho$, that is, the full set of honest players). Consequently, to formally define this notion, we first generalize the definition of quality (used in the definition of chain quality, see Definition 2.2) to consider "quality" w.r.t to any subset $S$ of the honest players.

*Warmup: fairness definition for static corruption.* As a warmup, let us consider how to define (approximate) fairness in a static corruption model where the adversary must declare corrupt nodes upfront — once we show how to do this, we then discuss how to extend the definition to an adaptive corruption model. Under a static corruption model, we say that a blockchain protocol satisfies $(T, \delta)$-approximate fairness, iff the following holds except with negligible probability over the protocol's execution: for any honest node's chain during the protocol execution, for any constant $\phi > 0$, for any subset $S$ of honest users such that $|S| = \phi \cdot n$ where $n$ denotes the total number of users, for any $T$ consecutive blocks $\mathsf{chain}[j+1..j+T]$ in chain, it holds that the fraction of blocks in $\mathsf{chain}[j+1..j+T]$ contributed by nodes in $S$ is at least $(1-\delta)\phi$.

*Fairness definition for adaptive corruption.* In general, the corruptions can be declared in an adaptive fashion, therefore nodes in any subset $S$ may become corrupt during the course of the window we care about. To define (approximate) fairness with adaptive corruptions, we need to allow the subset $S$ to change over time. We formalize the definition below.

- Let a *player subset selection*, $S(\mathsf{view}, r)$, be a function that given $(\mathsf{view}, r)$ outputs a subset of the players that are honest at round $r$ in view.
- We say that $S$ is a *$\phi$-fraction player subset selection* if $S(\mathsf{view}, r)$ always outputs a set of size $\phi n$ (rounded upwards) where $n$ is the number of players in view.
- Given a player subset selection $S$, we say that a *record m is $S$-compatible w.r.t. view and prefix* chain if there exists a player $j$

[5]The weaker liveness property from [8] only requires this is *all* honest players have m as their input; this weaker property is not enough for our purposes.

[6][18] only explicitly considered the case when $T_0$ is some slightly super-logarithmic function, but their proof actually only assumes that $T_0$ is sublinear. We also remark that any blockchain protocol which satisfies the security properties w.r.t. to a polynomial $T_0$ which potentially is super-linear can always be modified to satisfy security w.r.t. a sublinear $T_0$ by redefining the security parameter.

and round $r'$ such that $j$ is in $S(\text{view}, r')$, the environment provided m as an input to $j$ at round $r'$, and chain $\prec \text{chain}_i^{r'}(\text{view})$ where $\prec$ denotes "is a prefix of";

- Let $\text{quality}^{T,S}(\text{view}, \mu) = 1$ iff for every round $r$ and every player $i$ such that $i$ is honest in round $r$ of view, we have that among any consecutive sequence of $T$ records $\text{chain}_i^r(\text{view})[j+1 : j+T]$, the fraction of records that are $S$-compatible w.r.t. view and prefix $\text{chain}_i^r(\text{view})[: j]$ is at least $\mu$.

We now define fairness analogously to chain quality.

*Definition 3.1.* A blockchain protocol $\Pi$ has (approximate) *fairness* $(T_0, \delta)$ in $\Gamma$-environments, if for all $\Gamma$-compliant p.p.t. $(A, Z)$, every positive constant $\phi \leq 1 - \rho$, every $\phi$-fraction subset selection $S$, there exists some negligible function $\epsilon$ such that for every $\kappa \in \mathbb{N}$ and every $T \geq T_0$ the following holds:

$$\Pr\left[\text{view} \leftarrow \text{EXEC}^{\Pi}(A, Z, \kappa) : \text{quality}^{T,S}(\text{view}, (1-\delta)\phi)) = 1\right] \geq 1 - \epsilon(\kappa)$$

As a sanity check, note that the definition of $\text{quality}^{T,S}(\text{view}, \mu)$ collapses down to $\text{quality}^T(\text{view}, \mu)$ if $S$ is the full set of the honest players. As a consequence, $(T_0, \delta)$-fairness trivially implies $(T_0, (1-\delta)(1-\rho))$-chain quality (by considering $\phi = 1 - \rho$). Additionally, when $\rho \leq \frac{1}{2}$ which is the case we consider in this paper,

$$\begin{aligned}(1-\delta)(1-\rho) &= 1 - \delta - \rho + \delta\rho = 1 - [\delta + (1-\delta)\rho] \\ &\geq 1 - [2\delta\rho + (1-\delta)\rho] = 1 - (1+\delta)\rho\end{aligned}$$

Thus, no $\rho$-size coalition can get more than a factor $(1 + \delta)$ more than its "fair" share of blocks.

FACT 3.2. *If a blockchain protocol $\Pi$ satisfies $(T_0, \delta)$-fairness in $\Gamma$-environments, then it satisfies $(T_0, \mu)$-chain quality where $\mu = (1-\delta)(1-\rho) \geq 1 - (1+\delta)\rho$ in $\Gamma$-environments.*

# 4 THE FRUITCHAIN PROTOCOL

We now turn to formally defining our FruitChain protocol. Roughly speaking, the FruitChain protocol will be running an instance of $\Pi_{\text{nak}}(p)$ but instead of directly putting the records m inside the blockchain, the records are put inside "fruits" denoted $f$; these fruits themselves requires solving some proof of work—with a *different hardness parameter* $p_f$; additionally, we require a fruit to "hang" from a block which isn't too far from from the block which records the fruit—more specifically, the fruit needs to "point" to an earlier block in the chain which is not too far from the block containing it (and thus, the fruit could not have been mined "too" long ago); the *recency parameter* $R$ will be used to specify how far back a fruit is allowed to hang.

## 4.1 Valid Blocks, Fruits, and Blockchain

Towards formalizing the protocol, we first introduce some notation:

- We assume that the random oracle $H$ outputs strings of length at least $2\kappa$. Let d be a collision-resistant hash-function (technically, it is a family of functions, and the instance from the family is selected as a public-parameter; in the sequel we ignore this selection and simply treat it as a single function (for instance, selected using randomness $H(0)$.)
- Our protocol is parametrized by two "hardness" parameters $p = p, p_f = p_f$, and a recency parameter $R$. ($p$ is the mining hardness parameter for the underlying Nakamoto blockchain, and $p_f$ is the "fruit mining" hardness parameter, as mentioned above, the recency parameter will specify how far back a fruit is allowed to "hang"); the quantity $q = \frac{p_f}{p}$ will be useful in our analysis.

*Valid fruits.* A fruit is of the format $f = (h_{-1}; h'; \eta, \text{digest}; \text{m}; h)$ where each entry means the following:

- $h_{-1}$ points to the previous block's reference — this entry is an artifact of the fruit mining and block mining piggybacked on top of each other; a fruit actually does not care about this entry (but a block does). However the value still needs to be included for the fruit to be verified;
- $h'$ points to a (recently stablized) block that the fruit is hanging from — we call $h'$ the pointer of the fruit $f$;
- $\eta$ is a random nonce denoting the puzzle solution;
- digest is the digest of some fruit-set $F$ — this is an artifact since the fruit mining and block mining are piggybacked on top of each other. The block must contain a set of fruits denoted $F$, but the fruit does not care about the fruit-set, and therefore we include only its d that is necessary for checking that the fruit is correct;
- m is the record to be contained in the fruit; and
- $h$ is the hash or reference of the fruit.

We say that a *fruit* denoted $f = (h_{-1}; h'; \eta, \text{digest}; \text{m}; h)$ is valid iff

(i) $H(h_{-1}; h'; \eta; \text{digest}; \text{m}) = h$;
(ii) $[h]_{-\kappa:} < D_{p_f}$ where $[h]_{-\kappa:}$ denotes the last $\kappa$ bits of $h$.

We say that $F$ *is a valid fruit-set* if either $F = \emptyset$ or $F$ is a set of valid fruits.

*Valid blocks.* Since the block mining and the fruit mining are piggybacked on top of each other, a block looks very much like a fruit, except that a block must additionally include the actual fruit-set $F$. More specifically, a block is of the following format $\text{b} = ((h_{-1}; h'; \eta; \text{digest}; \text{m}; h), F)$ where each entry means the following:

- $h_{-1}$ points to the previous block's reference, this represents the chain that the block extends from;
- $h'$ is an artifact of the fruit mining and block mining piggybacked atop each other; a block actually does not care about this field (but a fruit does), but it still needs to be included for block verification;
- $\eta$ is a random nonce denoting the puzzle solution;
- digest is the digest of some fruit-set $F$ to be included in the block later;
- m is a record — the block also does not care about this field, and this is an artifact of the two piggybacked mining processes;
- $h$ is called the reference of the block, which is a hash of the previous fields; and
- $F$ is a fruit-set to be included in the block.

We say that a *block* denoted $\text{b} = ((h_{-1}; h'; \eta; \text{digest}; \text{m}; h), F)$, is valid iff

(i) digest $= \text{d}(F)$ where d is a collision-resistant hash function as mentioned earlier;
(ii) $F$ is a valid fruit-set;
(iii) $H(h_{-1}; h'; \eta, \text{d}(F); \text{m}) = h$;
(iv) $[h]_{:\kappa} < D_{p_1}$ where $[h]_{:\kappa}$ denotes the first $\kappa$ bits of $h$.

*Valid blockchain.* We say that a *chain* is valid iff

- $chain[0] = genesis$ where $genesis := ((0; 0; 0; 0; \bot; \mathsf{H}(0; 0; 0; 0, \bot)), \emptyset)$ is the "genesis" block;
- for all $i \in [\ell]$, $chain[i].h_{-1} = chain[i-1].h$, i.e., each block refers to the previous block's reference;
- for all $i \in [\ell]$, all $f \in chain[i].F$, there exists some $j \geq i - R\kappa$ such that the pointer of $f$ is $chain[j].h$.

*Recency of fruits.* Finally, we say that the *fruit* $f$ is recent *w.r.t. chain* if the pointer of $f$ is the reference of a block in $chain[-R\kappa :]$ (i.e., one of the last $R\kappa$ blocks in *chain*).

### 4.2 The FruitChain Protocol and Main Theorem

The FruitChain protocol denoted $\Pi_{\text{fruit}}$ is described in Figure 1. Henceforth, we say that $\Gamma^{p,p_f,R}_{\text{fruit}}(n, \rho, \Delta) = 1$ iff $\Gamma^{p}_{\text{nak}}(n, \rho, \Delta) = 1$. Moreover, we assume the following quantities are constants throughout this paper:

$$q := \frac{p_f}{p} = \Theta(1), \qquad R = \Theta(1)$$

We are now ready to state our main theorem.

THEOREM 4.1 (SECURITY OF FruitChain). *For any constant $0 < \delta < 1$, and any $p, p_f$, let $R = 17$, $\kappa_f = 2qR\kappa$, and $T_0 = 5\frac{\kappa_f}{\delta}$. Then the* FruitChain *protocol denoted $\Pi_{\text{fruit}}(p, p_f, R)$ satisfies*

- *$\kappa_f$-consistency;*
- *chain growth rate $(T_0, g_0, g_1)$ where $g_0 = (1-\delta)(1-\rho)np_f$, and $g_1 = (1+\delta)np_f$.*
- *fairness $(T_0, \delta)$.*

*in $\Gamma^{p,p_f,R}_{\text{fruit}}$-environments.*

*Proof of the main theorem.* In the interest of space, we provide the proof of our main theorem in our online full version [19].

## 5 FROM FAIRNESS TO INCENTIVE COMPATIBILITY

We remark that any secure blockchain protocol that satisfies $\delta$-approximate fairness (where $\delta < 0.3$) w.r.t $T(\kappa)$ length windows can be used as the ledger underlying a cryptocurrency system while ensuring $3\delta$-*incentive compatibility* if players (i.e. miners) only care about how much money they receive—that is, a miner's utility is the sum of the rewards and transaction fees it receives (potentially times some constant).[7]

Consider a crypto-currency which uses a blockchain protocol as the underlying ledger; we omit a formalization of what this means, but have in mind a system such as Bitcoin where rewards and transaction fees are somehow distributed among the miners of blocks—for instance, recall that in Bitcoin, the miner of a block receives a mining reward as well as all the transaction fees contained in the block it mined.

We say that *honest mining is a $\rho$-coalition-safe $\epsilon$-Nash equilibrium* if, with overwhelming probability, no $\rho' < \rho$ fraction coalition can gain more than a multiplicative factor $(1+\epsilon)$ in utility, no matter what transactions are being processed—formally, consider some environment providing transactions into the system. We restrict to a setting where the *total* rewards and transaction fees during the run of the system is some fixed constant $V$[8].

We now remark that if rewards and transaction fees are *evenly distributed* among the (miners of the) blocks in the $T(\kappa)$-length segment of the chain preceeding the block (and in the initial phase, before the chain is of length $T(\kappa)$, simply the first $T(\kappa)$ blocks) then it follows that honest mining is a $\rho$-coalition-safe $3\delta$-Nash equilibrium as long as the underlying blockchain satisfies $\delta$-approximate fairness w.r.t. $\rho$ attackers: as noted above, fairness implies that no matter what deviation the coalition performs, with overwhelming probability, the fraction of adversarial blocks in any $T(\kappa)$-length window of the chain is upperbounded by $(1+\delta)\rho$ and thus the total amount of compensation received by the attacker is bounded by $(1+\delta)\rho \cdot V$; in contrast, by fairness, if the coalition had been following the honest protocol, they are guaranteed to receive at least $(1-\delta)\rho \cdot V$; thus, the multiplicative increase in utility is $\frac{1+\delta}{1-\delta} \leq 1+3\delta$ when $\delta < 0.3$.[9]

To see why the "standard" bitcoin approach of giving all rewards and fees to the miner of the block does not work, consider an freshly mined (honest) block containing a transaction with a very high transaction fee. A coalition controlling a constant fraction of the computing power would have a huge incentive to "drop" this block and instead try to mine a new block which contains it. Fairness does not prevent such an attack, and indeed, even in our protocol such an attack will be successful with constant probability. (Indeed, it has been informally conjectured in the bitcoin community that $\epsilon$-incentive compatibility is impossible to achieve in the presence of transaction fees, due to exactly this reason. Our method of distributing the fees over a segment overcomes this "barrier".)

## 6 DISINCENTIVIZING POOLED MINING

An issue with the Bitcoin protocol (which relies on Nakamoto's blockchain protocol) is that the mining hardness is set so that the world (combined) finds a new block every 10 minutes—as shown in [18], the mining hardness needs to be set in such a way to ensure consistency. This not only leads to a long latency (which can be remedied by the Hybrid Consensus approach discussed above), but also leads to the issue that it may take a very long time for an individual miner to be successful in mining a block and consequently reap a reward for its work. In other words, the payments received by miners has a very *high variance.* This has lead to the creation of mining pools, where miners come together and pool their work and then share the reward once someone in the pool mines a block—such pooling decreases the variance. To prevent free-riding, miners submit "partial proofs of work" (that is, "near" solutions to the mining puzzles) that are significantly easier to find, and rewards are distributed (according to some distribution rule) among the contributors of the partial proofs-of-work.

[7]This may not always be a realistic assumption. For instance, a miner can care about what transactions get added into the blockchain etc, but following earlier approaches to modeling incentives in blockchains (e.g., [7]), we focus only on miners' monetary rewards.

[8]The analysis directly extends to a setting where the total rewards and fees are only guaranteed to be withing some multiplicative factor $(1+\delta')$ of $V$ at the cost of a degradation of the quality of the Nash equilibrium (i.e., increasing the $\epsilon$).

[9]Let us remark that an alternative approach would be to give the whole mining reward to the miner of a block (as in Bitcoin) but still distribute the transaction fees among the group of miners in a $T(\kappa)$-segment of the chain. This approach works by the same analysis as long as mining rewards are *fixed* throughout the experiment (which is not the case for e.g., Bitcoin where mining rewards decrease over time).

$\Pi_{\text{fruit}}(p, p_f, R)$: FruitChain **protocol**

**Initialize:** $chain := genesis$, $F = \emptyset$

Upon receiving a valid *fruit*: let $F := F \cup \{fruit\}$

Upon receiving a valid $chain'$, if $|chain'| > |chain|$: let $chain := chain'$

Every time step, upon receiving input m from the environment:

- let $F'$ be all fruits $f \in F$ that are recent w.r.t. *chain* and not already in *chain*;
- let $h'$ be the reference of $chain[pos]$ where $pos = max(1, |chain| - \kappa)$;
- let $h_{-1}$ be the reference of $chain[-1]$;
- Pick random $\eta \in \{0,1\}^{\kappa}$ and let $h := \mathsf{H}(h_{-1}; h'; \eta; \mathsf{d}(F'); \mathsf{m})$
- If $[h]_{-\kappa:} < D_{p_f}$ (i.e., we "mined a fruit"): let $fruit := (h_{-1}; h'; \eta; \mathsf{d}(F'); \mathsf{m}, h)$, $F := F \cup \{fruit\}$, and broadcast *fruit*
- If $[h]_{:\kappa} < D_p$ (i.e., we "mined a block"): let $chain := chain||((h_{-1}; h'; \eta, \mathsf{d}(F'); \mathsf{m}, h), F')$, and broadcast *chain*
- Output $\mathsf{extract}_{\text{fruit}}(chain)$ to $Z$, where $\mathsf{extract}_{\text{fruit}}(\cdot)$ is defined as below:

$\mathsf{extract}_{\text{fruit}}(chain)$:

On input a valid *chain*,

- first extract a sequence of *distinct* fruits from *chain*, where if the same fruit is included multiple times, only the first occurrence is included. The extracted fruits are ordered by the first block that contains the fruit; and for fruits in the same block, follow the order in which the fruits are serialized within the block.
- then, output the sequence of records m contained in the extracted sequence of fruits, where records contained in earlier fruits are extracted earlier.

**Figure 1: The** FruitChain **protocol. Nodes not only mine for blocks, but also fruits. Blocks confirm "recent" fruits; whereas fruits confirm transactions.**

An undesirable effect of such pools is that the pool operator effectively controls a large number of participants and potentially could get them to deviate; in a sense, the decentralized nature of the system gets lost.

We note that since the FruitChain protocol is parametrized by *two* mining hardnesses—the block hardness $p$, and the fruit hardness $p_f$—which are independent of each other, we can set $p$ appropriately to ensure consistency, but $p_f$ can be set to be much larger—for instance, as large as the probability of find a partial proof-of-work in mining pools—and consequently, we would reduce the variance of the rewards received by miners in exactly the same way as in mining pool, but now in a *fully decentralized* way.

Today, a solo miner (assuming one unit of typical commodity mining ASIC) would take 2 to 5 years to obtain its first reward [2]. With FruitChain, suppose we allocate space for 1000 fruits per block where each fruit is 80 bytes (same size as a Bitcoin puzzle solution), this would occupy roughly 8% of a 1MB block — however, this would allow a solo miner to get its first rewards 1000x faster, roughly on the order of a day (or days) rather than years.

*Acknowledgments.* This work is supported in part by NSF grants CNS-1217821, CNS-1314857, CNS-1514261, CNS-1544613, CNS-1561209, CNS-1601879, CNS-1617676, AFOSR Award FA9550-15-1-0262, an Office of Naval Research Young Investigator Program Award, a Microsoft Faculty Fellowship, a Packard Fellowship, a Sloan Fellowship, Google Faculty Research Awards, a VMWare Research Award, and a Baidu Research Award.

## REFERENCES


[1] 2016. Personal Communication with Iddo Bentov and Yuncong Hu and Siqiu Yao. (2016).

[2] 2017. http://www.coinwarz.com/calculators/bitcoin-mining-calculator. (2017).

[3] Boaz Barak, Ran Canetti, Yehuda Lindell, Rafael Pass, and Tal Rabin. 2005. Secure Computation Without Authentication. In *CRYPTO'05*.

[4] Miles Carlsten, Harry A. Kalodner, S. Matthew Weinberg, and Arvind Narayanan. 2016. On the Instability of Bitcoin Without the Block Reward. In *CCS*. 154–167.

[5] Phil Daian, Rafael Pass, and Elaine Shi. 2016. Snow White: Provably Secure Proofs of Stake. Cryptology ePrint Archive, Report 2016/919. (2016).

[6] Cynthia Dwork and Moni Naor. 1992. Pricing via processing or combatting junk mail. In *CRYPTO'92*. 139–147.

[7] Ittay Eyal and Emin Gün Sirer. 2014. Majority is not enough: Bitcoin mining is vulnerable. In *Financial Cryptography and Data Security*. Springer, 436–454.

[8] Juan Garay, Aggelos Kiayias, and Nikos Leonardos. 2015. The bitcoin backbone protocol: Analysis and applications. In *EUROCRYPT*.

[9] Joseph Y. Halpern and Rafael Pass. 2015. Algorithmic rationality: Game theory with costly computation. *J. Economic Theory* 156 (2015), 246–268.

[10] Aggelos Kiayias, Elias Koutsoupias, Maria Kyropoulou, and Yiannis Tselekounis. 2016. Blockchain Mining Games. In *EC*. 365–382.

[11] Aggelos Kiayias and Giorgos Panagiotakos. 2015. Speed-Security Tradeoffs in Blockchain Protocols. (2015).

[12] Aggelos Kiayias and Giorgos Panagiotakos. 2016. On Trees, Chains and Fast Transactions in the Blockchain. *IACR Cryptology ePrint Archive* 2016 (2016), 545.

[13] Aggelos Kiayias, Alexander Russell, Bernardo David, and Roman Oliynykov. 2016. Ouroboros: A Provably Secure Proof-of-Stake Blockchain Protocol. Cryptology ePrint Archive, Report 2016/889. (2016). http://eprint.iacr.org/2016/889.

[14] Yoad Lewenberg, Yonatan Sompolinsky, and Aviv Zohar. 2015. Inclusive Block Chain Protocols. In *Financial Crypto'15*.

[15] mtgox. 2010. https://bitcointalk.org/index.php?topic=2227. (2010).

[16] Satoshi Nakamoto. 2008. Bitcoin: A peer-to-peer electronic cash system. (2008).

[17] Kartik Nayak, Srijan Kumar, Andrew Miller, and Elaine Shi. 2016. Stubborn Mining: Generalizing Selfish Mining and Combining with an Eclipse Attack. In *EuroS&P*.

[18] Rafael Pass, Lior Seeman, and Abhi Shelat. 2017. Analysis of the Blockchain Protocol in Asynchronous Networks. In *Eurocrypt*.

[19] Rafael Pass and Elaine Shi. 2016. Fruitchains: A Fair Blockchain. Online Technical Report, https://eprint.iacr.org/2016/916.pdf. (2016).

[20] Rafael Pass and Elaine Shi. 2016. Hybrid Consensus. http://eprint.iacr.org/2016/917. (2016).

[21] Ayelet Sapirshtein, Yonatan Sompolinsky, and Aviv Zohar. 2016. Optimal Selfish Mining Strategies in Bitcoin. In *Financial Crypto'16*.

[22] Yonatan Sompolinsky and Aviv Zohar. 2015. Secure High-Rate Transaction Processing in Bitcoin. In *FC*. 507–527.

# Coordination Without Prior Agreement

Gadi Taubenfeld
The Interdisciplinary Center
P.O. Box 167
Herzliya, Israel 46150
tgadi@idc.ac.il

## ABSTRACT

Assuming that there is an a priori agreement between processes on the names of shared memory locations, as done in almost all the publications on shared memory algorithms, is tantamount to assuming that agreement has already been solved at the lower-level. From a theoretical point of view, it is intriguing to figure out how coordination can be achieved without relying on such lower-level agreement. In order to better understand the new model, we have designed new algorithms without relying on such a priori lower-level agreement, and proved space lower bounds and impossibility results for several important problems, such as mutual exclusion, consensus, election and renaming. Using these results, we identify fundamental differences between the standard model where there is a lower-level agreement about the shared register's names and the strictly weaker model where there is no such agreement.

## KEYWORDS

Shared memory; memory-anonymous algorithms; unnamed register; anonymous register; mutual exclusion; agreement; renaming.

## 1 INTRODUCTION

A central issue in distributed systems is how to coordinate the actions of asynchronous processes. In the context where processes communicate via reading and writing from shared memory, in almost all published concurrent algorithms it is assumed that the shared memory locations have global names which are a priori known to all the participating processes. From a theoretical point of view, it is intriguing to figure out what and how coordination can be achieved without relying on such lower-level agreement about the names of the memory locations.

We assume that all inter-process communications are via shared registers which are initially in a known state. Access to the registers is via atomic read and write operations. However, from the point of view of the processes, the registers *do not have global names*: the first register examined and the subsequent order in which registers are scanned may be different for each process. That is, a single register may be considered the fifth register by one process and the eighth by another. Even the order of the names may be different. Thus, for example, one process may scan four registers in order 3, 2, 1, 4 while another scans 2, 4, 1, 3.

We call algorithms that are correct for a model where the registers do not have global names, *memory-anonymous* algorithms. The lack of global names makes it convenient to think of each process as being assigned an initial register and an ordering of the registers which determines how it scans the registers. Our interest in such a weak computational model is of a theoretical nature; however, the *plasticity* of memory-anonymous algorithms – their ability to operate for any assigned ordering of the registers – may be found useful in practice. When using such algorithms, specific ordering can be assigned for reducing memory contention which may help in improving performance. Furthermore, various optimizations enable reordering memory references as it allows much better performance. Because of its plasticity, memory-anonymous algorithms may need to use only a small number of memory barriers to prevent reordering.

In order to better understand the new model, we have designed new memory-anonymous algorithms, proved space lower bounds and impossibility results for several important problems, which include mutual exclusion, consensus, election and renaming. Using these results, we identify fundamental differences between the standard model where there is a lower-level agreement about shared register's names and the *strictly weaker* model where there is no such agreement.

## 2 PRELIMINARIES

Our model of computation consists of a fully asynchronous collection of $n$ processes which communicate via atomic read/write registers that do not have global names. Thus, algorithms should be correct assuming a very powerful adversary, which can determine (essentially) the order in which processes access the registers.

The fact that the registers do not have global names implies that only multi-writer multi-reader (MWMR) registers are possible. A MWMR register can both be written and read by all the processes. With an *atomic* register, it is assumed that operations on the register occur in some definite order. That is, reading or writing an atomic register is an indivisible action. In the sequel, by *registers* we mean *atomic* registers. Asynchrony means that there is no assumption on the relative speeds of the processes. Each process has a unique identifier which is a positive integer. It is *not* assumed that the identifiers are taken from the set $\{1, ..., n\}$. Thus, a process does not a priori know the identifiers of the other processes.

A *symmetric algorithm* is an algorithm in which the processes are executing exactly the same code and the only way for distinguishing processes is by comparing identifiers. Identifiers can be written, read and compared, but there is no way of looking inside any


*PODC'17, July 25 27, 2017, Washington, DC, USA*
© 2017 ACM. 978-1-4503-4992-5/17/07...$15.00
DOI: http://dx.doi.org/10.1145/3087801.3087807

identifier. Thus, it is not possible to know whether an identifier is odd or even. Two variants of symmetric algorithms can be defined:

- *Symmetric with equality*, means that a process can determine if two identifiers are the same or not, but if they are different then nothing else can be determined.
- *Symmetric with arbitrary comparisons*, means that a process can learn something about identifiers if two unequal identifiers are compared. For example, comparisons can be defined that depend on a total order.

We assume that there is *no a priori agreement* between the processes regarding the *order* of their identifiers. Thus, throughout the paper, we assume that only comparisons for equality are allowed. Furthermore, a process will only compare its own identifier with another, and not compare it with a constant value.

In some cases, we will assume that processes may fail by crashing; that is, they fail only by never entering the algorithm or by leaving the algorithm at some point and thereafter permanently refraining from writing the shared registers. A process that crashes is said to be *faulty*, otherwise it is *correct*.

Several progress conditions have been proposed for algorithms in which processes may fail. *Wait-freedom* guarantees that *every* active process will always be able to complete its pending operations in a finite number of its own steps [14]. *Obstruction-freedom* guarantees that an active process will be able to complete its pending operations in a finite number of its own steps, if all the other processes "hold still" long enough [15]. Obstruction-freedom does not guarantee progress under contention.

In a model where participation is required, every correct process must eventually become active and execute its code. A more common and practical situation is one in which participation is not required. Throughout the paper, we will assume that participation is *not* required.

# 3 MEMORY-ANONYMOUS MUTUAL EXCLUSION

None of the published mutual exclusion algorithms (that I know of) using registers is memory-anonymous. Below we present the first memory-anonymous mutual exclusion algorithm for two processes.

## 3.1 The problem

The mutual exclusion problem is to design an algorithm that guarantees mutually exclusive access to a critical section among a number of competing processes [Dij65]. It is assumed that each process is executing a sequence of instructions in an infinite loop. The instructions are divided into four continuous sections: the remainder, entry, critical and exit. The exit section is required to be wait-free – its execution must always terminate. It is assumed that processes do not fail, and that a process always leaves its critical section. The *mutual exclusion problem* is to write the code for the entry and the exit sections in such a way that the following *two* basic requirements are satisfied.

- *Deadlock-freedom:* If a process is trying to enter its critical section, then some process, not necessarily the same one, eventually enters its critical section.
- *Mutual exclusion:* No two processes are in their critical sections at the same time.

Satisfaction of the above two properties is the minimum required for a mutual exclusion algorithm.

## 3.2 A result for two processes and its implications

We prove the following result:

THEOREM 3.1. *There is a memory-anonymous symmetric deadlock-free mutual exclusion algorithm for two processes using $m \geq 2$ registers if and only if $m$ is odd.*

In the standard model, where *there is* a lower-level a priori agreement regarding the registers names, the following three general properties hold:

- If a problem has a solution using $\ell$ registers then it also has a solution using $m$ registers, for every $m \geq \ell$. (Simply ignore $m-\ell$ of the registers. This requires a prior agreement on which $m-\ell$ registers should be ignored.)
- For every $n \geq 2$, if a problem has a solution for $n$ processes, with distinct identifiers taken from the set $\{1, ..., n\}$, using registers then it has a solution (not necessarily symmetric) using $n$ registers. (This follows from the fact that multi-writer registers can be wait-free implemented from single-writer registers.)
- For every $n \geq 2$, there is a symmetric mutual exclusion algorithm for $n$ processes using $n$ registers, which uses only comparisons for equality. (See [23].)

It follows immediately from Theorem 3.1, that these three properties do *not* hold for a model where there is *no* lower-level agreement regarding the registers names assuming comparisons for equality.

## 3.3 A memory-anonymous mutual exclusion algorithm

We present below a memory-anonymous deadlock-free mutual exclusion algorithm for two processes using $m$ registers, for any odd number of registers $m \geq 3$. The question whether there is an algorithm for more than two processes is open (at first glance this open problem looks simple, but it is not).

Each participating process scans the $m$ shared registers trying to write its identifier into each one of the $m$ registers. While accessing a register, a process may find that another process has already "visited" that register. In such a case, the process does not write into that register and continues to the next one. Once a process completes scanning the $m$ registers and possibly writing its identifier to some of them, it scans the registers again, this time only reading their values. If it finds that its identifier is written in all the $m$ registers, it safely enters its critical section. If its identifer is written in less than $\lceil m/2 \rceil$ registers, it gives up and sets the registers in which its name is written back to their initial values. If its identifer is written in at least $\lceil m/2 \rceil$ registers (but not in all), it starts all over again. On exiting its critical section, a process sets all the registers back to their initial values.

As the $m$ registers do not have global names, each process independently numbers them. We use the notation $p.i[j]$ to denote the $j^{th}$ register according to process $i$ numbering, for $1 \leq j \leq m$. Recall, that a process' identifier is a positive integer. The code of the algorithm appears in Figure 1.

Code of process $i$

```
Constants:
   m: an odd integer greater than 2                                  //m is the # of shared registers
Shared variables:
   p.i[1..m]: array of m atomic registers, initially all 0           //m ≥ 3 is odd
Local variables:
   myview[1..m]: array of m variables
   j: ranges over {1, ..., n}
1  repeat                                                            //begin entry code
2     for j = 1 to m do if p.i[j] = 0 then p.i[j] = i fi od          //scan and write
3     for j = 1 to m do myview[j] := p.i[j] od                       //read the shared array
4     if i appears in less than ⌈m/2⌉ of the entries of myview[1..m] then   //lose
5        for j = 1 to m do if p.i[j] = i then p.i[j] = 0 fi od       //clean up
6        repeat                                                      //wait for CS to be released
7           for j = 1 to m do myview[j] := p.i[j] od                 //read the shared array
8        until ∀j ∈ {1, ..., m} : myview[j] = 0                      //try again
9     fi
10 until ∀j ∈ {1, ..., m} : myview[j] = i                            //end entry code
11 critical section
12 for j = 1 to m do p.i[j] = 0 od                                   //exit code
```

**Figure 1: A memory-anonymous symmetric deadlock-free mutual exclusion algorithm for two processes**

In the first for loop (lines 2) process $i$ scans the $m$ registers trying to set them all to its identifier. If it does not succeed to set at least $\lceil m/2 \rceil$, it resets the registers with its identifier back to 0 (line 5) and then waits for the critical section to be released (lines 6–8). If it finds out that its identifier is written in all the $m$ registers, it safely enters its critical section (line 10). Otherwise, it go back to the beginning of the repeat loop (line 1) and starts all over again. In its exit code, process $i$ resets all the registers back to 0 (line 12).

## 3.4 Correctness proof

Below we present a correctness proof for the algorithm.

Theorem 3.2. *The algrithm satisfies mutual exclusion.*

Proof. Let $i$ and $j$ be the identifiers of the two processes. Assume that process $i$ is in its critical section, while process $i$ is in its entry code. Before $i$ enters its critical section the expression in line 10, $\forall j \in \{1, \ldots, m\} : myview[j] = i$ must be evaluated to true. This means that, before $i$ has entered its critical section, there is a single point in time where the value of each one of the $m \geq 3$ shared registers equals $i$. After that point, process $j$ might write once into one of the registers overwriting the $i$ value. Thus, process $j$, when executing line 4, will find that its identifier, $j$, appears in less that $\lceil m/2 \rceil$ of the entries of the shared array (actually, the value $j$ may appear in at most one entry) and will change back to 0 the single entry in which its identifier may appears (line 5). From that point on, as long as $i$ is in its critical section, the value $i$ will appear in at least $m - 1$ entries of the shared array, preventing $j$ for entering its critical section. □

Theorem 3.3. *The algorithm is deadlock-free.*

Proof. We show that if a process is trying to enter its critical section, then some process eventually enters its critical section. In the first for loop (lines 2) each process scans the $m$ registers trying to set those that are 0 to its identifier. If the process is running alone it will clearly succeed to set them all to its identifier and will enter its critical section. When there is contention (i.e., both processes are in their entry code) since $m \geq 3$ is an odd number, exactly one of the two processes must find that less than $\lceil m/2 \rceil$ of the registers are set to its identifier, will give up, wait in the inner repeat loop (lines 6–8), enabling the other process to write all the $m$ registers and to enter its critical section. In its exit code, a process resets all the registers back to 0 enabling a possibly waiting process to continue. Thus, it is not possible for both processes to simultaneously be in their entry codes forever. □

## 3.5 A general space lower bound

The result that there is a memory-anonymous symmetric deadlock-free mutual exclusion algorithm for two processes using $m \geq 2$ registers only if $m$ is odd is a special case of the following more general result. Two integers $x$ and $y$ are said to be *relatively prime* if their greatest common divisor is 1. We notice that a number is *not* relatively prime to itself.

Theorem 3.4. *There is a memory-anonymous symmetric deadlock-free mutual exclusion algorithm for $n$ processes using $m \geq 2$ registers only if for every positive integer $1 < \ell \leq n$, $m$ and $\ell$ are relatively prime.*

Proof. We assume to the contrary that there is a memory-anonymous symmetric deadlock-free mutual exclusion algorithm for $n$ processes using $m \geq 2$ registers such that for some positive integer $1 < \ell \leq n$, $m$ and $\ell$ are not relatively prime. This means that there is a number $1 < \ell \leq m$ such that $\ell$ divides $m$.

The lack of global names for the registers makes it convenient to think of each process as being assigned an initial register and an ordering of the registers which determines how it scans the registers when it runs alone. For example, if a process scans three registers, named 3,4 and 5, in the order 5445334 then the ordering would be 543, omitting duplications.

We arrange the registers as a unidirectional ring of size $m$, where the direction of the unidirectional ring corresponds to the direction in which the processes scan the registers. So, we pick up $\ell$ processes, and assign these $\ell$ processes the same ring ordering, though potentially different initial registers. That is, the processes scan the registers by "walking" around the ring in the same direction. The distance between two registers on the ring is the smallest number of registers between them plus 1. For each process, we assign an initial register such that the distance between any two neighbouring initial registers is exactly $m/l$. (Two initial registers are neighbours when there is no other initial register between them.)

We run the $\ell$ processes in lock steps. We first let each one of them take one step (in some order), and then let each one of them takes another step, and so on. Since only comparisons for equality are allowed, processes that take the same number of steps will be at the same state, and thus it is not possible to break symmetry. Thus, either all the processes will enter their critical sections at the same time violating mutual exclusion, or no process will ever enter its critical section violating deadlock-freedom. A contradiction. □

# 4 A MEMORY-ANONYMOUS OBSTRUCTION-FREE CONSENSUS ALGORITHM

The multi-valued consensus problem is to design an algorithm in which all non-faulty processes reach a common decision based on their initial opinions. It is impossible to solve consensus with a single crash failure using registers only (even in the classical model) [11, 16]. This implies that there is no wait-free consensus algorithm using registers. Below we focus on the design of an obstruction-free consensus algorithm.

The consensus problem is defined as follows: there are $n$ processes, and each process has some input value. The requirements of the consensus problem are that there exists a *decision value* $v$ such that: (1) *Agreement*: all non-faulty process that eventually decide, decide on the same value $v$, and (2) *Validity*: $v$ is the input value of at least one of the processes. We recall that obstruction-freedom requires that each process that runs alone, for sufficiently long time, must eventually decide.

When there are only two possible input values, the problem is called *binary* consensus. We solve the general *multi-valued* version of the problem. Our algorithm uses a key idea from an earlier algorithm, which uses single-writer registers and snapshot objects (and hence is not memory-anonymous) [5].

## 4.1 The consensus algorithm

The algorithm uses an array of $2n-1$ shared registers, where each register is defined as a record which has two fields: an *id* field that can store a process identifier and a *val* field which stores the preference of a process. Each participating process scans the $2n-1$ shared registers trying to write its identifier and preference into each one of the $2n-1$ registers. Before each write, the process scans the shared array and operates as follows: if its identifier and preference appears in all the $2n-1$ registers, it decides on its preference, and terminates; otherwise, if some preference appears in at least $n$ of the value fields, the process adopts this preference as its new value.

Afterwards, the process finds some arbitrary entry in the shared array that does not contain both its identifier and preference and writes the pair containing its identifier and preference into that entry. Once the process finishes writing it repeats the above steps until its identifier and preference appear in all the $2n-1$ registers, at which point it can decide on its current preference and terminate.

As in the previous section, we use the notation $p.i[j]$ to denote the $j^{th}$ register according to process $i$ numbering, for $1 \leq j \leq 2n-1$. The code of the algorithm appears in Figure 2.

After process $i$ sets its initial preference to its input (line 1), it executes the repeat loop (lines 2–8) until its identifier and preference appears in all the $2n-1$ registers. Within the repeat loop, it first copies the values of the shared array into the local array $myview[1..2n-1]$ (line 3). If some value appears in at least $n$ of the *val* fields of the entries of $myview[1..2n-1]$ (line 4), the process adopts this value as its preference, by writing this value into *mypref* (line 5). Then, the process finds some arbitrary entry in $myview[1..2n-1]$ that does not contain the pair $(i, mypref)$ (line 6) and writes this pair into that entry (line 7). Clearly, such an arbitrary entry exists. Once the process exits the repeat loop, it decides on the value of *mypref* and terminates.

**Remark:** Defining each register as a record which has two fields with *global* names, is done only for convenience. The two values in these fields can be encoded as a single value, removing the need for using more than one field. A similar comment applies also for the renaming algorithm presented in the next section.

**A note on obstruction-free election:** In the election problem, each participating process that terminates, outputs the identifier of some participating process before terminating. It is required that all the participants which terminate output the same identifier, which identifies the elected leader. Obstruction-freedom requires that each process that runs alone, for sufficiently long time, must eventually output a value and terminate. In asynchronous systems where processes communicate using registers, election is impossible with one faulty process even with registers which have global names [11, 19, 26].[1] It is straightforward to use the above consensus algorithm for constructing a memory-anonymous symmetric obstruction-free election algorithm: Each process simply uses its own identifier as its initial input.

## 4.2 Correctness proof

Below we present a correctness proof for the consensus algorithm.

THEOREM 4.1 (AGREEMENT UNDER OBSTRUCTION-FREEDOM). *Every participating process, that runs alone for sufficiently long time, eventually decides; and all the participating processes that decide, decide on the same value and terminate.*

[1] An algorithm that tolerates a single failure does not necessarily satisfies obstruction-freedom, and vice versa.

CODE OF PROCESS $i$ WITH INPUT $in_i$

**Shared variables:**
$p.i[1..2n-1]$: array of $2n-1$ atomic registers, initially all fields are 0

**Local variables:**
$myview[1..2n-1]$: array of $2n-1$ variables, each entry has two fields $id$ and $val$.
$mypref$: integer ; $j$: ranges over $\{1, ..., 2n-1\}$

```
1 mypref := in_i
2 repeat
3     for j = 1 to 2n − 1 do myview[j] := p.i[j] od                        //read the shared array
4     if ∃ value ≠ 0 which appears in at least n of the val fields of the entries of myview[1..2n − 1]
5         then mypref := value fi                                           //update preference
6     j := an arbitrary index k ∈ {1, ..., 2n − 1} such that myview[k] ≠ (i, mypref)   //search
7     p.i[j] := (i, mypref)                                                 // write
8 until ∀j ∈ {1, ..., 2n − 1} : myview[j] = (i, mypref)                     //my id appears everywhere
9 decide(mypref)                                                            //decide
```

**Figure 2: A memory-anonymous symmetric obstruction-free consensus algorithm**

PROOF. Let process $i$ be the first process to decide, and denote the value that $i$ decides on by $v$. This means that, before deciding, process $i$ has found that the value of each one of the $2n-1$ shared registers equals $(i, v)$. Each one of the other $n-1$ processes might write into one of the registers overwriting the $(i, v)$ value. Thus, *all* the other processes, when executing line 4, will find that $v$ appears in at least $n$ of the $val$ fields of the entries of $myview[1..2n-1]$, and each one of them will change its preference to $v$ (line 5). From that point on, the only possible decision value is $v$. Next, we show that each process eventually decides (and terminates) under obstruction-freedom (that is, if it runs alone for sufficiently long time). When a process, say process $j$, runs alone from some point on in a computation, $j$ will read the shared array (line 3) and set its preference to $v$ (if it is not $v$ already). From that point on, in each iteration of the repeat loop, process $j$ will set one entry of the shared array to $(j, v)$. Thus, after at most $2n-1$ iterations the values of all the $2n-1$ entries will equal $(j, v)$, and process $j$ will be able to exit the repeat loop, decide $v$ and terminate. □

THEOREM 4.2 (VALIDITY). *The decision value is the input of a participating process.*

PROOF. At each point the current preference of a process is either its initial input or a value (different from 0), it has read from the $val$ field of a shared register. Since a process may only write its preference into the $val$ field of a shared registers, the result follows. □

# 5 A MEMORY-ANONYMOUS OBSTRUCTION-FREE PERFECT RENAMING ALGORITHM

A *renaming* algorithm allows processes with initially distinct names from a large name space to acquire distinct new names from a small name space. A *perfect* renaming algorithm allows $n$ processes with initially distinct names from a large name space to acquire distinct new names from the set $\{1, ...n\}$. A perfect renaming algorithm is *adaptive* if, for any $1 \leq k \leq n$, when only $k$ processes participate, they acquire distinct new names from the set $\{1, ...k\}$. In asynchronous systems where processes communicate using atomic registers there is no perfect renaming algorithm which can tolerate a single failure even with registers which have global names [1, 19, 26]. We show that there is a memory-anonymous obstruction-free adaptive perfect renaming algorithm using registers.

It is straightforward to solve perfect renaming in a model where *there is* an a priori agreement on the names of the registers, given that there is a solution for the election problem. This is done as follows: $n-1$ (obstruction-free) election objects are used. The election objects are indexed $1,2,...,n-1$. Each process scans the objects, in order, starting with object number 1. At each step, the process applies the election operation, and either: moves to the next object if it is not elected in object $i < n-1$, stops if it is being elected, or stops if it not elected in object $n-1$. The process is assigned either the name equal to the index of the object on which its election operation has succeeded, or $n$ if it is not elected in all $n-1$ objects. This trivial solution requires a priori agreement on an ordering for the election objects, and hence would not work in a model where there is *no* a priori agreement on the registers names.

## 5.1 The perfect renaming algorithm

The basic idea, as in the above trivial solution, is for each process to participate in up to $n$ election "games", and to acquire a name according to the game in which it is elected. However, the solution does not require a priori agreement on an ordering for the election games. This is achieved by playing each one of these games in the same shared space. The algorithm uses an array of $2n-1$ shared registers, where each register is defined as a record which has *four* fields: an $id$ and $val$ fields, each can store a process identifier, a *round* field which can store a number between 1 to $n$, and a *history* field which stores a set of pairs of the form (*identifier, value*) where $value \in \{1, ..., n\}$.

CODE OF PROCESS $i$

**Shared variables:**

$p.i[1..2n-1]$: array of $2n-1$ registers, initially the fields *id, val, round,* and *history* are 0,0,0 and $\emptyset$, resp.

**Local variables:**

$myview[1..2n-1]$: array of $2n-1$ variables, each entry has four fields *id, val, round, history*
$mypref$: integer ; $j$: ranges over $\{1, ..., 2n-1\}$
$myround, mytemp$: ranges over $\{1, ..., n\}$, initially 1
$myhistory$: a set of pairs of the form (*identifier, value*) where $value \in \{1, ..., n\}$, initially $\emptyset$

```
1  repeat
2    mypref := i                                          //i tries to win in the current round
3    repeat                                     //in each round one process wins and gets a new name
4      for j = 1 to 2n − 1 do myview[j] := p.i[j] od                      //read the shared array
5      if ∃ j ∃ v : (i, v) ∈ myview[j].history                           //i already got new name!
6        then return(v) fi                                          //return new name and terminate
7      mytemp := max_{j∈{1,...,2n−1}} myview[j].round                     //finding the maximum round #
8      if mytemp > myround then                                             //i is lagging behind
9        j := an arbitrary index k ∈ {1, ..., 2n − 1} such that myview[k].round = mytemp
10       mypref := myview[j].val                                                   //catching up
11       myhistory := myview[j].history                                            //catching up
12       myround := myview[j].round fi                                             //catching up
13     if ∃ v ≠ 0 such that among the entries of myview[1..2n − 1] whose round fields equals myround
         v appears in at least n of the val fields of these entries
14       then mypref := v fi                                                 // change preference
15     j := an arbitrary index k ∈ {1, ..., 2n − 1} such that
         myview[k] ≠ (i, mypref, myround, myhistory)                                      //search
16     p.i[j] := (i, mypref, myround, myhistory)                                           //write
17   until ∀j ∈ {1, ..., 2n − 1} : myview[j] = (i, mypref, myround, myhistory)           //success
18   if mypref = i then return(myround) fi                          //return new name and terminate
19   myhistory := myhistory ∪ {(mypref, myround)}                                 //update history
20   myround := myround + 1                                                      //increment round
21 until myround = n                                                          //a single process left
22 return(n)                                                       //last process to acquire a name
```

**Figure 3: A memory-anonymous symmetric obstruction-free adaptive perfect renaming algorithm**

The algorithm precedes in rounds, where in each round the processes elect one of the participating processes as a leader. These rounds are *local* and do not require global synchronization. In each round, say $r$, each participating process scans the $2n-1$ registers trying to write its preference, which in this case is its identifier, into each one of the $2n-1$ registers. In addition, the process also writes into each one of the $2n-1$ registers a set which includes the history of all the processes that were elected in previous rounds. Eventually, the processes will agree on some value, say *id*, in round $r$ and *id* will identify the leader for round $r$. The process whose identity equals *id* will eventually be assigned the value $r$ as its new name. Once a process is elected in round $r$, it does not participate in later rounds. A process that notices that a leader is elected in around $r$, updates its history by adding the pair $(id, r)$ to its history, and continues to round $r+1$. After $n$ rounds, all the processes will be assigned new names. As before, we use the notation $p.i[j]$ to denote the $j^{th}$ register according to process $i$ numbering, for $1 \leq j \leq 2n-1$. The code of the algorithm appears in Figure 3.

After process $i$ sets its initial preference to its own identifier (line 2), it executes the inner repeat loop (lines 3–17) until its identifier and preference appears in all the $2n-1$ registers. Within the repeat loop, it first copies the values of the shared array into the local array $myview[1..2n-1]$ (line 4). It then checks if its identifier appears in the history of some process (line 5). If so, it means that it was elected as a leader in one of the previous rounds, in which case it returns the round number in which it was elected as its new name and terminates. Otherwise, if it sees that it is lagging behind (line 8), it is catching up by updating its preference, history and round number (lines 9-12). If some value appears in at least $n$ of the *val* fields of the entries of $myview[1..2n-1]$ whose *round* fields equals *myround* (line 13), the process adopts this value (identifier) as its new preference (line 14). Then, the process finds some arbitrary entry in $myview[1..2n-1]$ that does not contain the tuple $(i, mypref, myround, myhistory)$ (line 15) and writes it into that entry (line 16). Once the process exits the inner repeat loop, it first checks if it was elected in the current round, and if so it returns the round number and terminates (line 18). Otherwise, it updates its history (line 19) and round number (line 19). In case its round number reaches $n$, it exits the outer repeat loop, returns $n$ as its new name and terminates. Otherwise, it continues to the next round.

## 5.2 Correctness proof

Below we present a correctness proof for the renaming algorithm.

THEOREM 5.1 (TERMINATION UNDER OBSTRUCTION-FREEDOM). *Every participating processes, if it runs alone for sufficiently long time, acquires a new name and terminate.*

PROOF. Assume that at some point in time some a process, say process $i$, runs alone. One of the following four scenarios must happen:

(1) Process $i$ checks if its identifier appears in the history of some process (line 5). If so, it returns the round number in which it was elected as its new name and terminates (line 6).
(2) Process $i$, if needed, updates *once* its *mypref*, *myround* and *myhistory* variables (lines 10, 11, 12, 14). From that point on, in each iteration of the inner repeat loop (lines 3–17), process $i$ sets one entry of the shared array to $(i, mypref, myround, myhistory)$. Thus, after at most $2n-1$ iterations the values of all the $2n-1$ entries equal $(i, mypref, myround, myhistory)$, and process $i$ is able to exit the inner repeat loop. Once process $i$ exits the inner repeat loop, it checks if $mypref = i$, and if so it returns the round number and terminates (line 18).
(3) Process $i$ increments *mypref* by 1 (line 20). In case $mypref = n$, it exits the outer repeat loop, returns $n$ as its new name and terminates.
(4) Process $i$ continues alone to the next round. It first sets *mypref* to $i$ (line 2). From that point on, in each iteration of the inner repeat loop (lines 3–17), process $i$ sets one entry of the shared array to $(i, i, myround, myhistory)$. Thus, after at most $2n-1$ iterations the values of all the $2n-1$ entries equal $(i, i, myround, myhistory)$, and process $i$ is able to exit the inner repeat loop. Once process $i$ exits the inner repeat loop, since $mypref = i$, it returns the current round number as its new name and terminates (line 18).

This completes the proof. □

THEOREM 5.2 (UNIQUENESS). *Every participating processes acquires unique name from the set* $\{1, ...n\}$.

PROOF. Assume that process $i$ acquires the name $r$. This means that, at some point in time during round $r$ (before $i$ acquires the name $r$), for every $j \in \{1, ..., 2n-1\}$, $p.i[j].val = i$ and $p.i[j].round = r$. This happens immediately after some process (not necessarily $i$) has updated a shared register. Each one of the other $n-1$ processes might write into one of the $2n-1$ registers during round $r$ overwriting the value of a register. Thus, *all* the other processes, when executing line 13 during round $r$, will find that $v$ appears in at least $n$ of the *val* fields of the entries of $myview[1..2n-1]$, and each one of them will change its preference to $v$ during round $r$ (line 14). From that point on, the only possible leader for round $r$ is $i$. Thus, no other process will be assigned the value $r$. Since the number assigned to a process corresponds to the round at which it was elected or $n$ if not elected in the first $n-1$ rounds, the assigned name must be from the set $\{1, ...n\}$. □

THEOREM 5.3 (ADAPTIVITY). *For any* $1 \leq k \leq n$, *when only* $k$ *processes participate, they acquire new names from the set* $\{1, ...k\}$.

PROOF. If only $k < n$ processes participate, the algorithm will terminate after $k$ rounds. Since the number assigned to a process corresponds to the round at which it was elected (or $n$ if not elected in the first $n-1$ rounds), the assigned name must be from the set $\{1, ...k\}$. □

# 6 IMPOSSIBILITY RESULTS AND SPACE LOWER BOUNDS

We first address the following question: Is a model in which there is no agreement regarding the names of the registers *strictly weaker* than a model in which there is such agreement? The assumption that there is a lower-level a priori agreement regarding an object name can be viewed as an attribute of the object itself. A *named object* is an object for which there is an a priori agreement regarding its name, while an *unnamed object* (also called *anonymous* object) is an object for which there is no agreement regarding its name. Is it possible to implement a named register using unnamed registers? We prove the following result:

THEOREM 6.1. *A model in which there is no agreement regarding the names of the registers is strictly weaker than a model in which there is such agreement, even when assuming that processes never fail. Thus, it is not possible to implement a single named register using any number of unnamed registers, even when assuming that processes never fail.*

In the previous sections we have assumed that the number of processes, $n$, is finite and a priori known. Here we investigate the design of algorithms assuming *no a priori agreement* on the *number* of processes. Our results apply to both the case where the number of processes is finite but not a priori known, and the case where the number of processes is unbounded. We say that that the number of processes is *unbounded* when, in each run, the number of processes that are simultaneously active in any given point in time (i.e., in any state) is finite but can grow without bound.

We prove below three impossibility results for a model where the processes communicated via unnamed registers and there is no a priori known bound on number of processes. These results also hold for algorithms which are *not symmetric*. The results are for deadlock-free mutual exclusion, obstruction-free consensus and obstruction-free adaptive perfect renaming. The impossibility result for deadlock-free mutual exclusion does not hold when using named registers. Thus, the result for deadlock-free mutual exclusion implies Theorem 6.1. The impossibility proofs below are all based on covering arguments and have the same structure.

## 6.1 Preliminaries

For proving the impossibility results we will use the following notions and notations. An *event* corresponds to an atomic step performed by a process. A (global) *state* of an algorithm is completely described by the values of the (local and shared) registers and the values of the location counters of all the processes. A *run* is defined as a sequence of alternating states and events (also referred to as steps). For the purpose of the proofs below, it is more convenient to define a run as a sequence of events omitting all the states except the initial state. Since the states in a run are uniquely determined by the events and the initial state, no information is lost by omitting the states.

We will use $x$, $y$ and $z$ to denote runs. When $x$ is a prefix of $y$ (and $y$ is an *extension* of $x$), we denote by $(y - x)$ the suffix of $y$ obtained by removing $x$ from $y$. Also, we denote by $x; seq$ the sequence obtained by extending $x$ with the sequence of events $seq$. Saying that an extension $y$ of $x$ involves only processes from the set $P$ means that all events in $(y - x)$ are only by processes in $P$. Runs $x$ and $y$ are *indistinguishable* for process $p$, if the subsequence of all events by $p$ in $x$ is the same as in $y$, the initial values of the local registers of $p$ in $x$ are the same as in $y$, and the (current) values of all the shared registers in $x$ are the same as in $y$.

Process $p$ *covers* a register in run $x$, if $x$ can be extended by an event in which $p$ writes to some register. If every process in a set of processes $P$ covers a register in $y$ then $P$ is a set of *covering processes* in $y$. A *block write* by a set of covering processes $P$ is an execution in which each process in $P$ performs a single write (and nothing else). Notice that if process $p$ covers register *reg* in run $x$ then $p$ covers *reg* in any extension of $x$ which does not involve $p$. Also, if every process in $P$ covers a different register then the order of writes does not matter since the resulting runs are indistinguishable to all the processes.

## 6.2 An impossibility result for deadlock-free mutual exclusion

A deadlock-free mutual exclusion algorithm for an unbounded number of processes using named registers was presented in [17]. We prove that there is no such algorithm using unnamed registers. These possibility and impossibility results imply Theorem 6.1.

THEOREM 6.2. *There is no deadlock-free mutual exclusion algorithm using unnamed registers when the number of processes is not a priori known.*

PROOF. We assume to the contrary that there is a deadlock-free mutual exclusion algorithm using unnamed registers assuming that the number of processes is not a priori known, and show that this assumption leads to a contradiction.

A process must write at least once before it enters its critical section. Otherwise, we can let the process enter its critical section, and since it left no trace, if we let other processes run, by deadlock-freedom, one of them will also enter its critical section violating the mutual exclusion requirement.

Let $y$ be a run in which some process, say $q$, runs alone until it enters its critical section, and let $write(y, q)$ be the set of different registers to which $q$ has written in $y$. Let $P$ be a set of processes such that $q \notin P$ and $|P| = |write(y, q)|$. Since the number of processes is not a priori known (and thus can be as big as we need), we can always find such a set $P$, for any size of $write(y, q)$.

For each process $p \in P$, let $r.p$ denotes a run in which $p$ runs alone until it first covers some register. Since all the registers are unnamed, we can let each process scan the registers in an order which ensures that: (1) for each process $p \in P$, in $r.p$ process $p$ covers some register in $write(y, q)$, and (2) for each pair of processes $\{p, p'\} \subseteq P$, in $r.p$ and $r.p'$ processes $p$ and $p'$ cover different registers.

Since, for each $p \in P$ there are no writes in $r.p$, we can construct a run, called $x$, as follows: we pick an arbitrary process $p \in P$, and let it execute exactly the same steps as in $r.p$, then we pick another process from $P$ and repeat this procedure. We continue until each process in $P$ covers some register in $write(y, q)$. By construction, in $x$ the processes in $P$ together cover all the registers in $write(y, q)$. Let $x'$ be an extension of $x$ by a block write by $P$. By the deadlock-freedom property, there exists an extension $z$ of $x'$ in which only processes in $P$ take steps and some process in $P$ is in its critical section.

Next we construct a run, $\rho$, in which two processes are in their critical sections at the same time. We start the construction with the run $x$. Since no process writes a shared register in $x$, only processes in $P$ participate in $x$ and $q \notin P$, it follows that $x; y$ is a legal run. Let $w$ be an extension of $x; y$ by a block write by $P$. Since the block write by $P$ overwrites all the values written by process $q$ in $x; y$, it follows that $w$ and $x'$ are indistinguishable for all the processes $P$. Thus, any extension of $x'$ by processes in $P$ is also a possible extension of $w$. In particular, $\rho = w; (z - x')$ is a legal run. By construction at the end of $\rho$ two processes, $q \notin P$ and some process in $P$, are in their critical sections. A contradiction. □

## 6.3 An impossibility result and a space lower bound for obstruction-free consensus

In Section 4, we have presented an obstruction-free consensus for $n$ processes using unnamed registers, where $n$ is a (known) positive integer. We show that no such algorithm exists when the number of processes is not a priori known. Interestingly, it is shown in [25], how to construct an obstruction-free consensus algorithm using *named* registers when the number of processes is finite and not a priori known or even when the number of processes is unbounded. For a finite number of processes $n$, the question whether it is possible to solve obstruction-free consensus using $n - 1$ named registers is still open. We resolve this question for unnamed registers.

THEOREM 6.3. *There is no obstruction-free consensus algorithm (1) when the number of processes is not a priori known using (an unlimited number of) unnamed registers, and (2) for $n \geq 2$ processes using $n - 1$ unnamed registers.*

PROOF. We assume to the contrary that there is an obstruction-free consensus algorithm when the number of processes is not a priori known using unnamed registers (resp. for $n \geq 2$ processes using $n - 1$ unnamed registers), and show that this assumption leads to a contradiction.

A process that runs alone must write at least once before it decides. Otherwise, we let a process with input $v \in \{0, 1\}$ run alone until it decides $v$, Then (assuming the process never writes), we let a process with input $1 - v$ run alone until it decides on $1 - v$. This would violate the agreement requirement.

Let $y$ be a run in which some process, say $q$, with input 0 runs alone until it decides 0, and let $write(y, q)$ be the set of different registers to which $q$ has written in $y$. Let $P$ be a set of processes, all with input 1, such that $q \notin P$ and $|P| = |write(y, q)|$. Since the number of processes is not a priori known (resp. since there are $n$ processes and only $n-1$ registers), we can always find such a set $P$, for any possible size of $write(y, q)$.

For each process $p \in P$, let $r.p$ denotes a run in which $p$ runs alone until it first covers some register. Since all the registers are unnamed, we can let each process scan the registers in an order which ensures that: (1) for each process $p \in P$, in $r.p$ process $p$ covers some register in $write(y, q)$, and (2) for each pair of processes $\{p, p'\} \subseteq P$, in $r.p$ and $r.p'$ processes $p$ and $p'$ cover different registers.

Since, for each process $p \in P$, there are no writes in $r.p$, we can construct a run, called $x$, as follows: we pick an arbitrary process $p \in P$, and let it execute exactly the same steps as in $r.p$, then we pick another process in $P$ and repeat this procedure. We continue until each process in $P$ covers some register in $write(y, q)$. By construction, in $x$ the processes in $P$ together cover all the registers in $write(y, q)$. Let $x'$ be an extension of $x$ by a block write by $P$. By the obstruction-freedom and the validity properties, there exists an extension $z$ of $x'$ in which (1) only some process $p \in P$ takes steps and (2) $p$ decides 1.

Next we construct a run, $\rho$, in which two processes decide on different values. We start the construction with the run $x$. Since no process writes a shared register in $x$, only processes in $P$ participate in $x$ and $q \notin P$, it follows that $x; y$ is a legal run. Let $w$ be an extension of $x; y$ by a block write by $P$. Since the block write by $P$ overwrites all the values written by process $q$ in $x; y$, it follows that $w$ and $x'$ are indistinguishable for all the processes $P$. Thus, any extension of $x'$ by processes in $P$ is also a possible extension of $w$. In particular, $\rho = w; (z - x')$ is a legal run. By construction at the end of $\rho$, $q$ decides 0 and $p$ decides 1. A contradiction. □

Corollary 6.4. *There is no obstruction-free implementation of a single named register using any number of unnamed registers.*

Proof. The corollary follows immediately from Theorem 6.3 and the fact that it is possible to construct an obstruction-free consensus algorithm using *named* registers when the number of processes is finite and not a priori known [25]. □

**Remark:** The $k$-set consensus problem is to design an algorithm for $n$ processes, where each process starts with an input value from some domain, and must choose some participating process input as its output. All $n$ processes together may choose no more than $k$ distinct output values. The 1-set consensus problem, is the familiar consensus problem. It is possible to generalize Theorem 6.3, and prove that for every $k \geq 1$, there is no obstruction-free $k$-set consensus algorithm when the number of processes is not a priori known using (an unlimited number of) unnamed registers.

### 6.4 An impossibility result and a space lower bound for adaptive perfect renaming

In Section 5, we have presented an obstruction-free adaptive perfect renaming for $n$ processes using unnamed registers, where $n$ is a positive integer. Below we show that no such algorithm exists using only $n-1$ unnamed registers, or when the number of processes is not a priori known.

Theorem 6.5. *There is no obstruction-free adaptive perfect renaming algorithm (1) when the number of processes is not a priori known using (an unlimited number of) unnamed registers, and (2) for $n \geq 2$ processes using $n-1$ unnamed registers.*

Proof. We assume to the contrary that there is an obstruction-free adaptive perfect renaming algorithm when the number of processes is not a priori known using unnamed registers (resp. for $n \geq 2$ processes using $n-1$ unnamed registers), and show that this assumption leads to a contradiction.

A process that runs alone must write at least once before it decides. Otherwise, we let some process run alone until (by adaptivity) it acquires the new name 1. Then (assuming the process never writes), we let another process run alone until it also acquires the new name 1. This would violate the distinct new names requirement.

Let $y$ be a run in which some process, say $q$, runs alone until it acquires the new name 1, and let $write(y, q)$ be the set of different registers to which $q$ has written in $y$. Let $P$ be a set of processes, such that $q \notin P$ and $|P| = |write(y, q)|$. Since the number of processes is not a priori known (resp. since there are $n$ processes and only $n-1$ registers), we can always find such a set $P$, for any possible size of $write(y, q)$.

For each process $p \in P$, let $r.p$ denotes a run in which $p$ runs alone until it first covers some register. Since all the registers are unnamed, we can let each process scan the registers in an order which ensures that: (1) for each process $p \in P$, in $r.p$ process $p$ covers some register in $write(y, q)$, and (2) for each pair of processes $\{p, p'\} \subseteq P$, in $r.p$ and $r.p'$ processes $p$ and $p'$ cover different registers.

Since, for each process $p \in P$, there are no writes in $r.p$, we can construct a run, called $x$, as follows: we pick an arbitrary process $p \in P$, and let it execute exactly the same steps as in $r.p$, then we pick another process in $P$ and repeat this procedure. We continue until each process in $P$ covers some register in $write(y, q)$. By construction, in $y$ the processes in $P$ together cover all the registers in $write(y, q)$. Let $x'$ be an extension of $x$ by a block write by $P$. By the obstruction-free property and the adaptivity requirement, there exists an extension $z$ of $x'$ in which (1) only processes $P$ take steps and (2) the process in $P$ acquire the names 1 through $|P|$.

Next we construct a run, $\rho$, in which two processes acquire the name 1. We start the construction with the run $x$. Since no process writes a shared register in $x$, only processes in $P$ participate in $x$ and $q \notin P$, it follows that $x; y$ is a legal run. Let $w$ be an extension of $x; y$ by a block write by $P$. Since the block write by $P$ overwrites all the values written by process $q$ in $x; y$, it follows that $w$ and $x'$ are indistinguishable for all the processes $P$. Thus, any extension of $x'$ by processes in $P$ is also a possible extension of $w$. In particular, $\rho = w; (z - x')$ is a legal run. By construction at the end of $\rho$, process $q \notin P$ and some other process in $P$ both acquire the name 1. A contradiction. □

## 7 RELATED WORK

Our work is inspired by Michael O. Rabin's paper on solving the Choice Coordination Problem with $k$ alternatives ($k$-CCP) [21]. In the $k$-CCP, $n$ asynchronous processes must choose between $k$ alternatives. The agreement on a single choice is complicated by the fact that there is *no a priori* agreement on names for the alternatives. That is, each process has its own naming convention for the alternatives. Rabin has assumed that processes communicate by applying *read-modify-write* operations to $k$ shared registers which do not have global names. The $k$ different registers represent the $k$ possible alternatives. For the case of $k = 2$ and $t = n-1$ where $t$ is the possible number of faults, Rabin has presented a deterministic algorithm using $m = n+2$ symbols (for each register), proved a space lower bound of $m \geq (n/8)^{1/3}$ for deterministic algorithms, and contrasted these deterministic results with a randomized algorithm which, for $m$ symbols, terminates correctly with probability $1 - 1/2^{m/2}$. Because of the use of read-modify-write operations, *none* of the algorithmic ideas from [13, 21] were found useful in our case.

The mutual exclusion problem was first introduced by Edsger W. Dijkstra in [10]. Dijkstra's original definition requires the algorithm to satisfy only the requirements of mutual exclusion and deadlock-freedom as defined in Section 3. In [7, 8], it is shown that any deadlock-free mutual exclusion algorithm for $n$ processes using registers must use at least $n$ shared registers. Dozens of interesting mutual exclusion algorithms and lower bounds are described in details in [22, 24]. The election problem (sometimes called the one shot mutual exclusion problem) is a special case of the mutual exclusion problem where only one process is allowed enter once its critical section. This process is the elected leader.

The consensus problem was formally defined in [20]. The impossibility result that there is no consensus algorithm that can tolerate even a single crash failure was first proved for the asynchronous message-passing model in [11], and later has been extended for the shared memory model with atomic registers, in [16]. Many related impossibility results can be found in [2]. Two extensively studied progress conditions are wait-freedom [14] and obstruction-freedom [15]. It is shown in [15] that obstruction-free consensus is solvable using registers. In [5], an obstruction-free consensus algorithm (which is not memory-anonymous) using single-writer registers and snapshot objects is presented. Recently, it has been shown in [27], that any obstruction-free consensus algorithm for $n$ processes using registers must use at least $n - 1$ registers. The (one-shot) renaming problem was first solved for message-passing systems [1], and later for shared memory systems [4]. Several of the many papers on renaming are [3, 6, 9, 12, 18]. The impossibility result that there are no election algorithm and no perfect renaming algorithm that can tolerate a single crash failure was first proved for the asynchronous message-passing model in [1, 19], and later has been extended for the shared memory model in [26].

## 8 DISCUSSION

We have introduced several results for a model in which there is no lower-level agreement regarding the names of memory locations. The weak communication model considered, enables us to better understand the intrinsic limits for coordinating the actions of asynchronous processes.

We proved that unnamed registers (i.e, anonymous registers) are strictly weaker than named registers. Unnamed registers are the only non-trivial objects, that I know of, which are strictly weaker than the classical (named) atomic registers. It would be interesting to investigate the computational power of other unnamed objects, to consider models where, in addition to unnamed objects, a limited number of named objects are also available, and to explore models in which the number of objects and even their locations are not a priori agreed upon.

Several questions are left open: the existence of deadlock-free mutual exclusion algorithms for more than two processes, the existence of starvation-free mutual exclusion algorithms, finding tight space bounds for consensus and renaming, and finding solutions for additional problems under various progress conditions.

## REFERENCES


[1] H. Attiya, A. Bar-Noy, D. Dolev, D. Koller, D. Peleg, and R. Reischuk. Renaming in an asynchronous environment. *Journal of the Association for Computing Machinery*, 37(3):524–548, July 1990.

[2] H. Attiya and F. Ellen. *Impossibility Results for Distributed Computing*. Synthesis Lectures on Distributed Computing Theory. Morgan&Claypool, 2014. 162 pages.

[3] H. Attiya and A. Fouren. Algorithms adapting to point contention. *Journal of the ACM*, 50(4):144–468, 2003.

[4] A. Bar-Noy and D. Dolev. Shared memory versus message-passing in an asynchronous distributed environment. In *Proc. 8th ACM Symp. on Principles of Distributed Computing*, pages 307–318, 1989.

[5] J. Bowman. Obstruction-free snapshot, obstruction-free consensus, and fetch-and-add modulo k. Technical Report Technical Report TR2011-681, Dartmouth College, 2011.

[6] A. Brodsky, F. Ellen, and P. Woelfel. Fully-adaptive algorithms for long-lived renaming. *Distributed Computing*, 24(2):119–134, 2011.

[7] J. E. Burns and A. N. Lynch. Mutual exclusion using indivisible reads and writes. In *18th annual allerton conference on communication, control and computing*, pages 833–842, October 1980.

[8] J. N. Burns and N. A. Lynch. Bounds on shared-memory for mutual exclusion. *Information and Computation*, 107(2):171–184, December 1993.

[9] A. Castaneda, S. Rajsbaum, and M. Raynal. The renaming problem in shared memory systems: An introduction. *Computer Science Review*, 5(3):229–251, 2011.

[10] E. W. Dijkstra. Solution of a problem in concurrent programming control. *Communications of the ACM*, 8(9):569, 1965.

[11] M. J. Fischer, N. A. Lynch, and M. S. Paterson. Impossibility of distributed consensus with one faulty process. *Journal of the ACM*, 32(2):374–382, 1985.

[12] E. Gafni, M. Merritt, and G. Taubenfeld. The concurrency hierarchy, and algorithms for unbounded concurrency. In *Proc. 20th ACM Symp. on Principles of Distributed Computing*, pages 161–169, August 2001.

[13] D.S. Greenberg, G. Taubenfeld, and Da-Wei Wang Choice coordination with multiple alternatives. *In Proc. of the 6th International workshop on distributed algorithms*, LNCS 647, pages 54–68, 1992.

[14] M. P. Herlihy. Wait-free synchronization. *ACM Trans. on Programming Languages and Systems*, 13(1):124–149, January 1991.

[15] M. P. Herlihy, V. Luchangco, and M. Moir. Obstruction-free synchronization: Double-ended queues as an example. In *Proc. of the 23rd International Conference on Distributed Computing Systems*, page 522, 2003.

[16] M.C. Loui and H. Abu-Amara. Memory requirements for agreement among unreliable asynchronous processes. *Advances in Computing Research*, 4:163–183, 1987.

[17] M. Merritt and G. Taubenfeld. Computing with infinitely many processes. *Information and Computation*, 233:12 – 31, 2013.

[18] M. Moir and J. H. Anderson. Wait-free algorithms for fast, long-lived renaming. *Science of Computer Programming*, 25(1):1–39, October 1995.

[19] S. Moran and Y. Wolfstahl. Extended impossibility results for asynchronous complete networks. *Information Processing Letters*, 26(3):145–151, 1987.

[20] M. Pease, R. Shostak, and L. Lamport. Reaching agreement in the presence of faults. *Journal of the ACM*, 27(2):228–234, 1980.

[21] M. O. Rabin. The choice coordination problem. *Acta Informatica*, 17:121–134, 1982.

[22] M. Raynal. *Algorithms for mutual exclusion*. The MIT Press, 1986. Translation of: Algorithmique du parallélisme, 1984.

[23] E. Styer and G. L. Peterson. Tight bounds for shared memory symmetric mutual exclusion problems. In *Proc. 8th ACM Symp. on Principles of Distributed Computing*, pages 177–191, August 1989.

[24] G. Taubenfeld. *Synchronization Algorithms and Concurrent Programming*. Pearson / Prentice-Hall, 2006. ISBN 0-131-97259-6, 423 pages.

[25] G. Taubenfeld. Obstruction-free consensus for unbounded concurrency. Unpublished manuscript, 2017.

[26] G. Taubenfeld and S. Moran. Possibility and impossibility results in a shared memory environment. *Acta Informatica*, 33(1):1–20, 1996.

[27] L. Zhu. A tight space bound for consensus. In *Proceedings of the Forty-eighth Annual ACM Symposium on Theory of Computing*, STOC '16, pages 345–350, 2016.

# Ignore or Comply? On Breaking Symmetry in Consensus

Petra Berenbrink*
University of Hamburg
Hamburg, Germany
berenbrink@informatik.uni-hamburg.de

Andrea Clementi
Università di Roma Tor Vergata
Rome, Italy
clementi@mat.uniroma2.it

Robert Elsässer
University of Salzburg
Salzburg, Austria
elsa@cosy.sbg.ac.at

Peter Kling
University of Hamburg
Hamburg, Germany
peter.kling@uni-hamburg.de

Frederik Mallmann-Trenn†
École normale supérieure
Paris, France
Frederik.Mallmann-Trenn@ens.fr

Emanuele Natale
Max Planck Institute for Informatics
Saarbrücken, Germany
enatale@mpi-inf.mpg.de

## ABSTRACT

We study *consensus processes* on the complete graph of $n$ nodes. Initially, each node supports one up to $n$ different opinions. Nodes randomly and in parallel sample the opinions of constantly many nodes. Based on these samples, they use an *update rule* to change their own opinion. The goal is to reach *consensus*, a configuration where all nodes support the same opinion.

We compare two well-known update rules: 2-CHOICES and 3-MAJORITY. In the former, each node samples two nodes and adopts their opinion if they agree. In the latter, each node samples three nodes: If an opinion is supported by at least two samples the node adopts it, otherwise it randomly adopts one of the sampled opinions. Known results for these update rules focus on initial configurations with a limited number of colors (say $n^{\frac{1}{3}}$), or typically assume a bias, where one opinion has a much larger support than any other. For such biased configurations, the time to reach consensus is roughly the same for 2-CHOICES and 3-MAJORITY.

Interestingly, we prove that this is no longer true for configurations with a large number of initial colors. In particular, we show that 3-MAJORITY reaches consensus with high probability in $O(n^{3/4} \cdot \log^{7/8} n)$ rounds, while 2-CHOICES can need $\Omega(n/\log n)$ rounds. We thus get the first unconditional sublinear bound for 3-MAJORITY and the first result separating the consensus time of these processes. Along the way, we develop a framework that allows a fine-grained comparison between consensus processes from a specific class. We believe that this framework might help to classify the performance of more consensus processes.

**Keywords:** Distributed Consensus; Randomized Protocols; Majorization Theory; Leader Election

*This author is also affiliated with the Simon Fraser University, Burnaby, Canada.
†This author is also affiliated with the Simon Fraser University, Burnaby, Canada.


PODC '17, July 25-27, 2017, Washington, DC, USA

ACM ISBN 978-1-4503-4992-5/17/07...$15.00
https://doi.org/10.1145/3087801.3087817

## 1 INTRODUCTION

We study *consensus* (also known as agreement) processes resulting from executing a simple algorithm in a distributed system. The system consists of $n$ anonymous nodes connected by a complete graph. Initially, each node supports one opinion from the set $[k] := \{1, \ldots, k\}$. We refer to these opinions as *colors*. The system state is modeled as a *configuration* vector $c$, whose $i$-th component $c_i$ denotes the number (support) of nodes with color $i$. A consensus process is specified by an *update rule* that is executed by each node. The goal is to reach a configuration in which all nodes support the same color; the special case where nodes have pairwise distinct colors is leader election, an important primitive in distributed computing. We assume a severely restricted synchronous communication mechanism known as *Uniform Pull* [DGH+87, KSSV00, KDG03]. Here, in each discrete round, nodes independently pull information from some (typically constant) number of randomly sampled nodes. Both the message sizes and the nodes' local memory must be of size $O(\log k)$.

The so-called VOTER process (also known as POLLING), uses the most naïve update rule: In every round, each node samples one neighbor independently and uniformly at random and adopts that node's color. Two further natural and prominent consensus processes are the 2-CHOICES and the 3-*MAJORITY* process. Their corresponding update rules, as executed synchronously by each node, are as follows:

- 2-CHOICES: Sample two nodes independently and uniformly at random. If the samples have the same color, adopt it. Otherwise, ignore them and keep your current color.
- 3-MAJORITY: Sample three nodes independently and uniformly at random. If a color is supported by at least two samples, adopt it. Otherwise, adopt the color of one of them at random[1].

One reason for the interest in these processes is that they represent simple and efficient self-stabilizing solutions for *Byzantine agreement* [PSL80, Rab83]: achieving consensus in the presence of an adversary that can disrupt a bounded set of nodes each round [BCN+14, BCN+16, CER14, EFK+16]. Further interest stems from the fact that they capture aspects of how agreement

[1]Equivalently, the node may adopt the color of a fixed sample (the first, or second, or third).

is reached in social networks and biological systems [BSDDS10, CER14, FPM⁺02].

At first glance, the above processes look quite different. But a slight reformulation of 3-MAJORITY's update rule reveals an intriguing connection:

- 3-MAJORITY (alt.): Sample two nodes independently and uniformly at random. If the samples have the same color, adopt it. Otherwise, sample a new neighbor and adopt its color.

This highlights the fact that 3-MAJORITY is a combination of 2-CHOICES and VOTER: Each node $u$ performs the update rule of 2-CHOICES. If the sampled colors do not match, instead of keeping its color, $u$ executes the update rule of VOTER. Interestingly enough, both 3-MAJORITY and 2-CHOICES behave identical in expectation[2]. In comparison to VOTER, both 2-CHOICES and 3-MAJORITY exhibit a drift: they favor colors with a large support, for which it is more likely that the first two samples match. In particular, if there is a certain initial bias[3] towards one color, VOTER still needs linear time (in $n$) to reach consensus, while both 2-CHOICES and 3-MAJORITY can exploit the bias to achieve sublinear time. On the other hand, it is unknown how 2-CHOICES and 3-MAJORITY behave when they start from configurations having a large number of colors and no (or small) bias (see Section 1.1 for details).

In this paper, we compare the time 2-CHOICES and 3-MAJORITY require to reach consensus. In particular, we prove that there is a polynomial gap between their performance if the bias is small and the number of colors is large (say $\Omega\left(n^{1/3}\right)$). This result follows from our unconditional sublinear bound for 3-MAJORITY and an almost linear lower bound for 2-CHOICES. Details of our results and contribution are given in Section 1.2.

## 1.1 Related Work

Consensus processes are a quite general model that can be used to study and understand different flavors of "spreading phenomena", for example the spread of infectious diseases, rumors and opinions in societies, or viruses/worms in computer networks. Apart from the above mentioned processes, such spreading processes include the MORAN process [LHN05, DGRS14], contact processes, and classic epidemic processes [BG90, Lig99, Mor16]. This overview concentrates on results concerned with the time needed by VOTER, 2-CHOICES, and 3-MAJORITY to reach consensus. We also provide a short comparison of these processes and briefly discuss some of the slightly more distant relatives at the end of this section.

*VOTER.* Previous work provides strong results for the time to consensus of the VOTER process, even for arbitrary graphs. These results exploit an interesting duality: the time reversal of the VOTER process turns out to be the coalescing random walk process (see [HP01, AF02]). The expected runtime of VOTER on the complete graph and with nodes of pairwise distinct colors is $\Theta(n)$. This follows easily from results for more general graphs and the above mentioned duality: The authors of [CEOR13] provide the upper bound $O\left(\mu^{-1} \cdot (\log^4 n + \rho)\right)$ on the expected coalescing time. Here $\mu$ is the graph's spectral gap and $\rho = (d_{\text{avg}} \cdot n)^2/\sum_{u \in V} d^2(u)$, where $d_{\text{avg}}$ denotes the average degree. In [BGKMT16] the authors show that the expected time to consensus is bounded by $O(m/(d_{\min} \cdot \phi))$. Here, $m$ is the number of edges, $\phi$ the conductance, and $d_{\min}$ the minimal degree.

*2-CHOICES.* To the best of our knowledge, the only work that considers the case $k > 2$ for 2-CHOICES is [EFK⁺16]. The authors study the complete graph and show that 2-CHOICES reaches consensus with high probability in $O(k \cdot \log n)$ rounds, provided that $k = O(n^{\varepsilon})$ for a small constant $\varepsilon > 0$ and an initial bias of $\Omega\left(\sqrt{n \cdot \log n}\right)$. In [CER14, CER⁺15], the authors consider 2-CHOICES for $k = 2$ on different graphs. For random $d$-regular graphs, [CER14] proves that all nodes agree on the first color in $O(\log n)$ rounds, provided that the bias is $\Omega(n \cdot \sqrt{1/d + d/n})$. The same holds for arbitrary $d$-regular graphs if the bias is $\Omega(\lambda_2 \cdot n)$, where $\lambda_2$ is the second largest eigenvalue of the transition matrix. In [CER⁺15], these results are extended to general expander graphs.

*3-MAJORITY.* All theoretical results for 3-MAJORITY consider the complete graph. The authors of [BCN⁺14] assume that the bias is $\Omega(\min\{\sqrt{2k}, (n/\log n)^{1/6}\} \cdot \sqrt{n \log n})$. Under this assumption, they prove that consensus is reached with high probability in $O(\min\{k, (n/\log n)^{1/3}\} \cdot \log n)$ rounds, and that this is tight if $k \leq (n/\log n)^{1/4}$. The only result without bias [BCN⁺16] restricts the number of initial colors to $k = o(n^{1/3})$. Under this assumption, they prove that 3-MAJORITY reaches consensus with high probability in $O((k^2(\log n)^{1/2} + k \log n) \cdot (k + \log n))$ rounds. Their analysis considers phases of length $O(k^2 \log n)$ and shows that, at the end of each phase, one of the initial colors disappears with high probability. Note that this approach – so far the only one not assuming any bias – cannot yield sublinear bounds with respect to $k$.

Comparing the above processes on the complete graph for $k > 2$, we see that there are situations where VOTER is much slower than 2-CHOICES or 3-MAJORITY. Even with a linear bias, VOTER is known to have linear runtime. In contrast, whenever there is a sufficient bias towards one color, both 2-CHOICES and 3-MAJORITY can exploit this to achieve sublinear runtime[4]. However, to the best of our knowledge there are no unconditional results on 2-CHOICES and 3-MAJORITY. All but one results need a minimum bias (at least $\Omega\left(\sqrt{n \log n}\right)$), and the only approach that works without any bias restricts the number of colors to $k = o\left(n^{1/3}\right)$ [BCN⁺16].

A related consensus process is 2-MEDIAN [DGM⁺11]. Here, every node updates its color (a numerical value) to the median of its own value and two randomly sampled nodes. Without assuming any initial bias, the authors show that this process reaches consensus with high probability in $O(\log k \cdot \log\log n + \log n)$ rounds. This is seemingly stronger than the bounds achieved for 3-MAJORITY and 2-CHOICES without bias. However, it comes at the price of a complete order on the colors (our processes require colors only to be

[2] Simple calculations [BCN⁺14, EFK⁺16] show that, for both processes, if $x_i$ is the current fraction of nodes with color $i$ then the expected fraction of nodes with color $i$ after one round is $x_i^2 + (1 - \sum x_j^2) \cdot x_i$.

[3] The *bias* is the difference between the number of nodes supporting the most and second most common color.

[4] Interestingly enough, 2-CHOICES converges to the relative majority color whenever the initial bias is $\Omega(\sqrt{n \log n})$ [BGKMT16], while the lowest bias that 3-MAJORITY can cope with in order to converge to majority is $\Omega(\sqrt{k} \cdot \sqrt{n \log n})$ [BCN⁺14].

testable for identity). Moreover, 2-MEDIAN is not self-stabilizing for Byzantine agreement (unlike 3-MAJORITY and 2-CHOICES [BCN+16, EFK+16]): it cannot guarantee *validity*[5] [BCN+16]. Another consensus process is the *UNDECIDEDDYNAMICS*. Here, each node randomly samples one neighbor and, if the sample has a different color, adopts a special "undecided" color. In subsequent rounds, it tries to find a new (real) color by sampling one random neighbor. The most recent results [BCN+15] show that, for a large enough bias, consensus is reached with high probability in at most $O(k \log n)$ rounds. Slightly more involved variants yield improved bounds of $O(\log k \cdot \log n)$ [BFGK16, GP16, EFK+16]. However, observe that for $k = n$ all nodes become undecided with constant probability instead of agreeing on a color.

## 1.2 Contribution & Approach

In this work, we provide an upper bound on 3-MAJORITY and a lower bound on 2-CHOICES that solve two open issues: We give the first unconditional sublinear bound on any of these processes (an open issue from, e.g., [BCN+16]) and prove that there can be a polynomial gap between the performance of 3-MAJORITY and 2-CHOICES (see Theorem 1.1 below). One should note that this gap is in stark contrast not only to the expected behavior of both processes (which is identical) but also to the setting when there is a bias towards one color (where both processes exhibit the same asymptotic runtime $O(k \cdot \log n)$; see Section 1.1).

The following theorem states slightly simplified versions of our upper and lower bounds (see Theorem 3.1 and Theorem 4.1 for the detailed statements).

THEOREM 1.1 (SIMPLIFIED). *From an arbitrary configuration, 3-MAJORITY reaches consensus with high probability in $O(n^{3/4} \log^{7/8} n)$ rounds. When started from a configuration where each color is supported by at most $O(\log n)$ nodes, 2-CHOICES needs with high probability $\Omega(n/\log n)$ rounds to reach consensus.*

The lower bound for 2-CHOICES follows mostly by standard techniques, using a coupling with a slightly simplified process and Chernoff bounds. The proof of the upper bound for 3-MAJORITY is more involved and based on a combination of various techniques and results from different contexts. This approach not only results in a concise proof of the upper bound, but yields some additional, interesting results along the way. We give a brief overview of our approach in the next paragraph.

*Approach.* To derive our upper bound on the time to consensus required by 3-MAJORITY, we split the analysis in two phases: (a) the time needed to go from $n$ to $\approx n^{1/4}$ colors and (b) the time needed to go from $\approx n^{1/4}$ to one color. The runtime of the second phase follows by a simple application of [BCN+16] and is $\tilde{O}(n^{3/4})$. Bounding the runtime of the first phase is more challenging: we cannot rely on the drift from a bias or similar effects, and it is not clear how to perform a direct analysis in this setting (3-MAJORITY is geared towards biased configurations). To overcome this issue, we resort to a coupling between VOTER and 3-MAJORITY. Since the construction of such a coupling seems elusive, we use some machinery from majorization theory [MOA11] to merely prove the *existence* of the coupling (see next paragraph). As a consequence of (the existence of) this coupling, we get that the time needed by 3-MAJORITY to reduce the number of colors to a fixed value is stochastically dominated by the time VOTER needs for this (Lemma 3.2). This, finally, allows us to upper bound the time needed by 3-MAJORITY[6] to go from $\approx n$ to $\approx n^{1/4}$ colors by the time VOTER needs for this (which, in turn, we bound in Lemma 3.3 by $\tilde{O}(n/k)$).

The technically most interesting part of our analysis is the proof of the stochastic dominance between 3-MAJORITY and VOTER. It works for a wide class of processes (including VOTER and 3-MAJORITY), which we call *anonymous consensus* (AC-) processes (see Definition 2.1). These are defined by an update rule that causes each node to adopt any color $i$ with the same probability $\alpha_i$ that depends only on the current frequency of colors.

In the following, we provide a natural way to compare two processes. First, we define a way to compare two configurations $c$ and $c'$. We use *vector majorization* for this purpose: $c$ majorizes $c'$ ($c \succeq c'$) if the total support of the $j$ largest colors in $c$ is not smaller than that in $c'$ for all $j \in [k]$. In particular, note that a configuration where all nodes have the same color majorizes any other configuration. Let us write $P(c)$ for the (random) configuration obtained by performing one step of a process $P$ on configuration $c$. Consider two processes $P, P'$ and two configurations $c, c'$ with $c \succeq c'$. We say $P$ *dominates* $P'$ if, for all $j \in [k]$, the following holds:

The sum of the $j$ largest components of the vector $\mathbb{E}[\, P(c)\, ]$ is not smaller than that of $\mathbb{E}[\, P'(c)\, ]$.

Note that this definition is not restricted to AC-processes.

Our main technical result (Theorem 2.3) proves that, for two AC-processes, $P$ dominating $P'$ implies that the time needed by $P'$ to reduce the number of colors to a fixed value stochastically dominates the time $P$ needs for this. Note that while this statement might sound obvious, it is not true in general (if one of the processes is not an AC-process): 2-CHOICES dominates VOTER, but it is much slower in reducing the number of colors when there are many colors.

## 2 CONSENSUS MODEL & TECHNICAL FRAMEWORK

This section introduces our technical framework using concepts from majorization theory, which is used in Section 3 to derive the sublinear upper bound on 3-MAJORITY. After defining the model and general notation, we provide a few definitions and state the main result of this section (Theorem 2.3).

## 2.1 Model and Notation

We consider the *consensus problem* on the complete graph of $n$ nodes. Initially, each node supports one opinion (or color) from the set $[k] := \{1, 2, \ldots, k\}$, where $k \le n$. Nodes interact in synchronous, discrete rounds using the *Uniform Pull* mechanism [DGH+87]. That is, during every round each node can ask the opinion of a constant number of random neighbors. Given these opinions, it updates its own opinion according to some fixed update rule. The goal of

[5]Byzantine agreement requires that the system does not converge to a color that was initially not supported by at least one non-corrupted node.

[6]Note that for a large number of colors, a node executing 3-MAJORITY behaves with high probability like a node performing VOTER. Thus, it is relatively tight to bound 3-MAJORITY by VOTER in this parameter regime.

the system is to reach *consensus* (a configuration where all nodes support the same opinion).

Let $\mathbb{N} := \{1, 2, \dots\}$ and $\mathbb{N}_0 := \{0, 1, \dots\}$. We describe the system state after any round by an $n$-dimensional integral vector $c = (c_i)_{i \in [n]} \in \mathbb{N}_0^n$ with $\sum_{i \in [n]} c_i = n$. Here, the $i$-th component $c_i \in \mathbb{N}_0$ corresponds to the number of nodes supporting opinion $i$. If $k < n$, then $c_i = 0$ for all $i \in \{k+1, k+2, \dots, n\}$. We use $C := \{c \in \mathbb{N}_0^n \mid \sum_{i \in [k]} c_i = n\}$ to denote the set of all possible configurations.

Let $d \in \mathbb{N}$ and $x, y \in \mathbb{R}^d$. We define $\|x\|_1 := \sum_{i \in [d]} x_i$ and $\|x\|_2 := \left(\sum_{i \in [d]} x_i^2\right)^{1/2}$. Moreover, let $x^{\downarrow}$ denote a permutation of $x$ such that all components are sorted non-increasingly. We write $x \succeq y$ and say $x$ *majorizes* $y$ if, for all $l \in [d]$, we have $\sum_{i \in [l]} x_i^{\downarrow} \geq \sum_{i \in [l]} y_i^{\downarrow}$ and $\|x\|_1 = \|y\|_1$. For two random variables $X$ and $Y$ we write $X \preceq^{\text{st}} Y$ if $X$ is *stochastically dominated* by $Y$, i.e., $\Pr[X \geq x] \leq \Pr[Y \geq x]$ for all $x \in \mathbb{N}_0$. A function $f \colon \mathbb{R}^d \to \mathbb{R}$ is *Schur-convex* if $x \succeq y \Rightarrow f(x) \geq f(y)$. For a probability vector $\Theta \in [0, 1]^d$, we use $\text{Mult}(m, \Theta)$ to denote the multinomial distribution for $m$ trials and $d$ categories (the $i$-th category having probability $\Theta_i$).

## 2.2 Comparing Anonymous Consensus Processes

We first define a class of processes defined by update rules that depend only on the current configuration. The update rule states that each nodes adopts a color $i$ with the same probability $\alpha_i(c)$, where $c \in C$ is the current configuration. In particular, node IDs (including the sampling node's ID) do not influence the outcome. In this sense, such update rules are *anonymous*.

*Definition 2.1 (Anonymous Consensus Processes).* Given a distributed system of $n$ nodes, an *anonymous consensus process* $P_\alpha$ is characterized by a *process function* $\alpha \colon C \to [0, 1]^n$ such that $\sum_{i \in [n]} \alpha_i(c) = 1$ for all $c \in C$. When in configuration $c \in C$, each node independently adopts opinion $i \in [k]$ with probability $\alpha_i(c)$. We use the shorthand *AC-processes* to refer to this class.

Given an AC-process $P_\alpha$ and a fixed initial configuration, let[7] $P_\alpha(t)$ denote the configuration of $P_\alpha$ at time $t$. By Definition 2.1, $(P_\alpha(t))_{t \geq 0}$ is a Markov chain, since $P_\alpha(t)$ depends only on $P_\alpha(t-1)$. Another immediate consequence of Definition 2.1 is that $P_\alpha(t)$ conditional on $P_\alpha(t-1) = c$ is distributed according to $\text{Mult}(n, \alpha(c))$. In other words, the 1-step distribution of an AC-process is a multinomial distribution. Two important examples of AC-processes include Voter and 3-Majority:

- In the Voter process $P_{\alpha^{(\mathcal{V})}}$, each node samples one node (according to the pull mechanism) and (always) adopts that node's opinion. Thus

$$\alpha_i^{(\mathcal{V})}(c) = \frac{c_i}{n}. \tag{1}$$

- In the 3-Majority process $P_{\alpha^{(3M)}}$, each node samples independently and uniformly at random three nodes. If a color is supported by at least two of the samples, adopt it. Otherwise, adopt a random one of the sampled colors. Simple calculations (see [BCN+14]) show

$$\alpha_i^{(3M)}(c) = \frac{c_i}{n} \cdot \left(1 + \frac{c_i}{n} - \left\|\frac{c}{n}\right\|_2^2\right). \tag{2}$$

For any protocol $P$ starting with configuration $c \in C$ let $T_P^{\kappa}(c)$ denote the first time step where the number of remaining colors reduces to $\kappa$ where $\kappa \in \mathbb{N}$. The next definition introduces dominance between protocol. Intuitively, a protocol $P$ dominates another protocol $P'$ if their expected behavior preserves majorization.

*Definition 2.2 (Protocol Dominance).* Consider two (not necessarily AC-) processes $P, \tilde{P}$. We say $P$ dominates $\tilde{P}$ if $\mathbb{E}[P(c)] \succeq \mathbb{E}[\tilde{P}(\tilde{c})]$ holds for all $c, \tilde{c} \in C$ with $c \succeq \tilde{c}$.

Note that, in the case of AC-protocols, Definition 2.2 can be stated as follows: $P_\alpha$ dominates $P_{\tilde{\alpha}}$ if and only if $c \succeq \tilde{c} \Rightarrow \alpha(c) \succeq \tilde{\alpha}(\tilde{c})$ for all $c, \tilde{c} \in C$ with $c \succeq \tilde{c}$. With this, the main result of our framework can be stated as follows.

Theorem 2.3. *Consider two AC-Processes $P$ and $P'$ where $P$ dominates $P'$. Assume $P$ and $P'$ are started from the same configuration $c \in C$. Then, for any $\kappa \in \mathbb{N}$, the time needed by $P'$ to reduce the number of remaining colors to $\kappa$ dominates the time $P$ needs for this, i.e.,*

$$T_{P'}^{\kappa}(c) \succeq^{st} T_P^{\kappa}(c).$$

One should note that the statement of Theorem 2.3 is not true in general (i.e., for non-AC-processes). In particular, 2-Choices dominates Voter, but our upper bound on Voter (Section 3.2) and our lower bound on 2-Choices (Theorem 4.1) contradict the statement of Theorem 2.3.

## 2.3 Coupling two AC-Processes

In order to prove Theorem 2.3, we formulate a strong 1-step coupling property for AC-processes:

Lemma 2.4 (1-Step Coupling). *Let $P_\alpha$ and $P_{\tilde{\alpha}}$ be two AC-processes. Consider any two configurations $c, \tilde{c} \in C$ with $\alpha(c) \succeq \tilde{\alpha}(\tilde{c})$. Let $c'$ and $\tilde{c}'$ be the configurations of $P_\alpha$ and $P_{\tilde{\alpha}}$ after one round, respectively. Then, there exists a coupling such that $c' \succeq \tilde{c}'$.*

Proof. Consider the processes $P_\alpha$ and $P_{\tilde{\alpha}}$ with the configurations $c$ and $\tilde{c}$ from the theorem's statement. Let $Y = c'$ and $X = \tilde{c}'$ denote the configurations resulting after one round of $P_\alpha$ on $c$ and $P_{\tilde{\alpha}}$ on $\tilde{c}$, respectively. Let $\Theta := \alpha(c)$ and $\tilde{\Theta} := \tilde{\alpha}(\tilde{c})$. As observed earlier in Section 2.2, we have $Y \sim \text{Mult}(n, \Theta_1)$ and $X \sim \text{Mult}(n, \Theta_2)$. By the theorem's assumption, we have $\Theta \succeq \tilde{\Theta}$. Since, by Proposition A.1 (see Appendix A), the function $\Theta \to \mathbb{E}[\phi(\text{Mult}(n, \Theta))]$ is Schur-convex for any Schur-convex function $\phi$ for which the expectation exists, we get $X \preceq^{\text{st}} Y$.

Since the configuration space $C$ is a finite subset of $\mathbb{R}^n$, it is closed and so is $\{(x, y) \mid x \preceq y\}$. We now apply Theorem 2.6 (Strassen's Theorem, see Appendix A) to get that there exists a coupling between $X$ and $Y$ such that[8] $X \preceq Y$. This finishes the proof. □

[7]Recall that, with a slight abuse of notation we also write $P(c)$ for the (random) configuration obtained by performing one step of a process $P$ on configuration $c$.

[8]Observe that Strassen's Theorem gives us that $\Pr[X \preceq Y] = 1$. That is, $X \preceq Y$ holds *almost surely*. However, since $C$ is finite, this actually means that $\tilde{c}' = X \preceq Y = c'$ holds (surely).

Note that Theorem 2.3 is an immediate consequence of Lemma 2.4: Since $P$ dominates $P'$ (which is, for AC-processes, equivalent to $\alpha(c) \geq \tilde{\alpha}(\tilde{c})$ for all $c, \tilde{c}$ with $c \succeq \tilde{c}$) we can apply Lemma 2.4 iteratively to get Theorem 2.3. The fine-grained comparison enabled by Lemma 2.4 is based on three observations:

(1) The (pre-) order "$\preceq$" on the set of configurations naturally measures the closeness to consensus. Indeed, a configuration with only one remaining color is maximal with respect to "$\preceq$". Similarly, the $n$-color configuration is minimal.
(2) We can define a vector variant "$\preceq^{\mathrm{st}}$" of stochastic domination (see Definition 2.5) such that we have $\Theta_1 \preceq \Theta_2 \Rightarrow \mathrm{Mult}(m, \Theta_1) \preceq^{\mathrm{st}} \mathrm{Mult}(m, \Theta_2)$ (see [MOA11, Proposition 11.E.11] or Proposition A.1 in Appendix A).
(3) Consider two configurations $c, \tilde{c} \in C$ with $\alpha(c) \succeq \tilde{\alpha}(\tilde{c})$. Since $P_\alpha(c) \sim \mathrm{Mult}(n, \alpha(c))$ and $P_{\tilde{\alpha}} \sim \mathrm{Mult}(n, \tilde{\alpha}(\tilde{c}))$, the previous observations imply that one step of $P_\alpha$ on $c$ is stochastically "better" than one step of $P_{\tilde{\alpha}}$ on $\tilde{c}$. Our goal is to apply Lemma 2.4 iteratively to get Theorem 2.3. For this, we prove a coupling showing majorization between the resulting configurations. We achieve this via a variant of Strassen's Theorem (see Theorem 2.6 below), which translates *stochastic* domination among random vectors to the *existence* of such a coupling.

We now give a definition of stochastic majorization that is compatible with the preorder "$\preceq$" on the configuration space $C$ (cf., for example, [MOA11, Chapter 11]).

*Definition 2.5 (Stochastic Majorization).* For two random vectors $X$ and $Y$ in $\mathbb{R}^d$, we write $X \preceq^{\mathrm{st}} Y$ and say that $Y$ *stochastically majorizes* $X$ if $\mathbb{E}[\phi(X)] \leq \mathbb{E}[\phi(Y)]$ for all Schur-convex functions $\phi$ on $\mathbb{R}^d$ such that the expectations are defined.

We proceed by stating the aforementioned variant of Strassen's Theorem (Theorem A.2).

THEOREM 2.6 (STRASSEN'S THEOREM (VARIANT)). *Consider a closed subset $\mathcal{A} \subseteq \mathbb{R}^n$ such that the set $\{ (x, y) \mid x \preceq y \}$ is closed. For two random vectors $X$ and $Y$ over $\mathcal{A}$, the following conditions are equivalent:*

*(i) (Stochastic Majorization) $X \preceq^{st} Y$ and*
*(ii) (Coupling) there is a coupling between $X$ and $Y$ such that $\Pr[X \preceq Y] = 1$.*

PROOF. Consider the cone

$$C := \{ \phi\colon \mathcal{A} \to \mathbb{R} \mid \phi \text{ is Schur-convex} \}$$

of real-valued Schur-convex functions on $\mathcal{A}$. This cone implies a preorder "$\leq_C$" on $\mathcal{A}$ by the definition $x \leq_C y :\Leftrightarrow \phi(x) \leq \phi(y)$ for all $\phi \in C$. One can show that this preorder is the vector majorization "$\preceq$" (cf. [MOA11, Example 14.E.5])[9]. Now, "$\leq_C$" being equal to "$\preceq$" has two implications:

(a) The stochastic majorization "$\leq_C^{\mathrm{st}}$" implied by the preorder "$\leq_C$" is the stochastic majorization "$\preceq^{\mathrm{st}}$" from Definition 2.5 (cf. [MOA11, Definition 17.B.1]).
(b) Since a cone $C$ is complete if it is maximal with respect to functions preserving the preorder "$\leq_C$" (cf. [MOA11, Definition 14.E.2]), $C$ is complete (Schur-convex functions are by definition the set of all functions preserving the majorization preorder).

From (a) we get that Condition (i) is actually Condition (i) of Theorem A.2. The same holds for Condition (ii). From (b) we get that $C = C^* = C^+$ (cf. [MOA11, Proposition 17.B.3]), such that Conditions (i) and (ii) are equivalent by Theorem A.2. This finishes the proof. □

With this, Lemma 2.4 follows by a straightforward combination of the aforementioned machinery.

[9]Alternatively, one checks this manually: The direction $x \preceq y \Rightarrow x \leq_C y$ is trivial by the definition of Schur-convexity. For $x \leq_C y \Rightarrow x \preceq y$ consider the $n+1$ Schur-convex functions $z \mapsto \sum_{j \in [i]} z_j^{\downarrow}$ for $i \in [n]$ and $z \mapsto -\|z\|_1$.

# 3 UPPER BOUND FOR 3-MAJORITY

In this section, we provide a sublinear upper bound on the time needed by 3-MAJORITY to reach consensus with high probability. This is one of our main results and is formulated in the following theorem.

THEOREM 3.1. *Starting from any configuration $c \in C$, 3-MAJORITY reaches consensus w.h.p. in $O(n^{3/4} \log^{7/8} n)$ rounds.*

The analysis is split into two phases, each of which consists of $O(n^{3/4} \log^{7/8} n)$ rounds.

**Phase 1: From up to $n$ to $n^{1/4} \log^{1/8}$ colors.** This is the crucial part of the analysis. Instead of analyzing 3-MAJORITY directly, we use our machinery from Section 2.2 to show that 3-MAJORITY is not slower than VOTER (Lemma 3.2). Afterward, we prove that VOTER reaches $O(n^{1/4})$ colors in $O(n^{3/4} \log^{7/8} n)$ rounds (Lemma 3.3).

**Phase 2: From up to $n^{1/4} \log^{1/8} n$ to 1 color (consensus).** Once we reached a configuration with $n^{1/4} \log^{1/8} n$ colors, we can apply [BCN⁺16, Theorem 3.1] (see Theorem A.4 in Appendix A), a previous analysis of 3-MAJORITY. It works only for initial configurations with at most $k \leq n^{1/3-\epsilon}$ colors ($\epsilon > 0$ arbitrarily small). In that case, [BCN⁺16, Theorem 3.1] yields a runtime of $O\big((k^2 \log^{1/2} n + k \log n) \cdot (k + \log n)\big)$. Since the first phase leaves us with $O(n^{1/4})$ colors, this immediately implies that the second phase takes $O(n^{3/4} \log^{7/8} n)$ rounds.

This section proceeds by proving the runtime of Phase 1 in two steps: dominating the runtime of 3-MAJORITY by that of VOTER (Section 3.1) and proving the corresponding runtime for VOTER (Section 3.2). In the end, we can combine these results together with [BCN⁺16, Theorem 3.1] to prove Theorem 3.1.

PROOF OF THEOREM 3.1. Consider any initial configuration $c \in C$. By applying Lemma 3.3 for $k = n^{1/4}$, we get that VOTER reduces the number of remaining colors w.h.p. from initially at most $n$ to $n^{1/4}$ in $O(n^{3/4} \log^{7/8} n)$ rounds. By Lemma 3.2, the time it takes 3-MAJORITY to reach some fixed number of remaining colors is dominated by the time it takes VOTER to reach the same number of remaining colors. In particular, we get that 3-MAJORITY also reduces the number of remaining colors w.h.p. to $n^{1/4}$ in $O(n^{3/4} \log^{7/8} n)$ rounds. That is, the first phase takes $O(n^{3/4} \log^{7/8} n)$ rounds.

For the second phase, we apply [BCN+16, Theorem 3.1] (see Theorem A.4 in Appendix A) for $k = n^{1/4} = o\left(n^{1/3}\right)$. This immediately yields that the second phase takes $O(n^{3/4}\log^{7/8} n)$ rounds, finishing the proof. □

## 3.1 Analysis of Phase 1: 3-Majority vs. Voter

We prove the following lemma.

Lemma 3.2. *Consider* Voter *($\mathcal{V}$) and* 3-Majority *(3M) started from the same initial configuration $c \in C$. There is a coupling such that after any round, the number of remaining colors in* Voter *is not smaller than those in* 3-Majority. *In particular, the time* Voter *needs to reach consensus stochastically dominates the time needed by* 3-Majority *to reach consensus, i.e.,*

$$T^{\kappa}_{3M}(c) \leq^{st} T^{\kappa}_{\mathcal{V}}(c).$$

Proof. By Theorem 2.3, all we have to prove is $c \succeq \tilde{c} \Rightarrow \alpha^{(3M)}(c) \succeq \alpha^{(\mathcal{V})}(\tilde{c})$ (see Section 2.2). To this end, consider two configurations $c, \tilde{c} \in C$ with $c \succeq \tilde{c}$. Let $p := \alpha^{(3M)}(c)$ and $\tilde{p} := \alpha^{(\mathcal{V})}(\tilde{c})$. We have to show $p \succeq \tilde{p}$. Since these are probability vectors, we have $\|p\|_1 = 1 = \|\tilde{p}\|_1$. It remains to consider the partial sums for $k \in [n]$. For this, let $x := c/n$ and $\tilde{x} := \tilde{c}/n$. Remember that $p_i = x_i^2 + (1 - \|x\|_2^2) \cdot x_i$ (Equation (2)) and $\tilde{p}_i = \tilde{x}_i$ (Equation (1)). In the following, we assume (w.l.o.g.) $p = p^{\downarrow}$ and $\tilde{p} = \tilde{p}^{\downarrow}$ (this implies $x = x^{\downarrow}$ and $\tilde{x} = \tilde{x}^{\downarrow}$). We compute

$$\begin{aligned} \sum_{i=1}^{k} p_i - \sum_{i=1}^{k} \tilde{p}_i &= \sum_{i=1}^{k} x_i^2 + \sum_{i=1}^{k} x_i - \|x\|_2^2 \sum_{i=1}^{k} x_i - \sum_{i=1}^{k} \tilde{x}_i \\ &\geq \sum_{i=1}^{k} x_i^2 - \|x\|_2^2 \sum_{i=1}^{k} x_i. \end{aligned} \tag{3}$$

We have to show that this last expression is non-negative, which is equivalent to

$$\|x\|_2^2 \leq \left(\sum_{i=1}^{k} x_i^2\right) \Big/ \left(\sum_{i=1}^{k} x_i\right). \tag{4}$$

This holds trivially for $k = n$ (where we have equality). Thus, it is sufficient to show that $(\sum_{i=1}^{k} x_i^2)/(\sum_{i=1}^{k} x_i)$ is non-increasing in $k$. That is, for any $k \in [n-1]$ we seek to show the inequality

$$\frac{\sum_{i=1}^{k+1} x_i^2}{\sum_{i=1}^{k+1} x_i} = \frac{\sum_{i=1}^{k} x_i^2 + x_{k+1}^2}{\sum_{i=1}^{k} x_i + x_{k+1}} \leq \frac{\sum_{i=1}^{k} x_i^2}{\sum_{i=1}^{k} x_i}. \tag{5}$$

This inequality is of the form $\frac{A+x}{B+x} \leq \frac{A}{B}$, where $A, B, x > 0$. Rearranging shows that this is equivalent to $x \leq A/B$. Thus, Equation (5) holds if and only if $x_{k+1} \leq (\sum_{i=1}^{k} x_i^2)/(\sum_{i=1}^{k} x_i)$. This last inequality holds via $x_{k+1} \cdot \sum_{i=1}^{k} x_i = \sum_{i=1}^{k} x_i \cdot x_{k+1} \leq \sum_{i=1}^{k} x_i \cdot x_i = \sum_{i=1}^{k} x_i^2$, where we used $x = x^{\downarrow}$. This finishes the proof. □

## 3.2 Analysis of Phase 1: A Bound for Voter

We analyze the time the Voter process takes to reduce the number of remaining colors from $n$ to $k$. One should note that [BGKMT16] studies a similar process. However, their analysis relies critically on the fact that their process is lazy (i.e., nodes do not sample another node with probability 1/2), while our proof does not require any laziness.

We make use of the well-known duality (via time reversal) between the Voter process and *coalescing random walks*. In the coalescing random walks process there are initially $n$ independent random walks, one placed at each of the $n$ nodes. While performing synchronous steps, whenever two or more random walks meet, they coalesce into a single random walk. Let $T_C^k$ denote the number of steps it takes to reduce the number of random walks from $n$ to $k$ in the coalescing random walks process (the *coalescence time*). Similarly, let $T_{\mathcal{V}}^k$ denote the number of rounds it takes Voter to reduce the number of remaining colors from $n$ to $k$.

Lemma 3.3. *Consider an arbitrary initial configuration $c \in C$.* Voter *reaches a configuration $c'$ having at most $k$ remaining colors w.h.p. in $O(\frac{n}{k}\log n)$ rounds, i.e., $\Pr\left[T_{\mathcal{V}}^k = O(\frac{n}{k}\log n)\right] \geq 1 - 1/n$.*

Proof. We prove the lemma using the well-known duality (via time reversal) between the Voter process and *coalescing random walks*.

It is well-known (e.g., [AF02]), that $T_{\mathcal{V}}^1 = T_C^1$. This statement generalizes for all $k \in [n]$ (see Lemma A.5 in Appendix A for a proof) to

$$T_{\mathcal{V}}^k = T_C^k. \tag{6}$$

Thanks to the previous identity, we can prove the lemma's statement by proving that w.h.p. $T_C^k = O\left(\frac{n}{k}\log n\right)$. To this end, we show that $\mathbb{E}\left[T_C^k\right] = O(n/k)$. In order to get the claimed bound in concentration, we can apply the following standard argument. Consider the process as a sequence of phases, each one of length $2\mathbb{E}\left[T_C^k\right]$. We say that a phase is successful when the number of remaining random walks drops below $n/k$. Thanks to our bound in expectation above and the Markov inequality, we easily get that every phase has probability $\Omega(1)$ to be successful. So, with high probability, there will be at least one success within the first $O(\log n)$ phases.

Let $X_t$ denote the number of coalescing random walks at time $t$. We have $X_0 = n$ and $T_C^k = \min\{t \geq 0 \mid X_t \leq k\}$. We seek to apply drift theory (Theorem A.3 in Appendix A.2) to derive a bound on $\mathbb{E}\left[T_C^k\right]$. Next, we compute an upper bound on the value $\mathbb{E}[X_{t+1} - X_t \mid X_t = x]$.

Let us begin assuming that $k$ is any constant. It holds in general that $\mathbb{E}[X_{t+1} - X_t \mid X_t \geq 2] \leq -1/n$, since in expectation two random walks collide w.p. $1/n$ in a given time step. Hence we can directly apply[10] Theorem A.3 with parameters $h(x) = 1/n$ to reduce from $k$ random walks to 1, yielding the bound $\mathbb{E}\left[T_C^k\right] = O(n/k) = O(n)$, where in the latter equality we used that $k$ is constant.

We now consider the case where $k$ is larger than a big constant, say $k > 100$. Assume that in every time step the random walks move in two phases. Let $W_1$ denote an arbitrary set of $\lfloor X_t/2 \rfloor$ random walks and let $W_2$ denote the remaining ones. We first look at how the random walks in $W_1$ coalesce, then we consider the movement of the remaining walks $W_2$. Let $\mathcal{E}$ be the event that the walks in $W_1$ move onto more than $\lfloor X_t/4 \rfloor$ distinct nodes. This would imply that

[10]Technically, one would have to define a new random variable which is 0 whenever the number of random walks reduces to 1. We illustrate this technicality shortly, for case $k > 100$ below.

each walk in $W_2$ coalesces with one in $W_1$ with probability at least $\lfloor X_t/4 \rfloor/n$. We thus have

$$\mathbb{E}[X_{t+1} \mid X_t = x, \mathcal{E}] \le x - \lceil x/2 \rceil \cdot \frac{\lfloor x/4 \rfloor}{n} \le x - \frac{x^2}{10n}.$$

Moreover, conditioning on $\overline{\mathcal{E}}$ implies that there were at least $\lfloor X_t/2 \rfloor - \lfloor X_t/4 \rfloor$ collisions during the first phase. Thus,

$$\mathbb{E}\Big[X_{t+1} \mid X_t = x, \overline{\mathcal{E}}\Big] \le x - (\lfloor x/2 \rfloor - \lfloor x/4 \rfloor) \le x - \frac{x^2}{10n}.$$

Hence, by law of total expectation,

$$\mathbb{E}[X_{t+1} \mid X_t = x] = \mathbb{E}[X_{t+1} \mid X_t = x, \mathcal{E}]\Pr[\mathcal{E}] + \mathbb{E}\Big[X_{t+1} \mid X_t = x, \overline{\mathcal{E}}\Big]\Pr\Big[\overline{\mathcal{E}}\Big] \le x - \frac{x^2}{10n}.$$

In order to apply Theorem A.3, we define the random variables $(Y_t)_{t\ge 0}$ as follows

$$Y_t = \begin{cases} X_t & \text{if } X_t > k, \\ 0 & \text{otherwise.} \end{cases}$$

Let $T^* = \{t \ge 0 \mid Y_t = 0\}$. Since by construction we have $Y_t = X_t$ for $t < T_C^k$ and $Y_{T_C^k} = 0$ otherwise, it follows that

$$T_C^k = T^*. \tag{7}$$

Therefore,

$$\mathbb{E}[Y_{t+1} \mid Y_t = y, Y_t > k] \le y - \frac{y^2}{10n}.$$

We can thus apply Theorem A.3 for the random variables $(Y_t)_{t\ge 0}$ with $x_{\min} = k$, $x_{\max} = n$, and $h(x) = \frac{x^2}{10n}$, obtaining

$$\mathbb{E}[T^*] \le \frac{k}{k^2/(10n)} + \int_k^n \frac{1}{h(u)} \le \frac{10n}{k} + 10n\left(-\frac{1}{n} - \left(-\frac{1}{k}\right)\right) \le 20\frac{n}{k}. \tag{8}$$

Finally, from (6), (7) and (8) we get

$$\mathbb{E}\Big[T_{\mathcal{V}}^k\Big] = \mathbb{E}\Big[T_C^k\Big] = \mathbb{E}[T^*] \le 20\frac{n}{k}, \tag{9}$$

concluding the proof. □ □

## 4 LOWER BOUND FOR 2-CHOICES

This section gives an almost linear worst-case lower bound on the time needed by 2-Choices to reach consensus with high probability. It turns out that, when started from an almost balanced configuration, the consensus time is dictated by the time it takes for one of the colors to gain a support of $\Omega(\log n)$. To prove this result, we prove a slightly stronger statement, that captures the slow initial part of the process when started from configurations with a maximal load of $\ell$. Here we only provide a sketch of proof.

Theorem 4.1. *Let $\gamma$ be a sufficiently large constant. Consider the 2-Choices process starting from any initial configuration $c \in C$. Let $\ell := \max_i c_i(0)$ be the support of the largest color. Then, for $\ell' := \max\{2\ell, \gamma \log n\}$, it holds with high probability that no color has a support larger than $\ell'$ for $n/(\gamma\ell')$ rounds. In symbols,*

$$\Pr\left[\max_i c_i(t) > \ell' \text{ for some } t < \frac{n}{\gamma\ell'}\right] \le \frac{1}{n}. \tag{10}$$

*In particular, starting from the n-color configuration, it holds with high probability that no color has a support larger than $\gamma \log n$ for $\frac{n}{\gamma^2 \log n}$ rounds.*

Proof. Let $T_i = \min\{t \ge 0 \mid c_i(t) > \ell'\}$. For any fixed opinion $i \le k$ we show that $\Pr[T_i < n/(\gamma\ell')] \le 1/n^2$, so that, by a union bound over all opinions and using that $T = \min\{T_i \mid i \le k\}$, we obtain $\Pr[T < n/(\gamma\ell')] \le 1/n$. Intuitively, we would like to show that, conditioning on $c_i \le \ell'$, the expected number of nodes joining opinion $i$ is dominated by a binomial distribution with parameters $n$ and $p = (\ell'/n)^2$. The main obstacle to this is that naïvely applying Chernoff bounds for every time step yields a weak bound, since with constant probability at each round at least one color increases its support by a constant number of nodes. Instead, we consider a new process $\mathcal{P}$ in which the number $P(t)$ of nodes supporting color $i$ at time $t$ majorizes $c_i(t)$ as long as $P(t) \le \ell'$; we will then show that, after a certain time w.h.p. $P(t)$ is still smaller than $\ell'$ implying that $\mathcal{P}$ indeed majorizes the original process. Using the fact that in $\mathcal{P}$ we can simply apply Chernoff bounds over several rounds, we can finally get $c_i \le P(t) \le \ell'$ w.h.p..

Formally, process $\mathcal{P}$ is defined as follows. $P(0) := \ell$ and $P(t+1) = P(t) + \sum_{j\le n} X_j^{(t)}$, where $X_j^{(t)}$ is a Bernoulli random variable with $\Pr[X_i = 1] = p$ and, by a standard coupling, it is 1 whenever node $j$ sees two times color $i$ at round $t$ (note that the latter event happens with probability at most $p$ for any $t < T_i$). By definition, if $t < T_i$ it holds $c_i(t) \le \ell'$, which implies that the probability that any node in the original process gets opinion $i$ is at most $p$. Thus, we can couple 2-Choices and $P$ for $t \le T_i$ so that $c_i(t) \le P(t)$. This implies that

$$T' := \min\{t \ge 0 \mid P(t) \ge \ell'\} \le T_i. \tag{11}$$

In the remainder we show that $\Pr[T' < n/(\gamma\ell')] < 1/n^2$. For any round $t+1$, we define $\Delta_{t+1} := P(t+1) - P(t) = \sum_{i\le n} X_i$. Observe that $\Delta_{t+1} \sim \mathrm{Bin}(n,p)$. Let $t_0 = n/(\gamma\ell')$. In the following we bound

$$B := P(t_0) - P(0) = \sum_{i=1}^{t_0} \Delta_i.$$

Observe that $B \sim \mathrm{Bin}(t_0 \cdot n, p)$ and thus $\mathbb{E}[B] = t_0 \cdot n \cdot p$.

Using Chernoff bounds, e.g., [MU05, Theorem 4.4] we derive for any $\gamma \ge 18$

$$\begin{aligned}\Pr[P(t_0) \ge \ell'] &= \Pr[B \ge \ell' - \ell] \le \Pr\left[B \ge \max\left\{2\mathbb{E}[B], \frac{\gamma}{2}\log n\right\}\right] \\ &= \Pr\left[B \ge \mathbb{E}[B] \cdot \max\left\{2, 1 + \frac{\frac{\gamma}{2}\log n}{\mathbb{E}[B]}\right\}\right] \\ &\le \exp\left(-\frac{\frac{\gamma}{2}\log n}{3}\right) \le 1/n^3,\end{aligned} \tag{12}$$

where we used that

$$\begin{aligned}\max\left\{2\mathbb{E}[B], \frac{\gamma}{2}\log n\right\} &= \max\left\{2t_0 \cdot n \cdot p, \frac{\gamma}{2}\log n\right\} \\ &\le \max\left\{\frac{(\ell')^2}{\gamma\ell'}, \frac{\gamma}{2}\log n\right\} \\ &\le \max\left\{\frac{\ell'}{2}, \frac{\gamma}{2}\log n\right\} \le \frac{\ell'}{2} = \ell' - \ell.\end{aligned}$$

Putting everything together yields

$$\Pr\left[T < n/(\gamma\ell')\right] = \Pr[T < t_0] \tag{13}$$
$$\overset{(a)}{\leq} n \Pr[T_i < t_0]$$
$$\overset{(b)}{\leq} n \Pr\left[T' < t_0\right]$$
$$\overset{(c)}{\leq} n \Pr\left[P(t_0) \geq \ell'\right] \overset{(d)}{\leq} n^{-2}, \tag{14}$$

where in $(a)$ we used union bound over all colors, in $(b)$ we used (11), in $(c)$ we used that "$T' < t_0$" $\implies$ "$P(t_0) \geq \ell'$" and in $(d)$ we used (12). This completes the proof. □

## 5 LIMITATIONS OF 1-STEP COUPLING

In this section we show that there are configurations $c \preceq \tilde{c}$ such that $\alpha^{(hM)}(c) \not\preceq \alpha^{(h+1M)}(\tilde{c})$. This means that, Lemma 2.4 is not strong enough to derive Conjecture 6.1. Consider the configurations $x := (1/2, 1/6, 1/6, 1/6) \preceq (1/2, 1/2, 0, 0) =: \tilde{x}$ (for simplicity, we use the fraction vectors $x = c/n$). For symmetry reasons, we immediately get that $\alpha^{(h+1M)}(\tilde{c}) = (1/2, 1/2, 0, 0) = \tilde{c}$. However, even for $h = 3$, for the second configuration we get that the expected fraction of the nodes which adopt the first opinion after one step is

$$1 \cdot \binom{3}{0} \cdot \left(\frac{1}{2}\right)^3 + 1 \cdot \binom{3}{1} \cdot \left(\frac{1}{2}\right)^2 \cdot \frac{3}{6} + \frac{1}{3} \cdot \binom{3}{2} \cdot \frac{1}{2} \cdot \frac{3}{6} \cdot \frac{2}{6} = \frac{7}{12}. \tag{15}$$

The three terms of the sum on the left hand side correspond to the cases and probabilities for which the first color is adopted:

- all samples choose color 1 (probability to win is 1, number of cases $\binom{3}{0}$),
- two samples choose color 1 (probability to win is 1, number of cases $\binom{3}{1}$), or
- 1 sample chooses color 1 and the other samples choose different colors (probability to win is $1/3$, number of cases $\binom{3}{2}$).

Thus, for $n$ large enough, with high probability the configuration resulting from $(h + 1)$-MAJORITY will not majorize the one resulting from h−MAJORITY.

## 6 CONCLUSION & FUTURE WORK

This section briefly discusses some directions of future work and our conjecture that our framework might help to gain a better understanding of how different (AC-) processes compare to each other.

*Fault Tolerance.* As mentioned in the introduction, previous studies [BCN+14, BCN+16, CER14, EFK+16] show that 2-CHOICES and 3-MAJORITY are consensus protocols that can tolerate dynamic, worst-case adversarial faults. More in details, the protocols work even in the presence of an adversary that can, in every round, corrupt the state of a bounded set of nodes. The goal in this setting is to achieve a stable regime in which "almost-all" nodes support the same *valid* color (i.e. a color initially supported by at least one non-corrupted node). The size of the corrupted set is one of the studied quality parameters and depends on the number $k$ of colors and/or on the bias in the starting configuration. For instance, in [BCN+16] it is proven that, for $k = o\left(n^{1/3}\right)$, 3-MAJORITY tolerates a corrupted sets of size $O\left(\sqrt{n}/(k^{5/2}\log n)\right)$. A natural important open issue is to investigate whether our framework for AC-processes can be used to make statements about fault-tolerance properties in this (or in similar) adversarial models. We moderately lean toward thinking that our analysis is sufficiently general and "robust" to be suitably adapted in order to cope with this adversarial scenario over a wider range of $k$ and bias w.r.t. the relative previous analyses.

*Towards a Hierarchy.* Consider the process functions of the general $h$-MAJORITY process for arbitrary $h \in \mathbb{N}$. Intuitively, $h$-MAJORITY should be (stochastically) slower than $(h+1)$-MAJORITY. We strongly believe this result holds. However, naïvely applying our machinery to prove this does not work and needs to be amended. Our conjecture that such a "hierarchy" for h−MAJORITY for different $h \in \mathbb{N}$ holds is backed by the proof of Lemma 3.2 (which shows this for $h \in \{1, 2, 3\}$, since the VOTER process is actually equivalent to 1-MAJORITY and 2-MAJORITY).

CONJECTURE 6.1. *For $h \in \mathbb{N}$, we can couple $h$-MAJORITY and $(h+1)$-MAJORITY such that the latter never has more remaining colors than the former. In particular, $(h + 1)$-MAJORITY is stochastically faster than $h$-MAJORITY.*

However, as we have shown in Section 5 via a counterexample, it turns out that Lemma 2.4 is not strong enough to derive Conjecture 6.1. In fact, our failed attempts in adapting our approach may suggest that similar counterexamples exist for any majorization attempt that uses a total order on vectors.

## REFERENCES


[AF02] D. Aldous and J. Fill. Reversible markov chains and random walks on graphs, 2002. Unpublished. http://www.stat.berkeley.edu/~aldous/RWG/book.html.

[BCN+14] Luca Becchetti, Andrea E. F. Clementi, Emanuele Natale, Francesco Pasquale, Riccardo Silvestri, and Luca Trevisan. Simple dynamics for plurality consensus. In *26th ACM Symposium on Parallelism in Algorithms and Architectures, (SPAA)*, pages 247–256, 2014.

[BCN+15] Luca Becchetti, Andrea Clementi, Emanuele Natale, Francesco Pasquale, and Riccardo Silvestri. Plurality consensus in the gossip model. In *Proceedings of the 26th Annual ACM-SIAM Symposium on Discrete Algorithms (SODA)*, pages 371–390, 2015.

[BCN+16] Luca Becchetti, Andrea E. F. Clementi, Emanuele Natale, Francesco Pasquale, and Luca Trevisan. Stabilizing consensus with many opinions. In *Proceedings of the Twenty-Sixth Annual ACM-SIAM Symposium on Discrete Algorithms (SODA)*. SIAM, 2016.

[BFGK16] Petra Berenbrink, Tom Friedetzky, George Giakkoupis, and Peter Kling. Efficient plurality consensus, or: The benefits of cleaning up from time to time. In *Proceedings of the 43rd International Colloquium on Automata, Languages and Programming (ICALP)*, 2016. to appear.

[BG90] Carol Bezuidenhout and Geoffrey Grimmett. The critical contact process dies out. *The Annals of Probability*, pages 1462–1482, 1990.

[BGKMT16] Petra Berenbrink, George Giakkoupis, Anne-Marie Kermarrec, and Frederik Mallmann-Trenn. Bounds on the voter model in dynamic networks. In *ICALP*, 2016.

[BSDDS10] Ohad Ben-Shahar, Shlomi Dolev, Andrey Dolgin, and Michael Segal. Direction election in flocking swarms. In *Proc. of the 6th Int. Workshop on Foundations of Mobile Computing (DIALM-POMC)*, pages 73–80. ACM, 2010.

[CEOR13] Colin Cooper, Robert Elsässer, Hirotaka Ono, and Tomasz Radzik. Coalescing Random Walks and Voting on Connected Graphs. *SIAM Journal on Discrete Mathematics*, 27(4):1748–1758, 2013.

[CER14] Colin Cooper, Robert Elsässer, and Tomasz Radzik. The Power of Two Choices in Distributed Voting. In *Proc. ICALP*, pages 435–446, 2014.

[CER+15] Colin Cooper, Robert Elsässer, Tomasz Radzik, Nicolaás Rivera, and Takeharu Shiraga. Fast Consensus for Voting on General Expander Graphs. In *DISC*, pages 248–262, 2015.

[DGH+87] Alan Demers, Dan Greene, Carl Hauser, Wes Irish, John Larson, Scott Shenker, Howard Sturgis, Dan Swinehart, and Doug Terry. Epidemic algorithms for replicated database maintenance. In *Proc. of the 6th Ann. ACM Symposium on Principles of Distributed Computing (PODC)*, pages 1–12. ACM, 1987.

[DGM⁺11] Benjamin Doerr, Leslie Ann Goldberg, Lorenz Minder, Thomas Sauerwald, and Christian Scheideler. Stabilizing consensus with the power of two choices. In *Proceedings of the 23rd Annual ACM Symposium on Parallelism in Algorithms and Architectures, (SPAA)*, pages 149–158, 2011.

[DGRS14] Josep Díaz, Leslie Ann Goldberg, David Richerby, and Maria Serna. Absorption Time of the Moran Process. In *Approximation, Randomization, and Combinatorial Optimization. Algorithms and Techniques (APPROX/RANDOM 2014)*, volume 28, pages 630–642, 2014.

[EFK⁺16] Robert Elsässer, Tom Friedetzky, Dominik Kaaser, Frederik Mallmann-Trenn, and Horst Trinker. Efficient k-party voting with two choices. *CoRR*, abs/1602.04667, 2016.

[FPM⁺02] Nigel R. Franks, Stephen C. Pratt, Eamonn B. Mallon, Nicholas F. Britton, and David J.T. Sumpter. Information flow, opinion polling and collective intelligence in house-hunting social insects. *Philosophical Transactions of the Royal Society of London B: Biological Sciences*, 357(1427):1567–1583, 2002.

[GP16] Mohsen Ghaffari and Merav Parter. A polylogarithmic gossip algorithm for plurality consensus. In *Proceedings of the 2016 ACM Symposium on Principles of Distributed Computing*, pages 117–126. ACM, 2016.

[HP01] Y. Hassin and D. Peleg. Distributed probabilistic polling and applications to proportionate agreement. *Information and Computation*, 171(2):248–268, 2001.

[KDG03] David Kempe, Alin Dobra, and Johannes Gehrke. Gossip-Based Computation of Aggregate Information. In *Proc. of 43rd Ann. IEEE Symp. on Foundations of Computer Science (FOCS)*, pages 482–491. IEEE, 2003.

[KSSV00] Richard Karp, Christian Schindelhauer, Scott Shenker, and Berthold Vocking. Randomized rumor spreading. In *Proc. of the 41th Ann. IEEE Symp. on Foundations of Computer Science (FOCS)*, pages 565–574. IEEE, 2000.

[LHN05] E. Lieberman, C. Hauert, and M. Nowak. Evolutionary dynamics on graphs. *Nature*, 433(7023):312–316, January 2005.

[Lig99] Thomas M Liggett. *Stochastic interacting systems: contact, voter and exclusion processes.* Springer, 2099.

[LW14] Per Kristian Lehre and Carsten Witt. Concentrated hitting times of randomized search heuristics with variable drift. In *Proceedings of the 25th International Symposium on Algorithms and Computation (ISAAC)*, pages 686–697, 2014.

[MOA11] Albert W. Marshall, Ingram Olkin, and Barry C. Arnold. *Inequalities: Theory of Majorization and Its Applications.* Springer Series in Statistics. Springer, 2011.

[Mor16] Satoru Morita. Six susceptible-infected-susceptible models on scale-free networks. *Scientific reports*, 6, 2016.

[MU05] Michael Mitzenmacher and Eli Upfal. *Probability and Computing: Randomized Algorithms and Probabilistic Analysis.* Cambridge University Press, 2005.

[PSL80] Marshall Pease, Robert Shostak, and Leslie Lamport. Reaching agreement in the presence of faults. *Journal of the ACM*, 27(2):228–234, 1980.

[Rab83] Michael O. Rabin. Randomized byzantine generals. In *Proc. of the 24th Ann. Symp. on Foundations of Computer Science (SFCS)*, pages 403–409. IEEE, 1983.

[RS⁺77] Yosef Rinott, Thomas J Santner, et al. An inequality for multivariate normal probabilities with application to a design problem. *The Annals of Statistics*, 5(6):1228–1234, 1977.

# A AUXILIARY TOOLS

## A.1 Tools from Majorization Theory

PROPOSITION A.1 ([MOA11, PROPOSITION 11.E.11],[RS⁺77]). *For $N \in \mathbb{N}$ and a probability vector $\Theta \in [0,1]^l$, consider a random vector $X$ having the multinomial distribution* $\mathrm{Mult}(N,\Theta)$. *Let*

$$\phi\colon \left\{ x \in \mathbb{N}_0^l \;\middle|\; \sum_{i\in[l]} x_i = N \right\} \to \mathbb{R} \tag{16}$$

*be such that $\mathbb{E}[\phi(X)]$ exists. Note that this expected value depends on $\Theta$. Define the function $\psi$ on probability vectors as $\psi(\Theta) := \mathbb{E}[\phi(X)]$. If $\phi$ is Schur-convex, then so is $\psi$.*

THEOREM A.2 (STRASSEN'S THEOREM [MOA11, 17.B.6]). *Suppose that $\mathcal{A} \subseteq \mathbb{R}^n$ is closed and that $\leq_C$ is the preorder of $\mathcal{A}$ generated by the convex cone $C$ of real-valued functions defined on $\mathcal{A}$. Suppose further that $\{(x,y) \mid x \leq_C y\}$ is a closed set. Then the conditions*

*(i) $X \leq_C^{st} Y$ and*

*(ii) there exists a pair $\tilde{X}, \tilde{Y}$ of random variables such that*

*(a) $X$ and $\tilde{X}$ are identically distributed, $Y$ and $\tilde{Y}$ are identically distributed and*

*(b) $\Pr[\tilde{X} \leq_C \tilde{Y}] = 1$*

*are equivalent if and only if $C^+ = C^*$; i.e., the stochastic completion $C^+$ of $C$ is complete.*

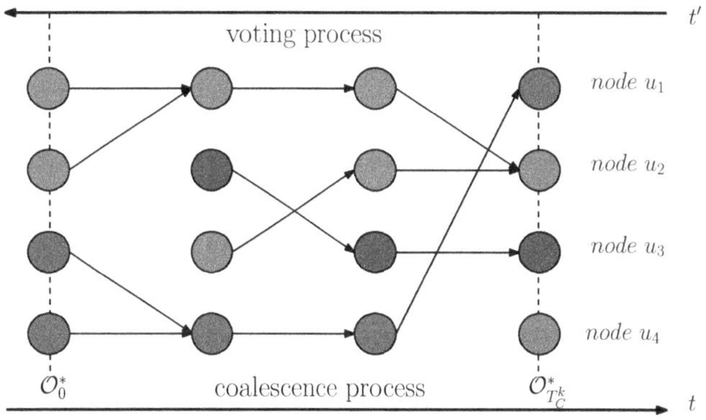


**Figure 1: In the coalescence process (left to right), we start with one token on each of the four nodes. Each token performs a random walk, and an arrow from $u$ to $v$ indicates the random walk destination. The shown random choices cause the number of tokens to reduce from four (left) to two (right, on the purple and red nodes). Using the same random choices for a voter process going from right to left, an arrow from $u$ to $v$ now indicates that $u$ pulls $v$'s opinion. This reduces the number of colors from four (right) to two (left). This is no coincidence as we show in Lemma A.5.**

## A.2 Tools from Drift Theory

THEOREM A.3 (VARIABLE DRIFT THEOREM [LW14, COROLLARY 1.(I)]). *Let $(X_t)_{t\geq 0}$, be a stochastic process over a state space $S \subseteq \{0\} \cup [x_{\min}, x_{\max}]$, where $x_{\min} \geq 0$. Let $h\colon [x_{\min}, x_{\max}] \to \mathbb{R}^+$ be a differentiable function. Then the following statements hold for the first hitting time $T := \min\{t \mid X_t = 0\}$. If $\mathbb{E}[X_{t+1} - X_t \mid \mathcal{F}_t; X_t \geq x_{\min}] \leq -h(X_t)$ and $\frac{d}{dx}h(x) \geq 0$, then*

$$\mathbb{E}[T \mid X_0] \leq \frac{x_{\min}}{h(x_{\min})} + \int_{x_{\min}}^{X_0} \frac{1}{h(y)}\,\mathrm{d}y.$$

## A.3 Tools for Consensus Processes

THEOREM A.4 ([BCN⁺16, THEOREM 3.1]). *Let $\varepsilon > 0$ be an arbitrarily small constant. Starting from any initial configuration with $k \leq n^{1/3-\varepsilon}$ colors, 3-MAJORITY reaches consensus w.h.p. in*

$$\mathrm{O}\Big((k^2 \log^{1/2} n + k \log n) \cdot (k + \log n)\Big)$$

*rounds.*

The following lemma uses the high-level idea of the proof presented in [AF02, Chapter 14] which only considers the case $k = 1$.

For the purposes of our proof we would only require a coupling with $T^k_{\mathcal{V}} \leq T^k_C$, but for the sake of completeness we show the stronger claim $T^k_{\mathcal{V}} = T^k_C$.

Lemma A.5. *For any graph $G = (V, E)$, there exists a coupling such that $T^k_C = T^k_{\mathcal{V}}$.*

Proof. For $t \in \mathbb{N}$ and for $u \in V$ define the random variables $Y_t(u)$ with $Y_t(u) \sim \text{uniform}(N(u))$, where uniform$(\cdot)$ denotes the uniform distribution and $N(u)$ denotes the neighborhood of $u$. Hence, $Y_t(u) = v$ means that $u$ pulls information from node $v$ in step $t$. In the Coalescence process, the random variable $Y_t(u) \in N(u)$, $t \in [0, T^k_C)$ captures the transition performed by the random walk which is at $u$ at time $t$ (if any). In other words, these random variables define the arrows in Figure 1. For the voter process $Y_t(u) = v$ means that in step $t$ node $u$ adopts the opinion of $v$.

Let $X(u) = (X_0(u) = u, X_1(u), \ldots, X_{T^k_C}(u))$ be the trajectory of the random walk starting at $u$. We can thus express

$$X_t(u) = \begin{cases} u & \text{if } t = 0 \\ Y_{t-1}(X_{t-1}(u)) & \text{otherwise.} \end{cases} \tag{17}$$

Thus, this trajectory $X(u)$ and the random variable $T^k_C$ are completely determined by the random variables $\mathcal{Y} = \{Y_t(u) : t \in \mathbb{N}, u \in V\}$.

Let $\mathcal{V}_{T^k_C}$ be the Voter process whose starting time $t' = 0$ equals the time $T^k_C$ of the coalescence process (see also Figure 1). Let $O^*_{T^k_C - t'}(u)$ be the opinion of $u$ at time $t'$ of $\mathcal{V}_{T^k_C}$. For every node $u \in V$ and $t' \in [0, T^k_C]$ we can thus express

$$O^*_{T^k_C - t'}(u) = \begin{cases} u & \text{if } t' = 0 \\ O^*_{T^k_C - (t'-1)}(Y_{T^k_C - t'}(u)) & \text{otherwise.} \end{cases} \tag{18}$$

Note that (18) constructs a coupling between the Voter process and the coalescence process through the common usage of the random variables $\mathcal{Y}$ in (17) and (18). In particular, by unrolling (17) and (18) we get

$$\begin{aligned} X_{T^k_C}(u) &= Y_{T^k_C - 1}(Y_{T^k_C - 2}(\ldots(Y_0(X_0(u)))\ldots)) \\ &\overset{(a)}{=} Y_{T^k_C - 1}(Y_{T^k_C - 2}(\ldots(Y_0(u))\ldots)) \\ O^*_0(u) &= O^*_{T^k_C}(Y_{T^k_C - 1}(Y_{T^k_C - 2}(\ldots(Y_0(u))\ldots))) \\ &\overset{(b)}{=} Y_{T^k_C - 1}(Y_{T^k_C - 2}(\ldots(Y_0(u)\ldots)), \end{aligned}$$

where and $(a)$ we used that $X_0(u) = u$ and in $(b)$ we used that $O^*_{T^k_C}(v) = v$ for all $v$. The above equations imply

$$X_{T^k_C}(u) = O^*_0(u). \tag{19}$$

Let $Z_t = \{X_t(u) : u \in V\}$ denote the positions of the remaining walks in the coalescence process at time $t$. Observe that $|Z_0| = n$, $|Z_{T^k_C}| \leq k$, by definition of $T^k_C$. We have, by (19), that

$$Z_{T^k_C} = \{X_{T^k_C}(u) : u \in V\} = \{O^*_0(u) : u \in V\} =: O^*_0. \tag{20}$$

From (20) we infer $|O^*_0| = |Z_{T^k_C}| \leq k$, which implies that

$$T^k_{\mathcal{V}} \leq T^k_C.$$

In the reminder we generalize the previous coupling to show that

$$T^k_{\mathcal{V}} = T^k_C.$$

In particular, we consider the Voter process for all starting position $\tau < T^k_C$ (all nodes have different colors at round $t$) and show that the resulting number of opinions is strictly more than $k$.

Let $\mathcal{V}_\tau$ be the Voter process that starts at time $\tau \in [0, T^k_C)$, and let $O^\tau_{T^k_C - t'}(u)$ be the opinion of $u$ at time $t'$ of $\mathcal{V}_\tau$. For every node $u \in V$ and $t' \in [0, \tau]$ we have

$$O^\tau_{\tau - t'}(u) = \begin{cases} u & \text{if } t' = \tau \\ O^\tau_{\tau - (t'-1)}(Y_{\tau - t'}(u)) & \text{otherwise.} \end{cases} \tag{21}$$

Similarly as before, by unrolling (17) and (21) we get

$$\begin{aligned} X_\tau(u) &= Y_{\tau-1}(Y_{\tau-2}(\ldots(Y_0(X_0(u)))\ldots)) \\ &\overset{(a)}{=} Y_{\tau-1}(Y_{\tau-2}(\ldots(Y_0(u))\ldots)) \\ O^\tau_0(u) &= O^\tau_\tau(Y_{\tau-1}(Y_{\tau-2}(\ldots(Y_0(u))\ldots))) \\ &\overset{(b)}{=} Y_{\tau-1}(Y_{\tau-2}(\ldots(Y_0(u)\ldots)), \end{aligned}$$

where and $(a)$ we used that $X_0(u) = u$ and in $(b)$ we used that $O^\tau_\tau(v) = v$ for all $v$. By defining $O^0_{T^k_C - t'} = \{O^0_{T^k_C - t'}(u) : u \in V\}$, from the above equations we get that

$$X_\tau(u) = O^\tau_0(u).$$

Hence,

$$Z_\tau = \{X_\tau(u) : u \in V\} = \{O^\tau_0(u) : u \in V\} =: O^\tau_0. \tag{22}$$

Since for all $\tau < T^k_C$ we have $|Z_\tau| > k$, from (22) it follows that $|O^\tau_0| = |Z_\tau| > k$ which yields the claim. □

# Life Beyond Set Agreement

David Yu Cheng Chan
Department of Computer Science
University of Toronto
10 King's College Road
Toronto, Ontario M5S3G4, Canada
davidchan@cs.toronto.edu

Vassos Hadzilacos
Department of Computer Science
University of Toronto
10 King's College Road
Toronto, Ontario M5S3G4, Canada
vassos@cs.toronto.edu

Sam Toueg
Department of Computer Science
University of Toronto
10 King's College Road
Toronto, Ontario M5S3G4, Canada
sam@cs.toronto.edu

## ABSTRACT

The *set agreement power* of a shared object $O$ describes $O$'s ability to solve set agreement problems: it is the sequence $(n_1, n_2, \ldots, n_k, \ldots)$ such that, for every $k \geq 1$, using $O$ and registers one can solve the $k$-set agreement problem among at most $n_k$ processes. It has been shown that the ability of an object $O$ to implement other objects is not fully characterized by its *consensus number* (the first component of its set agreement power) [1, 3, 14]. This raises the following natural question: is the ability of an object $O$ to implement other objects fully characterized by its *set agreement power*? We prove that the answer is no: every level $n \geq 2$ of Herlihy's consensus hierarchy has two objects that have the same set agreement power but are not equivalent, i.e., at least one cannot implement the other. We also show that every level $n \geq 2$ of the consensus hierarchy contains a *deterministic* object $O_n$ with some set agreement power $(n_1, n_2, \ldots, n_k, \ldots)$ such that being able to solve the $k$-set agreement problems among $n_k$ processes, for all $k \geq 1$, is not enough to implement $O_n$.

## KEYWORDS

asynchronous system, shared memory, set agreement, consensus hierarchy

## 1 INTRODUCTION

**Background and Motivation.** The most widely studied problem in distributed computing is consensus [8] and its natural generalization, $k$-set agreement [5]. With the $k$-set agreement problem, each process has a proposal value and must decide on one of the proposed values such that there are at most $k$ distinct decision values.

In this paper we consider distributed systems where asynchronous processes may apply operations to wait-free shared objects and fail by crashing [10]. The *$k$-set agreement number* of a shared object $O$ is the largest integer $n_k$ such that instances of $O$ and registers can solve the $k$-set agreement problem among $n_k$ processes, or it is $\infty$ if instances of $O$ and registers can solve the $k$-set agreement problem among any number of processes. Since 1-set agreement is just *consensus*, the 1-set agreement number of an object is its *consensus number* [10]. The *set agreement power* of an object $O$ is the infinite sequence $(n_1, n_2, \ldots, n_k, \ldots)$ where $n_k$ is the $k$-set agreement number of $O$ for all $k \geq 1$.[1] Thus $(n_1, n_2, \ldots, n_k, \ldots)$ describes the object $O$'s ability to solve set agreement problems among various numbers of processes: for all $k \geq 1$, $O$ can solve the $k$-set agreement problem among $n$ processes if and only if $n \leq n_k$.

Herlihy showed that instances of any object with consensus number $n$, together with registers, can implement in a wait-free manner any object that can be shared by up to $n$ processes [10]. The consensus number of an object, however, does not fully characterize its ability to implement other objects: there are objects $O$ and $O'$ that have the same consensus number but instances of $O$, together with registers, cannot implement $O'$ in a wait-free manner [1, 3, 14]. Since the consensus number of an object is only the *first* component of its set agreement power, this raises the following natural question: does the set agreement power of an object fully characterize its ability to implement other objects? To formulate this question more precisely, we define two objects to be *equivalent* if each can be implemented from instances of the other and registers in a wait-free manner. The question then is: are two objects equivalent if and only if they have the same set agreement power?

**Our Result.** In this paper, we show that the answer is no. In fact, we prove the following stronger result: every level $n \geq 2$ of the well-known consensus hierarchy [10] contains a pair of objects that have the same set agreement power but are not equivalent.[2] We also show that every level $n \geq 2$ of the consensus hierarchy contains a *deterministic* object $O_n$ with some set agreement power $(n_1, n_2, \ldots, n_k, \ldots)$ such that being able to solve the $k$-set agreement problems among $n_k$ processes, for all $k \geq 1$, is not enough to implement $O_n$.

## 2 ROADMAP OF THE PROOF

In Section 3, we introduce the *$n$-pseudo-abortable consensus ($n$-PAC)* object, which is a non-abortable and deterministic version of the abortable $n$-DAC object introduced in [9].

In Section 4, we consider the *$n$-DAC problem* defined in [9], and prove that for $n \geq 2$ the $(n+1)$-DAC problem *can* be solved using $(n+1)$-PAC objects, but *cannot* be solved using $n$-consensus objects, registers, and a strong version of 2-set agreement objects,

This work was partially supported by the Natural Sciences and Engineering Research Council of Canada.

*PODC'17, , July 25–27, 2017, Washington, DC, USA.*
© 2017 Association for Computing Machinery.
ACM ISBN 978-1-4503-4992-5/17/07...$15.00
http://dx.doi.org/10.1145/3087801.3087822

[1] In [7], $k$-set agreement number and set agreement power are called *$k$-set-consensus number* and *set consensus power*.
[2] Recall that an object $O$ is at level $n$ of the consensus hierarchy if instances of the object and registers can solve consensus among $n$, but not $n+1$, processes, i.e., the consensus number of $O$ is $n$.

denoted 2-SA objects. This implies:

for $n \geq 2$, the $(n+1)$-PAC object *cannot* be implemented using $n$-consensus objects, registers, and 2-SA objects. (1)

In Section 5, we introduce a combination of an $n$-PAC object and an $m$-consensus object, called the $(n, m)$-PAC object, and show that for all $m \geq 2$, $(n, m)$-PAC is at level $m$ of the consensus hierarchy. In particular, for all $n \geq 2$, the $(n+1, n)$-PAC object, denoted $O_n$, is at level $n$ of this hierarchy. By definition $O_n$ is at least as strong as the $(n+1)$-PAC object, therefore, by (1):

for $n \geq 2$, $O_n$ *cannot* be implemented using $n$-consensus objects, registers, and 2-SA objects. (2)

Finally, in Section 6, for all $n \geq 2$ we construct an object $O'_n$ such that: (a) $O'_n$ has the same set agreement power as $O_n$, and (b) $O'_n$ *can* be implemented by $n$-consensus objects, registers, and 2-SA objects. By (2) and (b):

$O_n$ cannot be implemented by $O'_n$ objects and registers. (3)

So every level $n \geq 2$ of the consensus hierarchy has two objects, namely, $O_n$ and $O'_n$, that are not equivalent to each other, even though they have the same set agreement power.

Let $(n_1, n_2, \ldots, n_k, \ldots)$ be the set agreement power of $O_n$. By construction, the set agreement power of $O'_n$ is $(n_1, n_2, \ldots, n_k, \ldots)$ as well. Thus, $O'_n$ and registers can solve the $k$-set agreement problem among $n_k$ processes, for all $k \geq 1$. By (3), this implies that the deterministic object $O_n$ *cannot* be implemented from arbitrary solutions to the $k$-set agreement problems among $n_k$ processes, for all $k \geq 1$, and registers.

## 3 PSEUDO-ABORTABLE CONSENSUS OBJECTS

In [9], Hadzilacos and Toueg introduced $n$-DAC objects that behave like $n$-consensus objects except for one key difference: operations can nondeterministically *abort* without taking effect as long as the following conditions are satisfied

- Every operation that aborts is concurrent with another operation.
- No crashed process may cause infinitely many aborts.

In this section, we define *n-pseudo-abortable consensus (n-PAC)* objects that behave similarly to $n$-DAC objects, but are deterministic and not abortable. Intuitively, for all $n \geq 1$, the $n$-PAC object simulates an $n$-DAC object by supporting two operations: PROPOSE$(v, i)$ and DECIDE$(i)$, where $i$ is an integer in $[1..n]$ that we call the *label* of the operation. A process can use these two operations to simulate a PROPOSE$(v)$ operation on an $n$-DAC object by first applying a PROPOSE$(v, i)$ operation and then applying a DECIDE$(i)$ operation with the same label $i$ on the $n$-PAC object. Whenever a PROPOSE$(v, i)$ operation is performed on an $n$-PAC object, the object simulates the invocation of a propose operation with value $v$ on the $i$-th port of the simulated $n$-DAC object, and returns **done**.[3] Whenever a DECIDE$(i)$ operation is performed, the $n$-PAC simulates the completion of the propose operation on the $i$-th port of the simulated $n$-DAC object, and returns the response.

Thus the propose and decide operations form matching pairs, with each decide operation needing a previous propose operation with the same label. If a DECIDE$(i)$ operation is performed without a matching PROPOSE$(-, i)$ operation performed beforehand, the $n$-PAC object becomes permanently upset. Similarly, if a pair of PROPOSE$(-, i)$ operations are performed without a DECIDE$(i)$ in between, the $n$-PAC object becomes permanently upset. Intuitively, this is because two operations were invoked concurrently on port $i$ of the $n$-DAC object.

A (sequential) *history* of an $n$-PAC object is a sequence of propose and decide operations applied to that object. We say that the history of an $n$-PAC object is *legal* if for all $i \in [1..n]$, the history of operations with label $i$ performed on the object is either empty or begins with a propose operation and alternates between propose and decide operations. Thus an $n$-PAC object becomes upset if and only if its history is not legal. For convenience, we say a PROPOSE$(-, i)$ operation on the $n$-PAC object *decides* a value $v'$ if it has a matching DECIDE$(i)$ operation that returns $v'$. Once an $n$-PAC object becomes upset, it returns the special value $\bot$ to all decide operations but still returns **done** to all propose operations.[4]

To simulate the fact that an $n$-DAC object can abort when operations are concurrent, an $n$-PAC object that is not upset behaves as follows: if there is an operation between a propose operation and its matching decide operation, then the decide operation returns $\bot$. So intuitively, an $n$-PAC object returns $\bot$ if it is upset or if it detects a concurrent operation.

We now describe the $n$-PAC object more precisely. The state of such an object consists of:

- A boolean *upset*, initially **false**.
- An array $V[1..n]$, initially all NIL. Intuitively, $V[i] = v$ if the last operation with label $i$ is a PROPOSE$(v, i)$ operation.
- A variable $L$, initially NIL. Intuitively, $L = i$ if the last operation is PROPOSE$(-, i)$.
- A variable *val*, initially NIL. Intuitively, *val* contains the consensus value.

The sequential behaviour of the $n$-PAC object is given by Algorithm 1.

From the above description, it is clear that the sequential specification of $n$-PAC can be formally given in terms of a set of states, a set of operations, a set of responses, and a state transition relation. For brevity, we omit this formal definition here. The $n$-PAC object is *linearizable* [11], i.e., the operations PROPOSE$(-, -)$ and DECIDE$(-)$ are *atomic*. Thus, we consider only sequential histories of this object.

An $n$-PAC object *is upset* if its variable *upset* = **true**.

OBSERVATION 3.1. *If an n-PAC object is upset at some time, it remains upset thereafter.*

In the full paper we show the following properties of $n$-PAC objects.

LEMMA 3.2. *An n-PAC object is upset at time t if and only if the history of all operations that have been performed on the object by time t is not legal.*

[3] The $n$-DAC has $n$ ports through which operations are applied; in contrast, our $n$-PAC object has no ports.

[4] We assume that processes do not propose the special values $\bot$ and NIL.

**Algorithm 1** Sequential specification of the $n$-PAC object

```
procedure PROPOSE(v, i) { 1 ≤ i ≤ n }
    if V[i] ≠ NIL then upset ← true
    if upset = false then
        L ← i
        V[i] ← v
    return done

procedure DECIDE(i) { 1 ≤ i ≤ n }
    if V[i] = NIL then upset ← true
    if upset = true then return ⊥
    if L ≠ i then
        temp ← ⊥
    else
        if val = NIL then val ← V[i]
        temp ← val
    L ← NIL
    V[i] ← NIL
    return temp
```

LEMMA 3.3. *If an n-PAC object is not upset at time t, then for all* $i \in [1..n]$,

$$V[i] = \begin{cases} v & \text{if, at time } t\text{, the last operation with label } i \text{ is a PROPOSE}(v, i) \text{ operation.} \\ \text{NIL} & \text{otherwise.} \end{cases}$$

LEMMA 3.4. *If an n-PAC object is not upset at time t,*

$$L = \begin{cases} i & \text{if, at time } t\text{, the last operation is PROPOSE}(-, i). \\ \text{NIL} & \text{otherwise.} \end{cases}$$

THEOREM 3.5. *An n-PAC object satisfies the following properties:*

(a) *Agreement: If a decide operation returns a value* $v \neq \bot$, *and another decide operation returns a value* $v' \neq \bot$, *then* $v = v'$.
(b) *Validity: If a decide operation returns a value* $v \neq \bot$, *then a propose operation proposes* $v$ *and decides* $v$.
(c) *Nontriviality: A decide operation op returns* $\bot$ *if and only if either (i) the n-PAC object is upset before op, or (ii) there is no operation before op, or the last operation before op is not a propose operation with the same label.*

## 4 THE $N$-DAC PROBLEM

In [9], Hadzilacos and Toueg introduced the $n$-DAC problem, where $n \geq 2$ processes start with binary inputs and are supposed to decide on a binary value; in addition, one of the $n$ processes is a distinguished process $p$ that can abort instead of deciding. An algorithm solves the $n$-DAC problem if every execution of the algorithm satisfies the following properties:

- **Agreement:** If a process $q$ decides $v$ and a process $q'$ decides $v'$, then $v = v'$.
- **Validity:** If a process decides $v$, then some process that does not abort has input $v$.
- **Termination:**
  (a) If the distinguished process $p$ takes infinitely many steps, then $p$ eventually decides or aborts.
  (b) If any process $q \neq p$ takes infinitely many steps solo (i.e., not interleaved with steps of other processes), then $q$ eventually decides.
- **Nontriviality:** If $p$ aborts, then some process $q \neq p$ took at least one step.

**Algorithm 2** Solving the $n$-DAC problem using a single $n$-PAC $\mathcal{D}$

```
Code executed by the distinguished process p:
𝒟.PROPOSE(v_p, p)
temp ← 𝒟.DECIDE(p)
if temp ≠ ⊥ then
    decide temp
else abort

Code executed by each process q ≠ p:
while true do
    𝒟.PROPOSE(v_q, q)
    temp ← 𝒟.DECIDE(q)
    if temp ≠ ⊥ then
        decide temp
        break
```

It is easy to solve the $n$-DAC problem with an $n$-PAC object: the processes numbered 1 to $n$ execute Algorithm 2, where $p$ is the distinguished process, and $v_q$ is the initial value of process $q$ ($1 \leq q \leq n$). The proof of the following theorem is straightforward and is given in the full paper.

THEOREM 4.1. *For all* $n \geq 2$, *the n-DAC problem can be solved using a single n-PAC object.*

We now define the *strong 2-set agreement object*, denoted 2-*SA*, that is designed to solve the 2-set agreement problem among any finite number of processes. The state of the 2-SA object is a set STATE, initially empty. The 2-SA object supports the PROPOSE($v$) operation, which adds $v$ to STATE if STATE contains fewer than 2 elements, and returns a value arbitrarily selected from STATE. Consequently, a 2-SA object responds to operations with at most two distinct values, corresponding to the *first* two distinct values proposed to the object.[5]

Algorithm 3 gives the sequential behaviour of the 2-SA object.

**Algorithm 3** Sequential specification of the 2-SA object

```
procedure PROPOSE(v)
    if |STATE| < 2 then STATE ← STATE ∪ {v}
    return arbitrary value from STATE
```

From the above, it is clear that the sequential specification of 2-SA can be formally given in terms of a set of states, a set of operations, a set of responses, and a state transition relation. The 2-SA object is linearizable, i.e., its PROPOSE($-$) operation is *atomic*.

[5]This object is "strong" because the 2-set agreement problem does not have this restriction: with the 2-set agreement problem, processes can decide *any* two of the proposed values.

It is straightforward to see that the 2-SA object solves the 2-set agreement problem among any finite number of processes, as required. A fortiori, the 2-SA object solves the $k$-set agreement problem among $n$ processes for all $k \geq 2$ and all $n \geq 1$.

In [9], it was shown that for all $n \geq 2$, the $(n+1)$-DAC problem cannot be solved using $n$-consensus objects and registers. We strengthen this result by showing the following:

THEOREM 4.2. *For all $n \geq 2$, the $(n+1)$-DAC problem cannot be solved using $n$-consensus objects, registers, and 2-SA objects.*[6]

PROOF. In the following, we use the bivalency technique introduced by Fischer et al. [8], and we assume the reader is familiar with the associated terminology. In particular, a configuration $C$ is *$v$-valent* (for $v \in \{0,1\}$) if starting from $C$ no process can decide $\overline{v} = 1 - v$; $C$ is *univalent* if it is either 0-valent or 1-valent; and $C$ is *bivalent* if it is not univalent [8, 10].

Assume, for contradiction, that there exists an algorithm $\mathcal{A}$ that solves the $(n+1)$-DAC problem among $n+1$ processes using only $n$-consensus objects, registers, and 2-SA objects. Let $I$ be the initial configuration where the input of the distinguished process $p$ is 1 and the input of every other process is 0.

The following standard claim still holds for the $(n+1)$-DAC problem:

CLAIM 4.2.1. *No configuration reachable from an $I$ is both 0-valent and 1-valent.*

PROOF. Suppose a configuration $C$ reachable from an $I$ is both 0-valent and 1-valent. There are $n+1 > 1$ processes, so some process $q$ is not the distinguished process $p$. By Termination (b) of the $(n+1)$-DAC problem, there exists a finite $q$-solo history $H$ such that $H$ is applicable to $C$ and $q$ decides some value $v \in \{0,1\}$ in $H(C)$. Then, since $q$ decides $v$ in $H(C)$, $H(C)$ is not $\overline{v}$-valent, where $\overline{v} = 1-v$. Thus $C$ is also not $\overline{v}$-valent, contradicting our assumption that $C$ is both 0-valent and 1-valent. □ Claim 4.2.1

CLAIM 4.2.2. *If $p$ aborts in a configuration $C$ that is reachable from initial configuration $I$, then $C$ is 0-valent.*

PROOF. Suppose, for contradiction, that $p$ aborts in a configuration $C$ that is reachable from $I$, but $C$ is not 0-valent. Then, there is a finite history $H$, applicable to $C$, such that some process decides 1 in $H(C)$. Since $p$ aborts in $C$, $p$ also aborts in $H(C)$, since aborting is irrevocable. Since $C$ is reachable from $I$, so is $H(C)$. This violates the Validity property of the $(n+1)$-DAC problem, since $p$ is the only process with input 1 in $I$. □ Claim 4.2.2

The above claim immediately implies:

OBSERVATION 4.2.3. *If $p$ aborts or decides in a configuration $C$ that is reachable from initial configuration $I$, then $C$ is univalent.*

CLAIM 4.2.4. *$I$ is bivalent.*

[6] Recall that an $n$-consensus object solves consensus among $n$ but not $n+1$ processes. A precise specification of the $n$-consensus object as a deterministic linearizable object, for $n \geq 2$, is given in [12, 13]: for the first $n$ propose operations, the $n$-consensus object returns the value of the first propose operation, and it returns a special value $\perp$ to any subsequent propose operation.

PROOF. Starting from $I$, let $p$ run solo until it either decides or aborts, which eventually happens by Termination (a). By Nontriviality, since $p$ is the only process that takes steps, $p$ does not abort. Furthermore, since $p$ is the only process that takes steps, $p$ does not know the input of any other process. Thus by Validity, $p$ decides its own input 1, so $I$ is not 0-valent.

Starting from $I$, let a process $q \neq p$ run solo until it decides, which eventually happens by Termination (b). Since $q$ is the only process that takes steps, $q$ does not know the input of any other process. Thus by Validity, $q$ decides its own input 0, so $I$ is not 1-valent.

Since $I$ is neither 0-valent nor 1-valent, $I$ is bivalent. □ Claim 4.2.4

CLAIM 4.2.5. *There is a bivalent configuration $C'$ that is reachable from $I$ such that for every history $H$ that is applicable to $C'$ and ends with a step of the distinguished process $p$, $H(C')$ is univalent.*

PROOF. Suppose, for contradiction, that the claim is false. In other words, for every bivalent configuration $C'$ that is reachable from $I$, there is a history $H$ such that $H$ is applicable to $C'$, $H$ ends with a step of $p$, and $H(C')$ is bivalent. Since $H(C')$ is itself a bivalent configuration that is reachable from $I$, a straightforward induction can be used to construct an infinite history that contains infinitely many steps of $p$ but never reaches a univalent configuration. Thus from Observation 4.2.3, $p$ takes infinitely many steps without deciding or aborting, violating Termination (a). □ Claim 4.2.5

CLAIM 4.2.6. *There is a configuration $C$ reachable from $I$, a process $q \neq p$, and steps $e_p$, $e'_p$ of $p$ and $e_q$ of $q$, such that $e_p$ and $e_q e'_p$ are applicable to $C$, $e_p(C)$ is $v$-valent and $e_q e'_p(C)$ is $\overline{v}$-valent for some $v \in \{0,1\}$.*

PROOF. Let $C'$ be a configuration as in Claim 4.2.5. Let $f_p$ be a step of $p$ that is applicable to $C'$. By Claim 4.2.5, $f_p(C')$ is univalent. Let $v \in \{0,1\}$ be such that $f_p(C')$ is $v$-valent.

SUBCLAIM 4.2.6.1. *There is a finite $p$-free history $H$ and a step $f'_p$ of $p$ such that $Hf'_p$ is applicable to $C'$, and $Hf'_p(C')$ is $\overline{v}$-valent.*

PROOF. Since $C'$ is bivalent, there is a configuration $C''$ that is reachable from $C'$ such that some process decides $\overline{v}$ in $C''$, and so $C''$ is $\overline{v}$-valent. Let $H'$ be a history such that $C'' = H'(C')$. There are two cases:

**Case 1.** $H'$ is $p$-free.
Then let $H = H'$, and $f'_p$ be a step of $p$ applicable to $C'' = H(C')$. Since $C''$ is $\overline{v}$-valent, so is $f'_p(C'') = Hf'_p(C')$. Thus $H$ is a finite $p$-free history and $f'_p$ is a step of $p$ such that $Hf'_p$ is applicable to $C'$, and $Hf'_p(C')$ is $\overline{v}$-valent as wanted.

**Case 2.** $H'$ is not $p$-free.
Then let $H$ be the longest $p$-free prefix of $H'$, and let $f'_p$ be the step of $p$ in $H'$ immediately after $H$. Thus $Hf'_p$ is a prefix of $H'$. Since $f'_p$ is a step of $p$ and $Hf'_p$ is applicable to $C'$, by Claim 4.2.5, $Hf'_p(C')$ is univalent. Then, since $Hf'_p$ is a prefix of $H'$ and $H'(C') = C''$, $C''$ is reachable from $Hf'_p(C')$. Finally, since $C''$ and $Hf'_p(C')$ are both univalent, and $C''$ is $\overline{v}$-valent and reachable from $Hf'_p(C')$, $Hf'_p(C')$ is also $\overline{v}$-valent.
□ Subclaim 4.2.6.1

SUBCLAIM 4.2.6.2. *The history $H$ of Subclaim 4.2.6.1 is not empty.*

PROOF. Suppose, for contradiction, that $H$ is empty. Thus there are two steps of $p$, $f_p$ and $f'_p$, such that $f_p(C')$ is $v$-valent and $f'_p(C')$ is $\overline{v}$-valent. Since processes are deterministic, $f_p$ and $f'_p$ are steps by $p$ on the same object $O$. Since $f_p(C')$ and $f'_p(C')$ have opposite valence, $O$ must be nondeterministic. Since the algorithm uses only $n$-consensus objects, registers, and 2-SA objects, and both $n$-consensus objects and registers are deterministic, $O$ is a 2-SA object. Thus the steps $f_p$ and $f'_p$ of $p$ are propose operations on the 2-SA object $O$. Furthermore, since $p$ is deterministic, the value proposed by $p$ in $f_p$ is the same as in $f'_p$. From the sequential specification of the 2-SA object (Algorithm 3), the state of the 2-SA object only records values that are proposed to it, not values that it returns. Thus the state of $O$ is the same in $f_p(C')$ as in $f'_p(C')$. Consequently, $f_p(C')$ and $f'_p(C')$ differ only in the state of $p$.

Now, let $q$ be a process other than $p$. By Termination (b), there exists a finite $q$-solo history $\hat{H}$ such that $\hat{H}$ is applicable to $f_p(C')$ and $q$ decides in $\hat{H}$. Since $f_p(C')$ and $f'_p(C')$ differ only in the state of $p$, $\hat{H}$ is also applicable to $f'_p(C')$. Thus $q$ decides the same value in $f_p\hat{H}(C')$ as in $f'_p\hat{H}(C')$, contradicting the fact that $f_p(C')$ and $f'_p(C')$ are univalent configurations with opposite valence. □ Subclaim 4.2.6.2

Let $H$ be a history as in Subclaim 4.2.6.1. By Subclaim 4.2.6.2, it is a non-empty history $H = h_1h_2\ldots h_k$, where $h_1, h_2, \ldots, h_k$ are steps of processes that are not $p$. Let $C_0, C_1, \ldots, C_k$ be the configurations such that $C_0 = C'$ and $C_i = h_i(C_{i-1})$ for all $i$, $1 \le i \le k$. For each $i$, $0 \le i \le k$, we now define a step $h_{p,i}$ of $p$ applicable to $C_i$. Let $h_{p,0} = f_p$, $h_{p,k} = f'_p$, and for $0 < i < k$, let $h_{p,i}$ be any step of $p$ that is applicable to $C_i$.

By Claim 4.2.5, $h_{p,i}(C_i)$ is univalent for all $i$, $0 \le i \le k$. Since $h_{p,0}(C_0) = f_p(C')$, $h_{p,0}(C_0)$ is $v$-valent. Then, since $h_{p,k}(C_k) = Hf'_p(C')$, $h_{p,k}(C_k)$ is $\overline{v}$-valent. Thus, there is some $i$, $0 \le i < k$, such that $h_{p,i}(C_i)$ is $v$-valent and $h_{p,i+1}(C_{i+1})$ is $\overline{v}$-valent. Let $C = C_i$, and let $q \ne p$ be the process that executes step $h_{i+1}$, $e_q = h_{i+1}$, $e_p = h_{p,i}$, and $e'_p = h_{p,i+1}$. Then we have that $e_p$ and $e_qe'_p$ are applicable to $C$, $e_p(C)$ is $v$-valent, and $e_qe'_p(C)$ is $\overline{v}$-valent, as wanted. □ Claim 4.2.6

Let configuration $C$, process $q$, steps $e_p$, $e'_p$, and $e_q$, and $v \in \{0, 1\}$ be as in Claim 4.2.6. Thus,

$$e_p(C) \text{ is } v\text{-valent, while } e_qe'_p(C) \text{ is } \overline{v}\text{-valent.} \tag{4}$$

Since processes are deterministic, $e_p$ and $e'_p$ access the same object $X$ and $e_q$ accesses some object $Y$.

CLAIM 4.2.7. *$X = Y$.*

PROOF. Suppose, for contradiction, that $X \ne Y$. Then the step $e_q$ of $q$ that is applicable to $C$ is also applicable to $e_p(C)$. There are two cases:

**Case 1.** $e_p = e'_p$.
Then $e_p$ and $e_q$ commute at $C$; i.e., $e_pe_q$ and $e_qe_p$ are both applicable to $C$, and $e_pe_q(C) = e_qe_p(C) = e_qe'_p(C)$. Since $e_pe_q(C)$ has the same valence as $e_p(C)$, this contradicts (4).

**Case 2.** $e_p \ne e'_p$.
Since $e_p \ne e'_p$, $X$ is a nondeterministic object, i.e., a 2-SA object. Furthermore, since processes are deterministic, the value proposed by $p$ to the 2-SA object $X$ is the same in $e_p$ as in $e'_p$. Then, since $e_q$ is an operation on $Y \ne X$, the state of $X$ is the same in $e_pe_q(C)$ as in $e_qe'_p(C)$. Consequently, $e_pe_q(C)$ and $e_qe'_p(C)$ differ only in the state of $p$.
By Termination (b), there exists a finite $q$-solo history $\hat{H}$ such that $\hat{H}$ is applicable to $e_pe_q(C)$ and $q$ decides in $e_pe_q\hat{H}(C)$. Since $e_pe_q(C)$ and $e_qe'_p(C)$ differ only in the state of $p$, $\hat{H}$ is also applicable to $e_qe'_p(C)$. Thus $q$ decides the same value in $e_pe_q\hat{H}(C)$ as in $e_qe'_p\hat{H}(C)$ contradicting (4). □ Claim 4.2.7

CLAIM 4.2.8. *$X$ is not a register.*

PROOF. Suppose, for contradiction, that $X$ is a register. There are two cases to consider:

**Case 1.** $e_p$ is a read step.
Since processes are deterministic, $e'_p$ is also a read step. Since $e_p$ is a read of $X$, the state of register $X$ is the same in $C$ as in $e_p(C)$. Thus, since $e_q$ is applicable to $C$, it is also applicable to $e_p(C)$. Thus the configurations $e_pe_q(C)$ and $e_qe'_p(C)$ are identical except possibly in the state of $p$. By Termination (b), there is a finite $q$-solo history $H$ such that $H$ is applicable to $e_pe_q(C)$ and $q$ decides in $e_pe_qH(C)$.
Since $e_pe_q(C)$ and $e_qe'_p(C)$ are identical except possibly in the state of $p$, and $H$ contains no steps of $p$, $H$ is also applicable to $e_qe'_p(C)$. Therefore $q$ decides the same value in $e_pe_qH(C)$ as in $e_qe'_pH(C)$. This contradicts (4).

**Case 2.** $e_p$ is a write step.
Since processes are deterministic, $e'_p = e_p$. Thus both $e_p$ and $e'_p$ write the same value into register $X$, and so configurations $e_p(C)$ and $e_qe'_p(C)$ are identical, except possibly in the state of $q$. By Termination (a), there is a finite $p$-solo history $H$ such that $p$ aborts or decides some value $u \in \{0, 1\}$ in $e_pH(C)$.
Since $e_p(C)$ and $e_qe'_p(C)$ are identical, except possibly in the state of $q$, and $H$ contains no steps of $q$, $H$ is also applicable to $e_qe'_p(C)$. Therefore $p$ aborts in both $e_pH(C)$ and $e_qe'_pH(C)$, or $p$ decides the same value $u \in \{0, 1\}$ in both $e_pH(C)$ and $e_qe'_pH(C)$. If $p$ aborts, then, by Claim 4.2.2, both $e_pH(C)$ and $e_qe'_pH(C)$ are 0-valent; if $p$ decides $u \in \{0, 1\}$, then both $e_pH(C)$ and $e_qe'_pH(C)$ are $u$-valent. This contradicts (4). □ Claim 4.2.8

CLAIM 4.2.9. *$X$ is not an $n$-consensus object.*

PROOF. Suppose, for contradiction, that $X$ is an $n$-consensus object. Let $e'_q$ be any step of $q$ that is applicable to $e_p(C)$. From (4), the configuration $C_v = e_pe'_q(C)$ and $C_{\overline{v}} = e_qe'_p(C)$ have valence $v$ and $\overline{v}$, respectively. Note that the consensus object $X$ is the only object whose state in $C_v$ may differ from its state in $C_{\overline{v}}$. Furthermore, since $C_v$ and $C_{\overline{v}}$ are configurations reached from $C$ via steps of $p$ and $q$ on $X$, each process that is not $p$ or $q$ has the same state in $C_v$ as in $C_{\overline{v}}$.

Let $q'$ be a process that is not $p$ or $q$; $q'$ exists, since there are $n + 1 > 2$ processes. Let $R$ be the set of $n - 2$ processes that are not $p$, $q$ or $q'$ (if $n = 2$ the set $R$ is empty). We construct a history $H$ that is applicable to $C_v$ as follows. Starting from $C_v$, let each process $r \in R$ (in some arbitrary order), run solo until *it is about to perform an operation on* $X$: this must happen because $r \neq p$, so by Termination(b), when $r$ runs solo it must eventually decide some value, but $r$ cannot distinguish between the univalent configurations $C_v$ and $C_{\overline{v}}$ with opposite valence without accessing $X$. Note that in history $H$, no process performs an operation on $X$, which is the only object whose state in $C_v$ may differ from its state in $C_{\overline{v}}$. Thus $H$ is also applicable to $C_{\overline{v}}$, each process $r \in R$ has the same state in $H(C_v)$ as in $H(C_{\overline{v}})$, and $X$ is the only object whose state in $H(C_v)$ may differ from its state in $H(C_{\overline{v}})$.

Starting from $H(C_v)$, let each process $r \in R$ take one step (in some arbitrary order), and let $C'_v$ be the resulting configuration. Similarly, starting from $H(C_{\overline{v}})$, let each process $r \in R$ take one step (in some arbitrary order), and let $C'_{\overline{v}}$ be the resulting configuration. Note that from the construction of $H$, every process $r \in R$ is about to perform an operation on $X$ at $H(C_v)$ and $H(C_{\overline{v}})$. Thus $X$ is the only object whose state in $C'_v$ may differ from its state in $C'_{\overline{v}}$. Furthermore, in both $C'_v$ and $C'_{\overline{v}}$, at least $n$ operations have been performed on $X$ (because every process, except possibly $q'$, has performed at least one operation on $X$). Since $X$ is an $n$-consensus object, after $n$ operations have been performed on it, $X$ is no longer useful in differentiating between configurations $C'_v$ or $C'_{\overline{v}}$: more precisely, any operation that is applied to $X$ after reaching configurations $C'_v$ or $C'_{\overline{v}}$ returns the special value $\perp$. Note also that $C'_v$ and $C'_{\overline{v}}$ are configurations with opposite valence.

Starting from $C'_v$, let $q'$ take steps solo until it decides some value $u \in \{0, 1\}$ (since $q' \neq p$, $q'$ must decide by Termination(b)), and let $H_{q'}$ be this solo history of $q'$. Since: (a) $X$ is the only object whose state may differ between $C'_v$ and $C'_{\overline{v}}$, and (b) after reaching configurations $C'_v$ or $C'_{\overline{v}}$, the $n$-consensus object $X$ returns $\perp$ to every operation, the solo history $H_{q'}$ of $q'$ is also applicable to $C'_{\overline{v}}$. Thus $q$ decides $u$ in both $H_{q'}(C'_v)$ and $H_{q'}(C'_{\overline{v}})$, contradicting the fact that $C'_v$ and $C'_{\overline{v}}$ have opposite valence. □ Claim 4.2.9

Claim 4.2.10. *$X$ is not a 2-SA object.*

Proof. Suppose, for contradiction, that $X$ is a 2-SA object. Thus $p$ and $q$ are both invoking propose operations on $X$. Let $v_p$ and $v_q$ be their respective proposal values. Since processes are deterministic, $e'_p$ also proposes $v_p$.

Subclaim 4.2.10.1. *There exists a value $\hat{v}$ such that $\hat{v}$ is in $X$.STATE in both $e_p(C)$ and $e_q e'_p(C)$.*

Proof. If $X$.STATE is not empty at $C$, we are done, since values are never removed from $X$.STATE. Otherwise, $X$.STATE contains $v_p$ in both $e_p(C)$ and $e_q e'_p(C)$. □ Subclaim 4.2.10.1

Now, let $q'$ be a process other than $p$ and $q$; $q'$ exists, since there are $n + 1 > 2$ processes. Let $\hat{v}$ be a value as in Subclaim 4.2.10.1, and let $\hat{H}$ be the finite history where, starting from $e_p(C)$, $q'$ runs solo while $X$ responds to all operations with $\hat{v}$, until $q'$ decides, which eventually happens by Termination (b). Since the state of $q'$ is the same in $e_p(C)$ as in $e_q e'_p(C)$, and $\hat{v}$ is in $X$.STATE in $e_q e'_p(C)$, this $q'$-solo history $\hat{H}$ is also applicable to $e_q e'_p(C)$. Thus $q'$ decides the same value in both $e_p\hat{H}(C)$ and $e_q e'_p\hat{H}(C)$. This contradicts (4). □ Claim 4.2.10

By Claims 4.2.8, 4.2.9, and 4.2.10, $X$ is not an $n$-consensus object, register, or 2-SA object, contradicting our assumption that Algorithm $\mathcal{A}$ uses only such objects. □ Theorem 4.2

Theorems 4.1 and 4.2 imply:

Theorem 4.3. *For all $n \geq 2$, $(n + 1)$-PAC objects cannot be implemented using $n$-consensus objects, registers, and 2-SA objects.*

# 5 $(N, M)$-PAC IS AT LEVEL $M$ OF THE CONSENSUS HIERARCHY

In this section, we first define a "boosted" version of the $n$-PAC object: for all $n \geq 1$ and $m \geq 1$, the $(n, m)$-PAC object is a combination of an $n$-PAC object $P$ and an $m$-consensus object $C$. The $(n, m)$-PAC object supports three operations:

- PROPOSEC$(v)$, which redirects the operation PROPOSE$(v)$ to $C$ and returns the response.
- PROPOSEP$(v, i)$, which redirects the operation PROPOSE$(v, i)$ to $P$ and returns the response.
- DECIDEP$(i)$, which redirects the operation DECIDE$(i)$ to $P$ and returns the response.

Note that for all $n \geq 1$ and $m \geq 1$, $(n, m)$-PAC objects are deterministic, since both $n$-PAC objects and $m$-consensus objects are deterministic.

Observation 5.1. *For all $n \geq 1$ and $m \geq 1$,*

(a) *An $(n, m)$-PAC object can be implemented using an $n$-PAC object and an $m$-consensus object.*
(b) *An $(n, m)$-PAC object can implement an $n$-PAC object.*
(c) *An $(n, m)$-PAC object can implement an $m$-consensus object.*

We now show that for $m \geq 2$, $(n, m)$-PAC objects are at level $m$ of the consensus hierarchy.

Theorem 5.2. *For all $n \geq 1$ and $m \geq 2$, $(n, m)$-PAC objects and registers cannot be used to solve the $(m + 1)$-consensus problem.*

Proof. By Observation 5.1(a), the $(n, m)$-PAC object can be implemented using an $n$-PAC object and an $m$-consensus object. Thus it suffices to show that, for all $n \geq 1$ and $m \geq 2$, the $(m + 1)$-consensus problem cannot be solved using only $n$-PAC objects, $m$-consensus objects, and registers.

As in the proof of Theorem 4.2, we use the bivalency technique and terminology introduced in [8]. Assume, for contradiction, that there exists a wait-free algorithm $\mathcal{A}$ that solves binary consensus among $m + 1$ processes using only $m$-consensus objects, registers, and $n$-PAC objects. We omit the proofs of Claims 5.2.1 to 5.2.5 since they are standard.

Claim 5.2.1. *The algorithm has an initial bivalent configuration $C_{init}$.*

Claim 5.2.2. *There is a bivalent configuration $C_{bi}$, reachable from $C_{init}$, such that if any process takes a step, the resulting configuration is univalent.*

Claim 5.2.3. *At $C_{bi}$, all $m + 1$ processes are about to perform an operation on the same object $\mathcal{D}$.*

Claim 5.2.4. *$\mathcal{D}$ is not a register.*

Claim 5.2.5. *$\mathcal{D}$ is not an $m$-consensus object.*

It remains to show that $\mathcal{D}$ is not an $n$-PAC object. To do so, we use the following two claims.

Claim 5.2.6. *There does not exist a pair of reachable univalent configurations $C$ and $C'$ with opposite valence such that (i) there is a process that has the same state in $C$ as in $C'$, (ii) there is an $n$-PAC object $D$ that is upset in both $C$ and $C'$, and (iii) every object other than $D$ has the same state in $C$ as in $C'$.*

Proof. Suppose, for contradiction, that there exists such a pair of configurations $C$ and $C'$. Let $p$ denote the process with the same state in $C$ as in $C'$, and let $D$ denote the $n$-PAC object that is upset in both $C$ and $C'$. Since $C$ and $C'$ have opposite valence, process $p$ must be undecided in both $C$ and $C'$. Consider a run $R$ starting from $C$ where $p$ takes steps solo until it decides (this must eventually happen by the Termination property of the consensus problem). Since $D$ is upset in $C$, all decide operations by $p$ on $D$ in $R$ return $\perp$. Furthermore, all propose operations by $p$ return **done**. Since $p$ has the same state in $C$ as in $C'$, and $D$ is upset in both $C$ and $C'$, it is clear that there is an identical $p$-solo run $R'$ that starts from $C'$. Thus $p$ decides the same value in both $R$ and $R'$, contradicting that $C$ and $C'$ have opposite valence. □ Claim 5.2.6

Claim 5.2.7. *There does not exist a pair of reachable univalent configurations $C$ and $C'$ with opposite valence such that (i) there are two processes that have the same state in $C$ as in $C'$, and (ii) with the possible exception of a single $n$-PAC object $D$, every object has the same state in $C$ as in $C'$.*

Proof. Suppose, for contradiction, that such a pair exists. Let $q_0$ and $q_1$ denote the two processes that have the same state in $C$ as in $C'$. Since $C$ and $C'$ have opposite valence, processes $q_0$ and $q_1$ must be undecided in both $C$ and $C'$. Let $D$ denote the $n$-PAC object whose state may be different in $C$ than in $C'$.

Construct a run $R$ starting from $C$ as follows:

(1) First let $q_0$ take steps solo until it is about to perform a DECIDE($i$) operation on $D$ for some label $i$.
This must eventually happen, since $D$ is the only object whose state in $C$ is not the same as its state in $C'$, and all PROPOSE($-,-$) operations on $D$ return the value **done** regardless of the state of $D$.
(2) Then let $q_1$ take steps solo until it is about to perform a DECIDE($i'$) operation on $D$ for some label $i'$.
By the same argument, this must eventually happen.

Since $q_0$ and $q_1$ have the same state in $C$ as in $C'$, and propose operations on $D$ always return **done**, it is clear that there is an identical run $R'$ that starts from $C'$.

Let $C_{clash}$ and $C'_{clash}$ denote the configurations resulting from $R$ and $R'$ respectively. Since $R$ is identical to $R'$, (i) $q_0$ and $q_1$ have the same state in $C_{clash}$ as in $C'_{clash}$, and (ii) all objects except possibly $D$ have states that are the same in $C_{clash}$ as in $C'_{clash}$. Note that $q_0$ and $q_1$ are about to perform a DECIDE($i$) operation and a DECIDE($i'$) operation on $D$, respectively, in both $C_{clash}$ and $C'_{clash}$. Furthermore, since they began from $C$ and $C'$ respectively, $C_{clash}$ and $C'_{clash}$ are univalent configurations with opposite valence. There are two cases:

**Case 1.** $i = i'$.
Consider the following configurations:

- The configuration $\overline{C}$ reached from $C_{clash}$ by letting first $q_0$ and then $q_1$ perform their DECIDE($i$) operations.
- The configuration $\overline{C}'$ reached from $C'_{clash}$ by letting first $q_0$ and then $q_1$ perform their DECIDE($i$) operations.

Since $C_{clash}$ and $C'_{clash}$ are univalent configurations with opposite valence, $\overline{C}$ and $\overline{C}'$ are univalent configurations with opposite valence. However, since two DECIDE($i$) operations were performed consecutively on the $n$-PAC object $D$, $D$ is upset in both $\overline{C}$ and $\overline{C'}$. Furthermore, when going from $C_{clash}$ to $\overline{C}$ and also when going from $C'_{clash}$ to $\overline{C}'$, $q_1$ received $\perp$ for its DECIDE($i$) operation because either this decide operation upsets $D$ or $D$ was already upset. Consequently, $q_1$ has the same state in $\overline{C}$ as in $\overline{C}'$. In other words, $\overline{C}$ and $\overline{C}'$ are a pair of reachable univalent configurations with opposite valence such that (i) there is a process, namely $q_1$, that has the same state in $\overline{C}$ as in $\overline{C}'$, (ii) there is an $n$-PAC object, namely $\mathcal{D}$, that is upset in both $\overline{C}$ and $\overline{C}'$, and (iii) every object other than $\mathcal{D}$ has the same state in $\overline{C}$ as in $\overline{C}'$. This contradicts Claim 5.2.6.

**Case 2.** $i \neq i'$.
From the sequential specification of an $n$-PAC object $D$ (given in Algorithm 1), it is clear that a DECIDE($i$) operation on $D$ returns $\perp$ if either $D$ is upset, or $i$ is not equal to the value of the variable $D.L$ of the state of $D$.
Consider the state of $D$ in configuration $C_{clash}$. If $D$ is upset, then both $q_0$ and $q_1$ can perform their decide operations on $D$ and receive $\perp$. Now suppose that $D$ is not upset in $C_{clash}$, and consider the value of $D.L$ in $C_{clash}$. Since $i \neq i'$, either $D.L \neq i$ or $D.L \neq i'$. Without loss of generality, suppose that $D.L \neq i$. Let $q_0$ perform DECIDE($i$). Since $D.L \neq i$, $q_0$ receives the reply $\perp$ from $D$. Moreover, from the sequential specification of $D$ shown in Algorithm 1, $q_0$'s decide operation either causes $D$ to become upset, or it sets $D.L$ to NIL. Now let $q_1$ perform DECIDE($i'$) on $D$. Since either $D$ is upset or $D.L =$ NIL $\neq i'$, $q_1$ also receives the reply $\perp$ from $D$.
From the above, we conclude that starting from configuration $C_{clash}$, there is an order in which $q_0$ and $q_1$ can each perform their decide operation such that they both receive $\perp$ from $D$. Let $\overline{C}$ be the resulting configuration.
By a symmetric argument, starting from $C'_{clash}$, there is an order in which $q_0$ and $q_1$ can each perform their decide operation such that they both receive $\perp$ from $D$. Let $\overline{C}'$ be the resulting configuration.
Since $C_{clash}$ and $C'_{clash}$ are univalent configurations with opposite valence, $\overline{C}$ and $\overline{C}'$ are univalent configurations with opposite valence. Furthermore, since $q_0$ and $q_1$ have the same state in $C_{clash}$ as in $C'_{clash}$, and both $q_0$ and $q_1$ receive the same response in going from $C_{clash}$ to $\overline{C}$ as in going from $C'_{clash}$ to $\overline{C}'$, they also have the same state in $\overline{C}$ as in $\overline{C}'$.
In other words, $\overline{C}$ and $\overline{C}'$ are a pair of reachable univalent configurations with opposite valence such that (i) there are two processes, namely $q_0$ and $q_1$, that have the same state in $\overline{C}$ as in $\overline{C}'$, and (ii) with the possible exception of a single

$n$-PAC object, namely $\mathcal{D}$, every object has the same state in $\overline{C}$ as in $\overline{C}'$.

Let $C_1 = C$ and $C_1' = C'$. Since we have proven that Case 1 never occurs, a straightforward induction on Case 2 allows us to construct for all $j > 1$ a pair of reachable univalent configurations $C_j$ and $C_j'$ with opposite valence such that (i) there are two processes, namely $q_0$ and $q_1$, that have the same state in $C_j$ as in $C_j'$ (so they are both undecided in $C_j$ and in $C_j'$), (ii) with the possible exception of a single $n$-PAC object, namely $\mathcal{D}$, every object has the same state in $C_j$ as in $C_j'$, and (iii) $C_j$ and $C_j'$ are reached from $C_{j-1}$ and $C_{j-1}'$, respectively, via runs in which both $q_0$ and $q_1$ take at least one step. Thus, this induction constructs runs in which both $q_0$ and $q_1$ take infinitely many steps without ever deciding — a violation of the Termination property of consensus. □ Claim 5.2.7

Claim 5.2.8. *$\mathcal{D}$ is not an $n$-PAC object.*

Proof. Suppose, for contradiction, $\mathcal{D}$ is an $n$-PAC object. Recall that by Claim 5.2.3, at $C_{bi}$, all $m+1$ processes are about to perform an operation on $\mathcal{D}$.

Subclaim 5.2.8.1. *At $C_{bi}$, every process is about to perform a decide operation on $\mathcal{D}$.*

Proof. Suppose, for contradiction, that some process $p_0$ is about to perform a propose operation on $\mathcal{D}$ at $C_{bi}$. Without loss of generality, suppose the resulting configuration $C_0$ is 0-valent. By Claim 5.2.2, there must exist another process $p_1$ such that if $p_1$ takes a step at $C_{bi}$, the resulting configuration $C_1$ is 1-valent. Consider the 1-valent configuration $C_1'$ reached by having $p_0$ take a step at $C_1$. Since propose operations always return **done**, $p_0$ has the same state in $C_0$ as in $C_1'$. Furthermore, since there are at least $m+1 > 2$ processes, there exists a process $p_2$ that is neither $p_0$ nor $p_1$, and since $p_2$ has not taken any steps since $C_{bi}$, $p_2$ has the same state in $C_0$ as in $C_1'$. Thus $C_0$ and $C_1'$ are a pair of reachable univalent configurations with opposite valence such that: (i) there are two processes, namely $p_0$ and $p_2$, that have the same state in $C_0$ as in $C_1'$, and (ii) with the possible exception of a single $n$-PAC object, namely $\mathcal{D}$, every object has the same state in $C_0$ as in $C_1'$. This contradicts Claim 5.2.7. □ Subclaim 5.2.8.1

Subclaim 5.2.8.2. *If a process performs a decide operation on $\mathcal{D}$ at $C_{bi}$, the reply of $\mathcal{D}$ is not $\bot$.*

Proof. Suppose, for contradiction, that a process $p_0$ performs a decide operation on $\mathcal{D}$ at $C_{bi}$ and receives $\bot$ from $\mathcal{D}$. Let $C_0$ be the resulting configuration. Without loss of generality, suppose that $C_0$ is 0-valent. By Claim 5.2.2, there exists another process $p_1$ such that if $p_1$ takes a step at $C_{bi}$, the resulting configuration $C_1$ is 1-valent. By Subclaim 5.2.8.1, this step of $p_1$ is a decide operation on $\mathcal{D}$, so either it sets $\mathcal{D}.L \leftarrow$ NIL, or $\mathcal{D}$ is upset in $C_1$. Consider the 1-valent configuration $C_1'$ reached by having $p_0$ perform its decide operation at $C_1$. Since either $\mathcal{D}.L$ = NIL, or $\mathcal{D}$ is upset in $C_1$, process $p_0$ receives $\bot$ for this decide operation. Thus $p_0$ has the same state in $C_0$ as in $C_1'$. The rest of the proof is now as in Subclaim 5.2.8.1. □ Subclaim 5.2.8.2

Recall that a DECIDE($i$) operation on $\mathcal{D}$ returns $\bot$ if either $\mathcal{D}$ is upset, or $i$ is not equal to the value of the variable $\mathcal{D}.L$ of the state of $\mathcal{D}$. Consequently, from Subclaim 5.2.8.1 and Subclaim 5.2.8.2, every process is about to perform a DECIDE($i$) operation at $C_{bi}$, such that $i = \mathcal{D}.L$ in $C_{bi}$. So, from Claim 5.2.2, there exist two processes $p_0$ and $p_1$ such that if $p_0$ performs DECIDE($i$) at $C_{bi}$, the resulting configuration $C_0$ is 0-valent, and if $p_1$ performs DECIDE($i$) at $C_{bi}$, the resulting configuration $C_1$ is 1-valent. Consider the following configurations:

- The 0-valent configuration $C_0'$ reached from $C_{bi}$ by first letting $p_0$ and then $p_1$ perform their DECIDE($i$) operations.
- The 1-valent configuration $C_1'$ reached from $C_{bi}$ by first letting $p_1$ and then $p_0$ perform their DECIDE($i$) operations.

Since two consecutive decide operations with the same label $i$ were performed, $\mathcal{D}$ is upset in both $C_0'$ and $C_1'$. Furthermore, since there are $m+1 > 2$ processes, there exists a process $p_2$ that is neither $p_0$ nor $p_1$, and since $p_2$ has not taken any steps since $C_{bi}$, $p_2$ has the same state in $C_0'$ as in $C_1'$. Thus $C_0'$ and $C_1'$ are a pair of reachable univalent configurations with opposite valence such that (i) there is a process, namely $p_2$, that has the same state in $C_0'$ as in $C_1'$, (ii) there is an $n$-PAC object, namely $\mathcal{D}$, that is upset in both $C_0'$ and $C_1'$, and (iii) every object other than $\mathcal{D}$ has the same state in $C_0'$ as in $C_1'$. This contradicts Claim 5.2.6. □ Claim 5.2.8

By Claim 5.2.4, Claim 5.2.5, and Claim 5.2.8, $\mathcal{D}$ is neither an $m$-consensus object, nor an $n$-PAC object, nor a register. This contradicts that algorithm $\mathcal{A}$ uses only such objects. □ Theorem 5.2

By Observation 5.1(c) and Theorem 5.2, we have:

Theorem 5.3. *For all $n \geq 1$, $m \geq 2$, $(n, m)$-PAC objects are at level $m$ of the consensus hierarchy.*

# 6 SET AGREEMENT POWER DOES NOT DETERMINE OBJECT EQUIVALENCE

We now prove the main result of this paper. This proof relies on *$(n, k)$-SA objects*, which allow up to $n$ processes to solve the $k$-set agreement problem [2, 6]. With an $(n, k)$-SA object, each of $n$ processes can apply a PROPOSE($v$) operation and receive a value that satisfies the $(n, k)$-set agreement problem requirements.

*Definition 6.1.* For each $n \geq 2$, let $O_n$ be the $(n+1, n)$-PAC object.

We now define an object $O_n'$ that "embodies" the set agreement power of $O_n$. Let $n \geq 2$, and $(n_1, n_2, \ldots, n_k, \ldots)$ be the set agreement power of $O_n$. Let $C_n$ be the collection of $(n_k, k)$-SA objects for all $k \geq 1$, i.e., $C_n = \bigcup_{k=1}^{\infty} \{(n_k, k)\text{-SA}\}$. The object $O_n'$ combines all the set agreement objects in $C_n$ as follows: for all $k \geq 1$, $O_n'$ supports the PROPOSE($v, k$) operation, which redirects the operation PROPOSE($v$) to the $(n_k, k)$-SA object of $C_n$, and returns that object's response. Note that, by construction and the definition of set agreement power, $O_n'$ has the same set agreement power as $O_n$, namely, $(n_1, n_2, \ldots, n_k, \ldots)$.

By Theorem 5.3, we have:

Observation 6.2. *For each $n \geq 2$, $O_n$ has consensus number $n$.*

From Theorem 4.3 and Observation 5.1(b), we also have:

Observation 6.3. *For each $n \geq 2$, $O_n$ cannot be implemented by n-consensus objects, registers, and 2-SA objects.*

Lemma 6.4. *For each $n \geq 2$, $O'_n$ can be implemented by n-consensus objects and 2-SA objects.*

Proof. Let $n \geq 2$ and $(n_1, n_2, \ldots, n_k, \ldots)$ be the set agreement power of $O_n$. Recall that $O'_n$ can be implemented by the objects in $C_n = \bigcup_{k=1}^{\infty}\{(n_k, k)\text{-SA}\}$. By Observation 6.2, $O_n$ has consensus number $n$, so $n_1 = n$. Thus the $(n_1, 1)$-SA object in $C_n$ can be implemented by an $n$-consensus object. In addition, for all $k \geq 2$, the $(n_k, k)$-SA object in $C_n$ can be implemented by the 2-SA object. So every object in the collection $C_n = \bigcup_{k=1}^{\infty}\{(n_k, k)\text{-SA}\}$ can be implemented by an $n$-consensus object or a 2-SA object. Thus $O'_n$ can be implemented by $n$-consensus objects and 2-SA objects. □ Lemma 6.4

Theorem 6.5. *For all $n \geq 2$, $O_n$ cannot be implemented by $O'_n$ objects and registers.*

Proof. Let $n \geq 2$. Suppose, for contradiction, that $O_n$ can be implemented by $O'_n$ objects and registers. So, by Lemma 6.4, $O_n$ can be implemented by $n$-consensus objects, 2-SA objects, and registers – contradicting Observation 6.3. □ Theorem 6.5

By Observation 6.2, $O_n$ is at level $n$ of the consensus hierarchy. Since $O'_n$ has the same set agreement power as $O_n$, it is also at level $n$ of the consensus hierarchy. So by Theorem 6.5, we have:

Corollary 6.6. *In every level $n \geq 2$ of the consensus hierarchy, there is a pair of objects, namely $O_n$ and $O'_n$, that have the same set agreement power but are not equivalent.*

Corollary 6.7. *In every level $n \geq 2$ of the consensus hierarchy, there is a* deterministic *object, namely $O_n$, that has set agreement power $(n_1, n_2, \ldots, n_k, \ldots)$ but cannot be implemented from arbitrary solutions to the k-set agreement problems among $n_k$ processes, for all $k \geq 1$, and registers.*

Proof. Let $n \geq 2$ and consider the objects $O_n$ and $O'_n$. Let $(n_1, n_2, \ldots, n_k, \ldots)$ be the set agreement power of $O_n$, and therefore of $O'_n$ as well. So $O'_n$ objects and registers can solve the $k$-set agreement problem among $n_k$ processes for all $k \geq 1$. Suppose, for contradiction, that $O_n$ can be implemented from arbitrary solutions of the $k$-set agreement problems among $n_k$ processes, for all $k \geq 1$, and registers. Thus $O_n$ can be implemented from $O'_n$ objects and registers – contradicting Theorem 6.5. □ Corollary 6.7

# 7 A RELATED RESULT

Qadri posed the following question in [13]: can $(m + 1)$-consensus objects and registers implement every deterministic object at level $m$ of the consensus hierarchy? Using PAC objects, we show that the answer is no. In fact, we show the following more general result:

Theorem 7.1. *For all $m \geq 2$ and $n \geq m+1$, level $m$ of the consensus hierarchy contains a deterministic object, namely the $(n + 1, m)$-PAC object, that cannot be implemented using n-consensus objects and registers.*

Proof. Let $m \geq 2$ and $n \geq m + 1$. Consider the deterministic object $(n + 1, m)$-PAC, which by Theorem 5.3, is at level $m$ of the consensus hierarchy. We claim that the $(n+1, m)$-PAC object cannot be implemented using $n$-consensus objects and registers. Suppose, for contradiction, that the $(n+1, m)$-PAC object can be implemented using $n$-consensus objects and registers. By Observation 5.1(b), the $(n + 1, m)$-PAC object can solve the $(n + 1)$-DAC problem, thus the $(n + 1)$-DAC problem can be solved using $n$-consensus objects and registers – contradicting Theorem 4.2. □ Theorem 7.1

# 8 CONCLUSION

This paper proves that the set agreement power of an object does not fully characterize its ability to implement other objects: every level $n \geq 2$ of the consensus hierarchy has objects that have the same set agreement power but are not equivalent (Corollary 6.6). The paper also shows that every level $n \geq 2$ of the consensus hierarchy has a *deterministic* object, namely $O_n$, with set agreement power $(n_1, n_2, \ldots, n_k, \ldots)$ such that being able to solve the $k$-set agreement problems among $n_k$ processes, for all $k \geq 1$, is not enough to implement $O_n$ (Corollary 6.7). This result seems to refute a conjecture mentioned in [7], namely that the "computational power" of a deterministic object can be captured by its set agreement power.

We say that an object $O$ is *equivalent to its set agreement power* if $O$ is equivalent to the collection of objects $C = \bigcup_{k=1}^{\infty}\{(n_k, k)\text{-SA}\}$, where $(n_1, n_2, \ldots, n_k, \ldots)$ is the set agreement power of $O$. Corollary 6.6 implies that there are objects that are *not* equivalent to their set agreement power. Consider now the *subset* $\mathcal{R}$ of objects that *are* equivalent to their set agreement power. In other work [4], we use a result of [7] to prove that the restriction of Herlihy's hierarchy to $\mathcal{R}$ is *robust* in the following sense [12]: in $\mathcal{R}$, for every positive integer $n$, any set of objects with consensus number at most $n$ cannot be used to implement any object with consensus number $n' > n$. In fact, we prove the following a more general result: roughly speaking, for any integer $\ell \geq 1$, if we classify objects in $\mathcal{R}$ based on the first $\ell$ components of their set agreement power sequence (i.e., if we place in the same class all the objects whose set agreement powers are identical for the first $\ell$ components), we obtain a classification that is also robust.

In [4] we also prove that the universe $\mathcal{U}$ of all shared-memory objects contains *uncountably* many objects with distinct computational power: the equivalence relation between objects (defined in Section 1) partitions $\mathcal{U}$ into uncountably many equivalence classes. Thus, the computational power of objects cannot be fully described by a countable scheme such as a finite vector of integers.

# ACKNOWLEDGMENTS

We thank the anonymous referees for their comments and suggestions. This work was partially supported by the Natural Sciences and Engineering Research Council of Canada.

# REFERENCES

[1] Yehuda Afek, Faith Ellen, and Eli Gafni. 2016. Deterministic Objects: Life Beyond Consensus. In *Proceedings of the 2016 ACM Symposium on Principles of Distributed Computing (PODC '16)*. ACM, New York, NY, USA, 97–106. https://doi.org/10.1145/2933057.2933116

[2] Elizabeth Borowsky and Eli Gafni. 1993. *The Implication of the Borowsky-Gafni Simulation on the Set-Consensus Hierarchy.* Technical Report 930021. UCLA Computer Science Dept.

[3] David Yu Cheng Chan, Vassos Hadzilacos, and Sam Toueg. 2017. Bounded Disagreement. In *20th International Conference on Principles of Distributed Systems (OPODIS 2016) (Leibniz International Proceedings in Informatics (LIPIcs))*, Panagiota Fatourou, Ernesto Jiménez, and Fernando Pedone (Eds.), Vol. 70. Schloss Dagstuhl–Leibniz-Zentrum fuer Informatik, Dagstuhl, Germany, Article 5, 16 pages. https://doi.org/10.4230/LIPIcs.OPODIS.2016.5

[4] David Yu Cheng Chan, Vassos Hadzilacos, and Sam Toueg. 2017. On the Number of Objects with Distinct Power and the Linearizability of Set Agreement Objects. Under submission.

[5] Soma Chaudhuri. 1993. More Choices Allow More Faults: Set Consensus Problems in Totally Asynchronous Systems. *Information and Computation* 105, 1 (1993), 132 – 158. https://doi.org/10.1006/inco.1993.1043

[6] Soma Chaudhuri and Paul Reiners. 1996. Understanding the Set Consensus Partial Order Using the Borowsky-Gafni Simulation (Extended Abstract). In *Proceedings of the 10th International Workshop on Distributed Algorithms (WDAG '96)*. Springer-Verlag, London, UK, UK, 362–379. http://dl.acm.org/citation.cfm?id=645953.675630

[7] Carole Delporte-Gallet, Hugues Fauconnier, Eli Gafni, and Petr Kuznetsov. 2017. Set-Consensus Collections are Decidable. In *20th International Conference on Principles of Distributed Systems (OPODIS 2016) (Leibniz International Proceedings in Informatics (LIPIcs))*, Panagiota Fatourou, Ernesto Jiménez, and Fernando Pedone (Eds.), Vol. 70. Schloss Dagstuhl–Leibniz-Zentrum fuer Informatik, Dagstuhl, Germany, 7:1–7:15. https://doi.org/10.4230/LIPIcs.OPODIS.2016.7

[8] Michael J. Fischer, Nancy A. Lynch, and Michael S. Paterson. 1985. Impossibility of Distributed Consensus with One Faulty Process. *J. ACM* 32, 2 (Apr 1985), 374–382. https://doi.org/10.1145/3149.214121

[9] Vassos Hadzilacos and Sam Toueg. 2013. On Deterministic Abortable Objects. In *Proceedings of the 2013 ACM Symposium on Principles of Distributed Computing (PODC '13)*. ACM, New York, NY, USA, 4–12. https://doi.org/10.1145/2484239.2484241

[10] Maurice Herlihy. 1991. Wait-free Synchronization. *ACM Trans. Program. Lang. Syst.* 11, 1 (Jan 1991), 124–149. https://doi.org/10.1145/114005.102808

[11] Maurice P. Herlihy and Jeannette M. Wing. 1990. Linearizability: A Correctness Condition for Concurrent Objects. *ACM Trans. Program. Lang. Syst.* 12, 3 (jul 1990), 463–492. https://doi.org/10.1145/78969.78972

[12] Prasad Jayanti. 1993. On the Robustness of Herlihy's Hierarchy. In *Proceedings of the Twelfth Annual ACM Symposium on Principles of Distributed Computing (PODC '93)*. ACM, New York, NY, USA, 145–157. https://doi.org/10.1145/164051.164070

[13] Ammar Qadri. 2017. *m*-Consensus Objects Are Pretty Powerful. In *20th International Conference on Principles of Distributed Systems (OPODIS 2016) (Leibniz International Proceedings in Informatics (LIPIcs))*, Panagiota Fatourou, Ernesto Jiménez, and Fernando Pedone (Eds.), Vol. 70. Schloss Dagstuhl–Leibniz-Zentrum fuer Informatik, Dagstuhl, Germany, 27:1–27:14. https://doi.org/10.4230/LIPIcs.OPODIS.2016.27

[14] Ophir Rachman. 1994. Anomalies in the Wait-free Hierarchy. In *Distributed Algorithms: 8th International Workshop, WDAG '1994 Terschelling, The Netherlands, September 29 – October 1, 1994 Proceedings*, Gerard Tel and Paul Vitányi (Eds.). Springer Berlin Heidelberg, Berlin, Heidelberg, 156–163. https://doi.org/10.1007/BFb0020431

# Brief Announcement: Hierarchical Consensus

Benjamin Bengfort
University of Maryland
College Park, Maryland 20742
bengfort@cs.umd.edu

Pete Keleher
University of Maryland
College Park, Maryland 20742
keleher@cs.umd.edu

## 1 INTRODUCTION

Strong consistency in geo-replicated storage systems requires fault-tolerance that guarantees consistency during node failure and communication partitions. Widely adopted distributed consensus protocols inspired by Paxos [4] usually handle such scenarios through leader re-election or conflict detection. However, due to increased communication load and decreasing availability, these strategies scale poorly [2]. Global, strong consistency is therefore often traded for weaker, localized consistency by implementing small consensus groups to coordinate object groups or tablets.

We introduce *Hierarchical Consensus*, an approach to generalizing consensus that allows us to scale groups beyond a handful of nodes, across wide areas. Hierarchical Consensus (HC) increases the availability of consensus groups by partitioning the decision space and nominating distinct leaders for each partition. Partitions eliminate distance by allowing decisions to be co-located with replicas that are responding to accesses. Partitions are coordinated by a root quorum that guarantees global consistency and fault tolerance. Hierarchical consensus is flexible locally, but improves upon prior approaches [1, 3, 5, 6] by balancing load, allowing fast replication across wide areas, and enabling consensus across large (>100) systems of devices.

Our default use case is in maintaining *linearizablity* across `read` and `update` operations used to support a wide-area object store or file system. We consider a set of processes (replicas) $P = \{p_i\}_{i=1}^{n}$ which are connected via an asynchronous network, whose connections are highly variable. The variability of a communication link between $p_i$ and $p_j$ is modulated by the physical distance of the link across the geographic wide area. Each process maintains the state of a set of objects, $O = \{o_i^v\}_{i=1}^{m}$, which are accessed singly or in groups at a given process and whose state is represented by a monotonically increasing version number, $v$. All replicas must maintain a consistent state of object versions and version history as well as dependencies that exist between different object's versions.

## 2 HIERARCHICAL CONSENSUS

Hierarchical consensus is a leader-oriented protocol [7] that maintains multiple subquorums, each of which elects a leader to coordinate decisions. Hierarchical consensus coordinates all managed processes by organizing them into a tier of quorums such that parent quorums manage the *decision space* and leaf quorums manage *access ordering*.

Each tier implements quorums that make decisions about fundamentally different operations. Hierarchical consensus considers the decision space as disjoint subsets of the object set, where accesses are occurring. Parent quorums therefore define subquorums as time-annotated disjoint subsets of the objects they maintain, $Q_{i,e} \subset O$. The set of subquorums, $Q$, is not a complete partition of $O$, but only represents the set of objects that are being accessed at time $e$.

The hierarchical consensus algorithm starts with a root quorum whose primary responsibilities are i) the mapping of objects to subquorums and ii) the mapping of replicas to subquorums. Each instance of such a map defines a distinct *epoch*, $e$, a monotonically increasing representation of the term of $Q_{i,e}$. Decisions that require a change of the decision space or changes the mapping of objects or replicas to subquorums requires a new *epoch*. The fundamental relationship between epochs is as follows: any access that happens in epoch $e \rightarrow e + 1$ (happens before). Alternatively, any access in epoch $e + 1$ *depends on* all accesses in epoch $e$.

All accesses to an object must be forwarded to the leader of the subquorum that maintains the object. Objects that are accessed together or who have application-specific, explicit dependencies (such as the set of objects included in a transaction) must be part of the same subquorum so that local accesses are totally ordered. Dependent objects that are not part of the same subquorum require either a change in epoch or a mechanism to allow *remote accesses*, which we will discuss in a following section. Accesses in different subquorums but in the same epoch happen concurrently from the global perspective (but are non-conflicting), though accesses in a specific subquorum are totally ordered locally.

### 2.1 Elections

Upon initialization all processes are independent, though fully connected, and must self-organize into a hierarchical structure. In order to maintain high availability, all participating processes elect a subset of the replicas to form the root quorum. In order to maintain correctness, the set of processes participating in root quorum leadership elections must intersect with the set of processes chosen to assign subquorums. To guarantee the intersection, $n - q + f$ votes is required to elect the root leader where $n$ is the number of processes, $q$ is the size of the root quorum and $f$ is the number of tolerated failures. In order to minimize the number of required consensus decisions, root leader candidates propose themselves along with $q - 1$ other processes to form the root quorum after a timeout in the random interval $t_r$.

In consensus groups of dozens or scores of members, the requirements for this election require the availability of the majority of


*PODC '17, July 25-27, 2017, Washington, DC, USA*

ACM ISBN 978-1-4503-4992-5/17/07.
https://doi.org/http://dx.doi.org/10.1145/3087801.3087853

processes in the system, not a simple three or five member consensus group. In a geo-replicated environment that intends to maintain linearizability, this is an onerous requirement that prevents progress. Therefore in order to ensure root quorum availability during partitions, the root quorum may elect leaders after a candidate timeout, $t_c$ occurs without a message from the leader. Because $t_c \ll t_r$, root elections are rare and only occur at initialization, when the entire root quorum is partitioned, or during a reconfiguration of the system.

In standard leader-oriented protocols, elections only occur after nodes detect that the leader has failed. In order to detect that the entire root quorum has failed, some heartbeat mechanism between all replicas is required. Rather than a broadcast from the root quorum to all other processes in the system, heartbeats are sent from the root quorum to leaders of the subquorums. Because subquorums are composed of $q$ replicas that are also sending heartbeats, any replica assigned to a subquorum can detect root node failure. This architecture creates an intersection between the root quorums and subquorums while minimizing the number of required messages. The primary benefit is localization of decision making to stable networks, so that the entire system can make progress in a geo-replicated environment. Secondarily, load is balanced across the system.

Once replicas are communicating in a hierarchy, we can solve the intersection problem between the root quorum and subquorums by allowing replicas to *delegate* their vote (Figure 1). Initially we propose that followers in a subquorum delegate their vote to their local leader. However, this delegation cannot last an entire epoch (or the possibility exists that no epoch change decisions are possible). To solve this, followers delegate their vote for a specific number of decisions, which expire, after which all replicas in the quorum vote as a single unit until the next epoch. For simplicity, leaders of the subquorums with delegated votes are also members of the root quorum, and no additional messages are required. This might make the root quorum too large, however, therefore we propose to investigate deepening the consensus hierarchy or using subsets of subquorum leaders in the root quorum similar to root quorum election.

## 2.2 Operation

The root consensus group coordinates all decision space changes. For example, assume each of two subquorums, $Q_1$ and $Q_2$, wants to give up a portion of its existing decision space and to add objects currently mapped to another subquorum. Reallocating subquorums requires a two phase consensus decision. Both subquorum leaders send change requests to the leader of the parent quorum, which may aggregate several requests into a single namespace change. While the parent quorum gets consensus to make the epoch change, subquorums can continue operating on their own decision space. Once the parent quorum updates the epoch, it communicates the change to all affected subquorums. Each subquorum independently decides when to transition to the new epoch. Subquorums in the new epoch can only access newly-gained objects once they have been released by the objects' owners in the last epoch.

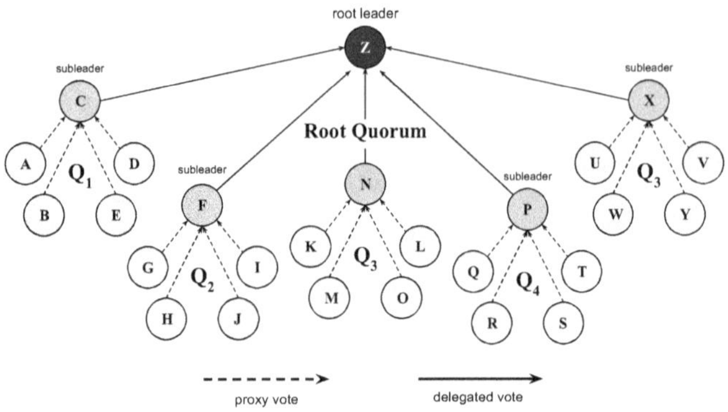


**Figure 1: Followers in subquorums guarantee intersection between the root and subquorums by delegating their votes to the subleader.**

## 2.3 Epochs and Ordering

Hierarchical consensus requires all accesses in each subquorum to be linearizable, guaranteed by serializing all accesses through the subquorum leader. Global linearizability is guaranteed by serializing epochs at the parent quorum, and limiting clients to access only one subquorum per epoch (relaxed below).

Let *interval* $i_e$ be the ordered set of accesses of the replicas in subquorum $Q_i$ during epoch $e$. We enforce linearizable ordering of all accesses in the entire system by ensuring that there must exist a total ordering of the intervals that produces the correct access results. Access results should be equivalent to any interval ordering such that all intervals in $e$ occur before intervals in $e + 1$ (our "interval ordering" invariant). This is because there is no cross-traffic between any $Q_i$ and $Q_j$, and therefore ordering interval $i_e$ before $j_e$ is exactly the same as ordering interval $j_e$ before $i_e$, for any $i$, $j$, and $e$.

The internal invariant requires $\forall_{x,y} : Q_{x,e} \rightarrow Q_{y,e+1}$. Ordering all accesses according to consensus-based log order and interval order satisfies both the internal invariant and linearizability while still allowing subquorums to operate independently within epochs. Given $Q_i$ and $Q_j$ within epochs $e = 1$ and $e = 2$, one possible interval order is $Q_{i,1} \rightarrow Q_{j,1} \rightarrow Q_{i,2} \rightarrow Q_{j,2}$.

*Remote Accesses:* By default we assume that the set of replicas *assigned* to subquorums are also disjoint, and that all accesses through a replica of a given subquorum are mapped to the local decision space. This is often reasonable. However, if an object is assigned to a decision space and a replica in another subquorum wishes to access it, the system must either disallow the access (our default approach) or take explicit notice that a dependency has been created between the subquorums.

The latter approach requires a serialization of all accesses currently within the remote quorum with respect to all accesses before the remote access in the local quorum. Assume a read access from $Q_k$ to $Q_i$ in epoch $e$; at the time of the read all accesses in $Q_i$ must $\rightarrow$ all accesses following the read. We accommodate this requirement by using the read endpoints to break interval $i_e$ into $i_{e.1}$ and $i_{e.2}$ at the point $Q_i$ receives the remote access, and interval $k_e$ into

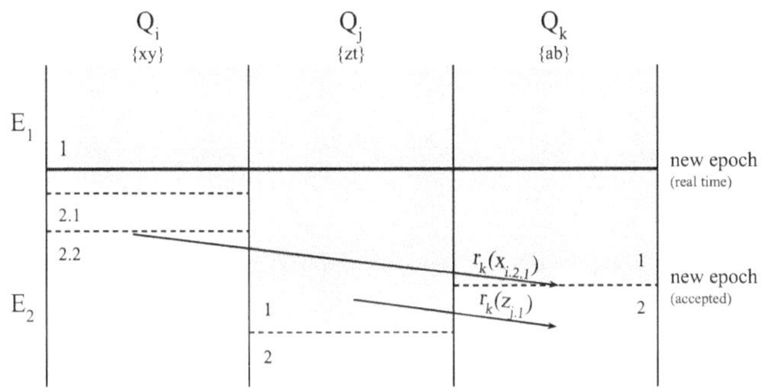


**Figure 2: The gray region shows the "fuzzy" boundary between epochs $E_1$ and $E_2$. $r_k(x_{2.1})$ reads the value of object $x$ from $Q_i$ into $Q_k$ and forces $Q_k$ to change epochs.**

$k_{e.1}$ and $k_{e.2}$ at the point $Q_k$ receives a response as shown in Figure 2. Our results are consistent with total interval ordering by incorporating $Q_{i.1} \rightarrow Q_{i.2}$. Remote accesses are expensive and the runtime system must weigh the cost of repeated remote accesses against the cost of epoch changes.

*Fuzzy Epochs:* Only subquorums involved in decision space changes need take notice of epoch changes. Other subquorums can move to a new epoch at no cost when informed of new epoch numbers from remote requests. Slow-responding subquorums therefore do not block decision space changes for other quorums. Safety is guaranteed because no writes in the next epoch depend on these writes. These "fuzzy epochs" (Figure 2) allow an epoch change to be implemented solely by the root quorum, allowing subquorums to move to the new epoch independently. This flexibility is key to coping with partitions and varying connectivity in the wide area.

*Linearizability:* The primary goal of hierarchical consensus is strong consistency in the form of a globally agreed upon linearizable ordering of read and update accesses. By combining the internal ordering invariant and subintervals on remote access, hierarchical consensus can be seen as defining the ordering of accesses in a grid (Figure 3). If traditional consensus can be seen as assigning operations to positions in a log, hierarchical consensus can be seen as assigning positions in a grid. The root quorum partitions the grid into major rows (each epoch) and major columns (each subquorum). Subquorums assign positions to cells in the current row, while remote accesses create new minor rows within each epoch. Once constructed, a global ordering is achieved that is maintained by *all* replicas, who read the grid left to right, top to bottom.

## 3 CORRECTNESS SKETCH

We assert that consensus at the leaf nodes is correct and safe because decisions are implemented using well-known leader-oriented consensus approaches. Hierarchical consensus therefore has to demonstrate linearizable correctness and safety between subquorums for a single epoch and between epochs. Briefly, linearizability requires that external observers view operations to objects as instantaneous events. Within an epoch, the subquorum coordinates read and write accesses, and thus guarantees linearizability for all replicas in that quorum. Remote accesses and the internal invariant also enforce linearizability of accesses between subquorums. Epoch

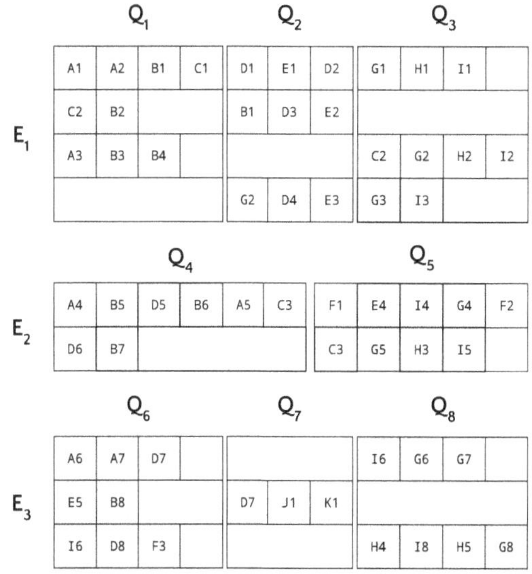


**Figure 3: Hierarchical consensus provides linearizability by ordering operations from left to right, top to bottom.**

transitions raise the possibility of objects being re-assigned from one subquorum to another, with each subquorum making the transition independently. Correctness is guaranteed by an invariant that acquiring subquorums delay accessing newly acquired objects until receiving notice that the releasing subquorum(s) have transitioned, *plus* a description of object versions at the point of this transition.

## 4 DISCUSSION

Hierarchical consensus flexibly allocates subquorums to dynamic object groupings. Multiple subquorums means both more leaders and less global communication, reducing the resource requirements for most nodes, preventing bottlenecks, and increasing throughput. Consensus decisions can also be localized to where the accesses are occurring, minimizing both distance and the effect of wide area network variability. Finally, hierarchical consensus does not arbitrarily assign consensus decisions to single objects or unrelated groups of objects, but to objects that are implicitly dependent on each other because of their associated accesses.

## REFERENCES

[1] Martin Biely, Zoran Milosevic, Nuno Santos, and Andre Schiper. 2012. S-Paxos: Offloading the Leader for High Throughput State Machine Replication. In *Reliable Distributed Systems (SRDS), 2012 IEEE 31st Symposium On*. IEEE, 111–120.
[2] H. Howard, D. Malkhi, and A. Spiegelman. 2016. Flexible Paxos: Quorum Intersection Revisited. *ArXiv e-prints* (Aug. 2016).
[3] Tim Kraska, Gene Pang, Michael J. Franklin, Samuel Madden, and Alan Fekete. 2013. MDCC: Multi-Data Center Consistency. In *Proceedings of the 8th ACM European Conference on Computer Systems*. ACM, 113–126.
[4] Leslie Lamport. 2001. Paxos Made Simple. *ACM Sigact News* 32, 4 (2001), 18–25.
[5] Yanhua Mao, Flavio Paiva Junqueira, and Keith Marzullo. 2008. Mencius: Building Efficient Replicated State Machines for WANs. In *OSDI*, Vol. 8. 369–384.
[6] Iulian Moraru, David G. Andersen, and Michael Kaminsky. 2013. There Is More Consensus in Egalitarian Parliaments. In *Proceedings of the Twenty-Fourth ACM Symposium on Operating Systems Principles*. ACM, 358–372.
[7] Diego Ongaro and John Ousterhout. 2014. In Search of an Understandable Consensus Algorithm. In *2014 USENIX Annual Technical Conference (USENIX ATC 14)*. 305–319.

# Brief Announcement: Statement Voting and Liquid Democracy

Bingsheng Zhang*
School of Computing and Communications
Lancaster University, UK
b.zhang2@lancaster.ac.uk

Hong-sheng Zhou
Department of Computer Science
Virginia Commonwealth University, USA
hszhou@vcu.edu

## ABSTRACT

The existing (election) voting systems, e.g., representative democracy, have many limitations and often fail to serve the best interest of the people in collective decision making. To address this issue, the concept of liquid democracy has been emerging as an alternative decision making model to make better use of "the wisdom of crowds". Very recently, a few liquid democracy implementations, e.g. Google Votes and Decentralized Autonomous Organization (DAO), are released; however, those systems only focus on the functionality aspect, as no privacy/anonymity is considered.

In this work, we, for the first time, provide a rigorous study of liquid democracy under the Universal Composability (UC) framework. In the literature, liquid democracy was achieved via two separate stages – delegation and voting. We propose an efficient liquid democracy e-voting scheme that unifies these two stages. At the core of our design is a new voting concept called *statement voting*, which can be viewed as a natural extension of the conventional voting approaches. We remark that our statement voting can be extended to enable more complex voting and generic ledger-based non-interactive multi-party computation. We believe that the statement voting concept opens a door for constructing a new class of e-voting schemes.

## CCS CONCEPTS

•**Security and privacy** → *Public key encryption; Mathematical foundations of cryptography; Distributed systems security;*

## KEYWORDS

E-voting, UC, Liquid democracy, Statement Voting

## 1 INTRODUCTION

Elections/Referendums provide people in each society with the opportunity to express their opinions in the collective decision making process. The existing election/voting systems can be mainly divided into two types, direct democracy and representative democracy. Although the former one treats every voter equally, it is not scalable; therefore, the latter one is widely used in most countries. However, representative democracy has many limitations and it often fails to serve the best interest of the people. For example, to make correct decisions, the voters have to invest tremendous effort to analyze the issues. The cost of identifying the best voting strategy is high, even if we assume that the voter has collected accurate information. What's worse, misinformation campaigns often influence the voters to select certain candidates which could be against the voters' own interests. In the past decades, the concept of liquid democracy [6] has been emerging as an alternative decision making model to make better use of collective intelligence. Liquid democracy is a hybrid of direct democracy and representative democracy, where the voters can either vote directly on issues, or they can delegate their votes to representatives who vote on their behalf. Due to its advantages, liquid democracy has received high attentions since the spread of its concept; however, there is no satisfactory solution in the form of either paper-voting or e-voting yet[1]. Is it possible to introduce new technologies to circumvent the implementation barriers to liquid democracy?

## 2 A NEW CONCEPT

We could approach the above problem via multiple angles. In this paper, we propose a new and clean concept: *statement voting*. Statement voting can be viewed as a natural extension of traditional candidate voting. Instead of defining a fixed election candidate, each voter can define a statement in his or her ballot but leave the vote "undefined" during the voting phase. During the tally phase, the (conditional) actions expressed in the statement will be carried out to determine the final vote. Single Transferable Vote (STV) is a special case of statement voting, where the voters rank the election candidates instead of naming only one candidate in their ballots. The ranked candidate list together with the STV tally rule can be viewed as an outcome-dependent statement. Roughly speaking, the statement declares that if my favorite candidate has already won or has no chance to win, then I would like to vote for my second favorite candidate, and so on. In terms of liquid democracy, the vote delegation can be expressed as a target-dependent statement, where a voter can define that his/her ballot is the same as the target voter's ballot. Of course, the target voter can also state whether he/she is willing to be delegated in the ballot. To obtain the basic intuition, let's first leave privacy aside and consider the following toy example.

*Example:* Each ballot is in the form of $(\mathsf{ID}, \mathtt{action}, \mathsf{target})$. If a voter $\mathsf{V}_i$ is willing to be delegated, he/she sets $\mathsf{ID} := \mathsf{V}_i$; otherwise, sets $\mathsf{ID} := \perp$. If $\mathsf{V}_i$ wants to delegate his/her vote to another voter $\mathsf{V}_j$, then the ballot is $B := (\mathsf{ID}, \mathtt{delegate}, \mathsf{V}_j)$. If $\mathsf{V}_i$ wants to directly

*This work is partially supported by EPSRC IoT Security Research Hub, EP/N023234/1.


*PODC '17, July 25-27, 2017, Washington, DC, USA*

ACM ISBN 978-1-4503-4992-5/17/07.
http://dx.doi.org/10.1145/3087801.3087868

[1]All the existing liquid democracy implementations, e.g., Google Votes and Decentralized Autonomous Organization (DAO) do not consider privacy/anonymity. This drawback prevents them from being used in serious elections. Here, we note that straightforword blockchain-based solutions cannot provide good privacy in practice. Although some blockchains such as Zerocash [1] can be viewed as a global mixer, they implicitly require anonymous channels. While in practice, all the implementations of anonymous channels suffer from time leakage, i.e., the user's ID is only hidden among the other users who are also using the system at the same time. Subsequently, the adversary can easily identify the user during quiet hours.

vote for $v_i$, then the ballot is $B := (\mathsf{ID}, \mathtt{vote}, v_i)$. Suppose there are seven ballots: $B_1 := (\mathsf{V}_1, \mathtt{delegate}, \mathsf{V}_7)$, $B_2 := (\mathsf{V}_2, \mathtt{vote}, v_2)$, $B_3 := (\mathsf{V}_3, \mathtt{vote}, v_3)$, $B_4 := (\perp, \mathtt{vote}, v_4)$, $B_5 := (\mathsf{V}_5, \mathtt{delegate}, \mathsf{V}_4)$, $B_6 := (\perp, \mathtt{delegate}, \mathsf{V}_3)$ and $B_7 := (\mathsf{V}_7, \mathtt{delegate}, \mathsf{V}_3)$. Here, the effective vote of $B_1$ is defined by $B_7$, which is further defined by $B_3$; note that $B_3$ votes for $v_3$; that means, $B_7$ votes for $v_3$ by following $B_3$. Now let's consider $B_6$: $B_6$ follows $B_3$; however, $B_6$ is not willing to be followed by anyone; as a result, $B_6$ also votes for $v_3$. Finally, let's consider $B_5$: $B_5$ follows $B_4$; however, $B_4$ is not willing to be followed by anyone; as a consequence, $B_5$ is re-defined as blank ballot, $\perp$. After interpreting the delegation statements, the final votes are $(v_3, v_2, v_3, v_4, \perp, v_3, v_3)$.

Careful readers may wonder why this type of natural voting idea has never appeared in the *physical* world. Indeed, it is typically not available in the real life. Different from the toy example, in the reality, the voters care about privacy and anonymity. To ensure anonymity, the voters are not willing to leave their identities in the ballots. If no identities (or equivalences) are included in the ballots, then it is difficult for voters to "follow" other voters' choices. The election committees might assign each voter a temporal ID to achieve anonymity, but a voter needs to obtain the target voter's temporal ID in order to delegate his vote. This requires secure peer-to-peer channels among all the voters, which is not practical. In "our design" paragraph in the Introduction, we will present the first *digital* construction for implementing full-fledged liquid democracy.

# 3 MODELING LIQUID DEMOCRACY VOTING

We for the first time provide a rigorous modeling for liquid democracy voting. More concretely, we model liquid democracy voting in the well-known Universal Composability (UC) framework, via an ideal functionality $\mathcal{F}_{\text{LIQUID}}$. The functionality interacts with a set of voters, trustees, and an auditor, and consists of preparation phase, voting/delegation phase, and tally phase. During the preparation phase, the trustees need to indicate their presence to $\mathcal{F}_{\text{LIQUID}}$, and the election/voting will not start until all the trustees have participated the preparation. During the voting/delegation phase, each voter can either directly vote for the candidate(s) or delegate his vote to another voter. In addition, each voter can use a flag $\alpha$ to indicate whether he is willing to be delegated. Note that, when all the trustees are corrupted, $\mathcal{F}_{\text{LIQUID}}$ leaks the voters' ballots to the adversary.

To model the privacy of mixing type of e-voting, we let $\mathcal{F}_{\text{LIQUID}}$ replace each voter's ID with a pseudonym. The functionality $\mathcal{F}_{\text{LIQUID}}$ then sorts the anonymized ballots lexicographically to hide the order correspondence and reveal them to the adversary. Note that this type of information leakage is consistent with the conventional paper-based voting system, where a voter submits his ballot to a ballot box and the ballot is mixed together with the other voters' ballots. To model end-to-end verifiability, we introduce an auditor Au who will verify whether the election result is mis-presented. Note that the auditor can be performed by any party, and here we model auditor as a single entity for simplicity.

We emphasize that in practice, virtually all threshold cryptographic systems suffer from selective failure attacks; namely, during the opening process of a threshold cryptographic system, the last several share holders can jointly see the content to be opened themselves before hand. Hence, they can decide if they want to

**Functionality $\mathcal{F}_{\text{LIQUID}}$**

The functionality $\mathcal{F}_{\text{LIQUID}}$ interacts with a set of voters $\mathbb{V} := \{\mathsf{V}_1, \ldots, \mathsf{V}_n\}$, a set of trustees $\mathbb{T} := \{\mathsf{T}_1, \ldots, \mathsf{T}_k\}$, an auditor Au, and the adversary $\mathcal{S}$. Let $\mathbb{V}_{\text{honest}}$, $\mathbb{V}_{\text{corrupt}}$ and $\mathbb{T}_{\text{honest}}$, $\mathbb{T}_{\text{corrupt}}$ denote the set of honest/corrupt voters and trustees, respectively. $\mathcal{F}_{\text{LIQUID}}$ is parameterized by an algorithm TallyProcess, a table Tab, and variables *result*, $T_1$, $T_2$, $T_3$, and $B_i$ for all $i \in [n]$.

Initially, set $result := \emptyset$, $T_1 := \emptyset$, $T_2 := \emptyset$, $T_3 := \emptyset$; for $i \in [n]$, set $B_i := \emptyset$.

**Preparation:**

(1) Upon receiving input (InitialTrustee, sid) from the trustee $\mathsf{T}_j \in \mathbb{T}$, set $T_1 := T_1 \cup \{\mathsf{T}_j\}$, and send a notification message (InitialTrusteeNotify, sid, $\mathsf{T}_j$) to the adversary $\mathcal{S}$.

(2) Upon receiving input (InitialVoter, sid, $\eta$) from the voter $\mathsf{V}_i \in \mathbb{V}$, if $|T_1| < k$, ignore the input.
Otherwise, send (InitialVoterNotify, sid, $\mathsf{V}_i$) to the adversary $\mathcal{S}$. If $|\mathbb{T}_{\text{corrupt}}| = k$, then additionally send a message (DelLeak, sid, $\mathsf{V}_i$, $\eta$) to the adversary $\mathcal{S}$.
Upon receiving (VoterID, sid, $\mathsf{V}_i$, $w_i$) from $\mathcal{S}$,
if $\mathsf{V}_i \in \mathbb{V}_{\text{corrupt}}$, then set $\mathsf{Tab}[i] := w_i$;
otherwise, if $\mathsf{V}_i \in \mathbb{V}_{\text{honest}}$ and $\eta = 0$, then set $\mathsf{Tab}[i] := \perp$;
else, generate random temporal ID $w'_i \leftarrow \{0,1\}^\lambda$, and set $\mathsf{Tab}[i] := w'_i$.

**Voting/Delegation:**

(1) Upon receiving input (Delegate, sid, $\mathsf{V}_j$) from the voter $\mathsf{V}_i \in \mathbb{V}$, if $|T_1| < k$, ignore the input. Otherwise, record $B_i := (\mathsf{Tab}[i], \mathtt{delegate}, \mathsf{Tab}[j])$; send a message (ExecuteNotify, sid, $\mathsf{V}_i$) to the adversary $\mathcal{S}$. If $|\mathbb{T}_{\text{corrupt}}| = k$, then additionally send a message (Leak, sid, $\mathsf{V}_i$, Delegate, $\mathsf{V}_j$) to the adversary $\mathcal{S}$.

(2) Upon receiving input (Vote, sid, $v_i$) from the the voter $\mathsf{V}_i \in \mathbb{V}$, where $v_i \in \mathcal{V}$ and $\mathcal{V}$ contains all possible votes, if $|T_1| < k$, ignore the input. Otherwise, record $B_i := (\mathsf{Tab}[i], \mathtt{vote}, v_i)$; send a message (ExecuteNotify, sid, $\mathsf{V}_i$) to the adversary $\mathcal{S}$. If $|\mathbb{T}_{\text{corrupt}}| = k$, then additionally send a message (Leak, sid, $\mathsf{V}_i$, Vote, $v_i$) to the adversary $\mathcal{S}$.

**Tally:**

(1) Upon receiving input (Mix, sid) from the the trustee $\mathsf{T}_j \in \mathbb{T}$, set $T_2 := T_2 \cup \{\mathsf{T}_j\}$. Send a notification message (MixNotify, sid, $\mathsf{T}_j$) to the adversary $\mathcal{S}$. If $|T_2| = k$, do
 - For $i \in [n]$, if $B_i$ is not defined, set $B_i := (\perp, \mathtt{vote}, \perp)$.
 - Sort $(B_1, \ldots, B_n)$ lexicographically to form a new ballot vector $(\tilde{B}_1, \ldots, \tilde{B}_n)$.

(2) Upon receiving input (Tally, sid) from the trustee $\mathsf{T}_j \in T_2$. Otherwise, set $T_3 := T_3 \cup \{\mathsf{T}_j\}$.
Send a notification message (TallyNotify, sid, $\mathsf{T}_j$) to $\mathcal{S}$.

(3) If $|T_3 \cap \mathbb{T}_{\text{honest}}| + |\mathbb{T}_{\text{corrupt}}| = k$,
send (Reveal, sid, $(\tilde{B}_1, \ldots, \tilde{B}_n)$) to $\mathcal{S}$.

(4) If $|T_3| = k$,
compute $result \leftarrow \mathsf{TallyProcess}((\tilde{B}_1, \ldots, \tilde{B}_n), \mathsf{Tab})$.

(5) Upon receiving input (ReadResult, sid) from a voter $\mathsf{V}_i \in \mathbb{V}$, if $result = \emptyset$, ignore the input.
Else, return (ResultReturn, sid, *result*) to $\mathsf{V}_i$.

**Figure 1: The voting functionality.**

actually open the content. However, surprisingly, this subtle issue was rarely modeled in the literature. For instance, the only previously known e-voting functionality [7] fails to address it. During the tally phase, the tally will be released if all the trustees agree to proceed. The formal description of the ideal functionality is depicted in Fig. 1 and Fig. 2.

TallyProcess

**Input:** a set of ballots $\mathcal{B} := (B_1, \ldots, B_n)$ and a set of voter labels $\mathcal{L} := (\mathsf{V}_1, \cdots, \mathsf{V}_n)$

**Output:** the tally result *result*

**Label Check:**

- Check the uniqueness of each label in $\mathcal{L}$. If there exist $i_1, \ldots, i_t \in [n]$, $i_1 \neq i_2 \neq \cdots \neq i_t$ s.t. $V_{i_1} = V_{i_2} = \cdots = V_{i_t}$, then replace all the labels $V_{i_1}, \ldots, V_{i_t}$ in $\mathcal{B}$ with $\perp$.

**Delegation statement interpretation:**

- For each ballot $B_i \in \mathcal{B}$, parse $B_i$ in form of either $(\mathsf{V}_i, \mathtt{delegate}, \mathsf{V}_j)$ or $(\mathsf{V}_i, \mathtt{vote}, v_i)$ and do the following:
  - If $B_i$ is in form of $(\mathsf{V}_i, \mathtt{delegate}, \mathsf{V}_j)$ and $\mathsf{V}_j \neq \perp$, try to locate a ballot $B_j$ in form of $(\mathsf{V}_j, \cdot, \cdot)$. If founded, replace $B_i := B_j$; otherwise, if $B_i$ is in form of $(\mathsf{V}_i, \mathtt{delegate}, \perp)$ set $B_i := (\mathsf{V}_i, \mathtt{vote}, \perp)$.
  - Repeat the above step, until $B_i$ is in form of $(\cdot, \mathtt{vote}, \cdot)$. If there is a delegation loop, define $B_i := (\perp, \mathtt{vote}, \perp)$.
- Denote the processed ballot set as $\mathcal{B}' := (B'_1, \ldots, B'_n)$.

**Tally computation:**

- Compute and return *result* $\leftarrow \mathsf{TallyAlg}(B'_1, \ldots, B'_n)$, where $\mathsf{TallyAlg}(\cdot)$ is the original tally algorithm.

**Figure 2: The extended tally processing algorithm.**

## 4 OUR DESIGN

Our toy example shows that it is possible to interpret the delegation statement by extending the tally algorithm. However, it is not immediately obvious about how to apply the same technique in conjunction with privacy. Before the voting/delegation phase, each voter can pick a temporal ID. However, the main challenge here is to distribute the temporal ID to the ones who need. The same as all existing end-to-end verifiable e-voting schemes, our design requires a publicly accessible consistent bulletin board, modeled as global functionality $\bar{\mathcal{G}}_{\rm BB}$. We let the voters post the re-randomizable RCCA encryption of their temporal ID on the $\bar{\mathcal{G}}_{\rm BB}$. If voter $\mathsf{V}_i$ wants to delegate his ballot to voter $\mathsf{V}_j$, he can include a re-randomized ciphertext of $\mathsf{V}_j$'s temporal ID. More specifically, $\mathsf{V}_i$ sets his ballot as $B_i := (w_i, \mathtt{delegate}, W_j)$, if he wants to delegate to $\mathsf{V}_j$; or he sets $B_i := (w_i, \mathtt{vote}, v_i)$, if he wants to vote for $v_i$; here $w_i$ is $\mathsf{V}_i$'s temporal ID and $W_j$ is the re-randomized ciphertexts of $\mathsf{V}_j$'s temporal ID. All the ballots will first be shuffled via a mix-net, and then all the trustees will jointly open those re-randomized ciphertexts inside the ballots. Subsequently, we can handle the delegation statement and compute the tally in the same way as the toy example. In the full version, we also show how to implement the liquid democracy voting scheme with re-randomizable threshold public key encryption (such as threshold ElGamal encryption) together with some necessary non-interactive proofs.

## 5 DISCUSSION AND FURTHER REMARKS.

In this work, we initiate the study of statement voting and liquid democracy. We remark that our statement voting concept can be significantly extended to support much richer ballot statements. It opens a door for constructing a new class of e-voting schemes. We also remark that this area of research is far from being completed, and our design and modeling ideas can be further improved. For example, if there is a delegation loop in which a set of voters delegate their votes to each other while no one votes, then what should be the "right" policy? Should the ballots be reset as blank ballots? This might not be ideal in reality. One possible approach is to extend the delegation statement to include a default vote. When a delegation loop exists, the involved ballots could be counted as their default votes. We finally remark that, voting policies can be heavily influenced by local legal and societal conditions. How to define "right" voting policy itself is a very interesting question. We believe our techniques here have the potential to help people to identify suitable voting policies which can further eliminate the barriers to democracy.

We remark that most non-trivial functionalities (including the e-voting functionality) cannot be UC-realized in the plain model [3–5]. Typically, we need trusted setup assumptions for UC secure e-voting systems, and the Common Reference String (CRS) model and the (Random Oracle) RO model are two common choices. In practice, if an e-voting system uses CRS, then we need to trust the party (parties) who generate(s) the CRS, which, in our opinion, is a stronger assumption than believing no adversary can break a secure hash function, e.g., SHA3. Therefore, we will realize our liquid democracy voting system in the RO model.

Alternative approach is as follows: we first use multiple party computation to generate a CRS; then we construct liquid democracy voting system by using the CRS. This approach has previously been used for constructing anonymous cryptocurrency Zerocash [1]; please see Ben-Sasson et al's recent effort [2]. We remark that, this approach might be problematic for cryptocurrency systems: typically a cryptocurrency system will last for many years and it is very difficult to ensure there is no attack on the CRS during this long time period. Interestingly, this limitation does not apply to liquid democracy voting systems. If there is an issue with the current CRS, we can use MPC to generate a new CRS.

## REFERENCES


[1] Eli Ben-Sasson, Alessandro Chiesa, Christina Garman, Matthew Green, Ian Miers, Eran Tromer, and Madars Virza. 2014. Zerocash: Decentralized Anonymous Payments from Bitcoin. In *2014 IEEE Symposium on Security and Privacy*. IEEE Computer Society Press, 459–474.

[2] Eli Ben-Sasson, Alessandro Chiesa, Matthew Green, Eran Tromer, and Madars Virza. 2015. Secure Sampling of Public Parameters for Succinct Zero Knowledge Proofs. In *2015 IEEE Symposium on Security and Privacy*. IEEE Computer Society Press, 287–304.

[3] Ran Canetti. 2001. Universally Composable Security: A New Paradigm for Cryptographic Protocols. In *42nd FOCS*. IEEE Computer Society Press, 136–145.

[4] Ran Canetti and Marc Fischlin. 2001. Universally Composable Commitments. In *CRYPTO 2001 (LNCS)*, Vol. 2139. Springer, Heidelberg, 19–40.

[5] Ran Canetti, Eyal Kushilevitz, and Yehuda Lindell. 2003. On the Limitations of Universally Composable Two-Party Computation without Set-up Assumptions. In *EUROCRYPT 2003 (LNCS)*, Vol. 2656. 68–86.

[6] Bryan Ford. 2002. Delegative Democracy. Manuscript. http://www.brynosaurus.com/deleg/deleg.pdf.

[7] Jens Groth. 2004. Evaluating Security of Voting Schemes in the Universal Composability Framework. In *ACNS 04 (LNCS)*, 46–60.

# Brief Announcement: Rapid Asynchronous Plurality Consensus

Robert Elsässer
University of Salzburg, Austria
elsa@cosy.sbg.ac.at

Tom Friedetzky
Durham University, U.K.
tom.friedetzky@dur.ac.uk

Dominik Kaaser
Universität Hamburg, Germany
dominik.kaaser@uni-hamburg.de

Frederik Mallmann-Trenn
École normale supérieure, France
Simon Fraser University, Canada
mallmann@di.ens.fr

Horst Trinker
University of Salzburg, Austria
horst.trinker@sbg.ac.at

## ABSTRACT

We consider distributed plurality consensus on a complete graph of size $n$ with $k$ initial opinions in the following asynchronous communication model. Each node is equipped with a random Poisson clock with parameter $\lambda = 1$. Whenever a node's clock ticks, it samples some neighbors uniformly at random and adjusts its opinion according to the sample.

Distributed plurality consensus has been deeply studied in the synchronous communication model. A prominent example is the so-called Two-Choices protocol, where in each round, every node chooses two neighbors uniformly at random, and if the two sampled opinions coincide, then that opinion is adopted. This protocol is very efficient when $k = 2$. If $k = O(n^{\varepsilon})$ for some small $\varepsilon$, we show that it converges to the initial plurality opinion within $O(k \cdot \log n)$ rounds, w.h.p., as long as the initial difference between the largest and second largest opinion is $\Omega\left(\sqrt{n \log n}\right)$. On the negative side, we show that there are cases in which $\Omega(k)$ rounds are needed, w.h.p.

To beat this lower bound, we combine the Two-Choices protocol with push-pull broadcasting. We divide the process into several phases, where each phase consists of a two-choices round followed by several broadcasting rounds. Our main contribution is a non-trivial adaptation of this approach to the above asynchronous model. If the support of the most frequent opinion is at least $(1 + \varepsilon)$ times that of the second-most frequent one and $k = O(\exp(\log n / \log \log n))$, then our protocol achieves the best possible run time of $O(\log n)$, w.h.p. Key to our adaptation is that we relax full synchronicity by allowing $o(n)$ nodes to be poorly synchronized, and the well synchronized nodes are only required to be within a certain time difference from one another. We enforce this "sufficient" synchronicity by introducing a novel gadget into the protocol. Other parts of the adaptation are made to work using arguments and techniques based on a Pólya urn model.

## KEYWORDS

Plurality Consensus; Distributed Randomized Algorithms; Asynchronicity


*PODC '17, July 25-27, 2017, Washington, DC, USA*

ACM ISBN 978-1-4503-4992-5/17/07.
https://doi.org/10.1145/3087801.3087860

## 1 INTRODUCTION

We consider the following plurality consensus process on the clique $K_n$ of size $n$. Initially, the nodes are partitioned into $k$ groups representing $k$ colors $C_1, \ldots, C_k$. We will denote the number of nodes having color $C_j$ as $c_j$. W.l.o.g., we assume that colors are ordered in descending order such that $c_1 \geq c_2 \geq \cdots \geq c_k$.

*Synchronous Model.* In the synchronous model we assume that the protocol operates in discrete rounds. In each round, the nodes may sample other nodes uniformly at random and then simultaneously change their opinion as a function of the observed samples. One prominent example here is the Two-Choices process [2] where in each round every node samples two nodes chosen uniformly at random, with replacement. If the chosen nodes' colors coincide, then the node adopts this color.

*Asynchronous Model.* In the continuous asynchronous model, every node is equipped with a random clock which ticks according to a Poisson distribution with parameter $\lambda = 1$. Whenever a node ticks, it samples nodes uniformly at random and updates its opinion based on the sampled values.

Instead of considering the asynchronous parallel process in continuous time, we rather analyze the process in the sequential model. In this sequential model, we assume that a discrete time is given by the sequence of ticks, and at any of the discrete time steps, a node is selected uniformly at random from the set of all nodes to perform its task. The two models lead to the same run time, see [4].

### 1.1 Our Contributions

We consider a modification of the Two-Choices protocol to design an efficient distributed voting algorithm, allowing a large number of different opinions in the asynchronous settings. So far, most work in this area concentrated on the synchronous communication model. As we see below, the Two-Choices protocol has certain limitations – even in this synchronous setting.

*Limits of the Two-Choices Approach.* The Two-Choices protocol seems to be very efficient if the number of colors is two [2]. The following result can be seen as an extension of Cooper et al. [2] on the complete graph to more than two opinions.

THEOREM 1.1. *Consider the synchronous model. Let $G = K_n$ be the complete graph with n nodes. Let $k = O(n^{\varepsilon})$ be the number of opinions for some small constant $\varepsilon > 0$. The Two Choices plurality consensus process converges with high probability*[1] *to $C_1$ within $O(n/c_1 \cdot \log n)$*

[1] The expression *with high probability* means a probability of at least $1 - n^{-\Omega(1)}$.

*rounds, if the initial bias is at least* $c_1 - c_2 \geq z \cdot \sqrt{n \log n}$ *for some constant z. Furthermore, if we assume that* $c_1 - c_2 = z \cdot \sqrt{n \log n}$ *for some constant z and* $c_2 = \cdots = c_k$*, then the Two-Choices protocol requires* $\Omega(n/c_1 + \log n)$ *rounds in expectation to converge.*

Interestingly, the required initial gap does not depend on the number of opinions present. Moreover, if $c_1 - c_2 = O(\sqrt{n})$, then $C_2$ wins with constant probability. To overcome the $\Omega(k)$ lower bound in general, we combine the Two-Choices process with a rumor spreading algorithm. We first consider this approach in the synchronous setting and denote the corresponding algorithm by `OneExtraBit`. For this, we investigate a slightly modified model called the *memory model*. In this model, we allow each node to transmit one additional bit. This allows us to reduce the run time from $O(n/c_1 \cdot \log n)$ to $O((\log(c_1/(c_1 - c_2)) + \log\log n) \cdot (\log k + \log\log n)) = O(\log^2 n)$, and the dominating color still wins with high probability, while the initial bias needs only to be slightly larger.

Theorem 1.2. *Consider the synchronous model. Let* $G = K_n$ *be the complete graph with n nodes. Let* $k = O(n^{\varepsilon})$ *be the number of opinions for some small constant* $\varepsilon > 0$*. Assume* $c_1 - c_2 \geq z \cdot \sqrt{n} \log^{3/2} n$ *for some constant z, then the plurality consensus process* `OneExtraBit` *on G converges within*

$$O((\log(c_1/(c_1 - c_2)) + \log\log n) \cdot (\log k + \log\log n))$$

*rounds to* $C_1$*, with high probability.*

Coming from a different angle, essentially the same result was obtained independently by Berenbrink et al. [1] and by Ghaffari and Parter [3]. To obtain our main result, we will generalize this approach to the asynchronous communication model.

Our main contribution is an adaptation of the algorithm `OneExtraBit` to the asynchronous setting. In the sequential asynchronous model, many nodes may remain *unselected* for up to $O(\log n)$ time, which implies that no algorithm can converge in $o(\log n)$ time. Thus, our aim is to construct a protocol that solves plurality consensus in $O(\log n)$ time. We show that if the difference between the numbers of the largest two opinions is at least $\Omega(c_2)$, where $c_2$ is the size of the second largest opinion, and $k = n^{O(1/\log\log n)}$, then our algorithm solves plurality consensus and achieves the best possible run time of $O(\log n)$, provided a node is allowed to communicate with at most constantly many other nodes in a step. Our result is formally stated in the following theorem.

Theorem 1.3. *Consider the asynchronous model. Let* $G = K_n$ *be the complete graph with n nodes. Let* $k = O(\exp(\log n/\log\log n))$ *be the number of opinions. Let* $\varepsilon > 0$ *be a constant. Assume* $c_1 \geq (1 + \varepsilon) \cdot c_i$ *for all* $i \geq 2$*, then the asynchronous plurality consensus process on G converges within time* $\Theta(\log n)$ *to the majority opinion* $C_1$*, with high probability.*

## 2 SYNCHRONOUS CONSENSUS

In order to achieve a polylogarithmic run time we combine the two-choices process with the speed of broadcasting. More specifically, the protocol consists of $\Theta(\log(n/c_1) + \log\log n)$ phases which in turn consist of two sub-phases: (i) one round of the Two-Choices process and (ii) several rounds of the so-called Bit-Propagation sub-phase in which each node that changed its opinion during the preceding two-choice step broadcasts its new opinion.

More precisely, we equip each node with an additional bit of memory which is set to True if and only if the node changed its opinion in the Two-Choices sub-phase. In the Bit-Propagation sub-phase, each node $u$ samples nodes randomly until a node $v$ with its bit set to True is found. Then $u$ adopts $v$'s opinion and sets its own bit to True, which means that subsequently any node sampling $u$ will set their bit as well.

The first sub-phase ensures that after the Two-Choices round the number of nodes holding opinion $C_1$ and having their bit set to True is concentrated around $c_1^2/n$. After the Bit-Propagation sub-phase all nodes will have their bit set, and the size of $C_j$'s support is concentrated around $c_j^2/x$, where $x$ is the total number of bits set after the Two-Choices sub-phase. This is enough to show that at the end of the phase after $O(\log(n/c_1))$ rounds the difference between $C_1$ and any opinion $C_j \neq C_1$ increases quadratically such that $c_1'/c_j' \geq (1 - o(1))c_1^2/c_j^2$. Due to the quadratic growth in the difference between $C_1$ and every other opinion, the number of required phases is only of order $\Theta(\log(n/c_1) + \log\log n)$. We assume that every node is aware of (upper bounds on) $n$ and $k$, allowing us to use these values within the algorithm, and in particular to run it in multiple phases of length $\Theta(\log k + \log\log n)$ each.

## 3 TOWARDS ASYNCHRONOUS CONSENSUS

Recall that the key to the speed of the synchronous algorithm is the combination of the two-choice process with an information dissemination process. However, this interweaving of these processes requires that the nodes execute the sub-phases simultaneously. While this is trivially the case in the synchronous setting, it is extremely unlikely in the asynchronous setting, since the numbers of ticks of different nodes may differ by up to $O(\log n)$.

To overcome this restriction, we adopt the following weaker notion of synchronicity. At any time we only require a $(1 - o(1))$ fraction of the nodes to be *almost synchronous*. This relaxes full synchronicity in three ways: First, nodes are only almost synchronous, meaning that for any two nodes their working times may differ by up to $\Delta = \Theta(\log n/\log\log n)$. Secondly, we allow $o(n)$ nodes to be poorly synchronized. Finally, we require this to hold only with high probability.

The above notion does not require the nodes to synchronize actively per se, since their number of ticks is to some extent concentrated even without active synchronization. However, it turns out that without synchronizing perpetually, the number of poorly synchronized nodes in each phase will become larger than the initial bias towards the plurality opinion $c_1 - c_2$ and could therefore influence the consensus significantly. We thus actively synchronize nodes at the end of each phase to decrease the fraction of poorly synchronized nodes such that their number is in $o(c_1 - c_2)$, resulting in a negligible influence of those nodes.

Once several technical challenges are resolved, the resulting weak synchronicity allows us to reuse the high-level structure of the synchronous algorithm. As in the synchronous case, the asynchronous protocol consists of one Two-Choices sub-phase and one Bit-Propagation sub-phase, the latter of which propagates the choices of the Two-Choices phase to all nodes in the network. In addition to these sub-phases we have a third sub-phase in which we synchronize nodes.

After executing the first two sub-phases, the relative difference between $C_1$ and any opinion $C_j \neq C_1$ increases quadratically and thus we only require $O(\log\log n)$ such phases. Each of the sub-phases has a length of $O(\log n/\log\log n)$, amounting to a total run-time of $O(\log n)$. While the asynchronous version may look very similar to the synchronous protocol, the analysis differs significantly from the synchronous case, in both approach and technical execution.

## 3.1 The Asynchronous Protocol

Our asynchronous protocol consists of two parts. The goal of the first part is to increase the number of nodes of color $C_1$ to at least $c_1 \geq (1-\varepsilon) \cdot n$ for some small constant $\varepsilon$. Once the execution of the first part has finished, the nodes execute a simple two-choices algorithm in an asynchronous manner, after which $C_1$ wins with high probability.

The algorithm operates in multiple phases. Each of these phases is split into three sub-phases. Each sub-phase consists of multiple blocks of length $\Delta$ each. During these sub-phases there are multiple blocks of instructions where nodes literally *do nothing*. These do-nothing-blocks are used, in combination with the following result on synchronicity, to ensure that a large fraction of nodes executes critical instructions at almost the same time. That is, for a large fraction of nodes we will show that these nodes execute instructions as if they were bulk synchronized, which they clearly are not.

The first phase is the Two-Choices sub-phase, which consists of two instructions, the Two-Choices step and the commit step. In the Two-Choices step, every node samples two neighbors uniformly at random. If and only if these neighbors' colors coincide, the node sets an intermediate color to the neighbors' colors. In the commit step, nodes change their color if they have their intermediate color set and then set their bit accordingly. The second phase is the Bit-Propagation sub-phase in which all nodes sample $O(\log n/\log\log n)$ times another node: As soon as node $u$ samples a node $v$ with a bit set, $u$ also sets its bit and adopts $v$'s color. At the beginning of the Bit-Propagation sub-phase, only a small fraction of the nodes will have their bit set. Their number grows to almost all nodes at the end. The crucial property is that among the nodes which have their bit set, a very large fraction supports $C_1$, while in the first round the number of nodes having their bit set may be as small as $n/k$ in expectation. By modeling the process as a Pólya urn process and by using martingale techniques, we show that the distribution of colors among the nodes which set a bit after the Two-Choices sub-phase remains almost unchanged at the end of the Bit-Propagation sub-phase – the purpose of the Bit-Propagation sub-phase is to grow the fraction of nodes supporting $C_1$. Finally, in the third phase, all nodes execute the so-called *Sync Gadget*. In this gadget, nodes adjust their *working time* in order to synchronize.

*Weak Perpetual Synchronization.* In the asynchronous algorithm, when a node is selected to tick, all operations are performed based on the node's current working time. In contrast, the real time of a node is used to always count the total number of ticks performed so far by this node. The Sync Gadget consists of a sampling sub-phase of length $\log^3 \log n$. During these ticks, every node samples a neighbor uniformly at random and collects the real time $T_u$ of the sampled neighbor $u$. Additionally, the node increments all real times sampled so far by 1 until a so-called jump step is executed. At the end of the phase at the jump step, after a proper waiting time, the node sets its working time to the median of the samples.

## 3.2 The Endgame

At the end of the first part, at least $(1-\varepsilon) \cdot n$ nodes have color $C_1$. We apply martingale techniques and drift theory to show that all nodes will have adopted $C_1$ before the first node finishes the execution of the second part of the algorithm, with high probability.

# 4 DISCUSSION

Our algorithm solves plurality consensus in the asynchronous setting in the best possible asymptotic run time in the setting where the number of opinions $k$ is bounded by $\exp(\log n/\log\log n)$. It remains an open question whether there exists an algorithm with the same run time allowing for $k = O(n^{\varepsilon})$ opinions; we note that even in the synchronous setting this questions is open.

We believe that the concept of weak synchronicity (including the Sync Gadget and the tactical waiting) as well as our analysis techniques may well prove to be of independent interest.

We showed our main result assuming independent Poisson clocks with parameter 1. However, our techniques should carry over to a much more general setting as well. Moreover, we assumed that once a node contacts another node, it receives that node's response without any delay. This assumption, however, might be unrealistic in real networks (or other models of asynchronicity). We may address this issue by extending our model to allow for response delays following some exponential distribution with constant parameter (which need not be 1, but must be independent of $n$).

Finally, we feel that the ideas presented here may be applicable to the adaptation of synchronous protocols to asynchronous settings for a much wider class of problems, perhaps even eventually leading to a generic framework.

# REFERENCES

[1] Petra Berenbrink, Tom Friedetzky, George Giakkoupis, and Peter Kling. 2016. Efficient Plurality Consensus, or: The benefits of cleaning up from time to time. In *Proc. ICALP '16*. 136:1–136:14.

[2] Colin Cooper, Robert Elsässer, and Tomasz Radzik. 2014. The Power of Two Choices in Distributed Voting. In *Proc. ICALP '14*. 435–446.

[3] Mohsen Ghaffari and Merav Parter. 2016. A Polylogarithmic Gossip Algorithm for Plurality Consensus. In *Proc. PODC '16*. 117–126.

[4] Damon Mosk-Aoyama and Devavrat Shah. 2008. Fast Distributed Algorithms for Computing Seperable Functions. *IEEE Transactions on Information Theory* 54, 7 (2008), 2997–3007.

# Brief Announcement: Object Oriented Consensus

Yehuda Afek
School of Computer Science, Tel-Aviv University
afek@tau.ac.il

James Aspnes
School of Computer Science, Yale University
james.aspnes@gmail.com

Edo Cohen
School of Computer Science, Tel-Aviv University
edocohen@tau.ac.il

Danny Vainstein
School of Computer Science, Tel-Aviv University
danvainstein@tau.ac.il

## ABSTRACT

We suggest a template that reveals the structure of many consensus algorithms as a generic procedure. The template builds on a new object, ***vacillate-adopt-commit*** which is an extension of the well known *adopt-commit* object. In addition we extend Aspnes's *conciliator* object to a new object that we call a ***reconciliator***. The consensus algorithm template works in rounds of alternating *vacillate-adopt-commit* and *reconciliator* operations. The *vacillate-adopt-commit* object observes the processors' preferences and suggests a preference output with a measure of confidence (*vacillate, adopt* or *commit*) on the preference. The *reconciliator* ensures termination, by providing new preferences for the processors. We show how several key consensus algorithms exactly fit our template. Here we demonstrate the decomposition of *Ben-Or's* randomized algorithm. The decomposition of the *Phase King Byzantine* and the *Paxos* algorithm are given in the full paper [1]. We analyze and compare our template based on *vacillate-adopt-commit* and *reconciliator* objects to previous work [3, 5], suggesting a decomposition of consensus based on *adopt-commit* and *conciliator* objects. We claim that the three return values of *vacillate-adopt-commit* more accurately describe existing algorithms.

## KEYWORDS

Distributed Algorithms; Consensus; Adopt-Commit;

## 1 INTRODUCTION

The consensus problem, introduced by Lamport, Pease and Shostak [6] resides at the heart of many distributed algorithms such as leader election, database transaction handling, resource allocation, ensuring storage replicas are mutually consistent and many more.

In the consensus protocol between $n$ processors, each with an input value, processors agree on a single common output which was the input to one of them. While consensus is trivial in a non-faulty synchronous environment, it is often more difficult in practice as most distributed networks are asynchronous and must be resilient to faults of various types.


*PODC'17, , July 25–27, 2017, Washington, DC, USA*

ACM ISBN 978-1-4503-4992-5/17/07.
http://dx.doi.org/10.1145/3087801.3087867

Gafni [5] proposed the *adopt-commit* object, an object fulfilling weaker guarantees than consensus, as a building block of consensus. Aspnes [3] further provided a detailed decomposition of consensus into *adopt-commit* and a complementary *conciliator* object which together form a generic framework describing consensus. In this work we extend these decompositions, into *vacillate-adopt-commit* and *reconciliator* objects, which describe the core of many existing consensus algorithms more accurately than the previous decomposition.

The paper is structured as follows. In Section 3, the consensus template is presented. In Section 4, we demonstrate how the decomposition applies to Ben-Or's consensus algorithm (in our full paper [1] we further apply our decomposition to the Paxos and Phase-King consensus algorithms). Section 5 explores the relation between *vacillate-adopt-commit* and *adopt-commit*, showing the latter is slightly weaker.

## 2 PRELIMINARIES

***Consensus*** guarantees the following three properties: ***Validity*** - The output value, $u$, was provided as an input to the object by some processor. ***Termination*** - The output is returned within a finite number of steps. ***Agreement*** - All processors invoking the object receive the same output value $u$.

***Adopt-commit*** is a weaker form of consensus which guarantees *validity* and *termination*. The object supports a single operation, *adopt-commit(v)* and returns some preference $u$ with a level of confidence, ***adopt*** or ***commit***. The object does not guarantee *agreement*, instead, *adopt-commit* holds the following guarantees: ***Coherence*** - If some processor receives $(commit, v)$, any other returned value (with either *commit* or *adopt*) must have the same value $v$. ***Convergence*** - If all processors invoke *adopt-commit(v)* with the same value $v$, the object must return $(commit, v)$ with the same value $v$ to all processors.

***Vacillate-adopt-commit*** is an extension of *adopt-commit* which supports a single operation, *vacillate-adopt-commit(v)* and returns some preference $u$ and a level of confidence, *vacillate, adopt* or *commit*. As opposed to *adopt-commit, vacillate-adopt-commit* adds a level of confidence and guarantees *validity, termination* and *convergence*. *Coherence* is modified to suit three levels of confidence, therefore, *vacillate-adopt-commit* guarantees ***coherence over adopt & commit*** - If any processor receives $(commit, v)$, then any other returned value is either $(commit, v)$ or $(adopt, v)$ (with the same value $v$) ***Coherence over vacillate & adopt*** - If no processor received *commit* and some processor received $(adopt, u)$, then every other processor receives either $(adopt, u)$ or $(vacillate, w)$ where $w$ may be any value.

The ***reconciliator*** object also supports a single operation, *reconciliator(v)* and only returns a preference $u$. The object guarantees that every value has a non-zero probability (that may depend on $n$, the number of processors) to be returned to all processors. In the *Byzantine* setting, the *reconciliator* guarantees to return the same value to all processors eventually (i.e., if called sufficiently many times). [1]

## 3 THE GENERIC FORM OF CONSENSUS

The thesis of this paper is that many well known consensus algorithms have the same basic structure consisting of two objects, *VAC*[2] that checks whether consensus has been reached or not and *reconciliator* that shakes up the preferences of the processors in case of a stalemate. We do not claim that this structure is necessarily better than using *AC* and *conciliators*, but that it more accurately reflects the existing structure of algorithms in the literature.

Informally, the generic consensus algorithms work in rounds. In each round, first the *VAC* is invoked to observe the system state and tell whether consensus has been reached. *VAC* returns to each processor one of three possible outputs: (1) ***(commit, v)*** which indicates that the system has reached an agreement on value v, (2) ***(adopt, v)*** which indicates that it is possible that some processors in the system have agreed on the value v, and (3) ***(vacillate, v)*** indicating that the system is in an indecisive state.

If a processor receives *(commit, v)*, it is guaranteed that no other processor receives a *vacillate* value and all outputs return with the same value, *v*. A processor receiving *(adopt, v)* is guaranteed that any other processor either received a *vacillate* value or received the same preference. Finally, if a processor receives *(vacillate, v)*, the only guarantee it has is that no other processor received a *commit* value.

We note the key difference between the *VAC* and *AC* objects. An adopt-commit object always returns a new value to be adopted by a process, but this is not consistent with the structure of many consensus protocols in the literature. Adding a third option, i.e., *vacillate*, accounts for situations where the algorithm does not force a process to update its preference.

The question is how termination of the consensus can be guaranteed if the collection of preferences is balanced and the VAC continually returns vacillate. For that purpose, the *reconciliator* is used to give each vacillating processor a new preference with a guarantee to provide a deciding set of preferences with some probability. That is, whenever a processor receives a *vacillate* value from the *VAC* object, the distributed *reconciliator* provides each processor with an alternate preference such that eventually enough processors will get the same preference leading to *VAC* eventually observing agreement. Pseudocode for the consensus template is given in Algorithm 1.

Note that *INIT* is a void function unless stated otherwise. Furthermore, note that the operation, *decide* $\sigma$, is followed by a halt operation, that is, the processor will decide upon its value and return. The argument *m* is the phase of the consensus process.

```
Consensus(v)
    m ← 0
    INIT()
    while true do
        m ← m + 1
        (X, σ) ← VAC(v, m)
        σ' ← reconciliator(σ, m)
        switch X do
            case vacillate: v ← σ'
            case adopt: v ← σ
            case commit: v ← σ and decide σ
        endsw
    end
```

**Algorithm 1:** Consensus Template

Next we prove that the template indeed achieves consensus, using the $VAC$ and *reconciliator* properties.

Lemma 3.1. *Algorithm 1 is a correct consensus algorithm.*

Proof. ***Agreement*** and ***validity*** follow from *VAC*'s *coherence* and *validity* respectively. ***Termination*** follows from the *convergence* property of the *reconciliator* object. □

## 4 DECOMPOSING BEN-OR'S ALGORITHM

In this section we show how Ben-Or's algorithm [4] can be described using our consensus template. Throughout this section the settings are asynchronous, message-passing model and the number of tolerated crash failures, *t*, is strictly smaller than $n/2$. Algorithms 2 and 3 are the *VAC*'s and *reconciliator*'s implementations, Lemmas 4.1 and 4.2 prove the implementations correctness, i.e., that they uphold the objects' guarantees.

```
Reconciliator(X, σ, m)
    return CoinFlip()
```

**Algorithm 2:** Ben-Or's *reconciliator* implementation

Lemma 4.1. *Algorithm 2 is a correct reconciliator implementation.*

Proof. ***Probabilistic convergence***: For any given value $v$, $\mathbb{P}$ (all processors finish with $v$ after the coin flip) $\geq \frac{1}{2^n} > 0$. □

Lemma 4.2. *Algorithm 3 is a correct vacillate-adopt-commit implementation.*

Proof. The proof is similar to the Ben-Or algorithm correctness proof found in the survey of Aspnes [2].

***Validity, termination*** and ***convergence*** follow easily from the implementation.

***Coherence over commit and adopt***, assume a process received $(commit, v)$. Therefore, it received more than $t$ $ratify$ messages, meaning a non-faulty processor sent out a $ratify$ message to all

[1] We note that the *reconciliator* weakens Aspnes' *conciliator* [3] definition in that it does not require *validity* (i.e., that the *reconciliator*'s returned value equals some processor's input). This is due to the fact that if all (non-Byzantine) processors' inputs are equal, the *VAC* is defined such that no processor will, anyhow, reach the *reconciliator*.

[2] Throughout the paper we abbreviate *vacillate-adopt-commit* as VAC and *adopt-commit* as AC.

```
VAC(v,m)
    send ⟨1, v⟩ to all
    wait to receive n − t ⟨1, ∗⟩ messages
    if received more than n/2 ⟨1, v⟩ messages then
        send ⟨2, v, ratify⟩ to all
    else
        send ⟨2, ?⟩ to all
    end
    wait to receive n − t ⟨2, ∗⟩ messages
    if received more than t ⟨2, v, ratify⟩ messages then
        return (commit, v)
    else if received a ⟨2, v, ratify⟩ message then
        return (adopt, v)
    else
        return (vacillate, v)
    end
```

**Algorithm 3:** Ben-Or's *vacillate-adopt-commit* implementation

other processors - therefore it is enough to show that every 2 $ratify$ messages have the same value, $v$ (since then all processes received atleast one $ratify$ message with the same value, $v$). Assume towards contradiction that this isn't the case - meaning messages $(2, v, ratify)$ and $(2, u, ratify)$ where $u \neq v$ had been sent. By the first $if$ statement, this means there's a processor that sent out both $u$ and $v$ which is a contradiction.

***Coherence over adopt and vacillate***, since every 2 $ratify$ messages have the same value, $v$, coherence follows. □

# 5 *VACILLATE-ADOPT-COMMIT* VS *ADOPT-COMMIT*

## 5.1 *Adopt-Commit* is Not Enough

The concept of decomposing consensus into separate objects is by no means original and was formally presented in [5]. Later work by Aspnes [3] described a framework of *adopt-commit* objects that detect agreement, and *conciliators* that ensure agreement with some probability. We argue that this decomposition breaches abstraction responsibilities. The consensus algorithm may be viewed as an iterative process which begins in some arbitrary state and terminates with an agreement upon a *valid* value. Under this interpretation, the framework of repetitive *adopt-commit* followed by *conciliator* fails to distinguish between the phases of the consensus procedure in which part of the participants have terminated and others have not. Due to this limitation and the *coherence* constraint, the *conciliator* must be aware of the global state of the consensus procedure in order to ensure *validity*.

In order to make our argument more concrete, we demonstrate how Ben-Or's consensus algorithm cannot be described by a sequence of *adopt-commit* alternating with *conciliator*, while it is naturally described as a sequence of repetitive *vacillate-adopt-commit* followed by *reconciliator*.

To demonstrate the problem with formulating Ben-Or's consensus protocol using a series of *adopt-commit* and *conciliator* objects,

$$U = A_{-1}; A_0; C_1; A_1; C_2; A_2; \ldots$$

(where $A, C$ denote *adopt-commit* and *conciliator* objects respectively), consider each round of Ben-Or's algorithm [4][3]. Let $P$ be a processor participating in the agreement process. $P$ experiences one of three possible outcomes: (1) not receiving any *ratify* message. (2) receiving up to $t$ *ratify* messages. (3) receiving more than $t$ *ratify* messages.

These outcomes correspond to vacillate, adopt, and commit, respectively. Option 1 fits a processor which received vacillate as it has no guarantees about other values received by other processors. Option 2 corresponds to *adopt* under the *VAC* framework, since by *coherence*, any processor that received $(adopt, v)$ is guaranteed that every other processor that received either *vacillate* or *commit*, also received the value $v$. Option 3 corresponds to *commit*, since any processor that received $(commit, v)$ is guaranteed that all other processors received either $(commit, v)$ or $(adopt, v)$.
However, using only *adopt-commit* objects is not enough in order to describe these three options.

It might be tempting to assume that two consecutive *adopt-commit* objects might resolve this entanglement as we have shown that *VAC* may be implemented using two *AC* objects.[4] We argue this is not the case, that is, we claim that the sequence of $U = A_{-1}; A_0^0; A_0^1; C_1; A_1^0; A_1^1; C_2; \ldots$ also fails to describe Ben-Or's consensus protocol. In order to describe option (2) the first *adopt-commit* must return *adopt* while the second returns *commit*. However, the decomposition framework described in [3] requires that upon reception of *commit* the processor immediately decides on the value received, whereas it is possible that in Ben-Or's protocol such a state is reached with value $u$ but a final agreement is achieved with value $u' \neq u$.

## 5.2 Relation Between *Vacillate-Adopt-Commit* and *Adopt-Commit*

In addition to the former section, we demonstrate in the full version of our paper [1] that one may easily simulate an *adopt-commit* object using a *VAC* object. On the other hand, one may successfully simulate *VAC* using two sequential calls to *adopt-commit* objects. In our opinion this further shows an inherent difference between the two objects.

## REFERENCES


[1] Yehuda Afek, James Aspnes, Edo Cohen, and Danny Vainstein. Object oriented consensus. In preparation, February 2017.

[2] James Aspnes. Randomized protocols for asynchronous consensus. *Distributed Computing*, 16(2-3):165–175, September 2003.

[3] James Aspnes. A modular approach to shared-memory consensus, with applications to the probabilistic-write model. *Distributed Computing*, 25(2):179–188, May 2012.

[4] Michael Ben-Or. Another advantage of free choice: Completely asynchronous agreement protocols (extended abstract). In *Proceedings of the Second Annual ACM SIGACT-SIGOPS Symposium on Principles of Distributed Computing, Montreal, Quebec, Canada, August 17-19, 1983*, pages 27–30, 1983.

[5] Eli Gafni. Round-by-round fault detectors (extended abstract): unifying synchrony and asynchrony. In *Proceedings of the seventeenth annual ACM symposium on Principles of distributed computing*, pages 143–152. ACM, 1998.

[6] Marshall Pease, Robert Shostak, and Leslie Lamport. Reaching agreement in the presence of faults. *Journal of the ACM (JACM)*, 27(2):228–234, 1980.


[3] We note that our description follows the presentation of Ben-Or's algorithm given in the survey paper of Aspnes [2]

[4] See [1] for detailed arguments.

# Greedy Routing and the Algorithmic Small-World Phenomenon*

Karl Bringmann
Max-Planck-Institute for Informatics
Saarbrücken, Germany
kbringma@mpi-inf.mpg.de

Ralph Keusch
Department of Computer Science
ETH Zürich, Switzerland
rkeusch@inf.ethz.ch

Johannes Lengler
Department of Computer Science
ETH Zürich, Switzerland
lenglerj@inf.ethz.ch

Yannic Maus†
Department of Computer Science
University of Freiburg, Germany
yannic.maus@cs.uni-freiburg.de

Anisur Rahaman Molla‡
School of Computer Sciences
NISER, Bhubaneswar, India
molla@niser.ac.in

## ABSTRACT

The algorithmic small-world phenomenon, empirically established by Milgram's letter forwarding experiments from the 60s [60], was theoretically explained by Kleinberg in 2000 [47]. However, from today's perspective his model has several severe shortcomings that limit the applicability to real-world networks. In order to give a more convincing explanation of the algorithmic small-world phenomenon, we study decentralized greedy routing in a more flexible random graph model (geometric inhomogeneous random graphs) which overcomes all previous shortcomings. Apart from exhibiting good properties in theory, it has also been extensively experimentally validated that this model reasonably captures real-world networks.

In this model, the greedy routing protocol is purely distributed as each vertex only needs to know information about its direct neighbors. We prove that it succeeds with constant probability, and in case of success almost surely finds an almost shortest path of length $\Theta(\log \log n)$, where our bound is tight including the leading constant. Moreover, we study natural local patching methods which augment greedy routing by backtracking and which do not require any global knowledge. We show that such methods can ensure success probability 1 in an asymptotically tight number of steps.

These results also address the question of Krioukov et al. [52] whether there are efficient local routing protocols for the internet graph. There were promising experimental studies, but the question remained unsolved theoretically. Our results give for the first time a rigorous and analytical affirmative answer.

*A full version of this paper, including all proofs and further discussion of the results, is available at http://arxiv.org/abs/1612.05539.

†Supported by ERC Grant No. 336495 (ACDC).

‡Most of the work was done while the author was at the Department of Computer Science, University of Freiburg, Germany. Research supported in part by ERC Grant No. 336495 (ACDC).



*PODC '17, July 25-27, 2017, Washington, DC, USA*

ACM ISBN 978-1-4503-4992-5/17/07...$15.00
https://doi.org/10.1145/3087801.3087829

## CCS CONCEPTS

• **Theory of computation** → *Routing and network design problems; Random network models;* • **Networks** → *Routing protocols;*

## KEYWORDS

small-world phenomenon; Milgram experiment; greedy routing; real-world networks; routing protocols; internet routing; random graph models

## 1 INTRODUCTION

The idea that everyone is connected to everybody else through six degrees of separation, also known as the *small world* phenomenon, was empirically established by the classic experiments of Milgram [60, 71]. Several random people were given a target person's name and address, and asked to send a letter to the target person by forwarding it to a personal acquaintance who is more likely to know the target person, iterating this process until the letter reached the target (or was lost). Among the more than 20% successful trials, Milgram reported an average distance of about 6. This showed not only that very short paths exist between two typical persons, but also that people are able to find them without global knowledge of the network, by greedily routing the letter.

In the last 50 years, this phenomenon inspired researchers in various disciplines such as sociology, physics, and experimental and theoretical computer science to study networks with small-world properties. The first theoretical explanation of the algorithmic small-world phenomenon was the seminal work of Kleinberg [47] who showed that greedy routing succeeds in $O(\log^2 n)$ steps on certain random graphs. However, as we will discuss in Section 1.1, his model has several severe shortcomings, that have not been resolved simultaneously in subsequent work [21, 33, 37, 58, 59]: routing succeeds only if a perfect lattice structure is contained in the network, the result is fragile with respect to small changes in the model, and the graph model is unrealistically homogeneous.

In order to give a more cogent theoretical explanation for Milgram's result, we study greedy routing in a more flexible and more convincing graph model: In *geometric inhomogeneous random graphs (GIRGs)* [17], every vertex draws independently a random position in a geometric space and a positive weight according to a power law which represents the node's influence. Two nodes are then more likely to connect if they have larger weights and if they are geometrically close.[1] We picked this model for the following reasons.

(i) GIRGs are a *natural extension of Kleinberg's model* that overcome its three main shortcomings.

(ii) Among the random graph models that have been proposed to model real-world networks, the GIRG model stands out because it not only *theoretically* reproduces structural properties of social, economical, and technological networks, but a special case of GIRGs (hyperbolic random graphs [11]) has also been extensively *experimentally validated* [11, 40, 56, 63, 69, 74]. E.g., Boguñá et al. [11] computed and studied a (heuristic) maximum likelihood fit of the internet graph into the hyperbolic random graph model, based on ideas from [49].

(iii) In general it is unclear how greedy routing generalizes to *inhomogeneous* geometric graphs. An ideal neighbor should optimize two objectives: being close to the target, and having large weight. Many possibilities have been suggested to resolve this conflict (e.g., in the physics community [44, 70]). Since GIRGs have a specific connection probability for each pair of vertices, there is a *natural interpretation of Milgram's instruction* to route to an "acquaintance who is more likely than you to know the target person" [71]: pick the neighbor most likely being adjacent to the target. Thus, Milgram's experiment has a natural analogon on GIRGs.

(iv) In the digital age, the area of routing protocols plays a more and more important role. Krioukov et al. [52] identified as a major open problem in this area "whether we can devise routing protocols for the internet that, having no full view of the network topology, can still efficiently route messages". This question stimulated further research on the embeddings from [11, 49], and by now routing on such graphs is experimentally well-studied [8–10, 24, 53, 54, 62, 63]. It turned out that greedy routing *works experimentally surprisingly well* on hyperbolic random graphs and GIRGs [53, 54, 62]. For example, the resulting greedy paths are only marginally longer than shortest paths in the network. Explaining these experimental findings theoretically was a driving question for many researchers in the theory community [16, 17, 20, 30, 39, 41, 46, 65], but it remained open.

We thus believe that studying greedy routing in GIRGs, in each step maximizing the connection probability to the target, gives a convincing theoretical explanation for Milgram's experiments, and addresses *at the same time* the question of Krioukov et al. We obtain the following results for any fixed source $s$ and target $t$ (for exact statements see Section 3).

- Greedy routing *succeeds* with probability $\Omega(1)$.

This is already surprising, as incorporating noisy positions in Kleinberg's model results in a tiny success probability, as we discuss in Section 1.1 below. The result is also best possible, as in GIRGs the target node is isolated with constant probability.

[1] Note that the geometric coordinates may capture more than just real world coordinates, like occupation and interests [57].

- A.a.s.[2], the *stretch*[3] of greedy routing in case of success is $1 + o(1)$. Hence, greedy routing is asymptotically optimal. In particular, since the average distance in the giant component of the GIRG model is *ultra-small*, i.e., $\Theta(\log \log n)$, so are the lengths of the greedy paths.

Arguably, $\Theta(\log \log n)$ is closer to six degrees of separation than Kleinberg's $O(\log^2 n)$, and average distances in modern networks are even smaller [4, 6]. All previous analyses of greedy routing in small-world models yielded at least $\Omega(\log n)$ steps, e.g. [34, 47].

- Our results are *robust* in the model parameters, i.e., they hold for all parameter choices of the model, in particular for any power law exponents in the natural range $(2, 3)$, cf. Section 1.1. Moreover, we show that nodes do not need to know exact weights and positions of their neighbors, but rather *rough approximations suffice* for all results.

Since constant success probability is too low for technical application, it is natural to ask whether there are patching methods that use backtracking to enforce success (if source and target are in the same component). We give an affirmative answer in a very strong sense:

- *Every patching method* that satisfies three natural criteria has *success probability 1* (conditional on $s$ and $t$ being in the same component), and still *has a.a.s. stretch* $1 + o(1)$.

This result gives (in our model) a strongly affirmative answer to Krioukov et al.'s question. Crucially, each node only needs to know the positions and weights of its direct neighbors and the geometric position of $t$, which we assume to be part of the message. Note that the greedy routing protocol is distributed and highly energy efficient since only one node needs to be awake at a time. Perhaps surprisingly, the same can be achieved for the patching protocols, so we can at the same time guarantee success and maintain the benefits of local protocols, with negligible additional costs.

Finally, our results explain many findings of the extensive experimental work which has been done on greedy routing in GIRGs. We postpone the discussion to Section 4.

## 1.1 Related Work and Choice of Model

*Kleinberg.* Kleinberg's model starts from an $n \times n$ lattice graph, i.e., we embed node $v = (i, j) \in [n] \times [n]$ at position $\mathsf{x}_v = (i/n, j/n)$ in the unit square and connect any two nodes $u, v$ in Manhattan distance $\|\mathsf{x}_u - \mathsf{x}_v\| \leq 1/n$ by an edge. Then we add for each node $u$ a constant number of additional long-range edges, where the other endpoint $v$ is chosen proportional to $\|\mathsf{x}_u - \mathsf{x}_v\|^{-\alpha \cdot 2}$ with decay parameter $\alpha$. This model has several shortcomings that limit the applicability to real-world networks and that are also present in subsequent work [21, 33, 37, 48, 58, 59]:

- Fragile Exponent: As shown by Kleinberg [47], his model is very fragile with respect to the decay parameter in exponent of the long-range probability distribution, since changing this distribution to $\|\mathsf{x}_u - \mathsf{x}_v\|^{-\alpha \cdot 2}$ for any $\alpha \neq 1$ increases the expected number of steps to $n^{\Omega(1)}$. This is reasonable for $\alpha < 1$, since in this regime most neighbors of most vertices lie very

[2] We say that an event holds a.a.s. if it holds with probability $1 - o(1)$ with $n \to \infty$.
[3] The stretch is the ratio of the lengths of the greedy path and the shortest path between source and target.

far and thus we cannot expect greedy routing to utilize locality. However, for $\alpha > 1$ there is no intuitive argument ruling out greedy routing in general. In particular, investigations of trajectories of bank notes in main cites of the USA suggest a value of $\alpha = 1.59 \pm 0.02$ [19].

- Perfect Lattice: Kleinberg's model assumes an underlying perfect lattice substrate. In this way, every vertex knows a priori a path to the target, which is an unrealistically strong assumption. In a more realistic model each vertex might choose a random position $\mathrm{x}_v$ in some geometric space, representing real-world coordinates, but also interests and occupation, followed by the same edge sampling procedure as in Kleinberg's model. It can be shown that in this adapted model with high probability greedy routing does not reach the target, essentially since in each step the current vertex has constant probability not to have any neighbor with smaller distance to the target. Thus, the unnatural assumption of a perfect lattice (or a similar globally known structure) is crucial for Kleinberg's result.
- Homogeneity: Kleinberg's graphs are homogeneous, i.e., all vertices have the same degree. In contrast, most real-world networks have been found to be *scale-free*, meaning that their degree distribution follows a power law $p(k) \sim k^{-\beta}$, typically with power law exponent $\beta$ in the range $(2, 3)$ [3, 27] (or at least a closely related distribution [61]).

Despite some effort to remove these shortcomings (see related work below) there is still no model which avoids all of them. Moreover, while the corresponding extensions of Kleinberg's model were developed in the context of routing protocols, GIRGs have been introduced as a model for real-world networks. Thus there is a much larger body of evidence (theoretical and experimental) that GIRGs resemble real-world networks than there is for any other graph model in this area.

*Geometric Inhomogeneous Random Graphs (GIRGs).* We now substantiate claims *(i)* and *(ii)* on page 2. Thereby, we further explain our reasons for picking the GIRG model.

*(i)* Let us first informally define GIRGs, a full definition is given below in Section 2.1. In a GIRG, each node $v$ is equipped with a random position $\mathrm{x}_v$ in an underlying geometry (for technical simplicity, we fix the $d$-dimensional torus) and with a *weight* $\mathrm{w}_v$ which is drawn according to a power law $p(w) \sim w^{-\beta}$ and represents the (expected) degree of vertex $v$ and thus its "connectedness". After drawing the positions and weights, all edges are picked independently. For two nodes $u$ and $v$, the probability $p_{uv}$ for the edge $\{u, v\}$ is increasing in the weights $\mathrm{w}_u$ and $\mathrm{w}_v$, and decreasing in $\|\mathrm{x}_u - \mathrm{x}_v\|$. More precisely, for fixed weights $p_{uv}$ is proportional to Kleinberg's distribution $\|\mathrm{x}_u - \mathrm{x}_v\|^{-\alpha \cdot d}$, where we want to choose $\alpha > 1$. In this sense, the GIRG model is a natural scale-free variant of Kleinberg's model that removes the implausible assumption of a perfect grid. As our results do not depend on the concrete choice of $\alpha$, we also overcome the problem of fragile exponents.

*(ii)* A large portion of the theoretical random graph literature of the last 10 years (e.g. [2, 5, 11, 13–17, 20, 25, 26, 29, 30, 39, 41, 43, 45, 46]) deals with the design and analysis of random graphs that have more and more of the experimentally observed properties of social, technological, and other real-world networks, e.g., sparsity, scale-freeness, small diameter, and high clustering. Most of these modern models come equipped with an underlying geometry, since locality naturally yields high clustering and, more generally, local community structure. This makes them candidates for analyzing geometric routing or other variants of greedy routing.

Since there are no comparative studies, it is hard to judge which of the proposed models is most realistic. However, GIRGs and their special case, hyperbolic random graphs, stand out, because this model has not only attracted theoretical research but has also been experimentally validated. On the theory side, it was proven for GIRGs and hyperbolic random graphs that they are sparse and scale-free [16, 30, 41], have constant clustering coefficient [17, 20, 41], a giant component and polylogarithmic diameter [16, 39, 46], and average distance $\frac{2 \pm o(1)}{|\log(\beta-2)|} \log\log n$, where $\beta$ is the power law exponent [16]. Furthermore, these graphs have entropy $O(n)$ [17], which coincides with the low entropy of the web graph [12]. Recently, researchers have started to design algorithms that run fast on hyperbolic random graphs [7, 38]. In terms of practical validation, Boguñá et al. [11] computed a (heuristic) maximum likelihood fit of the internet graph into the hyperbolic random graph model and demonstrated its quality by showing that greedy routing in the underlying geometry of the fit finds near-optimal shortest paths. This successful embedding of a real-world network validates the model experimentally, and was repeated and extended in [8, 63].

*Further Related Work.* For psychological work related to Milgram's experiments we refer to the survey by Schnettler [68]. The enormous amount of experimental and non-rigorous work on routing in real-world networks and random graphs is surveyed by Huang et al. [44]. Regarding theoretical work, a monograph by Watts summarizes the early work [72]. Let us highlight a few more recent theory papers on greedy routing and related decentralized routing schemes: Watts et al. [73] and Kleinberg [48] studied hierarchical network models that are well motivated by sociological principles. Alternatively, Fraigniaud et al. [35] augmented Kleinberg's model with long-range edges according to a power law. These approaches make the model somewhat more realistic, however, they still suffer from similar shortcomings as Kleinberg's original model, e.g., they either assume a perfect $b$-ary tree structure or a perfect lattice. On the other hand, after a long line of research [1, 28, 31, 32, 36, 55, 57] Fraigniaud et al. [34] replaced the lattice structure in Kleinberg's model with arbitrary connected base networks. They showed how these base networks can be augmented with long-range edges to make them navigable, which in the most general case means that variants of greedy routing succeed with a subpolynomial number of steps, provided that all nodes know the base network. Note that this available information is much less local than in our model, where each node only needs information about its direct neighbors. In particular, since every node knows in advance a path to the target, greedy routing succeeds with probability one. Arguably, all these networks were designed specifically for studying greedy routing, while our approach is rather to study greedy routing on a preexisting model for real-world networks. Also, none of the previous theoretical work showed ultra-small routing distance or considered patching strategies.

# 2 RANDOM GRAPH MODEL & GREEDY ROUTING

## 2.1 Geometric Inhomogeneous Random Graphs (GIRGs)

In this paper we study greedy routing in Geometric Inhomogenous Random Graphs (GIRGs), which is a model inspired by the classic Chung-Lu random graphs [22, 23]. A GIRG is a graph $G = (V, E)$ where both the set of vertices $V$ and the set of edges $E$ are random. Informally speaking, each vertex $v$ has a random position $\mathrm{x}_v$ in a geometric space $\mathbb{T}^d$ and a random weight $\mathrm{w}_v \in \mathbb{R}^+$, where the distribution of the weights follows a power law. For each pair of vertices we flip an independent coin to determine whether they are connected by an edge, where the probability to be connected increases with the weights and decreases with the distance of the vertices. We now give the formal definition of the model, following [51].

*Geometric space:* Let $d \in \mathbb{N}$ be some (constant) parameter. As our *geometric space* we use the $d$-dimensional torus $\mathbb{T}^d = \mathbb{R}^d/\mathbb{Z}^d$, which can be described as the $d$-dimensional cube $[0, 1]^d$ where opposite boundaries are identified with each other. As distance function we use the $\infty$-norm on $\mathbb{T}^d$. The choice of the geometric space is in the spirit of the classical random geometric graphs [64]. We prefer the torus to the hyper-cube for technical simplicity, as it yields symmetry. However, it is not hard to replace $\mathbb{T}^d$ by $[0, 1]^d$. Similarly, we may replace the $\infty$-norm by any other norm and obtain the same model since we allow constant factor deviations in the definition (EP) below.[4]

The set of vertices $V$ is then given by a Poisson point process on $\mathbb{T}^d$ with intensity $n$.[5] In particular, the expected number of vertices is $n$, and the positions of all vertices are uniformly at random in $\mathbb{T}^d$.

*Weights:* Let $2 < \beta < 3$ and $\mathrm{w}_{\min} > 0$ be fixed constants. Then for each vertex $v \in V$ independently we draw a weight according to a power law, i.e., with probability density function

$$f(w) := \Theta(w^{-\beta})$$

for $w \geq \mathrm{w}_{\min}$ and $f(w) = 0$ for $w < \mathrm{w}_{\min}$. Note that the probability that a random vertex has weight at least $w$ is proportional to $w^{1-\beta}$. The choice of the power law parameter ($2 < \beta < 3$) is standard [27].

*Edges:* Given the vertex set $V$ and all positions and weights, we connect vertices $u \neq v$ independently with probability $p_{uv}$, which depends on the weights $\mathrm{w}_u, \mathrm{w}_v$ and on the distance $\|\mathrm{x}_u - \mathrm{x}_v\|$. We require for some constant $\alpha > 1$ the following edge probability condition:

$$p_{uv} = \Theta\Big(\min\Big\{\|\mathrm{x}_u - \mathrm{x}_v\|^{-\alpha d} \cdot \big(\tfrac{\mathrm{w}_u\mathrm{w}_v}{n}\big)^{\alpha}, 1\Big\}\Big). \qquad \text{(EP)}$$

In particular, there exists a constant $c_1 > 0$ such that $p_{uv} = \Theta(1)$ if $u$ and $v$ are very close to each other, i.e., $\|\mathrm{x}_u - \mathrm{x}_v\|^d \leq c_1 \frac{\mathrm{w}_u\mathrm{w}_v}{n}$.

[4]Note that when embedding a real world network into the GIRG model, e.g., as in [11], the real world coordinates do not necessarily resemble the coordinates in the geometric space. It rather resembles an ambient space which additionally includes more parameters such as hobbies.

[5]A very similar model is obtained by placing $n$ points uniformly at random in $\mathbb{T}^d$, e.g. [17]. We prefer the Poisson point process since then the number of vertices in disjoint regions of $\mathbb{T}^d$ is independent. Also, all results are still valid for a non-uniform distribution, as long as the intensity fluctuates at most by constant factors.

The parameter $\alpha$ determines how fast the connection probability decays with increasing distance of the nodes. We also allow the *threshold case* $\alpha = \infty$, cf. [51]. The formula (EP) is chosen such that the expected degree of a vertex of weight $w$ is $\Theta(w)$. Moreover, for two vertices $u$ and $v$ of fixed weights, but with random positions, the connection probability is

$$\mathbb{E}_{\mathrm{x}_u,\mathrm{x}_v}[p_{uv} \mid \mathrm{w}_u, \mathrm{w}_v] = \Theta(\min\{\tfrac{\mathrm{w}_u\mathrm{w}_v}{n}, 1\}), \qquad (1)$$

as in the classic Chung-Lu random graphs.

Summarizing, the free parameters of the model are the intensity (i.e., the expected number of vertices) $n$, the minimum weight $\mathrm{w}_{\min}$, the power law parameter $2 < \beta < 3$, the dimension $d \in \mathbb{N}$, the decay parameter $\alpha > 1$, and the actual probability functions $p_{uv}$ which satisfy (*EP*).

## 2.2 Greedy routing

*Routing protocol:* We will evaluate the performance of greedy routing in a GIRG, which is the following process. A message $m$ should be sent from a starting vertex $s$ (source) to a target vertex $t$. The *address* of every vertex $v$ is the pair $(\mathrm{x}_v, \mathrm{w}_v)$. Then the routing proceeds in rounds and in every hop, the packet is sent from the current vertex $v$ to a neighbor $u$ which maximizes a given objective function $\phi$, cf. below. When a dead end is reached, the process stops and the packet is dropped. If $u = t$, then we say that the routing was *successful*. A pseudocode description is given with Algorithm 1 below.

**Algorithm 1** Greedy Routing Algorithm

```
function GREEDY(s, m)
    if s == t then deliver message m
    else
        v ← argmax{φ(u) | u ∈ Γ(s)}
        if φ(v) > φ(s) then GREEDY(v, m)
        else return failure
```

*Objective function:* It is natural and in spirit of Milgram's experiments [60, 71] that in every round the packet is sent to the neighbor $v$ which maximizes $p_{vt}$. Note that maximizing $p_{vt}$ is equivalent to maximizing the objective function

$$\phi(v) := \frac{\mathrm{w}_v}{n\|\mathrm{x}_v - \mathrm{x}_t\|^d}.$$

We observe that the target vertex $t$ globally maximizes $\phi$, which is a necessary condition for any reasonable objective function. In particular, if $\{s, t\} \in E$, then the routing will send the packet directly to the target.

We emphasize that each vertex only needs to know the positions and weights of its direct neighbors, and the geometric position of $t$ (which we assume to be part of the message). This goes in line with Milgram's experiment, where participants knew geometric positions and professions of their acquaintances and made their choices accordingly [60, 71].

## 3 RESULTS

We assume source $s$ and target $t$ to be random, but all results also hold if we condition on specific values for $x_s, x_t, w_s, w_t$. Proof sketches and intuitive reasons can be found in Section 6, for the formal proofs we defer to the full version [18].

*Success Probability.* As our first result we show that greedy routing from $s$ to $t$ succeeds with constant probability.

THEOREM 3.1. *Greedy routing succeeds with probability* $\Omega(1)$.

$\Theta(1)$ is in general the best possible success probability. Indeed, since in (EP) we allow any connection probability $\Theta(1)$ even if two vertices are very close, greedy routing may end in a vertex which is extremely close to $t$ but is not adjacent to $t$. If we assume connection probability 1 in such cases, then we get a better success probability. More precisely, assume that there is a constant $c_1 > 0$ such that the following condition holds:

$$p_{uv} = 1, \quad \text{if} \quad \|x_u - x_v\|^d \le c_1 \frac{w_u w_v}{n}. \qquad \text{(EP*)}$$

Then the failure probability decays exponentially with $w_{\min}$.[6]

THEOREM 3.2. *Suppose that* (EP*) *holds in addition to the model assumptions. Then:*

*(i) Greedy routing succeeds with probability* $1 - O\big(e^{-w_{\min}^{\Omega(1)}}\big)$, *where the hidden constants do not depend on* $w_{\min}$.
*(ii) If* $w_s = \omega(1)$ *and* $w_t = \omega(1)$, *then greedy routing succeeds a.a.s.*

The first part of this theorem is also almost-optimal. Indeed, the degree of a vertex $v \in V$ is distributed as a Poisson random variable with mean $\Theta(w_v)$, therefore $v$ is isolated with probability $O(e^{-\Theta(w_v)})$. If for example the weight of the target node is in the order of the minimum degree, i.e., $w_t = \Theta(w_{\min})$, then the success probability cannot be higher than $1 - O(e^{-\Theta(w_{\min})})$.

*Stretch.* One of the most crucial efficiency measures for routing protocols is the stretch, i.e., the ratio of the routing path's length compared to the length of a shortest path. Clearly, routing can only succeed if the source $s$ and the target $t$ are in the same component. In [16] it was proven that a.a.s. a GIRG possesses a giant connected component of linear size in which the average distance is $\frac{2\pm o(1)}{|\log(\beta-2)|} \log\log n$. We show that the number of steps of the greedy routing algorithm (until either the target is found or the routing stops) is a.a.s. equal to shortest path, up to a stretch of $1 + o(1)$.

THEOREM 3.3. *A.a.s. the number of steps needed by the greedy routing is at most* $\frac{2+o(1)}{|\log(\beta-2)|} \log\log n$.

Note that Theorems 3.1 and 3.3 together imply that even if we condition on greedy routing being successful, then still a.a.s. greedy routing needs at most $\frac{2+o(1)}{|\log(\beta-2)|} \log\log n$ steps. Since this agrees with the average distance in the giant component, it is optimal. In particular, for two random vertices $s, t$, if greedy routing between $s$ and $t$ is successful then a.a.s. the stretch is $1 + o(1)$.[7]

*Patching.* As outlined in the introduction, greedy routing may have practical applications. For these applications, it is not acceptable that the algorithm simply fails if it enters a local maximum. Therefore, several patching methods have been proposed. We show that *any* patching algorithm $A$ is efficient if it satisfies the following three basic conditions. For further discussions, see Section 5.

(P1) *(Greedy choices.)* If $A$ is at a vertex $v$ and visits an unexplored neighbor then it must choose the unexplored neighbor of largest objective. If $A$ visits a vertex $v$ for the first time, and $v$ has a neighbor of larger objective, then $A$ proceeds to the neighbor of $v$ with largest objective.

(P2) *(Poly-time exploration.)* If $A$ has explored $k$ vertices, and at least one of these vertices has an unexplored neighbor, then $A$ visits an unexplored vertex in at most $k^{O(1)}$ steps.

(P3) *(Poly-time exhaustive search.)* Assume that $A$ visits a vertex $v$ that has larger objective than all previously visited vertices, and let $S$ be the connected component of $v$ in $G[V_{\ge\phi(v)}]$, i.e., $S$ is the set of all vertices that can be reached from $v$ without touching vertices of worse objective than $v$. Then for all $1 \le k \le |S|$, $A$ visits at least $k$ vertices in $S$ in the next $k^{O(1)}$ steps (or finds $t$ in one of these steps).
If $\phi(s) = \Omega(1)$ then there exists a sufficiently slowly falling $\phi_0 = o(1)$ such that $A$ explores the connected component $S$ of $s$ in $G[V_{\ge\phi_0}]$ in $|S|^{O(1)}$ steps.

Condition (P2) ensures that the patching method is always successful if source $s$ and target $t$ are in the same component. The surprising result is that (P1)-(P3) are sufficient to ensure *efficient* routing, i.e., a.a.s. the stretch is $1 + o(1)$.

THEOREM 3.4. *Let $A$ be a routing algorithm satisfying (P1)-(P3). If $s$ and $t$ are in the same component*[8] *then $A$ successfully routes from $s$ to $t$ and a.a.s. takes at most* $\frac{2+o(1)}{|\log(\beta-2)|} \log\log n$ *steps.*

*Relaxations.* So far we assumed that the objective $\phi$ can be computed exactly, which may be unrealistic in practice. For example, in the Milgram experiment the participants can only estimate the objective values of their neighbors. Hence, we also study an approximate version of greedy routing, where the greedy algorithm uses an objective function $\tilde{\phi}$ which is only an approximation of $\phi$. This adds quite some *flexibility*: for any of the best $\min\{w_v, \phi(v)^{-1}\}^{o(1)}$ neighbors of a vertex $v$, there is a "good enough" approximation $\tilde{\phi}$ which puts this vertex to the top. In particular, it is not necessary to compute the optimal neighbor w.r.t. $\phi$, which may be costly. Moreover, the routing process is also very *robust*: for example, it is no problem if some of the edges fail during execution of the routing, since the current vertex can send the message to any other good neighbor instead.

THEOREM 3.5. *Let* $\tilde{\phi} : V \to \mathbb{R}$ *be a function which is maximized at $t$ such that* $\tilde{\phi}(v) = \Theta(\phi(v))$ *holds for all* $v \in V$. *Then Theorems 3.1, 3.2, 3.3, and 3.4 also hold for greedy routing with respect to* $\tilde{\phi}$ *instead*

[6]Here we assume that the model depends naturally on $w_{\min}$. In particular, we assume that a vertex of weight $w$ has expected degree $\Theta(w)$, where the hidden constants do not depend on $w_{\min}$.

[7]Technically speaking, here we use the slightly stronger statement that in the giant connected component, a.a.s. a $1 - o(1)$ fraction of all pairs of vertices have distance $\frac{2\pm o(1)}{|\log(\beta-2)|} \log\log n$. This statement is not explicitly formulated as a lemma in [16], but is in the proof of Theorem 5.9 in [16].

[8]That is, the a.a.s. statement holds conditioned on the event that $s$ and $t$ are in the same connected component.

*of* $\phi$.
*We may also replace* $\tilde{\phi}(v) = \Theta(\phi(v))$ *by the weaker assumption* $\tilde{\phi} = \Theta\left(\phi(v) \cdot \min\{w_v, \phi(v)^{-1}\}^{\pm o(1)}\right)$.

A consequence of Theorem 3.5 is that the results of this paper also hold for variations of the model. For example, most of the experimental work uses slightly different objective functions, e.g., they consider geometric routing on hyperbolic random graphs (see Section 4 for details). In [17] it was proven that one-dimensional GIRGs ($d = 1$) contain the model of hyperbolic random graphs as a special case, but still geometric routing in hyperbolic space is not exactly the same as greedy routing in our sense. Theorem 3.5 shows that the differences are negligible. Formally, *geometric* routing on hyperbolic random graphs induces an objective function $\phi_H$ on the corresponding GIRG, which falls into the class of objective functions considered in Theorem 3.5.

Corollary 3.6. *All results about success probability, path length, and patching algorithms also hold for geometric greedy routing in hyperbolic random graphs.*

## 4 COMPARISON WITH EXPERIMENTAL RESULTS

There are several recent papers which experimentally study 'greedy processes' in graphs with hidden metric spaces [9–11, 24, 53, 62]. In these papers, either GIRGs are sampled for various parameter combinations, sometimes under different names; or real networks (e.g., the internet graph) are embedded into the space $\mathbb{T}^d \times \mathcal{W}$, where $\mathcal{W}$ is the space of weights (mostly in the case $d = 1$, where $\mathbb{T}^d \times \mathcal{W}$ can be interpreted as hyperbolic disc [17, Theorem 7.3], cf. Corollary 3.6). Afterwards, in both settings, greedy routing algorithms are experimentally studied on these graphs. Thus our paper gives theoretical explanations for the observed effects, as we discuss in detail below.

In contrast, [9] and [10] study geometric greedy processes, i.e., the routing is degree-agnostic and uses only the distance in an homogeneous and isotropic space. It turns out that this geometric type of routing still works in some settings, but is far less efficient and robust (e.g., it completely fails for some values of $\beta \in [2, 3]$). This suggests that greedy routing as considered in this paper is superior to geometric routing. It remains for future work to compare both methods theoretically.

*Success Probability:* As the main contribution the aforementioned papers observe a large success probability of greedy routing for most studied combinations of parameters. This is explained by Theorem 3.1, which gives a general lower bound $\Omega(1)$ on the success probability. Often, the experimentally observed success probability is surprisingly large (i.e., larger than 97% in [11]). We believe that the reason for this observation is in Theorem 3.2 (i), where we show that the failure probability drops exponentially with the parameter $w_{\min}$ controlling the minimum expected degree. Thus, even with very moderate values of $w_{\min}$ it is not surprising to obtain large success probabilities.

*Trajectory of a Greedy Path:* In the experiments in [11, 53, 54, 62] a successful greedy path starting at a small degree node will first visit nodes of larger degrees and continue along this path until it reaches the core of the network; afterwards, the greedy path leaves the core towards nodes with smaller degrees but with much closer geometric distance to the target until it reaches its destination. When proving our main results, we confirm this observation formally and thus characterize accurately the trajectory of the routing path.

*Stretch:* Besides the success probability, the stretch of a greedy path, i.e., the quotient of a greedy paths length vs. the length of a shortest path, is an important measure to evaluate the usefulness of greedy routing in applications. Experiments revealed a surprisingly small stretch close to 1, both for embedded real graphs [11] and for sampled random graphs [53, 54, 62]. In Theorem 3.3 we prove formally that successful greedy routing has a stretch of $1 + o(1)$ in the case of success.

*Patching:* Patching has been experimentally found to be highly efficient, and to maintain an average stretch close to 1 [24, 44, 53, 54, 62]. However, most experiments in sampled models have been performed with a small number of vertices (e.g., $n = 1000$). Also, not all methods guarantee successful routing if $s$ and $t$ are in the same component. Interestingly, the gravity-pressure method considered in [24] shows good results, although it does not fall into our class of patching algorithms, and it suffers from the problems described in Section 5. So it remains open whether this algorithm is also theoretically efficient, or whether the good results were simulation artifacts (see also [67]).

As Theorem 3.4 shows, a broad class of natural patching algorithms are highly efficient, even if they boost the success probability to 100% for vertices in the same component. Most notably, we prove in Theorem 3.4 that a stretch of $1 + o(1)$ is not only achievable, but that it is guaranteed under the weak and natural assumptions (P1)-(P3).

## 5 PATCHING ALGORITHMS: DISCUSSION AND EXAMPLES

The naïve greedy protocol gets stuck if it enters a local optimum, which is not acceptable for technical applications. Several patching strategies have been suggested to overcome this issue, and experimental results showed that many of them work quite well in practice [24, 44, 53, 54, 62, 67]. We formally prove that in fact *any* patching strategy works well if it satisfies some basic conditions, namely (P1) *greedy choices*, (P2) *poly-time exploration*, and (P3) *poly-time exhaustive search*.

Note that all three conditions are natural: the first one is that the algorithm makes greedy choices whenever there is an obvious decision to be made. Note that still there are many choices left to the algorithm. For example, if it enters a local optimum, then it is free to decide if and how much it backtracks before continuing exploration. The second condition ensures that $A$ never gets stuck (or only for polynomial time). Finally, the third condition (P3) forces the algorithm to search exhaustively a connected set of "good" candidates in reasonable time before turning to less promising candidates. The second part of (P3) is concerned with the exceptional case $\phi(s) = \Omega(1)$ (for random $s$ and $t$ this only happens with probability $O(1/n)$) and is necessary to avoid trivialities: if $\phi(s) = \Omega(1)$ then there may be no (or only few) vertices of better objective than $s$, and the precondition of the first part of (P3) may never be fufillled. We remark that the requirement that $\phi_0$ is "sufficiently slowly falling" can be specified to $\phi_0 = (\log\log n)^{-o(1)}$.

The last condition (P3) does exclude some algorithms like the gravity-pressure algorithm introduced in [62]. This algorithm always visits the best neighbor $v'$ of the current search point $v$, even if $\phi(v') < \phi(v)$, and thus does not satisfy (P3). E.g., assume that the algorithm visits two consecutive vertices $v_1, v_2$ of increasing objective, and assume further that $v_2$ has exactly one more neighbor $u$ of very bad objective ($\phi(u) \ll \phi(v_1)$), while $v_1$ has other neighbors of better objective. Then continuing the search from $u$ before exploring the other neighbors of $v_1$ may be a bad strategy, and this is what (P3) rules out. For example, the gravity-pressure algorithm will prefer to visit any unexplored vertex over returning to $v_1$. So if $v_1$ lies on the only path to $t$ (which happens with probability $\Omega(1)$), then the algorithm may potentially explore large parts of the giant before returning to $v_1$, and thus before finding $t$. This may explain that the algorithm is especially vulnerable in sparse networks [67].

Generally, there are two relevant types of algorithms if the global structure is unknown to the vertices: either information about the routing history is stored in the message (e.g., the protocol SMTP for emails [66]); or for every message a small amount of information is stored in each vertex, yielding rather exploration than classical routing (e.g., flooding algorithms like [42, 50], the gravity pressure algorithm [62], or tree-based approaches [67]). In both cases, it is very easy to design a distributed routing algorithm that satisfies conditions (P1)-(P3), as we outline in the following.

For the first case, we may simply store the list of visited vertices in the message, and for each vertex $v$ we additionally store the objective of the best unexplored incident edge in the message (i.e., the objective of the best neighbor $u$ of $v$ for which the algorithm did not traverse the edge $uv$). Compared to SMTP this only increases the required memory by a single value per visited node. With this information, a trivial way to satisfy conditions (P1)-(P3) is to use the greedy algorithm if possible (i.e., if we are not in a local optimum), and otherwise explore the best unexplored edge that goes out from any visited vertex.

For the second case, a variant of depth-first search satisfies condition (P1)-(P3), in which the message and each visited vertex only need to store a constant number of pointers and objective values. More precisely, for a vertex $v \in V$ and a value $\Phi \in \mathbb{R}^+$ consider a greedy depth first search on the subgraph $G[V_{\geq\Phi}]$ of vertices which have objective at least $\Phi$, starting in $v$. "Greedy" here means that if there are several unexplored edges going out from a vertex, then the DFS algorithm picks the edge that leads to the vertex of highest objective. We call this algorithm (greedy) $\Phi$-DFS for short. Note that since $G[V_{\geq\Phi}]$ does not need to be connected, the $\Phi$-DFS does not necessarily visit all vertices in $G[V_{\geq\Phi}]$.

The idea is now the following. Whenever we encounter a vertex $v$ which has strictly larger objective than all previously visited vertices, then we start a $\phi(v)$-DFS at $v$. We do this recursively, so when in this $\phi(v)$-DFS we encounter another vertex $v'$ which has larger objective than all previously visited vertices (including the vertices visited during the $\phi(v)$-DFS), then we pause the $\phi(v)$-DFS, and start a $\phi(v')$-DFS in $v'$. It may happen that the $\phi(v')$-DFS is completed without success, i.e., that we return to $v'$ after recursively exploring all its better neighbors without finding $t$. In this case, we simply discard the $\phi(v')$-DFS and resume the paused $\phi(v)$-DFS. Note that we treat all vertices visited during the $\phi(v')$-DFS as unvisited for the resumed $\phi(v)$-DFS. However, we do store the best objective value that we have ever seen (regardless in which DFS we have seen them) in the message. This algorithm is distributed, i.e, there is no shared global memory, and no global stack of function calls is required to execute the algorithm. Moreover, at each time only one vertex is active, and each vertex only needs to know positions and weights of its direct neighbors.

# 6 PROOF SKETCHES AND THE TYPICAL TRAJECTORY OF A GREEDY PATH

In this section we describe the evolution of the basic greedy process and give a very rough outline of the proof ideas. At the same time, we describe the trajectory of a typical greedy path, which is also depicted in Figure 1 below. In this extended abstract we only describe the case where both the source $s$ and the target $t$ have constant weight and $\|\mathrm{x}_s - \mathrm{x}_t\| = \Omega(1)$. This case occurs with constant probability close to 1 and can be considered as the "typical" situation.

*Mean field analysis and typical trajectories:* If $s$ has small weight, then a.a.s. all its neighbors (if any) have relatively small weight as well and are located in a ball of small geometric distance around $\mathrm{x}_s$, which we call "region of influence" for illustrative purposes. Since the region of influence of $s$ is small and far away from $t$, all points in this region have the same distance from $t$, up to factors $(1 + o(1))$. In particular, all neighbors of $s$ have the same distance from $t$, up to factors $(1 + o(1))$. On the other hand, the weights of the neighbors fluctuate by non-negligible constant factors. (So do the distances *from* $s$, but they do not influence the objective values.) Therefore, the fluctuations of the weights dominate the fluctuations of the distances from $t$, and consequently, routing proceeds to a neighbor of $s$ with higher weight. Let $\overline{w}$ be a given weight. By (1), the expected number of neighbors of $s$ with weight at least $\overline{w}$ is

$$\Theta\left(n \int_{\overline{w}}^{\infty} f(w) \min\left\{\frac{w\mathrm{w}_s}{n}, 1\right\} dw\right) \approx \Theta\left(\int_{\overline{w}}^{\infty} \mathrm{w}_s w^{1-\beta} dw\right) = \Theta(\mathrm{w}_s \overline{w}^{2-\beta}).$$

Hence, setting $\overline{w} = \mathrm{w}_s^{1/(\beta-2)}$ we can expect that $s$ has a neighbor of weight roughly $\overline{w}$. We repeat the argument and observe that the routing exhibits a first phase in which the weight of the current node increases by an exponent $\approx 1/(\beta - 2) > 1$ within every step. This phase stops when a node $v$ with $\phi(v) \gtrsim \mathrm{w}_v^{-1/(\beta-2)}$ is reached. Since the weight increases by an exponent of $1/(\beta - 2)$ with every hop, this first phase needs only $\approx \log\log n/|\log(\beta - 2)|$ steps.

Once the routing reaches a node $v$ such that $\phi(v) \gtrsim \mathrm{w}_v^{-1/(\beta-2)}$, the relation between the current weight and the current objective changes, since now the region of influence of $v$ contains $t$. That does not mean that $v$ is adjacent to $t$ (in fact, this is very unlikely), but $v$ does have neighbors which are significantly closer to $t$. These neighbors typically have smaller weight than $v$, but the gain in distance is enough to have higher objective $\phi$. More precisely, let

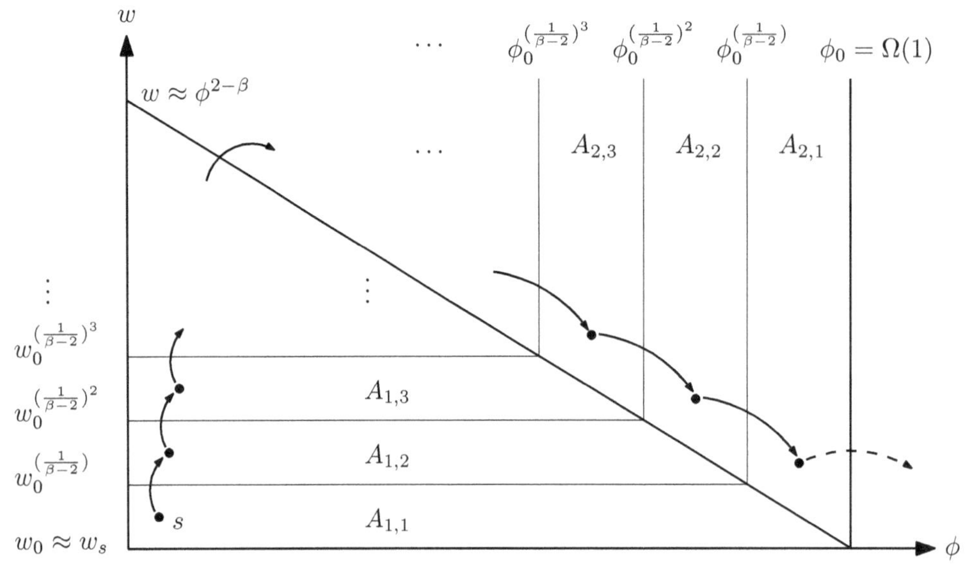


**Figure 1: A typical greedy path. Starting at $s$, the routing visits one vertex per layer. In the first phase, the weight increases exponentially, whereas in the second phase, the objective $\phi$ increases exponentially until a constant objective $\phi_0$ is reached. The two phases are given by the layers $A_{1,i}$ resp. $A_{2,i}$, and both phases consist of $\frac{1+o(1)}{|\log(\beta-2)|}\log\log n$ steps.**

$\delta := (\phi(v)^{1-\beta}n^{-1})^{1/d}$ and observe that by the definition of $\phi$

$$\|x_v - x_t\|^d = w_v\phi(v)^{-1}n^{-1} \geq \phi(v)^{1-\beta}n^{-1} = \delta^d$$

holds. Thus we have $\delta \leq \|x_v - x_t\|$. Next, we consider the set

$$A(v) := \{u \in V : w_u \geq \phi(v)^{-1} \wedge \|x_u - x_t\| \leq \delta\}.$$

We claim that with constant probability, $v$ has a neighbor in $A(v)$. By the Poisson point process, the expected number of vertices located in the ball of radius $\delta$ around $t$ is $\delta^d$. It follows that the expected number of vertices in the set $A(v)$ is

$$\Omega\left(n\int_{\phi(v)^{-1}}^{\infty} f(w)\delta^d dw\right) = \Omega\left(\phi(v)^{1-\beta}\int_{\phi(v)^{-1}}^{\infty} w^{-\beta}dw\right) = \Omega(1),$$

and it remains to verify that vertices in $A(v)$ are connected to $v$ with constant probability. Let $u \in A(v)$. By the triangle inequality we obtain $\|x_v - x_u\| = O(\|x_v - x_t\|)$. Next we use that the assumption $\phi(v) \gtrsim w_v^{-1/(\beta-2)}$ is equivalent to $w_v \gtrsim \phi(v)^{2-\beta}$, and deduce

$$\frac{w_u w_v}{n} \geq \frac{\phi(v)^{-1}w_v}{n} \gtrsim \delta^d \geq \|x_v - x_t\|^d = \Omega(\|x_v - x_u\|^d).$$

Then by (EP), indeed $v$ is connected to $u$ with constant probability and it follows that with constant probability, $v$ has a neighbor in $A(v)$. Finally, every node $u \in A(v)$ has significantly larger objective, i.e., it satisfies

$$\phi(u) \geq (\phi(v)\delta^d n)^{-1} \geq \phi(v)^{\beta-2},$$

and in this way we can hope for a neighbor $u$ of objective $\approx \phi(v)^{\beta-2}$. (Note that $\phi(v) < 1$, so indeed the objective increases.) Moreover, it can be shown that the best neighbor $u'$ again satisfies the relation $\phi(u') \gtrsim w_{u'}^{-1/(\beta-2)}$, so the argument can be repeated. Thus in this second phase, within every step the objective increases by the same exponent.

After $\approx \log\log n/|\log(\beta-2)|$ rounds, this second phase reaches a node $v$ of objective $\phi(v) = \Omega(1)$. At this point, in the case $\alpha < \infty$, we have $p_{vt} \geq (\phi(v)w_t)^{\alpha} = \Omega(1)$, so $v$ connects directly to $t$ with probability $\Omega(1)$. This sketch gives an idea why greedy routing succeeds with probability $\Omega(1)$ (Theorem 3.1), and why it only needs $\frac{2+o(1)}{|\log(\beta-2)|}\log\log n$ steps (Theorem 3.3). It also yields a typical trajectory of the greedy path, i.e., the routing consists of a first phase in which it merely increases weights and of a second phase in which the objective significantly increases and the distance to the target decreases.

*Main difficulties:* In the formal proofs of our statements we show that with sufficiently high probability, the routing does not deviate too much from the trajectory described above. For a single node $v$ it is not difficult, yet technical, to calculate the weight $w_u$ and the objective $\phi(u)$ of its best neighbor $u$. However, there is a major difficulty: the greedy algorithm only proceeds to $u$ when $u$ is *the best* neighbor of $v$. So if we want to compute the probability that the best neighbor of $u$ is again what we expect, then we need to compute a *conditional* probability, namely conditioned on $v$ having no better neighbor. Unfortunately, this introduces dependencies which are impossible to handle directly.

The main technical contribution of this paper is in overcoming these dependencies. The basic idea is to uncover the nodes by increasing objective. However, note that the greedy path $P_\phi$ in the graph $G_{\leq\phi}$ induced by nodes of objective at most $\phi$ does not need to coincide with the greedy path $P$ in $G$, since the nodes in $P_\phi$ may have a neighbor of objective larger than $\phi$, thus shortcutting the rest of $P_\phi$. Unfortunately, the number of nodes which lie on a greedy path in *some* $G_{\leq\phi}$ is so large that many of them have undesired properties. Thus we can not prove iteratively that all nodes on the temporary greedy paths have good properties, because they do not.

On the other hand, uncovering the next node on $P$ is impossible without introducing the aforementioned dependencies.

*Layer technique:* Instead of looking at individual nodes, we define carefully crafted layers $A_{1,i}$ for the first phase (defined via weights) and layers $A_{2,i}$ for the second phase (defined via objectives) such that the typical trajectory contains at most one node per layer. Then we consider the greedy path $P_i$ induced by the first $i$ layers and prove that with sufficiently high probability either $P_i$ has no node in the $i$-th layer or the first node $v \in P_i$ in the $i$-th layer has a neighbor $u$ outside the first $i$ layers with better objective than all neighbors *inside* the first $i$ layers (which we already have uncovered). Note that this is an event where we do not suffer from dependencies: the node $v$ is defined only in terms of the first $i$ layers, so we can determine $v$ without uncovering any parts of the remaining graph. At the same time, this approach deals with the problem of shortcuts because we only need to consider one vertex in each layer, rather than all vertices on the temporary greedy paths. Moreover, this vertex $v$ is allowed to have shortcuts to higher layers, which helps us again to avoid dependencies.

Due to the independence, the number of neighbors of $v$ in larger layers is Poisson distributed, and it suffices to show that its expectation is large. It is not hard to see that the above events together imply that greedy routing succeeds throughout all layers, and that it visits no layer twice. So we may apply a union bound over all layers, and obtain that the routing algorithms succeeds with probability $\Omega(1)$ and visits at most one node per layer. Note that we do not necessarily visit every layer, but since a.a.s. the stretch is $1 + o(1)$, we visit a.a.s. a $(1 - o(1))$-fraction of all layers. This proves Theorem 3.1. A more careful analysis along the same lines gives the relaxation result, Theorem 3.5. All other theorems also rely heavily on the layer technique, but require more tricks to handle the start and the end phase.

*Start and end phases:* It turns out that the failure probability of greedy routing is dominated by the first few steps (when the weight is still constant) and the last few steps (when the objective is constant). In each of these steps the algorithm has probability $\Omega(1)$ to fail. For example, in the typical case that $s$ has a constant weight, there is a constant probability that $s$ has no neighbors at all. However, the number of neighbors of $s$ is Poisson distributed with mean $\Theta(\mathrm{w}_s)$, so the probability to have no neighbor decays exponentially with $\mathrm{w}_s$. Similar considerations apply for the number of neighbors with better objective. For this reason the failure probability decays exponentially with $\mathrm{w}_{\min}$ (Theorem 3.2). The actual proof is much more tricky and is omitted in this extended abstract.

*Patching:* Finally, to prove the patching result (Theorem 3.4) we show three intermediate results.

(i) If we have explored $k$ nodes, starting from $s$, then with probability $1 - \exp\{-k^{\Omega(1)}\}$ at least one of these nodes is adjacent to a node of weight at least $k^{\Omega(1)}$. By condition (P2) it takes only $k^{O(1)}$ steps to explore $k$ nodes, so after a short exploration phase of $o(\log\log n)$ steps, a.a.s. we find a node of weight $\omega(1)$.

(ii) As in the purely greedy case, starting from a node of weight $\omega(1)$ a.a.s. we follow a typical trajectory of the greedy algorithm as described above, until we find a node $v$ with almost constant objective (say, with objective $\phi(v) \approx (\log\log\log n)^{-1}$). This middle phase is purely greedy and does not require patching. In particular, $v$ has better objective than any previously visited nodes.

(iii) We study the graph $G_{\geq\phi(v)}$ and find that a.a.s. it contains at most $O(\phi(v)^{-1})$ nodes and a giant component, which contains both the nodes $t$ and $v$. Thus by (P3) the algorithm explores the giant component of $G_{\geq\phi(v)}$ and finds $t$ in additional $o(\log\log n)$ steps.

## REFERENCES


[1] I. Abraham and C. Gavoille. 2006. Object location using path separators. In *Proceedings of the 25th annual ACM symposium on Principles of distributed computing (PODC)*. ACM, 188–197.

[2] W. Aiello, A. Bonato, C. Cooper, J. Janssen, and P. Prałat. 2008. A spatial web graph model with local influence regions. *Internet Mathematics* 5, 1-2 (2008), 175–196.

[3] R. Albert and A.-L. Barabási. 2002. Statistical mechanics of complex networks. *Reviews of modern physics* 74, 1 (2002), 47.

[4] L. Backstrom, P. Boldi, M. Rosa, J. Ugander, and S. Vigna. 2012. Four degrees of separation. In *Proceedings of the 4th Annual ACM Web Science Conference*. ACM, 33–42.

[5] A.-L. Barabási. 2012. Network science: Luck or reason. *Nature* 489, 7417 (2012), 507–508.

[6] S. Bhagat, M. Burke, C. Diuk, I. O. Filiz, and S. Edunov. 2016. Facebook Research, Three and a half degrees of separation. https://research.fb.com/three-and-a-half-degrees-of-separation/. (2016). Accessed: 2017-02-15.

[7] T. Bläsius, T. Friedrich, and A. Krohmer. 2016. Hyperbolic Random Graphs: Separators and Treewidth. In *European Symposium on Algorithms (ESA)*. 15:1–15:16.

[8] T. Bläsius, T. Friedrich, A. Krohmer, and S. Laue. 2016. Efficient Embedding of Scale-Free Graphs in the Hyperbolic Plane. In *European Symposium on Algorithms (ESA)*. 16:1–16:18.

[9] M. Boguñá and D. Krioukov. 2009. Navigating Ultrasmall Worlds in Ultrashort Time. *Physical Review Letters* 102, 5 (Feb. 2009), 058701.

[10] M. Boguñá, D. Krioukov, and K. C. Claffy. 2009. Navigability of complex networks. *Nature Physics* 5 (Jan. 2009), 74–80.

[11] M. Boguñá, F. Papadopoulos, and D. Krioukov. 2010. Sustaining the Internet with hyperbolic mapping. *Nature Communications* 1, 6 (Sept. 2010).

[12] P. Boldi and S. Vigna. 2004. The WebGraph framework I : compression techniques. In *13th International Conference on World Wide Web (WWW)*. 595–602.

[13] B. Bollobás, S. Janson, and O. Riordan. 2007. The phase transition in inhomogeneous random graphs. *Random Structures & Algorithms* 31, 1 (2007), 3–122.

[14] A. Bonato, J. Janssen, and P. Prałat. 2010. A geometric model for on-line social networks. In *1st International Workshop on Modeling Social Media (WOSM)*.

[15] M. Bradonjić, A. Hagberg, and A. G. Percus. 2008. The structure of geographical threshold graphs. *Internet Mathematics* 5, 1-2 (2008), 113–139.

[16] K. Bringmann, R. Keusch, and J. Lengler. 2016. Average Distance in a General Class of Scale-Free Networks with Underlying Geometry. *Preprint avaiable at arxiv:1602.05712* (2016).

[17] K. Bringmann, R. Keusch, and J. Lengler. 2016. Sampling Geometric Inhomogeneous Random Graphs in Linear Time. *Preprint available at arXiv:1511.00576* (2016).

[18] K. Bringmann, R. Keusch, J. Lengler, Y. Maus, and A. Molla. 2017. Greedy Routing and the Algorithmic Small-World Phenomenon. *Preprint available at arXiv:1612.05539* (2017).

[19] D. Brockmann, L. Hufnagel, and T. Geisel. 2006. The scaling laws of human travel. *Nature* 439, 7075 (2006), 462–465.

[20] E. Candellero and N. Fountoulakis. 2014. Clustering and the Hyperbolic Geometry of Complex Networks. In *11th International Workshop on Algorithms and Models for the Web Graph (WAW)*. 1–12.

[21] A. Chaintreau, P. Fraigniaud, and E. Lebhar. 2008. Networks become navigable as nodes move and forget. In *35th International Colloquium on Automata, Languages, and Programming (ICALP)*. 133–144.

[22] F. Chung and L. Lu. 2002. The average distances in random graphs with given expected degrees. *Proceedings of the National Academy of Sciences (PNAS)* 99, 25 (2002), 15879–15882.

[23] F. Chung and L. Lu. 2002. Connected Components in Random Graphs with Given Expected Degree Sequences. *Annals of Combinatorics* 6, 2 (2002), 125–145.

[24] A. Cvetkovski and M. Crovella. 2009. Hyperbolic Embedding and Routing for Dynamic Graphs. In *INFOCOM 2009. 28th IEEE International Conference on Computer Communications*. 1647 –1655.

[25] M. Deijfen, R. van der Hofstad, and G. Hooghiemstra. 2013. Scale-free percolation. *Annales de l'Institut Henri Poincaré, Probabilités et Statistiques* 49, 3 (2013), 817–838.

[26] P. Deprez, R. S. Hazra, and M. V. Wüthrich. 2015. Inhomogeneous long-range percolation for real-life network modeling. *Risks* 3, 1 (2015).

[27] S. N. Dorogovtsev and J. F. F. Mendes. 2002. Evolution of networks. *Advances in Physics* 51, 4 (2002), 1079–1187.

[28] P. Duchon, N. Hanusse, E. Lebhar, and N. Schabanel. 2006. Could any graph be turned into a small-world? *Theoretical Computer Science* 355, 1 (2006), 96–103.

[29] L. Ferretti, M. Cortelezzi, and M. Mamino. 2014. Duality between preferential attachment and static networks on hyperbolic spaces. *EPL (Europhysics Letters)* 105, 3 (2014), 38001.

[30] N. Fountoulakis. 2015. On the evolution of random graphs on spaces of negative curvature. *Journal of Complex Networks* (2015). http://arxiv.org/abs/1205.2923 To appear.

[31] P. Fraigniaud. 2005. Greedy routing in tree-decomposed graphs. In *European Symposium on Algorithms (ESA)*. Springer, 791–802.

[32] P. Fraigniaud. 2007. *Small Worlds as Navigable Augmented Networks: Model, Analysis, and Validation.* 2–1.

[33] P. Fraigniaud, C. Gavoille, and C. Paul. 2006. Eclecticism shrinks even small worlds. *Distributed Computing* 18, 4 (2006), 279–291.

[34] P. Fraigniaud and G. Giakkoupis. 2010. On the searchability of small-world networks with arbitrary underlying structure. In *42nd Annual ACM Symposium on Theory of Computing (STOC)*. 389–398.

[35] P. Fraigniaud and G. Giakkoupis. 2014. Greedy routing in small-world networks with power-law degrees. *Distributed Computing* 27, 4 (2014), 231–253.

[36] P. Fraigniaud, E. Lebhar, and Z. Lotker. 2006. A Doubling Dimension Threshold *Theta*(loglog*n*) for Augmented Graph Navigability. In *European Symposium on Algorithms (ESA)*. 376–386.

[37] M. Franceschetti and R. Meester. 2006. Navigation in small-world networks: A scale-free continuum model. *Journal of Applied Probability* (2006), 1173–1180.

[38] T. Friedrich and A. Krohmer. 2015. Cliques in hyperbolic random graphs. In *INFOCOM 2015. 34th IEE International Conference on Computer Communication.* 1544–1552.

[39] T. Friedrich and A. Krohmer. 2015. On the diameter of hyperbolic random graphs. In *42nd International Colloquium on Automata, Languages, and Programming (ICALP) (Lecture Notes in Computer Science)*.

[40] G. García-Pérez, M. Boguñá, A. Allard, and M. Á. Serrano. 2016. The hidden hyperbolic geometry of international trade: World Trade Atlas 1870–2013. *Scientific Reports* 6 (2016).

[41] L. Gugelmann, K. Panagiotou, and U. Peter. 2012. Random hyperbolic graphs: degree sequence and clustering. In *39th International Colloquium on Automata, Languages, and Programming (ICALP)*. 573–585.

[42] K. A. Harras, K. C. Almeroth, and E. M. Belding-Royer. 2005. Delay tolerant mobile networks (dtmns): Controlled flooding in sparse mobile networks. In *International Conference on Research in Networking*. Springer, 1180–1192.

[43] M. Heydenreich, T. Hulshof, and J. Jorritsma. 2016. Structures in supercritical scale-free percolation. *Preprint available at arXiv:1604.08180* (2016).

[44] W. Huang, S. Chen, and W. Wang. 2014. Navigation in spatial networks: A survey. *Physica A: Statistical Mechanics and its Applications* 393 (2014), 132–154.

[45] E. Jacob and P. Mörters. 2013. A spatial preferential attachment model with local clustering. In *Algorithms and Models for the Web Graph*. Springer, 14–25.

[46] M. Kiwi and D. Mitsche. 2015. A Bound for the Diameter of Random Hyperbolic Graphs. In *2015 Proceedings of the Twelfth Workshop on Analytic Algorithmics and Combinatorics (ANALCO)*. SIAM, 26–39.

[47] J. Kleinberg. 2000. The small-world phenomenon: an algorithm perspective. In *32nd Annual ACM Symposium on Theory of Computing (STOC)*. 163–170.

[48] J. Kleinberg. 2002. Small-world phenomena and the dynamics of information. *Advances in neural information processing systems* 1 (2002), 431–438.

[49] R. Kleinberg. 2007. Geographic Routing Using Hyperbolic Space. In *INFOCOM 2007. 26th IEEE International Conference on Computer Communications.* 1902 –1909.

[50] Y.-B. Ko and N. H. Vaidya. 2000. Location-Aided Routing (LAR) in mobile ad hoc networks. *Wireless networks* 6, 4 (2000), 307–321.

[51] C. Koch and J. Lengler. 2016. Bootstrap Percolation on Geometric Inhomogeneous Random Graphs. In *43rd International Colloquium on Automata, Languages, and Programming (ICALP)*. 147:1–147:15.

[52] D. Krioukov, K. Fall, A. Brady, et al. 2007. On compact routing for the Internet. *ACM SIGCOMM Computer Communication Review* 37, 3 (2007), 41–52.

[53] D. Krioukov, F. Papadopoulos, M. Boguñá, and A. Vahdat. 2009. Greedy forwarding in scale-free networks embedded in hyperbolic metric spaces. *SIGMETRICS Perform. Eval. Rev.* 37 (October 2009), 15–17. Issue 2.

[54] D. Krioukov, F. Papadopoulos, M. Kitsak, A. Vahdat, and M. Boguñá. 2010. Hyperbolic geometry of complex networks. *Phys. Rev. E* 82 (2010), 036106. Issue 3. https://doi.org/10.1103/PhysRevE.82.036106

[55] R. Kumar, D. Liben-Nowell, and A. Tomkins. 2006. Navigating Low-Dimensional and Hierarchical Population Networks. In *European Symposium on Algorithms (ESA)*. 480–491.

[56] V. Lehman, A. Gawande, B. Zhang, L. Zhang, R. Aldecoa, D. Krioukov, and L. Wang. 2016. An experimental investigation of hyperbolic routing with a smart forwarding plane in NDN. In *Quality of Service (IWQoS), 2016 IEEE/ACM 24th International Symposium on*. IEEE, 1–10.

[57] D. Liben-Nowell, J. Novak, R. Kumar, P. Raghavan, and A. Tomkins. 2005. Geographic routing in social networks. *Proceedings of the National Academy of Sciences (PNAS)* 102, 33 (August 2005), 11623–11628. https://doi.org/10.1073/pnas.0503018102

[58] G. S. Manku, M. Naor, and U. Wieder. 2004. Know the neighbor's neighbor: the power of lookahead in randomized P2P networks. In *36th Annual ACM Symposium on Theory of Computing (STOC)*. 54–63.

[59] C. Martel and V. Nguyen. 2004. Analyzing Kleinberg's (and other) small-world models. In *Proceedings of the 23th annual ACM symposium on Principles of distributed computing (PODC)*. ACM, 179–188.

[60] S. Milgram. 1967. The small world problem. *Psychology Today* 2, 1 (1967), 60–67.

[61] M. Mitzenmacher. 2004. A brief history of generative models for power law and lognormal distributions. *Internet mathematics* 1, 2 (2004), 226–251.

[62] F. Papadopoulos, D. Krioukov, M. Boguñá, and A. Vahdat. 2010. Greedy Forwarding in Dynamic Scale-Free Networks Embedded in Hyperbolic Metric Spaces. In *INFOCOM 2010. 29th IEEE International Conference on Computer Communications.* 1 –9.

[63] F. Papadopoulos, C. Psomas, and D. Krioukov. 2015. Network mapping by replaying hyperbolic growth. *Networking, IEEE/ACM Transactions on* 23, 1 (2015), 198–211.

[64] M. Penrose. 2003. *Random geometric graphs*. Vol. 5. Oxford University Press Oxford.

[65] U. Peter. 2014. *Random Graph Models for Complex Systems*. Ph.D. Dissertation. ETH Zurich.

[66] J. Postel. 1982. Simple mail transfer protocol. *Information Sciences* (1982).

[67] S. Sahhaf, W. Tavernier, D. Colle, M. Pickavet, and P. Demeester. 2013. Link failure recovery technique for greedy routing in the hyperbolic plane. *Computer Communications* 36, 6 (2013), 698–707.

[68] S. Schnettler. 2009. A structured overview of 50 years of small-world research. *Social Networks* 31, 3 (2009), 165–178.

[69] Y. Shavitt and T. Tankel. 2008. Hyperbolic embedding of internet graph for distance estimation and overlay construction. *IEEE/ACM Transactions on Networking (TON)* 16, 1 (2008), 25–36.

[70] H. P. Thadakamalla, R. Albert, and S. R. T. Kumara. 2007. Search in spatial scale-free networks. *New Journal of Physics* 9, 6 (2007), 190.

[71] J. Travers and S. Milgram. 1969. An experimental study of the small world problem. *Sociometry* (1969), 425–443.

[72] D. J. Watts. 2004. The "New" Science of Networks. *Annual Review of Sociology* 30 (2004), 243–270.

[73] D. J. Watts, P. S. Dodds, and M. E. J. Newman. 2002. Identity and search in social networks. *science* 296, 5571 (2002), 1302–1305.

[74] X. Zhao, A. Sala, H. Zheng, and B. Y. Zhao. 2011. Efficient shortest paths on massive social graphs. In *Collaborative Computing: Networking, Applications and Worksharing*. IEEE, 77–86.

# Triangle Finding and Listing in CONGEST Networks

Taisuke Izumi
Nagoya Institute of Technology
Gokiso-cho
Showa-ku, Nagoya, Aichi, Japan 466-8555
t-izumi@nitech.ac.jp

François Le Gall
Graduate School of Informatics, Kyoto University
Yoshida-Honmachi
Sakyo-ku, Kyoto, Japan 606-8501
legall@i.kyoto-u.ac.jp

## ABSTRACT

Triangle-free graphs play a central role in graph theory, and triangle detection (or triangle finding) as well as triangle enumeration (triangle listing) play central roles in the field of graph algorithms. In distributed computing, algorithms with sublinear round complexity for triangle finding and listing have recently been developed in the powerful CONGEST clique model, where communication is allowed between any two nodes of the network. In this paper we present the first algorithms with sublinear complexity for triangle finding and triangle listing in the standard CONGEST model, where the communication topology is the same as the topology of the network. More precisely, we give randomized algorithms for triangle finding and listing with round complexity $O(n^{2/3}(\log n)^{2/3})$ and $O(n^{3/4}\log n)$, respectively, where $n$ denotes the number of nodes of the network. We also show a lower bound $\Omega(n^{1/3}/\log n)$ on the round complexity of triangle listing, which also holds for the CONGEST clique model.

## CCS CONCEPTS

• **Theory of computation** → **Distributed algorithms**; **Graph algorithms analysis**;

## KEYWORDS

Distributed algorithms; graph algorithms; CONGEST model; triangle finding; triangle listing

## 1 INTRODUCTION

*Background.* The most standard way of modeling distributed networks is to use graphs, where vertices and edges respectively correspond to computing entities (e.g., nodes or processes) and communication channels. The graphical structure of networks naturally motivates, both practically and theoretically, the study of graph algorithms, i.e., in-network solving of combinatorial graph problems for the own topology of the network. In the last twenty years, research on distributed complexity theory has successfully investigated many fundamental graph problems such as independent set [1, 4], dominating set [21, 22], coloring [3, 25], minimum spanning trees [10, 11, 14, 15, 26, 32] shortest paths [19, 23, 24, 27], max-flow and min-cut [16, 17, 28]. The seminal textbook by Peleg [31] provides a good overview of those achievements.

A high-level perspective on distributed graph algorithms classifies problems into two categories according to their locality characteristics. Problems like minimum spanning trees, shortest paths or max-flow/min-cut mentioned above are classified as global problems because some node must (indirectly) communicate with a node $D$-hop away, where $D$ denotes the diameter of the network, which requires $\Omega(D)$ rounds. Since any problem can be solved within $O(D)$ rounds by a naive centralized approach if the communication bandwidth of each channel is unlimited, technical challenges on global problems appear only in the model of limited-bandwidth channels, the so-called CONGEST communication model where each channel has only $O(\log n)$-bit bandwidth. On the other hand, many local problems, like independent set, dominating set or coloring allow distributed (approximate) solutions within $o(D)$ rounds. Besides the limited bandwidth, a significant difficulty when designing distributed algorithms for local problems often consists in breaking the symmetry between nearby nodes.

*Triangle finding.* Triangle finding is an important counterpart of the perspective explained above. Since the distance-two information for a node $i$ is sufficient to find all triangles around $i$, it is a purely local task. Aggregating at each node the set of its 2-hop neighbors, however, takes $\Theta(d_{max})$ rounds in the CONGEST model, where $d_{max}$ denotes the maximum degree of the nodes. In the case of dense graphs, such an approach gives linear round complexity. In this sense, despite being a local problem, the underlying difficulty of triangle finding is similar to the difficulty encountered when working with global problems in the CONGEST model, that is, the lack of communication bandwidth. These particularities make triangle finding a difficult problem to handle with current techniques. As summarized in Table 1, recently some non-trivial upper bounds have been obtained by Dolev et al. [8] and then improved by Censor-Hillel et al. [6], but these upper bounds hold only in the much stronger CONGEST clique model (where at each round messages can even be sent between non-adjacent nodes) for which bandwidth management is significantly easier. No nontrivial upper bound is known in the standard CONGEST model. As far as lower bounds are concerned, the locality of triangle finding rules out many standard approaches used to obtain lower bounds on the complexity of global problems (e.g., the approaches from [13, 35]). The only known lower bounds have been obtained recently by Drucker et al. [9], but hold only for the much weaker broadcast CONGEST model, where at each round the nodes can broadcast only a single common message to all other nodes, under a (reasonable) conjecture in communication complexity theory. No nontrivial lower bound is known for triangle finding in the standard CONGEST model.


*PODC '17, July 25-27, 2017, Washington, DC, USA*

ACM ISBN 978-1-4503-4992-5/17/07...$15.00
https://doi.org/10.1145/3087801.3087811

Another, more practical, motivation for considering triangle finding is that for several graph problems faster algorithms are known over triangle-free graphs (we refer to [18, 33] for some examples in the distributed setting). The ability to efficiently check if the network is triangle-free, and more generally detect which part of the network is triangle-free, is essential when considering such algorithms in practice.

*Technical contribution.* In this paper, in addition to triangle finding we also consider the triangle listing problem, which requires that each triangle of the network should be output by at least one node (we refer to Section 2 for the formal definition). The triangle listing problem can be seen as a special case of motif finding, which is a popular problem in the context of network data analysis. It is obvious that triangle finding is not harder than triangle listing, since finding reduces to listing. In the literature mentioned above, triangle finding and triangle listing are not explicitly distinguished, but the algorithms by Dolev et al. [8] are actually for the listing version, while the algorithms by Censor-Hillel et al. [6] are based on an algebraic approach and only support finding. The lower bound by Drucker et al. [9] applies to triangle finding.

Our results are summarized in Table 1. The main contributions of this paper are a $O(n^{2/3}(\log n)^{2/3})$-round algorithm for triangle finding and a $O(n^{3/4}\log n)$-round algorithm for triangle listing, both in the CONGEST model. These two algorithms are the first algorithms with sublinear round complexity for triangle finding or listing applicable to the standard CONGEST model. The existence of sublinear-time algorithms shows, from an algorithmic perspective as well, that these two problems are indeed easier than global problems like diameter computation, which has a nearly linear-time lower bound in the CONGEST model [13]. Interestingly, this result contrasts with the known relations between triangle finding and diameter computation in the centralized setting, in which the best known algorithms for both problems rely on matrix multiplication and have the same complexity.

We also show that there exist networks of $n$ nodes for which any triangle listing algorithm requires $\Omega(n^{1/3}/\log n)$ rounds in the CONGEST model. Actually we show a stronger result: any triangle listing algorithm requires $\Omega(n^{1/3}/\log n)$ rounds even in the CONGEST clique model. This lower bound slightly improves the $\Omega(n^{1/3}/\log^3 n)$-round lower bound for triangle listing in the CONGEST clique model obtained recently by Pandurangan et al. [29]. Note that since the algorithm by Dolev et al. [8] has round complexity $O(n^{1/3}(\log n)^{2/3})$, these lower bounds are tight up to possible polylogarithmic factors in the CONGEST clique model. These lower bounds also have the following interesting consequence. They shows that triangle listing is strictly harder than triangle finding in the CONGEST clique model since, as already mentioned, $(n^{0.1572})$-round algorithms for triangle finding have been shown by Censor-Hillel et al. [6]. Actually, since the algorithms in [6] also count the number of triangles, these lower bounds thus even show that triangle listing is harder than counting in this model.

Our lower bound is shown by a simple information-theoretic argument on random graphs. By similar arguments (see Proposition 4.4 in Section 4), we can also show a $\Omega(n/\log n)$-round lower bound for local listing algorithms, where each node $i$ is required to output all the triangles containing $i$. This corollary implies that any triangle listing algorithm with sublinear complexity inherently requires some counter-intuitive mechanism that enables a triangle $t$ to be output by a node not contained in $t$. This is precisely how our $O(n^{3/4}\log n)$-round algorithm works.

*Other related works.* Distributed algorithms for triangle-freeness have recently also been considered in the setting of property testing [5] (see also [12]). Note that in property testing the goal is to decide whether either the network is triangle-free or it contains a large number triangles. Since there is no need to consider the case where the network may have only a small number of triangles, this property testing version is significantly easier than the problems studied in the present paper.

Triangle finding is a fundamental problem in the field of centralized algorithms as well. It has been known for a long time that this problem is not harder than Boolean matrix multiplication [20]. A few years ago Vassilevska Williams and Williams showed a converse reduction [36]: they proved that a subcubic-time algorithm for triangle finding can be used, in a combinatorial way, to construct a subcubic-time algorithm for Boolean matrix multiplication. This result, combined with recent developments [2, 7, 30, 37], have put triangle finding as a central problem in the recent theory of fine-grained complexity.

## 2 PRELIMINARIES

In this paper we consider undirected graphs. We will use $G = (V, E)$ to denote the graph considered, and write $n = |V|$ and $m = |E|$. In this section we present some of our notations, give details of our model and present some facts about hashing functions that will be used in Section 3.

*Graph-theoretic notations.* For any vertex $i \in V$, we denote $\mathcal{N}(i)$ the set of neighbors of $i$. For any finite set $X$, we will use the notation $\mathcal{E}(X)$ to represent the set of unordered pairs of elements in $X$, and use $\mathcal{T}(X)$ to represent the set of unordered triples of elements in $X$. We will write $\mathcal{E} = \mathcal{E}(V)$ and $\mathcal{T} = \mathcal{T}(V)$. Given a pair of vertices $\{j,k\} \in \mathcal{E}$, we write

$$\#(\{j,k\}) = \Big|\{l \in V \mid \{j,l\} \in E \text{ and } \{k,l\} \in E\}\Big|.$$

Given $t = \{j,k,l\} \in \mathcal{T}$, and $e \in \mathcal{E}$, we will write $e \in t$ when $e = \{j,k\}$, $e = \{j,l\}$, or $e = \{k,l\}$. For any $R \subsetneq \mathcal{T}$, we denote by $\mathcal{P}(R) \subseteq E$ the set of edges $e \in E$ such that $e \in t$ for some triple $t \in R$.

We define a triangle $t = \{j,k,l\} \in \mathcal{T}$ to be an unordered triple of vertices where any pair corresponds to an edge in $E$. Note that if $e$ is an edge of the graph, then $\#(e)$ represents the number of triangles containing $e$. We write $T(G)$ the set of all triangles contained in graph $G$.

*Communication Model.* In the paper we mainly consider the CONGEST communication model. The graph $G = (V, E)$ represents the topology of the network, executions proceed with round-based synchrony and each node can transfer one $O(\log n)$-bit message to each adjacent node per round. All links and nodes (corresponding to the edges and vertices of $G$, respectively) are reliable and suffers no faults. Each node has a distinct identifier from a domain $\mathcal{I}$. For simplicity we will assume $\mathcal{I} = V = [0, n-1]$, but this assumption is not essential and easy to remove as long as $|\mathcal{I}| = \mathrm{poly}(n)$. It is also assumed that each node can access infinite sequence of local

| Paper | Time Bound | Problem | Model |
|---|---|---|---|
| Dolev et al. [8] | $O(n^{1/3}(\log n)^{2/3})$<br>$O(d_{max}^3/n)$ | Listing | CONGEST clique |
| Censor-Hillel et al. [6] | $O(n^{0.1572})$ | Finding | CONGEST clique |
| This paper (Theorem 3.1) | $O(n^{2/3}(\log n)^{2/3})$ | Finding | CONGEST |
| This paper (Theorem 3.2) | $O(n^{3/4}\log n)$ | Listing | CONGEST |
| Drucker et al. [9] | $\Omega(\frac{n}{e^{\sqrt{\log n}}\log n})$ (conditional) | Finding | CONGEST broadcast |
| Pandurangan et al. [29] | $\Omega(\frac{n^{1/3}}{\log^3 n})$ | Listing | CONGEST clique |
| This paper (Theorem 4.1) | $\Omega(\frac{n^{1/3}}{\log n})$ | Listing | CONGEST clique |

**Table 1: Prior results on the round complexity of distributed triangle finding and listing and our new results, where $n$ denotes the number of nodes in the network.**

random bits, that is, the algorithm can be randomized. Initially, each node knows nothing about the topology of the network except the set of edges incident to itself and the value of $n$. All our upper bounds given in Section 3 hold for the CONGEST model.

The CONGEST clique model is a powerful variant of the CONGEST model. It allows an algorithm to transfer a $O(\log n)$-bit message per round between any two nodes not necessarily adjacent in $G$ at each round. This means that in this model the communication topology is the complete graph on the $n$ nodes, and the graph $G$ only takes the role of input instances to the algorithm. Except for the communication topology, all other features are common with the CONGEST model described in the above paragraph. The CONGEST clique model will be considered only in Section 4 when proving our lower bound (note that a lower bound for this model immediately holds for the CONGEST model as well).

*Triangle finding and listing in the CONGEST model.* In the triangle finding problem, at least one node must output a triangle if $T(G)$ is not empty, or all the nodes must output "not found" otherwise. In the triangle listing problem, the goal is that for each triangle in $T(G)$ at least one node in $V$ outputs it.

Formally, we describe the output of an algorithm for triangle finding or listing by an $n$-tuple $T = (T_0, T_1, \ldots, T_{n-1})$, where $T_i \subseteq T(G)$ is the output by node $i$. The algorithm can be deterministic or randomized. In the latter case, note that the condition on the $T_i$'s implies that any triple output at a node should corresponds to a triangle of $G$, and thus the algorithm should be one-sided error. Note also that we do not require that the $T_i$'s are mutually disjoint. We often use notation $T$ as the union of $T_i$ over all nodes if there is no ambiguity. We say that the algorithm solves the triangle finding problem if its output $T$ satisfies $T \cap T(G) \neq \emptyset$. We say that it solves the triangle listing problem if $T = T(G)$.

*Hash functions.* Let $\mathcal{X}$ and $\mathcal{Y}$ be two finite sets. For any integer $s \geq 1$, a family of hash functions $\mathcal{H} = \{h_1, h_2, \ldots, h_p\}$, where each $h_i$ is a function from $\mathcal{X}$ to $\mathcal{Y}$, is called *s-wise independent* if for any distinct $x_1, x_2, \ldots, x_s \in \mathcal{X}$ and any $y_1, y_2, \ldots y_s \in \mathcal{Y}$, a function $h$ sampled from $\mathcal{H}$ uniformly at random satisfies $\Pr[\bigwedge_{1\leq i\leq s} h(x_i) = y_i] = 1/|\mathcal{Y}|^s$. We will use the following lemma, which follows almost immediately from the definition of $s$-wise independence.

Lemma 2.1. *Let $\mathcal{H}$ be any 3-wise independent family of hash functions from $\mathcal{X}$ to $\mathcal{Y}$, and $h$ be a function sampled from $\mathcal{H}$ uniformly at random. Let $H(y) = \{x'' \in \mathcal{X} \mid h(x'') = y\}$. For any triple $(x, x', y) \in \mathcal{X} \times \mathcal{X} \times \mathcal{Y}$ we have*

$$\Pr\left[h(x) = h(x') = y \bigwedge \left|H(y)\right| \leq 4\left(2 + \frac{|\mathcal{X}| - 2}{|\mathcal{Y}|}\right)\right] \geq \frac{3}{4|\mathcal{Y}|^2}.$$

Proof. Let us write $Z = \{x'' \in \mathcal{X} \mid h(x'') = y\}$. For any $a \in \mathcal{X}$, let $Z_a$ be the indicator random variable corresponding to the event $a \in Z$. By the 3-wise independence property of $h$, we have

$$\begin{aligned} E\Big[|Z| \mid Z_x = Z_{x'} = 1\Big] &= 2 + \sum_{a\in\mathcal{X}\setminus\{x,x'\}} E[Z_a \mid Z_x = Z_{x'} = 1] \\ &= 2 + \frac{|\mathcal{X}| - 2}{|\mathcal{Y}|}. \end{aligned}$$

By Markov's inequality, we have

$$\Pr\left[|Z| > 4\left(2 + \frac{|\mathcal{X}| - 2}{|\mathcal{Y}|}\right) \,\Big|\, Z_x = Z_{x'} = 1\right] \leq \frac{1}{4}.$$

Since $\Pr[Z_x = Z_{x'} = 1] = 1/|\mathcal{Y}|^2$ holds, we obtain

$$\begin{aligned} &\Pr\left[Z_x = Z_{x'} = 1 \bigwedge |Z| \leq 4\left(2 + \frac{|\mathcal{X}| - 2}{|\mathcal{Y}|}\right)\right] \\ &= \Pr\left[|Z| \leq 4\left(2 + \frac{|\mathcal{X}| - 2}{|\mathcal{Y}|}\right)\Big| Z_x = Z_{x'} = 1\right] \times \Pr[Z_x = Z_{x'} = 1] \\ &\geq \frac{3}{4} \times \frac{1}{|\mathcal{Y}|^2}, \end{aligned}$$

as claimed. □

Note that using the standard construction by Wegman and Carter [38] we can encode $k$-wise independent hash functions using only $O(k \log |\mathcal{Y}|)$ bits.

## 3 UPPER BOUNDS

In this section we prove the following two theorems.

THEOREM 3.1. *Let $\delta > 0$ be any constant. In the CONGEST model there exists a randomized algorithm for triangle finding with round complexity $O(n^{2/3}(\log n)^{2/3})$, where $n$ denotes the size of the network, and success probability at least $1-\delta$.*

THEOREM 3.2. *In the CONGEST model there exists a randomized algorithm for triangle listing with round complexity $O(n^{3/4}\log n)$ and success probability at least $1-1/n$, where $n$ denotes the size of the network.*

Theorems 3.1 and 3.2 follow from three algorithms described in Propositions 3.3–3.5 below, which rely on the following concept of heavy triangles. Let $\varepsilon$ be any real number such that $0 \le \varepsilon \le 1$. We say that a triangle $t \in T(G)$ is *$\varepsilon$-heavy* if there exists an edge $e \in t$ such that $\#(e) \ge n^{\varepsilon}$. We define $T_{\varepsilon}(G) \subseteq T(G)$ as the set of all $\varepsilon$-heavy triangles in $T(G)$. The first proposition is almost trivial, and shows how to find an $\varepsilon$-heavy triangle by a straightforward sampling strategy:

PROPOSITION 3.3. *There exists a $O(n^{1-\varepsilon})$-round randomized algorithm $\mathcal{A}_1$ returning a set $T \subseteq T(G)$ such that, if $T_{\varepsilon}(G) \neq \emptyset$, then $T \cap T_{\varepsilon}(G) \neq \emptyset$ with probability $\Omega(1)$.*

PROOF. Algorithm $\mathcal{A}_1$ is as follows: First, each node $j \in V$ constructs a random set $S_j \subseteq \mathcal{N}(j)$ by including in $S_j$ each element of $\mathcal{N}(j)$ with probability $n^{-\varepsilon}$. If $|S_j| > 4n^{1-\varepsilon}$, node $j$ then does not send anything to its neighbors. Otherwise (i.e., if $|S_j| \le 4n^{1-\varepsilon}$), node $j$ then sends $S_j$ to each neighbor $k \in \mathcal{N}(j)$, and each such neighbor $k$ checks if there is a triangle containing $j$, $k$ and a third node in $S_j$, which can be done by computing locally the set $\mathcal{N}(k) \cap S_j$.

Observe that if $T_{\varepsilon}(G) \neq \emptyset$ then at least one $\varepsilon$-heavy triangle will be found with constant probability. Indeed, for each edge $\{j,k\} \in E$ such that $\#(\{j,k\}) \ge n^{\varepsilon}$, with constant probability at least one node adjacent to both $j$ and $k$ is included in $S_j$, and $S_j$ is small enough. □

The second proposition is about finding each $\varepsilon$-heavy triangle:

PROPOSITION 3.4. *There exists a $O(n^{1-\varepsilon/2})$-round randomized algorithm $\mathcal{A}_2$ returning a set $T \subseteq T(G)$ such that, for any triangle $t \in T_{\varepsilon}(G)$, this set $T$ contains $t$ with probability $\Omega(1)$.*

The third proposition is about finding each triangle that is not $\varepsilon$-heavy:

PROPOSITION 3.5. *There exists a $O(n^{1-\varepsilon} + n^{(1+\varepsilon)/2}\log n)$-round randomized algorithm $\mathcal{A}_3$ returning a set $T \subseteq T(G)$ such that, for any triangle $t \in T(G) \setminus T_{\varepsilon}(G)$, this set $T$ contains $t$ with probability $\Omega(1)$.*

Proposition 3.4 and especially Proposition 3.5 are the main technical contributions of this section. Their proofs are given in Subsections 3.1 and 3.2, respectively.

We now explain how Theorems 3.1 and 3.2 immediately follow from these three propositions.

PROOF OF THEOREM 3.1. The triangle finding algorithm simply applies Algorithm $\mathcal{A}_1$ and then Algorithm $\mathcal{A}_3$. From Propositions 3.3 and 3.5 we know that a triangle will thus be found with at least constant probability (if $G$ contains a triangle). For any constant $\delta$ the success probability can be amplified to $1-\delta$ by repeating this process $c$ times for a large enough constant $c$.

The round complexity of this algorithm is $O(n^{1-\varepsilon} + n^{1-\varepsilon} + n^{(1+\varepsilon)/2}\log n)$. Choosing $\varepsilon$ such that $n^{\varepsilon} = \frac{n^{1/3}}{(\log n)^{2/3}}$ gives the claimed upper bound. □

PROOF OF THEOREM 3.2. The triangle listing algorithm repeats $\lceil c\log n\rceil$ times the following process (here $c$ is a large constant): apply Algorithm $\mathcal{A}_2$ and then Algorithm $\mathcal{A}_3$.

We now show that this algorithm lists all the triangles of $G$. Let $t$ be a triangle in $T(G)$. From Propositions 3.4 and 3.5 we know that $t$ is found with at least constant probability at each step. If $c$ is large enough, repeating this process $\lceil c\log n\rceil$ times guarantees that $t$ is found with probability at least $1-1/n^4$. From the union bound, we can conclude that all triangles are found with probability at least $1-1/n$.

The round complexity of this algorithm is $O(((n^{1-\varepsilon/2} + n^{1-\varepsilon} + n^{(1+\varepsilon)/2}\log n)\log n)$. Choosing $\varepsilon$ such that $n^{\varepsilon} = \frac{n^{1/2}}{(\log n)^2}$ gives the claimed upper bound. □

### 3.1 Listing all $\varepsilon$-heavy triangles: Proof of Proposition 3.4

The goal of this subsection is to prove Proposition 3.4.

The main idea to find $\varepsilon$-heavy triangles is that each node $j$ will decide which information about $\mathcal{N}(j)$ it will send to each neighbor $a$ according to a hash function $h_a$ generated by $a$. More precisely, the function $h_a$ will be taken (by node $a$, and then distributed to all its neighbors) from a 3-wise independent family $\mathcal{H}$ of hash functions from $V$ to $\{0,1,\ldots,\lfloor n^{\varepsilon/2}\rfloor - 1\}$, and $j$ will send an edge $\{j,l\}$ to $a$ if $h_a(l) = 0$. The complete algorithm, which is Algorithm $\mathcal{A}_2$ claimed in Proposition 3.4, is described in Figure 1 and analyzed below.

We first prove the correctness of Algorithm $\mathcal{A}_2$. Let $t = \{j,k,l\}$ be any $\varepsilon$-heavy triangle of $G$. Let $\{j,k\}$ be the edge shared by at least $n^{\varepsilon}$ triangles and $A$ be the set of nodes such that $\{j,k,a\}$ forms a triangle for each $a \in A$. Consider the function $h_a \in \mathcal{H}$ chosen by node $a$. Applying Lemma 2.1 with $|\mathcal{X}| = n$ and $|\mathcal{Y}| = \lfloor n^{\varepsilon/2}\rfloor$, we obtain the inequality

$$\Pr\left[h_a(k) = h_a(l) = 0 \bigwedge |E_a^j \cup E_a^k| \le 8 + \frac{4n}{\lfloor n^{\varepsilon/2}\rfloor}\right] \ge \frac{3}{4n^{\varepsilon}}.$$

This bound implies that with probability at least $\frac{3}{4n^{\varepsilon}}$ node $a$ receives $\{j,k\}$ from $j$, $\{j,l\}$ from $j$ and $\{k,l\}$ from $k$ at Step 2, and thus $T_a$ (i.e., the output of node $a$) includes $t$ with the same probability. Since the events $t \notin T_a$ are mutually independent over all $a \in A$, we can bound the probability that no node in $A$ finds $t$ as follows:

$$\Pr\left[\bigcap_{a\in A} t \notin T_a\right] \le \left(1 - \frac{3}{4n^{\varepsilon}}\right)^{|A|} \le \left(1 - \frac{3}{4n^{\varepsilon}}\right)^{n^{\varepsilon}} \le e^{-\Omega(1)}.$$

The round complexity of Algorithm $\mathcal{A}_2$ is $O(n^{1-\varepsilon/2})$ since the hash function $h_i$ sent at Step 1 can be encoded using $O(\log n)$ bits, as explained in Section 2.

This concludes the analysis of Algorithm $\mathcal{A}_2$ and the proof of Proposition 3.4.

1. Each node $i \in V$ chooses a function $h_i\colon V \to \{0, 1, \ldots, \lfloor n^{\varepsilon/2} \rfloor - 1\}$ uniformly at random from a 3-wise independent family $\mathcal{H}$ of hash functions, and sends $h_i$ to all the nodes in $\mathcal{N}(i)$.
2. Each node $j \in V$ locally computes, for each node $a \in \mathcal{N}(j)$, the set of edges $E_a^j = \{\{j, l\} \in E \mid h_a(l) = 0\}$ and then sends $E_a^j$ to $a$ if $|E_a^j| \leq 8 + \frac{4n}{\lfloor n^{\varepsilon/2} \rfloor}$.
3. For any node $i \in V$, let $F_i$ be the set of edges received by $i$ at the first step. Node $i$ outputs all triples $\{j, k, l\}$ satisfying $\{j, k\}, \{j, l\}, \{k, l\} \in F_i$.

**Figure 1: Algorithm $\mathcal{A}_2$ finding any $\varepsilon$-heavy triangle in $O(n^{1-\varepsilon/2})$ rounds.**

## 3.2 Finding triangles that are not heavy: Proof of Proposition 3.5

The goal of this subsection is to prove Proposition 3.5. We first give a brief description of the main ideas underlying our algorithm before giving the full description of Algorithm $\mathcal{A}_3$.

*Key definition and outline of our approach.* For any set $X \subseteq V$, define the set

$$\Delta(X) = \mathcal{E}(V) \setminus \bigcup_{x \in X} \mathcal{E}(\mathcal{N}(x)),$$

which is the set of pairs of nodes that do not have a common neighbor in $X$. The following easy lemma shows how the set $\Delta(X)$ is related to finding triangles which are not $\varepsilon$-heavy.

Lemma 3.6. *Let $\varepsilon$ be any real number such that $0 \leq \varepsilon \leq 1$. Suppose that $X$ is a set obtained by including each node of $V$ into $X$ with probability $\frac{1}{9n^{\varepsilon}}$. Then, for any triangle $t \in T(G) \setminus T_{\varepsilon}(G)$, the three edges of $t$ are in $\Delta(X)$ with probability at least $2/3$.*

Proof. Let us consider any triangle $t \in T(G) \setminus T_{\varepsilon}(G)$. For each edge $e \in t$ we have $\#(e) < n^{\varepsilon}$. From the union bound, we obtain the inequality $\Pr_X\left[e \in \bigcup_{x \in X} \mathcal{E}(\mathcal{N}(x))\right] < \frac{1}{9}$. Thus, again from the union bound, $t$ has its three edges in $\Delta(X)$ with probability at least $2/3$. □

In view of Lemma 3.6, our strategy will be to take a set $X$ as in the lemma and then find the triangles with three edges in $\Delta(X)$ using the following approach: Each node $i \in V$ sends to all its neighbors the set $\mathcal{N}(i) \cap X$, in $O(|X|)$ rounds. Then each node $k \in V$ constructs for each $j \in \mathcal{N}(k)$ the set containing all nodes $l \in \mathcal{N}(k)$ such that $\{j, l\} \in \Delta(X)$, which can be done locally. Let us call this set $\mathcal{S}(j, k)$ for now – later it will be called $\mathcal{S}_V^X(j, k)$. Node $k$ then sends $\mathcal{S}(j, k)$ to neighbor $j$, who can report all triangles of the form $\{j, k, l\}$ with $\{j, l\} \in \Delta(X)$.

This approach works, but its round complexity depends on the size of the sets $\mathcal{S}(j, k)$. The crucial point is that we can show from a combinatorial argument that with high probability (on the choice of $X$) the average size of these sets is small. The main remaining issue is that, even if the average size is small, in general there exist pairs $(j, k)$ for which $\mathcal{S}(j, k)$ is large. We solve this issue by sending $\mathcal{S}(j, k)$ only when its size is close to the average and using a different strategy when its size exceeds the average. This latter strategy is based on a notion of "good" nodes. Roughly speaking, a node $j$ is good if it has only a small number of neighbors $k$ such that $\mathcal{S}(j, k)$ is large (see Definition 3.7 for the formal definition). The same combinatorial argument as above guarantees that most nodes are good (this is shown in Lemma 3.8 below). Triangles containing at least one good node are fairly easy to deal with, and we can deal with triangle containing three bad nodes by applying the same approach recursively on the subgraph induced by the bad nodes. Our final algorithm will thus be recursive: it will keep a set $U \subseteq V$, with initially $U = V$, and successively search for triangles in the subgraph of $G$ induced by $U$, removing the good nodes from $U$ at each step, until $U = \emptyset$.

*Further definitions and full description of Algorithm $\mathcal{A}_3$.* For any set $U \subseteq V$ and any nodes $j, k \in U$ such that $\{j, k\} \in E$, we define the set $\mathcal{S}_U^X(j, k) \subseteq U$ as follows:

$$\mathcal{S}_U^X(j, k) = \Big\{l \in U \mid \{j, l\} \in \Delta(X) \text{ and } \{k, l\} \in E\Big\}.$$

Note that this definition is asymmetric: we have $\mathcal{S}_U^X(j, k) \neq \mathcal{S}_U^X(k, j)$ in general. Let $r$ be any positive real number. For any node $j \in U$, we define the set

$$\mathcal{V}_{U,r}^X(j) = \Big\{k \in U \mid \{j, k\} \in E \text{ and } \left|\mathcal{S}_U^X(j, k)\right| > r\Big\}.$$

Finally, we will use the following concept of good nodes.

*Definition 3.7.* Let $U$ and $X$ be any subsets of $V$, and $r$ be any positive real number. A node $j \in U$ is $r$-good for $(U, X)$ if $\left|\mathcal{V}_{U,r}^X(j)\right| \leq r$.

The following crucial lemma shows an upper bound on the number of nodes which are not good, when $X$ is chosen as in Lemma 3.6.

Lemma 3.8. *Let $\varepsilon$ be any real number such that $0 \leq \varepsilon \leq 1$ and $X$ be a set chosen at random as in Lemma 3.6. Then, for any real number $r \geq \sqrt{54n^{1+\varepsilon}\log n}$, the following statement holds with probability at least $1 - 1/n$:*

*For any set $U \subseteq V$ there are at most $|U|/2$ nodes in $U$ that are not $r$-good for $(U, X)$.* (1)

Proof. Consider any pair $\{j, l\} \in \mathcal{E}$ such that

$$\#(\{j, l\}) \geq 27n^{\varepsilon}\log n.$$

We have

$$\Pr_X\left[\{j, l\} \notin \bigcup_{x \in X} \mathcal{E}(\mathcal{N}(x))\right] \leq \left(1 - \frac{1}{9n^{\varepsilon}}\right)^{27n^{\varepsilon}\log n} \leq \frac{1}{n^3}.$$

From the union bound we can thus conclude that with probability at least $1 - 1/n$ the following statement holds:

$$\#(\{j, l\}) < 27n^{\varepsilon}\log n \text{ for any pair } \{j, l\} \in \Delta(X). \tag{2}$$

We now show that Statement (2) implies Statement (1). Let us consider the number of ordered triples $(j, k, l) \in U \times U \times U$ such that $\{j, l\} \in \Delta(X)$, $\{j, k\} \in E$ and $\{k, l\} \in E$. If Statement (2) holds then this number is at most $27|U|^2 n^\varepsilon \log n$. This number of triples can also be computed in another way: it is equal to

$$\sum_{\substack{(j,k)\in U\times U \\ \text{s.t. } \{j,k\}\in E}} \left|\mathcal{S}_U^X(j,k)\right|.$$

Thus if Statement (2) holds we obtain the inequality

$$27|U|^2 n^\varepsilon \log n \geq \sum_{\substack{(j,k)\in U\times U \\ \text{s.t. } \{j,k\}\in E}} \left|\mathcal{S}_U^X(j,k)\right| \geq \sum_{j\in U} \left|\mathcal{V}_{U,r}^X(j)\right| r,$$

which implies that the number of nodes that are not $r$-good for $(U,X)$ is at most

$$27|U|^2 n^\varepsilon \log n \times \frac{1}{r^2} \leq \frac{27|U| n^{1+\varepsilon} \log n}{r^2}.$$

For any $r \geq \sqrt{54 n^{1+\varepsilon}\log n}$ we obtain the claimed upper bound. □

We now present an algorithm that lists all triangles of $G$ with three edges in $\Delta(X)$. The algorithm is denoted $\mathcal{A}(X,r)$ and described in Figure 2. We analyze it in the next proposition.

Proposition 3.9. *Assume that the set $X$ satisfies Statement (1). Then Algorithm $\mathcal{A}(X,r)$ terminates after $O(\log n)$ iterations of the while loop, has overall round complexity $O(|X| + r\log n)$, and its output $T \subseteq T(G)$ includes all the triangles of $G$ with three edges in $\Delta(X)$.*

Proof. Let us first show that Algorithm $\mathcal{A}(X,r)$ terminates after $O(\log n)$ iterations of the while loop. The assumption on the set $X$ implies that $|U \setminus U'| \leq |U|/2$ at Step 4.2 of each iteration of the while loop. Since we start with $|U| = n$, after at most $\log_2(n)+1$ iterations of the while loop the set $U$ becomes empty, at which point we exit the while loop.

We now analyze the overall round complexity of the algorithm by considering the complexity of each step. Step 1 requires only one round. Note that after Step 1 each node $k$ can locally compute the set $\mathcal{N}(k)\cap X$. Step 2 can then be implemented using at most $|X|$ rounds, since $|\mathcal{N}(k)\cap X| \leq |X|$. Step 4.1 can be implemented using at most $r$ rounds. Step 4.2 does not require any communication since the enough information has been obtained at Step 4.1 to compute $\mathcal{V}_{U,r}^X(k)$ locally. Step 4.3 only requires at most $r$ rounds, since $|\mathcal{V}_{U,r}^X(j)| \leq r$ for any $j \in U'$. Finally, Step 4.5 obviously requires only one round. The overall round complexity is thus at most

$$|X| + 1 + (\log_2(n)+1)(r+r+1) = O(|X| + r\log n).$$

We finally show that the algorithm lists all triangles of $G$ with three edges in $\Delta(X)$. First observe that for any set $U \subseteq V$, any triangle of $G$ with three nodes in $U$ and three edges in $\Delta(X)$ satisfies at least one of the following three properties (where $U' \subseteq U$ denotes the set of nodes that are $r$-good for $(U,X)$):

(a) it contains three distinct nodes $j,k,l \in U$ such that $\left|\mathcal{S}_U^X(j,k)\right| \leq r$ and $l \in \mathcal{S}_U^X(j,k)$;
(b) it contains two distinct nodes $j,k \in U$ such that $j \in U'$ and $k \in \mathcal{V}_{U,r}^X(j)$;
(c) all its three nodes are in $U \setminus U'$.

Indeed, if such a triangle does not satisfy Property (a) then the inequality $|\mathcal{S}_U^X(j,k)| > r$ holds for any two nodes $j$ and $k$ of the triangle (which means that $k \in \mathcal{V}_{U,r}^X(j)$). In that case it should satisfy either Property (b) or Property (c).

Algorithm $\mathcal{A}(X,r)$ starts with $U = V$ and decreases the set $U$ until it is empty. Let us consider what happens at each execution of the while loop, with the current set $U$. All triangles of type (a) are found at Step 4.1 and all triangles of type (b) are found at Step 4.3. The only remaining triangles are triangles of type (c). They are considered at the next execution of the while loop, where $U$ is replaced by $U \setminus U'$. □

We are now ready to present Algorithm $\mathcal{A}_3$ and give the proof of Proposition 3.5.

Proof of Proposition 3.5. Algorithm $\mathcal{A}_3$ is as follows. First each node selects itself with probability $\frac{1}{9n^\varepsilon}$. Then the nodes run Algorithm $\mathcal{A}(X,r)$ with $X$ being the set of selected nodes (note that each node $i$ of the network knows whether $i \in X$ or not, as required) and $r = \sqrt{54n^{1+\varepsilon}\log n}$, but stop as soon as the round complexity exceeds $c \times (n^{1-\varepsilon} + n^{(1+\varepsilon)/2}\log n)$ for some large enough constant $c$.

By construction, the round complexity of Algorithm $\mathcal{A}_3$ is

$$O(n^{1-\varepsilon} + n^{(1+\varepsilon)/2}\log n).$$

Let $t$ be any triangle in $T(G) \setminus T_\varepsilon(G)$, and let us show that Algorithm $\mathcal{A}_3$ finds $t$ with constant probability. Note that the expectation of the value $|X|$ is $\frac{1}{9}n^{1-\varepsilon}$. By Chernoff bound, we know that the probability that $|X| > \frac{2}{9}n^{1-\varepsilon}$ is negligible. Combining this observation with Lemmas 3.6 and 3.8, we conclude (using the union bound) that with probability $\Omega(1)$ the following three conditions hold: $X$ has size at most $\frac{2}{9}n^{1-\varepsilon}$, $X$ satisfies Statement (1), and $t$ has its three edges in $\Delta(X)$. From Proposition 3.9 we know that in this case algorithm $\mathcal{A}(X,r)$ stops within $O(n^{1-\varepsilon}+n^{(1+\varepsilon)/2}\log n)$ rounds and finds $t$. By choosing the constant $c$ large enough we can thus guarantee that the output of Algorithm $\mathcal{A}_3$ contains the triangle $t$ with probability $\Omega(1)$. □

# 4 LOWER BOUNDS

This section proves the following lower-bound theorem.

Theorem 4.1. *Let $\mathcal{A}$ be any triangle listing algorithm with error probability less than 1/32. Then there exists a probability distribution on inputs such that the expected round complexity of $\mathcal{A}$ is $\Omega(n^{1/3}/\log n)$.*

In this section we will write $V = \{0,1,\ldots,n-1\}$. Without loss of generality, the run of any algorithm $\mathcal{A}$ for triangle listing on any given instance $G = (V,E)$ can be described by two following steps:

(1) Each node $i$ locally constructs its initial state $\boldsymbol{\rho}_i$ according to $G$. This state depends on the set of edges incident to $i$, but is independent of all other edges.
(2) Each node $i$ construct its output $T_i$ from $\boldsymbol{\rho}_i$ and the transcript $\boldsymbol{\pi}_i$ of the communication received it receives during the execution of the algorithm.

To prove Theorem 4.1, we consider as input the random graph $G(n,1/2)$, which is the graph on $n$ nodes where each pair of nodes is independently taken as an edge with probability 1/2. Since $\boldsymbol{\rho}_i$, $\boldsymbol{\pi}_i$, and $T_i$ depend only on the algorithm $\mathcal{A}$ (and its random bits

1. Each node tells all its neighbors whether it is in $X$ or not.
2. Each node $k \in V$ sends the set $\mathcal{N}(k) \cap X$ to all its neighbors.
3. $U \leftarrow V$.
4. While $U \neq \emptyset$ do:
   - 4.1 Each node $k \in U$ sends the set $\mathcal{S}_U^X(j,k)$ to each neighbor $j \in \mathcal{N}(k) \cap U$ for which $|\mathcal{S}_U^X(j,k)| \leq r$. Each such neighbor $j$ then lists all triangles containing $j, k$ and a third node in $\mathcal{S}_U^X(j,k)$, by locally computing the set $\mathcal{S}_U^X(j,k) \cap \mathcal{N}(j)$.
   - 4.2 Each node $k \in U$ decides whether itself is $r$-good for $(U,X)$ or not. Let $U' \subseteq U$ denote the set of nodes that are $r$-good for $(U,X)$.
   - 4.3 Each node $j \in U'$ of the network sends the set $\mathcal{V}_{U,r}^X(j)$ to each neighbor $l \in \mathcal{N}(j) \cap U$. Each such neighbor $l$ then lists all triangles containing $j, l$ and a third node in $\mathcal{V}_{U,r}^X(j)$, by locally computing the set $\mathcal{V}_{U,r}^X(j) \cap \mathcal{N}(l)$.
   - 4.4 $U \leftarrow U \setminus U'$.
   - 4.5 Each node tells all its neighbors whether it is in $U$ or not.

**Figure 2: Algorithm $\mathcal{A}(X,r)$ that lists all triangles in $G$ with three edges in $\Delta(X)$. Here $X$ and $r$ are parameters of the algorithm: $X$ is a subset of nodes and $r$ is a positive real number. The set $X$ is given as follows: each node $i \in V$ knows whether $i \in X$ or not. The number $r$ is given to each node.**

if $\mathcal{A}$ is randomized) and the input $G$, we see all of them as random variables. For any pair $\{j,k\} \in \mathcal{E}$, let $\boldsymbol{e}_{\{j,k\}}$ be the random variable with value 1 if $\{j,k\}$ is an edge, and value 0 otherwise. Let $E = (\boldsymbol{e}_{\{0,1\}}, \boldsymbol{e}_{\{0,2\}}, \ldots, \boldsymbol{e}_{\{n-2,n-1\}})$ be the concatenation of these $|\mathcal{E}|$ random variables. The proof idea is to bound the amount of information in $\pi_i$ necessary to construct $T_i$ locally. We write $T = (T_0, T_1, \ldots, T_{n-1})$ and use the notation $w(T)$ to represent the node identifier $i$ such that $|T_i|$ is maximum (i.e., the index of the node that outputs the maximum number of triangles).

Our proof relies on the following graph-theoretic lemma, which is shown in [34].

Lemma 4.2. *If a graph $G$ contains $t$ triangles, then $G$ has at least $\frac{\sqrt{2}}{3}t^{2/3}$ edges.*

We first recall the definition of the entropy. For a random variable $X$ with domain $\mathcal{X}$ and probability distribution $p$, its entropy $H(X)$ is defined as $H(X) = -\sum_{x \in \mathcal{X}} p(x) \log p(x)$. The conditional entropy can be defined similarly. For any random variables $X$ and $Y$ the mutual information of $X$ and $Y$ is defined as $I(X;Y) = H(X) - H(X|Y)$. We will use in our proofs the following standard results from information theory about the mutual information.

Fact 1. *For any random variables $X$, $Y$, and $Z$, the following three properties hold:*

- *$I(X;Y) = I(Y;X)$,*
- *$I(X;Y) \leq H(X)$ (and $I(X;Y) \leq H(Y)$), and*
- *$I(X;Y) \geq I(X;(Y,Z)) - I(X;Z)$.*

Fact 2 (Data Processing Inequality). *For any three random variables $X, Y, Z$ such that $X$ and $Z$ are conditionally independent given $Y$, $I(X;Y) \geq I(X;Z)$.*

The key technical ingredient of our proof is the following lemma (the notation $\mathcal{P}$ is defined in Section 2).

Lemma 4.3. *For any node $i$, the inequality $I(E;T_i) \geq E[|\mathcal{P}(T_i)|]$ holds.*

The proof of Lemma 4.3 is based on an information-theoretic argument. The intuition is very simple: since the information $T_i$ completely reveals the information on the edges forming triangles in $T_i$, it must contain all the information on $\mathcal{P}(T_i)$.

We will write $M = |\mathcal{E}| = \frac{n(n-1)}{2}$ and $N = |\mathcal{T}| = \frac{n(n-1)(n-2)}{6}$.

Proof of Lemma 4.3. Since the random variables $\boldsymbol{e}_{\{j,k\}}$ are independent of each other, we have

$$\begin{aligned}
&I(E;T_i)\\
&= H(E) - H(E|T_i)\\
&= H(E) - \sum_{\{j,k\} \in \mathcal{E}} H(\boldsymbol{e}_{\{j,k\}}|T_i)\\
&= H(E) - \sum_{\{j,k\} \in \mathcal{E}} \sum_{R \subseteq \mathcal{T}} H(\boldsymbol{e}_{\{j,k\}}|T_i = R) \cdot \Pr[T_i = R]\\
&= M - \sum_{R \subseteq \mathcal{T}} \sum_{\{j,k\} \in \mathcal{E}} H(\boldsymbol{e}_{\{j,k\}}|T_i = R) \cdot \Pr[T_i = R]\\
&= M - \sum_{R \subseteq \mathcal{T}} \sum_{\{j,k\} \in \mathcal{E} \setminus \mathcal{P}(R)} H(\boldsymbol{e}_{\{j,k\}}|T_i = R) \cdot \Pr[T_i = R],
\end{aligned}$$

where the last equality comes from the assumption that Algorithm $\mathcal{A}$ never outputs a triple that is not a triangle (thus $\Pr[T_i = R] \neq 0$ only if $R \subseteq T(G)$, and conditioned to this event we have $\boldsymbol{e}_{\{j,k\}} = 1$ with probability 1 for any $\{j,k\} \in \mathcal{P}(R)$). Since $H(\boldsymbol{e}_{\{j,k\}}|T_i = R) \leq 1$ always holds, we conclude that

$$\begin{aligned}
I(E;T_i) &\geq M - \sum_{R \subseteq \mathcal{T}} (M - |\mathcal{P}(R)|) \cdot \Pr[T_i = R]\\
&\geq \sum_{R \subseteq \mathcal{T}} |\mathcal{P}(R)| \cdot \Pr[T_i = R] = E[|\mathcal{P}(T_i)|],
\end{aligned}$$

as claimed. □

Theorem 4.1 is proved by combining Lemma 4.2 and Lemma 4.3. The intuition is again fairly simple: In expectation, an instance of $G(n,1/2)$ contains $\Omega(n^3)$ triangles, and thus the average number of triangles output per node node is $\Omega(n^2)$. Thus node $w(T)$

outputs at least $\Omega(n^2)$ triangles and, from Lemma 4.2, we obtain $E[|\mathcal{P}(T_{w(T)})|] = \Omega(n^{4/3})$. Lemma 4.3 then gives the same lower bound for the mutual information between $E$ and $T_{w(T)}$, which then gives the lower bound $\Omega(n^{4/3})$ on the amount of communication received by node $w(T)$ during the execution of Algorithm $\mathcal{A}$. This implies the claimed $\Omega(n^{1/3}/\log n)$-round lower bound for triangle listing since $w(T)$ can receive at most $O(n \log n)$ bits of information per round.

Proof of Theorem 4.1. From Lemma 4.3, we have

$$I(E; T_{w(T)}) \geq E[|P(T_{w(T)})|].$$

By Lemma 4.2, for any $R \subseteq T(G)$ the inequality $|\mathcal{P}(R)| \geq \frac{\sqrt{2}}{3}|R|^{2/3}$ holds. We thus have

$$\begin{aligned} I(E; T_{w(T)}) &\geq E[|\mathcal{P}(T_{w(T)})|] \\ &= \sum_{R \subseteq \mathcal{T}} |P(R)| \cdot \Pr[T_{w(T)} = R] \\ &\geq \sum_{R \subseteq \mathcal{T}, |R| \geq \frac{N}{16n}} |\mathcal{P}(R)| \cdot \Pr[T_{w(T)} = R]. \\ &\geq \sum_{R \subseteq \mathcal{T}, |R| \geq \frac{N}{16n}} \frac{\sqrt{2}}{3}\left(\frac{N}{16n}\right)^{2/3} \cdot \Pr[T_{w(T)} = R] \\ &\geq \frac{\sqrt{2}}{3}\left(\frac{N}{16n}\right)^{2/3} \cdot \Pr\left[|T_{w(T)}| \geq \frac{N}{16n}\right]. \end{aligned}$$

The expected number of triangles in $G(n, 1/2)$ is $N/8$ and thus, since there cannot be more than $N$ triangles, with probability at least $1/15$ the number of triangles exceeds $N/16$. We conclude that the inequality $|T_{w(T)}| \geq N/(16n)$ necessarily holds if the number of triangles is at least $N/16$ and Algorithm $\mathcal{A}$ correctly lists all the triangles of the graph, which occurs with overall probability probability at least $1/15 - 1/32$. Consequently we obtain

$$I(E; T_{w(T)}) \geq \frac{\sqrt{2}}{3}\left(\frac{N}{16n}\right)^{2/3} \cdot \left(\frac{1}{15} - \frac{1}{32}\right) = \Omega(n^{4/3}). \quad (3)$$

From Fact 1 we have

$$\begin{aligned} H(\pi_{w(T)}) &\geq I(E; \pi_{w(T)}) \\ &\geq I(E; (\pi_{w(T)}, \rho_{w(T)})) - I(E; \rho_{w(T)}) \\ &\geq I(E; (\pi_{w(T)}, \rho_{w(T)})) - H(\rho_{w(T)}). \end{aligned} \quad (4)$$

Since the initial knowledge of each node $i$ is only the set of edges incident to itself, the inequality

$$H(\rho_i) \leq \sum_{j \neq i} H(e_{i,j}) = n - 1 \quad (5)$$

holds for each node $i \in V$. Since the output $T_{w(T)}$ is computed locally only from the transcript $\pi_{w(T)}$ and the initial state $\rho_{w(T)}$, the random variables $E$ and $T_{w(T)}$ are conditionally independent given $(\rho_{w(T)}, \pi_{w(T)})$. We can thus use Fact 2 in Inequality (4), which combined with Inequalities (3) and (5) gives

$$H(\pi_{w(T)}) \geq I(E; T_{w(T)}) - H(\rho_{w(T)}) = \Omega(n^{4/3}).$$

Since $H(\pi_i)$ lower bounds the average length of the transcript $\pi_i$, this implies that node $w(T)$ receives messages of average total length $\Omega(n^{4/3})$ bits. Since node $w(T)$ can receive only $O(n \log n)$ bits per round, we conclude that the expected round complexity of Algorithm $\mathcal{A}$ is $\Omega(n^{1/3}/\log n)$. □

The information-theoretic arguments of Lemma 4.3 can also be used to derive the following stronger lower bound mentioned in the introduction for local triangle listing, the setting where each node $i$ is required to output all the triangles containing $i$.

Proposition 4.4. *Let $\mathcal{A}$ be any local triangle listing algorithm with error probability less than $1/32$. Then there exists a probability distribution on inputs such that the expected round complexity of $\mathcal{A}$ is $\Omega(n/\log n)$.*

The proof of Proposition 4.4 is similar to the proof of Theorem 4.1 but does not even requires Lemma 4.2: we can immediately obtain the stronger bound $E[|\mathcal{P}(T_i)|] = \Omega(n^2)$ since for local triangle listing $T_i$ should include all the triangles containing $i$.

Proof of Proposition 4.4. The proof is almost similar to the proof of Theorem 4.1, except that we can derive the stronger lower bound

$$I(E; T_i) = \Omega(n^2) \quad \text{for any } i \in V, \quad (6)$$

instead of the lower bound (3). This new lower bound implies that $H(\pi_{w(T)}) = \Omega(n^2)$ and gives the claimed lower bound on the round complexity of the local triangle listing algorithm $\mathcal{A}$.

We now explain how to derive the lower bound (6). From Lemma 4.3 we get

$$\begin{aligned} I(E; T_i) &\geq E[|\mathcal{P}(T_i)|] \\ &= \sum_{R \subseteq \mathcal{T}} |\mathcal{P}(R)| \cdot \Pr[T_i = R] \\ &\geq \frac{M}{16} \cdot \Pr\left[T_i \text{ includes at least } M/6 \text{ triangles containing } i\right], \end{aligned}$$

since the quantity $|\mathcal{P}(R)|$ is lower bounded by the number of triangles in $R$ containing node $i$. The expected number of triangles in $G(n, 1/2)$ containing any fixed node is $M/8$ and thus, since there cannot be more than $M$ such triangles, with probability at least $1/15$ the number of triangles containing node $i$ exceeds $M/16$. Since in Algorithm $\mathcal{A}$ node $i$ correctly lists all the triangles containing $i$ with probability at least $1 - 1/32$, we conclude that $T_i$ includes at least $M/6$ triangles including $i$ with overall probability at least $1/15 - 1/32$. We thus obtain

$$I(E; T_i) \geq \frac{M}{16} \cdot \left(\frac{1}{15} - \frac{1}{32}\right) = \Omega(n^2),$$

as claimed □

## ACKNOWLEDGMENTS

FLG was partially supported by MEXT KAKENHI (24106009) and JSPS KAKENHI (15H01677, 16H01705, 16H05853). TI was partially supported by JSPS KAKENHI (15H00852, 16H02878) and JST-SICORP Japan-Israel Bilateral Program "ICT for a resilient society".

## REFERENCES

[1] Noga Alon, Laszlo Babai, and Alon Itai. 1986. A Fast and Simple Parallel Algorithm for the Maximal Independent Set Problem. *Journal of Algorithms* 7, 4 (1986), 567–583.

[2] Nikhil Bansal and Ryan Williams. 2012. Regularity Lemmas and Combinatorial Algorithms. *Theory of Computing* 8, 1 (2012), 69–94.

[3] Leonid Barenboim and Michael Elkin. 2013. *Distributed Graph Coloring: Fundamentals and Recent Developments.* Morgan & Claypool.

[4] Leonid Barenboim, Michael Elkin, Seth Pettie, and Johannes Schneider. 2016. The Locality of Distributed Symmetry Breaking. *J. ACM* 63, 3 (2016), 20:1–20:45.

[5] Keren Censor-Hillel, Eldar Fischer, Gregory Schwartzman, and Yadu Vasudev. 2016. Fast Distributed Algorithms for Testing Graph Properties. In *Proceedings of the International Symposium on Distributed Computing (DISC).* Springer, 43–56.

[6] Keren Censor-Hillel, Petteri Kaski, Janne H. Korhonen, Christoph Lenzen, Ami Paz, and Jukka Suomela. 2015. Algebraic Methods in the Congested Clique. In *Proceedings of the ACM Symposium on Principles of Distributed Computing (PODC).* ACM, 143–152.

[7] Artur Czumaj and Andrzej Lingas. 2009. Finding a Heaviest Vertex-Weighted Triangle Is not Harder than Matrix Multiplication. *SIAM J. Comput.* 39, 2 (2009), 431–444.

[8] Danny Dolev, Christoph Lenzen, and Shir Peled. 2012. "Tri, Tri Again": Finding Triangles and Small Subgraphs in a Distributed Setting. In *Proceedings of the International Symposium on Distributed Computing (DISC).* Springer, 195–209.

[9] Andrew Drucker, Fabian Kuhn, and Rotem Oshman. 2014. On the Power of the Congested Clique Model. In *Proceedings of the ACM Symposium on Principles of Distributed Computing (PODC).* ACM, 367–376.

[10] Michael Elkin. 2004. A Faster Distributed Protocol for Constructing a Minimum Spanning Tree. In *Proceedings of the ACM-SIAM Symposium on Discrete Algorithms (SODA).* SIAM, 359–368.

[11] Michael Elkin. 2006. An Unconditional Lower Bound on the Time-Approximation Trade-off for the Distributed Minimum Spanning Tree Problem. *SIAM J. Comput.* 36, 2 (2006), 433–456.

[12] Pierre Fraigniaud, Ivan Rapaport, Ville Salo, and Ioan Todinca. 2016. Distributed Testing of Excluded Subgraphs. In *Proceedings of the International Symposium on Distributed Computing (DISC).* Springer, 342–356.

[13] Silvio Frischknecht, Stephan Holzer, and Roger Wattenhofer. 2012. Networks Cannot Compute Their Diameter in Sublinear Time. In *Proceedings of the ACM-SIAM Symposium on Discrete Algorithms (SODA).* SIAM, 1150–1162.

[14] Robert G. Gallager, Pierre A. Humblet, and Philip M. Spira. 1983. A Distributed Algorithm for Minimum-Weight Spanning Trees. *ACM Transactions on Programming Languages and Systems (TOPLAS)* 5, 1 (1983), 66–77.

[15] J.A. Garay, S. Kutten, and D. Peleg. 1993. A Sub-Linear Time Distributed Algorithm for Minimum-Weight Spanning Trees. In *Proceedings of the IEEE Symposium on Foundations of Computer Science (FOCS).* IEEE, 659–668.

[16] Mohsen Ghaffari, Andreas Karrenbauer, Fabian Kuhn, Christoph Lenzen, and Boaz Patt-Shamir. 2015. Near-Optimal Distributed Maximum Flow: Extended Abstract. In *Proceedings of the ACM Symposium on Principles of Distributed Computing (PODC).* ACM, 81–90.

[17] Mohsen Ghaffari and Fabian Kuhn. 2013. Distributed Minimum Cut Approximation. In *Proceedings of the International Symposium on Distributed Computing (DISC).* Springer, 1–15.

[18] Juho Hirvonen, Joel Rybicki, Stefan Schmid, and Jukka Suomela. 2014. Large Cuts with Local Algorithms on Triangle-Free Graphs. *CoRR* abs/1402.2543 (2014). http://arxiv.org/abs/1402.2543

[19] Stephan Holzer and Roger Wattenhofer. 2012. Optimal Distributed All Pairs Shortest Paths and Applications. In *Proceedings of the ACM Symposium on Principles of Distributed Computing (PODC).* ACM, 355–364.

[20] Alon Itai and Michael Rodeh. 1978. Finding a Minimum Circuit in a Graph. *SIAM J. Comput.* 7, 4 (1978), 413–423.

[21] Fabian Kuhn, Thomas Moscibroda, and Roger Wattenhofer. 2016. Local Computation: Lower and Upper Bounds. *J. ACM* 63, 2 (2016), 17:1–17:44.

[22] Fabian Kuhn and Roger Wattenhofer. 303–310. Constant-Time Distributed Dominating Set Approximation. *Distributed Computing* 17, 4 (303–310), 2005.

[23] Christoph Lenzen and Boaz Patt-Shamir. 2015. Fast Partial Distance Estimation and Applications. In *Proceedings of the ACM Symposium on Principles of Distributed Computing (PODC).* ACM, 153–162.

[24] Christoph Lenzen and David Peleg. 2013. Efficient Distributed Source Detection with Limited Bandwidth. In *Proceedings of the ACM Symposium on Principles of Distributed Computing (PODC).* ACM, 375–382.

[25] Nathan Linial. 1992. Locality in Distrubuted Graph Algorithms. *SIAM J. Comput.* 21, 1 (1992), 193–201.

[26] Zvi Lotker, Boaz Patt-Shamir, Elan Pavlov, and David Peleg. 2005. Minimum-Weight Spanning Tree Construction in $O(\log \log n)$ Communication Rounds. *SIAM J. Comput.* 35, 1 (2005), 120–131.

[27] Danupon Nanongkai. 2014. Distributed Approximation Algorithms for Weighted Shortest Paths. In *Proceedings of the ACM Symposium on Theory of Computing (STOC).* ACM, 565–573.

[28] Danupon Nanongkai and Hsin-Hao Su. 2014. Almost-Tight Distributed Minimum Cut Algorithms. In *Proceedings of the International Symposium on Distributed Computing (DISC).* Springer, 439–453.

[29] Gopal Pandurangan, Peter Robinson, and Michele Scquizzato. 2016. Tight Bounds for Distributed Graph Computations. *CoRR* abs/1602.08481 (2016). http://arxiv.org/abs/1602.08481

[30] Mihai Patrascu. 2010. Towards Polynomial Lower Bounds for Dynamic Problems. In *Proceedings of the ACM Symposium on Theory of Computing (STOC).* ACM, 603–610.

[31] David Peleg. 2000. *Distributed Computing: A Locality-Sensitive Approach.* Society for Industrial and Applied Mathematics.

[32] David Peleg and Vitaly Rubinovich. 2000. A Near-Tight Lower Bound on the Time Complexity of Distributed Minimum-Weight Spanning Tree Construction. *SIAM J. Comput.* 30, 5 (2000), 1427–1442.

[33] Seth Pettie and Hsin-Hao Su. 2015. Distributed Coloring Algorithms for Triangle-Free Graphs. *Information and Computation* 243 (2015), 263–280.

[34] Igor Rivin. 2002. Counting Cycles and Finite Dimensional $L^p$ Norms. *Advances in Applied Mathematics* 29, 4 (2002), 647 – 662.

[35] Atish Das Sarma, Stephan Holzer, Liah Kor, Amos Korman, Danupon Nanongkai, Gopal Pandurangan, David Peleg, and Roger Wattenhofer. 2012. Distributed Verification and Hardness of Distributed Approximation. *SIAM J. Comput.* 41, 5 (2012), 1235–1265.

[36] Virginia Vassilevska Williams and Ryan Williams. 2010. Subcubic Equivalences between Path, Matrix and Triangle Problems. In *Proceedings of the IEEE Symposium on Foundations of Computer Science (FOCS).* IEEE, 645–654.

[37] Virginia Vassilevska Williams and Ryan Williams. 2013. Finding, Minimizing, and Counting Weighted Subgraphs. *SIAM J. Comput.* 42, 3 (2013), 831–854.

[38] Mark N. Wegman and J. Lawrence Carter. 1981. New Hash Functions and Their Use in Authentication and Set Equality. *J. Comput. System Sci.* 22, 3 (1981), 265 – 279.

# Asynchronous Shared Channel

Gianluca De Marco
University of Salerno
Dipartimento di Informatica
Italy
demarco@dia.unisa.it

Grzegorz Stachowiak
University of Wrocław
Instytut Informatyki
Poland
gst@cs.uni.wroc.pl

## ABSTRACT

In this work we address the question whether a simple shared channel could be efficiently utilized, that is, with a constant throughput and linear packet latency. A shared channel (also called a multiple access channel), introduced nearly 50 years ago in the context of the Ethernet [36], is among the most popular and widely studied models of communication and distributed computing. In a nutshell, a number of stations is able to communicate by transmitting and listening to a shared channel, and a message is successfully delivered to all stations if and only if its source station is the only transmitter at a time. Despite of a vast amount of work in the last decades, many fundamental questions remain open, such as: What is the impact of asynchrony on channel utilization? How important is the knowledge/estimate of the number of contenders? Could non-adaptive protocols (i.e., random codes) be asymptotically as efficient as adaptive protocols? In this work we present a broad picture of results answering the abovementioned questions for a fundamental problem of contention resolution, in which each of the contending stations needs to broadcast successfully its message. We show that adaptive algorithms *or* algorithms with the knowledge of contention size $k$ (i.e., random codes with knowledge of $k$) achieve constant channel throughput and linear message latency even for very weak channels, i.e., with feedback restricted to simple acknowledgments and in the absence of synchronization. This asymptotically optimal performance cannot be extended to other settings — we prove that there is *no* non-adaptive algorithm without the knowledge of contention size $k$ achieving throughput $\omega((\log\log k)^2/(\log k))$ and/or admitting latency $o(k\log k/(\log\log k)^2)$. This means, in particular, that coding (even random) with acknowledgments is not very efficient on a shared channel without synchronization or estimate of contention size. We also present a non-adaptive algorithm with no knowledge of contention size that almost matches these two complexities. More specifically, it achieves latency $O(k\log^2 k)$ and channel utilization $\Omega(1/\log^2 k)$ even if stations do not switch off after successful transmissions (and thus, could disturb other stations in succeeding), and could be improved by factor $\Theta(\log\log k)$ if stations switch off after acknowledgment. Despite the absense of a collision detection mechanism, our algorithms are also efficient in terms of energy. The maximum number of channel accesses (including transmissions and listenings) for our non-adaptive solutions, with and without knowledge of $k$, is respectively $O(\log k)$ and $O(\log^2 k)$ whp. Regarding the adaptive algorithm, we argue that a simple modification of our protocol preserves constant throughput and linear latency while achieving $O(\log k)$ maximum number of channel accesses per station whp.

**Keywords:** shared channel; multiple-access channel; contention resolution; distributed algorithms; randomized algorithms; lower bound.

## 1 INTRODUCTION

A shared channel, also called a multiple access channel, is one of the fundamental communication models considered in the literature. The formal model that is taken as the basis for theoretical studies is defined as follows, cf. the surveys by Gallager [24] and Chlebus [5].

**Stations.** A set of $k$ stations are connected to the same multi-point transmission medium. Stations are anonymous, that is, they have no ID labels to uniquely distinguish them. There is no central control: every station acts autonomously by means of a distributed algorithm.

**Communication.** Stations can communicate by transmitting and receiving messages on the shared channel in synchronous *rounds*. If $m \le k$ stations transmit at the same round, then the result of the transmission depends on the parameter $m$ as follows: if $m = 0$, the channel is *silent* and no packet is successfully transmitted; if $m = 1$, the packet owned by the singly transmitting station is *successfully transmitted* on the channel and therefore delivered to all the other stations; finally, if $m > 1$, simultaneous transmissions interfere with one another (we say that a *collision* occurs) and as a result no packet is heard by the other stations.

No special signal is heard in case of collision, making impossible to distinguish between an occurred collision and the case where no station transmits; it is called a setting *without collision detection.*[*] The only feedback a station can hear is when it actually transmits successfully, in which case it gets an *aknowledgement.*

**Contention resolution problem.** Each station possesses a packet, which can be transmitted in a single round. The aim is to let each of the $k$ stations to transmit successfully its packet. A *contention resolution* algorithm is a distributed algorithm that schedules the transmissions for each of the $k$ participating stations guaranteeing

[*]By contrast, in a *collision detection* setting, not considered in this paper, the channel elicits a *feedback* (interference noise) in case of collision, allowing to deduce that two or more stations tried to transmit at the same time.

This work was supported by the Polish National Science Centre grant DEC-2012/06/M/ST6/00459.



*PODC '17, July 25-27, 2017, Washington, DC, USA*



ACM ISBN 978-1-4503-4992-5/17/07...$15.00
https://doi.org/10.1145/3087801.3087831

that every station eventually transmits individually (i.e., without interfering with other stations) on the channel.

**Static vs dynamic scenarios.** The vast majority of the literature on contention resolution problem produced so far either assumed the (simplified) *static* situation in which the $k$ stations are all activated at the very beginning (and therefore start simultaneously their transmitting schedules) [1, 4, 13, 27–29, 33] or that the activation times are restricted to statistical (when packet arrivals are determined by a Poisson distribution) or adversarial-queueing models [2, 9, 25, 35–37].

Inspired by the inherently decentralized nature of the multiple access model, in this paper we focus on a more general and realistic *dynamic* scenario, in which the stations with packets could get awake (i.e., start their local executions of a distributed algorithm) in *arbitrary times*, i.e., the sequence of activation times, also called a *wake-up schedule*, is totally determined by a worst-case adversary. This scenario, sometimes also called asynchronous, reflects the more realistic situation in which the stations are geographically far apart or totally independent, and consequently each activation time is locally determined and cannot be known or even approximately predicted by other stations. Throughout the paper, "switched on", "activated", "woken up" and their derived terms are used interchangeably to mean the action, controlled by a worst-case adversary, by which a station wakes up and starts executing the algorithm.

**Timing.** Although the communication is in synchronous rounds (the clocks of all the stations tick at the same rate) there is *no global clock* and *no system-based synchronization*: each station starts its local clock in the round in which it wakes up, without knowing anything about the round numbers ticked by the other clocks.

It is interesting that in the static model there is no distinction between the model with a global clock and that without it. Indeed, here one can assume that a global clock is available: all stations are activated simultaneously and therefore their clocks, starting at the same time, will always tick the same round numbers. In this sense, the dynamic model considered in this work is more general and challenging than the static one.

**Performance measures.** Since the activation times can be arbitrarily distant from each other, we measure the efficiency of a station in terms of its *latency*, i.e., the number of rounds necessary for a station to transmit its packet successfully, measured since its activation time. The complexity of an algorithm, called an *algorithm latency* (or simply a *latency* if understood from the context) is measured by the maximum latency over all awaken stations. A *throughput*, also called a *channel utilization*, is defined as the worst-case ratio between the contention size $k$ (which corresponds to the minimum number of rounds needed for the stations to transmit singly to the channel) and the algorithm latency. We express the latency and throughput as functions of the contention size $k$. In technical results, we will focus on analyzing latency for any contention size parameter $k$, as the channel utilization easily follows from it.

**Algorithms.** We seek *randomized* algorithms that allow every station to transmit successfully its packet, regardless of the activation times. Note that the choice of randomized solutions is forced since in the absence of unique IDs there is no deterministic way of breaking the symmetry among the *identical* stations on the shared channel.

All our asymptotic bounds are to be understood as high probability bounds, that is, they hold *with high probability* (in short: *whp*). We say that an event for an algorithm holds whp, when for a predefined parameter $\eta > 0$, the parameters of the algorithm can be chosen, so that for any contention size $k$ the event holds with probability at least $1 - 1/k^{\eta}$.

## 1.1 Previous work and our contribution

Contention resolution on a shared channel has a very long and rich history, including communication tasks, scheduling, fault-tolerance, security, energy, game-theoretical and many other aspects, which is impossible to condense into a short space. The first theoretical papers on channel contention resolution date back to the 70's and considered mainly deterministic solutions. We refer the reader to the full version of this paper for a more complete account of such a bibliography.

Concerning randomized solutions, which represent the topic of the present paper, Greenberg, Flajolet and Ladner [28] and Greenberg and Ladner [29] presented an algorithm with collision detection working in $2.14k + O(\log k)$ rounds with high probability without any *a priori* knowledge of the number $k$ of contenders. Recently, Fernández Anta, Mosteiro and Ramon Muñoz [1] obtained the same asymptotic (optimal) bound in the model without collision detection with a non-adaptive algorithm that also ignores any knowledge about contention size $k$. *This shows that in the static model, i.e., when all the packets arrive at the same time, there is no asymptotic difference in the time complexity between adaptiveness and non-adaptiveness, even in the absence of any knowledge about channel contention.*

The first formalization of the dynamic model, is due to Gąsieniec, Pelc and Peleg [26], who introduced it for the wakeup problem, where the goal is simply to get one successful transmission. They introduced many interesting variations concerning synchrony and knowledge both for deterministic and randomized algorithms. Further developments specific for randomized solutions were provided in [32]. The contention resolution problem has been also studied in the more general framework of multi-hop radio networks, particularly in the context of problems such as (multi-)broadcast, gossip and others in the so-called blindfold model, i.e. in total absence of knowledge about topology and network parameters [10, 13, 16, 17]. Developments where similar issues on selecting stations (included broadcasting in multi-hop radio networks) under many assumptions, mainly regarding knowledge and synchrony, can be found in [6–8, 11, 12, 14, 18–23].

As for the contention resolution problem in the dynamic scenario, considered in this paper, Bender et al. [3] very recently designed an adaptive algorithm *with collision detection* that, without any given bound on parameter $k$, exhibits constant throughput, linear latency and $O(\log\log^* k)$ expected transmissions.

**Our contribution.** We pursue the study on contention resolution further by considering both adaptive and non-adaptive protocols in the more general setting when stations with packets awake at arbitrary times and in the more severe model without collision detection. The wake-up times are determined by a worst-case adversary. Upon waking up, each station starts its protocol from the beginning and a global clock is not available (an upper bound for

**Table 1: Currently best results on latency in randomized contention resolution (the result marked with (*) holds if switch-off upon aknowledgement is allowed)**

| synchrony | collision det. | settings | upper bound | lower bound |
|---|---|---|---|---|
| static | no | non-adaptive and $k$ unknown | $O(k)$ [1] | $\Omega(k)$ |
| | yes | adaptive and $k$ unknown | $O(k)$ [3] | $\Omega(k)$ |
| dynamic | no | adaptive or $k$ known | $O(k)$ [this paper] | $\Omega(k)$ |
| | no | non-adaptive and $k$ unknown | $O(k\log^2 k)$, $O\left(k\frac{\ln^2 k}{\ln\ln k}\right)$ (*) [this paper] | $\Omega\left(k\frac{\log k}{(\log\log k)^2}\right)$ [this paper] |

the case with global clock has been given recently for the deterministic setting [21]). Our results can be summarized as follows (cf. Table 1 for a comparison with the static model in the most severe settings, i.e. non-adaptivity without collision detection and with $k$ unknown).

If the protocol is adaptive or a linear upper bound on $k$ is given *a priori* to the stations, then the contention resolution can be done optimally (in asymptotic sense); we provide two corresponding algorithms working whp with latency $O(k)$ and constant channel utilization.

If the protocol is non-adaptive and no linear upper bound is known on $k$, then we show a time complexity separation with the previous cases by proving that there is *no* non-adaptive randomized algorithm without any linear upper bound on $k$ achieving $o\left(k\frac{\log k}{(\log\log k)^2}\right)$ latency and $\omega\left(\frac{(\log\log k)^2}{\log k}\right)$ channel utilization whp.

We finally give a non-adaptive algorithm with no linear upper bound on $k$, i.e., universal random code, with latency $O(k\log^2 k)$ and $\Omega\left(\frac{1}{\log^2 k}\right)$ channel utilization, whp, which almost match our lower bounds for the same setting. We also show that if we allow switch-off upon acknowledgment then this algorithm/code guarantees even better latency $O(k\frac{\log^2 k}{\log\log k})$ and $\Omega\left(\frac{\log\log k}{\log^2 k}\right)$ channel utilization, whp.

*Our contribution implies that, in contrast with the static model, in the dynamic counterpart there is separation, in terms of time complexity and channel utilization, between non-adaptive algorithms ignoring k and algorithms that either are adaptive or know k. It also implies a separation between the static and dynamic models, in case of non-adaptive algorithms without a good estimate of the number k of contenders.* It is interesting to note that, compared with the Bender et al. [3] protocol, our adaptive algorithm exhibits the same optimal performances both on latency and throughput even in the more severe setting without collision detection. As for energy efficiency, we argue that a simple modification of the protocol, while preserving the same contant throughput and linear latency, allows us to achieve an $O(\log k)$ maximum number of channel access (counting both transmissions and listenings) whp. As for our non-adaptive solutions, with and without knowledge of $k$, the energy cost is respectively $O(\log k)$ and $O(\log^2 k)$ whp. We remind the reader to the full version of the paper for details on the analysis of the energy cost.

Given the generality of the shared channel as a *symmetry breaking* model, we believe that our contribution and newly developed techniques could shed light on the complexity of other distributed computing problems.

**Our approach.** The first and key finding is that in order to utilize the channel efficiently, against some non-synchronized sequence of activation times, any "universally efficient" (i.e., efficient for any contention size) *non-adaptive* contention resolution algorithm has to schedule the probabilities of transmissions in the first $\Theta(k\log k/(\log\log k)^2)$ rounds in such a way that they sum up to $\Omega(\log k/\log\log k)$, cf., Lemma 5.3 in Section 5.1. (Recall that we do not require from the algorithms that these probabilities are independent in rounds, which make our lower bound on latency more general.) This was not the case for previous analysis of simplified static scenarios (i.e., when stations start the protocol at the same time) or simpler problems such as wakeup (i.e., waiting for the first successful transmission). We later show that some slightly more subtle selection of the activation times pumps-up the sum requirement to $\Omega(\log^2 k/(\log\log k)^2)$ over the first $\Theta(k\log k/(\log\log k)^2)$ rounds, cf., Lemma 5.6. This occurs to be sufficient to prove the corresponding overlinear lower bound on latency and a sub-constant upper bound on channel utilization, cf., Theorem 5.1.

Second, we found out that such an effect doesn't hold if we know some linear upper bound on $k$, as slowly increasing probabilities, starting from the level of $1/k$ and ending at $(\log k)/k$, guarantees the existence of many rounds with a sum of probabilities of alive stations being smaller than 1 regardless of how the activation times are located (cf., Lemmas 3.3 to 3.6 in Section 3). This, together with the property that the transmission probability of a single station is at least $(\log k)/k$, implies that each station succeeds in linear time with high probability (cf., Lemma 3.2 and the final proof of Theorem 3.1). Note that in this case the sum of transmission probabilities of a station during the first $\Theta(k)$ rounds is also $\Omega(\log k)$, however the knowledge of $k$ (or its linear upper bound) allows to schedule them in such a way that the pumping-up technique from the lower bound mentioned above (for non-adaptive solutions *without* knowledge of $k$) does not work.

Third, adaptiveness moderates the effect of pumped-up sums, as it allows to elect the first leader quickly using known solutions to the wake-up problem, the leader could coordinate the selection of another successful station which becomes a new leader, and so on. The leaders provide time synchronization, which allows to run known efficient protocols for synchronized activation times (static scenarios). For details see Section 4.

Finally, in the most severe setting of non-adaptive algorithms with no a priori knowledge, sub-linearly decreasing probabilities allow to find a linear fraction of rounds with $O(1)$ sum of transmission probabilities, cf., Section 5.2. This, together with the fact that a station itself transmits with sub-linearly decreasing probability $(\log j)/j$ in round $j$, guarantees successful transmission with high probability in a slightly super-linear time period, namely $O(k \log^2 k/(\log\log k))$ rounds.

**Structure of the paper.** After some conventions and notations (Section 2), we give asymptotically optimal algorithms: non-adaptive with known contention size (Section 3) and adaptive without known contention size (Section 4). Our lower bound shows a separation of settings allowing efficient channel utilization from the ones incurring substantial costs (Section 5.1). It is almost matched by our last algorithm (Section 5.2).

## 2 CONVENTIONS AND FREQUENTLY USED NOTATION

The activity of every station is articulated into synchronous rounds counted by a local clock. Each station can measure the time only on the base of this local numbering. By convention, we assume that a station is activated at round 0 of its local clock and can start its transmitting schedule from the next round: i.e., at each round $1, 2, 3, \ldots$ a station can decide the probability of transmission.[†]

Although there is no global time accessible to the stations, in our analysis we need also to refer to an *absolute* time which measures the time elapsed since the first activation and allows us, in particular, to consider all the stations that are simultaneously active at any given time of the computation. Therefore, besides to the local numbering of rounds, we will also use a *global numbering* (not visible to the stations) that conventionally starts at the time when the first station (or group of stations) wakes up.

To clarify the relationship between local and global numbering of rounds for different stations, consider the following situation. A station $u_1$ is the first station to be activated. After 4 rounds, stations $u_2$ and $u_3$ are activated. After two more rounds, $u_4$ is activated. In this case, the local numbering of $u_1$ (the first to be activated) coincides with the global numbering. But the global numbering is 4 steps ahead of the local numberings of $u_2$ and $u_3$, and it is 6 steps ahead of the local numbering of $u_4$.

Given a time $t$ of the global numbering, we denote by $\hat{A}[t]$ the set of stations activated until time $t$. Some stations may however cease to be active during the protocol, therefore we use notation $A[t]$ for the set of stations that are active at time $t$ and by $q_v[t]$ the transmission probability of station $v$ at time $t$. Moreover, we define the *sum of transmission probabilities* at time $t$ as follows: $\sigma[t] = \sum_{u \in A[t]} q_u[t]$.

The notation introduced so far will be used both for adaptive and non-adaptive algorithms. We now introduce some definitions specific for *non-adaptive* algorithms. When dealing with non-adaptive algorithms, we will also need to express the transmission probability of a station at any round of its *local clock*: $p(i)$ denotes the probability that an arbitrary station transmits at the $i$th round of its local clock. More precisely, without loss of generality, we can assume that each station $v$ chooses randomly, in advance, the sequence of rounds in which it schedules the transmissions. Recall that the assignment of transmissions to rounds does not need to be independent over the rounds.

Notice that in $p(i)$ we do not need to specify the station which this probability refers to. Indeed, for non-adaptive algorithms, the probability that a station transmits at the $i$th round of its local clock depends only on the local round index $i$ (recall that the stations are anonymous). We also define the *sum of transmission probabilities of an arbitrary station* up to local time $i$: $s(i) = \sum_{j=1}^{i} p(j)$. Let $t_v$ denote the global number of the round in which station $v$ is activated. Note that if $v$ is active in round $t$, its transmission probability in this round is $q_v[t] = p(t - t_v)$. We define $\hat{\sigma}[t] = \sum_{v \in \hat{A}[t]} p(t - t_v)$. It is easy to see that $\hat{\sigma}[t] \geq \sigma[t]$, due to the ranges of sums defining these two values.

When the time appears as argument of a function (like $p(i)$, $s(i)$, $A[t]$, $q_u[t]$), to avoid confusion, we have used parenthesis for local rounds and square brackets for global rounds. We will continue using such a convention throughout the paper.

## 3 A NON-ADAPTIVE ALGORITHM FOR KNOWN CONTENTION

In this section we give a non-adaptive algorithm achieving latency $O(k)$ whp in the case when the number of contenders $k$, or a linear upper bound on $k$, is given to the stations as a part of the input.

**Protocol 1** NonAdaptiveWithK$(k, c)$

**for** $l = 0, 1, 2, \ldots, \log\log k$ **do**
  **for** $c\varphi(l)$ rounds **do** transmit with prob. $\frac{2^l}{2k}$
  **end for**
**end for**

Recall that we allow the stations to wake up arbitrarily, and the stations do not need to have any ID's. An additional advantage of our algorithm is that it is uniform, i.e., transmissions are independent over rounds.

The main idea of construction of this algorithm is to start with transmission probability $\Theta(1/k)$, that assures a small interference from other stations and a constant probability of successful transmission in $k$ rounds. Since for this probability stations tend to transmit successfully and drop out from the set of potential transmitters, this probability can be increased with time without raising the total probability sum $\sigma[t]$. Stations end this increase, when the probability reaches $\Theta(\log k/k)$, and transmitting with this probability assures success whp in time $O(k)$.

For every integer $0 \leq l \leq \log\log k$, we let $\varphi(l) = \frac{k}{2^l}$ if $l < \log\log k$, and $\varphi(l) = k$ if $l = \log\log k$. Any station, starting from the time at which it is activated, executes NonAdaptiveWithK$(k, c)$. It takes two parameters in input, the number $k$ of stations and a constant $c$ that determines the probability of success: we'll see that the larger $c$ the larger $\eta$ and, consequently, the probability of success.

The following performance guarantee follows directly from the inspection of the pseudo-code.

FACT 3.1. *For any given integer constant $c > 0$, the number of rounds needed for any station to execute* NonAdaptiveWithK$(k, c)$ *is less than $3c \cdot k = O(k)$.*

[†]The probabilities of transmission need not be independent: we follow the general definition of randomized algorithms as random distributions over deterministic algorithms, and, in case of adaptiveness, they may depend also on the history of the channel feedback.

Hence, from now on we may focus on proving correctness, as expressed in the following theorem.

THEOREM 3.1. *Any station executing Protocol 1, for a sufficiently large constant c, will eventually transmit its message successfully whp.*

As stated by Fact 3.1, each station is able to transmit only for slightly less than $3c \cdot k$ rounds following its activation. Hence there are altogether at most $3c \cdot k^2$ rounds in which transmissions from these $k$ stations can occur. This set of rounds can be partitioned into disjoint intervals consisting of subsequent rounds at which some active stations can choose to transmit. These intervals are called *time frames* (there can be many of them). In the proofs we concentrate on the time frame in which some station $v$ can transmit. The rounds of this time frame will be numbered $1, 2, 3, \ldots$ Since there are altogether at most $3c \cdot k^2$ rounds in which a transmission can occur, the following fact holds.

FACT 3.2. *For any choice of the activation times, any time frame lasts at most $3ck^2$ rounds.*

For any round $t$, let us define $\mathcal{E}[t]$ as the event that $\sigma[t] < 1$.

LEMMA 3.2. *If event $\mathcal{E}[t]$ holds, then the probability that a given station $v$ transmits successfully in round $t$ is larger than $q_v[t]/4$.*

Our next goal will be to show that actually this favorable situation of having rounds $t$ such that the sum $\sigma[t] < 1$, recurs whp for the whole time of the algorithm's execution. Indeed, in Lemma 3.6 we will show that events $\mathcal{E}[t]$ simultaneously occur for all rounds $t$ of a given time frame. Before being able to prove such a claim, we need three preparatory lemmas.

In the first of these lemmas we consider a scenario in which the sum of transmission probabilities $\sigma[\iota]$ is less than 1 for rounds $\iota < t$, i.e., $\mathcal{E}[\iota]$ occur before round $t$. We show that during the $c\varphi(l)$ rounds preceding round $t$, for any $0 < l \leq \log\log k$, many stations that at time $t$ are involved in some iteration $\lambda \geq l$ of the outer for-loop of the protocol, will transmit successfully whp, and therefore switch off by round $t$.

Let $U$, $|U| \leq k$, be the set of all the stations executing the algorithm in a given frame. For any integer $l \in [0, \log\log k]$ and time round $t \geq 0$, we define $T^l[t] \subseteq U$ to be the subset of stations $v$ (not necessarily still active) that at round $t$ have assigned a transmission probability $q_v[t] = 2^l/(2k)$. In other words, it includes all the stations that have been activated in some round $t' \leq t$ and would transmit with probability $2^l/(2k)$ if still active (i.e. if not switched off due to a successful transmission) at round $t$.

Let $c$ be chosen so that $\eta = (c-8)^2/(32c) + 4$.

LEMMA 3.3. *Let $0 < l \leq \log\log k$ be an integer. Let $t$ and $t'$ be time rounds such that $t' = t - c\varphi(l)$ and assume that the events $\mathcal{E}[1], \mathcal{E}[2], \ldots, \mathcal{E}[t-1]$ hold. Then, if $T' \subseteq \bigcup_{\lambda \geq l} T^\lambda[t]$ and $|A[t'] \cap T'| \leq x$ for some $x > 0$, then $|A[t] \cap T'| \leq \max\{x/2, \sqrt{k}\}$ with probability at least $1 - k^{-\eta-4}$.*

PROOF. Let us consider rounds $\iota \in [t', t-1]$. Notice that since $l > 0$, all the stations from $T'$ must have joined the protocol before round $t'$. This means that during the interval $[t', t-1]$ the number of stations in $|A[\iota] \cap T'|$ cannot increase (it can only decrease as stations can switch-off after successful transmissions).

If $x \leq \sqrt{k}$, then $|A[t] \cap T'| \leq |A[t'] \cap T'| \leq x \leq \sqrt{k}$ and there is nothing to prove. So hereafter we assume that $x > \sqrt{k}$ and our aim will be to prove that $|A[t] \cap T'| \leq x/2$ with probability at least $1 - k^{-\eta-4}$.

To any execution of the algorithm, we can attribute the following 0-1 sequence $\rho$, of length $c\varphi(l)$, corresponding to the sequence of rounds $t', t'+1, \ldots, t-1$. For any round $\iota$, $t' \leq \iota \leq t-1$, the corresponding $(\iota - t' + 1)$th position of $\rho$ is assigned as follows.

- If $|A[\iota] \cap T'| > x/2$ and there is no successful transmission from $A[\iota] \cap T'$ at time $\iota$, then we have a 0 on the position corresponding to $\iota$.
- When $|A[\iota] \cap T'| > x/2$ and there is a successful transmission from $A[\iota] \cap T'$ at time $\iota$, then we assign 1 at this position with probability $x2^l/16k$ in the following way. First observe that the probability of such a successful transmission is $p \geq x2^l/16k$ (indeed, there are more than $x/2$ stations in $A[\iota] \cap T'$ and each of them transmits successfully with probability at least $q_v(\iota)/4 = 2^l/8k$ by Lemma 3.2). In order to assign 1 to the position corresponding to $\iota$ with probability *exactly* $x2^l/16k$, we make an additional independent draw which produces 1 with probability $(1/p)x2^l/16k$ and 0 otherwise.
- Finally, if $|A[\iota] \cap T'| \leq x/2$ then the position is set by tossing a coin where 1 is output with probability $x2^l/16k$.

Notice that each position of $\rho$ is set to 1 with probability *exactly* $x2^l/16k$ independently of the values in the other positions. Let $X$ be the random variable defined as the number of ones in $\rho$. If $X \geq x/2$, then $|A[t] \cap T'| \leq x/2$. Indeed, by hypothesis we have that $|A[t'] \cap T'| \leq x$ and recalling that $f(\iota) = |A[\iota] \cap T'|$ is monotonically decreasing in the interval $[t', t-1]$, we must have at least $x/2$ successful transmissions, i.e., $|A[t] \cap T'| \leq |A[t'] \cap T'| - x/2 \leq x - x/2 = x/2$.

Therefore, the probability that $|A[t] \cap T'| \leq x/2$ is at least the probability that $X \geq x/2$. An estimate of the latter probability will complete the proof. The random variable $X$ expresses the number of successes in $c\varphi(l) \geq ck/2^l$ mutually independent experiments, in each of which the probability of success is $x2^l/16k$. Therefore $\mathbb{E}(X) \geq cx/16$. [‡] Hence,

$$\begin{aligned}
\Pr(X < x/2) &\leq \Pr(X \leq \mathbb{E}(X) \cdot 8/c) \\
&\leq \exp[-\mathbb{E}(X)(1 - 8/c)^2/2] \text{ (by the Chernoff bound)} \\
&\leq \exp[-\sqrt{k}(c-8)^2/(32c)] \text{ (recalling that } x > \sqrt{k}) \\
&< k^{-(c-8)^2/(32c)} = k^{-\eta-4}.
\end{aligned}$$

□

Our next milestone will be to use Lemma 3.3 to show that when the events $\mathcal{E}[1], \mathcal{E}[2], \ldots, \mathcal{E}[t-1]$ hold, then $\mathcal{E}[t]$ also holds whp. This will be done in the two following lemmas. First, we define the more complex events $\mathcal{A}^l[t]$ and prove that their intersection implies event $\mathcal{E}[t]$, c.f., Lemma 3.4. Second, we apply this fact to upper bound the sought conditional probability in Lemma 3.5.

Let $t \geq 0$ be a round index and $0 \leq l \leq \log\log k$. Event $\mathcal{A}^l[t]$ holds if and only if $|A[t] \cap T^l[t]| \leq \max\{|T^l[t]|/2^l, \sqrt{k}\}$. Let $\mathcal{A}[t]$

[‡]Notice that for this inequality to hold, it is sufficient that $c\varphi(l) = ck/2^l$ for every $l = 0, 1, \ldots, \log\log k$. The reason why the algorithm uses $c\varphi(l) = ck$ rounds in its last iteration, corresponding to $l = \log\log k$, will be clear in the final proof of Theorem 3.1 on page 6.

be the event that holds if and only if all events $\mathcal{A}^l[t]$ hold, for $0 \leq l \leq \log\log k$.

LEMMA 3.4. *For every round t, if event $\mathcal{A}[t]$ holds then $\mathcal{E}[t]$ holds.*

PROOF. Fix a round $t$ and assume that for $l = 0, 1, \ldots, \log\log k$, events $\mathcal{A}^l[t]$ hold. We have to show that $\sigma[t] < 1$. Indeed,

$$\begin{aligned}\sigma[t] &= \sum_{l=0}^{\log\log k} |A[t] \cap T^l[t]| \cdot 2^l/2k \\ &\leq \sum_{l=0}^{\log\log k} |T^l[t]|/2k + \sum_{l=0}^{\log\log k} \sqrt{k} \cdot 2^l/2k \\ &\quad \text{(by the hypothesis that } \mathcal{A}[t] \text{ holds)} \\ &< |U|/2k + 1/2 < 1.\end{aligned}$$

□

For any event $\mathcal{A}$ we denote by $\bar{\mathcal{A}}$ the negation of $\mathcal{A}$.

LEMMA 3.5. *For every round t,*

$$\Pr\left(\overline{\mathcal{E}[t]} \,\middle|\, \mathcal{E}[1] \wedge \mathcal{E}[2] \wedge \cdots \mathcal{E}[t-1]\right) < k^{-\eta-3}(\log\log k + 1).$$

LEMMA 3.6. *Given any time frame F, all events $\mathcal{E}[t]$, for every $t \in F$, simultaneously occur with probability larger than $1 - k^{-\eta}/2$.*

PROOF. Let $F$ be any time frame. We want to prove that $1 - \Pr(\mathcal{E}[1] \wedge \mathcal{E}[2] \wedge \cdots \wedge \mathcal{E}[|F|])$ is less than $k^{-\eta}/2$.

Hence,

$$\begin{aligned}&1 - \Pr(\mathcal{E}[1] \wedge \mathcal{E}[2] \wedge \cdots \wedge \mathcal{E}[|F|]) \\ &= \sum_{t=1}^{|F|} \Pr\left(\overline{\mathcal{E}[t]} \,\middle|\, \mathcal{E}[1] \wedge \mathcal{E}[2] \wedge \cdots \mathcal{E}[t-1]\right) \cdot \\ &\quad \Pr(\mathcal{E}[1] \wedge \mathcal{E}[2] \wedge \cdots \mathcal{E}[t-1]) \\ &\leq \sum_{t=1}^{|F|} \Pr\left(\overline{\mathcal{E}[t]} \,\middle|\, \mathcal{E}[1] \wedge \mathcal{E}[2] \wedge \cdots \mathcal{E}[t-1]\right) \\ &\leq 3c \cdot k^2 \cdot \Pr\left(\overline{\mathcal{E}[t]} \,\middle|\, \mathcal{E}[1] \wedge \mathcal{E}[2] \wedge \cdots \mathcal{E}[t-1]\right) \text{ (by Fact 3.2)} \\ &\leq 3c \cdot k^2 \cdot k^{-\eta-3}(\log\log k + 1) \text{ (by Lemma 3.5)} \\ &< k^{-\eta}/2,\end{aligned}$$

for sufficiently large $k$. □

The last lemma tells us that, whp, $\sigma[t] < 1$ holds for all rounds $t$ within a time frame. Due to this inequality, we are now able to show that in each of the last $ck$ rounds, station $v$ — if still awake — transmits successfully with probability $\Omega(\log k/k)$. This, in turn, assures that $v$ transmits successfully, whp, in one of these final rounds (provided it didn't do so earlier). Now we prove Theorem 3.1, which concludes this section.

**Proof of Theorem 3.1** Let us focus on some station $v$ active in some time frame. We will prove that $v$ manages to transmit successfully, whp. Let $R$ be the set of the last $ck$ rounds executed by $v$ correspondent to the final iteration of the inner for-loop. While it is active, station $v$ transmits in any round $t \in R$ with probability $q_v[t] = p(t - t_v) = \log k/(2k)$.

In order to prove the theorem, we need to show that $v$ transmits successfully in one of these rounds whp. The probability that station $v$ does not transmit successfully during the rounds in $R$ is upper bounded by the probability that a station does not transmit successfully in a round $t \in R$ if all events $\mathcal{E}[t]$ for $t \in R$ hold or that there exists a round $t \in R$ such that $\mathcal{E}[t]$ does not hold.

By Lemma 3.2, in any round $t \in R$ such that event $\mathcal{E}[t]$ holds, the active station $v$ transmits successfully with probability larger than $q_v[t]/4 = \log k/(8k)$. So, assuming that for every round $t \in R$ event $\mathcal{E}[t]$ holds, station $v$ does not manage to transmit successfully with probability less than $(1 - \log k/(8k))^{ck} < e^{-c\log k/8}$, which is smaller than $k^{-\eta}/2$ if we take constant $c$ sufficiently large.

By Lemma 3.6 the probability that there exists a round $t \in R$ such that event $\mathcal{E}[t]$ does not hold is also smaller than $k^{-\eta}/2$. Hence, the probability that station $v$ does not transmit successfully is less than $k^{-\eta}/2 + k^{-\eta}/2 = k^{-\eta}$. This concludes the proof of Theorem 3.1. □

# 4 AN ADAPTIVE ALGORITHM FOR UNKNOWN CONTENTION

The lack of knowledge of contention's size, or even its linear approximation, creates an additional challenge to the algorithm. In Section 5 we will show that, for non-adaptive algorithms, this makes the problem complexity provably higher. However, adaptive algorithms could overcome this obstacle. We now describe a protocol `AdaptiveNoK` which resolves the contention with constant throughput and linear latency without any knowledge of contention size.

The algorithm works by alternating between two modes: *leader election mode* and *dissemination mode*. The first mode aims at getting a synchronized subset of stations and electing a leader. The task of the leader will be to coordinate the computation in the dissemination mode, which aims at the actual contention resolution among the synchronized subset of stations defined in the previous execution of the leader election mode.

**Protocol 3** `DecreaseSlowly` *(for a station u)*

$q \leftarrow$ some constant $> 0$
$i \leftarrow 0$
**while** $u$ is active **do**
  transmit with probability $q \cdot \frac{1}{2q+i}$
  **if** transmission is successful **then**
    switch-off
  **end if**
  $i \leftarrow i + 1$
**end while**

During the dissemination mode the leader has also the task to send periodically a message `<D mode>` which informs newly awaken stations about the mode currently executed. A formal description of the modes and actions can be found in the pseudocode of Protocol 2 in the full version in the Appendix. A newly awaken station first listens for 4 rounds in order to determine the current mode of the system: if during these rounds the station gets message `<D mode>`, then it knows that the current system's mode is the dissemination mode, otherwise it infers that it is in the leader election mode. A station can only start the computation in leader election mode, so any newly awaken station just waits until it finds 4 consecutive rounds without getting the `<D mode>` message. In the *leader election mode* the stations execute a wake-up protocol, whose goal is to get just one successful transmission. For such a task, we use protocol DecreaseSlowly introduced in [32] (cf. Protocol 3). Once a successful transmission appears in some round $t$, the station which transmitted in $t$ becomes the *leader*, it sets up a new variable time_counter to 0, and then the *dissemination mode* starts. At this point the leader and all other stations that were alive at $t$, are synchronized. Let us denote by $C$ such a *synchronized* subset of stations. We can assume that a global clock (represented by variable time_counter initiated by the leader) starts for all the stations in $C$ at the round in which the leader was elected. This allows us to use a contention resolution protocol SUniform for the synchronized model with unknown $k$. For this task, we can use one of the protocols (One-Fail Adaptive or Exp Back-on/Back-off) in [1], which guarantee that all stations transmit successfully within $O(k)$ rounds after the synchronization round whp.

During an execution of SUniform, all stations from set $C$ switch off directly after a successful transmission (are not active anymore), while all stations which are currently waking up are waiting until the end of this particular execution of SUniform. To make it possible that the stations can distinguish between both modes after waking up, the algorithm SUniform is executed in odd rounds only, while even rounds are devoted to performing the following kind of coordination: in rounds $t = 4x$ for $x \in \mathbb{N}$, all alive stations from set $C$ and the leader transmit a message. We distinguish two cases depending on the outcome of such a transmission:

- If the leader does not receive an acknowledgment, it knows that there are still some stations in $C$ which have not succeeded in transmitting a message. Consequently, in rounds $t = 4x + 2$ for $x \in \mathbb{N}$, it broadcasts the <D mode> message, informing that the system is still in dissemination mode.
- If the leader receives an acknowledgment, then it knows that it was the only transmitter (all stations in $C$ successfully transmitted and switched off). In this case, no message will be transmitted in rounds $t = 4x + 2$ for $x \in \mathbb{N}$, (which causes the system to change its mode to *leader election*: all newly awaken stations do not get any message in 4 consecutive rounds and therefore infer that the current mode is leader election). Finally, the leader switches off itself.

The correctness and the time complexity of this algorithm will be proved in Theorem 4.3. The first step is to show that protocol DecreaseSlowly wakes up the system in $O(k)$ rounds whp. In [32], an algorithm *Decrease Slowly* has been presented which completes the wakeup in $O(k \log k)$ rounds whp. In the following theorem, we show that actually this algorithm can complete the wakeup in $O(k)$ rounds whp.

Theorem 4.1. *Algorithm* DecreaseSlowly *finishes wake-up in $O(k)$ rounds whp.*

The following lemma shows that once a station enters the leader election mode, i.e., after it has found 4 consecutive rounds without receiving the <D mode> message, it reaches a successful transmission within $O(k)$ rounds whp. The final theorem will further consider the time spent to enter the leader election mode.

Lemma 4.2. *A station $u$ sends successfully whp in $O(k)$ rounds after entering the computation in leader election mode.*

Theorem 4.3. *Algorithm* AdaptiveNoK *solves the contention resolution problem with latency $O(k)$ whp.*

# 5 NON-ADAPTIVE ALGORITHMS FOR UNKNOWN CONTENTION

## 5.1 A lower bound

The aim of this subsection is to prove the following theorem stating a lower bound on non-adaptive algorithms without the knowledge of $k$.

Theorem 5.1. *There is no non-adaptive contention resolution algorithm with no knowledge of contention size $k$ with latency of $o(k \log k/(\log\log k)^2)$ rounds whp.*

For the sake of contradiction, in the following we will assume that there is a non-adaptive algorithm $\mathcal{A}$ which, without having any information on contention size $k$, solves the Contention Resolution problem for any number $k$ of stations, with latency of $o\left(k\frac{\log k}{(\log\log k)^2}\right)$ rounds whp.

In the following, we will use the term *instance* to denote a schedule assigning to each station the time at which it becomes activated. Our aim will be to show existence of an instance of the problem such that whp algorithm $\mathcal{A}$ does not make *any* successful transmission on this instance within the first $\Omega\left(k\frac{\log k}{(\log\log k)^2}\right)$ rounds. This obviously contradicts the assumption on the latency of algorithm $\mathcal{A}$. We stress out the following interesting polarization that we have discovered and make use of here, and which does not take place in the simpler setting with synchronization – if one tries to solve contention resolution (i.e., to have *all* stations successful) using too short codes with acknowledgment (even random), there will be *not even a single successful round. In other words, if the algorithm is too greedy in terms of channel utilization, it may not achieve even a single successful transmission.*

Remind that for algorithm $\mathcal{A}$ we can define a sequence of probabilities $p(1), p(2), p(3), \ldots$ of transmissions of station's message in its local rounds $1, 2, 3, \ldots$ counting from its activation. This sequence is the same for all executions and across all stations, due to $\mathcal{A}$ being non-adaptive. Namely, any station transmits its message with probability $p(1)$ in the first round after it has been activated. If it has not transmitted successfully before, the transmission occurs with probability $p(i)$ for $i > 1$ in the $i$th round after its activation. Note that the transmission in a round $i$ does not have to be necessarily an event independent on the transmissions in previous rounds; in this sense our proof is more general than many other lower bounds in the literature of shared channel which hold under assuming such independence over rounds.

Without loss of generality we can assume $p(1) > 0$. Moreover, since the stations do not know parameter $k$, the contention size, probabilities $p(i)$ do not depend on $k$. We emphasize that, in view of our contradictory hypothesis, all the following definitions and results hold for a non-adaptive algorithm $\mathcal{A}$ which, without knowing $k$, solves the contention resolution problem for *any number $k$* of contending stations, with a time complexity of $o\left(k\frac{\log k}{(\log\log k)^2}\right)$ whp.

There are the following two parameters related to algorithm $\mathcal{A}$. Let $I$ be an arbitrary instance in which exactly $k$ stations are activated. Let $\tau(I)$ be the minimum time needed for algorithm $\mathcal{A}$ to assure any activated station transmits successfully in instance $I$ whp at least $1 - n^{-\eta}$. Let $\tau(k) = \max_I\{\tau(I)\}$ where the maximum is taken over all instances $I$ of activating $k$ stations. A straightforward consequence of our contradictory assumption is that $\tau(k) = o\left(k\frac{\log k}{(\log\log k)^2}\right)$. We also define $\varsigma(k) = s(\tau(k)) = \sum_{i\in[1,\tau(k)]} p(i)$.

The proof of the lower bound consists of two parts. In the first part we show a dependance of successful transmissions (or more specifically, the lack of them) from the sum of transmission probabilities in rounds. More precisely, the following lemma shows that if in any round up to some $T \le k^2$ the sum $\hat{\sigma}[t]$ of transmission probabilities of stations awaken by this round is $\Omega(\log k)$ then there is no successful transmission by round $T$ whp $1 - 1/k$. Recall, from Section 2, that $\hat{\sigma}[t] = \sum_{v\in\hat{A}[t]} p(t - t_v)$. Note that no successful transmission by round $\tau(k)$ whp $1-1/k$ contradicts the assumption on latency $\tau(k)$, whp, of algorithm $\mathcal{A}$.

Lemma 5.2. *Fix an arbitrary instance. Assume that for any round $t \in [1,T]$, with $T \le k^2$, it holds that $\hat{\sigma}[t] \ge \gamma\log k$ for some sufficiently large constant $\gamma > 0$. Then, no station transmits successfully by round $T$ whp $1 - 1/k$.*

From now on, we can consider $\gamma$ being fixed.

In the second part of the proof, we focus on constructing an instance of activation times such that we could use Lemma 5.6 and block successful transmissions whp. The construction of the problem instance assuring the lower bound on the algorithm will be based on the inequality $\varsigma(k) = \Omega(\log^2 k/(\log\log k)^2)$ proved in the key Lemma 5.6, transformed later into the lower bound on $\hat{\sigma}[t]$ in Lemma 5.7. In order to prove that key lemma, we first formulate a weaker inequality that $\varsigma(k)$ has to fulfill. This lemma can be proved by activating station $v$ in round 1 and all other stations in random rounds in $[1,\tau(k)]$. Since $v$ transmits successfully in these rounds, the inequality in Lemma must hold.

Lemma 5.3. $\varsigma(k) = \Omega(\log k/\log\log k)$.

Proof. We will construct for $\mathcal{A}$ a random instance for which the first station $v$ activated in this instance transmits successfully with probability smaller than $1 - 1/k^\eta$ if $\varsigma(k)$ is not $\Omega(\log k/\log\log k)$ for sufficiently large $k$. Because of this, the contention resolution problem would not be solved whp.

Let station $v$ be activated among the earliest possible group of stations, i.e., at round 1 of the instance, and let us draw $k-1$ different random rounds from time interval $[1,\tau(k)]$ in which the other $k-1$ stations are switched on.

Station $v$ chooses at random the rounds in which it is going to transmit (this choice can be done at the moment $v$ is activated, as the algorithm is non-adaptive). The number of such rounds in time period $[1,\tau(k)]$ is a random variable $X$. Since $E(X) = \varsigma(k)$, by Markov's inequality we have

$$\Pr(X < 2\varsigma(k)) > 1/2\,. \tag{1}$$

The activation times of the other $k-1$ stations are distributed uniformly at random among the $\tau(k) = O(k\log k)$ rounds. Each station transmits with probability $p(1)$ at the first round it switches on. The probability of no successful transmission for station $v$ during the interval $[1,\tau(k)]$ is at least

$$\Omega\left(\frac{1}{(\log k)^X}\right).$$

Hence, this probability (that $v$ does not transmit successfully) is negligible, i.e., at most $1/k^\eta$ for some constant $\eta > 0$, only when $X = \Omega(\log k/\log\log k)$. By Equation (1), it follows that $\varsigma(k) = \Omega(\log k/\log\log k)$, or otherwise station $v$ does not transmit successfully whp. □

In the following lemma we show that the sum of probabilities in a round could be indeed made $\Omega(\log n)$ over the period slightly shorter that the ultimate length $\tau(k)$; we will extend it even further later on.

Lemma 5.4. *There is a constant $c_1 > 0$ and integer $k_0$ such that for $k > k_0$ there is an instance $I(k)$ such that $\hat{\sigma}[t] \ge \gamma\log k$ in rounds $t \in [1, \tau(k/(c_1\log k\log\log k))]$.*

Using the activation times from Lemma 5.4 for half of stations, we can extend the statement of Lemma 5.3 by proving that the probabilities of transmissions concentrate in some suffix of the considered period $[1,\tau(k)]$. In this argument we randomly activate the other half in this suffix.

Lemma 5.5. *For some constant $c_2 > 0$, we have*

$$\varsigma(k) - \varsigma(k/(c_2\log k\log\log k)) = \Omega(\log k/\log\log k).$$

Using Lemma 5.5 in a telescopic way, we can increase the requirement on the sum of transmission probabilities of a single station over the considered period $\tau(k)$.

Lemma 5.6. $\varsigma(k) = \Omega(\log^2 k/(\log\log k)^2)$.

We now transform the lower bound on transmission probabilities of a station over the considered period $[1,\tau(k)]$, proved in Lemma 5.6, into the lower bound on the sums of transmission probabilities in rounds. Using Lemma 5.6 one can construct an instance $J(k)$ for which no successful transmissions are likely.

Lemma 5.7. *There is an instance $J(k)$ for sufficiently large integers $k$ such that for some constant $c^* > 0$, the lower bound $\hat{\sigma}[t] \ge \gamma\log k$ holds in rounds $t \in [1, c^* k\log k/(\log\log k)^2]$.*

The proof of the main result is now straightforward.

**Proof of Theorem 5.1.** The contradiction is obtained by applying Lemma 5.2 to the rounds specified in Lemma 5.7. Since no station transmits in instance $J(k)$ whp $1 - 1/k$, station $v$ cannot achieve latency $o(k\log k/(\log\log k)^2)$ whp. □

## 5.2 Algorithm SublinearDecrease($b$)

In this section we describe a non-adaptive protocol, that we call SublinearDecrease($b$), that resolves the conflicts without having any a priori knowledge on the number $k$ of contenders. This protocol is parametrized by integer

**Protocol 4** `SublinearDecrease`($b$)

```
for j = 3, 4, 5, 6, ..., ∞ do
    for ℓ = 1, 2, 3 ..., b do
        transmit with probability (ln j)/j
    end for
end for
```

$b > 0$. In step $t = (j-3)\cdot b + \ell$, for integers $j \geq 3$ and $1 \leq \ell \leq b$, a station transmits (independently) with probability $\frac{\ln j}{j}$, cf., Protocol 4. As in Section 3, the value of constant $b > 0$, taken as input, depends only on constant $\eta > 0$ (cf., the definition of whp given in Section 1) and determines how close to 1 we want the notion of *high probability* to be.

The main idea of construction of this algorithm is to start with a high probability of transmission and then to reduce this probability gradually. This reduction has to be done very carefully. If we reduce too fast, then we do not achieve successful transmissions of stations whp. If we reduce too slowly, then stations can ba activated gradually during a long period of time in which no successul transmissions occur whp.

#### 5.2.1 *Analysis of protocol* `SublinearDecrease`($b$).

**Introduction and notations.** From now on we fix any station $v$ with the aim of proving that it transmits within a given time from its activation whp. Recall from the previous sections that $p(i)$ denotes the probability of transmission in the $i$th round counting from $v$'s activation, and $s(i) = p(1) + p(2) + \cdots + p(i)$.

In round $t$ of the protocol each station $u$ transmits with probability $q_u[t]$ which is equal to $p(t - t_u) = p(i)$, where $i$ is the $i$th round number according to the local clock of $u$, or it is 0 if the station $u$ transmitted successfully before. As in the previous sections, the sum of probabilities of transmissions $q_u[t]$ of all awaken stations that can send a message in round $t$ is denoted by $\sigma[t]$. Notice that $\sigma[t]$ depends on the particular execution of the protocol as, during the execution, the stations that successfully transmitted switch off and this reflects in a variation of the value $\sigma[t]$. As we already argued in Subsection 5.1, the maximum possible value of $\sigma[t]$ is $\hat{\sigma}[t]$ which is the sum of probabilities $p(t - t_u)$ without taking into account the switching off of stations after successful transmissions. The value $\hat{\sigma}[t]$, unlike $\sigma[t]$, depends only on the instance, i.e. the wake-up times, (not on the random choices of the stations) and, of course, $\hat{\sigma}[t] \geq \sigma[t]$ for all rounds $t$.

**Analysis.** We will prove that any station $v$ transmits successfully with high probability with latency $O(k\log^2 k)$. The transmission probability sequence $p(i)$ in the algorithm is chosen so that during $\Theta(k\log^2 k)$ rounds following the spontaneous wake-up of $v$, the total sum of all values $p(i)$ for all stations and all these rounds is $O(k\log^2 k)$. We will prove, that we can set constants hidden behind these "$\Theta$" and "$O$" so that, by counting argument, during (at least) half of these rounds $t$ we have $\sigma[t] \leq 1$, i.e., the sum of transmission probabilities of stations awaken by round $t$ is at most 1. Since in each such round station $v$ transmits successfully with probability $\Omega(1/(k\log k))$, this half of rounds assure that $v$ transmits successfully whp. More details follow.

All the following results refer to an execution of protocol `SublinearDecrease`($b$) for an arbitrary value of its input parameter $b$. We start with the following technical facts derived using Calculus.

FACT 5.1. *For a sufficiently large i, we have*

$$s(i) < 2b\ln^2(i/b).$$

FACT 5.2. *If $r = 8k\ln^2 k$, then $2k\ln^2 r < r/2$ for sufficiently large $k$.*

LEMMA 5.8. *Let $r = 8k\ln^2 k$. In at least $br/2$ rounds $t \in [1, br]$ the sum of transmission probabilities of active stations, $\hat{\sigma}[t]$, is smaller than 1.*

PROOF. By Fact 5.1 and Fact 5.2, it follows that $k \cdot s(br) < 2bk\ln^2 r < br/2$ for sufficiently large $k$. Consequently, the total sum of transmission probabilities of active stations in the first $br$ rounds after activation of station $v$ is smaller than $br/2$. Thus, in at least $br/2$ rounds $t \in [1, br]$ the sum $\hat{\sigma}[t]$ is smaller than 1. □

Lemma 5.8 holds for an arbitrary value of the input parameter $b$. In order to conclude the proof of Theorem 5.9, we will show that, for a suitable choice of the constant parameter $b$, protocol `SublinearDecrease`($b$) allows any station to transmit successfully within $br$ rounds, for $r = 8k\ln^2 k$, whp.

THEOREM 5.9. *For a sufficiently large constant b, the protocol* `SublinearDecrease`($b$) *solves the contention resolution problem with latency $O(k\ln^2 k)$ and channel utilization $\Omega\left(\frac{1}{\ln^2 k}\right)$ whp.*

PROOF. Consider any station $v$. Let $r = 8k\ln^2 k$. For any round $t \in [1, br]$, we have $\sigma[t] \leq \hat{\sigma}[t]$ and $p(t - t_v) \geq p(br) = \ln r/r$. By Lemma 5.8, there are at least $br/2$ rounds $t \in [1, br]$ in which $\sigma[t] \leq \hat{\sigma}[t] < 1$. We are in the same hypothesis of Lemma 3.2 from Section 3, therefore the probability of successful transmission of $v$ in round $t$ is at least $p(t - t_v)/4$. Hence, the probability that $v$ will not manage to transmit successfully in rounds $1, 2, \ldots, br$, is at most $\left(1 - \frac{p(br)}{4}\right)^{br/2} = \left(1 - \frac{\ln r}{4r}\right)^{br/2} < e^{-(b/8)\ln r} < k^{-b/8}$. This last value can be made smaller than $k^{-\eta-1}$ by choosing $b$ sufficiently large. Next, we apply union bound over all contending stations $v$ to argue that *all k* of them transmit successfully with latency at most $br$ with probability at least $1 - k^{-\eta}$. Hence, we have proved that protocol `SublinearDecrease`($b$) guarantees latency $br = O(k\ln^2 k)$ whp. □

**Analysis of** `SublinearDecrease`($b$) **with acknowledgments.** If we allow each station to switch off after getting an acknowledgment of its successful transmission during execution of `SublinearDecrease`($b$), we could improve performance guarantees by factor $\Omega(\log\log k)$.

We will show, again by a counting argument, that in (at least) half of the first $\Theta(k\log^2 k/\log\log k)$ rounds following a station $v$'s wake-up, the upper bound $\sigma[t] = O(\log\log k)$ holds. Then, for some constants hidden in "$\Theta$" and "$O$", in each round belonging to this half, if $\sigma[t] \geq 1$ then a successful transmission occurs in this round with probability $\Omega(\log\log k/\log^2 k)$. This will imply many successful transmissions of stations, and consequently in (at least) half of rounds $t$ in this half, the value of $\sigma[t]$ will drop below 1 whp. This quarter of rounds alone assures successful transmission of $v$ whp if it does not happen otherwise, because in each of them the awaken station $v$ transmits successfully with probability $\Omega(1/(k \log k \log\log k))$.

THEOREM 5.10. *For a sufficiently large $k$ and constant $b$,* `SublinearDecrease(b)` *with acknowledgment solves the contention resolution problem with latency* $O\left(k \frac{\ln^2 k}{\ln\ln k}\right)$ *and channel utilization* $\Omega\left(\frac{\ln\ln k}{\ln^2 k}\right)$ *whp.*

## 6 CONCLUSIONS AND OPEN PROBLEMS

We provided a comprehensive study of shared channel settings with respect to which parameters allow asymptotically optimal channel utilization and which do not. Several questions and directions remain open. One is to shrink the gap between lower and upper bounds for channel utilization for non-adaptive algorithms, which is nearly quadratic. The complexity of deterministic contention resolution is another open problem, for which only solutions with over-quadratic latency are known so far.

**Acknowledgments.** We would like to thank Darek Kowalski for many stimulating discussions on the topic and problems considered in this paper.

## REFERENCES


[1] A. Fernández Anta, M.A. Mosteiro, J. Ramon Muñoz, Unbounded Contention Resolution in Multiple-Access Channels, *Algorithmica* 67 (2013) 295 - 314.

[2] M.A. Bender, M. Farach-Colton, S. He, B.C. Kuszmaul, and C.E. Leiserson, Adversarial contention resolution for simple channels, in *Proceedings, 17th Annual ACM Symposium on Parallel Algorithms (SPAA)*, 2005, pp. 325 - 332.

[3] M. A. Bender, T. Kopelowitz, S. Pettie, and M. Young, Contention resolution with log-logstar channel accesses, in *Proceedings of the forty-eighth annual ACM symposium on Theory of Computing (STOC)*, 2016, Cambridge, MA, USA, pp. 499-508.

[4] J. Capetanakis, Tree algorithms for packet broadcast channels. *IEEE Transactions on Information Theory* 25 (1979) 505 - 515.

[5] B.S. Chlebus, Randomized communication in radio networks. A chapter in "Handbook on Randomized Computing," P.M. Pardalos, S. Rajasekaran, J.H. Reif, and J.D.P. Rolim, (Eds.), Kluwer Academic Publishers, 2001, vol. I, pp. 401 - 456.

[6] B. S. Chlebus, G. De Marco, M. Talo, Naming a Channel with Beeps, *Fundamenta Informaticae*, 153 (3), pp. 199-219, 2017.

[7] B. S. Chlebus, G. De Marco, D. R. Kowalski, Scalable wake-up of multi-channel single-hop radio networks, *Theoretical Computer Science*, vol. 615, pp. 23-44, 2016.

[8] B. S. Chlebus, G. De Marco, D. R. Kowalski, Scalable Wake-up of Multi-channel Single-Hop Radio Networks in *Proceedings, 18th International Conference on Principles of Distributed Systems (OPODIS 2014)*, Cortina d'Ampezzo, Italy, December 16-19, 2014.

[9] B.S. Chlebus, D.R. Kowalski, and M.A. Rokicki, Adversarial Queuing on the Multiple Access Channel. *ACM Transactions on Algorithms* 8 (2012).

[10] B.S. Chlebus, L. Gasieniec, A. Gibbons, A. Pelc, and W. Rytter, Deterministic broadcasting in unknown radio networks, *Distributed Computing* 15 (2002) 27-38.

[11] M. Chrobak, L. Gasieniec, and D.R. Kowalski, The wake-up problem in multihop radio networks, *SIAM Journal on Computing* 36 (2007) 1453 - 1471.

[12] B.S. Chlebus, L. Gasieniec, D. Kowalski, and T. Radzik, On the wake-up problem in radio networks, in *Proceedings, 32nd International Colloquium on Automata, Languages and Programming (ICALP)*, 2005, pp. 347 - 359.

[13] M. Chrobak, L. Gasieniec, and W. Rytter, Fast broadcasting and gossiping in radio networks, *Journal of Algorithms* 43 (2002) 177 - 189.

[14] B.S. Chlebus and D. Kowalski, A better wake-up in radio networks, in *Proceedings, 23rd ACM Symp. on Principles of Distributed Computing (PODC)*, 2004, 266 - 274.

[15] A.E.F. Clementi, A. Monti, and R. Silvestri, Distributed broadcast in radio networks of unknown topology, *Theoretical Computer Science* 302 (2003) 337 - 364.

[16] G. De Marco, Distributed Broadcast in Unknown Radio Networks, *19th Annual ACM-SIAM Symposium on Discrete Algorithms (SODA 2008)*, San Francisco, California, USA, January 2008.

[17] G. De Marco, Distributed Broadcast in Unknown Radio Networks. *SIAM J. Comput.* 39(6): 2162-2175 (2010)

[18] G. De Marco, D. Kowalski, Contention Resolution in a Non-synchronized Multiple Access Channel, *27th Annual IEEE International Symposium on Parallel and Distributed Processing, (IPDPS 2013)* Cambridge, MA, USA, May 2013.

[19] G. De Marco, D. R. Kowalski, Searching for a Subset of Counterfeit Coins: Randomization vs Determinism and Adaptiveness vs Non-Adaptiveness, *Random Structures and Algorithms*, vol. 42 (1), pp. 97-109, 2013.

[20] G. De Marco, D. R. Kowalski, Towards Power-Sensitive Communication on a Multiple-Access Channel. *30th International Conference on Distributed Computing Systems (ICDCS 2010)*, Genoa, Italy, May 2010.

[21] G. De Marco, and D. Kowalski, Fast Nonadaptive Deterministic Algorithm for Conflict Resolution in a Dynamic Multiple-Access Channel, *SIAM J. Comput.*, 44 (3) 2015, 868 - 888.

[22] G. De Marco, and D. Kowalski, Contention Resolution in a Non-Synchronized Multiple Access Channel *Theoretical Computer Science*, 2017, to appear.

[23] G. De Marco, M. Pellegrini, G. Sburlati, Faster deterministic wakeup in multiple access channels. *Discrete Applied Mathematics* 155(8): 898-903 (2007)

[24] Robert G. Gallager. A perspective on multiaccess channels. IEEE Trans. Information Theory, 31 (2): 124–142, 1985.

[25] L.A. Goldberg, P.D. MacKenzie, M. Paterson, A. Srinivasan. Contention resolution with constant expected delay. Journal of the ACM, 47 (6): 1048–1096, 2000.

[26] L. Gasieniec, A. Pelc, and D. Peleg, The wakeup problem in synchronous broadcast systems, *SIAM Journal on Discrete Mathematics* 14 (2001) 207 - 222.

[27] A.G. Greenberg and S. Winograd, A lower bound on the time needed in the worst case to resolve conflicts deterministically in multiple access channels, *Journal of ACM* (JACM) 32 (1985) 589 - 596.

[28] A.G. Greenberg, P. Flajolet, R. E. Ladner, Estimating the multiplicities of conflicts to speed their resolution in multiple access channels, *Journal of the ACM* (JACM) 34 Issue 2, (1987) 289 - 325.

[29] A.G. Greenberg and R. E. Ladner, Estimating the multiplicities of conflicts in multiple access, In *Proc. of the 24th Annual Symp. on Foundations of Computer Science (FOCS)* (Tucson, AZ.). IEEE, New York, 1983, 383-392.

[30] J.F. Hayes, An adaptive technique for local distribution, *IEEE Transactions on Communications* 26 (1978) 1178 - 1186.

[31] P. Indyk, Explicit constructions of selectors and related combinatorial structures, with applications, in *Proceedings, 13th ACM-SIAM Symposium on Discrete Algorithms (SODA)*, 2002, pp. 697 - 704.

[32] T. Jurdzinski and G. Stachowiak, Probabilistic algorithms for the wakeup problem in single-hop radio networks, *Theory Comput. Syst.*, 38 (3) 2005, pp. 347-367.

[33] J. Komlós and A.G. Greenberg, *An Asymptotically Optimal Nonadaptive Algorithm for Conflict Resolution in Multiple-Access Channels*, IEEE Trans. on Information Theory, vol. 31, (2), (1985), pp. 302 - 306

[34] D. Kowalski, On selection problem in radio networks, in *Proceedings, 24th ACM Symposium on Principles of Distributed Computing (PODC)*, 2005, pp. 158 - 166.

[35] P. Kumar and L. Merakos. Distributed control of broadcast channels with akcnowledgement feedback: Stability and performance. In CDC'84, 1984.

[36] R.M. Metcalfe and D.R. Boggs, Ethernet: distributed packet switching for local computer networks, *Communications of the ACM* 19 (1976) 395 - 404.

[37] P. Raghavan and E. Upfal. Stochastic contention resolution with short delays. Siam Journal on Computing, 28 (2): 709–719, 1999.

[38] B.S. Tsybakov and V.A. Mikhailov, Free synchronous packet access in a broadcast channel with feedback, *Prob. Inf. Transmission* **14** (1978) 259 - 280. (Translated from Russian original in *Prob. Peredach. Inf.*, 1977.)

# Self-organized Segregation on the Grid*

Hamed Omidvar
University of California, San Diego
homidvar@ucsd.edu

Massimo Franceschetti
University of California, San Diego
mfrances@ucsd.edu

## ABSTRACT

We consider an agent-based model in which two types of agents interact locally over a graph and have a common intolerance threshold $\tau$ for changing their types with exponentially distributed waiting times. The model is equivalent to an unperturbed Schelling model of self-organized segregation, an Asynchronous Cellular Automata (ACA) with extended Moore neighborhoods, or a zero-temperature Ising model with Glauber dynamics, and has applications in the analysis of social and biological networks, and spin glasses systems. Some rigorous results were recently obtained in the theoretical computer science literature, and this work provides several extensions. We enlarge the intolerance interval leading to the formation of large segregated regions of agents of a single type from the known size $\epsilon > 0$ to size $\approx 0.134$. Namely, we show that for $0.433 < \tau < 1/2$ (and by symmetry $1/2 < \tau < 0.567$), the expected size of the largest segregated region containing an arbitrary agent is exponential in the size of the neighborhood. We further extend the interval leading to large segregated regions to size $\approx 0.312$ considering "almost segregated" regions, namely regions where the ratio of the number of agents of one type and the number of agents of the other type vanishes quickly as the size of the neighborhood grows. In this case, we show that for $0.344 < \tau \leq 0.433$ (and by symmetry for $0.567 \leq \tau < 0.656$) the expected size of the largest almost segregated region containing an arbitrary agent is exponential in the size of the neighborhood. This behavior is reminiscent of supercritical percolation, where small clusters of empty sites can be observed within any sufficiently large region of the occupied percolation cluster. The exponential bounds that we provide also imply that complete segregation, where agents of a single type cover the whole grid, does not occur with high probability for $p = 1/2$ and the range of tolerance considered.

## CCS CONCEPTS

•**Computing methodologies** → **Self-organization;**

*A full version of this paper with complete proofs can be found in [32]. This work was partially supported by Army Research Office (ARO), award number W911NF-15-1-0253.


*PODC'17, July 25-27, 2017, Washington, DC, USA*

DOI: http://dx.doi.org/10.1145/10.1145/3087801.3087826

## KEYWORDS

Agent-based Model; Asynchronous Cellular Automata; Zero-temperature Ising Model; Unperturbed Schelling Segregation; Distributed Algorithm; Self-organized Segregation; Percolation Theory; First Passage Percolation; Exponential Segregation

## 1 INTRODUCTION

### 1.1 Background

In social and biological networks as well as other complex networks, agents only interact with a small subset of nodes located in their local neighborhood. These local interactions, however, lead to global outcomes whose analysis is of much interest. To study such behaviors, we consider an agent-based model with two types of agents initially located at random on the vertices of a grid. Each agent is assumed to be able to only communicate with at most a logarithmically small subset of the agents in its local neighborhood to detect their types. This information is then used to determine a boolean state of each agent. Given a common threshold parameter $\tau$, an agent is called *happy* if the fraction of same type agents in its neighborhood is at least $\tau$. Unhappy agents then, asynchronously change their types according to a Poisson clock, if this will make them happy. As such, the model can be thought of as a distributed algorithm in which each agent gathers local information and then acts independently of the others. Simulations of the model, for a wide range of intolerance parameter $\tau$, show that when the system reaches a stable state, large regions of spontaneously self-segregated agents tend to appear in the network (see Figure 1).

In the context of the social sciences, the above model is known as an unperturbed Schelling model of segregation in an open system [33, 34]. In computation theory, mathematics, complexity theory, theoretical biology and microstructure modeling, the model is known as a two-dimensional, two-state Asynchronous Cellular Automata (ACA), with extended Moore neighborhoods and exponential waiting times [10]. In statistical physics, it is analogous to the Ising model with zero temperature, where spins align along the direction of the local field [9, 36]. Similar models also arise in epidemiology [12, 20], economics [22], engineering and computer sciences [13, 25]. Mathematically, all of these models fall in the general area of interacting particle systems, or contact processes, and exhibit phase transitions [26, 28].

Several variants have also appeared in the literature, such as models with agents that have a small probability of acting differently than what the general rule prescribes (e.g., perturbed Schelling model), models where agents have multiple intolerance levels, multiple agent types, different agent distributions, or time-varying intolerance [3, 4, 6, 29, 30, 35, 38–41].

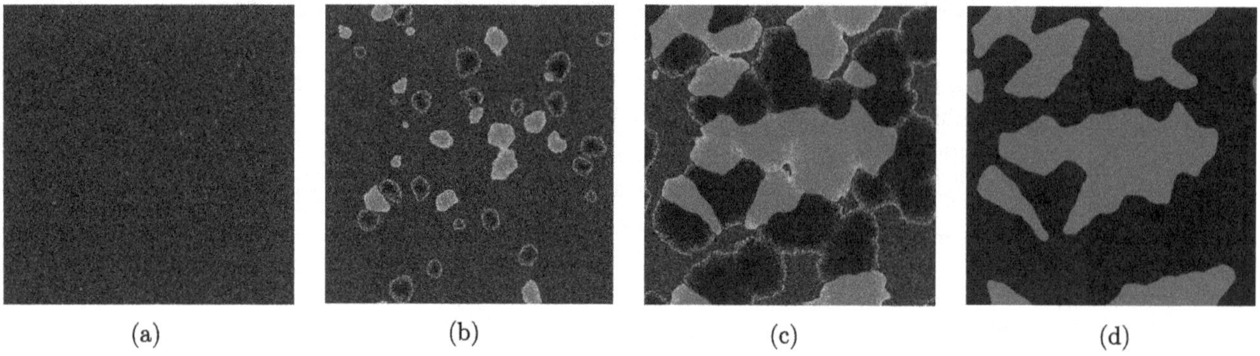

**Figure 1: Self-segregation arising over time for a value of the intolerance $\tau = 0.42$ on a grid of size $1000\times1000$ and neighborhood radius 10 (size 441). Green and blue indicate areas of "happy" agents of type (+1) and (-1), respectively. White and yellow indicate areas of "unhappy" agents of type (+1) and (-1) respectively. Initial configuration (a), intermediate configurations (b)-(c), final configuration (d). When the process terminates all agents are happy but large segregated regions can be observed.**

## 1.2 Contribution

We consider the case of two types of agents placed uniformly at random on a two-dimensional grid according to a Bernoulli distribution of parameter $p = 1/2$ and having a single intolerance level $0 < \tau < 1$, and study the range of intolerance leading to the formation of large segregated regions. Even in the one-dimensional setting, rigorous results appeared only recently.

Brandt et al. [7] considered a ring graph and a Kawasaki dynamical model of evolution, which assumes that a pair of unhappy agents swaps their locations if this will make both of them happy. In this setting, letting the neighborhood of an agent be the set of nearby agents that is used to determine whether the agent is happy or not, they showed that for an intolerance level $\tau = 1/2$, the expected size of the largest segregated region containing an arbitrary agent in steady state is polynomial in the size of the neighborhood. Barmpalias et al. [2] showed that there exists a value of $\tau^* \approx 0.35$, such that for all $\tau < \tau^*$ the initial configuration remains static with high probability (w.h.p.), while for all $\tau^* < \tau < 1/2$ the size of the largest segregated region in steady state becomes w.h.p. exponential in the size of the neighborhood. On the other hand, for all $\tau > 1/2$ the system evolves w.h.p. towards a state with only two segregated components.

In the Glauber dynamical model of evolution, which assumes that unhappy agents simply flip their types if this will make them happy, the behavior is similar, but symmetric around $\tau = 1/2$, with a first transition from a static configuration to exponential segregation occurring at $\tau \approx 0.35$, a special point $\tau = 1/2$ with the largest segregated region of expected polynomial size, then again exponential segregation until $\tau \approx 0.65$, and finally a static configuration for larger values of $\tau$.

In a two-dimensional grid graph on a torus, the case $\tau = 1/2$ is open. Immorlica et al. [21] have shown the existence of a value $\tau^* < 1/2$, such that for all $\tau^* < \tau < 1/2$ the expected size of the largest segregated region is exponential in the size of the neighborhood. This shows that segregation is expected in the small interval $\tau \in (1/2 - \epsilon, 1/2)$. Barmpalias et al. [5] have shown that for $\tau > 3/4$ and $\tau < 1/4$ the initial configuration remains static w.h.p.

Our main contribution is depicted in Figure 2. We consider the Glauber dynamics for the two-dimensional grid graph on a torus. First, we enlarge the intolerance interval that leads to the formation of large segregated regions from the known size $\epsilon > 0$ to size $\approx 0.134$, namely when $0.433 < \tau < 1/2$ (and by symmetry $1/2 < \tau < 0.567$), the expected size of the largest segregated region is exponential in the size of the neighborhood. Although the proof of this first result shares some similarities with the one given in [21], it is generally different, as explained in section 2.3. Second, we further extend the interval leading to large segregated regions to size $\approx 0.312$. In this case, the main contribution is to consider "almost segregated" regions, namely regions where the ratio of the number of agents of one type and the number of agents of the other type quickly vanishes as the size of the neighborhood grows, and show that for $0.344 < \tau \leq 0.433$ (and by symmetry for $0.567 \leq \tau < 0.656$) the expected size of the largest almost segregated region is exponential in the size of the neighborhood.

As shown for the one dimensional case in [2] and conjectured for the two-dimensional case in [5], we show that as the intolerance parameter gets farther from one half, in both directions, the average size of both the segregated and almost segregated regions gets larger. This means that higher tolerance in our model does not necessarily lead to less segregation. On the contrary, it can increase the size of the segregated areas. This result is depicted in Figure 3. The intuitive explanation is that highly tolerant agents are seldom unhappy in the initial configuration, and small segregated regions of opposite types that can ignite a cascading effect are likely to start from far apart, and may grow larger before meeting at their boundaries.

Finally, the exponential upper bound that we provide on the expected size of the largest segregated region implies that complete segregation, where agents of a single type cover the whole grid, does not occur w.h.p. for the range of intolerance considered. In contrast, Fontes et al. [15] have shown the existence of a critical probability $1/2 < p^* < 1$ for the initial Bernoulli distribution of the agents such that for $\tau = 1/2$ and $p > p^*$ the Glauber model on the $d$-dimensional grid converges to a state where only one type of agents are present. This shows that complete segregation occurs w.h.p. for

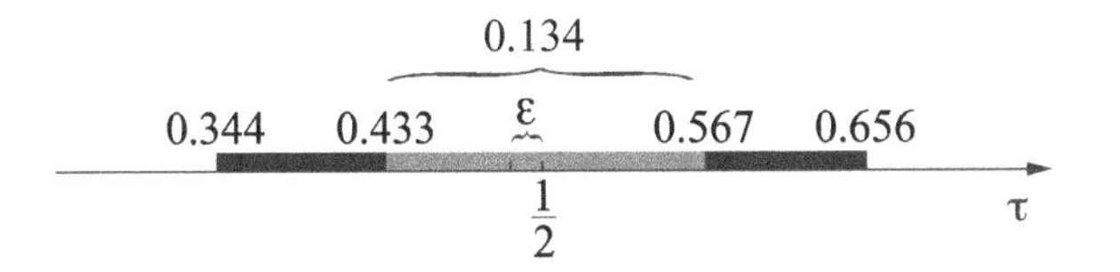


**Figure 2: We enlarge the width of the intolerance interval for which the expected size of the largest segregated region containing an arbitrary agent is exponential in the size of the neighborhood from the known value $\epsilon > 0$ to $\approx 0.134$ (grey region). We also show that the expected size of the largest almost segregated region containing an arbitrary agent is exponential in the size of the neighborhood for an intolerance interval of width $\approx 0.312$ (grey plus black region).**

$\tau = 1/2$ and $p \in (1-\epsilon, 1)$. Morris [31] has shown that $p^*$ converges to 1/2 as $d \to \infty$. Caputo and Martinelli [8] have shown the same result for $d$-regular trees, while Kanoria and Montanari [23] derived it for $d$-regular trees in a synchronous setting where flips occur simultaneously, and obtained lower bounds on $p^*(d)$ for small values of $d$. The case $d = 1$ was first investigated by Erdös and Ney [14], and Arratia [1] has proven that $p^*(1) = 1$.

### 1.3 Techniques

Our proofs are based on a typicality argument showing a self-similar structure of the neighborhoods in the initial state of the process, and on the identification of geometric configurations igniting a cascading process leading to segregation. To show the cascading effect, we make use of some tools from percolation theory, including the exponential decay of the radius of the open cluster below criticality [18], concentration bounds on the passage time [24] (see also [11, 37]), and on the chemical distance between percolation sites [17]. We also make frequent use of renormalization, and correlation inequalities for contact processes [27].

The paper is organized as follows. In section 2 we introduce the model, state our results, and give a summary of the proof construction. In section 3 we study the initial configuration and derive some properties of the sub-neighborhoods of the unhappy agents. In section 4 we study the dynamics of the segregation process and derive the main results. Concluding remarks are given in section 5.

## 2 MODEL AND MAIN RESULTS

### 2.1 The Model

*Initial Configuration.* We consider an $n \times n$ grid graph $G_n$ embedded on a torus $\mathbb{T} = [0,n) \times [0,n)$, an integer $w \in O(\sqrt{\log n})$ called *horizon*, and a rational $0 \leq \tau \leq 1$ called *intolerance*. All arithmetic operations over the coordinates are performed modulo $n$, i.e., $(x,y) = (x+n, y) = (x, y+n)$. We place an agent at each node of the grid and choose its type independently at random to be (+1) or (-1) according to a Bernoulli distribution of parameter $p = 1/2$.

A *neighborhood* is a connected sub-graph of $G_n$. A *neighborhood of radius* $\rho$ is the set of all agents with $l_\infty$ distance at most $\rho$ from a central node, and is denoted by $\mathcal{N}_\rho$. The *size* of a neighborhood is the number of agents in it. The *neighborhood of an agent* $u$ is a neighborhood of radius equal to the horizon and centered at $u$, and is denoted by $\mathcal{N}(u)$.

*Dynamics.* Let $\tau = \lceil \tilde{\tau} N \rceil / N$, where $\tilde{\tau} \in [0,1]$ and $N = (2w+1)^2$ is the size of the neighborhood of an agent. The integer $\tau N$ represents the minimum number of agents of the same type as $u$ that must be present in $\mathcal{N}(u)$ to make $u$ happy.

For every agent $u$, we let $s(u)$ be the ratio between the number of agents of the same type as $u$ in its neighborhood and the size of the neighborhood. We assign an independent Poisson clock with unit rate to each agent. If $s(u) \geq \tau$ then $u$ is labeled *happy*, otherwise it is labeled *unhappy*. When the clock rings, the agent will flip its type if and only if it is unhappy and the flip will make it happy. We assume that this change is immediately broadcasted to the neighborhood of $u$. It follows that one can also think of the graph as an extended grid, where agents are located at the vertices and there are additional edges between each node in the grid and the nodes in its neighborhood. The distributed process running at each agent is illustrated in Algorithm 1. Two observations are now in order. First, for $\tau < 1/2$, flipping the type of an unhappy agent would always make it happy, but this is not the case for $\tau > 1/2$. Second, given the memoryless property of the exponential distribution is memoryless, this model is equivalent to a Glauber model, where an unhappy agent is selected uniformly at random and decides whether or not its type should be flipped.

**Data:** $\mathcal{N}(u)$;
**Result:** Agent $u$ decides to flip its type or not;
reset local time $t$;
choose $t^*$ according to an exponential distribution with unit mean;
**while** *1* **do**
  **if** $t \geq t^*$ **then**
    calculate $s(u)$;
    **if** $s(u) < \tau$ **and** $1 - s(u) + 1/N \geq \tau$ **then**
      flip type of $u$;
      broadcast the new type to $\mathcal{N}(u)$;
      reset local time $t$;
      choose $t^*$ according to an exponential distribution with unit mean;
    **end**
  **end**
**end**

**Algorithm 1:** Distributed algorithm running on each agent $u$.

*Termination.* The process continues until there are no unhappy agents left, or there are no unhappy agents that can become happy by flipping their type. By defining a Lyapunov function to be the sum over all agents $u$ of the number of agents of the same type as $u$ present in its neighborhood, it is easy to argue that the process indeed terminates.

*Segregation.* The *monochromatic region* of an agent $u$ is the neighborhood with largest radius containing agents of a single type and that also contains $u$ when the process stops. Let $\epsilon > 0$ and $N = (2w+1)^2$. The *almost monochromatic region* of an agent $u$, is the neighborhood with largest radius such that the ratio of the number of agents of one type and the number of agents of the other type is bounded by $e^{-N^{\epsilon}}$ and that also contains $u$ when the process stops.

Throughout the paper we use the terminology *with high probability* (w.h.p.) meaning that the probability of an event approaches one as $N$ approaches infinity.

## 2.2 The Results

To state our results, we let $\tau_1 \approx 0.433$ be the solution of

$$\frac{3}{4}\left[1 - H\left(\frac{3}{4}\tau_1\right)\right] - [1 - H(\tau_1)] = 0, \tag{1}$$

where $H$ is the binary entropy function

$$H(\tau_1) = -\tau_1 \log_2 \tau_1 - (1-\tau_1)\log_2(1-\tau_1), \tag{2}$$

and $\tau_2 \approx 0.344$ be the solution of

$$\tau_2 = \frac{1}{2}\left[\frac{3}{4} - \frac{1}{6}\left(\frac{3}{4} - \frac{1}{2}(3 - 8\tau_2)\right)(16\tau_2 - 5) - \frac{1}{4}\left(\frac{1}{8} - \frac{1}{6}(16\tau_2 - 5)\right)\right]. \tag{3}$$

We also let $M$ and $M'$ be the sizes of the monochromatic and almost monochromatic regions of an arbitrary agent, respectively.

We consider values of the intolerance $\tau \in (\tau_2, 1-\tau_2) \setminus \{1/2\}$. Most of the work is devoted to the study of the intervals $(\tau_2, \tau_1]$ and $(\tau_1, 1/2)$, a symmetry argument extends the analysis to the intervals $(1/2, 1-\tau_1)$ and $[1-\tau_1, 1-\tau_2)$. The following theorems show that segregation occurs for values of $\tau$ in the grey region of Figure 2, where we expect an exponential monochromatic region, and in the black region of Figure 2, where we expect an exponential almost monochromatic region.

**Theorem** 1. *For all $\tau \in (\tau_1, 1-\tau_1) \setminus \{1/2\}$ and for sufficiently large $N$, we have*

$$2^{a(\tau)N - o(N)} \leq \mathbb{E}[M] \leq 2^{b(\tau)N + o(N)}, \tag{4}$$

*where $a$ and $b$ are decreasing functions of $\tau$ for $\tau < 1/2$ and increasing for $\tau > 1/2$.*

**Theorem** 2. *For all $\tau \in (\tau_2, \tau_1] \cup [1-\tau_1, 1-\tau_2)$ and for sufficiently large $N$, we have*

$$2^{a(\tau)N - o(N)} \leq \mathbb{E}[M'] \leq 2^{b(\tau)N + o(N)}, \tag{5}$$

*where $a$ and $b$ are decreasing functions of $\tau$ for $\tau < 1/2$ and increasing for $\tau > 1/2$.*

The numerical values for $a(\tau)$ and $b(\tau)$ computed in the proofs of the above theorems are plotted in Figure 3. For $\tau \in (\tau_1, 1-\tau_1)\setminus\{1/2\}$, as the intolerance gets farther from one half in both directions, larger monochromatic regions are expected.

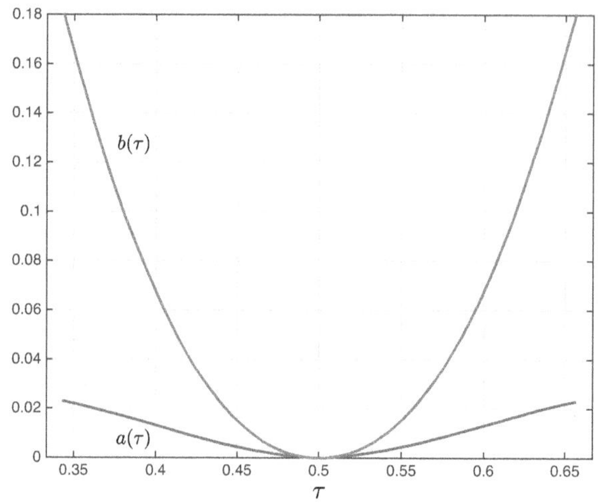


**Figure 3: Exponent multipliers $a(\tau)$ and $b(\tau)$ for the lower bound and upper bounds on the expected size of the largest segregated region $\mathbb{E}[M]$, and the expected size of the largest almost segregated region $\mathbb{E}[M']$.**

## 2.3 Proof construction

The main idea of the proof is to identify a local initial configuration that can potentially trigger a cascading process leading to segregation. We then bound the probability of occurrence of such a configuration in the initial state, and of the conditions to trigger segregation.

To identify this local configuration, we study the relationship between the typical neighborhood of an unhappy agent and the sub-neighborhoods contained within this neighborhood, showing a self-similar structure. Namely, the fraction of agents of the same type, when scaled by the size of the neighborhood, remains roughly the same (Proposition 1). We then define a *radical region* that contains a nucleus of unhappy agents (Lemma 1), and using the self-similar structure of the neighborhoods we construct a geometric configuration where a sequence of flips can lead to the formation of a neighborhood of agents of the same type inside a radical region (Lemma 2). Finally, we provide a lower bound for the probability of occurrence of this configuration in the initial state of the system (Lemma 3), which can initiate the segregation process.

The second part of the proof is concerned with the process dynamics, and shows a cascading effect ignited by the radical regions that leads to the formation of exponentially large segregated areas. We consider an indestructible and impenetrable structure around a radical region called a *firewall* and show that once formed it remains static and protects the radical region inside it from vanishing. Conditioned on certain events occurring in the area surrounding the radical region, including the formation of the initial configuration described in the first part of the proof, we show that an agent close to the radical region will be trapped w.h.p. inside an exponentially large firewall whose interior becomes monochromatic, see Figure 4(a).

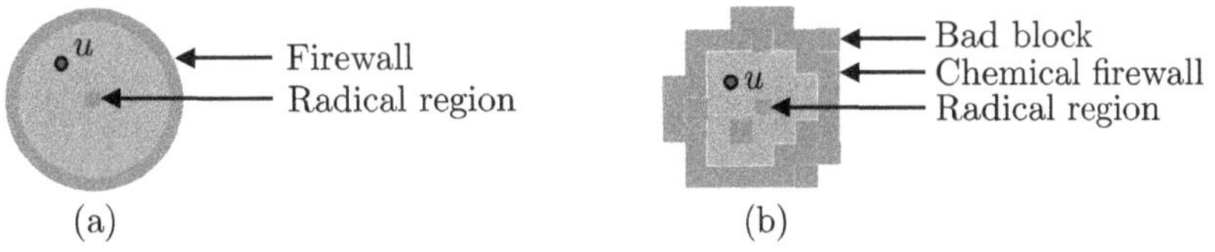


**Figure 4: An arbitrary agent $u$ that is close to a radical region will be trapped inside a firewall of exponential size whose interior will eventually become monochromatic (a), or almost monochromatic (b).**

We then obtain a lower bound on the joint probability of the conditioning events and this leads to a lower bound on the probability that an agent is eventually contained in a monochromatic region of exponential size. Since the lower bound holds for both type of agents, we expect to have both types of exponential monochromatic regions in a large area by the end of the process. This leads to an exponential upper bound on the expected size of the largest monochromatic region of each type. To perform our computations, we rely on a bound on the passage time on the square lattice [24] (see also [11, 37]) to upper bound the rate of spread of other monochromatic regions outside the firewall, and ensure that they do not interfere with its formation during the dynamics of the process.

The construction described above works for all $\tau_1 < \tau < 1/2$. For smaller values of $\tau$, agents are more tolerant and this may cause the construction of a firewall to fail, since tolerant agents do not easily become unhappy and flip their types igniting the cascading process. In order to overcome this difficulty, we introduce a *chemical firewall* through a comparison with a Bernoulli site percolation model, see Figure 4(b). This firewall is constructed through renormalization and is made of *good* blocks that occur independently and with probability above the critical threshold for site percolation on the square grid. Using a theorem in [17] on the chemical distance between good blocks, we show that they form a large circuit and isolate its interior. Finally, using the exponential decay of the size of the clusters of bad blocks [18], we show that the region inside the chemical firewall becomes *almost monochromatic*, namely for all $\tau_2 < \tau < 1/2$, we expect the formation of exponentially large regions where the ratio of number of agents of one type and the number of agents of the other type quickly vanishes.

All results are extended to the interval to $1/2 < \tau < 1 - \tau_2$ using a symmetry argument.

Compared to the proof in [21], our derivation differs in the following aspects. The definition of radical region is fundamentally different from the viral nodes considered in [21], and the identification of the radical regions gives us an immediate understanding of the arrangement of the agents in the initial configuration in terms of self-similarity arising at different scales. Our definition of an annular firewall that forms quickly enough eliminates the need for additional arguments from first passage percolation that are used [21], it allows for a wider range of intolerance parameters, and it is easily generalized to the notion of chemical firewall using the results from [17]. The renormalization argument used to study the growth of the monochromatic regions is also different from [21] and work for a wider range of the intolerance. Finally, the idea of considering almost monochromatic regions is new, and so are the approaches that we use from percolation theory to argue the existence of the chemical firewall and the size of the minority clusters.

Finally, we rigorously apply a variation of the Fortuin-Kasteleyn-Ginibre (FKG) inequality, that we prove in the Appendix, to show positive correlation of certain events, while in [21] it is often informally argued that similar correlations exist in their setting.

## 3 TRIGGERING CONFIGURATION

We start our analysis considering the initial configuration of the system. Proposition 1 shows a similarity relationship between the neighborhood of an agent and its sub-neighborhoods. This relationship is exploited in Lemma 2 to construct an initial configuration of agents that can trigger the segregation process. Lemma 3 provides a bound on the probability of occurrence of this triggering configuration.

Let $\mathcal{N}(u)$ be the neighborhood of an arbitrary agent $u$ containing $N$ agents. Consider a sub-neighborhood $\mathcal{N}'(u) \subset \mathcal{N}(u)$ containing $N'$ agents and let $\gamma$ be the scaling factor $N'/N$. Let $W$ and $W'$ be the random variables representing the number of (-1) agents in $\mathcal{N}(u)$ and $\mathcal{N}'(u)$ respectively. The following proposition shows that, conditioned on $W$ being less than $\tau N$, $W'$ is very close to the rescaled quantity $\gamma\tau N$, with overwhelming probability as $N \to \infty$.

**Proposition** 1. *For any $\epsilon \in (0, 1/2)$ and $c \in \mathbb{R}^+$ there exists $c' \in \mathbb{R}^+$ for all $N$ such that*

$$P\left(|W' - \gamma\tau N| < cN^{1/2+\epsilon}|W < \tau N\right) \geq 1 - e^{-c'N^{2\epsilon}}.$$

The proof is omitted due to space limitations and can be found in [32].

We now identify a configuration that has the potential to trigger a cascading process. For any $\epsilon, \epsilon' \in (0, 1/2)$ let $\hat{\tau} = \tau[1 - 1/(\tau N^{1/2-\epsilon})]$ and define a *radical region* to be a neighborhood of radius $(1 + \epsilon')w$ containing less than $\hat{\tau}(1 + \epsilon')^2 N$ agents of type (-1). We also define an *unhappy region* to be a neighborhood of radius $\epsilon' w$, containing at least $\lfloor \tau\epsilon'^2 N - N^{1/2+\epsilon} \rfloor$ unhappy agents of type (-1).

**Lemma** 1. *A radical region $\mathcal{N}_{(1+\epsilon')w}$ contains an unhappy region $\mathcal{N}_{\epsilon' w}$ at its center w.h.p.*

The proof is omitted due to space limitations and can be found in [32].

A radical region is *expandable* if there is a sequence of at most $(w + 1)^2$ possible flips inside it that can make the region $\mathcal{N}_{w/2}$ at its center monochromatic.

We consider a geometric configuration where a radical region, its unhappy region, and neighborhoods $\mathcal{N}_{w/2}$ and $\mathcal{N}_\rho$ with $\rho > 3w$, are all co-centered. We let $u^+$ be a (+1) agent and

$$T(\rho) = \inf\{t : \exists u^+ \in \mathcal{N}_\rho \text{ that is unhappy}\}. \quad (6)$$

The next lemma shows that the radical region in this configuration is expandable w.h.p., provided that $\epsilon'$ is large enough and no (+1) agent at the location of any agent in $\mathcal{N}_\rho$ is unhappy. The main idea is that the (-1) agents in the unhappy region at the center of the radical region can trigger a process that leads to a monochromatic (+1) region of radius $w/2$.

**Lemma 2.** *For all $\epsilon' > f(\tau)$ where*

$$f(\tau) = \frac{3(\tau - 0.5) + \sqrt{9(\tau - 0.5)^2 - 7(\tau - 0.5)(3\tau + 0.5)}}{2(3\tau + 0.5)}, \quad (7)$$

*there exists w.h.p. a sequence of at most $(w+1)^2$ possible flips in $\mathcal{N}_{(1+\epsilon')}$ such that if they happen before $T(\rho)$, then all the agents inside $\mathcal{N}_{w/2}$ will become of type (+1).*

The proof is omitted due to space limitations and can be found in [32, Lemma 5].

Using Lemma 2 we obtain an exponential bound on the probability of having an expandable radical region inside a sufficiently large neighborhood.

**Lemma 3.** *Let $r = 2^{[1-H(\tau')]N/2-o(N)}$, where $\tau' = (\tau N - 2)/(N-1)$. Let*

$$C = \{\mathcal{N}_r \text{ contains an expandable radical region at } t = 0\}.$$

*For every $\epsilon' > f(\tau)$ and sufficiently large $N$, we have*

$$P(C) \geq 2^{-[1-H(\tau')](2\epsilon'+\epsilon'^2)N-o(N)}.$$

The proof is omitted due to space limitations and can be found in [32, Lemma 6].

## 4 THE SEGREGATION PROCESS

We now consider the dynamics of the segregation process and show that for all $\tau \in (\tau_1, 1/2)$ the expected size of the monochromatic region in steady state is exponential, while for all $\tau \in (\tau_2, \tau_1]$ the expected size of the almost monochromatic region is exponential.

### 4.1 Monochromatic region

We need the following definitions. A *firewall* of radius $r$ and center $u$ is a set of agents of the same type contained in an annulus

$$A_r(u) = \left\{y : r - \sqrt{2}w \leq \|u - y\| \leq r\right\},$$

where $\|.\|$ denotes Euclidean distance and $r \geq 3w$. By [32, Lemma 9], once formed a firewall of sufficiently large radius remains static, and since its width is $\sqrt{2}w$ the agents inside the inner circle are not going to be affected by the configurations outside the firewall. We can now give the first part of the proof of Theorem 1.

**Proof of Theorem 1** (for $\tau_1 < \tau < 1/2$). First, we derive the lower bound in the theorem letting

$$a(\tau) = [1 - (2\epsilon' + \epsilon'^2)][1 - H(\tau')], \quad (8)$$

where $\epsilon' > f(\tau)$, and $\tau' = (\tau N - 2)/(N-1)$.

We consider neighborhoods $\mathcal{N}_\rho$, $\mathcal{N}_{\rho/2}$, and $\mathcal{N}_r$, with

$$\rho = 2^{[1-H(\tau')]N/2}$$

and $r < \rho/8$, all centered at node $u$ as depicted in Figure 5. We let $u^+$ be a (+1) agent, and consider the following event in the initial configuration

$$A = \left\{\forall v \in \mathcal{N}_\rho,\ u^+ \text{ is happy at the location of } v\right\}. \quad (9)$$

By [32, Lemma B.3], we have

$$P(A) \longrightarrow 1, \text{ as } N \longrightarrow \infty. \quad (10)$$

We then consider a firewall of radius $2r$ centered anywhere inside $\mathcal{N}_r$, let $\kappa > 0$ so that $\kappa r N^{1/2}$ is the sum of the number of agents in it and the number of agents in a line of width $w+1$ that connects its center to its boundary and includes $\mathcal{N}_{w/2}$ at its center. Consider the event

$$B = \left\{T(\rho/2) > 2\kappa r N^{1/2}\right\},$$

where $T(\rho)$ is defined in (6). By [32, Lemma 7], we can choose $r$ proportional to $\rho/(N^2)$ so that

$$P(B|A) \longrightarrow 1, \text{ as } N \longrightarrow \infty. \quad (11)$$

With this choice, we also have

$$r = 2^{[1-H(\tau')]N/2-o(N)},$$

and if we consider the event

$$C = \{\mathcal{N}_r \text{ contains an expandable radical region at } t = 0\},$$

by Lemma 3, we have for $N$ sufficiently large

$$P(C) \geq 2^{-[1-H(\tau')](2\epsilon'+\epsilon'^2)N-o(N)}. \quad (12)$$

Finally, call a *region of expansion* any neighborhood whose configuration is such that by placing a neighborhood $\mathcal{N}_{w/2}$ of type (+1) agents anywhere inside it, all the (-1) agents on the outside boundary of $\mathcal{N}_{w/2}$ become unhappy with probability one. Consider a neighborhood $\mathcal{N}_{4r}$ also centered at $u$ and the event

$$D = \{\forall t < T(\rho/2),\ \mathcal{N}_{4r} \text{ is a region of expansion}\}.$$

By [32, Lemma 8], we have

$$P(D) \longrightarrow 1, \text{ as } N \longrightarrow \infty. \quad (13)$$

We now note that $A, B, C, D$ are increasing events with respect to a partial ordering on their outcomes. More precisely, consider two outcomes of the sample space $\omega, \omega' \in \Omega$ such that $\omega, \omega' \in E$ where $E$ is an event. We define a partial ordering on the outcomes such that $\omega' \geq \omega$ if for all time steps, the set of agents of type (+1) in $\omega$ is a subset of the set of agents of type (+1) in $\omega'$. Event $E$ is increasing if $1_E(\omega') \geq 1_E(\omega)$ where $1_E$ is the indicator function of the event $E$. According to this definition, $A, B, C, D$ are increasing events. By combining (10), (11), (12), and (13), and using a version of the FKG inequality adapted to our dynamic process, as described in Lemma A.2, it follows that for $N$ sufficiently large

$$\begin{aligned} P(A \cap B \cap C \cap D) &\geq P(A)P(B)P(C)P(D) \\ &\geq P(A)P(B \cap A)P(C)P(D) \\ &= P(B|A)[P(A)]^2 P(C)P(D) \\ &= 2^{-[1-H(\tau')][2\epsilon'+\epsilon'^2]N-o(N)}. \end{aligned} \quad (14)$$

Since by [32, Lemma 10], we have that conditioning on $A, B, C, D$, at the end of the process w.h.p. agent $u$ will be part of a monochromatic region with radius at least $r$, it follows that (14) is also a lower bound for the probability that the monochromatic neighborhood of agent $u$ will have size of at least proportional to $r^2$. The desired lower bound on the expected size of the monochromatic region now easily follows by multiplying (14) by the size of a neighborhood of radius $r$.

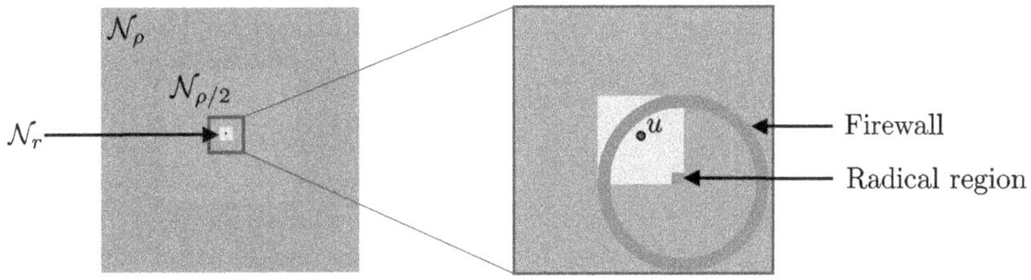


**Figure 5: Neighborhoods described in the proof of Theorem 1.**

Next, we show the corresponding upper bound, letting

$$b(\tau) = \left[\frac{3}{2}(1+\epsilon')^2\right][1 - H(\tau')],$$

and $\epsilon'$ and $\tau'$ as defined above. For any $\delta > 0$, consider a neighborhood $\mathcal{N}_{\rho'}$ such that

$$\rho' = 2^{(1+\epsilon')^2[1-H(\tau')]N/2+\delta N/2},$$

Divide $\mathcal{N}_{\rho'}$ into blocks of size $\mathcal{N}_\rho$ in the obvious way. Let $M_{+1}$ and $M_{-1}$ denote the events of $\mathcal{N}_{\rho'}$ being monochromatic of type (+1) and (-1) respectively. Also let $E_{+1}$ and $E_{-1}$ be the events of having a monochromatic region of type (+1) and (-1) inside a firewall of radius $2r$ centered anywhere inside $\mathcal{N}_{\rho'}$. We have that for $N$ sufficiently large

$$\begin{aligned} P(M_{+1} \cup M_{-1}) &\leq P(M_{+1}) + P(M_{-1}) \\ &= P(M_{+1} \cap E^C_{-1}) + P(M_{-1} \cap E^C_{+1}) \\ &\leq P(E^C_{-1}) + P(E^C_{+1}) \\ &= 2P(E^C_{-1}) \\ &\leq 2(1 - 2^{-[1-H(\tau')](2\epsilon'+\epsilon'^2)N - o(N)})^{\rho'^2/\rho^2} \\ &= e^{-2^{\delta N - o(N)}}. \end{aligned} \tag{15}$$

By considering the set of all the neighborhoods of radius $\rho'$ sharing agent $u$, by the union bound the probability that at least one of them will be monochromatic of only one type is also bounded by (15). We now consider the expected size of the monochromic region of agent $u$, that is bounded as

$$\mathbb{E}[M] \leq \sum_{m=1}^{n} m^2 p_m,$$

where $p_m$ denotes the probability of having a monochromatic region of size $m^2$ containing $u$. We let

$$\rho'' = 2^{[(1+\epsilon')^2(1-H(\tau')]N/2+o(N)},$$

and divide the series into two parts

$$\begin{aligned} \mathbb{E}[M] &\leq \sum_{m=1}^{\rho''} m^2 p_m + \sum_{m=\rho''+1}^{n} m^2 p_m \\ &\leq 2^{[\frac{3}{2}(1+\epsilon')^2(1-H(\tau')]N/2+o(N)} + \sum_{m=\rho''+1}^{n} m^2 p_m, \end{aligned} \tag{16}$$

where the first inequality follows from $p_m \leq 1$. Since by (15) for all $m \geq \rho'$, the probability of having a monochromatic region of size $m^2$ containing $u$ has at most a double exponentially small probability, the tail of the remaining series in (16) converges to a constant, while for sufficiently large $N$ the sum of the first $\rho' - \rho'' - 1$ terms is smaller than the first term of (16), and the proof is complete. □

## 4.2 Almost monochromatic region

We turn our attention to the case where $\tau \in (\tau_2, \tau_1]$. We define an $m$-block to be a neighborhood of radius $m/2$ with $m = 2w^3 + 2w$. Let $\mathcal{I}$ be the collection of all the possible intersections of a $\mathcal{N}_{w/2}$ neighborhood with an $m$-block on the grid in the initial configuration. Also, let $W_I$ be the random variable representing the number of (-1)'s in $I$, and $N_I$ be the total number of agents in $I$.

For any $\epsilon \in (0, 1/2)$, a *good block* is an $m$-block such that for all $I \in \mathcal{I}$ we have $W_I - N_I/2 < N^{1/2+\epsilon}$. The $m$-blocks that do not satisfy this property are called *bad blocks*. An *r-chemical path* is the union of a circuit of good blocks contained in the set $\mathcal{N}_{3r} \setminus \mathcal{N}_r$, where $r > 5w^3$, and a path of good blocks from the center of $\mathcal{N}_r$ to the circuit, such that the total length of the circuit and the path is proportional to $r$. An agent, or a neighborhood, is said to be at the center of an $r$-chemical path if it is located at the center of $\mathcal{N}_r$. A *chemical firewall* with radius $r$ is a circuit of $2w^3$-blocks around the center of the $r$-chemical path which are monochromatic and contained in the $r$-chemical path. By [32, Lemma 9], it is easy to see that the above structure acts as a firewall.

An *r-expandable radical region* of type (-1) is a radical region such that it has an expandable radical region at its center and such that it is located at the center of an $r$-chemical path.

With the above definitions, we can proceed to the first part of the proof of Theorem 2 (for $\tau_2 < \tau \leq \tau_1$).

**Proof of Theorem 2** (for $\tau_2 < \tau \leq \tau_1$). First we derive the lower bound in which

$$a(\tau) = [1 - (2\epsilon' + \epsilon'^2)][1 - H(\tau')], \tag{17}$$

where $\epsilon' > f(\tau)$, and $\tau' = (\tau N - 2)/(N - 1)$.

We consider neighborhoods $\mathcal{N}_\rho$, $\mathcal{N}_{\rho/2}$, and $\mathcal{N}_r$, with $\rho = 2^{[1-H(\tau')]N/2}$ and $r < \rho/8$, all centered at node $u$ as depicted in Figure 6. We let $\rho = 2^{[1-H(\tau')]N/2}$, and $u^+$ be a (+1) agent. Consider the following event in the initial configuration

$$A = \{\forall v \in \mathcal{N}_\rho, u^+ \text{ is happy at the location of } v\}.$$

By [32, Lemma B.3] , we have

$$P(A) \to 1, \text{ as } N \to \infty. \tag{18}$$

We then consider a chemical firewall of radius $2r$ centered anywhere inside $\mathcal{N}_r$, let $\kappa > 0$ so that $\kappa r N^{3/2}$ is an upper bound on the total number of agents in the $2r$-chemical path containing it, and consider the event

$$B = \{T(\rho/2) > 2\kappa r N^{3/2}\},$$

where $T(\rho)$ is defined in (6). By [32, Lemma 7] , we can choose $r$ proportional to $\rho/(N^3)$ so that

$$P(B|A) \longrightarrow 1, \text{ as } N \longrightarrow \infty. \quad (19)$$

With this choice, we also have

$$r = 2^{[1-H(\tau')]N/2-o(N)},$$

and if we consider the event

$$C = \{\mathcal{N}_r \text{ contains a } 2r\text{-expandable radical region at } t = 0\},$$

by Lemma 3 and [32, Lemma 13] and the FKG inequality, since $\epsilon' > f(\tau)$ we conclude that for sufficiently large $N$

$$P(C) \geq 2^{-[1-H(\tau')][2\epsilon'+(\epsilon')^2]N-o(N)}, \quad (20)$$

and there is a $2r$-expandable radical region surrounding $u$. Let us divide the grid into $m$-blocks in the obvious way. Let the *radius* of a bad cluster be defined as

$$\sup\{\Delta(0,x) : x \in \text{bad cluster}\}.$$

where $\Delta$ denotes the $l_1$ distance. Let

$$D = \{\nexists \text{ clusters of bad blocks with radius greater than } N^2 \text{ blocks in } \mathcal{N}_{4r}\}.$$

We show that,

$$P(D) \longrightarrow 1, \text{ as } N \longrightarrow \infty. \quad (21)$$

Finally, let $\epsilon \in (0, 1/2)$ and let $N_B$ and $N_G$ denote the total number of bad blocks sharing at least one agent with $\mathcal{N}_r$ and good blocks contained in $\mathcal{N}_r$ respectively and let

$$E = \{N_B/N_G < e^{-N^{\epsilon}} \text{ in } \mathcal{N}_r\}.$$

We also show,

$$P(E) \longrightarrow 1, \text{ as } N \longrightarrow \infty. \quad (22)$$

See Figure 6 for a visualization of the neighborhoods defined above.

Now it is easy to see that the events $A$, $B$, $C$, $D$, and $E$ are increasing. By combining (18), (19), (20), (21), and (22), and using a version of the Fortuin-Kasteleyn-Ginibre (FKG) inequality adapted to our dynamic process described in Lemma A.2, it follows that for $N$ sufficiently large

$$\begin{aligned} P(A \cap B \cap C \cap D \cap E) &\geq P(A)P(B)P(C)P(D)P(E) \quad (23) \\ &\geq P(A)P(A \cap B)P(C)P(D)P(E) \\ &= P(B|A)[P(A)]^2 P(C)P(D)P(E) \\ &= 2^{-[1-H(\tau')](2\epsilon'+(\epsilon')^2)N-o(N)}. \quad (24) \end{aligned}$$

Using [32, Lemma 17], we have that conditioning on $A, B, C, D, E$, at the end of the process w.h.p. agent $u$ will be part of an almost monochromatic region with radius at least $r$, it follows that (24) is also a lower bound for the probability that the monochromatic neighborhood of agent $u$ will have size of at least proportional to $r^2$. The desired lower bound on the expected size of the monochromatic region now easily follows by multiplying (24) by the size of a neighborhood of radius $r$. The second part of the proof follows the same argument as the second part of the proof of Theorem 1. □

### 4.3 Extension to the interval $1/2 < \tau < 1 - \tau_2$

We call *super-unhappy agents* the unhappy agents that can potentially become happy once they flip their type. While for $\tau < 1/2$ unhappy agents can alway become happy by flipping their type, for $\tau > 1/2$ this is only true for the super-unhappy agents. It follows that for $\tau > 1/2$ super-unhappy agents act in the same way as unhappy agents do for $\tau < 1/2$.

We let $\bar{\tau} = 1 - \tau + 2/N$. A *super-unhappy agent* of type (-1) is an agent for which $W < \bar{\tau}N$ where $W$ is the number of (-1) agents in its neighborhood. The reason for adding the term $2/N$ in the definition is to account for the strict inequality that is needed for being unhappy and the flip of the agent at the center of the neighborhood which adds one agent of its type to the neighborhood. A *super-radical region* is a neighborhood $\mathcal{N}_S$ of radius $S = (1 + \epsilon')w$ such that $W_S < \bar{\tau}'(1 + \epsilon')^2 N$, where $\epsilon \in (0, 1/2)$ and

$$\bar{\tau}' = \left(1 - \frac{1}{\bar{\tau}N^{1/2-\epsilon}}\right)\bar{\tau}.$$

By replacing $\tau$ with $\bar{\tau}$, "unhappy agent" with "super-unhappy agent" and "radical region" with "super-radical region," it can be checked that all proofs extend to the interval $1/2 < \tau < 1 - \tau_2$.

## 5 CONCLUDING REMARKS

We studied self segregation arising in a system of interacting agents evolving according to a distributed algorithm. Similar algorithms are used in different fields to model various physical processes evolving on graphs. Rigorous results appeared only recently in the computer science literature. We extended them, and provided a wider range of the threshold parameter used to determine the local state of each agent that leads to the formation of large segregated regions in a grid graph. We also extended the definition of segregation to include almost monochromatic regions. The structure of these regions is reminiscent of percolation clusters, where small clusters of empty sites can be observed within any sufficiently large region of the occupied percolation cluster, and has led us to develop novel proof techniques based on the chemical distance between agents of the same type.

The main lesson learned from our study is that even a small amount of intolerance can lead to segregation at the large scale. We point out, however, that the model used to obtain this result is somewhat naturally biased towards segregation because agents can flip their type when a sufficiently large number of their neighbors are different from themselves, but they never flip when a large number of their neighbors are of their same type. Variations where agents could potentially flip in both situations, namely they are "uncomfortable" being both a minority or a majority in a largely segregated area, would be of interest. Another direction of further study could be the investigation of how the parameter of the initial distribution of the agents influences segregation, since it is only known that complete segregation occurs w.h.p. for $\tau = 1/2$ and $p \in (1 - \epsilon, 1)$, while we have shown that for $0.344 < \tau < 1/2$ and $p = 1/2$ the size of the monochromatic region is at most exponential in the size of its neighborhood, w.h.p. Finally, we point out that

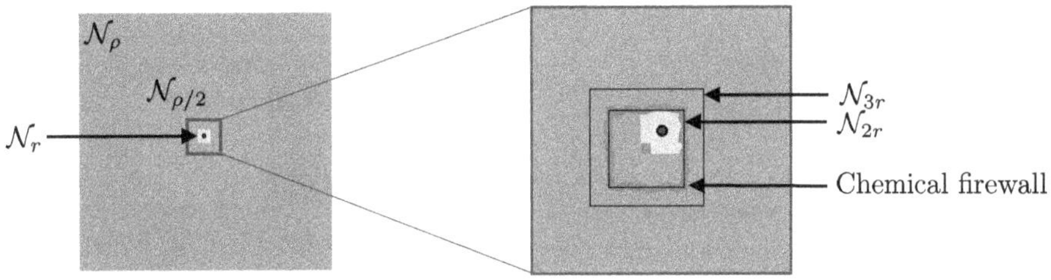


**Figure 6: Neighborhoods described in the proof of Theorem 2.**

for $\tau = 1/2$ and for $\tau \in [1/4, \tau_2] \cup [1 - \tau_2, 3/4]$ the behavior of the model is unknown.

## ACKNOWLEDGMENT

The authors thank Prof. Jason Schweinsberg of the Mathematics Department of University of California at San Diego for providing invaluable feedback on earlier drafts of the paper and for suggesting some improved proofs. This work was partially supported by Army Research Office (ARO), award number W911NF-15-1-0253.

## REFERENCES

[1] Richard Arratia. 1983. Site recurrence for annihilating random walks on $\mathbb{Z}^d$. *The Annals of Probability* (1983), 706–713.

[2] George Barmpalias, Richard Elwes, and Andy Lewis-Pye. 2014. Digital morphogenesis via Schelling segregation. In *Foundations of Computer Science (FOCS), 2014 IEEE 55th Annual Symposium on*. IEEE, 156–165.

[3] George Barmpalias, Richard Elwes, and Andy Lewis-Pye. 2015. Minority population in the one-dimensional Schelling model of segregation. *arXiv preprint arXiv:1508.02497* (2015).

[4] George Barmpalias, Richard Elwes, and Andy Lewis-Pye. 2015. Tipping points in 1-dimensional Schelling models with switching agents. *Journal of Statistical Physics* 158, 4 (2015), 806–852.

[5] George Barmpalias, Richard Elwes, and Andrew Lewis-Pye. 2016. Unperturbed Schelling segregation in two or three dimensions. *Journal of Statistical Physics* (2016), 1–28.

[6] Prateek Bhakta, Sarah Miracle, and Dana Randall. 2014. Clustering and mixing times for segregation models on $\mathbb{Z}^d$. In *Proceedings of the Twenty-Fifth Annual ACM-SIAM Symposium on Discrete Algorithms*. Society for Industrial and Applied Mathematics, 327–340.

[7] Christina Brandt, Nicole Immorlica, Gautam Kamath, and Robert Kleinberg. 2012. An analysis of one-dimensional Schelling segregation. In *Proceedings of the forty-fourth annual ACM symposium on Theory of computing*. ACM, 789–804.

[8] Pietro Caputo and Fabio Martinelli. 2006. Phase ordering after a deep quench: the stochastic Ising and hard core gas models on a tree. *Probability theory and related fields* 136, 1 (2006), 37–80.

[9] C. Castellano, S Fortunato, and V. Loreto. 1969. Statistical physics of social dynamics. *Reviews of Modern Physics* 81, 2 (1969), 591–646.

[10] B Chopard and M Droz. 1998. *Cellular automata*. Springer.

[11] Michael Damron, Jack Hanson, Philippe Sosoe, and others. 2014. Subdiffusive concentration in first-passage percolation. *Electron. J. Probab* 19, 109 (2014), 1–27.

[12] Moez Draief and Laurent Massouli. 2010. *Epidemics and rumours in complex networks*. Cambridge University Press.

[13] David Easley and Jon Kleinberg. 2010. *Networks, crowds, and markets: Reasoning about a highly connected world*. Cambridge University Press.

[14] P. Erdos and P. Ney. 1974. Some problems on random intervals and annihilating particles. *The Annals of Probability* 2, 5 (1974), 828–839.

[15] Luiz Renato Fontes, RH Schonmann, and Vladas Sidoravicius. 2002. Stretched exponential fixation in stochastic Ising models at zero temperature. *Communications in mathematical physics* 228, 3 (2002), 495–518.

[16] Cees M Fortuin, Pieter W Kasteleyn, and Jean Ginibre. 1971. Correlation inequalities on some partially ordered sets. *Communications in Mathematical Physics* 22, 2 (1971), 89–103.

[17] Olivier Garet and Régine Marchand. 2007. Large deviations for the chemical distance in supercritical Bernoulli percolation. *The Annals of Probability* (2007), 833–866.

[18] GR Grimmett. 1999. Percolation, second ed. *Springer* 321 (1999).

[19] Theodore E Harris. 1977. A correlation inequality for Markov processes in partially ordered state spaces. *The Annals of Probability* (1977), 451–454.

[20] Herbert W Hethcote. 2000. The mathematics of infectious diseases. *SIAM review* 42, 4 (2000), 599–653.

[21] Nicole Immorlica, Bobby Kleinberg, Brendan Lucier, and Morteza Zadomighaddam. 2017. Exponential Segregation in a Two-Dimensional Schelling Model with Tolerant Individuals. *ACM-SIAM Symposium on Discrete Algorithms (SODA 2017), to appear.* (2017).

[22] Matthew O Jackson and Alison Watts. 2002. On the formation of interaction networks in social coordination games. *Games and Economic Behavior* 41, 2 (2002), 265–291.

[23] Yashodhan Kanoria, Andrea Montanari, and others. 2011. Majority dynamics on trees and the dynamic cavity method. *The Annals of Applied Probability* 21, 5 (2011), 1694–1748.

[24] Harry Kesten. 1993. On the speed of convergence in first-passage percolation. *The Annals of Applied Probability* (1993), 296–338.

[25] Jon Kleinberg. 2007. Cascading behavior in networks: Algorithmic and economic issues. *Algorithmic game theory* 24 (2007), 613–632.

[26] Thomas Liggett. 2012. *Interacting particle systems*. Vol. 276. Springer Science & Business Media.

[27] Thomas M Liggett. 2010. Stochastic models for large interacting systems and related correlation inequalities. *Proceedings of the National Academy of Sciences* 107, 38 (2010), 16413–16419.

[28] Thomas M Liggett. 2013. *Stochastic interacting systems: contact, voter and exclusion processes*. Vol. 324. Springer Science & Business Media.

[29] Hildegard Meyer-Ortmanns. 2003. Immigration, integration and ghetto formation. *International Journal of Modern Physics C* 14, 03 (2003), 311–320.

[30] Markus M Mobius and TS Rosenblat. 2000. The formation of ghettos as a local interaction phenomenon. *Unpublished manuscript, Harvard University* (2000).

[31] Robert Morris. 2011. Zero-temperature Glauber dynamics on $\mathbb{Z}^d$. *Probability theory and related fields* 149, 3-4 (2011), 417–434.

[32] Hamed Omidvar and Massimo Franceschetti. 2017. Self-organized segregation on the grid. *arXiv preprint arXiv:1705.08586* (2017).

[33] Thomas C Schelling. 1969. Models of segregation. *The American Economic Review* 59, 2 (1969), 488–493.

[34] Thomas C Schelling. 1971. Dynamic models of segregationfi. *Journal of mathematical sociology* 1, 2 (1971), 143–186.

[35] Christian Schulze. 2005. Potts-like model for ghetto formation in multi-cultural societies. *International Journal of Modern Physics C* 16, 03 (2005), 351–355.

[36] Dietrich Stauffer and Sorin Solomon. 2007. Ising, Schelling and self-organising segregation. *The European Physical Journal B-Condensed Matter and Complex Systems* 57, 4 (2007), 473–479.

[37] Michel Talagrand. 1995. Concentration of measure and isoperimetric inequalities in product spaces. *Publications Mathematiques de l'IHES* 81, 1 (1995), 73–205.

[38] H Peyton Young. 2001. *Individual strategy and social structure: An evolutionary theory of institutions*. Princeton University Press.

[39] Junfu Zhang. 2004. A dynamic model of residential segregation. *Journal of Mathematical Sociology* 28, 3 (2004), 147–170.

[40] Junfu Zhang. 2004. Residential segregation in an all-integrationist world. *Journal of Economic Behavior & Organization* 54, 4 (2004), 533–550.

[41] Junfu Zhang. 2011. Tipping and Residential Segregation: A Unified Schelling Model*. *Journal of Regional Science* 51, 1 (2011), 167–193.

# A FKG-HARRIS INEQUALITY

The following is Theorem 4 in [27] which is originally by Harris [19]. Let $\sigma_t$ be the configuration of the agents on the grid at time $t$. $\mathbb{E}^{\sigma_0}[X]$ is the expected value of the random quantity $X$, when the initial state of the system is $\sigma_0$. A probability distribution $\mu$ on

$\{0,1\}^{\mathbb{Z}^d}$ is said to be positively associated if

$$\mathbb{E}[f(\sigma)g(\sigma)] \geq \mathbb{E}[f(\sigma)]\mathbb{E}[g(\sigma)]$$

for all increasing $f$ and $g$.

THEOREM A.1 (HARRIS). *Suppose the process satisfies the following two properties: (a) Individual transitions affect the state at only one site. (b) For every continuous increasing function $f$ and every $t > 0$, the function $\sigma_0 \longrightarrow \mathbb{E}^{\sigma_0}[f(\sigma_t)]$ is increasing. Then if the initial distribution is positively associated, so is the distribution at all later times.*

The following is a version of the FKG inequality [16] in our setting. The original inequality holds for a static setting and is extended here to our time-dynamic setting using Theorem A.1.

LEMMA A.2 (FKG-HARRIS). *Let $A$ and $B$ be two increasing events defined on our process on the grid. We have*

$$P(A \cap B) \geq P(A)P(B).$$

PROOF. Suppose $A$ and $B$ are increasing random variables which depend only on the states of the sites $v_1, v_2, ..., v_k$ and first time step. We proceed by induction on $k$. First, let $k = 1$. Let $\omega(v_1)$ be the realization of the site $v_1$. We also have

$$(1_A(\omega_1) - 1_A(\omega_2))(1_B(\omega_1) - 1_B(\omega_2)) \geq 0,$$

for all pairs of vectors $\omega_1$ and $\omega_2$ from the sample space. Let $p(\omega_i) = P(\omega(v_1) = \omega_i)$ for $i = 1, 2$. We have

$$\begin{aligned} 0 &\leq \sum_{\omega_1,\omega_2} (1_A(\omega_1) - 1_A(\omega_2))(1_B(\omega_1) - 1_B(\omega_2))\, p(\omega_1)p(\omega_2) \\ &= 2\left(P(A \cap B) - P(A)P(B)\right), \end{aligned}$$

as required. Suppose now that the result is valid for values of $n$ satisfying $k < n$. Then

$$\begin{aligned} P(A \cap B) &= \mathbb{E}\left[P\left(A \cap B|\omega(v_1), ..., \omega(v_{n-1})\right)\right] \\ &\geq \mathbb{E}\left[P\left(A|\omega(v_1), ..., \omega(v_{n-1})\right) P\left(B|\omega(v_1), ..., \omega(v_{n-1})\right)\right], \end{aligned}$$

since, given $\omega(v_1), ..., \omega(v_{n-1})$, $1_A$ and $1_B$ are increasing in the single variable $\omega(v_n)$.

Now since $P\left(A|\omega(v_1), ..., \omega(v_{n-1})\right)$ and $P\left(B|\omega(v_1), ..., \omega(v_{n-1})\right)$ are increasing in the space of the $n-1$ sites, it follows from the induction hypothesis that

$$\begin{aligned} P(A \cap B) &\geq \mathbb{E}\left[P\left(A|\omega(v_1), ..., \omega(v_{n-1})\right)\right] \mathbb{E}\left[P\left(B|\omega(v_1), ..., \omega(v_{n-1})\right)\right] \\ &= P(A)P(B). \end{aligned} \tag{25}$$

Next, suppose $A$ and $B$ are increasing random variables which depend only on the states of the sites in the first $k$ time steps. We proceed by induction on $k < K$ such that $K$ denotes the final time step over all the realizations. First, let $k = 0$. Let $\omega(t_0)$ be the configuration of the graph at the first time step. We have

$$P(A \cap B) \geq P(A)P(B),$$

by the above result. Suppose now that the result is valid for all values of $k$ satisfying $k < K$. Then, we have

$$\begin{aligned} P(A \cap B) &= \mathbb{E}\left[P\left(A \cap B|\omega(t_0), ..., \omega(t_{K-1})\right)\right] \\ &\geq \mathbb{E}\left[P\left(A|\omega(t_0), ..., \omega(t_{K-1})\right) P\left(B|\omega(t_0), ..., \omega(t_{K-1})\right)\right], \end{aligned}$$

by Theorem A.1 since our process satisfies the conditions of this theorem (see [19, 27]) and given $\omega(t_0), ..., \omega(t_{K-1})$, $1_A$ and $1_B$ are increasing in $\omega(t_K)$. Now since $P\left(A|\omega(t_0), ..., \omega(t_{K-1})\right)$ and $P\left(B|\omega(t_0), ..., \omega(t_{K-1})\right)$ are increasing in the space of the configurations of the graph in the first $K-1$ time steps, it follows from the induction hypothesis that

$$\begin{aligned} P(A \cap B) &\geq \mathbb{E}\left[P\left(A|\omega(t_0), ..., \omega(t_{K-1})\right)\right] \mathbb{E}\left[P\left(B|\omega(t_0), ..., \omega(t_{K-1})\right)\right] \\ &= P(A)P(B). \end{aligned}$$

□

# Brief Announcement: Efficient Self-Stabilizing 1-Maximal Matching Algorithm for Arbitrary Networks*

Michiko Inoue
Nara Institute of Science and Technology
Ikoma, Nara, Japan
kounoe@is.naist.jp

Fukuhito Ooshita
Nara Institute of Science and Technology
Ikoma, Nara, Japan
f-ooshita@is.naist.jp

Sébastien Tixeuil
UPMC Sorbonne Universités
LIP6 - CNRS 7606, IUF
Paris, France
sebastien.tixeuil@lip6.fr

## ABSTRACT

We present a new self-stabilizing 1-maximal matching algorithm that works under the distributed unfair daemon for arbitrarily shaped networks. Our algorithm is efficient (its stabilization time is $O(e)$ moves, where $e$ denotes the number of edges in the network). Besides, our algorithm is optimal with respect to identifiers locality (we assume node identifiers are distinct up to distance three, a necessary condition to withstand arbitrary networks).

## CCS CONCEPTS

• **Theory of computation → Distributed algorithms**;

## KEYWORDS

self-stabilization, 1-maximal matching, distributed unfair daemon, arbitrary network

**Table 1: Self-stabilizing matching algorithms. ID denotes identifier, $n$ denotes the number of nodes, $e$ denotes the number of edges, $\delta$ denotes the maximum degree, $D$ denotes the diameter, and $k$ is a positive integer.**

| Ref. | Matching | Topology | ID | Daemon | Complexity |
|---|---|---|---|---|---|
| [2] | maximum | tree | global | distributed | $O(n^2)$ moves |
| [12] | maximum | tree | local | central | $O(n^4)$ moves |
| [5] | maximum | tree | local | distributed | $O(n \cdot D)$ moves |
| [3] | maximum | bipartite | local | central | $O(n^2)$ rounds |
| [10] | maximal | arbitrary | local | central | $O(e)$ moves |
| [13] | maximal | arbitrary | local | distributed | $O(e)$ moves |
| [6] | maximal | arbitrary | local | distributed | $O(\delta n)$ rounds |
| [14] | 1-maximal | arbitrary | global | distributed | $O(2^n \delta n)$ moves |
| [4] | 1-maximal | arbitrary | global | distributed | $O(n^3)$ moves |
| [8] | 1-maximal | tree, cycle* | local | central | $O(n^4)$ moves |
| [1] | 1-maximal | no $3k$ cycle | local | central | $O(e)$ moves |
| [11] | 1-maximal | no $3k$ cycle | local | distributed | $O(e)$ moves |
| Proposed | 1-maximal | arbitrary | local | distributed | $O(e)$ moves |

* cycle (no $3k$)

## 1 INTRODUCTION

*Self-Stabilization* [7] is a versatile technique to withstand any kind of transient failure that may occur in computer networks, *e.g.*, caused by memory corruption, erroneous initialization, or topology change.

A *matching* in an undirected graph $G = (V, E)$ is a subset $M$ of $E$ such that each node in $V$ is incident to at most one edge in $M$. A maximal matching $M$ is *1-maximal* if, for any $e \in M$, any matching cannot be produced by removing $e$ from $M$ and adding two edges to $M - \{e\}$. A 1-maximal matching is a $\frac{2}{3}$-approximation of the maximum matching, and expected to produce more matching pairs than a maximal matching ($\frac{1}{2}$-approximation is guaranteed).

Self-stabilizing matching algorithms have been well studied [9]. Table 1 summarizes the results. Self-stabilizing maximum matching algorithms are considered for restricted classes of networks, while maximal matching algorithms are considered for arbitrary networks. In case of 1-maximal matching, some algorithms [4, 14] work for arbitrary networks using global identifiers, while some algorithms [1, 8, 11] work for restricted classes of networks (arbitrary networks without cycle whose length is a multiple of 3) using local identifiers implemented by distance 2 node coloring.

To this paper, there appears to be a trade-off for self-stabilizing 1-maximal matching between efficiency ($O(e)$ moves, local identifiers [11]) and generality (arbitrary networks [4]). These algorithms can run with a distributed daemon, where a distributed daemon may select any number of nodes simultaneously. The time complexities for these algorithms are measured in *moves*. A move is the execution of one algorithm action by one node.

We close the complexity gap between previous solutions, and present a self-stabilizing 1-maximal matching algorithm that is both efficient and general. Our solution preserves the better complexity of $O(e)$ moves and local identifiers, yet considers arbitrary networks and the unfair distributed daemon, demonstrating that previous restrictions were unnecessary to preserve complexity results.

While our identifiers are local, we assume *distance 3 node coloring* rather than *distance 2 node coloring* [11]. This assumption is necessary for arbitrary networks because no self-stabilizing 1-maximal matching algorithm exists for rings with length of a multiple of 3 with distance 2 node coloring [8]. Our protocol is thus optimal with respect to structural information for the considered problem.

In this paper, we consider self-stabilizing algorithms for a distributed system that consists of multiple asynchronous processes. Its topology is represented by an undirected connected graph $G = (V, E)$ where a node in $V$ represents a process, and an edge in $E$ represents the interconnection between the processes. We assume

*This work was supported by JSPS KAKENHI Grant Numbers 26330084 and 15H00816. Part of this work was carried out while the third author was visiting NAIST thanks to Erasmus Mundus TEAM program.


*PODC '17, July 25-27, 2017, Washington, DC, USA*

ACM ISBN 978-1-4503-4992-5/17/07.
https://doi.org/10.1145/3087801.3087840

that nodes have colors that are unique within distance three in order to implement "pointer to neighbor" variables. A node is a state machine that changes its state by actions. Each node has a set of actions, and a collection of actions of nodes is called a *distributed algorithm*. We consider *state-reading model* and an *unfair distributed daemon*. For more detailed definitions, readers can refer related works including [11].

## 2 ALGORITHM

### 2.1 MM1D

Our proposed algorithm MM1DG is based on our previous algorithm MM1D [11]. MM1D works for arbitrary networks without cycle whose length is a multiple of 3. In MM1D, a node is said to be *free* if it has no matching partner, otherwise it is said to be *matched.*

A node $i$ has three variables; `stage`$_i$, `m-ptr`$_i$, `i-ptr`$_i$. The variable `m-ptr`$_i$ is a matching pointer that points to its partner, while the variable `i-ptr`$_i$ is an invitation pointer that is used to invite a neighboring node to make a new match. There are ten stages of a node where 4 stages mean the node is *free* and 6 stages mean the node is *matched.*

A free node tries to make a new match with another free node, and two matched nodes try to increase the number of matches by breaking the current match and making new matches with free nodes. A basic scenario to make a new match is that one node invites another node and the invited node accepts the invitation.

When one match is replaced with two new matches, a matched node changes its stages `faithful`, `curious`, `open`, possibly `promise`, `confirmed`, `ready` in this order, and finally goes back to `faithful` if it gets a new matching partner. On the other hand, a free node changes its stage from `single`, `approved`, or `single`, `proposing`, `discouraged`, `approved` in this order and finally becomes `faithful` if it gets a matching partner. When a node makes a new match, it becomes `faithful`, and then becomes `curious` if it finds a free neighboring node. Once both matched nodes become `curious`, they can move to `open`. That shows the invited free node is ready to approve the invitation.

However, it does not always work well. The invited node may make a match with a different node. In this case, nodes cancel the progress of making new matches. A node also may reset its state. If a node finds itself in some invalid state, it will reset the state.

Though the above cancel and reset may influence the neighboring nodes, nodes carefully proceed actions to make a new match by loosely synchronizing with its neighboring nodes and the influence of cancel or reset is minimized.

### 2.2 MM1DG

We extend MM1D to be applicable to arbitrary networks. We first strengthen the assumption of an available coloring from distance 2 node coloring to distance 3 node coloring. This is a minimal assumption for silent 1-maximal matching self-stabilizing algorithm since there is no silent 1-maximal matching self-stabilizing algorithm with distance 2 node coloring [8].

There are two situations where MM1D could not work well for general graphs. (1) When two matched nodes invite free neighboring nodes to migrate into them, they may invite the same free node.

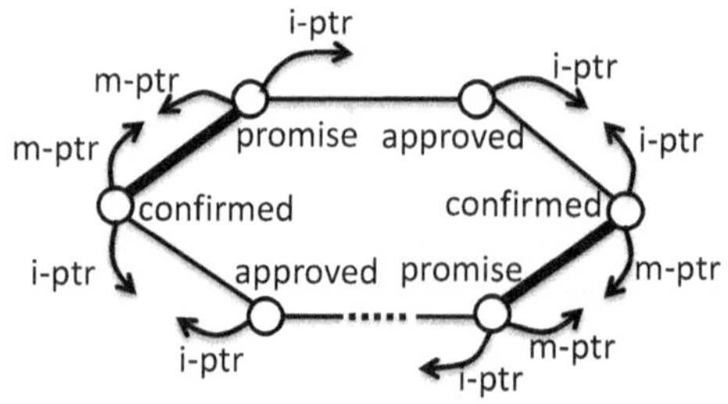


**Figure 1: Deadlock configuration**

It is not supposed for MM1D because MM1D assumes no cycle of length of three. (2) There is a deadlock configuration as shown in Fig. 1, where a `confirmed` node waits for a `promise` node to be `confirmed`, the `promise` node waits for an `approved` node to approve its invitation, and the `approved` node waits a `confirmed` to be `ready`. To overcome these situations, we introduce two extensions to MM1D and get MM1DG.

#### 2.2.1 *Choosing different nodes for migration.*

For matched nodes to invite different free nodes for migration, two additional pointers $\alpha_i$ and $\beta_i$ are introduced for each node $i$, where $\alpha_i$ and $\beta_i$ point to free neighboring nodes with the smallest identifier and the second smallest identifier respectively. The values of $\alpha_i$ and $\beta_i$ are updated when node $i$ becomes `faithful` (when it has a new match) or while it is `faithful` if its circumstance is changed and it needs to be updated. The `faithful` stage means that a node has a matching partner and does not invite any free node to migration.

Let $i$ and $j$ be matched nodes. They decide inviting nodes for migration only when $\alpha_i \neq \perp$, $\alpha_j \neq \perp$ and there are at least two unique identifiers among $\alpha_i$, $\beta_i$, $\alpha_j$ and $\beta_j$. Node $i$ determines which node it will invite using the following function $target(i,j)$ where $j$ is $i$'s current partner and $unique()$ returns the number of unique identifiers among parameters.

```
target(i,j) {
    if (α_i ≠⊥ ∧α_j ≠⊥ ∧unique(α_i, β_i, α_j, β_j) ≥ 2) {
        if ((α_i ≠ α_j)
            ∨(α_i = α_j ∧ β_i =⊥)
            ∨(α_i = α_j ∧ β_i ≠⊥ ∧β_j ≠⊥ ∧i < j))
        return α_i
        else return β_i
    } else
        return ⊥
}
```

We claim that $target(i,j)$ and $target(j,i)$ are different if they are not $\perp$. The claim clearly holds if $\alpha_i \neq \alpha_j$. Let us assume $\alpha_i = \alpha_j$. If $\beta_i = \perp$, $\beta_j \neq \perp$ holds from $unique(\alpha_i, \beta_i, \alpha_j, \beta_j) \geq 2$ and thus $target(i,j) = \alpha_i$ and $target(j,i) = \beta_j$ are different. The claim similarly holds if $\beta_j = \perp$. If $\beta_i \neq \perp$ and $\beta_j \neq \perp$, the node with the smaller identifier chooses $\alpha$-value and the other chooses $\beta$-value. That is, if $i < j$ w.l.o.g, $target(i,j) = \alpha_i (= \alpha_j)$ and $target(j,i) = \beta_j (\neq \alpha_j)$ hold. Consequently the claim holds.

In MM1D, a node $i$ cancels its invitation for migration and goes back to `faithful` only if (1) an invited node has made a match with another node and (2) node $i$ is already in open or later stage

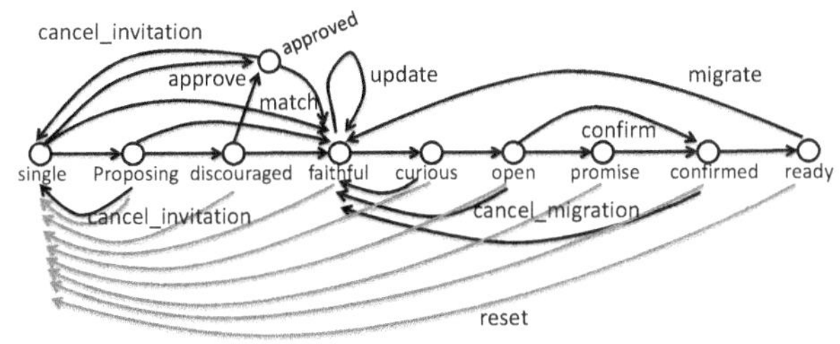


**Figure 2: Transitions of stages**

and a partner node has gone back to `faithful` by cancelling. In MM1DG, in addition to these conditions, node $i$ cancels if (3) node $i$ is still in `curious` but $target(i, j)$ is not consistent with current $\alpha_i$, $\beta_i$, $\alpha_j$ and $\beta_j$. That happens when a partner node $j$ updates values $\alpha_j$ and $\beta_j$. The last cancel policy enables matched nodes to invite different node for migration.

*2.2.2 Deadlock avoidance.* To avoid a deadlock as mentioned, the order of moves is controlled in MM1DG. When two matched nodes $i$ and $j$ try to migrate to new partners, they are loosely synchronized in MM1D. Once both nodes become `curious` they independently change their stages to `open`, possibly `promise`, and `confirmed`, and finally they are synchronized at `confirmed` stage. However, if MM1D is applied to a graph with a cycle of length of a multiple of 3, it may get deadlock as shown in Fig. 1. In MM1DG, if both matched nodes are inviting their neighboring nodes for migration, a node that is inviting a node with a smaller identifier becomes `open` first. The other node has to wait for its partner to become `confirmed`. The assumption of distance 3 node coloring ensures that no deadlock situation happens.

This is proved by contradiction. Assume there is a deadlock like Fig. 1, where each of `approved` (free) nodes is being invited from `promise` and `confirmed` nodes. The length of cycle is not 3 since matched nodes do not invite the same free node. Let us consider a node that has the smallest identifier among `approved` nodes. Since it has the smallest identifier and matched nodes invite a different node, its neighboring nodes becomes `confirmed` prior to their matched node. That contradicts with the deadlock configuration.

# 3 CORRECTNESS

With the mentioned extension, MM1DG does not fall into a deadlock configuration even for arbitrary networks and 1-maximal matching is guaranteed in any terminal configuration.

THEOREM 3.1. *A 1-maximal matching is constructed in any terminal configuration of MM1DG for arbitrary networks.*

In MM1DG, each node changes its stages as shown in Fig. 2 where vertices represent stages and arcs represents actions to change stages. Action `update` is newly introduced to MM1DG and updates values of $\alpha_i$ and $\beta_i$ for a node $i$. We can see that every action except `update`, `migrate`, `cancel_invitation`, `cancel_migration`, and `reset` moves stages to the right in Fig. 2. It can be proved that the number of moves of `update`, `migrate`, `cancel_invitation`, `cancel_migration`, and `reset` is $O(e)$ in any execution, and the following theorem holds.

THEOREM 3.2. *MM1DG is silent and takes $O(e)$ moves to construct 1-maximal matching for any graphs under an unfair distributed daemon.*

# 4 CONCLUSION

We proposed a 1-maximal matching algorithm MM1DG that is silent and works for any arbitrary networks under a distributed unfair daemon. Our solution does not trade generality for efficiency, as it maintains best time complexity and is optimal with respect to structural knowledge, closing the complexity gap appearing in previous works. Two natural open questions arise from our work:

(1) There exists a trivial $\Omega(n)$ lower bound for the number of moves. Our algorithm is thus optimal in trees and rings, but what about other topologies?
(2) The move from distance 2 coloring to distance 3 coloring for 1-maximal matchings call for a generalization for self-stabilizing $k$-matchings (where $k \geq 1$).

# REFERENCES

[1] Yuma Asada, Fukuhito Ooshita, and Michiko Inoue. 2016. An Efficient Silent Self-Stabilizing 1-Maximal Matching Algorithm in Anonymous Networks. *J. Graph Algorithms Appl.* 20, 1 (2016), 59–78. https://doi.org/10.7155/jgaa.00384
[2] Jean R. S. Blair and Fredrik Manne. 2003. Efficient self-stabilizing algorithms for tree networks. In *Proceedings of 23rd International Conference on Distributed Computing Systems*. IEEE, 20–26. https://doi.org/10.1109/ICDCS.2003.1203448
[3] Subhendu Chattopadhyay, Lisa Higham, and Karen Seyffarth. 2002. Dynamic and self-stabilizing distributed matching. In *Proceedings of the twenty-first annual symposium on Principles of distributed computing*. ACM, 290–297. https://doi.org/10.1145/571825.571877
[4] Johanne Cohen, Khaled Maâmra, , George Manoussakis, and Laurence Pilard. 2016. Polynomial self-stabilizing maximal matching algorithm with approximation ratio 2/3. In *International Conference on Principles of Distributed Systems*.
[5] Ajoy K. Datta, Lawrence L. Larmoreand, and Toshimitsu Masuzawa. 2015. Maximum Matching for Anonymous Trees with Constant Space per Process. In *Proceedings of International Conference on Principles of Distributed Systems*. 1–16.
[6] Stéphane Devismes, Toshimitsu Masuzawa, and Sébastien Tixeuil. 2009. Communication efficiency in self-stabilizing silent protocols. In *Proceedings of 23rd International Conference on Distributed Computing Systems*. IEEE, 474–481. https://doi.org/10.1109/ICDCS.2009.24
[7] Edsger W. Dijkstra. 1974. Self-stabilizing Systems in Spite of Distributed Control. *Commun. ACM* 17, 11 (1974), 643–644. https://doi.org/10.1145/361179.361202
[8] Wayne Goddard, Stephen T Hedetniemi, Zhengnan Shi, et al. 2006. An Anonymous Self-Stabilizing Algorithm for 1-Maximal Matching in Trees. In *Proceedings of International Conference on Parallel and Distributed Processing Techniques and Applications*. 797–803.
[9] Nabil Guellati and Hamamache Kheddouci. 2010. A survey on self-stabilizing algorithms for independence, domination, coloring, and matching in graphs. *J. Parallel and Distrib. Comput.* 70, 4 (2010), 406–415. https://doi.org/10.1016/j.jpdc.2009.11.006
[10] Su-Chu Hsu and Shing-Tsaan Huang. 1992. A self-stabilizing algorithm for maximal matching. *Inform. Process. Lett.* 43, 2 (1992), 77–81. https://doi.org/10.1016/0020-0190(92)90015-N
[11] Michiko Inoue, Fukuhito Ooshita, and Sébastien Tixeuil. 2016. An Efficient Silent Self-stabilizing 1-Maximal Matching Algorithm Under Distributed Daemon Without Global Identifiers. In *International Symposium on Stabilization, Safety, and Security of Distributed Systems*. Springer, 195–212.
[12] Mehmet Hakan Karaata and Kassem Afif Saleh. 2000. Distributed self-stabilizing algorithm for finding maximum matching. *Computer Systems Science and Engineering* 15, 3 (2000), 175–180.
[13] Fredrik Manne, Morten Mjelde, Laurence Pilard, and Sébastien Tixeuil. 2009. A new self-stabilizing maximal matching algorithm. *Theoretical Computer Science* 410, 14 (2009), 1336–1345. https://doi.org/10.1016/j.tcs.2008.12.022
[14] Fredrik Manne, Morten Mjelde, Laurence Pilard, and Sébastien Tixeuil. 2011. A self-stabilizing 2/3-approximation algorithm for the maximum matching problem. *Theoretical Computer Science* 412, 40 (2011), 5515–5526. https://doi.org/10.1016/j.tcs.2011.05.019

# Brief Announcement: Secure Self-Stabilizing Computation

Shlomi Dolev
Department of Computer Science,
Ben-Gurion University of the Negev
Beersheva, Israel 84105
dolev@cs.bgu.ac.il

Karim Eldefrawy
SRI International
Menlo Park
California, USA
karim@csl.sri.com

Juan Garay
Yahoo Research
Sunnyvale
California, USA
garay@yahoo-inc.com

Muni Venkateswarlu Kumaramangalam
Department of Computer Science,
Ben-Gurion University of the Negev
Beersheva, Israel 84105
muni@cs.bgu.ac.il

Rafail Ostrovsky
Department of Computer Science and
Department of Mathematics,
University of California
Los Angeles, USA
rafail@cs.ucla.edu

Moti Yung
Snap & Columbia University
New York, USA
moti@cs.columbia.edu

## ABSTRACT

Self-stabilization refers to the ability of systems to recover after temporal violations of conditions required for their correct operation. Such violations may lead the system to an arbitrary state from which it should automatically recover. Today, beyond recovering functionality, there is a need to recover security and confidentiality guarantees as well. To the best of our knowledge, there are currently no self-stabilizing protocols that also ensure recovering confidentiality, authenticity, and integrity properties. Specifically, self-stabilizing systems are designed to regain functionality which is, roughly speaking, desired input output relation, ignoring the security and confidentiality of computation and its state. Distributed (cryptographic) protocols for generic secure and privacy-preserving computation, e.g., secure Multi-Party Computation (MPC), usually ensure secrecy of inputs and outputs, and correctness of computation when the adversary is limited to compromise only a fraction of the components in the system, e.g., the computation is secure only in the presence of an honest majority of involved parties. While there are MPC protocols that are secure against a dishonest majority, in reality, the adversary may compromise *all components* of the system for a while; some of the corrupted components may then recover, e.g., due to security patches and software updates, or periodical code refresh and local state consistency check and enforcement based on self-stabilizing hardware and software techniques. It is currently unclear if a system and its state can be designed to *always* fully recover following such individual asynchronous recoveries. This paper introduces *Secure Self-stabilizing Computation* which answers this question in the affirmative. Secure self-stabilizing computation design ensures that secrecy of inputs and outputs, and correctness of the computation are automatically regained, even if at some point the *entire system is compromised.* We consider the distributed computation task as the implementation of virtual global finite satiate machine (FSM) to present commonly realized computation. The FSM is designed to regain consistency and security in the presence of a minority of Byzantine participants, e.g., one third of the parties, and following a temporary corruption of the entire system. We use this task and settings to demonstrate the definition of *secure self-stabilizing computation.* We show how our algorithms and system autonomously restore security and confidentiality of the computation of the FSM once the required corruption thresholds are again respected.

The first author is partially Supported by the Rita Altura Trust Chair in Computer Sciences, by Lynne and William Frankel Center for Computer Sciences, by a grant of the Ministry of Science, Technology and Space, Israel and the National Science Council (NSC) of Taiwan, and by a grant of the Ministry of Science, Technology and Space, Israel, and the Ministry of Foreign Affairs, Italy.
The fifth author's research is supported in part by NSF grant 1619348, US-Israel BSF grant 2012366, by DARPA Safeware program, OKAWA Foundation Research Award, IBM Faculty Research Award, Xerox Faculty Research Award, B. John Garrick Foundation Award, Teradata Research Award, and Lockheed-Martin Corporation Research Award. The views expressed are those of the authors and do not reflect position of the Department of Defense or the U.S. Government.

*PODC '17, July 25-27, 2017, Washington, DC, USA*

ACM ISBN 978-1-4503-4992-5/17/07.
https://doi.org/http://dx.doi.org/10.1145/3087801.3087864

## CCS CONCEPTS

• **Security and privacy → Privacy-preserving protocols**; *Public key encryption*; *Security requirements*;

## KEYWORDS

Self-stabilization; Secure multi-party computation; Security and privacy;

**ACM Reference format:**
Shlomi Dolev, Karim Eldefrawy, Juan Garay, Muni Venkateswarlu Kumaramangalam, Rafail Ostrovsky, and Moti Yung. 2017. Brief Announcement: Secure Self-Stabilizing Computation. In *Proceedings of PODC '17, Washington, DC, USA, July 25-27, 2017,* 3 pages.
https://doi.org/http://dx.doi.org/10.1145/3087801.3087864

## 1 PRELIMINARIES

**System and Network Model.** We consider a system of $n$ parties $p_1, \ldots, p_n$ with a completely connected semi synchronous network, that interactively and continuously computes a function $f(.)$ over a finite field $\mathbb{F}$ (below we use a Mealy FSM as an example of $f(.)$). Each party has a True Random Number Generator (TRNG). To simplify the presentation we first assume that the system is set up by a Configuration Authority (*CA*) that initializes each party $p_i$ with a pair of public- and private-key, $PK_{p_i}$ and $SK_{p_i}$ respectively; each party is also initialized with public-keys of other parties in the system. Each party's private-key, and the *CA*'s public-key, $PK_{CA}$ are stored in a secure hardware module that only allows the party to decrypt or to sign messages with its private-key, or to verify signatures by the *CA* using its public-key. Each pair of parties shares private secure authenticated communication channels that can be established based on the initial setup. In fact, the use of TRNG suffices to establish the required keys. Parties can repeatedly establish fresh public and private keys (unknown to the non-present adversary), and agree on the keys (by using Byzantine agreement over each declared public key), and then establish genuine symmetric keys for each pair of the participants and secure broadcast channels from scratch. Alternatively, parties may receive the symmetric keys as a part of the inputs.

The parties periodically receive some global input in secret shared format from an external client (or the environment in general), and use that input in the computation of $f(.)$. The parties are not aware of their state history i.e., they do not know whether they are corrupted or not. The parties exchange messages in sequence of rounds to communicate and compute the function $f(.)$. In each *round*, every party in the system receives messages, performs local computation and sends messages. We consider both synchronous and semi-synchronous network settings during the system implementation. In a synchronous system, all the $n$ parties are synchronized via a global clock and perform a given event on a common clock pulse that occurs periodically. Whereas in a semi-synchronous system, time-bounded events happen in real-time. An event needs to be completed before its time elapses. A self-stabilizing Byzantine clock synchronization [7] can facilitate a (logical) global clock pulse when the system has only semi-synchronous promise. Moreover, it can be used to announce a common round number, that in-turn can be used to start establishing the keys and repeatedly perform the given global FSM transition.

**Mixed Adversarial Model.** There is a central *mixed adversary* with bounded computational power that is actively trying to prevent the success of the computation. The adversary may corrupt up to $n$ parties corrupting some parties *passively*, to learn their internal information, and/or even *actively*, causing them to deviate arbitrarily from prescribed protocol steps. Because parties are periodically recovered/reset/rebooted to a consistent/clean state (using a hardware watchdog mechanism that is designed to automatically recover following any (time-count) corruption), the adversary is not able to maintain corruption of all the $n$ parties indefinitely. An underlying assumption is that, once the adversary loses control over a party it is unable to immediately compromise the party again.

## 2 STANDARD SELF-STABILIZING VS SECURE SELF-STABILIZING COMPUTATION

**Standard Self-Stabilization.** A self-stabilizing system can be started in any possible global state (possibly due to the occurrence of transient unpredictable faults) and is guaranteed to converge to a consistent state and correct operation. If a system is self-stabilizing, then the system must satisfy the following properties [4]:

- *Convergence:* For any arbitrary inconsistent configuration $c_r$, there exists a safe (legal, arbitrary but consistent) configuration $c_f$ after a finite number of rounds, i.e., starting from any arbitrary configuration, the system is guaranteed to eventually reach a stable legal configuration from which the execution is legal, fulfilling the task requirement.
- *Closure:* Once a system reaches a stable state, the system is guaranteed to stay in the stable state provided that no further unexpected fault happens.

**Secure Computation.** Secure Multi-Party Computation (MPC) enables $n$ parties to jointly and securely compute a function $f(.)$ of their private inputs, even in the presence of adversarial behavior (typically modeled as a fraction of $t$ parties that can be passively or actively corrupted). MPC ensures that while computing $f(.)$ and when corruption is less than $t$, parties inputs' remain private, except what is revealed by the output of the computation (*privacy*). MPC also guarantees the correctness of the output of the computation (*correctness*) [10].

**Secure Self-Stabilizing Computation.** Existing secure MPC protocols [5, 10, 11] guarantee privacy (computation state, inputs and outputs) and correctness of computation only when there are a limited number of corrupted parties. However, in reality, a powerful adversary may even compromise all the parties of a system. The aim of introducing *Secure Self-stabilizing Computation* is to specify the requirements for automatically recovering secrecy of computation state, inputs and outputs, and correctness of a computation even if an entire system is compromised for a finite time. Consider a self-stabilizing system of $n$ parties that perform a computation in a distributed fashion while maintaining the input secrecy and correctness of the output. We assume that the system does not necessarily have an initial state to start with, i.e., it may begin its execution from any arbitrary configuration $c_r$ and does not necessarily stop. An external client or environment, e.g., sensors or a physical process, etc., supplies inputs to the system and reconstructs output(s) from the individual outputs of the parties. Over a long period of time, the considered mixed adversary may corrupt a large number of the parties and may even compromise all the $n$ parties for a finite time. When the system is fully exposed, after a finite number of rounds $r_x$, $n_x$ parties may recover independently due to some proactive measures, such as security patches and software updates, anti-virus updates, periodical code refreshing based on self-stabilizing hardware and software techniques. From the above *closure property*, ensuring no further corruption, the asynchronous independent recovery establishes local consistency of the recovered parties (for example, see [2, 6] for a self-stabilizing infrastructure that guarantees a safe recovery of a party even in the presence of Byzantine faults). Due to the independent recovery and the *closure property*, the system gradually recovers *itself* autonomously to exhibit the needed behavior. From the *convergence* property, the system may converge to a safe arbitrary consistent configuration $c_f$, after $r_f$ ($r_f \geq r_x$) rounds, recovering enough number of parties $n_f$, $n_f \geq n_x$, from Byzantine behavior. The independent recovery continues until the required secure computation requirements (thresholds) hold again. Once the threshold requirements are respected again, the system automatically regains confidentiality of state and inputs/outputs, and security of the computation.

## 3 SECURE SELF-STABILIZING COMPUTATION OF AN INTERACTIVE FSM

In a nutshell, we use a global clock (obtained by e.g., [7]) to establish a consistent state of the FSM among all the non-Byzantine participants, and then compute transitions using the (secret shared) inputs to obtain (secret shared) outputs. To achieve this, we first harvest randomness from the true random source that each participant owns. Next, we use a secure MPC protocol to check whether the state shares held by all the participants represent a legitimate state (using, say, the Berlekamp-Welch algorithm [1] to eliminate corrupted state shares contributed by the Byzantine participants). If the state is valid, then another MPC instance uses the (secret shared) state and the inputs (represented by secret shares, with the same redundancy against Byzantine participants as the state redundancy) to compute the (secret shares of the) next state and output. In-case the state is found invalid by the first MPC, is followed by assignment of state secret shares of a default state and then continues as in the previous case. The process is described in more details below.

Note that we have two kinds of rounds, one is a clock pulse, and the other is a round of the FSM transition, say starting whenever the clock pulse number is zero, the FSM transition round consists of so many clock pulses to allow (in short): (a) establishing new keys (a1. using true random source the parties obtain fresh public and private keys, a2. sending the public key of each participant to all other participants, a3. agree on each public key using Byzantine agreement [3, 9], a4. establishing a fresh symmetric key between any two participants), (b) using verifiable secret sharing scheme [8] on the secret shares of the current FSM state, (c) executing a secure multi-party computation for enforcing a correct FSM state, both in the polynomial degrees for the representation of each portion of the FSM state and the well formation of the state, (d) applying the transition table, that is shared (hardwired) among the participants, compute a circuit in secure MPC that will compute the next FSM state and the output.

Let $F$ be a publicly known interactive Mealy finite state machine (FSM) $F = \{ST, S_0, \Gamma, \Lambda, T, O\}$ with a finite set of states $ST$, and initial state $ST_0$, a finite input alphabet $\Gamma$, a finite output alphabet $\Lambda$, a transition function $T : ST \times \Gamma \longrightarrow ST$ mapping pairs of a state and an input symbol to the corresponding next state, and an output function $O : ST \times \Gamma \longrightarrow \Lambda$ mapping pairs of a state and an input symbol to the corresponding output symbol. Computation of the FSM is delegated to the $n$ parties. Every party has two arithmetic circuits (consisting of addition and multiplication gates) that represent the functions $T$ and $O$, *Transition Circuit (TC)* and *Output Circuit (OC)* respectively. The input is distributed to the parties in a secret shared form [12], denoting $[x]_{p_i}$ as the share of party $p_i$ of secret $x$. The parties are in agreement (and have necessary software) to execute an MPC protocol $\Pi$ which can perform any computation represented as addition and multiplication gates using secret shared inputs. Parties are in possession of a circuit representation of a (fault tolerant) error detection algorithm ($\xi$), e.g., the Berlekamp-Welch algorithm [1], that if given evaluations of an univariate polynomial $P(.)$ of degree $t$, can interpolate it as long as there are enough correct points given (we use $\xi$ to securely verify that the secret encoded by some shares is one of the legitimate states of $F$). Let $S_0$ also denote the default state of the FSM, while $\zeta$ denotes the current state of the FSM. Algorithm 1 is executed when each of the parties, $p_i$, receives a share of a new input ($\tau$).

**Algorithm 1:** Secure Self-stabilizing Computation of FSM $F = \{ST, S_0, \Gamma, \Lambda, T, O\}$

```
Each p_i receives a share of the secret shared input [τ]_{p_i}
Each p_i obtains some random seed r_{p_i} from its TRNG
Each p_i participates in Π to compute ξ with [τ]_{p_i} as input
  and r_{p_i} as its randomness
if computation of ξ succeeds then
    Each p_i computes via Π the TC with [ζ]_{p_i} and [τ]_{p_i} and
      outputs [T(ζ, τ)]_{p_i}
    Each p_i computes via Π the OC with [ζ]_{p_i} and [τ]_{p_i} and
      outputs [O(ζ, τ)]_{p_i}
else
    Each p_i computes via Π the TC with [S_0]_{p_i} and [τ]_{p_i} and
      outputs [T(S_0, τ)]_{p_i}
    Each p_i computes via Π the OC with [S_0]_{p_i} and [τ]_{p_i} and
      outputs [O(S_0, τ)]_{p_i}
end if
```

Algorithm 1 ensures that whenever the conditions for stabilization hold, e.g., less than one third of the participants are Byzantine, the adversary's knowledge concerning the state of the FSM is lost, as the adversary cannot obtain the arriving input, and therefore cannot use the revealed state for computing the current state. In particular, when the graph of the transition function of the FSM is a complete graph, then in the eyes of the adversary any state is possible after the first transition following the system convergence. Similarly, when the transition function graph forms an expander, the knowledge concerning the FSM state is totally lost after a number of steps that is logarithmic in number of the FSM states.

## REFERENCES


[1] Elwyn R. Berlekamp. 1984. *Algebraic Coding Theory.* Aegean Park Press.

[2] Alexander Binun, Mark Bloch, Shlomi Dolev, Ramzi Martin Kahil, Boaz Menuhin, Reuven Yagel, Thierry Coupaye, Marc Lacoste, and Aurélien Wailly. 2014. Self-Stabilizing Virtual Machine Hypervisor Architecture for Resilient Cloud. In *2014 IEEE World Congress on Services, SERVICES 2014, Anchorage, AK, USA, June 27 - July 2, 2014.* 200–207.

[3] Ran Cohen, Sandro Coretti, Juan A. Garay, and Vassilis Zikas. 2016. Probabilistic Termination and Composability of Cryptographic Protocols. In *Advances in Cryptology - CRYPTO 2016 - 36th Annual International Cryptology Conference, Santa Barbara, CA, USA, August 14-18, 2016, Proceedings, Part III.* 240–269.

[4] Shlomi Dolev. 2000. *Self-Stabilization.* MIT Press.

[5] Shlomi Dolev, Karim El Defrawy, Joshua Lampkins, Rafail Ostrovsky, and Moti Yung. 2016. Proactive Secret Sharing with a Dishonest Majority. In *Security and Cryptography for Networks - 10th International Conference, SCN 2016, Amalfi, Italy, August 31 - September 2, 2016, Proceedings.* 529–548.

[6] Shlomi Dolev and Yinnon A. Haviv. 2012. Stabilization Enabling Technology. *IEEE Trans. Dependable Sec. Comput.* 9, 2 (2012), 275–288.

[7] Shlomi Dolev and Jennifer L. Welch. 2004. Self-stabilizing clock synchronization in the presence of Byzantine faults. *J. ACM* 51, 5 (2004), 780–799.

[8] Paul Feldman. 1987. A Practical Scheme for Non-interactive Verifiable Secret Sharing. In *Proceedings of the 28th Annual Symposium on Foundations of Computer Science (SFCS '87).* IEEE Computer Society, Washington, DC, USA, 427–438.

[9] Juan A. Garay and Yoram Moses. 1998. Fully Polynomial Byzantine Agreement for $n > 3t$ Processors in $t + 1$ Rounds. *SIAM J. Comput.* 27, 1 (1998), 247–290.

[10] O. Goldreich, S. Micali, and A. Wigderson. 1987. How to Play ANY Mental Game. In *Proceedings of the Nineteenth Annual ACM Symposium on Theory of Computing (STOC '87).* ACM, New York, NY, USA, 218–229.

[11] Ueli Maurer. 2006. Secure multi-party computation made simple. *Discrete Applied Mathematics* 154, 2 (2006), 370 – 381. Coding and Cryptography.

[12] Adi Shamir. 1979. How to Share a Secret. *Commun. ACM* 22, 11 (Nov. 1979), 612–613.

# Brief Announcement: Stateless Computation

Danny Dolev*
Hebrew University of Jerusalem
dolev@cs.huji.ac.il

Michael Erdmann
Carnegie Mellon University
me@cs.cmu.edu

Neil Lutz†
Rutgers University
njlutz@rutgers.edu

Michael Schapira‡
Hebrew University of Jerusalem
schapiram@cs.huji.ac.il

Adva Zair
Hebrew University of Jerusalem
adva.zair@mail.huji.ac.il

## ABSTRACT

We present and explore a model of *stateless* and *self-stabilizing* distributed computation, inspired by real-world applications such as routing on today's Internet. Processors in our model do not have an internal state, but rather interact by repeatedly mapping incoming messages ("labels") to outgoing messages and output values. While seemingly too restrictive to be of interest, stateless computation encompasses both classical game-theoretic notions of strategic interaction and a broad range of practical applications (e.g., Internet protocols, circuits, diffusion of technologies in social networks). Our main technical contribution is a general impossibility result for stateless self-stabilization in our model, showing that even modest asynchrony (with wait times that are linear in the number of processors) can prevent a stateless protocol from reaching a stable global configuration. Furthermore, we present hardness results for verifying stateless self-stabilization. We also address several aspects of the computational power of stateless protocols. Most significantly, we show that short messages (of length that is logarithmic in the number of processors) yield substantial computational power, even on very poorly connected topologies.

## KEYWORDS

self-stabilization; network protocols; best-response dynamics

## 1 MOTIVATION

One of our main motivating examples is routing with the Border Gateway Protocol (BGP). BGP establishes routes between the independently administered networks that make up the Internet, and can be regarded as the glue that holds the Internet together. A BGP-speaking router continuously (1) receives update messages from each of its neighbors, announcing routes to different destinations (IP address prefixes) on the Internet, (2) selects the best available route to each destination (according to its local preferences), and (3) propagates its newly selected routes to neighboring BGP routers. An important and extensively studied desideratum is for this decentralized route-selection process to converge to a stable routing configuration from *any* initial configuration of the routing system [10].

While BGP route selection involves maintaining state, in terms of internal memory, this is for the sole purpose of recording the last route-advertisement (per IP prefix) received from each neighbor. Indeed, BGP's route-selection can be modeled as a function that maps the most recent messages received from neighbors to routing choices (see [10]). BGP is a prominent example for environments in which all nodes repeatedly "best respond" to each other's most recent choices of actions. Other examples of "best-response dynamics" [11] include additional network protocols [15], diffusion of technologies in social networks [18], circuits with feedback loops, and more, as discussed in [8, 13, 14]. Such environments, and others, fall within our framework of stateless computation, in which computational nodes are modeled as not having an internal state (i.e., memory), but rather interact by repeatedly mapping incoming messages to outgoing messages and output values. Since such applications are inherently ongoing and susceptible to transient faults, we focus on *self-stabilizing* protocols.

Because output is separated from communication in our model, it permits two very natural notions of self-stabilization. The first is *label stabilization*, which requires that, regardless how the system is initialized, its entire configuration must eventually reach an "equilibrium," at which the nodes' messages and outputs can no longer change. This is a strong requirement that corresponds to *silent stabilizing* algorithms [6] in the literature. The second notion is *output stabilization*, which requires (again, regardless of initialization) that each node's output will eventually stop changing. This weaker notion is actually a type of *pseudo-stabilization*, which is sufficient for many applications of self-stabilizing algorithms [2]. There is a large body of literature on stateful self-stabilization, including on the design of silent stabilizing algorithms (e.g., [1, 3, 12, 16]), instability in the presence of crashes (e.g., [9]), and the surprising computational power of pseudo-stabilizing

*Danny Dolev is Incumbent of the Berthold Badler Chair in Computer Science, The Rachel and Selim Benin School of Computer Science and Engineering, Edmond J. Safra Campus. This work was supported in part by the HUJI Cyber Security Research Center in conjunction with the Israel National Cyber Bureau in the Prime Minister's Office.
†Research supported in part by NSF Grant 1445755.
‡Michael Schapira is supported by the Israeli Center for Research Excellence (I-CORE) in Algorithms.


*PODC '17, July 25-27, 2017, Washington, DC, USA*

ACM ISBN 978-1-4503-4992-5/17/07.
https://doi.org/http://dx.doi.org/10.1145/3087801.3087854

algorithms, even with a constant number of states (e.g., [17]). These topics are covered in detail in [5]. On the topic of statelessness in self-stabilizing algorithms, [7] describes a way to design self-stabilizing algorithms by prepending a stateless stage to executions of otherwise stateful protocols.

The immediate precursor of our work is [14], which analyzes convergence of self-independent and bounded-recall dynamics, including best-response dynamics, in asynchronous environments. Our main result, which demonstrates label instability in the presence of multiple stable states, strengthens the historyless case of that work's main result in two ways. First, unlike the model of [14], our model of stateless computation allows the messages sent between nodes to be distinct from the nodes' outputs. Second, the negative results in that work permit the adversarial scheduler to impose arbitrarily long delays. Here, we show that an oscillation can occur even when the asynchrony is significantly more "fair," imposing delays that are at most linear in the number of nodes. This extension answers open questions posed in [14] and requires a valency argument that is substantially different from and more delicate than the argument used in that work. Similarly, our hardness results for testing self-stabilization build on those of [8, 14] by extending them to the broader class of stateless protocols and to linearly fair schedules.

## 2 MODEL

Consider a distributed network of size $n$, in which every node (processor) receives an external input, $x_i$. The nodes are connected by some set of directed communication links, and they compute a global function, $f(x_1, \dots, x_n)$, by repeatedly sending messages along these links. We abstract the communication model and refer to a message from one node to another as a *label* on the directed edge representing their communication link; an edge's label reflects the most recent message sent along that link. Edge labels are assumed to come from a finite *label space*. We consider computation in which nodes have no internal *state*. Instead, each node is equipped with a *reaction function* that maps the profile of labels on its incoming edges to (1) a profile of labels on its outgoing edges (2) an output value, based on the node's input. Given a network topology, a protocol specifies a label space and a collection of reaction functions.

We study *self-stabilizing* distributed systems, which enjoy an important robustness property: the ability to recover from any transient fault, provided that the processor code and input remain intact. The notion of self-stabilization was introduced in a seminal paper by Dijkstra [4]. A system is self-stabilizing if, regardless of its initialization, it is guaranteed to arrive and remain at a global "legitimate state" in a finite number of steps. We consider two definitions of a legitimate state. From an algorithmic perspective, when computing $f$ on input $(x_1, \dots, x_n)$, a legitimate state is a configuration in which the output value of every node is $f(x_1, \dots, x_n)$. A stronger legitimacy condition requires not only correct outputs, but also that the system is at a fixed point of the reaction functions, meaning that no label can possibly change. We call self-stabilization under the former condition *output stabilization* and under the latter *label stabilization*. In practice, label stabilization can be translated to a reduction in communication overhead and bandwidth. Hence, such a property is clearly appealing in the context of algorithm design for distributed networks.

We model the asynchronous nature of distributed environments as a (possibly adversarial) *schedule* that determines which nodes will be *activated* in each time step. Upon activation, a node updates its outgoing labels and output by applying its reaction function to its current incoming labels and input. We quantify limited asynchrony by considering *$r$-fair* schedules, in which $r$ is the maximum number of consecutive time steps a node might have to wait between activations. We say that a protocol is *output* (or *label*) *$r$-stabilizing* if it is output (or label) stabilizing under all $r$-fair schedules.

## 3 RESULTS

We embark on a systematic exploration of stateless computation. Two broad questions arise naturally from a distributed computing viewpoint: (1) Under what conditions may stateless protocols be self-stabilizing? and (2) What is the computational power of our model, and what are its limitations?

### Self-stabilization in Stateless Computation

Our main technical result establishes that multiple stable labelings induce potential instability in our model, even under relatively fair schedules of node activation. In particular, our result states that the existence of two stable labelings implies that a stateless protocol on $n$ nodes cannot be label $(n-1)$-stabilizing in our model, regardless of the network topology. This result implies that an oscillation can occur even under schedules that are $(n-1)$-fair, which is a relatively "mild" level of asynchrony. Showing that nonconvergence can occur even within this highly restricted class of schedules—as opposed to schedules in which nodes may be held inactive for arbitrarily long durations (see [19])—involves a very nuanced valency argument. Specifically, the proof of our nonconvergence result relies on two new ingredients: (1) defining a global state-transition space in a manner that captures *all* $(n-1)$-fair system dynamics; and (2) applying a valency argument to a carefully chosen *subset* of this space so as to obtain the impossibility result. We also show that the $n-1$ bound is tight by exhibiting an $(n-2)$-stabilizing protocol that has two stable labelings. As stateless computation encompasses best-response dynamics (assuming unique best-responses), our impossibility result implies new nonconvergence results for the broad range of environments that fall within this category, including BGP routing, congestion control, asynchronous circuits, and diffusion of technologies, as discussed and formalized in [13, 14].

*Hardness of Testing Self-stabilization.* We present two complementary hardness results, establishing that determining whether a protocol is $r$-stabilizing is hard in terms of both computation and communication. We prove that determining whether a protocol is $r$-stabilizing is PSPACE-hard, and requires at least exponential number of bits of communication. As these results are proven with respect to *all* possible values of $r$, our proofs are applicable even when assuming synchronized communication (i.e., for $r = 1$).

### Power of Stateless Computation

We next turn our attention to the question of the computational power of stateless computation. We focus on synchronous computation and consider two complexity measures: the *round complexity*, defined as the maximum number of rounds (time units) it takes the protocol to converge, and the *label complexity*, defined as the length of the labels in binary encoding. We provide straightforward general upper bounds on the label complexity and round complexity of any function $f$, showing that a linear number of rounds and linear label length are sufficient to compute any function, regardless of the network topology. We show that there exist hard functions that require labels of linear length, matching the general upper bound. We thus investigate what functions can (and cannot) be computed when the label complexity is restricted. Our results show that, even on sparsely connected networks, stateless computation is sufficiently powerful to solve a nontrival range of computational problems in a manner that is both robust to transient faults and frugal in terms of message length.

*Output-stabilizing Protocols.* Our investigation into output-stabilizing protocols reveals that even in the seemingly simplest network topologies, such as the unidirectional and bidirectional rings, stateless computation is quite powerful. We show that protocols on the unidirectional ring have the same computational power as branching programs of polynomial size, L/poly. On the bidirectional ring, we show that protocols with polynomial round complexity essentially have the same computational power as Boolean circuits of polynomial size, i.e., they can decide the languages in P/poly. Our results imply that proving super-logarithmic lower bounds in the output-stabilizing scheme is linked to resolving fundamental open questions in complexity theory.

*Label-stabilizing Protocols.* We present a general method for proving lower bounds on the label complexity of label-stabilizing protocols on arbitrary graphs, and we utilize this method to prove a linear lower bound and a logarithmic lower bound on the label complexity of protocols on ring topologies for specific functions (equality and majority, respectively).

## 4 CONCLUSION

We believe that we have but scratched the surface in our exploration of stateless computation. We view the further investigation of stateless computation as an important research direction with both theoretical and practical implications and thus leave the reader with several exciting avenues for future research: (1) Identifying necessary and sufficient conditions on the reaction functions for self-stabilization. (2) Exploring the computational power of stateless computation in the presence of asynchrony. (3) Extending our research to specific network topologies such as the hypercube, torus, trees, etc. (4) Understanding the implications of randomized reaction functions for self-stabilization and computation.

## REFERENCES

[1] Afek, Y., Kutten, S., and Yung, M. Memory-efficient self stabilizing protocols for general networks. In *International Workshop on Distributed Algorithms* (1990), Springer, pp. 15–28.
[2] Burns, J. E., Gouda, M. G., and Miller, R. E. Stabilization and pseudo-stabilization. *Distributed Computing 7*, 1 (1993), 35–42.
[3] Cournier, A. A new polynomial silent stabilizing spanning-tree construction algorithm. In *International Colloquium on Structural Information and Communication Complexity* (2009), Springer, pp. 141–153.
[4] Dijkstra, E. W. Self-stabilization in spite of distributed control. In *Selected writings on computing: a personal perspective*. Springer, 1982, pp. 41–46.
[5] Dolev, S. *Self-Stabilization*. MIT Press, 2000.
[6] Dolev, S., Gouda, M. G., and Schneider, M. Memory requirements for silent stabilization. *Acta Informatica 36*, 6 (1999), 447–462.
[7] Dolev, S., Kahil, R. M., and Yagel, R. Stateless stabilization bootstrap (extended abstract). In *Stabilization, Safety, and Security of Distributed Systems: 16th International Symposium, SSS 2014, Paderborn, Germany, September 28 – October 1, 2014. Proceedings* (Cham, 2014), P. Felber and V. Garg, Eds., Springer International Publishing, pp. 180–194.
[8] Engelberg, R., Fabrikant, A., Schapira, M., and Wajc, D. Best-response dynamics out of sync: complexity and characterization. In *Proceedings of the fourteenth ACM conference on Electronic commerce* (2013), ACM, pp. 379–396.
[9] Fekete, A., Lynch, N., Mansour, Y., and Spinelli, J. The impossibility of implementing reliable communication in the face of crashes. *J. ACM 40*, 5 (Nov. 1993), 1087–1107.
[10] Griffin, T. G., Shepherd, F. B., and Wilfong, G. The stable paths problem and interdomain routing. *IEEE/ACM Transactions on Networking (ToN) 10*, 2 (2002), 232–243.
[11] Hart, S. Adaptive heuristics. *Econometrica 73*, 5 (2005), 1401–1430.
[12] Huang, S.-T., and Chen, N.-S. A self-stabilizing algorithm for constructing breadth-first trees. *Information Processing Letters 41*, 2 (1992), 109–117.
[13] Jaggard, A. D., Lutz, N., Schapira, M., and Wright, R. N. Dynamics at the boundary of game theory and distributed computing. *CoRR abs/1509.02955* (2015).
[14] Jaggard, A. D., Schapira, M., and Wright, R. N. Distributed computing with adaptive heuristics. In *Innovations in Computer Science - ICS 2010, Tsinghua University, Beijing, China, January 7-9, 2011. Proceedings* (2011), B. Chazelle, Ed., Tsinghua University Press, pp. 417–443.
[15] Karp, B., and Kung, H.-T. Gpsr: Greedy perimeter stateless routing for wireless networks. In *Proceedings of the 6th annual international conference on Mobile computing and networking* (2000), ACM, pp. 243–254.
[16] Kosowski, A., and Kuszner, L. A self-stabilizing algorithm for finding a spanning tree in a polynomial number of moves. In *International Conference on Parallel Processing and Applied Mathematics* (2005), Springer, pp. 75–82.
[17] Mayer, A., Ofek, Y., Ostrovsky, R., and Yung, M. Self-stabilizing symmetry breaking in constant-space (extended abstract). In *Proceedings of the Twenty-fourth Annual ACM Symposium on Theory of Computing* (New York, NY, USA, 1992), STOC '92, ACM, pp. 667–678.
[18] Morris, S. Contagion. *The Review of Economic Studies 67*, 1 (2000), 57–78.

# Towards Efficient Verification of Population Protocols

Michael Blondin
Technische Universität München
blondin@in.tum.de

Javier Esparza
Technische Universität München
esparza@in.tum.de

Stefan Jaax
Technische Universität München
jaax@in.tum.de

Philipp J. Meyer
Technische Universität München
meyerphi@in.tum.de

## ABSTRACT

Population protocols are a well established model of computation by anonymous, identical finite state agents. A protocol is well-specified if from every initial configuration, all fair executions of the protocol reach a common consensus. The central verification question for population protocols is the *well-specification problem*: deciding if a given protocol is well-specified. Esparza et al. have recently shown that this problem is decidable, but with very high complexity: it is at least as hard as the Petri net reachability problem, which is EXPSPACE-hard, and for which only algorithms of non-primitive recursive complexity are currently known.

In this paper we introduce the class $WS^3$ of well-specified strongly-silent protocols and we prove that it is suitable for automatic verification. More precisely, we show that $WS^3$ has the same computational power as general well-specified protocols, and captures standard protocols from the literature. Moreover, we show that the membership problem for $WS^3$ reduces to solving boolean combinations of linear constraints over $\mathbb{N}$. This allowed us to develop the first software able to automatically prove well-specification for *all* of the infinitely many possible inputs.

## CCS CONCEPTS

• **Networks → Protocol testing and verification**; • **Theory of computation → Logic and verification**;

## KEYWORDS

population protocols; automated verification; termination

## 1 INTRODUCTION

Population protocols [1, 2] are a model of distributed computation by many anonymous finite-state agents. They were initially introduced to model networks of passively mobile sensors [1, 2], but are now also used to describe chemical reaction networks (see e.g. [7, 19]).


*PODC '17, July 25-27, 2017, Washington, DC, USA*

ACM ISBN 978-1-4503-4992-5/17/07...$15.00
http://dx.doi.org/10.1145/3087801.3087816

In each computation step of a population protocol, a fixed number of agents are chosen nondeterministically, and their states are updated according to a joint transition function. Since agents are anonymous and identical, the global state of a protocol is completely determined by the number of agents at each local state, called a configuration. A protocol computes a boolean value $b$ for a given initial configuration $C_0$ if in all fair executions starting at $C_0$, all agents eventually agree to $b$ — so, intuitively, population protocols compute by reaching consensus under a certain fairness condition. A protocol is *well-specified* if it computes a value for each of its infinitely many initial configurations (also called *inputs*). The predicate computed by a protocol is the function that assigns to each input the corresponding consensus value. In a famous series of papers, Angluin *et al.* [1, 2] have shown that well-specified protocols compute exactly the predicates definable in Presburger arithmetic [1–4].

In this paper we search for efficient algorithms for the *well-specification problem*: Given a population protocol, is it well-specified? This is a question about an infinite family of finite-state systems. Indeed, for every input the semantics of a protocol is a finite graph with the reachable configurations as nodes. Deciding if the protocol reaches consensus for a fixed input only requires to inspect one of these graphs, and can be done automatically using a model checker. This approach has been followed in a number of papers [6, 8, 20, 24], but it only shows well-specification for some inputs. There has also been work in formalizing well-specification proofs in interactive theorem provers [10], but this approach is not automatic: a human prover must first come up with a proof for each particular protocol.

Recently, the second author, together with other co-authors, has shown that the well-specification problem is decidable [13]. That is, there is an algorithm that decides if for all inputs the protocol stabilizes to a boolean value. The proof uses deep results of the theory of Petri nets, a model very close to population protocols. However, the same paper shows that the well-specification problem is at least as hard as the reachability problem for Petri nets, a famously difficult problem. More precisely, the problem is known to be EXPSPACE-hard, and all known algorithms for it have non-primitive recursive complexity [22]. In particular, there are no stable implementations of any of these algorithms, and they are considered impractical for nearly all applications.

For this reason, in this paper we search for a class of well-specified protocols satisfying three properties:

(a) *No loss of expressive power*: the class should compute all Presburger-definable predicates.

(b) *Natural*: the class should contain most protocols discussed in the literature.
(c) *Feasible membership problem*: membership for the class should have reasonable complexity.

The class *WS* of all well-specified protocols obviously satisfies (a) and (b), but not (c). So we introduce a new class $WS^3$, standing for *Well-Specified Strongly Silent* protocols. We show that $WS^3$ still satisfies (a) and (b), and then prove that the membership problem for $WS^3$ is in the complexity class DP; the class of languages $L$ such that $L = L_1 \cap L_2$ for some languages $L_1 \in$ NP and $L_2 \in$ coNP. This is a dramatic improvement with respect to the EXPSPACE-hardness of the membership problem for *WS*.

Our proof that the problem is in DP reduces membership for $WS^3$ to checking (un)satisfiability of two systems of boolean combinations of linear constraints over the natural numbers. This allowed us to implement our decision procedure on top of the constraint solver Z3 [9], yielding the first software able to automatically prove well-specification for *all* inputs. We tested our implementation on the families of protocols studied in [6, 8, 20, 24]. These papers prove well-specification for some inputs of protocols with up to 9 states and 28 transitions. Our approach proves well-specification for all inputs of protocols with up to 20 states in less than one second, and protocols with 70 states and 2500 transitions in less than one hour. In particular, we can automatically prove well-specification for *all* inputs in less time than previous tools needed to check *one single large input*.

The verification problem for population protocols naturally divides into two parts: checking that a given protocol is well specified, and checking that a given well-specified protocol computes the desired predicate. While in this paper we are concerned with well-specification, our implementation is already able to solve the second problem for all the families of protocols described above. This is achieved by adding to the second system of constraints used to check well-specification further linear constraints describing the sets of input configurations for which the protocol should return *true* or *false*. An extension of the software that, given a protocol and an arbitrary Presburger predicate, checks whether the protocol computes the predicate, requires to solve implementation problems related to Presburger arithmetic, and is left for future research.

The paper is organized as follows. Section 2 contains basic definitions. Section 3 introduces an intermediate class $WS^2$ of silent well-specified protocols, and shows that its membership problem is still as hard as for *WS*. In Section 4, we characterize $WS^2$ in terms of two properties which are then strengthened to define our new class $WS^3$. We then show that the properties defining $WS^3$ can be tested in NP and coNP, and so that membership for $WS^3$ is in DP. Section 5 proves that $WS^3$-protocols compute all Presburger predicates. Section 6 reports on our experimental results, and Section 7 presents conclusions.

## 2 PRELIMINARIES

*Multisets.* A *multiset* over a finite set $E$ is a mapping $M : E \to \mathbb{N}$. The set of all multisets over $E$ is denoted $\mathbb{N}^E$. For every $e \in E$, $M(e)$ denotes the number of occurrences of $e$ in $M$. We sometimes denote multisets using a set-like notation, e.g. $\{\!\{f, g, g\}\!\}$ is the multiset $M$ such that $M(f) = 1$, $M(g) = 2$ and $M(e) = 0$ for every $e \in E \setminus \{f, g\}$. The *support* of $M \in \mathbb{N}^E$ is $[\![M]\!] \stackrel{\text{def}}{=} \{e \in E : M(e) > 0\}$. The *size* of $M \in \mathbb{N}^E$ is $|M| \stackrel{\text{def}}{=} \sum_{e \in E} M(e)$. Addition and comparison are extended to multisets componentwise, i.e. $(M + M')(e) \stackrel{\text{def}}{=} M(e) + M'(e)$ for every $e \in E$, and $M \leq M' \stackrel{\text{def}}{\iff} M(e) \leq M(e)$ for every $e \in E$. We define multiset difference as $(M \ominus M')(e) \stackrel{\text{def}}{=} \max(M(e) - M'(e), 0)$ for every $e \in E$. The empty multiset is denoted $\mathbf{0}$, and for every $e \in E$ we write $\boldsymbol{e} \stackrel{\text{def}}{=} \{\!\{e\}\!\}$.

*Population protocols.* A *population* $P$ over a finite set $E$ is a multiset $P \in \mathbb{N}^E$ such that $|P| \geq 2$. The set of all populations over $E$ is denoted by $\mathrm{Pop}(E)$. A *population protocol* is a tuple $\mathcal{P} = (Q, T, \Sigma, I, O)$ where

- $Q$ is a non-empty finite set of *states*,
- $T \subseteq Q^2 \times Q^2$ is a set of *transitions* such that for every $(p, q) \in Q^2$ there exists at least a pair $(p', q') \in Q^2$ such that $(p, q, p', q') \in T$,
- $\Sigma$ is a non-empty finite *input alphabet*,
- $I : \Sigma \to Q$ is the *input function* mapping input symbols to states,
- $O : Q \to \{0, 1\}$ is the *output function* mapping states to boolean values.

Following the convention of previous papers, we call the populations of $\mathrm{Pop}(Q)$ *configurations*. Intuitively, a configuration $C$ describes a collection of identical finite-state *agents* with $Q$ as set of states, containing $C(q)$ agents in state $q$ for every $q \in Q$, and at least two agents in total.

Pairs of agents[1] interact using transitions. For every $t = (p, q, p', q') \in T$, we write $(p, q) \mapsto (p', q')$ to denote $t$, and we define $\mathrm{pre}(t) \stackrel{\text{def}}{=} \{\!\{p, q\}\!\}$ and $\mathrm{post}(t) \stackrel{\text{def}}{=} \{\!\{p', q'\}\!\}$. For every configuration $C$ and transition $t \in T$, we say that $t$ is *enabled* at $C$ if $C \geq \mathrm{pre}(t)$. Note that by definition of $T$, every configuration enables at least one transition. A transition $t \in T$ enabled at $C$ can *occur*, leading to the configuration $C \ominus \mathrm{pre}(t) + \mathrm{post}(t)$. Intuitively, a pair of agents in states $\mathrm{pre}(t)$ move to states $\mathrm{post}(t)$. We write $C \xrightarrow{t} C'$ to denote that $t$ is enabled at $C$ and that its occurrence leads to $C'$. A transition $t \in T$ is *silent* if $\mathrm{pre}(t) = \mathrm{post}(t)$, i.e., if it cannot change the current configuration.

For every sequence of transitions $w = t_1 t_2 \cdots t_k$, we write $C \xrightarrow{w} C'$ if there exists a sequence of configurations $C_0, C_1, \ldots, C_k$ such that $C = C_0 \xrightarrow{t_1} C_1 \cdots \xrightarrow{t_k} C_k = C'$. We also write $C \to C'$ if $C \xrightarrow{t} C'$ for some transition $t \in T$, and call $C \to C'$ a *step*. We write $C \xrightarrow{*} C'$ if $C \xrightarrow{w} C'$ for some $w \in T^*$. We say that $C'$ is *reachable from* $C$ if $C \xrightarrow{*} C'$. An *execution* is an infinite sequence of configurations $C_0 C_1 \cdots$ such that $C_i \to C_{i+1}$ for every $i \in \mathbb{N}$. An execution $C_0 C_1 \cdots$ is *fair* if for every step $C \to C'$, if $C_i = C$ for infinitely many indices $i \in \mathbb{N}$, then $C_j = C$ and $C_{j+1} = C'$ for infinitely many indices $j \in \mathbb{N}$. We say that a configuration $C$ is

- *terminal* if $C \xrightarrow{*} C'$ implies $C = C'$, i.e., if every transition enabled at $C$ is silent;
- a *consensus configuration* if $O(p) = O(q)$ for every $p, q \in [\![C]\!]$.

[1] While protocols only model interactions between two agents, $k$-way interactions for a fixed $k > 2$ can be simulated by adding additional states.

For every consensus configuration $C$, let $O(C)$ denote the unique output of the states in $[\![C]\!]$. An execution $C_0C_1\cdots$ *stabilizes* to $b \in \{0,1\}$ if there exists $n \in \mathbb{N}$ such that $C_i$ is a consensus configuration and $O(C_i) = b$ for every $i \geq n$.

*Predicates computable by population protocols.* Every *input* $X \in \mathrm{Pop}(\Sigma)$ is mapped to the configuration $I(X) \in \mathrm{Pop}(Q)$ defined by

$$I(X)(q) \stackrel{\text{def}}{=} \sum_{\substack{\sigma\in\Sigma \\ I(\sigma)=q}} X(\sigma) \text{ for every } q \in Q.$$

A configuration $C$ is said to be *initial* if $C = I(X)$ for some input $X$. A population protocol is *well-specified* if for every input $X$, there exists $b \in \{0,1\}$ such that every fair execution of $\mathcal{P}$ starting at $I(X)$ stabilizes to $b$. We say that $\mathcal{P}$ *computes* a predicate $\varphi$ if for every input $X$, every fair execution of $\mathcal{P}$ starting at $I(X)$ stabilizes to $\varphi(X)$. It is readily seen that $\mathcal{P}$ computes a predicate if and only if it is well-specified.

*Example 2.1.* We consider the majority protocol of [3] as a running example. Initially, agents of the protocol can be in either state $A$ or $B$. The protocol computes whether there are at least as many agents in state $B$ as there are in state $A$. The states and the input alphabet are $Q = \{A, B, a, b\}$ and $\Sigma = \{A, B\}$ respectively. The input function is the identity function, and the output function is given by $O(B) = O(b) = 1$ and $O(A) = O(a) = 0$. The set of transitions $T$ consists of:

$$\begin{aligned} t_{AB} &= (A,B) \mapsto (a,b) \\ t_{Ab} &= (A,b) \mapsto (A,a) \\ t_{Ba} &= (B,a) \mapsto (B,b) \\ t_{ba} &= (b,a) \mapsto (b,b) \end{aligned}$$

and of silent transitions for the remaining pairs of states. Transition $t_{AB}$ ensures that every fair execution eventually reaches a configuration $C$ such that $C(A) = 0$ or $C(B) = 0$. If $C(A) = 0 = C(B)$, then there were initially equally many agents in $A$ and $B$. Transition $t_{ba}$ then acts as tie breaker, resulting in a terminal configuration populated only by $b$. If, say, $C(A) > 0$ and $C(B) = 0$, then there were initially more $A$s than $B$s, and $t_{Ab}$ ensures that every fair execution eventually reaches a terminal configuration populated only by $A$ and $a$.

## 3 WELL-SPECIFIED SILENT PROTOCOLS

Silent protocols[2] were introduced in [12]. Loosely speaking, a protocol is silent if communication between agents eventually ceases, i.e. if every fair execution eventually stays in the same configuration forever. Observe that a well-specified protocol need not be silent: fair executions may keep alternating from a configuration to another as long as they are consensus configurations with the same output.

More formally, we say that an execution $C_0C_1\cdots$ is *silent* if there exists $n \in \mathbb{N}$ and a configuration $C$ such that $C_i = C$ for every $i \geq n$. A population protocol $\mathcal{P}$ is *silent* if every fair execution of $\mathcal{P}$ is silent, regardless of the starting configuration. We call a protocol that is well-specified and silent a *$WS^2$-protocol*, and denote by $WS^2$ the set of all $WS^2$ protocols.

[2] Silent protocols are also referred to as *protocols with stabilizing states* and silent transitions are called *ineffective* in [17, 18].

*Example 3.1.* As explained in Example 2.1, every fair execution of the majority protocol is silent. This implies that the protocol is silent. If, for example, we add a new state $b'$ where $O(b') = 1$, and transitions $(b,b) \mapsto (b',b'), (b',b') \mapsto (b,b)$, then the protocol is no longer silent since the execution where two agents alternate between states $b$ and $b'$ is fair but not silent.

Being silent is a desirable property. While in arbitrary protocols it is difficult to determine if an execution has already stabilized, in silent protocols it is simple: one just checks if the current configuration only enables silent transitions. Even though it is was not observed explicitely, the protocols introduced in [1] to characterize the expressive power of population protocols belong to $WS^2$. Therefore, $WS^2$-protocols can compute the same predicates as general ones.

Unfortunately, a slight adaptation of [14, Theorem 10] shows that the complexity of the membership problem for $WS^2$-protocols is still as high as for the general case:

Proposition 3.2. *The reachability problem for Petri nets is reducible in polynomial time to the membership problem for $WS^2$. In particular, membership for $WS^2$ is* EXPSPACE*-complete.*

To circumvent this high complexity, we will show in the next section how $WS^2$ can be refined into a smaller class of well-specified protocols with the same expressive power, and a membership problem of much lower complexity.

## 4 A FINER CLASS OF SILENT WELL-SPECIFIED PROTOCOLS: $WS^3$

It can be shown that $WS^2$-protocols are exactly the protocols satisfying the two following properties:

- Termination: for every configuration $C$, there exists a terminal configuration $C'$ such that $C \xrightarrow{*} C'$.
- Consensus: for every initial configuration $C$, there exists $b \in \{0,1\}$ such that every terminal configuration $C'$ reachable from $C$ is a consensus configuration with output $b$, i.e. $C \xrightarrow{*} C'$ implies $O(C') = b$.

We will introduce the new class $WS^3$ as a refinement of $WS^2$ obtained by strengthening Termination and Consensus into two new properties called LayeredTermination and StrongConsensus. We introduce these properties in Section 4.1 and Section 4.2, and show that their decision problems belong to NP and coNP respectively.

Before doing so, let us introduce some useful notions. Let $\mathcal{P} = (Q, T, \Sigma, I, O)$ be a population protocol. For every $S \subseteq T$, $\mathcal{P}[S]$ denotes the *protocol induced by* $S$, i.e. $\mathcal{P}[S] \stackrel{\text{def}}{=} (Q, S \cup T', \Sigma, I, O)$ where $T' \stackrel{\text{def}}{=} \{(p,q,p,q) : p,q \in Q\}$ is added to ensure that any two states can interact. Let $\to_S$ denote the transition relation of $\mathcal{P}[S]$. An *ordered partition* of $T$ is a tuple $(T_1, T_2, \ldots, T_n)$ of nonempty subsets of $T$ such that $T = \bigcup_{i=1}^n T_i$ and $T_i \cap T_j = \emptyset$ for every $1 \leq i < j \leq n$.

### 4.1 Layered termination

We replace Termination by a stronger property called LayeredTermination, and show that deciding LayeredTermination belongs to NP. The definition of LayeredTermination is inspired by the typical structure of protocols found in the literature. Such protocols are organized in layers such that transitions of higher layers cannot be enabled by executing transitions of lower layers. In particular, if the protocol reaches a configuration of the highest layer that does not enable any transition, then this configuration is terminal. For such protocols, TERMINATION can be proven by showing that every (fair or unfair) execution of a layer is silent.

*Definition 4.1.* A population protocol $\mathcal{P} = (Q, T, \Sigma, I, O)$ satisfies LAYEREDTERMINATION if there is an ordered partition

$$(T_1, T_2, \ldots, T_n)$$

of $T$ such that the following properties hold for every $i \in [n]$:

(a) For every configuration $C$, every (fair or unfair) execution of $\mathcal{P}[T_i]$ starting at $C$ is silent.

(b) For every configurations $C$ and $C'$, if $C \xrightarrow{*}_{T_i} C'$ and $C$ is terminal in $\mathcal{P}[T_1 \cup T_2 \cup \cdots \cup T_{i-1}]$, then $C'$ is also terminal in $\mathcal{P}[T_1 \cup T_2 \cup \cdots \cup T_{i-1}]$.

*Example 4.2.* The majority protocol satisfies LAYEREDTERMINATION. Indeed, consider the ordered partition $(T_1, T_2)$, where

$$T_1 = \{(A, B) \mapsto (a, b), (A, b) \mapsto (A, a)\}$$
$$T_2 = \{(B, a) \mapsto (B, b), (b, a) \mapsto (b, b)\}.$$

All executions of $\mathcal{P}[T_1]$ and $\mathcal{P}[T_2]$ are silent. For every terminal configuration $C$ of $\mathcal{P}[T_1]$, we have $[\![C]\!] \subseteq \{A, a\}$ or $[\![C]\!] \subseteq \{B, a, b\}$. In the former case, no transition of $T_2$ is enabled; in the latter case, taking transitons of $T_2$ cannot enable $T_1$.

As briefly sketched above, LAYEREDTERMINATION implies TERMINATION. In the rest of this section, we prove that checking LAYEREDTERMINATION is in NP. We do this by showing that conditions (a) and (b) of Definition 4.1 can be tested in polynomial time.

We recall a basic notion of Petri net theory recast in the terminology of population protocols. For every step $C \xrightarrow{t} C'$ and every state $q$ of a population protocol, we have $C'(q) = C(q) + \text{post}(t)(q) - \text{pre}(t)(q)$. This observation can be extended to sequences of transitions. Let $|w|_t$ denote the number of occurrences of transition $t$ in a sequence $w$. We have $C'(q) = C(q) + \sum_{t \in T} |w|_t \cdot (\text{post}(t)(q) - \text{pre}(t)(q))$. Thus, a necessary condition for $C \xrightarrow{w} C'$ is the existence of some $\boldsymbol{x} : T \to \mathbb{N}$ such that

$$C'(q) = C(q) + \sum_{t \in T} \boldsymbol{x}(t) \cdot (\text{post}(t)(q) - \text{pre}(t)(q)). \quad (1)$$

We call (1) the *flow equation* for state $q$.

PROPOSITION 4.3. *Let $\mathcal{P} = (Q, T, \Sigma, I, O)$ be a population protocol. Deciding whether an ordered partition $(T_1, T_2, \ldots, T_n)$ of $T$ satisfies condition (a) of Definition 4.1 can be done in polynomial time.*

PROOF. Let $i \in [n]$ and let $U_i$ be the set of non silent transitions of $T_i$. It can be shown that $\mathcal{P}[T_i]$ is non silent if and only if there exists $\boldsymbol{x} : U_i \to \mathbb{Q}$ such that $\sum_{t \in U_i} \boldsymbol{x}(t) \cdot (\text{post}(t)(q) - \text{pre}(t)(q)) = 0$ and $\boldsymbol{x}(q) \geq 0$ for every $q \in Q$, and $\boldsymbol{x}(q) > 0$ for some $q \in Q$. Therefore, since linear programming is in P, we can check for the (non) existence of an appropriate rational solution $\boldsymbol{x}_i$ for every $i \in [n]$. □

We show how to check condition (b) of Definition 4.1 in polynomial time. Let $U \subseteq T$ be a set of transitions. A configuration $C \in \text{Pop}(Q)$ is $U$-*dead* if for every $t \in U$, $C \xrightarrow{t} C'$ implies $C' = C$. We say that $\mathcal{P}$ is $U$-*dead from* $C_0 \in \text{Pop}(Q)$ if every configuration reachable from $C_0$ is $U$-dead, i.e. $C_0 \xrightarrow{*} C$ implies that $C$ is $U$-dead. Finally, we say that $\mathcal{P}$ is $U$-*dead* if it is $U$-dead from every $U$-dead configuration $C_0 \in \text{Pop}(Q)$.

PROPOSITION 4.4. *Let $\mathcal{P} = (Q, T, \Sigma, I, O)$ be a population protocol. Deciding whether an ordered partition $(T_1, \ldots, T_n)$ of $T$ satisfies condition (b) of Definition 4.1 can be done in polynomial time.*

PROOF. Let $i \in [n]$ and let $U \stackrel{\text{def}}{=} T_1 \cup T_2 \cup \cdots \cup T_{i-1}$. $\mathcal{P}[T_i]$ satisfies condition (b) if and only if $\mathcal{P}[T_i]$ is $U$-dead. The latter can be tested in polynomial time through the following characterization: $\mathcal{P}[T_i]$ is *not* $U$-dead if and only if there exist $t \in T_i$ and non silent $u \in U$ such that for every non silent $u' \in U$:

$$\text{pre}(u') \not\leq \text{pre}(t) + (\text{pre}(u) \ominus \text{post}(t)). \quad □$$

Propositions 4.3 and 4.4 yield an NP procedure to decide LAYEREDTERMINATION. Indeed, it suffices to guess an ordered partition and to check whether it satisfies conditions (a) and (b) of Definition 4.1 in polynomial time.

COROLLARY 4.5. *Deciding if a protocol satisfies LAYEREDTERMINATION is in* NP.

## 4.2 Strong consensus

To overcome the high complexity of reachability in population protocols, we strengthen CONSENSUS by replacing the reachability relation in its definition by an *over-approximation*, i.e., a relation $\dashrightarrow$ over configurations such that $C \xrightarrow{*} C'$ implies $C \dashrightarrow C'$. Observe that the flow equations provide an over-approximation of the reachability relation. Indeed, as mentioned earlier, if $C \xrightarrow{*} C'$, then there exists $\boldsymbol{x} : T \to \mathbb{N}$ such that $(C, C', \boldsymbol{x})$ satisfies all of the flow equations. However, this over-approximation alone is too crude for the verification of protocols.

*Example 4.6.* For example, let us consider the configurations $C = \llparenthesis A, B \rrparenthesis$ and $C' = \llparenthesis a, a \rrparenthesis$ of the majority protocol. The flow equations are satisfied by the mapping $\boldsymbol{x}$ such that $\boldsymbol{x}(t_{AB}) = \boldsymbol{x}(t_{Ab}) = 1$ and $\boldsymbol{x}(t_{Ba}) = \boldsymbol{x}(t_{ba}) = 0$. Yet, $C \xrightarrow{*} C'$ does not hold.

To obtain a finer reachability over-approximation, we introduce so-called traps and siphons constraints borrowed from the theory of Petri nets [11, 15, 16] and successfully applied to a number of analysis problems (see e.g. [5, 15, 16]). Intuitively, for some subset of transitions $U \subseteq T$, a $U$-trap is a set of states $P \subseteq Q$ such that every transition of $U$ that removes an agent from $P$ also moves an agent into $P$. Conversely, a $U$-siphon is a set $P \subseteq Q$ such that every transition of $U$ that moves an agent into $P$ also removes an agent from $P$. More formally, let ${}^{\bullet}R \stackrel{\text{def}}{=} \{t \in T : [\![\text{post}(t)]\!] \cap R \neq \emptyset\}$ and $R^{\bullet} \stackrel{\text{def}}{=} \{t \in T : [\![\text{pre}(t)]\!] \cap R \neq \emptyset\}$. $U$-siphons and $U$-traps are defined as follows:

*Definition 4.7.* A subset of states $P \subseteq Q$ is a $U$-*trap* if $P^{\bullet} \cap U \subseteq {}^{\bullet}P$, and a $U$-*siphon* if ${}^{\bullet}P \cap U \subseteq P^{\bullet}$.

For every configuration $C \in \text{Pop}(Q)$ and $P \subseteq Q$, let $C(P) \stackrel{\text{def}}{=} \sum_{q \in P} C(q)$. Consider a sequence of steps $C_0 \xrightarrow{t_1} C_1 \xrightarrow{t_2} \cdots \xrightarrow{t_n} C_n$

where $t_1, \ldots, t_n \in U$. It follows from Definition 4.7 that if some transition $t_i$ moves an agent to a $U$-trap $P$, then $C_j(P) > 0$ for every $j \geq i$. Similarly, if some transition $t_i$ removes an agent from a $U$-siphon, then $C_j(P) > 0$ for every $j < i$. In particular:

Observation 4.8. *Let $U \subseteq T$, and let $C$ and $C'$ be configurations such that $C \xrightarrow{*}_U C'$. For every $U$-trap $P$, if $C'(P) = 0$, then ${}^\bullet P \cap U = \emptyset$. For every $U$-siphon $P$, if $C(S) = 0$, then $P^\bullet \cap U = \emptyset$.*

We obtain a necessary condition for $C \xrightarrow{*}_U C'$ to hold, which we call potential reachability:

*Definition 4.9.* Let $C, C'$ be two configurations, let $\boldsymbol{x} : T \to \mathbb{N}$, and let $U = [\![\boldsymbol{x}]\!]$. We say that $C'$ is *potentially reachable from* $C$ *through* $\boldsymbol{x}$, denoted $C \overset{\boldsymbol{x}}{\dashrightarrow} C'$, if

(a) the flow equation (1) holds for every $q \in Q$,
(b) $C'(P) = 0$ implies ${}^\bullet P \cap U = \emptyset$ for every $U$-trap $P$, and
(c) $C(P) = 0$ implies $P^\bullet \cap U = \emptyset$ for every $U$-siphon $P$.

*Example 4.10.* Let us reconsider Example 4.6. Let $U = [\![\boldsymbol{x}]\!] = \{t_{AB}, t_{Ab}\}$ and $P = \{A, b\}$. Recall that $t_{AB} = (A, B) \mapsto (a, b)$ and $t_{Ab} = (A, b) \mapsto (A, a)$. We have $P^\bullet \cap U = U$ which implies that $P$ is a $U$-trap. This means that Definition 4.9(b) is violated as $C'(P) = 0$ and ${}^\bullet P \cap U = U \neq \emptyset$. Therefore, $\langle A, B \rangle \overset{\boldsymbol{x}}{\dashrightarrow} \langle a, a \rangle$ does not hold.

We write $C \dashrightarrow C'$ if $C \overset{\boldsymbol{x}}{\dashrightarrow} C'$ for some $\boldsymbol{x} : T \to \mathbb{N}$. As an immediate consequence of Observation 4.8, for every configurations $C$ and $C'$, if $C \xrightarrow{*} C'$, then $C \dashrightarrow C'$. This allows us to strengthen Consensus by redefining it in terms of potential reachability instead of reachability:

*Definition 4.11.* A protocol satisfies StrongConsensus if for every initial configuration $C$, there exists $b \in \{0, 1\}$ such that every terminal configuration $C'$ potentially reachable from $C$ is a consensus configuration with output $b$, i.e. $C \dashrightarrow C'$ implies $O(C') = b$.

Since the number of $U$-traps and $U$-siphons of a protocol can be exponential in the number of states, checking trap and siphon constraints by enumerating them may take exponential time. Fortunately, this can be avoided. By definition, it follows that the union of two $U$-traps is again a $U$-trap, and similarly for siphons. Therefore, given a configuration $C$, there exists a unique maximal $U$-siphon $P_{\max}$ such that $C(P_{\max}) = 0$, and a unique maximal $U$-trap $P'_{\max}$ such that $C(P'_{\max}) = 0$. Moreover, $P_{\max}$ and $P'_{\max}$ can be computed in linear time by means of a simple greedy algorithm (see e.g. [11, Ex. 4.5]). This simplifies the task of checking traps and siphons constraints, and yields a coNP procedure for testing StrongConsensus:

Proposition 4.12. *Deciding if a protocol satisfies StrongConsensus is in* coNP.

Proof. Testing whether a protocol *does not* satisfy StrongConsensus can be done by guessing $C_0, C, C' \in \text{Pop}(Q)$, $b \in \{0, 1\}$, $q, q' \in Q$ and $\boldsymbol{x}, \boldsymbol{x}' : T \to \mathbb{N}$, and testing whether

(a) $C_0$ is initial, $C$ is terminal, $C'$ is terminal, $q \in [\![C]\!]$, $q' \in [\![C']\!]$, $O(q) \neq O(q')$, and
(b) $C_0 \overset{\boldsymbol{x}}{\dashrightarrow} C$ and $C_0 \overset{\boldsymbol{x}'}{\dashrightarrow} C'$.

Since there is no *a priori* bound on the size of $C_0, C, C'$ and $\boldsymbol{x}, \boldsymbol{x}'$, we guess them carefully. First, we guess whether $D(p) = 0$, $D(p) = 1$ or $D(p) \geq 2$ for every $D \in \{C_0, C, C'\}$ and $p \in Q$. This gives enough information to test (a). Then, we guess $[\![\boldsymbol{x}]\!]$ and $[\![\boldsymbol{x}']\!]$. This allows to test traps/siphons constraints as follows. Let $U \stackrel{\text{def}}{=} [\![\boldsymbol{x}]\!]$, let $P_{\max}$ be the maximal $U$-trap such that $C(P_{\max}) = 0$, and let $P'_{\max}$ be the maximal $U$-siphon such that $C_0(P'_{\max}) = 0$. Conditions (b) and (c) of Definition 4.9 hold if and only if ${}^\bullet(P_{\max}) \cap U = \emptyset$ and $(P'_{\max})^\bullet \cap U = \emptyset$, which can be tested in polynomial time. The same is done for $\boldsymbol{x}'$. If (a) and siphons/traps constraints hold, we build the system $\mathcal{S}$ of linear equations/inequalities obtained from the conjunction of the flow equations together with the constraints already guessed. By standard results on integer linear programming (see e.g. [23, Sect. 17]), if $\mathcal{S}$ has a solution, then it has one of polynomial size, and hence we may guess it. □

## 4.3 $WS^3$-protocols

We say that a protocol belongs to $WS^3$ if it satisfies LayeredTermination and StrongConsensus. Since $WS^3 \subsetneq WS^2 \subsetneq WS$ holds, every $WS^3$-protocol is well-specified. Recall that a language $L$ belongs to the class DP [21] if there exist languages $L_1 \in$ NP and $L_2 \in$ coNP such that $L = L_1 \cap L_2$. By taking $L_1$ and $L_2$ respectively as the languages of population protocols satisfying LayeredTermination and StrongConsensus, Corollary 4.5 and Proposition 4.12 yield:

Theorem 4.13. *The membership problem for $WS^3$-protocols is in* DP.

# 5 $WS^3$ IS AS EXPRESSIVE AS $WS$

In a famous result, Angluin *et al.* [3] have shown that a predicate is computable by a population protocol if and only if it is definable in Presburger arithmetic, the first-order theory of addition [1, 3]. In particular, [1] constructs protocols for Presburger-definable predicates by means of a well-known result: *Presburger-definable* predicates are the smallest set of predicates containing all threshold and remainder predicates, and closed under boolean operations. A *threshold predicate* is a predicate of the form

$$P(x_1, \ldots, x_k) = \left( \sum_{i=1}^{k} a_i x_i < c \right),$$

where $k \geq 1$ and $a_1, \ldots, a_k, c \in \mathbb{Z}$. A *remainder predicate* is a predicate of the form

$$P(x_1, \ldots, x_k) = \left( \sum_{i=1}^{k} a_i x_i \equiv c \pmod{m} \right),$$

where $k \geq 1$, $m \geq 2$ and $a_1, \ldots, a_k, c, m \in \mathbb{Z}$. Here, we show that these predicates can be computed by $WS^3$-protocols, and that $WS^3$ is closed under negation and conjunction. As a consequence, we obtain that $WS^3$-protocols are as expressive as $WS$, the class of all well-specified protocols.

*Threshold.* We describe the protocol given in [1] to compute the threshold predicate $\sum_{i=1}^{k} a_i x_i < c$. Let

$$v_{\max} \stackrel{\text{def}}{=} \max(|a_1|, |a_2|, \ldots, |a_k|, |c| + 1)$$

and define

$$f(m,n) \stackrel{\text{def}}{=} \max(-v_{\max}, \min(v_{\max}, m+n))$$
$$g(m,n) \stackrel{\text{def}}{=} (m+n) - f(m,n)$$
$$b(m,n) \stackrel{\text{def}}{=} (f(m,n) < c)$$

The protocol is $\mathcal{P}_{\text{thr}} \stackrel{\text{def}}{=} (Q, T, \Sigma, I, O)$, where

$$Q \stackrel{\text{def}}{=} \{0,1\} \times [-v_{\max}, v_{\max}] \times \{0,1\}$$
$$\Sigma \stackrel{\text{def}}{=} \{x_1, x_2, \ldots, x_k\}$$
$$I(x_i) \stackrel{\text{def}}{=} (1, a_i, a_i < c) \text{ for every } i \in [k]$$
$$O(\ell, n, o) \stackrel{\text{def}}{=} o \text{ for every state } (\ell, n, o),$$

and $T$ contains

$$(1,n,o),(l,n',o') \mapsto (1, f(n,n'), b(n,n')), (0, g(n,n'), b(n,n'))$$

for every $n, n' \in [-v_{\max}, v_{\max}]$, $\ell, o, o' \in \{0,1\}$. Intuitively, a state $(\ell, n, o)$ indicates that the agent has value $n$, opinion $o$, and that it is a leader if and only if $\ell = 1$. When a leader $q$ and a state $r$ interact, $r$ becomes a non leader, and $q$ increases its value as much as possible by substracting from the value of $r$. Moreover, a leader can change the opinion of any non leader.

Proposition 5.1. *$\mathcal{P}_{thr}$ satisfies StrongConsensus.*

Proof. Let $\text{val}(q) \stackrel{\text{def}}{=} n$ for every state $q = (\ell, n, o) \in Q$, and let $\text{val}(C) \stackrel{\text{def}}{=} \sum_{q \in Q} C(q) \cdot \text{val}(q)$ for every configuration $C \in \text{Pop}(Q)$. The following holds for every $C, C' \in \text{Pop}(Q)$:

(a) If $(C, C', \boldsymbol{x})$ is a solution to the flow equations for some $\boldsymbol{x} : T \to \mathbb{N}$, then $\text{val}(C) = \text{val}(C')$.
(b) If $C, C'$ are terminal, $C$ and $C'$ contain a leader, and $\text{val}(C) = \text{val}(C')$, then $O(C) = O(C')$.

Suppose for the sake of contradiction that $\mathcal{P}$ does not satisfy StrongConsensus. There exist $C_0, C, C' \in \text{Pop}(Q)$, $q, q' \in Q$ and $\boldsymbol{x}, \boldsymbol{x}' : T \to \mathbb{N}$ such that $C_0 \xrightarrow{\boldsymbol{x}} C$, $C_0 \xrightarrow{\boldsymbol{x}'} C'$, $C_0$ is initial, $C$ and $C'$ are terminal consensus configurations, $q \in [\![C]\!]$, $q' \in [\![C']\!]$ and $O(q) \neq O(q')$. Note that $(C_0, C, \boldsymbol{x})$ and $(C_0, C', \boldsymbol{x}')$ both satisfy the flow equations. Thus, by (a), $\text{val}(C) = \text{val}(C_0) = \text{val}(C')$. Since $C_0$ is initial, it contains a leader. Since the set of leaders forms a $U$-trap for every $U \subseteq T$, and $(C_0, C, \boldsymbol{x})$ and $(C_0, C', \boldsymbol{x})$ satisfy trap constraints, $C$ and $C'$ contain a leader. By (b), $C$ and $C'$ are consensus configurations with $O(C) = O(C')$, which is a contradiction. □

Proposition 5.2. *$\mathcal{P}_{thr}$ satisfies LayeredTermination.*

Proof. Let $L_0 \stackrel{\text{def}}{=} \{(1,x,0) : c \leq x \leq v_{\max}\}$, $L_1 \stackrel{\text{def}}{=} \{(1,x,1) : -v_{\max} \leq x < c\}$, $N_0 \stackrel{\text{def}}{=} \{(0,0,0)\}$ and $N_1 \stackrel{\text{def}}{=} \{(0,0,1)\}$. It can be shown that the following ordered partitions satisfy layered termination for $c > 0$ and $c \leq 0$ respectively:

$$T_1 \stackrel{\text{def}}{=} \{t \in T : \text{pre}(t) \neq \wr q, r \wr \text{ for all } q \in L_0, r \in N_1\},$$
$$T_2 \stackrel{\text{def}}{=} T \setminus T_1, \text{ and}$$
$$S_1 \stackrel{\text{def}}{=} \{t \in T : \text{pre}(t) \neq \wr q, r \wr \text{ for all } q \in L_1, r \in N_0\},$$
$$S_2 \stackrel{\text{def}}{=} T \setminus S_1.$$ □

*Remainder.* We give a protocol for the remainder predicate

$$\sum_{i=1}^{k} a_i x_i \equiv c \pmod{m}.$$

The protocol is $\mathcal{P}_{\text{rmd}} = (Q, T, \Sigma, I, O)$, where

$$Q \stackrel{\text{def}}{=} [0, m) \cup \{\text{true}, \text{false}\}$$
$$\Sigma \stackrel{\text{def}}{=} \{x_1, x_2, \ldots, x_k\}$$
$$I(x_i) \stackrel{\text{def}}{=} a_i \bmod m \text{ for every } i \in [k]$$
$$O(q) \stackrel{\text{def}}{=} \begin{cases} 1 \text{ if } q \in \{c, \text{true}\} \\ 0 \text{ otherwise} \end{cases}$$

and where $T$ contains the following transitions for every $n, n' \in [0, m)$ and $b \in \{\text{false}, \text{true}\}$:

$$(n, n') \mapsto (n + n' \bmod m, n + n' \bmod m = c) \quad \text{and}$$
$$(n, b) \mapsto (n, n = c).$$

In the the full version of this paper[3] we show that $\mathcal{P}_{\text{rmd}}$ belongs to $WS^3$ by adapting the proof for $\mathcal{P}_{\text{thr}}$.

*Negation and conjunction.* Let $\mathcal{P}_1 = (Q_1, T_1, \Sigma, I_1, O_1)$ and $\mathcal{P}_2 = (Q_2, T_2, \Sigma, I_2, O_2)$ be $WS^3$-protocols computing predicates $\varphi_1$ and $\varphi_2$ respectively. We may assume that $\mathcal{P}_1$ and $\mathcal{P}_2$ are defined over identical $\Sigma$, for we can always extend the input domain of threshold/remainder predicates by variables with coefficients of value zero. The predicate $\neg\varphi_i$ can be computed by replacing $O_i$ by the new output function $O_i'$ such that $O_i'(q) \stackrel{\text{def}}{=} \neg O_i(q)$ for every $q \in Q_i$. To compute $\varphi_1 \wedge \varphi_2$, we build an asynchronous product where steps of $\mathcal{P}_1$ and $\mathcal{P}_2$ can be executed independently.

More formally, the *conjunction* of $\mathcal{P}_1$ and $\mathcal{P}_2$ is defined as the population protocol $\mathcal{P} \stackrel{\text{def}}{=} (Q, S, I, \Sigma, O)$ such that $Q \stackrel{\text{def}}{=} Q_1 \times Q_2$, $S \stackrel{\text{def}}{=} S_1 \cup S_2$, $I(\sigma) \stackrel{\text{def}}{=} (I_1(\sigma), I_2(\sigma))$ and $O(p,q) \stackrel{\text{def}}{=} O_1(p) \wedge O_2(q)$ where

$$S_1 \stackrel{\text{def}}{=} \{(p,r),(p',r') \mapsto (q,r),(q',r') : (p,p',q,q') \in T_1, r, r' \in Q_2\},$$
$$S_2 \stackrel{\text{def}}{=} \{(r,p),(r',p') \mapsto (r,q),(r',q') : (p,p',q,q') \in T_2, r, r' \in Q_1\}.$$

In the full version of this paper. we show that $\mathcal{P}$ is in $WS^3$ since terminal/consensus configurations, flow equations, and traps and siphons constraints are preserved by projections from $\mathcal{P}$ onto $\mathcal{P}_1$ and $\mathcal{P}_2$.

[3] https://arxiv.org/abs/1703.04367

| Threshold | | | |
|---|---|---|---|
| $v_{\max}$ | $\|Q\|$ | $\|T\|$ | Time |
| 3 | 28 | 288 | 8.0 |
| 4 | 36 | 478 | 26.5 |
| 5 | 44 | 716 | 97.6 |
| 6 | 52 | 1002 | 243.4 |
| 7 | 60 | 1336 | 565.0 |
| 8 | 68 | 1718 | 1019.7 |
| 9 | 76 | 2148 | 2375.9 |
| 10 | 84 | 2626 | timeout |

| Remainder | | | |
|---|---|---|---|
| $m$ | $\|Q\|$ | $\|T\|$ | Time |
| 10 | 12 | 65 | 0.4 |
| 20 | 22 | 230 | 2.8 |
| 30 | 32 | 495 | 15.9 |
| 40 | 42 | 860 | 79.3 |
| 50 | 52 | 1325 | 440.3 |
| 60 | 62 | 1890 | 3055.4 |
| 70 | 72 | 2555 | 3176.5 |
| 80 | 82 | 3320 | timeout |

| Flock of birds [6] | | | |
|---|---|---|---|
| $c$ | $\|Q\|$ | $\|T\|$ | Time |
| 20 | 21 | 210 | 1.5 |
| 25 | 26 | 325 | 3.3 |
| 30 | 31 | 465 | 7.7 |
| 35 | 36 | 630 | 20.8 |
| 40 | 41 | 820 | 106.9 |
| 45 | 46 | 1035 | 295.6 |
| 50 | 51 | 1275 | 181.6 |
| 55 | 56 | 1540 | timeout |

| Flock of birds [8] | | | |
|---|---|---|---|
| $c$ | $\|Q\|$ | $\|T\|$ | Time |
| 50 | 51 | 99 | 11.8 |
| 100 | 101 | 199 | 44.8 |
| 150 | 151 | 299 | 369.1 |
| 200 | 201 | 399 | 778.8 |
| 250 | 251 | 499 | 1554.2 |
| 300 | 301 | 599 | 2782.5 |
| 325 | 326 | 649 | 3470.8 |
| 350 | 351 | 699 | timeout |

| Majority | | |
|---|---|---|
| $\|Q\|$ | $\|T\|$ | Time |
| 4 | 4 | 0.1 |

| Broadcast | | |
|---|---|---|
| $\|Q\|$ | $\|T\|$ | Time |
| 2 | 1 | 0.1 |

**Table 1: Results of the experimental evaluation where $|Q|$ denotes the number of states, $|T|$ denotes the number of non silent transitions, and the time to prove membership for $WS^3$ is given in seconds.**

## 6 EXPERIMENTAL RESULTS

We have developed a tool called Peregrine[4] to check membership in $WS^3$. Peregrine is implemented on top of the SMT solver Z3 [9].

Peregrine reads in a population protocol $\mathcal{P} = (Q, T, \Sigma, I, O)$ and constructs two sets of constraints. The first set is satisfiable if and only if LayeredTermination holds, and the second is unsatisfiable if and only if StrongConsensus holds.

For LayeredTermination, our tool Peregrine iteratively constructs constraints checking the existence of an ordered partition of size $1, 2, \ldots, |T|$ and decides if they are satisfiable. To check that the execution of a layer is silent, the constraints mentioned in the proof of Proposition 4.3 are transformed using Farkas' lemma (see e.g. [23]) into a version that is satisfiable if and only if all the executions of the layer are silent. Also, the constraints for condition (b) of Definition 4.1 are added.

For StrongConsensus, Peregrine initially constructs the constraints for the flow equation for three configurations $C_0, C_1, C_2$ and vectors $\boldsymbol{x}_1$ and $\boldsymbol{x}_2$, with additional constraints to guarantee that $C_0$ is initial, $C_1$ and $C_2$ are terminal, and $C_1$ and $C_2$ are consensus of different values. If these constraints are unsatisfiable, the protocol satisfies StrongConsensus. Otherwise, Peregrine searches for a $U$-trap or $U$-siphon to show that either $C_0 \xrightarrow{\boldsymbol{x}_1} C_1$ or $C_0 \xrightarrow{\boldsymbol{x}_2} C_2$ does not hold. If, say, a $U$-siphon $S$ is found, then Peregrine adds the constraint $C_0(S) > 0$ to the set of initial constraints. This process is repeated until either the constraints are unsatisfiable and StrongConsensus is shown, or all possible $U$-traps and $U$-siphons are added, in which case StrongConsensus does not hold. We use this refinement-based approach instead of the coNP approach described in Proposition 4.12, as that could require a quadratic number of variables and constraints, and we generally expect to need a small number of refinement steps.

We evaluated Peregrine on a set of benchmarks: the threshold and remainder protocols of [2], the majority protocol of [3], the broadcast protocol of [8] and two versions of the flock of birds[5] protocol from [6, 8]. We checked the parametrized protocols for increasing values of their primary parameter until we reached a timeout. For the threshold and remainder protocols, we set the secondary parameter $c$ to 1 since it has no incidence on the size of the protocol, and since the variation in execution time for different values of $c$ was negligible. Moreover, we assumed that all possible values for $a_i$ were present in the inputs, which represents the worst case.

All experiments were performed on the same machine equipped with an Intel Core i7-4810MQ CPU and 16 GB of RAM. The time limit was set to 1 hour. The results are shown in Table 1. In all cases where we terminated within the time limit, we were able to show membership for $WS^3$. Generally, showing StrongConsensus took much less time than showing LayeredTermination, except for the flock of birds protocols, where we needed linearly many $U$-traps.

As an extension, we also tried proving correctness after proving membership in $WS^3$. For this, we constructed constraints for the existence of an input $X$ and configuration $C$ with $I(X) \xrightarrow{\boldsymbol{x}} C$ and $\varphi(X) \neq O(C)$. We were able to prove correctness for all the protocols in our set of benchmarks. The correctness check was faster than the well-specification check for broadcast, majority, threshold and both flock of birds protocols, and slower for the remainder protocol, where we reached a timeout for $m = 70$.

## 7 CONCLUSION AND FURTHER WORK

We have presented $WS^3$, the first class of well-specified population protocols with a membership problem of reasonable complexity (i.e. in DP) and with the full expressiveness of well-specified protocols. Previous work had shown that the membership problem for the general class of well-specified protocols is decidable, but at least EXPSPACE-hard with algorithms of non primitive recursive complexity.

[4] Peregrine and benchmarks are available from https://gitlab.lrz.de/i7/peregrine/.

[5] The variant from [8] is referred to as *threshold-n* by its authors.

We have shown that $WS^3$ is a natural class that contains many standard protocols from the literature, like flock-of-birds, majority, threshold and remainder protocols. We implemented the membership procedure for $WS^3$ on top of the SMT solver Z3, yielding the first software able to automatically prove well-specification of population protocols for *all* (of the infinitely many) inputs. Previous work could only prove partial correctness of protocols with at most 9 states and 28 transitions, by trying exhaustively a *finite* number of inputs [6, 8, 20, 24]. Our algorithm deals with all inputs and can handle larger protocols with up to 70 states and over 2500 transitions.

Future work will concentrate on three problems: improving the performance of our tool; automatically deciding if a $WS^3$-protocol computes the predicate described by a given Presburger formula; and the diagnosis problem: when a protocol does not belong to $WS^3$, delivering an explanation, e.g. a non-terminating fair execution. We think that our constraint-based approach provides an excellent basis for attacking these questions.

## ACKNOWLEDGMENTS

We wish to thank David de Frutos Escrig and Pierre Ganty for pointing out some mistakes in an earlier version of this paper.

## REFERENCES

[1] Dana Angluin, James Aspnes, Zoë Diamadi, Michael J. Fischer, and René Peralta. 2004. Computation in networks of passively mobile finite-state sensors. In *Proc. 23rd Annual ACM Symposium on Principles of Distributed Computing (PODC)*. 290–299. https://doi.org/10.1145/1011767.1011810

[2] Dana Angluin, James Aspnes, Zoë Diamadi, Michael J. Fischer, and René Peralta. 2006. Computation in networks of passively mobile finite-state sensors. *Distributed Computing* 18, 4 (2006), 235–253. https://doi.org/10.1007/s00446-005-0138-3

[3] Dana Angluin, James Aspnes, and David Eisenstat. 2006. Stably computable predicates are semilinear. In *Proc. 25th Annual ACM Symposium on Principles of Distributed Computing (PODC)*. 292–299. https://doi.org/10.1145/1146381.1146425

[4] Dana Angluin, James Aspnes, David Eisenstat, and Eric Ruppert. 2007. The computational power of population protocols. *Distributed Computing* 20, 4 (2007), 279–304. https://doi.org/10.1007/s00446-007-0040-2

[5] Konstantinos Athanasiou, Peizun Liu, and Thomas Wahl. 2016. Unbounded-Thread Program Verification using Thread-State Equations. In *IJCAR (Lecture Notes in Computer Science)*, Vol. 9706. Springer, 516–531.

[6] Ioannis Chatzigiannakis, Othon Michail, and Paul G. Spirakis. 2010. Algorithmic Verification of Population Protocols. In *Proc. 12th International Symposium on Stabilization, Safety, and Security of Distributed Systems (SSS)*. 221–235.

[7] Ho-Lin Chen, Rachel Cummings, David Doty, and David Soloveichik. 2014. Speed Faults in Computation by Chemical Reaction Networks. In *DISC (Lecture Notes in Computer Science)*, Vol. 8784. Springer, 16–30.

[8] Julien Clément, Carole Delporte-Gallet, Hugues Fauconnier, and Mihaela Sighireanu. 2011. Guidelines for the Verification of Population Protocols. In *ICDCS*. IEEE Computer Society, 215–224.

[9] Leonardo Mendonça de Moura and Nikolaj Bjørner. 2008. Z3: An Efficient SMT Solver. In *TACAS (Lecture Notes in Computer Science)*, Vol. 4963. Springer, 337–340. Z3 is available at https://github.com/Z3Prover/z3.

[10] Yuxin Deng and Jean-François Monin. 2009. Verifying Self-stabilizing Population Protocols with Coq. In *Proc. 3rd IEEE International Symposium on Theoretical Aspects of Software Engineering (TASE)*. 201–208. https://doi.org/10.1109/TASE.2009.9

[11] Jörg Desel and Javier Esparza. 1995. *Free choice Petri nets*. Cambridge University Press.

[12] Shlomi Dolev, Mohamed G. Gouda, and Marco Schneider. 1999. Memory requirements for silent stabilization. *Acta Informatica* 36, 6 (1999), 447–462.

[13] Javier Esparza, Pierre Ganty, Jérôme Leroux, and Rupak Majumdar. 2015. Verification of Population Protocols. In *Proc. 26th International Conference on Concurrency Theory (CONCUR)*. 470–482.

[14] Javier Esparza, Pierre Ganty, Jérôme Leroux, and Rupak Majumdar. 2016. Model Checking Population Protocols. In *FSTTCS (LIPIcs)*, Vol. 65. 27:1–27:14.

[15] Javier Esparza, Ruslán Ledesma-Garza, Rupak Majumdar, Philipp J. Meyer, and Filip Niksic. 2014. An SMT-Based Approach to Coverability Analysis. In *CAV (Lecture Notes in Computer Science)*, Vol. 8559. Springer, 603–619.

[16] Javier Esparza and Stephan Melzer. 2000. Verification of Safety Properties Using Integer Programming: Beyond the State Equation. *Formal Methods in System Design* 16, 2 (2000), 159–189.

[17] Othon Michail, Ioannis Chatzigiannakis, and Paul G. Spirakis. 2011. Mediated population protocols. *Theor. Comput. Sci.* 412, 22 (2011), 2434–2450.

[18] Othon Michail, Ioannis Chatzigiannakis, and Paul G. Spirakis. 2012. Terminating Population Protocols via Some Minimal Global Knowledge Assumptions. In *Stabilization, Safety, and Security of Distributed Systems - 14th International Symposium, SSS 2012, Toronto, Canada, October 1-4, 2012. Proceedings*. 77–89.

[19] Saket Navlakha and Ziv Bar-Joseph. 2015. Distributed information processing in biological and computational systems. *Commun. ACM* 58, 1 (2015), 94–102. https://doi.org/10.1145/2678280

[20] Jun Pang, Zhengqin Luo, and Yuxin Deng. 2008. On Automatic Verification of Self-Stabilizing Population Protocols. In *Proc. 2nd IEEE/IFIP International Symposium on Theoretical Aspects of Software Engineering (TASE)*. 185–192. https://doi.org/10.1109/TASE.2008.8

[21] Christos H. Papadimitriou. 2007. *Computational complexity*. Academic Internet Publ.

[22] Sylvain Schmitz. 2016. The complexity of reachability in vector addition systems. *SIGLOG News* 3, 1 (2016), 4–21.

[23] Alexander Schrijver. 1986. *Theory of Linear and Integer Programming*. John Wiley & Sons.

[24] Jun Sun, Yang Liu, Jin Song Dong, and Jun Pang. 2009. PAT: Towards Flexible Verification under Fairness. In *Proc. 21st International Conference on Computer Aided Verification (CAV)*. 709–714. https://doi.org/10.1007/978-3-642-02658-4_59

# Clocked Population Protocols

James Aspnes*
Yale University, Department of Computer Science.
james.aspnes@gmail.com

## ABSTRACT

Population protocols are required to converge to the correct answer, and are subject to a fairness condition that guarantees eventual progress, but generally have no internal mechanism for detecting when this progress has occurred. We define an extension to the standard population protocol that provides each agent with a clock signal that indicates when the agent has waited long enough. To simplify the model, we represent "long enough" as an infinite time interval, and treat a clocked population protocol as operating over transfinite time. This gives a clean theoretical model that we show how to translate back into finite real-world executions where the clock ticks whenever the underlying protocol is looping or stuck.

Over finite time intervals, the protocol behaves as in the standard model. At nonzero limit ordinals $\omega$, $\omega \cdot 2$, etc., corresponding to clock ticks, the protocol switches to a limit of previous configurations supplemented by an signal registering in an extra component in some of the agents' states. Using transfinite times means that we can represent fairness over sequences of transitions that may include clock ticks with the same definition as over smaller intervals. Using arbitrary ordinals allows using times like $\omega^2$ or $\omega^3$ to represent convergence that depends on detecting convergence repeatedly at lower levels.

We show that a clocked population protocol running in less than $\omega^k$ time for any fixed $k \geq 2$ is equivalent in power to a nondeterministic Turing machine with space complexity logarithmic in the size of the population. A consequence of this equivalence is that any symmetric predicate that can be computed in less than $\omega^k$ time can be computed in less than $\omega^2$ time, which requires only finitely many clock ticks.

## 1 INTRODUCTION

A **population protocol** [1] consists of a collection of finite-state agents that interact in pairs. If the scheduling of these interactions is random, population protocols or the closely-related model of chemical reaction networks can, with high probability, perform computations limited only by the number of distinct configurations of the population as a whole [2, 16]. But in the standard model, scheduling is adversarial, and as a result standard population protocols with a complete interaction graph can only compute predicates definable in first-order Presburger arithmetic [3], a restriction that allows addition, parity, and majority, but that removes even such basic operations as multiplication.

The fundamental limitation of population protocols that yields this result is that while a population protocol is only required to converge to the correct answer in the limit, individual agents cannot determine when this convergence occurs. This makes it difficult to compose population protocols sequentially, and puts even such basic programming tools as nested loops out of reach. One of the key tools in showing that randomized population protocols can perform more sophisticated computations is a **phase clock** that allows the population to detect, with high probability, when enough time has elapsed that its current task is complete.

An explicit mechanism used to detect termination is the **absence detector** of Michail and Spirakis [14]. The absence detector acts like an extra agent in the population, that provides a bit-vector indicating the presence or absence of each other state in the population. Michail and Spirakis show that an absence detector can be implemented by a weaker object called a **cover-time service**, which provides an upper bound on the cover time of a random walk, allowing an agent to deduce when it has successfully encountered every other agent in the system. They show that with a cover-time service, the power of a population protocol with $n$ agents lies between SPACE($\log n$) and NSPACE($\log n$), when both are restricted to symmetric inputs. We can think of this cover-time service, like the internal clocks of randomized population protocols and chemical reaction networks, as instances of a family of possible clock mechanisms whose function is to tell a protocol when it has waited long enough to converge.

We propose an extension to the population protocol model that makes such clocks explicit without committing to any specific implementation: a **clock** oracle that signals to one or more agents when the population has either converged or started looping, a condition formally modeled by reaching a configuration that will recur infinitely often in the future. Such **clocked population protocols** are capable of carrying out any computation that is feasible for a Turing machine with equivalent storage capacity: specifically, with a population of size $n$, whose state can be represented in $\Theta(\log n)$ space, a clocked population protocol can compute any symmetric predicate on the agents' initial states that can be computed by a nondeterministic Turing machine that also uses $\Theta(\log n)$ space

An advantage of showing that clocked population protocols have power equivalent to **NL** is that we can use closure results on **NL** to program clocked population protocols. For example, the Immerman-Szelepcsényi Theorem [12, 17] and the resulting collapse of the logspace hierarchy mean that clocked population protocols can not only compute **NL** predicates, but can effectively use **NL** computations as subroutines. We use this fact to demonstrate that many

*Supported in part by NSF grants CCF-1637385 and CCF-1650596.


*PODC '17, July 25-27, 2017, Washington, DC, USA*

ACM ISBN 978-1-4503-4992-5/17/07...$15.00
http://dx.doi.org/10.1145/3087801.3087836

natural extensions of the clocked population protocol model turn out to be equivalent in power.

An issue that arises in clocked population protocols is how to keep track of time. At the lowest level, we still have **protocol transitions** in which individual pairs of agents encounter one another and update their state as defined by the standard transition relation. But at a higher level, we have **clock transitions** where some of the agents in a configuration receive **ticks** that indicate that a clock cycle has completed. We would like to have a method for indexing events in a protocol that clearly distinguishes between protocol transitions and clock ticks. The method we use is to assign each event to an **ordinal number**, a generalization of the natural numbers that includes transfinite elements.

In this representation, the ordinary passage of time is represented by finite intervals, while clock ticks occur at limit ordinals $\omega$, $\omega \cdot 2$, $\omega \cdot 3$, etc. A typical time for an event might be something like $\omega \cdot 3 + 28$. This is an event that follows 3 clock ticks—each arriving after what might a very long sequence of ordinary protocol transitions—followed by 28 ordinary protocol transitions. By using ordinals, we allow for the possibility of introducing "higher-order" clock ticks, indicating longer intervals $\omega^2$, $\omega^3$, and so forth, during which even infinitely many lower-order clock ticks still leave the protocol stuck. The use of ordinal arithmetic for this purpose allows us to define a consistent rule for what configurations are eligible to appear at these times (essentially any configuration that occurs without bound in the interval leading up to the limit ordinal), as well as a straightforward extension of the usual global fairness condition for standard population protocols to clocked population protocols.

Though the transfinite-execution model is not something one could reasonably expect to implement in practice, we show that it is equivalent to a finite-execution model where clock ticks are delivered once the protocol reaches a terminal strongly-connected component in an appropriately-defined graph. In addition to giving a practical rule for deciding when to send in a clock tick, this also shows that output-stable clocked population protocols compute symmetric functions in **P**, and that output-stable clocked population protocols that finish in less than $\omega^k$ time for any fixed, finite $k$, compute symmetric functions in **NL**. Together with the converse result on simulating **NL**, this in fact shows that a transfinite clock hierarchy based on counting layers of increasingly patient clocks never gets off the ground: any protocol that finishes in less than $\omega^k$ time computes the same function as a protocol that finishes after receiving finitely many first-order clock ticks.

The goal of this work is to explore the effect of adding clocks to population protocols, and to this end we consider primarily the simplest model with a complete interaction graph and a generic clock. We consider some variants on the clock mechanism and show that for the most part they compute the same functions. In the conclusion, we briefly discuss additional possible extensions of the model.

## 1.1 Other related work

Adding a clock is not the only way to increase the power of the standard population protocol model. The **community protocol** model of Guerraoui and Ruppert [10], which allows agents to remember the identities of a constant number of other agents, boosts the power of a system with $n$ agents to decide any language in NSPACE($n \log n$). The still stronger **mediated population protocol** model of Chatzigiannakis *et al.* [8], which stores information on edges between agents, boosts this power still further to NSPACE($n^2$) [6]. It is also possible to expand the space in each agent, which is $O(1)$ in the standard model. Chatzigiannakis *et al.* [7] have shown that even a modest extension to $\Theta(\log n)$ bits per agent allows computations of symmetric predicates in **NSPACE**($n \log n$) (as in the community protocol model), while smaller extensions up to $o(\log \log n)$ still limit population protocols to the semilinear predicates computable in the standard model.

Unfortunately, the substantial computational power of these extensions argues against their practical application. In contrast, the merely **NL** $\subseteq$ **P** power of previous mechanisms for detecting termination inside a population protocol or similar model [2, 14, 16] suggests that such mechanisms are more likely to be realizable in a physical system that runs for a reasonable amount of time. We consider the present work to be firmly in this tradition, even though for purposes of analysis we find it convenient to model the intervals between clock ticks using transfinite time.

The idea of modeling computation over transfinite time has precedent in work on transfinite Turing machines [11] as a model for **supertasks** [18], a concept extensively studied in the philosophical literature. A supertask is a task that involves an infinite number of steps (often taken as occurring over decreasing time intervals whose sum converges to a finite bound), and the problem of characterizing sensible outcomes of supertasks goes as far back as Zeno's Paradox. In a sense, clocked population protocols are carrying out supertasks, but our choice for the behavior of these systems in the limit is less open to controversy, because it is implied by the goals of the model. Our purpose is only to represent waiting long enough that further waiting will have no effect on the possible outcomes of a protocol. Were we actually modeling infinite computations, a different limit definition (for example, taking the limit of each agent's state separately) might be more appropriate.

## 1.2 Ordinals and ordinal arithmetic

In this section, we give a brief overview of the **ordinal numbers**, a generalization of the natural numbers that include infinite values. More details on the ordinals can be found in any textbook on set theory, for example in Chapter 2 of Jech [13].

Formally, an ordinal number is an equivalence class over totally-ordered sets $(S, \leq)$ that are **well-ordered**, meaning that every subset $T$ of $S$ has a least element. A standard construction due to von Neumann [19] represents each ordinal as the set of all smaller ordinals, so that 0 is represented by the empty set $\emptyset$, $1 = \{0\}$, $2 = \{0, 1\}$. The finite ordinals $0, 1, 2, \ldots$ are the **natural numbers**. The first infinite ordinal, denoted $\omega$, is just the set of all finite ordinals $\{0, 1, 2, \ldots\}$.

In this representation, $\alpha \leq \beta$ if $\alpha$ is a subset of $\beta$, $\alpha < \beta$ if $\alpha$ is an element of $\beta$, the minimum of a set of ordinals is just their common intersection, the **successor** $\alpha + 1$ of an ordinal $\alpha$ is represented by $\alpha \cup \{\alpha\}$, and the supremum of a set of ordinals is their union. For example, $\omega + 1$ is represented by $\{0, 1, 2, \ldots; \omega\}$, $\omega + 2$ by

$\{0, 1, 2, \ldots; \omega, \omega + 1\}$, and so on. Not every ordinal is a successor. An ordinal (like 0 or $\omega$) that is not a successor of any other ordinal is called a **limit ordinal**.

We adopt the usual convention that arbitrary ordinals are denoted by lowercase Greek letters, while finite ordinals are denoted by lowercase Latin letters.

Ordinal arithmetic is defined using operations on the corresponding ordered sets. Addition corresponds to concatenation: the ordinal $\omega+\omega$ consists of two copies of $\omega$ laid end-to-end, and is represented in set form by $\{0, 1, 2, \ldots; \omega, \omega + 1, \omega + 2, \ldots\}$. Addition involving infinite ordinals is not commutative in general: $1+\omega = \omega$, since there is a one-to-one map that preserves the order type, but $\omega + 1 \neq \omega$. Note that if $\beta \neq 0$, $\alpha + \beta$ is a limit ordinal if and only if $\beta$ is.

Multiplication is defined recursively by the rule that $\alpha \cdot 0 = 0$, $\alpha \cdot (\beta + 1) = \alpha \cdot \beta + \alpha$, and, when $\gamma$ is a limit ordinal, $\alpha \cdot \gamma = \sup_{\beta<\gamma} \alpha \cdot \beta$, which can be represented in set form by $\bigcup_{\beta\in\gamma} \alpha \cdot \beta$.[1] It is also possible to define multiplication using order types by applying lexicographic order to $\alpha \times \beta$, with the least-significant value provided first. Like addition, multiplication is generally not commutative when one or both operands are infinite: for example, $\omega \cdot 2$ consists of two copies of $\omega$ laid end-to-end, and is equal to $\omega + \omega$, but $2 \cdot \omega$ consists of $\omega$ copies of 2 laid end-to-end, and is equal to $\omega$.

Exponentiation is defined similarly to multiplication, with $\alpha^0 = 1$, $\alpha^{\beta+1} = \alpha^\beta \cdot \alpha$, and $\alpha^\gamma = \sup_{\beta<\gamma} \alpha^\beta$. Note that exponentiation involving infinite ordinals can produce results that look strange compared to what happens with natural numbers: for example, $2^\omega = \omega < \omega^2$ and $\omega^\omega$ is order-isomorphic to the set of all *finite* sequences of natural numbers ordered first by increasing size and then lexicographically (or to the set of all infinite sequences that are eventually all 0). Both $2^\omega$ and $\omega^\omega$ are countable.

As with finite ordinals, division by nonzero ordinals is possible. Specifically, if $\alpha$ and $\beta$ are ordinals, and $\beta \neq 0$, then there are unique ordinals $\gamma$ and $\rho$ such that $\alpha = \beta \cdot \gamma + \rho$ and $\rho < \beta$.

**Cantor's Normal Form Theorem** (see [13, Theorem 2.26]) says that any ordinal $\alpha$ has a unique representation $\alpha = \omega^{\beta_1} \cdot k_1 + \cdots + \ldots \omega^{\beta_n} \cdot k_n$, where $n$ is finite, $\alpha \geq \beta_1 > \beta_2 > \cdots > \beta_n$ are ordinal numbers, and $k_1, \ldots, k_n$ are nonzero natural numbers. In effect, the normal form theorem says that any ordinal number can be represented as a sequence of finite coefficients indexed by larger and larger powers of $\omega$, which for our purposes will represent increasing durations of waiting for convergence. Most of the ordinal numbers we will be dealing with in this work will be small, with representations typically of the form $\omega \cdot k + \ell$. But occasionally it will be useful to consider larger ordinals.

## 2 MODEL

We use a variant of the standard population protocol model that extends the state of each agent to include an extra flag to signal a clock tick.

In the standard model [1], a population protocol is described by a tuple $\langle X, Y, Q, I, O, \delta\rangle$, where $X$ and $Y$ are the input and output alphabets, $Q$ is the state space for agents, $I : X \to Q$ and $O : Q \to Y$ are functions translating inputs to states and extracting outputs from states, and $\delta : Q \times Q \to Q \times Q$ is a **transition function** used to update the states of two agents that interact with each other. A **population** consists of $n$ agents organized as the nodes of a directed **interaction graph**. A **configuration** specifies the state of each agent. A **step** consists of taking two agents $u$ and $v$ such that $uv$ is an edge in the interaction graph, and updating their states according to $\delta$. It is assumed that which pair of agents interact at each step is controlled by an **adversary**, but the adversary is restricted the **global fairness condition** that if some configuration $C_1$ occurs infinitely often, and there is a step that transforms $C_1$ into $C_2$, then $C_2$ also occurs infinitely often.

In the present work, we will assume that the interaction graph is complete: any agent may interact with any other agent at any time. But our extension to the standard model applies equally well to a more restricted interaction graph.

### 2.1 Adding the clock

We would like to add a mechanism for detecting the passage of time to this model, in the form of an oracle that provides extra information to the agents. We do so by extending the state of each agent to include a clock bit that is provided as input to $\delta$ and that may be set to 1 by the external clock. By convention, we will not allow a protocol to use the clock bits for its own purposes. We enforce this by requiring that $\delta$ always outputs states in which the clock bits are set to 0.

This effectively gives $\delta$ the type $Q \times \{0, 1\} \times Q \times \{0, 1\} \to Q \times Q$, where the extra bits represent the clock bit at each agent. This is similar to the approach taken by Fischer and Jiang in their work on self-stabilizing leader election with the $\Omega?$ oracle [9]. However, changes to the clock bits are more restricted than in this and subsequent work applying oracles to population protocols (e.g., [4, 5]). The role of the clock bit on an agent is to act as a inbox for clock ticks, set by special clock transitions that occur only when the protocol is looping or stuck, and reset only by subsequent protocol transitions involving the agent.

To save space, we represent a state in which a clock bit is set typographically using a prime (or "tick") symbol. So a state $A$ does not have the clock bit set, but the corresponding state $A'$ does.

### 2.2 Clocked executions

The idea of the clock is that the system only delivers a clock tick when the protocol has run long enough that anything that could still happen has already happened.

Applying a simple induction to the global fairness condition shows that if $C_1$ is a configuration that occurs infinitely often, then any configuration $C_2$ that is **reachable** from $C_1$ by zero or more transitions also occurs infinitely often. Because the number of configurations is finite, this means that any execution of a standard population protocol eventually converges to some terminal strongly-connected component (SCC): a set of configurations $S$ such that all configurations in the set are reachable from all of the others, and no transition leaves the set. Once a protocol has reached such a set, no further progress is possible. The standard model says that a protocol **stably computes** a predicate if, in this terminal SCC, all configurations produce the correct output at all agents.

[1] This is an example of **transfinite recursion**, which generalizes ordinary recursion by requiring a rule for handling limit ordinals. Typically a recursively-defined value at a limit ordinals will itself be a limit (supremum in this case) of values at smaller ordinals.

We would like to define the clock to fire only once we have reached a set that is a terminal SCC with respect to protocol transitions. While it would be possible to do so directly, doing so by taking a limit over an infinite execution fragment gives the same result in a way that interacts more cleanly with the fairness condition. Later we will recover a graph-theoretic interpretation of this definition, to make the behavior of clocked population protocols easier to reason about.

Let $\alpha$ be a limit ordinal. A set of times $T$ is **cofinal** in $\alpha$ if, for any $\beta < \alpha$, there is some $\gamma$ in $T$ such that $\beta \leq \gamma < \alpha$. For example, the times $2, 4, 8, 16, \ldots$ are cofinal in $\omega$. We will use this concept to define the set of configurations that may occur (possibly with clock bits set) at time $\alpha$.

We say that configurations $C_1$ and $C_2$ are **equivalent**, written $C_1 \sim C_2$, if the only difference between them is in the clock bits. We refer to the part of a configuration that omits the clock bits as the **protocol configuration**; two configurations are equivalent if and only if they have the same protocol configurations.

An **execution** $\Xi$ of length $\alpha$ consists of a sequence of configurations $C_\beta$ indexed by the ordinals $\beta < \alpha$ satisfying certain consistency constraints. A configuration $C$ is **enabled** following $\Xi$ if:

(1) $\alpha = 0$ and $C$ is the initial configuration,
(2) $\alpha = \gamma+1$ and $C$ follows from an application of the transition function to two agents in the configuration $C_\gamma$ that appears at time $\gamma$, or
(3) $\alpha$ is a nonzero limit ordinal, and the set of times at which configurations equivalent to $C$ occur is cofinal in $\alpha$.

An execution is **valid** if each configuration $C_\beta$ is enabled following the prefix of $\Xi$ of length $\beta$. Henceforth we will only consider valid executions.

Note that we only consider executions that have a length. This avoids complications that would arise from executions indexed over all of the ordinals (for example, such executions would not be definable as sets in the usual Zermelo-Fraenkel set theory).

The definition of enabled configurations at successor ordinals matches the standard model. The definition at (small) nonzero limit ordinals captures the intuition of waiting long enough to reach a terminal SCC, because the only configurations enabled at time $\omega \cdot k$ are those that appear infinitely often during the preceding standard execution, which are precisely those in the set to which the protocol converges.

Which of the enabled configurations occurs at each nonzero limit ordinal $\alpha$ is chosen by the adversary, the same as at successor ordinals. At limit ordinals, in addition to choosing from all configurations cofinal in $\alpha$, the equivalence condition allows the adversary to apply clock bits to any subset of the agents, including the empty subset. To make the clock bits useful requires imposing restrictions on this choice, which we do by extending the standard global fairness condition to transfinite intervals.

## 2.3 Fairness in clocked executions

We define an execution to be **fair** if, for any ordinal $\alpha$, if the set of times at which a configuration $C$ is enabled is cofinal in $\alpha$, then $C$ occurs cofinally in $\alpha$. We define an execution fragment to be fair if the same condition holds for any $\alpha$ less than or equal to the length of the execution fragment.

A standard execution consists of times less than $\omega$, and restricting attention to this interval yields the standard fairness condition, since on $\omega$, occurring infinitely often and occurring cofinally coincide. But over longer intervals, having $C$ occur infinitely often when it is enabled infinitely often is not enough.

For example, suppose that $C_1 \to C_2$, and $C_1$ occurs infinitely often over both the intervals $[0, \omega)$ and $[\omega, \omega \cdot 2)$. We do not wish the clock tick at time $\omega$ to change the effect of the fairness condition, but if we only require $C_2$ to occur infinitely often in the entire execution, it is possible for it to do so only in $[0, \omega)$ (or only in $[\omega, \omega \cdot 2)$), yielding an execution that is unfair by the standard definition within this interval. Cofinality prevents this, and indeed we can show that the extended definition is equivalent to the standard definition over all intervals of length $\omega$:

Lemma 2.1. *Let $\Xi$ be a fair execution. Then if $C_1 \to C_2$, and $C_1$ occurs infinitely often in some interval $[\alpha, \alpha + \omega)$, $C_2$ also occurs infinitely often in $[\alpha, \alpha + \omega)$.*

Proof. Let $\alpha + k_1 < \alpha + k_2 < \ldots$ enumerate the times at which $C_1$ appears in $[\alpha, \alpha + \omega)$. Because the sequence $k_1, k_2, \ldots$ is infinite, it is unbounded in $\omega$, thus $\alpha + k_1, \alpha + k_2, \ldots$ is cofinal with $\alpha + \omega$. So $C_2$ is enabled at times $a + k_i + 1$, which are also cofinal in $\alpha + \omega$. Fairness then implies that $C_2$ occurs at times cofinal in $\alpha + \omega$.

Suppose that only finitely many of those times occur in $[\alpha, \alpha+\omega)$. Then there is some largest time $\alpha + k < \alpha + \omega$ at which $C_2$ occurs. But then there is no time $\beta$ with $\alpha + k < \beta < \alpha + \omega$ at which $C_2$ occurs, and $C_2$ does not occur cofinally in $\alpha + \omega$, a contradiction. So $C_2$ occurs infinitely often in $[\alpha, \alpha + \omega)$. □

In addition to generalizing the standard definition, our definition also forces the adversary to eventually set the clock bits. Consider an adversary that never sets a clock bit. In the interval $[0, \omega^2)$, at each time $\omega, \omega \cdot 2, \omega \cdot 3, \ldots$, there is some enabled configuration $C'_{\omega \cdot k}$ that includes clock bits. Since there are only finitely many possible such configurations, there is some specific configuration $C'$ that is enabled at infinitely many times of the form $\omega \cdot k$. These times are cofinal in $\omega^2$, so $C'$ must also occur cofinally in $\omega^2$. It follows that in $\omega^2$, the clock ticks infinitely often.

Note that this does not provide any particular guarantee on when the clock bits arrive: just as the adversary may delay a protocol transition for any finite amount of steps, the adversary may similarly delay a particular limit configuration over any finite number of limit times. But it cannot do so forever.

## 3 TRANSITION GRAPHS

Working directly with transfinite executions is awkward. In this section, we give an alternative characterization of a clocked population protocol's executions based on paths through a directed **transition graph**, where each node in the graph represents a configuration and each edge represents either a transition between configurations or the delivery of a clock tick taking some configuration to an equivalent configuration.

The transition graph is constructed recursively, where each layer $G_k$ of the recursion adds transitions that can occur at times that are a multiple of $\omega^k$. The bottom layer $G_0$ contains an edge for all transitions that can occur in one time unit, as the result of applying the protocol's transition relation $\delta$ to two agents. We write $C_1 \to_0 C_2$ if such an edge appears in $G_0$, and write $C_1 \to_0^* C_2$ if there is a (nonempty) directed path from $C_1$ to $C_2$ in $G_0$. Similarly, we will write $C_1 \to_k C_2$ or $C_1 \to_k^* C_2$ if there is a single edge or directed path, respectively, from $C_1$ to $C_2$ in $G_k$.

To construct $G_{k+1}$ from $G_k$, we add edges representing the arrival of clock ticks at multiples of $\omega^k$. To do so, we need to detect when some configuration in $G_k$ might occur cofinally in an interval $[\alpha, \alpha + \omega^k)$ in a fair execution.

At minimum, we need $C \to_k^* C$, so that $C$ can occur infinitely often. But this is not enough: we also need it to be the case that the fairness condition does not drive us to a state $C_2$ from which we cannot return to $C$. This essentially means that no such state $C_2$ can be reachable from $C$ at all, or in other words that $C$ is an element of a terminal strongly-connected component in $G_k$.

Formally, define $G_{k+1} = (V_{k+1}, E_{k+1})$, where $V_{k+1} = V_k$ is the set of all configurations of the protocol (including clocked configurations), and $E_{k+1} = E_k \cup \{(C, C') \mid C \sim C' \text{ and } C \text{ is in a terminal SCC in } G_k\}$. We will refer to the edges in $E_{k+1} \setminus E_k$ as level $k+1$ edges.

The full transition graph $G$ is just the union of all $G_k$ for $k \in \mathbb{N}$. Note that if we restrict ourselves to configurations of a fixed size, all but a finite number of these graphs are identical, because at some point we run out of edges to add. But for simplicity we will imagine each $G_k$ is an infinite graph that represents all possible population sizes, so $G$ will in general be a limit $\bigcup_{k=0}^{\infty} G_k$. Fortunately, we do not have to go past $\omega$ to compute $G$, since we only consider protocols with finite populations.

THEOREM 3.1. *Given a clocked population protocol, let $G_0, G_1, \ldots$ be the family of transition graphs defined as above, and consider some fair execution $\Xi$.*

*The following hold for any configurations $C$ and $D$:*

1. *If $C$ occurs at time $\alpha$, and $D$ occurs at time $\beta \in [\alpha, \alpha + \omega)$, then there is a path from $C$ to $D$ in $G_k$.*
2. *If $C$ occurs cofinally in $\Xi$ over some interval $[\alpha, \alpha + \omega^k + 1)$, then $D$ occurs cofinally over the same interval if and only if there is a path from $C$ to $D$ in $G_k$.*
3. *If $D$ occurs in $[\alpha, \alpha + \omega^{k+1})$, then $D$ occurs cofinally in $[\alpha, \alpha + \omega^{k+1})$ if and only if $D$ is in a terminal strongly-connected component of $G_k$.*

PROOF. By induction on $k$.

When $k = 0$, $G_0$ consists only of transitions that do not involve clock bits, and the interval $[\alpha, \alpha + \omega^{k+1})$ contains only successor ordinals. We can show:

1. There is a path in $G_0$ from $C$ to each configuration $C_\beta$ with $\alpha \le \beta < \alpha + \omega^{k+1} = \alpha + \omega$. The proof is by induction on $\beta$. The base case is $\beta = \alpha$; use the empty path. For the induction step, go from $\beta$ to $\beta + 1$ by extending the path from $C = C_\alpha$ to $C_\beta$ by the edge from $C_\beta$ to $C_{\beta+1}$.
2. If there is no path from $C$ to $D$ in $G_0$, then let $\beta$ be some time at which $C$ occurs in $[\alpha, \alpha + \omega)$. Then from the preceding claim, $D$ does not occur in $[\beta, \beta + \omega) = [\beta, \alpha + \omega)$ and in particular there is no time $\gamma$ such that $\beta < \gamma < \alpha + \omega$ at which $D$ occurs. So $D$ does not occur cofinally in $[\alpha, \alpha + \omega)$.

   Alternatively, suppose there is a path from $C$ to $D$ in $G_0$. We will show that $D$ occurs cofinally in $[\alpha, \alpha + \omega)$ by induction on $d(C, D)$. If $d(C, D) = 0$, then $D = C$ and the result holds trivially. If $d(C, D) > 0$, let $B$ be the last configuration on a shortest path from $C$ to $D$ in $G_0$. Then by the induction hypothesis, $B$ occurs cofinally in $[\alpha, \alpha + \omega)$. For each time $\gamma$ at which $B$ occurs, $D$ is enabled at time $\gamma + 1$, so $D$ is enabled cofinally in $[\alpha, \alpha + \omega)$, and because the execution is fair, it must occur cofinally as well.
3. Let $S$ be the strongly-connected component of $G_0$ that contains $D$. If $S$ is not terminal, there is an outgoing edge from $S$ to some configuration $B$, such that there is no path from $B$ to $D$ (since $B$ is not in the same strongly-connected component). By the preceding claim, if $D$ occurs cofinally in $[\alpha, \alpha + \omega)$, then so does $B$. But then, since there is no path from $B$ to $D$, $D$ cannot occur cofinally in $[\alpha, \alpha + \omega)$.

   Conversely, suppose there is no outgoing edge from $S$. From (1), once $D$ occurs at some time $\beta \in [\alpha, \alpha + \omega)$, only configurations $B$ reachable from $D$ can occur in $[\beta, \alpha + \omega) = [\beta, \beta + \omega)$. Since there are only finitely many such $B$, one of them occurs infinitely often and thus cofinally in $[\beta, \beta + \omega)$. But since $B$ is in the same SCC as $D$, there is a path from $B$ to $D$, and so $D$ occurs cofinally in $[\beta, \beta + \omega)$ (and thus $[\alpha, \alpha + \omega)$ by (2).

For larger $k$, suppose that the claim holds for $k - 1$. We will essentialy repeat the argument for the base case $G_0$, but now we must deal with limit ordinals and edges corresponding to limit transitions. Fortunately we can refer to the preceding arguments to handle the successor ordinal cases.

1. For the first claim, we will again show by induction on $\beta \in [\alpha, \alpha + \omega^{k+1})$ that there is a path in $G_k$ from $C = C_\alpha$ to $C_\beta$. The base case $\beta = \alpha$ and the induction step for successor ordinals $\beta + 1$ are the same as for $k = 0$. This leaves the case where $\beta$ is a limit ordinal.

   Expand $\beta$ as $\alpha + \omega^k \cdot q + \rho$, where the quotient $q$ is finite and the remainder $\rho < \omega^k$. We will first argue by induction on $q$ that there is a path in $G_k$ from $C_\alpha$ to $C_{\alpha + \omega^k \cdot q}$. If $q = 0$, this is trivial. Otherwise, by the induction hypothesis on $q$ there exists a path in $G_k$ from $C_\alpha$ to $C_{\alpha + \omega^k \cdot (q-1)}$. For $C_{\alpha + \omega^k \cdot q}$ to be enabled at $\alpha + \omega^k \cdot q$, there must be a configuration $C^* \sim C_{\alpha + \omega^k \cdot q}$ that occurs cofinally in $[\alpha + \omega^k \cdot (q-1), \alpha + \omega^k \cdot q)$. From the induction hypothesis on $G_{k-1}$, this can only be the case if $C^*$ appears in a terminal SCC of $G_{k-1}$, in which case there is an edge in $G_k$ from $C^*$ to $C_{\alpha + \omega^k \cdot q}$. In addition, the occurrence of $C^*$ in this interval also implies that there is a path in $G_{k-1}$ form $C_\alpha$ to $C^*$. Stitching this path and edge onto the previous path gets us the claimed path in $G_k$ to $C_{\alpha + \omega^k \cdot q}$.

   We still have to deal with finding an extension from $C_{\alpha + \omega^k \cdot q}$ to $C_\beta = C_{\alpha + \omega^k \cdot q + \rho}$, but as $\rho < \omega^k$, $\beta \in [\alpha + \omega^k \cdot q, \alpha + \omega^k \cdot q + \omega^k)$, and the induction hypothesis on $G_k$ implies that such a path exists.
2. If there is no path from $C$ to $D$ in $G_k$, the argument reduces to the preceding claim as in the $G_0$ case.

If there is a path from $C$ to $D$ in $G_k$, we again use induction on the length $\ell$ of the path to show that every configuration on the path occurs cofinally in $[\alpha, \alpha + \omega^{k+1})$. This holds trivially when $\ell = 0$. for larger $\ell$, let $B$ be the last configuration on the path before $D$. From the induction hypothesis on $\ell$ we have that $B$ occurs cofinally in $[\alpha, \alpha + \omega^{k+1})$. Let $m \le k$ be the smallest value such that a $B \to D$ edge appears in $G_m$.

If $m = 0$, then there is a protocol transition from $B$ to $D$, and fairness gives that $D$ occurs cofinally in $[\alpha, \alpha + \omega^{k+1})$, since it is enabled in every successor to a time at which $B$ occurs. For larger $m$, we have from the definition of $G_m$ that $B \sim D$, and $B$ appears in a terminal SCC in $G_{m-1}$. Now apply part (3) to show that $B$ occurs cofinally in any interval $[\gamma, \gamma + \omega^{m-1}]$ such that $B$ occurs at time $\gamma$. Each such interval enables $D$ at time $\gamma + \omega^m$, and because the set of times $\gamma$ is cofinal in $[\alpha, \alpha + \omega^{k+1})$, so is the set of times $\gamma + \omega^m$ at which $D$ is enabled. So fairness says $D$ occurs cofinally in $[\alpha, \alpha + \omega^{k+1})$.

(3) If the SCC $S$ of $G_k$ containing $D$ is not terminal, then there is some path from $D$ to a configuration $B$ not in $S$, so from (1) we reach $B$ and can't return.

Alternatively, if $S$ is terminal, then some state $B \in S$ occurs in infinitely many intervals $[\alpha + \omega^k \cdot \ell, \alpha + \omega^k \cdot (\ell + 1))$. It is not necessarily the case that $B$ is in a terminal SCC in $G_{k-1}$, but there is some configuration reachable from $B$ that is, and since there are only finitely many possible configurations, one of these configurations $A$ must be cofinal in $[\alpha + \omega^k \cdot \ell, \alpha + \omega^k \cdot (\ell + 1))$. That configuration $A$ is in the same SCC $S$ in $G_k$ as $D$, because there is a path to it from $D$ in $G_k$ and $S$ is terminal. So for each interval $[\alpha + \omega^k \cdot \ell, \alpha + \omega^k \cdot (\ell + 1))$ in which $A$ occurs, $D$ is enabled at $\alpha + \omega^k \cdot (\ell + 1)$, and since these times occur cofinally in $[\alpha, \alpha + \omega^{k+1})$, by fairness, so does $D$.

□

Transition graphs give a translation between transfinite executions and the finite executions they represent. In this translation, transition along edges not in $G_0$ correspond to clock interrupts that cut off a looping computation and advance it to some future limit configuration. Each "phantom" sequence of transitions that is omitted when this occurs in effect acts as a certification that when a clock signal of a given level arrives, the current configuration could have recurred forever. By recognizing terminal SCCs directly, the transition graph approach gives an alternative certification that can be implemented in finite time on a conventional computer. We can also imagine implementing these clock ticks in practice by delivering a tick from some external source after a sufficiently long time interval, on the assumption that any reasonable physical implementation of a population protocol would converge with high probability in a bounded number of transitions.

## 3.1 Computation of transition graphs

Because population protocols preserve the number of agents, each graph $G_k$ is made up of non-communicating subgraphs $G_k^n$ for each population size $n$. Assuming the interaction graph of a population is complete (so that we can represent configurations with the same population counts as a single vertex), we can compute these subgraphs (and their limits!) efficiently, and use them to answer questions about population protocols running on particular inputs or input sizes.

THEOREM 3.2. *For any population protocol with $m$ agent states and a complete interaction graph, the transition graphs $G_0^n, \dots G_{n^{4m}}^n = G^n$ can be computed in time polynomial in $n$.*

PROOF. Given $m$ different agent states, there are fewer than $n^{2m}$ vertices in each $G_k^n$, where the 2 comes from the clock bit. For fixed $m$, this is polynomial in $n$.

Computing the edges in $G_0^n$ can easily be done in polynomial time by examining the transition function. Computing the added edges in $G_{k+1}^n$ requires finding the terminal SCCs of $G_k^n$, a linear-time operation using standard graph algorithms. Since $G_{k+1}^n = G_k^n$ implies $G_\ell^n = G_k^n$ for all $\ell \ge k$, we must add at least one edge to $G_{k+1}^n$ at each step to keep going; after fewer than $n^{4m}$ steps we will have either added all possible edges or reached the limit; in either case, $G_{n^{4m}}^n = G$. □

It follows that, in polynomial time, we can answer any questions about reachability, output-stability, and so forth that can be determined by applying standard graph algorithms to $G^n$. In particular, given an output-stable clocked population protocol that decides some language $L$, we can compute $G^n$, and for any input configuration determine the output in any terminal SCC reachable from some initial configuration $C$. This puts computation by clocked population protocols firmly in **P**, even if we allow unbounded transfinite time (in real life, arbitrarily deep layers of clocks) for them to complete.

But we can say more than this. The same argument that shows that computing $G_k^n$ can be done in time polynomial in $n$ also shows:

THEOREM 3.3. *For any population protocol with a complete interaction graph and any fixed $k$, whether there is a path from $C$ to $D$ in the transition graph $G_k^n$ can be computed in nondeterministic $O(\log n)$ space.*

PROOF. Because of the nondeterminism, this problem reduces to testing if there is an edge from $C$ to $D$ in $G_k^n$. Internally, we represent $C$ and $D$ as a list of agent counts (thus taking $O(\log n)$ space to store each), although a logspace machine is smart enough to convert a vector of agents states into such a list and store the result if needed.

For $k = 0$, this just involves checking if the counts of each state in $C$ and $D$ differ by an amount that is consistent with some transition in $\delta$, which is easily done in space $O(\log n)$.

For larger $k$, we make heavy use of the Immerman-Szelepcsényi Theorem [12, 17], which says that **NL** = **coNL** and more generally implies that $\mathbf{NL}^{\mathbf{NL}} = \mathbf{coNL}^{\mathbf{NL}} = \mathbf{NL}$ [12]. This means that as long as we recurse only to bounded depth, we can use **NL** subroutines in a **NL** or **coNL** computation and stay in **NL**.

In particular, to determine if $C \to D$ appears in $G_k^n$, we must check (a) if it is already in $G_{k-1}^n$, and if not, check (b) if $C \sim D$ and $C$ is in a terminal SCC of $G_k^n$. Testing if $C \sim D$ is trivial. Testing if

$C$ is in a terminal SCC requires testing for all $B$ such that there is a path from $C$ to $B$ in $G^n_{k-1}$ if there is also a path from $B$ to $C$ in $G^n_{k-1}$.

Fortunately, checking if there is a path from $C$ to $B$ in $G^n_{k-1}$ is easily done in $\mathbf{NL}^{\mathbf{NL}} = \mathbf{NL}$ (guess each step of the path nondeterministically, and call the **NL** oracle for edges in $G^n_{k-1}$ to verify that each step is an edge), and similarly testing for the non-existence of a path from $B$ to $C$ is easily done in $\mathbf{coNL}^{\mathbf{NL}} = \mathbf{NL}$. This leaves the universal quantifier over $B$, which puts the problem of detecting if $C$ is in a terminal SCC in $\mathbf{coNL}^{\mathbf{NL}}$, which is again equal to **NL**. □

Just as Theorem 3.2 puts all languages computed by clocked population protcols in **P**, Theorem 3.3 puts all languages computed by clocked population protocols using at most $\omega^k$ time in **NL**. In §4.2, we will use this to show that for any fixed $k$, a clocked population protocol that runs in time $\omega^k$ can be replaced by a clocked population protocol that runs in time $\omega^2$: one level of clock ticks is always enough.

# 4 PROGRAMMING A CLOCKED POPULATION PROTOCOL

Clocked population protocols are more powerful than standard population protocols. In this section, we give some applications of this extra power.

## 4.1 Leader election

Standard population protocols support leader election from an initially uniform state by fratricide: initially, each agent starts in a **leader** state $L$, and the transition rule $(L, L) \to (L, F)$ eventually turns all but one leader into a **follower**. But the winning leader cannot detect that this condition has occurred, and previous protocols that have used leader election as an initial stage have had to include a mechanism for restarting the computation after each remaining candidate is eliminated.

With a clock, the eventual leader can detect that it has won, because it can only receive a clock tick in a terminal SCC of the transition graph, and the only terminal SCCs are the one-leader configurations. But we can do even better than this. Fischer and Jiang [9] demonstrated that a standard population protocol cannot elect a leader starting from an arbitrary initial state, and proposed an $\Omega$? oracle that eventually signals when there is no leader in the current configuration. We can get the same effect by using clock ticks.

Consider a protocol with three states: **leader** $L$, **candidate** $C$, and **follower** $F$. We use the following transition table:

$$\begin{aligned} L, L &\to L, F \\ L, C &\to L, F \\ C, C &\to C, F \\ F', x &\to C, x \\ C', x &\to L, x \end{aligned}$$

As usual, we assume that the initial configuration does not have any clock bits set. But we place no other restriction on the states of the agents. Note that we are using the convention defined earlier that $F'$ (for example) is the state $F$ with the clock bit set.

Theorem 4.1. *Starting from any initial configuration with no clock bits set, the above protocol produces in time bounded by $\omega^2$ an agent in state $L'$. Furthermore, if an agent reaches state $L'$ in the above protocol, it is the only agent in the population in state $L'$ or $L$.*

Proof. Let $G_k$ be the transition graphs for this protocol from §3. Examining the transition relation shows that terminal SCCs in $G_0$ come in three varieties (up to symmetry): a configuration $C_F$ consisting of all followers, and configuration $C_C$ containing a single candidate and the rest followers, and a configuration $C_L$ containing a single leader and the rest followers. In each case, no agent in these stable configurations has a clock bit set.

If we reach $C_F$, then a configuration with some $F'$ is enabled at time $\omega$ and at each multiple of $\omega$ thereafter until $F'$ appears. By fairness, eventually there is some $\omega \cdot \ell$ at which at least one $F'$ does so. The next transition involving this agent falls produces a configuration with at least one candidate, and the rest of the agents followers. The terminal SCC reachable from such a configuration consists of $C_C$.

If we reach $C_C$, then a configuration with $C'$ is again enabled at each following multiple of $\omega$ until it occurs. When it does so, the next transition produces a single leader, and we reach the stable configuration $C_L$ after finitely many steps.

If we reach $C_L$, then the same argument as before shows that after some time $\omega \cdot \ell$, $L'$ appears.

Combining these cases shows that $L'$ appears after $\omega \cdot \ell < \omega^2$ time, where $\ell$ is some finite (though unbounded) quantity.

It remains to show that when $L'$ occurs, no other agent is in state $L$ or $L'$. Under the assumption that no clock bits are set in the initial configuration, $L'$ can only occur at a limit ordinal $\alpha$ before which a configuration containing $L$ or $L'$ occurs cofinally. But since multiple leaders are eliminated after finitely many steps, and no transition (including clock-tick transitions) ever increases the number of leaders, any configuration that occurs cofinally over a non-finite interval has at most one leader. □

## 4.2 Computing symmetric predicates in NL

Because agents with the same state are indistinguishable, the configuration of a population protocol with a complete interaction graph can be summarized by giving counts of the numbers of agents in each state. This essentially limits the population to storing data in unary, in the form of counters, and effectively limits population protocols to space logarithmic in the size of the population. Following the general approach of the universal randomized population protocol with a leader of Angluin *et al.* [2], we can represent a counter machine in the style of Minsky [15] by using the unique leader $L$ remaining from the preceding construction as a finite-state controller, and expressing counter values up to $n$ as the sum of bits scattered across all $n$ agents. But where Angluin *et al.* were limited by the need to build a randomized **phase clock** internally out of the agents themselves, by using an external clock we can eliminate the possibility of failure and compute any symmetric predicate in **NL** on the initial agent states.

Minsky's construction shows that counter machines can simulate Turing machines, but it requires that the finite-state controller be able to test a counter for zero in addition to incrementing or decrementing it. Incrementing a counter that is not already at its maximum value consists of executing the transition $(L_1, 0) \to (L_2, 1)$ (where we omit extraneous parts of the states from the description), while decrementing a counter consists of execution $(L_1, 1) \to (L_2, 0)$. In both cases, if there is not agent with the appropriate value 0 or 1, the operation never happens.

This is a problem for standard population protocols, because they have no mechanism to detect when they have stalled. But it is not a problem with clocks: a protocol that converges to a fixed configuration will remain in that configuration at the next clock tick, and the fairness condition enforces that a clock tick is eventually delivered to the leader. So the leader can test for 0 by attempting to decrement a counter and waiting until it either succeeds or fails. (If it succeeds, an increment will restore the previous state, allowing non-destructive tests.)

A transition relation that uses clock ticks to support a decrement operation that moves the leader from state $L_1$ to $L_2$ if successful and to $L_3$ can be as simple as this:

$$L_1, 1 \to L_2, 0$$
$$L_1', x \to L_3, x$$

(Here $x$ represents an arbitrary state, and transitions involving pairs not described are assumed to have no effect.)

Each such counter can count up to $n$, where increments and decrements that do not hit the bounds take $< \omega$ time and those that hit the bounds take $< \omega^2$ time. By using multiple counters as separate digits, we can represent values up to $n^c$ for any fixed $c$. The costs of increment and decrement operations may now be only $< \omega^2$ given the need to detect overflow or underflow on lower-order digits.

Given an $n^c$-bounded counter, we can use it to represent a $(c \lg n)$-bit stack for binary values, where popping from the stack is done by division by two (repeatedly decrement the counter twice if possible, and increment an auxiliary counter for each pair), and pushing to the stack is done by the reverse operation of multiplying by two and adding the new value. Two such stacks make a Turing machine tape, and the leader agent can act as the finite-state controller.

For the input tape, count the number of agents in each input state, and use a counter to represent the input tape head position. We can then pretend that the input tape is sorted (because we can only compute symmetric languages). If the TM controller asks what symbol lies under the current head position, we can sum up the counter values for each possible symbol until the total exceeds the simulated head position.

So far this gets us the symmetric languages in **L**. To get **NL**, we allow the leader to both make nondeterministic choices and to reset the computation to the beginning after reaching a rejecting state. Nondeterminism does not require modifying the transition function to be nondeterministic; instead, we can use the nondeterministic scheduling of which agent the leader meets next as a supply of nondeterminism, and observe that fairness gives that if there exists an accepting computation path, we will eventually find it. By mapping all other states that the accepting state to a rejecting output, we get an output-stable simulation of a nondeterministic logspace machine.

Careful accounting of the counter operations shows that the time per step of this machine is $< \omega^2$. Because we converge to a terminal SCC (either an accepting state or an endless loop of rejecting computation paths) in finitely many steps, the total time to reach an output-stable configuration is also $< \omega^2$. In the next section, we show that it is possible to detect when an output-stable configuration occurs.

### 4.3 Detecting stable outputs

The ability to simulate **NL** predicates means that we can detect when a clocked population protocol has reached an output-stable configuration, provided it does so in time $< \omega^k$ for some fixed $k$. This means that unlike standard population protocols, we can compose clocked population protocols sequentially, using the output of one protocol as the input to the next.

Here is the idea: At any time, the leader may nondeterministically choose to test for an output-stable configuration. To do so, the leader switches to transitions of the form $(L, x) \to (L, \hat{x})$, where $\hat{x}$ represents a "frozen" version of state $x$. Eventually, no more unfrozen agents remain, and the protocol enters a configuration that is stable until the next clock tick.

Upon receiving a clock tick, the leader can tell that it has successfully frozen all the agents, and proceeds to the verification step. The frozen configuration $C$ will be output-stable if every configuration reachable from it in $< \omega^k$ time has the same uniform output on all agents. We now observe that the **NL** simulation of the preceding section allows the leader to perform an **NL** computation of its choosing on the frozen state in $< \omega^2$ time, so we need only find a way to test output-stability in **NL**. Using an **NL** machine, we can nondeterministically guess the common output $x$. The question then becomes, is there a sequence of transitions starting from the frozen state that gives some agent a different output $y \neq x$? The existence of such a sequence is testable in **NL** by Theorem 3.3: we nondeterministically guess a bad configuration $D$ and then apply the theorem to check if $D$ is reachable from $C$ in $< \omega^k$ time. But what we want to know is that no such sequence exists. This question is in **coNL**, which puts output-stability in $\mathbf{L}^{\mathbf{coNL}}$. But this class is equal to **NL** by the Immerman-Szelepcsényi Theorem.

This means that whenever the leader freezes the configuration, it can use the procedure of the preceding section to try one branch of the **NL** computation that tests output-stability (note that this will require additional state in the agents separate from the frozen states). If the configuration is in fact output-stable and the protocol picks the right branch, we are done. If not, the leader reverses the freezing process and restarts the underlying protocol.

### 4.4 Reduction to $< \omega^2$ time

We can also apply Theorem 3.3 to not only detect convergence of a population protocol that runs in $< \omega^k$ time but to reduce its cost to $< \omega^2$ time. Given a protocol that runs in $< \omega^k$ time, we know that it computes a symmetric function in **NL**. We can thus ignore the original protocol and simulate the protocol using the method of §4.2 to compute the same predicate, output-stably, in time $< \omega^2$. Adding the convergence detector of §4.3 gives us the ability to detect when the output has stabilized: if we fire it only after clock ticks, we can guarantee that it runs only finitely many times using $< \omega^2$ time each, for a total cost that is still $< \omega^2$. So we can in fact compute any predicate that is stably computable by a clocked population protocol that runs in $< \omega^k$ time for any fixed $k$ in $< \omega^2$ time.

We summarize this result as:

THEOREM 4.2. *Any predicate computable by a clocked population protocol in $< \omega^k$ time, for fixed k, is computable in $< \omega^2$ time.*

# 5 RELATION TO OTHER ORACLES

The clock ticks added in the clocked population protocol model are a kind of oracle, providing the protocol with information ("you are stuck") that it cannot obtain for itself. We have seen that for the purposes of leader election, clock ticks are at least as powerful as the Ω? oracle of Fischer and Jiang. A natural question is whether other kinds of oracles can be simulated using clock ticks or vice versa.

## 5.1 Higher-order clock ticks

We think of the multiples of $\omega$ as the smallest clock interval in the system, while multiples of larger ordinals like $\omega^2$ represent longer intervals. The clock mechanism by itself does not allow the agents to distinguish between a tick that arrives at a multiple of $\omega$ that is not a multiple of $\omega^2$ from one that arrives at a multiple of $\omega^2$. An obvious extension is to add $2, 3, \ldots, k$ values to the existing 0 and 1 clock values so that a clock tick $i$ is delivered only at times that are multiple of $\omega^i$.

But this is not necessary. Having elected a unique leader, we can use it together with a counter implemented across the other agents to simulate such higher-order clock ticks for multiples of $\omega^k$ up to the maximum value of the counter.

Let $x$ represent the value in the counter. Initially, $x$ is 0. When the leader receives a clock tick, it increments $x$ and then resets it to zero. (As part of the reset operation, it may also copy the counter value somewhere else for later use.)

THEOREM 5.1. *Using the above mechanism, the leader increments the counter to k following a clock tick only at times that are multiples of $\omega^k$.*

PROOF. By induction on $k$. The base case is $k = 0$; all limit ordinals are multiples of $\omega^{0+1} = \omega$, so the hypothesis holds trivially.

For larger $k$, observe that $x = k$ can occur at $\alpha$ if and only if configurations with $x = k$ are cofinal in $\alpha$. Each such configuration must occur at a time that is a multiple of $\omega^k$. Expand $\alpha$ as $\omega^{k+1} \cdot \beta + \omega^k \cdot q + \rho$, where $q$ is finite and $\rho < \omega^k$. If either $\gamma$ or $\rho$ is nonzero, there there exists a time $\nu$ less than $\alpha$ such that no multiples of $\omega^k$ occur after $\nu$. But then configurations with $x = k$ are not cofinal in $\alpha$. It follows that $q = \rho = 0$ and $\alpha$ is a multiple of $\omega^{k+1}$. □

Note that these higher-order clock ticks are not the strongest we can imagine: for example, when the leader sees $x = 2$, it may be that the current time is $\omega^3$ or some even larger power of $\omega$. It is not clear whether providing an exact measure of the exponent would give a protocol more power directly, although if $k$ is bounded by a constant, we can extend the transition graph construction from §3 to enforce this constraint within the transition graph model, and compute the same predicates as a clocked population-protocol with these stronger higher-order ticks using the same approach as in Theorem 4.2.

## 5.2 Absence detectors

The **absence detector** of Michail and Spirakis [14] allows agents to determine precisely which states are present in the population at the time of encountering the detector. This allows construction of counters as in §4.2, and generally allows computation of symmetric predicates in **NL**.

Clock ticks are weaker than absence detectors in the sense that delivery of a clock tick can only indicate that no progress can be made. This can be used to test for the absence of a particular state $q$ by a leader that changes state if it encounters a $q$, but only if no other activity is ongoing in the population. This suggests simulating an absence detector directly by applying the same freezing-and-unfreezing method used in §4.3, but the cost of triggering this mechanism routinely during the execution of a larger protocol might be high.

On the other hand, it is straightforward to modify the transition graph construction of §3 to include an absence detector, and an **NL** machine that has access to the entire population count can easily implement an absence detector while simulating a population protocol. So the fact that clocked population protocols can compute functions in **NL** gives them the same computational power as a population protocol with an absence detector.

# 6 CONCLUSIONS

We have shown that allowing an external clock to deliver ticks to a stuck population protocol extends its power dramatically, giving it the ability to compute any symmetric predicate in **NL**. This generalizes previous results [1, 14, 16] that obtained similar power using more specialized mechanisms to detect convergence.

By using a model of transfinite executions over time intervals represented using ordinal arithmetic, we showed that the transition rules and fairness condition of the standard model extend in a straightforward way to these clocked population protocols. We also gave a representation of these transfinite executions using paths over finite transition graphs, demonstrating that this model both corresponds to a clock mechanism that could be implemented in practice in finite time, that the added power still remains plausibly within **P**, and that clocked population protocols have a capability for introspection, allowing clocked population protocols to compute properties of the executions of other clocked population protocols and related models by applying **NL** computations to their transition graphs.

Our results apply to population protocols with complete interaction graphs, the weakest form of the standard model. An interesting question is how clock bits and their representation in terms of transfinite fair executions would interact with population protocols with less symmetric interaction graphs, or even with other distributed computing models providing by their own eventual progress guarantees.

## ACKNOWLEDGMENTS

I would like to thank the anonymous referees for their many helpful comments, including a suggestion to consider in more detail direct simulations of absence detectors, a topic not examined in earlier versions of this paper.

## REFERENCES


[1] Dana Angluin, James Aspnes, Zoë Diamadi, Michael J. Fischer, and René Peralta. 2006. Computation in networks of passively mobile finite-state sensors. *Distributed Computing* (March 2006), 235–253.

[2] Dana Angluin, James Aspnes, and David Eisenstat. 2008. Fast computation by population protocols with a leader. *Distributed Computing* 21, 3 (Sept. 2008), 183–199.

[3] Dana Angluin, James Aspnes, David Eisenstat, and Eric Ruppert. 2007. The computational power of population protocols. *Distributed Computing* 20, 4 (Nov. 2007), 279–304.

[4] Joffroy Beauquier, Peva Blanchard, and Janna Burman. 2013. Self-stabilizing leader election in population protocols over arbitrary communication graphs. In *International Conference On Principles Of Distributed Systems*. Springer, 38–52.

[5] Joffroy Beauquier, Peva Blanchard, Janna Burman, and Oksana Denysyuk. 2016. On the Power of Oracle Ω? for Self-Stabilizing Leader Election in Population Protocols. In *International Symposium on Stabilization, Safety, and Security of Distributed Systems*. Springer, 20–35.

[6] Ioannis Chatzigiannakis, Othon Michail, Stavros Nikolaou, Andreas Pavlogiannis, and Paul G Spirakis. 2010. All symmetric predicates in NSPACE (n 2) are stably computable by the mediated population protocol model. In *International Symposium on Mathematical Foundations of Computer Science*. Springer, 270–281.

[7] Ioannis Chatzigiannakis, Othon Michail, Stavros Nikolaou, Andreas Pavlogiannis, and Paul G. Spirakis. 2011. Passively mobile communicating machines that use restricted space. *Theor. Comput. Sci.* 412, 46 (2011), 6469–6483. https://doi.org/10.1016/j.tcs.2011.07.001

[8] Ioannis Chatzigiannakis, Othon Michail, and Paul G Spirakis. 2009. Mediated population protocols. In *International Colloquium on Automata, Languages, and Programming*. Springer, 363–374.

[9] Michael Fischer and Hong Jiang. 2006. Self-stabilizing leader election in networks of finite-state anonymous agents. In *International Conference On Principles Of Distributed Systems*. Springer, 395–409.

[10] Rachid Guerraoui and Eric Ruppert. 2009. Names trump malice: Tiny mobile agents can tolerate byzantine failures. In *International Colloquium on Automata, Languages, and Programming*. Springer, 484–495.

[11] Joel David Hamkins and Andy Lewis. 2000. Infinite time Turing machines. *The Journal of Symbolic Logic* 65, 02 (2000), 567–604.

[12] Neil Immerman. 1988. Nondeterministic Space is Closed Under Complementation. *SIAM J. Comput.* 17, 5 (1988), 935–938. https://doi.org/10.1137/0217058

[13] Thomas Jech. 2002. *Set Theory: The Third Millenium Edition: revised and expanded*. Springer.

[14] Othon Michail and Paul G Spirakis. 2015. Terminating population protocols via some minimal global knowledge assumptions. *J. Parallel and Distrib. Comput.* 81 (2015), 1–10.

[15] Marvin L. Minsky. 1961. Recursive unsolvability of Post's problem of "Tag" and other topics in theory of Turing machines. *Annals of Mathematics* 74, 3 (Nov. 1961), 437–455.

[16] David Soloveichik, Matthew Cook, Erik Winfree, and Jehoshua Bruck. 2008. Computation with finite stochastic chemical reaction networks. *natural computing* 7, 4 (2008), 615–633.

[17] Róbert Szelepcsényi. 1988. The method of forced enumeration for nondeterministic automata. *Acta Informatica* 26, 3 (1988), 279–284. https://doi.org/10.1007/BF00299636

[18] James F. Thomson. 1954. Tasks and super-tasks. *Analysis* 15, 1 (1954), 1–13.

[19] Johann v. Neumann. 1923. Zur Einführung der transfiniten Zahlen. *Acta Universitatis Szegediensis* 1 (1923), 199–208.

# A Distributed Learning Dynamics in Social Groups

L. Elisa Celis
École Polytechnique Fédérale de Lausanne (EPFL)
elisa.celis@epfl.ch

Peter M. Krafft
Massachusetts Institute of Technology
pkrafft@csail.mit.edu

Nisheeth K. Vishnoi
École Polytechnique Fédérale de Lausanne (EPFL)
nisheeth.vishnoi@epfl.ch

## ABSTRACT

We study a distributed learning process observed in human groups and other social animals. This learning process appears in settings in which each individual in a group is trying to decide over time, in a distributed manner, which option to select among a shared set of options. Specifically, we consider a stochastic dynamics in a group in which every individual selects an option in the following two-step process: (1) select a random individual and observe the option that individual chose in the previous time step, and (2) adopt that option if its stochastic quality was good at that time step. Various instantiations of such distributed learning appear in nature, and have also been studied in the social science literature. From the perspective of an individual, an attractive feature of this learning process is that it is a simple heuristic that requires extremely limited computational capacities. But what does it mean for the group – *could such a simple, distributed and essentially memoryless process lead the group as a whole to perform optimally?* We show that the answer to this question is *yes* – this distributed learning is highly effective at identifying the best option and is close to optimal for the group overall. Our analysis also gives quantitative bounds that show fast convergence of these stochastic dynamics. We prove our result by first defining a (stochastic) infinite population version of these distributed learning dynamics and then combining its strong convergence properties along with its relation to the finite population dynamics. Prior to our work the only theoretical work related to such learning dynamics has been either in deterministic special cases or in the asymptotic setting. Finally, we observe that our infinite population dynamics is a stochastic variant of the classic multiplicative weights update (MWU) method. Consequently, we arrive at the following interesting converse: the learning dynamics on a finite population considered here can be viewed as a novel distributed and low-memory implementation of the classic MWU method.

## CCS CONCEPTS

• **Theory of computation → Theory and algorithms for application domains**; • **Human-centered computing →** *Collaborative and social computing theory, concepts and paradigms*; Social networks; • **Applied computing →** Sociology;


*PODC '17, July 25-27, 2017, Washington, DC, USA*

ACM ISBN 978-1-4503-4992-5/17/07...$15.00
https://doi.org/10.1145/3087801.3087820

## KEYWORDS

Natural algorithms, computational social science, social sampling, multiplicative weight updating, distributed learning

## 1 INTRODUCTION

A powerful assumption – often leveraged in biology, ecology, and evolutionary psychology in order to reason about why humans, animals, and other biological organisms behave in certain ways – is to suppose that behavior is tuned to alleviate evolutionary pressure. This assumption provides deductive power because once a behavior is assumed to be optimally or near-optimally solving *some* problem, one can then attempt to discover *which* problem the system might be solving through the *computational lens*. We study this phenomenon in the context of social behavior. In particular, we consider a class of distributed social learning dynamics which are at once conspicuous in daily life, oft discussed in the social science literature, and also empirically verified; yet are also simple to the point that they appear perhaps suboptimal. Consider the setting consisting of a social group of $N$ individuals presented with a set of $m$ options of different quality. The quality of each option is assumed to be an independent random variable whose parameters are unknown to the individuals and remain fixed over time. At each time step each individual selects one option and observes a stochastic indicator of that option's quality. The goal of the *individual* is to identify the best option.

The distributed learning dynamics then boils down to *individuals copying or imitating the behavior of others* in an effort to solve this problem. Such dynamics roughly have the following two steps: At each time step, each individual independently decides which option to select by first

(1) **Sampling** – observing the choice of a random member of the group at the last time step, and then
(2) **Adopting** – deciding whether or not to adopt the recommended option as a function of the *most recent* (stochastic) signal of that option's quality.

Instances of such two-stage distributed learning dynamics in social settings have been widely proposed and validated with data in the literature on human choice behavior (e.g., [7, 10, 29, 32, 34]) and animal behavior (e.g., [40, 43]). They are cognitively simple because individuals need not maintain any history of previous observations; rather they only use the most recent quality signal of one option. Furthermore, as with many other distributed protocols observed in nature (e.g., [27, 35]), each step requires only limited communication with other group members. In light of the fact that such distributed learning processes are ubiquitous, the question arises – why? To answer this, we need to understand the following: *What does such a distributed learning dynamics imply for the group as a whole?*

## Our Contribution

We consider a general model that captures a wide variety of distributed learning dynamics in social settings as defined above (see Section 2.1 for a formal definition) and study two fundamental algorithmic questions:

- *do such learning dynamics (despite each individual having a limited memory) have the potential to successfully converge to the best option for the collective population?* and if so,
- *how efficient are such dynamics?*

We prove that the answer to the first question is *yes* and provide quantitative bounds for the second in the most general case in which the population is finite and both the sampling and adopting step are stochastic.

In general, due to the fact that populations are finite and there is stochasticity in both steps, the social learning dynamics may be chaotic, with no single option dominating, and the popularity of options rising and falling over time. However, we prove that social learning leads the population, as a whole, to be competitive – pretty quickly – as compared to the best strategy in *hindsight*; i.e., the dynamics have low *regret* (see section 2.1). Prior to our work, many instances of such social learning dynamics have been proposed and validated (see, e.g., [39] for an exposition), and, even though on the surface there seem to be several related processes, the only theoretical work has been either in deterministic special cases or in the asymptotic setting where both the size of the population and time goes to infinity; such results (see [12, 22] and Section 3) effectively focus on deriving asymptotic (large deviation) bounds. To the best of our knowledge, ours is the first rigorous analysis of this distributed learning dynamics in a realistic setting when the size of the group is finite.

Key to our results are the following two realizations which we can use to understand the emergent behavior of the distributed learning dynamics:

- In the infinite population limit, by rewriting the underlying stochastic equations of the distributed learning dynamics, the individuals are effectively implementing a *stochastic* variant of the classic multiplicative weights update (MWU) method [4] at the group-level.[1]
- While the finite population distributed learning dynamics can be approximated with its infinite population limit for *short* times, to ensure that the regret bounds remain valid for longer times, further new ideas are required. Here, we show how we can appeal to the strong convergence properties of the infinite population stochastic dynamics to ascertain that the regret remains bounded for all times in the finite population case.

Computationally, contrasting with typical implementations of the MWU method, in the learning dynamics we consider, no individual keeps track of the weights. Rather, the popularity of the options in the previous time step serve as a proxy for weights, and suffice to propel the process forward. Thus, we arrive at the following interesting conclusion – *the learning dynamics in social groups considered here can inform novel, low-memory, low-communication, distributed implementations of the MWU algorithm in the stochastic setting*; perhaps appropriate for low-power devices in distributed settings such as sensor networks or the internet-of-things.

[1]This stochastic process is not to be mistaken with the standard deterministic MWU or its continuous time limit, the replicator dynamics.

# 2 MODEL, OUR RESULTS AND OVERVIEW

## 2.1 The Model

The learning environment we consider consists of a set of $N$ individuals repeatedly choosing among $m$ options during a sequence of $T$ discrete time steps. Each option has an unknown underlying quality, $\eta_1 \geq \eta_2 \geq \cdots \geq \eta_m \in [0,1]$, which represents the probability that the option is "good" at any given time step; we let $R_j^t$ = Bernoulli($\eta_j$) be the indicator random variable for the event that option $j$ is good at time $t$. The goal of each individual is to select the best option. Now, let $X_{ij}^t \in \{0,1\}$ be the indicator random variable for the event that individual $i$ chooses to adopt option $j$ at time $t$. The distributed learning dynamics we consider is a two-stage model:

**(1) Sampling.** First, individuals select which option to consider, and then they choose whether or not to adopt that option. To obtain an option to consider at time $t+1$, with probability $\mu$ individual $i$ selects an option $j \in [m]$ to consider uniformly at random, and with probability $(1-\mu)$ individual $i$ selects an option $j \in [m]$ proportional to its current popularity:

$$Q_j^t = \frac{\sum_{i=1}^N X_{ij}^t}{\sum_{k=1}^m \sum_{i=1}^N X_{ik}^t}$$

is the fraction of the population that adopts option $j$ at time $t$, and we assume $Q_j^0 = \frac{1}{m}$ for all $j$.[2] Note that this can be implemented in a distributed manner as suggested in the introduction by letting $i$ select a companion $i' \in \{1,\ldots,N\}$ uniformly at random, and observing the choice of individual $i'$ at time $t$. The parameter $\mu > 0$ is small and represents a fraction of the population which may take independent decisions; its role is to ensure that the population does not get stuck in a bad option.

**(2) Adopting.** In the second stage, after choosing an option $j$ to consider, individual $i$ must then decide whether to commit to this option or to sit out during this time step. Individual $i$ observes the most recent quality signal associated with $j$, namely $R_j^{t+1}$ and decides to adopt the option with probability $f_i(R_j^{t+1}) \in \{0,1\}$ where $f_i$ is a stochastic function such that $\mathbb{E}[f_i(1)] > \mathbb{E}[f_i(0)]$. Hence, for each $i$, we can express $f_i$ in the following form:

$$f_i(R_j^{t+1}) = \begin{cases} 1 & \text{with probability } \beta_i \text{ if } R_j^{t+1} = 1 \\ 1 & \text{with probability } \alpha_i \text{ if } R_j^{t+1} = 0 \\ 0 & \text{otherwise.} \end{cases}$$

Here, $\alpha_i \leq \beta_i$ are parameters of the model and represent how sensitive individuals are to the most recent signal of goodness as compared to the weight they give to the recommendation. For simplicity in the exposition, we assume that all $f_i$ are identical, and drop the index $i$. This assumption is not essential for our results –

[2]In the absence of prior knowledge, we initialize at the point where all options are equally popular. This also simplifies the exposition, but is not crucial to our results – our results hold from arbitrary initial conditions.

we omit the details. Thus, the two relevant parameters are $0 \leq \alpha \leq \beta \leq 1$.

**Examples of the model.** Many instances of social learning in the social sciences and economics literature can be interpreted as special cases of the distributed learning dynamics introduced above. Here we give two concrete examples – one direct and one indirect; see more discussion in Section 3. The simplest such example [31] corresponds exactly to our model when $\alpha = 1 - \beta$ for some $\beta \geq \frac{1}{2}$ when $\eta_1 > \frac{1}{2} = \eta_2 = \cdots = \eta_m$. The authors validate this model using observational data on the decisions of amateur investors on an online platform in which users are able to copy the actions of others.

Another instance, which takes a bit of explanation, appears in the economics literature [22]. We present it here because it illustrates two common ways in which more general-looking models, specifically ones with continuous-valued rewards and reward differences across individuals, can often be reinterpreted in such a way that our framework applies. The authors consider a learning setting where $m = 2$ and rewards $r_j^t$ are drawn from a continuous-valued distribution $\mathcal{F}_j$. Furthermore, their model incorporates player-specific stochastic shocks, so that if $\epsilon_{ij}^t \sim \mathcal{G}$ is the size of the shock to player $i$ on option $j$ at time $t$, then the reward to player $i$ is $r_j^t + \epsilon_{ij}^t$. The sampling step (1) is similar, except that $\mu = 0$. In the adoption step (2), if player $i$ sampled player $i'$, then player $i$ adopts option 1 if $r_1^t + \epsilon_{i1}^t + \epsilon_{i'1}^t > r_2^t + \epsilon_{i2}^t + \epsilon_{i'2}^t$, and adopts option 2 otherwise. To convert this to our setting, let $R_1^t$ (and $R_2^t$) be the indicator random variable for the event that $r_1^t > r_2^t$ (and $r_1^t < r_2^t$); this occurs with some probability $p$ (and $1 - p$) and defines our parameters $\eta_1 = p > 1 - p = \eta_2$.[3] Note that in the adoption step, we can replace $\epsilon_{i1}^t + \epsilon_{i'1}^t - \epsilon_{i2}^t - \epsilon_{i'2}^t$ by a continuous random variable $\xi$. Then $\beta = \mathbb{P}\left[\xi > r_2^t - r_1^t | r_1^t > r_2^t\right]$ and $\alpha = \mathbb{P}\left[\xi > r_2^t - r_1^t | r_2^t > r_1^t\right]$. As the $\epsilon_{ij}^t$s are i.i.d., $\xi$ has zero mean and is symmetric, hence $\alpha < \beta$ and our results apply. The authors consider the infinite population version of this model where a constant fraction of the population updates at each time step, and analyze its asymptotic properties as $T \to \infty$.

## 2.2 Our Results and Overview

In order to explain our results for the distributed learning dynamics we first need to quantify a measure of optimality. In the remainder of the paper we let $\alpha = 1 - \beta$. This just simplifies the reading and has no impact on the statements of the theorem – the same bounds hold with a dependence on $\frac{\beta}{\alpha}$ as opposed to $\frac{\beta}{1-\beta}$. Let $Q_j^t$ be the random variable which measures the fraction of individuals that chose option $j$ at time $t$, as defined above. Wishfully, we might like to prove that as $t$ becomes large, $Q_j^t$s, for all $j \neq 1$ are close to zero (assuming $\eta_1 > \eta_2$). However, simple examples show that this may not be the case; the stochastic process is non-monotone, even when there is a significant gap between $\eta_1$ and $\eta_2$, and may step away significantly from $Q_1^t \approx 1$ even for large $t$. Instead, we consider the average expected performance of the group when compared to that of the best option:

$$\text{Regret}_N(T) := \eta_1 - \frac{1}{T}\sum_{t=1}^{T}\sum_{j=1}^{m}\mathbb{E}[Q_j^{t-1}R_j^t].$$

As the name suggests, this is nothing but the average regret of this process; namely, the difference between the group's expected average reward if all individuals who adopted an option select the optimal $j = 1$, and the group's expected average reward selected according to the distributed learning process up to time $T$. The following is the main technical contribution of the paper; see Theorem 4.5 for a formal statement of this result.

***Distributed learning achieves near-optimal regret in a social group.*** *For a range of parameters $1/2 \leq \beta \leq e/(e+1)$, $\mu$ a small constant, $N$ roughly at least $m^{1/\delta^2}$ and for all $T \geq \frac{\ln m}{\delta^2}$, $\text{Regret}_N(T)$ is at most $6\delta$ where $\delta = \ln\left(\frac{\beta}{1-\beta}\right)$.* Thus, the closer $\beta$ is to $1/2$, the better the regret.

The proof of the above result relies on the following connection between our distributed learning dynamics in a finite population and what can be thought of as an infinite population variant of the distributed learning dynamics. The latter can also be seen as a stochastic variant of the MWU method (see Theorem 4.9) which we explain below. Consider $m$ experts where expert $j$ generates a stochastic reward $R_j^{t+1}$ at time $t$ that is 1 with probability $\eta_j$ and 0 otherwise. In this setting, a *single* player maintains weight $W_j^t$ for option $j$ at time $t$, which is updated multiplicatively in the following manner:[4]

$$W_j^{t+1} := \underbrace{\left((1-\mu)W_j^t + \frac{\mu}{m}\sum_{k=1}^{m} W_k^t\right)}_{\text{deterministic sampling}} \underbrace{\beta^{R_j^{t+1}}(1-\beta)^{1-R_j^{t+1}}}_{\text{stochastic rewards}}$$

and $W_j^0 = 1$ for all $j$. We arrive at this update equation by the (non-rigorous) thought process that in the infinite population case, we can replace the stochastic quantities by their expectation in the sampling stage: in this case, the expected fraction of individuals picking the option $j$ in the sampling stage of the social learning dynamics is proportional to $(1-\mu)W_j^t + \frac{\mu}{m}\sum_{k=1}^{m} W_k^t$. This gives us the first term in the right-hand side above. The second term is just $f(R_j^{t+1})$ with respect to parameter $\beta$. We note that, since the rewards are stochastic, it is not the standard adversarial MWU setting and, since all the information is known to the population as a whole, it is also not the standard setting of stochastic bandits.

Even though these weight update equations are arrived at by a heuristic calculation, we can prove that for *short* time periods, there is a coupling between the infinite and the finite distributed learning dynamics such that the stochastic trajectories corresponding to the weights in the infinite population case remain close to that of the finite population case.

***Infinite vs. finite population distributed social learning.*** *If $(P_j^t)_{j=1}^m$ is the probability distribution induced by the weights $W_j^t$*

[3]Note that in their model the $R_1^t$ and $R_2^t$ are correlated as exactly one of them is 1 in every time step; however independence across $t$ remains which suffices for our results.

[4]It is worth noticing the similarity between the weights update (in particular the first term) and that used in the result of Christiano et al. [18] who developed a variant of the MWU method in the design of a fast algorithm for a flow problem.

*after time t for a given sequence of rewards, then for all j,* $1 - \frac{5^t}{\sqrt{N}} \le P_j^t/Q_j^t \le 1 + \frac{5^t}{\sqrt{N}}$.

The proof of this crucially relies on the fact that $\mu$ is strictly positive. On the other hand, the fact that $\mu > 0$ also makes the analysis quite messy. Note that the closeness deteriorates very quickly and, in particular, the bound becomes uninteresting after about $\log N$ time steps. On the other hand, for fixed $t$, as $N \to \infty$, the trajectories of the two processes are identical; put another way, the distributed learning process over infinite populations is identical to the corresponding stochastic MWU method. This is typically the kind of asymptotic result that exists in the literature. The more interesting and challenging direction is to show convergence when $N$ is large, but *fixed*, and $T$ goes to infinity.

In order to leverage this connection between infinite and finite population variants of the distributed learning dynamics, we first analyze the corresponding regret of the stochastic MWU method, which is defined to be

$$\text{Regret}_\infty(T) := \eta_1 - \frac{1}{T}\sum_{t=1}^{T}\sum_{j=1}^{m}\mathbb{E}[P_j^{t-1}R_j^t].$$

We can establish the following regret bound in this case; see Theorem 4.4.

***Infinite population distributed social learning dynamics achieves near-optimal regret.*** *For a range of parameters* $1/2 \le \beta \le e/(e+1)$, $\mu$ *a small constant, and for all* $T \ge \frac{\ln m}{\delta^2}$, $\text{Regret}_\infty(T)$ *is at most* $3\delta$ *where* $\delta = \ln\left(\frac{\beta}{1-\beta}\right)$.

The proof of this obtained by adapting the proof of the MWU method to take into account stochastic rewards.

At this point we would be done except that the closeness between the probability distributions of finite and infinite distributed learning dynamics holds only for short times – if we run the process for about $\frac{\ln m}{\delta^2}$ steps, then for the probability distributions to be close we would need $N \ge m^{O(1/\delta^2)}$. What about when $T \ge \frac{\ln m}{\delta^2}$? To tackle this problem, we need a new idea. The first observation is that, in fact, the regret bound for the infinite population case can be made stronger: roughly, *as long as the starting distribution has enough entropy, the regret becomes small in about the same number of steps.* Thus, we can break $T$ into epochs of size approximately $\frac{\ln m}{\delta^2}$ and observe that at the beginning of each epoch, each option will have about $\mu/m$ probability – again we need crucially that $\mu > 0$. Thus, we can show convergence starting from such a probability distribution in $\frac{\ln(m/\mu)}{\delta^2}$ iterations. As a consequence, in each epoch, we can bound the regret by about $6\delta$ for slightly larger $N$. Rewriting it a different way, having a finite population will have an additive error term of approximately $\frac{m^{1/\delta^2}}{\sqrt{N}}$ to the regret obtained by the infinite population. Thus, we rely on the strong *attractive* properties of the infinite population stochastic dynamics to obtain quantitative regret bounds for the finite population social learning dynamics. This contributes to the growing set of connections between using attractors of dynamical systems to analyze stochastic processes[8, 38, 49, 50]. Details of the proof of Theorem 4.5 appear in Section 4.3.

# 3 RELATED WORK

There is a growing body of work in theoretical computer science, and distributed computing theory in particular, that studies problems arising in the sciences through the computational lens; see, e.g., [1, 17, 19, 27, 35, 46]. Such studies have also on occasion contributed back to computer science by providing insights into existing techniques, or giving rise to novel bio-inspired algorithms. Our work touches upon both of these aspects.

Among related studies in the sciences, while dynamics that *only* have a sampling step [14, 23] or *only* an adoption step [30] have been studied, combining both has been shown empirically to result in a better strategy [34]. Indeed, in line with these observations, one can formally see from our analysis that if we only have sampling ($\beta = 1 - \alpha = 1$) or only have adoption ($\mu = 1$), the process does not always converge to the best option. Hence, both steps of the process seem crucial, and many models in sociology and economics are such distributed two-step processes [5, 15, 22, 31, 41]. While some models a priori look different, many can be captured by our formulation; for example, models that have continuous rewards but whose adoption rule depends on whether the reward is above or below a threshold [11, 12, 26] can be converted to a binary reward structure in a standard way. Similarly, differences across individuals can be captured in the functions $f_i$ (see the second example in Section 2.1). While some of these models consider the aggregate popularity of options over time, many (including models for human behavior, e.g., [31]) consider only the current popularity. In the economics literature, some similar finite population models have been studied, many of which also fall into our framework. Their analysis has only been *asymptotic* as $N, T \to \infty$; such results (see, e.g., [9, 12, 22]) effectively focus on deriving large deviation bounds. In contrast, the main technical contribution of our work includes quantitative bounds of the social learning dynamics for finite populations ($N < \infty$). Asymptotic and infinite-population results follow as corollaries.

There has been a large body of work on the distributed consensus problem; see for instance [3, 6] and the references therein. The goal in such problems is for all individuals to agree on a single opinion, and various distributed dynamics for doing so have been proposed and analyzed. Our setting differs in that there is additional information – the repeated stochastic signals associated to the quality of each opinion.

In evolutionary game theory, similar-looking deterministic imitator dynamics have been considered (see [37, 44] for an overview). A key difference with this work is the learning environment – we are not attempting to select a strategy in a game, rather are trying to identify the best option of out a collection. Hence, the reward of an individual depends on her choice $j$, while in evolutionary game theory the reward of an individual depends on the choices of *the entire population*. In this setting one can still consider the regret of an individual (see, e.g., [13]). While fast convergence of similar dynamics has been shown for some special cases (e.g., potential games [21] and selfish routing [24]), for general games we cannot expect to always converge quickly unless $PPAD \subseteq P$. In fact, it has been shown that in some games, versions of the replicator dynamics may converge to outcomes that are not optimal, or not even equilibria [26, 42].

The fact that an MWU-like method emerges from a simple distributed behavior of individuals in a social setting, is somewhat reminiscent of unrelated results that arise in the context of biological evolution [16] and task allocation among ants [47]. The MWU algorithm [4], or its well-known continuous time limit, the replicator dynamics [45, 48] can also be seen as a special case of our distributed learning dynamics if we remove the randomness from *both* the sampling and adopting steps *and* the rewards (effectively taking the process to a deterministic and infinite setting). However, as-is, MWU-type dynamics are different because each individual must effectively maintain full weights (or a mixed strategy vector) at every time step. Furthermore, the lack of stochasticity and the infinite population setting avoid the key technical hurdles in the analysis of our model.

Our results suggest that the distributed learning dynamics in finite populations can be viewed as a novel distributed and approximate implementation of the MWU method. While parallelized implementations for solving multi-armed bandit problem exist (see, e.g., [2, 25, 28, 33, 36]), in such works each node explicitly maintains a weight vector on all options. The most distinctive aspect of the distributed MWU interpretation of the learning dynamics we consider is that no such memory is required - the weights are represented implicitly by the popularity of the various options, and the sampling and adopting processes require almost no memory. This difference distinguishes our distributed learning dynamics from prior work on distributed MWU or bandit methods.

# 4 TECHNICAL DETAILS AND PROOFS

## 4.1 Basic Facts

We first recall a few theorems and definitions that will be useful in our proofs.

THEOREM 4.1 (**CHERNOFF-HOEFFDING BOUNDS [20]**). *Let $Z_1, \ldots, Z_n$ be independent Bernoulli random variables with mean $\gamma_i$. Let $\gamma := \frac{1}{n}\sum_{i=1}^n \gamma_i$. When $0 < \delta \leq 1$, we have $\mathbb{P}\left[\left|\frac{1}{n}\sum_{i=1}^n Z_i - \gamma\right| > \gamma\delta\right] \leq 2\exp\left(-n\gamma\delta^2/3\right)$.*

*Definition 4.2.* For real numbers $A$, $B$, and $c \geq 0$, the notation $A \overset{c}{\sim} B$ denotes $\frac{1}{c} \leq \frac{A}{B} \leq c$.

FACT 4.3. *For fixed $0 \leq \delta \leq 1$ and for all $0 \leq x \leq 1$, $e^{\delta x} \leq 1 + (e^\delta - 1)x$.*

## 4.2 The Infinite Population Distributed Learning Dynamics

Consider the following stochastic process: $W_j^0 := 1$ for all $1 \leq j \leq m$. For $t > 0$ and for all $1 \leq j \leq m$

$$W_j^{t+1} := \left((1-\mu)W_j^t + \frac{\mu}{m}\sum_{k=1}^m W_k^t\right)\beta^{R_j^{t+1}}(1-\beta)^{1-R_j^{t+1}}. \quad (1)$$

This definition parallels the two-step finite population distributed learning dynamics and can be thought of as an infinite population distributed learning dynamics: $W_j^{t+1}$ is first updated according to $W_i^t$ (with weight $1-\mu$) and with uniform additive factor $\sum_{k=1}^m W_k^t/m$ (with weight $\mu$), and then (stochastically) as the corresponding function of $\beta$ and $R_j^{t+1}$. The stochasticity is now solely with respect to the $R_j^t$s. Now, consider the following probability distribution corresponding to these weights, $P_j^t := \frac{W_j^t}{\sum_{k=1}^m W_k^t}$, which corresponds to the fraction of the (infinite) population that has adopted option $j$ at time $t$.

Let $\delta := \ln\left(\frac{\beta}{1-\beta}\right)$, and note that we can re-write the above as

$$W_j^{t+1} := (1-\beta)\left((1-\mu)W_j^t + \frac{\mu}{m}\sum_{k=1}^m W_k^t\right)e^{\delta R_j^{t+1}}.$$

This now takes a more standard form as a multiplicative update; the $(1-\beta)$ term can be ignored as it is cancels out in $P_j^t$, so the main difference with the standard MWU is the $\frac{\sum_{k=1}^m W_k^t}{m}$ term that takes up a $\mu$ fraction of the weight. One can think of this as a regularizing term and bears some similarity to what was considered in the recent breakthrough result on computing flows [18].

Assuming that $\eta_1 \geq \eta_j$ for all $j \neq 1$, the optimal strategy for the population is to select option 1. If they did this, then the average expected gain of the population is $\eta_1$. On the other hand, the average expected gain of the population over $T$ iterations while following this stochastic process is $\frac{1}{T}\sum_{t=1}^T\sum_{j=1}^m \mathbb{E}\left[P_j^{t-1}R_j^t\right]$. We now proceed to understand how the latter compares to the former - in other words, bound the regret of the infinite population stochastic process. Formally, in the remainder of this subsection, we prove the following result:

THEOREM 4.4 (REGRET OF INFINITE POPULATION DISTRIBUTED LEARNING DYNAMICS). *Let $\eta_1 > \eta_2 \geq \cdots \geq \eta_m$, let $\frac{1}{2} < \beta \leq \frac{e}{e+1}$ (and hence $0 < \delta \leq 1$), and let $6\mu \leq \delta^2$. Let $P^0$ be the uniform distribution on $\{1, \ldots, m\}$ and $\{P^t\}_{t=1}^T$ be the probability distributions produced by the infinite population distributed learning dynamics with stochastic rewards $\{R^t\}_{t=1}^T$. Then for $T \geq \frac{\ln m}{\delta^2}$, the average expected regret after T steps is*

$$\text{Regret}_\infty(T) = \eta_1 - \frac{1}{T}\cdot\sum_{t=1}^T\sum_{j=1}^m \mathbb{E}\left[P_j^{t-1}R_j^t\right] \leq 3\delta.$$

*Furthermore, $\frac{1}{T}\sum_{t=1}^T \mathbb{E}\left[P_1^{t-1}\right] \geq 1 - \frac{3\delta}{\eta_1-\eta_2}$.*

The proof of Theorem 4.4 appears in Section 5

## 4.3 Main Result: Regret of the Distributed Learning Dynamics in Finite Populations

THEOREM 4.5 (REGRET OF THE DISTRIBUTED LEARNING PROCESS IN FINITE POPULATIONS). *Let $\eta_1 > \eta_2 \geq \cdots \geq \eta_m$, let $\frac{1}{2} < \beta \leq \frac{e}{e+1}$ (and hence $0 < \delta \leq 1$), let $6\mu \leq \delta^2$, and let $\delta'' := \sqrt{\frac{60m\ln N}{(1-\beta)\mu N}}$, $c := \frac{240m}{(1-\beta)\mu}$, and $N$ is such that*

$$\frac{N}{\ln N} \geq \frac{\left(c\frac{4m}{\mu(1-\beta)}\right)^{\frac{2\ln 5}{\delta^2}}}{\delta''^2} \text{ and } N^{10} \geq \frac{24m\ln m}{\mu(1-\beta)\delta^3}.$$

*Let $Q^0$ be the uniform distribution on $\{1, \ldots, m\}$ and $\{Q^t\}_{t=1}^T$ be the probability distributions produced by the finite population distributed learning dynamics with stochastic rewards $\{R^t\}_{t=1}^T$, then* *for* $\frac{N^{10}}{m\delta} \geq T \geq \frac{\ln m}{\delta^2}$, *the average expected regret after* $T$ *steps is* $\eta_1 - \frac{1}{T} \cdot \sum_{t=1}^{T} \sum_{j=1}^{m} \mathbb{E}\left[Q_j^{t-1} R_j^t\right] \leq 6\delta$.

Here, $N^{10}$ is arbitrary and can be made as large as required at the expense of constants.

In order to prove this result, we first give an analysis which holds for $T = \frac{\ln m}{\delta^2}$, and then show how to leverage this result for large $T$.

*4.3.1* ***Small*** *T.* To conduct the analysis, we first set up some definitions and which correspond to the two different stages of the finite population distributed learning process, and show that, in each step, the finite population dynamics is approximated by the infinite population distributed learning dynamics/MWU stochastic process.

**Stage 1.** Let $D_j^t$ denote the number of people committed to option $j$ at time $t$ and let $Q_j^t := \frac{D_j^t}{\sum_{k=1}^m D_k^t}$ be the probability distribution capturing the relative popularity of option $j$ at time $t$. Let $\mathcal{S}_j^{t+1} \subseteq [N]$ denote the set of people who select $j$ after the first stage in the sampling process in step $t+1$ and let $S_j^{t+1} := |\mathcal{S}_j^{t+1}|$. Let $Y_{ij}^{t+1}$ be the indicator random variable for the event that $i$ chooses $j$ in stage one at time step $t+1$. Note that these $\left\{Y_{ij}^{t+1}\right\}_{i=1}^{N}$ are independent conditioned on everything up to time $t$ with

$$\mathbb{P}\left[Y_{ij}^{t+1} = 1 \,\middle|\, t\right] = \left((1-\mu)Q_j^t + \frac{\mu}{m}\right) \geq \frac{\mu}{m}. \tag{2}$$

Since $S_j^{t+1} = \sum_{i=1}^{N} Y_{ij}^{t+1}$, it follows from linearity of expectation that $\mathbb{E}\left[S_j^{t+1} \,\middle|\, t\right] = \left((1-\mu)Q_j^t + \frac{\mu}{m}\right) N$.

Proposition 4.6. *Let* $t \geq 0$ *be fixed. For* $\delta' := \sqrt{\frac{30m\ln N}{\mu N}} \leq \frac{1}{2}$, *with probability at least* $1 - \frac{2m}{N^{10}}$ *(conditioned on everything up to time t), for all j* $S_j^{t+1} \overset{1+2\delta'}{\sim} \left((1-\mu)Q_j^t + \frac{\mu}{m}\right) N$. *Thus, we deduce that (unconditionally) with probability* $1 - \frac{2m}{N^{10}}$, $S_j^{t+1} \geq \frac{\mu N}{2m}$ *for all j.*

Proof. The proof follows from Chernoff-Hoeffding bound (Theorem 4.1), noting that $\gamma \geq \frac{\mu}{m}$ from (2), and taking a union bound over all $j \in [m]$. For the latter part, note that for any fixed $t$ and for all $j$, with probability at least $1 - \frac{2m}{N^{10}}$, $S_j^{t+1} \geq \frac{1}{1+2\delta'} \frac{\mu N}{m}$. Since $\delta' \leq \frac{1}{2}$, this implies that with probability at least $1 - \frac{2m}{N^{10}}$, we have $S_j^{t+1} \geq \frac{\mu N}{2m}$. □

**Stage 2.** There are two outcomes for each option $j$: $R_j^{t+1} = 1$ and $R_j^{t+1} = 0$. Let $Z_{ij}^{t+1}$ be the indicator random variable for the event that $i$ commits to $j$ in stage two of the process. Note that

$$\mathbb{P}\left[Z_{ij}^{t+1} = 1 \,\middle|\, \mathcal{S}_j^{t+1}, R_j^{t+1}, t\right] = \beta^{R_j^{t+1}} (1-\beta)^{1-R_j^{t+1}} \geq (1-\beta) \tag{3}$$

if $i \in \mathcal{S}_j^{t+1}$ since $\beta \geq 1/2$, and $\mathbb{P}\left[Z_{ij}^{t+1} = 1 \,\middle|\, \mathcal{S}_j^{t+1}, R_j^{t+1}, t\right] = 0$ otherwise. Let $D_j^{t+1} = \sum_{j \in \mathcal{S}_j^{t+1}} Z_{ij}^{t+1}$. It follows from linearity of expectation that $\mathbb{E}\left[D_j^{t+1} \,\middle|\, \mathcal{S}_j^{t+1}, R_j^{t+1}, t\right] = S_j^{t+1} \beta^{R_j^{t+1}} (1-\beta)^{1-R_j^{t+1}}$.

Proposition 4.7. *Let* $t \geq 0$ *be fixed. For* $\delta'' := \sqrt{\frac{60m\ln N}{(1-\beta)\mu N}} \leq \frac{1}{2}$, *with probability greater than* $1 - \frac{4m}{N^{10}}$ *(conditioned on everything up to time* $t, \mathcal{S}_j^{t+1}, R_j^{t+1}$*), for and all j* $D_j^{t+1} \overset{1+2\delta''}{\sim} S_j^{t+1} \beta^{R_j^{t+1}} (1-\beta)^{1-R_j^{t+1}}$.

Proof. The proof again follows from Chernoff-Hoeffding bound (Theorem 4.1), noting that $\gamma \geq 1-\beta$ from (3), and taking a union bound over all $j \in [m]$. Here we have also used Theorem 4.6 that $S_j^{t+1} \geq \frac{\mu N}{2m}$ for large enough $N$ for all $j$ with probability at least $1 - \frac{2m}{N^{10}}$. □

Combining Theorem 4.6 and Theorem 4.7 we obtain the following.

Proposition 4.8. *Let* $t \geq 0$ *be fixed. Let* $\delta'' := \sqrt{\frac{60m\ln N}{(1-\beta)\mu N}}$. *With probability greater than* $1 - \frac{6m}{N^{10}}$ *(conditioned on everything up to time* $t, R_j^{t+1}$*)*

$$D_j^{t+1} \overset{1+6\delta''}{\sim} \left((1-\mu)Q_j^t + \frac{\mu}{m}\right) N \beta^{R_j^{t+1}} (1-\beta)^{1-R_j^{t+1}}.$$

Proof. Follows directly from Theorem 4.6 and Theorem 4.7 and noting that $\delta' \leq \delta'' \leq \frac{1}{2}$. Thus

$$(1+2\delta')(1+2\delta'') \leq 1 + 2\delta' + 2\delta'' + 4\delta'\delta'' \leq 1 + 6\delta''.$$

□

Now we establish a relationship between the probability distributions $P^t$ and $Q^t$. Note that both processes start with $P^0 = Q^0$. Let $\delta_t := 5^t \delta''$.

Lemma 4.9. *There is a coupling such that* $P_j^t \overset{1+\delta_t}{\sim} Q_j^t$ *with probability at least* $1 - \frac{6tm}{N^{10}}$ *for all choices of* $\{R_j^t\}$*s.*

Proof. As suggested by our notation, we couple $P_j^t$ and $Q_j^t$ so that the realizations of the $R_j^t$s is the same in both processes for all $j$ and all $t$.

The proof proceeds by induction on $t$. The statement holds when $t = 0$ as, by definition, $P^0 = Q^0$. Assume it holds for $t$. Thus, with probability at least $1 - \frac{6tm}{N^{10}}$, $P_j^t \overset{1+\delta_t}{\sim} Q_j^t$. Let us condition on this event. Recall that

$$P_j^{t+1} = \frac{\left((1-\mu)P_j^t + \frac{\mu}{m}\right) \beta^{R_j^{t+1}} (1-\beta)^{1-R_j^{t+1}}}{\sum_{k=1}^m \left((1-\mu)P_k^t + \frac{\mu}{m}\right) \beta^{R_k^{t+1}} (1-\beta)^{1-R_k^{t+1}}}.$$

Thus, with probability at least $1 - \frac{6tm}{N^{10}}$,

$$P_j^{t+1} \overset{(1+\delta_t)^2}{\sim} \frac{\left((1-\mu)Q_j^t + \frac{\mu}{m}\right) \beta^{R_j^{t+1}} (1-\beta)^{1-R_j^{t+1}}}{\sum_{k=1}^m \left((1-\mu)Q_k^t + \frac{\mu}{m}\right) \beta^{R_k^{t+1}} (1-\beta)^{1-R_k^{t+1}}}.$$

Here we used induction for both the numerator and the denominator. From Theorem 4.7, we know that

$$D_j^{t+1} \overset{1+6\delta''}{\sim} \left((1-\mu)Q_j^t + \frac{\mu}{m}\right) N \beta^{R_j^{t+1}} (1-\beta)^{1-R_j^{t+1}}$$

for all $j$ with probability at least $1 - \frac{6m}{N^{10}}$. Thus, we obtain that with probability at least $1 - \frac{6(t+1)m}{N^{10}}$

$$P_j^{t+1} \overset{(1+\delta_t)^2(1+6\delta'')^2}{\sim} \frac{D_j^{t+1}}{\sum_{k=1}^m D_k^{t+1}} = Q_j^{t+1}.$$

Now note that, assuming that $\delta_t = 5^t\delta'' \le 1$ and $\delta'' \le \frac{1}{40}$, $(1+\delta_t)^2(1+6\delta'')^2 \le (1+3\delta_t)(1+13\delta'') \le 1+3\delta_t+13\delta''+39\delta''\delta_t \le 1+4\delta_t+13\delta'' \le 1+5^{t+1}\delta'' = 1+\delta_{t+1}$ for $t \ge 2$. For $t=1$ the bound can be checked by a direct calculation. □

Hence, for any fixed set of $R_j^t$s, the trajectories $P^t$ and $Q^t$ remain close. Thus, using Theorem 4.4 and Theorem 4.9, we obtain that $\eta_1 - \left(1+5^T\delta''\right)\frac{1}{T}\sum_{t=1}^T\sum_{j=1}^m \mathbb{E}\left[Q_j^{t-1}R_j^t\right] - \frac{6T^2m}{NT} \le \frac{\ln m}{\delta T} + 2\delta$. Here, the first negative term in the left hand side of the equation occurs when Theorem 4.9 applies and the second negative term is when it does not. Rearranging, we obtain $\eta_1 - \frac{1}{T}\sum_{t=1}^T\sum_{j=1}^m \mathbb{E}\left[Q_j^{t-1}R_j^t\right] \le \frac{\ln m}{\delta T} + 2\delta + 5^T\delta'' + \frac{6mT}{N^{10}}$. Since $\delta'' := \sqrt{\frac{240m\ln N}{(1-\beta)\mu N}} \le \sqrt{\frac{c\ln N}{N}}$ for $c = \frac{240m}{(1-\beta)\mu}$. Thus, when $T = \frac{\ln m}{\delta^2}$, $5^T\delta'' \le \frac{m^{\frac{\ln 5}{\delta^2}}\sqrt{c\ln N}}{\sqrt{N}}$. Hence, when $N$ is such that

$$\frac{N}{\ln N} \ge \frac{cm^{\frac{2\ln 5}{\delta^2}}}{\delta''^2} \text{ and } N^{10} \ge \frac{6m\ln m}{\delta^3}, \tag{4}$$

then

$$\text{Regret}_N(T) = \eta_1 - \frac{1}{T}\sum_{t=1}^T\sum_{j=1}^m \mathbb{E}\left[Q_j^{t-1}R_j^t\right] \le 5\delta. \tag{5}$$

This concludes the proof of Theorem 4.5 when $T = \frac{\ln m}{\delta^2}$.

*4.3.2* ***Large*** *T.* For large $T$ we need one new ingredient; here we focus on this additional aspect. We first need a slight generalization of Theorem 4.4 to handle $P^0$ that are not uniform. This is similar to the version of MWU with *restricted distributions* as in Theorem 2.4 in [4].

Theorem 4.10 (Regret of Infinite Population Distributed Learning Dynamics with Nonuniform Start). *Let $\eta_1 \ge \eta_2 \ge \cdots \ge \eta_m$, let $\frac{1}{2} < \beta \le \frac{e}{e+1}$ (and hence $0 < \delta \le 1$), and let $6\mu \le \delta^2$. Let $P_j^0 \ge \zeta$ for all $j \in \{1,\ldots,m\}$ and $\{P^t\}_{t=1}^T$ be the probability distributions produced by the MWU process with stochastic rewards $\{R^t\}_{t=1}^T$. Then for $T \ge \frac{\ln(1/\zeta)}{\delta^2}$, the average expected regret after T steps is $\text{Regret}_\infty(T) = \eta_1 - \frac{1}{T}\cdot\sum_{t=1}^T\sum_{j=1}^m \mathbb{E}\left[P_j^{t-1}R_j^t\right] \le 3\delta$.*

The proof closely follows from that of Theorem 4.4, and we omit the details.

Similarly, the results in Section 4.3.1 for small $T$ follow analogously with nonuniform start. This just requires us to chose $N$ slightly bigger in particular, instead of (4), we would need $N$ such that $\frac{N}{\ln N} \ge \frac{c\left(\frac{1}{\zeta}\right)^{\frac{2\ln 5}{\delta^2}}}{\delta''^2}$ and $N^{10} \ge \frac{6\ln m}{\zeta\delta^3}$. This gives that the regret of the finite population distributed learning dynamics is at most $5\delta$ when $T = \frac{\ln(1/\zeta)}{\delta^2}$. We now complete the proof of Theorem 4.5 for large $T$, by breaking the time into epochs consisting of $\frac{\ln(1/\zeta)}{\delta^2}$ time steps. In each epoch, we couple an infinite population distributed learning dynamics with the finite population distributed learning dynamics such that the starting points are identical at the beginning of each epoch, and both observe the same sequence of rewards $R_j^t$s.

It remains to lower bound $\zeta$ appropriately. From Theorem 4.8, it follows that for any $t$, with probability at least $1-\frac{6m}{N^{10}}$, for all $j$ $Q_j^t \ge \frac{\mu(1-\beta)}{4m}$. We let $\zeta := \frac{\mu(1-\beta)}{4m}$, and hence our epochs are of length $\frac{\ln\left(\frac{4m}{\mu(1-\beta)}\right)}{\delta^2}$. This gives us regret $\eta_1 - \frac{1}{T}\sum_{t=1}^T\sum_{j=1}^m \mathbb{E}\left[Q_j^{t-1}R_j^t\right] \le 5\delta + \frac{Tm}{N^{10}}$. The additive term of $\frac{Tm}{N^{10}}$ is precisely due to the fact that with probability $\frac{6m}{N^{10}}$, the above inequality will not be satisfied, in which case the regret could be at most 1 for that epoch. Finally, note that $N^{10}$ is arbitrary and can be made as large as required at the expense of constants. This concludes the proof of Theorem 4.5.

## 5 PROOF OF THEOREM 4.4

Let us define the potential function $\Phi^T := \sum_{j=1}^m W_j^T$, and recall that $e^\delta = \frac{\beta}{1-\beta}$. Then,

$$\begin{aligned}
\Phi^T &= \sum_{j=1}^m W_j^T \\
&= (1-\beta)\sum_{j=1}^m\left((1-\mu)W_j^{T-1} + \frac{\mu}{m}\sum_{k=1}^m W_k^{T-1}\right)e^{\delta R_j^T} \\
&= (1-\beta)\Phi^{T-1}\sum_{j=1}^m\left((1-\mu)P_j^{T-1} + \frac{\mu}{m}\right)e^{\delta R_j^T} \\
&\le (1-\beta)\Phi^{T-1}\sum_{j=1}^m\left((1-\mu)P_j^{T-1} + \frac{\mu}{m}\right)\left(1+(e^\delta-1)R_j^T\right) \\
&= (1-\beta)\Phi^{T-1}\left(1+(e^\delta-1)\sum_{j=1}^m\left((1-\mu)P_j^{T-1}+\frac{\mu}{m}\right)R_j^T\right) \\
&\le (1-\beta)\Phi^{T-1}\left(1+\mu(e^\delta-1)+(1-\mu)(e^\delta-1)\sum_{j=1}^m P_j^{T-1}R_j^T\right).
\end{aligned}$$

Here, the first inequality follows from the assumption that $0 \le R_j^T \le 1$ and Fact 4.3. The last inequality follows from the assumption that $0 \le R_j^T \le 1$.

Now, we let $\delta' := \frac{(1-\mu)(e^\delta-1)}{1+\mu\delta}$ and, using the inequality $\delta \le e^\delta - 1$, obtain that

$$\begin{aligned}
\Phi^T &\le (1-\beta)(1+\mu(e^\delta-1))\Phi^{T-1}\times \\
&\quad\left(1+\frac{(1-\mu)(e^\delta-1)}{1+\mu\delta}\sum_{j=1}^m P_j^{T-1}R_j^T\right) \\
&\overset{1+\delta'x\le e^{\delta'x}}{\le} (1-\beta)(1+\mu(e^\delta-1))\Phi^{T-1}e^{\delta'\sum_{j=1}^m P_j^{T-1}R_j^T} \\
&\overset{\Phi^0=m}{\le} (1-\beta)^T(1+\mu(e^\delta-1))^T m e^{\delta'\sum_{t=1}^T\sum_{j=1}^m P_j^{t-1}R_j^t}.
\end{aligned}$$

On the other hand,

$$\Phi^T \ge (1-\beta)^T(1-\mu)^T e^{\delta\sum_{t=1}^T R_1^t}.$$

Combining the lower bound and upper bound and taking logarithms we obtain

$$\delta\sum_{t=1}^T R_1^t \le \ln m + T\ln\left(\frac{1+\mu(e^\delta-1)}{1-\mu}\right) + \delta'\sum_{t=1}^T\sum_{j=1}^m P_j^{t-1}R_j^t.$$

Thus,

$$\delta\sum_{t=1}^T R_1^t - \delta'\sum_{t=1}^T\sum_{j=1}^m P_j^{t-1}R_j^t \le \ln m + T\ln\left(\frac{1+\mu(e^\delta-1)}{1-\mu}\right).$$

Now, for $\mu \leq \frac{1}{2}$ we know that $\frac{1}{1-\mu} \leq 1 + 2\mu$. Also, $1 + \mu(e^{\delta} - 1) \leq 1 + \mu(e - 1)$. Thus, as $\mu \leq \frac{1}{2}$, $\frac{1+\mu(e^{\delta}-1)}{1-\mu} \leq (1 + (e - 1)\mu)(1 + 2\mu) \leq 1 + (e + 1)\mu + 2(e - 1)\mu^2 \leq 1 + 2e\mu \leq 1 + 6\mu$. Hence, using the inequality $\ln(1 + x) \leq x$ for all $x \geq 0$, we obtain

$$\ln\left(\frac{1 + \mu(e^{\delta} - 1)}{1 - \mu}\right) \leq 6\mu.$$

Further, using the fact that $e^{\delta} - 1 \leq \delta + \delta^2$ for $0 \leq \delta \leq 1$, which is implied by the assumption that $\beta \leq \frac{e}{1+e}$, it can be seen that

$$\delta' = \frac{(1 - \mu)(e^{\delta} - 1)}{1 + \mu\delta} \leq \frac{(1 - \mu)\delta(1 + \delta)}{1 + \mu\delta} \leq \delta(1 + \delta).$$

Therefore,

$$\delta\left(\sum_{t=1}^{T} R_1^t - (1 + \delta)\sum_{t=1}^{T}\sum_{j=1}^{m} P_j^{t-1}R_j^t\right) \leq \ln m + 6\mu T.$$

Note that $\sum_{t=1}^{T}\sum_{j=1}^{m} P_j^{t-1}R_j^t \leq T$, hence, the above implies that

$$\delta\left(\sum_{t=1}^{T} R_1^t - \sum_{t=1}^{T}\sum_{j=1}^{m} P_j^{t-1}R_j^t\right) \leq \ln m + (\delta^2 + 6\mu)T.$$

Taking expectations and dividing by $T\delta$ we obtain the following regret bound.

$$\eta_1 - \frac{1}{T}\cdot\sum_{t=1}^{T}\sum_{j=1}^{m}\mathbb{E}\left[P_j^{t-1}R_j^t\right] \leq \frac{\ln m}{\delta T} + \left(\delta + \frac{6\mu}{\delta}\right).$$

Assuming $6\mu \leq \delta^2$ we obtain

$$\eta_1 - \frac{1}{T}\cdot\sum_{t=1}^{T}\sum_{j=1}^{m}\mathbb{E}\left[P_j^{t-1}R_j^t\right] \leq \frac{\ln m}{\delta T} + 2\delta.$$

Thus, for $T \geq \frac{\ln m}{\delta^2}$, we obtain the desired bound

$$\text{Regret}_{\infty}(T) \leq 3\delta.$$

From this we can derive the lower bound on the probability that the best option $j = 1$ is selected as stated in the second part of the theorem. Firstly, it follows (as $R_j^t$ is independent of $P_j^{t-1}$) that for all $T \geq 1$

$$\eta_1 - \frac{1}{T}\cdot\sum_{t=1}^{T}\sum_{j=1}^{m}\eta_j\,\mathbb{E}\left[P_j^{t-1}\right] \leq \frac{\ln m}{\delta T} + 2\delta.$$

Thus,

$$\eta_1\left(1 - \frac{1}{T}\cdot\sum_{t=1}^{T}\mathbb{E}\left[P_1^{t-1}\right]\right) - \frac{\eta_2}{T}\cdot\sum_{t=1}^{T}\sum_{j=2}^{m}\mathbb{E}\left[P_j^{t-1}\right] \leq \frac{\ln m}{\delta T} + 2\delta.$$

From this we obtain

$$(\eta_1 - \eta_2)\left(1 - \frac{1}{T}\cdot\sum_{t=1}^{T}\mathbb{E}\left[P_1^{t-1}\right]\right) \leq \frac{\ln m}{\delta T} + 2\delta,$$

and consequently for $T \geq \frac{\ln m}{\delta^2}$,

$$\frac{1}{T}\sum_{t=1}^{T}\mathbb{E}\left[P_1^{t-1}\right] \geq 1 - \frac{3\delta}{\eta_1 - \eta_2}.$$

This completes the proof.

## 6 CONCLUSION AND FUTURE WORK

In this work we study a fundamental distributed learning dynamics prevalent in various social and biological contexts and provide the first convergence and regret bounds for it in the finite population setting. The connection between this learning dynamics and the MWU method suggests a novel distributed and essentially memoryless implementation of the MWU method. Another interpretation of our result comes by looking at the infinite population limit of the distributed learning dynamics; while an individual can be effectively solving a stochastic multi-armed bandit problem, the population as a whole is solving a full-information version of the problem, and hence can be very efficient on the group-level.

Several important directions remain open. The first is to extend our results to the social network setting where individuals can only sample in step (1) from their neighbors. The question here would be whether, and to what extent, the efficiency of the group remains as a function of the network topology. It would also be interesting to explore the distributed learning algorithms when the parameters controlling the quality of the options ($\eta_i$s) are allowed to change, or when there is dependence across options and time (e.g., when the options represent stocks). Lastly, we note that as an algorithm designer, if we were to implement these learning dynamics as a distributed approximation to the stochastic version of MWU method, we can optimize $\beta$ to attain the usual $O\left(\sqrt{\ln m/T}\right)$ regret; in the distributed learning dynamics, we are constrained by the behavior of the group – the regret bound will only be as good as the $\beta$ they use. This naturally raises the question of whether human groups match the ideal values for $\beta$, perhaps in a context-specific manner, to achieve good regret bounds.

## ACKNOWLEDGMENTS

The authors would like to thank Ashish Goel for useful discussions, and the BIRS-CMO 2016 Workshop on Models and Algorithms for Crowds and Networks, where part of this work was done. The first author was supported in part by an SNF Project Grant (205121_163385).

## REFERENCES

[1] Yehuda Afek, Noga Alon, Omer Barad, Eran Hornstein, Naama Barkai, and Ziv Bar-Joseph. A biological solution to a fundamental distributed computing problem. *Science*, 331(6014):183–185, 2011.
[2] Animashree Anandkumar, Nithin Michael, Ao Kevin Tang, and Ananthram Swami. Distributed algorithms for learning and cognitive medium access with logarithmic regret. *IEEE Journal on Selected Areas in Communications*, 29(4):731–745, 2011.
[3] Dana Angluin, James Aspnes, Zoë Diamadi, Michael J. Fischer, and René Peralta. Computation in networks of passively mobile finite-state sensors. *Distributed Computing*, 18(4):235–253, 2006.
[4] Sanjeev Arora, Elad Hazan, and Satyen Kale. The multiplicative weights update method: a meta-algorithm and applications. *Theory of Computing*, 8(1):121–164, 2012.
[5] Abhijit V Banerjee. A simple model of herd behavior. *The Quarterly Journal of Economics*, pages 797–817, 1992.
[6] L. Becchetti, A. Clementi, E. Natale, F. Pasquale, and L. Trevisan. Stabilizing consensus with many opinions. In *Proceedings of the Twenty-seventh Annual ACM-SIAM Symposium on Discrete Algorithms*, SODA '16, pages 620–635, Philadelphia, PA, USA, 2016. Society for Industrial and Applied Mathematics.
[7] Bret Alexander Beheim, Calvin Thigpen, and Richard McElreath. Strategic social learning and the population dynamics of human behavior: The game of Go. *Evolution and Human Behavior*, 35(5):351–357, 2014.
[8] Michel Benaïm, Josef Hofbauer, and Sylvain Sorin. Stochastic approximations and differential inclusions. *SIAM J. Control and Optimization*, 44(1):328–348, 2005.

[9] Michel Benaïm and Jörgen W Weibull. Deterministic approximation of stochastic evolution in games. *Econometrica*, 71(3):873–903, 2003.

[10] Ginestra Bianconi and Albert-László Barabási. Bose-Einstein condensation in complex networks. *Physical Review Letters*, 86(24):5632, 2001.

[11] Ken Binmore and Larry Samuelson. Muddling through: Noisy equilibrium selection. *journal of economic theory*, 74(2):235–265, 1997.

[12] Jonas Björnerstedt and Jörgen Weibull. Nash equilibrium and evolution by imitation. Technical report, Research Institute of Industrial Economics, 1994.

[13] Avrim Blum, MohammadTaghi Hajiaghayi, Katrina Ligett, and Aaron Roth. Regret minimization and the price of total anarchy. In *Proceedings of the fortieth annual ACM symposium on Theory of computing*, pages 373–382. ACM, 2008.

[14] Robert Boyd and Peter J Richerson. *Culture and the evolutionary process*. University of Chicago Press, 1988.

[15] Antonio Cabrales. Stochastic replicator dynamics. *International Economic Review*, 41(2):451–481, 2000.

[16] Erick Chastain, Adi Livnat, Christos Papadimitriou, and Umesh Vazirani. Algorithms, games, and evolution. *Proceedings of the National Academy of Sciences*, 111(29):10620–10623, 2014.

[17] Bernard Chazelle. Natural algorithms and influence systems. *Commun. ACM*, 55(12):101–110, December 2012.

[18] Paul Christiano, Jonathan A. Kelner, Aleksander Madry, Daniel A. Spielman, and Shang-Hua Teng. Electrical flows, laplacian systems, and faster approximation of maximum flow in undirected graphs. In *Proceedings of the 43rd ACM Symposium on Theory of Computing, STOC 2011, San Jose, CA, USA, 6-8 June 2011*, pages 273–282, 2011.

[19] Alejandro Cornejo, Anna Dornhaus, Nancy Lynch, and Radhika Nagpal. Task allocation in ant colonies. In *International Symposium on Distributed Computing*, pages 46–60. Springer, 2014.

[20] Devdatt P Dubhashi and Alessandro Panconesi. *Concentration of measure for the analysis of randomized algorithms*. Cambridge University Press, 2009.

[21] Peter Duersch, Jörg Oechssler, and Burkhard Schipper. Once beaten, never again: Imitation in two-player potential games. Technical report, University of California, Davis, Department of Economics, 2011.

[22] Glenn Ellison and Drew Fudenberg. Word-of-mouth communication and social learning. *The Quarterly Journal of Economics*, pages 93–125, 1995.

[23] David M Estlund. Opinion leaders, independence, and condorcet's jury theorem. *Theory and Decision*, 36(2):131–162, 1994.

[24] Simon Fischer and Berthold Vöcking. On the evolution of selfish routing. In *European Symposium on Algorithms*, pages 323–334. Springer, 2004.

[25] Yi Gai and Bhaskar Krishnamachari. Decentralized online learning algorithms for opportunistic spectrum access. In *Global Telecommunications Conference (GLOBECOM 2011), 2011 IEEE*, pages 1–6. IEEE, 2011.

[26] John Gale, Kenneth G Binmore, and Larry Samuelson. Learning to be imperfect: The ultimatum game. *Games and Economic Behavior*, 8(1):56–90, 1995.

[27] Mohsen Ghaffari, Cameron Musco, Tsvetomira Radeva, and Nancy A. Lynch. Distributed house-hunting in ant colonies. In *Proceedings of the 2015 ACM Symposium on Principles of Distributed Computing, PODC 2015, Donostia-San Sebastián, Spain, July 21 - 23, 2015*, pages 57–66, 2015.

[28] Daniel Golovin, Matthew Faulkner, and Andreas Krause. Online distributed sensor selection. In *Proceedings of the 9th ACM/IEEE International Conference on Information Processing in Sensor Networks*, pages 220–231. ACM, 2010.

[29] Boris Granovskiy, Jason M Gold, David JT Sumpter, and Robert L Goldstone. Integration of social information by human groups. *Topics in Cognitive Science*, 7(3):469–493, 2015.

[30] Joseph Henrich. Cultural transmission and the diffusion of innovations: Adoption dynamics indicate that biased cultural transmission is the predominate force in behavioral change. *American Anthropologist*, 103(4):992–1013, 2001.

[31] Peter M Krafft, Julia Zheng, Wei Pan, Nicolás Della Penna, Yaniv Altshuler, Erez Shmueli, Joshua B Tenenbaum, and Alex Pentland. Human collective intelligence as distributed bayesian inference. *arXiv preprint arXiv:1608.01987*, 2016.

[32] Coco Krumme, Manuel Cebrian, Galen Pickard, and Alex Pentland. Quantifying social influence in an online cultural market. *PLoS ONE*, 7(5):e33785, 2012.

[33] Keqin Liu and Qing Zhao. Decentralized multi-armed bandit with multiple distributed players. In *Information Theory and Applications Workshop (ITA), 2010*, pages 1–10. IEEE, 2010.

[34] Richard McElreath, Adrian V Bell, Charles Efferson, Mark Lubell, Peter J Richerson, and Timothy Waring. Beyond existence and aiming outside the laboratory: Estimating frequency-dependent and pay-off-biased social learning strategies. *Philosophical Transactions of the Royal Society B: Biological Sciences*, 363(1509):3515–3528, 2008.

[35] Cameron Musco, Hsin-Hao Su, and Nancy Lynch. Ant-inspired density estimation via random walks. In *Proceedings of the 2016 ACM Symposium on Principles of Distributed Computing*, pages 469–478. ACM, 2016.

[36] Naumaan Nayyar, Dileep Kalathil, and Rahul Jain. On regret-optimal learning in decentralized multi-player multi-armed bandits. *arXiv preprint arXiv:1505.00553*, 2015.

[37] Martin A Nowak. *Evolutionary dynamics*. Harvard University Press, 2006.

[38] Robin Pemantle. When are touchpoints limits for generalized pólya urns? *Proceedings of the American Mathematical Society*, pages 235–243, 1991.

[39] Alex Pentland. *Social Physics: How Good Ideas Spread-The Lessons from a New Science*. Penguin, 2014.

[40] Stephen C Pratt, David JT Sumpter, Eamonn B Mallon, and Nigel R Franks. An agent-based model of collective nest choice by the ant Temnothorax albipennis. *Animal Behaviour*, 70(5):1023–1036, 2005.

[41] Alan R Rogers. Does biology constrain culture? *American Anthropologist*, 90(4):819–831, 1988.

[42] Larry Samuelson and Jianbo Zhang. Evolutionary stability in asymmetric games. *Journal of economic theory*, 57(2):363–391, 1992.

[43] Thomas D Seeley and Susannah C Buhrman. Group decision making in swarms of honey bees. *Behavioral Ecology and Sociobiology*, 45(1):19–31, 1999.

[44] Karl Sigmund et al. *Evolutionary Game Dynamics: American Mathematical Society Short Course, January 4-5, 2011, New Orleans, Louisiana*, volume 69. American Mathematical Soc., 2011.

[45] John Maynard Smith. *Evolution and the Theory of Games*. Cambridge university press, 1982.

[46] Damian Straszak and Nisheeth K Vishnoi. IRLS and slime mold: Equivalence and convergence. *Invited at the Innovations in Theoretical Computer Science*, 2017.

[47] Hsin-Hao Su. *Algorithms for Fundamental Problems in Computer Networks*. PhD thesis, ETH Zürich, 2015.

[48] Peter D Taylor. Evolutionarily stable strategies with two types of player. *Journal of applied probability*, pages 76–83, 1979.

[49] Nisheeth K Vishnoi. The speed of evolution. In *Proc. 26th Annual ACM-SIAM Symp. Discret. Algorithms (SODA)*, pages 1590–1601, 2015.

[50] Nicholas C Wormald. Differential equations for random processes and random graphs. *The annals of applied probability*, pages 1217–1235, 1995.

# Brief Announcement: Population Protocols for Leader Election and Exact Majority with $O(\log^2 n)$ States and $O(\log^2 n)$ Convergence Time*

Andreas Bilke
Dept Computer Sciences, University of Salzburg
Salzburg, Austria
abilke@cosy.sbg.ac.at

Colin Cooper
Dept Informatics, King's College London
London WC2R 2LS, U.K.
colin.cooper@kcl.ac.uk

Robert Elsässer
Dept Computer Sciences, University of Salzburg
Salzburg, Austria
elsa@cosy.sbg.ac.at

Tomasz Radzik
Dept Informatics, King's College London
London WC2R 2LS, U.K.
tomasz.radzik@kcl.ac.uk

## ABSTRACT

We consider the model of population protocols, which can be viewed as a sequence of random pairwise interactions of $n$ agents (nodes). During each interaction, two agents $v$ and $w$ selected uniformly at random update their states on the basis of their current states, and the whole system should in long run converge towards a desired global final configuration. We study population protocols for two problems: the leader election and the exact majority voting. Both protocols use $\Theta(\log^2 n)$ states per agent and run in $O(\log^2 n)$ rounds (the number of interactions divided by $n$), w.h.p. and in expectation, improving on the running time of the $\Theta(\log^2 n)$-state protocols proposed recently by Alistarh *et al.* [SODA 2017]. Our protocols are based on the idea of agents counting their local interactions and rely on the probabilistic fact that the uniform random selection would limit the divergence of the individual counts.

## CCS CONCEPTS

• **Theory of computation → Distributed algorithms**;

## KEYWORDS

Population protocols; leader election; exact majority

## 1 INTRODUCTION

The computation of a *population protocol* [4] is a (perpetual) sequence of pairwise interactions between agents (nodes). The system consists of a set $V$ of $n$ nodes and a *scheduler* which keeps selecting pairs of nodes for interaction. The objective is that the whole system eventually stabilizes in (converges to) a configuration which has some desired target property. We assume a complete communication graph and the random uniform scheduler. That is, each pair of nodes has equal probability to be selected for interaction in the current step, independently of previous interactions.

The *leader election* starts with all nodes in the same initial state and the goal is to converge to a configuration with exactly one agent in a distinguished 'leader' state. The (two-opinion) *exact majority voting* starts with each node in one of two states $q_A$ and $q_B$, representing two distinct opinions/votes $A$ and $B$. Initially $a_0$ nodes hold opinion $A$ and $b_0$ nodes hold opinion $B$, and we assume $a_0 \neq b_0$. The goal is that eventually all nodes will have the opinion of the initial majority. The exact majority voting has to guarantee the correct answer even if $|a_0 - b_0| = 1$.

A population protocol is defined by a set of states $S$, a set of outputs $\Gamma$, a deterministic transition function $\delta : S \times S \longrightarrow S \times S$, which shows how the two interacting agents change their states, and an *output function* $\gamma : S \longrightarrow \Gamma$. For the exact majority voting, $\Gamma = \{A, B\}$, and a protocol should eventually reach a step $t$ such that in each step $t' \geq t$, each node $v \in V$ is in a state $q(v, t)$ such that $\gamma(q(v, t))$ is the initial majority opinion. For leader election protocols, the output values are $L$ and $F$, indicating the leader or a follower. The goal is to reach a step such that in all subsequent steps exactly one (and the same) node outputs $L$. The *completion (convergence) time* of a protocol is a random variable denoting the round when the system stabilizes on the desired property. The objectives in design of population protocols are to keep the number of states and the convergence time as low as possible.

**Previous work.** Draief and Vojnović [8] and Mertzios *et al.* [9] analyse four-state exact-majority protocols, where throughout the computation each node has either a 'strong' opinion $A$ or $B$ (as in the initial configuration), or their 'weak' version $a$ or $b$. Two opposite strong opinions cancel each other and change into weak opinions, if they interact. The strong opinions which are still alive keep 'converting' the passive opposite opinions. Mertzios *et al.* [9] prove that the expected convergence time of such a protocol is $O(n^5)$ for any graph and $O((n \log n)/|a_0 - b_0|)$ for complete graphs. Draief and Vojnović [8] derive a $2n(\log n + 1)/|a_0 - b_0|$ upper bound on the expected convergence time as well as upper bounds for cycles, stars and Erdős-Rényi graphs.

Alistarh *et al.* [3] achieve a $O(\text{polylog}\, n)$-time exact majority protocol by starting with multiplying all initial strong opinions by $r$,

*Full version available at https://arxiv.org/abs/1705.01146.


*PODC '17, July 25-27, 2017, Washington, DC, USA*

ACM ISBN 978-1-4503-4992-5/17/07.
https://doi.org/10.1145/3087801.3087858

where $1 \le r \le n$. That is, initially each node contains either $r$ opinions (tokens) $A$ or $r$ opinions $B$. The imbalance between the strong opinions remains at $|a_0 - b_0|r$ throughout the computation, speeding up both the canceling of strong opinions and the converting of weak opinions of the initial minority. On complete graphs this protocol converges in expected $O((n \log n)/(|a_0 - b_0|r) + \log n \log r)$ time and w.h.p.[1] in $O((n \log^2 n)/(|a_0 - b_0|r) + \log^2 n)$ time, requiring $r + O(\log n \log r)$ states. Thus this protocol needs $|a_0 - b_0| = \Omega(n/\text{polylog}\, n)$ or $\Omega(n/\text{polylog}\, n)$ states to achieve $O(\text{polylog}\, n)$ time. This protocol is modified in Alistarh *et al.* [1] to achieve $O(\log^3 n)$ time, w.h.p. and in expectation, with $O(\log^2 n)$ states.

A suite of polylog -time population protocols for various functions, including exact majority, was proposed by Angluin *et al.* [5], but they require a unique predefined leader to synchronize the progress of computation. Their exact-majority protocol runs w.h.p. in $O(\log^2 n)$ time with constant number of states, but may fail with some small probability. The protocols in [5] are based on the idea of alternating *cancellations* and *duplications* of tokens. In the context of exact majority, the cancellations stop when the number of strong opinions is reduced w.h.p. to less than $cn$, for a small constant $c < 1$. This is then followed by interactions which ensure that w.h.p. all remaining strong opinions duplicate. One phase of canceling and duplicating of strong opinions takes $O(\log n)$ time and is repeated $O(\log n)$ times, boosting the imbalance between $A$ and $B$ to $\Theta(n)$.

Berenbrink *et al.* [6] consider population protocols for *plurality consensus*, which generalizes the majority voting problem to $k \ge 2$ opinions. Their results imply $O(\log n)$ time (w.h.p.) for complete graphs and $k = 2$, but this bound requires a polynomial number of states and the $\Theta(n)$ initial imbalance between the opinions.

The most recent population protocols for leader election are due to Alistarh and Gelashvili [2], who showed a protocol with $O(\log^3 n)$ states and $O(\log^3 n)$ time (in expectation and w.h.p.) and Alistarh *et al.* [1], who showed a protocol with $O(\log^2 n)$ states and $O(\log^{5.3} n)$ expected and $O(\log^{6.3} n)$ w.h.p. convergence time. Doty and Soloveichik [7] showed that any leader election protocol with constant number of states has at least linear expected convergence time. Subsequently, Alistarh *et al.* [1] showed that any leader-election or exact-majority protocol with $O(\log \log n)$ states has $\Omega(n/\text{polylog}\, n)$ expected time.

**Our contributions.** We present an exact-majority protocol for complete graphs which converges in $O(\log^2 n)$ time w.h.p. and in expectation, and uses $O(\log^2 n)$ states. Our protocol is based on the idea of alternating cancellation and duplication of opinions introduced in [5], but achieves all necessary synchronization without a leader. We present also a leader-election protocol which has the same $O(\log^2 n)$ asymptotic running time and the number of states. Our protocols improve on the time of the recent protocols proposed in [1] while requiring the same $O(\log^2 n)$ number of states.

Both our protocols are based on nodes maintaining their *local clocks* – the counters of their own interactions – which remain sufficiently closely synchronized due to the uniform random selection of interactions. $O(\log^2 n)$ states mean that each node can keep count of up to $O(\log^2 n)$ interactions. Both protocols use an $O(\log n)$-time asynchronous push-pull broadcast protocol to spread information throughout the system and to pull the local clocks together, if they start diverging. Our leader election protocol uses also a technique for simulating Bernoulli trials in a population protocol. The nodes count the number of successes within the same logarithmic number of trials and one can show that with constant probability the maximum number of successes occurs at a unique node. Such a node will become the leader. Since with constant probability two or more nodes have the same maximum number of successes, we need a process of testing which of these two cases has happened and restart the protocol in the latter case.

[1] w.h.p. – *with high probability* of at least $1 - n^{-\alpha}$ for a constant $\alpha > 0$.

## 2 EXACT MAJORITY PROTOCOL

The state of each node $v$ consists of the current opinion $v.vote \in \{A, B, \emptyset\}$ held by $v$, the counter of the interactions $v.time$ and three boolean values $v.doubled$, $v.done$ and $v.fail$. The time counter increases by 1 with each interaction of $v$ and is viewed as a pair of counters $v.phase$ and $v.step$: the first one counts $P = \log n + 1$ phases and the second one counts $\tau = C \log n$ steps in the current phase, where $C$ is a suitably large constant. The variables $v.doubled$, $v.done$ and $v.fail$, all initialized to *false*, indicate, respectively, whether the opinion held by $v$ has been already duplicated in the current phase, whether node $v$ has decided that its current opinion $v.vote$ is the majority opinion, and whether $v$ has realized that something has gone wrong. We say that $v$ is in a *fail* state, if $v.fail = true$, and in a *done* state, if $v.done = true$ and $v.fail = false$. Otherwise $v$ is in a *normal state*. The counter $v.time$ counts only to $C \log^2 n$, so the number of states is $O(\log^2 n)$.

We want the local times at the nodes to remain w.h.p. consistent throughout the computation, implying that each interaction is between two nodes in the same part or in two consecutive parts of the same phase, or one node in the last part of a phase while the other in the first part of the next phase. This would require the local clocks not to differ by more than $c \log n$, for some constant $0 < c \ll C$. However, since the number of interactions per node reaches $\Theta(\log^2 n)$, we should expect that eventually there will be nodes with clocks differing by $\omega(\log n)$. To keep the clocks close together, if the clocks of two interacting nodes are still consistent but at different phases, then the node at the lower phase jumps to the end of its phase. Such adjustments guarantee that w.h.p. for each phase $p$, there is a (global) time step $T$ such that each node is in phase $p$ and at step at most $c \log n$ within this phase.

Assuming that all nodes are in the beginning part of the same phase $p$, that is, for each node $v$, $v.phase = p$ and $v.step \in [0, c \log n)$, the computation during this phase proceeds w.h.p. in the following way. A node $v$ is in the *canceling stage* when its steps are in $[c \log n, (C/2 - c) \log n)$, and in the *doubling stage* when the steps are in $[(C/2 + 2c) \log n, (C - 5c) \log n)$. At the time when the first node $u$ reaches the next phase $p + 1$, all other nodes are w.h.p. at the end of phase $p$, that is, at steps in $[(C - 5c) \log n, C \log n)$. The push-pull broadcast started by $u$ brings all nodes up to phase $p + 1$ and at some point they all are in the beginning part of this phase. If there is already a node in state *done* or *fail*, then w.h.p. each node will be in one of these two states within $cn \log n$ (global) interactions, again by the asynchronous push-pull broadcast. If two interacting nodes are in normal states, then they participate in the canceling and doubling stages. For example, if both nodes are in the canceling stage of the same phase and have opposite votes, then they change to the no-vote $\emptyset$. If both nodes are in the doubling stage, exactly one of them has a vote and this vote has not been duplicated yet in this phase, then this vote is duplicated now: the copies and shared between the two nodes and the variables *doubled* are set.

If a node at the end of a phase has a vote not duplicated during this phase and all nodes are in normal states, then w.h.p. the minority opinion has been already eliminated. Such a node changes to state *done*. The *done* state propagates through the system, but may change to the *fail* state, if there are still two opposite votes. Two interacting nodes change into *fail* also when their local clocks are too far apart. The *fail* state propagates through the system and does not change to any non-*fail* state. The nodes in the *fail* state switch to a slow back-up four-state exact majority protocol.

The proof that w.h.p. $O(\log^2 n)$ time is sufficient to eliminate the minority opinion is based on the following invariant. When all nodes are in the beginning part of the same phase $p$ and all are still in normal states, then the difference between the number of opinions $A$ and $B$ is equal to $2^p |a_0 - b_0|$.

## 3 LEADER ELECTION

Our leader election protocol consists of two parts. The first part is an $O(\log n)$-time process of selecting leader candidates. This is done by all nodes performing w.h.p. the same $\Theta(\log n)$ number of Bernoulli trials and the leader candidates are the nodes which collect the maximum number of successes. At least one candidate is selected and exactly one candidate is selected with constant probability.[2]

The second part of the protocol is a process of testing whether there is exactly one candidate. This process consists of $O(\log n)$ *test phases* and each phase takes w.h.p. $O(\log n)$ time and gives either negative or non-negative answer. If there is exactly one candidate, then w.h.p. each test phase gives the non-negative answer. If there are two or more candidates, then each phase gives the negative answer with constant probability, so the first negative answer is obtained w.h.p. within $O(\log n)$ phases. The first phase with the negative answer causes the restart of the whole computation: the push-pull broadcast moves all nodes back to the beginning of the first part. When $\Theta(\log n)$ consecutive phases give only non-negative answers, then w.h.p. there is exactly one candidate, so each candidate declares itself the leader. In the low-probability event that two or more candidates declare themselves leaders, direct duels between leaders leave eventually only one surviving leader.

Since the first part of (each restart of) our protocol selects a unique candidate with constant probability, the number of restarts is constant in expectation. The number of test phases between two consecutive restarts can be bounded by a geometric random variable with constant expected value. These random variables are independent, so the total number of test phases (over all restarts) is w.h.p. $O(\log n)$ and the total time is w.h.p. $O(\log^2 n)$.

The state of each node includes a pair $\langle X, G \rangle$, where $X$ is the set to which the node belongs – $A$ or $B$, or $N$ for "not defined" – and $G \in \{0, 1, N\}$ supports Bernoulli trials. The number of states is $O(\log^2 n)$ because in the first part of the protocol each node counts its $O(\log n)$ Bernoulli trials and the successes in those trials. Moreover, in the second part each node counts its interactions up to $O(\log^2 n)$.

[2] *Constant probability* means here probability $p$ for a constant $0 < p < 1$.

**Selecting leader candidates.** The first part of the protocol can be viewed (roughly) as consisting of five phases: (i) partitioning of the nodes into two sets $A$ and $B$, (ii) setting the binary values $G$, (iii) waiting to ensure that w.h.p. each node has decided the set ($A$ or $B$) and the $G$ value, (iv) $C \log n$ Bernoulli trials at each node, and (v) eliminating from the leader contention all nodes with the number of successes less than the maximum.

At the beginning, each node has $\langle X, G \rangle = \langle N, N \rangle$. Every node, based on its interactions with other nodes, joins either set $A$ or $B$ (the first phase) and sets its $G$-value to either 0 or 1 (the second phase). W.h.p. for each of the four combinations of the set $A$ or $B$ and the $G$-value 0 or 1, the number of nodes having this combination will be $\Theta(n)$. The $B$ nodes perform $C \log n$ independent Bernoulli trials: each meeting with an $A$ node is a trial and the success is a meeting with an $A$ node which has the $G$ value 1. Each node with the maximum number of successes is a leader candidate. At least one node becomes a leader candidate but with constant probability there may be two or more candidates.

**Testing the number of leader candidates.** In each test phase, each leader candidate broadcasts a message of one of two types, say either message 1 or message 2. The general idea is that if there are two (or more) leader candidates, then with constant probability, in the same test phase one candidate broadcasts message 1 and some other candidate broadcasts message 2. The nodes realize that different types of messages are in the system and the whole protocol is restarted. The test phase gives the non-negative outcome, if there is only one leader candidate or if all leader candidates decide to broadcast the same message. The non-negative outcome leads to the next test phase. The limit on the number of test phases is set at $C \log n$. If a leader candidate does not recognize any other leader candidates during $C \log n$ phases, then it declares itself as the leader.

See the full version of this work for detailed descriptions and analysis of our protocols.

## ACKNOWLEDGMENTS

Partially supported by EPSRC, Grant No.: EP/M005038/1 and FWF (Austrian Science Fund), Grant No.: P27613.

## REFERENCES

[1] Dan Alistarh, James Aspnes, David Eisenstat, Rati Gelashvili, and Ronald L. Rivest. 2017. Time-Space Trade-offs in Population Protocols. In *Proc. SODA 2017*. 2560–2579.
[2] Dan Alistarh and Rati Gelashvili. 2015. Polylogarithmic-Time Leader Election in Population Protocols. In *Proc. ICALP 2015*. 479–491.
[3] Dan Alistarh, Rati Gelashvili, and Milan Vojnovic. 2015. Fast and Exact Majority in Population Protocols. In *Proc. PODC 2015*. 47–56.
[4] Dana Angluin, James Aspnes, Zoë Diamadi, Michael J. Fischer, and René Peralta. 2006. Computation in networks of passively mobile finite-state sensors. *Distributed Computing* 18, 4 (2006), 235–253.
[5] Dana Angluin, James Aspnes, and David Eisenstat. 2008. Fast computation by population protocols with a leader. *Distributed Computing* 21, 3 (2008), 183–199.
[6] Petra Berenbrink, Tom Friedetzky, Peter Kling, Frederik Mallmann-Trenn, and Chris Wastell. 2016. Plurality Consensus via Shuffling: Lessons Learned from Load Balancing. *CoRR* abs/1602.01342 (2016).
[7] David Doty and David Soloveichik. 2015. Stable leader election in population protocols requires linear time. In *Proc. DISC 2015*. 602–616.
[8] Moez Draief and Milan Vojnovic. 2010. Convergence Speed of Binary Interval Consensus. In *Proc. INFOCOM 2010*. 1792–1800.
[9] George B. Mertzios, Sotiris E. Nikoletseas, Christoforos L. Raptopoulos, and Paul G. Spirakis. 2014. Determining Majority in Networks with Local Interactions and Very Small Local Memory. In *Proc. ICALP 2014*. 871–882.

# Brief Announcement: Byzantine-Tolerant Machine Learning

Peva Blanchard
Swiss Federal Institute of Technology, Lausanne
peva.blanchard@epfl.ch

El Mahdi El Mhamdi*†
Swiss Federal Institute of Technology, Lausanne
elmahdi.elmhamdi@epfl.ch

Rachid Guerraoui
Swiss Federal Institute of Technology, Lausanne
rachid.guerraoui@epfl.ch

Julien Stainer‡
Swiss Federal Institute of Technology, Lausanne
julien.stainer@epfl.ch

## ABSTRACT

We report on *Krum*, the first *provably* Byzantine-tolerant aggregation rule for distributed Stochastic Gradient Descent (SGD). Krum guarantees the convergence of SGD even in a distributed setting where (asymptotically) up to half of the workers can be malicious adversaries trying to attack the learning system.

## CCS CONCEPTS

**•Mathematics of computing → Stochastic processes;** *Differential calculus;* **•Hardware → Robustness; •Theory of computation → Machine learning theory;**

## KEYWORDS

Distributed Stochastic Gradient Descent ; Adversarial Machine Learning

## 1 INTRODUCTION

The increasing amount of data involved as well as the growing complexity of models has led to learning schemes that require a lot of computational resources. As a consequence, most industry-grade machine-learning implementations are now distributed [1]. For example, as of 2012, Google reportedly used 16.000 processors to train an image classifier [8]. However, distributing a computation over several machines induces a higher risk of failures, including crashes and computation errors. In the worst case, the system may undergo *Byzantine* failures [5], i.e., completely arbitrary behaviors of some of the machines involved. In practice, such failures may be due to stalled processes, or biases in the way the data samples are distributed among the processes.

A classical approach to mask failures in distributed systems is to use a state machine replication protocol [11], which requires however state transitions to be applied by all processes. In the case of distributed machine learning, this constraint can be seen in two ways: either *(a)* the processes agree on a sample of data based on which they update their local parameter vectors, or *(b)* they agree on how the parameter vector should be updated. In case *(a)*, the sample of data has to be transmitted to each process, which then has to perform a heavyweight computation to update its local parameter vector. This entails communication and computational costs that defeat the entire purpose of distributing the work. In case *(b)*, the processes have no way to check if the chosen update for the parameter vector has indeed been computed correctly on real data (a Byzantine process could have proposed the update). Byzantine failures may easily prevent the convergence of the learning algorithm. Neither of these solutions is satisfactory in a realistic distributed machine learning setting.

In fact, most learning algorithms today rely on a core component, namely *stochastic gradient descent* (SGD) [4]. In a machine learning setting, a cost function – depending on the *parameter vector* – is minimized based on stochastic estimates of its gradient. Distributed implementations of SGD [12] typically take the following form: a single parameter server is in charge of updating the parameter vector, while worker processes perform the actual update estimation, based on the share of data they draw from un unknown distribution. The parameter server executes synchronous rounds, during each of which, the parameter vector is broadcast to the workers. In turn, each worker computes an estimate of the update to apply (an estimate of the *gradient*), and the parameter server aggregates their results to finally update the parameter vector. Today, this aggregation is typically implemented through averaging [10], or variants of it [6,12].

The motivation of this work is the question of how a distributed SGD can be devised to tolerate $f$ Byzantine processes among the $n$ workers. We provide the first provable answer to this question.

*Contributions.* We first show that no linear combination (current approaches) of the updates proposed by the workers can tolerate a *single* Byzantine worker. A non-linear, *distance-based* choice function, that chooses, among the proposed vectors, the vector "closest to everyone else" (for example by taking the vector that minimizes the sum of the distances to every other vector), might look appealing. Yet, such a distance-based choice tolerates only a single Byzantine worker. Two Byzantine workers can collude, one helping the other to be selected, by moving the barycenter of all the vectors farther from the "correct area". We formulate a Byzantine resilience property capturing sufficient conditions for

*E.M. El Mhamdi's work is funded by the Swiss National Science Foundation under the grant 200021_169588 TARBDA (*a Theoretical Approach to Robustness in Biological Distributed Algorithms*).
†Corresponding author.
‡P. Blanchard and J. Stainer are supported in part by the European ERC Grant 339539

*PODC '17, July 25-27, 2017, Washington, DC, USA*

ACM ISBN 978-1-4503-4992-5/17/07.
http://dx.doi.org/10.1145/3087801.3087861

the parameter server's choice to tolerate $f$ Byzantine workers. Essentially, to guarantee that the cost will decrease despite Byzantine workers, we require the parameter server's choice *(a)* to point, on average, to the same direction as the gradient and *(b)* to have statistical moments (up to the fourth moment) bounded above by a homogeneous polynomial in the moments of a correct estimator of the gradient. One way to ensure such a resilience property is to consider a *majority-based* approach, looking at every subset of $n - f$ vectors, and considering the subset with the smallest diameter. While this approach is more robust to Byzantine workers that propose vectors far from the correct area, its exponential computational cost is prohibitive. Interestingly, combining the intuitions of the *majority-based* and *distance-based* methods, we can choose the vector that is somehow the closest to its $n - f$ neighbors. Namely, the one that minimizes a distance-based criteria, but only within its $n - f$ neighbors. This is the main idea behind our choice function we call *Krum*[1]. We show (using techniques from multi-dimensional stochastic calculus) that our Krum function satisfies the resilience property aforementioned and the corresponding machine learning scheme converges. An important advantage of the Krum function is that it requires $O(n^2 \cdot d)$ local computation time, where $d$ is the dimension of the parameter vector. This contrasts with the prohibitive $O(n^d)$ cost of approximate agreement [9]. (In deep learning, the dimension $d$ of the parameter vector may take values in the hundreds of billions.)

## 2 MODEL

We consider a general distributed system consisting of a parameter server[2] [1], and $n$ workers, $f$ of them possibly Byzantine. Computation is divided into (infinitely many) synchronous rounds. During round $t$, the parameter server broadcasts its parameter vector $x_t \in \mathbb{R}^d$ to all the workers. Each correct worker $p$ computes an estimate $V_p^t = G(x_t, \xi_p^t)$ of the gradient $\nabla Q(x_t)$ of the cost function $Q$, where $\xi_p^t$ is a random variable representing, e.g., the sample drawn from the dataset. A Byzantine worker $b$ proposes a vector $V_b^t$ which can be arbitrary (see Figure 1).

The parameter server computes a vector $F(V_1^t, \dots, V_n^t)$ by applying a deterministic function $F$ to the vectors received. We refer to $F$ as the *choice function* of the parameter server. The parameter server updates the parameter vector using the following SGD equation: $x_{t+1} = x_t - \gamma_t \cdot F(V_1^t, \dots, V_n^t)$. We assume that the correct (non-Byzantine) workers compute unbiased estimates of the gradient $\nabla Q(x_t)$. More precisely, in every round $t$, the vectors $V_i^t$'s proposed by the correct workers are independent identically distributed random vectors, $V_i^t \sim G(x_t, \xi_i^t)$ with $\mathbb{E}G(x_t, \xi_i^t) = \nabla Q(x_t)$. This can be achieved by ensuring that each sample of data used for computing the gradient is drawn uniformly and independently, as classically assumed in the literature of machine learning [3]. The Byzantine workers have full knowledge of the system, including the choice function $F$, the vectors proposed by the other workers and can collaborate with each other [7].

[1] Krum, in Greek Κρούμος, was a Bulgarian Khan of the end of the eighth century, who undertook offensive attacks against the Byzantine empire. Bulgaria doubled in size during his reign.

[2] The parameter server is assumed to be reliable. Classical techniques of state-machine replication can be used to avoid this single point of failure.

## 3 BYZANTINE RESILIENCE

In most SGD-based learning algorithms used today [3,4], the choice function consists in computing the average of the input vectors. Lemma 3.1 below states that no linear combination of the vectors can tolerate a single Byzantine worker. In particular, averaging is not robust to Byzantine failures.

**Figure 1: The gradient estimates of correct workers (black dashed arrows) are distributed around the actual gradient (blue solid arrow) of the cost function (thin black curve). A Byzantine worker can propose an arbitrary vector (red dotted arrow).**

Lemma 3.1. *Consider a choice function $F_{lin}$ of the form: $F_{lin}(V_1, \dots, V_n) = \sum_{i=1}^n \lambda_i \cdot V_i$, where the $\lambda_i$'s are non-zero scalars. Let $U$ be any vector in $\mathbb{R}^d$. A single Byzantine worker can make $F$ always select $U$. In particular, a single Byzantine worker can prevent convergence.*

Intuitively, the choice function should output a vector $F$ that is not too far from the "real" gradient $g$, more precisely, the vector that points to the steepest direction of the cost function being optimized. This is expressed as a lower bound (condition *(i)*) on the scalar product of the (expected) vector $F$ and $g$. If $\mathbb{E}F$ belongs to the ball centered at $g$ with radius $r$, then the scalar product is bounded below by a term involving $\sin\alpha = r/\|g\|$. Condition *(ii)* is more technical, and states that the moments of $F$ should be controlled by the moments of the (correct) gradient estimator $G$. The bounds on the moments of $G$ are classically used to control the effects of the discrete nature of the SGD dynamics [3]. Condition *(ii)* allows to transfer this control to the choice function.

*Definition 3.2 ($(\alpha, f)$-Byzantine Resilience).* Let $0 \le \alpha < \pi/2$ be any angular value, and any integer $0 \le f \le n$. Let $V_1, \dots, V_n$ be any independent identically distributed random vectors in $\mathbb{R}^d$, $V_i \sim G$, with $\mathbb{E}G = g$. Let $B_1, \dots, B_f$ be any random vectors in $\mathbb{R}^d$, possibly dependent on the $V_i$'s. Choice function $F$ is said to be $(\alpha, f)$-Byzantine resilient if, for any $1 \le j_1 < \dots < j_f \le n$, the vector $F = F(V_1, \dots, \underbrace{B_1}_{j_1}, \dots, \underbrace{B_f}_{j_f}, \dots, V_n)$ satisfies *(i)* $\langle \mathbb{E}F, g \rangle \ge (1 - \sin\alpha) \cdot \|g\|^2 > 0$ and *(ii)* for $r = 2, 3, 4$, $\mathbb{E}\|F\|^r$ is bounded above by a linear combination of terms $\mathbb{E}\|G\|^{r_1} \dots \mathbb{E}\|G\|^{r_{n-1}}$ with $r_1 + \dots + r_{n-1} = r$.

## 4 THE KRUM FUNCTION

The barycentric choice function $F_{bary} = \frac{1}{n}\sum_{i=1}^n V_i$ can be defined as the vector in $\mathbb{R}^d$ that minimizes the sum of squared distances to the $V_i$'s $\sum_{i=1}^n \left\|F_{bary} - V_i\right\|^2$. Lemma 3.1, however, states that this approach does not tolerate even a single Byzantine failure. One could try to define the choice function in order to select, *among* the $V_i$'s, the vector $U \in \{V_1, \dots, V_n\}$ that minimizes the sum $\sum_i \|U - V_i\|^2$. Intuitively, vector $U$ would be close to every proposed vector, including the correct ones, and thus would be close to the "real" gradient. However, all Byzantine workers but one may propose vectors that are large enough to move the total barycenter far away from the correct vectors, while the remaining Byzantine worker proposes this barycenter. Since the barycenter always minimizes the sum of squared distance, this last Byzantine worker is certain to have its vector chosen by the parameter server. This situation is depicted in Figure 2. In other words, since this choice function takes into account all the vectors, including the very remote ones, the Byzantine workers can collude to force the choice of the parameter server.

**Figure 2: Selecting the vector that minimizes the sum of the squared distances to other vectors does not prevent arbitrary vectors proposed by Byzantine workers from being selected if $f \geq 2$. If the gradients computed by the correct workers lie in area $C$, the Byzantine workers can collude to propose up to $f - 1$ vectors in an arbitrarily remote area $B$, thus allowing another Byzantine vector $b$, close to the barycenter of proposed vectors, to be selected.**

Our approach to circumvent this issue is to preclude the vectors that are too far away. More precisely, we define our *Krum* choice function $\text{Kr}(V_1, \ldots, V_n)$ as follows. For any $i \neq j$, we denote by $i \to j$ the fact that $V_j$ belongs to the $n - f - 2$ closest vectors to $V_i$. Then, we define for each worker $i$, the *score* $s(i) = \sum_{i \to j} \left\| V_i - V_j \right\|^2$ where the sum runs over the $n - f - 2$ closest vectors to $V_i$. Finally, $\text{Kr}(V_1, \ldots, V_n) = V_{i_*}$ where $i_*$ refers to the worker minimizing the score, $s(i_*) \leq s(i)$ for all $i$.[3]

Lemma 4.1. *The Krum Function $\text{Kr}(V_1, \ldots, V_n)$, where $V_1, \ldots, V_n$ are $d$-dimensional vectors, is computed in $O(n^2 \cdot d)$ time at the parameter server.*

*Resilience.* Proposition 4.2 below states that, if $2f + 2 < n$ and the gradient estimator is accurate enough, (its standard deviation is relatively small compared to the norm of the gradient), then the Krum function is $(\alpha, f)$-Byzantine-resilient, where angle $\alpha$ depends on the ratio of the deviation over the gradient. When the Krum function selects a correct vector (i.e., a vector proposed by a correct worker), the proof of this fact is relatively easy, since the probability distribution of this correct vector is that of the gradient estimator $G$. The core difficulty occurs when the Krum function selects a Byzantine vector (i.e., a vector proposed by a Byzantine worker), because the distribution of this vector is completely arbitrary, and may even depend on the correct vectors. In a very general sense, this part of our proof is reminiscent of the geometric median technique and is discussed in details in the full paper [2].

Proposition 4.2. *Let $V_1, \ldots, V_n$ be any independent and identically distributed random $d$-dimensional vectors s.t $V_i \sim G$, with $\mathbb{E}G = g$ and $\mathbb{E}\left\|G - g\right\|^2 = d\sigma^2$. Let $B_1, \ldots, B_f$ be any $f$ random vectors, possibly dependent on the $V_i$'s. If $2f + 2 < n$ and $\eta(n, f)\sqrt{d} \cdot \sigma < \|g\|$, where $\eta(n, f) = \begin{cases} O(n) & \text{if } f = O(n) \\ O(\sqrt{n}) & \text{if } f = O(1) \end{cases}$, then the Krum function $\text{Kr}$ is $(\alpha, f)$-Byzantine resilient where $0 \leq \alpha < \pi/2$ is defined by $\sin \alpha = \frac{\eta(n,f) \cdot \sqrt{d} \cdot \sigma}{\|g\|}$.*

*Convergence.* The SGD equation is expressed as follows: $x_{t+1} = x_t - \gamma_t \cdot \text{Kr}(V_1^t, \ldots, V_n^t)$, where at least $n - f$ vectors among the $V_i^t$'s are correct, while the other ones may be Byzantine. For a correct index $i$, $V_i^t = G(x_t, \xi_i^t)$ where $G$ is the gradient estimator. We define the *local standard deviation* $\sigma(x)$ by $d \cdot \sigma^2(x) = \mathbb{E}\left\|G(x, \xi) - \nabla Q(x)\right\|^2$.

Proposition 4.3. *We assume that (i) the cost function $Q$ is three times differentiable with continuous derivatives, and is non-negative, $Q(x) \geq 0$; (ii) the learning rates satisfy $\sum_t \gamma_t = \infty$ and $\sum_t \gamma_t^2 < \infty$; (iii) the gradient estimator satisfies $\mathbb{E}G(x, \xi) = \nabla Q(x)$ and $\forall r \in \{2, \ldots, 4\}$, $\mathbb{E}\|G(x, \xi)\|^r \leq A_r + B_r\|x\|^r$ for some constants $A_r, B_r$; (iv) there exists a constant $0 \leq \alpha < \pi/2$ such that for all $x$ $\eta(n, f) \cdot \sqrt{d} \cdot \sigma(x) \leq \|\nabla Q(x)\| \cdot \sin \alpha$; (v) finally, beyond a certain horizon, $\|x\|^2 \geq D$, there exist $\epsilon > 0$ and $0 \leq \beta < \pi/2 - \alpha$ such that $\|\nabla Q(x)\| \geq \epsilon > 0$ and $\frac{\langle x, \nabla Q(x) \rangle}{\|x\| \cdot \|\nabla Q(x)\|} \geq \cos \beta$. Then the sequence of gradients $\nabla Q(x_t)$ converges almost surely to zero.*

Proposition 4.3 basically says that in the presence of Byzantine workers, the parameter vector $x_t$ almost surely reaches a basin around points where the gradient is small ($\|\nabla Q\| \leq \eta(n, f) \cdot \sqrt{d} \cdot \sigma$), i.e., points where the cost landscape is "almost flat".

Note that the convergence analysis is based only on the fact that function $\text{Kr}$ is $(\alpha, f)$-Byzantine resilient. The detailed proof of convergence, as well as its qualitative interpretation, can be found in the full paper [2].

*Acknowledgment.* We are very grateful to Lê Nguyen Hoang for fruitful discussions.

## REFERENCES

[1] M. Abadi, P. Barham, J. Chen, Z. Chen, A. Davis, J. Dean, M. Devin, S. Ghemawat, G. Irving, M. Isard, et al. Tensorflow: A system for large-scale machine learning. In *Proceedings of the 12th USENIX Symposium on Operating Systems Design and Implementation (OSDI). Savannah, Georgia, USA*, 2016.
[2] P. Blanchard, E. M. El Mhamdi, R. Guerraoui, and J. Stainer. Byzantine-tolerant machine learning. *arXiv preprint arXiv:1703.02757*, 2017.
[3] L. Bottou. Online learning and stochastic approximations. *Online learning in neural networks*, 17(9):142, 1998.
[4] L. Bottou. Large-scale machine learning with stochastic gradient descent. In *Proceedings of COMPSTAT'2010*, pages 177–186. Springer, 2010.
[5] L. Lamport, R. Shostak, and M. Pease. The byzantine generals problem. *ACM Transactions on Programming Languages and Systems (TOPLAS)*, 4(3):382–401, 1982.
[6] X. Lian, Y. Huang, Y. Li, and J. Liu. Asynchronous parallel stochastic gradient for nonconvex optimization. In *Advances in Neural Information Processing Systems*, pages 2737–2745, 2015.
[7] N. A. Lynch. *Distributed algorithms*. Morgan Kaufmann, 1996.
[8] J. Markoff. How many computers to identify a cat? 16,000. *New York Times*, pages 06–25, 2012.
[9] H. Mendes and M. Herlihy. Multidimensional approximate agreement in byzantine asynchronous systems. In *Proceedings of the forty-fifth annual ACM symposium on Theory of computing*, pages 391–400. ACM, 2013.
[10] B. T. Polyak and A. B. Juditsky. Acceleration of stochastic approximation by averaging. *SIAM Journal on Control and Optimization*, 30(4):838–855, 1992.
[11] F. B. Schneider. Implementing fault-tolerant services using the state machine approach: A tutorial. *ACM Computing Surveys (CSUR)*, 22(4):299–319, 1990.
[12] S. Zhang, A. E. Choromanska, and Y. LeCun. Deep learning with elastic averaging sgd. In *Advances in Neural Information Processing Systems*, pages 685–693, 2015.

[3] If two or more workers have the minimal score, we choose the vector of the worker with the smallest identifier.

# Brief Announcement: Certified Multiplicative Weights Update

## Verified Learning Without Regret

Alexander Bagnall
Ohio University
ab667712@ohio.edu

Samuel Merten
Ohio University
sm137907@ohio.edu

Gordon Stewart
Ohio University
gstewart@ohio.edu

## ABSTRACT

The Multiplicative Weights Update method (MWU) is a simple yet powerful algorithm for learning linear classifiers, for ensemble learning à la boosting, for approximately solving linear and semidefinite systems, for computing approximate solutions to multicommodity flow problems, and for online convex optimization, among other applications.

In this brief announcement, we apply techniques from interactive theorem proving to define and prove correct the first formally verified implementation of MWU (specifically, we show that our MWU is no regret). Our primary application – and one justification of the relevance of our work to the PODC community – is to verified multi-agent systems, such as distributed multi-agent network flow and load balancing games, for which verified MWU provides a convenient method for distributed computation of approximate Coarse Correlated Equilibria.

## CCS CONCEPTS

•**Theory of computation** → **Program verification;** *Algorithmic game theory; Convergence and learning in games;* Multi-agent learning; Network games; •**Software and its engineering** → *Distributed systems organizing principles;*

## KEYWORDS

The Multiplicative Weights Update Method; Interactive Theorem Proving; Coq

## 1 INTRODUCTION

The Multiplicative Weights Update method (MWU, [1, 6]) solves the general problem of "combining expert advice", in which an agent repeatedly chooses which action, or "expert", to play against an adaptive environment. The agent, after playing an action, learns from the environment both the cost of that action and of other actions it could have played in that round. The environment, in turn, may adapt in order to minimize environment costs. MWU works by maintaining a weighted distribution over the action space, in which each action initially has equal weight, and by updating weights with a linear or exponential loss function to penalize poorly performing actions.


*PODC'17, July 25-27, 2017, Washington, DC, USA*

ACM ISBN 978-1-4503-4992-5/17/07.
DOI: http://dx.doi.org/10.1145/3087801.3087852

This simple algorithm performs remarkably well: In number of rounds logarithmic in the size of the action space, MWU's expected cost approaches to within a small bound $\epsilon$ that of the best fixed action the agent could have chosen in hindsight (MWU has bounded external regret). In [1], Arora, Hazan, and Kale showed that MWU has wide-ranging connections to numerous problems in computer science, including optimization, linear and semidefinite programming, and machine learning (cf. boosting [4]).

Our work targets another important application of MWU that is perhaps of greater interest to the PODC community: the approximate solution of multi-agent games, especially as such games relate to the construction of distributed systems. It is well known (cf. [7, Chapter 4]) that no-regret algorithms converge, in expectation when played by multiple independent agents, to a large equilibrium class known as Coarse Correlated Equilibria (CCEs). CCEs may not be socially optimal, but for some games (e.g., Roughgarden's smooth games [8]) the social, or objective, cost of such equilibrium states can be bounded with respect to the optimal cost (the Price of Anarchy, or POA, of the game). Our broader research program, the CAGE project:

https://github.com/gstew5/cage

seeks to use such results and others from algorithmic game theory and distributed optimization to build distributed systems – e.g., distributed network routers and load balancers – that have verified convergence and correctness properties by design.

*Contributions.* In promotion of the first part of our broader research program, this brief announcement reports on the design, construction, and verification of the first formally certified implementation of the MWU algorithm, available open-source on the CAGE project's website.

By *verified*, we mean our MWU implementation has mechanically checked convergence bounds and correctness proof within an interactive theorem prover (specifically, Ssreflect [5], an extension of the Coq [2] system). By *convergence* and *correctness*, we mean that we prove both that MWU produces the right answer (functional correctness wrt. a high-level functional specification), but also that it does so with external regret bounded by a function of the number of iterations of the protocol (convergence).

As we've mentioned, MWU has broad application across a number of subdisciplines of computer science, including linear programming, optimization, and machine learning. Our work uses MWU to implement no-regret dynamics, a general strategy for computing the CCEs of multi-agent games. By formally proving correctness and convergence results for our implementation of MWU, we demonstrate a new architecture for formal verification of (a subclass of) distributed systems: represent the system as a game, prove POA bounds for the game, then compose the POA results

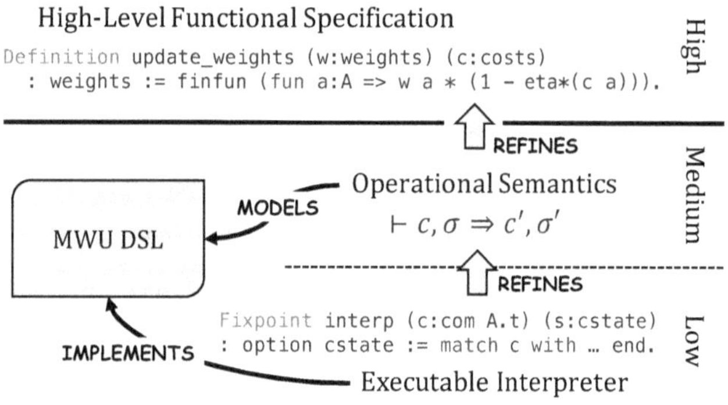


Figure 1: MWU Architecture

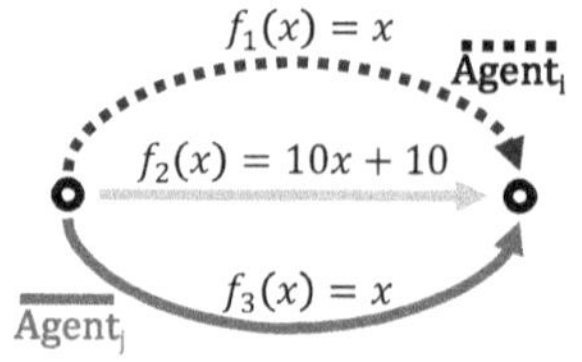


**Figure 2: Routing game with source $s$, sink $t$, and affine cost functions $f_e(x) = a_e x + b_e$ where $x$ is the amount of traffic on an edge $e$. Solutions of the game are assignments of players to source-sink paths. An optimal solution minimizes the total cost to all players.**

with our general proof of correctness and convergence of MWU – which drives any such game to an approximate CCE, or $\epsilon$-CCE – to yield correctness and performance results of the overall system. Section 3 sketches how these pieces fit together when applied to problem of distributed routing with affine latency functions.

## 2 MWU IMPLEMENTATION AND PROOF

Our implementation and proof of MWU (Figure 1) were designed to be extensible. At a high level, the structure of the proof follows the program refinement methodology, in which a high-level mathematical but inefficient specification of the MWU algorithm (High-Level Functional Specification) is gradually made more efficient by a series of refinements to various features of the program (for example, by replacing an inefficient implementation of a key-value map with a more efficient balanced binary tree).

For each such refinement, we prove that every behavior of the lower-level program is one of the acceptable behaviors of the higher-level program it refines. Thus specifications proved for all behaviors of the high-level program also apply to each behavior at the low level. By behavior here, we mean the trace of action distributions output by MWU as it interacts with, and receives cost vectors from, the environment.

In order to make our MWU implementation and proof extensible, we factor the lower implementation layers (Medium and Low) into an interpreter and semantics over a domain-specific language specialized to MWU-style algorithms. The DSL defines commands for updating the weights table as well as commands for interacting with the environment, in the style of process calculi or message-passing concurrency.

At the top level, the convergence theorem we prove of our high-level functional MWU is:

**Theorem** perstep_weights_boundedregret :
(expCostsR – OPTR)/T ≤ etaR + (ln size_A) / (etaR*T).

Here expCostsR is the expected cost of MWU on a sequence of cost vectors, OPTR is the cumulative cost of the best fixed action, etaR is the algorithm's exploration parameter $\eta$ (required to lie in the range $(0, 1/2]$), ln size_A is the natural log of the size of the action space $A$, and T is the number of time steps.

The exploration parameter $\eta$ controls how quickly actions are penalized in MWU's update rule $w^{t+1}(a) = w^t(a) \cdot (1 - \eta \cdot c^t(a))$, and can therefore be tuned to balance exploration of the state space versus exploitation of cost information learned from the environment. Since our MWU interpreter performs exact rational arithmetic (in fact, dyadic rational arithmetic for performance), we require that $\eta$ be representable as a dyadic rational number.

As a second consequence of our use of exact arithmetic, our verified MWU uses the linear scaling term $1 - \eta \cdot c(a)$ to update the weight of action $a$ in each round, where $c(a)$ denotes the cost of $a$ in the previous round. A variant of the algorithm uses the exponential scaling term $exp(-\eta \cdot c(a))$, which we cannot represent exactly in our executable version of MWU. One could use the Taylor-series approximation of $e^x$ to approximate $exp(-\eta \cdot c(a))$ at each update step, but only at the expense of additional reasoning about approximation error bounds in the rest of the proof.

## 3 APPLICATIONS

No-regret algorithms such as MWU can be used to drive multi-agent systems toward the $\epsilon$-CCEs of arbitrary games. Although the CCEs of general games may have high social cost, those of *smooth* games, as identified by Roughgarden [8], have robust Price of Anarchy (POA) bounds that extend even to $\epsilon$-CCEs.

Our generic algorithm for proving bounds on the social cost of games like multi-agent affine routing has the following steps:

(1) Prove that the game is $(\lambda, \mu)$-smooth, for smoothness parameters $\lambda$ and $\mu$. The smoothness parameters are specific to the game. In affine routing, $\lambda = \frac{5}{3}$ while $\mu = \frac{1}{3}$.
(2) Use smoothness from (1) to prove robust POA bounds for the game. For example, the POA of an $\epsilon$-CCE of a $(\lambda, \mu)$-smooth game is $\frac{(1+\epsilon)\lambda}{1-(1+\epsilon)\mu}$. The POA of affine routing wrt. $\epsilon$-CCEs is therefore approximately 5/2.
(3) Prove that $N$ agents each running verified MWU together drive the system to an $\epsilon$-CCE. This proof follows directly from the per-agent regret bound that results from each agent running our verified MWU.
(4) Compose the results in (2) and (3) to prove overall bounds on the social cost of the resulting state.

We illustrate with an application – distributed routing – in which we let multiple agents independently run our verified MWU to drive each other toward an $\epsilon$-CCE.[1] In a simple version of the distributed routing game with affine latency functions (Figure 2), $N$ routing agents each choose a path from a global source vertex $s$ to a global sink vertex $t$ (a generalization of this game allows $s$ and $t$ to differ across players). Latency over edge $e$, modeled by an affine cost function $f_e(x) = a_e x + b_e$, scales in the amount of traffic $x$ over that edge. An optimal solution minimizes the total cost to all agents. Roughgarden [8] showed that such games are $(\frac{5}{3}, \frac{1}{3})$-smooth, implying a robust POA bound of 5/2; thus even $\epsilon$-CCEs as produced by MWU are bounded with respect to the socially optimal solutions of the game.

In Coq, we represent games as pairs $(A,C)$ of

- a finite type $A$, the strategy or action space; and
- a cost function $C(i,s) : \mathbb{Q}$, which for a given player $i \in [0,N)$ returns the cost to that player of state $s$, a strategy profile of type $[0,N) \rightarrow A$ mapping players to strategies.

As an example game, consider a simplified version of resource (congestion) games [3] in which agents may choose to use (or not use) just a single resource.[2] The cost to a player of this game is the total number of players using the resource, assuming the player chooses to use the resource, and 0 otherwise.

In Coq, we represent this game's strategy space $A$ as the inductive data type Resource $\triangleq$ RYes | RNo in which the constructor RYes indicates that the agent chose to use the resource and RNo otherwise.[3] The cost function for Resource is:

$$C_{\mathsf{Resource}}(i,s) = \textbf{if } s_i \textbf{ is } \mathsf{RYes} \textbf{ then } \mathsf{traffic}\ s \textbf{ else } 0$$

where traffic $s$ equals the total number of agents who used the resource in state $s$.

From basic games such as (Resource, $C_{\mathsf{Resource}}$) we build more complicated ones using a language of game combinators (functions mapping games to games). For example, the product combinator over games – which can be thought of informally as running two games in parallel – takes as input games $(A,C_A)$ and $(B,C_B)$ and produces as output the new game $(A \times B, C_{A\times B})$ over states mapping players to ordered pairs $(a,b)$. The cost function $C_{A\times B}$ of the resulting game sums the costs with respect to $C_A$ and $C_B$. To prove smoothness of both basic games such as (Resource, $C_{\mathsf{Resource}}$) and of derived games, we developed a library of smoothness preservation proofs following the structure of our language of game combinators. In the product game, for example, if $(A,C_A)$ is $(\lambda_A,\mu_A)$-smooth and $(B,C_B)$ is $(\lambda_B,\mu_B)$-smooth, then $(A \times B, C_{A\times B})$ is $(\max(\lambda_A,\lambda_B), \max(\mu_A,\mu_B))$-smooth. We prove smoothness of basic games such as (Resource, $C_{\mathsf{Resource}}$) by mechanizing the standard paper-and-pencil proofs (e.g., [8, 2.3.1] for congestion games).

In our implementation of the affine routing games of Figure 2, we model each edge $e$ in the network as a Resource under application of a second combinator, $\mathsf{Affine}(a_e, b_e, C_{\mathsf{Resource}})$, which maps the $C_{\mathsf{Resource}}$ cost function to the more general

$$C_e(i,s) = \textbf{if } s_i \textbf{ is } \mathsf{RYes} \textbf{ then } a_e * (\mathsf{traffic}\ s) + b_e \textbf{ else } 0.$$

The resulting game over edge $e$ has cost 0 if an agent does not use edge $e$ in state $s$, and cost $a_e*(\mathsf{traffic}\ s) + b_e$ otherwise.

[1] The project website includes a second application, to distributed load balancing.

[2] We generalize below to multiple resource games with arbitrary affine cost functions.

[3] We define a new inductive type RYes | RNo as opposed to letting Resource equal the isomorphic bool for technical reasons related to Coq's typeclass resolution.

We generalize from games over a single edge to those over all source-sink paths in a network in two steps:

First, we construct an $m$-edge game, in which the agents are free to use any subset of the Resources modeling the graph's edges, by building the product of $m$ affine resources:

$$T \triangleq \begin{cases} & \mathsf{Affine}(a_{e_1}, b_{e_1}, C_{\mathsf{Resource}}) \\ \times & \mathsf{Affine}(a_{e_2}, b_{e_2}, C_{\mathsf{Resource}}) \\ & \vdots \\ \times & \mathsf{Affine}(a_{e_m}, b_{e_m}, C_{\mathsf{Resource}}) \end{cases}$$

The associated cost function of the game over type $T$ is the sum of the individual $\mathsf{Affine}(a, b, C_{\mathsf{Resource}})$ cost functions.

Second, to transform the unrestricted game over type $T$ – in which players are free to choose any subset of the edges – to one in which the players may choose only valid paths, we apply a final combinator to $T$ that limits the strategy space to those actions satisfying a predicate, $\mathsf{isValidPath}(G, s, t)$, specifying the set of valid paths from source $s$ to sink $t$ under a particular topology $G$.

All the combinators we apply in the affine routing game preserve smoothness. To prove that the game thus implemented by $N$ agents each running MWU converges to an optimal routing configuration, it's therefore sufficient to compose our MWU proof with the robust POA guarantee we have proved generically for all smooth games.

*Conclusion.* This brief announcement reports on the first formally verified implementation of Multiplicative Weights Update, a simple yet powerful algorithm for approximately solving Coarse Correlated Equilibria (CCE), among many other applications. We prove our MWU implementation correct via a series of program refinements with respect to a high-level implementation of the algorithm. As part of the larger CAGE project, we use our certified MWU to prototype a new architecture for verified distributed systems in which MWU generically drives game-based distributed systems with robust Price of Anarchy bounds to socially optimal CCEs.

## ACKNOWLEDGMENTS

We thank the PODC reviewers for their comments on an earlier draft. The research was supported in part by NSF award #1657358.

## REFERENCES


[1] Sanjeev Arora, Elad Hazan, and Satyen Kale. 2012. The Multiplicative Weights Update Method: a Meta-Algorithm and Applications. *Theory of Computing* 8, 1 (2012), 121–164.

[2] Yves Bertot and Pierre Castéran. 2013. *Interactive theorem proving and program development: Coq'Art: the calculus of inductive constructions.* Springer Science & Business Media.

[3] George Christodoulou and Elias Koutsoupias. 2005. The price of anarchy of finite congestion games. In *Proceedings of the 37th annual ACM Symposium on Theory of Computing.* ACM, 67–73.

[4] Yoav Freund and Robert E Schapire. 1995. A decision-theoretic generalization of on-line learning and an application to boosting. In *European conference on computational learning theory.* Springer, 23–37.

[5] Georges Gonthier, Assia Mahboubi, and Enrico Tassi. 2015. *A small scale reflection extension for the Coq system.* Technical Report. INRIA.

[6] Nick Littlestone and Manfred K Warmuth. 1989. The weighted majority algorithm. In *Proceedings of the 30th Annual Symposium on Foundations of Computer Science.* IEEE, 256–261.

[7] Noam Nisan, Tim Roughgarden, Eva Tardos, and Vijay V Vazirani. 2007. *Algorithmic Game Theory.* Vol. 1. Cambridge University Press.

[8] Tim Roughgarden. 2009. Intrinsic robustness of the price of anarchy. In *Proceedings of the 41st annual ACM Symposium on Theory of Computing.* ACM, 513–522.

# Author Index

www.ingramcontent.com/pod-product-compliance
Lightning Source LLC
LaVergne TN
LVHW080525210926
848481LV00022B/2940
*9781450352055*